IARIA

ACHI 2020

The Thirteenth International Conference on Advances in Computer-Human Interactions

November 21 – 25, 2020

Valencia, Spain

ACHI 2020 Editors

Jaime Lloret Mauri, Polytechnic University of Valencia, Spain
Diana Saplacan, University of Oslo – Oslo, Norway
Klaudia Çarçani, Østfold University College – Halden, Norway
Prima Oky Dicky Ardiansyah, Iwate Prefectural University, Japan
Simona Vasilache, University of Tsukuba, Japan

Printed from e-media with permission by:

Curran Associates, Inc.
57 Morehouse Lane
Red Hook, NY 12571

Some format issues inherent in the e-media version may also appear in this print version.

International Academy, Research, and Industry Association (IARIA)
412 Derby Way
Wilmington, DE 19810

Phone: (408) 893-6407
Fax: (408) 527-6351

petre@iaria.org

Additional copies of this publication are available from:

Curran Associates, Inc.
57 Morehouse Lane
Red Hook, NY 12571 USA
Phone: 845-758-0400
Fax: 845-758-2633
Email: curran@proceedings.com
Web: www.proceedings.com

Table of Contents

ACHI 2020

Forward

The Thirteenth International Conference on Advances in Computer-Human Interactions (ACHI 2020) covered a wide range of human-computer interaction related topics such as graphical user interfaces, input methods, training, recognition, and applications

The conference on Advances in Computer-Human Interaction, ACHI 2020, was a result of a paradigm shift in the most recent achievements and future trends in human interactions with increasingly complex systems. Adaptive and knowledge-based user interfaces, universal accessibility, human-robot interaction, agent-driven human computer interaction, and sharable mobile devices are a few of these trends. ACHI 2020 brought also a suite of specific domain applications, such as gaming, social, medicine, education and engineering.

The event was very competitive in its selection process and very well perceived by the international scientific and industrial communities. As such, it is attracting excellent contributions and active participation from all over the world. We were very pleased to receive a large amount of top quality contributions.

We believe that the ACHI 2020 contributions offered a large panel of solutions to key problems in all areas of human-computer interaction.

We take here the opportunity to warmly thank all the members of the ACHI 2020 technical program committee as well as the numerous reviewers. The creation of such a broad and high quality conference program would not have been possible without their involvement. We also kindly thank all the authors that dedicated much of their time and efforts to contribute to the ACHI 2020. We truly believe that thanks to all these efforts, the final conference program consists of top quality contributions.

This event could also not have been a reality without the support of many individuals, organizations and sponsors. In addition, we also gratefully thank the members of the ACHI 2020 organizing committee for their help in handling the logistics and for their work that is making this professional meeting a success.

We hope the ACHI 2020 was a successful international forum for the exchange of ideas and results between academia and industry and to promote further progress in the human-computer interaction field.

ACHI 2020 Chairs

ACHI 2020 General Chair
Jaime Lloret Mauri, Polytechnic University of Valencia, Spain

ACHI 2020 Steering Committee
Flaminia Luccio, University Ca' Foscari of Venice, Italy
Lasse Berntzen, University College of Southeast, Norway

ACHI 2020 Publicity Chair
Lorena Parra, Universitat Politecnica de Valencia, Spain

ACHI 2020 Advisory Committee
Leslie Miller, Iowa State University - Ames, USA
Uttam Kokil, Kennesaw State University Marietta, USA

ACHI 2020
Committee

ACHI 2020 General Chair
Jaime Lloret Mauri, Polytechnic University of Valencia, Spain

ACHI 2020 Steering Committee
Flaminia Luccio, University Ca' Foscari of Venice, Italy
Lasse Berntzen, University of South-Eastern Norway, Norway

ACHI 2020 Publicity Chair
Lorena Parra, Universitat Politecnica de Valencia, Spain

ACHI 2020 Advisory Committee
Leslie Miller, Iowa State University - Ames, USA
Uttam Kokil, Kennesaw State University Marietta, USA

ACHI 2020 Technical Program Committee
Mostafa Alani, Tuskegee University, USA
Marran Aldossari, University of North Carolina at Charlotte, USA
Rawan Alghofaili, George MasonUniversity, USA
Obead Alhadreti, Umm Al-Qura University, Al-Qunfudah, Saudi Arabia
Prima Oky Dicky Ardiansyah, Iwate Prefectural University, Japan
Ahmad Azadvar, Ubisoft Entertainment Sweden A.B. - Ubisoft Massive / Malmo University, Sweden
Catalin-Mihai Barbu, University of Duisburg-Essen, Germany
Lasse Berntzen, University of South-Eastern Norway, Norway
Ganesh D. Bhutkar, Vishwakarma Institute of Technology (VIT), Pune, India
Cezary Biele, National Information Processing Institute, Poland
Christos J. Bouras, University of Patras, Greece
Christian Bourret, UPEM - Université Paris-Est Marne-la-Vallée, France
James Braman, The Community College of Baltimore County, USA
Pradeep Buddharaju, University of Houston - Clear Lake, USA
Idoko John Bush, Near East University, Cyprus
Minghao Cai, University of Alberta, Canada
Klaudia Carcani, Østfold University College, Norway
Stefan P Carmien, University of York, UK
Meghan Chandarana, NASA Langley Research Center (LaRC), USA
Lara Jessica da Silva Pontes, University of Debrecen, Hungary
Andre Constantino da Silva, Federal Institute of São Paulo - IFSP, Brazil
Lea Daling, Cybernetics Lab IMA & IfU - RWTH Aachen University, Germany
Antonio Diaz Tula, University of São Paulo, Brazil
Verena Distler, University of Luxembourg, Luxembourg

Krzysztof Dobosz, Silesian University of Technology - Institute of Informatics, Poland
Margaret Drouhard, University of Washington, USA
Ahmed Elkaseer, Karlsruhe Institute of Technology, Germany
Pardis Emami-Naeini, Carnegie Mellon University, USA
Stefano Federici, University of Perugia, Italy
Jicheng Fu, University of Central Oklahoma, USA
Somchart Fugkeaw, Mahidol University - Nakhonpathom, Thailand
Pablo Gallego, Independent Researcher, Spain
Dagmawi Lemma Gobena, Addis Ababa University, Ethiopia
Benedikt Gollan, Research Studios Austria FG mbH, Austria
Bernard Grabot, INP-ENIT, France
Denis Gracanin, Virginia Tech, USA
Andrina Granic, University of Split, Croatia
Ibrahim A. Hameed, Norwegian University of Science and Technology (NTNU), Norway
Ragnhild Halvorsrud, SINTEF Digital, Norway
Haikun Huang, University of Massachusetts, Boston, USA
Maria Hwang, Fashion Institute of Technology (FIT), New York City, USA
Sara Ibarra Vargas, Institución Universitaria Pascual Bravo, Colombia
Gökhan İnce, Istanbul Technical University, Turkey
Francisco Iniesto, Institute of Educational Technology - The Open University, UK
Jamshed Iqbal, University of Jeddah, Saudi Arabia
Angel Jaramillo-Alcázar, Universidad de Las Américas, Ecuador
Oluwafemi Akintunde Jeremiah, Towson University, Maryland, USA
Sofia Kaloterakis, Utrecht University, Netherland
Yasushi Kambayashi, Nippon Institute of Technology, Japan
Ahmed Kamel, Concordia College, USA
Simeon Keates, Edinburgh Napier University, UK
Suzanne Kieffer, Université catholique de Louvain, Belgium
Si Jung "SJ" Kim, University of Nevada, Las Vegas (UNLV), USA
Susanne Koch Stigberg, Østfold University College, Norway
Uttam Kokil, Kennesaw State University Marietta, USA
Daniel Kostrzewa, Silesian University of Technology, Poland
Josef Krems, Chemnitz University of Technology, Germany
Shiro Kumano, NTT (Nippon Telegraph and Telephone Corporation), Japan
Wen-Hsing Lai, National Kaohsiung University of Science and Technology, Taiwan
Monica Landoni, Università della Svizzera italiana, Switzerland
Maria Teresa Llano Rodriguez, Goldsmiths - University of London, UK
Tsai-Yen Li, National Chengchi University, Taiwan
Wenjuan Li, The Hong Kong Polytechnic University, Hong Kong
Fotis Liarokapis, Masaryk University, Czech Republic
Zhicong Lu, University of Toronto, Canada
Flaminia Luccio, Universita' Ca' Foscari Venezia, Italy
Sergio Luján-Mora, University of Alicante, Spain
Yan Luximon, The Hong Kong Polytechnic University, Hong Kong

Ben Steichen, California State Polytechnic University, Pomona, USA
Han Su, RA - MIT, USA
Federico Tajariol, University Bourgogne Franche-Comté, France
Sheng Tan, Trinity University, Texas, USA
Jiro Tanaka, Waseda University, Japan
Cagri Tanriover, Intel Corporation (Intel Labs), USA
Ranjeet Tayi, User Experience - Informatica, San Francisco, USA
Tom Torsney-Weir, Swansea University, UK
Carlos Toxtli Hernandez, West Virginia University, USA
David Unbehaun, University of Siegen, Germany
Simona Vasilache, University of Tsukuba, Japan
KatiaVega, University of California, Davis, USA
Konstantinos Votis, Information Technologies Institute | Centre for Research and Technology Hellas, Greece
Zhanwei Wu, Shanghai Jiao Tong University, China
Shuping Xiong, KAIST, South Korea
Panpan Xu, Bosch Research, Sunnyvale, USA
Sunny Xun Liu, Stanford University, USA
Ye Zhu, Cleveland State Unviersity, USA

Copyright Information

For your reference, this is the text governing the copyright release for material published by IARIA.

The copyright release is a transfer of publication rights, which allows IARIA and its partners to drive the dissemination of the published material. This allows IARIA to give articles increased visibility via distribution, inclusion in libraries, and arrangements for submission to indexes.

I, the undersigned, declare that the article is original, and that I represent the authors of this article in the copyright release matters. If this work has been done as work-for-hire, I have obtained all necessary clearances to execute a copyright release. I hereby irrevocably transfer exclusive copyright for this material to IARIA. I give IARIA permission or reproduce the work in any media format such as, but not limited to, print, digital, or electronic. I give IARIA permission to distribute the materials without restriction to any institutions or individuals. I give IARIA permission to submit the work for inclusion in article repositories as IARIA sees fit.

I, the undersigned, declare that to the best of my knowledge, the article is does not contain libelous or otherwise unlawful contents or invading the right of privacy or infringing on a proprietary right.

Following the copyright release, any circulated version of the article must bear the copyright notice and any header and footer information that IARIA applies to the published article.

IARIA grants royalty-free permission to the authors to disseminate the work, under the above provisions, for any academic, commercial, or industrial use. IARIA grants royalty-free permission to any individuals or institutions to make the article available electronically, online, or in print.

IARIA acknowledges that rights to any algorithm, process, procedure, apparatus, or articles of manufacture remain with the authors and their employers.

I, the undersigned, understand that IARIA will not be liable, in contract, tort (including, without limitation, negligence), pre-contract or other representations (other than fraudulent misrepresentations) or otherwise in connection with the publication of my work.

Exception to the above is made for work-for-hire performed while employed by the government. In that case, copyright to the material remains with the said government. The rightful owners (authors and government entity) grant unlimited and unrestricted permission to IARIA, IARIA's contractors, and IARIA's partners to further distribute the work.

Engagement Estimation for an E-Learning Environment Application

Win Shwe Sin Khine
School of Information Science
Japan Advanced Institute of
Science and Technology
Ishikawa, Japan
Email: winshwesinkhine@jaist.ac.jp

Shinobu Hasegawa
Research Center for
Advanced Computing Infrastructure
Japan Advanced Institute of
Science and Technology
Ishikawa, Japan
Email: hasegawa@jaist.ac.jp

Kazunori Kotani
School of Information Science
Japan Advanced Institute of
Science and Technology
Ishikawa, Japan
Email: ikko@jaist.ac.jp

Abstract—**In this study, we conducted an estimation of engagement through virtual learning environment by using facial images. We aim to improve student learning rates and get a better understanding of them through facial expressions. Nowadays, computation power and memory capacity are available for analysis on large scale datasets. As a result, deep learning techniques can effectively extract useful features from the given dataset over traditional approaches. Unfortunately, deep learning-based methods require a massive amount of labeled data. Although there are many face datasets for face related problems, such as face detection and face recognition, it is still limited to facial expressions. To overcome this limitation, we use the advantages of the style transfer technique to obtain the basic features of the face and eliminate the features that are not useful for engagement estimation. In our experiment, we use the Visual Geometry Group-16 (VGG-16) face model to extract the prominent basic features of the face and eliminate the non-related features by differing peak and neutral frames. We demonstrated the practical use of our method through the efficiency of detecting student engagement. The results show that our proposed method provides 50% accuracy in engagement estimation.**

Keywords–E-learning; Engagement; Fine-tuning.

I. INTRODUCTION

Since Information Technology (IT) is incredibly improving in the 21st century, the usage of the virtual system is gradually increasing. Therefore, it is essential to maintain good experience and communication between users and the system. Human-Computer Interaction (HCI) becomes a significant concern in the IT field. From historical statistics, we know that, since the 1980s, there is a significant drop out rate, numerically between 25% and 60% shows by (see Larson and Richards [1]) for the participants in the learning system because students are extremely bored and not interested in their lectures. Maintaining the students' willingness, alternatively, is called engagement. Besides, interaction with a virtual system becomes important in HCI. As a result, it is a widely discussed topic in the educational area.

Learning methods of the adequate level of e-learning based on facial expressions can be divided into two categories. They are traditional hand-crafted based and deep-learning-based methods. The hand-crafted based methods typically consist of feature extraction and classification stages. In the feature extraction stage, appearance or geometric features are extracted by using traditional methods, such as Gabor filters [2], Local Binary Patterns (LBP) [3], Histograms of Oriented Gradients (HOG) [4]. Furthermore, the appearance features are depending on environmental settings, such as lighting, background, pose, and many other sensitive effects. On the other hand, geometric features are depending on prominent facial features and curvature of the face. The problem is that, when researchers use hand-crafted feature extraction methods, they need to set the constant environmental settings to get a stable result. However, facial expressions are depending on many variables and factors. Therefore, hand-crafted feature extraction is not feasible to extract facial features in the wild.

To overcome the difficulties of hand-crafted feature extraction methods, deep-learning-based feature extraction methods have been adopted. They provide impressive performance in face-related tasks, such as face detection, face recognition, facial expression recognition, and engagement estimation.

This paper is organized as follows; Section 2 focuses on the relevant study of facial expressions recognition related to deep-learning-based methods. Section 3 describes the dataset of this study. Section 4 presents the method used to conduct experiments in this study and discusses the obtained result. Section 5 summarizes our findings, draws conclusions based on our research objectives, and suggests potential improvements to this study.

II. LITERATURE REVIEWS

Mayya et al. [5] designed a deep neural network architecture called Deep Convolution Neural Network (DCNN) to learn features for recognizing six basic facial expressions from a single image. 96% recognition rate is achieved based on Extended Cohn-Kanade (CK++) and Japanese Female Facial Expressions (JAFFE) datasets, which are Action Unit (AU)-coded expression datasets. They discovered that more layers in the deep convolution neural network increases the ability to extract more features of an image when compared to few layers.

Jain et al. [6] designed a similar architecture with Mayya et al. [5]. However, the difference between these two models is that they use residual blocks after the convolution layer to prevent the degrading problem in which the gradient line cannot learn the data properly. It also saturates the accuracy at some point of time and finally degrades the model performance. Alternatively, it is a so-called gradient varnishing problem. Therefore, they used two residual blocks, which can help prevent the degrading problem and improve the accuracy. After that, they trained the model with CK++ and JAFFE datasets and obtained 95% of recognition rates, a result that is close to Mayya's model.

He and Zhang [7] designed a model consisting of two networks. The first network is a binary positive or negative classification model which is used to disintegrate the emotions into a binary class, and serves as an extra input to the second one for specific emotion recognition. When the input patches are fed into the network, the first model gives a positive or negative result to the second network and serves as prior knowledge. The second model extracts the features from input patches and gives the classification result based on the learned features and the prior binary result. From the study, they achieved up to 64% of overall accuracy using the Image Emotion Dataset, which contains downloaded images from Flickr and Instagram with searching eight emotions as keywords.

Chen et al. [8] developed a model for recognition of basic emotions with a limited amount of training images. It consists of three parts. The first part is the extraction of face-related features with deep face model VGG-16 [9]. The results of VGG-16 show that the adopted model obtained high performance in feature extraction. However, some features are not necessary for the recognition of facial expressions. Therefore, in the second part, they used k-means clustering to cluster all frames into two groups, such as peak-like frames and neutral-like frames. After clustering, they used the semi-classification method like Support Vector Machine (SVM++) to determine the clustered groups and retrieved the critical peak and neutral frames which are closer to the centers. After getting keyframes, they calculated differences between the key peak frame and the key neutral frame in order to eliminate the face identity information. Finally, in the last part, they perform multi-classification for basic classified emotions. Their experimental results show that their model achieved 78.4% of recognition rate using the Binghamton University 3D Facial Expression (BU3DFE) dataset.

Sabri and Kurita [10] show that the performance of the Convolution Neural Network (CNN) is dependent on the labeled data. With a limitation of labeled data, it is not feasible for CNN learn and extract information from the data. To get the general property of CNN, Koch et al. [11] proposed a Siamese network that can learn unfamiliar features by utilizing extra information about the relationship between input pairs. However, compared to the features representations that are explicitly learned by the model, the learned features by the Siamese network produces results lower than the average. Therefore, a triplet network model is introduced by Wang and Gupta [12] to overcome this problem. It consists of three input vectors instead of two in the Siamese network. Their results are comparable to the ones that are explicitly learned by the model. Moreover, the triplet network does not require the class labels of the processing input. Inspired by the benefits of the Siamese and Triple network models, Sabri and Kurita [10] use three data frames in their approach. The data frames consist of the onset, neutral, and apex of spatio-temporal data. They are used for the estimation of facial expression intensity against the basic emotions. Their study shows that it obtained the accuracy of up to 86% on the Cohn-Kanade (CK) facial expression dataset.

III. DAiSEE: Dataset for Affective States in E-Environment

To train our model, we utilize DAiSEE, which is a multi-labeled classification dataset. The number of interactions with computers has greatly increased in recent years, and the interaction between users and computers has become more significant than in the past. The interaction of the user with the system can change the response that the system returns, depending on the level of engagement of each user. Based on this effect, Gupta et al. [13] simulated the environment and constructed DAISEE dataset for testing the developed model. The dataset is used to recognize human affective states, which are based on how much users of an online system are engaged or satisfied while using the system. The examples of the application are online shopping, health care system, e-advertisement, online learning system, and others.

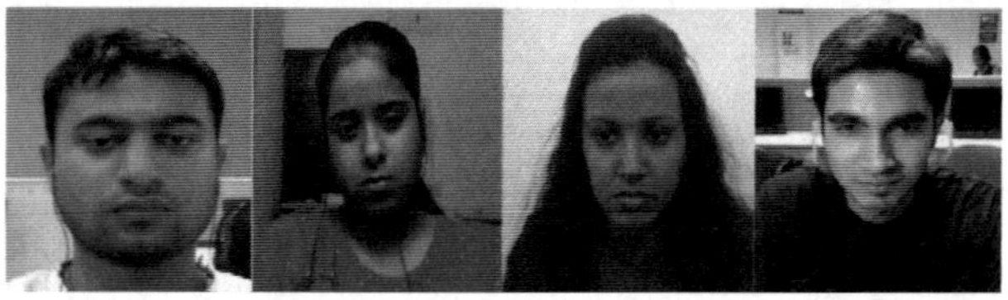

Figure 1. Examples images from DAiSEE dataset with engagement levels 0 (leftmost), 1, 2 and 3 (rightmost) respectively

DAiSEE consists of 9,068 videos with 10 seconds duration that is captured from 112 users for recognizing user affective states, such as boredom, confusion, engagement, and frustration. Gupta et al. [13] defined that levels of labels have four states ranging the values from 0 to 3. The engagement values '0', '1', '2' and '3' namely refer to 'very low level', 'low', 'high' and 'very high' level of engagement respectively. The example images with different engagement levels from the DAiSEE dataset are shown in Figure 1.

IV. The Applied Method

In this section, we describe the applied methods in the implementation stage. Figure 2 shows our proposed model.

Training a deep convolution neural network requires a massive amount of labeled data. If the labels are not enough for training, the model cannot learn properly on unknown data and lead to an over-fitting problem. Since research topics related to face, such as face detection and recognition, have been developed from a few decades ago, the techniques and learning methods to solve these types of problems are nearly optimum. Besides, there are different types of large scale face datasets for evaluation of these methods. Unfortunately, these datasets are useful for face detection and recognition but not for engagement. To overcome this issue, we use the transfer learning technique, which can transfer the learned features from one specific problem to another if both problems are similar. For example, face recognition and engagement recognition are quite similar to each other, because both are recognition based on the face. In face recognition that is based

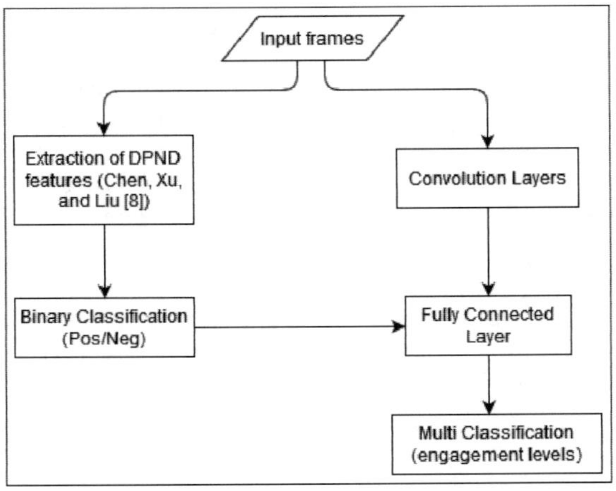

Figure 2. The proposed system design

on the deep learning method, it needs to extract prominent face features for classification. The outcome is similar to engagement recognition, that classifies the level of engagement based on facial expressions; it also requires prominent facial features that are changing in image sequences. As a result, we can transfer learned features from face problems to engagement estimation problems.

For a base model, we used the VGG-16 face model, which is pre-trained on large-scaled face datasets, comprising 2.6 million images. Parkhi et al. [9] collected the face images and classified them into 2,622 classes of celebrities. The based-model achieved over 98% accuracy in face recognition. Recognizable results of the VGG-16 model proved that it could learn face features for face recognition by all means. Inspired by the advantage of the VGG-16 model, we adopted the VGG-16 model for the extraction of deep representations of input frames.

Unfortunately, features that are extracted by the model for face recognition may contain face identity information, which is useful for face recognition but not for engagement estimation, because VGG-16 is explicitly trained for recognizing faces. Therefore, it is necessary to eliminate face-related information. We used the technique from Chen et al. [8] to eliminate face identity information. In their method, they used Deep Peak Neutral Difference (DPND) features for training the model. In DPND features, they removed face identity information by finding the differences between key peak and key neutral frames. The reason is that appearances are changing only in the face in different frames. As a result, by finding differences among these keyframes, we can obtain the features for recognition of engagement only.

After we obtained the extracted features, the features are classified into binary class, namely positive and negative classes. In parallel, we fed the same input to convolution layers to extract features and used the binary classification result to assist the final multi-classification. The result is for recognizing levels of engagement, ranging values from 0 to 3.

A. Preprocessing

DAiSEE dataset provides the videos with 10 seconds duration in which students' facial expressions are recorded while playing lectures. To feed these videos to the model, they are converted into frames sequences by using Fast Forward Motion Picture Experts Group (FFmpeg) [14] video converter. It converts the videos into frame sequences with 30 frames per second (fps) and gives 300 frames per video. In Gupta et al. [13], they defined each video with engagement labels. Therefore, each frame sequence that is extracted from videos is also labeled the same as videos.

B. Extraction of Deep Representations of Frames

Inspired by the advantages of the VGG-16 face model, which is developed by Parkhi et al. [9], we used their model as a based development of our model network to extract prominent features of the face. In the architecture of the VGG-16 model, it uses five blocks of convolution layers, followed by max-pooling layers.

After constructing the model, the input frames are fed into the network; it converts the images into matrix representation and passes it to convolution layers. At the convolution layers, it does pairwise multiplication with kernels throughout the whole matrix to get the general features of the entire image and gives the feature maps as an outcome. This result is passed to max-pooling layers to reduce the dimension of feature maps, followed by non-linear activation, so-called Rectified Linear Unit (relu), to return the result. The activation unit activates the neuron if the inputs are greater than zero; otherwise, it does not activate and returns zero as a result. In the configuration of the VGG-16 model, the input image is limited to 224 by 224 dimensions. The 3 by 3 as kernels are used and defined as the first block of the convolution layer. Similar to the first block, the next four convolution blocks are designed and followed by fully connected layers to perform multi-classification.

1) Extraction Features by VGG-16 Model with Engagement Labels: In the first step, before inputting the frames into the VGG-16 model, we used the same processing steps of the VGG-16 model by Parkhi et al. [9]. In their study, they fed the model with cropped 224 by 224 patches of input images from four corners and centers. They also performed data-augmentation of horizontal flipping with a 50% probability during training. For our study, we performed the preprocessing steps similar to Parkhi's study and visualized the result of preprocessing, as shown in Figure 3.

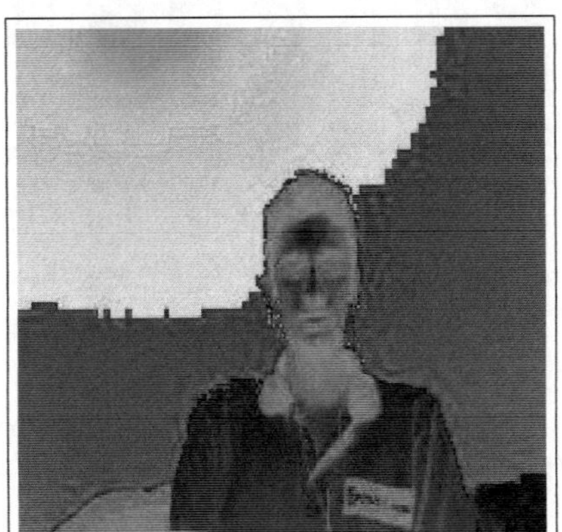

Figure 3. Visualization Preprocessing Result of VGG-16

In order to get a better understanding of extracted features from convolution layers, the feature maps are visualized from the first and last convolution blocks, as shown in Figures 4 and 5, respectively. In visualization, all feature maps of the first and last blocks of convolution layers are visualized as 8 by 8 square images. The result shows that some feature maps are focusing on the foreground, whereas the others are focusing on the background. According to the visualization result, the feature maps of the first convolution layer still have the input shapes, and we can guess what feature maps look like by looking at the visualization of feature maps. However, visualization of the last block of the convolution layer shows that a deeper layer of deep neural network extracts more general features rather than the shallow layers for classification. It implies that if we want to get more general deep representations, we have to use the result from deeper layers. Therefore, we compared the discrimination capabilities of fully connected layers, namely 'fc6' and 'fc7', adopted by Parkhi et al. [9].

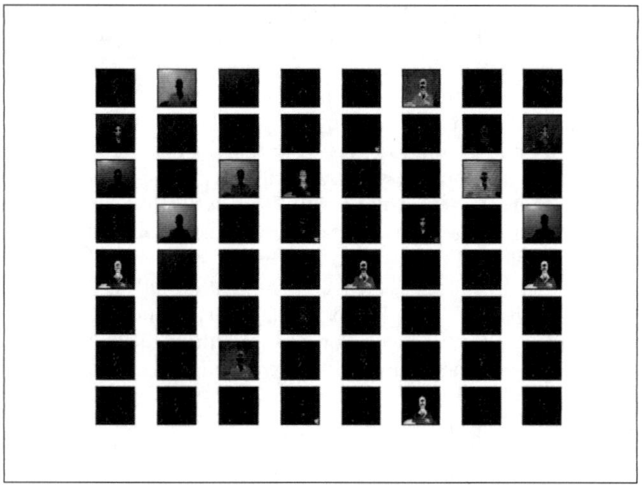

Figure 4. Visualization of Feature Maps from Convolution Layer (1st block)

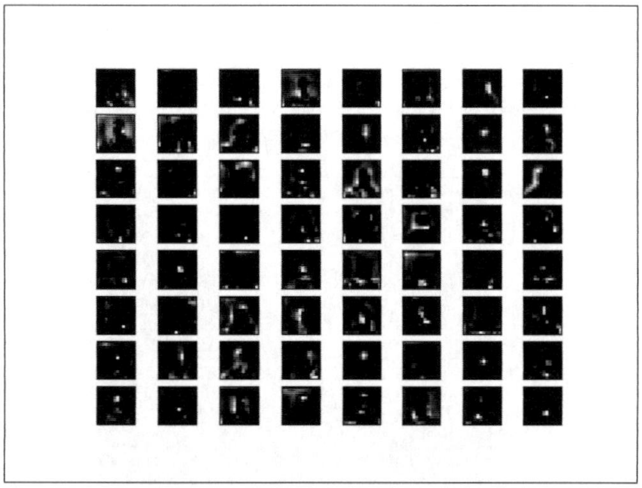

Figure 5. Visualization of Feature Maps from Convolution Layer (5th block)

For the evaluation of the model, we used 8,100 images for training and 2,100 images for testing. DAiSEE has 16 million frames from 112 users, which supports deep learning models. However, our purpose is to reuse the extracted features from the pre-trained model, such as VGG-16, for transferring the prior information and saving training time instead of learning from scratch. Therefore, we restricted our dataset to be small based on our purpose, and 0.005% samples of the original dataset are randomly selected from the video sequences. The randomized numbers of training images and validation are shown in Table I.

TABLE I. SAMPLES SET STRUCTURE

Train Labels	*# of samples*	*Validation Labels*	*# of samples*
Label 0	300	**Label 0**	**0**
Label 1	**0**	Label 1	600
Label 2	3600	Label 2	900
Label 3	4200	Label 3	600

Randomized selection of samples from the dataset cannot fairly cover all the labels. According to Table I, there are no samples sequences of engagement label '1' for training and label '0' for validation. So that, randomized samples from both sets are combined into a set and utilized leave-one-out of the v-fold cross-validation method [15]. It splits the dataset into a 'v' number of subsets and uses one subset for validation. The remaining subsets are for training the model. We repeated the process up to 10-fold. 9 fold is used for training the model, and the remaining is for validated the model. The results of 10-fold cross-validation are shown in Table II. We obtained an accuracy of around 50% for both training and validation.

TABLE II. LOSS AND ACCURACY OF FINE-TUNING VGG-16 MODEL WITH 10-FOLD CROSS VALIDATION

# of epoch	*train_loss*	*train_accuracy*	*val_loss*	*val_accuracy*
1	1.1204	0.4625	0.9317	0.4725
2	0.9471	0.4654	0.9250	0.4422
3	0.9398	0.4657	0.9091	0.4471
4	0.9309	0.4690	0.8864	0.4588
5	0.9233	0.4696	0.9083	0.4657
6	0.9246	0.4620	0.9006	0.4588
7	0.9223	0.4618	0.8804	**0.4784**
8	0.9188	0.4669	0.8933	0.4824
9	0.9114	**0.4747**	0.9353	0.4745
10	0.9168	0.4703	0.8839	0.4765

TABLE III. LOSS AND ACCURACY OF DEEP REPRESENTATIONS FROM 'FC6' DENSE LAYER

# of epoch	*train_loss*	*train_accuracy*	*val_loss*	*val_accuracy*
1	1.5751	0.4728	4.0148	0.4657
2	8.3836	**0.4814**	13.4151	0.4657
3	13.8168	0.4764	14.5101	0.4765
4	14.3863	0.4748	14.8962	0.4814
5	14.5621	0.4796	14.9514	0.4549
6	14.6212	0.4723	14.8178	**0.4941**
7	14.7216	0.4719	14.7799	0.4814
8	14.7823	0.4749	14.5372	0.4853
9	14.7558	0.4769	14.7691	0.4843
10	14.8142	0.4748	14.7804	0.4843

To determine which layers are suitable to extract more general features, we followed the usage from Parkhi et al. [9]. The fully connected layers, namely, 'fc6' and 'fc7', are considered as candidate layers. They are the last two layers before the final classification for deep representations. We utilized linear Support Vector Machine (SVM) to investigate the abilities of the facial expressions classification and compared the results from these two dense layers. The results are shown in Tables III and IV for 'fc6' and 'fc7' layers, respectively. Based on

TABLE IV. LOSS AND ACCURACY OF DEEP REPRESENTATIONS FROM 'FC7' DENSE LAYER

# of epoch	*train_loss*	*train_accuracy*	*val_loss*	*val_accuracy*
1	11.1773	0.4644	13.8237	0.4716
2	12.5062	0.4667	13.7523	0.4637
3	12.4247	0.4700	13.5395	0.4696
4	12.4178	0.4666	13.6752	**0.4892**
5	13.6556	0.4664	14.6021	0.4716
6	13.9989	0.4658	14.2492	0.4824
7	13.9343	**0.4745**	14.1655	0.4657
8	14.0053	0.4686	14.2087	0.4745
9	13.9698	0.4690	14.1892	0.4706
10	13.9838	0.4667	14.3439	0.4853

the results, deep representations from 'fc6' dense layers can extract more general features. Therefore, they are used in the next section.

C. Clustering of Peak and Neutral Frames

According to our proposed method, we obtained deep representations for engagement estimation from the 'fc6' layer of the VGG-16 model. We discovered that the detection of peak and neutral frames are essential to assist in the estimation process. In order to determine the peak and neutral frames, firstly, all of the frames are clustered into two groups. A first group is a peak-like group, and the second one is a neutral-like group. In this case, the number of clusters is known, numerically 2, which categorizes the frames into peak and neutral. Therefore, the k-means method is used for the clustering task because of its simplicity and optimum if the number of k is known.

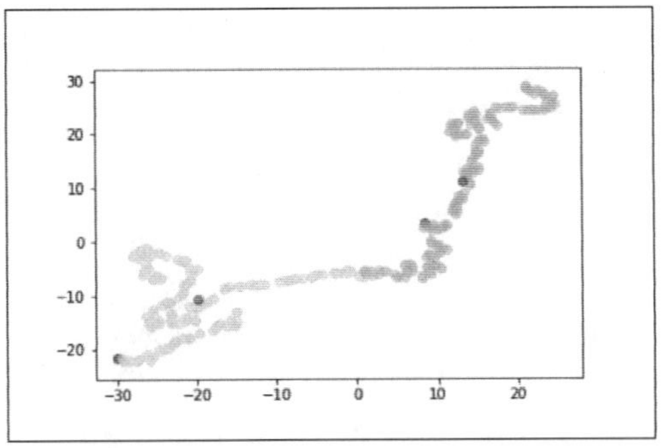

Figure 6. k-means cluster for peak and neutral frames where red: centers, black: sample, green: cluster 0, blue: cluster 1

Figure 7. Samples from k-means cluster 0 (left) and cluster 1 (right)

However, deep representations which are obtained from the 'fc6' layer of VGG-16 have 4,096 dimensions. It is not feasible to perform clustering as the data are in the form of a high dimension. Therefore, before the clustering method is performed, it is crucial to make dimension reduction in dealing with this high dimensional data. The dimension reduction technique is performed by using t-Distributed Stochastic Neighbor Embedding (t-SNE), which is a non-linear feature extraction method. The non-linear feature extraction method calculates the probability distributions of similarity of points in both high and low dimensions. It also minimizes the difference between these two distributions by using Kullback-Leibler divergence [16]. The reason for choosing the t-SNE method is because of the non-linear property of deep representations. In the VGG-16 model, Rectified Linear-Unit (relu) activation units are used to select the suitable neurons in the network to propagate the data. Besides, relu is a limited type of non-linear function due to the selection of maximum value between 0 and x (input). It serves as a linear function if the inputs are negative values, whereas it will be a non-linear function for positive inputs. Therefore, after applying non-linear activation units to filter the neuron. As a result, the output feature maps have non-linear properties. It is comprised of 4,096 dimensions. These dimensions are reduced from 4096 to 2, and the clustering results are shown in Figure 6. In addition, the samples from the experimental result of two clusters are reconstructed and visualized in Figure 7. In Figure 7, after k-means clustering, the first frame of a video sequence is classified as cluster 0. Generally, facial expressions of the student at the beginning of the lectures seem to be relaxed and have neutral expressions. As the lecture continued, based on their engagement levels, facial expressions of the students changed. We discovered that in cluster 1, the student is looking at the camera and seems to be interested in the lecture. Therefore, the frames in the cluster 1 are classified as peak frames, whereas the others in the cluster 0 are classified as neutral frames.

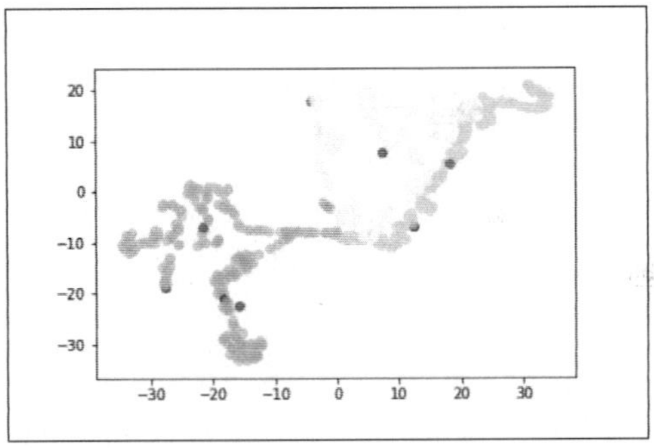

Figure 8. k-means cluster for peak and neutral frames where red or dark blue: centers, black: samples, green and yellow: cluster 0, blue and pink: cluster 1

Figure 9. Samples from k-means cluster 0

The way for expressing internal feelings depends on people and their characteristics. Each person expresses six basic

Figure 10. Samples from k-means cluster 1

emotions in different ways. For example, the first person shows happiness with a smiling face, whereas the second one expresses with laughing. In an alternative word, it is conditioning on individual differences. Therefore, individual differences among different people are also considered in clustering for peak-like and neutral-like groups. The same procedures are performed, and the experimental results are shown in Figure 8. After clustering, peak and neutral frames are grouped together based on their respective features. Besides, the samples from each cluster are also shown in Figures 9 and 10 for both cluster 0 and cluster 1. Based on the visualization result, persons from cluster 0 in Figure 9 are looking at the camera directly and seem to be listening to their lectures. Their faces express normal expressions compared to samples from cluster 1. However, in Figure 10, the person in the right image shows that his eyes were looking away from the camera and did not concentrate on the lectures. Therefore, according to their facial expressions, cluster 1 can be classified as a group of peak frames, whereas cluster 0 can be classified as a group of neutral frames.

V. Conclusion and Future Work

To conclude our study, we discovered that the deep learning-based methods require a large scale of labeled data. However, in some problems, obtaining the desired dataset for training is impossible. In order to overcome the dataset limitation, the transfer learning technique is performed to train the proposed model. The process consists of two steps. In the first stage, fine-tuning the pre-trained model is performed. Moreover, the benefit of the VGG-16 model, such as a higher face recognition rate, is used to assist in engagement estimation and to reduce the process of computational time and resources while training the model. In our experimental result, we achieved the result of fine-tuning up to 50% of accuracy. Although the results still have gaps to make improvements. Fortunately, we discovered that these results could be compared with the ones that are obtained from explicitly training for engagement estimation without using transfer learning.

For a second stage of the model, elimination of face identity information is performed. All frames are divided into two groups: peak-like frames and neutral-like frames. So to dealing with this problem, k-means clustering is performed. The frame is clustered based on individual differences because of the differences in expressing their internal emotions. According to our result, k-means clustering shows that it performed well to divide the same people characteristic into the same group. We also obtained the peak-like and neutral-like frames clusters based on individual differences. In the future, we will improve our proposed model to handle more levels of facial expressions on online learning engagement.

Acknowledgment

This work was supported by IMAGICA GROUP. We would like to express our sincere gratitude to their support during our research project.

References

[1] R. W. Larson and M. H. Richards, “Boredom in the middle school years: Blaming schools versus blaming students,” American journal of education, vol. 99, 1991, pp. 418–443, ISSN: 0195-6744.

[2] T. R. Almaev and M. F. Valstar, “Local gabor binary patterns from three orthogonal planes for automatic facial expression recognition,” in 2013 Humaine Association Conference on Affective Computing and Intelligent Interaction. IEEE, 2013, pp. 356–361, ISSN: 0769550487, URL: https://ieeexplore.ieee.org/ [accessed: 2020-02-23].

[3] W.-L. Chao, J.-J. Ding, and J.-Z. Liu, “Facial expression recognition based on improved local binary pattern and class-regularized locality preserving projection,” Signal Processing, vol. 117, 2015, pp. 1–10, ISSN: 0165-1684.

[4] Z. Luo, L. Liu, J. Chen, Y. Liu, and Z. Su, “Spontaneous smile recognition for interest detection,” in Chinese Conference on Pattern Recognition. Springer Singapore, 2016, pp. 119–130, ISBN: 978-981-10-3002-4 , URL: https://link.springer.com/ [accessed: 2020-02-23].

[5] V. Mayya, R. M. Pai, and M. M. Pai, “Automatic facial expression recognition using dcnn,” Procedia Computer Science, vol. 93, 2016, pp. 453–461, ISSN: 1877-0509.

[6] D. K. Jain, P. Shamsolmoali, and P. Sehdev, “Extended deep neural network for facial emotion recognition,” Pattern Recognition Letters, vol. 120, 2019, pp. 69–74, ISSN: 0167-8655.

[7] X. He and W. Zhang, “Emotion recognition by assisted learning with convolutional neural networks,” Neurocomputing, vol. 291, 2018, pp. 187–194, ISSN: 0925-2312.

[8] J. Chen, R. Xu, and L. Liu, “Deep peak-neutral difference feature for facial expression recognition,” Multimedia Tools and Applications, vol. 77, 2018, pp. 29 871–29 887, ISSN: 1380-7501.

[9] O. M. Parkhi, A. Vedaldi, A. Zisserman et al., “Deep face recognition.” in bmvc, vol. 1, no. 3. British Machine Vision Association, 2015, p. 1–12, URL: https://ora.ox.ac.uk/ [accessed: 2020-02-23].

[10] M. Sabri and T. Kurita, “Facial expression intensity estimation using siamese and triplet networks,” Neurocomputing, vol. 313, 2018, pp. 143–154, ISSN: 0925-2312.

[11] G. Koch, R. Zemel, and R. Salakhutdinov, “Siamese neural networks for one-shot image recognition,” in ICML deep learning workshop, vol. 2. Lille, 2015, URL: http://www.cs.toronto.edu/ [accessed: 2020-02-23].

[12] X. Wang and A. Gupta, “Unsupervised learning of visual representations using videos,” in Proceedings of the IEEE International Conference on Computer Vision, December 2015, pp. 2794–2802, URL: http://openaccess.thecvf.com/ [accessed: 2020-02-23].

[13] A. Gupta, A. D’Cunha, K. Awasthi, and V. Balasubramanian, “Daisee: Towards user engagement recognition in the wild,” CoRR, vol. abs/1609.01885, 2016.

[14] “FFmpeg,” URL: https://www.ffmpeg.org/ [accessed: 2020-02-23].

[15] P. Burman, “A comparative study of ordinary cross-validation, v-fold cross-validation and the repeated learning-testing methods,” Biometrika, vol. 76, 1989, pp. 503–514, ISSN: 1464-3510.

[16] S. Kullback and R. A. Leibler, “On information and sufficiency,” The annals of mathematical statistics, vol. 22, 1951, pp. 79–86, ISSN: 0003-4851.

Facial Mimicry Training Based on 3D Morphable Face Models

Oky Dicky Ardiansyah Prima, Hisayoshi Ito
Graduate School of Software and Information Science, Iwate Pref. Univ.
Takizawa, Japan
email: {prima, hito}@iwate-pu.ac.jp

Takahiro Tomizawa
Hitachi Ind. & Ctrl. Solutions
Yokohama, Japan
email: Takahiro.tomizawa.ax@hitachi.com

Takashi Imabuchi
Office of Regional Collaboration, Iwate Pref. Univ.
Takizawa, Japan
email: t_ima@ipu-office.iwate-pu.ac.jp

Abstract— **The recent techniques of automated facial expression recognition from facial images have achieved human perception levels. The application of this technology is expected not to be limited to facial expression analysis, but also to evaluate how well someone mimics another person's expression. Facial mimic training will help people improve their interpersonal communication and that, in turn, will improve their work performance. This study proposes a self-learning-based expression training system using a simple 3D Morphable Face Model (3DMM). The proposed system analyzes faces of a subject and a given picture of a person who the subject is mimicking. The 68 facial landmarks for both faces are detected automatically and are used to fit a 3DMM using a deformation transfer technique. Our experiment shows that the proposed system accurately measures the similarity of facial appearance between subjects and their corresponding mimic targets. Thus, the proposed system can be used as a facial mimicry training tool to improve social communication.**

Keywords-mimicry; expression training; emotion; image processing.

I. INTRODUCTION

Non-verbal (unspoken) communication plays an important role in providing additional information and cues over verbal communication. Facial expression is a type of non-verbal (spoken) communication that involves subtle signals of the larger communication process. For example, a smile, typically with the corners of the mouth turned up and the front teeth exposed, may indicate joy. Frowning, typically by turning down the corners of the mouth, forms an expression of disapproval.

While culture differences might cause differences in the absolute level of emotional intensity, the basic facial expressions such as happiness, surprise, sadness, fear, disgust, and anger are similar throughout the world [1]. The Facial Action Code System (FACS), which is based on the anatomical basis of facial movement, is a traditional measure to analyze facial expressions [2]. Individual facial muscle movements are encoded by FACS from slightly different instantaneous changes in facial appearance. Each Action Unit (AU) is described in the FACS manual.

Early attempts have been conducted to automate facial expressions using FACS. Bartlett et al. [3] applied computer image analysis to classify the basic elements that comprise complex facial movements. Their method classified six upper facial actions with 91% accuracy by combining three approaches: holistic spatial analysis, measurement of local facial features, and estimation of motion flow fields. However, this method was not fully automated, such as the initial facial alignment needs mouse clicks at the center of each eye. Tian et al. [4] developed an Automatic Face Analysis (AFA) system, which recognizes changes in facial expression into AUs. Initial detections of facial features, such as lips, eyes, brows and cheeks were done using template matching [5]. AFA has achieved around 96% recognition rates for upper and lower AUs, whether they occur alone or in combinations.

With the recent computer vision techniques, the conventional procedure to recognize facial expressions such as face detection, face alignment, facial feature extraction, and expression classification can be done in realtime. Affdex [6], one of the most widely used face analysis systems, provides a cross-platform realtime multi-face expression recognition. It uses Support Vector Machine (SVM) to train 10,000 manually coded facial images [7]. Affdex can achieve acceptable accuracy to detect facial expressions that are expressed externally on a face where certain parts of the face change significantly.

Automated facial expression recognition has been used in the development of humanoid robots to enable them to mimic human-like emotions [8]. Mimicking emotion is the act of imitating the facial expression of others and it is considered central for social interactions. The humanoid robot can be used as an experiment tool to construct a communication model of mimicry. A sophisticated model of mimicry will be useful to train people to improve social interactions through non-verbal communication [9].

Recently, 3D morphable models (3DMM) [10] have been widely used to create virtual faces in some software application programs, such as Augmented Reality (AR) and messaging apps. The advanced computer vision techniques have enabled to fit the model to the corresponding facial image. Moreover, it is possible to design virtual characters that can express different emotions such as compound emotions that are a mix of basic emotion expressions. Now, "Animoji"s exist, which are animated emoticons created by mirroring one's own facial expressions.

This study proposes a self-learning-based facial mimicry training system based on 3DMM to measure how close a person can mimic another person's facial expressions. The

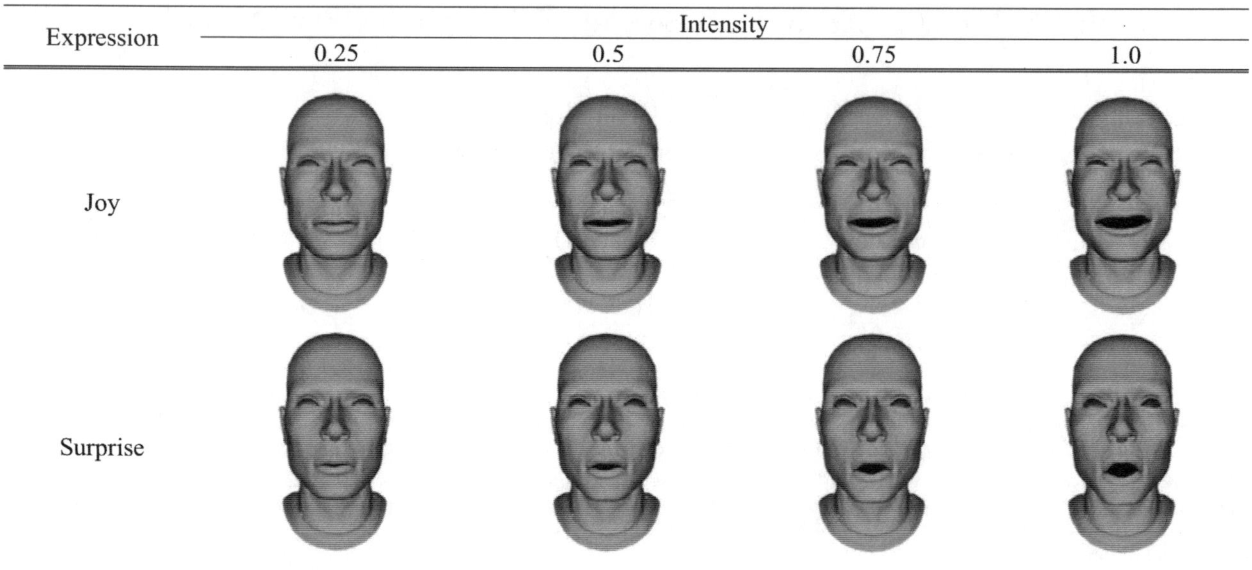

Figure 1. Some facial expressions generated using 3DMM.

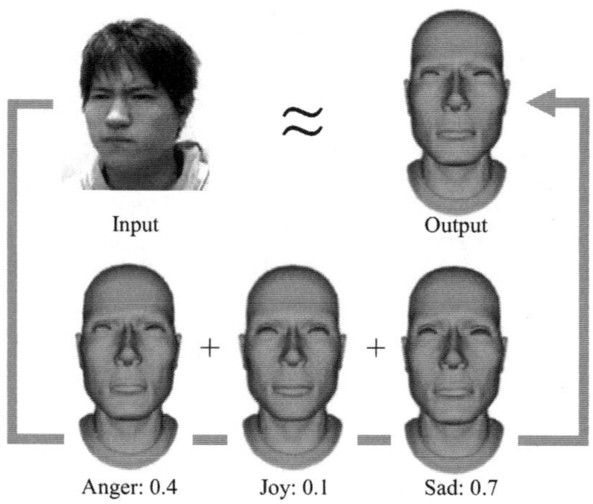

Figure 2. A corresponding 3DMM for a subject.

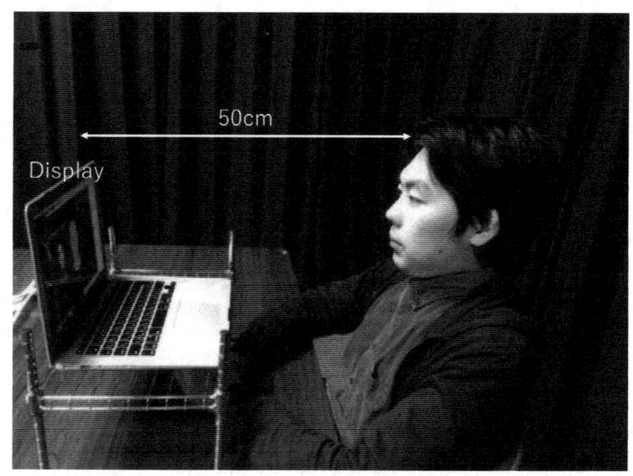

Figure 3. The experiment setup in this study.

proposed system uses blended emotive expressions of the models to find the most similar shape that matches a given facial image. This paper is organized as follows. Section II discusses known approaches to facial expression imitation. Section III introduces our proposed facial mimicry training system. Section IV shows the experiment results of the proposed system. Finally, Section V gives a short conclusion and highlights the most important outcomes of this paper.

II. Related Work

3DMM is a well-established technique in computer graphics that produces expressive and plausible animations. This technique has been used to clone expressions from one face mesh to another. The cloning processes take two steps: determining surface points in the target correspond to vertices in the source model and transfer motion vectors from vertices of the source model to the target model. Sumner and Popović [10] proposed deformation transfer for triangle meshes, where the cloning process does not require the source and the target model to share a number of vertices or triangles. Figure 1 demonstrates deformations of faces [10] based on their expressions where the expression intensity varies from 0 to 1.0.

To fit 3DMM into a facial image, some points of 3DMM are associated to the corresponding landmark points in the facial image [11]. Extracting landmark points from facial images can be done using automated facial landmarks tools, such as Dlib library [12]. Those 2-dimensional (2D) landmarks are mapped into 3-dimensional (3D) using a 2D-to-3D registration method by referring to 3D facial points. The

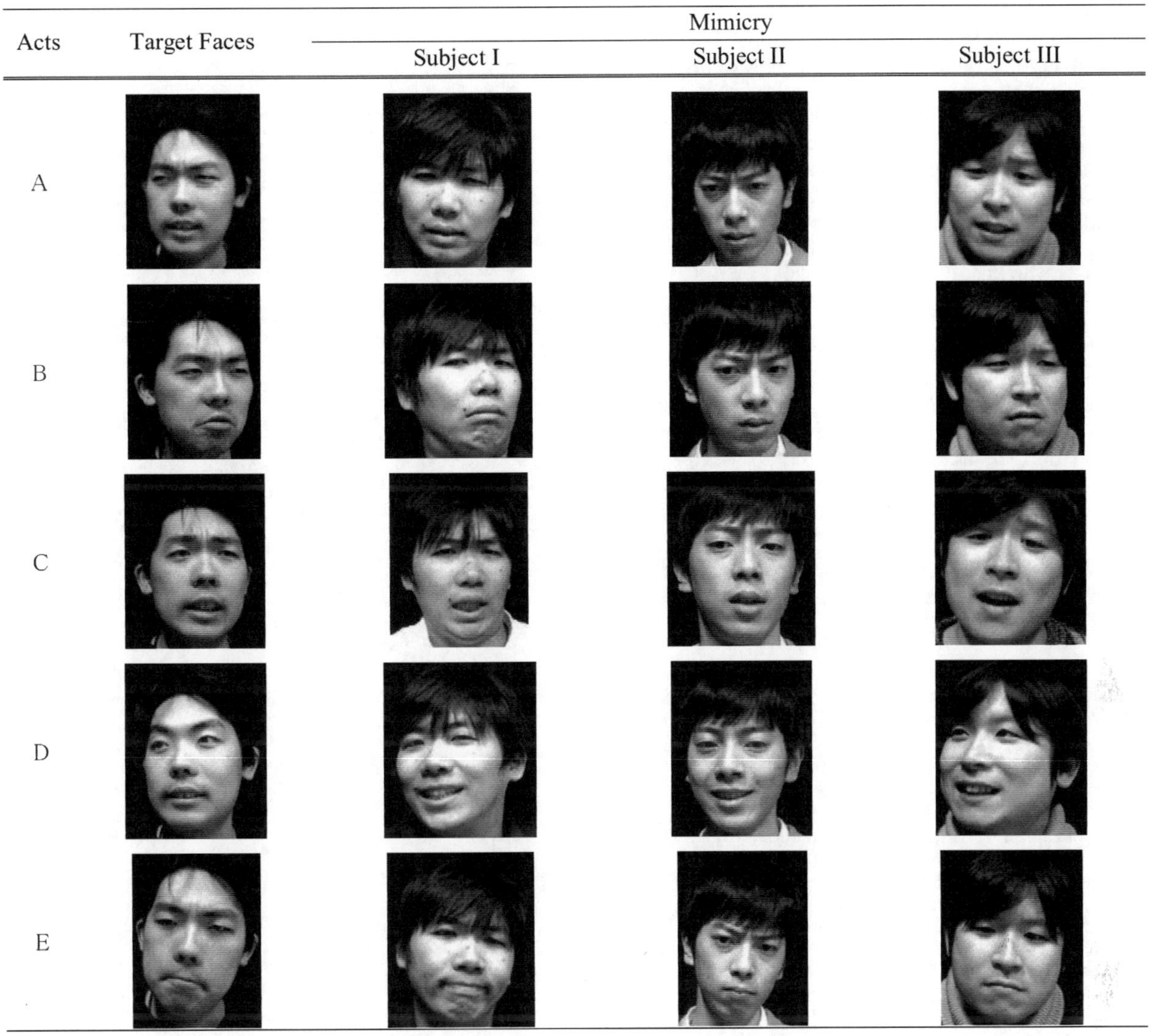

Figure 4. Results of mimicry training performed by three subjects.

resulted 3D landmarks are used for head-pose normalization. Figure 2 shows 3DMM imitating a subject's expression by blended emotive expressions.

III. Facial Mimicry Training

Our facial mimicry training system uses Dlib library to automatically annotate 68 landmarks from the facial image. These landmarks are associated to 3D face points [13] and then the head pose is calculated. SolvePnP library is used to solve the Perspective-n-Point (PnP) problem to perform 2D-to-3D registration [14].

Figure 3 shows the experimental setup in this study. The system uses a built-in webcam to capture the subject's face. The subject selects a target face to mimic from the database. While mimicking the target faces, subjects are instructed to adjust their head posture to match the target faces. When the subjects feel that they have precisely mimicked the target face, they press the "analyze" button to analysis the score for the mimicry. During the experiment, we did not specify the time required by each subject to mimic a target face. The resulted 3DMM for the subject is outputted along with the 3DMM for each emotive expression that makes up the result. The score for the mimicry is calculated as the correlation coefficient between the 3D points of the generated 3DMM for the subject and the target.

IV. Result

Three male subjects (mean age 21.7 years) were recruited for the experiments. All subjects agreed to participate and signed the consent forms, to allow their data to be used in publications of this research. Figure 4 shows the results of mimicry training performed by the subjects.

Table I to III show the correlation coefficients of the resulted mimics by the three subjects against the target faces. There are high correlations among the 3DMM of target faces and subjects' faces mimicking those target faces (values shown on gray background). Here, the correlation coefficients are above 0.98 for 3DMM of the target faces and their mimicries. When subjects were mimicking different faces, the correlation coefficients are below 0.94. These results show that, although most different places in the changes in facial expressions only occur at the upper part of the face (eyes and eyebrows) and the lower part of the face (lips), there is significant correlation between 3DMM and their mimicries.

V. Conclusion and Future Work

In this study, we have demonstrated that our self-learning-based facial mimicry training system is able to measure how close a person can mimic another person's facial expressions. By using this tool, users can train themselves to closely mimic someone's face interactively by referring to the expression intensity of each 3DMM constructing the blended 3DMM. In our further study, we will confirm the performance of the training system using a fine 3DMM that is generated from a large three-dimensional face dataset [15].

TABLE I. CORRELATION COEFFICIENTS OF THE RESULTED MIMICS BY THE SUBJECT I AGAINST THE TARGET FACES.

		Target Faces				
		A	B	C	D	E
Mimicries	A	0.994	0.908	0.894	0.913	0.873
	B	0.913	0.991	0.907	0.925	0.899
	C	0.881	0.891	0.987	0.926	0.923
	D	0.905	0.917	0.931	0.993	0.929
	E	0.87	0.891	0.923	0.924	0.997

TABLE II. CORRELATION COEFFICIENTS OF THE RESULTED MIMICS BY THE SUBJECT II AGAINST THE TARGET FACES.

		Target Faces				
		A	B	C	D	E
Mimicries	A	0.988	0.908	0.892	0.906	0.867
	B	0.913	0.994	0.906	0.923	0.896
	C	0.88	0.888	0.985	0.926	0.927
	D	0.894	0.91	0.924	0.989	0.925
	E	0.847	0.872	0.908	0.906	0.985

TABLE III. CORRELATION COEFFICIENTS OF THE RESULTED MIMICS BY THE SUBJECT III AGAINST THE TARGET FACES.

		Target Faces				
		A	B	C	D	E
Mimicries	A	0.997	0.912	0.899	0.915	0.877
	B	0.919	0.995	0.911	0.928	0.901
	C	0.895	0.903	0.998	0.935	0.93
	D	0.912	0.924	0.934	0.997	0.929
	E	0.866	0.888	0.921	0.921	0.996

References

[1] P. Ekman et al., "Universals and cultural differences in the judgments of facial expressions of emotion," *Journal of Personality and Social Psychology*, 53(4), pp.712-717, 1987.

[2] M. S. Bartlett, J. C. Hager, P. Ekman, and T. J. Sejnowski, "Measuring facial expressions by computer," Psychophysiology, Cambridge University Press, 36(2), pp. 253–263, 1999.

[3] M. Bartlett, J. Hager, P. Ekman, and T. Sejnowski, "Measuring Facial Expressions by Computer Image Analysis," *Psychophysiology*, vol. 36, pp. 253-263, 1999.

[4] Y. L. Tian, T. Kanade, and J. F. Cohn, "Recognizing lower face action units for facial expression analysis." Proceedings - 4th IEEE International Conference on Automatic Face and Gesture Recognition, FG 2000, 23(2), pp. 484–490, 2000.

[5] Y. Tian, T. Kanade, and J. F. Cohn, "Dual-State Parametric Eye Tracking," Proc. International Conference on Automatic Face and Gesture Recognition, pp. 110- 115, Mar. 2000.

[6] D. McDuff et al., "AFFDEX SDK: A cross-platform real-time multi-face expression recognition toolkit," Conference on Human Factors in Computing Systems, pp. 3723–3726, 2016. https://doi.org/10.1145/2851581.2890247

[7] M. Magdin, L. Benko, and Š. Koprda, "A case study of facial emotion classification using affdex," Sensors, 19(9), pp. 1–17, 2019. https://doi.org/10.3390/s19092140

[8] H. Miwa et al., "Effective emotional expressions with Emotion Expression Humanoid Robot WE-4RII - Integration of humanoid robot hand RCH-1," 2004 IEEE/RSJ International Conference on Intelligent Robots and Systems (IROS), 3(4), pp. 2203–2208, 2004.

[9] K. Ito and Y. Nishimua, "An Interaction Analysis of System Usage: User-Instructor Interaction on the System named 'iFace'," *The Transactions of Human Interface Society*, 16(1), pp. 51–62, 2014. (in Japanese)

[10] R. W. Sumner and J. Popović, "Deformation Transfer for Triangle Meshes," *ACM Transactions on Graphics*, 23(3), pp. 399-405, 2004.

[11] H. Dai, N. Pears, W. Smith, and C. Duncan, "A 3D Morphable Model of Craniofacial Shape and Texture Variation," In 2017 IEEE International Conference on Computer Vision (ICCV), pp. 3085–3093, 2016.

[12] V. Kazemi and J. Sullivan, "One millisecond face alignment with an ensemble of regression trees," Proceedings of the IEEE Conference on Computer Vision and Pattern Recognition (CVPR 2014), pp. 1867–1874, 2014.

[13] X. Zhang. Face 3D Model File in CSV. [Online]. Available: https://xiaohaionline.com/wp-content/uploads/2017/10/average-face3d.csv [retrieved: March, 2020]

[14] X. X. Lu, "A Review of Solutions for Perspective-n-Point Problem in Camera Pose Estimation," In First International Conference on Advanced Algorithms and Control Engineering, pp. 1–8, 2018. https://doi.org/doi :10.1088/1742-6596/1087/5/052009

[15] B. Eggerr et al., "3D Morphable Face Models -- Past, Present and Future," ArXiv Preprint ArXiv:1909.01815, 2019.

A Perspective-Corrected Stylus Pen for 3D Interaction

Rintaro Takahashi, Katsuyoshi Hotta, Oky Dicky Ardiansyah Prima, Hisayoshi Ito
Graduate School of Software and Information Science, Iwate Prefectural University
152-52 Sugo Takizawa, Japan
email: { g231r019, g236q004}@s.iwate-pu.ac.jp, {prima, hito}@iwate-pu.ac.jp

***Abstract*—Compared to traditional flat displays, the three-dimensional (3D) spherical display allows us to see images more naturally from any directions. This display can show not only surface information data, such as digital globes, but also 3D objects. Some user interfaces, such as multi-touch and gesture interfaces, have been implemented on this display. In this study, we propose a novel perspective-corrected stylus pen that can be used for 3D interaction with the display. The stylus pen has six Degrees of Freedom (6DoF) and can be used as pointing and drawing device in the 3D space within the spherical display. Therefore, the user can see the auxiliary line from the pen tip from a different angle. We demonstrated the stylus in terms of accuracy, pointing stability and how users can correctly perceive it in the 3D space. Some applications, such as selecting objects inside a virtual fish tank, were presented to show the usability of the proposed stylus.**

Keywords-VR; 3D stylus; spherical display; virtual reality; perception.

I. INTRODUCTION

In recent years, non-planar displays have been actively developed. These displays can display images that are more effective and immersive than flat displays. Non-planar displays can be broadly classified into three types: curved, cylindrical, and spherical. Curved displays have already been put to practical use in mobile devices. They provide excellent visibility even at the edges of the screen. Therefore, some additional information can be put on the edge of the screen. Cylindrical displays are expected to be new digital signages which can effectively display advertisements. Spherical displays, on the other hand, can display images from any angle. These displays can display not only surface information data, such as digital globes, but can also display three-dimensional (3D) objects inside.

Many efforts have been conducted to produce spherical displays. These include a combination of multiple small flat display panels (Geo-Cosmos [1]), synchronized rotating Light-Emitting Diode (LED) strips [2], and a projection mapping system using a Digital Light Processing (DLP) projector [3]. PufferSphere [4], a commercially projector-based spherical display, has a multitouch interface allowing human interaction with the display, such as pointing and rotating.

The spherical display can be enhanced to represent 3D objects [5]. The 3D experiences can be achieved by using monocular (motion parallax) or binocular (stereoscopic) cues. Motion parallax is a type of depth perception cue in which objects that are closer appear to move faster than objects that are further. Stereoscopic vision refers to the sense of depth derived from the two eyes. Fafard et al. [6] indicate that users' performance in various 3D interactions, such as pattern alignment, distance estimation, 3D selection, and 3D manipulation is consistently better when stereo cues are included.

3D interactions with the 3D sphere display need a device that capable to define its 3D location (*x*, *y*, *z*) with respect to the center of the display and its posture information (*pitch*, *yaw*, *roll*). Hereafter, information of 3D location and posture is simply called Six Degrees of Freedom (6DoF).

Currently, several input devices equipped with 6DoF sensors have been developed. The Touch™ Haptic Device [7] is a motorized device that applies force feedback on the user's hand, allowing them to feel virtual objects and producing true-to-life touch sensations as user manipulates on-screen 3D objects. This device acquires the 6DoF information from a sensor attached to the pen tip. The DodecaPen [8] is a stylus pen which obtains its 6DoF with sub-millimeter accuracy using multiple Augmented Reality (AR) markers arranged on a dodecahedron mounted on the stylus. Both styluses [7][8], however, are designed to work on a flat surface where the working area is limited.

A stylus pen for the spherical display must be able to acquire the 6DoF information of the pen tip when touching the surface of the display. The arm for the Touch™ Haptic Device limits its working range, especially when working on the opposite side of the spherical display surface. This problem also applies to DodecaPen because the AR markers of the stylus will be hidden when working on the lower part of the spherical display.

In this study, we propose a stylus pen which is suitable for a spherical display. Measurement of the 6DoF information is done using two sensors. Here, the 3D location (*x*, *y*, *z*) of the pen tip on the display surface is measured by an infrared (IR) camera installed at the bottom of the display. The posture information (*pitch*, *yaw*, *roll*) of the stylus pen is obtained using a gyro sensor. We believe that the new stylus pen's strategy for measuring 6DoF information is effective in capturing this information when the pen tip is touching the display surface.

This paper is organized as follows. Section II describes related works in the development of 3D spherical displays. Section III introduces our approach to implement the perspective-corrected stylus pen. Section IV describes our experiment results in terms of accuracy, stability and visual perception. Finally, Section V presents our conclusions and future works.

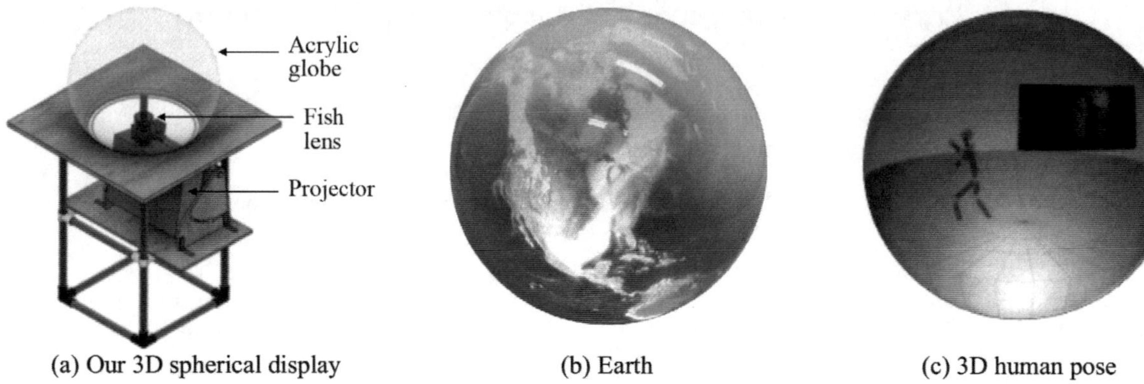

Figure 1. Our 3D spherical display (a) and some contents (b), (c) projected onto the display.

II. Related Work

There are some companies producing spherical displays, such as Global Imagination [3], PufferSphere [4], and ArcScience [9]. These displays were mainly intended to show earth surface data and 360-degree videos. Therefore, there are more like digital globes than displays.

To our knowledge, SnowGlobe is the first published 3D spherical display [10]. This display was implemented by reflecting a projected image off a hemispherical mirror, allowing for a seamless curvilinear display surface. However, it had non-uniform resolution and the mirror caused a blind spot. Spheree is a spherical, multi-projector perspective-corrected display that supports 3D representation using parallax-based 3D depth cues [11]. Uniform resolution is mostly achieved because each projector covers a small area on the display. CoGlobe is a large 3D spherical display for multiple users [12]. It uses a multi-camera OptiTrack system for tracking users' heads and multiplex viewpoints using modified active shutter glasses.

For this study, we have built a 3D spherical display similar to Spheree, but only using a fish-eye lens-equipped single projector (Figure 1). A 4k projector was used to generate a high-resolution image onto the display, comparable with that of Spheree. Our display is capable of supporting monoscopic and stereoscopic displays.

III. Perspective-Corrected Stylus Pen

The proposed stylus pen can find its 6DoF information on any location on the display. As shown in Figure 2, the 3D location (*x*, *y*, *z*) of the pen tip on the display surface is measured with an IR camera. This camera captures the blob (the image of the light reflected from the IR LEDs) of the pen tip. An ellipse is then fitted to the blob, and the center of the ellipse is calculated as the position of the pen tip on the display surface. The posture information (*pitch*, *yaw*, *roll*) of the stylus pen is obtained using a gyro sensor.

In order to simplify the design of the stylus pen, we use a mobile phone with a pen tip attached. The advantage of using a mobile phone is that we can use the built-in gyro information, and send that information to the computer that controls the spherical display. Using this information, the computer calculates the posture of the stylus pen and projects the auxiliary line from the pen tip according to the user's viewpoint. Here, we used VIVE Tracker [13] to track the user's head and define the viewpoint. Users can point out an object inside the spherical display using the auxiliary line from the pen tip, as shown in Figure 3.

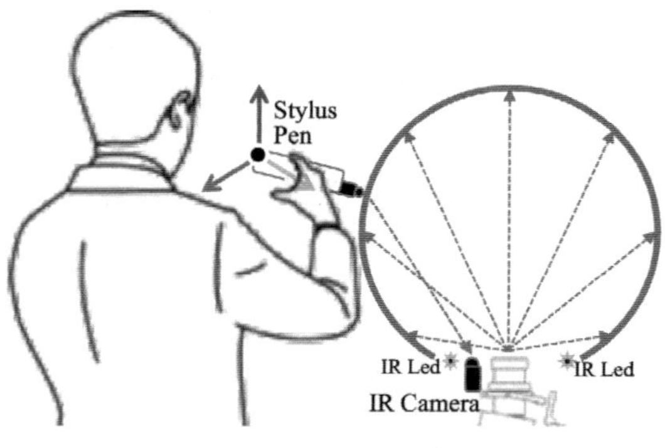

Figure 2. Our proposed stylus pen.

IV. Experimental Results

We evaluate the proposed stylus pen in terms of accuracy, pointing stability, and user experience. For the experiments, we built a spherical display with a diameter of 51 cm. The coordinate systems of the display, stylus pen and user's viewpoint are calibrated using the VIVE tracker. The display system runs on a desktop computer with a 3.6 GHz CPU, 32 GB RAM, and a GTX980Ti graphics card. An iPhone 7 (iOS 13) is used to get the posture information for the stylus pen.

A. Accuracy

Twelve arbitrary locations on the display surface were selected and the stylus pen was used to point to the center of the display from each location. The resulting 6DoF information of the stylus pen on each location was validated against the true 6DoF information (ground truth) as the vector

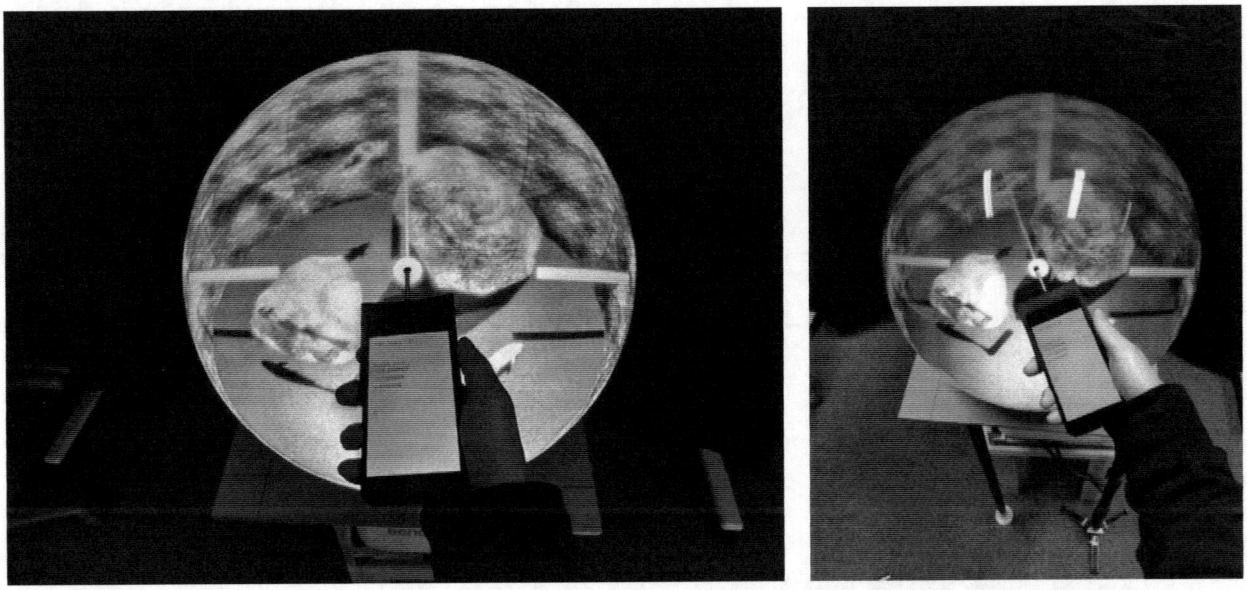

Figure 3. Our working perspective-corrected stylus pen.

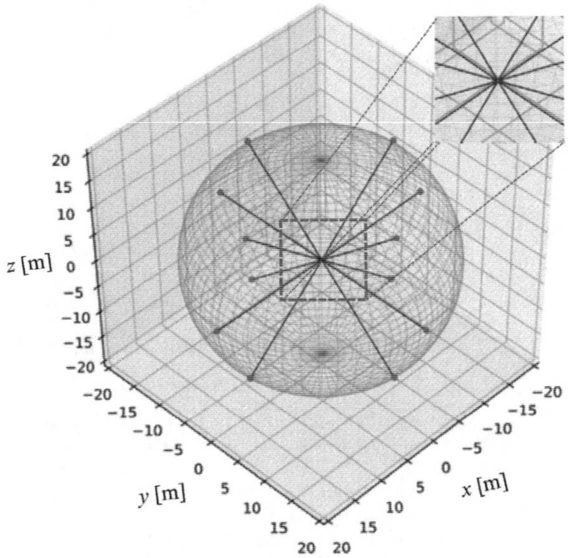

Figure 4. The resulting auxiliary lines from the pen tip and their corresponding ground truths.

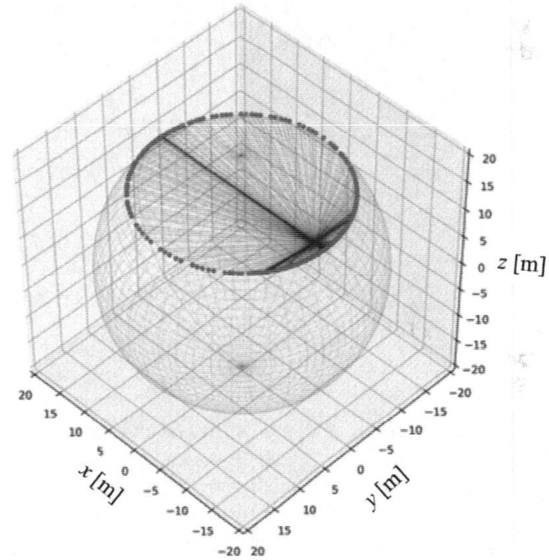

Figure 5. Intersection points of the auxiliary lines from the pen tip and the display surface.

connecting the display center to that location. Overall, the accuracy was achieved with an average of 1.08 degrees. The ground truth vectors (red lines) and auxiliary lines from the pen tip (blue lines) are shown in Figure 4. We considered that our stylus pen is accurate to do 3D interactions within the spherical display. In practical use, most users are not aware of the differences within this range.

B. Pointing Stability

The stylus pen was rotated horizontally from 0 to 180 degrees at a location toward the display. For each angle, the intersection (red dot) of the auxiliary line (blue line) from the pen tip with the display surface was calculated. The resulting points were observed to be horizontally distributed (Figure 5), indicating the pointing stability of the stylus pen. The error distribution is shown in Figure 6.

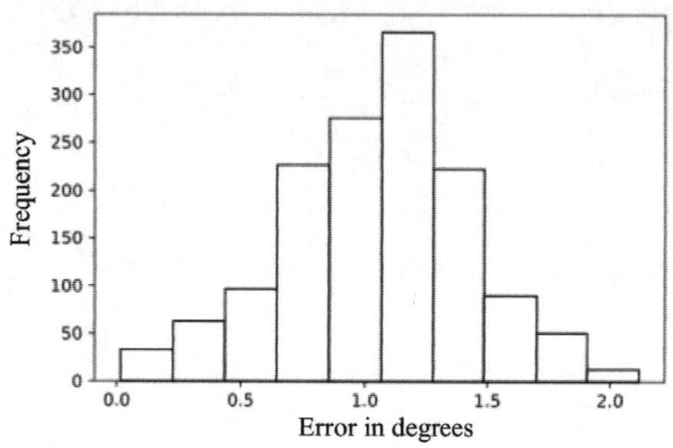

Figure 6. Histogram of the error distribution during the pointing stability test.

Figure 7. The virtual fish tank used for the visual perception evaluation.

C. *Visual Perception*

In order to perform a visual evaluation, an experiment was performed in which a virtual fish tank was drawn on a spherical display and the subject was instructed to use a stylus pen to touch the fish from multiple directions (Figure 7). Three users participated in the experiment. All of them managed to touch all fishes in the spherical display. This result shows that the proposed stylus pen can be perceived in the same way as the real one.

V. CONCLUSION

In this study, we have proposed a novel perspective-corrected stylus pen that can be used to interact with a 3D spherical display. A mobile phone with a pen tip attachment is used to build the stylus pen. The use of a mobile phone does not only make it easier to obtain posture information from the built-in gyro, but also has advantages, such as simplifying the design. The location where the stylus pen touches is detected by the IR camera installed in the spherical display. Our experiments have confirmed the high accuracy of the proposed stylus and show that it can be used to perform natural 3D interactions. We are working on putting a pressure sensor inside the stylus pen to enable the user to control the length of the auxiliary line from the pen tip by applying varying levels of pressure to the screen surface. In the future, the proposed stylus pen will be extended for use in virtual surgical training on a spherical display.

REFERENCES

[1] GK Design Group, http://www.gk-design.co.jp/en/works/309/. [retrieved: February, 2020]

[2] T. Crespel, P. Reuter, and X. Granier, "A low-cost multitouch spherical display: hardware and software design," Display Week 2017, May 2017, Los Angeles, California, United States. pp.619- 622, 10.1002/sdtp.11716 . hal-01455523.

[3] S. W. Utt, P. C. Rubesin, and M. A. Foody, "Display system having a three-dimensional convex display surface," US Patent 7,352,340. 2005.

[4] Pufferfish Ltd. pufferfishdisplays.co.uk, 2002. [retrieved: February, 2020]

[5] G. Hagemann, Q. Zhou, I. Stavness., O. D. A. Prima, and S. Fels, "Here's looking at you: A Spherical FTVR Display for Realistic Eye-Contact," ISS 2018 - Proceedings of the 2018 ACM International Conference on Interactive Surfaces and Spaces, pp. 357-362, 2018. https://doi.org/10.1145/3279778.3281456

[6] D. Fafard et al., "FTVR in VR: Evaluating 3D performance with a simulated volumetric fish-tank virtual reality display," Conference on Human Factors in Computing Systems, pp. 1–12, 2019. https://doi.org/10.1145/3290605.3300763

[7] The Touch™ Haptic Device, 3D Systems, https://www.3dsystems.com/haptics-devices/touch. [retrieved: February, 2020]

[8] P. C. Wu et al., "DodecaPen: Accurate 6DoF tracking of a passive stylus," UIST 2017 - Proceedings of the 30th Annual ACM Symposium on User Interface Software and Technology, pp.365–374, 2017. https://doi.org/10.1145/3126594.3126664

[9] L. Thomas, F. Christopher, and L. Jonathan, "A self-contained spherical display system," In ACM Siggraph 2003 Emerging Technologies, 2003.

[10] J. Bolton, K. Kim, and R. Vertegaal, "SnowGlobe: A spherical fish-tank VR display," In Conference on Human Factors in Computing Systems – Proceedings, pp. 1159–1164, 2011. https://doi.org/10.1145/1979742.1979719.

[11] F. Ferreira et al., "Spheree: A 3D perspective-corrected interactive spherical scalable display," 2014. https://doi.org/10.1145/2614066.2614091.

[12] Q. Zhou et al., "CoGlobe - a co-located multi-person FTVR experience," ACM SIGGRAPH 2018 Emerging Technologies, SIGGRAPH 2018, 2018. https://doi.org/10.1145/3214907.3214914.

[13] VIVE Tracker, https://www.vive.com/eu/vive-tracker/ [retrieved: February, 2020]

Toward Automated Analysis of Communication Mirroring

Kumiko Hosogoe, Miyu Nakano
Faculty of Social Welfare,
Iwate Prefectural University
Takizawa, Japan
email: hosogoe@iwate-pu.ac.jp, g221r007@s.iwate-pu.ac.jp

Oky Dicky Ardiansyah Prima, Yuta Ono
Graduate School of Software and Information Science,
Iwate Prefectural University
Takizawa, Japan
email: prima@iwate-pu.ac.jp, g231q005@s.iwate-pu.ac.jp

***Abstract*—Mirroring is a technique in which someone unconsciously reflects other people's behavior, such as gestures and facial expressions. This technique can help us to build rapport with others by making communication more effective and reflective. Due to the developments in computer vision, human behavior observation based on vision cameras has become viable. Moreover, the wide spread of omnidirectional cameras has made it possible to observe more people at the same time, making it easier to analyze face-to-face conversation scenes. In this study, we propose a framework to perform a time series analysis based on Dynamic Time Warping (DTW) to determine whether communication mirroring has been established. The framework uses human pose estimation techniques to track hand gestures of two persons during a conversation. The framework will detect all gestures that are similar to the trained gestures. Our experiments show that the DTW was able to detect mirroring acts having distinct gestures. However, detections of similarities of weak gestures are challenging.**

Keywords-communication mirroring; communication mirroring; human pose estimation; DTW; 360 degree camera.

I. INTRODUCTION

Gestures are forms of nonverbal communication that use body movements instead of words. These movements include the hand, head, or other parts of the body. Gestures enable to produce more intuitive communication and flexible interactions. Using gestures to reflect the behavior of the talking partner can create a strong connection during the conversation. These techniques are called mirroring, from a communication perspective. Mirroring can improve rapport with others. It happens very naturally when people are talking [1]. The ability to mirror others nonverbally facilitates empathy. Although many people have an ability to empathize with others, only a few people have excellent natural empathy.

Many studies have been conducted in conversation scene analyses. Most of them are multimodal, using cues produced by audio and video recordings [2]. Traditionally, analyzing this data involves works of manual coding of the repeating behavior, its duration, and response latency. BECO2, an integrated behavior coding system, has been widely used in universities in Japan to train students to perform behavior analysis [3]. With this system, observers can record and analyze the occurrence and duration of behaviors by pressing keyboard keys corresponding to those in each category.

Audio and video processing techniques have contributed to performing conversation scene analyses effectively. On the one hand, audio processing can reveal non-verbal behaviors, including utterances, acts of stressing, and speaking rate based on the speech signals. On the other hand, video processing can measure facial information and gestures. Otsuka and Araki [4] introduce Voice Activity Detection (VAD) to determine the presence/absence of utterances from speech signals. An omnidirectional camera-microphone system was used to partition an input audio stream into homogeneous segments according to the speaker's identity as being captured by the camera. This diarization is vital to identify different speakers' turns in a conversation.

Advanced computer vision applications have enabled the estimation of human posture from a single image [5][6]. These approaches are more flexible than those based on a depth camera. Depending on the Field of View (FOV) of the cameras, human posture from multiple targets can be effectively measured [7]. With an omnidirectional camera, it is possible to take photos of people as if it were taken from the front, even if they talk to face each other. Derivation of human posture from images opens up new ways to recognize gestures. The extracted gestures can be used to identify specific responses during a conversation. However, even with the same gestures, the length and speed of these gestures are different. Dynamic Time Warping (DTW) is a promising technique that can measure the similarity between two temporal sequences of gestures [8]. It enables a non-linear mapping of one signal to another by minimizing the distance between them.

This study proposes a framework for automatically detecting the presence of mirroring motion in hand gestures during a conversation between two people using an omnidirectional camera. The framework converts the video image obtained from the omnidirectional camera into a panoramic image and extracts the posture information of the conversation participants from the video. The Graphical User Interface (GUI) allows observers to select gestures as training data. The training data is used to estimate similarity to gestures found in the observed data. Detection of communication mirroring is done by thresholding the similarity of hand gestures between participants.

This paper is organized as follows. Section II describes related works on behavior coding and gesture analysis based on computer vision techniques. Section III introduces our proposed framework to analyze the presence of communication mirroring. Section IV describes our experimental setting and its results. Finally, Section V presents our conclusions.

II. Related Work

Traditional methods to measure nonverbal behavior rely on the manual coding system. Since there are a lot of ambiguities on judging a particular action, many observers tend to perform in an inconsistent manner, thus degrading the quality of the measurements. Jaana et al. [8] developed an automated behavior analysis system using a single omnidirectional camera. This system analyzed facial expressions, head nodding, utterances based on facial landmarks extracted from facial images captured by the camera. Schneider et al. [9] proposed a gesture recognition system using human postures obtained from a single camera, using a human pose estimation framework, OpenPose [5]. This system utilized DTW to classify the time-series data. Although this method yielded promising results, it has limitations in case of attempting to classify more similar gestures. For general-purpose gesture recognition, the Gesture Recognition Toolkit (GRT) is a cross-platform open-source C++ library designed to make real-time machine learning and gesture recognition more accessible [10].

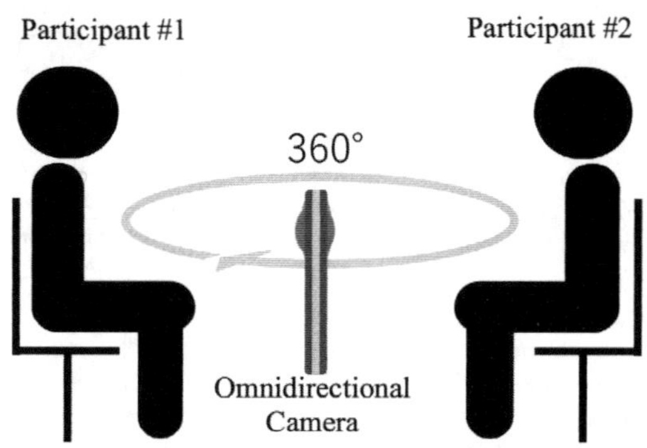

Figure 1. Experimental setting.

III. Communication Mirroring Detection

We build a framework to detect communication mirroring that occurs in a conversation scene, as shown in Figure 1. The omnidirectional camera captures an image of the whole bodies of the two communication participants.

A. Panoramic Image Projection

The omnidirectional camera produces two fisheye images to represent a 360° image. These images are combined and warped into a panoramic image, as shown in Figure 2, so that the information in the image can be interpreted directly. The panoramic image displays a 360° image as a rectangular image.

B. Pose Estimation

We use the OpenPose framework [5] to estimate the body posture of the communication participants. The skeletal information of the hands is extracted for the analysis. This information consists of six body joints, such as the wrist, elbow, shoulder, and neck. We normalize each joint to achieve translation and scale invariance [8]. Normalization is done by taking the neck joint as the origin of the coordinate system and subtracting this coordinate from all other joints.

C. Training

We provide a GUI to allow observers to select the typical movement of the participant, which can be considered as a gesture. The automatic data trimming will remove images that

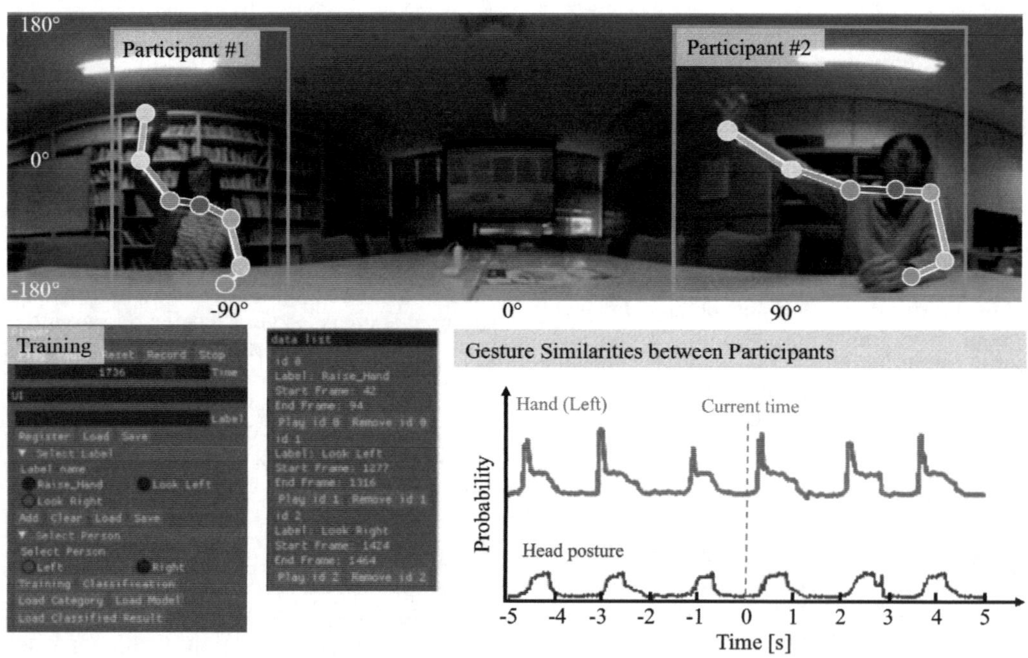

Figure 2. The user interface of our framework.

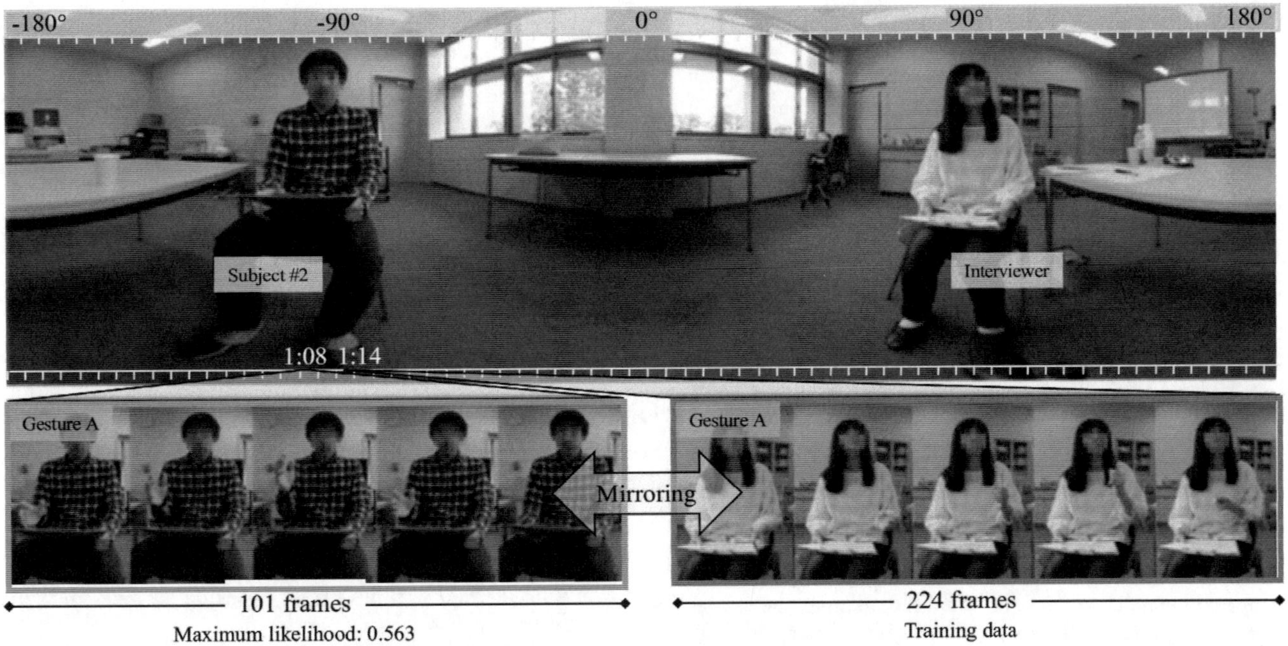

Figure 3. The successful case of similar gestures detected in Experiment 1.

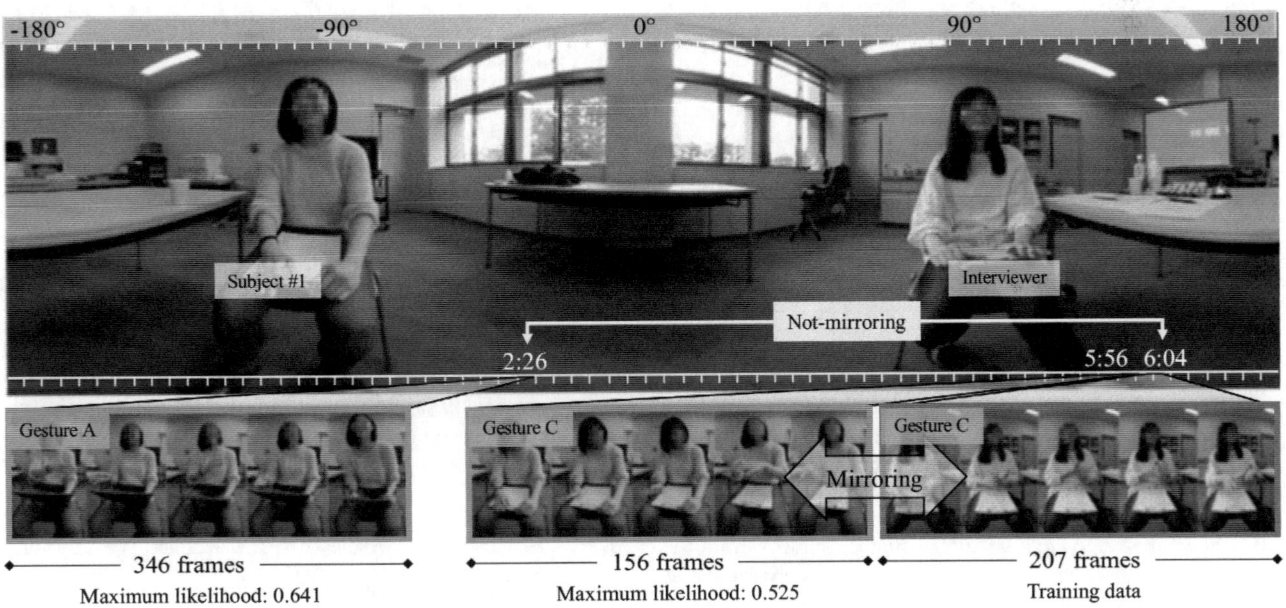

Figure 4. An example of weak gestures that failed to classify.

do not contain body movements from the start to the end of the training.

D. Detection

We apply maximum likelihood from the warping distance to estimate the similarity between the training data created from a participant and the hand movement data of another participant in a conversation. Here, we present a graphical representation to determine the maximum likelihood threshold. Finally, we use the threshold in order to detect gestures that resemble the training data.

IV. EXPERIMENT AND RESULT

In this study, two experiments were conducted, involving two subjects and an interviewer. All participants in the experiments agreed to participate and signed the consent forms to allow their data to be used in publications of this research. Each subject was interviewed face to face, at which

TABLE I. MAXIMUM LIKELIHOOD BETWEEN GESTURES OF THE SUBJECT AND THE INTERVIEWER FOR EXPERIMENT 1.

No.	Subject's Gesture	Interviewer's Gesture	Maximum Likelihood
1.	A	A	0.563
2.	B	B	0.688
3.	C	C	0.660
4.	D	D	0.558

Accuracy: 100%

TABLE II. MAXIMUM LIKELIHOOD BETWEEN GESTURES OF THE SUBJECT AND THE INTERVIEWER FOR EXPERIMENT 2.

No.	Subject's Gesture	Interviewer's Gesture	Maximum Likelihood
1.	A	C	0.641
2.	B	B	0.582
3.	C	C	0.525

Accuracy: 67%

point the interviewer randomly imitated the subject's gestures approximately five seconds after recognizing the subject's gesture. Subjects had not previously been informed that the interviewer imitated his or her gestures during the interview. We used RICOH THETA S to record the interview scenes in 1,920×1080 pixels panoramic image frames. Skeletal information was obtained from each frame by using the OpenPose framework [5].

A. Experiment 1

The interviewer imitated four subject's hand gestures: A, B, C, and D. This data was trained using the GRT [10] to predict the corresponding gestures performed by the subject. Table I shows the maximum likelihood between the gestures of the subject and the interviewer. All gestures performed by the interviewer have the maximum likelihood with the corresponding subject's gesture. A successful case of similar gestures detected in this experiment is shown in Figure 3.

B. Experiment 2

During the interview, the subject was excitedly speaking and performing subtle gestures. The interviewer imitated three of them (A, B, and C) and trained this data using the GRT [10]. However, gesture A performed by the interviewer did not resemble that of the subject. Table II shows the maximum likelihood between the gestures of the subject and the interviewer. Gesture A of the subject was determined as Gesture C performed by the interviewer, as shown in Figure 4.

From the above results, we have shown that our proposed framework for detecting the presence of mirroring motion in hand gestures yielded promising results. Some subtle gestures, however, were difficult to classify. In our experiment, we did not make a detailed analysis to optimize the warping window size for the DTW calculation [11]. This issue could be addressed in future research to improve the results.

V. CONCLUSION

In this study, we have proposed a framework to determine whether communication mirroring has been established from the recorded video scenes. Our experiments show that the DTW was able to detect mirroring acts having distinct gestures. The proposed framework will provide a new indication for developing an integrated behavioral analysis system that will enable the assessment of communication mirroring.

ACKNOWLEDGMENT

We thank the faculty of Social Welfare, Iwate Prefectural University, Japan, for funding this project.

REFERENCES

[1] Z. Jiang-Yuan and G. Wei, "Who Is Controlling the Interaction? The Effect of Nonverbal Mirroring on Teacher-Student Rapport," US-China Education Review, A(7), pp. 662–669, 2012.

[2] D. Jayagopi, D. Sanchez-Cortes, K. Otsuka, J. Yamato, and D. Gatica-Perez, "Linking speaking and looking behavior patterns with group composition, perception, and performance," ICMI'12 - Proceedings of the ACM International Conference on Multimodal Interaction, pp. 433–440, 2012.

[3] Behavior coding system, DKH Co. Ltd., https://www.dkh.co.jp/product/behavior_coding_system/ [retrieved: February 20, 2020]

[4] K. Otsuka and S. Araki, "Audio-visual technology for conversation scene analysis," NTT Technical Review, 7(2), pp. 1-9, 2009.

[5] Z. Cao, T. Simon, S. E. Wei, and Y. Sheikh, "Realtime multi-person 2D pose estimation using part affinity fields," Computer Vision and Pattern Recognition, pp. 1-9, 2017.

[6] R. A. Guler, N. Neverova, and I. Kokkinos, "DensePose: Dense Human Pose Estimation In The Wild," In Proceedings of the IEEE Conference on Computer Vision and Pattern Recognition, pp. 7297–7306, 2018.

[7] D. Scaramuzza, "Omnidirectional camera," In Encyclopedia of Computer Vision, 2012.

[8] Y. Jaana, O. D. A. Prima, T. Imabuchi, H. Ito, and K. Hosogoe, "The development of automated behavior analysis Software," Proc. SPIE 9443, Sixth International Conference on Graphic and Image Processing (ICGIP), pp. 1-5, 2014.

[9] P. Schneider, R. Memmesheimer, I. Kramer, and D. Paulus, "Gesture Recognition in RGB Videos Using Human Body Keypoints and Dynamic Time Warping," Lecture Notes in Computer Science, vol. 11531, pp. 281–293, 2019.

[10] N. Gillian and J. A. Paradiso, "The gesture recognition toolkit," Journal of Machine Learning Research, 15, pp. 3483–3487, 2014.

[11] C. A. Ratanamahatana and E. Keogh, "Everything you know about Dynamic Time Warping is Wrong," In Proceedings of the 3rd Workshop on Mining Temporal and Sequential Data, pp. 1–11, 2004.

Simple Generative Adversarial Network to Generate Three-axis Time-series Data for Vibrotactile Displays

Shotaro Agatsuma
Graduate School of Systems and Information Engineering,
University of Tsukuba, Japan
e-mail: agatsuma@saga-lab.org

Junya Kurogi
Faculty of Engineering,
Kumamoto University, Japan
e-mail: kurogi@saga-lab.org

Satoshi Saga
Faculty of Advanced Science and Technology,
Kumamoto University, Japan
e-mail: saga@saga-lab.org

Simona Vasilache
Faculty of Engineering, Information and Systems,
University of Tsukuba, Japan
e-mail: simona@cs.tsukuba.ac.jp

Shin Takahashi
Faculty of Engineering, Information and Systems,
University of Tsukuba, Japan
e-mail: shin@cs.tsukuba.ac.jp

Abstract—**Various kinds of vibrotactile information have been recorded from real textures and used to present high-quality tactile sensations via tactile displays. However, it is unrealistic to collect large amounts of vibrotactile data under many different conditions. Thus, we develop a method whereby recorded data can be changed to represent conditions differing from those at the time of initial recording. In the first step, we construct a data generation model using a Generative Adversarial Network (GAN). The model makes simple calculations and generates unknown data from recorded acceleration data obtained by rubbing real objects. The model can generate three-axis, time-series data. To evaluate the quality of the data generated, we devised a string-based tactile display and presented generated vibrotactile information to users. Users reported that the generated data were indistinguishable from real data.**

Keywords–Acceleration; Generative Adversarial Networks; Vibrotactile Display.

I. Introduction

Currently, various tactile displays have been developed, and a lot of applications that enable users to touch virtual objects are released. The quality of such applications is measured by the extent of realism felt when the virtual objects are touched. It is difficult to create realistic tactile sensations. In particular, realistic surface reproduction is challenging because touching is bidirectional, thus affected by object condition. If the object surface, physical characteristics, or rubbing speed differ between the contactor and the contacted object, the induced phenomena differ. To ensure high-quality tactile sensation, it is necessary to collect and analyze data under various conditions [1][2]. However, many conditions were not addressed in the cited works. For example, Strese et al. [2] collected six types of data (accelerations, pressures, temperatures, images, sounds, and magnetic field powers) for 108 textures, under various conditions, using a pen-type device. However, there are many more than 108 textures, and not all rubbing directions or contact angles were explored.

To solve this problem, our method eliminates the need for vibrotactile signal data from real objects; vibrotactile stimulation is created employing existing recorded data on real textures. We do not collect data from real objects; we generate alternative data under conditions different from those at the times of the original recordings. This reduces the cost of data collection and greatly expands the utility of vibrotactile displays.

In the first step, we generate vibrotactile acceleration data by acceleration data collected from rubbing real objects. The generated data can be used as output signals for vibrotactile displays [3][4]. Today, accelerometers are both small and inexpensive; a collection of acceleration data is simple. Thus, we use the data to generate new data with the aid of a Generative Adversarial Network (GAN) [5]. GANs generate images that find many applications in super-resolution [6] and audio synthesis; some sounds are very similar to the human voice [7][8]. GANs can generate high-quality time-series data. Our data generation model is based on WaveGAN [7], which was developed for audio synthesis. We generate nine types of time-series data based on real textures. We create data spectrograms to evaluate realism. We perform a user study employing a vibrotactile display to evaluate whether the vibrotactile stimuli were realistic. We explored whether it was possible to mix the characteristics of two textures by combining two types of label data in the input.

Our principal contribution is that we generate time-series data using a GAN originally developed for audio synthesis. The training data of the model are accelerations recorded by rubbing real objects. Our model has a simpler architecture than an earlier model [9], and thus requires fewer computational resources. We generate three-axis time-series data for vibrotactile displays that require more than two datasets [3]. The three-axis data facilitate the analysis and recognition of tactile signals.

The structure of this paper is as follows. This section describes the purpose of our research and our approach. In Section II below, we review related work. Section III describes our model architecture; Section IV deals with data generation. Section V describes the user study. Section VI presents a preliminary experiment on multi-label (merged) data generation. Section VII draws conclusions and describes our future plans.

II. Related Work

Vibrotactile displays reproduce real textures, including the mechanical vibrations of actuators [10], electrostatic forces [11], and so on. Some real-object data are available, but a complete dataset would be unimaginably large. We initially use a GAN to generate data based on the three-axis accelerations of real textures. GANs are machine-learning models generating images that may be simple or complex; the latter include super-high-resolution images [6] and images translated from other images [12]. A GAN features a generator and a discriminator that, respectively, generate and classify training and test data. The discriminator accurately classifies the two types of data. The generator creates data that the discriminator cannot initially classify. After repetitive training of the generator and the discriminator, the generator generates data that are almost the same as the training data.

A few scholars have used GANs to generate data for tactile displays. Ujitoko et al. [9] employed a GAN generating time-series data equivalent to texture images. The model featured an encoder and a generator that, respectively, transformed texture images into labeled vectors and generated spectrograms using the recoded accelerations and the labels. The spectrograms were transformed into tactile signals for pen-type vibrotactile displays. The model generated nine types of high-quality, one-axis time-series data that only found applications in simple (i.e., pen-type) vibrotactile displays. It appeared that the computational demand was high; the model featured many neural networks. Our model is simpler than the model, and we generate three-axis acceleration data that are available for more types of situations (e.g., displaying, analyzing, and recognizing the vibrotactile signals) than one-axis data. We employ a GAN originally developed for audio synthesis; some such GANs generate high-quality sounds [7][8]. Acceleration data, like sounds, are time-series data. Specifically, we employed the WaveGAN of Donahue et al [7]. The model architecture is simple. However, Donahue et al. were concerned that spectrograms served as both inputs and outputs; it was thought that spectrogram inversion might compromise quality. Thus, we did not use spectrograms.

III. The Architecture of our GAN

Table I shows the architecture of our GAN. " C " refers to the several classes of training data. " n " refers to batch size. The table shows the architecture of the generator and the discriminator, and the input and output layers; the intermediate layers are hidden layers. The input data propagate to the output layer. The kernel shapes of each convolutional layer are shown, as are the output data shapes of all layers.

As mentioned above, we employed WaveGAN. However, WaveGAN generates only a single data type. We thus additionally implemented a conditional GAN [13] that generates class-specified data by attaching class labels c to the training data. In this GAN, all data are associated with a class label c and a noise z. This allowed us to generate many types of data using one-hot vectors as labels. The vectors have values of either zero or one, and their lengths are the same as the number of classes. Each class vector has the value of one and all others have values of zero The model applies convolution to each axis, and the convolution operates three-acceleration data but only in the time direction.

We describe the details of the generator and the discriminator. The inputs of the generator are random noise vectors based on uniform -1 to 1 distributions. The vector length is 1×100 and is combined with a label vector when input. The output depends on the training data. The discriminator inputs

TABLE I. THE ARCHITECTURE OF OUR GAN.

Generator	Kernel Size	Output Shape
Input : Uniform(-1,1)+C		(n, 100+C)
Dense	(100+C, 49152)	(n, 49152)
Reshape		(n, 3, 16, 1024)
LeakyReLU (α = 0.2)		(n, 3, 16, 1024)
Trans Conv2D (Stride = (1, 4))	(1, 25, 512, 1024)	(n, 3, 64, 512)
LeakyReLU (α = 0.2)		(n, 3, 64, 512)
Trans Conv2D (Stride = (1, 4))	(1, 25, 256, 512)	(n, 3, 256, 256)
LeakyReLU (α = 0.2)		(n, 3, 256, 256)
Trans Conv2D (Stride = (1, 4))	(1, 25, 128, 256)	(n, 3, 1024, 128)
LeakyReLU (α = 0.2)		(n, 3, 1024, 128)
Trans Conv2D (Stride = (1, 4))	(1, 25, 64, 128)	(n, 3, 4096, 64)
LeakyReLU (α = 0.2)		(n, 3, 4096, 64)
Trans Conv2D (Stride = (1, 4))	(1, 25, 1, 64)	(n, 3, 16384, 1)
Output : Tanh		(n, 3, 16384, 1)

Discriminator	Kernel Size	Output Shape
Input : Training data or Generated data		(n, 3, 16384, 1+C)
Conv2D (Stride = (1, 4))	(1, 25, 1+C, 64)	(n, 64, 4096, 64)
LeakyReLU (α = 0.2)		(n, 64, 4096, 64)
Phase Shuffle		(n, 64, 4096, 64)
Conv2D (Stride = (1, 4))	(1, 25, 64, 128)	(n, 64, 1024, 128)
LeakyReLU (α = 0.2)		(n, 64, 1024, 128)
Phase Shuffle		(n, 64, 1024, 128)
Conv2D (Stride = (1, 4))	(1, 25, 128, 256)	(n, 64, 256, 256)
Phase Shuffle		(n, 64, 256, 256)
LeakyReLU (α = 0.2)		(n, 64, 256, 256)
Conv2D (Stride = (1, 4))	(1, 25, 256, 512)	(n, 64, 64, 512)
LeakyReLU (α = 0.2)		(n, 64, 64, 512)
Phase Shuffle		(n, 64, 64, 512)
Conv2D (Stride = (1, 4))	(1, 25, 512, 1024)	(n, 3, 16, 1024)
LeakyReLU (α = 0.2)		(n, 3, 16, 1024)
Reshape		(n, 49152)
Output : Dense	(49152, 1)	(n, 1)

are either training or generated data. The outputs are data that have been manipulated by the discriminator layers. We use the WGAN-GP [14] as a loss function; the discriminator outputs are used to calculate losses. We employed PhaseShuffle (Donahue et al. [7]) to generate data effectively. The phases of the layer activations are perturbed using $-n$ to n samples before being input to the next layer. We used the weight initialization method of He et al. [15] to each convolution layer in both models.

IV. Data Generation

We generated data using the model described above and confirmed that the data exhibited the characteristics of training data. We first used an earlier dataset to explore whether the model could generate similar data. Second, we used acceleration data collected by rubbing real textures with an index finger. We explored whether the model was valid when the methods used to collect training data differed.

A. Data Generation Using Lehrstuhl Für Medientechnik Haptics Texture Database

1) Training Settings: We used nine textural, three-axis acceleration datasets (Figure 1) from the Lehrstuhl Für Medientechnik (LMT) Haptic Texture Database [16] as training data; these were the data employed by Ujitoko et al. [9]. The data were collected by rubbing various textures in one direction using a pen-type device; the sampling rate was 10 kHz.

Table II shows the hyperparameters used to train the model. The discriminator input was normalized to a value between -1 to 1. We extracted 6,000 random datasets, each containing 16,384 sequential points, for each texture, and employed these for training. We generated a three-axis time-series dataset featuring 16,384 sequential points. We trained the model for

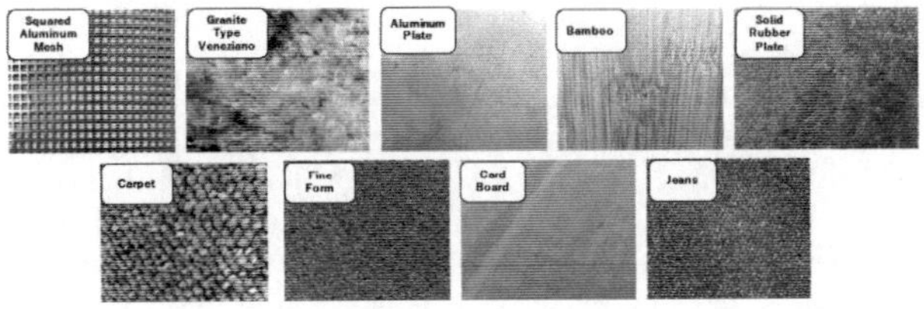

Figure 1. Textures that were chosen from the LMT Haptic Texture Database for this experiment.

40 epochs using a Windows PC with two GPUs (NVIDIA GTX1080 Ti); training required about 47 hours. We found that we succeeded in training the model quickly using the general-purpose GPU and a PC.

TABLE II. THE HYPERPARAMETERS USED.

Name	Value
Batch size	64
Phase Shuffle	2
Loss	WGAN-GP
WGAN-GP λ	10
Generator updates per discriminator	2
Optimizer	Adam (α = 1e-4, β 1 = 0.5, β 2 = 0.9)

2) Results: We drew spectrograms of the training and generated data (Figure 2) to determine whether they were similar. We extracted three classes. The three spectrograms on the left show training data (Ground Truths); the three on the right display the generated data. We computed the spectrograms in a wave format using a 256-point short-time Fourier transform (STFT) with a Hamming window of 256 and a hop size of 128. All values were normalized to between 0 and 1. The spectrograms show that the generated data exhibited the characteristics of training data. In particular, the generated "Bamboo" data were indistinguishable from the training data. Therefore, the model well-learned the characteristics of the training data. However, the generated data did not reproduce the characteristics of "Granite Type Veneziano"; the generated data differed from the training data.

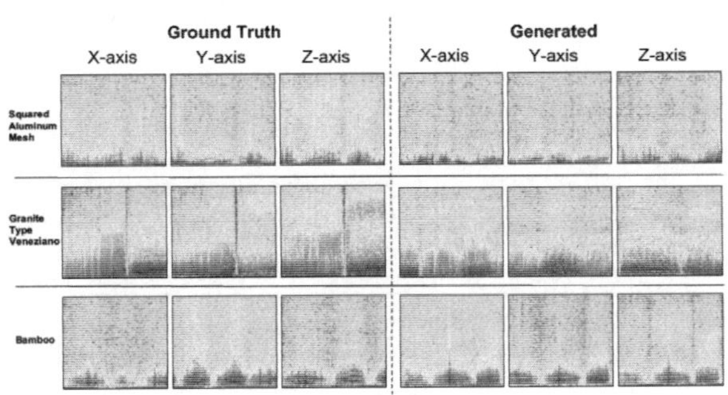

Figure 2. Spectrograms of each labeled class in the LMT Haptic Texture Database.

B. Data Generation Using Real Texture Data

1) Training Settings: We obtained three-axis acceleration data by rubbing nine textures (Figure 3) with an index finger bearing a three-axis accelerometer. "Artificial Grass" was a spiky artificial grass. "Cloth" was a silky cloth. "Carpet" was a hard carpet. "Cork Sheet" was a plate-like cork. "Punched Plastic Sheet" was a smooth punched plastic plate. "Tile" was a patterned tile. "Place Mat 01, 02, and 03" were placemats made from different materials. Figure 4 shows an overview of the data collection. The collector was one of the authors (male, 24 years of age). All textures were traced from left to right for 6 seconds at about 5 cm/s. The sampling rate was about 1 kHz. A metronome was used to ensure that the speed was approximately constant. The angle between the finger and each texture was about 45°. Each texture was sampled 80 times. We removed the first and last 1,000 points of sequential data.

We used the hyperparameters employed above (Table II). We created about 40,000 data points from 10 repeats of each collected data because the collected data lengths were shorter than 16,384 points. We extracted 6,000 random datasets each of 16,384 three-axis, time-series sequential points from the data on each texture; these served as training data. We trained the model for 40 epochs using the PC described above; training required about 46 hours, and was thus relatively fast even though the data differed from those in the LMT Haptics Texture Database.

Figure 3. The Sampled Textures.

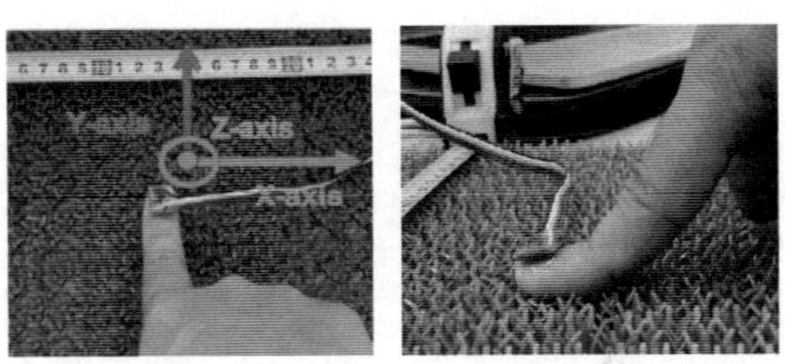

Figure 4. Overview of data collection.

2) Results: Figure 5 shows sample spectrograms prepared in a manner similar to dataset generation. The data exhibit the characteristics of training data; all generated and training data were identical. Therefore, we found that the model can generate data effectively, even using the training data that is different from the LMT Haptics Texture Database.

V. THE USER STUDY

To evaluate the quality of data generated by our model, we presented vibrotactile stimuli to users. We employed the collected data described above as training data. Ten participants (eight males and two females, age 22-24 years) were enrolled. The work was approved by the Ethics Committee of the University of Tsukuba (authorization number 2019R299) and written informed consent was obtained from all participants.

We performed two user studies. First, we explored whether vibrotactile stimuli based on generated data could be distinguished from those based on training data. The more difficult this was, the more effectively our model learned the data

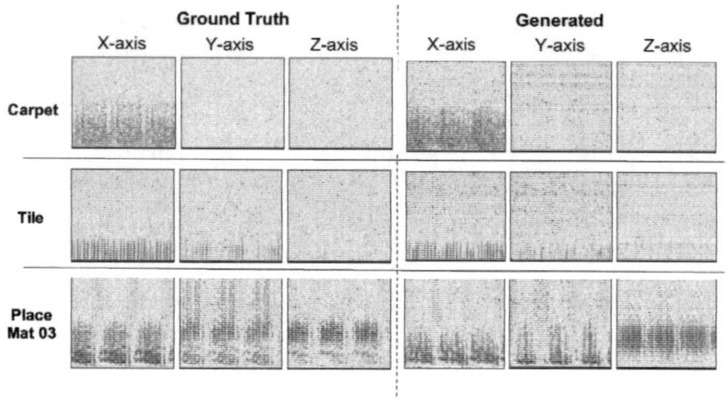

Figure 5. Spectrograms for each labeled class of collected data. The spectrogram settings are the same as those of Figure 2.

characteristics. Second, we explored the realism of vibrotactile stimuli based on training and generated data. We used the task design of Ujitoko et al. [9] and the vibrotactile display proposed by Saga et al. [3] (Figure 6 left). A finger pad was connected via threads to four motors on the four corners of the tablet. The strings were wound to deliver vibrotactile stimuli; the X-axis and Y-axis vibrations were independently controlled. This was appropriate because our model generated three-axis time-series data. The generated data is not only applied for 1-axis vibrotactile displays but also used for vibrotactile displays that need more types of data like it. We used the first 4,000 training and generated data points to present vibrotactile sensations; we were careful to ensure that data repetition did not affect sensation.

A. Procedure of the User Studies

Figure 6 shows an overview of the user studies and the vibrotactile display employed. Each participant placed an index finger on the pad and moved the finger from left to right on the surface of the display over two different predefined paths; s/he received vibrotactile stimuli created by test or generated data and was asked to identify the path that employed generated data. S/he then rubbed the real texture and scored realism using a Visual Analog Scale [17]. To control movement speed, we used a guide bar (on a screen) to indicate where to move. Each participant followed the movement of the bar; the finger moved at approximately 5 cm/s. The display order of training and generated trial data were randomized. We performed 10 repeat experiments for each texture; thus, each participant performed 90 tests. We explored participant views via a questionnaire. All experiments were concluded in approximately 1 hour.

Figure 6. Left: An overview of the experiments. Right: The string-based vibrotactile display.

B. Result and Discussion

The top panel of Figure 7 shows the correct identification frequencies ("Correct answer rates") of stimuli created using generated data. A value close to 50% indicated that a participant failed to distinguish training from generated data. Thus, the closer the value to 50%, the more effective the model. All values were about 50%. It was not possible to distinguish the training from the generated data. When completing the questionnaires, most participants indicated that they could not distinguish the data. Thus, the model generated data very similar to real acceleration data. The correct answer rates of most participants were 40-60% for each texture. Notably, seven participants exhibited 50% correct answer rates for "Carpet" (a rough texture).

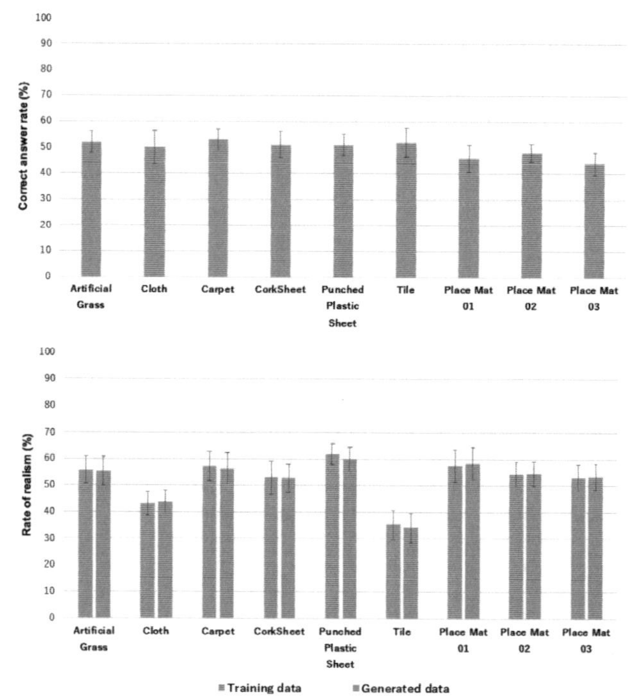

Figure 7. Top: The correct answer rate for each texture. Bottom: The realism of each texture.

The bottom panel of Figure 7 deals with realism; the values are the averages of all answers. If the values for generated data are close to those for training data (as was indeed the case for all textures), the two types of data were similar. The paired Student's t-test revealed no significant difference between the training and generated data for any texture; vibrotactile stimuli created using generated data were as realistic as those prepared to employ training data. In contrast, significant differences between training and generated data were evident for some textures in the work of Ujitoko et al. [9]. Our model may generate higher-quality data.

The realism scores were 50-70% for all textures except "Cloth" and "Tile." Saga et al. [3] reported realism scores of 50-70% using the vibrotactile display that we employed to present real textures. Thus, our vibrotactile display performed well. Turning to the two textures with lower values: "Cloth" scored poorly because the vibrotactile display did not reproduce the stimuli well. The display preferentially reproduces rough textures (the fingertip vibrations are large) and, thus, not silky textures such as "Cloth". In the future, we will use a different display. The "Tile" value was low because the stimuli were weak, explained by the fact that the accelerations were small. The "Tile" featured a gutter (Figure 3) that affected changes in acceleration; these were small because the gutter was shallow and fingertip vibration thus very low. This will be improved by changing the data collection method and the display. The bottom panel of Figure 7 reveals almost no difference between the realism of generated and training data, even for " Tile " (Figure 5). Therefore, it appears that the model succeeded in generating data effectively.

VI. DATA GENERATION WITH THE MERGED LABEL

We explored whether the model generated unknown data when we varied the input label; we performed a preliminary experiment. We merged two input labels and generated data. Before we generated data for "Place Mat 03", we merged the label for data generation based on " Tile " with the "Place Mat 03" input label. In the "Tile" label, the index for "Tile" ranged from 0 to 1. The "Place Mat 03" index was 1.

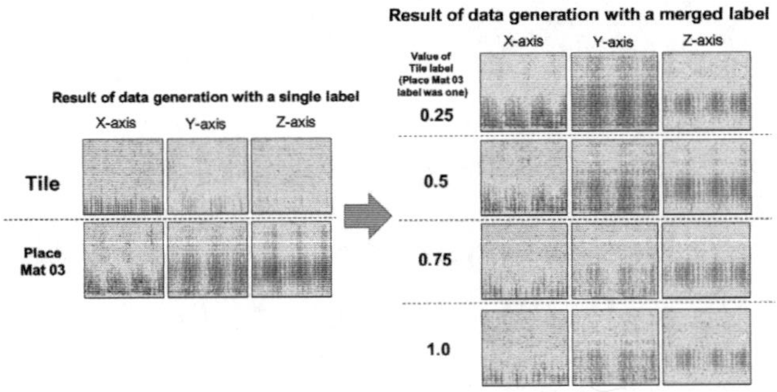

Figure 8. Spectrograms of all labeled generated signals.

Figure 8 shows the results. The two images on the left show the data generated using the standard single labels. The four images on the right show the data generated using multiple labels. The spectrograms change as the label values vary. The greater the value of the "Tile" label, the more mixed the data characteristics become, especially on the X-axis. Thus, the model is likely to generate unknown data if we manipulate the input label. We will determine what types of data the model generates under various conditions.

VII. CONCLUSIONS AND FUTURE WORK

We used GANs to generate vibrotactile signals. Our GAN is based on WaveGAN [7] and a conditional GAN [13]. We generated three-axis time-series data; earlier work created only one-axis data. The model is smaller than the earlier model. The training was complete in about 46 hours using a general-purpose GPU and PC. Three-axis data can be used for vibrotactile displays that are more elaborate than one-axis pen-type displays. In the user study, we found that vibrotactile stimuli based on generated data were as realistic as stimuli based on training data. In the future, we will deliver real textures using higher-quality vibrotactile displays than the ones used by Saga et al. [3]. We will also explore whether the model can generate unknown data when we manipulate the input label; our preliminary experiment suggests that this is likely. We will examine the data generated when we merge three or more labels.

ACKNOWLEDGMENT

This work was partly supported by JSPS KAKENHI 18H04104G1 (Grant-in-Aid for Scientific Research (A)) and 19K2287900 (Grant-in-Aid for challenging Exploratory Research).

REFERENCES

[1] A. Abdulali and S. Jeon, "Data-Driven Modeling of Anisotropic Haptic Textures: Data Segmentation and Interpolation," in Haptics: Perception, Devices, Control, and Applications: 10th International Conference. Springer International Publishing, 2016, pp. 228–239.

[2] M. Strese, Y. Boeck, and E. Steinbach, "Content-based Surface Material Retrieval," in 2017 IEEE World Haptics Conference (WHC). IEEE, 2017, pp. 352–357.

[3] S. Saga and K. Deguchi, "Lateral-force-based 2.5-dimensional tactile display for touch screen," in Haptics Symposium 2012. IEEE, 2012, pp. 15–22.

[4] Y. Cho, A. Bianchi, N. Marquardt, and N. Bianchi-Berthouze, "RealPen: Providing Realism in Handwriting Tasks on Touch Surfaces using Auditory-Tactile Feedback," in Proceedings of the 29th Annual Symposium on User Interface Software and Technology, ser. UIST '16. ACM, 2016, pp. 195–205.

[5] I. Goodfellow et al., "Generative Adversarial Nets," in Advances in neural information processing systems. Curran Associates, Inc., 2014, pp. 2672–2680, and Pouget-Abadie, Jean and Mirza, Mehdi and Xu, Bing and Warde-Farley, David and.

[6] C. Ledig et al., "Photo-Realistic Single Image Super-Resolution Using a Generative Adversarial Network," in Proceedings of the IEEE conference on computer vision and pattern recognition. IEEE, 2017, pp. 4681–4690.

[7] C. Donahue, J. McAuley, and M. Puckette, "Adversarial Audio Synthesis," in International Conference on Learning Representations, 2019. [Online]. Available: https://openreview.net/forum?id=ByMVTsR5KQ [accessed: 2020-02-29]

[8] J. Engel et al., "GANSynth: Adversarial Neural Audio Synthesis," in International Conference on Learning Representations, 2019. [Online]. Available: https://openreview.net/forum?id=H1xQVn09FX [accessed: 2020-02-29]

[9] Y. Ujitoko and Y. Ban, "Vibrotactile Signal Generation from Texture Images or Attributes using Generative Adversarial Network," in International Conference on Human Haptic Sensing and Touch Enabled Computer Applications. Springer, 2018, pp. 25–36.

[10] K. Minamizawa, Y. Kakehi, M. Nakatani, S. Mihara, and S. Tachi, "TECHTILE toolkit: A prototyping tool for designing haptic media," in Proceedings of the 2012 Virtual Reality International Conference, ser. VRIC '12. ACM, 2012, p. 26.

[11] H. Tomita, S. Saga, H. Kajimoto, S. Vasilache, and S. Takahashi, "A Study of Tactile Sensation and Magnitude on Electrostatic Tactile Display," in 2018 IEEE Haptics Symposium (HAPTICS). IEEE, 2018, pp. 158–162.

[12] P. Isola, J.-Y. Zhu, T. Zhou, and A. A. Efros, "Image-to-Image Translation with Conditional Adversarial Networks," in Proceedings of the IEEE conference on computer vision and pattern recognition. IEEE, 2017, pp. 1125–1134.

[13] M. Mirza and S. Osindero, "Conditional Generative Adversarial Nets," arXiv preprint arXiv:1411.1784, 2014.

[14] I. Gulrajani, F. Ahmed, M. Arjovsky, V. Dumoulin, and A. C. Courville, "Improved Training of Wasserstein GANs," in Advances in Neural Information Processing Systems 30. Curran Associates, Inc., 2017, pp. 5767–5777.

[15] K. He, X. Zhang, S. Ren, and J. Sun, "Delving Deep into Rectifiers: Surpassing Human-level Performance on Imagenet Classification," in Proceedings of the IEEE international conference on computer vision. IEEE, 2015, pp. 1026–1034.

[16] M. Strese, C. Schuwerk, A. Iepure, and E. Steinbach, "Multimodal Feature-Based Surface Material Classification," IEEE transactions on haptics, vol. 10, no. 2, IEEE, 2016, pp. 226–239.

[17] K. A. Lee, G. Hicks, and G. Nino-Murcia, "Validity and reliability of a scale to assess fatigue," Psychiatry research, vol. 36, no. 3, Elsevier, 1991, pp. 291–298.

Rendering Method of 2-Dimensional Vibration Presentation for Improving Fidelity of Haptic Texture

Junya Kurogi

Faculty of Engineering, Kumamoto University
2-39-1, Kurokami, Chuo-ku, Kumamoto, Japan
Email: kurogi@saga-lab.org

Satoshi Saga

Faculty of Advanced Science and Technology,
Kumamoto University,
2-39-1,Kurokami, Chuo-ku, Kumamoto, Japan
Email: saga@saga-lab.org

***Abstract*—In recent years, touchscreens have been used all over the world, however, most of them are without realistic haptic feedback. Some of them have feedback, but most of them have vibration direction limited to one direction. Here we propose a novel rendering method for direction-controlled 2-dimensional vibration display to present texture information. In this paper, we proposed a dimension-controlled rendering method of texture information that enables vibration control in the X and Y-axis precisely by using lateral force. Further, to improve the fidelity for large-scaled texture, we proposed to combine image features information of the textures. We held an experiment to evaluate the fidelity of the proposed method. The result shows that the proposed method can present randomized textures and large periodic textures more precisely than the conventional method.**

Keywords–Haptic Rendering; Vibrotactile display.

I. INTRODUCTION

In recent years, touchscreens have been used all over the world due to the spread of smartphones and the like, however many of them do not have realistic vibrotactile feedback. At the research level, several haptic devices using a liquid crystal panel have been developed. For example, Chubb et al. developed a haptic device employing friction change induced by squeeze film effect[1], and Konyo et al. proposed vibration frequency control and virtual pointer [2]. Wang et al. developed a sliding system using shear force [3]. These vibration stimuli realize high reproducibility, though, the direction of the vibration is limited to one-dimension. This is because it has been found that receptors transmitting vibrational stimulus in the skin cannot discriminate the direction of vibration[4]. For this reason, the direction of vibration has not been regarded as much importance in the tactile research so far, and most of them have employed one-dimensional vibration.

However, there is some distribution of the receptors in the skin. Thus, the input signals from multiple receptors may induce discrimination of multi-dimensional vibration. In this paper, we propose a rendering method to reproduce biaxial acceleration information through our lateral-force-displaying device using X–axis and Y-axis vibration information. We report the results of experiments on the reproducibility of tactile sensation by comparing the conventional method and proposed one. We propose a novel rendering method to display multi-dimensional vibration. Further, to improve the fidelity for large-scaled texture, we proposed to combine image features information of the textures. We held an experiment to evaluate the fidelity of the proposed method. The result suggests that the proposed method can present randomized textures and periodic textures more precisely than the conventional method.

II. PRESENTATION OF TACTILE TEXTURE INFORMATION USING VIBRATION

Many researchers are considering methods of presenting tactile texture information using vibration information from various viewpoints [5], [6]. Romano et al. proposed a method for recording texture on a tablet by recording acceleration, position, and contact force overtime when touching a texture with a dedicated tool [7]. Saga et al. proposed a simpler recording/playing method by omitting the measurement of pressure and using a compensation method when reproducing vibration [8]. They reproduce the sense of direct touch by recording vibration information with fingers and reproducing the recorded information by using the shearing force presentation device.

III. METHODS

We extend the method of Saga et al. and propose a method to accurately record the vibration information on the X and Y axes and reproduce it on our device.

A. Recording phase

The triaxial acceleration sensor (ADXL - 335) is fixed to the finger with tape and the acceleration information is recorded from several textures. Since Saga et al. recorded acceleration information by the audio input, it was recorded as one-dimensional data. In this research, to accurately acquire three-dimensional data, acceleration information was processed by a microcontroller, Arduino, which packs three-axis information as one packet and transmitted to a PC using serial communication. On the PC, packed vibration information was unpacked and recorded by the Processing application.

The acceleration is sampled at 1 kHz. To accurately present the recorded vibration direction and reproduce faithful vibrations, using correct vibrations which are suitable for the user ’s movement direction is essential. Therefore, when recording vibration information, we stored vibration separately not in one direction but two directions, X and Y-axis. This makes it possible to more accurately reproduce vibrations not only for textures that give similar vibrations regardless of the direction in which the fingers are moved but also for textures with significantly different vibrations depending on the direction in which the fingers are moved.

B. Display phase

Reproduction of vibration is carried out by using pre-recorded vibrations in two directions and a shearing force presenting device. In the presentation phase, vibration patterns are generated by using the vibration information of these two directions.

The compensation method used by Saga et al. resampled the acceleration by using the ratio of the moving speed of the finger during recording and playing. In our proposed method, we use a new compensation method extended the method of Saga et al. in this experiment. The compensation method is described below.

First, information to be recorded and reproduced is defined (The superscript $\mathbf{D}$ $=X,Y$represents the direction of movement, r and p represent the phase of record or play).

$$\mathbf{a}_r^{\mathscr{D}}(t_r) = \begin{pmatrix} a_{rx}^{\mathscr{D}} \\ a_{ry}^{\mathscr{D}} \end{pmatrix} \quad (1)$$

The t_r shows the elapsed time in the recording phase. The finger position $\mathbf{X}_p$ during playing phase is obtained, and the finger movement speed is derived from the following value.

$$\mathbf{X}_p(t_p) = \begin{pmatrix} x_p \\ y_p \end{pmatrix} \quad (2)$$

At this time, the moving speed of the finger during playing phase ($\dot{\mathbf{x}}_\mathbf{p}$) is calculated using the moving distance in unit time ΔT.

$$\dot{\mathbf{x}}_\mathbf{p} = \frac{\Delta \mathbf{X}_p(t_p)}{\Delta T} = \begin{pmatrix} \frac{\Delta x_p}{\Delta T} \\ \frac{\Delta y_p}{\Delta T} \end{pmatrix} \quad (3)$$

Because the elapsed time between frames during recording and playing phase should be the same, the presented vibration is calculated using the ratio of recording speed $\dot{\mathbf{x}}_\mathbf{r}$ and playing speed $\dot{\mathbf{x}}_\mathbf{p}$.

$$\mathbf{a}_p^{\mathscr{D}}(t_{p_{n+1}}) = \mathbf{a_r}^{\mathscr{D}}(t_{p_n} + \frac{|\dot{\mathbf{x}}_\mathbf{p}(t_{p_n})|}{|\dot{\mathbf{x}}_\mathbf{r}(t_{p_n})|}\Delta T) \quad (4)$$

In this experiment, the moving speed in the recording phase, $\dot{\mathbf{x}}_\mathbf{r}$ = 5 cm/s. In the playing phase, the vibration is presented using the $\mathbf{a}_p^{\mathscr{D}}(t_{p_{n+1}})$ (Eq. 5), which is a linear joint of a^X anda^Y . As shown in Figure 1, depending on the movement direction, switch the acceleration information. If the movement vector of the user' s finger is (α, β), the presented acceleration $\mathbf{a}_p(t_{p_{n+1}})$ is obtained using the following formula

$$\mathbf{a}_p(t_{p_{n+1}}) = \left|\frac{\alpha}{\sqrt{\alpha^2+\beta^2}}\right| \mathbf{a}_r^X(t_{p_{n+1}}) + \left|\frac{\beta}{\sqrt{\alpha^2+\beta^2}}\right| \mathbf{a}_r^Y(t_{p_{n+1}}) \quad (5)$$

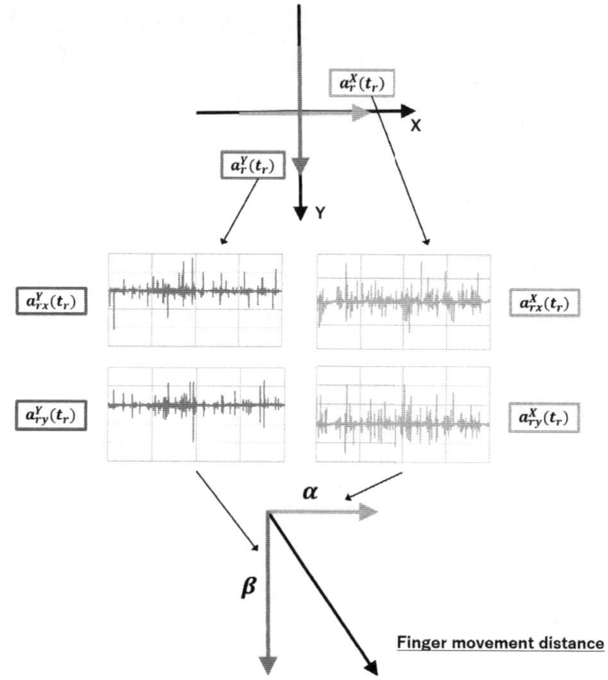

Figure 1. Presentation method of vibration according to the movement direction of the finger

IV. SUPERPOSITION INFORMATION OF IMAGE FEATURES

The proposed method has a problem that tactile reproducibility decreases for a texture having a certain spatial frequency (e.g., tiled-floor). Hence the fidelity of the texture decreases. We considered that the problem is caused by the periodicity and continuity of the presented vibration. Therefore, we propose to combine another rendering method to resolve this problem by employing image information.

A. Recording of image features

To solve the problem in displaying larger periodic textures, we propose a vibration presentation method using image features. The parameters of feature points, such as size and angle, are considered to represent some texture information. Therefore, our method extracts the information contained in the texture image, processes it into a one-dimensional form that can be used for augmenting vibration. The procedure of presenting the actual vibration information and image information by augmentation is shown below. OpenCV is used for image processing. The procedure is described below;

1) Acquire features from texture images using AKAZE
2) Extract the size information representing the diameter of the important region around the feature
3) Obtains one-dimensional information by averaging information in each of the x-axis and y-axis directions and then normalizing
4) Augment the size information corresponding to the display position on the vibration information and presented

As large periodic textures, we used a self-made texture of a tile pattern made of polylactic acid (PLA). Figure 2 shows

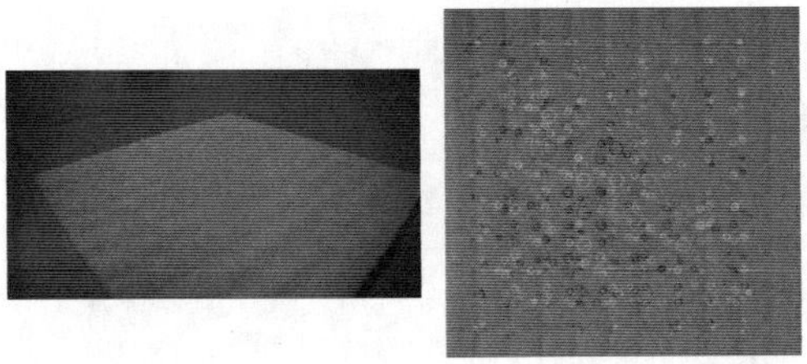

Figure 2. (left)self-made texture : (right)image future

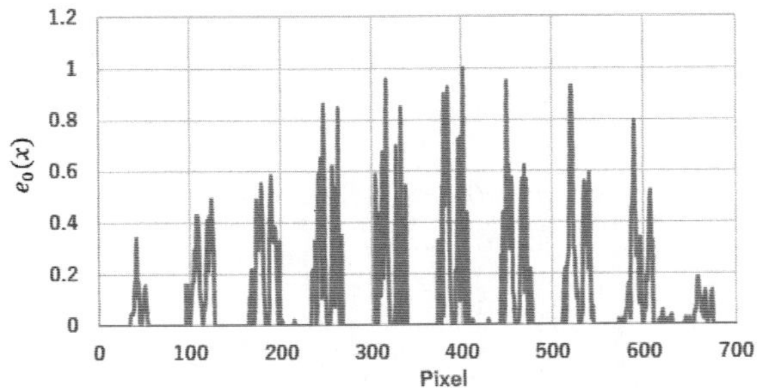

Figure 3. Image features extracted from self-made tile texture

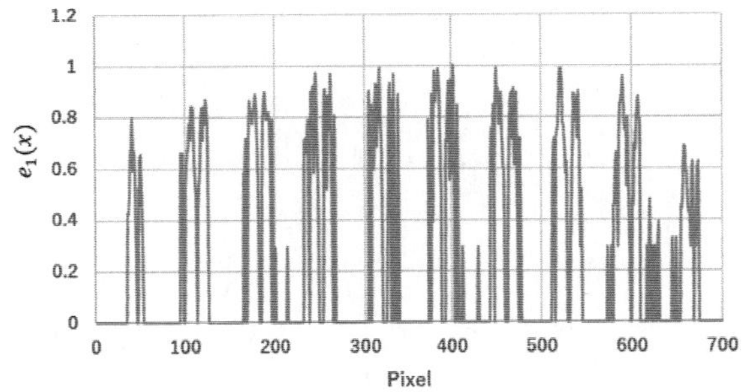

Figure 4. Image features with logarithmic function

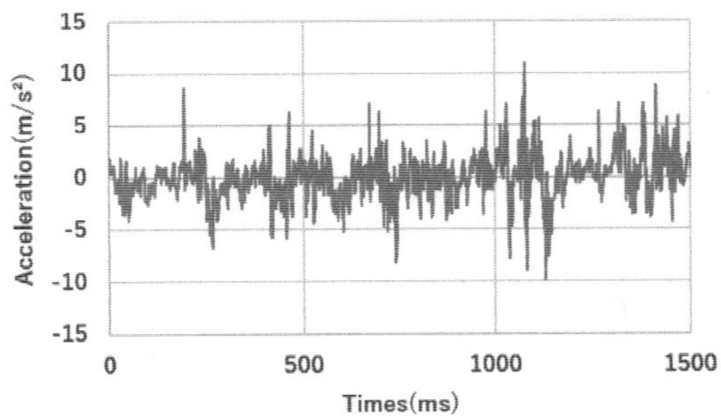

Figure 5. The vibration information before the image feature is superimposed

the result of the extraction of image features from the image of the self-made texture.

Image features can also be acquired for textures with other certain spatial frequencies in the same way, and by superimposing image features corresponding to finger positions on texture vibration information, it is effective for textures with low tactile reproducibility vibration is presented. Figure 3 shows one-dimensional image features extracted from a self-made tile texture ($e_0(x)$). Further, to avoid the diminishing of vibration at no feature area, we also prepared normalized features after applying a logarithmic function to the image features ($e_1(x)$). Figure 4 shows a normalized image features($e_1(x)$).

B. Presentation of vibration information using image feature

The presented vibration is calculated by the following equation. ax, ay is the presentation vibration on the x-axis and y-axis, and e is the size information of the image feature to be superimposed.

$$a(x,y) = a_x e(x) + a_y e(y) \tag{6}$$

By using this presentation method, it is possible to emphasize and present only the characteristic parts of the texture. Figure 5 shows the vibration information before the image feature is augmented, and Figure 6 shows the vibration information after the image feature is augmented. Figure 7 shows the vibration information after the augmentation of $e_1(x)$.

V. EXPERIMENT

A. Experiment preparation

We used 10 textures for an experiment. The textures are the following; soft artificial grass1 which is close to natural grass, artificial grass2 which is harder than natural grass, stiff carpet1, soft carpet2, self-made tiled texture, 40 coarse sandpaper, three types of placemats with different feels, and punched plastic plates. Figure 8 shows the image of the texture used in the experiment.

Participants were 6 healthy men aged 22 to 24. During this experiment, they wear eye masks to block visual information and headphones to block external sounds. They were all right-handed, and they used their right index fingers for rubbing movement.

B. Experiment procedure

We compared several rendering methods of vibration for each texture. 5 stages Likert scale were used for evaluation.

1) Ask the subject to touch the sample texture placed on the weighing scale and train them so that the pressing force to be kept about 50 gf for 5 minutes
2) Have they touch the real texture for 10 seconds to learn the tactile sensation
3) Ask them to touch the texture presented on the display for 10 seconds and evaluate it in five steps how much the texture have fidelity
4) Change the presentation method and have it evaluated in the same way as steps 2 and 3.
5) Only when the texture to be displayed was a large periodic texture, a method of augmenting image features is also used, and the user is asked to select whis is the better method for fidelity, $e_0(x)$ or$e_1(x)$
6) After completing steps 2 to 5 for all ten types of textures, we finished the experiment.

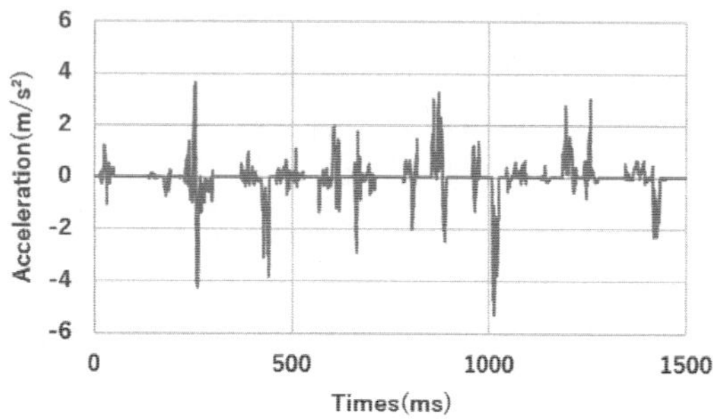

Figure 6. The vibration information after the image feature is superimposed

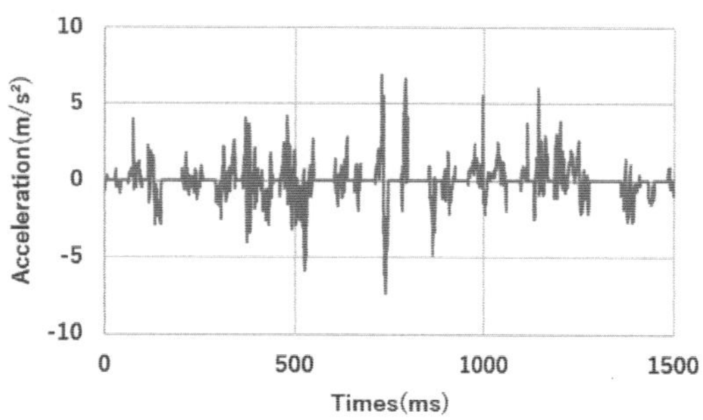

Figure 7. the vibration information after the image feature to which the logarithmic function is applied is superimposed

To eliminate the influence of the order effect, experiments are conducted by changing the order of presenting patterns for each subject.

VI. RESULTS AND DISCUSSION

A. *Reality of virtual texture*

The results of reality evaluation of the virtual texture are shown in Figure 9.

The proposed two-dimensional vibration rendering method was evaluated higher than the one-dimensional vibration presentation in artificial grass 2, carpet 2, placemat 1, and placemat 2 (Figure 9). However, as a result of Tukey ' s test, no significant difference was obtained for textures other than artificial grass 2. We consider the reasons as follows. Among the textures that were highly evaluated for the two-dimensional vibration presentation, the following textures, artificial turf 2, sandpaper, and mat 2, have random spatial frequencies. Also, although no significant difference was obtained between sandpaper and mat 2, both scores exceeded 3.0. This suggests that our two-dimensional vibration presentation method is good at presenting textures with random spatial frequencies. With soft textures,such as artificial grass 1, carpet, and mat 3, there was no significant difference between the one-dimensional and two-dimensional vibration presentations. Our proposed method records vibrations in the X-axis and Y-axis directions and selects and presents vibrations by the direction of finger movement, making it easier to generate random-period vibrations than one-dimensional vibrations it is conceivable that. In particular, since the display surface is

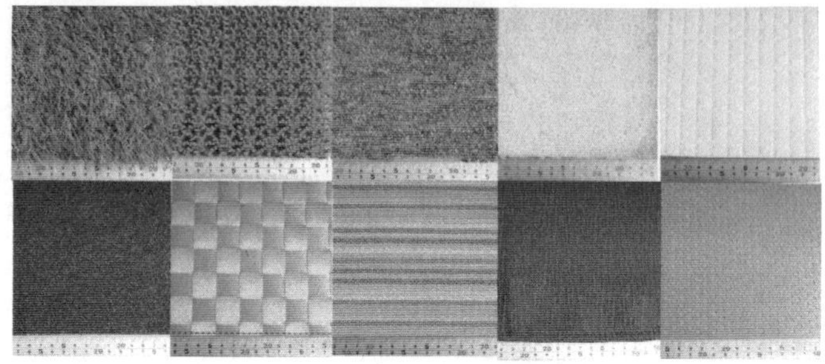

Figure 8. Texture used in experiment

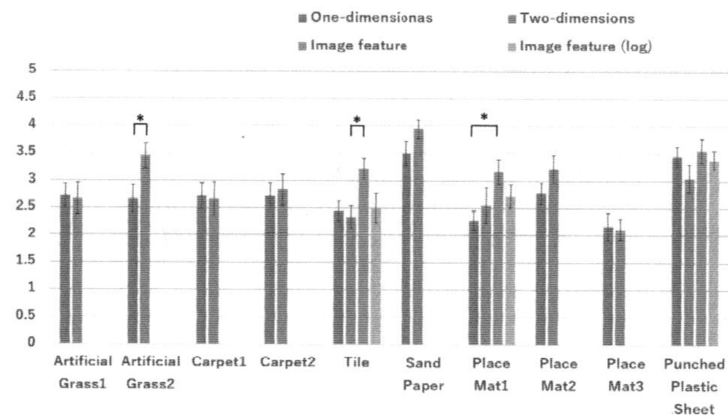

Figure 9. Result of reality evaluation

a hard material, it can be said that the evaluation of a texture having a hard random spatial frequency tends to be high. This may be related to the perception of softness due to the change in the contact area between the finger and the texture.

B. *Evaluation of image feature superposition method*

From Figure 9, as you can see that for some textures, the presentation method that augments image features on vibration information is highly evaluated.

From the two results, the proposed two-dimensional rendering method is suitable for presenting materials with random spatial frequencies (artificial grass 2 and sandpaper 2). In other words, it is not suitable for presenting materials with certain spatial frequencies (e.g., tile). We will discuss the reasons for this result. In the proposed method, independent vibrations are presented on the X-axis and the Y-axis, and it is speculated that vibrations with random periods are likely to occur, depending on the direction in which the finger is moved since the subject can freely move the finger during the experiment. However, it is difficult to present a periodic vibration. Also, the larger the period of the real texture, the easier it is for the users to recognize the periodicity. Therefore, the reality of the virtual texture tends to be lower when compared to the real texture. For these reasons, the users felt fidelity on materials with random spatial frequencies. On the other hand, they couldn ' t feel fidelity on materials with large periodic patterns. Since the texture of tiles, place mat1 and punched plastic sheet has large periodic patterns, it is considered difficult to reproduce it with the two-dimensional rendering method.

However, from the results of the image feature-based rendering method, we found the method can display large periodic

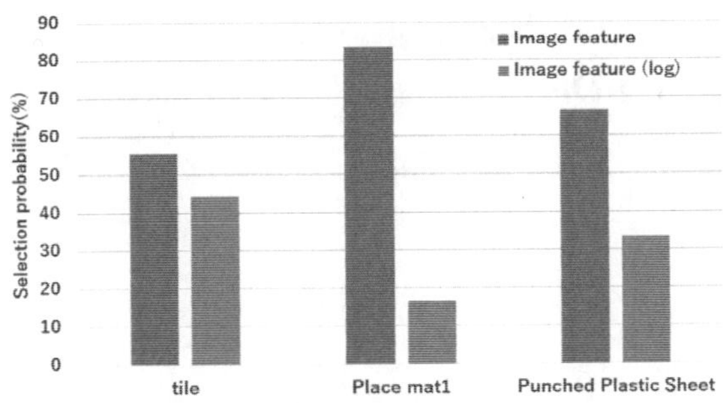

Figure 10. Result of reality evaluation

patterns. By using the image feature, we can emphasize the characteristic part of the texture. Figure 10 shows the result of selecting the higher evaluation one of the two image feature augmentation methods.

The method that did not apply the logarithmic function($e_0(x)$) in all three textures received higher ratings. We consider the reason for this result. The method using a logarithmic function for image features ($e_1(x)$) reduced loss of vibration information but also reduced feature enhancement. In particular, since place mat1 has the longest distance between features among the three textures, that the periodicity of the features seemed to contribute more to the fidelity than the magnitude of the vibration. Also, the score of the punched plastic sheet texture exceeds 3.0 even in the case of a two-dimensional vibration presentation, although the texture has a certain spatial frequency. This is probably because the distance between feature points of the texture is small and it is difficult to recognize a constant period. This indicates that the two-dimensional vibration presentation method is not good at presenting textures that have a constant and large period.

VII. CONCLUSION

We proposed a method to record the vibration of a texture tracing using a three-axis acceleration sensor and reproduce it as faithfully as possible in two dimensions. Experiments show that our proposed method is suitable for displaying textures with random spatial frequencies. In addition, we proposed a presentation method that combines image features, and succeeded in improving the reproducibility of textures that are difficult to present.

ACKNOWLEDGMENT

This work was partly supported by JSPS KAKENHI 18H04104G1 (Grant-in-Aid for Scientific Research (A)) and 19K2287900 (Grant-in-Aid for challenging Exploratory Research).

REFERENCES

[1] E. C. Chubb, J. E. Colgate, and M. A. Peshkin, "Shiverpad: A glass haptic surface that produces shear force on a bare finger," IEEE Transactions on Haptics, vol. 3, no. 3, 2010, pp. 189–198.

[2] M. Konyo, H. Yamada, S. Okamoto, and S. Tadokoro, "Alternative display of friction represented by tactile stimulation without tangential force," in International Conference on Human Haptic Sensing and Touch Enabled Computer Applications. Springer, 2008, pp. 619–629.

[3] D. Wang, K. Tuer, M. Rossi, and J. Shu, "Haptic overlay device for flat panel touch displays," in Haptic Interfaces for Virtual Environment and Teleoperator Systems, 2004. HAPTICS'04. Proceedings. 12th International Symposium on. IEEE, 2004, p. 290.

[4] A. Brisben, S. Hsiao, and K. Johnson, "Detection of vibration transmitted through an object grasped in the hand," Journal of Neurophysiology, vol. 81, no. 4, 1999, pp. 1548–1558.

[5] K. Minamizawa, Y. Kakehi, M. Nakatani, S. Mihara, and S. Tachi, "Techtile toolkit: a prototyping tool for design and education of haptic media," in Proceedings of the 2012 Virtual Reality International Conference. ACM, 2012, p. 26.

[6] Y. Visell, A. Law, and J. R. Cooperstock, "Toward iconic vibrotactile information display using floor surfaces," in EuroHaptics conference, 2009 and Symposium on Haptic Interfaces for Virtual Environment and Teleoperator Systems. World Haptics 2009. Third Joint. IEEE, 2009, pp. 267–272.

[7] J. M. Romano and K. J. Kuchenbecker, "Creating realistic virtual textures from contact acceleration data," IEEE Transactions on Haptics, vol. 5, no. 2, 2012, pp. 109–119.

[8] S. Saga and R. Raskar, "Simultaneous geometry and texture display based on lateral force for touchscreen," in World Haptics Conference (WHC), 2013. IEEE, 2013, pp. 437–442.

Alarm Sound Classification System in Smartphones for the Deaf and Hard-of-Hearing Using Deep Neural Networks

Yuhki Shiraishi
and Takuma Takeda

Faculty of Industrial Technology
Tsukuba University of Technology, Japan
Email: yuhkis@a.tsukuba-tech.ac.jp

Akihisa Shitara

Graduate School of Library, Information and Media Studies
University of Tsukuba, Japan
Email: theta-akihisa@digitalnature.slis.tsukuba.ac.jp

Abstract—**For the deaf and hard-of-hearing to be able to go out safely, they must be able to recognize alarm sounds (horns, bicycle bells, ambulance sirens, etc.) among various environmental sounds. Therefore, it is crucial to be able to transmit these kinds of sounds to such people, even in noisy environmental conditions. In this paper, we propose and develop an alarm sound classification system using deep neural networks. The system works on smartphones that can always be carried by the users when they are going out. Besides, we performed evaluation experiments to verify the effectiveness of the system using the 5-fold cross-validation method. Furthermore, we evaluate the classification rate for unlearned data and re-evaluate one by adding data downloaded from the web. We also discuss the limitations of the system to improve it and make it more useful.**

Keywords*–*Alarm sound; Classification; Deaf and hard-of-hearing; Neural network; Smartphone.

I. INTRODUCTION

Over 5% of the world's population (466 million people) has disabling hearing loss as stated in [1]. In order for these people to be able to go out safely, they must be able to recognize alarm sounds (horns, bicycle bells, ambulance sirens, etc.) directly linked to a safe and secure life, among various environmental sounds. Therefore, there is need for a system that distinguishes these specific alarm sounds from environmental sounds and transmits them to those with disabling hearing loss.

In recent years, Deep Neural Networks (DNNs) have been attracting attention; DNNs automatically learn alarm sounds to be recognized, and they automatically acquire the features of these sounds. With DNNs, high-precision classification is expected even when the sound quality is affected because of the movement of objects or noisy environments.

In this research, we develop an alarm sound classification system using DNN (Figure 1). As a result, hearing-impaired people will be able to recognize alarm sounds and go out safely. Our aim is to build a system that uses a smartphone because the users carry smartphones when they go out.

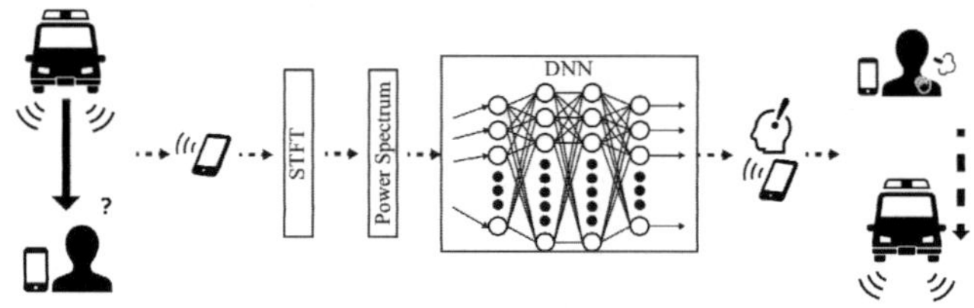

Figure 1. Alarm sound classification and transmission systems.

In this paper, we propose an alarm sound classification system using DNN and confirm essential classification performance. Moreover, we develop a smartphone application that recognizes the siren of an ambulance, the bell of a bicycle, etc., and sends it to the user. We perform evaluation experiments to verify the effectiveness of the system using the 5-fold Cross-Validation (CV) method. Furthermore, we evaluate the classification rate for unlearned data and re-evaluate one by adding data downloaded from the web. We also discuss the limitations of the system to improve it and make it more useful in the future.

II. RELATED WORK

Ontenna [2] is an interface that focuses on vibration, which lets the user recognize sounds by real-time vibration. The system was created to recognize sound, so there is no system to tell the user the type and direction of the sound. However, the Ontenna system is tiny and lightweight. In the system, a sound of 0–90 dB was converted into 256 steps of vibration and light intensity. The sound feature is transmitted to the user through some kinds of vibration.

Google Live Transcribe [3] is mainly for voice recognition, but can also recognize environmental sounds. The only alert sound supported by the system is the horn of the car. Moreover, since the main feature of the system is voice recognition, there is no ability to communicate with the user via a vibration or through pop-up notifications.

Wavio SeeSound [4] can send sounds to the user via vibration and pop-up notifications. However, the system works indoors and does not support outdoor use.

Takeda et al. [5] proposed a system for classifying alarm sounds using a multilayer perceptron neural network. However, the alarm system only targets straightforward beep sounds in oxygen concentrators.

Nicholas et al. [6] present the first mobile audio sensing framework built from coupled deep neural networks that simultaneously perform everyday audio sensing tasks. However, the target sounds are from diverse acoustic environments such as bedrooms, vehicles, or cafes. The classification ratio is at most about 90%, which is inadequate for safety alarm recognition.

Meanwhile, Jain et al. [7] examine how Deaf and Hard-of-Hearing (DHH) people think about sounds in the home, and they explore potential concerns. Findlater et al. [8] conducted an online survey with 201 DHH participants to investigate preferences for mobile and wearable sound awareness systems. The reviewed studies support the importance of alarm sound classification systems.

III. Development System

In this system, the classification and transmission application run on a smartphone without internet connection. Since users of this system are DHH or people with disabling hearing loss, a non-sound notification system is required. Therefore, the developed system displays the names of alarm sounds on the screen when such sounds occur.

The basic flow of the proposed system is as follows:

1) Collect environmental sounds with a smartphone.
2) Notify smartphone when an alarm sound is identified.

Deep learning is used as a classification method. To create learning data, we collected sound data such as ambulance sirens, horns, and bells, to be classified and transmitted. We pre-collected these sounds in a real environment using smartphones. The reason why we collected the data in the real environment instead of using the pure tone of the warning sound is to make full use of the generalization ability of deep learning.

We performed data reduction and data screening on the alarm sound data collected in various environments, and we created a learning database.

Keras [9] was used for implementing deep learning algorithms. Keras was a wrapper library for Tensorflow [10], and now Keras is officially integrated into Tensorflow. Besides, it supports not only Linux servers but also Android and iOS, which makes possible application development more straightforward.

Figure 2 shows a snapshot of the ongoing developed application. Presently, the application works only on the iPhone, which is programmed using the Swift programming language. By using Apple's neural network library, we can import the learned weight data using Keras to iPhone.

IV. Classification Algorithm

The alarm classifying flow consists of the following three steps.

1) Continuous collection of environmental sounds.
2) If volume data exceeding the threshold is detected, record audio data for a certain period.
3) Specify the alarm class (horns, bicycle bells, ambulance sirens, etc.) of the recorded audio data.

Besides, because the nature of the alarm sound tends to be monotonous, we apply the Short-Time Fourier Transform (STFT)

$$STFT(t,\omega) = \int_{-\infty}^{\infty} x(\tau)h(\tau - t)e^{-j\omega\tau}d\tau, \quad (1)$$

where $x(t)$ is sound data, and $h(t)$ is a window function to the sound data collected by the above threshold processing.

After STFT, the power spectrum of STFT is converted to the log scale, which is used as an input to the DNN. Finally,

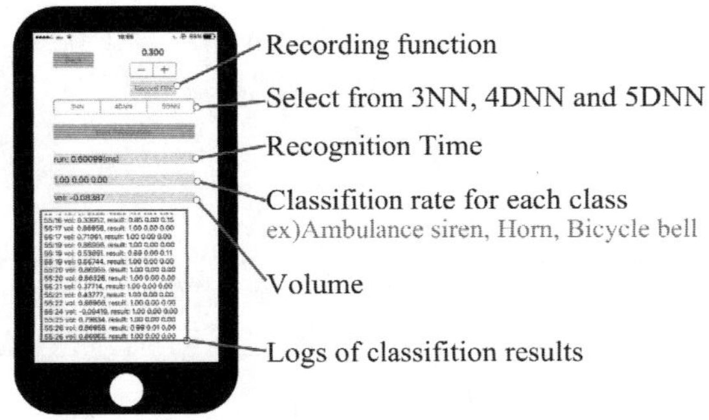

Figure 2. Snapshot of develop smartphone application.

real-time classification is performed by applying an integrated process to the one-time classification results that DNN has repeatedly determined for all audio data.

ReLU (2) is used for the activation function, Softmax cross entropy (3) is used for the error function, and Adam [11] is used for the learning algorithm, where t_k is the correct label (one-hot expression), and y_k indicates the network output.

$$f(u) = max(u, 0) \quad (2)$$

$$E = -\sum_k t_k \log y_k \quad (3)$$

The operation of the classification application is as follows:

1) Use a smartphone microphone and collect sound every 1024 frames using 32-bit single-precision floating-point numbers (-1.0 to 1.0).
2) When the absolute value of the buffered single-precision floating-point buffer exceeds the threshold value (0.3), identification processing starts.
3) Multiply the buffer by 2^{31} and change the buffer range to a 32-bit integer type, then execute STFT.
4) Input of logarithmic power spectrum to DNN.
5) Display the classification result on the screen.

In a real environment, the target sound would continue to resonate so that the classification result would be displayed multiple times for one occurrence of the target sound. Therefore, considering the importance of desired alarm sounds, the final classification result is determined by the following algorithm (called integrated judgment process). As a result, the classification ratio and reliability are expected to be improved.

1) Evaluate sounds continuously (more than once to less than ten times).
2) If there is more than one classification result from a specific sound other than noise,
   a) Calculate the sum of outputs.
   b) The largest of the noise exclusions is used as the final classification result.
3) If all classification results are noise,
   a) Regard the final classification result as noise.

Figure 1 shows the flow of the entire operation up to the classification result determination.

TABLE I. 5-FOLD CV FOR 5 TYPES OF ALARMS.

Number of layers	*Classification rate*
3	0.9845
4	0.9867
5	0.9924

TABLE II. CLASSIFICATION RESULTS IN A NOISY ENVIRONMENT (BEFORE APPLYING THE INTEGRATED JUDGMENT PROCESS).

	TP	*FP*	*FN*	*TN*	*Prec.*	*Recall*	*F-value*	*Max vol[dB]*
Horn	545	0	87	2232	1.00	0.86	0.92	98.1
Bicycle bell	502	0	113	2249	1.00	0.81	0.98	127.7
Ambulance	572	1	56	2336	0.99	0.91	0.95	90.0
Fire alarm	631	1	57	2176	0.99	0.91	0.95	93.2
Noise	298	262	2	2563	0.53	0.99	0.69	100.3

V. EXPERIMENTS

A. *Basic performance of the classification system*

In addition to the two types of manually collected sound data (ambulance sirens and bicycle bells), we downloaded a total of 18 horn sound data from the web page [12]. We also manually recorded fire alarm sounds during evacuation drills. Furthermore, we added a noise class to handle cases where sounds other than the target sounds are generated. We collected six types of noises: footsteps, car driving sounds, voices, door opening/closing sounds, hitting desks, and rubbing plastic bags.

Training and evaluation were performed on 3-layer NN, 4-layer DNN, and 5-layer DNN. We performed STFT with 1024 frame for the 44.1 kHz 32 bit sound. We carried out a 5-fold CV for 25 000 pieces of training and evaluation data (5000 pieces $\times$ 5 classes) with a maximum of 1000 epochs (input layer: 513, hidden layer: 128, output layer: 5).

A 5-fold CV is described as follows. First, we divide all data into five groups. Next, data from one group are used for the test and the data from the other four groups are used for the learning. Finally, the learning process is repeated five times by using five different test groups.

Table I shows the experimental results. The classification results in the table are above 98% for all NN/DNNs. In the following experiments, we used the five-layer DNN because it gives the highest classification rate.

B. *Performance in a noisy environment*

Next, the experiment was performed in a noisy environment of 50.5 to 100.3 dB. In this study, we assumed that the noise originating from outdoors was mainly the noise of cars, and repeatedly evaluated the noise from driving cars 100 times (after applying the integrated judgment process). At that time, we recorded the maximum volume of each target sound.

Table II shows the classification results before applying the integrated judgment process, and Table III shows the results after applying the integrated judgment process. After applying the judgment process, it was possible to classify these sounds with an average F-measure of more than 99% in a real environment.

C. *Performance for unlearned horn sounds*

In this algorithm, we performed feature extraction and identification using STFT. In particular, since the quality of horn sounds differs depending on the type, the frequency characteristics also differ. Therefore, there is concern that generalizability of the performance of new types of horn sounds is perhaps low.

TABLE III. CLASSIFICATION RESULTS IN A NOISY ENVIRONMENT (AFTER APPLYING THE INTEGRATED JUDGMENT PROCESS).

	TP	*FP*	*FN*	*TN*	*Prec.*	*Recall*	*F-value*	*Max vol[dB]*
Horn	100	0	0	400	1.00	1.00	1.00	98.1
Bicycle bell	100	0	0	400	1.00	1.00	1.00	127.7
Ambulance	100	0	1	400	1.00	0.99	0.99	90.0
Fire alarm	100	0	1	400	1.00	0.99	0.99	93.2
Noise	100	2	0	398	0.99	1.00	0.99	100.3

TABLE IV. UNLEARNED HORN CLASSIFICATION (BEFORE APPLYING THE INTEGRATED JUDGMENT PROCESS).

	TP	*FN*	*Classification rate*
Horn 1	62	16	0.79
Horn 2	43	11	0.80
Horn 3	42	8	0.84
Horn 4	55	23	0.71
Horn 5	67	8	0.89
Horn 6	36	29	0.55
Horn 7	50	33	0.60

Therefore, we examined the classification in the case of a new type of horn sound (20 times $\times$ 7 types) different from the learning data in a noisy environment. The results are shown in Tables IV and V.

As a result, by applying the integrated judgment process, we were able to obtain a classification rate of over 95% for unknown horn sounds.

D. *Adding new type of data from the web*

In addition to the five types of sound data collected so far (car horn, ambulance siren, bicycle bell, fire alarm, noise), we downloaded different car horns and ambulance sounds from the web page [13]. We also downloaded different bicycle bells from other web pages [14] (because the bicycle bells are not included in the [13]). We collected 428 car horn sounds, 929 ambulance siren sounds, and 169 bicycle bell sounds as new collections. Furthermore, the data was manually separated into the noisy and relatively clear data. Table VI shows the characteristics (types, numbers, and the range of sound time) of all obtained relatively clear data.

Using the CV method (5-fold, 1000 epochs) with 77 183 training and evaluation data (21 180 car horns, 28 684 ambulance sirens, 9819 bicycle bells, 12 500 fire alarms, 5 000 noises), training and evaluation were performed (input layer: 513, hidden layer: 128, output layer: 5). The classification results are shown in Table VII.

Table VII shows that the classification rates were above 94% for all NN/DNNs. However, the five-layer DNN has the highest classification rate, about 97%.

VI. LIMITATIONS OF THE DEVELOPED SYSTEM

First, we discuss data collection. The data set downloaded from the web has some problems: It includes 1) the noisy data, 2) the unlabeled data, and 3) the mixed sound data for one target (including no sound time). It is also challenging to collect significant amounts of sound data manually. This is because making a real alarm sound for acquiring such data can confuse others even when it is not truly dangerous. Crowdsourcing is a solution because crowd workers could

TABLE V. UNLEARNED HORN CLASSIFICATION (AFTER APPLYING THE INTEGRATED JUDGMENT PROCESS).

	TP	*FN*	*Classification rate*
Horn 1	20	0	1.00
Horn 2	20	0	1.00
Horn 3	20	0	1.00
Horn 4	20	0	1.00
Horn 5	20	0	1.00
Horn 6	20	1	0.95
Horn 7	20	1	0.95

TABLE VI. ALL DATA FOR LEARNING AND EVALUATION

	Types of alarm		*Number of each*	*Time range[sec]*
Conventional Data	Horn	18	4	6-20
	Bicycle bell	7		1-10
	Ambulance	18		1-2
Additional Data	Horn	151	1-2	0-4
	Bicycle bell	120		0-4
	Ambulance	103		0-76

record the alarm sound in daily life; other crowd workers would only label the alarm sound when they have time.

Second, in terms of the recognition response timing, a fast response time is vital because of the dangerous circumstances surrounding the sounding of alarms. There is a method to determine the recognition timing when the sound is approaching from a distance based on inverse calculation using the sound speed. However, it is difficult to distinguish the alarm sound from other environmental sounds. This problem might be solved by notifying users when the big alarm sounds occur, which happens in a hazardous situation, e.g., when the car sound is very close to the user. In this case, the way of notification is crucial.

Finally, with DHH it is difficult for people to notice the direction of the sound source. Even when the system recognizes a type of alarm sound, determining the direction of the source of that sound could be another problem. This problem could be resolved by using a microphone array and direction estimate algorithms. The mode of notifying the user of the sound direction is also essential.

VII. CONCLUSION

In this paper, we have proposed and developed an alarm sound classification system using DNNs based on smartphones. Besides, we performed evaluation experiments to verify the effectiveness of the system using the 5-fold CV, and the classification rates were above 98% for all NN/DNNs. We also proposed an integrated judgment process and made it possible to classify the types of alarms with an average F-measure of more than 99% in a real environment by using the integrated process. By applying the integrated judgment process, we were able to obtain a classification rate of over 95% for unknown horn sounds. Furthermore, even after adding the different sound data (428 car horn sounds, 929 ambulance siren sounds, and 169 bicycle bell sounds), the classification rates were above 94% for all NN/DNNs; the five-layer DNN has the highest classification rate, about 97%. We also discussed the limitations of the developed system and the expectations of the improved system by overcoming these limitations.

TABLE VII. 5-FOLD CV USING ADDITIONAL DATA.

Number of layers	*classification rate*
3	0.9367
4	0.9498
5	0.9714
6	0.9710

ACKNOWLEDGMENT

The authors would like to thank Mr. N. Hata and Mr. K. Yano, who have partially worked on the project. This work was partially supported by JSPS KAKENHI Grant Numbers #16K16460, #19K11411, and Promotional Projects for Advanced Education and Research in NTUT. One of the authors, T. Takeda, is now working at NEC Fielding, Ltd., Japan. We would like to thank Editage (www.editage.com) for English language editing.

REFERENCES

[1] World Health Organization, "Deafness and hearing loss," March 2019, URL: https://www.who.int/news-room/fact-sheets/detail/deafness-and-hearing-loss [accessed: 2020-02-06].

[2] Fujitsu, "Ontenna," 2020, URL: https://ontenna.jp/en/ [retrieved: February, 2020].

[3] Google Android, "live transcribe," 2 2020, URL: https://www.android.com/accessibility/live-transcribe/ [retrieved: February, 2020].

[4] Wavio, "See sound," 7 2019, URL: https://www.see-sound.com [retrieved: February, 2020].

[5] F. Takeda, Y. Shiraishi, and T. Sanechika, "Alarm sound classification system of oxygen concentrator by using neural network," International Journal of Innovative Computing, Information and Control, Special Issue on Innovative Computing Methods in Management Engineering, vol. 3, no. 1, 2007, pp. 211–222.

[6] N. D. Lane, P. Georgiev, and L. Qendro, "Deepear: Robust smartphone audio sensing in unconstrained acoustic environments using deep learning," in Proceedings of the 2015 ACM International Joint Conference on Pervasive and Ubiquitous Computing, ser. UbiComp '15. New York, NY, USA: Association for Computing Machinery, 2015, p. 283–294. [Online]. Available: https://doi.org/10.1145/2750858.2804262

[7] D. Jain, A. Lin, R. Guttman, M. Amalachandran, A. Zeng, L. Findlater, and J. Froehlich, "Exploring sound awareness in the home for people who are deaf or hard of hearing," in Proceedings of the 2019 CHI Conference on Human Factors in Computing Systems, ser. CHI '19. New York, NY, USA: Association for Computing Machinery, 2019, pp. 1–13. [Online]. Available: https://doi.org/10.1145/3290605.3300324

[8] L. Findlater, B. Chinh, D. Jain, J. Froehlich, R. Kushalnagar, and A. C. Lin, "Deaf and hard-of-hearing individuals' preferences for wearable and mobile sound awareness technologies," in Proceedings of the 2019 CHI Conference on Human Factors in Computing Systems, ser. CHI '19. New York, NY, USA: Association for Computing Machinery, 2019, pp. 1–13. [Online]. Available: https://doi.org/10.1145/3290605.3300276

[9] Keras Google group., "Keras," 9 2019, URL: https://keras.io [retrieved: February, 2020].

[10] Google, "Tensorflow," 1 2020, URL: https://www.tensorflow.org [retrieved: February, 2020].

[11] D. P. Kingma and J. Ba, "Adam: A method for stochastic optimization," arXiv preprint arXiv:1412.6980, 2014.

[12] Mitsubasankowa, "Mitsubasankowa," 2005, URL: http://www.mskw.co.jp/car/car-horn/ [retrieved: February, 2020].

[13] J. Salamon, C. Jacoby, and J. P. Bello, "A dataset and taxonomy for urban sound research," in 22nd ACM International Conference on Multimedia (ACM-MM'14), Orlando, FL, USA, Nov. 2014, pp. 1041–1044, URL:https://urbansounddataset.weebly.com/ [retrieved: February, 2020].

[14] freesound, "freesound," 2005, URL: https://freesound.org/browse/ [retrieved: February, 2020].

Sensor Glove Approach for Japanese Fingerspelling Recognition System Using Convolutional Neural Networks

Tomohiko Tsuchiya*, Akihisa Shitara†, Fumio Yoneyama*, Nobuko Kato* and Yuhki Shiraishi*
*Faculty of Industrial Technology, Tsukuba University of Technology, Japan
Email: {a193102, yonefumi, nobuko, yuhkis}@a.tsukuba-tech.ac.jp
†Graduate School of Library, Information, and Media Studies, University of Tsukuba, Japan
Email: theta-akihisa@digitalnature.slis.tsukuba.ac.jp

Abstract—**We have developed a Japanese fingerspelling recognition system based on a sensor glove, using deep learning, to achieve smooth communication between the deaf and hard-of-hearing, and hearing people. In this study, we conducted evaluation experiments using a convolutional neural network to recognize 76 characters of Japanese fingerspelling. In the developed system, we have adopted a sensor glove that is light and cheap. Additionally, the target Japanese fingerspelling alphabet includes 35 characters for dynamic fingerspelling, which require both finger and wrist movement. The experimental results demonstrated that the average recognition rate of the developed system was approximately 70.0%. Based on these results, we have discussed the peculiarity of Japanese fingerspelling and potential improvements to sensor gloves and algorithms.**

Keywords–Sign language; Japanese fingerspelling; Sensor glove; Recognition; Convolutional neural network.

I. INTRODUCTION

In recent years, there has been an increased interest in research on speech recognition and information technology devices with voice input functions. Various applications, such as KoeTra [1] and UDtalk [2], as well as cloud-speech-to-text services [3], have been released to provide information accessibility to the Deaf and Hard-of-Hearing (DHH) based on speech recognition. As a result, the DHH can read text corresponding to vocalizations.

However, it is difficult for hearing people to read sign language. Some research on information accessibility systems for sign language recognition has been reported [4]–[11]. However, compared to information accessibility systems based on speech recognition, the development of a practical sign language recognition system is still in progress.

As a primary communication method, sign language is used in everyday conversations among the DHH. Sign language recognition has different characteristics than speech recognition. It is difficult for hearing people to learn and read sign languages. Therefore, a system for converting sign language into voice information or text information (i.e., a sign language recognition system) is necessary (see Figure 1).

A sign language recognition system must recognize the position, direction, and shape of the hands, as well as motion. Methods for recognizing sign language can be roughly classified into recognition using cameras [4] [5] [9], which are non-contact-type sensors, and recognition using sensor gloves, which are contact-type sensors [6] [7] [10] [11]. Luzhnica et al. [6] reported a recognition accuracy of 98.5% for sign language using a sensor glove; however, they only considered approximately 30 recognition candidate classes, which is insufficient for practical use.

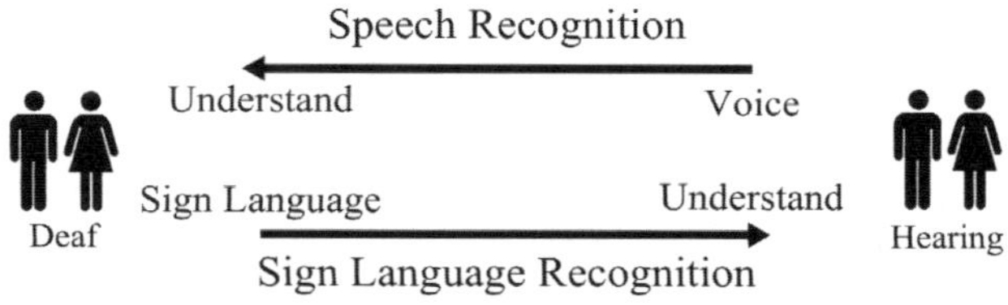

Figure 1. Information accessibility system.

TABLE I. NUMBERS OF FINGERSPELLING CHARACTERS IN DIFFERENT COUNTRIES.

Language	*Dynamic*	*Static*	*Sum*
American	2	24	26
French	3	23	26
Japanese	35	41	76

In recent years, technologies based on deep learning have attracted significant attention. Deep learning, which increases the number of hidden layers in a neural network, is a type of machine learning that can contribute to improving recognition rates. For example, to improve hand gesture recognition accuracy based on image recognition, various techniques for applying deep learning have been reported [4].

In this study, as a first step toward sign language recognition to facilitate communication with the DHH, we attempted to recognize the Japanese FingerSpelling (JFS) recognition system. JFS is composed of representations of Japanese characters, using only the fingers.

A camera, which is a non-contact-type sensor, is difficult to use for sign language recognition in everyday life because hands must be captured by the camera. Additionally, cameras are easily affected by environmental factors. In contrast, hand shape recognition using contact sensors, such as sensor gloves, is easy to perform because sensors can be attached directly to the hands.

We were motivated by the goal of improving recognition accuracy by adopting conductive fiber weaving technology [12], which can reduce the weight and cost of sensor gloves and simplify hand movements (see Figure 2).

In our experiments, we evaluated our developed system by classifying 76 JFS characters, including dynamic (non-static) fingerspelling characters, which are a unique feature of JFS compared to other fingerspelling systems, as shown in Table I. Evaluation experiments were conducted using a Convolutional

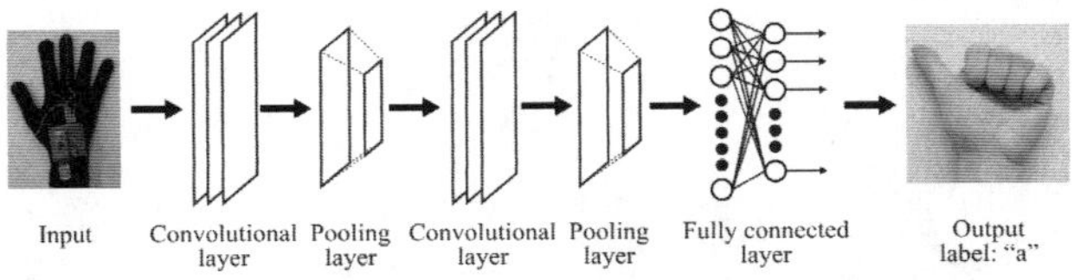

Figure 2. Recognition diagram.

Neural Network (CNN) as a learning model (this type of model performed best in previous studies) to perform data reduction by calculating moving averages of the data acquired from gyro sensors. In these evaluation experiments, all 76 characters of JFS were included as recognition targets, as well as dullness, semi-voiced sounds, diphthongs, and long vowels. Evaluation experiments were conducted using all collected data under a variety of experimental conditions.

In Section II, we present the related works. In Section III, our developed system is detailed. In Section IV, the experimental method is described. In Section V, experimental results are presented, and their implications and limitations are discussed. In Section VI, the conclusions are provided.

II. Related Work

In past research on fingerspelling recognition, two main types of sensors have been proposed to recognize a series of operations in fingerspelling: contact-type sensor gloves and non-contact-type cameras for image recognition.

A. Image recognition

Several methods for recognizing hand shapes based on processing images of fingerspelling captured by cameras have been proposed. Mukai et al. [8] reported that fingerspelling recognition targeting 41 characters without movement in Japanese sign language resulted in an average recognition accuracy of 86%. They used a classification tree and machine learning based on a support vector machine to classify individual images. Hosoe et al. [9] employed deep learning to perform recognition and achieved a recognition rate of 93%, but only for static fingerspelling. Jalal et al. [5] reported a recognition rate for American Sign Language (ASL) images of 99% based on a deep learning algorithm, but only for static fingerspelling (i.e., excluding "J" and "Z"). Therefore, recognition accuracy cannot be considered sufficient for the practical recognition of JFS. Additionally, very few recognition results for dynamic fingerspelling (i.e., the fingers move when expressing a character) have been reported.

B. Sensor glove recognition

Several methods for recognizing hand shapes based on measurement data acquired by contact-type sensor gloves have been proposed. This method can be used to measure finger bending, hand position, and directional data. The measurement data are then sent to a personal computer and a classification algorithm is used to recognize hand shapes. Cabrera et al. [10] paired the Data Glove 5 Ultra [13] sensor glove with an acceleration sensor and acquired information regarding the degree of flexion of each finger, as well as wrist direction. They conducted test classification using 24 static fingerspelling characters in ASL, excluding "J" and "Z." Their neural network

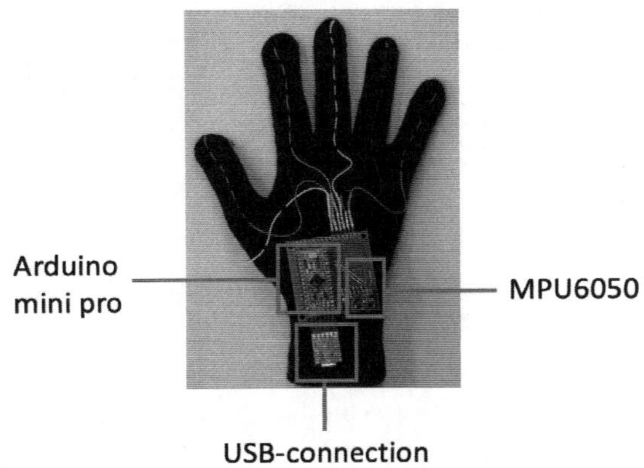

Figure 3. Prototype sensor glove.

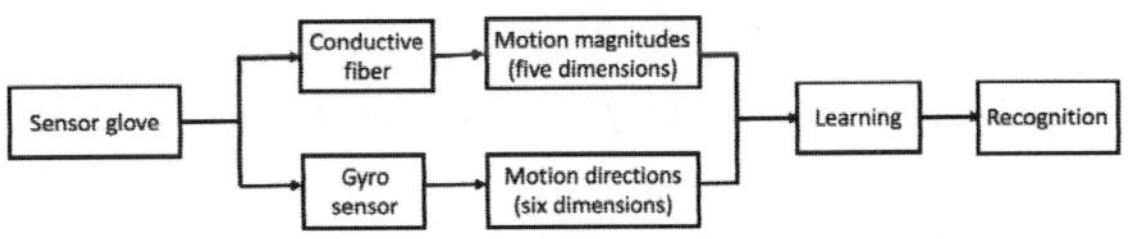

Figure 4. Software structure.

was trained using 5 300 patterns and achieved a recognition rate of 94.07% for 1 200 test patterns. Mummadi et al. [11] proposed a sensor glove prototype with multiple embedded small inertial sensors. They collected French sign language fingerspelling data from 57 people and achieved an average recognition rate of 92% with an F value of 91%. Among various methods for performing JFS recognition, the conductive fiber braid method [12] uses gloves woven with conductive fibers instead of bending sensors. Additionally, such gloves can recognize hand shapes and hand movements by incorporating directional gyro sensor. However, the recognition rate for JFS ("a", "i", "u", "e", "o") based on Euclidean distance has been reported to be only 60%.

III. System Development

In this study, to achieve smooth communication in real-world environments, we designed a system for communicating information using lightweight and comfortable sensor gloves to recognize fingerspelling with high accuracy in real time. The developed system consists of a sensor value measurement unit and recognition unit. Figure 3 presents the JFS recognition system developed in this study. Figure 4 presents the corresponding software architecture.

A. Sensor glove

To recognize fingerspelling efficiently based on hand, finger, and wrist data, it is necessary to detect motion magnitudes and directions using a sensor glove. In this study, we adopted a hand shape recognition technique using conductive fiber sensor gloves, which are more comfortable, less expensive, and lighter than traditional sensor gloves. Motion direction is detected using a gyro sensor. Motion magnitudes are detected based on resistance changes in the conductive fibers in the

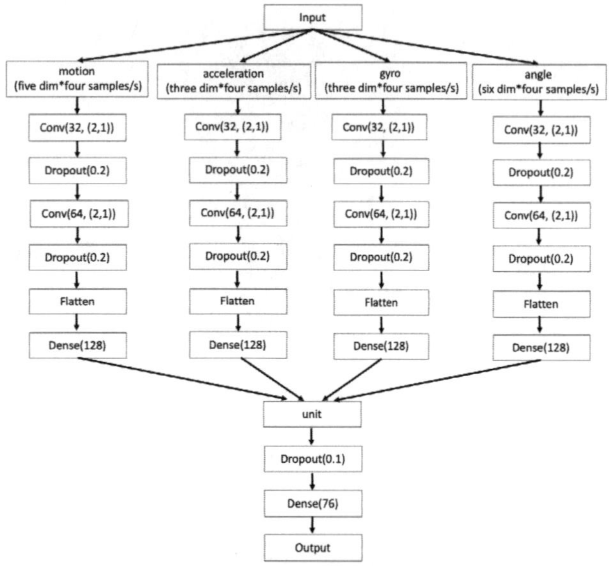

Figure 5. Architecture of the convolutional neural network.

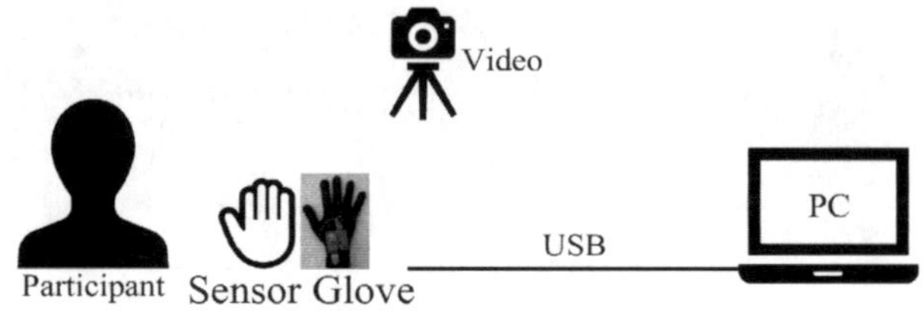

Figure 6. Data acquisition experiment.

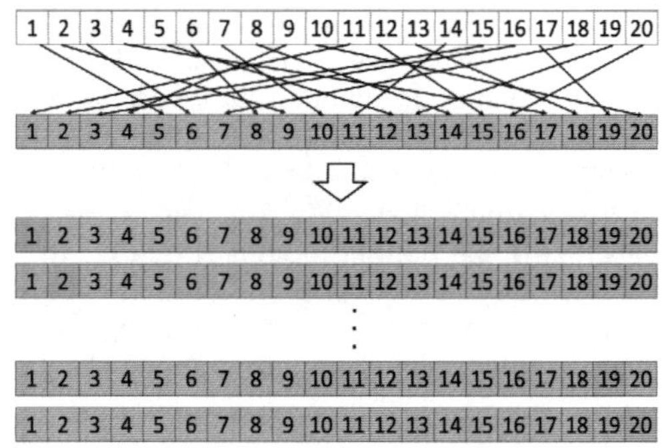

Figure 7. Twenty-fold cross validation by shuffling data.

gloves. The motion detection board is an Arduino board and the measurement values from the sensor glove are transferred from the detection board to a PC, where they are saved in comma-separated-value format. Machine learning and motion recognition are performed using Python implementations on a PC. Sensor readings for JFS motion from the data gloves have different scales depending on the wearer. Therefore, the data are subjected to linear normalization in consideration for differences in movement. Additionally, because the activation function and likelihood function of the proposed system are based on probabilities, as a pretreatment for network inputs, we perform scale conversion to a range of zero to one.

Motion magnitudes are detected based on resistance changes in the conductive fibers during flexion and extension of the fingers. We use partial pressure values to calculate input voltages based on (1).

$$V_{in} = \frac{R_1}{R_1 + R_2} * V_{out} \tag{1}$$

In this equation, V_{in} is the estimated motion magnitude, V_{out} is the reference voltage, R_1 is the variable resistance of the conductive fibers, R_2 is a fixed resistance. When a finger is stretched, the resistance value of the conductive fiber increases. When a finger is bowed, the resistance value of the fiber decreases.

B. Recognition algorithm

In this study, we adopted a CNN. This type of network has achieved high recognition rates in previous studies. The CNN and k-fold cross validation were implemented using open-source libraries called TensorFlow [14] and scikit-learn [15]. We adopted the RMSprop training algorithm [16]. The activation function is a rectified linear unit, as shown in (2). The error function is the cross-entropy function shown in (3), where t_k is the correct label (one-hot expression) and y_k expresses the network output.

$$f(u) = max(u, 0) \tag{2}$$

$$E = -\sum_k t_k \log y_k \tag{3}$$

CNNs are often used for image recognition and can generally achieve high recognition rates. Convolutional layers and pooling layers are the main features of CNNs. These layers are updated as their feature values are extracted during the training process. We transform the measurement data acquired by the sensor glove into two dimensions based on training and evaluation trials. The motion magnitudes, accelerations, and gyro readings are branched at the time of input. Through the CNN (typical layer size of 32 to 64 nodes), these data are coupled using "Flatten" and "Dense" operations (128 nodes). Finally, by using an additional Dense operation (76 nodes) corresponding to the number of JFS characters, outputs are generated. Figure 5 presents a system overview of the CNN. In the CNN, inputs are initially separated based on the physical meanings of each signal. The separated signals are eventually combined to recognize JFS characters.

IV. Experimental Method

A. Data collection

To target 76 JFS characters, we recruited 20 participants (from 20 to 27 years old). In our experiments, each participant wore a sensor glove and performed the motions of finger-spelling characters in sequence for 1 s at a time according to directions provided by a moderator. As shown in Figure 6, video was also recorded to capture the motions of the wrists and fingers of the participants. For each 1 s motion, at a

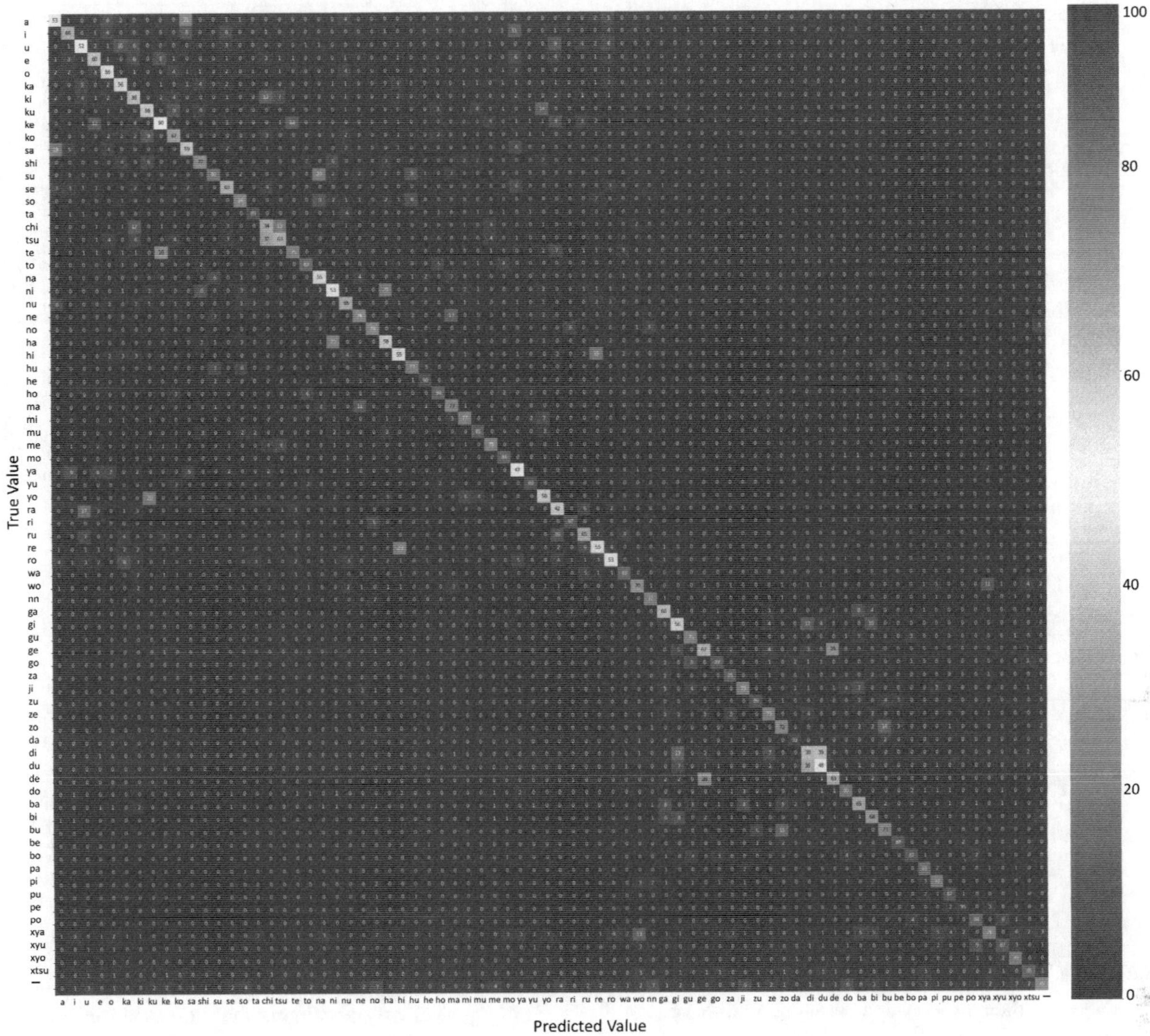

Figure 8. Confusion matrix.

rate of 200 samples per second, the sensor gloves captured five dimensions of motion magnitude data, three dimensions of acceleration data, and three dimensions of gyro data for a total of 11 dimensions. Data labeling was conducted manually at the same time as data collection. This series of motions was repeated five times. Therefore, with five repetitions per participant, 76 JFS characters, and 200 samples per second for 1 s, a total of 76 000 motion measurement data were collected for each participant. We were able to collect a total of 1 520 000 data samples for all 20 participants. These experiments were conducted with approval from the Tsukuba University of Technology Research Ethics Committee (Approval number: H30-17).

To overcome several of the issues in previous works, we performed extensive data cleaning and feature selection operations. To prevent gyro drift, we used Madgwick filters [17], which calculate angles from the values of acceleration and gyro sensors in real time. This allowed us to calculate three angle dimensions from the acceleration and gyro data. To clarify hand directions, the angles were converted into sine and cosine data. The resulting six dimensions were combined with the motion magnitudes (five dimensions) and motion directions (six dimensions) mentioned above to generate a total of 17 dimensions. Next, we conducted a review of the sampling frequency. Although 200 samples per second can be acquired without leakage, noise and training time are included

TABLE II. TWENTY-FOLD CROSS VALIDATION RESULTS.

k	Learning data (%)	Validation data (%)
1	93.6	65.0
2	94.1	75.5
3	94.8	68.7
4	93.1	69.7
5	94.2	66.3
6	93.9	73.2
7	92.9	67.9
8	93.5	71.1
9	93.0	67.4
10	94.6	70.5
11	93.4	71.6
12	93.0	66.1
13	94.6	68.9
14	94.3	70.3
15	93.0	69.7
16	93.4	68.4
17	92.9	71.3
18	93.1	71.1
19	94.5	74.2
20	94.5	72.4
Average	93.7	70.0

TABLE III. MISRECOGNITION PATTERNS.

Teacher	a	sa	ku	yo	ke	te	ki	chi	chi
Prediction	sa	a	yo	ku	te	ke	chi	ki	tsu
Rate (%)	21.0	19.0	14.0	20.0	12.0	28.0	12.0	12.0	34.0
Teacher	tsu	ni	ha	ne	ma	hi	re	wo	xya
Prediction	chi	ha	ni	ma	ne	re	hi	xya	wo
Rate (%)	32.0	20.0	22.0	13.0	11.0	19.0	23.0	11.0	13.0
Teacher	gi	di	ge	de	di	du	zo	bu	
Prediction	di	gi	de	ge	du	di	bu	zo	
Rate (%)	12.0	13.0	29.0	20.0	39.0	35.0	14.0	15.0	

in these samples. Therefore, the number of data was reduced by calculating a moving average to achieve a final value of 4 samples/s.

B. Evaluation experiments

The collected data were evaluated using a CNN (Figure 5) and k-fold cross validation (k = 20). In our evaluation experiments, data shuffling was performed using Google Colaboratory [18]. The number of folds for k-fold cross validation was set to 20 according to the number of participants. Additionally, confusion matrices and accuracy rates were generated using 20-fold cross validation of all data shuffling evaluations (see Figure 7).

V. RESULTS AND DISCUSSION

The experimental results of 20-fold cross-validation are listed in Table II. This table reveals an average recognition rate of approximately 70.0%.

As shown in Figure 8 and Table III, various misrecognition patterns occurred. We believe these patterns occurred because the conductive fibers are firmly attached to the sensor gloves. We confirmed that the hand directions for "ha" and "ni, " which are JFS characters, varied among participants. Additionally, "ne" and "ma" appear to be confused based on both hand bending and finger bending.

Figure 9 presents sample input data leading to misrecognition for the JFS characters "te" and "ke". By analyzing the data, it was confirmed that close contact between the fingers caused these errors. Notably, the thumb sometimes contacted the forefinger. Additionally, depending on the participant, the hand may be widely opened or the fingers may be in close contact.

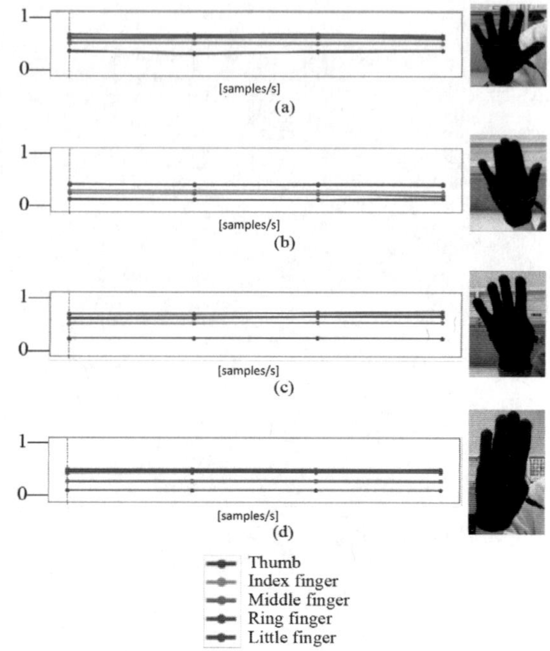

Figure 9. Example input data (only five dimensions): (a) predict "te" as "te" correctly, (b) predict "te" as "ke" incorrectly, (c) predict "ke" as "te" incorrectly, (d) predict "ke" as "ke" correctly.

Figure 10 presents examples of acquiring data from two participants using the sensor glove for dynamic fingerspelling. This figure clearly highlights the individual differences in fingerspelling between participants, particularly in the strength of finger bending (including noisy signals), timing of hand move movement, and shape of the fingers. Therefore, it is necessary to improve recognition algorithms and data glove devices (e.g., detecting hand movement periods and constructing more robust glove devices).

Based on the aforedescribed results, we determined that recognition errors largely occurred based on variance in the flexion and direction of the fingers. We also confirmed that finger expressions vary based on individual differences, which can be attributed to different home and social environments, making recognition more difficult.

However, JFS is widely used for displaying proper names and technical terms. Therefore, the recognition of JFS is essential for realizing a Japanese sign language recognition system.

VI. CONCLUSIONS AND FUTURE WORK

In this study, to realize smooth communication between the DHH and hearing people, we adopted a lightweight sensor glove, developed an effective convolutional neural network

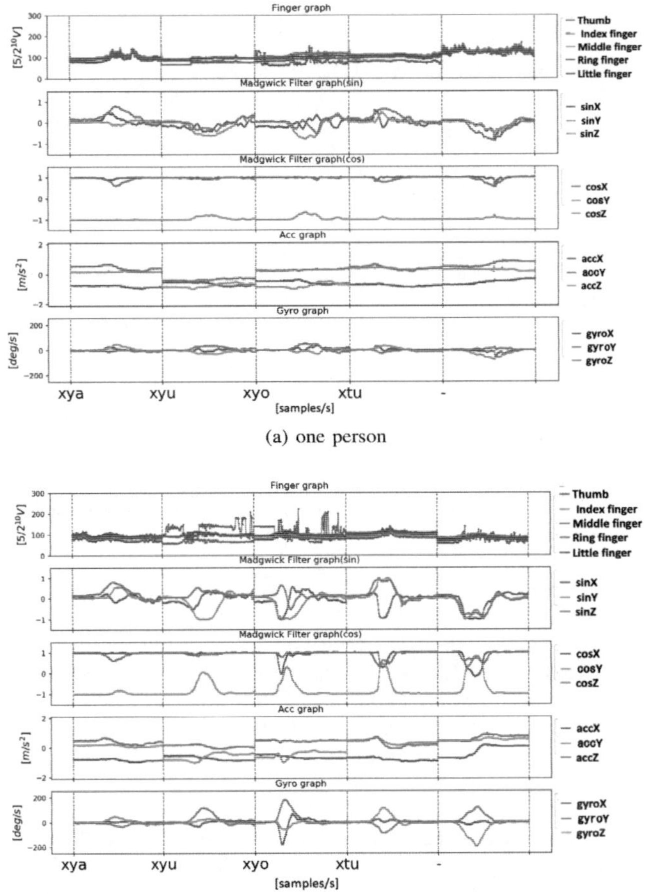

(a) one person

(b) another person

Figure 10. Example of acquiring data.

model, implemented a JFS recognition system, and evaluated the performance of the developed system. JFS data collection experiments with 20 participants and 76 target JFS characters were repeated five times. Data were acquired at a rate of 200 samples per second for 11 input dimensions. Angle data were then transformed by applying a Madgwick filter to gyro readings and converted into the sine and cosine space, which increased the total number of input dimensions to 17. However, the data acquired at 200 samples per second contained various issues, including noisy signals. To solve this problem, we calculated moving averages to reduce the frequency to 4 samples/s.

Finally, a 20-fold cross validation evaluation experiment was conducted. The average recognition rate was approximately 70.0% and the maximum recognition rate was approximately 75.5%. It was determined that the firm attachment of conductive fibers was a significant cause of misrecognition.

In future work, we will construct improved sensor gloves and investigate methods to handle various problems, such as individual differences and hand movement detection. To this end, we are planning additional experiments for data collection under more controlled conditions. Additionally, we will conduct continuous fingerspelling recognition experiments.

ACKNOWLEDGMENT

This work was partially supported by JSPS KAKENHI Grant Number #19K11411 and the Promotional Projects for Advanced Education and Research in NTUT. We would like to thank Editage (www.editage.com) for English language editing.

REFERENCES

[1] "KoeTra," 2015, URL: https://www.koetra.jp/en/ [retrieved: February,2020].

[2] "UDtalk," 2015, URL: https://udtalk.jp/ [retrieved: February,2020].

[3] "speech-to-text," 2019, URL: https://cloud.google.com/speech-to-text [retrieved: February,2020].

[4] S. Gattupalli, A. Ghaderi, and V. Athitsos, "Evaluation of deep learning based pose estimation for sign language recognition," in Proceedings of the 9th ACM International Conference on PErvasive Technologies Related to Assistive Environments, 2016, pp. 1–7.

[5] M. A. Jalal, R. Chen, R. K. Moore, and L. Mihaylova, "American sign language posture understanding with deep neural networks," in 2018 21st International Conference on Information Fusion (FUSION). New York, NY, USA: IEEE (Institute of Electrical and Electronics Engineers), July 2018, pp. 573–579.

[6] G. Luzhnica, J. Simon, E. Lex, and V. Pammer, "A sliding window approach to natural hand gesture recognition using a custom data glove," in 2016 IEEE Symposium on 3D User Interfaces (3DUI). New York, NY, USA: IEEE (Institute of Electrical and Electronics Engineers), March 2016, pp. 81–90.

[7] K. Murakami and H. Taguchi, "Gesture recognition using recurrent neural networks," in Proceedings of the SIGCHI conference on Human factors in computing systems, 1991, pp. 237–242.

[8] N. Mukai, N. Harada, and Y. Chang, "Japanese fingerspelling recognition based on classification tree and machine learning," in 2017 Nicograph International (NicoInt). New York, NY, USA: IEEE (Institute of Electrical and Electronics Engineers), June 2017, pp. 19–24.

[9] H. Hosoe, S. Sako, and B. Kwolek, "Recognition of jsl finger spelling using convolutional neural networks," 05 2017, pp. 85–88.

[10] M. E. Cabrera, J. M. Bogado, L. Fermin, R. Acuna, and D. Ralev, "Glove-based gesture recognition system," in Adaptive Mobile Robotics. World Scientific, 2012, pp. 747–753.

[11] C. K. Mummadi, F. P. P. Leo, K. D. Verma, S. Kasireddy, P. M. Scholl, and K. Van Laerhoven, "Real-time embedded recognition of sign language alphabet fingerspelling in an imu-based glove," in Proceedings of the 4th International Workshop on Sensor-Based Activity Recognition and Interaction, ser. iWOAR '17. New York, NY, USA: Association for Computing Machinery, 2017, pp. 1–6. [Online]. Available: https://doi.org/10.1145/3134230.3134236

[12] R. Takada, J. Kadomoto, and B. Shizuki, "A sensing technique for data glove using conductive fiber," in Extended Abstracts of the 2019 CHI Conference on Human Factors in Computing Systems, ser. CHI EA '19. New York, NY, USA: Association for Computing Machinery, 2019, pp. 1–4. [Online]. Available: https://doi.org/10.1145/3290607.3313260

[13] "5DT Data Glove 5 Ultra," 2019, URL: https://5dt.com/ [retrieved: February,2020].

[14] "TensorFlow," 2019, URL: https://www.tensorflow.org [retrieved: February,2020].

[15] "scikit-learn," 2019, URL: https://scikit-learn.org/stable/index.html [retrieved: February,2020].

[16] G. Hinton, N. Srivastava, and K. Swersky, "Lecture 6e-rmsprop: Divide the gradient by a running average of its recent magnitude. coursera neural networks mach learn. 2012."

[17] S. O. H. Madgwick, A. J. L. Harrison, and R. Vaidyanathan, "Estimation of imu and marg orientation using a gradient descent algorithm," in 2011 IEEE International Conference on Rehabilitation Robotics. New York, NY, USA: IEEE (Institute of Electrical and Electronics Engineers), June 2011, pp. 1–7.

[18] E. Bisong, "Google colaboratory," in Building Machine Learning and Deep Learning Models on Google Cloud Platform. Springer, 2019, pp. 59–64.

Closing the Loopholes: Categorizing Clients to Fit the Bureaucratic Welfare System

Johanne Svanes Oskarsen

Department of Informatics
Gaustadalléen 23B, 0373 Oslo
University of Oslo
Email: johansos@ifi.uio.no

***Abstract*—Categorizing clients is an essential part of the work in public services traditionally done by street-level bureaucrats. However, in the Norwegian Labour and Welfare Administration, this work has been distributed between supervisors, the front-line workers interacting with clients, and central unit caseworkers, who make decisions regarding financial welfare benefits on behalf of the bureaucracy. In cases regarding disability benefits, supervisors do the work of *closing loopholes* in clients' cases to improve the client's chances for being granted benefits, before a caseworker further processes the case. Both knowledge about the bureaucratic system with its laws and rules and knowledge about the client's situation is vital to do this work well. Digitalization or automation of case management processes and the increased use of self-service solutions may make this work more difficult. Thus, it may hinder the individual assessment that clients have a right to. This paper contributes to a growing interest in public services in Computer-Supported Cooperative Work (CSCW) by giving a detailed account of the work that street-level bureaucrats do to represent citizens' cases digitally.**

Keywords–Categorization; Representations; Street-level Bureaucracy; Work; Digitalization.

I. INTRODUCTION

In public welfare organizations, a central part of the work is to categorize citizens so that they can receive the further treatment and financial benefits they are entitled to. This work is done by street-level bureaucrats — the employees who, through encounters with citizens, "render services, provide support, or make judgments about how citizens fit the laws and practices" of the organization they represent [1] (p. 237). A key characteristic of street-level bureaucrats is the opportunity to use discretion in their work, as they are unable to work "according to the highest standards of decision making" [1] due to lack of time, information or other resources. Their work is complicated by nature and can rarely be reduced to "programmable formats"— as they meet with and make decisions for real people with individual issues and concerns.

In CSCW and related fields, the use of digital systems in public service organizations has gained increased attention, both when it comes to the street-level bureaucrats' work [2] and with the notion of *participatory citizenship* and cooperation between employees and clients [3]–[6]. A common anticipation when introducing digital case management systems or automating work is that professionals will spend less time on routine tasks and thus have more time to do work that the systems can not do, typically referred to as more *meaningful*. However, this is not necessarily the case, as digital or automated systems may leave residual tasks, or introduce new tasks that add on the employees' or users' workload [7]–[9]. For street-level bureaucrats, the expected outcome may be that they can spend their time and resources on complex cases that require human intervention or work that is more social. Still, research shows that not only may digital systems add new tasks — street-level bureaucrats may end up doing a very different job. Classification systems meant to systematize front-line workers in employment services have been shown to lead to their work becoming more administrative than social, and the use of classification systems may "benefit the system rather than the client" [10] (p. 400). The work of front-line professionals may also change as a consequence of introducing new digital self-service solutions for citizens because administrative tasks are moved from the bureaucracy to the citizens themselves, and thus the bureaucrat's role is no longer tied to specialized fields of knowledge, but rather to a support role for the citizen to *become digital* [11].

In this paper, we examine a particular part of the work that the supervisors in the agency do: the work of *closing loopholes* in preparatory casework to make sure the client will fit into the category that the front-line worker consider is the correct one when the case is processed further. Though the metaphor is not precisely used as it is in the ordinary language, it represents an association with suspicion and deception that the supervisors ascribe the bureaucratic system. The paper is structured as follows. Section 2 presents the background for the study, both the research project and the scientific background. Section 3 describes the theoretical grounding in street-level bureacuracy and categorization, while Section 4 describes the methods used. Section 5 presents the findings, before they are discussed in Section 6.

II. BACKGROUND

The study is part of an ongoing research project on how citizens' cases are represented and processed in the bureaucratic system, both by people in the local office, people in central units, and computer systems. The aim of the project is to explore how clients of welfare services is and can be represented digitally to ensure that they receive the good they are entitled to. In the Norwegian Labour and Welfare Administration (NAV), citizens must belong to a category to get the treatment they need. These categories include "unemployed" to get help seeking jobs, "sick" to get sickness benefits, or as in the cases described later, "permanently disabled" to receive permanent disability benefits. The categorization of people in public organizations is not a new phenomenon [1][12][13], but the modern-day public organizations have developed, both in terms of internal organization, increased managerial control, and with the use of Information and Communication Technologies (ICTs). Where street-level bureaucrats traditionally could make many decisions concerning their clients using discretion, their work has been distributed between several employees in NAV.

In questions regarding financial welfare benefits, the work of categorization is distributed between the client's supervisor and a central unit caseworker. The supervisor is an employee working in a local agency office who interacts with the client and does the preparatory categorization work, while the central unit caseworker processes the case and make the decision on whether the client fits with the supervisor's selected category and is thus entitled to welfare benefits. They can only assess the case with the documentation available in computer systems, and the local supervisor's written assessment of the client's case. As the supervisors know the clients after having been involved in their case over time, they work to make sure the clients' cases meet the bureaucratic system in the best way possible. Therefore, they do work to present the case to an unknown person representing the bureaucratic system — the caseworker — in a way that they find beneficial to the client. For the processing of cases, then, digital information from various actors such as doctors, course organizers and specialists surrounding the clients is becoming increasingly important in the further processing of the cases, along with the supervisor's knowledge of the bureaucratic system.

Within CSCW, categorization and representation of people has not been explored much. However, both social workers' work practice and the notion of participatory citizenship has been described, as well as employee's "intermediary" role in public encounters between citizen and state [2]–[5][14]. Through an ethnographic study, Bolous-Rødje investigated the work practice of welfare workers in municipal jobcentres in Denmark, with an emphasis on how they use computational artefacts to assess citizens and identify *perfect pathways*. She describes a work environment very similar to that of NAV, where work is "carried out in a highly politically driven organization, with constantly changing institutional demands" [2] (p. 843). Ehrlich and Cash [14] discussed how technological developments would decrease the need for people acting as intermediaries between users and companies, as the information that people need will be available through the Internet. Their point is, however, that people who have an intermediary role, such as tech support or librarians, have a different expertise and competence with customization, formulation and source validation that regular people do not have. They are trained to uncover the user's "real" problems, find relevant information and customize that information to the user's problem [14]. Borchorst et al. [4] transfer the concept of intermediaries into public service provision, and describes how front-line professionals serve as intermediaries between citizens and the services they encounter face-to-face when they need to "construct identities" in order to fit within the bureaucratic system to get the service they need. Thus, when introducing digital self-service, the role that intermediaries have in today's public encounters will change. The authors state that finding ways of designing interfaces that conform better with the citizens' situations is a major design challenge, but that human contact should not be replaced. Instead, they argue that finding ways to re-configure processes and thus empowering citizens is key [4].

III. METHODS

This case study deals with the phenomenon of representations of people in computer systems, where NAV is used as an instrumental case to illustrate this [15]. An important aspect is how the representations can enable automated case processing in the future, as well as what cannot be automated. The five participants in the study are all front-line employees at a local NAV office, who interacts with citizens and thus represents the bureaucracy at the street level. We have interviewed all participants, and each interview was recorded and transcribed. Furthermore, we have used ethnographic methods for data collection through a combination of observation and interviews. The observation has been participatory as we have asked questions and discussed work and cases with the participants along the way. During the fieldwork, we have also spoken to other employees and attended internal meetings where they discussed client's cases and their work. All the people involved have been aware that we are researchers, and consent has been given orally in these cases. Observations have not been recorded, and the data from the observations are based on field notes. The reason for this is that the participants work in open offices where other than the participants are also located. All participants who have been recorded have signed a consent form, but not the clients mentioned. Therefore, it is important to emphasize that none of the cases mentioned here are precisely described as they are in reality, but they are based on real cases. Elements such as age, occupation, and diagnoses have been blurred or changed, and all the names mentioned are pseudonyms. The data in the study was collected from August 2019 to January 2020. The project is reported to the Norwegian Center for Research Data and follows its requirements for safe storage.

IV. THEORETICAL GROUNDING

Citizens come to street-level bureaucracies as unique individuals with different personalities, experiences, and circumstances [1]. For them to receive treatment or help from the bureaucracy, the complex citizen must transform into a client, which is more manageable for the bureaucratic system. People are therefore placed in one of a small number of categories defined by the bureaucracy itself as if all people somehow fit a standardized definition with a set of characteristics and an associated slot in the system. These client characteristics often do not exist outside the process that gives rise to them; the social process it is to make a human being into a client [1]. Prottas [12] (p. 289) views clients as both consumers of the bureaucracy's output or services and as the *raw material* that the bureaucracy processes. In typical public service bureaucracies, it is not the goods that are distributed between clients, but clients that are distributed between the goods, and therefore the work of categorizing and processing people is very central. Becoming a client belonging to a category with an associated process is thus a prerequisite for being able to receive the goods you are entitled to. Clients are therefore viewed as the organization's raw material: as something that must be transformed or processed in order to become consumers of the goods [12]. In some cases, categorization of people is a simple routine task and is done without particular human involvement on the part of the bureaucracy. Other times, it is complex, requiring someone to receive, evaluate, interpret, and act upon information from and about citizens [12]. In this process, highlighting or ignoring specific attributes of the citizen to determine which category they belong to is central. It is not all attributes that are important in all further processes. For example, NAV distinguishes between medical factors and social factors that may prevent a citizen from working. Social factors include challenges related to things such as not speaking the language, unhappiness at work, and sickness in the family. In cases of citizens receiving sickness benefits, for example, only the medical factors should be taken into account when processing the case.

The work of the street-level bureaucrats thus lies in transforming the human being into a client with certain characteristics or attributes that are crucial to the further process. The work and decisions of the street-level bureaucracy are naturally bound to and directed by the client's "real" characteristics and the bureaucracy's own rules, but "a considerable margin of discretion remains," according to Prottas [12] (p. 291). Categorization in institutions and bureaucracies differs from other categorization because one wants both to reduce complexity by categorizing and then use the category to determine possible actions and further processes [10]. Categorizing involves both a label and a process: The client's label defines what treatment it can get, and this label simultaneously binds the bureaucracy itself to a process of tasks, and therefore categorization has not only implications for the client itself but also the bureaucracy [12]. According to Lipsky [1], it is not certain that the citizens themselves agree with the categorization done by the street-level bureaucrat since their perception of reality is often different. The citizen sees himself as a human being with individual needs, challenges, and expectations of treatment that fit their understanding of their unique situation, as they are encouraged by society. The street-level bureaucrats who decide on the categorization, on the other hand, want to reduce human complexity to determine which categories of action suits their problems [1]. Categorizing is, therefore, a powerful tool that can be of great importance to the citizens of the welfare state; it is not only retrospective but also prospective.

V. Findings

In this section, we present the findings by using illustrative examples from the data. We describe here the work of closing loopholes by supervisors in the local NAV office, and how this work is done as an attempt to make sure the outcome in the case will be what the supervisors believe is correct.

A. Closing loopholes around unclear diagnoses

A supervisor in the sickness benefits department, Jon, has taken on the task of writing a work-ability assessment document for one of his colleagues who works in the work assessment allowance department. Jon's colleague finds this assessment particularly difficult to write as it is not a straightforward case easily categorized in the slot they are aiming for. Though the client is currently receiving work assessment allowance (a different financial welfare benefit) and thus is not Jon's client or in his department, he can still write the assessment. His colleague has asked him this favor as she believes he does a good job formulating the document in a way that favors the client. Jon is an experienced employee, having worked in the agency for nearly 20 years in various departments with different positions. The case at hand belongs to a middle-aged woman working in a job that is quite physically demanding, but that she likes and masters. Both her physical and mental health, however, are poor. She has a long history of thorough medical examinations, but except for a mental diagnosis, it is not clear what is the reason for her physical challenges. She has been on sick leave for years, though working part-time for a while. Thus, she has first been a client receiving sickness benefits, then work assessment allowance, and now hopefully moving on to receive disability benefits, as she is considered to have a permanent impaired ability to work by her supervisor and doctor. They believe she can work part-time 40 percent, which means she can be considered to be 60 percent disabled. The client's supervisor is clear about this: though she finds the case difficult, it is still apparent to her that the client should be granted a disability benefit. She has known the client for years, following her journey through sickness, employment measures, and disagreements with her employer. However, as the work-ability assessment can only be based on the available documentation, the state office may disagree. To be granted a disability benefit, everything must have been tried and tested out to examine any options for full-time working.

Jon explains that writing a good assessment document takes time, and he often starts by writing a draft containing the most important information, before going back several times to tweak formulations and change the wording. His task in this case, according to himself, is to write pro disability benefits by "closing the loopholes" that may cause the state caseworker to refuse the client's application for disability benefits. Jon's loyalty thus lies with the client and his colleague. He trusts that his colleague has assessed this case the right way. To write the assessment document, Jon starts by finding the relevant documentation in the client's case. In the archiving system, he finds the doctor's assessment and the final report from the employment measure organizer. In the system that facilitates dialogue between the client and her supervisor, he finds a summary of the latest meeting between the client and supervisor. He uses this documentation as a basis for what he intends to write in the assessment document but emphasizes what the client's supervisor tells him about the case as well. She has been in and out of his office during the time he has been working on the case, discussing the case and answering any of Jon's questions.

B. Closing loopholes by adding or reformulating information

In a different department, Mia, a supervisor working with young adults receiving work assessment allowance, tells a story about another disability benefits case. One of her clients is a young woman who has had cancer. She has been through treatment and is considered to be recovered from cancer, but she is suffering from fatigue and is struggling to get back to work because of this. The client has been in an employment measure after recovering but had to quit due to exhaustion. Mia finds it evident that this client has the right to be granted a disability benefit so that she can focus on getting well without worrying about her finances. She says the client will most likely be able to work in the future, but that, as of this moment, she is unable due to medical reasons. As all other financial benefits are temporary, Mia argues that disability benefits will enable the client to focus on getting well instead of worrying about her finances. The client applied for disability benefits months back after Mia had written a work-ability assessment she believed to be bulletproof. Both Mia and the client's doctor agreed that she was so ill that she was currently unable to work. The state caseworkers, however, disagreed. They justified the rejection by arguing that the client had not tried out everything, and their advisory consultant doctor did not consider the client to be so sick that she could not do anything work-related. Mia found this assessment weak, and thus began her quest to convince the state caseworkers she was right. As the work-ability assessment can only be a little less than 5000 characters, she forwarded additional documentation that she did not have room for in the original document, like the epicrisis from the hospital where the client was receiving treatment. The processing time in the disability benefits cases is normally about five months, but Mia spent another three to four months to argue in her client's favor. In the end, the state caseworkers granted the client disability benefits.

Another supervisor describes a similar case. The supervisor, Anne, wants to discuss one of her client's further possibilities with the others in her team so that she can ensure that the client gets the best possible further case progress. Anne's client has been documented by doctors to be very ill, but the central unit caseworkers rejected his application for disability benefits. Anne believes the caseworkers have misjudged the case, as they justified the refusal by explaining that the client had to see if the treatment he received could work positively and possibly lead to him being healthy enough to work in the future. After the rejection, Anne spoke with the client's doctor, who stated that the treatment the client was receiving was only a way to keep the disease at bay and relieve the client's pain, and as such, the doctor said that nothing would change for the client's health in the future. The colleagues agree with Anne's assessment and believe that if the caseworkers are informed of the correct description of the treatment the user receives, they will grant him disability benefits. Anne and her colleagues want to make the further case process as quick as possible for the client. Therefore, they agree that Anne should ask the client not to use his right of appeal to complain about the previous rejection, as it will stop the temporary financial benefit the client is receiving today. Instead, the client should submit a new disability benefits application after Anne's colleague has written a new work ability assessment. This way, the client can retain the temporary benefit he receives today until he is granted the disability benefit. In other words, the supervisors have come up with a plan for how they will close the loopholes in the case by specifying that the treatment the client receives will not change anything regarding his illness. Also, they have put together a strategy for how the holes in the previous work ability assessment should not affect the client's finances until they have set the record straight.

VI. Discussion

The clients in the agency are categorized into the bureaucratic system by a set of characteristics. In the case of disability benefits, the client must be between 18 and 67 years of age, they must have been a member of the National Insure scheme for three years prior to their sickness, the sickness or disability must be the main reason their earning capacity is reduced, appropriate treatment or employment measures must have been tried, and their earning capacity must be permanently reduced by at least 50 percent due to sickness or disability. The two former requirements can quite easily be ticked off in a scheme. The last three requirements, however, demands an assessment by someone. To be granted disability benefits today is described to be very difficult by the supervisors in the NAV office. From a political point of view, the line of work is strong, and all Norwegian citizens should work as much as they can. For citizens who are sick or disabled to such an extent that they cannot work full time, their work ability must be clarified to examine how much they are capable of working. Disability benefits are intended to replace the income of people who have a permanent disability due to illness or injury. Since disability benefits cost society a great deal, it is important for the agency that the work ability of clients who may be entitled to disability benefits is thoroughly assessed and that all possibilities for working are explored. This means that the clients must have been through various employment measures, which can be e.g., education or courses, and that they have tried the treatment their doctor recommends based on the illness or injury they are living with. If everything has been tried and the work ability is still considered to be permanently reduced, the client can be considered to be entitled to disability benefits. The number of measures or treatments a client must take is individual and is often evaluated by NAV based on medical certificates and documentation from medical treatment. The medical certificates or documentation typically include a diagnosis — which is a code that consists of one letter and two numbers. Some diagnoses are classified as a sickness diagnosis (a clear diagnosis where the doctor has identified disease or injury). In contrast, others are so-called symptom diagnoses — unclear diagnoses explaining the patient's symptoms rather than the sickness itself. Clients who have a chronic illness that is known to prevent them from having a permanent job, e.g., dementia, may not need to go through many measures to be considered for disability benefits. Others, who may have unclear diagnoses, often need to go through more. It is these measures and treatments that help close loopholes in a case initially.

The work of assembling the key information needed in a work ability assessment starts long before the actual document is opened. First of all, the client, supervisor, and doctor need to have a common understanding of the client's case: they have to agree that what is best for the client is to apply for a disability benefit. Thus, the client must already have tried any and all other options for work there is, and treatment for whatever disease or disability they suffer from. Further, the client must partake in a clarification measure to get an outsider's perspective on the work ability. When all the actors involved agree that a disability benefit is the best solution for the client, the client and supervisor must have a meeting discussing the matter together. This meeting is the client's opportunity to influence the outcome by explaining how the disease or disability affects his or her life, emphasizing why he or she cannot work the usual 100 percent. Next, to ensure that the advisors in the office assess cases somewhat in a similar matter, the case might be brought up for discussion in a joint meeting with other advisors and managers. These meetings typically occur every week and is a chance for the advisors to get others' views on the case and to ensure that similar cases are handled in a somewhat similar manner.

After there is a consensus between the involved actors that the work ability is assessed as permanently reduced, the supervisor must write a work ability assessment before the client can send in the digital application for disability benefits. In the work ability assessment, the supervisor must present the case in such a way that the caseworker understands that everything the local agency office considers appropriate has been tried, even though the client may not have tried all possible measures. The supervisor's job here is to speak the client's case, and close any loophole that may cause the caseworker to reject the client's application. The *loophole issue* seems to stem from a basic belief in the bureaucratic system and society in general that some people do not want to work, and thus, it is important to screen out those who would try to *trick the system*. From the supervisors' point of view, caseworkers look for potential loopholes in the work ability assessments that may cause them to reject the client's application. All the caseworkers who write work ability assessments regularly have a similar approach to writing them, as they follow the same recipe. They have a template document on their computer that they use as a basis, and fill in the information they consider relevant from other electronic documents. This is typically medical certificates, summaries from conversations between the supervisor and the client, and reports from labor marked initiatives in which the client has partaken. To do this job, they find the user's case files in the archiving system and the case management system that facilitates dialogue between supervisor and client by using the client's social security in the search field. The information in the systems is usually sorted by date so that the most recent information is immediately visible. However, to find the relevant documentation, they often need to browse through several documents. Every loophole must be closed, or else specifically mentioned why it has not been tried. The documentation that makes up the basis for the supervisor's assessment of the case is made mainly by doctors or other medical personnel, as well as people working in the private companies that organize employment and clarification measures that the client has partaken in.

The supervisors describe the work of closing loopholes both as overseeing that the client has been through any necessary measures for exploring options for working and as the work of assembling and presenting the key information in the case in a 5000-character document: the work ability assessment. In this document, the facts in the case are presented with the supervisor's subsequent assessment of the clients opportunities for a working life or lack thereof. When the case is sent for processing in the central unit, the caseworker uses this document as a basis for his or her assessment of the case, together with the user's digital application and other available documentation that the work ability assessment is based on. A loophole in the work ability assessment is described as, for instance, missing information about the illness, labour market measures, or a lacking assessment that may cause the central unit caseworker to reject the application for disability benefits. Thus, the supervisors do some parts of their work to ensure that their clients' cases are assessed in what they consider is the right way further in the bureaucratic system. This is done to make up for the fact that other caseworkers and computer systems do not know the client as they do, and do not have the same knowledge about the client. They speak their clients' case when it meets the bureaucratic system.

In Jon's case, two aspects of the case may be considered as loopholes: the fact that the client does not have a clear sickness diagnosis, and the fact that he finds the clarification measure report a bit lacking. Thus, his job of closing loopholes concerns writing about these aspects in such a way that the central unit caseworker may not see them as loopholes. Therefore, he puts a strong emphasis on all the examinations that the client has partaken in with the aim of getting a final diagnosis and figuring out what treatment may be fitting. Also, he avoids mentioning what he finds lacking in the clarification measure report but puts emphasis on the organizer's assessment. The two latter cases illustrate the importance of solid supervisor work. Both of the client's applications were rejected by the central unit caseworkers because they believed some aspects in the cases were not appropriately explored, and that the client's health might change in the near future. However, the supervisors were sure that additional existing information would change the outcome. In the former case, the supervisor was right. As the whole team agreed on the latter case, the client's application will likely be approved after the supervisor reformulates the wording about the medical treatment. Thus, more information and a richer description of the clients' cases were needed to close loopholes.

The supervisors in the local agency offices work with *people* and their cases, whereas the caseworkers in the central unit only ever work with the *cases* that belong to the people. When a case is sent for further processing, important aspects about the clients disappear, as only the information that is crucial to the outcome in the *case* is sent. The supervisors can, in face-to-face encounters with the clients, see things such as how they function in social settings and whether their disease is hurting. Such things can only be described to the caseworkers, but they cannot see it for themselves. Therefore, the supervisors do their best to make sure the caseworker assesses the case in what they consider to be the right way. If they believe a client is entitled to disability benefits, they work to close any potential loophole. We see this as an attempt to ensure that the individual client is represented as just that: a unique individual, not like a person who automatically fits into a standardized category [1]. However, the digital systems in use today do not support this work: the information in the clients' cases is distributed between three systems; the archiving system, the case management system, and the system that facilitates dialog between client and the agency. To make case processing more efficient, only the most relevant information in the case should be included in the work ability assessment. As some clients may have had a case in the NAV system for many years, the supervisors emphasize how difficult it is to decide what information is crucial.

The work of closing loopholes has arisen as a result of redistributing the work of the traditional street-level bureaucrat among several different people. As the decision-making authority concerning financial welfare benefits has been moved out of the local office, front-line employees cannot make these decisions for their clients any longer. The supervisor who meets the client does the work of closing loopholes to represent the client as best as possible when facing the bureaucratic system. The caseworker in the central unit represents the bureaucratic system with its laws and rules. They act to a greater extent based on pressure from management, and political and socio-economic goals, to reduce the number of citizens receiving disability benefits. By granting disability benefits, they also bind the bureaucracy to a further, expensive process [10][12]. From a political point of view, therefore, as few as possible should be placed in the "disabled" category. The supervisors, who know the clients, have a vast knowledge of the bureaucratic system; they also often know which aspects of a case should be highlighted in further processing. Thus, they speak the client's case by closing loopholes. The work of assembling the key information and closing loopholes can be quite a time-consuming activity for the supervisors. They may not know what information might make a difference when the case is further processed, and because the supervisor needs to search for the information in three different case management systems. Wording and formulations may also be of importance, as was illustrated in Anne's case.

Furthermore, since public welfare services are working on getting as many users as possible into using self-services, the client does some parts of the bureaucracy's prior work himself [8]. Will the clients eventually have to do the work of closing loopholes? As most citizens may not have a deep understanding of the bureaucratic system, they will have challenges with representing their case, free of loopholes, to the caseworkers who are making the decision. The categorization work described in this paper is complex and difficult, even for experienced supervisors. As the caseworkers always look for potential loopholes, the client should have an understanding of what these might be if he or she is to assemble the case.

REFERENCES

[1] M. Lipsky, Street-Level Bureaucracy, 30th Anniversary Edition: Dilemmas of the Individual in Public Services, 2010.

[2] N. Boulus-Rødje, "In Search for the Perfect Pathway: Supporting Knowledge Work of Welfare Workers," Computer Supported Cooperative Work (CSCW), vol. 27, no. 3, Dec. 2018, pp. 841–874. [Online]. Available: https://doi.org/10.1007/s10606-018-9318-0

[3] N. G. Borchorst and S. Bødker, ""You probably shouldn't give them too much information" – Supporting Citizen-Government Collaboration," in ECSCW 2011: Proceedings of the 12th European Conference on Computer Supported Cooperative Work, 24-28 September 2011, Aarhus Denmark, S. Bødker, N. O. Bouvin, V. Wulf, L. Ciolfi, and W. Lutters, Eds. Springer London, 2011, pp. 173–192.

[4] N. G. Borchorst, B. McPhail, K. L. Smith, J. Ferenbok, and A. Clement, "Bridging Identity Gaps—Supporting Identity Performance in Citizen Service Encounters," Computer Supported Cooperative Work (CSCW), vol. 21, no. 6, Dec. 2012, pp. 555–590. [Online]. Available: https://doi.org/10.1007/s10606-012-9163-5

[5] N. G. Borchorst, S. Bødker, and P.-O. Zander, "The boundaries of participatory citizenship," in ECSCW 2009, I. Wagner, H. Tellioğlu, E. Balka, C. Simone, and L. Ciolfi, Eds. Springer London, 2009, pp. 1–20.

[6] N. L. Holten Møller, G. Fitzpatrick, and C. A. Le Dantec, "Assembling the Case: Citizens' Strategies for Exercising Authority and Personal Autonomy in Social Welfare," Proceedings of the ACM on Human-Computer Interaction, vol. 3, no. GROUP, Dec. 2019, pp. 244:1–244:21. [Online]. Available: https://doi.org/10.1145/3361125

[7] L. Bainbridge, "Ironies of Automation," IFAC Proceedings Volumes, vol. 15, no. 6, Sep. 1982, pp. 129–135. [Online]. Available: http://www.sciencedirect.com/science/article/pii/S1474667017628970

[8] G. Verne and T. Bratteteig, "Do-it-yourself Services and Work-like Chores: On Civic Duties and Digital Public Services," Personal Ubiquitous Comput., vol. 20, no. 4, Aug. 2016, pp. 517–532. [Online]. Available: http://dx.doi.org/10.1007/s00779-016-0936-6

[9] L. Gasser, "The Integration of Computing and Routine Work," ACM Trans. Inf. Syst., vol. 4, no. 3, Jul. 1986, pp. 205–225. [Online]. Available: http://doi.acm.org/10.1145/214427.214429

[10] D. Caswell, G. Marston, and J. E. Larsen, "Unemployed citizen or 'at risk' client? Classification systems and employment services in Denmark and Australia," Critical Social Policy, vol. 30, no. 3, Aug. 2010, pp. 384–404. [Online]. Available: https://doi.org/10.1177/0261018310367674

[11] A. S. Pors, "Becoming digital – passages to service in the digitized bureaucracy," Journal of Organizational Ethnography, vol. 4, no. 2, Jan. 2015, pp. 177–192. [Online]. Available: https://doi.org/10.1108/JOE-08-2014-0031

[12] J. M. Prottas, "The Power of the Street-Level Bureaucrat in Public Service Bureaucracies," Urban Affairs Quarterly, vol. 13, no. 3, Mar. 1978, pp. 285–312. [Online]. Available: https://doi.org/10.1177/107808747801300302

[13] G. C. Bowker and S. L. Star, Sorting Things Out: Classification and Its Consequences. MIT Press, Aug. 2000, google-Books-ID: xHlP8WqzizYC.

[14] K. Ehrlich and D. Cash, "The Invisible World of Intermediaries: A Cautionary Tale," Computer Supported Cooperative Work (CSCW), vol. 8, no. 1, Mar. 1999, pp. 147–167. [Online]. Available: https://doi.org/10.1023/A:1008696415354

[15] R. E. Stake, "Qualitative Case Studies," in The Sage handbook of qualitative research, 3rd ed. Thousand Oaks, CA: Sage Publications Ltd, 2005, pp. 443–466.

BEACON: A CSCW Tool for Enhancing Co-Located Meetings Through Temporal and Activity Awareness

Ole-Edvard Ørebæk, David Aarlien, Fahad Faisal Said, Karoline Andreassen, Klaudia Carcani
Østfold University College, Halden, Norway
Emails: {oleedvao, davidaa, fahads, karolan, klaudia.carcani}@hiof.no

***Abstract*—This paper explores how enhancement of temporal awareness and activity awareness affects co-located meetings' effectiveness and efficiency. Our focus is meetings happening as part of a project where cooperation is essential for its fulfillment. As a case study, we investigated group work in university projects. In a preliminary study, we found that individuals deviate from topics due to the lack of structure, which results in time wasted on irrelevant discussions. Agendas are essential in order to conduct a productive meeting. In order to investigate this issue, a prototype, "BEACON", was developed with two components. The first component is a desktop dashboard revolving around creating and managing meeting agendas, as well as having an integrated co-writing noting tool that contributes to temporal awareness. The second component is a status-based artifact that uses color and sound as notifications of defined time limits for different activities in the meeting agenda and contributes to activity awareness. An evaluation with a group of 6 persons was conducted. The findings showed that enhancing temporal and activity awareness through displayed shared notes and a clearly presented agenda during the meeting contributed to generate more ideas and keep the discussions focused. Participants expressed that the artifact's colors dictated the pace of the meeting positively, influencing them to optimize the available time and reach conclusions. Thus, we conclude that the enhancement of temporal and activity awareness in a workspace-like meeting setting can increase meeting effectiveness and be an incentive of better cooperation within a project.**

***Keywords*–awareness meetings; CSCW; temporal awareness; activity awareness; design study.**

I. INTRODUCTION

Organizations nowadays work quite often with project groups, where a set of people come together from different departments to achieve a specific goal. Examples could be the launch of a new product, producing a common report, writing a common document, etc. In these cases, people need to cooperate in order to achieve the final goal. An important part of this cooperation are group meetings. These are used as touchpoints where important things are discussed, and decisions that will push the project forward are made. Meetings are an integral part of the everyday working life of employees who attend approximately 3.2 meetings per week. However, the quality of these meetings is evaluated as poor in 41.9% of the cases [1].

People feel that meetings are not as productive as they would like [2]. They lose track of the context of the topics discussed, resulting in poor decision making [3]. Furthermore, it appeared that agendas have an essential role in structuring group meetings [4]-[7]. Thus, new ways to enhance meeting efficiency and effectiveness are needed as a way of contributing to the cooperation.

Context-Based Workplace awareness [8] was defined as establishing an awareness of the workplace and the activities occurring within it, regardless of distance in space and time. This type of awareness has been studied in situations where people are distributed and ways to remain aware of others' activities in the workplace are needed. In this paper, we explore context-based workplace awareness, specifically, its subtypes of temporal awareness and activity awareness in the context of meetings and study how meeting efficiency and effectiveness can be influenced by the enhancement of these types of awareness.

Through an interaction design process, we developed a prototype that we call BEACON. It consists of a desktop dashboard that supports creating and managing meeting agendas, as well as having an integrated co-writing noting tool that contributes to temporal awareness. The second component is a status-based artifact that uses color and sound as notifications of defined time limits for different activities in the meeting agenda.

BEACON was further used to investigate how technology that enhances context-based temporal and activity awareness can affect meeting effectiveness and efficiency?

In Section 2 of this article, we present the conceptual grounding for our work. In Section 3, we present a short description of the design process of the prototype and its evaluation. In Section 4, we present the findings of the evaluation. In Section 5, we discuss our findings in relation to temporal and activity awareness. Finally, in Section 6, we conclude the study and outline possible directions for future work.

II. CONCEPTUAL GROUNDING

Computer Supported Cooperative Work (CSCW), as defined by [9], is "the field which aims to understand the nature and characteristics of cooperative work with the objective of designing adequate computer-based technologies". This type of technology has previously been referred to as groupware [10], where the focus was on the group of people working together. However, Schmidt and Bannon [9] argue that the focus should not be only on groups but on cooperative ensembles which can be people or organizations that come together to work on a common goal. These are usually dissolved after the goal has been achieved. Project work fits this description of cooperative work.

Moreover, Schmidt and Bannon argue that cooperative work requires ensembles to be distributed in time and space. This is the case with project work where members work on their own. However, their common encounters in meetings are relevant, which is why we in this paper study meetings as a cooperative work activity in need of technological support.

A. Meeting Effectiveness and Efficiency

We live in a world where it is common that workers in service-oriented organizations spend a considerable part of their time in meetings. However, meetings are not as productive as participants would like, and participants often engage in discussions that deviate from the meeting focus. Garcia et al. [4] imply that despite the importance of meetings, participants often feel that time is wasted because meeting goals could not be reached (low effectiveness), or because the meeting lasted significantly longer than planned (low efficiency). Symptoms of a bad meeting are stated as low group participation, bad decision-making processes, free riders and lack of group attention.

A study by Nixon and Littlepage [11] examined the relationship between certain group meeting procedures and their correlation with the studied subjects' perceived effectiveness of the meetings. The meeting effectiveness was measured by goal attainment and decision satisfaction. The results suggested that among other things; open communication, focus on tasks, exploration of options, analysis of decision consequences, temporal integrity, and agenda integrity might be important effectiveness-related processes. More detailed aspects contained in these processes include (in no particular order); that all members participate in the meeting, that options are discussed before final decisions are made, as well as the consequences of these options, that the agendas are followed during the meeting and that the goals are clear and well defined, being focused and committed to the meeting in terms of time and effort, being prepared for the meeting and having access to the relevant meeting information like, e.g., the agenda, that the meetings are more satisfying than frustrating, that notes are taken of the decisions made during the meeting, and that the meeting start and end on time.

In a study by Davison [2], a method for measuring meeting success was proposed. The factors of this method were quite similar to the procedures explored in Nixon and Littlepage's [11] study, with emphasis on, e.g., communication, discussion-quality and how result-oriented and time-efficient the meeting was. Thus, looking for how many of these meeting procedures are present in group meetings might also give an indication of how effective and/or efficient they are.

B. Context-Based Workplace Awareness

A largely discussed concept in CSCW is the concept of awareness [10][12]-[14]. Awareness within CSCW was initially discussed by Heath and Luff in their seminal paper, "Collaboration and control: Crisis management and multimedia technology in London Underground" [15]. A relevant definition of awareness comes from Dourish and Bellotti [16]. They described it as "an understanding of the activities of others, which provides a context for your own activity", and outlined the importance of awareness information in coordinating group activities. This definition of awareness has in the CSCW community been referred to as "social awareness".

Bardram and Hansen [8] discussed in their work another type of awareness which they called context-based workplace awareness. They defined context-based workplace awareness as establishing an awareness of the workplace and the activities occurring within it, regardless of distance in space and time. Thus, focusing not only on what others in your immediate surroundings are doing but also having an awareness of the activities that happen in a specific workplace by focusing on the spatial, temporal and activity-related dimensions.

The part "context-based" of the term was used by Bardram and Hansen [8] to define that the awareness they are discussing is often based on context. Their definition of *context* was derived from Dey at al. [17] who defined it as "information that characterizes a situation related to the interaction between users, applications, and the surrounding environment". Dey et al. [17] also outlined in their paper several categories of context. Of these, status (also referred to as activity) is the most relevant to our study. Status encompasses characteristics of the relevant entity of focus that can be sensed. The entity can here refer to anything from an individual or group of people, to software components or applications. In a separate study, Borges et al. [18] proposed a conceptual framework for analyzing the context in the form of presented information in groupware applications. Of the outlined information types that encompass the context were *scheduled tasks*, defined as identifying tasks through representing their characteristics, and *completed tasks*, defined as providing an understanding of previously completed tasks and their contexts.

Bardram and Hansen [8] argued that context-based workplace awareness is central when attempting to establish coordination in workplaces. Based on the works of Nixon and Littlepage [11] and Davison [2], it is quite apparent that many of the outlined factors that indicate meeting effectiveness and efficiency are related to coordinating the meeting participants around different aspects of the meeting. Thus, coordination is an important factor when discussing meeting effectiveness and efficiency. In this study, we explore how enhancing certain aspects of context-based workplace awareness might be relevant when attempting to improve meetings' effectiveness and efficiency.

As methods of how context can be utilized in applications, Dey et al. [17] proposed the concept of context-aware functions in the form of three categories. The first category, *presenting information and services*, contains two functions, the first is displaying context information to the user and the second is proposing a set of relevant actions to the user based on the current context. The second category, *automatically executing a service*, is described as applications that will perform certain commands or reconfiguring the system for the users triggered by context changes in the system. The third and last category, *attaching context for later retrieval*, is defined as applications that tags relevant context information data, in which the users can later retrieve. These three proposed functions are thus useful when designing a technological solution that aims to enhance context-based workplace awareness.

While the aim of the study was to look into how meeting effectiveness and efficiency was influenced when enhancing workplace awareness, we should as well state that as meetings happen in co-located places (different from the study setting Bardram and Hansen [8]), the influence of context-based workplace awareness has not been studied before in a meeting "context". Thus, this paper also contributes as an example of discussing context-based workplace awareness in settings where participants are indeed seated together, but cooperation can still be enhanced through context-based elements.

Bardram and Hansen [8] described several types of awareness as part of context-based workplace awareness. Of these, we thoroughly present temporal awareness and activity awareness below, as well as their relation to the contexts of status, scheduled tasks, and completed tasks.

C. Temporal Awareness

Temporal awareness is defined as an awareness of the progress of activities over time in terms of past, present, and future and outlines the importance of schedules for coordination, as well as being aware of events in the past, which often can be important when making decisions in the present or planning the future [8]. This is very relevant to group meetings as they often have a limited timeframe. Planning and managing the tasks/activities according to the available time is, therefore, important in order to avoid problems, such as those highlighted by Garcia et al. [4] and achieve the meeting's objective(s).

As stated above, our context is a "meeting" where people come together to discuss issues that relate to a cooperative project. In order to increase the temporal awareness in meetings, we investigate the concept of agendas. According to the Cambridge dictionary [19], an agenda is described as "a list of matters to be discussed at a meeting". In other words; An agenda can implicitly be used as a method of describing the activities and establishing the structure of a meeting. Multiple studies have concluded that the use of agendas is essential for improving the effectiveness and efficiency of group meetings [4][5][7][20]. Furthermore, a study [21] in the area of Group Support Systems (GSS) discussed that meeting structure has a positive influence on information sharing between group members in decision-making situations, and highlighted how group members need cues and indicators, e.g., boldfaced text to be able to share initially unshared information. Using the context of scheduled and completed tasks, presenting such agendas by describing upcoming and completed activities during the meeting can be used as a method for increasing temporal awareness.

Yamane [22] conducted a study in the context of his lectures where students were given "course preparation assignments" aiming to prepare them prior to the lectures in order to establish thoughts and opinions on the course matter. This was an attempt to increase the effectiveness of the discussion in the lecture, which was documented to be very successful. Thus, presenting meeting information in a way that allows group members to prepare thoughts and opinions about the discussion topics before the meeting, might be a good method of promoting discussions.

D. Activity Awareness

Activity awareness is defined as an awareness of specific activities and their surrounding context, irrespective of who is performing them [8]. As group meetings naturally contain several different activities, e.g., in the form of tasks, this type of awareness becomes quite relevant. In our study, to simplify the types of activities in a group meeting, we group them to three levels of abstraction; high, medium, and low. We define high-level as the activity of conducting the meeting as a whole, medium as activities related to the meeting's overarching goal (e.g., topic discussions), and low-level as any activity contained within a medium-level activity, such as communication and discussion within a specific topic.

In a study by Haller et al. [23], a digitally enhanced meeting room was developed to promote group creativity by combining digital and paper media through pen-based interfaces. The results indicated that having digital tools simulating pen and paper helped improve group collaboration. Integrating a note system where group members can make notes and share with the rest of the group, might, therefore, have a positive effect on how the members collaborate as well as increase the awareness of low-level activities.

In a study by Janicik and Bartel [24], it was discussed how temporal planning affects coordination and task performance in groups and found that temporal planning had a positive relationship with task performance. In another study [25], different design strategies for supporting collaborative activities were proposed. Among these, deadlines were suggested as a method of enhancing activity awareness and prompting coordination by presenting progress, specifically as a status reminder. Another study [26] that revolved around patterns in group interaction when regarding time limits and task types on the quality and quantity of the group performance, suggested that sessions with short time limits generate ideas at a higher rate despite a reduction on the quality of such content produced. Based on these studies, having a method of planning the meeting's activities in terms of time and presenting the time limits as a status reminder during the meeting might make a positive impact on the meeting's effectiveness.

III. METHODS

As mentioned in the introduction, we chose student projects as a case study. The study was conducted in a university college in Norway.

We took a design process approach for our research [27] and went through the four phases of *Informing*, *Visioning*, *Prototyping*, and *Evaluating*. Initially, we conducted research for design to design the prototype and then we conducted research through design by using the prototype to answer our research question. In the first part, we collected data that showed the need for a digital tool that could support meeting efficiency. We then designed and developed a prototype based on these needs and conducted a thorough investigation into relevant literature as a means for answering the research question through an evaluation. Hence, we shortly present our design journey and explain in detail the evaluation process and its respective findings.

A. Informing and Visioning

In order to understand the students' needs in a meeting situation, an observation of a group meeting was conducted early on. Additionally, the informing-phase included individual interviews with two students and one expert. Collected data were analyzed with a qualitative interpretive approach [5] from a CSCW perspective, where we tried to identify the groups' needs in relation to the cooperation among participants and the overall meeting efficiency.

Findings showed that there was a lack of a consistent flow in the activities discussed despite having a good leader that stimulated the discussion. Decisions were made by just a few of the participants without being documented. However, when they utilized a collaborative writing platform on the common display (google docs), the participants seemed to be more active in discussing and expressing ideas based on what the activity required. The fact that the group's discussions were lacking in structure seemed to reduce the quality of the meeting, but the use of a common medium for information sharing and collective decision-making notes seemed to improve it.

The findings presented above were, through an initial literature investigation, associated with "awareness" as a major concept in CSCW. Further investigation in the CSCW literature regarding awareness brought us in the context-based workplace awareness and the respective sub-types such as temporal and activity awareness as closely related to the needs for increasing meeting efficiency that was our initial aim. Thus, our aim became designing a digital solution that supports context-based workplace awareness and investigates how that would influence meeting effectiveness and efficiency.

Based on our findings in the informing phase both from the empirical data and the look at the literature, we took the role of designers and had a brainstorming session, and a design workshop [27] where various design concepts for possible prototypes were discussed. Through different sketches and use of different materials, we explored how the solution would look and what kind of features would promote temporal and activity awareness. Based on the final sketches we built a prototype that we named "BEACON". The name was inspired by the concept of a beacon, a light set up in a high or prominent position as a warning, signal, or celebration [28].

B. Prototype

The prototype Beacon consists of two components, a desktop Dashboard and an Artifact. Figure 1 illustrates the prototype in a meeting setting.

Figure 1. Stylised illustration of how the prototype is intended to be used.

1) Desktop Dashboard: This component utilizes the first context-aware function, *presenting information and services*, as described by Day et al. [17]. It presents to users medium-level meeting activities in the form of an agenda, as well as their descriptions and time durations. It also utilizes the third context-aware function, *attaching context information for later retrieval*, through an interactive co-writing noting tool for each activity that allows the participants to later retrieve previously recorded low-level activities. Adobe XD was used to create the dashboard with four base pages:

- **Home screen:** Shows recent projects, current group members, and meetings that have been conducted. Users can create a new meeting agenda from here.
- **Agenda creation:** Includes a form section for the creation of agendas, such as agenda title, description, date, as well as the agenda's activities that each has a title, description, and priority (1 - 5). The higher the priority, the more time will be allocated to the activity.
- **In-session screen:** Shows which activity is active, in addition to the noting functionality. This is shown in Figure 2.
- **Meeting review screen:** Gives the users the ability to review the activities they have discussed in a structured manner, with the option to edit the notes of each one.

2) Status-based Artifact: This component is a 3D printed artifact (shown in Figure 3) designed to present the status of defined time limits of high- and medium-level activities in the meeting. The artifact has a built-in speaker and two

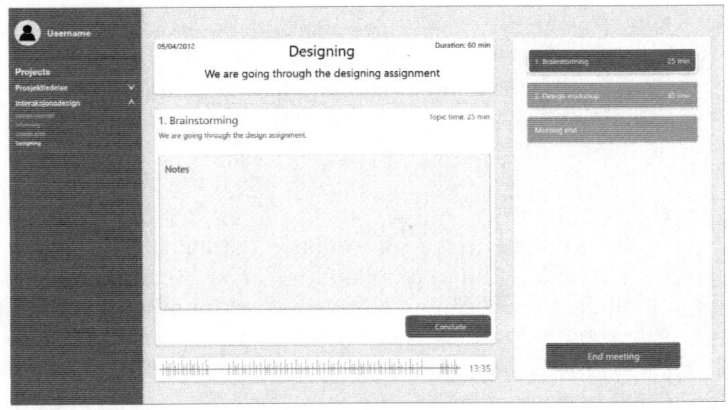

Figure 2. Screenshot of the desktop dashboard in the "in-session" phase.

light sources that each can display different colors. The top light source represents the time left of meetings' high-level activities (the meeting as a whole), and the bottom light source represents the time left of medium-level activities (e.g., topic discussions). The speaker is used to audibly notify the participants when different time limits have been reached. Figure 3 illustrates the artifact component of the prototype. The defined colors of the light sources indicate the following:

- **Green:** More than half of the activity's allocated time remains.
- **Yellow:** Half of the activity's allocated time remains.
- **Red:** Only about 10% of the activity's allocated time remains.
- **Blue:** The activity's allocated time has been used up and any further time spent on this activity is considered *overtime*. The speaker sounds a notification when this phase is reached.

The choice of colors is inspired by a study on the relationship between color and emotion [29]. The transition between colors occurs instantly. When high and medium-level activities are concluded the relevant light source resets to green. This is especially relevant for medium-level activities.

Figure 3. The artifact component of the prototype.

The second context-aware function, *automatically executing a service* [17], is the core concept of this component. The component will dynamically change its colors based on context changes, such as the time duration of the activity. These changes are both triggered by time events and user input. E.g., the allocated time of remaining medium-level activities can increase if the current activity is concluded before the time is up, or the allocated times can be reduced if and the more the current activity is spent in overtime. These increases of reductions in allocated times are calculated based on defined activity priorities and the remaining time of the high-level activity.

C. Evaluation

We will refer to this subsection as "Evaluation" to adhere to the interaction design process phases. However, the evaluation in this paper relates to the testing of our prototype, collecting data about the testing and further analyzing it. The evaluation phase helped us explore the research question raised in this paper.

Due to limitations in time and resources, we conducted the evaluation with a small group of people as a pilot study. The evaluation was conducted in the form of a usability test in a controlled setting involving users [27]. We investigated how users utilize, interact with, and feel about the prototype, and how the presence of the prototype impacted the efficiency and effectiveness of the meeting.

We observed a group of 6 students having a meeting in a university group room. The observation was followed with a structured interview in which each participant in the meeting was asked about his/her experience of using the tool in the meeting.

The process of the evaluation started with the researches explaining how the evaluation would be completed, with an explanation on how the artifact and desktop dashboard operates. They were informed that the researchers would manually control the artifact's colors and sound notifications (Wizard of Oz approach [27]) based on their time used during the meeting and that they should try to pay attention to these types of changes. Since Adobe XD could not support writing directly in text boxes in the prototype tab, we utilized a google docs document mimicking the desktop dashboard. They were however told to use the desktop dashboard when they needed to read the activity titles and descriptions, and when concluding medium-level activities.

Task enactment: The subjects were beforehand given four activities in the form of discussion topics, with additional instructions for how to interact with the prototype. As described in Subsection C, the desktop dashboard can be used to assign priorities to the activities, which the group leader was told to do before the meeting.

Observing users' reaction: During the task enactment, all four of the researchers took notes on how the users reacted to certain predicted scenarios and other unexpected reactions to the prototype.

User satisfaction structured interview: An interview including nine structured questions were created for understanding how the participants felt about using the prototype and how they perceived the prototype to influence meeting efficiency and effectiveness through enhancing context-based workplace awareness. Questions related to the prototype were therefore mostly stated as "How did you feel...". Questions related to awareness was more investigative without using CSCW terminology as that would most likely just confuse the interviewees.

The whole observation was video recorded to prevent data loss. The interviews were audio-recorded and further transcribed. Figure 4 shows the evaluation setup with the prototype in a group room.

Figure 4. Evaluation observation in process.

The data collected was then analyzed with a qualitative interpretative approach [30] in two phases. Initially, all the researchers looked at the video-recording and the notes taken during the observation. The aim was to reflect on meeting efficiency by interpreting participants' behavior in relation to the features of the prototype. The first round of interpretations was then refined with the data from the interview transcript. That helped us in refining the initial interpretations, finding contradiction among what was said, and what was observed and further explore behaviors with uncertain interpretations. The results of this first analysis are presented in Section 4.

The second phase was a qualitative interpretative analysis of our findings from the perspective of context-based workplace awareness and its subtypes, such as temporal awareness and activity awareness and their influence in the meeting efficiency and/or effectiveness. The data from the interview was in this phase primarily used for interpretation and sensemaking. Iterative rounds of discussions with all researchers concluded in what is presented in Section 5.

IV. FINDINGS

Our selected group of participants found the prototype interesting and were generally excited about the opportunity to test it. Participants agreed that knowledge of the content of the discussions presented in a structured manner prior to the meeting helped to form ideas and express opinions with ease. The participants also agreed that the colors of the artifact had an impact on how the discussion dynamic played out.

One thing to note is that the participants never naturally used up the allocated time suggested from the dashboard. As a result, the artifact's function for indicating overtime (blue light) was not activated due to the early conclusions of the activities. To test the function for overtime, an additional topic ("bonus activity") was added, with a stricter time constraint than what the participants thought to be necessary.

The findings are separated into two sections, the artifact and the dashboard, where we elaborate on the specific results of the evaluation.

A. Dashboard

1) Agenda: As mentioned at the start of this section, knowing the activities beforehand and having the activities and their descriptions structurally listed was agreed by all participants as being helpful with forming ideas, which made it easier to state their individual opinions. It was also expressed by participants 1, 2, 3, and 6 that knowing the activity sequence within the meeting had a similar effect of helping them prepare their opinions. It was observed that the participants would often reread the activities' titles and descriptions. Participants 1 and 5 said that the option to reread the activity's titles and descriptions was helpful in reminding them of what the initial discussion was about. They also said that this additionally helped them to keep their thoughts and opinions relevant to the topic.

2) Noting: The participants frequently used the noting function of the prototype during the activities for multiple purposes. Generally, they used it to record each participant's take on the topic. It was also observed that the fourth activity was controversial for all participants as the atmosphere seemed to become more tense and focused as they had strong and partially biased opinions on the topic. To overcome this the group used the recorded data in the noting tool to systematically exclude the less agreed upon opinions, until a consensus by majority vote was reached. At the end of each activity, the group would analyze what was written in the notes and continued to the next activity when all members agreed to do so.

3) Meeting review: As described in the Prototype-section, the desktop dashboard also provided a meeting review of the completed activities at the end of the meeting. It was observed that the group used this feature briefly to review the contents and conclusions of the meeting's activities, as well as confirming that nothing was missing and that the conclusions should remain. One of the participants suggested after the evaluation that "It could be helpful to have some sort of agree/disagree button to click on each activity to make the process faster".

B. Artifact

1) Colors of the Artifact: Participants 1, 3, and 5 expressed the colors made a positive impact on controlling the pace and engagement of the discussion. Participant 4 said it made them more aware of the time left. It was also mentioned by participants 1 and 5 that the time-pressure made them feel that things moved faster, and a conclusion had to be met regardless of incidental disagreement between participants. These views coincided with what was observed by the researchers, who noted that the members actively responded to the color changes even in the middle of discussions. For instance, when the color of the activity status was green; the discussion was perceived to be relaxed and open. When the participants noticed the color of the activity status had changed to yellow; they became more focused on moving towards a conclusion without becoming stressed. The color change to red was perceived to make the participants stressed to reach a conclusion.

However, it was expressed by almost all of the participants that the color red was thought to be indicating the end of an activity, even though they were explained beforehand that red is meant to represent a low amount of time before a recommended activity change. Another observation was that the participants only seemed to express notice of the color change after about 1-2 minutes after it had changed. In the "bonus activity" it was observed that the participants became aware of the activity running on overtime when the color changed to blue and asked the researchers if they had to stop working on the activity. The researchers told the participants to continue their discussion if they wished to do so, which they chose to do for a few minutes.

2) Sound Notifications: As mentioned in Section 3.B, the artifact had the function of playing soundbites as an indication of, e.g., activity change. Activity change was only reached in the "bonus activity" and it was observed that the sound notification was not immediately noticed by the participants. The sound was also not significantly mentioned by any of the participants in the interview answers. The melody that was played after the participants agreed that the meeting was over, was observed to make them uplifted as they laughed and smiled in reaction. The group also mentioned in the interview that a helpful implementation could be a short ping when the color of the activity status would change to keep the awareness present. One participant mentioned the possibility of integrating a voice that informs users how much time is left. The use of vibrations was also suggested by another participant in a casual discussion after the meeting.

V. Discussion

A. Temporal Awareness

As mentioned in Section 4, the participants stated that knowing the activities and their sequence before and during the meeting, helped them prepare by generating thoughts/ideas, which made it easier to express them in the discussions. In other words; The temporal awareness of knowing about activities in the future was helpful for preparing in advance, and that in the moment of the activities these past preparations made it easier to contribute. This appeared to make the discussions more effective and/or efficient by reducing the time spent in generating these thoughts/ideas during the activities. This seems to coincide with what Yamane [22] suggested in his study. Being prepared before meetings in terms of role and information was also listed by Nixon and Littlepage [11] as a procedure that might be related to meeting effectiveness and efficiency. Backing up this argument; The evaluated group meeting, in regard to this, certainly seemed more efficient than the group observed in the informing phase, where several minutes were used just acquiring knowledge about the task at hand.

An interesting and unexpected observation made by the researchers was one of the ways the participants used the prototype's noting tool. In the fourth activity, the discussions between the participants were quite heated and there was a significant amount of disagreement and differing opinions on the discussed topic. To solve this the group, without any guidance from the researchers, wrote down each participant's opinion. This could potentially have given the rest of the group members a cue [21] to discuss why some of the opinions were more "valid" than others in regard to the discussed topic. One could argue that providing these cues "forced" the members to defend their argument by presenting initially unshared information about their opinion, which could have resulted in other members adjusting their opinion/stance and therefore, led to a more thorough exploration of options. The participants then proceeded to systematically narrow down the opinions until a conclusion was made by the majority vote. This is a small example of temporal awareness as the recorded opinions can be considered records of past low-level activities used to solve the task in the present. Somewhat similarly, the meeting review feature was also used briefly by the participants as a method of control checking if what was previously concluded was still agreed upon. This is another example of how the notes can contribute to temporal awareness by allowing the participants to view what had previously been discussed. Coincidentally, exploring different options properly before a final decision is made is outlined by Nixon and Littlepage [11] as something that might indicate meeting effectiveness and efficiency.

We argue that removing the common noting tool would reduce the quality of the discussions as the participants would have fewer means of properly exploring options. It could, however, be argued that the group leader was the primary reason for the noting tools good use, meaning that the noting tool's efficiency might be depended on how well the users can apply it. Regardless, it seemed that when the noting tool was put to good use, it enhanced the awareness of the low-level activities in the discussion. This could confirm our assumptions made in the conceptual grounding on the basis of Haller et al. [23], that group collaboration could be enhanced by integrating a noting system where participants can share their thoughts with the rest of the group.

B. Activity Awareness

During the meeting, the information about the high- and medium-level activities presented through the agenda appeared to help the participants to stay on track in the discussions. Specifically, the opportunity to reread the title and descriptions of activities appeared to be useful, as participants 1 and 5 expressed that this helped them remember what the initial activity was about. This could be an indication of something that improved the effectiveness and efficiency of the meeting, as Garcia et al. [5] specified that lack of group focus is a sign of a bad meeting, and Nixon and Littlepage [11] mentioned how participants being focused and committed to the meeting might be a factor indicating meeting effectiveness and efficiency.

In the interview, several of the participants expressed that the colors of the artifact made them more aware of the status of the meeting in terms of activity time limits and encouraged them to come to a conclusion before the time was up. This aligns with the researchers' observations that the participants seemed aware of the status of medium- and high-level activities even when predominantly working on low-level activities. Raising activity awareness through presenting the status of activity time limits using colors seemed to be effective as the participant 1 explicitly mentioned that the pace of the meeting was controlled positively by this feature. This was also implicitly mentioned by participants 3 and 5. It was also observed that the participants would not recognize the status change before 1-2 minutes had passed, which likely changed the current pace as soon as it was identified. It could, therefore, be argued that the state of the color changed too quickly, and a gradual change over time could facilitate the pace even more.

In terms of the sound notifications of recommended topic changes, this was never naturally observed during the meeting, as the participants concluded the topics before this notification could initiate. The only time this was observed was during the "bonus topic", where the participants at first did not notice the notification until the sound was replayed by the researchers with higher volume. This gives the indication that such a notification sound should be clear and easily identifiable, in which the sound used during the evaluation apparently was not. However, the fact that the topics were always concluded before the recommended time was up, and thus the meeting was also ended with time to spare, could be an indication that the meeting was efficient. This coincides with both Nixon and Littlepage [11], as well as Davison [2], who both outlined the potential importance of temporal integrity. The time allocated to each topic was also indirectly defined by the participants themselves through giving each topic a priority, as described in Section 3.C. This aligns with the study by Janicik and Bartel [24], who proposed that there is a correlation between specific time duration and task performance. As also described in Section 5, Kelly and McGrath [26] suggested that having short time limits results in a faster pace but might lead to lower result quality. As mentioned earlier in this section, the participants perceived the awareness of activity status to result in a higher pace, which coincided with what the researchers observed. The quality of conclusions/results, however, were not significantly investigated.

VI. Conclusion and Future Work

Our findings, based on the observation and interviews compared to the conceptual grounding, indicate a positive effect on decision making in group meetings when temporal and activity awareness are enhanced. Specifically, The participants came prepared for the meeting, and it seemed that the foreknowledge of activities was beneficial for the effectiveness and efficiency of the discussions. A central focus for increasing the awareness of the meeting structure was the agenda, and especially the topic titles and descriptions, which were reread several times by the participants during the discussions. They expressed that this helped them keep the discussions relevant to the ongoing topics, which in turn might have made the discussion more effective and/or efficient. The most impactful observation for the awareness of discussion was the use of the noting tool. The tool was often used as a common area to record thoughts and seemed to be useful and effective in that the participants could keep track of the explored and, therefore, unexplored options/information until a conclusion was reached. In addition, the status-based artifact seemed to be dictating the pace of the meeting. For instance, the activity status colors of yellow and red were perceived to motivate the group to move towards a conclusion at a quicker rate compared to green, which seemed to have a more relaxed atmosphere.

Hence, our findings show promising results on how the prototype can aid group meetings in terms of effectiveness and/or efficiency through enhancing temporal and activity awareness in the meeting. The responses from the participants were generally quite positive.

While the findings of the study seem promising, the prototype was only tested in one meeting. In order to gain more insight into its true effects on group meeting efficiency and effectiveness, the prototype would have to be tested in several meetings of different settings, as well as with different participants. It would be especially relevant to investigate the prototype in the setting of an organizational meeting, as this would provide more insight into how generalizable the prototype is in more and less professional settings. The effectiveness and efficiency would also have to be measured with a more reliable method, and the findings of meeting participants using the prototype would have to be compared with the findings of participants not using it in order to see if there is a significant difference. The prototype should also be further developed, so all of its features are fully functional and not controlled through a "Wizard of Oz"-approach. This should make for a more natural experience, and thus produce more accurate results.

Beyond this, we also collected more data during the evaluation regarding insight into possible improvements to the design of the prototype. One such improvement could be looking into design alternatives for the artifact, as it was observed that it was not naturally visible at the center of the table due to being low in height. This is suboptimal as it can prevent the participants from receiving the presented context information, and thus not generating awareness. We also believe that gradually changing the colors of the artifact is another possible improvement for enhancing awareness, as this would give a more accurate feel of the status of activities, as opposed to instant color change. Lastly, adding more functionalities to the noting tool could be beneficial.

REFERENCES

[1] S. Kauffeld and N. Lehmann-Willenbrock, "Meetings Matter Effects of Team Meetings on Team and Organizational Success," Small Group Research, vol. 43, Apr. 2012, pp. 130–158.

[2] R. Davison, "An instrument for measuring meeting success," Information & management, vol. 32, no. 4, 1997, pp. 163–176.

[3] L. K. Michaelsen, L. D. Fink, and A. Knight, "Designing effective group activities: Lessons for classroom teaching and faculty development," To improve the academy, vol. 16, no. 1, 1997, pp. 373–397.

[4] A. C. B. Garcia, J. Kunz, and M. Fischer, "Meeting details: Methods to instrument meetings and use agenda voting to make them more effective," in meeting of the Center for Integrated Facility Engineering, Stanford (no. TR147), 2003.

[5] A. C. Bicharra Garcia, J. Kunz, and M. Fischer, "Cutting to the chase: improving meeting effectiveness by focusing on the agenda," in Proceedings of the 2004 ACM conference on Computer supported cooperative work, 2004, pp. 346–349.

[6] H. Bang, S. Fuglesang, M. Ovesen, and D. Eilertsen, "Effectiveness in top management group meetings: The role of goal clarity, focused communication, and learning behavior," Scandinavian journal of psychology, vol. 51, Jun. 2010, pp. 253–61.

[7] R. J. Garmston, "Results-oriented agendas transform meetings into valuable collaborative events," The Learning Professional, vol. 28, no. 2, 2007, p. 55.

[8] J. E. Bardram and T. R. Hansen, "Context-based workplace awareness," Computer Supported Cooperative Work (CSCW), vol. 19, no. 2, 2010, pp. 105–138.

[9] K. Schmidt and L. Bannon, "Taking cscw seriously," Computer Supported Cooperative Work (CSCW), vol. 1, no. 1-2, 1992, pp. 7–40.

[10] T. Gross, "Supporting effortless coordination: 25 years of awareness research," Computer Supported Cooperative Work (CSCW), vol. 22, no. 4-6, 2013, pp. 425–474.

[11] C. T. Nixon and G. E. Littlepage, "Impact of meeting procedures on meeting effectiveness," Journal of Business and Psychology, vol. 6, no. 3, 1992, pp. 361–369.

[12] C. Heath, M. S. Svensson, J. Hindmarsh, P. Luff, and D. Vom Lehn, "Configuring awareness," Computer Supported Cooperative Work (CSCW), vol. 11, no. 3-4, 2002, pp. 317–347.

[13] C. Heath and P. Luff, "Documents and professional practice: "bad" organisational reasons for "good" clinical records," in Proceedings of the 1996 ACM conference on Computer supported cooperative work, 1996, pp. 354–363.

[14] P. Luff, C. Heath, and D. Greatbatch, "Tasks-in-interaction: paper and screen based documentation in collaborative activity," in Proceedings of the 1992 ACM conference on Computer-supported cooperative work, 1992, pp. 163–170.

[15] C. Heath and P. Luff, "Collaboration and controlcrisis management and multimedia technology in london underground line control rooms," Computer Supported Cooperative Work (CSCW), vol. 1, no. 1-2, 1992, pp. 69–94.

[16] P. Dourish and V. Bellotti, "Awareness and coordination in shared workspaces," in Proceedings of the 1992 ACM conference on Computer-supported cooperative work, 1992, pp. 107–114.

[17] A. K. Dey, G. D. Abowd, and D. Salber, "A conceptual framework and a toolkit for supporting the rapid prototyping of context-aware applications," Human–Computer Interaction, vol. 16, no. 2-4, 2001, pp. 97–166.

[18] M. Borges, P. Brezillon, J. Pino, and J.-C. Pomerol, "Bringing context to cscw," in 8th International Conference on Computer Supported Cooperative Work in Design, vol. 2. IEEE, 2004, pp. 161–166.

[19] "AGENDA | meaning in the cambridge english dictionary." [Online]. Available: https://dictionary.cambridge.org/dictionary/english/agenda [retrieved: Feb., 2020].

[20] H. Bang, S. L. Fuglesang, M. R. Ovesen, and D. E. Eilertsen, "Effectiveness in top management group meetings: The role of goal clarity, focused communication, and learning behavior," Scandinavian Journal of Psychology, vol. 51, no. 3, 2010, pp. 253–261.

[21] B. E. Mennecke, "Using group support systems to discover hidden profiles: An examination of the influence of group size and meeting structures on information sharing and decision quality," International Journal of Human-Computer Studies, vol. 47, no. 3, 1997, pp. 387–405.

[22] D. Yamane, "Course preparation assignments: A strategy for creating discussion-based courses," Teaching Sociology, vol. 34, no. 3, 2006, pp. 236–248.

[23] M. Haller et al., "The nice discussion room: Integrating paper and digital media to support co-located group meetings," in Proceedings of the SIGCHI Conference on Human Factors in Computing Systems, 2010, pp. 609–618.

[24] G. A. Janicik and C. A. Bartel, "Talking about time: Effects of temporal planning and time awareness norms on group coordination and performance." Group Dynamics: Theory, Research, and Practice, vol. 7, no. 2, 2003, p. 122.

[25] J. M. Carroll, D. C. Neale, P. L. Isenhour, M. B. Rosson, and D. S. McCrickard, "Notification and awareness: synchronizing task-oriented collaborative activity," International Journal of Human-Computer Studies, vol. 58, no. 5, 2003, pp. 605–632.

[26] J. R. Kelly and J. E. McGrath, "Effects of time limits and task types on task performance and interaction of four-person groups." Journal of personality and social psychology, vol. 49, no. 2, 1985, p. 395.

[27] P. Rogers, H. Sharp, and J. Preece, Interaction Design, beyond human–computer interaction, fourth edition ed. West Sussex, PO19 8SQ, United Kingdom: John Wiley & Sons Ltd, 2015.

[28] "Beacon | Definition of Beacon by Lexico." [Online]. Available: https://www.lexico.com/en/definition/beacon [retrieved: Feb., 2020].

[29] K. NAz and H. Epps, "Relationship between color and emotion: A study of college students," College Student J, vol. 38, no. 3, 2004, p. 396.

[30] H. K. Klein and M. D. Myers, "A set of principles for conducting and evaluating interpretive field studies in information systems," MIS quarterly, 1999, pp. 67–93.

Designing Personal Health Records for Cognitive Rehabilitation

Klaudia Çarçani
Faculty of Computer Science
Østfold University College
Halden, Norway
email: klaudia.carcani@hiof.no

Miria Grisot
Department of Informatics
University of Oslo
Oslo, Norway
email: miria.grisot@uio.no

Harald Holone
Faculty of Computer Science
Østfold University College
Halden, Norway
email: harald.holone@hiof.no

***Abstract*—Personal Health Records (PHRs) are digital tools that give people the possibility to have access and control over their health data. They are usually used in situations when the patient is home or in casual encounters between the patient and the healthcare practitioner. Current related literature does not discuss much in terms of PHR usage in hospitals and possible implications for designing such PHRs. In this paper, we present the case of cognitive rehabilitation in a rehabilitation hospital. Patients in rehabilitation should take a leading role in their treatment as a prerequisite for more beneficial rehabilitation. We have analyzed the cognitive rehabilitation case and present a set of six design implications for designing a PHR for the patients in cognitive rehabilitation during their time at the hospital. We discuss these implications from a Computer Supported Cooperative Work (CSCW) perspective, where the PHR has been conceptualized as hybrid information spaces compounded by personal and Common Information Spaces (CIS). We found, that in cognitive rehabilitation, an important element for designing a PHR is its role not only in creating the possibility of sharing information between the patient and the healthcare practitioners, but, at the same time, offering some mechanisms for coordination between them as an incentive of recognizing patients work in the division of labor and helping the patient take more control over his/her rehabilitation.**

Keywords-PHR; cognitive rehabilitation; coordination mechanisms; patients empowerment; CIS.

I. INTRODUCTION

Personal Health Records (PHRs) are defined as "digital tools that allow people to access and coordinate their lifelong health information and make appropriate parts of it available to those who need it" [1]. PHRs emerged from the need of patients to take control of their health information and contribute to it [2]. Commonly, patient health information has been stored in Electronic Medical Records (EMR), which are used by healthcare practitioners to facilitate the management of patient's treatment and also as a cooperative tool with other healthcare practitioners [3]. However, despite an increasing requirement in health policies in recognizing patients' role as being active participants in their care, patients still do not have access to EMRs and their own health information. Often, the only way they get access is by obtaining a paper copy of their records. Thus, patients collect paper documents and create their own big paper folder that they usually bring over in consultations. This practice has limitations in terms of how the information is stored, retrieved, and shared. In response to these limitations, PHRs emerged around two decades ago to give patients the possibility to have access to their health data and also be able to generate more health information that they can share with whoever they want.

PHRs have been discussed in the literature under different lenses, and different types of PHRs have been developed. The CSCW field has contributed to increasing the understanding of the cooperative work in healthcare and introducing a set of digital artifacts that facilitate cooperation [4], offering in this way, better services to the persons in need. From a CSCW perspective, the PHR is a collaborative tool between patients and healthcare practitioners. The PHR has been conceptualized as an information space of a hybrid nature [5]-[7] representing a tool that integrates personal and interpersonal/common information spaces. In this paper, we follow this line of work and are interested in both the design of PHRs and their conceptualization as collaborative tools. Therefore, we address the following research question: *"How to design a PHR for cognitive rehabilitation?" and "How can this contribute to conceptualize PHRs?"*

Specifically, we analyze the collaborative use of a PHR in the hospital context, while patients are still hospitalized. PHRs are mostly designed to support the collaboration between the patient and health practitioners when the patient is home or when s/he has casual encounters with the healthcare practitioners. We argue that, in order to support collaborative work in the hospital context, the PHR needs to be designed differently. In addition, we also argue that PHRs need to accommodate the specific needs of the patient's clinical problem. Hence, in this paper, we identify and discuss implications for the design of a PHR in the case of patients in cognitive rehabilitation in a rehabilitation hospital. In this context, patients have to actively participate in care practices (not only receive care). Cognitive rehabilitation is a special rehabilitation program that is usually offered in rehabilitation hospitals to patients who suffer from some cognitive impairments after Acquired Brain Injury (ABI) caused mainly from stroke or accidents [8]. We have investigated the cognitive rehabilitation process in the Cognitive Unit (CU) of a rehabilitation hospital in Norway and defined a set of implications for the design of a PHR in such a setting. We discuss the PHR design implications in relation to the current conceptualization of PHRs within CSCW research and contribute to a better understanding of such tools.

In Section II, a description of our main concepts is presented. Section III gives an overview of how the data was collected and analyzed. Section IV is a detailed presentation of the practice of cognitive rehabilitation as a summary of our empirical study. Section V presents a set of implications for designing a PHR used in cognitive rehabilitation grounded in our empirical findings. In Section VI, we discuss the implications for design with a more conceptual perspective drawn from the existing conceptual discussion of PHRs in CSCW.

II. Conceptual Grounding

In this section, we present more in-depth the main concepts for this paper. Initially, we present PHRs and how they have been defined and described in the literature. Further, we present how PHRs have been conceptualized in CSCW as a hybrid information space. Moreover, we focus on the CIS as a concept and finally describe the concept of coordination mechanisms as a parameter of CIS and relevant for our discussion later in the paper.

A. Personal Health Records

PHRs have been defined generally as Internet-based, lifelong health records that are controlled by the individual and are meant to promote the individual's engagement in his or her health and healthcare [1]. PHRs should be controlled by the patients who should as well enter at least part of the information. Davidson et al. [1] in a PHRs literature review found that there are different types of PHRs. One type of PHRs are those tethered to EMR. In that configuration, part of the PHR information is provided and maintained by healthcare providers. A patient can access the EMR and mostly read through the information, but it is usually not common to have the possibility to edit or change the data in the EMR, even when that is needed, required, and liable for the patient. This does not mean the patient will access the EMR and change the description of their diagnosis. However, the patient can contribute by describing more details about his/her situation, which will then help the doctor make a better diagnosis. Other type of PHRs are those fully controlled by patients, who enter and maintain their own health data [1]. This health data can be brought over to be discussed with the healthcare practitioners during consultations, and the collaboration and interaction happen outside of the PHR. Another type are PHR platforms/ecosystems. They are supposed to be a mix between standalone PHRs and tethered to EMR PHRs, but with a distinction to be untethered from a specific healthcare provider. PHR platforms are supposed to give the patient the freedom to use the PHR independent of where s/he is receiving the treatment. An example of PHR platforms from the Norwegian healthcare has been described by Vassilakopoulou et al. [7]. Helsenorge.no is a patient platform where the patient can find part of his/her health data arriving from different health settings. The aim of helsenorge.no is to give patients a space/platform where they can find health data such as diagnosis (epicrise), have the possibility to communicate electronically with their General Practitioner (GP), check their vaccine history, their medicine, etc. and possibly more services in the future.

PHRs are considered to have the potential to contribute to patients' empowerment by implying changes in the way healthcare is delivered and give patients the possibility of being more involved and getting more control over their care [2]. However, their usage is still low, and there is limited research on how PHRs can empower the patients in having more control and being involved in their care.

Creating PHRs is associated with multifaced socio-technical problems attributed to their role of connecting multiple parties and social actors [9]. From a patient perspective, a PHR is valuable for accessing information and sharing health information with the ones s/he wants. From a healthcare practitioner perspective, the usage of a PHR could contribute to better coordination with the patient and the possibility to access information that surpasses organizational boundaries.

B. PHR as Hybrid Informations Spaces

Researchers in CSCW have been discussing how to conceptualize PHRs. Cabitza et al. [6] argue that conceptualizing PHRs as tools that can just support the flow of information mitigates their full potential to be more collaboration and communication oriented. Thus, they suggest framing PHRs as hubs where patients and healthcare practitioners meet to enhance a collaborative relationship. Cabitza et al. [6] have defined the concept of InterPersonal Health Record (IPHR) as a hybrid electronic record that merges the typical EMR and PHR related features that aim at enhancing "relationships, communication, and collaboration between citizens/patients and their healthcare practitioners" [6]. The emphasis on the interpersonal aims to highlight the involvement in the management of care of both patients and healthcare providers. Cabitza and Gesso [5] describe MEDICONA as an example of an IPHR. MEDICONA implements the concept of a shared record among different user types, in addition to electronic messaging [5] and is described as an IPHR. Further, they discuss how the IPHR can be conceptualized as a CIS, where patients and healthcare practitioners can access the information that they need regarding health management in a common space. This conceptualization is compatible with Lahtiranta et al. [10] health spaces defined as collaborative information space for patients and health providers, which are not limited only to healthcare-related encounters.

Unruh and Pratt [11] identify a set of functional requirements for an information space designed explicitly for patients' cooperation with clinicians. They define explicit representations and increased interaction as a way that CIS can facilitate cooperation between patients and their clinicians.

Recently, Vassilakopoulou et al. [7] have conceptualized PHRs as information spaces of a hybrid character. They state that "PHR can be more than a private tool, serving as CIS that straddles work and non-work contexts, bringing together participants – patients and professionals – in a collaborative relation". Thus, considering PHR as personal information space (serving sensitive health information management need) and CIS (stressing the cooperative dimension of the patient- healthcare practitioners' relations). They have analyzed and discussed two cases of a PHR: a) MyHealth, which gives the possibility to the patient to access and store personal health information, and supports electronic exchanges between patients and healthcare providers. Moreover, it offers connections to several existing systems and the possibility for other applications to connect and extend the core functionality [7], and b) MyBook, which facilitates information sharing between the patient and his/her GP [7]. The cases described, such as MEDICONA, MyHealth, and MyBook, are examples of PHRs which facilitate communication, awareness through records, and collaboration based on the information shared in the common space. However, this literature considers mainly cases when the patient is outside of the hospital and has only occasional health encounters with the healthcare practitioner. The literature on PHRs has not yet addressed the use of PHRs in hospital/clinical context. In this context, it is assumed that patients do not need to have access to their health data as they are in close contact with clinicians. However, as patients are asked to cooperate/work together with clinicians (and not just receive care), they also need tools that enable them to take up this role. Thus, the case described in this paper contributes to the conceptualization of PHRs in a hospital setting in a context where the patient has to actively participate in the care practices (not only receive care).

C. Common Information Spaces

In CSCW, PHRs have been defined as CIS or hybrid information spaces. While personal information spaces refer to patients' individual needs in managing health information that is personal to them, the concept of CI has been discussed in CSCW. In this subsection, we will present a deeper understanding of CIS as a concept.

CIS is a conceptual framework in CSCW which highlights the relationship between actors, artifacts, information, and cooperative work [12]. The aim is to provide an analytical tool that can inform developing systems that can support cooperative work [12].

CIS "encompasses artifacts that are accessible to a cooperative ensemble as well as the meaning attributed to these artifacts by the actors" [12]. In cooperative work settings, actors are interdependent. This requires that they coordinate who is doing what, when, and why [13]. Thus, what is called articulation work takes an important role. Articulation work as the supra type of work, which is necessary for the division of labor [12][14], can be facilitated by the usage of artifacts or mechanisms of interaction [15]. According to Schmidt and Bannon [12], CIS is necessary for distributed cooperative work to maintain some form of shared and locally and temporally created understanding about objects in the CIS.

An important characteristic of CIS is the openness and closure and the need for a balance between the malleability of information and the need for some closure to allow for translation among communities. In making this possible, a balance of interpretations among different webs of significance (as called by Bossen, representing people from different groups) is needed [13]. Hence, CIS requires a new type of articulation work, which makes possible the coordination of interpretations.

In healthcare, there are some examples of CIS, such as [16] in which the influence of the physical position of artifacts used in a CIS in a hospital is investigated. In [17], CIS were investigated in emergency teams in hospitals.

Bossen [13] describes seven parameters of CIS such as the degree of distribution; the multiplicity of webs of significance; the multiplicity and intensity of means of communication; the level of required articulation work; the web of artifacts; the immaterial mechanisms of interaction and the need for precision and promptness of interpretation. Bossen [13] as well build his analysis of CIS in a hospital ward.

A relevant parameter for this paper is the "web of artifacts" described as material mechanisms of coordination to make possible cooperation among the distributed actors and having a better overview of the state of the work possible. Based on this definition, a PHR as a material artifact in the hand of the patient in which the patient can communicate, collaborate, cooperate with the healthcare practitioners, is a mechanism which materializes a CIS between the patient and healthcare practitioners.

In the literature, different types of artifacts that support a CIS are described. Bossen refers to the web of artifacts as material coordination mechanisms by referencing to coordination mechanisms as defined by Schmidt and Simonee [15]. However, Bannon and Bødker [18] have discussed that what is defined as boundary objects from Star and Strauss [19] can be as well used as a means for sharing items in the CIS. Thus, another type of web of artifact in CIS. The concept of boundary objects and coordination mechanisms have differences, as discussed in [20]. In this paper, we are particularly interested in coordination mechanisms and will get back to this concept in our discussion.

D. Coordination Mechanisms

Coordination mechanisms have been defined [15] as "a specific organizational construct, consisting of a coordinative protocol imprinted upon a distinct artifact, which, in the context of a certain cooperative work arrangement, stipulates and mediates the articulation of cooperative work to reduce the complexity of articulation work of that arrangement." Thus, coordination mechanisms are artifacts which aim to reduce the complexity of the division of labor in a cooperative work setting and make cooperation possible. The concept of the coordination mechanism, as defined, describes a material artifact. This approach has been considered narrow by Bossen [13], who emphasizes that organizational structures and division of labor also facilitate coordination of work since they explicate who does what and when. Hence, as another parameter of CIS, Bossen lists the immaterial mechanisms of interaction for these other constructs, which facilitate articulation of cooperative work. Coordination mechanisms aim to coordinate activities among semi-autonomous actors who should have a certain level of consensus in order to get the job done [20].

The PHRs that have been described in the literature as CIS [5] [21] [22] or hybrid information spaces [7] show mostly cases of artifacts that offer a space where the information is shared, and communication and collaboration are supported, thus resembling coordination mechanisms. However, they lack an aspect of a more cooperative relationship between the patient and the healthcare practitioners, where the patient has an active role in his/her care by taking over tasks and work in the division of labor. Moreover, cases of CIS discussed in healthcare [13][16] [17] are mostly focusing on hospital wards and describing the need for sharing information among healthcare practitioners. The patient's voice and visibility in the process lacks. Hence, in this paper, we describe, in the next section, a case of a hospital ward where the CIS also involves the patient. Moreover, the requirements for a PHR are not only communication and sharing information but entering a cooperative relationship where the patient and the healthcare practitioners supporting him/her are interdependent on each other.

III. DESCRIPTION OF THE COGNITIVE REHABILITATION EXISTING PRACTICES

We studied the process of cognitive rehabilitation in the CU of a rehabilitation hospital in Norway. The unit is specialized exclusively for offering cognitive rehabilitation. Cognitive rehabilitation is a special rehabilitation program that is offered to people that suffer from cognitive impairments after an Acquired Brain Injury (ABI). ABI is brain damage acquired after birth. The causes of ABI can be "from a traumatic brain injury (i.e., accidents, falls, assaults, etc.) and non-traumatic brain injury (i.e., stroke, brain tumors, infection, poisoning, hypoxia, ischemia, metabolic disorders or substance abuse)". The cognitive rehabilitation aims to support the patients in therapeutic manners, thus, either improving his/her functions in daily life or helping the patients to find alternative ways for compensating the lost functions through additional aids. Rehabilitation, as defined by the Norwegian Health Authorities [23], requires a multidisciplinary team that works together with the patient during rehabilitation. The multidisciplinary team involves different healthcare practitioners.

In our study in cognitive rehabilitation, the multidisciplinary team is usually compounded by the medical doctor, a nurse, an occupational therapist, a physiotherapist, a psychologist, a social worker, and a speech therapist. This team assists the patient throughout the 5 five weeks of rehabilitation at the hospital. Each offers specialized care to the patient based on their domain of knowledge.

Rehabilitation is based on the goal-setting theory. This theory is defined broadly as a process in which the patient and members of the multidisciplinary team agree on a set of rehabilitative goals to be achieved during the rehabilitation program [24]. Goal-setting is not only an administrative tool, but it is considered a clinical intervention [24]. It has been shown that setting personal goals increases the possibilities of behavior change by increasing motivation (the desire to act in a particular way) [25].

In the CU, the rehabilitation process is built based on the goal-setting theory. Thus, a patient, in collaboration with the multidisciplinary team, has to decide on a set of goals that s/he wants to work with during rehabilitation. Goals are mostly long term. As the time stay at the hospital is only for five weeks, the patient and the multidisciplinary team during the first week should agree on the things to prioritize for those five weeks and decide on a set of sub-goals for each main goal. The sub-goals should be SMART (Specific, Measurable, Achievable, Realistic, and Timely). As rehabilitation targets the increase in the patient's functional level in his/her daily life, the involvement of the patient in defining the rehabilitation goals is essential. The first week at the hospital, the patient meets with all the members of the multidisciplinary team one by one. In the ideal scenario, the patient comes already with a set of predefined goals, written by himself/herself. However, in many cases, the patient is not able to define his/her rehabilitation goals, and the multidisciplinary team members should help him/her. If the patient is not cooperating with the team, it is a risk that not relevant and specific goals would be set, and the result of the rehabilitation will be mitigated. The refining of goals comes together with the definition of a set of interventions that the patient would go through at the hospital to be able to achieve the goals. Interventions are defined as "an act performed for, with or on behalf of a person or population whose purpose is to assess, improve, maintain, promote or modify health, functioning or health conditions" [26]. It is absolutely relevant to the involvement of the patient in the process, so the patient later understands why s/he is doing different activities at the hospital.

The goals, respective sub-goals, and the interventions for each sub-goal are stipulated in a document called the goal plan document. This document is originated in the hospital EMR as part of the patient record. The goal plan is conceptualized to be shared with the patient as the main document of coordination between the team and the patient in rehabilitation. The document is designed to show the goals, sub-goals, and interventions, the team member that is responsible together with the patient for a specific intervention, and some more mechanisms that can help keep track of how the patient is advancing during rehabilitation. As the document is in the hospital EMR, the patient cannot access it. So, a printed version is given to the patient from the start. The electronic document is then shown during a meeting where all the multidisciplinary team, the patient, and if willing any of the patient's kin would go through the goals and agree on the final version. The final version will then be printed out and given to the patient.

During the time at the hospital, the patient receives a weekly plan every beginning of the week. The weekly plan involves all the activities that the patient should do during the week. The weekly plan is not part of the patient records in the EMR. It is maintained in a shared word document and printed out for each of the patients. If changes are made, the team member that implements the change can print another version or, in some cases, the patients write over the paper. The activities in the weekly plans should relate to any of the interventions in the goal plan and consequently contribute to the patient's sub-goals. This connection is very important to be highlighted for the patient as part of his/her rehabilitation process. However, the restriction that the current procedure and materiality of the artifacts imposes is not exploring the whole potential.

When the five weeks of rehabilitation are finished, the patient returns home. S/he can continue rehabilitation by his/her own or receives additional help from local rehabilitation therapists. The plan on how the patient should continue rehabilitation home has been made since s/he was at the hospital. The therapists at the hospital have established some connections with local therapists. It is important that the patient continues training with rehabilitation goals and sub-goals and keeps us with respective interventions as taught at the hospital.

IV. Methods

A. Data collection

The data that we have analyzed for this paper has been collected in two phases under the umbrella of the same project called "Patient Empowerment in Cognitive rehabilitation through the use of technology", which is a joint research initiative between a rehabilitation hospital and a university college in Norway.

Initially, as part of the initiative in boosting patients' involvement in their rehabilitation, the hospital decided to redesign the goal plan document and the procedures surrounding it. To redesign the document, a Participatory Design (PD) approach with workshops was taken in April-May 2018. First, the first author of this paper facilitated three workshops with a total of 10 patients, asking how to redesign the goal plan document (Figure 2) to make them want to engage more in their rehabilitation (more in detail this has been reported in another publication [27]). Second, the first author of this paper organized two PD workshops with the multidisciplinary team at the CU (20 participants). The healthcare practitioners were presented with a list of requirements from the patients' workshops and were invited to discuss these requirements and propose a new design of the document which would fulfill patients' requirements and, at the same time, fit within their routines and procedures. With the data collected, a redesigned document (as shown in Figure 2) was launched in June 2018 and has been in use ever since. Data collected where audio recordings of the workshops and designs of the new goal plan version from each of the participants. All participants signed a consent form before the workshops, and the data collected has been stored in safe locations at the hospital premises.

In the second phase, ethnographic observations of the rehabilitation process at the CU from an extended period of 6 months, August-December 2018, were conducted. Together with the CU management, we decided that for the ethnographic observations, the researcher (first author here) should shadow each of the health practitioners in the multidisciplinary team for a short period of time. This would minimize the stress of the patients and would give us the possibility to investigate the illness journey of more patients. The first author shadowed two occupational therapists respectively for 4 and 3 working days (8 hours shift during the day shift because in the afternoon most of the patients would go in their homes and no rehabilitation activities were planned at the unit) and participated in activities with 12 patients, one nurse for 6 days and met 5 patients, one physiotherapist for 4 days and met 8 patients, one speech therapist, one social worker for 4 days and met 8 patients and one psychologist for 1 day and met 1 patient. Handwritten notes where taken while observing. These notes where expanded with details at the end of each day when transcribed digitally. Digital notes were saved in a folder in the safe hospital network that the first author can access through an encrypted laptop given by the hospital. The staff member asked the patients for consent before the researcher would participate in any patient-staff meeting. This was documented by signing a consent form.

B. Analysis

Overall, a qualitative interpretative research approach [28] was adopted. First, the data collected were analyzed with the aim of defining a list of implications for designing a PHR for patients in cognitive rehabilitation. Second, reflections on these implications with the theoretical lenses of hybrid information spaces [7] were conducted. The principles defined by Klein and Myers [28] were used to do an interpretive analysis of the data collected in the two phases described in the previous section. We describe the process more in detail below.

Initially, the first author analyzed the audio-recorded data from the workshops and the designs of the patients and staff. Considering that the design requirements that emerged during the workshops were focused on the redesign of the goal plan document, which is a patient health record, the first author interpreted them with the perspective of possible design implications for a PHR. Moreover, the implications for design that emerged during the first iteration of interpretative analysis were supplemented and refined while analyzing notes from the observation period. The first author used a grounded theory approach to analyze the observation notes and defined a set implications for designing a PHR in cognitive rehabilitation in a hospital.

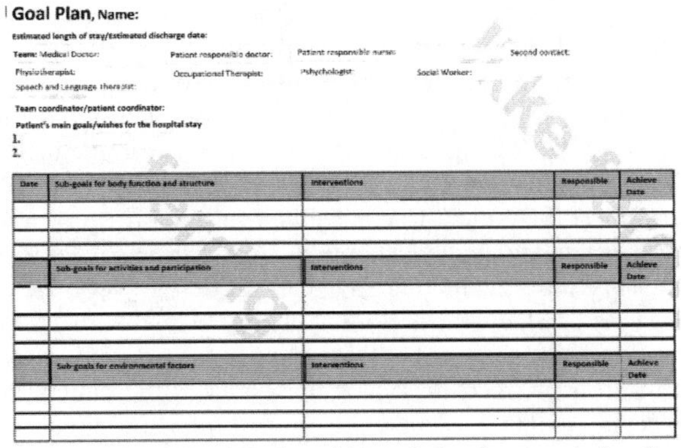

Figure 1. A translated version of the goal plan document before the redesign.

The list of implications was then discussed and refined with the other two authors who took a critical stance toward the findings. In the discussion, we (the three authors) reflected on implications for design, which were considered desirable for both the patients and staff.

V. IMPLICATIONS FOR DESIGN FOR A PHR IN COGNITIVE REHABILITATION

The case of cognitive rehabilitation in a rehabilitation hospital and, to a certain extent, rehabilitation in general either in the hospital or in the local communities has its own specificities. Below we present a list of implications for designing a PHR for cognitive rehabilitation.

1) Enhance the existing shared artifacts – The goal plan document and the weekly plans are an example of artifacts that are already implemented at the hospital and support cooperation and coordination between the patient and the multidisciplinary team, as presented in Section III. These artifacts are special to the rehabilitation process and the organization of care based on the goal-setting theory. From our data, we found that patients and the multidisciplinary team consider the goal plan an important element of the rehabilitation. Thus, designing a PHR for cognitive rehabilitation at the hospital should take into consideration these good practices in place and enhance the experience.

The goal plan document is compatible with the definition of PHRs, as stated in Davidson et al. [1]. With goal-setting as not only an administrative tool but as a clinical intervention [24], the document represents a health record that is supposed to be controlled by the individual and is meant to promote the individual's engagement in his/her health and healthcare [1]. The goal plan document is a limited version of a PHR as the patient cannot directly generate information (write goals or add appointments suggestions in the weekly plan), and every change in the health record is mediated by health professionals. Control allocation has been defined as a design tension when designing PHRs by Vassilakopoulou et al. [7]. However, the goal plan is still a special and good practice in clinical rehabilitation where the patient is supposed to not only receive care but co-construct care together with the multidisciplinary team. The team and the patient consider problematic that the goal plan is in the EMR of the hospital. The paper version that is given to the patient limits the options for using the goal plan. In the workshop and during observation, all the team members and the patients pointed to the need for digitalizing the goal plan and giving control to the patient. One other important insight is that the team would like a PHR for the patient, but they as well require this PHR to be tethered to the EMR [1] to avoid double work in reporting.

2) *Implement elements of coordination* – During the workshops, we found from both the patients and the team that when defining goals, the best scenario would be to see the patients themselves writing their rehabilitation goals. In this scenario, the multidisciplinary team would check the goals the patient has defined, then discuss them with the patient in a meeting. During the meeting, the staff participating would then change the goals based on what is discussed with the patient. The patient could then access the document and make additional changes. Finally, both team and patient, if agreed, would sign the final version of the goals during the so-called 'goal meeting'.

However, during observations, we found that the patient involvement in defining his/her goals is mitigated because s/he doesn't have direct access to the goal plan. The team compensates for the lack of patient involvement, but this can influence the result of the rehabilitation.

An Occupational Therapist during an in-situ interview stated that "an important aim of the treatment is to increase patients' knowledge on how to set rehabilitation goals and get to know which activities they can do to achieve the goals". Thus, rehabilitation is not only a matter of giving a service to the patients, but it is about increasing patients' health-literacy as a way to achieve self-management of their own condition. As a way to give patients more control over their rehabilitation and increase health literacy, we found that patients and the team members consider relevant assigning patients a role in the division of labor of the treatment and make this explicitly stated.

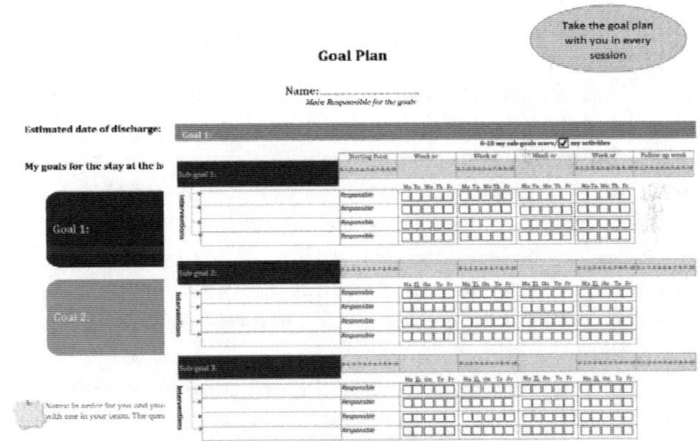

Figure 2. The redesigned goal plan document.

PHRs give people the possibility to look into and generate some of their health data and as well communicate and collaborate with a healthcare practitioner [1]. From the analysis of our data, we find that a PHR in cognitive rehabilitation should support not only common information and communication but also a cooperative work relationship between the patient and the multidisciplinary team. Hence, the PHR should facilitate the tasks that the patient should do and coordinate these patient's tasks with the tasks of the healthcare practitioners.

3) *Support different representations* – As stated above, rehabilitation goals can be divided into sub-goals, and for each sub-goal, there is a set of interventions. This tree structure is seen differently by the patient and the multidisciplinary team perspective. For the patients, the rehabilitation goals relate to the need for functioning in everyday life and should be articulated in that way. For the multidisciplinary team, the decision on rehabilitation goals and interventions is influenced by rehabilitation theories [29]-[31]. Thus, different representations of the same information are needed. During the PD workshops, we found that a classification of goals as defined by the International Classification of Functioning, Disability, and Health (ICF) [32] (as in Figure 1) was preferred more from the team. However, patients in workshops expressed that they did not relate to the classification of goals based on ICF and that "did not make sense" to them. One patient said, "is easier.. I want to have my goals, sub-goal and interventions… is that simple". Hence, designing a PHR for cognitive rehabilitation while the patient is at the hospital requires that the health information shared with the patient should be explicitly represented in a way that the patient can understand.

The case of a representation of a health record in a format that relates more to healthcare practitioners is very common. PHRs should surpass this downside of the current way of delivering healthcare and support an explicit representation of the information for the patients – in a way that facilitates how they interpret the information. The label of this implication for design is adapted from Unruh and Pratt [11]. Such an implication for design is not unique to cognitive rehabilitation, but it is of extreme relevance in the case of cognitive rehabilitation due to the cognitive impairments that the patients in this patient group face.

4) *Integrate elements that can support enhanced interactions* – "We want to be asked how we feel in relation to our rehabilitation goals every week," said one of the patients in the workshops. While at the hospital encounters between the patient and healthcare practitioners is quite intense, our participants in the workshops expressed that they would like to have more encounters with the multidisciplinary team where they can share their opinion on how rehabilitation is progressing. It is relevant to consider this when designing a PHR that supports cognitive rehabilitation. The PHR should integrate elements that can support the patient to have their say in rehabilitation and share their feedback with the multidisciplinary team.

However, in interactions, the two sides that should interact should agree. We found that the team agrees that more interactions with the patient to ask about their perception of achieving goals would benefit the patient. This, however, would require changes in their routines, and they cannot be overwhelmed with data and consultation sessions (in analogy with Tang and Lansky [33]). For example instead of asking the patient every week on how they feel the PHR can support the patient to enter this information every week in his/her health data and be able to have maybe a meeting of discussing the information saved in the PHR every second week with one from the multidisciplinary team members. The interaction with the team will increase as the patient is giving feedback. Moreover, the encounter between the patient and the team member would be more meaningful as the discussion can be facilitated by the information kept track in the PHR on which both sides have agreed and share a common interpretation.

Thus, in cognitive rehabilitation, a PHR that can support and enhance interactions is needed. Moreover, the PHR should be flexible enough to support the negotiation of these interactions. This implication for design is more specific to the case of using PHRs in hospitals where the patient has more possibilities of encounters with the healthcare practitioners.

5) *Facilitating for personal spaces and having the possibility to negotiate boundaries for cooperation and coordination* – We found that patients' rehabilitation is individual. A PHR that aims to support the patient in cognitive rehabilitation should take into consideration the possibility of adapting to specific health information needs for the patient. During the workshops, patients expressed that they would like to have the possibility to keep notes and possibly share some of these notes later with the nurse or someone from the multidisciplinary team. During the observations, we saw patients writing and personalizing the goal plan and weekly plans, as well as other health information given at the hospital. The PHR should offer the patient this additional functionality to enable personalization that can fit the need for personal information spaces.

However, a patient's private space is challenged by the need for cooperation and coordination with the multidisciplinary team. For example, before setting the goals, patients are asked about their life. They receive a file that aims to find out more about their life before and after injury in the attempt to define better rehabilitation goals. Patient information, in this case, can be private, and the patient decides how much to put on the common space. However, not sharing part of this information would undermine the collaboration with the team and the definition of better rehabilitation goals. Thus, a PHR for cognitive rehabilitation in hospital should create the possibility for the patient to a) have personal spaces b) have the possibility to negotiate the boundaries of public and private spaces of information shared and decide where the boundaries stand and c) integrate elements that would motivate patients in expanding boundaries when the discloser of the information can improve rehabilitation.

6) *Support continuity after the hospitalization period* – This requirement surpasses the boundaries of the hospital, but it is necessary to bring up because continuing the rehabilitation therapies started at the hospital is determinative for rehabilitation success.

The rehabilitation is more related to what Wagner et al. [34] describe as the patient's Self-Management and Behavioral Change Support, which needs support for continuity. The patient should have the possibility to continue using a goal plan when moving from the hospital to home. Also, the patient should have the possibility to carry his/her own medical history from the time at the hospital and share that further with others that s/he considers relevant such as kin or local rehabilitation specialists. This is relevant since, in rehabilitation, the patient is not 'cured' once s/he leaves the hospital. Continuity of care is very important in the rehabilitation journey. The rehabilitation is considered finished when the patient achieves a desirable level of function [23].

Finally, the PHR design implications listed here are recommended for the case of cognitive rehabilitation in a rehabilitation hospital. The first two implications for design are special for cognitive rehabilitation. Instead, design implications 3-6 are not exclusive for a PHR in cognitive rehabilitation, but they have become specifically relevant for a PHR in cognitive rehabilitation.

VI. Discussion: A Conceptual Understanding of a PHR in Cognitive Rehabilitation

PHRs are considered tools that facilitate patients' involvement and give them more control over their health information [2]. Moreover, a PHR shows the invisible work that the patient does in managing his/her personal health records [7]. Our case shows that this is especially important in rehabilitation, where the patient should have higher control over his/her health information, be actively involved, and become the one leading his/her own rehabilitation. This is not only a need but a necessity for the success of rehabilitation [29]. Thus, PHRs are tools that can make a difference in the outcome of the care for patients that have passed the acute phase and are in need of rehabilitation. This paper contributes to the design and construction of a PHR in cognitive rehabilitation specifically, but we also present insights that can be relevant in rehabilitation in general. While in the previous section, we described a set of implications for design that should be taken into consideration in designing a PHR for cognitive rehabilitation based on the analysis of our empirical case, in this section, we will take a more conceptual perspective and discuss the conceptual implications of our study.

A. Hybrid Information Spaces

Vassilakopoulou et al. [7], in their paper, have argued for a conceptualization of PHRs as hybrid information spaces serving personal health information management needs (private information spaces) and facilitating information sharing between patients and healthcare professionals (CIS). We argue that a PHR designed for patients in cognitive rehabilitation also works as a hybrid information space as it is partly personal and partly common. We discuss these two aspects in the following subsections.

1) PHR in cognitive rehabilitation as a CIS - Cognitive rehabilitation involves several actors from different disciplines working together with the patient in an interdependent cooperative relationship and using a series of artifacts to facilitate their collaboration and interpretations. While the multidisciplinary team members have a high level of awareness of the other webs of significance in the team (so a nurse is aware of what an occupational therapist does), the situation differs for the patients. Due to the patients' challenges in cognition, there is a higher need for interpretative articulation work despite physical closeness [18]. Thus, in this setting the CIS includes a) the information that is stipulated in the goal plan b) the information that the patient receives from each of the multidisciplinary team members as part of the rehabilitation therapies and c) the information the patient generates during rehabilitation such as notes or patient journey stories which are then shared with the team. The patient and the multidisciplinary team member have to interpret this information shared in the common space in order to do their part of the work.

Two coordination artifacts [13] are used to facilitate the sharing of the information in the common space between the patient and the multidisciplinary team: the goal plan document and the weekly plan. However, patients and the team have different needs for their interpretative work. The team has a higher understanding of the information. However, they as well are new in the CIS, which is created in the case of a new patient. Thus, they need to put more effort into interpreting the patient's individual and personal needs and goals. In rehabilitation, there are artifacts in place for sharing common information. Thus, enhancing the practice of these existing artifacts by moving from paper to digital should be considered when designing the PHR. Our findings show that a PHR needs to be a flexible tool in order to facilitate the interpretation of the common information. For instance, changes in CIS openness and closeness is important to adapt to each of the patients' requirements regarding the continuity of their rehabilitation and integration with information from other rehabilitation settings (outside of the hospital).

2) PHR in cognitive rehabilitation as a Personal Information Space - The rehabilitation process is individual and closely related to the specifics of the patients. A patient receives personalized information regarding his/her rehabilitation. One of the most important requirements is that patients are able to construct personal interpretations of this information that they can use on their own to continue rehabilitation. Providing the patients with a tool that facilitates the personal health information management based on their individual needs is of a strong relevance in rehabilitation where the increased awareness of patients toward their rehabilitation treatment is the core part of the treatment itself.

Thus, our findings show that in addition to supporting and enabling a common space for information sharing, the PHR should also be designed for personalization.

B. *PHR in cognitive rehabilitation as a coordination mechanism*

Coordination of activities, as described above, is relevant in rehabilitation. Having a CIS would give access to the same information, but it will not make sure that this will be used in a cooperative way between the patient and the multidisciplinary team. For example, when defining the rehabilitation goals, a PHR conceptualized as a CIS will give the possibility to have the goals shared. However, it will not guarantee that these goals would be written or initiated by the patient. To create a cooperative procedure that would support the process of rehabilitation and give patients a more explicit role in their rehabilitation, the PHR should integrate a requirement that the patients write the first version of the rehabilitation goals, and then the team looks at it and maybe approves the goals. Bossen [13] has described a set of parameters of CIS. Among the parameters are the web of artifacts, described as mechanisms that support the cooperation and facilitate interpretations in the CIS [18]. Bossen [13] further refers to this as coordination mechanisms described by Schmidt and Simonee [15]. Coordination mechanisms are not only means for sharing items in a CIS. They have the characteristics of supporting the coordination of activities in a cooperative setting where cooperative work between interdependent actors is happening. We have described coordination mechanisms in Section 2.D. In analogy to the characteristics of coordination mechanisms, the actors that are seeking cooperation - the patient and the multidisciplinary team - are interdependent in rehabilitation. They are as well interdependent in defining the goal plan and keeping track of activities during rehabilitation. Moreover, consensus is required between the patient and the team in order to do the interventions in rehabilitation. Thus, in cognitive rehabilitation, coordinating activities is needed in addition to accessing the CIS.

So, designing a PHR in cognitive rehabilitation accounts for a coordination mechanism between the patient and his/her multidisciplinary team. This will contribute to making explicit the patient contribution in his/her rehabilitation, increase the level of awareness regarding the activities that happen as part of his/her treatment, and as well influence patient's health literacy, involvement, participation in decision-making, and self-management.

Hence, we conclude that a PHR in cognitive rehabilitation can be conceptualized as a hybrid information space [7]. However, within the hybrid information space, our findings also show that the PHR should also work as a coordination mechanism [15] that recognizes the patient's position as part of the division of labor, supports the process of rehabilitation, and empowers the patient. The PHR as a coordination mechanism would vary based on the diagnosis, patient's ability, the scale of willingness to be involved in his/her treatment, and the medical practitioners' commitment to supporting the patient. How much coordination and on what tasks the patient can take charge should be considered in individual cases. However, starting by discussing and recognizing the PHR as a coordination mechanism contributes to making the patient role in his/her care more active than just the receiver of care. A feeling of involvement, even in small tasks, will increase the perceived empowerment. The conceptualization of the PHR as a coordination mechanism also puts the burden on the staff as an important element in the coordination. Thus, the patient can feel safer and not left alone.

VII. Conclusion and Future Work

In this paper, we presented the case of cognitive rehabilitation. We defined a set of implications for design of a PHR for a patient in cognitive rehabilitation such as: Enhance the existing shared artifacts; Implement elements of coordination; Support different representations; Integrate elements that can support enhanced interactions; Facilitating for personal spaces and having the possibility to negotiate boundaries for cooperation and coordination; Support continuity after the hospitalization period.

Moreover, we discussed the design of a PHR for cognitive rehabilitation in hospitals under the current conceptualization of PHRs within CSCW as hybrid information spaces compounded by personal information space and CIS. We conclude that a PHR in cognitive rehabilitation can be conceptualized as a hybrid information space [7]. However, its development as a coordination mechanism that recognizes the patient's position as part of the division of labor will support the process of rehabilitation and empower the patient. The analysis of our case also contributes to the design of PHRs in the context of the hospital. Cognitive rehabilitation represents a very special case of hospitalization. Thus, as part of our future work, we want to investigate further if the implications for design for this specific case of hospitalization can be replicated in other cases or not. Moreover, the implications for design presented in this paper will be the bases for developing a PHR for cognitive rehabilitation as part of an inter-regional funded project by 2021.

References

[1] E. J. Davidson, C. S. Østerlund, and M. G. Flaherty, "Drift and shift in the organizing vision career for personal health records: An investigation of innovation discourse dynamics," Information and Organization, vol. 25, no. 4, pp. 191-221, 2015/10/01/, 2015.

[2] C. Pagliari, D. Detmer, and P. Singleton, "Potential of electronic personal health records," BMJ, vol. 335, no. 7615, pp. 330-333, 2007.

[3] J. E. Bardram and C. Bossen, "A web of coordinative artifacts: collaborative work at a hospital ward," Proceedings of the International ACM SIGGROUP conference on Supporting group work, pp. 168-176, 2005.

[4] G. Fitzpatrick and G. Ellingsen, “A Review of 25 Years of CSCW Research in Healthcare: Contributions, Challenges and Future Agendas,” Computer Supported Cooperative Work (CSCW), vol. 22, no. 4, pp. 609-665, 2013.

[5] F. Cabitza and I. Gesso, "Trying to Fill the Gap between Persons and Health Records," Proceedings of the International Joint Conference on Biomedical Engineering Systems and Technologies, vol. 5. SCITEPRESS: Science and Technology Publications Lda, pp. 222-229, 2014.

[6] F. Cabitza, C. Simone, and G. De Michelis, “User-driven prioritization of features for a prospective InterPersonal Health Record: Perceptions from the Italian context,” Computers in Biology and Medicine, vol. 59, pp. 202-210, 2015.

[7] P. Vassilakopoulou, M. Grisot, and M. Aanestad, “Between Personal and Common: the Design of Hybrid Information Spaces,” Computer Supported Cooperative Work (CSCW), vol. 28, no. 6, pp. 1011-1038, 2019.

[8] S. Sunnaas. "Sunnaas Rehabilitation Hospital – a way forward," retreived: 02/2020; https://www.sunnaas.no/Documents/Brosjyrer/Sunnaas_Rehabilitation_Hospital_a_way_forward.pdf, 2013.

[9] D. W. Simborg, “The limits of free speech: the PHR problem,” Journal of the American Medical Informatics Association, vol. 16, no. 3, pp. 282-283, 2009.

[10] J. Lahtiranta, J. S. Koskinen, S. Knaapi-Junnila, and M. Nurminen, “Sensemaking in the personal health space,” Information Technology & People, vol. 28, no. 4, pp. 790, 2015.

[11] K. T. Unruh and W. Pratt, "The Invisible Work of Being a Patient and Implications for Health Care:“[the doctor is] my business partner in the most important business in my life, staying alive.,” Ethnographic Praxis in Industry Conference Proceedings, vol. 1. Oxford, UK: Blackwell Publishing Ltd, pp. 40-50, 2008.

[12] K. Schmidt and L. Bannon, “Taking CSCW seriously,” Computer Supported Cooperative Work (CSCW), vol. 1, no. 1-2, pp. 7-40, 1992.

[13] C. Bossen, "The parameters of common information spaces: The heterogeneity of cooperative work at a hospital ward," Proceedings of the 2002 ACM conference on Computer supported cooperative work, pp. 176-185, 2002.

[14] A. Strauss, S. Fagerhaugh, B. Suczek, and C. Wiener, “Social organization of medical work,” Chicago: University of Chicago Press, 1985.

[15] K. Schmidt and C. Simonee, “Coordination mechanisms: Towards a conceptual foundation of CSCW systems design,” Computer Supported Cooperative Work (CSCW), vol. 5, no. 2-3, pp. 155-200, 1996.

[16] P. G. Scupelli, Y. Xiao, S. R. Fussell, S. Kiesler, and M. D. Gross, “Supporting coordination in surgical suites: physical aspects of common information spaces,” Proceedings of the SIGCHI Conference on Human Factors in Computing Systems, pp. 1777-1786, 2010.

[17] Z. Zhang, A. Sarcevic, and C. Bossen, "Constructing Common Information Spaces across Distributed Emergency Medical Teams," Proceedings of the 2017 ACM Conference on Computer Supported Cooperative Work and Social Computing, pp. 934-947, 2017.

[18] L. Bannon and S. Bødker, "Constructing common information spaces," Proceedings of the Fifth European Conference on Computer Supported Cooperative Work, Springer, Dordrecht, pp. 81-96, 1997.

[19] S. L. Star and A. Strauss, “Layers of silence, arenas of voice: The ecology of visible and invisible work,” Computer supported cooperative work (CSCW), vol. 8, no. 1-2, pp. 9-30, 1999.

[20] K. Çarçani and H. Holone, “Boundary Objects or Coordination Mechanisms?,” Selected Papers of the IRIS, vol. 9 (2018). 4, 2019.

[21] F. Cabitza and C. Simone, “Computational Coordination Mechanisms: A tale of a struggle for flexibility,” Computer Supported Cooperative Work (CSCW), vol. 22, no. 4, pp. 475-529, August 01, 2013.

[22] F. Cabitza, “Remain Faithful to the Earth: Reporting Experiences of Artifact-Centered Design in Healthcare,” Computer Supported Cooperative Work (CSCW), vol. 20, no. 4, pp. 231-263, October 01, 2011.

[23] LOVDATA, "Regulations on habilitation and rehabilitation, individual plan and coordinator," 14/04/2019, M. o. J. a. E. Planning, ed., 2019.

[24] D. T. Wade, "Goal setting in rehabilitation: an overview of what, why and how," SAGE Publications Sage UK: London, England, 2009.

[25] J. J. Evans, “Goal setting during rehabilitation early and late after acquired brain injury,” Current opinion in neurology, vol. 25, no. 6, pp. 651-655, 2012.

[26] WHO, "International Classification of Health Interventions (ICHI)," 2018.

[27] K. Çarçani and H. Holone, “Participatory Design “Method Story”: The Case of Patients Living with Mild Acquired Cognitive Impairments,” ACHI 2019, The Twelfth International Conference on Advances in Computer-Human Interactions, Athens, Greece. IARIA, pp. 210 to 217, 2019.

[28] H. K. Klein and M. D. Myers, “A set of principles for conducting and evaluating interpretive field studies in information systems,” MIS quarterly, pp. 67-93, 1999.

[29] B. A. Wilson, F. Gracey, J. J. Evans, and A. Bateman, “Neuropsychological rehabilitation: Theory, models, therapy and outcome,” Cambridge University Press, 2009.

[30] B. A. Wilson, “Towards a comprehensive model of cognitive rehabilitation,” Neuropsychological rehabilitation, vol. 12, no. 2, pp. 97-110, 2002.

[31] E. C. Haskins, K. D. Cicerone, and L. E. Trexler, “Cognitive rehabilitation manual: Translating evidence-based recommendations into practice,” ACRM Publishing, 2012.

[32] WHO, "International Classification of Functioning, Disability and Health (ICF)," 2011.

[33] P. C. Tang and D. Lansky, “The missing link: bridging the patient–provider health information gap,” Health Affairs, vol. 24, no. 5, pp. 1290-1295, 2005.

[34] E. H. Wagner, B. T. Austin, and M. Von Korff, “Organizing care for patients with chronic illness,” The Milbank Quarterly, pp. 511-544, 1996.

A Digital Tabletop Tool for Teacher-Student Supervision to Support Student Learning

Samgwa Quintine Njanka
Faculty of Computer Science
Østfold University College
Halden, Norway
email: samgwa.q.njanka@hiof.no

Shubodha Acharya
Faculty of Computer Science
Østfold University College
Halden, Norway
email: shubodha.acharya@hiof.no

Prameet Bhakta Acharya
Faculty of Computer Science
Østfold University College
Halden, Norway
email: prameet.acharya@hiof.no

Abstract **- Effective integration of technology into teaching and learning is becoming an essential competency for teachers. General classroom lectures are important for understanding the course material, but providing other opportunities like well-structured individual or group supervision sessions for students is indispensable. This will ensure the full mastery of the subject matter and expand the scope of learning experiences. Following a pilot demonstration of 15 students and 3 supervisors, interviews were conducted and the feedback showed the benefits of group supervision for these students. Students noted many positive benefits in support of a collaborative learning environment using a digital platform, while supervisors followed suit in the same perspective. This article, therfefore, describes the use of a digital tabletop board as a learning platform to facilitate individual/group supervision of students. After establishing the design requirements, we proceeded with prototyping, providing a series of sketches illustrating how users might progress through a task using the product under development and, lastly, the finished product with two major functionalities: notes taking and recording during a supervision session. The prototype was tested and analysed. The users indicated that the recording would help playback the supervision session. Also, in terms of usability, the interface was perceived as not different from that of the desktop paradigm, hence, user-friendly. Also, in terms of usability, the interface was perceived as not different from that of the desktop paradigm, hence, user-friendly. Teachers, on the other hand, noted the website created will provide notes or audio record for the students and even serves as announcement platform from the supervisors to the students on the class schedule. This would facilitate the achievement of course objectives and would enhance learning.**

Keywords – Digital tabletop; teachers; students; cooperation; CSCW; CSCL.

I. INTRODUCTION

The quality of education is a major concern of all educational goals. Continuous support for students in individual or group supervision sessions has been defined as one of the most effective ways to improve and sustain the quality of learning [1].

Fixed-time schedule classes may not be effective enough for students to understand the whole lectures. However, other means can be employed to tackle this issue; for instance, organizing individual or group sessions with the help of a guidance counselor or an instructor. The supervision can take place in a convenient environment, be it inside the classroom, library, maker space, or the lab.

Individual or group supervision sessions between a teacher and students served to expand the scope of learning experiences, providing several unique opportunities for mentoring that are not available during general classroom lectures. Supervision, according to Ogunsaju [12], is a way of stimulating, guiding, improving, refreshing, encouraging and overseeing certain groups by supporting them in their learning process. It is a dual relationship, in which both students and teachers should engage. However, if the student and teacher do not engage in a cooperative way, the supervision benefits would diminish. Thus, the learning process will be undermined and both the teacher and the students will waste their time [2].

With the rapid development of emerging technologies, the integration of digital learning platforms has an influence on improving learning experience. However, during supervision sessions, paper notebooks methods are usually part of the process, and most of the communication is handled verbally. Thus, in this paper, we explored the need for a technology that can support cooperation in supervision sessions among teachers and students and, consequently, increase the learning possibilities of students. We designed a digital solution and tested it. The respective findings are presented in this paper. The paper is a work in progress and more research will be done looking into cooperation and technology in this individual encounter among students and teachers and how to prompt learning and reduce waste of time.

The rest of the paper is structured as follows. In Section II, we describe the background of the study. In Section III, we present the design process from data gathering to designing the prototype. In Section IV, we present the evaluation of the prototype and findings from participants or potential users on the importance of the device during their supervision sessions. Finally, we conclude in Section V which links the major findings with the relevant literature of the study.

II. BACKGROUND

Students find it challenging to commit to verbal information discussed with the teacher. The theory of constructivism believes learners construct knowledge individually or in groups based on prior experience or repetition of new information. Also, knowledge is the outcome of collaborative construction in a socio-cultural context mediated by discourse. Learning is fostered through interactive processes of information sharing, negotiation, and discussion [4]. This theory acknowledges individual differences and believes students can construct knowledge through various learning resources and activities. Still, this theory acknowledges collaborative learning with which students can learn from each other as well as construct correct and meaningful knowledge. In addition, teachers remain facilitators in a constructivist learning environment [5], hence, playing an important part in the construction of knowledge together with the students. Instead of a paternalistic perspective, where the teacher leads and the student executes, in this paper, we discuss for more balanced power relations, especially during supervision sessions as individual time among students and teachers, being these individual students or students working together in a group project. This perspective has been discussed in Computer Supported Cooperative Work (CSCW) and Computer Supported Cooperative Learning (CSCL) [9].

Literature relating to class size is also important for this study; a lecture is usually a large class containing approximately 25-100 students at any time. During lectures, learning is instructor-directed, questions may be encouraged, but discussions are kept minimal [6]. Therefore, the large size and the physical distance between instructor and students could pose a challenge towards the formation of a healthy teacher-student relationship. It is safe to conclude that students learn very well and feel more positive in smaller classrooms than large lecture halls. The notion of supervision sessions in this regard cannot be overemphasized because it further enhanced learning [7].

There has been a lot of activity in creating tools that utilize learning analytics, with a focus on educational technology [8].

The collaborative approach to education has been shown to develop critical thinking, deepen the level of understanding, and increase shared understanding of the course material [10]. CSCL facilitates collaboration by using computer-mediated communication tools to enable new communication methods between teachers and students. However, the nature of CSCL has to be taken into account from the first planning stages when designing the model because it can be a drawback instead of a benefit. While there has been extensive research on the benefits and drawbacks of collaborative learning approaches in higher education [11], there has been less research on how the choice of collaborative tools affects cooperative processes and collaborative outcomes. This paper aimed at designing a digital learning platform that students will find easy to work with and that will further enhance learning.

III. DESIGN PROCESS

In this paper, we explore how to facilitate learning in supervision sessions through the help of technology. Thus, we took an interaction design process approach to explore the needs of students and teachers in supervision and then designed a digital tool that could support and increase the learning potential of such sessions. We describe the interaction design process below.

A. Informing phase

As a primary source of data collection, we conducted interviews with 15 undergraduate students and 3 professors based on the challenges faced during a supervision session.

For the students, the interview aim was to find out how often do they take supervision from their teachers, whether they use technology during supervision sessions, and if supervision is really important to them.

For the professors, the aim was to find out how often do they supervise students and what spaces do they use, do they keep track of progress on each student's work during supervision, what could be improved from their past experience on technological perspective and, lastly, how do they like to share the lesson of supervision session with the student that could not attend the supervision session. A consent form was signed from all the participants in the study.

We found that students prefer to have more cooperative supervision sessions that can integrate technology. The need for technology should support easy access to lecture materials. On the other hand, teachers want to improve their supervision experience by replacing the old method of chalk, talk, and paper experience with new technology. They also stated that they embrace the notion of recording the supervision session as a means for facilitating students to remember by referring back to it.

B. Design

Based on the findings, we decided to design a tabletop solution that could be used during supervision.

The top of the table would be an interactive screen in which an application that can be used during supervision could be started. The application we designed had the following functionalities:

1. A pen-based touch board where both the supervisor and the students could write notes or make sketches about things that are discussed during supervision. This functionality would help to improve the current situation of paper and chalk and, at the same time, afford a more sustainable way of having these notes in a common space, which will be later saved in the students and teacher folder (Figure 1).
2. Another important functionality is the recording button which, if pressed, will record the sessions. This is helpful in the situation when the students forget about the verbal information, and maybe they might not understand at the moment and want to came back to it. By repetition of the recordings, the student will have a higher chance of processing and internalizing the information (Figure 1).

3. Saving the notes on the cloud on specific folders for the students will improve the situations when papers are lost, and sometimes students do not have access to them (Figure 2).

The idea of a tabletop interface was inspired by the setting where supervision happens, namely, in a room where all the students are sitting around the table together with the teacher. Moreover, the tabletop metaphor which covers the whole table area serves as a mean for expanding the collaboration space among the student and the teacher. While making schemas and writing on a piece of paper is more or less a personal activity which can be shared with others, in the case of a tabletop, this surface is expanded. This helps in making the students and teachers more equal during supervision and can motivate cooperation.

C. Prototype

The prototype for the app was developed in ADOBE XD and testing was done through the Wizard of Oz technique.

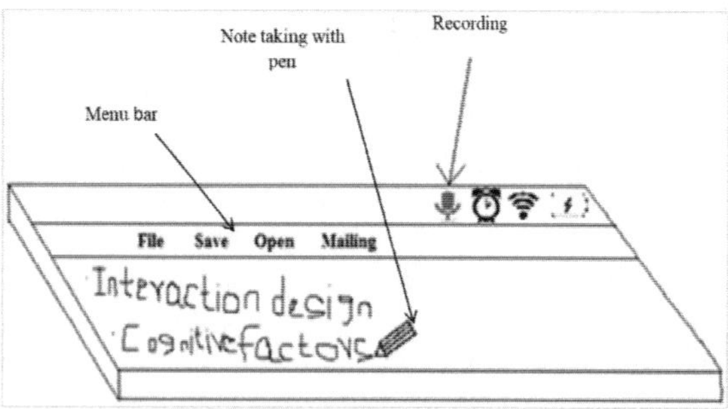

Figure 1. Interface for Note-taking and recording.

Figure 1 shows where both the supervisor and the students could write notes, record, or make sketches about things that are discussed during supervision.

Figure 2. Saving files /File locations.

Figure 2 indicates the process of saving the notes in specific folders either on the device hard disk, cloud (internet) or Tabletop (Website) during or after supervision.

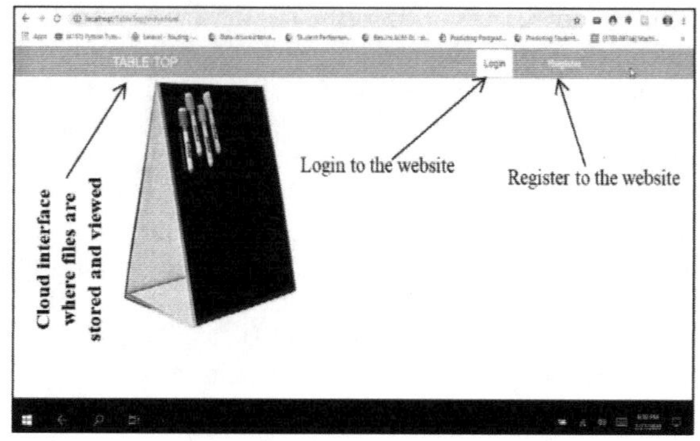

Figure 3. Accessing files on Tabletop (Website).

Figure 3 indicates that, for students to have access to the websites (Tabletop), they must log in with their username and password.

D. Evaluation

A number of tests were conducted with a few students and teachers to evaluate usability, accessibility, cooperation, and learning enhancement.

We conducted observations in two supervision sessions of one lecturer's office with 2 students at one time and one student another time. We initially installed the prototype on the lecturer's office tabletop. The users were briefed on the basic functionalities of the prototype prior to usage. For testing, we used the Wizard of Oz technique by installing a projector that projected the application on the tabletop, while one of the team members faked the touch-based interaction with the tabletop. The idea of testing was not to look into details of the solution, but focus on the user experience and the set of functionalities that we had integrated. The two sessions were video recorded, and hand-written notes from the first author were taken on site. Moreover, after the supervision, we interviewed in-situ the teacher and the students regarding their experience with the prototype in terms of cooperation during supervision. The video recordings, the notes, and interview answers were then analyzed to make sense of the user experience. The analysis is in its initial phases, and the findings presented below are based on the answers of the users regarding their experience with the prototype.

IV. FINDINGS

From the evaluation, we received a lot of feedback.

1) Students - appreciated the recording functionality by stating that, if you are not taking down notes, you can just launch the audio recording to avoid being lost in the course of the discussion. Furthermore, the information on the cloud will help students who could not make it for the supervision.

2) Lecturer –indicated that it would be beneficial to have the possibility to post assignments in this group space and make it work as a social platform for communication with regards to announcements concerning supervision schedule. In addition, the lecturer was asked to rate the digital tabletop with regards to learning enhancement and indicated that it serves as a collaborative platform whereby students play an active role instead of being passive.

Generally, students currently find it challenging to manage information either from the classroom lectures or in an individual or group session. Conceptualizing and designing a digital tabletop with the functionalities of note-taking and recording can help enhance learning and collaboration.

V. DISCUSSION

The paper described how a digital tool was designed to enhance cooperation in supervision sessions.

In conceptualizing the design space, an instructing interaction type was used in this prototype, where users issue instructions to the system. This can be done in several ways, including typing in commands or selecting options from menus in a windows environment. Literature indicates that knowledge is constructed through prior experience or repetitive studying of recorded materials and also when students gather as groups. Learning is fostered through interactive processes of information, negotiation and discussion.

Additionally, student and lecturer interaction is not only confined to lecture rooms where the large classroom size and the physical distance between lecturer and students could pose a challenge towards the formation of a healthy teacher-student relationship. Supervision sessions are often offered. This setting contributes to motivating the students and has an impact on learning.

A successful supervision session is the creation of a cooperative and transformative learning environment between the supervisor and the students. The supervisor should guide and facilitate the students, allowing them to create their own learning process as they move through the phases of collaborative activities [13]. Supervisors should give up some control, and students must take on more responsibility so as to establish and nurture a collaborative community of learners. This is where our prototype can contribute. It can enhance the supervision experience by increasing cooperation. Cooperation can further be the foundation for learning. Our solution was designed mostly as a proof of concept, and, through this paper, we want to open up the discussion of technologies that can enhance cooperation in supervisions.

In the future, we will continue exploring different kinds of technological solutions that can support both cooperation and learning during supervision.

REFERENCES

[1] A. Naz, R. N. Awan, and A. Nasreen, "A comparative study of instructional supervision in public and private schools of the Punjab," Journal of Educational Research, vol. 12, no. 2, pp. 53-267, 2009.

[2] H. Borko and V. Mayfield, "The roles of the cooperating teacher and university supervisor in learning to teaching," vol. 11, no. 5, pp. 501-518,1995.

[3] R. S. Earle, "The integration of instructional technology into public education: Promises and challenges," Educational Technology, vol. 1, no. 42, pp. 5–13, 2002.

[4] D. Jonassen, "Objectivism versus constructivism: Do we need a new philosophical paradigm?," Technology: Research and Development, vol. 3, no. 39, pp. 5–14, 1991.

[5] A. Hirumi, "Student-centered, technology- environments (SCenTRLE): Operationalizing constructivist approaches to teaching and learning," Journal of Technology and Teacher Education, vol. 10, pp. 497–537, 2002.

[6] G. V. Glass and M. L. Smith, "Meta-analysis of research on class size and achievement," Educational evaluation and policy analysis, vol. 1, no. 1, pp. 2-16, 1979.

[7] M. L. Smith and G. V. Glass, "Meta-analysis of research on class size and its relationship to attitudes and instruction," American Educational Research Journal, vol. 4, no. 17, pp. 419-433, 1980.

[8] J. Il-Hyun, K. Dongho, and Y. Meehyun, "Analyzing the Log Patterns of Adult Learners in LMS Using Learning Analytics," In Proceedings of the Fourth International Conference on Learning Analytics And Knowledge (LAK '14). ACM, New York, NY, pp.183–187, 2014.

[9] K. Rob, "Cooperation, coordination and control in computer-supported work," Communications of the ACM 34, no.12, pp. 83–88, 1991.

[10] D. W. Johnson and R. T. Johnson, "Making cooperative learning work," Theory Into Practice. vol. 2, no. 38, pp. 67–73, 1999.

[11] P. Resta and T. Laferrière, "Technology in support of collaborative learning," Educational Psychology Review. vol. 1, no. 19, pp. 65–83, 2007.

[12] S. Ogunsaju, "Educational Supervision Perspective and Problem," 1983.

[13] W. E. Rowe, "Enhancing student learning experience through group supervision using a digital learning platform," Royal Roads University, 2016.

A Simple System for the Complicated Cases?

Using Service Design Methods to Visualize Work Practice

Kathinka Olsrud Aspvin
Department of Informatics
University of Oslo
Oslo, Norway
e-mail: kathino@ifi.uio.no

Guri B. Verne
Department of Informatics
University of Oslo
Oslo, Norway
e-mail: guribv@ifi.uio.no

Abstract— **This paper presents a study of work practice at the Norwegian Agency for Quality Assurance in Education (NOKUT), a Norwegian agency working with recognition of foreign education. Through ethnographic field studies and methods from service design, we explore, analyze and visualize the steps of a digital case handling practice. We show how cases and case handling practice vary in complexity due to different circumstances, and how levels of complexity are not dependent on the type of case handling system used. Further, we discuss how this rich variety of cases would benefit from different levels of digital system support in order to support and not hamper the case handling process.**

Keywords- CSCW; Practice; Ethnography; Service Design; Visualization.

I. Introduction

Governments and the public sector are continually working on digitalization. Both external public services and internal systems supporting the work performed by employees are being digitalized, resulting in new information technology (IT) systems and work practices. This digitalization is affecting IT systems and government employees across agencies, such as labor and welfare, healthcare, taxes, customs and education [1]-[5].

The Norwegian Agency for Quality Assurance in Education (NOKUT) is currently digitalizing their systems for case handling, an ongoing process since the agency digitalized case handling in 2016. NOKUT is “an independent expert body” under the Ministry of Education and Research. The agency’s work consists of accreditation of higher education in Norway, such as universities, university colleges and vocational schools. Additionally, NOKUT works with recognition of foreign education, making it possible for people with education from other countries to apply for recognition of their education in order to work or continue studies in Norway. The digitalized case handling of the Department of Foreign Education is the topic for this paper.

Recognizing foreign education is cooperative work between the NOKUT case handler and an applicant, where the applicant is responsible for providing his or her certificates and diplomas and the case handler for providing and translating documents for assessing the qualifications the applicant claims to have. However, the case handlers’ work practice [6] varies considerably, mostly due to the circumstances involved for each application in retrieving documents and assessing education from foreign educational institutions. NOKUT’s case handling systems support both workflow and accountability of the case handlers’ work as they make the case handlers work and progress visible for colleagues and management [7]. Digital case handling often introduces more standardization and less flexibility for the case handlers, which necessitates negotiations and adaptions to fit the IT system with their use [4].

Investigating and understanding actual work practice as a basis for designing computer support is a central interest for the field of computer supported cooperative work (CSCW) [8]. A work practice is a regularly occurring activity that is constituted by some rules and principles that will be adapted by the practitioner to the circumstances of the actual work situation [6]. Theoretical knowledge and practical work are united in the practice, and the knowledge involved in mastering a practice is what makes it possible to adapt the work to meet the changing circumstances in the actual work situation [6].

Digital interaction between case handlers and applicants/citizens is a topic for CSCW and related research fields [2][9]-[12]. Service design [13] offers a perspective for understanding case handling as a service and provides methods for describing the service as a customer journey. Such journeys traditionally focus on the citizen as the customer, using customer journey mapping to improve public services [14], both by mapping actual experience journeys, and by visualizing an ideal interaction with services [15]. Journey mapping can also be used to visualize other processes, such as case handling, which is the focus in this paper. Case handlers are not customers in a traditional sense. However, they are users of IT systems developed to support their work practices, and their processes are important for understanding case handling practice.

This paper reports from a study of the case handling processes for digital applications to NOKUT, and how the case handling systems support the work of case handlers. Service design methods are used for analyzing the case handling practice. The case handling is explored through an ethnographic approach [16]. The research questions for this study are:

RQ 1: What are the communalities and differences between the various case handling processes?

RQ 2: How do the digitalized case handling systems support the case handlers’ processing of different cases?

The rest of this paper is structured as follows. Section II describes the methodology and methods used. Section III describes NOKUT and the different case handling processes. Section IV discusses the results of the study. Section V suggests some implications for design for supporting the most complex case handling practice. The last section offers some concluding remarks.

II. Methodology and Methods

The study was conducted as an ethnographically inspired case study where the main methods for data collection have been participant observation, interviews and document studies. The fieldwork took place as weekly visits to NOKUT offices, with averagely one day a week over four months during the fall of 2019.

We had free access to NOKUT employees and spent our time in their open office landscapes. We attended internal meetings, and shadowed and interviewed case handlers while they were performing their work. As such, we became part of the work environment, talking and socializing with NOKUT employees.

The interviews with case handlers and section heads were carried out as informal, unstructured interviews of various length, often taking place spontaneously during the fieldwork. These conversations were focused on understanding case handling practice. The interviews were not recorded as such conversations were often impromptu. Instead, notes were taken with pen and paper. Finding and starting a recording device whenever a "promising" conversation started would have been disrupting for the contact established in the situation. This means that we have few verbatim quotes from the case handlers, although some particularly interesting quotes were memorized and written down as soon as possible.

Document studies were carried out to understand NOKUT's goals and responsibilities as well as their working plans.

Methods from service design have been used for both describing the case handlers' work and for analyzing the steps that the case handling consists of. The service design method journey mapping was used to analyze case handling practice. Co-creating journey maps offers methods for analyzing the case handling for the different application types together with the case handlers. A visualization of the casework as a journey map is co-created to illustrate the differences and commonalities between the case handling for the different application types.

The design methods "touchstone tours", "contextual inquiry" and "journey mapping" were used to explore, describe and analyze different aspects of the work of the case handlers with the different application types. As these methods are rarely used as part of a case study, they are described in detail below.

A. *Touchstone Tour*

In order to understand the physical space in which the case handlers of the Department of Foreign Education perform their work, two walking touchstone tours [17] of NOKUTs offices were carried out. The first tour was with a section head, the second with a case handler. The aim of the tours was to gain insight into what a workday looks like for a NOKUT employee, focusing on what objects they interact with and the rooms they use for different activities. Both tours took 15-20 minutes from start to finish. Photos were taken during the tours, and we took notes using pens and paper.

B. *Contextual Inquiry*

Contextual inquiries involve the researcher taking on the role of novice, while the expert (in this case the case handlers) performs a task [18]. The novice asks questions in order to understand and clarify what is happening, and the two people together form a common understanding of the issues at hand. We focused on which IT systems were used, how they were used, what steps make up the actual application processing, which people were involved in specific decisions and what tools were used in order to give applicants a final answer. This method was employed over our four months at NOKUT, with seven different case handlers across the two sections, in sessions of varying lengths (30 min - 3 hours). Notes were taken with a pen and paper throughout the sessions.

C. *Co-creating Journey Maps*

Journey mapping is a service design method that presents events or touchpoints in chronological order to visualize a process [15]. In order to map the case handling practices, two case handlers from the different sections took part in co-creating a journey map [13], based on the insights gathered. The journey map was drawn concentrating on the core steps of the practice. Post-it notes and markers were used on a whiteboard to simultaneously analyze the case handling practice for all three types of applications. The case handlers were asked questions during the mapping process in order to clarify statements and placements of post-it notes. The case handlers used the provided materials to analyze the journey an application takes from when it enters NOKUT's digital application systems to when the applicant receives a reply.

D. *Ethics*

We signed a standard non-disclosure agreement with NOKUT, which they also use for external consultants. We did not collect personal data about the case handlers or managers as our focus was on collecting data about the case handling process and their use of system support in their work.

In the fieldwork, we could observe applications to NOKUT, but did not collect any data about the applicants nor the applications. Pen and paper were used for interviews and observations. According to Norwegian rules for research ethics, this kind of data collection does not necessitate evaluation by an ethical board, as it does not involve personal data.

Our introduction to the NOKUT employees took place in meetings, where we presented the project and discussed voluntary participation. The study was endorsed from the manager of one of the sections, and all participants in the study are NOKUT employees. We were given a work desk in one of the sections, where we were free to contact the case handlers and other employees. As most interviews happened spontaneously, we did not use consent forms for each individual person interviewed. Consent for an interview was granted orally. We have no indication of any case handlers or section heads wanting to withdraw from the study.

III. CASE HANDLING AT NOKUT

NOKUT consists of five Departments: the Departments for Quality Assurances and Legal Affairs, Evaluation and Analysis, and Foreign Education work with accreditation and recognition of Norwegian and foreign education respectively. There are two administrative departments for Administration and Communication. NOKUT's Department of Foreign Education is comprised of four Sections: the two sections described here are the Section for Recognition of Higher Education and the Section for Recognition of VET and TVET, where VET stands for "Foreign Tertiary Vocational Education" and TVET for "Foreign Vocational Education and Training". Additionally, the Department houses a Section for Interview-based Procedures and a Section for Information about Foreign Education.

Three types of applications are managed at the Department for Foreign Education:

- Recognition of Foreign Higher Education involves recognition of education from universities and university colleges.
- Recognition of VET involves recognition of vocational education completed after upper secondary education; usually training that takes between 6 months and two years.
- Recognition of TVET recognizes vocational training and education on levels comparable to Norwegian upper secondary education, and craft or journeyman's certificates. This recognition is only available for applicants from five Eastern European countries and is limited to 17 professions.

Applications for Recognition of Foreign Higher Education are processed at the correspondingly named section, while the Section for Recognition of VET and TVET processes both application types concerning vocational education.

Two IT systems, ESAM and Public 360°, are used for supporting the case handlers' work. ESAM is a custom-built case handling system developed by NOKUT's section for information and communication technology (ICT) in cooperation with hired consultants. The system was first customized for applications for recognition of higher education and has since been expanded to include VET applications. NOKUT's goal is that ESAM will be used for handling all applications, with a possible long-term goal of automating much of case handling. TVET applications are still processed using 360°; an off the shelf general case handling and archival system originally used for all case handling at NOKUT. 360° is still used as an archival system for all applications, but for TVET applications, it is the only digital case handling system.

A. *Case handling takes place in several sections*

The actual case handling of the applications varies a lot, from relatively simple and standardized, to very complicated and involving many steps. However, there are some key similarities between how applications are managed across the two sections of the Foreign Education Department.

Case handlers mostly work alone on applications. They might ask co-workers for advice or discuss particularly tricky cases with others, but in general, each application has one case handler who works on the case alone. Managers and co-workers are involved with quality assurance of the process and the resulting decision letter to the applicant.

Not all case handlers work with all kinds of cases: both in higher education and in VET and TVET, there are area experts who have knowledge about education within a particular geographical area. Some areas are "easy" and can be managed by everyone, while some areas are only managed by area experts. Some case handlers in the Section for Recognition of VET and TVET only work with VET, some work only with TVET, some do both. No case handler works in both sections, so case handling for higher education and VET and TVET are completely separate.

All applications are managed through one of the two IT systems, ESAM or 360°. Since 2016, case handling is digitized, and applicants are encouraged to apply through an online application portal.

Apart from these key similarities, there is a lot of variation in the actual case handling practice. The main difference lies in how different types of applications have differing levels of complexity. Recognition of higher education relies heavily on international networks and databases comparing (usually) well-documented education. On the other hand, recognition of VET and TVET requires complicated evaluation of professional skills that are not related to international standards, such as ECTS-credits. Here, expert committees, old curriculum and translation of local documents are required parts of the case handling practice, increasing the level of complexity. This also results in widely different processing times: cases of recognition of higher education have an average processing time of 7.5 hours, while a VET or TVET application can take anywhere from 21 to 329 days.

In addition to the two sections that carry out case handling of applications, there are other departments and sections at NOKUT that are important to case handling, such as the Section of Interview-based Procedures, which the case handlers also refer to as "the Refugees Section". They work with applicants who cannot document their education, or whose documents come from areas the Norwegian government "does not trust". This mostly includes conflict areas like Yemen and Syria. Applicants who apply for recognition of higher education can be forwarded to this section, but not applicants within the VET and TVET systems.

Another important collaborator is the Switch Board / Reception / Information Centre, where a collection of NOKUT employees handles direct contact with applicants and the general public. NOKUT case handlers are not directly available to applicants through phone calls or personal e-mail, unless the case handler explicitly encourages this. Most communication with applicants goes through the online application portal, but some applicants still call NOKUT with various queries. The communication between case handlers and the employees who answer phone calls is therefore an important line of communication.

B. Different steps for the different applications

Some elements of the case handling are at the core of all application processing, while other aspects belong to edge cases. In the journey map workshop, the case handlers agreed on, and numbered, stages 1 through 4 as the common core stages for all application management:

1. The application arrives in either ESAM or 360° and is selected by or given to a specific case handler. The application is looked through and the case handler makes sure all required documents are included.
2. The actual evaluation of the education takes place. This includes different steps and levels of complexity depending on the circumstances and type of application.
3. Quality assurance of the proposed outcome of the evaluation is performed, either by a co-worker, a manager or both.
4. A decision letter is sent to the applicant. This could be a rejection of the application or an approval of the foreign education. Additionally, it could include a recommendation to apply for another type of recognition or the forwarding of the case to the Section for Interview-based Procedures.

Figure 1 shows the result of the journey map that was co-created together with the case handlers of the two sections, using post-its and markers on a whiteboard.

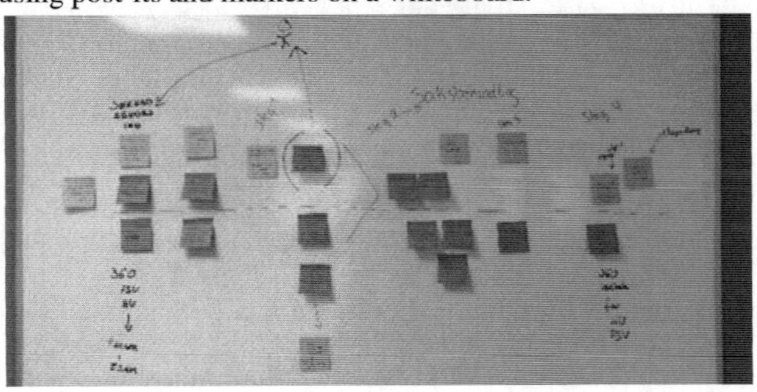

Figure 1. The first version of the journey map illustrating the steps of the case handling.

This figure was re-worked for the final journey map shown in Figure 2. This re-worked journey map illustrates the differences and similarities between the case handling processes. There are three application handling processes for the three application types higher education, VET and TVET. The first step shows that the application is received and selected by a case handler. The document check is shown as a separate step, as it often resulted in communication back and forth with an applicant, or even the rejection of an application if the required documentation was not produced.

The third section, evaluation and recognition, is the main part of the case handling, consisting of only one step for Higher Education applications, and up to four steps for TVET. The only step in this section that the three application types have in common is what the case handlers call "system evaluation". This involves evaluation of the level, the scope and the duration of the education. For higher education applications, this is the only step. For VET and TVET, this is only the beginning. VET additionally recognizes the professional profile of applicants, while TVET applications must be checked against NOKUTs existing precedence database. If no similar cases have been processed previously, case handlers must obtain the foreign curriculum for the education. The curriculum then needs to be translated and processed before being evaluated by expert professionals, who decide whether the education can be equated to its Norwegian counterpart.

The last step involves deciding on the case and includes quality assurance. The quality assurance step is usually more of a formality, as the outcome is rarely changed based on this feedback. Finally, a decision letter is dispatched to the applicant.

C. Differences in complexity

Case handling of applications for recognition of foreign higher education is, in most cases, straightforward. If applicants provide documentation of higher education, international standards for higher education, such as the European Credit Transfer and Accumulation System (ECTS) from the Bologna process [19], makes recognizing equivalent education relatively easy. It requires mostly a recognition of credits, level of higher education (Bachelor's, Master's or PhD) and the amount of time spent on the studies. Online portals list accredited foreign education for most countries. Additionally, as most countries provide a service similar to NOKUT, recognition of foreign education can be standardized between neighboring countries, or regions with similar education systems. This highly regulated practice leaves less room for interpretation for case handlers and reduces complexity and processing time, which averages to only 7.5 hours for a case.

Processing applications to VET and TVET shows greater variety and involves more steps. In order to recognize foreign vocational education and training, case handlers need to have the specific curriculum from the teaching institution, time period and qualification that the applicant has documented in their application. While applicants need to provide documentation of their education, they are not responsible for providing the documentation of their curriculum. Finding the curriculum can be challenging: case handlers describe visiting libraries and public archives in other countries and exploring old basements in public buildings looking for documents. There they would scan or take pictures of as much relevant documentation as possible. Finding curriculum also involves cooperation with people working in foreign libraries or archives, who can obtain

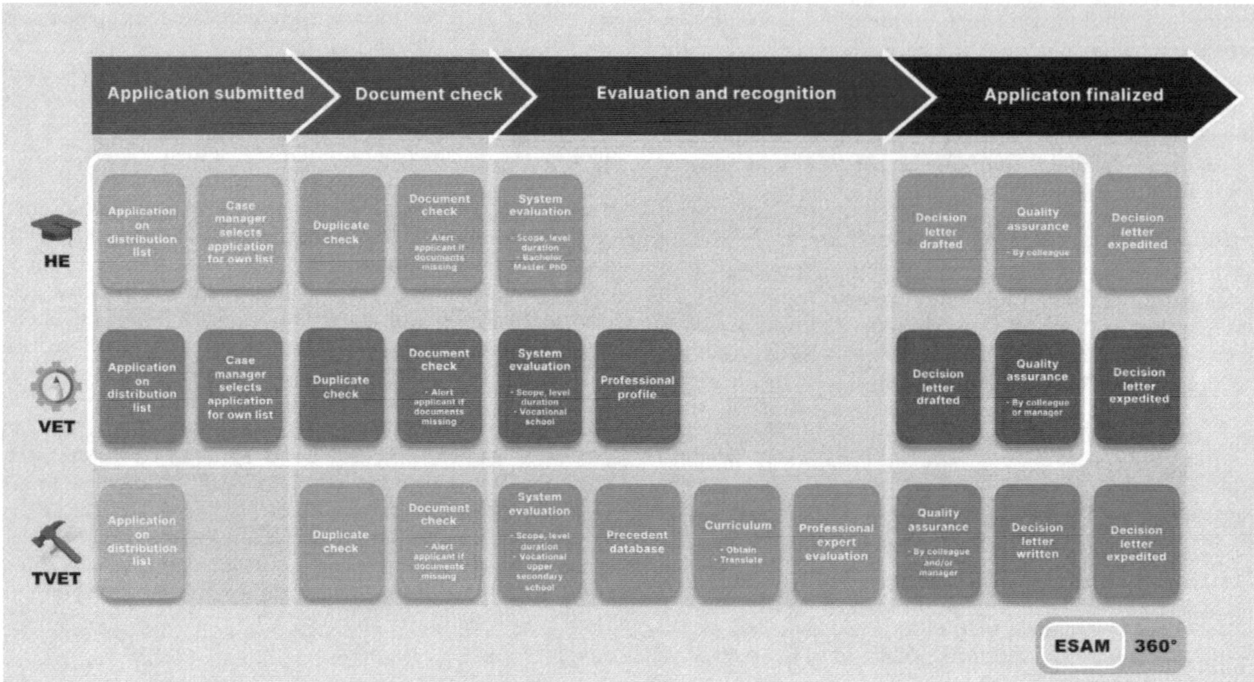

Figure 2. The final journey map illustrates the differences and similarities between the three case handling processes.

"helpful" curricula without anyone from NOKUT needing to travel. In these cases, case handlers have a network of contacts who can be contacted via email or telephone. In some ex-Soviet states local- or state archives have been burned, making it impossible to find documentation of old curricula. In these cases, the education cannot be recognized. These steps add considerable variety and complexity to case handling and processing time.

If a case handler manages to locate the curriculum, the documents need to be translated into Norwegian before experts can evaluate whether the qualification would equal a similar qualification in Norway. Some foreign curricula can be several hundred pages, while an equivalent Norwegian curriculum can be 3-5 pages. Recognition of TVET is not carried out by many other countries, meaning international standards, databases and networks are limited. Translation work followed by external professional expert evaluations without internal support further prolongs processing time and increase complexity, resulting in some TVET cases taking almost a year to process.

While this case handling practice is complex, it is currently performed using a case handling system that offers zero system support. While ESAM provides extensive system support and is developed to closely "guide" case handlers through pre-defined steps in the application process for higher education and VET applications, 360° offers no such support. Case handlers for TVET use their well-established practice and "know how" to process the applications as required, given the specific circumstances of each case.

D. Levels of complexity in practice

Several case handlers at the Section for Recognition of VET and TVET made comments along the line of "it's not always like this" or "usually we would do it like that, but because of X we have to do it like this", demonstrating how practice is not just "rule-following" [6]. The level of detailed understanding needed to know how to process an application showed great skill from the case handlers on when to follow the rules and when to adapt to circumstances, in line with Schmidt [6]. While the basic steps of case handling can be defined and followed, a lot of the practice builds on "know-how" developed over time and through experience. The case handlers are aware of these differences in complexity. One newly hired case handler in the Section for Recognition of VET and TVET described how she had been instructed to focus on VET applications, to "get to grips with the basics". When working with VET cases she would have the benefit of them being less complex, in addition to system support from the custom build ESAM system.

The case handlers at NOKUT had such a "feel" for what decisions to make, which is not explicitly described in the "standard practice". While some degree of complexity was present in all case handling practice, recognition of higher education was closer to "rule-following" than the VET and TVET applications. The journey map (Figure 2) visualizes case handling steps from the "simple" higher education recognition, through the more complex VET recognition and ending in the most complex TVET recognition. The extra case handling steps that are identified for VET and TVET consist of the most varied case handling for this kind of education and visualize an increasing level of complexity.

IV. Discussion

Insight gained from ethnographic studies can be complex and come in many forms [16]. Deep situational understanding and learning is why the methodology lends itself to researching complex socio-technical environments and practices, but also makes findings difficult to synthesize or summarize. Deep insight into the use situation and the user's actual work practices is a prerequisite for technology design within CSCW. Findings should be shared with fellow researchers, participants and other collaborators in order to better design technologies that support cooperative work [8]. In order to design such systems, both designers and workers need to understand and be able to communicate about practices relevant to the systems. By analyzing the case handling at NOKUT as a service, the practice of processing applications can be visualized as a series of activities with a fixed start- and endpoint. The benefit of visualization is to communicate different information about the steps and the complexity of the corresponding case handling process.

Journey mapping is not the only way to visualize complexity. Methods such as giga-mapping [20] could lend itself to visualizing the complexity by mapping all relevant stakeholders or systems in a practice, but would not ease a reader's understanding of the different steps that make up the process. Service blueprints have been used for visualizing processes, including both organizational and customer perspectives [15], but would in our case show both NOKUT's internal processes as well as frontstage events towards the applicants. The overall result can be cluttered and focus too much on existing systems to support the needs of case handlers. In contrast, by co-creating a journey map with the case handlers, their practice is the focus of the visualization. The co-creation helps both case handlers and researchers to understand and agree on what the practice looks like and can contribute to a shared language and understanding between them. Additionally, the relative simplicity of the visual expression of the journey map and the singular focus on case handling practice reveals complexities in the practice that are vital to designing appropriate systems.

Schmidt [6] writes that "understanding work practices as a basis for systems design has become a practical necessity". We argue that using service design methods in conjunction with an ethnographical approach can boost researchers' understanding of a work practice, by providing a framework for visualizing it. In utilizing journey mapping, complexities in practice can be highlighted, providing further insights that are valuable for designing systems appropriate to supporting the practice.

V. Implications for the Design of Case Handling Support

The objective of CSCW research is to gain insight into actual work practices for designing better digital support [8]. NOKUT's case handling process for higher education is relatively simple and is represented by fewer steps for evaluation and recognition than VET and TVET in Figure 2. The application handling processes can be ordered according to a level of complexity from low (higher education), to middle (VET) and high (TVET), mirrored in the number of steps in Figure 2 for each type of application. While the case handling processes for VET and TVET contain more steps than for higher education, the process still starts and ends with the same basic steps. When developing the new system for case handling, ESAM, the in-house developers started with higher education. The first version of the system could handle the "straight forward" applications and supported the steps that all applications go through. Later, the system was expanded to also include handling of VET applications. The case handling process of the TVET applications is however supported by using a general document archival system, 360°, with no specialized process support.

Thus, the most complex cases currently have the least amount of system support. Because these case handling processes have such varied steps and rules, and require very varied skills, such as nurturing international networks of helpful contacts to find a curriculum document in a basement archive in a foreign state, it would be almost impossible to design detailed system support for all possible steps in a case handling process. Such a system would risk being cumbersome and time-consuming in use as it would need to represent several possible steps and actions for a case handler to take, where many would be irrelevant in most cases. It could additionally hamper case handling as it may require navigating irrelevant choices and ticking off irrelevant boxes. In line with Røhnebæk [4], it would require negotiation and various workarounds [21] to use and we argue it would offer case handlers little real support for their work.

We suggest instead that an expansion of ESAM to include management of TVET applications should mirror the current case handling practice, by providing a minimal structure of support to give case handlers "room" to process applications as best, based on the circumstances and complexity of the actual case. By keeping the support minimal, case handlers won't be hampered by unnecessary steps when using the system. They have already proved their capability to manage applications with only generic archival system support, and we believe trying to create a system that closely supports all the possible circumstances of a TVET application would be too cumbersome and thereby unbeneficial. Case handlers of the most complex cases would benefit from a system where the steps that make up the work process are represented with more room for variety and minimal structured system support.

However, if in the future, more countries change their practices and start recognizing VET or TVET educations, international resources and standards for such educations may develop. These new circumstances could affect NOKUT's case handling practices by reducing the level of complexity for these cases. This again could affect the suitable level of system support.

VI. Conclusion

Through field studies within an ethnography-inspired case study, supplemented with methods from service design, we explored, analyzed and visualized the case handling practices at NOKUT for recognizing foreign education. These visualizations show that the case handling processes for different types of educations contain almost similar steps in the beginning and end of the case handling process but vary for the central steps of evaluation and recognition, based on the circumstances and types of education recognized.

We argue that service design can be complimentary to ethnographic studies in analyzing and visualizing complex practices, given that the practice lends itself to being explored as a service. By exposing variations and complexities, service design methods contribute to understanding actual work practices, which provide a sound foundation for systems design in CSCW.

NOKUT receives applications for recognition through an online portal but uses different IT systems to manage the different types of applications. This use of different case handling systems does not fundamentally affect the steps of the case handling process. Applications processed within the same section (VET and TVET) do not have the same case handling practice, because the academic and professional assessments are not the same. Applications with complex academic and professional assessments have a longer average processing time. Applications with a less standardized case handling practice have more steps in the assessment process and have a longer average processing time. The level of complexity in the type of application processed, rather than the type of IT systems, is what affects the complexity of the case handling.

When developing new system support for the most complicated cases, we suggest a design that provides a minimal structure of support to give case handlers "room" to process applications as best based on the case handlers' experience and the rich variety and circumstances of the cases.

We purpose this approach to systems design can be useful in other development of case handling systems, where designing system support for all circumstances and complexities in case handling practice would be both cumbersome, expensive, time-consuming and unnecessary.

Future research on digitalization of work processes could include whether visualizing complexity of the case handling process could be important for assessing which case handling practices are eligible for automation.

Acknowledgments

Many thanks go to NOKUT for their cooperation in conducting this study, and for allowing us access to their offices and practices. We would like to thank all the case handlers and section managers for their time and patience. We would further like to thank Lars T. Moen for his encouragement and assistance in digitalizing the final journey map.

References

[1] N. Boulus-Rødje, "In search for the perfect pathway: supporting knowledge work of welfare workers," Computer Supported Cooperative Work (CSCW), vol. 27, pp. 841-874, Dec 2018, doi:10.1007/s10606-018-9318-0.

[2] N. G. Borchorst and S. Bødker, "You probably shouldn't give them too much information – supporting citizen-government collaboration", Proc. ECSCW 2011, pp. 173-192, 2011.

[3] M. Grisot and P. Vassilakopoulou, "The Work of Infrastructuring: A Study of a National eHealth Project", Proc. ECSCW 2015, pp. 205-221, 2015.

[4] M. Røhnebæk, "Standardized Flexibility: The Choreography of ICT in Standardization of Service Work," Culture Unbound, vol. 4, 2012, pp. 679-698.

[5] G. Verne and T. Bratteteig, "Do-it-yourself services and work-like chores: on civic duties and digital public services", Personal and Ubiquitous Computing, vol. 20, pp. 517-532, 2016, doi:10.1007/s00779-016-0936-6.

[6] K. Schmidt, "The concept of 'practice': what's the point?", In C. Rossitto, L. Ciolfi, D. Martin, and B. Conein (Eds.), Proc. COOP 2014, pp. 427-444, Springer International Publishing, 2014.

[7] J. Bowers, G. Button, and W. Sharrock, "Workflow from within and without: technology and cooperative work on the print industry shopfloor". In H. Marmolin, Y. Sundblad, and K. Schmidt (Eds.), Proc. ECSCW 1995, pp. 51-66, Dordrecht, Springer Netherlands, 1995.

[8] K. Schmidt, and L. Bannon, "Taking CSCW seriously: supporting articulation work", Computer Supported Cooperative Work (CSCW), 1992, vol. 1, pp. 7-40.

[9] T. Bratteteig and G. Verne, "Conditions for Autonomy in the Information Society: Disentangling as a public service", Scandinavian Journal of Information Systems, 2012, vol. 24, pp 51-72.

[10] G. Verne and T. Bratteteig, "Do-it-yourself services and work-like chores: on civic duties and digital public services", .Personal and Ubiquitous Computing, 2016, vol. 20, pp. 517-532. doi:10.1007/s00779-016-0936-6.

[11] I. Lindgren, C. Ø. Madsen, S. Hofmann, and U. Melin, "Close encounters of the digital kind: A research agenda for the digitalization of public services", Government Information Quarterly, 2019, vol 36, pp. 427-436, doi:https://doi.org/10.1016/j.giq.2019.03.002.

[12] C. Ø. Madsen and P. Kræmmergaard, "The efficiency of freedom: Single parents' domestication of mandatory e-government channels", Government Information Quarterly, 2015, vol. 32, pp. 380-388. doi:https://doi.org/10.1016/j.giq.2015.09.008

[13] M. Stickdorn, M. E. Hormess, A. Lawrence, and J. Schneider, This is service design doing, online companion, pp. 45-47, O'Reilly Media, Inc, 2018, [retrieved: Januar, 2020].

[14] R. Halvorsrud, M. Røhne, E.G. Celius, S.M. Moen, and F. Strisland, "Application of Patient Journey Methodology to Explore Needs for Digital Support, A Multiple Sclerosis Case Study", Proc. SHI 2019, pp. 148-153, 2019.

[15] R. Halvorsrud, K. Kvale, and A. Følstad, "Improving service quality through customer journey analysis", Journal of service theory and practice, 2016, vol. 26, pp. 840-867.

[16] M. Crang and I. Cook, Doing Ethnographies, Sage Publications, 2007, pp. 132-133.

[17] B. Hanington and B. Martin, Universal methods of design: 100 ways to research complex problems, develop innovative ideas, and design effective solutions, Rockport Publishing, 2012.

[18] J. Preece, Y. Rogers and H. Sharp, Interaction Design: Beyond Human-Computer Interaction, John Wiley & Sons, 2015, pp. 366 - 367.
[19] European Higher Education Area and Bologna Process, http://www.ehea.info/index.php, [retrieved: January, 2020].
[20] B. Sevaldson, "GIGA-mapping: Visualisation for complexity and systems thinking in design", Proc. NORDES 2011, 2011.
[21] L. Gasser, "The integration of computing and routine work", ACM Trans. Inf. Syst., vol. 4, 1986, pp. 205-225, doi:http://doi.acm.org/10.1145/214427.21442.

Cross-Use of Digital Learning Environments in Higher Education: A Conceptual Analysis Grounded in Common Information Spaces

Diana Saplacan
Department of Informatics, Digitalization - Design of Information Systems
Oslo, Norway
e-mail: diana.saplacan@ifi.uio.no

***Abstract*—This paper addresses the cross-use of different Digital Learning Environments (DLE) in Higher Education (HE). The paper aims to analyze DLEs and their use in a HE organizational entity through the lens of Common Information Spaces (CIS), a concept grounded in Computer Supported Cooperative Work (CSCW). In general, CSCW literature focuses on individual systems regarded as CIS. Moreover, the research shows that DLEs are often analyzed from an educational perspective, and less from a *cooperative work* perspective. However, a teaching/learning context can be viewed as a co-dependent cooperative work arrangement, where the exchange of information and knowledge is performed *through*- and *with* the help of DLEs. In this way, DLEs should be rather viewed as being part of a complex cooperative ensemble rather than analyzed as individual CIS. This paper sheds light on such complex information spaces, where the information spaces are formed through clusters of DLEs, rather than individual DLE units. Finally, the contribution of the paper consists of addressing the cross-use of DLEs from a CIS perspective, moving beyond looking at DLEs just through an educational perspective.**

Keywords-Digital Learning Environments (DLE); Higher Education (HE); Computer-Supported Cooperative Work (CSCW); Common Information Spaces (CIS); information spaces.

I. INTRODUCTION

This paper presents the cross-use of different Digital Learning Environments (DLE) in a Higher Education (HE) organizational entity. DLEs are defined here as digital platforms, websites or specific webpages used by course instructors and students in a course for exchanging information or knowledge, relevant for their learning, respectively teaching, within the frame of the course. In a course, a course instructor can use one or more such DLEs: for instance, the course instructor can use both a dedicated Learning Management System (LMS), the email system, the HE website, and a social media platform or channel dedicated to the course. Each of these is considered individually as a DLE when they are used for the purpose of teaching/learning. We will call in this paper the individual DLE as a DLE unit. Therefore the terminology used here is not LMS but rather DLEs. They all together form a Common Information Space (CIS) in that specific course, for the course attendees, and the course instructor. However, the complexity of understanding these information spaces increase when each of the course instructors start using several DLEs in their courses, some of them being officially the HE institutions' DLEs, whereas some of them are not.

Nevertheless, students may attend several such courses, where each of the course instructors may have their own set of dedicated DLEs. The students usually have very little power regarding the decision on what DLEs to use. At the same time, there are cases when the course attendees themselves suggest to the course instructors to use some *new* web platforms or the *latest* social media platform, in the course. Through this paper, we wish to understand the complexities that come along with this dynamic use of DLEs. Specifically, we want to understand: *what challenges do they set for the students, respectively for the course instructors;* how *do DLE translate as CIS: what type of CIS are they, how are those represented, and used in a HE setting?* Specifically, the paper discusses and analyzes DLEs through the lenses of Common Information Spaces (CIS) (*compare to* Communication Spaces [1]).

The rest of this paper is organized as follows. We continue with the background of this study in Section II. Section III posits this paper on a theoretical level, elaborating on the concept of Common Information Spaces (CIS), giving a detailed account of the existent literature discussing CIS, including relevant definitions, examples, and characteristics. We continue then by introducing the methods in Section IV. Section V summarizes the findings, whereas Section VI discusses them through the lens of CIS. Finally, Section VII concludes the paper and gives directions for further work. The acknowledgments close the article.

II. BACKGROUND

DLEs are often analyzed from an educational perspective, and less from a cooperative or collaborative perspective. Analyzing DLE in a HE organizational entity through the concept of CIS is interesting because it challenges the traditional view on DLE as educational platforms and less as cooperative or collaborative platforms. This perspective is grounded on several arguments.

First, we argue that DLE should be seen as cooperative platforms and as CIS since multiple stakeholders usually use them: Course Instructors (CI), Students (S), administrative staff (ADM), junior and senior researchers, and nevertheless by the IT department (IT) for maintaining, securing or updating them. There are many cases when one individual in an organization takes multiple roles: CI are asked to take courses at the same HE institution, students work part-time as teaching or research- assistants, or senior CI are both researchers using various research platforms and at the same time teaching personnel.

Second, a HE organization usually has its own official DLEs that were either bought through a formal agreement or built in-house for many years. These can cover a range from LMS to web publishing systems, to examination systems, or submission systems. Some of these DLEs official systems to the HE organization might also be official at a national level, not only at a local level. The official DLE's are required by the Norwegian law to be universally designed [2][3]. However, although there are official DLEs that are usually used by multiple internal stakeholders (CI, S, ADM, IT), there are also non-official DLEs, i.e., DLEs that are not quality ensured, secured, maintained, or tracked by the organization itself, but by external stakeholders, such as privately-owned companies, perhaps located in another country. One such example is social media platforms owned by private companies. In this case, the platforms are not primarily LMSs. However, these can be used by a HE organizational entity as DLEs to support communication, exchange files, knowledge, and information.

Third, etymologically, teaching can be defined as showing something to someone by informing or instructing, directing, guiding, sharing, delivering, or making someone aware of some specific knowledge, communicating or informing someone about something [4], while learning refers to acquiring knowledge or skill(s) through teaching, an exchange of experiences, or as a result of studying [5]. Learning is strongly connected to teaching and the individual's experience.

Fourth, although much focus is on teaching and learning in HE institutions, these entities are after all public organizations with their own procedures, rules, regulations, dedicated laws, own organizational structures, and employees. They are workplaces similar to other public institutions: The Tax Office, Public Hospitals, or National Employment Agency. In the Nordic countries, many of these institutions' procedures and ways of interaction with their "clients" are very much automated, digitalized, or in the process of automation and digitalization. Along the same lines, HE processes and ways of interaction between different stakeholders are aimed to be automated and digitalized. For instance, in Sweden, the application process to universities is done through an online website [6], where the prospective students can apply online to educational programs or extra curriculum courses, at least twice a year, with some standards deadlines (April, 15th and October, 15th). The website functions as a national database where any citizen can apply to any university programs or courses, as long as they fulfill the requirements. The whole process is smooth. In Norway, an almost similar digital platform exists [7].

Nevertheless, once accepted to a program or a course, being it campus-, distance-, or Internet-based, the students will be asked to use new digital platforms. Moreover, in Sweden and Norway, much of the teaching, even the campus-based one, make use of various DLEs. Nevertheless, employees at these institutions will use additional human resources platforms, the type of Enterprise Resource Planning (ERP) systems to plan their resources (teaching staff, courses, budget), such as SAP [8], Microsoft Sharepoint [9] or Box [10]; time schedule systems that have to be synchronized with teaching staff, courses, class-, laboratory- or group rooms; or in some cases digital examination platforms, that have to be secured, and limit the individuals taking the exam to navigate the web or reach to other external resources during the examination time. Moreover, email is usually extensively used for communication within and outside of these organizational entities.

As such, HE institutions are more than educational entities that *produce* or prepare individuals for taking part in the workforce, but as complex and dynamic cooperative assemblages, where interactions, different negotiations amongst various stakeholders, communication, and cooperative work arrangements take place. Computer Supported Cooperative Work (CSCW) emerged from the need to study group work and office automation [11]. As indicated by Schmidt and Bannon [12], CSCW is conceived as "*an endeavor to understand the nature and requirements of cooperative work to design computer based technologies for cooperative work arrangements*" (emphasis in original). A subfield of CSCW is Computer-Supported Collaborative Learning (CSCL). As shown in a CSCL study, information technology, such as DLEs, can support collaborative learning; however, the users need to overcome some challenges that come along with the use of these technologies [13].

Nevertheless, these information technologies also change the behaviors and practices of learners and teachers [13]. However, CSCL focuses in general on mediated communication technology between teachers and students, and not on seeing DLEs as part of large organizations, where DLEs can be seen as information spaces. Moreover, seeing learning/teaching as a form of *cooperative work* is interesting because, according to Schmidt [14], cooperative work refers to co-dependent work that has to be done by an ensemble of people together, (either for achieving a product or a service), which otherwise would not be able to be achieved by individual persons. *Cooperative work,* (comp. to *collaborative work* which is positively laden [12]), refers to the interdependent relations that develop due to the manifested practices that take place, which very often require some form of *coordination* as well, e.g., so-called *coordinative practices* [15]. At the same time, a learning/teaching relation in a HE context is usually a co-dependent one: the teacher's responsibility is to provide relevant knowledge in a course that the students can learn; at the same time, the students need to deliver assignments, take exams or in some form show that they have achieved the learning outcomes. In this way, such a setting can be regarded as a cooperative setting.

Finally, the paper emphasizes the use of multiple systems and how these are viewed as clusters of CIS, rather than individual systems. All in all, HE organizational entities viewed through the lens of cooperative work helps us in seeing beyond educational setting and reflecting on the complexity of the use of multiple virtual information spaces used in HE organizational entities, and on the need of coordinative practices for enabling a successful cooperative work, i.e., a successful exchange of knowledge in teaching/learning context.

III. Literature Review: On CIS

This section gives an extensive overview of CIS, by defining the concept, grounding it in examples, illustrating the specific characteristics, and explaining how the concept will be later used in the paper.

A. *Defining CIS*

The concept of CIS was first used in Schmidt, and Bannon's [12] work on "Taking CSCW seriously." The authors used the terminology along with the definition of articulation work, saying that CIS is one of the aspects supporting articulation work, together with workflow [12]. According to them, a CIS is necessary for distributed cooperative work, to maintain some form of 'shared' and locally and temporarily created understanding about the objects in the CIS. Usually, such a CIS is actively created, accessed, maintained, manipulated, and shared at various degrees, amongst multiple actors or stakeholders.

A CIS has the aim to allow the members of a cooperative ensemble to cooperate and interact without formal constraints, such as procedures or conventions [12]. A CIS also aims to bring "people and information together, through artifacts (...) and interpersonal communication, and they help ensure uniformity of information" [16].

TABLE I. Seven CIS Parameters From Bossen [17]

#	CIS Parameter	Explanation
1	degree of distribution	physical distribution of the cooperative work;
2	the multiplicity of the web of significance	several webs of significance are included in CIS;
3	degree of the needed articulation work	articulation work may vary depending on the character of the cooperative work;
4	multiplicity and intensity of means of communication	face to face communication, but also other communication means available and/or necessary during the cooperative work;
5	web of artifacts	all the artifacts included in the cooperative work;
6	immaterial means of interaction	habits, procedures, the structure of the organization, division of labor, etc. that decrease the need for coordination;
7	need for precision and promptness of interpretation, in the cooperative work.	the need for precision for the available information; this parameter is especially important in time- or safe-critical situations;

Moreover, CIS "indicate spaces that support distributed cooperative work as an alternative to procedural or workflow type arrangements" [18]. A CIS goes beyond a personal information space, where the individual producer of an object is also the 'consumer' of an object, i.e., the meaning that an individual attributed to an object is interpreted by the *same* individual [12].

A CIS also includes a common developed vocabulary [12]. CIS are containers and carriers of information [19]. Finally, Bossen [17] developed and formulated seven parameters of CIS. He argued that CIS is too loosely defined and that the proposed parameters can be used as an analytical framework for CIS [17]. These are represented in Table I.

B. *Examples of CIS*

A shared database is not necessarily a CIS, following [12]. The objects represented in a database are "*carriers* of representations," and not objects *per se* [12] if the actors do not have direct access to the material objects as artifacts. For instance, if the actors have access to a product X, or to a file Y, both outside of the database system, then they can build a common and shared understanding of how these objects should be represented in a database system. In other words, the actors can give a *common* interpretation of the material objects. Hence, a CIS embeds a coherent and interpretative aspect of the material objects represented in a database, compared to database objects that are rather "*carriers* of representations" [12].

A clear example of a CIS given by the authors is a whiteboard, where several members of the cooperative ensemble jointly scribble, modify, draw, or erase things written on the whiteboard [12]. Each member of the cooperative ensemble interprets the objects on the whiteboard individually. However, the scope is to achieve a common and shared meaning.

An excellent example of a CIS is when a department develops its own "set of meanings for key terms" (Savage, 1987, p. 6) in [12]. For instance, in a HE institution, the meaning of a *seminar* or *laboratory assignment* may be different based on different educational departments or courses. A laboratory assignment in a programming course means perhaps the development of a program by coding in an ordinary classroom environment, while laboratory assignment in biology or chemistry can possibly mean a form of experimenting in a specially dedicated lab, where specific tools and instruments are available. In this sense, CIS has a physical character.

Other examples of CIS are documents and artifacts used in an organization, supporting the cooperation between the cooperative ensemble members [12].

However, we have seen that lately, with the advanced web or software solutions available, these documents or artifacts can be represented virtually: virtual post-its or virtual dash-boards shared between members of an organization. Trello, Microsoft Team, Slack, or Google Drive are a few examples of CIS where objects of a CIS are co-created by several members of the cooperative ensemble. Such a system should: "in addition to services facilitating the creation, modification, transmission, etc. of messages, provide services supporting the cross-referencing, cataloging and indexing of the accumulating stock of messages", but they should also support the inclusion of external items [12].

A more extreme example of CIS is the web (www), where some pages are produced by several entities that do not necessarily are tangential to each other, however, a heterogeneous group of consumers of the CIS access information produced by several of them [19]. According to the study, this is a paradox example of CIS, which is both *internally closed* to the producers, however *open and accessible* for many.

C. *Characteristics of CIS*

Besides the seven parameters of CIS identified by Bossen [17], the literature has identified a couple of other parameters of characteristics specific to CIS. We briefly illustrate each of those, as follows.

1) Dialectic Nature of CIS

Bannon and Bødker [19] argue that putting information in common and interpreting it was not sufficiently discussed [19]. Their paper argues for a dialectical nature of CIS: CIS is both *open* and *closed,* and they are often both *portable* and *immutable*, containing *malleable information items* while *supporting the cooperative work*".

2) Hybrid Information Spaces: In-between Private and Common

CISs are also characterized by some sort of malleability: "open for some yet closure for others" [19]. Such an example of *hybrid* information spaces is illustrated in [18]. These are framed as information spaces that are in-between private and common [18]. Such an example is the Personal Health Records (PHR) studied in MyBook and MyHealth Norwegian projects [18]. PHR are considered to be *hybrid information spaces,* partially because the patients have to input and track their personal health data, but some of this data is also shared with medical staff [18]. Hence, they can be shared across roles and boundaries [18]. This can trigger dilemmas along how and with whom the information is shared, who owns it, in which ways it is accessible and for whom, and how these are regulated amongst the patient and the medical staff [18]. The authors recommend the regionalization of hybrid information spaces, such that the systems are designed in such a way that they can both be private and preserve the user's autonomy and control, but also shared (hybrid), with the aim of cooperative work [18].

Nevertheless, CIS should be mediated by human mediators, that support both those members of the cooperative ensemble who create, modify, or develop (*producers*) the common information, and those that use this information (*consumers*) [19].

3) Scalability and Multiplicity of CIS

One study added to Bossen's CIS parameters, the following ones: collaboration's scalability and information spaces' multiplicity [17]. Collaboration scalability includes the number of participants involved, and the phases necessary for achieving the collaborative work [17]. The information spaces' multiplicity refers to the number of entities and artifacts that intersect in the collaborative work and form the CIS [17].

4) Multiple Centers, Peripheries and Overlapping Areas

Information always belongs to a place, although the place does not necessarily need to be geographically fixed [20]. Following [20], CIS is described as having both *multiple centers* and *peripheries* but also *overlapping areas.*

5) CIS Objects Re-producing Fragmentation

Rolland et al. conceptualizing CIS across heterogeneous contexts [21]. They presented the idea of CIS as malleable and open objects, which are achieved in practice [21]. They also emphasized the idea of large scale CIS reproducing fragmentation [21]. One of the earlier studies [22] *(forthcoming)* also proves this fragmentation.

6) Temporality of CIS

CIS distributed across time and space is characterized by physical separation of cooperative members, limited access and control over the shared material, and more strict division of tasks [19].

A study investigated CIS across distributed medical teams in *emergency, time-critical, episodic, and heterogeneous cooperative situations* [23]. Having a shared understanding of these emergency cooperative settings is necessary. Munkvold and Ellingsen [24] talk about CIS use in a hospital ward while they introduce the temporal dimension of CIS, when several users are involved with their own trajectories, and intersected trajectories. Moreover, Bertelsen and Bødker [20] problematized cooperation and CIS in *massively distributed information spaces*, a case on a wastewater plant. The authors challenge the idea of CIS that provides access to *everything everywhere* [20].

7) Physical Aspects

The study from [16] investigated the physical aspects of objects part of a physical CIS in emergencies. The CIS part of the emergency rooms is artifacts, including electronic records, equipment, or whiteboards, supporting the staff work [16]. However, the study stresses that the information available on these CIS's is determined not only on the quality of the information, or how timely it is disposed of but also how easy it is for the staff to interact with it [16]. For instance, the study illustrated that the height and the place where the displays in the hospital are placed determines the coordination work the staff, and how much they engage with each other. Bossen [17] presented a similar case from a hospital ward. Another study that explored distributed information spaces in a hospital setting from Mexico city is the study presented in [25]. Specifically, the authors explore the physical mobility, moving beyond the desktop metaphor [26].

CIS in a shared workspace is characterized by the physical co-location of the cooperative ensemble' members, real-time sharing of resources, and sometimes ad-hoc co-handling tasks [19]. However, cooperative work does not always take place in the same shared location: the *cooperative work might exceed the temporal and local boundaries* [19]. This also puts additional requirements and changes in the design of a CIS. The information shared in a distributed CIS has to be packaged and belong to a context [19].

8) Communication Means in CIS

Hjelle [27] illustrates an example of information spaces used in an oil and gas company. He analyzes the case through Bossen's seven parameters of CIS [17]. The author points out that the best interaction is done through face to face communication [27]. The study concludes that not all of the seven parameters [17] are equally significant. However, many tools seem to be used to facilitate the cooperation, although they are not always cooperation tools, communication tools used to facilitate the cooperation when face to face meetings are not possible [27].

Sometimes, information technologies used in organizational settings are discussed as *communication spaces* instead. However, CIS and communication spaces are different, although they might have some similarities in common [1][28]. While communication spaces focus very much on the communication takes place across distributed or non-distributed spaces, CIS focus instead on how information is created, shared, maintained, and achieved. At the same time, CIS may include various communication spaces.

D. CIS in This Study

The CIS literature covers, in general, a few studies from hospital wards (see [14][17][21][22]), and in organizations, such as oil and gas companies [27], or wastewater plants [20]. However, many of these studies focused very much on the physical CIS, except for the study from [18], who focused on the hybrid and mobile information spaces. To our knowledge, it seems that CIS was not so far studied in HE institutions and that DLEs were much more often regarded from an educational perspective rather than a CSCW perspective. This study aims to bring new insights on both DLEs seen through the lens of CIS and CSCW literature, but also to the CSCW community on how DLEs can be regarded as CIS and the complexity of analyzing those as such. We continue in the next section with the method, and after that, we present the findings before we discuss those.

IV. METHOD

A. Participants and Setting

We have interviewed several experts, with an area of expertise in pedagogics and universal design. We define experts as senior researchers, with an area of knowledge in either pedagogics or universal design and a subdomain of informatics, such as human-computer interaction, interaction design, computer-supported cooperative work, or computer-supported collaborative learning. All of the participants had several years of experience of being course instructors. We will use, therefore, interchangeably the notions of experts, course instructors, or teachers, referring to the same participants.

The interviews were performed in several stages of the study. In this paper, we illustrate some findings from the interviews conducted with the interviewees having their background in pedagogics (n=3). However, similar findings are also presented in the rest of the interviews (see [22], [29]).

Finally, the interviewees were recruited through personal contact. The author had no relation to the participants since before.

B. Data Collection and Analysis

The interviews lasted about one hour- one hour and fifteen minutes each. These were transcribed verbatim by the author (SD). The data were analyzed in several steps, as recommended by [30]. Some photos were also taken during the interviews, on artifacts shown by the participants. These did not contain any personal or sensitive data.

The analysis was done through systematic text condensation [30]. 12 Excel spreadsheets were used for documenting all the steps throughout the process. The analysis was done in four steps: (step 1) the data was fully read to get a sense of what the data was talking about (themes: n_1=6, prioritized themes n_1=4); (step 2) identifying and categorizing meaning units (codes n_1=130 for the first theme, n_2=124 for the second theme, n_3=125 for the third theme, and n_4=39 for the fourth theme); (step 3) condensing the codes into meanings (n_1=23, n_2=13, n_3=25, and n_4=9); these subcategories were then organized in categories (n_1=7); (step 4) finally, during the last step, the author has synthesized the condensates into concepts (n_1=3). The resulted concepts were: cross-platform use of DLE, user diversity in Higher Education, universal design, and organizational tensions. This paper focuses solely on the cross-platform use of DLEs. However, the theme of user diversity and universal design were covered in [29].

C. Ethical Considerations

All the participants were given detailed information about the study, the possibility to ask questions prior- and during the study, and they could withdraw at any time without providing any explanation and without any consequences for them. The participation was based on free will. All the participants were willing to participate in the study signed informed consent before taking part in the study. The study follows the ethical guidelines from the Norwegian Center for Research Data (NSD) ref. Nr: 55087). This work was performed on the Tjenster for Sensitive Data (TSD) facilities, owned by the University of Oslo, Norway, operated and developed by the TSD service group at the University of Oslo, IT-Department (USIT) (project number: p400).

V. Findings

The participants mentioned 23 DLEs. The minimum number of DLEs used by the participants was 5, whereas the maximum was 16 out of 23. It seems that the youngest of the interviewee was more prone to use digital technology in class, together with her students. The same interviewee used social media platforms and considering using instant messenger in her communication with students, arguing that these were the preferred communication channels by the students.

The official publishing system was used by two out of three participants. However, one of the interviewees used it only for information related to her area of work, research, and publications, but not in a teaching/learning context. The interviewee considered the HE's official web publishing system more as an administrative tool rather than being a dedicated tool for teaching/learning.

Moreover, only two participants used the official examination system, whereas the third participant was aware of it, but did not find it appropriate to use it together with its course-takers. However, email and the new official DLEs introduced at the HE institution were used by all interviewees.

Further, one of the interviewees used three simulation environments, as the leading DLE platforms, in his teaching, although another DLE was the official institutional platform. These simulation environments were mandatory to be used by the students during the course. While some of the students were against using these external simulation tools, some felt motivated in using real-world scenarios in simulated environments. Teaching specific and generic skills by using these external simulations environments and DLEs was the main argument for using those. However, the students were required to make their submissions in the official DLEs, across the semester. But a final official examination at the end of the semester was required to be done in a third system, i.e., in the official examination system.

Two of the interviewees were using two other digital systems each in their teaching. Only one participant used cloud-based storage. The same participant also used additional plug-ins in the official DLEs.

Further, one of the participants expressed the need for a participatory tool and keeping track of things in a DLE. Therefore, she chose a publicly available database system-like online tool for recording each years' course participants' entries.

Table II gives an overview of the systems in use, as described by the participants. Another inventory of DLEs used by other participants taking part in the same study was done in our earlier published work (see more in [22], *forthcoming*).

TABLE II. Overview Over The Digital Learning Environments And Tools

#	**Participant (CI)** / **Systems used in a HE Organizational Entity**	**#1**	**#2**	**#3**
1	Publishing system		X	X
2	Internally and externally used submission and assessment system	X		X
3	External quiz and input system 1			X
4	External quiz and input system 2			X
5	External quiz and input system 3			X
6	Email	X	X	X
7	New DLE system	X	X	X
8	Third-party application			X
9	Social media platform 1			X
10	Web service for forum discussions and wikis		X	
11	MOOC or MOOC like platform		X	
12	Examination platform	X		X
13	Virtual game environment 1	X		
14	Virtual game environment 2	X		
15	Virtual game environment 3	X		
16	Learning Analytics	X		X
17	Specialized analysis software 1	X		
18	Specialized analysis software 2	X		
19	Specialized video analysis software 1			X
20	Specialized video analysis software 2			X
21	Cloud-based storage			X
22	Different variants of messenger applications			X
23	The third-party plugin used in the official DLE system			X

The official DLE was described by one of the participants as being an administrative tool rather than supporting learning. The system was also described as not being user-friendly and being cumbersome; however, it was also described as being easy to access and manipulate if one is familiar with such tools. At the same time, it seems to be a complex system to navigate, and that many of the student users complained about navigation issues. She also mentioned that non-regular students, i.e., older employees at the HE who are asked to use the official DLE, have a hard time using it. She described how the systems are nowadays designed as dashboards. According to the participant, these are often seen by international students that lack digital skills as a "dump place," where the course instructor "dumps" course material and information rather than as a DLE that provides opportunities for learning.

"(...) for some of the students, they were not used to it, and they were not introduced to it in the way I would like to do it, it was just like a.., sort of a repository, like a "dump place," where all this information about the course, slides, whatever the material teachers wanted to use, it was kind of thrown into that, in an organized way - which is good. For them, this was not a discussion platform; it was not a place where they could express their views or interact with the materials where they would say: okay, I would want it in

this way, or I would post my idea or view in an idea or knowledge in a discussion. They did not perceive technology as something that offers them the possibility to express, learn, engage, and be an active participant in this case in a learning activity. And I think it is an important function of the technology, to provide a platform, for those that either does not have a possibility or the attitude to do this face-to-face in plenary, for various reasons, or for those that are at a distance. So this is an opportunity. I think it is a missed opportunity if we do not present it and use it as teachers, or those who introduce it in the right way." (Participant, Interview)

Finally, one participant was pledging for digital natives being prone to like dynamic DLE than others, and therefore they might find the official web publishing system as being *out of date*. However, she was complaining that there are (perhaps too) many functionalities available in the official DLE, that there are anomalies in these functionalities, i.e., a chat functionality available in the system for all class, but not inside the groups, that the system is characterized of high complexity, that it can be perceived as overwhelming at times, that it is rich in functionalities, and has a U.S. based design geared towards assessment. She mentioned that the system requires to have a pedagogical rationale when planning a course to be able to make the most use of it.

"It's often that the students, like the natives, they come to the University, first-year students and they know they will be using learning platform, digital learning platforms, because most of them have used it in high school, or even in lower grades, while students coming from other parts of the world, don't have this ingrained experience, or simply experience of using the technology in this way. And I think there is always a gap there that often creates difficulties for the other group, not because they are not good performers, or good learners, or interest or motivated, because they simply need, a different encounter- start encounter with technology." (Participant, Interview)

VI. Discussion

This section presents a regionalization of DLEs units in categories and clusters of information spaces. Based on our findings, shown earlier in Table II, DLEs are re-grouped in this section into official systems, third-party applications, and specialized software applications, quiz input systems, virtual games environments, and social media platforms. The classification is made based on each DLE unit's own primary purpose. The reason for regionalizing DLEs in these categories is to illustrate that the majority of the DLEs in use are non-official systems, but also to showcase their distribution across different domains requiring a different set of skills for using those. After that, a discussion on DLEs as information spaces follows.

A. *Regionalization of the DLEs Units in Categories and Clusters of Information Spaces*

Information always belongs to a *place*, or for that matter, to *space*, as it was also proved in the illustrated examples [20]. In line with [20], this study also proves that information can belong to some *overlapped areas* and *multiple centers*, i.e., see for instance the information distributed or shared through the official systems; or to *peripheries*, such as the information belonging to the quiz input systems, social media, virtual game environments, or specific specialized software systems that are used solely in particular courses. Such regionalization is needed to show the high use of non-official systems and the cross-use distribution amongst official and non-official DLEs.

Figure 1 shows a heat-map on the regionalization of DLEs from Table II. The black line distinguishes between the official systems, i.e., the system that is official to the HE organizational entity, such that they are proposed, indicated, maintained, and secured by the HE organization itself. We organized the DLEs units used by the participants in six categories: official systems (dark green), third party applications (pink), social media (blue), quiz input systems (yellow), virtual games environments (orange), and specialized software applications (light green).

The set of official DLEs {#1, #2, #6, #7, #12} is represented by five DLEs. However, we can observe that only five out of 23 DLEs in use are official systems, whereas the majority of the systems, precisely 18 of them, are not official ones, i.e., neither maintained nor secured by the HE organization personnel. Next, we can observe that six DLEs used to subscribe to the *third-party applications* category. Examples of these are the use of a third-party application (#8), web service for forum discussions and wikis (#10), MOOC or MOOC like platform (#11), learning analytics (#16), cloud-based storage (#21), and third party plugin used in the official DLE system (#23). Several specialized software applications were used – the set represented by {#17, #18, #19, #20}. Virtual game environments were used in a number of three: the set composed of {#13, #14, #15}, as well as quiz input systems – the set represented by {#3, #4, #5}. Finally, only two social media platforms were mentioned as used by the participants in their students-teaching/learning HE context, the set composed of {#9, #22}.

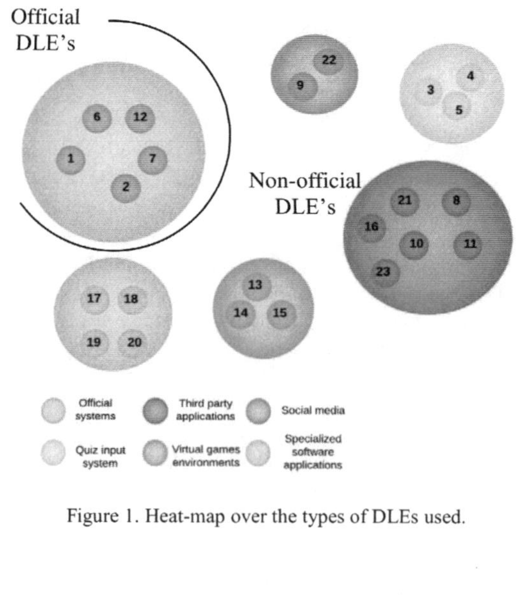

Figure 1. Heat-map over the types of DLEs used.

Further, Figure 2 illustrates a heat-map over the DLEs handled by each of the interviewees, including their types, which is color-coded. It indicates a regionalization of DLEs units based on an *individual regionalization* for each of the participants.

We can observe from Figure 2 that participant #3 used all five official systems, participant #2 used only three of them, whereas participant #1 used four of them. However, it seems that only participant #3 used social media and quiz input systems, and only participant #1 used virtual games environments. Participant #3 was also the youngest amongst the interviewees, which can perhaps be one of the reasons for being more prone to adopt DLEs. However, this is less important. More interesting is to look at the variation of the range itself, because it means that if a student takes all three courses, at the same time, from these three course instructors, the students will have slightly different CIS clusters for each of the courses (Figure 2). Such a situation may take place since all of the participants belonged to the same HE organizational entity.

At the same time, we can observe that each course's CIS is formed out of at least two DLEs units, and a maximum of five. This means that the student's virtual information space is not solely formed out of a single DLE unit, but of at least two. As many as DLE units are included in the information space, as more fragmented, the information space becomes. Nevertheless, once with the fragmentation, more coordinative practices are also needed: the student, as well as the course instructor, needs perhaps to have an account on each of these information spaces, to log in, to log out, to download or upload course material, to share, read or write information to space, etc. This may contribute to fragmented information awareness [22].

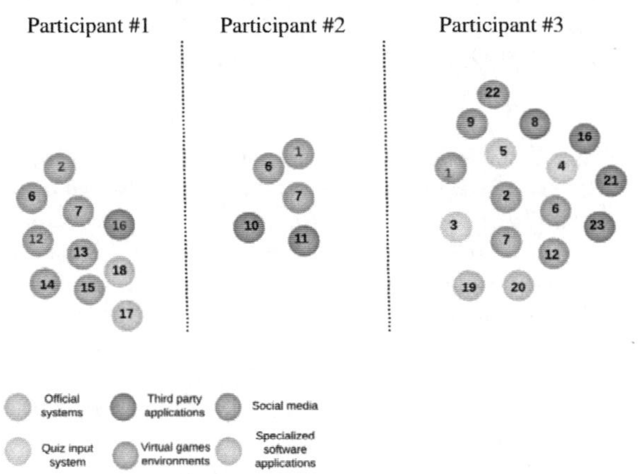

Figure 2. Heat-map over each of the participants' DLEs units used.

B. *DLEs as Information Spaces*

This subsection analyzes DLEs as information spaces, based on the Bossen's seven parameters [17] of CIS and the CIS's characteristics (Section III).

The physical distribution of the cooperative work (parameter #1 in [17]) across space and time calls for the need of a number of DLEs, both common and hybrid information spaces. However, what is essential to do is not to disregard the amount of *articulation work*, which is a "supra-type of work" (see [12], [31]–[33]) that comes once an information technology or system is introduced in an organization, to facilitate the work. In the examples presented earlier in the previous sub-section, it seems that often the CI is the decision-maker on what DLEs units are to be used in the course as CIS. Thus, the CI is often the decision-maker of the information spaces to be used by students. In some cases, students also suggest some new channels of communication as DLEs units to be included in the course's CIS. However, as the literature shows, it seems that it is very much overlooked or underestimated the disadvantages of adopting specific interfaces, the decision is mostly based on intuition, rather than on a thorough or elaborated process [34]. Nevertheless, according to Bossen's parameter #3 on articulation work, this depends on the character of cooperative work [17]. We argue that the amount of articulation work required by information spaces is given not only by the cooperative work but also by the number of DLEs units included in an information space, being it *hybrid* of *common*.

A *hybrid* information space composed by DLEs units refers to the information space created by both the private or peer group notes of a course attendant or course instructor and the information that is put in common in such an information space. For instance, the CIS that participant #3 is using is, in fact, a cluster of DLEs units, or individual hybrid information spaces, such as social media platforms. A social media platform used both as a DLE unit and as a CIS is a hybrid information space, in this sense. The cluster of information spaces used by participant #3, together with her students, is hence a hybrid one.

Further, the information spaces' multiplicity [17] is given by the number of entities or artifacts that intersect in the collaborative work and form the CIS. In the illustrated examples on the cross-use of DLEs, we can say that the students' or course instructors' information spaces' multiplicity is given by the number of DLEs units used in a course. However, while this number of DLE unit types (e.g., official systems, third party applications, social media, etc.), varies between 2 and 5, for the students or course attendants taking courses from all the three course instructors, the number of DLE units in use may vary up to 23.

Moreover, multiplicity is also given by the multiple webs of significances (parameter #2 in [17]) of the users: students and by the course instructors, each having different backgrounds, skills, different levels in digital literacy, etc. The web of significance is given by the number of users (students, CI) and the context the DLE units are used within. The multiplicity and intensity of the means of communication (parameter #4 in [17]) are illustrated by the majority of DLEs units, as many of them include some form of communication channels, especially the official systems and social media. Moreover, the web of artifacts (parameter #5 in [17]) distributed across different DLEs units form the students' respectively, the course instructors' information space. The web of artifacts is also given by all the resources provided by the CI, and by all assignments or submissions provided by the students.

The immaterial means of interaction (parameter #6 in [17]) consists of all the habits, procedures, and division of labor shared amongst the stakeholders. When these routines are well known to all of the stakeholders, the coordinative work will decrease [17]. However, as shown in [35], the lack of procedures and rules around a newly adopted groupware system puts particular demands on the quality control of the data gathered, the privacy of the organization and the individuals' using the system, and it can become a liability to the organization, rather than an asset. Similarly, in the case of students that do not know how to use DLEs as their common or hybrid information space, the articulation work for making the work *work* will most likely increase on the teacher's side. Specifically, one of the participants explained how she had to do some coordinative work in the form of articulation work when students with a lower digital literacy did not know how to use or navigate the information spaces, although she explained during class where the web of artifacts is available and how to use those. As one of the participants specified, "*students coming from other parts of the world, don't have this ingrained experience, or simply experience of using the technology in this way.*" (Participant, Interview).

In terms of needs of precision (parameter #7 in [17]), the participants did not express any concern regarding time- or safe critical issues for the availability of information. Perhaps the *deadlines* can be regarded as such, but other than that, there are not such critical time aspects. However, compared to physical information spaces, such as a whiteboard during a class filled with notes co-created through discussion by students and CI, that's is dynamic, momentary, and transitory, in a way – it will be deleted by the end of the class, virtual information spaces are seemingly slightly different. Virtual CIS and their objects seem to have a more extended temporality, i.e., the course material objects are available online over a more extended period of time throughout the semester, rather than only for one hour during the class. Moreover, virtual information spaces, such as DLEs units forming clusters of information spaces, seem to be more malleable and plastic than the physical ones: while they still keep their constant variable over time, they can yet be changed, updated, modified, deleted, and re-created. However, they are still present in the system. Their temporality, in this sense, can, in a way, be episodic.

Finally, the dialectic nature of DLEs clusters forming the hybrid or CIS is given by the openness and closeness of the DLEs units. For instance, we can notice the dialectic feature for the DLEs used by participant #1 and #3. The findings show that both participants use both official systems, being those closed (e.g., system #7, #9) or open (e.g., system #1), and other external systems – they also closed (e.g., #9, #13) or open (e.g., #3, #4, #10).

C. Cross-use of DLEs

Each of the DLE units can be considered as CIS or hybrid information spaces, based on two conditions: 1) the functionalities they provide, and 2) the perspective from which they are analyzed (student/CI). The clusters of information spaces, as shown in the figures (Figure 1 and 2), are indicated based on the data collected from the CI. However, for the students, the information spaces may cross different information spaces regions, depending on which courses they take, and the DLEs CI use in their teaching.

Several studies from the existent literature showed (see, for example, [35]-[36]), the introduction or integration of information technology or information technology devices in various organizations with the purpose of office automation [11] challenges the respective organizations their local procedures, rules, habituated practices, and coordinative practices. Similarly, our study shows some of the challenges posed when un-official DLEs are used: the information becomes fragmented across different information spaces, the distribution of DLEs may cross different information spaces regions, for the students; the degree of articulation work increases with the number of DLEs in use; the multiplicity and intensity of the means of interactions depends on the type and number of DLEs used, as well as on the number of users;

Finally, using such complex information spaces that are formed out of DLE units and clusters of DLEs give some freedom and flexibility to its users, but it also puts some responsibilities or expectations on them, such as collective expectations on one's availability at all the time, everywhere, increased commitment in communication, changed practices and norms, or experiencing an intensified communication, similarly to the findings from [37].

VII. Conclusion and Future Work

This paper has presented DLEs viewed through the lens of CIS. The research question addressed was: *what challenges do they set for the students, respectively, for the course instructors;* how *do DLE translate as CIS: what type of CIS are they, how are those represented, and used in a HE setting?* Specifically, the article has focused on how DLEs can be designated as complex information spaces. DLEs are often seen, analyzed, and discussed about as educational environments. Moreover, it seems that CIS addressed in educational settings seem not commonly explored. The contribution of the paper consists of discussing the cross-use of DLEs from a CIS perspective, moving beyond looking at DLEs just through an educational perspective. This makes the contribution of the article interesting and relevant. As future work, it would be interesting to investigate the articulation work necessary to be performed when large DLEs clusters are in use, and how these affect the work and performance of CI and students. Moreover, addressing these information spaces from a universal design perspective would be both interesting, relevant, and timely.

ACKNOWLEDGMENTS

I would like to warmly express my thanks to project partners, to the participants, and especially to Klaudia Carçani for allocating time on discussing early drafts of this paper.

REFERENCES

[1] P. G. T. Healey, G. White, A. Eshghi, A. J. Reeves, and A. Light, "Communication Spaces," vol. 17, no. 2, pp. 169–193, Apr. 2008, doi: 10.1007/s10606-007-9061-4.

[2] K. Knarlag, "Nye krav til universell utforming av IKT - Universell utforming av læringsmiljø - Universell utforming - Universell.no," [in English: New requirements to the universal design of ICT - Universal Design of Learning Environments, Universal Design] 10-Feb-2017.

[3] Kommunal- og moderniseringsdepartementet, "Forskrift om endring i forskrift om universell utforming av informasjons- og kommunikasjonsteknologiske (IKT)-løsninger - Lovdata," [in English: Ministry of Local Government and Regional Development, Regulations on amendments to regulations on universal design of information and communication technology (ICT) solutions, Law data] 20-Sep-2017.

[4] Oxford Eng, Dictionary, "teach, v.," Oxford University Press, 2020.

[5] Oxford Eng. Dictionary, "learn, v.," Oxford University Press, 2020.

[6] Swedish Council for Higher Education, "antagning.se," Antagning.se, 2020. [Online]. Available from https://www.antagning.se/se/start, 25.02.2020.

[7] Kompetanse Norge, "utdanning.no," utdanning.no, 2020. [in English: Competence, Norway]. [Online]. Available from https://utdanning.no/front, 25.02.2020.

[8] "SAP" SAP. [Online]. Available from https://www.sap.com/index.html, 25.02.2020.

[9] "What is SharePoint?" [Online]. Available from https://support.office.com/en-us/article/what-is-sharepoint-97b915e6-651b-43b2-827d-fb25777f446f, 25.02.2020.

[10] "Box" [Online]. Available from https://www.box.com/en-gb/home, 25.02.2020.

[11] J. Grudin, "Computer-Supported Cooperative Work: history and focus," Comp., vol. 27, no. 5, pp. 19–26, May 1994, doi: 10.1109/2.291294.

[12] K. Schmidt and L. Bannon, "Taking CSCW seriously," CSCW, vol. 1, no. 1, pp. 7–40, Mar. 1992, doi: 10.1007/BF00752449.

[13] H. Jeong, C. E. Hmelo-Silver, and K. Jo, "Ten years of Computer-Supported Collaborative Learning: A meta-analysis of CSCL in STEM education during 2005–2014," Educ. Res. Rev., vol. 28, p. 100284, Nov. 2019, doi: 10.1016/j.edurev.2019.100284.

[14] K. Schmidt, "The Concept of 'Work' in CSCW," CSCW, vol. 20, no. 4, pp. 341–401, Oct. 2011, doi: 10.1007/s10606-011-9146-y.

[15] K. Schmidt, Cooperative Work and Coordinative Practices. London: Springer London, 2011.

[16] P. G. Scupelli, Y. Xiao, S. R. Fussell, S. Kiesler, and M. D. Gross, "Supporting coordination in surgical suites: physical aspects of common information spaces," in Proc. intern. conf. on Hum. fact. in comp. sys. - CHI '10, Atlanta, Georgia, USA, 2010, p. 1777, doi: 10.1145/1753326.1753593.

[17] C. Bossen, "The parameters of common information spaces:: the heterogeneity of cooperative work at a hospital ward," in Proc. of the 2002 ACM conf. on CSCW '02, New Orleans, Louisiana, USA, 2002, p. 176, DOI: 10.1145/587078.587104.

[18] P. Vassilakopoulou, M. Grisot, and M. Aanestad, "Between Personal and Common: the design of hybrid information spaces," CSCW, vol. 27, no. 3, pp. 1085–1112, Dec. 2018, doi: 10.1007/s10606-017-9304-y.

[19] L. Bannon and S. Bødker, "Constructing Common Information Spaces," 1997, vol. ECSCW, pp. 81–96.

[20] O. W. Bertelsen and S. Bødker, "Cooperation in massively distributed information space," Bonn, Germany, 2001, vol. ECSCW, pp. 1–17, doi: 10.1007/0-306-48019-1.

[21] K. H. Rolland, V. Hepsø, and E. Monteiro, "Conceptualizing common information spaces across heterogeneous contexts: mutable mobiles and side-effects of integration," in Proc. of the 2006 20th anniversary conf. on CSCW '06, Banff, Alberta, Canada, 2006, pp. 493–500, DOI: 10.1145/1180875.1180951.

[22] D. Saplacan, J. Herstad, and Z. Pajalic, "Use of digital learning environments: A study about fragmented information awareness," Interact. Des. Archit. J. IDxA, *forthcoming*, p. 20, 2020.

[23] Z. Zhang, A. Sarcevic, and C. Bossen, "Constructing Common Information Spaces across distributed emergency medical teams," in Proc. ACM Conf. on CSCW and Soc. Comp. - CSCW '17, Portland, Oregon, USA, 2017, pp. 934–947, DOI: 10.1145/2998181.2998328.

[24] G. Munkvold and G. Ellingsen, "Common Information Spaces along the illness trajectories of chronic patients," in ECSCW 2007, 2007, pp. 291–310.

[25] V. M. González et al., "Understanding mobile work in a distributed information space: implications for the design of ubicomp technology," in Proc. Lat. Amer. conf. on HCI - CLIHC '05, Cuernavaca, Mexico, 2005, pp. 52–63, doi: 10.1145/1111360.1111366.

[26] V. Bellotti and S. Bly, "Walking away from the desktop computer: distributed collaboration and mobility in a product design team," in Proc. ACM Conf. on CSCW '96, New York, NY, USA, 1996, pp. 209–218, doi: 10.1145/240080.240256.

[27] T. E. Hjelle, "Information spaces in large-scale Org.," COOP 2008 Proc. 8th Int. Conf. Des. Coop. Syst., pp. 265–273, 2008.

[28] A. Clement and I. Wagner, "Fragmented Exchange: disarticulation and the need for regionalized communication spaces," in Proc. 4th Euro. Conf. on CSCW, ECSCW '95: 10–14 Sep. 1995, Stockholm, Sweden, H. Marmolin, Y. Sundblad, and K. Schmidt, Eds. Dordrecht: Springer Netherlands, 1995, pp. 33–49.

[29] D. Saplacan, "Situated ability: A case from Higher Education on digital learning environments," Lect. Notes Comput. Sci. Springer, 2020, *in press*, HCII.

[30] K. Malterud, "Systematic text condensation: a strategy for qualitative analysis," Scand. J. Public Health, vol. 40, no. 8, pp. 795–805, Dec. 2012, doi: 10.1177/1403494812465030.

[31] L. Suchman, "Supporting articulation work," in Computerization and Controversy (2Nd Ed.), R. Kling, Ed. Orlando, FL, USA: Academic Press, Inc., 1996, pp. 407–423.

[32] I. Hampson and A. Junor, "Invisible work, invisible skills: interactive customer service as articulation work," New Tech. Work Employ., vol. 20, no. 2, pp. 166–181, 2005, doi: 10.1111/j.1468-005X.2005.00151.x.

[33] A. Strauss, "The Articulation of Project Work: An Organizational Process," Sociol. Q., vol. 29, no. 2, pp. 163–178, 1988.

[34] J. Grudin, "Why CSCW applications fail: problems in the design and evaluation of organizational interfaces," in Proc. ACM Conf. on CSCW '88, New York, NY, USA, 1988, pp. 85–93, doi: 10.1145/62266.62273.

[35] W. J. Orlikowski, "Learning from Notes: organizational issues in groupware implementation," in Proc. ACM Conf.on CSCW '92, New York, NY, USA, 1992, pp. 362–369, doi: 10.1145/143457.143549.

[36] W. J. Orlikowski, "The duality of technology: rethinking the concept of technology in organizations," Organ. Sci., vol. 3, no. 3, pp. 398–427, Aug. 1992, doi: 10.1287/orsc.3.3.398.

[37] M. Mazmanian, W. J. Orlikowski, and J. Yates, "The autonomy paradox: the implications of mobile email devices for knowledge professionals," Org. Sci., vol. 24, no. 5, pp. 1337–1357, Feb. 2013, doi: 10.1287/orsc.1120.0806.

Being a Reflexive Insider: The Case of Designing Maritime Technology

Yushan Pan
Faculty of Engineering, Ocean Operations Department
Norwegian University of Science and Technology
Ålesund, Norway
Email: yushan.pan@ntnu.no

***Abstract*—This article reports a long-term, multiple-site ethnographic study in which the author cooperated with a heterogeneous group in designing remote-control systems for maritime operations since 2015. The paper reports how the participants were assembled in a network that represented their interests in balancing the relationship between a design and its use. The author asserts that if Computer Supported Cooperative Work (CSCW) research aims to shed light on other disciplines, CSCW researchers should be reflexive insiders that first position themselves in such disciplines. Different from the first generation of CSCW researchers, members of the new generation are trained in multiple disciplines, and they have the ability to use their expertise in reducing the gap between CSCW research and engineering practices in various fields. Thus, through reflexive practice, CSCW researchers could connect communities of practice, thus narrowing the distance between humanity and engineering. The paper moves the historical debate on the relationship between ethnography and design toward a new focus on reflective insiders as a method used to support CSCW research outside the CSCW community.**

Keywords- CSCW; engineering design; reflectivity; practice–research gap.

I. INTRODUCTION

The literature shows that current maritime technology does not purely support cooperative work among operators on board [1]. The current design of operator–vessel interaction follows the principles of engineering design, including cognitive ergonomics and human factors [2]. The fundamental principle is to focus on the design applicability, the scope of the technical process, and the system structures to support the efficacy of machine use [3]. Operators are subjects in experimental work conducted to verify that a design is successful. However, the social aspects of human–vessel interaction have been largely dismissed. Moreover, operators are not encouraged to articulate their requirements, and the system design team is composed of a variety of specialists acting in the capacity of consultants to the project.

If the above are the facts, then how could CSCW researchers contribute to the design of maritime technology as a completely foreigner who shares few common interests with engineering designers? Shifting the focus from machines to humans challenges, the design of cooperative systems to support maritime operations, which is indeed how to position a CSCW researcher in the maritime field. However, very few previous studies have addressed how researchers could successfully conduct CSCW research outside the CSCW community. For example, scholars have tried to extend collaborative computing in a design approach to shaping the design processes to help users articulate their requirements with other specialists in systems design in both the aviation and maritime domains [4]–[6]. Thus, it was worthwhile discussing how CSCW could be extended beyond the classic discussion about the relationship between ethnography and design [7] to the collaborative effort of computer scientists and social scientists [8].

This movement in CSCW research has been debated for several years [9]. Moreover, current CSCW design has moved beyond single disciplines, such as sociology and computer science to establish itself and well in a new field. However, in the key literature on the intervention of design in CSCW [9], little attention has been paid to intervention in CSCW research [9]. Even when intervention is addressed, it is not clear that how, when and what could be intervened. Although a few studies address how CSCW research could help in design technologies, mainly in the healthcare field, the difference is that the work practices of health workers require CSCW researchers to communicate with developers who, in most cases, share similar a background, such as computer science, software engineering, and so on.

However, the story is changed if CSCW researchers work with people who have different background but focus on control engineering and automation. The priority is given to expertise outside CSCW, and interactive experiences of computation and cooperative work are less vital. Operators are affected by usefulness and usability issues in the given technology. Moreover, different priorities in the design process challenge CSCW researchers, who must design systems in cooperation with foreigners outside the CSCW world. In protecting his or her own academic interest CSCW researchers have to find ways to make sense of CSCW insights beyond their own discipline [1]. As a member of new generation of CSCW researchers, the author has multidisciplinary education, and he is interdisciplinary by training. This generation of CSCW researchers can reveal the design site and the object of study, and they play roles in supporting technology design. Thus, the research question of the present work can be formulated as: *how to shorten the distance between CSCW research and its practice in engineering design in terms of CSCW researchers' roles in engineering project?*

This article is structured as follows: first, in Section II, the case is presented – designing remote control systems as a fundamental background of the article. In Section III, reflexivity as theoretical basis and methods used are presented. In Section IV, the article describes how participants were recruited in designing remote control with respect to CSCW insights. In Section V, the author reflects on his own experience in conducting CSCW research in the maritime domain, which is relevant for maritime studies. In doing so, the author discusses contribution to CSCW research, which moves the historical debate on the relationship between ethnography and design toward a new focus on reflexive insiders as a method used to support CSCW research. The paper concludes in Section VI.

II. The Case: Designing Remote-Control Systems

Traditionally, maritime technology is designed in the fields of mechanical engineering, electrical engineering, electronic engineering, and even computer engineering. In these fields, the focus is on control systems, machinery, and the automation of maritime vehicles of any kind. The design process is purposeful, systemic, and iterative. Engineering designers conduct their work in various constraint conditions to find possible solutions for problems that are usually limited to the given scenarios. Engineering designers communicate with a small group of users, for whom the design follows a positivist paradigm with the intention to test a system. Design requirements are usually based on three principles: corporate, technology, and social [10]. The primary principle is that the corporation needs to generate design requirements in line with the company's organisational structures, strategic vision, and available resources, based mainly on the knowledge and expertise of the engineering designers. This principle does not change until social aspects challenge the company's frame through markets. The second principle, which Gershenson and Stauffer [11] termed technology, is the knowledge of engineering principles, material properties, and physical laws [3]. The user's requirements are considered last. The requirements of the third principle are weighted to optimise the trade-off with the requirements of the first two principles and to align with the needs of the users, such as the "must-be need" and the "attractive need".

Thus, in line with the principles, engineering designers consider artefacts important for remote-control systems. In addition, engineering designers narrow design specifications to comply with reliability, ergonomics (i.e., human factors), manufacturability, control ability which similar to software engineers, who use models to automatically synthesise an executable code [12]. The philosophy underlying all solutions is technology-centred design. That is, using a certain algorithm to represent situational awareness [26] [29], systems are expected to represent information as accurately as possible in human decision-making [25][26]. The common sense that underpins these previous studies is the assumption that the systems will be well-designed to support human tasks, such as drawing patterns, creating models, and making sense of a machine's actions. Through a well-structured technology-centred experiment, as in most engineering design work, engineering designers expect that human factor specialists [21][22] could investigate whether or not interfaces could be built to satisfy the operators. If so, what kinds of "human error" could be investigated? Hopefully, the results could be used to reform the systems according to a better vision. As a consequence of this approach, operators are expected, oddly enough, to be re-trained in the skills needed in the autonomous future [18]. The rest, without protection against the failures, errors, and faults caused by technology, which cannot be called human errors, is treated as regulation and policy issues [24][25]. Politicians, societies and ship owners require clarification of potential liabilities introduced by autonomous technology, such as collisions [21].

However, the cost of shipping may not be reduced as expected. Instead, it might increase significantly because of infinite maintenance and change in remote-control systems, which will displease operators. When changes are introduced, people quickly learn their characteristics and discover how to get the best from them. When autonomous technology and remote control are introduced, people react the same.

III. Theoretical Concept and Methods

A. *Reflexivity*

Calas and Smircich [27, p.240] define reflexivity as the '*constant assessment of the relationship between "knowledge" and "the ways of doing knowledge"*'. Through 'reflexivity' researchers could pay attention to '*the way different kinds of linguistic, social, political, and theoretical elements are woven together in the process of knowledge development during which empirical materials is constructed, interpreted and written (p.9)*'. In doing reflexivity study, interpretation is used as a tool to produce scientific knowledge [23]. Doing interpretation, we experience reflection '*we become observers of our own practice* [24]'. Reflexivity suggests a complexification of thinking and experience, or thinking about experience [24]. It is a process of exposing or questioning our ways of doing. In the discussion of third wave HCI, Bødker [25] calls a crucial and conventional understandings of reflexivity. Reflexivity, in her means, is unlike positivism. Instead, it is an intervention for data gathering and a chew how data gathering impacts the quality of the data itself. At the end, reflexive practices could find structural patterns in what they have observed, and in turn, to extend the theory they used. However, reflexivity has had difficulty found a place in HCI and in CSCW literature. Due to its subjectivity of the method use, it is hard for reflexivity researchers to open their work to future scrutiny. However, Geirbo [26] states reflexivity itself is important as methodological considerations which can guide researchers to entre a community, phenomenon or practice that are foreign to the researchers. In the present, it is possible for the researcher to share sensemaking between the practitioners and the ethnographer in terms of gaining performative knowledge of professional knowledge. The researcher has the capability to articulate and analyse that performative knowledge gained through an insider-role [27].

In this effort, it is possible to bridge the practice-research gap by enacting researcher-practitioner roles across community boundaries, developing and disseminating new knowledge, and engaging field professionals outside of CSCW community.

Thus, in line with this specific theoretical concept, a CSCW researcher is able to be reflexive on how his/her ethnographic account will affect the research process. This action could help other CSCW peers gain a better understanding of the choice the researcher has made during the entire research process including the design, data collection, and interpretation phases. By reporting and discussing the theoretical struggles of interpretive empirical research could also help fulfil the principles of 'dialogue [28]' in between the fieldwork material with the reflectivity thinking and engineering design practice. As the core of 'dialogue' interpretation is relating back to the experience in terms that the CSCW peers can understand what the researcher has seen, what the researcher has been experienced, and how evaluate that work. In turn, they could sense the socio-technical gap within CSCW research itself as well as the gap between humanity and engineering in general.

B. Methods

For a long time, the role of CSCW researcher in the maritime domain is questioned. The CSCW researcher struggled to answer this question because CSCW contributions might not remain in its own area, which is *interpretive ethnography*, but might extend to in a foreign context where the CSCW researcher would have to change his/her tone and voice so those living there could understand the researcher. Although the initial question in 2015 of the author's research was "What is going on in designing maritime technology?" when he did fieldwork at sea, he asked questions about how maritime technology is produced, assembled, and maintained. Although remote-control systems are designed on land, the author sees himself not only as part of land-based maritime design teams that he observes and interviews, and then writes about. His fieldwork began from the first year when he was a doctoral student at the University of Oslo, and it continued after his doctorate degree. The author has not stayed on one site to understand the design of maritime technology. Instead, multi-sites [29] were visited both at sea and on land to observe and interview the people who will be users of remote-control systems. Importantly, seminars, workshops, and conferences were included where shipowners and their colleagues, such as engineering designers, and policymakers, as well as other relevant participants celebrate their technical achievements. Although the research project requires a long-term engagement in the maritime domain, luckily the heterogeneous group has not changed much since 2015. A group of professionals, such as operators, engineering designers, educators, and ship owners are involved in the study. The present work is a long-range project to observe and interview them in different places both at sea and on land in European countries. An online platform was established where engineering designers could share information via email and videoconferences, chat, and leave comments on documents. Those topics that the author does not understand in the hope that someone will explain were commented and observed. In addition, the author interacts with many of engineering designers through individual emails and videoconferences to construct an ethnography of their experiences in design work. A few new participants joined his study, but others have remained since the beginning. Thus, informed consent is not required but only verbally introduce the research work to newcomers when the author works with them. A few of them withdrawal their participation due to starting a new career path. However, they keep in touch from time to time in case any questions need to be followed up.

A table illustrates the research activities since 2015 (see Table I). All interviews, seminar and workshops were noted without audio-recordings due to ethical considerations. At sea and land-based simulator room the observation was recorded by videos. However, the author did not transcribe all videos. Instead, only the ones which are relevant to engineering design process were transcribed since the difference between cooperative work of seafarers at sea and on land is vital.

TABLE I. RESEARCH ACTIVITIES SINCE 2015

Settings	Methods		
	Interview[a]	*Observation[b]*	*Year*
At Sea, on board	72	1838	Autumn 2015-Spring 2016
Land-based Simulator room	18	48	Autumn 2016
Conferences on sites	4	-	Autumn 2017 – Autumn 2019
Seminar	8	-	Autumn 2016-Spring 2018
Workshops	7	63	Autumn 2016-Autumn 2019
Emails	232	-	Autumn 2015 – Spring 2020
Videoconferences	4	-	Spring 2018 – Autumn 2020

a. Number of interviews
b. Hours of observation

The data analysis has been ongoingly conducted since 2015. Thematically indexing words was conducted such as cooperative work, design, remote-control, systems collaboration, team's cooperation, remote-control and so forth. Themes were also identified. However, these themes are used to describe not only remote-control system design but also other work of the project, which is also focused on investigation and design in the maritime domain in general. The purpose in data analyses are offering an ethnographic account of the practice and associations orchestrated by crossing multiple sites both offline and online, particularly in the case of a remote-control system. Moreover, the aim is directing attention to the researcher's relf-reflectivity [30] to bridge the gulf between what Dourish [31] called the sociotechnical gap and Ackerman's definition of "the divide between what we know we must support socially and what we can support technically" [32] without any pre-conditions. Simply put, this paper addresses the gap between CSCW research and CSCW practice in industrial contexts.

IV. The Development of CSCW Research in Designing Remote-Control Systems

In the maritime domain, operators are rarely involved in the design process. As previously mentioned, operators are used as subjects for testing purposes when a product is developed. Educators are also rarely involved because they teach operators without considering their concerns about technology. Moreover, CSCW researchers are rarely involved in a maritime design project because their expertise is invisible in the engineering field. Furthermore, shipowners are rarely consulted in design projects too for various reasons. Thus, in this study, a group of stakeholders was assembled to balance their interests in design toward a sustainable solution for all through a CSCW perspective.

A. Unheard opinions

In 2016, challenges were coming up. The operators thought the author (a CSCW researcher, and hereafter the researcher will be used) was an engineering designer. They thought that the researcher was only concerned about examining their work. However, that was untrue since a CSCW researcher who was also trained as ethnographer. The purpose of CSCW researcher to be on board was not to evaluate any work but to observe what is going on. The CSCW researcher also wanted to interview operators. Based on those findings, the CSCW researcher would work with engineering designers to design remote-control systems.

After above explanation, the operators were worried that what the researcher observed and heard would be documented as 'evidences' to change the vessel design to automatic shipping. It seems they thought the researcher was a spy who studied them and would try to create a technology that would replace human operators. Although the purpose of being on board was explained and they had given informed consent to participate the research study, the author still was misunderstood. However, later on they apologised and added that they indeed really hope someday their expertise and knowledge could be acknowledged rather than overlooked in designing remote-control. Since then, the researcher noticed that not everyone welcomes remote control.

On board, one of the operators expressed his worry that he does not believe the systems can do what he is good at. His experience at sea cannot be simply cloned into a machine. He felt anxiety that shipowners just want to save costs and do not care operators. The researcher did not know how to respond to them at that time. The researcher could not promise them that they would be assisted rather than replaced by the remote-control system. The researcher also was not able to say that their expertise would be acknowledged and used in designing maritime technology. Because the engineering designers would adopt a concept called "human-in-the-loop" anyway, which means that machines interact without human assistance. Human operators are just a backup if a problem arises.

This worry was not unique. In 2018, the same worry about remote control was expressed by maritime educators. These educators expressed their worry at a conference on upgrading the skills of maritime operators for digitalisation in the future. In a panel discussion, several educators questioned remote control operations and worried that no one knows how to teach since no one has experiences on remote-control. Although educators believe re-training themselves are needed, they do not believe simulator-based system is the best solution. In addition, although the educators said they might be re-trained, systematic training is not available. Simply put, remote-control systems have not yet been delivered to users. The work is conducted in engineering design firms. Only engineering designers run the design work. However, engineering designers assume that they have the knowledge of remote-control and that it is less important to observe current maritime operations or take into account the concerns of others. The researcher engaged with a design workshop at a company in autumn 2018, asking what was the purpose of remote control? One engineering designer replied that remote control is aiming at replacing human beings on board due to most unsafe operations are human errors. Human operators must be relocated on land to build up new abilities to control an object that they do not touch. Only one concern was given – cybersecurity issue.

The answer was not convinced the researcher since the skills the engineering designer refers to is not clear. The researcher asked the engineering designer that what are the new skills and how cybersecurity will look like and who will able to take responsibility in control vessels. A solid answer was not given. Instead, the engineering designer assumes that skills are about interaction. Operators need to take responsibility to handle any problems and make decisions if needed. In order to convince the researcher, the engineering designer guided the researcher to a lab, in which a huge screen is presented. On the screen much information was presented. An engineer sitting front of the screen brought out four small screens to simulate a case for the researcher. The case was about a vessel being remote controlled but now under attack by unknown hackers. The engineer said he would lose control of the vessel, and he was now trying to solve the problem. The solution was to protect the user interfaces through developed software. Using the mouse, the engineer opened a software application and ran it to protect his user interfaces. The engineer believed that it is a method for remote-control and such method no operators have a chance to learn it. It is not surprising that engineers expect to train everyone to use the new technology. However, it was strange for the researcher that operators need to be trained in clicking a software application to protect the safety of the vessel.

How about the weather, waves, and swimmers in the fjord? If the simulation is not real, why do educators worry about training? At least, operators could become familiar with the interaction styles in the new technology. However, although the educators were eager to welcome remote-control systems, they mentioned many times that their goal was to obtain educational funding, not the outcomes of their teaching and the students' learning. They said nothing about learning how to interact with computers. This was nothing new in maritime studies. When discussing this issue with an educator at another conference in 2019, the educator replied that simulator-based training is computer games. No true operations at all. The whole shipping industry misunderstand a basic question: *What learning outcome and what level we expect to achieve in simulator-based training.*

Interestingly, the educator knew it might be questionable to accept the engineer's proposal to conduct training by means of simulators. However, the entire maritime domain seems to follow the shipowners and engineering designers wishes. The educator cannot challenge that value. Although the researcher tried to play a mediating role between the engineers and operators, there were invisible hands pushing engineering work to be conducted as fast as possible.

B. Assembling participants

The above scenario indicates that intervening directly in the design process was difficult. This situation was not like an empirical study that is conducted before the actual design process is begun. In the maritime domain, engineering designers assume that software and computer systems follow mathematical models although this assumption is incorrect [33]. In 2019, by chance, the researcher engaged in observing the application process regarding innovative educational programmes for maritime studies. There was a call for applications by nautical science departments at universities to use a bottom-up approach to position students in the centre in designing new study programmes. The objective of the call was to establish an ecosystem to support lifelong relationships among technology, engineering companies, educational institutions, and, most importantly, operators. Because the CSCW researcher was engaged with the educators and invited engineering designers during the application process, the researcher wanted to contribute to making the voices of operators heard. However, it did not happen because the researcher would like to see how they would react to such a call. In CSCW research, balancing outsider–insider role and avoid inserting the researcher's biases into the project is vital. Although CSCW insights may help design technology, it is unclear that whether those insights would pose difficulties for engineering designers, challenge their professional expertise, or even interfere with their work on the ground. The same applies to working with educators. In addition to using CSCW insights to shape technology design, the intention is to scrutinise the usefulness of such insights outside the CSCW community. The power relations between different stakeholders could be balanced by their own interests rather than by an external force, such as the role of researcher in the present project. Thus, instead of interviewing the stakeholders as most ethnographers would have done, a few challenging, structured questions were asked with aim of fostering a new way of thinking about design, which is an approach sought by the researcher.

When participated in a design workshop again in 2019, the engineering designers were asked how they understand a bottom-up approach in design process. There were no clear answers. However, no one doubts that a user in engineering designers' eyes is the person who pay for the project – the shipowners. During the dialogue in the workshop, the operators were not mentioned even once. The researcher reflects that multidisciplinary design is a challenge and requires the reconciliation of diverging design perspectives [34]. Although in CSCW community, software engineers and CSCW researchers in software design projects can share and integrate their viewpoints in the design process, such design process could still miss important aspects of the design problem [35]. If that were the case in the CSCW community, it would also apply to the engineering field [36]. Engineering designers lack the ability to demonstrate the effects of their design concepts because of their insufficient thinking and reflection about such effects. In line with these arguments, in 2019, a question in a panel discussion at an academic conference on ship design was posed, addressing the overlooked operators in technology design. This time, the replies were engineering is about designing functions for the needs of products, not people who use it. In most cases, training is even important because engineers believe people need to be taught in order for properly using a product.

For the researcher, it is a circular relationship: "shipowner–engineering designer–shipowner". Similar to the article, "Located accountabilities in technology production", Suchman reflected on her experience in addressing a similar problem as "a central dilemma of CSCW researchers' participation in increasingly complex divisions of labour and professional specialisation were the layers of mediation between each of us and the consequences of our work" [37]. Although it is the responsibility of the researcher to the process of technology production, his/her participation, of course, broke the relationship into pieces. The question to the engineering designer was about investigating whether they wanted to take the responsibility to trace the usefulness of the production. However, they simply handed off the production after delivery, and they might have never revisited it until someone requested updates or changes. In the present study, one of the engineering designers discussed the following with the CSCW researcher privately after the conference: *The whole industry works in a mechanism like a design-test-deliver-maintenance loop. It is about business. Our motto is that users know very little about what they do and what they want.* The researcher cannot agree with this statement. Bannon [38] warned that users are as professional as anyone else about their workplace and tasks in designing computer systems. They have an insiders' overview of their work and the tools (including technology) that assist them.

The researcher is challenged in thinking about how to assemble different insights to propose a balance of design and use. According to Suchman, she dwelt uncomfortably in the distance between design and use for many years in the 1980s. The balance between design and use forced her to think about her role in technology design projects. She concluded that she, as an anthropologist of technology, could only translate her practice into design terms. However, because of the division of professional labour, the problem was caused by neither her ability nor the design team [37].

After studying the maritime domain for several years, the researcher felt differently. As a member of new generation in

CSCW research, the origin of the problem is known: the mismatch of design problems across multiple disciplines, such as design, science, and engineering. The researcher also knew where, when, and how to contribute to the project to benefit everyone. However, he could not. The reason was not the capability but the role of the researcher in the project. There was simply no chance to intervene in the design process from the very beginning. Because of rapid marketing changes in the shipping industry and technological development, technology companies would like to respond quickly to the expectations of shipowners. Thus, the researcher will always intervene late in the project. The researcher is expected to focus on how their studies could be used in future projects based on the results of investigating current technology.

However, the situation was changed on this occasion. Although no one has actually developed remote control, for various reasons, the researcher could intervene in an early stage to learn how to position themselves in potential projects. In this case, the researcher must be sensitive about the ongoing discussion in the industry as well as the intersection between engineering departments at research institutions and project funding organisations.

Thus, when continually asking if engineering designers can predict the future of remote control, none of them could reply. Instead, the chief engineering designer said it is sadly too few chances for them to learn from the operators. They know where to gain knowledge, however, they choose to ignore the chance. When continually asking and inviting operators to design workshops, however, actually getting even one participant is challenge due to various reasons. Although the operators did not accept the invitation, they seemed happy that their messages were delivered through the study. In mail inbox of the researcher, there was an email from one of the operators, saying that if the researcher would like to ask any questions, please contact the operator in Sep 2017. The operator would love to share his ideas and opinions. In addition, the operator told the researcher that he had started a land-based job and had continued his academic path, seeking a master's degree in computer science. He wanted to work in an engineering company in the future to design systems for vessels. This sounded like an extra bonus. At least, the researcher did not expect the research work to influence others' lives. However, to some degree, it seems the researcher not only managed to get engineering designers to accept that other opinions are also important in technology design. The researcher also inspired operators to share their experience and expertise with others. The researcher unconsciously stepped in the project to play both roles of designer (i.e., in guiding engineering designers) and user (i.e., in inspiring operators). On several occasions, the researcher formatted and reformatted the ideas and opinions of operators, educators, engineering designers, and even his own reflections into a dialogue between investigation and design [28].

C. Reflexivity as an intervention tools in assembling shipowners

Including only operators, educators, and engineering designers in this study was not enough. As previously mentioned, design requirements are given by shipowners. Without their participation, design work is unrealistic, and there would be problems if requirement conflicts arose between operators, educators, and shipowners. Indeed, the researcher has documented results in various formats. However, considering the differences between traditions in CSCW research across the Atlantic, it is notable that a few previous studies concentrated on how cooperative technologies could be created with a focus on articulation work of users [39], as in the European CSCW tradition. Some studies focused on how to intervene in the design process and how intervention is implemented in design [9]. In interviews with Volker Wulf and Myriam, Lewkowicz, Richter and Koch [40] observed that the term practice-based CSCW was descriptive. Although Lewkowicz argued that the importance of CSCW was that it enabled designers and social scientists to use same communication channel. The CSCW researcher of the present work does not fully agree because according to many CSCW studies, at least in European CSCW research, the true design process is conducted by engineering designers. It is questionable how intervention could be implemented realistically without a monitor. Moreover, most CSCW research has evaluated the outcome of design, and there are few studies on the subsequent effects on organizational changes in connection with CSCW research.

Bratteteig and Wagner [41] in the field of participatory design asked the following question: What is a result of participatory design? They argued, "Ideally, a project outcome should be evaluated in a real-use situation when users have had a chance to integrate it into whatever they are doing and (eventually) develop a new form of practice". As a participant in designing remote control systems, did the researcher improves the knowledge of the systems that are supposed to be designed? Through his activities to assemble participants, did he introduce a better "tool" for all stakeholders in the projects, inspiring them to understand that all their voices were important, but no one had a priority. Like the reply by the chief engineering designer, they acknowledged that without information from operators, it was impossible to ensure the quality of remote-control systems in the future. The educators replied similarly. The researcher therefore interviewed three shipowners at their offices at different times from August 2019 to February 2020. The aim was to enable shipowners to develop a realistic expectation of remote control. In doing so, several cases in video format based on the fieldwork in 2015 and 2018 both at sea and in simulators were showed. The shipowners expressed their astonishment after they watched those videos. They saw a great difference between realistic operations and training using simulators. Although they all invest money on training courses for the operators, after the videos they expressed their uncertainties when they addressed the usefulness of the training programmes. It seems no one was sure that there was a link between training and real work in ensuring safer operation. However, everyone wanted to hear from the operators, at least the most experienced ones, and recognise their voices in decision-making about technology design, including decisions about material artefacts on board (e.g., dynamic positioning systems).

In February 2020, when talking with the operators and the educator in a seminar at Athens, both were offered a chance to participate in the design of remote control. A positive answer was given this time: '*if that could happen, it would be great that we were not just treated as tools. We do not need to bind ourselves to the terms and conditions offered by engineering designers through their productions. We will not outsource our decision-making and capabilities to someone who has no knowledge of our business. We are the core elements of technology.*'

Now operators, educators, and shipowners gather in public and in private to discuss their opinions regarding design. One example is the joint calls for proposals funded by the Education, Audio-Visual and Culture Executive Agency (EACEA) of the European Commission, the European Shipowner Association and the European Transportation Workers' Foundation. The calls are for a bottom-up approach, learner-centred, lifelong action plan involving education, research, shipping, and maritime technology, which are addressed as vital and mandatory [42] [43]. It seems timely for the maritime domain to respond to such calls rather than me working to re-assemble them.

V. Being a Reflexive Insider

The researcher continues to be active in the maritime domain. The researcher values making changes according to the feedback on what have been seen and where he must intervene to improve maritime technology. The intention of this value is twofold: 1) deploy useful CSCW research in an engineering-oriented field; 2) contributing CSCW research with practical feedback from the front line in engineering work. If the CSCW work on assembling participation and mediating outcomes between social and engineering phrases is a practical activity, then the reflection on the role and the contribution of the researcher to the CSCW community is the highest achievement.

A. Interest-driven CSCW research in maritime design

Nygaard and Bergo [44] suggested that designers, particularly participatory designers, take sides in considering the following: 1) improving the knowledge on which systems are built while aiming to build a better "tool" for users [45]; 2) enabling people to develop realistic expectations and reducing resistance to change [46]; 3) increasing workplace democracy by giving the members of an organization the right to participate in decisions that are likely to affect their work [47]. Differing from their wishes, the researcher does not taken side with the operators, educators, shipowners, or engineering designers. However, the first two suggestions are firmly followed.

Eyal [48] warned that researchers must consider carefully who are experts and lay experts. As an outsider in the maritime domain, the judgement of experts is made by the researcher might not be convincing. Although all stakeholders have an interest in improving maritime technology, "better" is understood differently. For example, operators and educators believe that their experience and expertise are vital in remote control. Engineering designers strongly rely on their procedure-based design process. Shipowners seek to effectively invest in a project and reap the benefits. All these interests involve few or no political conflicts. How could the researcher dare to say who is a better participant in designing remote control systems? The only thing for sure is that the researcher can balance these interests and explore a design point that involves all stakeholders, such as designing organizational frameworks for actions and designing industrial relations context [41]. However, differ from participatory designers who discuss political and policy contexts in design projects, the researcher is particularly interested in collaborating with engineering designers to inspire them and the researcher himself to bridge the gap between CSCW research and CSCW design practice. Some CSCW researchers focus on recognising various materials that have different qualities depending on how they are used in specific places as intervention areas. However, regardless of how the material is bounded through time and space in cooperative work among stakeholders, it is completely static, irrespective of the execution of the coordination it prescribes. CSCW researchers have to consider that materials not only stipulate articulation work (e.g., a standard operating procedure in a social order) as invention [49] but also need to think that materials can be inscribed as a result of the delegation of social roles to nonhumans [50] as well as humans. In this manner, the CSCW researchers can identify different aspects of interest in a design project and find the most appropriate way to represent it in various formats for different stakeholders without changing the meaning. Although the formats are different, the core interest of the present project is held by the researcher; thus, it is a "win-win" situation [51] rather than maximising the complexity of remote control systems. Thus, the researcher is a spokesperson who addresses interactive relations among operators, artefacts, maritime technology, engineering designers, educators, and shipowners to improve their cooperation in such actor networks.

Importantly, as maritime technology becomes increasingly computer supported, the researcher has the responsibility to ensure the final design benefits all stakeholders. By doing so, CSCW insights into designing maritime technology should be best used to change the mechanism of design in the maritime domain, including information technology [52]. That is, the insights of stakeholders do not pertain only to requirement specifications that inform design. By representing their interests, the researcher should trigger a *modus operandi* for intervening in the project by taking specific actions regarding when, where, and what forms in the design process to support interactive relationships between actors – in social-technical associations between humans and nonhumans. Such interactions are badly needed in engineering-oriented fields.

B. *Insider roles across communities*

Regarding whether CSCW researchers could potentially address the sociotechnical gap, the CSCW community is divided. Some believe it is possible, but others think that it will take a long time to achieve the division of what we knew socially and what we can support technically. Although some researchers advocate intervention [9] as a solution, their peers are uncertain about how to follow the "the guidelines" [24] because of the lack of reflexivity in interpretive writing. In the present study, the researcher worked in a heterogeneous group. The work of CSCW goes beyond researcher's own accounts of epistemological and theoretical bases. It is crucial to understand not only the nature of the ethnographic encounter and its methodology but also the datasets collected in engineering design work. Instead of tending to discuss people as the objects of study through so-called participant observation, the point is that the researcher shall take his own embodied experiences in the context of personal relationships to gain and exchange knowledge with stakeholders. It is not just a matter of methodology, such as writing detailed field notes and showing videos about practices. It is also a matter of relational epistemology. If a CSCW study is inherently experiential, then it loses the voice of the author in its writing, which limits our insights into the data and our ability to use them in design. The constant assessment of the relationship between knowledge and "the ways of doing knowledge" must be undertaken.

Positioning CSCW insights in engineering projects also concerns relationships with stakeholders, which are reciprocal [53]. In Beaulieu's [53] definition, the value of relationships in different fields in ethnographic studies goes beyond the central notion of face-to-face interaction to the co-presence with the ethnographer during the research. As the present study shows, the relationships among the stakeholders and between the stakeholders and the researcher had nothing to do with negotiating conflicts of interest. The relationship among them was based on self-interest and then was extended to integrate their willingness to participate in the network of actors. They all want their interests to be traceable and consistently represented by someone. The researcher of the present study coincidentally crossed various sites and moments during the research to formulate representations that were useful to all, which was successful. Perhaps another researcher could do the same.

Thus, a few years after completing the research work, the researcher does not perceive that he has a value-neutral stance in research work in the maritime domain. The researcher would argue that CSCW researchers should make themselves explicit to stakeholders so that the latter can better understand their own interests, which, as well as their reasons and motivations, are articulated by the researcher. In this manner, the researcher makes explicit his ideological assumptions to allow other CSCW peers to see the worlds in which the researcher is embedded. Moreover, the CSCW peers could build their own interpretations of the case study of remote-control technology and the indication to reflect on their own assumptions and mindsets. The purpose is mainly to triangulate the sources of evidence with other peers although they use different contexts. Regardless of whether the context is the maritime domain or the healthcare domain, they all work with and in a heterogeneous group. How should they share their reflexive insiders' views of epistemology and methodology in deploying CSCW insights in the design process [26]? It is not a matter that only the CSCW researcher must address. It is also a matter of how CSCW researchers communicate with others. In the present study, the researcher, engineering designers, and shipowners did not share the same mindsets in learning from experience. Thus, a dialogue between the three forms of knowledge helped promote mutual improvement and anchor the relevance of the CSCW research in policy making for design projects in the maritime domain. The CSCW researcher of the present work influences epistemological assumptions and the previous experience in the field influences the dialogic process. It is likely that the best is to position people in the centre in designing the usefulness of technology. Through the dialogue between stakeholders with whom the research engaged, it was possible for peers to investigate and criticise the accounts of interventions, thereby assessing whether the interpretations were valid.

C. *Connecting Communities of Practice*

Because of the researcher's unique background in software engineering, CSCW, and sociology, his enrolment in a group designing maritime technology was more than seeking to improve current design practices in multidisciplinary fields. To make sense of the problems the researcher faced in the maritime domain by creating something new. As a practitioner–researcher in systems design, CSCW research is different when it is used in the engineering field not only because it was new but also because it was a foreign element that was usually rejected by a group of professionals. The nature of the work practice of a professional community is to transform the status quo by new ways of working and interacting rather than accommodate a completely new element. CSCW insights are examples in the present study.

Jackson et al. [54] proposed that CSCW has fewer concerns about translating its theoretical knowledge into forms and instruments that are useable by wider communities. The researcher of the present study faces similar challenges in working in designing maritime technology, in which remote control systems are only one of several design projects. The new generation of CSCW researchers may be different from first-generation. They know about human-centred computing, they know how to do fieldwork, and they even know how to translate their findings into special formats to communicate with systems developers [1]. However, they miss long-term engagement and design sensitive analysis in dealing with their reflections on how they connect different communities. Most CSCW research is iterative enough of its design process and does not challenge the lack of voices of confessional reflection [30] in their community. When researchers seek intervention as a bridge between research and practice, they might fall into their existing cognitive knowledge and create their own artificial worlds and seek their own language in doing design. They focus on exploring the inner symbolic space of a paradigm, and they try to convince others to believe that their languages are universal and useful. This might be wrong. If they do not accept procedure-oriented engineering design, is it correct to assume that CSCW can provide a solution? Suchman [55] suggested that we might need to find a customised solution rather than a universal solution. The challenge of this idea is not only the cognitive aspect of engineering design and CSCW research. It requires the development of radically new forms of scientific inquiry.

In this article, the researcher has reported and discussed his theoretical struggles in interpretive empirical research to fulfil the forms of scientific inquiry in connecting communities of practice. In a heterogeneous group, the collaboration in designing remote control is not a straightforward process. When reading the CSCW literature, the researcher always turn on his software engineer mode to review praxis [40][77]. It is a challenge. Even though the researcher holds two sets of knowledge—CSCW and software engineering—, he should have different perspectives on what he has read, and he should consider them equal contributions to his knowledge. However, in a heterogeneous group, this inner attribute of the researcher becomes both he and others. Because the designer of remote control systems is not the researcher and most work still depends on control engineering principles, inquiry requires extensive empirical data and practical concerns as well as a theoretical framework that might be perceived as disconnected from social construction [56]. Thus, as a researcher who was uniquely trained in two fields and is now working in the complete unstructured maritime domain becomes a challenge. The researcher needs to give his peers the tools to criticise his accounts of the work practice in the workplace. He also needs to engineering designers the tools to investigate the usefulness of the contribution from CSCW point of view to them. In the present work, although no one forced the researcher to make notes and work-in-progress drafts available to all members of the project, he realises that opening the datasets helped fulfil hermeneutic cycles and multiple interpretations. In interviewing the engineering designers, the CSCW perspective of maritime technology led to further discussion. Thus, multiple interpretations of the benefits and why the project should design alternatives became possible. The CSCW approach made it possible for the engineering designers to discuss the situation and to switch from a cooperative project where everyone had his own spot to engage in truly collaborative work. Moreover, both the engineering designers and the researcher recognised the value of reflectivity even though it might differ among them. However, it is important in the discipline of design between CSCW and engineering. The engineering designers found a way forward to be comfortable with the various interests and reflected on them in a dialogue to find a solution.

VI. CONCLUSION

In this article, a case study of reassembling participation to improve the design of remote-control systems with respect to all stakeholders is presented. In addition to the contribution of practical knowledge to the maritime domain, the reflective writing in this article offers a view of how CSCW insights and engineering practices were transformed during the engagement of the researcher in designing maritime technology. In the last seven years, the CSCW interpretation of designing maritime technology suffered from blind spots. However, following the interpretive research and the knowledge and experience gained in CSCW research, the reward was not effecting change. Instead, the rewards were the better understanding of the challenges and opportunities related to bridging the gaps between applying CSCW insights and conducting research in CSCW inside and outside the CSCW community to make real contributions to other fields. As a result, the article suggests that the development of CSCW insights in the engineering fields should have a strong focus on the participation of stakeholders who not only use technology but also those who fund and develop technology. Thus, CSCW researchers could learn more about self-reflection and self-revelation in the contribution to the industry and possibly positively influence policymakers to rethink framework development in the engineering field. In conducting research in the maritime domain, the researcher found that the best way is to reflect and reveal one's own research findings and activities to enable combining them in a wider scientific discourse. If intervention is an unavoidable condition of CSCW research, by being there, the researcher already connected communities of practice, thus making a difference by affecting the practice he studies. The case in this paper, the translation of the research work, the qualitative inquiry the paper developed, and the reflective materials the researcher wrote are tools that could serve both the community and the community from which CSCW insights emerge. The rest is up to others who want to confirm their own values to balance their position with the CSCW insights in their own work. As a result, the gap between research and practice both inside and outside CSCW research could be reduced.

REFERENCES

[1] Y. Pan, "From field to simulator: visualizing ethnographic outcomes to support systems developers," University of Oslo, 2018.

[2] L. Deng, G. Wang, and S. Yu, "Layout Design of Human-Machine Interaction Interface of Cabin Based on Cognitive Ergonomics and GA-ACA," Comput. Intell. Neurosci., pp.1-12, 2016.

[3] G. Pahl, W. Beitz, J. Feldhusen, and K.-H. H. Grote, Engineering design: A systematic approach, 3rd ed. Springer-Verlag London, 2007.

[4] J. A. Hughes, D. Randall, and D. Shapiro, "From ethnographic record to system design - Some experiences from the field," Comput. Support. Coop. Work, 1, 3, pp. 123–141, 1992.

[5] Y. Pan and S. Finken, "Visualising Actor Network for Cooperative Systems in Marine Technology," in HCC'16, 2016, pp. 178–190.

[6] Y. Pan and S. Finken, "From Offshore Operation to Onshore Simulator: Using Visualized Ethnographic Outcomes to Work with Systems Developers," Informatics, 5, 1, pp. 1-12, 2018.

[7] R. Bentley and D. Randall, "Tutorial notes," in CSCW 2004, 2004.

[8] K. Schmidt and L. J. Bannon, "Taking CSCW Seriously. Supporting Articulation Work," J. Collab. Comput. Work Pract., 1, 1, pp. 7–40, 1992.

[9] P. Bjørn and N. Boulus-Rødje, "The Multiple Intersecting Sites of Design in CSCW Research," Comput. Support. Coop. Work CSCW An Int. J., 24, 4, pp. 319-351, 2015.

[10] X. Li, Z. Zhang, and A.-K. Saeema, "The sources and methods of engineering design requirement," Adv. Transdiscipl. Eng., 1, pp. 1–10, 2014.

[11] J. A. Gershenson and L. A. Stauffer, "The creation of a taxonomy for manufacturability design requirements," in 7th ASME Design Technical Conferences, 1995, pp. 305–314.

[12] W. Brace and K. Thramboulidis, "From requirements to design specifications - a formal approach," in International Design Conference, 2010, pp. 639–650.

[13] DNV GL, "Remote-controlled and autonomous ships," 2018.

[14] T. Porathe, J. Prison, and Y. Man, "Situation awareness in remote control centres for unmanned ships," in Human factors in ship design & operations, 2014. pp. 1-8.

[15] R. Rylander and Y. Man, "Autonomous safety on vessels," 2016.

[16] M. A. Ramos, I. B. Utne, and A. Mosleh, "On factors affecting autonomous ships operators performance in a shore control center," in PSAM 14, 2018, pp. 1–12.

[17] M. Wahlström, J. Hakulinen, H. Karvonen, and I. Lindborg, "Human factors challenges in unmanned ship operations - insights from other domains," in 6th International AHFE Conferences, 2015, pp. 1038–1045.

[18] Unkonwn, "Research on the Impacts of Marine Autonomous Surface Ship on the Seafarer's Career and MET," 2018.

[19] Danish Maritime Authority, "Analysis of regulatory barriers to the use of autonomous ships," 2017.

[20] A. Komianos, "The Autonomous Shipping Era. Operational, Regulatory, and Quality Challenges," TransNav, Int. J. Mar. Navig. Saf. Sea Transp., 12, 2, pp. 335-348, 2018.

[21] T. K. Lee, "Liability of autonomous ship: The Scandinavian perspecive: How the liability regimes shall be regulated in the Scandinavian region?," University of Oslo, 2016.

[22] M. B. Calas and L. Smircich, "Re-writing gender into organizational theorizing: directions from feminist perspectives," M. R. M. Hughes, Ed. Thousand Oaks: Sage, 1992, pp. 227–253.

[23] M. Burawoy, "The extended case method," Sociol. Theory, 16, 1, pp. 4–33, 1998.

[24] J. Malaurent and D. Avison, "Reflexivity: A third essential 'R' to enhance interpretive field studies," Inf. Manag., 54, 7, pp. 920-933, 2017.

[25] S. Bødker, "When second wave HCI meets third wave challenges," in NordiCHI 2006, pp. 1-8.

[26] H. C. Geirbo, "Knowing through relations. On the epistemology and methodology of being a relflexive insider," Interacation Des. Archit., 38, 107–123, 2018.

[27] W. J. Orlikowski and J. J. Baroudi, "Study information technology in organizations: research approaches and assumptions," Infor.Syst.Res, 2, 1, pp. 1–28, 1991.

[28] D. Randall, "Investigation and Design," in Social Informatics - A practice-based perspective on the design and use of IT artifacts, V. Wulf, V. Pipek, D. Randall, M. Rohde, K. Schmidt, and G. Stevens, Eds. Oxford: Oxford University Press, 2018, pp. 221–241.

[29] G. E. Marcus, Ethnography through thick and thin. Princeton, NJ: Princeton University Press, 1998.

[30] J. A. Rode, "Reflexivity in digital anthropology," in SIGCHI CHI, 2011, pp.123-132.

[31] P. Dourish, "Implications for design," in SIGCHI CHI, 2006, pp. 541–550.

[32] M. S. Ackerman, "Intellectual challenge of CSCW: the gap between social requirements and technical feasibility," Human-Computer Interact., 15, 2, pp. 179-203, 2000.

[33] R. Turner, Computational artifacts: Towards a philosophy of computer science. Colchester: Springer Nature, 2018.

[34] A. Dittmar and P. Forbrig, "Integrating personas and use case models," in INTERACT 2019, 2019, pp. 666–686.

[35] W. E. Mackay, "Educating multi-disciplinary desi in Tales of the Disappearing Computer, 2003.

[36] Q. Peng and J.-B. Martens, "Design requirements of tools supporting reflection on design impact," in INTERACT 2019, 2019, pp. 609–622.

[37] L. Suchman, "Located accountabilities in technology production," Scand. J. Inf. Syst., 14, 2, pp. 1–15, 2002.

[38] L. J. Bannon, "From human factors to human actors: the role of psychology and human-computer interaction studies in system design," in Design at work: cooperative design of computer systems, R. M. BAECKER, J. GRUDIN, W. A. S. BUXTON, and S. B. T.-R. in H. I. GREENBERG, Eds. Morgan Kaufmann, 1992, pp. 25–44.

[39] P. Bjørn, L. Ciolfi, M. Ackerman, G. Fitzpatrick, and V. Wulf, "Practice-based CSCW research: ECSCW bridging arocss the Atlantic," in CSCW '16, 2016, pp. 210–219.

[40] A. Richter and M. Koch, "Interviews with Volker Wulf and Myriam Lewkowicz on 'The European Tradition of CSCW,'" Bus. Inf. Syst. Eng., 60, 2, pp. 175–179, 2018.

[41] T. Bratteteig and I. Wagner, "What is a participatory design result?," in PDC'16, 2016, pp. 141–150.

[42] European Commission, "Centres of vocational excellence," European Union Official Website, 2019. [Online]. Available: https://eacea.ec.europa.eu/erasmus-plus/actions/centres-of-vocational-excellence_en. [Accessed: 03-Feb-2020].

[43] E. Commission, "Improving impact and broadening stakholder engagement in support of transport research and innovation," European Union Official Webpage, 2019. [Online]. Available: https://cordis.europa.eu/programme/id/H2020_MG-4-10-2020. [Accessed: 03-Feb-2020].

[44] K. Nygaard and O. T. Bergo, "The trade unions-New users of research," Pers. Rev., 4, 2, pp. 5–10, 1975.

[45] E. Balka, P. Bjorn, and I. Wagner, "Steps toward a typology for health informatics," in CSCW, 2008, pp. 515-524.

[46] P. Bachrach and M. S. Baratz, "Power and Its Two Faces Revisited: A Reply to Geoffrey Debnam," Am. Polit. Sci. Rev., pp. 1-4, 1975.

[47] G. Bjerknes and T. Bratteteig, "User participation and democracy: A discussion of Scandinavian research on system development," Scand. J. Inf. Syst., 7, 1, pp. 258–266, 1995.

[48] G. Eyal, The crisis of expertise. Cambridge, UK: Polity, 2019.

[49] K. Schmidt, "Of maps and scripts - the status of formal constructs in cooperative work," in SIGGROUP GROUP, 1997, pp. 138–147.

[50] K. Schmidt and I. Wagner, "Ordering systems: coordinative practices and artefacts in architectural design and planning," Comput. Coop. Work, 13, 5, pp. 349–408, 2004.

[51] S. Bødker and P.-O. Zander, "Participation in design between public sector and local communities," in 7th C&T, 2015, pp. 49–58.

[52] I. Di Loreto and K. L. H. Ting, "Sense and sensibility: Designing a museum exhibition with visually impaired people," Interact. Des. Archit., 38, pp. 155–183, 2018.

[53] A. Beaulieu, “From co-location to co-presence: Shifts in the use of ethnography for the study of knowledge,” Soc. Stud. Sci., 40, 3, pp. 453-470, 2010.

[54] S. J. Jackson, S. B. Steinhardt, and A. Buyuktur, “Why CSCW needs science policy (and vice versa),” in CSCW’13, 2013, pp. 1113–1124.

[55] L. A. Suchman, Human-Machine Reconfiguration. Plans and Situated Actions, 2nd ed. Cambridge, UK: Cambridge University Press, 2007.

[56] L. Mathiassen and A. Sandberg, “How a professionally qualified doctoral student bridged the practice-research gap: A confessional account of Collaborative Practice Research,” Eur. J. Inf. Syst., 34, 3, pp. 695-726, 2013.

Smart Home Techniques for Young People with Functional Disabilities

Daniel Einarson
Department of Computer Science
Kristianstad University
Kristianstad, Sweden
e-mail: daniel.einarson@hkr.se

Marijana Teljega
Department of Computer Science
Kristianstad University
Kristianstad, Sweden
e-mail: marijana.teljega@hkr.se

***Abstract*—A purpose behind the United Nation's Agenda 2030 is that no one shall be left behind, which implies that support for vulnerable people shall be seen as clearly significant. In that context, assistive technologies serve purposes of improving disabled individuals' inclusiveness and overall well-being. This contribution covers ongoing experiments on techniques developed for Smart Homes, where the outcomes of such developments are targeted towards young people with functional disabilities, in order to provide them with independence in their own living space.**

Keywords - Smart Homes; IT-based support systems; Sustainable Development; Quality of Life; Assistive technologies.

I. INTRODUCTION

The expression 'leave no one behind' is a cornerstone of United Nation's (UN) Agenda 2030, so that even the most vulnerable people are guaranteed an acceptable level of quality of life. Matters of *leaving no one behind* are covered in a discussion paper of the United Nation Development Program (UNDP). Here, several key factors and the meaning behind those are discussed, such as *discrimination*, based on, for instance, *age, social class and disability* [1]. To be even more precise, the *disability* aspect is further elaborated on through several of the Agenda 2030's Sustainable Development Goals, their targets, and indicators [2]. Here, for instance, target 4.5 relates to appropriate access to education, 10.2 relates to reduced inequalities with respect to income, and 16.7 relates to societal inclusiveness, all with perspective in the situations of disabled people.

The Convention on the Rights of Persons with Disabilities (CRPD) is intended as an instrument to achieve human rights for disabled people concerning a multitude of aspects, such as, making their own free decisions in their lives and being active members of society. To meet that, the necessity of research on, and development of, assistive technologies, as well as the availability of those, is proclaimed [3]. Furthermore, through the program *Global Cooperation on Assistive Technology* [4], the World Health Organization (WHO) points out that not only is assistive technology a tool to ensure quality of life for disabled people, but also, such technology shall be a human right. In that context, Information Technology (IT), as an example of a technology, has a rather minor role in the context of sustainable development, and has been more seen as a complementary tool [5]. Still, IT has also been claimed to be a driving force in contexts of *quality of life* [6].

At the Department of Computer Science, Kristianstad University, Sweden, there have been ongoing experiments during several years, with specific focus on developing IT-based support systems for people with functional disabilities. Especially, focus has been on younger students at specific secondary schools, with support for an independent living for those students. Thus, the context of Smart Home-techniques has been especially emphasized, where the experiments have been conducted as research projects, as well as served as examples of project-based teaching and learning Computer Science courses material. At the core of the work stand the questions on how to develop techniques, and arrange techniques to support differently-abled persons in their daily living. This, in turn, should have consequences on grades of societal inclusiveness, as pointed out by high level actions, such as, UN's Agenda 2030, CRPD, and WHO's Global Cooperation on Assistive Technology.

This contribution will cover IT-based techniques experimented on prototype systems. Such systems and techniques especially address assistance in the daily living of young people with functional disabilities, and, thus, should contribute to the quality and the sustainability aspects of life for those people.

The contribution is outlined as follows: Section II will provide a description of the case, while Section III will discuss related work. Section IV will give a brief overview of the methods of use, and the results of the work will be presented in Section V, Section VI, Section VII, and Section VIII. Section IX will provide discussions on the work, and, finally, Section X will present conclusions and further work.

II. DESCRIPTION OF THE CASE

Riksgymnasiet is a secondary school in Sweden for students aged 16 to 19 years old who have different kinds of functional disabilities. Sweden has four such schools, where one of those is positioned in Kristianstad, in the very south of Sweden. The students may come from different parts in Sweden and have accommodations arranged close to the school.

In 2012, a study was performed by researchers at Computer Science, Kristianstad University (CS@HKR), at Riksgymnasiet at Kristianstad, with the purpose of investigating possible IT-based support systems to be used by students in their daily living at that school. In parallel with that study, a prototype system was developed, where the end users (i.e., students at Riksgymnasiet) were able to turn on and off the light of lamps from apps developed for smart phones in their rooms [7]. The studies showed that the end users (as well as support staff at Riksgymnasiet), were satisfied with the prototype system, and that they also had further desires from such a system. For instance, they wanted to have support for different kinds of practical activities that, at that time, needed a personal assistant's cooperation.

Among other things, researchers at CS@HKR observed that it was impossible for the students to pull down blinds, and put on fans by themselves to protect themselves from the sunshine and heat in their rooms. Furthermore, the air quality was questionable and could gain from being controlled. Such conclusions formed the basis for further investigations and technical development of a support system, in order to increase the degree of independence of the end users' accommodation. Apps, as well as other user units, should be developed to control devices in the homes. While several solutions exist today for Smart Home-techniques for use by the common public, it should be noticed that it is also especially important to regard the diversity of the end users' needs.

III. RELATED WORK

There exist several examples of academic approaches to Smart-Home systems for people in home settings (for instance, the *Home Aware Research Initiative* at Georgia Tech, [8], and Washington State University's initiative, *Integrative Training in Health-Assistive Smart Environments*, [9]). The work of this specific contribution is especially motivated by, on one hand, the possible applicability of the emerging flora of new techniques, and, on the other hand, by the end-users' need for participatory customization to meet a diversity of needs.

Today, there are several examples of commercialized Smart Home-systems for the common public, such as to control lamps and washing machines remotely through the use of apps. Often, those are not integrated as one in the same system, even though, for instance, *Apple* provides large scale solutions in that direction. Still, in contexts of diversity in disabilities, requirements of integrating off-the-shelf components with customized solutions may be hard to overcome.

The result of the Brundtland's commission [10] has provided a view on sustainable development that today is widely acknowledged. First, that view concerns not only environmental aspects, but also economic and social aspects. Second, as a temporal dimension, sustainable development concerns the sustainability of today, as well as of tomorrow (or, more precisely, meeting today's needs, without compromising the needs of tomorrow).

Seen from a sustainability perspective, commercial products certainly correspond well to economic aspects. Projects, as covered in this contribution, developed for Smart Homes to support people with specific needs, and, thus, in the context of assistive technologies, typically relate to social aspects of sustainable development. Research at CS@HKR indicates experiences from the development of several systems in the domain of eHealth to provide support for people with specific needs. Hence, investigations especially point out social aspects on sustainable development. Examples of these include:

- Internet of Things-based support systems for parents with Attention Deficit Hyperactivity Disorder (ADHD) and Autism [11], where prototype systems were developed, for instance, to remind the parents of things to carry with them when leaving their home, through tagging the things and matching that against a 'remember map'.
- Food supply systems for elderly people [12], where, among other things, a Smart Phone app was developed to filter in and filter out food choices of the day, based on e.g., nutrition aspects and allergies.
- Support systems for people with cognitive disorders [13]. Prototypes were developed to support children with a communication support for them to move freely outdoors.

Studies behind these examples have been performed on the bases of participatory action research [13], tested on potential end-users [12], and with careful investigations of the daily living of stakeholders [11]. However, the above examples are typically time-limited research projects, that is, with no sustainability in time and with a need for further follow up strategies.

It can clearly be seen that 'following up' needs to take place at several meetings for feedback-information from the end users. Especially, disabilities may also mean diversity and, therefore, a need for customizing solutions. The question of what matters to people is presented by Greenhalgh et al. [14] and, putting that work in the context of this contribution would mean that 'following up' would put focus on the needs of the end users as a driver for the technical solutions. In that context, the observation that *science of assisted living is still in its infancy* is especially interesting and certainly needs more attention.

Meurer et al. [5] take a conceptual approach to the sustainability of the design of IT-based projects for support for the continuing living for elderly at home. Here, among other things, sustainability relates to a temporal scale and the approach problematizes around the typical time limits that apply to research-related projects. In the context of [5], a sustainable development shall be seen on the basis of a multidimensional space, with aspects, such as, outcomes at *levels of individuals*, and implications at *levels of organizations*. Here, it is claimed that the effect of developing a research project tends to end when a project is over, and, thus, will not correspond to a sustainable development.

IV. METHODS

While early initiatives were taken to understand the living situation of the young students at Riksgymnasiet, later experiments were mainly done at the lab at CS@HKR. Here, development processes have typically been prototype-based, which is an efficient way of testing out ideas, reject ideas, and build new solutions upon previous successful experimentations.

V. SYSTEM DESCRIPTION

A system overview is captured by Figure 1, illustrating the main system architectural parts. The *User Controlled Units* correspond to the communication from end user's point of view (such as apps), while the *Home Devices* correspond to devices to be controlled (such as lamps). Communication flows wirelessly (typically based on techniques such as Bluetooth and Wi-Fi) through a server and a database with information regarding current user units and home devices.

Figure 1. Smart Home system overview.

In the sequel, user units, home devices, and the usability of those, will be described in more detail. Techniques have been experimented on, and developed by, researchers and by students at CS@HKR under the researchers' supervision.

VI. USER CONTROLLED UNITS

Different kinds of user units have been developed to be able to control the system, as outlined in Figure 2. The use of those will be further described in this section.

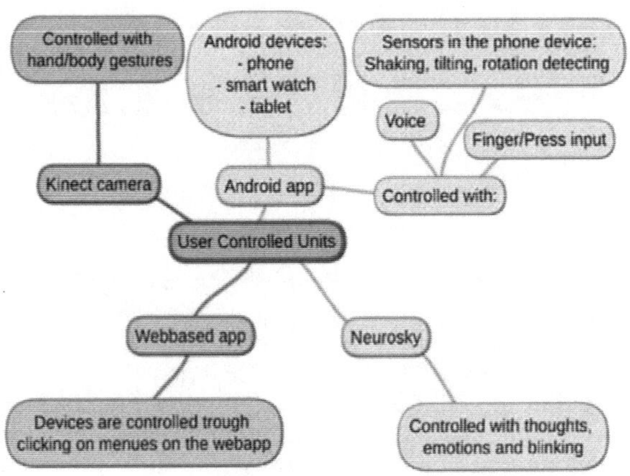

Figure 2. User Unit overview.

A. Smart Phone Apps

Apps for Smart Phones have been especially developed based on Google's Android platform. The apps have been developed to control Smart Home-devices through pushing buttons on common user interfaces, such as illustrated in Figure 3. Their use at Riksgymnasiet, as shown by experiments done there [7], was regarded as quite 'cool' by the end users. Still, even though the interaction form in itself is common today, the usability is a challenge that needs to be addressed. This concerns both the clarity of the details of the user interface as well as usefulness in cases of different grades of functional disabilities.

To open up for further possibilities, voice recognition has also been introduced. For instance, the spoken command '*Turn on the light*', implies an answer from the Smart Home, '*I heard you said turn on light*', followed by the light being turned on. Experiments like this have been performed in order to provide a variety of forms of communication, based on a diversity of needs. Yet, another example is based on the use of sensors of a Smart Phone when shaking and rotating it. The three-axials accelerometer of Android phones corresponds to a 3D space, to compute and form different commands.

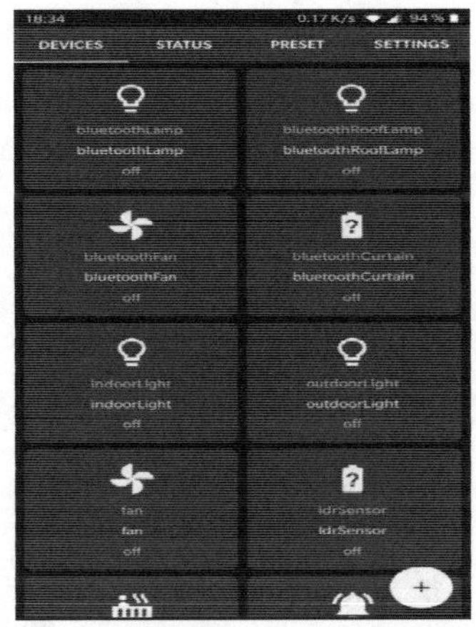

Figure 3. Smart Phone User Interface example.

B. Camera based interfaces for capturing gestures

Preliminary gesture languages have been developed where the gestures are captured by a Kinect camera [15] and interpreted through software especially developed to recognize the different language elements. Even though the Kinect camera originally was developed for computer gaming reasons, it can be used generally to notice movements in a 3D space, see Figure 4.

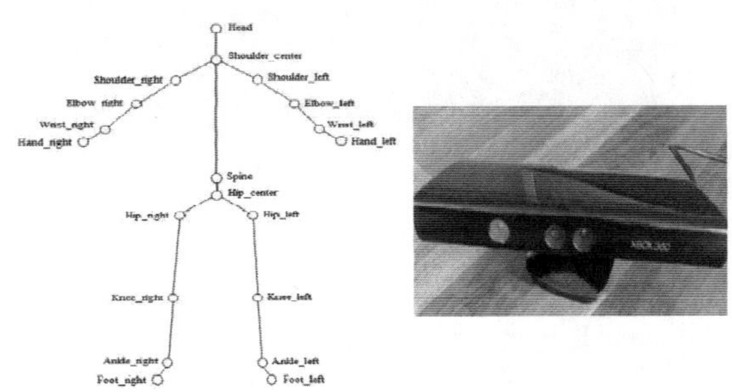

Figure 4. Detection of skeleton joints (skeleton picture from [16]).

Here, the camera has been used to notice simple up-down or left-right hand movements to control lights, fans, or a curtain. The technique records each joint on the body/skeleton to represent 3D coordinates *(x, y, z)*, which, then are further converted to commands. There are 20 joints for one person, can be used to interpret more complex gesture recognition commands [17].

The joint detection was done with the camera's depth image information. To map each one of them is a complex work, where each one is composed of 3D coordinates; for example, the right-hand 3D coordinates are: *(x1, y1, z1)*, *(x2, y2, z2)*, *(x3, y3, z3)*.

C. *The NeuroSky brainwave interface*

To meet even harder degrees of disabilities, experiments have been introduced with NeuroSky brainwave headsets, see Figure 5. The control of home devices is triggered by thoughts, emotions and blinking. One experiment was done with different combinations of specifically chosen thoughts to form commands that can be used to control the window curtain. The result was showing that a combination of two specific thought tasks could be used to form two commands with 97% accuracy performance, and that three specific thought tasks could form three commands with 92% accuracy performance [18].

Figure 5. The NeuroSky BrainWave Headset.

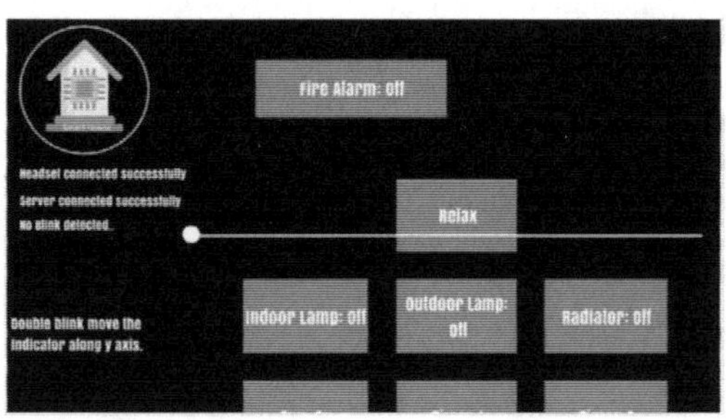

Figure 6. A NeuroSky controlled menu.

The experiment showed that the strongest two thought tasks are when a person is counting backwards, and the second one is when a person is imagining and focusing on the point between the ears in the head. It was suggested to continue with this experiment by using eye blinking to build several more commands.

Another experiment on the NeuroSky headset was the use of relaxing modes to move an indicator along the y-axis, which gets a user into a desired part of a menu. Well inside the menu, the user can choose to blink once to turn on or off the chosen device (for example the lamp) or blink twice to continue moving inside the menu, as illustrated in Figure 6, and exemplified by students at CS@HKR through a short video-clip [19].

D. *Web-based interface*

Although the previously presented user-side units of a possible Smart Home can provide good opportunities to control the home's devices, the information about the state of the home is rather limited. Through a web-based user interface, not only more detailed information is provided, but also additional practical possibilities to control Smart Home devices. Figure 7 illustrates that devices, such as lamps, fans, and blinds in several different rooms may be controlled from a web-based user interface. Furthermore, Figure 7 shows that additional information about, for example, air quality (temperature, humidity, carbon dioxide, etc.) can be summarized by a more complete interface.

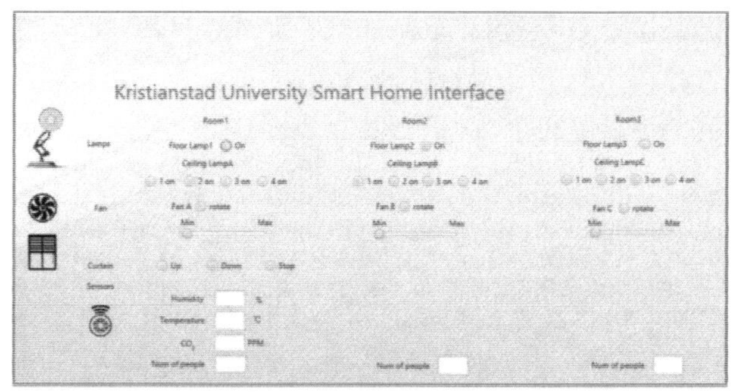

Figure 7. A web-based user interface.

The scale of a web-based user interface is not only beneficial for additional usability for an end-user (if this is useful to the user in terms of their capabilities), it also provides opportunities for supporting organizations to communicate with the Smart Home remotely. That is, a person with special needs can receive support remotely and, therefore, this can contribute to being independent of the physical presence of personal assistants. Such insights also indicate many additional opportunities in the development of IT-based support for Smart Homes.

VII. HOME DEVICES

While the previous section on user units mainly presented the 'left part' of the system, as outlined in Figure 1, the 'right part' corresponds to the devices of the Smart Home, that is, things to be observed or manipulated. For experimentation reasons, both for research and for examples in student projects, real as well as simulated devices have been used.

The actions of devices are mainly triggered through user commands, but, in some cases, activities are triggered by inbuilt intelligence. Examples on this include a fan that is turned on when the temperature exceeds a certain level.

A. *Real devices*

Real devices correspond to devices that may be used in common homes, see Figure 8. This includes, for instance, lamps or fans from IKEA (as is also the case in the experiments performed). Adapters have been used here to convert from high- to low level voltages. Furthermore, blinds have been fitted with a machinery to be able to be lifted up and down remotely.

At the endpoints of the devices (lamps, fans, etc.), microprocessors have been attached, which furthermore have been programmed to fulfill the specific tasks of controlling the devices (turning on, pulling down, etc.). The microprocessors, in turn, carry communication devices for remote communication based on, e.g., Bluetooth or Wi-Fi.

Figure 8. Examples on physical devices. Pictures from lab and from [20].

Furthermore, sensors have been used for detection of quality of air, based on humidity, temperature, and carbon dioxide. Moreover, sensors based on ultrasonic sound have been experimented on to catch the number of entrances and exits in and out of a room.

B. *Simulated devices*

For experimentation reasons, a small scaled model of a house has been used by students, as shown in Figure 9. From the point of view of techniques for a Smart Home, this house still has a wide range of functionalities that, in several cases, may be scaled up into real life contexts. Table 1 provides an overview of those.

Figure 9. A small scaled model of a house.

TABLE I. FUNCTIONALITIES IN A SMART HOME

	Functionality	***Description***
1	Automatic fire alarm	This signal is simulated with a switch
2	Housebreaking alarm	This input is realized by using a magnetic switch mounted at the house door
3	Water leakage alarm	This signal is simulated with a switch
4	Temperature indoors	This signal is realized using an analog temperature sensor mounted inside the house (on the first and the second floor
5	Temperature outdoors	This signal is realized using a digital temperature sensor mounted outside the house
6	Stove On	This signal is simulated with a switch on the front panel
7	Window open	This signal is simulated with a switch
8	2 Timers	This output signal is simulated with an LED lamp on the front panel
9	Lighting indoors	This function is realized with a lamp mounted inside the house
10	Lighting outdoors	This function is realized with a lamp mounted outside the house
11	Power cut	This input is realized by controlling the presence of supply voltage
12	Electricity consumption	This input is realized by measuring the supply voltage deliver to the house (an analog signal)
13	Twillight automatic system	This input is realized by Light-to-Voltage sensor (outdoors)
14	Fan	This function is realized with a fan mounted on the house's loft
15	Radiator	Four power resistors are connected in series to realize the heating of the house. The resistors are mounted in pairs, two at each long side wall

From Table 1, some functionalities are merely simulated by switches at a processor board (such as, *Window open*), while others have potentials to be connected to a prototype system. For instance, *Lighting indoors* may be manipulated through a smart phone-app, and *Temperature indoors*, may be used to trigger actions of *Fan*, and *Radiator*.

VIII. FURTHER INVESTIGATIONS

Several concepts have been experimented on, in addition to the above-mentioned techniques. Those increase the potential for a possible full-scaled development of Smart Home-support systems. Here, system development has typically been done through student projects, and student thesis work at CS@HKR. Examples include:

- Usability aspects of Smart Phone User Interfaces (UI). The UI not only have to be attractive in their shape, but, e.g., must also meet the complexities of a possible growing number of devices of a Smart Home.
- Scheduling Smart Home-functionalities, where events can be activated through time points set at, e.g., Google Calendar.
- Security aspects of Smart Homes, which, of course, constitute a fundamental matter to protect the individuals' integrity.

- Spatial awareness, that is, a system's awareness of where the users, as well as devices, are positioned in a Smart Home
- Simulations of devices, such as Media players, and Microwave ovens.

The core purpose of the techniques presented in this contribution has a focus on the independence of the living of the end users, that is, in our case, young people with different kinds of functional disabilities. Although the projects listed above and in previous sections show promising results so far, they need to be critically examined from several perspectives.

With a diversity of disabilities, supporting techniques certainly must be customized to suit specific needs. Moreover, the degrees of independence a system contributes with must be examined, based on a conceptualized framework. For instance, a fan may be controlled from a distance through an app and, therefore, provide a significant degree of value, while controlling a washing machine from an app may bring less value, since it still must be loaded with clothes. Here, concepts should relate to the degree of independence and the degree of external assistance that is still needed even with the support of the developed system.

IX. DISCUSSIONS

High level organizations, such as UN and WHO, have stated ambitions concerning especially vulnerable people, where it is pointed out that *no one shall be left behind*. Furthermore, actions such as *Agenda 2030* and *Global Cooperation on Assistive Technology*, addresses the situation of disabled people, where the quality of life of those people and their societal inclusiveness are especially emphasized.

As research and development organizations, academia certainly has a role to play here, where, on one hand, the situations and specific needs of the disabled people should be studied and concretized, and, on the other hand, solutions should be found and developed. Moreover, bridging a gap between need and solution can probably only be done through participatory research, that is, research where representatives of the end-users act cooperatively with researchers and developers, and only then.

This contribution has had a starting point in observations of the living situation of young students at Riksgymnasiet in Kristianstad, Sweden. The technical prototypes that have been developed from that starting point have yet only been executed in lab environments. Still, this has brought a level of maturity of the techniques and skills in handling those, which may contribute well to possible future participatory research projects.

Several examples on technical solutions have been tested out and put into contexts of complete Smart Home prototype systems. Different kinds of user-controlled units are used here to observe or manipulate different kinds of home devices. Even though prototypes may be stable at preliminary levels, putting those in real world contexts certainly will require several exhaustive test cases. Still, so far, the work seems to show clear potential in serving as an example of a useful assistive technology.

X. CONCLUSIONS AND FURTHER WORK

This contribution has presented experiments that have been ongoing over several years regarding the development of IT-based solutions to support people (especially young people) with functional disabilities in their housing, through technologies for Smart Home. User units for a variety of disabilities have been developed and prototyped together with devices related to Smart Homes. The state of the prototypes is mostly at the level of labs, that is, they need to be further tested out in contexts they are intended to be used, that is, the housings of disabled people.

In addition, the development of such prototype systems has been discussed in the context of sustainable development. This has partly been done with respect to Agenda 2030 and especially on a level of usefulness for the individuals. For the individuals, sustainability especially corresponds to how well the outcome of projects may work over time. Further work needs studies of the core technical aspects, as well as the usefulness of the end user-related aspects.

The covered techniques and the systems/subsystems need in many cases be further investigated for the sake of achieving a mature and trustworthy level. From a system perspective, several qualities must be especially studied, such as, robustness, performance, and security. Still, such qualities may solely relate to sustainability from a perspective of the system in itself.

For the sake of sustainability in use, an iterative process involving end users and support organizations for collaboration and participation must be further initiated. Initiatives for further collaboration between researchers at CS@HKR and the Riksgymnasiet have been taken, and a mutual interest in future collaborations has been shown. A form of such collaborations should also emphasize a conceptualization of grades of independence that technical support may provide. Solutions should be useful for purposes of independence in the daily living, not only motivated by the functionality of the technique itself.

ACKNOWLEDGMENT

Acknowledgments to the students and staff at Riksgymnasiet who were involved in and have contributed to the first studies behind this contribution. Also, many thanks to all the students over the years who have contributed with experiments and system development in project-based courses and thesis work in the study programs in Computer Science at Kristianstad University.

REFERENCES

[1] S. Renner, L. Bok, N. Igloi and N. Linou, "What does it mean to leave no one behind?" A UNDP discussion paper and framework for implementation, 2018.

[2] United Nations Statistics Division, "SDG Indicators" Availabe from: https://unstats.un.org/sdgs/metadata/ 2020.02.23.

[3] United Nations Convention on the Rights of Persons with Disabilities, "United Nations Convention on the Rights of Persons with Disabilities," 2006, Article available from: https://www.un.org/development/desa/disabilities/convention-on-the-rights-of-persons-with-disabilities.html 2020.02.23.

[4] Global Cooperation on Assistive Technology, “Disability and rehabilitation,”World Health Organization, Available from: https://www.who.int/disabilities/technology/gate/en/ 2020.02.23.

[5] J. Meurer, C. Müller, C. Simone, I. Wagner and V. Wulf, “Designing for Sustainability: Key Issues of ICT Projects for Ageing at Home”, Computer Supported Cooperative Work (CSCW), 27, pp. 495–537, 2018.

[6] D. Hornung, C. Müller, I. Shklovski, T. Jakobi and V. Wulf, “Navigating Relationships and Boundaries: Concerns around ICT-uptake for Elderly People”, Technology Use Challenges for Older Adults, CHI-2017, Denver USA, 2017.

[7] Z. Demant, “Interaktivt hus”, Bachelor Thesis in Computer Science, Kristianstad University (in Swedish), 2012.

[8] J. A. Kientz et al., “The Georgia Tech Aware Home”, Research Landscapes , CHI-2008, Florence, Italy, 2008.

[9] Washington State University, “Integrative Training in Health-Assistive Smart Environments”, Availabe from: http://igert.eecs.wsu.edu/index.html/ 2020.02.23.

[10] G. H. Brundtland, “Our Common Future: The World Commission on Environment and Development”. Oxford: Oxford University Press, 1987.

[11] D. Einarson, P. Sommarlund and F. Segerström, “IoT-Support Systems for Parents with ADHD and Autism”, International Conference on Computational Systems & Information Technology for sustainable Solution, csitss, 2016.

[12] D. Einarson and D. Saplacan, “The Active Ageing Approach to Quality of Life for Elderly People through Order and Distribution Chains”, International Conference on Computational Systems & Information Technology for sustainable Solution, csitss2016, 2016.

[13] D. Saplacan and D. Einarson, "A Participatory Action Research Approach to Developing Assistive Technologies for People Suffering from Cognitive Disorders," in Living Knowledge Conference, Copenhagen, 2014.

[14] T. Greenhalgh et al., “What matters to older people with assisted living needs? A phenomenological analysis of the use and non-use of telehealth and telecare”, Social Science & Medicine, 93, pp. 86-94, 2013.

[15] D. Levac, D. Espy, E. Fox, S Pradhan and J. E. Deutch, “"Kinect-ing" With Clinicians: A Knowledge Translation Resource to Support Decision Making About Video Game Use in Rehabilitation”, Innovative Technologies Special Series, Physical therapy, Volume 95, Number 3, pp. 426-440, 2015.

[16] A. Shingade and A. Ghotkar, “Animation of 3D Human Model Using Markerless Motion Capture Applied To Sports”, International Journal of Computer Graphics & Animation (IJCGA), Vol.4, No.1, pp. 27-39, 2014.

[17] L. Huynh et al. “Robust classification of human actions from 3D data”, 2012 IEEE International Symposium on Signal Processing and Information Technology, San Juan, PR, USA, pp. 263-268, 2012.

[18] M. Teljega, “Automatic control of a window blind using EEG signals”, Master thesis of Science in Computer Science with specialization in Embedded Systems, Kristianstad University, 2018.

[19] S. Dehghani, E Haol, A. Abdulal and N. Cunha, “The art of turning on the light with the power of the mind”, Kristianstad University News, in Swedish, Available from: https://www.hkr.se/nyheter/2020/konsten-att-tanda-en-lampa-med-tankens-kraft, 2020.02.23.

[20] The Application of PWM Capture (Data Acquisition) and Ultrasonic Sensors, Aimagin blog, Available from http://aimagin.com/blog/pwm-capture-data-acquisition-and-ultrasonic-sensor, 2020.03.25.

Exploring Engagement in Distributed Meetings during COVID-19 Lock-down

Fahad Said
Faculty of Computer Sciences
Østfold University College
Halden, Norway
Email: fahads@hiof.no

Klaudia Carcani
Faculty of Computer Sciences
Østfold University College
Halden, Norway
Email: klaudia.carcani@hiof.no

***Abstract*—Meetings are an important part of articulation work in cooperative groups. Thus, engagement in meetings influences cooperation. In the case of distributed cooperative meetings, engagement is influenced by the spatial distance among members. Building on the existing literature, we introduce a framework for analyzing engagement in distributed cooperative meetings and study the phenomenon specifically for the period of the nationwide lock-down due to COVID-19, where remote meetings were the only choice. We interviewed 11 professionals experiencing home office during the nationwide lockdown, documenting their experiences on engagement in distributed cooperative meetings, and conducted five participant observations in meetings with 8, 4, 6, 4, and 13 subjects as a direct investigation of engagement. Findings suggest that the use of social cues, meeting facilitator and personal interest are influential factors that regulate engagement in distributed meetings. The suggested framework has potential for detecting engagement, as we discuss the implications of our findings for digital meeting platforms. This paper contributes in the field of Computer supported cooperative work and Human Computer Interaction, with discussions and future research in how to detect, obtain, and sustain engagement in the context of cooperative work.**

Keywords–Engagement; CSCW; Digital Meeting Platforms; Distribued Cooperation Work; Distributed Meetings; Attention; COVID-19; HCI; Participation; Conversation roles.

I. INTRODUCTION

Meetings have become a standard arena to come together, discuss, and divide the labor for upcoming work in most workplaces, being those in organizations ranging from small to medium to large, or the public sector [1]. Until recent times, meetings have been associated with a physical location, where participants can coordinate and interact more fluently [2]. Due to the increase in Information and Communication Technologies, the perception of meetings has changed, as people participate in virtual meetings. Participation in virtual meetings is optimal when physical alternatives are exhausted [3].

"The need for group decision making has never been so important", as a single individual's perspective on their work is limited in isolation [4]. Due to a diverse specialization and demand for expertise, people are increasingly cooperating to achieve a common objective [5]. Despite the use of supportive technologies for cooperative work, meetings are the most popular and optimal way for group decision applications [6].

Recent developments in supporting meetings have worked exclusively on technologies that support access to meeting content to distributed participants. However, to the extent of our knowledge, there has been little research on technologies that support the activity of discussion and decision making in settings where participants in the meeting are involved in cooperative work, where they articulate, delegate, and coordinate tasks. We will refer to these meetings as cooperative meetings. Researchers within the field of Human-Computer Interaction (HCI) and Computer Supported Cooperative Work (CSCW) have been exploring strategies and tools to support group meetings through teleconferencing technology [7]–[10]. Engagement is deemed important in multi-party interactions as it operates as a key component and condition to assure that a participant is immersed and receptive to shared information [11]. Frank et al. [12] outlined engagement as a key factor for meeting success. Furthermore, one must understand what influences a user's engagement in meetings in order to operate cooperative sessions productively.

In the early months of 2020, multiple countries enforced nationwide shutdowns due to the ongoing COVID-19 pandemic, reducing physical interactions to a minimum. A significant number of workers around the world were immediately faced with technology as the only option to do work. Meetings are now operated using digital tools, such as Skype, Zoom, Microsoft teams, etc. Previously, these digital tools were considered to only be a secondary option. The co-located cooperative meetings were now moved into the digital realm, into what we define as distributed cooperative meetings. In this context, we do not include educational lectures, conferences, and informative meetings as they are not of direct relevance for our study.

Considering the immediate shift towards distributed cooperative meetings amid in the lock-down, and the relevance of engagement in these sessions, we investigate these research questions:

RQ1: What is influencing engagement in distributed cooperative meetings?

RQ2: How to enhance engagement in distributed cooperative meetings?

We have investigated engagement as a concept and how it has been defined in the relevant literature. Moreover, we have explored how previous research has discussed the factors that influence engagement in the context of physical and distributed meetings. Based on a critical reflection of the literature, we have conceptualized a two-dimensional framework of engagement in distributed cooperative work. Our data collection is based on 11 semi-structured interviews with professionals involved in cooperative work within different workplaces along with participant observations of five distributed cooperative meetings. The findings provide insight into engagement on two parallel dimensions. The first being on the interaction between humans in the cooperative space, and the second focuses on the interaction between the human and the digital platform that provides the distributed meeting, which affects engagement on the first level. The findings contribute to the fields of HCI and CSCW by discussing the elements of engagement that should be taken into consideration in the development of future technologies and research that can support distributed work. The research questions are aimed at distributed cooperative meetings as they are the only option for work for the time being, but they are also essential for organizations operating distributed cooperative work as part of an accelerated digital transformation.

The rest of the paper is structured as follows: In Section II, we review related work on the different perspectives of meetings and engagement. In Section III, we present a framework that will be used to analyze engagement in distributed cooperative work based on critical reflection from the previous section. In Section V, we present a qualitative evaluation from participant observations and interviews. This will lead to discussions about the effects of distributed meetings on one's engagement in Section VI, followed by implications for development with theoretical grounds in Section VII.

II. BACKGROUND

In this section, we present a review of the literature related to our main concepts. As CSCW is the field concerned with cooperative work, we initially present how meetings have been studied in CSCW. We then present engagement as a concept and how it has been discussed in HCI. Furthermore, we outline how engagement in meetings has been previously studied.

A. Meetings and CSCW

Meetings take an important part of our workdays. They are used to coordinate with colleagues with whom we cooperate toward common goals either in the same sites or when we are distributed in different sites [13]. Computer Supported Cooperative Work (CSCW) according to Bannon and Schmidt is the endeavor to understand the nature and characteristics of cooperative work, with the aim of designing technology. Interdependence is an important topic within CSCW as people engage in cooperative work when they are mutually dependent and are required to cooperate in order to get the work done [5].

In the context of cooperative work, a distributed group is characterised by work activity where members' work is not co-located with the support of technology [14]. Distributed cooperative work concerns the support of people's interdependence of work with others as they aim to complete tasks in meetings [7]. Thus, we define distributed cooperative work as group activity characterized by spatial and temporal distance, supported by CSCW technology. The style and specifications of said technology depend on the nature of the cooperation between members. According to Mills [15], space and time are dimensions within CSCW that a system should adapt to, as they are uncontrollable constraints for remote, cooperative work.

Previous studies claim that CSCW can save resources while improving interaction [16]. In a cooperative work setting, meetings can be used to distribute labor and discuss progress. We will refer to these meetings where all participants contribute to discuss and divide labor as cooperative meetings.

Joris et al. [17] argued that physical attendance in face-to-face meetings aids in reaching a shared understanding during distributed meetings. Related work suggests that human interactions depend on physical presence as a mode of communication. Hence, thousands of people worldwide travel for business daily [18]. However, during the lock-down, the normal way of doing cooperative work has been compromised. Topics that have been discussed previously in last-minute meetings with colleagues become an invitation for a distributed meeting, with digital meeting platforms that use rich media to provide representations of participants in a virtual room [19]. In addition to video calls, there are options to send messages and files, along with screen sharing, which has been outlined to be important in the context of content sharing [15]. Zoom has gained a rise in popularity at the time this study was conducted, due to its simplicity in configurations [19]. Figure 1 illustrates how the interface operates in a distributed cooperative meeting for two people.

Figure 1. Zoom as the digital meeting platform to illustrate the interface for distributed cooperative work.

Rodden and Blair [20] claimed that the majority of CSCW applications are fundamentally distributed, stressing the importance of assessing the support these systems provide [21]. Previous work also shows the use of group support systems to empower cooperation, whether it be in co-located [22] or distributed applications [23].

Finally, in our study, we have focused on investigating engagement and its relevance in distributed cooperative meetings, where we explore aspects of engagement that are relevant to get work done.

B. Engagement

Engagement is derived from social and cognitive psychology. Doherty and Doherty's [24] review of engagement encountered 102 definitions used in HCI. The most-cited definition of engagement is that of Sidner et al. [25]: *"By engagement, we mean the process by which two (or more) participants establish, maintain and end their perceived connection."*

This framing implicitly places the definition within the context of a conversation between at least two agents, where both parties involved in the engagement are active and receptive participants in a continuous, synchronous process with a clearly defined beginning and end. This is relevant in the context of meetings where the underlying context is that of a multi-party conversation. Cooperation within group meetings requires participants to interact with each other by participation, especially in the context of the workplace.

In the analysis of conversation, Goffman [26] defined different roles in face-to-face conversations: the participant who makes the utterance is labeled a speaker, and the listener is referred to as an addressee. Sidner et al.'s definition of engagement in this context implies that the speaker and the addressee are actively engaged in the conversation. Dobrian et al. [27] claim that engagement is a reflection of user involvement and interaction. This is also supported by Glas and Pelachaud [28] who argue that involvement and engagement are closely related. The more involved the user is, the stronger the interaction with other participants. Based on this, we can argue that a participant that takes the role as a speaker exhibits involvement and is therefore engaged.

Goffman introduces side participants, who are not addressed

by the speaker. Researchers have conceptualized a state of engagement without inheriting the role of the speaker or addressee, focusing on exhibiting attentive behavior in the conversation. While involvement in the context of engagement appeals to the speaker and addressee, passive participation in the conversation includes side participants as well. In cooperative work, a speaker would want to ensure that all participants are understanding the message directed towards an addressee [29]. Clark [30] emphasizes the importance of side participants as they shape how speakers and addressees act to one another. In order to achieve engagement for side participants, we look for factors that contribute to participation. Peters et al. [31] argues that selective attention is necessary to establish engagement, explaining further that the level of attention regulates the level of engagement, creating a lower threshold for involvement at a later point in the conversation. Turner [11] argues that engagement is the state in which one is immersed, accompanied by positive emotions. Findings from a study by O'Brien and Toms [32] show that participants lose their mental surroundings when concentrating in an activity, showing a form of engagement. Furthermore, personal interest, attention, control, motivation, and feedback are established attributes of engagement, which can lead to direct involvement at a later point [33]. These factors are suggested to establish a precedent for increased participation at a later point [34].

While we have presented engagement above in the context of a conversation, in the field of HCI, engagement has been discussed extensively on how users engage with the technology and the content provided to them. However, engagement has been addressed differently in HCI throughout the years, found mostly as "user engagement". Bouvier et al. [35] state that definitions of engagement are used broadly, and are dependent on context. This is also supported by Salam and Chetouani [36] as their findings suggest that the mental and/or emotional state of the user varies depending on the context of the interaction, meaning the definition of engagement varies as well. Within this field, engagement as a concept has multiple angles to consider as engagement has been defined in the context of the qualities of an interface [37], and as a state of captivation and immersion in social media [38]. In both cases, engagement has been interpreted as a state, where interest is captured, with control over an individual's attention, and keeping them in a state of immersion [39]. Doherty and Doherty [24] associate an engaged agent with commitment, intent, attention, immersion, and motivation. Meaning that engagement is not a state that occurs in isolation. Engaged agents that are labeled to be motivated are said to include reasons for action.

Engagement has also been studied in the context of gaming [40], education [41], [42], administration [43], creativity [44], and other applications using modern day technology [45].

C. Engagement in meetings (multiparty settings)

Related work has outlined that engagement can be boost using meeting structure accompanied by a facilitator. [46]. Sauer and Kauffeld [47] study suggested that meeting facilitators should ensure active interaction from all participants in the session. In addition, technology should be able to coordinate the interactions, by identifying the current speaker [48]. Frank et al.'s [12] study on engagement detection in meetings presented indicators of engagement using attributes, such as physical motions, facial expressions, and vocal responses.

Frank et al. associates disengagement with distractions and lack of attention [12]. Furthermore, the author presents a form of relaxed engagement with side participants, characterised by observant behavior, receptive to information shared without direct involvement. The study outlines apparent attributes of engagement, accompanied by a feeling of excitement and constant commitment to content. Furthermore, Frank et al.'s study outlined similar attributes of engagement to that of O'Brien and Toms [32].

Previous literature emphasized the importance of engagement in face-to-face settings. It is therefore essential to investigate elements that influence engagement in remote settings. Distributed meetings provide flexibility for participants in terms of saving resources and traveling time [49], and have been traditionally viewed as support for cooperation, in addition, these systems should be enabling when doing cooperative work [20]. The use of these systems has increased since their development as they save time and money, however, some researchers have focused on challenges and limitations to improve its usability in several applications [50] [51].

Mark et al. [51] considers engagement in addition to mental presence to be determining factors for remotely based teams to operate optimally.

Related work has highlighted the effects of the barriers and limitations of the technology used. For instance, poor audio quality(background noise, poor speakers) leads to disruptions in the flow of conversation [52]. It may also be challenging to know who is active in the room by just looking at the screen. Kuzminykh and Rintel's findings show that participants are attentive to social information such as facial expressions to confirm their engagement to what has been said, addressing also the challenges of finding them through a video feed [49]. Another underlying theme within studies concerning engagement in distributed engagement is trust. According to Jarvenpaa and Leidner [3], shared experiences and consistent social norms influence trust between group members in co-located settings. These are factors that are partially diminished in virtual meetings. The authors suggest that groups need to create norms and give feedback to invite interaction and reduce isolation.

Looking back at Kuzminykh and Rintel's study, lack of identifying non-verbal cues make it difficult to shift speakers naturally compared to a physical meeting, according to one of their interviewees, as they have to be addressed directly in remote meetings [49]. Based on their findings, Kuzminykh and Rintel argue that remote participation would contribute to a sense of engagement, as well as assessment to shared information by demonstrating purposeful attentive actions. Most participants in Mark et al.'s study relied on video feeds of their remote participants [2]. Cutler et al. suggests that technology must correctly visualize who is speaking and where they are located, so that meeting participants can get a sense of the current speaker [16].

Due to the freedom of using distributed systems, multitasking occurs in the current session. Multitasking has a significant impact in participating relationships in virtual as well as physical meetings [53]. It can enhance the meeting experience when it comes to distributed cooperative work, as it can provide benefits, such as effectiveness and efficacy [51]. However, this comes at the cost of participation, level of attention and thus, engagement [54].

Video feeds allow participants to express understanding by using gestures and nodding which do not disrupt the meeting, but rather enhance the experience. Isaacs and Tangs' findings show that in contrast to audio, video interactions make it easier for participants to come to an agreement [55].

In addition, their findings show that turn-taking is easier to do with video compared to audio. Sharing documents live in distributed systems seemed to strengthen coordination and direct attention to relevant discussion areas and to some degree, increase participation [2].

III. A FRAMEWORK TO ANALYZE ENGAGEMENT IN DISTRIBUTED COOPERATIVE WORK

Considering a lack of a definition for engagement and analysis of engagement in distributed work, we conducted a critical reflective analysis of the background literature presented above and propose a definition for engagement accompanied with a framework for analyzing engagement in distributed meetings.

We define engagement in distributed cooperative work as: *A process using technology as a medium where at least two parties involved are established as active and receptive participants in a continuous, synchronous process with a clearly defined beginning and end.*

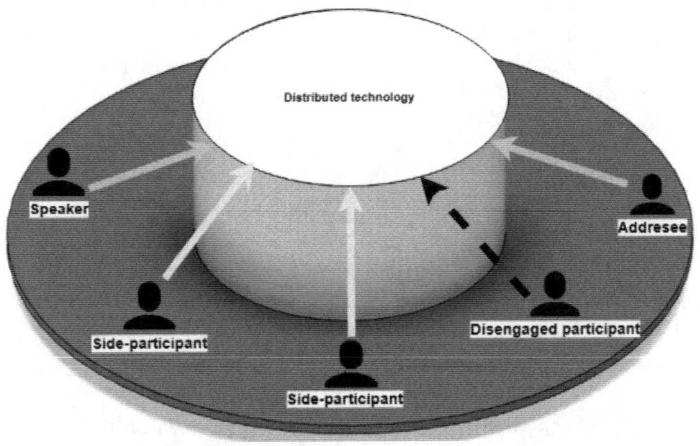

Figure 2. Illustration of the proposed engagement framework for analyzing engagement in distributed cooperative work

Figure 2 is an illustration of the framework for analyzing engagement in distributed cooperative work with the technology at the center of all interactions between participants. By active participants, we refer to participants that take the role of the speaker, who addresses participant(s) during a turn. Due to being addressed by the speaker, the addressee is active as well. Receptive agents operate as side participants, being immersed and attentive to the conversation between the speaker and the addressee(s). Furthermore, we adopt Frank et. al's [12] definition of relaxed engagement as passive engagement illustrated in figure 2 with yellow arrows from side participants. Involved engagement will be interpreted as direct engagement, illustrated by the green arrows which are exclusive to the speaker and addressee. A disengaged participant is illustrated with black dotted arrows as they are still be connected to the technology but not immersed in the meeting like the side participants. There are two dimensions within engagement in distributed cooperative work. Figure 2 is inspired by Goffman's [26] description of conversation roles, and illustrates the level of engagement between the user, their peers, and the technology. The first dimension is about the interaction between the participants themselves through the distributed system (green area), which is influenced by the content of the meeting, other participants' behavior, social norms, trust, and personal interest. The second dimension (white area) is about the influence of technology towards the user's engagement, which is influenced by factors such as video feed, microphone usage, and internet connection.

The speaker is initially engaged and will primarily use the digital meeting platform's inputs (web camera, microphone, or messages) as a medium to communicate with other users. The same applies when other functions within the system (written messages and screen sharing) are in use, regardless of context. A participant shows passive engagement by expressing non-verbal responses to the conversation (nodding, facial expression). On the other hand, one can be in a state of disengagement by late responses as a result of their mental absence or even possibly, technical disruptions.

IV. METHODOLOGY

This section begins with the process of how data was collected. The second part pertains to the analysis of the findings concerning to the research questions defined in section I.

A. Data Collection

Due to the exploratory nature of this study, we have taken a qualitative approach to investigate this matter during the nationwide lock-down for authenticity. We applied two data collection methods: semi-structured interviews and participant observations, which we will explain in detail below. Figure 3 summarizes the data collection process.

Method	Size	Description	Average time
Interview	11 participants	Semi-structed	18 minutes
Observation	Five sessions 4-8 participants	Participant Observation	2 hours

Figure 3. Summary of the data collection process using semi-structured interviews and participant observations.

Semi-structured interviews provide an in-depth understanding of exploratory topics [56]. We conducted 10 semi-structured interviews with professionals working in Norway and 1 interview with a subject working in the United States. All interviewees were working in national and global organizations and operated at a home office. The selection of the interviewees was made carefully to fit the target group of the research. We recruited interviewees through the personal contacts of both authors.

The interview guide we created was divided into main topics with a set of sub-questions and probes, with themes such as the frequency of cooperative sessions, nature of work, norms during meetings, the transition to operating cooperative work in remote settings, multitasking and it's implications on their engagement. In addition, we asked questions about the interviewee's experiences using digital meeting platforms and their level of involvement, and engagement from their peers as well as themselves. Furthermore, we asked interviewees about their use of multimedia extensions such as, video feed, screen sharing, and messages. Follow-up questions had been also planned to further investigate specific episodes. The structure of the interview was inspired by the theoretical ground above, investigating factors that influenced one's engagement in the two levels outlined from our suggested framework. During the interview, the first author adapted to the flow of the session based on the answers of the interviewee. We transcribed the interviews using verbatim transcription guidelines.

In order to capture the natural engagement of participants in distributed cooperative meetings, we used also participant observations as a second method for collecting data. Participants observations is a technique in which the researcher enters the research setting and is involved with her/his user group activities as well [57]. The first author took the participant role in the observation of five online meetings, the structure of which resembles distributed cooperative work sessions, where a group of co-workers had to coordinate activities within a shared project. The first author was an active meeting participant. As the first authors was the one involved in the observations, we have chosen to write about the application of this method in a personal matter. We find the personal perspective to be helpful in the reflections and analysis on how the method was applied and what impact it had on engagement in cooperative work meetings. Thus, when referring to the observations, we will use the auto-ethnographic storytelling first person "I", to report on the process. In the next subsection, where we present the process of analyzing raw data, we return to the analytical "we".

The sessions that I participated in were groups and teams that had recently had a transition to digital, remote meetings due to social distancing. All of the groups would normally have cooperative work in co-located environments. Participants in the meetings were familiar with each other as they had been working for almost one year, and had already established social norms, which had been translated to the digital realm. I kept handwritten notes during the meetings, which were expanded furthermore after each session. In addition, for each meeting I drew a schema of each participant and kept the notes for the engagement of each of the specific participants in the meeting. This was done in analogy with the theoretical framework presented above. I chose to use traditional note taking to collect data because participants commented that they would not feel as comfortable participating while being recorded. Furthermore, the recording would increase the awareness of being monitored, which could significantly alter the level of engagement that would normally be in natural sessions.

The number of participants I observed were respectively 8, 4, 6, 4, and 13. Since I was an established and familiar member of these groups, the people involved did not alter their threshold to participate in the sessions due to my presence. I took notes in instances where one participant assumed the role as the main speaker, as well as how the addressee was receiving information. I documented the behavior of side participants that were reacting to the dialogue between the main speaker and the addressee and also made note of the time between dialogue exchanges. When the response time was relatively high, I identified the reason to why a member of the meeting was absent. The same was applied to immersive dialogue between multiple participants. In some cases, I evaluated my own engagement when multitasking between data collection and the content of the meeting itself.

The participant's eye gaze and head movement as an addressee, speaker, and side participant when using live video feed was also documented. On the other hand, I documented participants that did not use video feed, focusing on their vocal responses and interaction with the chat platform. Participating in the meetings and observing the others behavior and their engagement was challenging but helped me in achieving a more realistic scenario and build a critical self-reflection of my own engagement along with the others in the meetings.

In summary, the two selected data collection methods complemented each other and gave us a wider overview of the issues we investigate in this paper. The results of the data collection and analysis will be presented in the next section.

B. Data Analysis

After collecting data from interviews and observations, we used open coding and grounded theory as our analysis method. Grounded theory allows researchers to systematically break down raw data and conceptualize theories from findings that can be interesting for discussion or future work [58]. In addition, the method is beneficial in generalizing findings and ensures credibility in the emerging theory [59].

As the study had two research questions, the first step was to review the notes the from observations along with the transcripts from the interviews by looking for similarities and relevance towards our theoretical background. This was done by remarking codes on data from our observations and expressions made by our interviewees that were deemed relevant. On our first iteration, we created 13 codes covering aspects within participation, levels of engagement, and the use of technology. Using our established understanding of raw data, we continued expanding our analysis by reviewing the results in multiple iterations, ending up with 26 codes. We created five categories addressing the first research question and four categories aimed towards the second one. Our categories were grouped through continuous analysis and reflection to themes which are further presented in our findings below.

V. FINDINGS

In this section, we present the findings in an attempt to address our research questions from Section I. Firstly, we cover elements that influence engagement in meetings among participants (RQ1). Then we present elements of technology that influence the engagement (RQ2). We end this section with a set of strategies to encourage engagement retrieved from the data collection in Section IV.

A. Elements that influence meeting engagement

Here we address our first research question by presenting factors that affect an individual's interaction with other participants, and how that can stimulate or disrupt their respective meeting engagement.

1) Personal interests: Eight interviewees express that the content of the meeting has an influence on their participation in the meeting with varying degrees. They state that they are invested in topics and discussions that concern them by answering direct questions or waiting for a mediator to address them personally. Findings also show that a comprehension of what is being discussed contributes to more involvement. A priority for the meeting facilitator is for the topics to be relevant for all participants, specifically remote settings. It was noted in all five observations that the speaker tends to address a participant by announcing their name first, in order to gain their attention.

For two interviewees, if the interactions of the session do not reflect their expectations in terms of context, then there would be less engagement as a result. Remote participation requires incentive, compared to physical meetings, where social factors and norms can almost force a contribution according to one interviewee, noting that eye contact is an incentive to engage. The observations correlate with this when two participants directed their gaze towards the screen as the current speaker focused on the camera lens.

2) Turn Taking: Findings from the interviews show that involvement occurs when members provide a signal to take the role as the next speaker. This is done by either communicating it to others visually or by using the meeting facilitator. The latter being used the most in our observations, which is also verified by one interviewee that implied the importance of a meeting facilitator as their group depended on one person to lead the conversation. This varies based on the size of participants in the session, which was the case for four interviewees. Having too many participants in the session decreases the threshold for involvement. Turn taking helps coordinate speaker roles, and guides the discussion towards a goal, which also avoids derailing away from the current topic that can be a potential cause for disengagement.

3) Structure in the meeting: Agendas, systems, and norms make it easier to participate in meetings. This has been the case in four observations as participants notified each other on the order of the agenda when others start to derail from the current topic. There is also a set of constraints in terms of time per topic. The importance of a facilitator that moderates the meeting by keeping control of these rules has been essential for members. As one interviewee explained, the mediator sets the scene for the meeting. According to two interviewees, the facilitator is the most engaged person in the meeting, furthermore, seven interviewees expressed that one to one communication in such arenas provides comfort in involvement. For all interviewees, it is normal to use a mute function to ensure that one participant can speak at a time without disruptions. One interviewee explains that using the chat function to signalize that you want to speak is an alternative. This was also confirmed in the observations, when one participant forgot to mute their microphone, three other participants sent a message in the common chat, instructing them to activate the mute function. The chat was also used for turn taking, as the participants were required to write their names to provide a signal to not just the facilitator, but the rest of the participants. Clarification on who is to be given the role as the speaker provides convenience to anyone who wants to speak at any given time. In addition, the session's duration has an impact as longer discussions can disrupt the focus if a conclusion is not met, which leads to loss of interest, withheld progress, and disengagement.

B. Technology factors influencing engagement

This part of the analysis focuses on the technical aspects of digital meetings that influence the engagement in meetings, addressing the second research question from Section I. We have identified the use of video, messaging, and compatibility between participants through the digital meeting platform as factors.

1) Visibility: Nine interviewees claimed that the use of the camera feed in their meetings enhances engagement operating as an indicator of their mental presence. Findings also show that a majority of interviewees would prefer a video feed of all participants in the meeting in order to participate more, as it helps regulate their tone, observe their reaction, and response to what is being said.

One can tell that a participant is less engaged using eye gaze to interpret the direction of where the focus is. A video presentation creates presence, ensures that that participant is present, and establishes an incentive to engage as all attention will be locked to the one who is speaking at the time as explained by one of our interviewees.

On the other hand, two interviewees argued that the use of video can be inconvenient as what is being recorded in the background can turn into distractions themselves. Partial use of the camera or the digital platform's inability to visualize all participants on one display can lead to uncertainty for some participants, which discourages them to express their thoughts. In our interviews, we discovered that taking turns using video simplifies the process and creates more transparency to the meeting compared to physical meetings.

It seems easier to read people and change the setting of the meeting based on their reactions. However, for some, it seems that there is still a limitation to the use of video as poor visuals restricts small reactions. Furthermore, depending on the platform being used, the display of the speaker is scaled to be larger so that it becomes the focus of the display for all participants, making it clear who always has control.

It can seem difficult to engage naturally when there is no video feed as one interviewee pointed out if they were to not use audio as a backup. A simple nod from the head, hand gestures, and even facial expressions helped some continue speaking. In three of our observations, we notice multiple participants using gestures with their thumbs to confirm the tasks they have been articulated. Four interviewees have experienced live sharing of files with others, explaining that it helps other members look at relevant content at the same time.

2) Communication between members: There are a variety of exchanges between members during a meeting. Everything from vocal responses to messages in the chat area on the same platform. Writing a message to participants while another member is speaking does not seem to disrupt the flow, but rather create room for positive responses. Six interviewees have experienced that writing a short message builds on a discussion and clarifies misunderstandings so that the debate is still relevant to the topic.

However, most interviewees present the chat function only as a supplement in these sessions, primarily for turn taking and troubleshooting. Images, GIFS, and illustrations invite interaction, even in lenient moments during group meetings. This was also the case in three of our observations.

Three interviewees feel that there are limitations to adequately expressing themselves due to the fear of not being understood. A lack of confirmation from other participants in larger meetings led to shorter and more concise sentences.

Disruption of the conversation due to a problem with the internet effects the organic flow of the conversation greatly for some interviewees and repeated incidents discourage participation, which leads to disengagement. As conversations become stunted, members deviate from what has been said and resolve to do other activities. This has been the case in two of our observations.

3) Trust: The freedom of being able to do other things during a meeting has been expressed by most interviewees in the form of multitasking. In some cases, participants and interviewees used programs such as Microsoft Word to take notes of what is being said, which can disengage one from active participation, while others have been on social media and other irrelevant websites after being disengaged.

The duration of being mentally absent creates uncertainty and distrust according to three interviewees. Remote members rely on each other to be attentive to the topic at hand, however, in distributed meetings, trust may decrease as one cannot be certain of what others are doing. Members do not know if the reactions from others are genuine, which can lead to constraints in engagement on their part. Being a listener appears to be a heavier responsibility for speakers in digital meetings, as they require confirmation to maintain their level of engagement.

C. Strategies to encourage engagement

This part of the analysis pertains to suggestions and strategies from participants based on experiences that contribute to enhancing and sustaining engagement in distributed meetings.

For most interviewees, being able to see all faces provides comfort and a lower threshold to participate in the meeting. In addition, the technology should minimize background noises or notify that one should be in a quiet location. Seven interviewees suggested that the digital platform should disable all notifications on the computer during the session. One interviewee suggested that the platform should show all participants on the same display, in order to encourage users to turn on their video feed. Indicating that some programs may not have this feature yet. Notifying participants of who is the next speaker can help enhance the flow in cooperative work. Technologies that enhance the conversation experience through virtual reality has also been suggested. One interviewee suggested measuring engagement from the meeting and provide oversight over which members need guidance or more encouragement after analyzing reports of retina graphs for instance.

Social norms in meetings can help reduce distrust among distributed groups. As mentioned earlier, a mediator can enhance engagement in meeting through constant interaction, good content, direct questions and turn taking. One interviewee created temporal constraints for tasks in an online session, informing them that one participant will present their work at random. Two interviewees suggested that the meeting duration could be shorter, which would give incentive to provide additional input and discourage derailing as there are constraints.

VI. DISCUSSION

In this section, we discuss our findings regarding elements that influence engagement in distributed cooperative meetings in relation to elements of engagement found in the literature.

Based on our findings, indicators of engagement from our suggested framework have an influence on the cooperative nature of meeting participants. Speakers show commitment to being involved as they become the center of the meeting. Most participants are engaged in the meeting when the topic concerns them personally. Personal interest, feedback, and motivation operate as incentives for engagement. This is compatible with the attributes of engagement outlined by O'Brien and Toms [32] and thus serve as mechanisms for the facilitator to sustain engagement with side participants. While the relationship between the meeting participant's involvement and engagement is not conclusive, Glas and Pelachaud argue that the concept of these two to be closely related [28]. Meeting participants inhabit direct engagement through involvement when initiating an utterance. Based on this reflection, involvement is an indicator of engagement in the context of meetings. In addition, speakers are sharing their resources with the rest of the group, which promotes productivity.

In our observations, side participants exhibit passive engagement using non-verbal cues from their video feed, which verifies Liu et al.'s [29] view on participation. This form of remote participation leads to engagement, which is compatible with Kuzminykh and Rintel's [49] findings on attentive actions in video meetings. We see that head nodding and non-verbal, reactive responses from the video feed foreshadow involvement, confirming Isaacs and Tang's claim on video interactions [55].

We find that there is a higher threshold for involvement when there are multiple parties in the digital room, specifically when there are challenges acquiring reactive information as a speaker. Furthermore, some groups that prefer to only use audio and chat over video, that still maintain a certain level of presence in the meeting, partially contradicting Tang and Isaacs's study [55].

The implications of being disengaged due to multitasking support the results from Lyons and Kim's study, implying that multitasking has a negative impact on engagement [53]. Another indicator of disengagement is the lack of visibility from video feed. Participants that do not use video lack the social presence required to interact with others, creating barriers for reaching shared understanding. Most attendants that used audio could not demonstrate engagement unless they were addressed by the facilitator. Op den Akker et al.'s [52] study emphasizes the need for feedback from participants in order to coordinate turn taking and topic management, two characteristics of meeting structure which have an impact on a participant's level of engagement in meetings [60].

We found that the facilitator has an influential role in prompting attendants in the meeting. This coincides to the recommendations and strategies for meeting facilitators to engage participants from Sauer and Kauffeld's study [47]. Four observations illustrated that the meeting facilitator was the one coordinating the meeting. One session in our observations show that there was no clear meeting facilitator, however, there were only four participants using video and established routines for turn taking. This may indicate that the need for a facilitator is dependent on the size of participants, however, this could also be due to the level of trust and social relationships between participants.

In our findings, interviewees expressed the need for feedback on their contribution from other participants. Jarvenpaa and Leidner's perception of shared experiences in this context indicates that social norms play an important role in enhancing engagement [3]. However, turn-taking norms in the meetings accompanied by a focused view of the current speaker as suggested by Bohus and Horvitz [48] and Cutler et al. [16] complies with the required meeting structure in disturbed meetings, which encourages participation. Based on this, we argue that if facilitators did not institute strategies of turn taking, then it would be difficult for them to control the floor [55].

The findings highlight conflicting opinions of participants deviating from the meeting platform due to multitasking. Some participants use other applications due to loss of interest in the meeting, while others have other tasks they would want to complete while attending the meeting. Mark et al.'s findings are closely related when it comes to these perspectives [51]. Lyon and Kim's results correlate with our observations, as the participants that seemed to be mentally absent were looking downwards, away from the screen. [53].

The findings indicate that distractions caused by audio problems disrupt the flow in the conversation, leading to frustration and a loss of engagement. Our observations confirm this as participants were less active after a series of audio problems occurred. This is listed as one common problem that people experience in Yankelovich et al.'s [50] study of telepresence. However, it seems that such problems can be solved relatively quickly by other participants who use the messaging function for troubleshooting.

A. Implications for engagement in distributed meetings

Our study presents a set of elements that can influence engagement in distributed cooperative work. Moreover, we presented a framework, based on extensive theory for investigating engagement in distributed cooperative work. The findings and suggestions contribute as implications for developing future technology that aim to facilitate distributed cooperative meetings.

One implication for development is finding methods to conceptualize the context of the current speaker along with the topic. Ørebæk et al.'s [10] study developed a prototype that enhances the context of the current topic of the meeting with temporal constraints. This can appeal to a predictable and sustainable structure for those who need a sense of context to maintain engagement. Furthermore, there is potential for augmenting the meeting platforms by regulating turn-taking in an interactive matter.

Digital tools should also address multitasking, by handling notifications outside of the meeting. Alternatively, a facilitator can implement methods that allow groups to do work while maintaining the interdependence of cooperation. To the extent of our knowledge, there is a functionality within digital meeting platforms that creates breakout rooms. Using these rooms, the meeting participants are separated from each other, with the intention of returning to the meeting after a duration and thereafter continue doing cooperative work where they can provide feedback. We suggest that CSCW tools support meeting facilitators in order to keep track of when participants can work on their tasks during the session.

A study by Ståhl [61] explored experiences of VR(Virtual Reality) in project meetings. To the extent of our knowledge, there is no clear relationship between virtual reality and engagement. However, based on our findings, we see a need to visualize expressions so that speakers can adjust the dialogue to maintain engagement.

As for interaction between participants, trust between remote participants can contribute to an increase in participation, and thus engagement. Szewc [62] suggests that managers should maintain frequent contact with members. Our findings on the facilitators' role in cooperative work support this.

VII. CONCLUSION AND FUTURE WORK

In this paper, we investigated the concept of engagement in the distributed cooperative work setting. We introduced a thorough review of the literature on engagement and engagement in meetings, followed by a proposed framework for analyzing engagement in distributed meetings. The framework was used later in gathering empirical data. From the findings, we can state that the framework is promising and can contribute as a conceptual ground for studying engagement in cooperative meetings. Moreover, the framework for investigating engagement in distributed meetings shows potential for adjusting today's digital meeting platforms. Engagement in meetings is an important factor for groups to be able to do cooperative work in a productive matter, especially when there are no alternatives during the lock-down. The list of factors that influence engagement in distributed cooperative meetings can be used to design future technology that can support these specific meetings, contributing in this way both in HCI and CSCW.

The aim was not to exhaust the issue of engagement in distributed cooperative meetings, but rather open discussions into developing and assessing digital meeting platforms that address the relevant issues within distributed cooperative work. The number of interviews and the observations can be considered as a limitation, but was adjusted due to the situation. In addition, it would be beneficial to explore engagement based on the nature of the meeting. Thus, in the future, we plan to investigate more on this issue and possibly observe a group meeting in both co-located and remote settings and comparing how engagement elements might differ in this setting.

REFERENCES

[1] C. M. Fox and J. H. Brockmyer, "The Development of the Game Engagement Questionnaire: A Measure of Engagement in Video Game Playing: Response to Reviews," Interacting with Computers, vol. 25, no. 4, Jul. 2013, pp. 290–293, publisher: Oxford Academic.

[2] G. Mark, J. Grudin, and S. E. Poltrock, "Meeting at the desktop: An empirical study of virtually collocated teams," in ECSCW'99, 1999, pp. 159–178.

[3] S. L. Jarvenpaa and D. E. Leidner, "Communication and trust in global virtual teams," Journal of computer-mediated communication, vol. 3, no. 4, 1998, p. JCMC346.

[4] E. McFadzean and A. O'Loughlin, "Five strategies for improving group effectiveness," Strategic Change, vol. 9, no. 2, 2000, pp. 103–114.

[5] K. Schmidt and K. Schmidt, "Riding a Tiger, or Computer-Supported Cooperative Work (1991)," in Cooperative Work and Coordinative Practices. London: Springer London, 2008, pp. 31–44, series Title: Computer Supported Cooperative Work.

[6] S. Rogelberg, J. Allen, L. Shanock, C. Scott, and M. Shuffler, "Employee satisfaction with meetings: A contemporary facet of job satisfaction," Human Resource Management, vol. 49, Mar. 2010, pp. 149–172.

[7] K. Schmidt, "Taking cscw seriously: Supporting articulation work (1992)," in Cooperative Work and Coordinative Practices. Springer, 2008, pp. 45–71.

[8] T. Robertson, J. Li, K. O'Hara, and S. Hansen, "Collaboration Within Different Settings: A Study of Co-located and Distributed Multidisciplinary Medical Team Meetings," Computer Supported Cooperative Work (CSCW), vol. 19, no. 5, Oct. 2010, pp. 483–513.

[9] I. Rae, G. Venolia, J. C. Tang, and D. Molnar, "A Framework for Understanding and Designing Telepresence," in Proceedings of the 18th ACM Conference on Computer Supported Cooperative Work & Social Computing - CSCW '15. Vancouver, BC, Canada: ACM Press, 2015, pp. 1552–1566.

[10] O.-E. Ørebæk, D. Aarlien, F. F. Said, K. Andreassen, and K. Carcani, "BEACON: A CSCW Tool for Enhancing Co-Located Meetings Through Temporal and Activity Awareness," Mar. 2020, pp. 243–250.

[11] P. Turner, "The anatomy of engagement," in Proceedings of the 28th Annual European Conference on Cognitive Ergonomics - ECCE '10. Delft, Netherlands: ACM Press, 2010, p. 59.

[12] M. Frank, G. Tofighi, H. Gu, and R. Fruchter, "Engagement detection in meetings," arXiv preprint arXiv:1608.08711, 2016.

[13] S. Kauffeld and N. Lehmann-Willenbrock, "Meetings Matter: Effects of Team Meetings on Team and Organizational Success," Small Group Research, vol. 43, no. 2, Apr. 2012, pp. 130–158, publisher: SAGE Publications Inc.

[14] G. Mark, "Conventions and Commitments in Distributed CSCW Groups," Computer Supported Cooperative Work (CSCW), vol. 11, no. 3-4, Sep. 2002, pp. 349–387.

[15] K. L. Mills, "Computer-supported cooperative work," in Encyclopedia of Library and Information Sciences (2nd Edition). Marcel Dekker, 2003, pp. 666–677.

[16] R. Cutler et al., "Distributed meetings: A meeting capture and broadcasting system," in Proceedings of the tenth ACM international conference on Multimedia, 2002, pp. 503–512.

[17] J. de Rooij, R. Verburg, E. Andriessen, and D. den Hartog, "Barriers for shared understanding in virtual teams: A leader perspective," The Electronic Journal for Virtual Organizations and Networks, vol. 9, 2007, pp. 64–77.

[18] P. L. Mokhtarian and I. Salomon, "Emerging travel patterns: Do telecommunications make a difference," In perpetual motion: Travel behaviour research opportunities and application challenges, 2002, pp. 143–182.

[19] M. Mohanty and W. Yaqub, "Towards seamless authentication for zoom-based online teaching and meeting," 2020.

[20] T. Rodden and G. Blair, "CSCW and Distributed Systems: The Problem of Control," in Proceedings of the Second European Conference on

Computer-Supported Cooperative Work ECSCW '91. Dordrecht: Springer Netherlands, 1991, pp. 49–64.

[21] T. Rodden and G. S. Blair, "Distributed systems support for computer supported cooperative work," Computer Communications, vol. 15, no. 8, 1992, pp. 527–538.

[22] J. Lee, "Sibyl: a tool for managing group decision rationale. proceedings of the conference on computer supported cooperative work, (cscw 90)," ACM, New York, 1990, p. 28.

[23] C. Heath and P. Luff, "Collaborative activity and technological design: Task coordination in london underground control rooms," in Proceedings of the Second European Conference on Computer-Supported Cooperative Work ECSCW'91, 1991, pp. 65–80.

[24] K. Doherty and G. Doherty, "Engagement in HCI: Conception, Theory and Measurement," ACM Computing Surveys, vol. 51, no. 5, Jan. 2019, pp. 1–39.

[25] C. L. Sidner, C. Lee, C. Kidd, N. Lesh, and C. Rich, "Explorations in engagement for humans and robots," Artificial Intelligence, volume 166, issues 1-2, August 2005, pp. 140-164, 2005.

[26] E. Goffman, Forms of Talk. University of Pennsylvania Press, 1981.

[27] F. Dobrian et al., "Understanding the impact of video quality on user engagement," ACM SIGCOMM Computer Communication Review, vol. 41, no. 4, 2011, pp. 362–373.

[28] N. Glas and C. Pelachaud, "Definitions of Engagement in Human-Agent Interaction," in International Workshop on Engagment in Human Computer Interaction, Xi'an, China, Sep. 2015, pp. 944–949.

[29] P.-J. Liu, J. M. Laffey, and K. R. Cox, "Operationalization of technology use and cooperation in CSCW," in Proceedings of the ACM 2008 conference on Computer supported cooperative work - CSCW '08. San Diego, CA, USA: ACM Press, 2008, p. 505.

[30] H. H. Clark, Using language. Cambridge university press, 1996.

[31] C. Peters, G. Castellano, and S. de Freitas, "An exploration of user engagement in HCI," in Proceedings of the International Workshop on Affective-Aware Virtual Agents and Social Robots - '09. Boston, Massachusetts: ACM Press, 2009, pp. 1–3.

[32] H. L. O'Brien and E. G. Toms, "The development and evaluation of a survey to measure user engagement," vol. 61, no. 1. Wiley Online Library, 2010, pp. 50–69.

[33] H. L. O'Brien, P. Cairns, and M. Hall, "A practical approach to measuring user engagement with the refined user engagement scale (UES) and new UES short form," International Journal of Human-Computer Studies, vol. 112, Apr. 2018, pp. 28–39.

[34] C. Peters, S. Asteriadis, K. Karpouzis, and E. de Sevin, "Towards a real-time gaze-based shared attention for a virtual agent," in Workshop on Affective Interaction in Natural Environments, ACM International Conference on Multimodal Interfaces (ICMI'08), 2008, pp. 574–580.

[35] P. Bouvier, E. Lavoué, and K. Sehaba, "Defining Engagement and Characterizing Engaged-Behaviors in Digital Gaming," Simulation & Gaming, vol. 45, no. 4-5, Aug. 2014, pp. 491–507, publisher: SAGE Publications Inc.

[36] H. Salam and M. Chetouani, "A multi-level context-based modeling of engagement in human-robot interaction," in 2015 11th IEEE international conference and workshops on automatic face and gesture recognition (FG), vol. 3. IEEE, 2015, pp. 1–6.

[37] W. Quesenbery and W. I. Design, "Dimensions of usability: Defining the conversation, driving the process," in UPA 2003 Conference, 2003, pp. 23–27.

[38] A. Jaimes, M. Lalmas, and Y. Volkovich, "First international workshop on social media engagement (some 2011)," in ACM SIGIR Forum, vol. 45, no. 1. ACM New York, NY, USA, 2011, pp. 56–62.

[39] M. Chen, B. E. Kolko, E. Cuddihy, and E. Medina, "Modeling but NOT measuring engagement in computer games," in Proceedings of the 7th international conference on Games + Learning + Society Conference, ser. GLS'11. Madison, Wisconsin: ETC Press, Jun. 2011, pp. 55–63.

[40] E. A. Boyle, T. M. Connolly, T. Hainey, and J. M. Boyle, "Engagement in digital entertainment games: A systematic review," Computers in Human Behavior, vol. 28, no. 3, May 2012, pp. 771–780.

[41] C. Beer, K. Clark, and D. Jones, "Online student engagement," 2010, pp. 75–86.

[42] B. De Carolis, F. D'Errico, N. Macchiarulo, and G. Palestra, "Engaged Faces: Measuring and Monitoring Student Engagement from Face and Gaze Behavior," ser. WI '19 Companion. Thessaloniki, Greece: Association for Computing Machinery, Oct. 2019, pp. 80–85.

[43] D. L. Strom, K. L. Sears, and K. M. Kelly, "Work engagement: The roles of organizational justice and leadership style in predicting engagement among employees," Journal of leadership & organizational studies, vol. 21, no. 1, 2014, pp. 71–82.

[44] N. Bryan-Kinns and F. Hamilton, "Identifying mutual engagement," Behaviour & Information Technology, vol. 31, no. 2, 2012, pp. 101–125.

[45] H. A. Voorveld, G. van Noort, D. G. Muntinga, and F. Bronner, "Engagement with social media and social media advertising: The differentiating role of platform type," Journal of advertising, vol. 47, no. 1, 2018, pp. 38–54.

[46] N. Lehmann-Willenbrock, S. G. Rogelberg, J. A. Allen, and J. E. Kello, "The critical importance of meetings to leader and organizational success," Organizational Dynamics, vol. 47, no. 1, Jan. 2018, pp. 32–36.

[47] N. C. Sauer and S. Kauffeld, "The Structure of Interaction at Meetings: A Social Network Analysis," Zeitschrift für Arbeits- und Organisationspsychologie A&O, vol. 60, no. 1, Jan. 2016, pp. 33–49.

[48] D. Bohus and E. Horvitz, "Dialog in the open world: platform and applications," in Proceedings of the 2009 international conference on Multimodal interfaces, ser. ICMI-MLMI '09. Cambridge, Massachusetts, USA: Association for Computing Machinery, Nov. 2009, pp. 31–38.

[49] A. Kuzminykh and S. Rintel, "Classification of Functional Attention in Video Meetings," in Proceedings of the 2020 CHI Conference on Human Factors in Computing Systems. Honolulu HI USA: ACM, Apr. 2020, pp. 1–13.

[50] N. Yankelovich, W. Walker, P. Roberts, M. Wessler, J. Kaplan, and J. Provino, "Meeting central: making distributed meetings more effective," in Proceedings of the 2004 ACM conference on Computer supported cooperative work - CSCW '04. Chicago, Illinois, USA: ACM Press, 2004, p. 419.

[51] G. Mark, S. Poltrock, and J. Grudin, "Virtually collocated teams in the workplace," in CHI'00 Extended Abstracts on Human Factors in Computing Systems, 2000, pp. 370–370.

[52] R. op den Akker, D. Hofs, H. Hondorp, H. op den Akker, J. Zwiers, and A. Nijholt, "Supporting engagement and floor control in hybrid meetings," in Cross-Modal Analysis of Speech, Gestures, Gaze and Facial Expressions. Springer, 2009, pp. 276–290.

[53] K. Lyons, H. Kim, and S. Nevo, "Paying attention in meetings: Multitasking in virtual worlds," in First Symposium on the Personal Web, Co-located with CASCON, vol. 2005, 2010, p. 7.

[54] K. K. Stephens and J. Davis, "The Social Influences on Electronic Multitasking in Organizational Meetings," Management Communication Quarterly, vol. 23, no. 1, Aug. 2009, pp. 63–83, publisher: SAGE Publications Inc.

[55] E. A. Isaacs and J. C. Tang, "What video can and cannot do for collaboration: a case study," Multimedia systems, vol. 2, no. 2, 1994, pp. 63–73.

[56] B. L. Leech, "Asking questions: Techniques for semistructured interviews," PS: Political science and politics, vol. 35, no. 4, 2002, pp. 665–668.

[57] B. B. Kawulich, "Participant observation as a data collection method," in Forum qualitative sozialforschung/forum: Qualitative social research, vol. 6, no. 2, 2005.

[58] B. G. Glaser, A. L. Strauss, and E. Strutzel, "The discovery of grounded theory; strategies for qualitative research," Nursing research, vol. 17, no. 4, 1968, p. 364.

[59] M. El Hussein, S. Hirst, and V. Salyers, "Using Grounded Theory as a Method of Inquiry: Advantages and Disadvantages," The Qualitative Report, vol. 19, Jan. 2014, pp. 1–15.

[60] N. Lehmann-Willenbrock, J. A. Allen, and D. Belyeu, "Our love/hate relationship with meetings: Relating good and bad meeting behaviors to meeting outcomes, engagement, and exhaustion," Management Research Review, vol. 39, no. 10, Jan. 2016, pp. 1293–1312, publisher: Emerald Group Publishing Limited.

[61] O. Ståhl, "Meetings for real—experiences from a series of VR-based project meetings," in Proceedings of the ACM symposium on Virtual reality software and technology - VRST '99. London, United Kingdom: ACM Press, 1999, pp. 164–165.

[62] J. Szewc, "Selected Success Factors of Virtual Teams: Literature Review and Suggestions for Future Research," International Journal of Management and Economics, vol. 38, no. 1, Oct. 2014, pp. 67–83.

An Analysis of Independent Living Elderly's Views on Robots

A Descriptive Study from the Norwegian Context

Diana Saplacan, Jo Herstad, Zada Pajalic*
Department of Informatics, University of Oslo;
*Faculty of Health Studies, VID Specialized University;
Oslo, Norway
e-mail: {diana.saplacan; jo.herstad}@ifi.uio.no; {Zada.Pajalic}@vid.no;

Abstract—**This study illustrates the independent living elderly's (≥65 years) views on robots. The data was documented through audio recordings of interviews, photos, and written logs. The analysis was done through qualitative manifest and latent content analysis. The results of the analysis were sorted into three categories: aging during the technological renaissance, domestic robots, and the elderly's expectations of robots. The overall resulted theme was: integrating robots in the elderly's everyday life. The results were discussed through the lenses of the Sense-of-Coherence (SOC) theoretical construct and its belonging elements: *comprehensibility*, *manageability*, and *meaningfulness*. The relevance of this paper contributes to giving an understanding of the domestic robots' requirements specifications and the elderly's expectation of human-robot interaction.**

Keywords-robot; comprehensibility; manageability; meaningfulness; healthy aging; independent living elderly; Norway; Sense-of-Coherence (SOC) theory; salutogenesis; elderly; human-robot interaction, domestic robots.

I. INTRODUCTION

We were interested in this study to investigate how robots are seen by the independent living elderly, before integrating the robots in their homes. Specifically, the study aimed to illustrate the elderly's (≥65 years) views on robots. The research question addressed in this study was: what is the elderly's understanding of robots, and how can these be better integrated into their daily lives?

Studies show that western countries face an increase in individuals' lifespan, and this, in turn, puts pressure on the healthcare systems [1]. Non-digital personal health records have been earlier widely used [2]. However, lately, the elderly prefer to live independently in their homes. To support the elderly's independent living, various welfare technologies have been used. In the past years, robots for supporting independent living got special attention [3][4]. In general, most of the elderly have a hard time accepting and learning new modern technologies. At the same time, earlier research shows that the elderly are not interested in devices designed especially for their age group [5]. However, modern technologies often let the elderly feeling they cannot keep up with those; their design does not always suit the elderly. For instance, a study from the U.K. talked about the mismatch between the technologies and services that are available for supporting the elderly's needs and their real needs [6]. The authors mean that, for designing and providing better technologies, we first need to understand in-depth the elderly's needs [6].

Further, Koelen et al. [7] say that in the next couple of years, it will be not only vital aging in place, i.e., aging in the home of choice, but also "healthy aging." According to Eriksson [8], every individual, even those considered healthy, might have moments when they feel ill. Furthermore, there are still uncertainties about how robots could accommodate aging in place since these technologies are still in development. Moreover, we are still not sure how these technologies could be better integrated into the elderly's homes since they already have a hard time accepting the existing technologies.

The rest of the paper is structured as follows. This section continues by giving a background on this study. Section II presents the theoretical construct of Sense-of-Coherence (SOC) and its elements of *comprehensibility, manageability,* and *meaningfulness.* Section III presents our data collection and analysis methods, the setting of the study, and the participants. Section IV presents our findings. Section V continues with a discussion by using the theoretical construct and its elements presented earlier in Section II. Section VI presents the conclusion. Acknowledgments close the paper.

A. *Background*

This study is part of the Multimodal-Elderly Care Systems (MECS) project. MECS aims to develop knowledge around a caring safety robot alarm for the elderly. The elderly are defined as old adults (≥ 65 years), according to gerontology [9][10]. The insights gotten during this study are intended to contribute to the design of the MECS safety alarm robot. However, before going further, we want to define the concepts of a *robot* as a welfare technology.

Welfare is defined as something *doing* or *being* well [11]. Within the Nordic countries, The Nordic Welfare Center describes the notion of *welfare technology* as technology either compensating due to a disability or supporting it [12]. This definition of welfare technologies includes: "assistive devices, consumer goods, home adaptation solutions, educational equipment, tools" [12]. Among such examples, there are games consoles used for rehabilitation and physical therapy, mobile care systems, smart home environments, and automation solutions, robot vacuum cleaners, and safety alarms connected to a healthcare system. Amongst these technologies, a safety alarm robot can be considered as a welfare technology of the future. A *robot* is defined as a programmable machine that can conduct a complex set of actions on its own [13][14]. The term was coined from the Czech "robota" in the '20s and had the meaning of "forced labor" [13]. Robots are similar to other types of modern technologies, wearables, or personal devices. Besides, this type of welfare technology also has the *motion element* which is needed to be taken into consideration [15].

We have seen that the digitalization of care services for the elderly can be done with wearable sensors and through self-monitoring devices, or personal safety alarms. While body sensor networks are considered intrusive and often not readily accepted, users would instead opt for self-monitoring devices [16]. These include ambient intelligence techniques [17], such as wearables, or mobile devices, as shown in Chiauzzi et al., Petersen et al., and Laidlaw et al. [18]–[20]. Besides, personal alarms are usually used in the form of bracelets or pendant alarms. For instance, almost 20% of the total safety alarm installations used in the U.K. were necklace alarms [6]. Very few of these or other devices were actively used by the elderly [6]. However, these types of alarms can be effective in detecting falls among the elderly, if these are used effectively [21]. It seems like the elderly use of this type of assistive living technologies is often done in wrong ways, such as pressing the button of a pendant alarm when feeling lonely instead of when needing medical help [6]. These types of devices also are often not used when showering, while most of the falls amongst the elderly happen while they shower.

Moreover, these types of devices are not afforded by some of the users, whereas for some, other alternatives should be considered when personal devices are likely to be misused, or not used at all [21]. One alternative is the use of robots, through "connected and secure assistive robots ecosystems" [22]. However, introducing robots in the homes of the elderly requires scrutiny, both of the user and the current use of modern technologies, of the *home* context, and of the technology itself. Previous studies show that a few robots for the independent living elderly are available on the market, whereas the use of robots in homes has excellent potential and could prolong independent living [23][24].

Furthermore, Norway, a welfare state, has its healthcare system partially subsidized by the government [25]. For instance, elderly people that are over 90 years old and may live in nursing homes cost the state around 800 000 Norwegian crowns (NOK) per year (ca 84 000 euros, or 98 000 US dollars) per individual [25]. However, only half of the elderly wish to live in such nursing homes, while some choose to stay in their own homes, and others wish to move in accommodation facilities for the elderly [25]. Furthermore, according to Ramm [26], at the start of 2013, 13% of Norway's population was 65 years old or older, whereas, by 2050, this percentage is forecasted to increase to 21%.

In addition, a similar study of quantitative nature was performed in Norway. The study was based on 1000 phone survey interviews lasting, on average, about 13-14 minutes each [28]. The focus of the research was mainly on the use of Information Communication Technologies (ICT's) and did not include any questions regarding robots [28]. Helsevakta (eng. Health Watch, HW) is another example of a project that was created for investigating the challenges that are met in healthcare [29]. The study was performed in Trondheim, Norway showing so far that the Norwegian healthcare system was not prepared for the upcoming demographic challenges, such as an increasing number of the elderly [29]. Extensive empirical qualitative studies on integrating robots in the homes of the independent living elderly, from the Norwegian context, have not so far been identified.

II. THEORETICAL LENSES

We chose to discuss our findings through the theoretical lenses of Aaron Antonovsky's work [30]. The theoretical construct was chosen to discuss the findings. Antonovsly was a sociologist that challenged the pathologic view on healthcare, focusing on salutogenesis [29][30]. Salutogenesis is viewed as a health promoter [32]. His theoretical model is based on the Sense-of-coherence (SOC) of an individual. He defined it as:

> "a global orientation that expresses the extent to which one has a pervasive, enduring though dynamic feeling of confidence that (1) the stimuli, deriving from one's internal and external environments in the course of living are structured, predictable and explicable; (2) the resources are available to one to meet the demands posed by these stimuli; and (3) these demands are challenges, worthy of investment and engagement" (Antonovsky, 1987, p. 19 in Super et al. [33]).

The theoretical construct includes three elements: *comprehensibility*, *manageability*, and *meaningfulness*. *Comprehensibility,* as an element of SOC, is illustrated as the motivation behind the challenge of coping with the situation at hand. *Manageability* is depicted as the availability of resources to cope with the situation, whereas *meaningfulness* is represented as understanding the challenge [30]. The theoretical construct, however, was developed to reflect on how one can deal with life stressors [33]. We borrowed these concepts for this study since robots are seen as assistive technologies for independent and healthy living. We argue that having such lenses when designing and integrating these technologies in the elderly's home, could be beneficial for reflecting over the process of understanding their views on technologies. The concepts are also beneficial to understand the acceptance of modern technologies by the elderly.

There are a few studies that have the same salutogenic perspective on health using Aaron Antonovky's theory. According to [32], studies based on this theoretical construct seem to be quantitative, and just a few qualitative ones are available. Some similar studies are from Lahttiranta et al. [34][35]. Another similar study is from Svaneus [36], where the author takes the approach towards health as "homelike being-in-the-world." The author also asserts that this perspective on modern technologies can be made visible through *medical technologies* [36] – in our case, the robots used in the homes of independent living elderly. We argue that it is essential to make visible the salutogenic approach inbuild in a safety alarm robot for the elderly. Moreover, yet again, the question we ask is: how do they understand the concept of a robot, in order to better integrate it into their daily lives?

III. Method

The present study had a qualitative inductive research design. Next, we present the study context, participants, and data collection.

A. *Study context*

The study was performed in the southern-east part of Norway, in the area of Oslo. Norway has a population of approximately 5.2 million inhabitants [37], where the elderly represent about 14.6% of this number [38]. In Oslo, the capital area, live about 660 000 inhabitants. This study has been performed in a subarea of the old Oslo district area. The district has a total population of roughly 53 000, out of which nearly 3000 are senior citizens over 67 years old. Some of these citizens have home-care; some live in the nursery cares, whereas some live in accommodation facilities for the independently living elderly. The accommodation facilities usually include apartments that can be rented individually by the elderly, or together with their partner. The facilities also include a reception available 24/7, where at least two personnel staff are available at all times. The facilities also include a gym, a restaurant available for non-residents, an open area where various social events are taking place, and a library. The building is equipped with various sensors: WiFi, light and heating sensors, motion sensors, but also tablets installed in each of the apartments. The residents can use computer tablets, for instance, for seeing the menu available at the restaurant in the building, ordering food, or navigating the Internet. Similar studies have been performed in such accommodation facilities, but none of them involving robots [39]–[44].

B. *Participants*

The participants in this study were recruited through an accommodation facility, which has 91 apartments. Ninety (90) residents were living as of April 2017. Fifty-two (52) of them were females, with an average age of 84, and 38 males, with an average age of 80. The residents were spending at the time, on average, around 577 days, in the accommodation facility – according to an internal document.

Sixteen participants participated in three group interviews and one pilot interview. Four researchers involved in this project (two senior researchers and two junior researchers, including the authors SD, HJ) had a meeting with the two management representatives at our partner organization, before the first two group interviews. We documented the meeting through a log report, followed by a visit of the junior researchers (including author SD) at the elderly's facilities, and a presentation about the project held for the elderly and the employees (including the authors SD, HJ). Some of the elderly signed up for the group interviews at the presentation, whereas others joined during the presentation itself. The participants were self-selected, i.e., entered the study based on voluntary choice. For the third group interview, the elderly were informed approximately one month before the activity, and they participated, this time as well, voluntarily. The third group interview was part of a half-day workshop. Two of the participants taking part in the first group interviews also took part in the third group interview.

The participants' background was mixed: they have worked in the public sector (library, university, military, other public authorities), arts and handcraft, and industry (including office work that requires the use of computers, but also factory work). All were over 67 years old, with ages ranging up to 90 years old. Some of the participants used walkers and some wheelchairs. During the interviews, they explained that several of them experienced balance problems, and they sometimes fall. Three hundred five (305) falls were reported amongst all the facility's residents between 2015-2017. Other health-related issues pointed out were: impaired or weak vision and hearing and memory loss. Table I below gives an overview of the participants and their background experience with computers.

TABLE I. Overview Participants.

#	Gender (Female F, male M)	Age	Comment on the participants' work experience (Not available N/A)
1	F	>65	Public sector
2	F	84	Arts and Craft
3	M	81	Arts and Craft
4	M	>65	Worked with computers.
5	F	94	Private- and public sector. Worked with computers.
6	F	>65	Public sector
7	F	90	Private sector
8	F	>65	N/A
9	F	>65	She worked previously in the private sector.
10	M	>65	N/A
11	M	>65	N/A
12	M	>65	N/A
13	F	89	Public sector.
14	M	>65	Public sector.
15	M	>65	Public sector.
16	F	90	Public sector. She had experience with computers before.

C. *Data collection*

Our primary data gathering method was group interviews. A research interview aims to develop an understanding of the investigated phenomena surrounding the persons and situations in their contexts and social reality [45]. All three group interviews were semi-structured. All the interviews included some demographic questions, where the participants were asked to share, based on free will, their name, age, and background. Moreover, the interviews contained questions regarding the participants' familiarity with digital technology, including smartphones, computers, and robots. The author (SD) has also participated in multiple meetings, one public discussion, together with the author (HJ). Further, we give details on group interviews one and two, a pilot interview that took place after the first two group interviews, and a third group interview. The pilot interview and the third group interview was based on the findings first two group interviews. Some photos from the group interviews are illustrated in Figure 1.

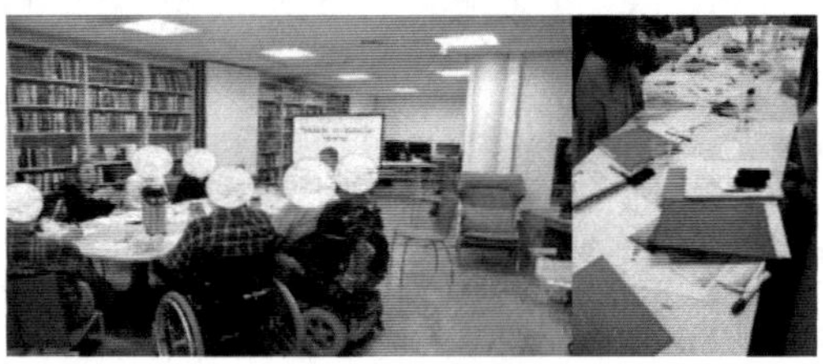

Figure 1. Sample photos from group interviews 1 and 3.

All the details regarding the group interviews and the pilot interview are available in Table II below.

TABLE II. OVERVIEW OF THE DATA COLLECTION.

Group interview #	Number of participants and their gender	Time for data collection	Type and duration of data collected
1	5 females, 2 males	Spring 2017	Interview 60 minutes, Photos
2	2 female 3 males	Spring 2017	Interview 60 minutes, Photos
1 Individual Pilot	1 female	Spring 2017	Interview 60 minutes, Photos
3 (part of a half-day workshop)	1female 2 males	Spring 2017	Interview 45 minutes, Photos
Total	16 participants (9 Female and 7 Males)		

D. *Analysis*

The textual data was fully transcribed. The author (SD) has listened to the audio recording and written logs for the two parallel-group interviews, and the pilot interview, immediately after those took place, to help her remember better the context. She also took unstructured notes during the first and third group interview. After listening through the transcriptions, the authors have discussed their understanding of the data, making the analysis more reliable. The data was transcribed verbatim and was coded through open-coding. The authors have later decided to leave the data for a while before coming back to it. At this stage, both conscious and unconscious reflection took place. After a few months of an incubation stage, we have chosen to analyze the data by using qualitative manifest and latent content analysis [46]. The analysis was performed through the following steps: first, the whole transcripts were read through several times to get a sense of the content. The next step was decontextualization of text with the identification of meaning units. We identified in total (n= 132) meaning units. The next step was condensation and coding of meaning units (n = 13). The systematic grouping of codes to sub-categories and categories, with reflective discussions with the aim of the study as the base, was performed together by authors (SD, PZ). The analyzing process towards the formation of categories was the result of manifest content analysis. The latent analysis started with the reading of the transcript again and trying to capture what text was talking about. The result of the final step was the theme "Integrating robots and welfare technology in the elderly's everyday life." The process between the group interviews is shown in Figure 2.

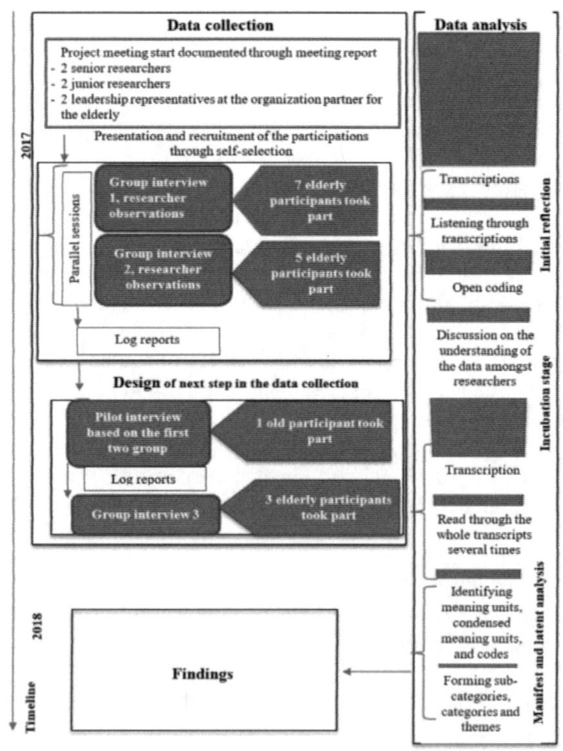

Figure 2. Overview of the process.

E. Ethical considerations

The project was conducted accordingly to the ethical guidelines from the Norwegian Center for Research Data (NSD) Ref. Nr: 50689). This work was performed on the Services for Sensitive Data (TSD) facilities, owned by the University of Oslo, Norway, operated and developed by the TSD service group at the University of Oslo, IT-Department (USIT). The participants were self-selected. The participants were given detailed information about the study, and they could withdraw at any time without giving any explanation and without any consequences for them. All the participants willing to participate signed informed consent before taking part in the study.

IV. FINDINGS

A. Integrating welfare technology in the everyday life of the elderly

The overall theme of this study that emerged is: "*Integrating welfare technology in the elderly's everyday life.*". The theme comprises the elderly's daily experiences with personal devices (smartphones, computers) and modern technologies used in homes (sensors in a smart home, semi-autonomous robots). In general, the use of personal devices by the elderly would be minimal and limited to their needs, such as using internet banking, for checking the account balance. Some of the participants did not own a smartphone, and some even a mobile phone, *but* a fixed home phone. Only a few of the participants owned both a smartphone and a tablet. These participants were also those who were highly interested in the use of modern technologies and to influence rules or policies, at some level. They were often engaged in other types of organizations for the elderly. Although some of them were highly engaged with this type of personal devices, the majority had limited knowledge about the use of robots in homes. The general impression was that they could not follow up with the fast development of technologies. In general, they felt left out, as one participant expressed it: *"for me, it goes too fast... for me, it goes too fast... I cannot keep up with it.. unfortunately"*.

The findings also showed that, besides the fast technological advancements, the elderly need to keep up with, the authorities need to develop legislation accordingly, at the same pace, in order to have a functioning and inclusive society. They viewed this as especially important when trying to introduce domestic robots in their homes. Detailed results are presented descriptively, as follows.

B. Aging during the technological renaissance

We started by asking the participants to talk about their relationship to the use of modern technology (e.g., computers, tablets, and smartphones) in their homes. The majority of the participants answered that they use modern technologies for checking their bank account balance – internet banking was a common motivation for using computers. Regarding the autonomous technology used in homes, they would recognize this type of electronic technology from the building they were living in, as it has light and motion detection sensors.

The majority would describe their interactions as being limited to computers for writing emails and checking the account balance, TV, phone (home phone, mobile phone, smartphone), and printers. However, one of the participants expressed a high interest in "*everything new.*" This participant also used more advanced terms that their peers did not know about, such as *cloud computing* and *bitcoin*. Bitcoin, for instance, had to be explained by one of the female participants to others as "*valuta in the cloud.*" The same participant confessed that she uses modern technology for solving crosswords, sending emails, search on Google, and using Facebook.

Regarding the price of modern technologies, such as robots, the elderly found those expensive. Hence, they did not recognize themselves as being the *right* target-group/consumer group. They were also reluctant to robots that are big due to taking too much space in their apartments, usually consisting of a small living room integrated with an open kitchen, a small bedroom, and a bathroom. Robots were viewed by them in general as inferior, subordinates to people, as one participant says: "he is *just* a robot." Specifically, companion robots, such as an AIBO robot, were not interesting enough for the participants, as they were "*nothing to cuddle with,*" as one participant described it. They rated robots from a cost-benefit perspective, always seeking a *practical perspective/benefit*. However, they admitted that such a robot could decrease some of the feelings of loneliness. The participants agreed that a companion robot could supply some daily dialogical interaction-when they do not have anyone else to talk to.

Four of the participants (two males and two females) pointed out that they cannot follow and keep up with the fast development of modern technology, feeling surpassed. They expressed feelings of hopelessness, exclusion, and technological illiteracy, as one of them pointed out:

> *"I feel like I am in another world, you know.. I do not know so much about these things we discuss now... and this has to do with the [world] we grew up within... a different one, yes. What I mean is that we start getting so old, that there is so much surpassing us. We are not able to keep up the pace. However, the authorities do not take this into account."*

In general, they felt anxious about dealing with modern technologies, due to *fear of doing something wrong,* or *failure.* This, despite the majority that was willing to learn about modern technologies. In this sense, they mentioned that having an own pre-understanding and familiarity towards those (e.g., having used modern technologies before), and a *clear objective of the use*, as one points out: *"When I should learn something new, I am asking – what's the point?"*, is imperative. They also specified that they often rely on help from their family members (children and grandchildren). However, to trust a robot, they mentioned that they need to have some control over it. They suggested that this could be done through, for instance, control via voice recognition. One female participant pointed out that such a safety alarm robot would make her feel safe in situations where they do not have the safety alarm wristband on them, such as when using the shower. The robot should also have *predictable* ways of moving in order to feel safe around it.

C. *Domestics robots*

At the start of the discussions, the participants did not know "*what a robot is*" and said that they had seen robots only on TV. However, immediately after starting the conversation about the robots, they were wondering if an autonomous vacuum cleaner or a lawnmower is counted as robots. They found this type of home appliances, so-called *domestic robots*, more familiar for them, and could place them in their understanding. However, some of them were familiar with industrial robots: robots that are used in factories and robots used in hospitals.

Their description of the robots used in homes fitted under the description of *assistive* and *servant robots*, as a female participant points out, about what a robot should do:

"*To fix the TV when it gets stuck. Or the computer when something went wrong. It would have been nice to have such a robot for this*". Another participant explained: *"The robots have to have a practical aim. I think many feel ill and do not have the energy to bring food from downstairs... This could be something a robot could do."*

When we showed pictures of various robots, we also showed pictures of *companion* robots. It was clear that the elderly sought some practical attributions of the robots, and they were less interested in safety alarm robots. The majority of the participants agreed that the robots need to have some practical function for them to use those. Only one participant brought attention to the implications of introducing such a robot in their homes, such as potentially reducing their physical activity. Regarding the appearance of a robot versus the functionality, it was a difference between the female and male participants: whereas for the female participants, the robot appearance was necessary, for the male participants were not. However, both female and male participants agreed that functionality is more important than appearance.

Among the functionalities of the *domestic robots*, they named that they would like to have semi-autonomous robots (e.g., servant robots, assistive robots) that help them clean or wash the floor. To be able to interact with the robot via voice recognition, and specifically being able to interact in Norwegian, were essential for the participants. Physical interaction, such as having a stop button, was also vital to them. The feedback received from the robots should be, according to them, auditive, visible, and visual, as they have learned from their interaction with the industrial robots, i.e., signalizing with red and green blinking lamps.

Besides these types of functionalities, robot navigation within the elderly's homes has also been discussed. The participants found problematic the robot-human encounter, especially if they had to move with the help of a walker, or a wheelchair. They were also concerned about the obstacles they had in their homes, such as furniture. Some of the participants compared the behavior of a robot when navigating inside the home, with the driving of a car – the robot should behave in a similar fashion when encountering humans.

D. *The elderly's expectations of the legislation and regulations around robots*

The participants pointed out some expectations regarding the well-functioning of laws and regulations in practice. For instance, one female participant gave an example where the laws and regulations at a national level do not always match on an organizational level. She ended: "*It is not ready... the laws are not ready yet.. for these.. which is quite advanced.*". The same participant, in a later interview, says that, although the laws and regulations are not fully developed, *they* still have to *adapt* to the use of modern technology, because "*the authorities do not allow resignation.*" In addition to their perceived control regarding laws and regulations, the participants also expressed the need for having *autonomy* over the robot itself.

Although the focus of the MECS project is around developing a safety alarm robot, for the majority of the participants, it seemed important that the robot would help them with physical activities in homes.

V. DISCUSSION

Integrating robots in the homes of the elderly should be done gradually, where the acceptance of these technologies is taken into consideration. Studies support this idea, saying that these types of technologies cannot be introduced only when the elderly need extensive care [47]. Moreover, domestic robots, such as care robots, should not be introduced in the home of the elderly, solely to reduce society's care burden with the aging of the population, as shown by [48]. However, integrating robots in their homes means that these technologies also need to be comprehensible, manageable, and meaningful, for the elderly. We base further our discussion on the SOC from Aaron Antonovsky earlier described (Section 2).

A. *Comprehensibility and manageability of robots in the homes of the elderly*

This study shows that the majority of the participants used modern technology for simple everyday tasks, such as checking the bank account balance. However, not many of them felt that they were skilled enough to using these technologies. This indicates that the elderly do have limited *comprehensibility* of these technologies. They were familiar mostly with robots used in the industry.

Moreover, they were unsure if an autonomous vacuum cleaner or a lawnmower are also robots. This indicates their limited understanding (comprehensibility) of domestic robots. They also considered using in-motion technologies, such as robots, only if this type of technology had a practical benefit. This indicates that they sought some manageability in those.

A study showed that people are afraid of interacting with technology that they do not understand [49]. While the participants mentioned the importance of using their natural language in the interaction with robots, Sciutti et al. [49] emphasize the importance of mutual understanding: not only concerning language, but the robots should consider the people around them. In literature, robots are being portrayed as agential actors with emotions and autonomy [50]. If we strictly refer to a robot, a robot is autonomous through, for instance, independently moving around. In this case, the additional element to be considered and understood by the elderly is the motion element. This adds to the complexity of the manageability of a robot. After all, a care robot, an in-motion technology, would be a new element in the elderly's homes that will move around. Facilitations and adjustments of the home, to adapt the robot would probably need to be made. This is nevertheless a question of autonomy: of the person him- or herself, and the technology. In the case of in-motion technologies, such as robots, the elderly may loose from his-/her autonomy if they cannot master the robot.

Further, the participants also indicated that they could not keep up with the technological advancements, as they often were afraid of doing something wrong when they interact with it. To be able to interact independently with such systems, they suggested being able to interact with the robots via voice recognition. Moreover, they specifically suggested that this should be available in their mother tongue, Norwegian. This indicates that such systems should be manageable by them, in their mother tongue (manageability). At the same time, studies recommend that it should be of high priority to make scalable care systems that support voice recognition [1]. They recommend systems that are socially aware, but at the same time, that do not need the user to interact with the system continuously [1].

Moreover, another study showed that the robots used in hospitals were expected to be able to talk [51]. However, even advanced build-in ways of interactions, such as talking, may still not lead to the acceptance of a robot [51]. Based on the findings presented in this study, we consider that this point is also valid for robots used for supporting the elderly's independent living in their own homes.

Further, introducing new emerging technology for health monitoring in the home may change the relationship amongst people interacting with them [1]. This type of system may have implications beyond the intended use [1]. For the elderly to feel well, it also needs to be considered the broader context of use, including the need for social connectivity [52]. The need for voice interaction could be one aspect of social exchange. However, as one study shows, people may tolerate robots in different ways, depending on the context [51]. Robots, for instance, used in hospitals in different settings, were viewed as: "an alien, a hospital worker, a colleague, a machine, or a mixture of these" [51].

In the same way, this is confirmed by the current study: a robot that would be able to talk might be easier understood by the elderly. However, being able to interact with the robots through voice does not guarantee that domestic robots will be accepted. Although they may be manageable by the elderly, it does not mean that it also will be meaningful for them. However, for integrating these types of technologies, it is not enough to be comprehensible and manageable. These also need to be meaningful.

B. *Meaningfulness in the robots for the elderly*

"When I should learn something new, I am asking – what is the point?" asked one of the participants. Besides finding the welfare technologies and robots *useful* for their health monitoring, the elderly also need to find them *meaningful*. Older adults need to be motivated and get enough time to learn how to use new digital tools [53]. Further, the elderly seem to dislike devices that are "off-putting," i.e., reminding them of medical instruments and monitoring instead of feeling personal and appropriate for their dis-/un-ability (Lehoux et al. in Procter et al. [6]). We have also seen that technologies can support aging in place, through monitoring [52]. However, this solution is somehow limited: monitoring is supporting in the first place the caregiver, not the elderly [52]. Integrating these technologies in their homes also means that they should be *meaningful* for the elderly in the first place.

The present study showed that the participants were familiar with domestic robots, such as semi-autonomous vacuum cleaner, and lawnmower robots. The functionality of robots was more important than appearance, but the appearance had some importance for the female participants. When it comes to robot appearance, literature often discusses the anthropomorphic robotic looks [50][54] [55]–[58]. The literature also talks about the notion of the uncanny valley, defined as the look of a robot that may set expectations on its functionality as well [59]. Further, an early study since 2004 was conducted about the use of robots in professional settings on how people would collaborate on tasks with human-like vs. machine-like robots [54]. The study concluded that the participants felt more responsibility when using a machine-like robot, as they saw it more as a tool that helps them fulfilling a task [54]. Furthermore, studies show that human-like robots were preferred in stressful or complex situations, where the participants have to delegate responsibility due to stress and work overload, but also where such robots could perform/process better and faster than a person [54]. At the same time, functionality and appearance are interconnected. We have shown that the elderly saw the robots mostly as *servant robots* and that the robots that looked more humanoid-like were "*nothing to cuddle with*," as one participant said. If a safety alarm robot would be designed as a machine-like robot, this, on the other hand, could potentially put more responsibility on the elderly as they would feel more responsible towards the robot. However, they seem to find servant robots more meaningful.

Studies talk about the "domestication" of technology when integrating it into daily lives [53]. To be able to manage these technologies and give them meaning, the elderly seem to adapt them to their own. Small details of the devices' design are significant for the configurability and adaptability of the devices' to the elderly's individual needs [6]. For instance, bricolage is often used to adapt to technological devices to individual needs [6]. This is a way of *domesticating* and integrating the technology in their homes, in such a way that it becomes meaningful for them. According to [53], domestication is a prerequisite for integrating technological devices in the elderly's daily lives. This is also talked about sometimes as *appropriation.* Procter et al. [6] suggest the possibility of customizing the technology itself as a solution to this. This could perhaps contribute to some degree to the meaningfulness of the robots and yet ease the integration of those in their homes.

C. *Integration of robots viewed through the Sense-of-Coherence*

'*The authorities do not allow resignation*,' as the elderly specified about adopting new robots. However, comprehensible, manageable, and meaningful welfare technologies and robots seem to be still not enough for achieving consistency, e.g., a *sense of coherence*. These should also be aligned with political legislation and regulations. Developing policies by promoting the sense of coherence is done in time, but it requires synergies amongst individuals, groups, organizational- and societal levels [60]. Earlier, the emphasis on the alignment between technologies and governmental regulation was put through the (technical) standardization. Such an example is enabling the exchange of patient records all over Europe (Read in Hanseth et al. [61]). The technology was, at the time, predicted to have a vast potential to improve the Norwegian health care system [61].

Further, The Norwegian Social Ministry has since early 2000, a salutogenic approach on elderly *home* care: they listed 16 regulations regarding the quality of life and well-being for the elderly [62]. Amongst the listed prioritized areas were: *autonomy, self-worth,* and *ways of living*. However, at the time, this referred to homecare (comp. to *independent living*). Besides, in a Norwegian report from 2011 [63], it is pointed out that welfare technology should support, amongst others, self-help, independence, having own control despite eventual impairments [63]. This was in line with the Active Ageing framework from 2002 [64]. Active Ageing was at the time defined as: '[...] the process of optimizing opportunities for health, participation, and security in order to enhance the quality of life as people age.' [64]. However, 'healthy aging' replaced the old term framed in 2002 and is the new framework for 2015-2030 [65]. The new policy focuses on the diversity of people, independently of their health status (whether considering them healthy or not). Light et al. [66] supports this indirectly by addressing the technologies as *enabling,* instead of *'assistive.'* The authors also say that this approach will ease tensions amongst national policies.

Finally, in the independent living accommodations for the elderly, based on our empirical data, it seems we still deal with the same issues: political, institutional, and standardization issues. As another participant pointed out, *"It is not ready...' the laws are not ready yet.. for this.. which is quite advanced".* While the global or national standards are already there, we still lack standardization that prioritizes less knowledgeable users, such as independent living elderly with reduced ICT literacy. With the integration of new *living technologies*, such as in-motion robots, in the elderly's homes, we should perhaps consider SOC. We argue that the elderly could achieve a greater SOC, as a result of an increased comprehension, manageability, and eventually meaningfulness of robots. This could facilitate the integration of these technologies in their homes. We also admit that there might be other individual or external factors that contribute to SOC.

VI. CONCLUSION

In this work, we have presented views of the elderly on robots. To analyze the data, we have used a qualitative inductive approach by using the content and latent manifest analysis method. The analysis resulted in three categories: aging during the technological renaissance, domestic robots, and the elderly's expectations of legislation and regulations on robots. The overall resulted theme was integrating robots in everyday life. We have later discussed our findings through the lenses of the SOC theory and its concepts of comprehensibility, manageability, and meaningfulness.

Through this study, we have contributed to the understanding of the integration of robots in the homes of the elderly. We have brought concrete examples of how the elderly seek to understand (*comprehend*) and to be able *to manage* welfare robots. We also drew attention upon the importance of having meaningful technologies for them – that are not only useful (for them and their caregivers).

Further, studies show that in the coming years, people will not only live longer but also be more preoccupied with their "*meaning, purpose, and well-being*" in their later stages of life, while "looser family ties" will be more common [67]. This may yet put more pressure on the welfare system provided by the society's public services [67]. As the authors show, this "*self-empowering*" care approach for the elderly, in Norway, is predicted to be *mostly home-based*, but *enabled by* governments, through municipalities, vendors of welfare technologies, and residents and their families [67]. In another study, it is explained that the population aging, as a global phenomenon, would be addressed through "home-based care and multidisciplinary care," by *meeting the demands of the elderly* for living longer at home [68]. However, aldeen Al-Halhouli et al. [69] notified that while "smart house systems" are taking shape, the elderly "do not have *extra time to learn* new technologies" [69]. We have argued in this paper that we should consider the elements from SOC: *comprehensibility, manageability, and meaningfulness,* for better *integration* of robots in the independent living elderly's homes.

ACKNOWLEDGMENT

We wish to heartfully thank our project funders-The Research Council of Norway IKT Plus Program (Grant agreement no: 247697); our project partners and the participants; the project manager, J. Tørresen; colleagues T. Schulz, and R. Soma for our time at KO++; and the master students V. Søyseth and M. Søyland.

REFERENCES

[1] J. E. Bardram, C. Bossen, and A. Thomsen, "Designing for transformations in collaboration: A study of the deployment of homecare technology," in Proc. of the 2005 International ACM SIGGROUP Conf. on Supporting Group Work, New York, NY, USA, 2005, pp. 294–303.

[2] D. Detmer, M. Bloomrosen, B. Raymond, and P. Tang, "Integrated personal health records: transformative tools for consumer-centric care," BMC Med. Inform. Decis. Mak., vol. 8, p. 45, Oct. 2008.

[3] D. Fischinger et al., "Hobbit, a care robot supporting independent living at home: First prototype and lessons learned," Robot. Auton. Syst., vol. 75, pp. 60–78, Jan. 2016.

[4] S. A. McGlynn, S. Kemple, T. L. Mitzner, C.-H. A. King, and W. A. Rogers, "Understanding the potential of PARO for healthy older adults," Int. J. Hum.-Comp. Stud., vol. 100, pp. 33–47, Apr. 2017.

[5] A. Light, T. W. Leong, and T. Robertson, "Ageing well with CSCW," in ECSCW 2015: Proc. of the 14th Euro. Conf. on CSCW, 19-23 Sep. 2015, Oslo, Norway, Springer, Cham, 2015, pp. 295–304.

[6] R. Procter et al., "The day-to-day co-production of ageing in place," CSCW, vol. 23, no. 3, pp. 245–267, Jun. 2014.

[7] M. Koelen, M. Eriksson, and M. Cattan, "Older people, sense of coherence and community," in The Handb. of Salutogen., M. B. Mittelmark, S. Sagy, M. Eriksson, G. F. Bauer, J. M. Pelikan, B. Lindström, and G. A. Espnes, Eds. Cham: Springer Intern. Pub., 2017, pp. 137–149.

[8] M. Eriksson, "The Sense of Coherence in the salutogenic model of health," in The Handbook of Salutogenesis, M. B. Mittelmark, S. Sagy, M. Eriksson, G. F. Bauer, J. M. Pelikan, B. Lindström, and G. A. Espnes, Eds. Cham: Springer Intern. Pub., 2017, pp. 91–96.

[9] P. B. Baltes and J. Smith, "New frontiers in the future of aging: from successful aging of the young old to the dilemmas of the fourth age," Gerontology, vol. 49, no. 2, pp. 123–135, Apr. 2003.

[10] D. Field and M. Minkler, "Continuity and change in social support between young-old and old-old or very-old age," J. Gerontol., vol. 43, no. 4, pp. P100-106, Jul. 1988.

[11] OED, "welfare, n.," OED Online. Oxford University Press, 2017, Retrieved Feb. 2020.

[12] Nordic Centre for Welfare and Social Issues, "Welfare technology." Nordic Centre for Welfare and Social Issues, Retrieved Feb. 2020.

[13] OED, "robot", Oxford Dictionaries | English. Oxford University Press, 2017, Retrieved Feb. 2020.

[14] E. Oborn, M. Barrett, and A. Darzi, "Robots and service innovation in health care," J. Health Serv. Res. Policy, vol. 16, no. 1, pp. 46–50, Jan. 2011.

[15] D. Saplacan and J. Herstad, "A quadratic anthropocentric perspective on feedback - Using proxemics as a framework," Conf. Proceed. of BritishHCI 2017, Sunderland, U.K., pp. 1-6, Jul. 2017.

[16] J. M. Alcalá, J. Ureña, Á. Hernández, and D. Gualda, "Assessing human activity in elderly people using non-intrusive load monitoring," Sensors, vol. 17, no. 2, , p. 351-368, Feb. 2017.

[17] G. Acampora, D. J. Cook, P. Rashidi, and A. V. Vasilakos, "A survey on ambient intelligence in healthcare," Proc. IEEE, vol. 101, no. 12, pp. 2470–2494, Dec. 2013.

[18] E. Chiauzzi, C. Rodarte, and P. DasMahapatra, "Patient-centered activity monitoring in the self-management of chronic health conditions," BMC Med., vol. 13, pp. 1-6, Apr. 2015.

[19] M. Petersen and N. F. Hempler, "Development and testing of a mobile application to support diabetes self-management for people with newly diagnosed type 2 diabetes: a design thinking case study," BMC Med. Inform. Decis. Mak., vol. 17, no. 1, pp. 1-10, Jun. 2017.

[20] R. Laidlaw et al., "Using participatory methods to design an mHealth intervention for a low income country, a case study in Chikwawa, Malawi," BMC Med. Inform. Decis. Mak., vol. 17, pp. 1-12, Jul. 2017.

[21] K. Johnston, K. Grimmer-Somers, and M. Sutherland, "Perspectives on use of personal alarms by older fallers," Int. J. Gen. Med., vol. 3, pp. 231–237, Aug. 2010.

[22] P. Caleb-Solly, "A brief introduction to … Assistive robotics for independent living," Perspect. Public Health, vol. 136, no. 2, pp. 70–72, Mar. 2016.

[23] S. Bedaf, G. J. Gelderblom, and L. De Witte, "Overview and categorization of robots supporting independent living of elderly people: What activities do they support and how far have they developed," Assist. Technol. Off. J. RESNA, vol. 27, no. 2, pp. 88–100, 2015.

[24] S. Bedaf and L. de Witte, "Robots for Elderly Care: Their Level of Social Interactions and the Targeted End User," Stud. Health Technol. Inform., vol. 242, pp. 472–478, 2017.

[25] Samfunnkunskap.no, "Welfare state" 2018. [Online]. Retrieved Feb. 2020.

[26] J. Ramm, "Health and care. Use of services among the elderly," ssb.no, 2013. [Online]. Retrieved Feb. 2020

[27] D. Slettemeås, "Eldres bruk av digitale verktøy og internett: En landsdekende undersøkelse av mestring, støttebehov, motivasjon og hindringer," Deltasenteret, Statens Institutt for frobruksforskning (SIFO), 5–2014, Jun. 2014.

[28] B. A. Farshchian, T. Vilarinho, and M. Mikalsen, "From episodes to continuity of care: a study of a call center for supporting independent living," CSCW, vol. 26, no. 3, pp. 309–343, Jun. 2017.

[29] A. Antonovsky, "The salutogenic model as a theory to guide health promotion," Health Promotion International, vol. 1, 11 vols. Oxford University Press, Great Britain, pp. 11–18, 1996.

[30] C. Benz, T. Bull, M. Mittelmark, and L. Vaandrager, "Culture in salutogenesis: the scholarship of Aaron Antonovsky," Glob. Health Promot., vol. 21, no. 4, pp. 16–23, Dec. 2014.

[31] S. Suominen and B. Lindstrom, "Salutogenesis," Scand. J. Public Health, vol. 36, no. 4, pp. 337–339, Jun. 2008.

[32] S. Super, M. a. E. Wagemakers, H. S. J. Picavet, K. T. Verkooijen, and M. A. Koelen, "Strengthening sense of coherence: opportunities for theory building in health promotion," Health Promot. Int., vol. 31, no. 4, pp. 869–878, Dec. 2016.

[33] J. Lahtiranta, J. S. S. Koskinen, S. Knaapi-Junnila, and M. Nurminen, "Sensemaking in the personal health space," Inf. Technol. People, vol. 28, no. 4, pp. 790–805, Nov. 2015.

[34] J. Lahtiranta and J. S. S. Koskinen, "Electronic health services for cardiac patients: a salutogenic approach," Finn. J. EHealth EWelfare, vol. 5, pp. 96–93, 2013.

[35] H. Dreyfus, Being-in-the-world: A Commentary on Heidegger's Being and Time, Division I. Massachusetts Institute of Technology, 1991.

[36] F. Svenaeus, "The relevance of Heidegger's philosophy of technology for biomedical ethics," Theor. Med. Bioeth., vol. 34, no. 1, pp. 1–15, Feb. 2013.

[37] ssb, "Next million reached set to be the fastest," ssb.no, 2017. [Online]. Retrieved Feb. 2020.

[38] Statistics Norway, "Population," (Statistik sentralbyrå, ssb.no, 17-Nov-2016. [Online]. Retrieved Feb. 2020.

[39] S. G. Joshi, "Designing for capabilities: A phenomenological approach to the design of enabling technologies for older adults," 2017.

[40] A. Woll, "Use of welfare technology in elderly care," University of Oslo, Oslo, Norway, 2017.

[41] S. G. Joshi and T. Bratteteig, "Assembling fragments into continuous design: On participatory design with old people," in Nordic Contributions in IS Research, 2015, pp. 13–29.

[42] S. G. Joshi and T. Bratteteig, "Designing for prolonged mastery. On involving old people in participatory design," Scand. J. Inf. Syst., vol. 28, no. 1, Jul. 2016.

[43] S. G. Joshi, "Designing for experienced simplicity. Why analytic and imagined simplicity fail in design of assistive technology," Int. J. Adv. Intell. Syst., vol. 8, no. 3 and 4, pp. 324–338, Dec. 2015.

[44] R. B. Rosseland, "Exploring movement-absed rhythmic interaction with senior citizens," University of Oslo, Department of Informatics, Faculty of mathematics and natural sciences, Oslo, Norway, 2018.

[45] M. Dalen, Intervju som forskningsmetode: en kvalitativ tilnærming, 2. utg. Oslo: Universitetsforl, 2013.

[46] U. H. Graneheim and B. Lundman, "Qualitative content analysis in nursing research: concepts, procedures and measures to achieve trustworthiness," Nurse Educ. Today, vol. 24, no. 2, pp. 105–112, Feb. 2004.

[47] S. A. Ballegaard, J. Bunde-Pedersen, and J. E. Bardram, "Where to, Roberta?: Reflecting on the role of technology in assisted living," in Proc. of the 4th Nordic Conf. on HCI: Changing Roles, New York, NY, USA, 2006, pp. 373–376.

[48] A. Vercelli, I. Rainero, L. Ciferri, M. Boido, and F. Pirri, "Robots in elderly care," Digit. - Sci. J. Digit. Cult., vol. 2, no. 2, pp. 37–50, Mar. 2018.

[49] A. Sciutti, M. Mara, V. Tagliasco, and G. Sandini, "Humanizing Human-Robot Interaction: On the importance of mutual understanding," IEEE Technol. Soc. Mag., vol. 37, no. 1, pp. 22–29, Mar. 2018.

[50] E. Cheon and N. M. Su, "Configuring the user: 'Robots have needs too,'" in Proc. of the 2017 ACM Conf. on CSCW and Soc. Comp., New York, NY, USA, pp. 191–206, 2017.

[51] S. Ljungblad, J. Kotrbova, M. Jacobsson, H. Cramer, and K. Niechwiadowicz, "Hospital robot at work: Something alien or an intelligent colleague?," in Proc. of the ACM 2012 Conf. on CSCW, New York, NY, USA, pp. 177–186, 2012.

[52] Y. Riche and W. Mackay, "PeerCare: supporting awareness of rhythms and routines for better aging in place," CSCW, vol. 19, no. 1, pp. 73–104, Feb. 2010.

[53] J. Meurer, C. Müller, C. Simone, I. Wagner, and V. Wulf, "Designing for sustainability: Key issues of ICT projects for ageing at home," ECSCW 2018, pp. 1-44, 2018.

[54] P. J. Hinds, T. L. Roberts, and H. Jones, "Whose Job is It Anyway? A Study of Human-robot Interaction in a Collaborative Task," Hum-Comput Interact, vol. 19, no. 1, pp. 151–181, Jun. 2004.

[55] J. Fink, "Anthropomorphism and human likeness in the design of robots and Human-Robot Interaction," in Soc. Rob., S. S. Ge, O. Khatib, J.-J. Cabibihan, R. Simmons, and M.-A. Williams, Eds. Springer Berlin Heidelberg, pp. 199–208, 2012.

[56] F. Eyssel, D. Kuchenbrandt, S. Bobinger, L. de Ruiter, and F. Hegel, "'If you sound like me, you must be more human': on the interplay of robot and user features on human-robot acceptance and anthropomorphism," in Proc. of the 7th annual ACM/IEEE intern. conf. on HRI, pp. 125–126, 2012.

[57] C. Bartneck, D. Kulić, E. Croft, and S. Zoghbi, "Measurement instruments for the anthropomorphism, animacy, likeability, perceived intelligence, and perceived safety of robots," Int. J. Soc. Robot., vol. 1, no. 1, pp. 71–81, Jan. 2009.

[58] K. Yogeeswaran et al., "The interactive effects of robot anthropomorphism and robot ability on perceived threat and support for robotics research," J. Hum.-Robot Interact., vol. 5, no. 2, pp. 29–47, Sep. 2016.

[59] M. Mori, "The uncanny valley [From the Field]," IEEE Robot. Autom. Mag., vol. 19, no. 2, pp. 98–100, Jun. 2012.

[60] M. Eriksson and M. B. Mittelmark, "The Sense of Coherence and its measurement," in The Handbook of Salutogenesis, M. B. Mittelmark, S. Sagy, M. Eriksson, G. F. Bauer, J. M. Pelikan, B. Lindström, and G. A. Espnes, Eds. Cham (CH): Springer, pp. 97-106, 2017.

[61] O. Hanseth, K. Thoresen, and L. Winner, "The politics of networking technology in health care," CSCW, vol. 2, no. 1, pp. 109–130, 1993.

[62] T. Bratteteig and I. Eide, "Becoming a good homecare practitioner: Integrating many kinds of work," CSCW, vol. 26, no. 4, pp. 563–596, Dec 2017.

[63] Norwegian Government Security and Service Organisation (G.S.S.O), "Innovation in care (Original Title: Innovasjon i Omsorg)," NOU (Norway's public investigations), Oslo, Norway, 2011:11, 2011.

[64] WHO, "Active ageing: a policy framework," World Health Organization, 2002, Retrieved Feb. 2020.

[65] WHO, "What is Healthy Ageing?," Ageing and life course, 2018. [Online]. Retrieved Feb. 2020.

[66] A. Light et al., "What's special about aging," ACM Interactions, vol. 23, Number 2. pp. 66–69, 2016.

[67] B. Bygstad and G. Lanestedt, "Expectations and realities in welfare technologies: A comparative study of Japan and Norway," Transform. Gov. People Process Policy, vol. 11, no. 2, pp. 286–303, Apr. 2017.

[68] H. Arai et al., "Toward the realization of a better aged society: Messages from gerontology and geriatrics," Geriatr. Gerontol. Int., vol. 12, no. 1, pp. 16–22, Jan. 2012.

[69] A. 'aldeen Al-Halhouli et al., "LEGO Mindstorms NXT for elderly and visually impaired people in need: A platform," Technol. Health Care Off. J. Eur. Soc. Eng. Med., vol. 24, no. 4, pp. 579–585, Jul. 2016.

Uses of Interactive Devices such as Artificial Intelligence Solutions for the Improvement of Human-Computer Interactions through Telemedicine Platforms in France

Bourret Christian
Dicen-IdF Research Team
University of Paris East Marne-la-Vallée (UPEM)
Val d'Europe, France
e-mail: christian.bourret@u-pem.fr

Depeyrot-Ficatier Thérèse
Dicen-IdF Research Team
University of Paris East Marne-la-Vallée (UPEM)
Val d'Europe, France
e-mail: t.depeyrot@ndv-consulting.com

Abstract—**The health sector, like all sectors of our society, is strongly impacted by digital transformations. We propose to consider it through new uses of Interactive Devices in the scope of Artificial Intelligence (AI) solutions for the improvement of Human-Computer Interactions, principally through Telemedicine Platforms in France. First of all, we define our scientific position and the methodology used. Secondly, we present the use of data in telemedicine and Artificial Intelligence data processing. Furthermore, we consider observations of AI applications in telemedicine, through cases analysis. We then analyze the effects of the combination of the two technologies. We discuss the main challenges of this digital transformation with the risk of a "solutionist" and "technocentric" approach, sometimes forgetting that health is above all based on a human dimension and interactions. We also outline the question of territories. Finally, we give a conclusion focusing on the main challenges undertaken as well as provide some perspectives.**

Keywords - Artificial Intelligence; Telemedicine Platform; Territories; Healthcare; Digital Transformation; France.

I. Introduction

Health is an essential sector in the digital transformation of our entire society, using interactive devices. The Isaac's report [1] clearly highlighted the main challenges of this transformation, with digital technology enabling the transition from curative to more predictive medicine. More recently, Villani's report [2] stressed the importance of Artificial Intelligence (AI), particularly in the health sector. The question of health is linked to the territories, in particular with the subject of social and territorial inequalities in health [3], with the concern of "medical deserts", with issues of traceability of care acts and health pathways, with the possible contributions of telemedicine.

In this paper, we propose first to examine the background of the transformation of the healthcare system and the current context of the development of telemedicine platforms and AI. We clarify the scope and the objectives of the survey that deals with the production and use of healthcare data on telemedicine platforms. Then, we intend to address, through an example, the issue of the AI solutions to implement better Human-Computer Interactions in telemedicine. To get a relevant picture of the recent situation, we choose the examples amongst new worldwide trends and French implementations. During teleconsultations, there are no physical examinations, so they seem somewhat like tele regulation and are required to reduce uncertainty in diagnosis. We intend to identify how combining AI and telemedicine may specifically support and improve the process of a remote medical consultation. Finally, we try to bring out the main findings concerning technical approaches as well as other considerations.

The transformation of the French healthcare system has become vital due to the combination of demographic evolution and the epidemiologic transition. With the decrease of infectious diseases that have led to the model of hospital, important changes have been brought with the rise of degenerative diseases and multi chronical pathologies. In this context, the patients are more and more involved in their healthcare pathway. They use search engines to get information on Internet, they share opinions and feelings on social networks, they interact on platforms to obtain medical appointments and they take charge of their healthcare records.

With the implementation of Healthcare Information Systems (HIS) in doctors' offices or hospitals, important volumes of medical data are produced. They gave rise to the implementation of data warehouses for archiving them in secure ways and managing their use. With multi-chronic pathologies, data for analysis are not only medical parameters but they come from different sources, on issues such as nutrition, habits and behavior, environment, etc. This wide scope of data is produced by the interactions of patients on digital platforms, characterized as social technical devices. Moreover, the chronic patients' healthcare requires the coordination of all the healthcare providers in the hospitals and in the ambulatory system. The different stakeholders have to exchange information for the organization of their patients' healthcare pathways and the monitoring. Medical data are produced and recorded in the different Electronic Healthcare Records (EHR) on proprietary software and in the "*Dossier médical partagé*" (DMP) in France, used till recently as repositories. But the priority is to enable data retrieval and sharing. Healthcare coordination should be based on interactive devices and updated data.

In this paper, after an introduction, in Section 2, we first define our scientific position and the methodology used. Then, in Section 3, we present the use of data in telemedicine and Artificial Intelligence data processing. In Section 4, we consider observations on AI applications in telemedicine through cases analysis. In Section 5, we then analyze the effects of the combination of the two technologies. After a discussion in Section 6, finally, we give a conclusion focusing on main challenges tackled and perspectives for future works.

II. Scientific Position and Methodology

In a research-action approach, this paper associates two researchers, one with a university position and the other with a more consulting position and implication in experimental activities on the deployment of interactive devices, such as AI and telemedicine projects in the territories. Their complementarity allows for a back and forth between theory and practice, by comparing practical results with theoretical issues, to produce knowledge for action.

We position our research within the interdisciplinary field of information and communication sciences, in the perspective outlined by F. Bernard [4], proposing to articulate the four dimensions of links and relationships (interactions in a systemic dimension), meaning, knowledge and action. We insist on the complementarity of information and communication, stressing both the importance of information to shape organizations and data for their management and development, and also of communication to foster change [5], by promoting cooperative dynamics, articulating the project and storytelling dimensions of all actors [6], both human and socio-technical devices. We propose an approach that we call Information and Communication Organizing Ecosystems (ICOE). The notion of "organizing" was proposed by Weick [7], focusing on processes, and interdependence of interactions, to study human activity by means of "sensemaking recipe" in a set of dynamics to try to grasp the complexity of organizations. For us, information and communication contribute to the shaping and ecosystems, which can be organizations, companies, groups or territories. We thus articulate the approaches of Economic Intelligence and Quality [8], in the wake of Wilensky [9], when he speaks of organizational intelligence, without forgetting the innovation dimension in process approaches [10]. In the wake of Goffman [11], we particularly mobilize the notion of situation (situations of activity, management, information, communication, etc.) with all the ambivalence of technology [12]. Tensions exist between those who are in favor of new uses of digital technology to improve patient services, such as G. Vallancien [13] and those who fear regression, rationalization meaning rationing or "uberization" (standardization and precarization of the health professions), such as the National Board of Doctors or *Conseil National de l'Ordre des Médecins en France* [14]. By favoring the "situational and interactionist semiotics" reading the grid proposed by A. Mucchielli [15], we analyze situations of activity, also integrating the dimension of emotions and leadership [16] and trust building in complex projects [17]. The aim is to promote new services for patients and healthcare professionals, with the importance of information (data uses) and communication with a strong territorialization and proximity dimension, with the emergence of new professions such as data scientist or human data interfaces [18], with specificities in the health sector.

III. The Use of Data in Telemedicine and the AI Data Processing

We intend to examine the use of healthcare data on telemedicine platforms and then, the AI solutions that could improve the process. The recent trend in new technologies is melding telemedicine with AI. Figure 1 gives an idea of the advance of those two technologies. For getting a comprehensive overview of the context, we can observe the expected expansion in telemedicine and AI in the twenty next years through the following chart extracted from a study of the English National Health System (NHS).

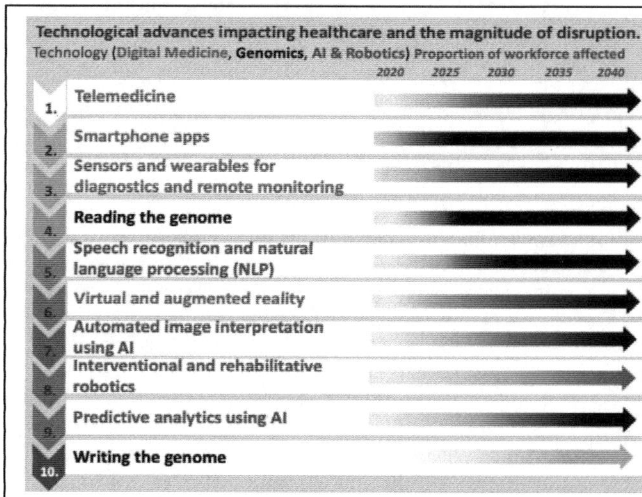

Figure 1. Top 10 digital healthcare technologies and their projected impact on the NHS workforce from 2020 to 2040 [19].

A. The Use of Data in Telemedicine

According to the French regulation definition (telemedicine decree: 2010), five situations or types of telemedicine can be distinguished: tele consultation, tele expertise, tele monitoring (for chronic diseases), tele assistance and medical answers for emergency regulation. The types of patients addressed by telemedicine are:

- Every patient in contact with their general practitioner within their healthcare pathway,
- The dependent elderly,
- Patients with chronic diseases: diabetes, heart failure, renal failure, Chronic Obstructive Pulmonary Disease (COPD), etc.
- Outpatients after surgery in hospital.

In terms of technological structure, a telemedicine platform is a connecting device, where the central data repository is related to interfaces. For teleconsultations, there are instantly interactions between the patients and the doctors, who receive measurements and answers, as well as view and analyze patient health data through a web portal. The portal is customized for the exchanges between stakeholders: patients and professionals, according to the medical specialties. It can be accessed from a computer browser or also from a smartphone on a mobile app with an ergonomic workflow interface. The integration of algorithms for a preliminary analysis of medical data and imaging is now expanding. The platform has to support the entire process chain for providing services:

- The medical appointment, linked to calendaring,
- The collect of the patient's agreement,
- The stakeholders' authentication,
- The diagnosis and medical report,
- The prescription (for drugs, etc.),
- The data recording,
- The billing and payment processes.

Usually, booking a telemedicine appointment is possible through this interface where it can be scheduled. The waiting line may be displayed on a dashboard, and a virtual space organized as a waiting room for the patients. Sometimes documents can be exchanged beforehand (questionnaire, measurements, medical imaging, etc.). Recording the National Healthcare Insurance card is the usual way to check the identity of the patient. Some other forms can be found like the patients' agreement and the eligibility questionnaire. The payment system and the online prescriptions can be supplied through the portal. Additional services consist of the integration of the EHR for adding data and the report of the teleconsultation, with eventually the telemedicine video record.

The Healthcare Insurance Fund may provide a financial aid to physicians for purchasing the following connected devices: oxymeter, stethoscope, dermatoscope, otoscope, glucometer, electrocardiogram (ECG), doppler device, echograph, device for blood pressure measure, camera, tools for ocular and hearing tests and equipment for breathing functional exploration. As a socio technical device, a telemedicine platform contributes to the transformation of the healthcare system mainly with an extended use of data through Human-Computer Interactions. As there is no physical presence for the patient and consequently no auscultation, the doctors have to secure their medical acts by whatever means possible. Different types of data are needed for improving the general process that includes mainly assessment, diagnosis and medical prescription. Data have to be retrieved and completed for the anamnesis, the medical case history. The diagnosis that is sometimes based on medical imaging requires decision support systems, as prescription too.

B. AI Data Processing and Solutions

1) Machine learning, deep learning: With the implementation of EHR in hospitals and the extension of Information Systems (IS) for the healthcare production, medical data began to be mass produced; then, the data management could develop with the creation of algorithms. As data mass production reduces the limitation in the use of statistical rules, AI devices are more and more reliable with deep learning. They were first learning algorithms, with data analysis (neural networks) and the capability for the machine to deduct rules to get a result. AI applications were especially numerous for the analysis of medical imaging, allowing the development of diagnosis support systems, for example in cardiology or ophthalmology, with satisfactory rates of reliability. Genetics is now providing huge amounts of data, which paves the way to the search for predictive models. Thus, AI solutions strengthen the evolution towards a personalized, preventive, predictive and participative medicine.

2) Mass production of healthcare data: Human-Computer Interactions increased with the patients' empowerment, as they access more frequently social technical devices; they not only use various search engines to get relevant information, but mainly digital platforms on computers or smartphones to know the conditions and costs of healthcare, getting on line appointments or healthcare appreciations, discussing on forums, using connected objects or contributing to design innovative products. Data can also be retrieved from the informal exchanges on the social media that have become at the origin of useful information related to healthcare (behavior, habits, ways of living, feelings). In a more global approach towards the determinants of healthcare, information lead to new perspectives in retrieving more data and crossing them to build algorithms that could help to improve the patients' healthcare. The data integrates not only medical, but social, psycho-social information to obtain the signs of any evolution in the living conditions of a person and the risks of degradation.

3) Different uses of AI: The following figure displays the main uses of AI in healthcare:

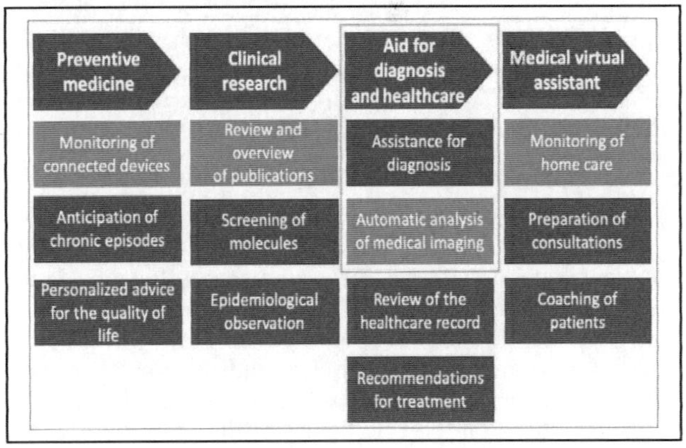

Figure 2. Typology of AI uses in healthcare (the mature uses are pointed out in green) [20].

Through the main characteristic of AI, which is to manage huge amounts of data and provide quick results, we try to clear the applications that would especially enhance the value of the telemedicine process, combining data retrieval, data analysis and the decision support system.

- *Retrieval of the Appropriate Information*: AI applications can retrieve the patients' information automatically, from EHR and other sources. Basically, machine learning can help to analyze clinical data in a patient's EHR to provide patient care recommendations.
- *Automatic Analysis of Medical Imaging:* AI solutions are especially relevant for analyzing huge masses of data from medical imaging. In 2018, DeepMind developed a software using a neural network learning system for detecting ophthalmic pathologies from scanner eye retina imaging [21]. The detection focuses on age-related macular degeneration (AMD), diabetic retinopathy, glaucoma or retinal detachment. DeepMind obtained a precision of around 94% for the AI application it developed. Such AI solutions in medical imaging can provide aid for diagnosis, which helps to secure them.
- *AI Advice for Prescriptions*: Machine learning algorithms may recommend treatment options and solutions for the patients.
  They help the doctors when recommending prescriptions by taking into account the existing ones, checking and validating prescriptions to make sure that the drugs prescribed are compatible with the patient's data.

IV. The Observation of AI Applications in Telemedicine

A. The Analysis of New Trends for AI in Telemedicine

Some applications for telemedicine now use machine learning to help the medical professionals with diagnostic support based on symptoms and patient health data. New trends pivot on the capabilities and benefits of AI in combining high speed data retrieval from very different sources, analysis of huge amounts of data and its results with the decision support system. AI solutions may be used for the patients' orientation, helping to screen patients in telemedicine as they do for emergency calls.

B. Data Collection before a Consultation

Lemonaid Health, an AI application before virtual video consultations: Lemonaid provides video consultations with medical professionals [22]. It uses machine learning at the beginning of the process with the evaluation of the patient's state of healthcare. The patient has to complete a questionnaire online that includes medical history, current medicines, allergies and regular symptoms. An AI model of screening based on the complexity of the case analyzes the information obtained to categorize the patient and orientate him to the suitable healthcare provider. Doctors evaluate the situation, usually during a video consultation available with an assigned healthcare professional.

C. Personalized Diagnosis Support

The telemedicine application Ada Health (Germany): A diagnosis support for telemedicine [22] uses a machine learning AI application to provide personalized diagnosis support. The patient has first to complete his medical profile in an initial survey. A chatbot uses a series of questions to identify possible symptoms.

D. A Case Example of Telemedicine Using AI

1) MédecinDirect: MédecinDirect is a telemedicine platform [23] that provides medical advice and remote consultations through contracts with companies and mutual funds for their stockholders. Facing the increase of the activity in remote medical consultations, MédecinDirect uses AI solutions in order to keep the quality level and to reduce the length of time for providing an answer. They fulfill two major aims: improving the anamnesis and securing both the diagnosis and the prescribed treatment.

2) Analysis Based on the Reasons for the Consultation: The healthcare practitioners have to ask different questions for the clarification of symptoms and to retrieve the patients' medical history, without omitting to get important information. Built on the use of a great number of exchanges recorded on the platform, the analysis aims at standardizing the different healthcare professionals' answers. After the analysis of the major reason for the consultation from natural language, AI solution proposes to the doctor a complete set of relevant questions in order to better define the medical case history. A conversational agent may be integrated into the process of asking questions.

E. Decision Support System

AI is used for creating an inference engine that enables the provision of medical recommendations to doctors for the exclusion of serious risks, for making diagnosis and assisting medical prescription.

V. The effects of combining telemedicine and AI technologies

A. The Impacts for the Doctors

The processes are noticeably different between remote medical consultations and consultations with the physical presence of the patients. This fact explains how some doctors are still reluctant to the practice of telemedicine. AI and telemedicine are complementary. AI really contributes to securing the whole process of a teleconsultation. First, getting accurate information about the patient's state of health helps the professionals in their assessment. Then, any information improving the decision-making and enabling to confirm the appropriate diagnosis is really valued. Finally, the prescription is much more reliable if the doctors get all the information about the patients' other drugs and prescribed medicine. AI algorithms have to be trustworthy, especially since they are used for healthcare. The use of AI solutions may be time saving for doctors. They can give them more time for doctor-patient interaction. So AI may be a real help for doctors in the teleconsultation process, but some challenges have still to be solved [24]; it introduces a risk due to an insufficient accuracy in the results of AI. Retrieving significant amount of data for the training procedure in order to create reliable algorithms is very important. The data retrieval and their standardization are very important factors facilitating faith in the algorithms created.

B. The New Scopes for the Patients

The present development of teleconsultations seems to result not only of recent changes in regulation and of the context of "medical desertification", but also of the patients' current needs.

Some policy holders have access to telemedicine platforms with their healthcare insurance contracts; more patients want to avoid waiting for a medical consultation going to the doctor's office and use such platforms for getting information fast and accurately. With the empowerment for their healthcare, patients are more involved in digital processes, like booking online for medical appointments or filling in information forms before consultations. They also communicate about their patients' experience on social media and forums, so that they contribute to producing data that can be retrieved for AI in healthcare. This observation leads to the questioning concerning the evolution towards digital medicine, with direct access for patients to the information automatically produced by AI, and less human interactions with the healthcare professionals.

VI. Discussion

The interactive devices studied (AI, telemedicine) are certainly very promising and should constitute major levers of the digital transformation to make the health system evolve from a purely curative and fee-for-service medicine to a more preventive medicine, as envisaged by the Isaac's report [1].

We have already highlighted in the wake of J. Ellul [11], the ambivalence of technology and the tensions between technophiles and technophobes. In France, the Descartes' country, engineers have always occupied a privileged place, with the risk of technological "solutionism" drifting away from technocentric approaches, with tools too often developed without real consultation with users, whether they are health professionals or patients and their families. The integration of new project management methods (known as "agile", integrating users into the various stages of project development) such as the method for developing trust in complex projects, for instance the Fears - Attractions - Temptations (FAcT)-Mirror method proposed by G. Le Cardinal [17], are interesting approaches. These tools also renew territorial approaches to health and in particular those of health inequalities, which can have an individual, social (isolation and poverty) and collective dimension, concerning not only individuals, but the collective dimension of territories, the question of "medical deserts", territories without health professionals, these "medical deserts" being also "digital deserts" [3] with specific work on AI and rurality, data and weakened territories or smart cities and smart territories.

Another essential aspect is the evaluation of the impact of these new devices and their added value in improving services for both health professionals, patients and their families. This is another area of research we are working to propose, still in an approach based on information and communication issues, a more contributory evaluation by integrating the expectations and emotions of all stakeholders, tool designers, users: health professionals, patients and their families. These patients are gradually affirming their role with the notion of "health democracy" enshrined in the law on "Patients' rights and the quality of the health system" of March 2002.

All these developments imply a new "territorialization" of health management, with an affirmation over the past thirty years of "healthcare interface organizations" (healthcare networks, multi-professional healthcare centers, home hospitalization, etc.) to overcome the barriers between urban medicine and the hospitalization sector, or new territorial groups of urban medicine, with whom there are still challenges of coordination and traceability of acts.

All these digital transformations are also reflected in the affirmation of new coordination professions [25] and also to give meaning to data, not only data scientist but also human data mediation [18]. But if we have outlined the challenges of the digital transformation of the health system through the implementation of new devices, mainly AI and telemedicine, we must not forget the whole human dimension of healthcare, well emphasized by M.J. Thiel, with the suffering and anxiety of illness and the end of life [26].

VII. Conclusion

With the rise of more uses in telemedicine, we are witnessing a new step in the transformation of the healthcare system, with major challenges to overcome.

The digital process in telemedicine is a Human-Computer Interaction, both requiring and producing data. It contributes to the increase of the volume of healthcare data and therefore to the possible development of AI. Telemedicine is based on data exchanges between the stakeholders and data processing. Data collection in this case is even more important than when there is physical presence in a medical consultation. The doctors have to act without any information from the patient's auscultation. The relevant information must be available, thus the necessity to gather as much data as possible, i.e., recent information, then, to select the required information and to get support when making a decision.

The use of AI strengthens the requirements of the information systems interoperability, as data are collected from different sources where their meaning may be different. Data entered into an AI system should be complete and accurate. A healthcare data normalization engine, curated and versioned data sets for the terminologies could be used. But in order to improve the quality of the available data, especially with large-scale data sources, we would need some of the standardization tools for curating the data that do not yet exist [27][28]. A standard terminology, such as the Systematized Nomenclature for Human and Veterinary Medicine (SNOMED) Clinical Terms achieves semantic interoperability. Archetypes provide the shared meaning of data with the specifications of its format.

Furthermore, the implementation of AI solutions highlights the complex ethical questions about the use of medical and behavioral personal data, with the upcoming extension to genetics. From an ethical point of view, beyond the patients' free consent, the use of their healthcare data mandates a differentiated exploitation according to their sensitivity.

The future trends may be the temptations to use AI for services to patients without any human interaction, in answer to their various questions about the seriousness of the symptoms, how to understand, what to do, when seeing a doctor is essential. We have outlined the risk of any only "solutionist' approach, as medicine is managing human beings and not only materials or connected objects. The challenges are very important and shape the whole future of our society. Health is an essential sector to observe the issues and challenges of the digital transformation of our entire society.

REFERENCES

[1] H. Isaac, "From a curative health system to a preventive model using digital tools"/"D'un système de santé curatif à un modèle préventif grâce aux outils numériques", Paris: Renaissance numérique, 2014, http://fr.slideshare.net/RenaissanceNumerique/lb-sante-preventive-renaissance-numerique-1.

[2] C. Villani, "Giving meaning to artificial intelligence: for a national and European strategy"/"Donner du sens à l'intelligence artificielle : pour une stratégie nationale et européenne", Paris: French Government, 2018, https://www.enseignementsup-recherche.gouv.fr/cid128577/rapport-de-cedric-villani-donner-un-sens-a-l-intelligence-artificielle-ia.html.

[3] C. Bourret, "Tackle the challenge of Social and Territorial Inequalities in Health (ISTS) by meeting interface and telehealth organizations in a « digital humanism » approach to health?"/"Relever le défi des Inégalités Sociales et Territoriales en Santé (ISTS) par la rencontre des organisations d'interface et de la télésanté dans une approche d'« humanisme numérique » en santé ?", Contemporary Trends in Organizational Communication / Tendances contemporaines en communication organisationnelle, in S. Alemanno, C. Le Moënne, and G. Gramaccia, Revue Française des Sciences de l'Information et de la Communication September 2016, http://rfsic.revues.org/2013, DOI : 10.4000/rfsic.2013.

[4] F. Bernard, "Information and Communication Sciences (ICS) as a discipline of openness and decompartmentalization"/ "Les SIC une discipline de l'ouverture et du décloisonnement", in A. Bouzon, Organizational communication in debate. Fields, concepts, perspectives / La communication organisationnelle en débat. Champs, concepts, perspectives, Paris: L'Harmattan, 2006, pp. 33 – 46.

[5] V. Carayol, "Organizational communication. An allagmatic perspective"/"Communication organisationnelle. Une perspective allagmatique", Paris: L'Harmattan, 2004.

[6] N. D'Almeida, "Organisations between projects and stories" /"Les organisations entre projets et récits", in A. Bouzon, Organizational communication in debates. Fields, concepts and perspectives / La communication organisationnelle en débats. Champs, concepts et perspectives, Paris: L'Harmattan, 2006, pp. 145 – 158.

[7] K. E. Weick, "The Social Psychology of Organizing", New York: McGraw-Hill, 1979.

[8] C. Bourret, "Economic Intelligence Meeting Quality Prospects in France with Particular Focus on Healthcare Issues", Journal of Business and Economics, New York: Academic Star Publishing Company, 2015, vol. 6, n° 8, pp. 1487 - 1502.

[9] H. L. Wilensky, "Organizational Intelligence: knowledge and policy in government and industry", New York: Basic Books Publishers, 1967.

[10] J. P. Caliste and C. Bourret, "Contribution to a typological analysis of processes: from compliance to agility" / "Contribution à une analyse typologique des processus : de la conformité à l'agilité", 10th International Congress Qualia / 10ème Congrès International Qualita, Université de Technologie de Compiègne, 2013.

[11] E. Goffman, "The Neglected Situation", in J.J. Gumperz and D. Hymes, The Ethnography of Communication, American Anthropologist, Washington DC, 1964, pp. 133 – 137.

[12] J. Ellul, "The technique or challenge of the century"/"La technique ou l'enjeu du siècle", Paris: Economica, 1990.

[13] G. Vallancien, "Medicine without a doctor. Digital technology at the service of the patient"/"La médecine sans médecin. Le numérique au service du malade", Paris: Gallimard, Coll. Le Débat, 2015.

[14] National Board of Physicians / Conseil National de l'Ordre des Médecins, "Health Uberization Risk"/"Risque d'ubérisation de la santé", 2015, https://www.lequotidiendumedecin.fr/archives/uberisation-de-la-sante-lordre-veut-verifier-la-conformite-des-prestations-medicales-en-ligne.

[15] A. Mucchielli, "Situation and Communication"/"Situation et communication", Nice: Les éditions Ovadia, 2010.

[16] D. Goleman, R. Boyatzis, and A. Mc Kee, "Primal Leadership: Realizing the Power of Emotional Intelligence", 2002 /"L'intelligence émotionnelle au travail", Pearson Education, France, 2010.

[17] G. Le Cardinal, J. F. Guyonnet, B. Pouzoullic, and J. Rigby, "Intervention Methodology for complex problems: The FAcT-Mirror method", European Journal of Operational Research, Elsevier, n° 132, 2001, pp. 694-702.

[18] A. Nesvijevskaia, "Big Data Phenomenon in Companies: Project Process, Value Generation and Human Mediation – Data"/"Phénomène Big Data en entreprise : processus projet, génération de valeur et Médiation Homme– Données", Ph-D in Information and Communication Sciences / Doctorat en Sciences de l'Information et de la Communication, G. Chartron, Paris: CNAM, 2019.

[19] "Preparing the healthcare workforce to deliver the digital future", February 2019, The Topol Review, Health Education England.

[20] "Artificial intelligence – latest developments and perspectives for France"/"Intelligence artificielle - État de l'art et perspectives pour la France", Pôle interministériel de Prospective et d'Anticipation des Mutations économiques, February 2019.

[21] S. Ravindran, "How artificial intelligence is helping to prevent blindness", Nature Outlook, April 2019.

[22] K. Sennaar, "Artificial intelligence in Telemedicine and Telehealth", February 2019, https://emerj.com/ai-sector-overviews/artificial-intelligence-in-telemedicine-and-telehealth/.

[23] "Teleconsultation: an AI tool for maximizing the medical time"/"Téléconsultation: un outil d'intelligence artificielle pour optimiser le temps médical", November 2018,

https://web.babbler.fr/document/show/teleconsultation-un-outil-dintelligence-artificielle-pour-optimiser-le-temps-medical/newsroom#/.

[24] D. Pacis, E. Subido, and N. Bugtai, "Trends in telemedicine utilizing artificial intelligence", AIP Conference Proceedings 1933, 040009, February 2018, https://doi.org/10.1063/1.5023979.

[25] C. Bourret, "New Intermediation Jobs in Health Interface Organizations"/"Nouveaux métiers d'intermédiation dans les organisations d'interface en santé", Health Ecosystem: New Modes of Information Regulation / "Ecosystème de santé : nouveaux modes de régulation de l'information", in D. Dufour-Coppolani and P. Hassanaly, Information, Data and Documents / Information, Données et Documents (I2D), n° 3, 2016, pp. 32-33.

[26] M. J. Thiel, "Where is medicine going? Meaning of medical representations and practices"/"Où va la médecine ? Sens des représentations et pratiques médicales", Strasbourg: Presses Universitaires de Strasbourg, 2003.

[27] S. Shilo, H. Rossman, and E. Segal, "Axes of a revolution: challenges and promises of big data in healthcare", Nat Med 26, 29–38, 2020, doi:10.1038/s41591-019-0727-5.

[28] M. Matheny, S. T. Israni, M. Ahmed, and D. Whicher, "Artificial Intelligence in Health Care: The Hope, the Hype, the Promise, the Peril", National Academy of Medicine (NAM) Washington, D.C., 2019.

Decision-making in Game Development Process - A Systematic Review

Régis Batista Perez
Cesar School
Recife, Brazil
email: rbp@cesar.school

Leandro Marques do Nascimento
UFRPE
Recife, Brazil
email: leandro.marques@ufrpe.br

Alberto de Lima Medeiros
Cesar School
Recife, Brazil
email: alm@cesar.school

Tiago Beltrão Lacerda
Cesar School
Recife, Brazil
email: tbl@cesar.school

***Abstract*—Game development is a field that has been continuously researched. The current state of the art of game development has been applied in many fields, from education to design research. This work has the objective of identifying, evaluating, and interpreting published research that examines how decision-making impacts the game development process. To achieve that, a systematic review of current literature was conducted. In this review, 36 works were identified as primary studies. The studies were then classified according to research focus and the use of game development the authors focused on. The review investigates what it is known about the challenges and opportunities in the use of decision-making in game development. The results show data about game development, gaps in current research and models of successful implementation.**

***Keywords*—game development; decision-making; systematic review.**

I. INTRODUCTION

Before, software products usually were developed to solve a problem or provide a service, whereas games were considered a form of entertainment, with no inherent value or usefulness beyond the scope of providing user experience [1]. Nowadays, the video games industry is worth billions of dollars [3] and the current state of the art of game development has been applied in many fields like education [7][37], design research [22], alleviating anxiety [38] and combating dementia [39].

However, to develop a game is simultaneously an advanced software product and a complex work of creativity and art [2]. This merger of disciplines makes video game production an interesting process to study from many different perspectives, but it also poses several challenges for the game development community.

This work is organized as follows: in Section II, we present a brief discussion about the work theme: basic concepts of game development and decision-making. Section III presents the applied protocol to conduct this review. In Section IV, the results of this review are shown. In Section V, the results are discussed. In Section VI, we conclude this work.

II. GAME DEVELOPMENT AND DECISION-MAKING

Decision-making can affect the software development process at every stage: from requirements analysis, to product delivery, to the consumer. Although a game is a software, its development process has more phases and involves more stakeholders than commercial automation software, for example. Because it has more phases and more stakeholders, therefore, the game development process has more decisions being made all the time.

Several papers cite how these decisions impact the game development process. These works include: user experience [16][23], gameplay [15], monetization models [35], project and code quality [4][11][34], sales [9][21], social media [24] and the gaming industry as a whole [1][13][25].

Seeking to understand how to optimize this decision-making, researchers have been analyzing the game development process using data on: gameplay [15][28][32], artificial intelligence behavior [30], sales [9][21], rates game completion [30], among others.

III. APPLIED PROTOCOL

Our review methodology is composed of eight steps: (1) development of the protocol, (2) definition of search questions (3) definition of search questions, (4) identification of inclusion and exclusion criteria (5) search for relevant studies, (6) critical assessment, (7) extraction of data, and (8) synthesis. The steps applied to the study contained herein are presented below.

The objective of this review is to identify primary studies that focus on game development process and the use of decision-making. The following question helps identifying primary studies:

- How does decision-making impact the game development?

From this central question, other secondary questions were developed to help in the comprehension of the problem:

- Which tools can be applied to evaluate the accuracy of decision-making in game development?
- What are the opportunities and challenges in adopting of decision-making in game development?

A. Inclusion and Exclusion Criteria

For this review, we considered studies that were published starting from year 2017. The following studies were also excluded:

- Studies not published in the English language;
- Studies that were unavailable online;
- Studies not based on research and that express only the official opinions of governments and field experts;
- Call for works, prefaces, conference annals, handouts, summaries, panels, interviews and news reports.

B. Search Strategies

The databases considered in the study are in the list below:

- ACM Digital Library;
- IEEE Xplore;

- ScienceDirect – Elsevier.

Combinations of terms were created to guarantee that relevant information would not be excluded when querying different search engines and databases. As a result, three search strings were created:

- String 1: "decision-making" AND "game development"
- String 2: "decision-making" AND "game development" AND (tools OR evaluate)
- String 3: "game development process"

We noted that to use the complementary string "and decision-making" did not increase the results. In the process of extracting information from the databases, the search strings were used separately in each database. The searches were performed in August 2019.

The results of each search were grouped together, according to database and were, later, examined closer in order to identify duplicity. Tables I - III show the number of studies found in each database, with the string utilized in the search.

TABLE I. NUMBER OF STUDIES FOUND IN EACH DATABASE FOR STRING 1

Database	Number of studies
ACM Digital Library	2
IEEE Xplore	5
ScienceDirect – Elsevier	105

TABLE II. NUMBER OF STUDIES FOUND IN EACH DATABASE FOR STRING 2

Database	NUmber of studies
ACM Digital Library	20
IEEE Xplore	2
ScienceDirect – Elsevier	101

TABLE III. NUMBER OF STUDIES FOUND IN EACH DATABASE FOR STRING 3

Database	Number of studies
ACM Digital Library	8
IEEE Xplore	4
ScienceDirect – Elsevier	33

C. Studies Selection Process

This section describes the selection process from the beginning, namely, from the initial search using the Search Strategies described above to identification of primary studies.

At the first step, 261 works were found with the initial research strings. Duplicated works were removed and, for title analysis, 143 works were selected. After the title analysis, 75 works were selected for abstract analysis. In the end, 36 works were selected based on the abstract analysis for full read. Table IV presents the number of studies filtered in each step of the selection process.

D. Quality Assessment

In the quality assessment stage, works passed through a critical analysis. In this stage, the complete studies were read and analyzed, instead of only the titles or abstracts. After this, the last studies that were considered uninteresting for the review were eliminated, resulting in the final set of works.

TABLE IV. NUMBER OF STUDIES FILTERED IN EACH STEP OF SELECTION PROCESS

Phase of Selection Process	Number of Studies
1. Databases Search	261
2. Title Analysis	143
3. Abstract Analysis	75
4. Full read	36

Six questions were used to help in the quality assessment. Those questions helped determine the relevance, rigor, and credibility of the work being analyzed. The questions were:

- Question 1: Does the study examine how decision-making can improve the game development process?
- Question 2: Does the study present aspects related with challenges or opportunities in adopting decision-making in game development process?
- Question 3: Does the study present tools to evaluate the accuracy of decision-making in game development process?
- Question 4: Is the context of the study adequately described?
- Question 5: Does the study contribute to research in game development and decision-making?
- Question 6: Does the study contribute to research in game development in any way?

Of the 75 studies that were analyzed in the quality assessment stage, 36 passed to the stage of Data Extraction and Synthesis and were thus considered the primary studies. The quality assessment process will be presented in detail in the result section, along with the assessment of the 36 remaining studies.

IV. RESULTS

In this paper, 36 primary studies were identified [1] – [36]. Each one deals with on a wide array of research topics and utilize a wide set of exploration models for each different scenario.

According to the studies above, it was identified that are opportunities to research decision-making in many phases of game development process: user experience [16][23], gameplay [15], monetization models [35], project and code quality [4][11][34], sales [9][21], social media [24], requirements analysis [32] and the gaming industry as a whole [1][13][25].

A. Quantitative Analysis

The research process that was developed resulted in 36 primary studies. As Table V shows, they were written by 130 authors, linked to institutions based in 20 different countries, distributed on five continents, and were published between 2017 and 2019.

In regards to the country of origin, most of the publications came from the United States of America, Netherlands, Canada and Brazil (five publications), followed by Finland (four works), Australia (three works), Arab Emirates, Pakistan, Spain, Taiwan and the United Kingdom (two works). Each of the other remaining countries had only one publication.

Figure 1 shows the percentage of participation of each continent in the primary studies. The tag "Global" is for the studies with more than one country or continent involved in the research.

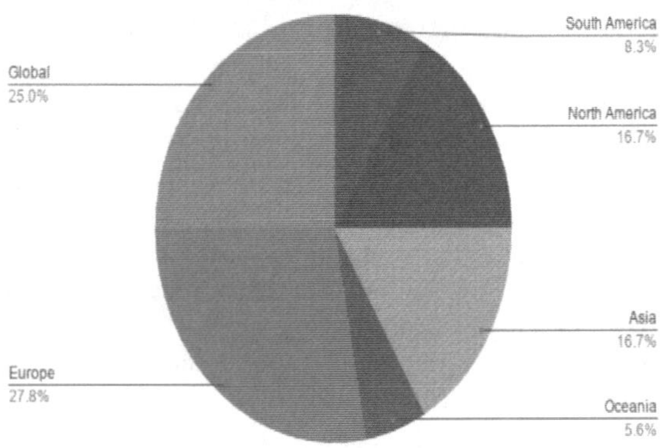

Figure 1. Participation of each continent

The large number of countries that have publications on the subject of game development and decision-making show how widespread the topic is globally.

Table VI shows what type of research was conducted in the primary studies. Figure 2 presents the percentage of each type of research.

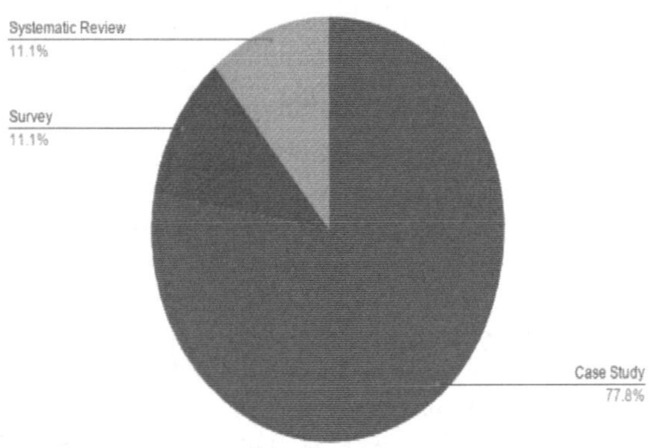

Figure 2. Type of research

B. *Quality Analysis*

As it was described in section D - Quality Assessment - each of the primary studies was assessed according to six quality criteria that relate to rigor and credibility as well as to relevance. If considered as a whole, these six criteria provide a trustworthiness measure to the conclusions that a particular study can bring to the review. The classification for each of the criteria used a scale of positives and negatives.

TABLE V. COUNTRIES AND NUMBER OF AUTHORS

Study	Country	Authors (number)
[1]	Finland	3
[2]	Sweden	4
[3]	United Arab Emirates	4
[4]	Canada (a), Pakistan (b), United Arab Emirates (c)	4(1a + 1b + 2c)
[5]	Pakistan	3
[6]	United States of America	5
[7]	Brazil	7
[8]	United States of America	1
[9]	Jordan	3
[10]	United States of America	1
[11]	Brazil (a), Canada (b), Egypt (c)	6 (4a+1b+1c)
[12]	Austria (a), United Kingdom (b)	4(3a+1b)
[13]	Netherlands	1
[14]	Brazil (a), Canada (b)	4 (2a+2b)
[15]	Netherlands (a), Canada (b)	3 (1a+2b)
[16]	Brazil	5
[17]	Australia	1
[18]	Australia	4
[19]	Norwegen	2
[20]	Netherlands	4
[21]	Canada	3
[22]	Spain	5
[23]	Spain (a), Netherlands (b)	5 (3a + 2b)
[24]	Finland	4
[25]	United Kingdom (a), Italy (b)	8 (7a + 1b)
[26]	Brazil	3
[27]	Taiwan	3
[28]	United States of America	5
[29]	Japan	2
[30]	India	2
[31]	United States of America	2
[32]	Netherlands	1
[33]	Finland	6
[34]	Taiwan (a), United States of America (b)	3 (2a + 1b)
[35]	Australia (a), Switzerland (b)	6 (5a+ 1b)
[36]	Finland	3
Total		130

Table VII presents the results of the evaluation. Each row represents a primary work and the columns 'Q1' to 'Q6' represent the 6 criteria defined by the questions used on quality assessment: decision-making and game development, challenges and opportunities, tools to evaluate decision-making impacts, context, contribution for decision-making and game development, and contribution for game development in any way, respectively. For each criteria, '1' represents the positive answer and '0' the negative one.

All studies that were analyzed in this step had positive answers for questions 1 and 2 because, as previously stated in the research methodology part, these questions represent inclusion and exclusion criteria. Consequently, all studies with negative answers to at least one of these criteria were already removed during selection stage.

All studies that were analyzed provided information on the context of the work and contributed in some way to research game development. Only 17 of 36 studies answered the question 3 about tools to evaluate accuracy of decision-making in game development. The same fraction, 17 of 36 studies, obtained the maximum score (6) in quality analysis.

TABLE VI. TYPE OF RESEARCH

Study	Type
[1]	Survey
[2]	Systematic Review
[3]	Systematic Review
[4]	Case Study
[5]	Case Study
[6]	Case Study
[7]	Case Study
[8]	Case Study
[9]	Survey
[10]	Case Study
[11]	Case Study and Survey
[12]	Case Study
[13]	Systematic Review
[14]	Case Study
[15]	Case Study and Survey
[16]	Case Study and Survey
[17]	Systematic Review
[18]	Case Study
[19]	Survey and Interviews
[20]	Case Study
[21]	Case Study
[22]	Systematic Review
[23]	Case Study
[24]	Survey
[25]	Case Study
[26]	Case Study
[27]	Case Study
[28]	Case Study
[29]	Case Study
[30]	Case Study
[31]	Case Study
[32]	Case Study
[33]	Case Study
[34]	Case Study
[35]	Case Study
[36]	Case Study

TABLE VII. QUALITY ANALYSIS OF PRIMARY STUDIES

Study	Q1	Q2	Q3	Q4	Q5	Q6	Total
[1]	1	1	0	1	1	1	5
[2]	1	1	0	1	1	1	5
[3]	1	1	0	1	1	1	5
[4]	1	1	1	1	1	1	6
[5]	1	1	1	1	1	1	6
[6]	1	1	0	1	1	1	5
[7]	1	1	0	1	1	1	5
[8]	1	1	1	1	1	1	6
[9]	1	1	0	1	1	1	5
[10]	1	1	0	1	1	1	5
[11]	1	1	0	1	1	1	5
[12]	1	1	1	1	1	1	6
[13]	1	1	1	1	1	1	6
[14]	1	1	1	1	1	1	6
[15]	1	1	1	1	1	1	6
[16]	1	1	0	1	1	1	5
[17]	1	1	0	1	1	1	5
[18]	1	1	0	1	1	1	5
[19]	1	1	0	1	1	1	5
[20]	1	1	0	1	1	1	5
[21]	1	1	1	1	1	1	6
[22]	1	1	0	1	1	1	5
[23]	1	1	0	1	1	1	5
[24]	1	1	0	1	1	1	5
[25]	1	1	0	1	1	1	5
[26]	1	1	1	1	1	1	6
[27]	1	1	1	1	1	1	6
[28]	1	1	1	1	1	1	6
[29]	1	1	1	1	1	1	6
[30]	1	1	1	1	1	1	6
[31]	1	1	0	1	1	1	5
[32]	1	1	1	1	1	1	6
[33]	1	1	1	1	1	1	6
[34]	1	1	1	1	1	1	6
[35]	1	1	1	1	1	1	6
[36]	1	1	0	1	1	1	5
Total	36	36	17	36	36	36	-

V. DISCUSSION

After the analysis and data extraction steps performed on the primary works, it was possible to identify some aspects related to how decision-making impacts the game development process.

In the first place, it is possible to conclude that decision-making impacts all stages of game development process, from requirements analysis to user experience, consequently affecting game sales and industry survival. All primary works were published after 2017, therefore, this research field is very active.

The systematic review also found it difficult to find open data from the gaming industry, since some databases cited in the articles (SteamDB and SteamSpy [21][29]) are Application Programming Interfaces (API) that do data mining in the Steam store.

In addition to keeping research on game development in vogue, one of the advantages of the present work was to show a well-documented and detailed research process, easy to be replicated and tested.

As a disadvantage in relation to the researched works, we noticed that there is no interaction with the developers as well as the industry can hinder the results. However, we tried to collect data directly from them at the beginning of this work using social networks and other means of contact, which unfortunately, did not result in a relevant amount of data. This fact corroborates the statement about the difficulty of collecting data from the gaming industry.

A. How decision-making is impacting game development?

This review illustrated that decision-making impacts every stage of the game development process, as pros decision-making can provide: improved performance, quality, sales and user experience. The negative impacts are: to affect the artistic spectrum of game development as it may limit the creative process.

B. Which tools can be applied to evaluate the accuracy of decision-making in game development?

In this review, it was noticed the lack of research about the tools that have been applied to evaluate the accuracy of decision-making in game development. Only 17 of 36 studies showed or briefly identified some type of tool. The identified tools are: playtesting data, postmortem documents, Halstead complexity measures; learning performance, conclusion of activities performance, SteamSpy and SteamDB, game telemetry, virtual reality, heat analysis, artificial intelligence behavior, requirement analysis, tests analysis, project quality analysis and monetization model analysis.

C. What are the opportunities and challenges in adopting of cloud computing in decision-making tools?

The key decision-making challenge in the game development process is to control the process to meet scope, time, and budget, while not limiting the creative process and user experience. One opportunity found in this review was the lack of work addressing how to improve the game sequence development process using decision-making during this process. Also other opportunities were identified: artificial intelligence, education, serious games, social media, lack of open data about games and to analyze more games.

VI. CONCLUSION

The main objective of this work was to conduct a search and analysis of the adoption of decision-making to improve the game development process. To that goal, a systematic review was conducted, briefly analyzing 261 papers and deeply analyzing 36 papers in order to discuss topics about the usage of decision-making. During the analysis phase, it was realized that the decision-making has been widely applied in many steps of game development process.

As future works, we intend to conduct further studies related to how game development companies and game developers apply decision-making in game sequels development.

REFERENCES

[1] G. J. Kasurinen and M. Palacin-Silva, "What Concerns Game Developers?," pp. 15–21, 2017.

[2] H. Engström, B. B. Marklund, P. Backlund, and M. Toftedahl, "Game development from a software and creative product perspective a quantitative literature review approach", Entertainment Computing, pp. 10-22, 2018, doi: https://doi.org/10.1016/j.entcom.2018.02.008.

[3] N. B. Ahmad, S. A. R. Barakji, T. M. A. Shahada, and Z. A. Anabtawi, "How to Launch A Successful Video Game: A Framework", Entertainment Computing, pp. 1-11, 2017, doi: http:// dx.doi.org/10.1016 /j.entcom.2017.08.001.

[4] F. Ahmed, M. Zia, H. Mahmood, and S. Al Kobaisi, "Open Source Computer Game Application: An Empirical Analysis of Quality Concerns", Entertainment Computing, pp. 1-10, 2017, doi: http://dx.doi.org/10.1016/ j.entcom.2017.04.001.

[5] A. Fatima, T. Rasool, and U. Qamar, "GDGSE: Game Development with Global Software Engineering" 2018 IEEE Games, Entertainment, Media Conference (GEM), pp. 288-292, 2018.

[6] T. Machado, D. Gopstein, A. Nealen, O. Nov, and J. Togelius, "AI-assisted game debugging with Cicero", pp. 9-17, 2018 IEEE Congress on Evolutionary Computation (CEC).

[7] B. Pacheco et al., "What Where?! A game for learning art, history and architecture", 978-1-5386-2376-3/17/$31.00. pp. 159-163, 2017 IEEE.

[8] R. Small, "Mods and Convergence Culture:Connecting character creation, user interface, and participatory design", SIGDOC'18, August 3-5,pp. 1-2, 2018. https://doi.org/10.1145/3233756.3233943.

[9] M. Arafat, A. Qusef, and S. Al-Taher, "Steam's Early Access Model: A Study on Consumers' Perspective", pp. 336-342, 2019 IEEE Jordan International Joint Conference on Electrical Engineering and Information Technology (JEEIT).

[10] R. Castillo, "Computer Games As Learning Tools:Teachers Attitudes & Behaviors",CHI PLAY'18 Extended Abstracts, Oct. 28–31, pp. 95-101, 2018, Melbourne, Australia. https://doi.org/10.1145/3270316.3270611.

[11] R. Santos et al., "Computer Games Are Serious Business and so is their Quality: Particularities of Software Testing in Game Development from the Perspective of Practitioners", ESEM '18, October 11–12, pp. 1-10, 2018, Oulu, Finland. https://doi.org/10.1145/3239235.3268923

[12] J. Pirker, I. Lesjak, A. Punz, and A. Drachen, "Social Aspects of the Game Development Process in the Global Gam Jam", ICGJ 2018, March 18, pp. 9-16, 2018, San Francisco, CA, USA. https://doi.org/10.1145/3196697.3196700

[13] F. Zhao, G. Nian, H. Jin, L. T. Yang, and Y. Zhu, "A Hybrid eBusiness Software Metrics Framework for Decision Making in Cloud Computing Environment," IEEE Syst. J., vol. 11, no. 2, pp. 1049–1059, 2017.

[14] C. Politowski, L. Fontouraa, F. Petrillob, and Y. Guéhéneucb, "Learning from the past: A process recommendation system for video game projects using postmortems experiences", Information and Software Technology, pp. 103-118, 2018. https://doi.org/10.1016/j.infsof.2018.04.003.

[15] G. Wallner, N. Halabi, and P. Mirza-Babaei, "Aggregated Visualization of Playtesting Data". In CHI Conference on Human Factors in Computing Systems Proceedings (CHI 2019), May 4–9,pp.1-12, 2019. https://doi.org/10.1145/3290605.3300593.

[16] S. Martins, G. Cabral, D. Junior, E. Haendel, and G. Cabral, "Lessons learned about the development of digital entertainment tools for experiments on Resources Division", Computers in Human Behavior, pp. 523-534, 2017, doi: 10.1016/j.chb.2017.01.023.

[17] A. Pyae, "Understanding the Role of Culture and Cultural Attributes in Digital Game Localization", Entertainment Computing, pp.105-116, 2018, doi: https://doi.org/10.1016/j.entcom.2018.02.004.

[18] Y. Tim , P. Hallikainen , S. Pan, and T. Tamm, "Actualizing Business Analytics for Organizational Transformation: A Case Study of Rovio Entertainment", European Journal of Operational Research, pp. 642-655, 2018, doi: https://doi.org/10.1016/j.ejor.2018.11.074.

[19] M. N. Giannakos and L. Jaccheri, "From players to makers: An empirical examination of factors that affect creative game development", International Journal of Child-Computer Interaction, pp. 27-36, 2018, https://doi.org/10.1016 /j.ijcci.2018.06.002.

[20] I. Soute, T. Vacaretu, J. Wit, and P. Markopoulos, "Design and Evaluation of RaPIDO, A Platform for Rapid Prototyping of Interactive Outdoor Games", ACM Trans. Comput.-Hum. Interact. 24, 4, Article 28, pp. 1-30, 2017. https://doi.org/10.1145/3105704.

[21] D. Lin, C. Bezemer, and A. Hassan, "An empirical study of early access games on the Steam platform", Empir Software Eng, pp. 1-29, 2017, DOI 10.1007/s10664-017-9531-3

[22] C. Alonso-Fernández, A. Calvo-Morata, M. Freire, I. Martínez-Ortiz, and B. Fernández-Manjón, "Applications of data science to game learning analytics data: A systematic literature review", Computers & Education 141, 2019. 103612, https://doi.org/10.1016/j.compedu.2019.103612.

[23] M. Teruela, N. Condori-Fernandez, E. Navarro, P. González, and P. Lago, "Assessing the impact of the awareness level on a co-operative game", Information and Software Technology, pp. 89-116, 2018.https://doi.org/10.1016/j.infsof.2018.02.008.

[24] M. Sjöblom, M. Törhönen, J. Hamari, and J. Macey, "Content structure is king: An empirical study on gratifications, game genres and content type on Twitch", Computers in Human Behavior 73, pp. 161-171, 2017. http://dx.doi.org/10.1016/j.chb.2017.03.036.

[25] I. Cabras et al., "Exploring survival rates of companies in the UK video-games industry: An empirical study", Technological Forecasting & Social Change, Volume 117, April 2017, pp. 305-314, 2017. http://dx.doi.org/10.1016/j.techfore.2016.10.073

[26] T. Kohwalter, L. Murta, and E. Clua, "Filtering irrelevant sequential data out of game session telemetry though similarity collapses", Future Generation Computer Systems, pp. 108-122, 2018. https://doi.org/10.1016/j.future.2018.03.004.

[27] C. Chen and T. Hsu, "Game development data analysis visualized with virtual reality", Proceedings of IEEE International Conference on Applied System Innovation, pp. 682-686, 2018.

[28] M. Young, A. McCoy, J. Hutson, M. Schlabach, and S. Eckels. "Hot under the collar: The impact of heat on game play", Applied Ergonomics 59, pp. 209-214, 2017. http://dx.doi.org/10.1016/j.apergo.2016.08.035

[29] E. Bailey and K. Miyata, "Improving video game project scope decisions with data: An analysis of achievements and game completion rates", Entertainment Computing, 2019, doi: https://doi.org/10.1016/ j.entcom.2019.100299.

[30] A. Sehrawat and G. Raj, "Intelligent PC Games: Comparison of Neural Network Based AI against Pre-Scripted AI". 2018 International Con-

ference on Advances in Computing and Communication Engineering (ICACCE-2018) Paris, France 22-23 June , pp. 378-384, 2018.

[31] A. Copenhaver and C. Ferguson, "Selling violent video game solutions: A look inside the APA's internal notes leading to the creation of the APA's 2005 resolution on violence in video games and interactive media", International Journal of Law and Psychiatry 57, pp. 77–84, 2018. https://doi.org/10.1016/j.ijlp.2018.01.004.

[32] M. Daneva, "Striving for balance: A look at gameplay requirements of massively multiplayer online role-playing games", The Journal of Systems and Software 134, pp. 54–75, 2017. http://dx.doi.org/10.1016/j.jss.2017.08.009.

[33] E. Annanperä et al., "Testing Methods for Mobile Game Development A case study on user feedback in different development phases", 978-1-5386-6298-4/18/$31.00 ©2018 IEEE.

[34] J. Liu, J. Chang, and J. Chia-An Tsai, "The Role of Sprint Planning and Feedback in Game Development Projects: Implications for Game Quality", The Journal of Systems & Software, pp. 79-91, 2019. doi: https://doi.org/10.1016/j.jss.2019.04.057

[35] D. King et al., "Unfair play? Video games as exploitative monetized services: An examination of game patents from a consumer protection perspective", Computers in Human Behavior, pp. 131-143, 2019. doi: 10.1016/j.chb.2019.07.017

[36] K. Alha, E. Koskinen, J. Paavilainen, and J. Hamari, "Why Do People Play Location-Based Augmented Reality Games: A Study on Pokémon GO", Computers in Human Behavior, pp.114-122, 2018. doi: 10.1016/j.chb.2018.12.008

[37] L. Grace et al., "Factitious: Large Scale Computer Game to Fight Fake News and Improve News Literacy", In Extended Abstracts of the 2019 CHI Conference on Human Factors in Computing Systems (CHI EA '19). Association for Computing Machinery, New York, NY, USA, Paper CS05, 1–8.

[38] L. Tabbaa et al., "Bring the Outside In: Providing Accessible Experiences Through VR for People with Dementia in Locked Psychiatric Hospitals", Proceedings of the SIGCHI Conference on Human Factors in Computing Systems, pp. 1–15, 2019.

[39] L. Wijnhoven et al., "The effect of the video game Mindlight on anxiety, symptoms in children with an Autism Spectrum Disorder", BMC Psychiatry 15, 138 (2015)

Human Factors in Exhaustion and Stress of Japanese Nursery Teachers: Evidence from Regression Model on a Novel Dataset

Tran Phuong Thao*, Midori Takahashi†, Nobuo Shigeta*,
Mhd Irvan*, Toshiyuki Nakata‡, and Rie Shigetomi Yamaguchi§

University of Tokyo
7-3-1, Hongo, Bunkyo, Tokyo, 113-8656, Japan
Email: *{tpthao, shigeta, irvan}@yamagula.ic.i.u-tokyo.ac.jp
†midorit@p.u-tokyo.ac.jp
‡nakata.toshiyuki@sict.i.u-tokyo.ac.jp
§yamaguchi.rie@i.u-tokyo.ac.jp

***Abstract*—Japan is well known for one of the highest suicide rates in the world, and suicide is the third cause of death after cancer and accidents. The most common reason for suicide comes from overwork and stress-related issues. Researchers have found that education is listed in the top 6 job categories that are highly affected by overwork and stress. In this paper, we investigate the human factors that influence the exhaustion and stress levels of nursery teachers, which is one of the top social issues in the education system of Japan. We are the first to own a novel dataset that contains the data of nursery teachers in Tokyo including demographics, working schedule, and stress and exhaustion information. The data was collected using survey-based and real-time approaches with professional devices. We built a regression model in machine learning with t-test in statistics and divided the effect levels of the factors into three levels: normal, nearly-significant, and significant. We found the following results. First, we found the evidence that working on Thursday and Friday affects both exhaustion and stress. Interestingly, although working on Friday is more exhaustive than on Thursday, working on Thursday is more stressful than on Friday. Surprisingly, we found that while working on Saturday does not affect either exhaustion or stress, working on Sunday is a factor affecting the stress (but not exhaustion) of the participants. Furthermore, gender, weight, and height do not appear as affecting factors. Also, people who are less than 30 years old get more easily stressed than the other ages.**

Keywords–Machine Learning; Multiple (Linear) Regression; Student's T-test (t-test); Human Factors.

I. INTRODUCTION

Japan is well known for having one of the highest suicide rates in the developed world. Japanese culture has a long history of considering certain types of suicides honorable, especially during military service. According to the National Police Agency (Government of Japan), 24,025 people died by suicide in Japan in 2015; and among those, 2,159 (12.0%) were suicides due to overwork and stress-related issues [1]. Y. Takashi et al. [2] studied 18 most common job categories and found that education/learning support is listed in the top 6 job categories that are highly affected by overwork and stress.

A. Motivation

Based on the data mentioned above, we ask the question: why does education/learning support have such a very high rank of overwork and stress rates? It is even higher than some other job categories that were believed to have high overwork and stress rates, such as scientific research, professional, and technical services, or information and communications. Furthermore, while a national initiative towards the prevention of overwork and stress-related issues becomes a challenge, Japan is encountering another big social issue in education that is the massive demand for nursery teachers [3][4]. According to the Ministry of Health, Labor and Welfare in Japan, the number of children on the waiting lists of nursery schools was over 20,000 between 2009 and 2016 [5]. Especially, this problem is serious in large cities like Tokyo. In 2016, more than 35% of the children on waiting lists lived in Tokyo [6]. So, we ask another question: Is there a relation between these two social issues in Japan, especially in Tokyo? More concretely, what are the factors influencing the exhaustion and stress of nursery teachers?

B. Contribution

In this work, we investigate human factors that affect the stress and exhaustion of Japanese nursery teachers:

- To the best of our knowledge, we are the first to collect a novel dataset related to the exhaustion and stress measurements of the nursery teachers in Tokyo. Our dataset was collected using a survey-based approach (i.e., questionnaire) and a real-time approach with the help of professional devices.
- Many people thought (but did not have evidence) that working on the days of the week that are before and close to weekends is more exhaustive and stressful than on the other days, and we are the first to find the evidence about it. We built a regression model in machine learning, applied the t-test, and found that the teachers working on Thursday and Friday tend to get exhausted and stressed. Moreover, while working on Friday is more exhaustive than on Thursday, working on Thursday is more stressful than on Friday.
- We also found that, while working on Saturday does not affect either the exhaustion or the stress, working on Sunday is a factor affecting the stress but not the exhaustion, although both Saturday and Sunday are weekend. Furthermore, gender, weight, and height do not appear as effecting factors; but people under 30 years old get stressed easier than the others.

C. Roadmap

The rest of this paper is organized as follows. The related work is described in Section II. The procedure is presented in Section III. The model is given in Section IV. The experiment and discussion are analyzed in Sections V. Finally, the conclusion is drawn in Section VI.

II. Related Work

In this section, we introduce related work about factor analysis in exhaustion and stress.

A. Exhaustion and Stress in Education

A. Rudman et al. [7] studied the influences of burnout during nursing education in health and professional development, and quality of care. They monitored the burnout of a national sample of nursing students during their years in higher education and at follow-up one year post-graduation, and found that the burnout during education is an important concern to the future clinical performance. A. Antoniou et al. [8] investigated the occupational stress and professional burnout of teachers in primary and secondary education. They showed that the teachers in primary education and the female teachers experience higher levels of stress compared to those in secondary education and male teachers, respectively. Furthermore, female teachers experience lower personal accomplishment than male teachers. N. Barkhuizen et al. [9] analyzed the relationship between burnout and work engagement in higher education. They found that job demands contributed to burnout while job resources contributed to work engagement. Dispositional optimism strongly affects perceptions of job resources, burnout, work engagement, ill-health, and organizational commitment. L. Flook et al. [10] analyzed the Mindfulness-Based Stress Reduction course (mMBSR) for teachers. They showed that the course has a good effect on the participants with significant reductions in psychological symptoms and burnout, improvements in classroom and performance on a computer task of affective attentional bias, and an increase in self-compassion. In contrast, control group participants showed declines in cortisol functioning and significant increases in burnout. Contrary to our work, none of the related work analyzed the stress and exhaustion for nursery teachers.

B. Exhaustion and Stress in Other Fields

N. Khamisa et al. [11] analyzed the nature of relationships between work-related burnout, job satisfaction, and general health of nurses. They showed that lack of support was associated with burnout, patient care was associated with job satisfaction, and staff issues were associated with general health of nurses. Furthermore, burnout is more strongly related to job satisfaction than general health. M. Mikolajczak et al. [12] analyzed whether parental burnout is affected by overwhelming exhaustion related to parental roles, emotional distance with children, and sense of ineffectiveness in parental roles. They showed that parental burnout is a multi-determined syndrome mainly predicted by three sets of factors: parent's stable traits, parenting, and family-functioning. P. Gkorezis et al. [13] studied Machiavellian leadership (a person's tendency to be unemotional, lacking in concern for conventional morality and more inclined to engage in interpersonal manipulation) in employees' emotional exhaustion. They showed that Machiavellian leadership has both direct and indirect effect on employees' emotional exhaustion through organizational cynicism. W. Liang et al. [14] analyzed whether the stress itself affects other issues (i.e., the problematic smartphone used among college students). Stress measurement is used as a factor not a target function like our goal. G. Mark et al. [15] analyzed three email use patterns, such as duration, interruption habit, and batching in affecting workplace productivity and stress. They tracked email usage of 40 information workers for 12 workdays and found that the longer daily time spent on email, the lower productivity and the higher stress. Furthermore, people who primarily check email through self-interruptions report higher productivity with longer email duration compared to those who rely on notifications. A. Barbarin et al. [16] investigated whether health information technology can support overweight or obese women in addressing emotion and stress-related eating. They showed that the factors (participants' needs) are holistic health goal development, building motivation to achieve goals, and assistance with handling stress. J. Adriaenssens et al. [17] analyzed the influence of changes over time in work and organizational characteristics on job satisfaction, work engagement, emotional exhaustion, turnover intention and psychosomatic distress in emergency room nurses. They found that changes in job demand, control, and social support predicted job satisfaction, work engagement, and emotional exhaustion. In addition, changes in reward, social harassment, and work agreements predicted work engagement, emotional exhaustion, and intention to leave, respectively.

III. Procedure

We collaborated with the Center of Early Childhood Development, Education, and Policy Research (CEDEP) at the University of Tokyo, Japan. CEPDEP helped contact 36 nursery teachers, who are working in seven nursery schools located in different wards in Tokyo. All the teachers agreed to participate in our measurement and signed the Privacy Policy agreement about their personal data.

A. Demographics

A paper-based questionnaire is prepared and distributed to the participants. The questions related to the demographics include:

- Gender: It is a single-choice question with two answer options (male and female).
- Age: The inputs are integers. The valid values are from 15 to 65 (years old), which are the allowed working ages by the Japanese government.
- Weight and height: The inputs are integers. The units are kilogram (kg) and centimeter (cm), respectively.

The distribution of gender, age, weight, and height are given in Tables I, II, III, and IV, respectively.

B. Working Days

All the measurements were conducted in 2019. Since there were not enough devices for all the participants to use at the same time, the data of each participant was collected in different periods. Each day in the measurement period is transformed to the corresponding day of the week (Monday to Sunday). The distribution is given in Table V. The first column represents the participant ID (36 participants in total). The second column represents the measurement periods. Some

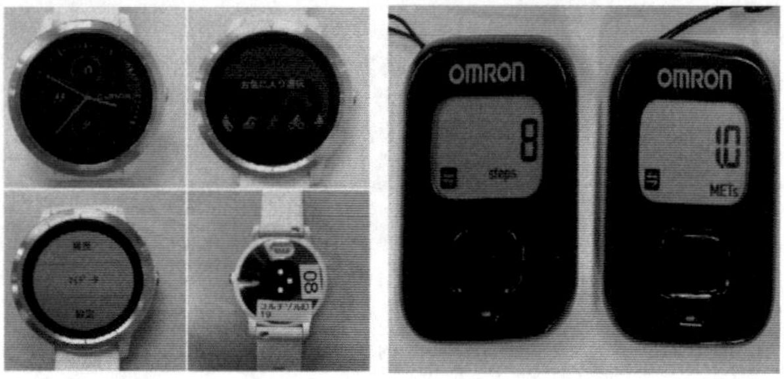

Figure 1. Garmin (Left) and Omron (Right) Devices

participants have discontinuous measurement periods which are presented in different rows. The third to ninth columns represent the number of weekdays extracted from the measurement periods.

C. Stress and Exhaustion Measurement

Professional devices were used to measure the stress and exhaustion. The devices were given to the participants only in the corresponding measurement periods that were designed for each participant, as mentioned in Section III-B. The teachers were required to wear the devices during the working time in the nursery schools only, and had to return them before leaving the schools.

To measure the stress, we used Garmin smartwatches (Vivoactive 3), as depicted in Figure 1 (left). Garmin is a technology company specializing in wearable technology products, such as activity trackers and smartwatches [18]. The devices measured the stress from 1 to 100. 1 to 25 represents the resting states, 26 to 50 represents the low stress, 51 to 75 represents the medium stress, and 76 to 100 represents the high stress. The devices determine the stress based on the heart-rate variability. From the heart rate data, the device extracts the interval between each heartbeat. If the variable length of time in between each heartbeat is fast, it reflects the autonomic nervous system of the user's body. The lower the variability between beats, the higher the stress levels, whereas an increase in variability indicates less stress. We can read the stress directly from the devices or logging in the accounts from the Application Programming Interface (API) webpage of Garmin.

To measure the exhaustion, we used Omron devices (Active Style Pro HJA-750C), as depicted in Figure 1 (right). Omron is an electronics company that is well-known for medical equipment devices [19]. The devices measure the total calories burned and the Basal Metabolic Rate (BMR). These values are then used to calculate the exhaustion. More details are explained in Section IV.

TABLE I. DISTRIBUTION OF GENDER

Value	#Participants	Percentage
1 (Male)	6	16.67%
0 (Female)	30	83.33%
Total	36	100%

TABLE II. DISTRIBUTION OF AGE

Value	#Participants	Percentage
$\leq$ 29	16	44.44%
30 to 39	10	27.78%
$\geq$ 40	10	27.78%
Total	36	100%

TABLE III. DISTRIBUTION OF WEIGHT

Weight	#Participants	Percentage	Weight	#Participants	Percentage
44	1	2.78%	56	1	2.78%
45	2	5.56%	57	1	2.78%
46	3	8.33%	58	1	2.78%
47	2	5.56%	60	1	2.78%
48	3	8.33%	63	3	8.33%
49	2	5.56%	65	1	2.78%
50	2	5.56%	66	1	2.78%
51	4	11.11%	68	1	2.78%
53	3	8.33%	70	1	2.78%
55	2	5.56%	73	1	2.78%
Total	#Participants = 36 (100%)				

TABLE IV. DISTRIBUTION OF HEIGHT

Height	#Participants	Percentage	Height	#Participants	Percentage
150	1	2.78%	160	5	13.89%
152	1	2.78%	161	2	5.56%
153	1	2.78%	162	1	2.78%
154	1	2.78%	163	1	2.78%
155	1	2.78%	165	2	5.56%
156	1	2.78 %	167	1	2.78%
157	6	16.67%	168	3	8.33%
158	4	11.11 %	177	2	5.56%
159	2	5.56%	179	1	2.78%
Total	#Participants = 36 (100%)				

IV. MODEL

Let f denote the model for both the exhaustion and stress:

$$f = demog + wdays \tag{1}$$

where $demog$ and $wdays$ denote the features extracted from demographics and working weekdays, respectively.

A. Variables

The explanatory variables related to $demog$ consist of gender, age, weight, and height. For the gender, the input values are normalized to binary numbers, such as male: 1 and female: 0. For the age, the input values are grouped into three features (i.e., $\leq$ 29, 30 to 39, and $\geq$ 40 (years old)), and are normalized to binary numbers for each feature. For the weight and height, the variables use the original input values.

The explanatory variables related to $wdays$ are the seven days in a week (Monday to Sunday) which are extracted from the measurement period. For each weekday, the variable is a binary number, such as working on that day: 1 and not working on that day: 0. In summary, there are 13 variables (11 binary variables and 2 continuous variables).

B. Target functions

For the exhaustion, the target function is defined as follows:

$$f_1 = \frac{wkcal}{bmr} \tag{2}$$

where $wkcal$ denotes the calories burned during the working time for each weekday (Monday to Sunday); and bmr

TABLE V. DISTRIBUTION OF MEASUREMENT PERIOD (IN 2019)

#Part.	Measurement Period	Mon	Tue	Wed	Thu	Fri	Sat	Sun
01	5/29-5/31	0	1	1	1	0	0	0
02	5/29-5/31	0	1	1	1	0	0	0
03	5/29-5/31	0	1	1	1	0	0	0
04	5/29-5/31	0	1	1	1	0	0	0
05	5/29-5/31	0	1	1	1	0	0	0
06	5/29-5/31	0	1	1	1	0	0	0
07	6/06-6/08	0	0	0	1	1	1	0
08	6/03-6/12	2	2	2	1	1	1	1
09	6/07-6/09	0	0	0	0	1	1	1
10	6/06-6/07	0	0	0	1	1	0	0
11	6/06-6/07	0	0	0	1	1	0	0
12	5/27-6/12	3	3	3	2	2	2	2
13	6/06-6/07	0	0	0	1	1	0	0
14	6/06-6/07	0	0	0	1	1	0	0
15	6/06-6/07	0	0	0	1	1	0	0
16	6/06-6/07	0	0	0	1	1		0
17	6/12	0	0	1	0	0	0	0
18	6/13-6/14	0	0	0	1	1	0	0
	6/17-6/18	1	1	0	0	0	0	0
19	6/12-6/14	0	0	1	1	1	0	0
20	5/27-6/18	4	4	3	3	3	3	3
21	5/27-6/18	4	4	3	3	3	3	3
22	6/12-6/15	0	0	1	1	1	1	0
23	5/27-7/08	7	6	6	6	6	6	6
24	6/12-6/14	0	0	1	1	1	0	0
25	6/19-6/21	0	0	1	1	1	0	0
	6/23-6/24	1	0	0	0	0	0	1
26	6/19-6/20	0	0	1	1	0	0	0
	6/24	1	0	0	0	0	0	0
27	6/19	0	0	1	0	0	0	0
	6/21	0	0	0	0	1	0	0
28	6/19-6/21	0	0	1	1	1	0	0
29	6/19-6/21	0	0	1	1	1	0	0
30	6/19-6/21	0	0	1	1	1	0	0
31	6/19-6/21	0	0	1	1	1	0	0
32	6/19-6/21	0	0	1	1	1	0	0
33	6/19-6/21	0	0	1	1	1	0	0
34	6/20-6/21	0	0	0	1	1	0	0
35	6/20-6/22	0	0	0	1	1	1	0
36	6/19-6/21	0	0	1	1	1	0	0

denotes the BMR, which is the body's metabolism. BMR represents the required calories to keep one's body functioning at rest (a constant for each person). Thus, we calculate the exhaustion by the rate of total calories burned everyday and the BMR. For each weekday, $wkcal$ is calculated as the average of calories burned in all the working days that can be transformed to this weekday. More concretely, suppose that the measurement period is n days $\{d_1, \cdots, d_n\}$. For each weekday $w \in$ {Monday, $\cdots$, Sunday}, $wkcal$ is calculated as $wkcal = \mathsf{average}(\mathsf{CaloriesBurned}(d_i))$ for all $\forall i$ such that $\mathsf{WeekDay}(d_i) = w$.

For the stress, the target function is defined as follows:

$$f_2 = wsl \tag{3}$$

where wsl dennotes the stress for each weekday. wsl is calculated as the average of stress levels in all the working days that can be transformed to the weekday: $wsl = \mathsf{average}(\mathsf{StressLevel}(d_i))$ for all $\forall i$ such that $\mathsf{WeekDay}(d_i) = w$.

C. Factor Determination

After constructing the model, the (multiple) linear regression is applied for each target function. The linear regression is used instead of the logistic regression because the exhaustion and stress have continuous values. Formally, suppose y_p is the predicted value. y_p is determined as:

$$y_p(w, x) = w_0 + w_1 x_1 + \cdots + w_n x_n \tag{4}$$

where $(x_1, \cdots, x_n)$ are the variables and n is the number of variables. The algorithm designates the vector $w = (w_1, \cdots, w_n)$ as the coefficients and w_0 as the intercept (i.e., the constant which is the expected mean value of y_p when all x's are 0). To estimate w and w_0, we use the Ordinary Least Squares (OLS) method which fits the model with coefficients to minimize the residual sum of squares between the observed targets in the dataset and the targets predicted by the linear approximation:

$$\min_x \; || \; xw - y \; ||_2^2 \tag{5}$$

The t-test is then applied to find the factors whose p-values are less than or equal to 0.05. The factors are categorized as follows:

- $0.01 < p \leq 0.05$: normal affecting factors
- $0.001 < p \leq 0.01$: nearly-significant affecting factors
- $p \leq 0.001$: significant affecting factors

In the experiment result, besides the p-value, we also show the t-value which measures the size of the difference relative to the variation in the sample data, the coefficients w_i of the linear equation, and 95% of Confidence Interval (CI) which is an estimated range of values that may contain the true mean of the population.

V. EXPERIMENT

The program is written in Python 3.7.4 on a computer MacBook Pro 2.8 GHz Intel Core i7, RAM 16 GB. The regression model is executed using *scikit-learn* library 0.21. The t-test is applied using *statsmodels* library 0.10.

A. Data Pre-processing and Statistics

1) Cronbach's Alpha (α): Cronbach's α is used to measure the Internal Consistency (IC) or the reliability of the questions that have multiple Likert-scale sub-questions. Suppose a quantity which is a sum of K components is measured as: $X = Y_1 + Y_2 + \cdots + Y_K$. The value α is defined as follows:

$$\alpha = \frac{K}{K-1}\left(1 - \frac{\sum_{i=1}^{K} \sigma_{Y_i}^2}{\sigma_X^2}\right) \tag{6}$$

where σ_X^2 denotes the variance of the observed total test scores and $\sigma_{Y_i}^2$ denotes the variance of the component i for the current sample of persons. The values of α can be interpreted as follows: $\alpha \geq 0.9$ (excellent IC), $0.9 > \alpha \geq 0.8$ (good IC), $0.8 > \alpha \geq 0.7$ (acceptable IC), $0.7 > \alpha \geq 0.6$ (questionable IC), $0.6 > \alpha \geq 0.5$ (poor IC), and $0.5 > \alpha$ (unacceptable IC). For our dataset containing the working weekdays (Table V), we can ask the same type of question. We run the Cronbach α test on the set of 36 rows (36 participants) and 7 columns (Monday to Sunday) in the table. For the participants that have more than one row, the values are summed for each working weekday. The number of sub-questions is $K = 7$. The sum of the item variances is $\sum_{i=1}^{K} \sigma_{Y_i}^2 = 10.49$. The variance of total scores is $\sigma_X^2 = 67.01$. Therefore, $\alpha = \frac{7}{7-1}(1 - \frac{10.49}{67.01}) = 0.98$ (excellent IC). This indicates that the data for working days is reliable.

2) Noise Removal: Each participant has different working weekdays. In Table V, 122 samples are extracted as the number of working weekdays of the 36 participants. For the exhaustion measurement, we used all the 122 samples for the learning dataset and applied the regression to the dataset. For the stress measurement, there are nine samples that have zero or untraceable stress levels. We thus considered them as data outliers, and removed them from the dataset. We applied the regression on the remaining $122 - 9 = 113$ samples.

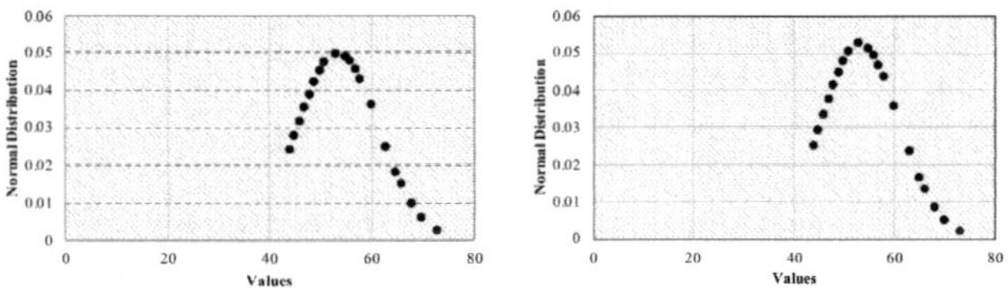

(a) Exhaustion (b) Stress

Figure 2. Normal Distribution Curves (Weight)

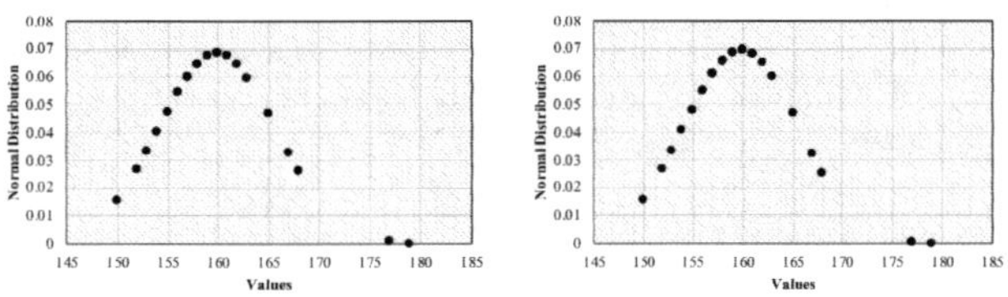

(a) Exhaustion (b) Stress

Figure 3. Normal Distribution Curves (Height)

3) Distribution: As mentioned in Section IV-A, the model consists of 13 variables (11 binary variables and 2 continuous variables). The distributions are separately calculated on 122 samples for the exhaustion and 113 samples for the stress. The distribution of binary variables is given in Table VI. In some variables, the values may have a low distribution. For instance, the variables Monday, Tuesday, Saturday, and Sunday have less than 10% of the distribution for the binary value '1' (or 'yes'). This may raise the question whether this kind of variables will affect the result and should be removed from the dataset. However, for the linear regression model, it is not necessary to remove such variables because the influences of any variable, which is even strong or weak, will be reflected in the t-test's result. For the continuous variables, the distribution scores are described in Table VII and the distribution curves are given in Figures 2 (weight) and 3 (height). The curve shapes for the exhaustion and the stress look the same but in fact, are different. All the variables have bell curves and the skewness in $[-2, +2]$; this indicates that the variables are valid for normal (Gaussian) distribution.

B. Main Experimental Results

1) Exhaustion: The regression is applied to 122 samples. The result is shown in Table VIII. Two factors were found:

- Friday: *significant affecting factor* ($p = 0.001$). The positive coefficient (0.2541) indicates that the teachers who work on Friday tend to get exhausted. If the coefficient is negative, the variable and the target function will have an inverse effect (e.g., the teachers who do NOT work on Friday tend to get exhausted).
- Thursday: *nearly-significant affecting factor* ($p = 0.004$). The positive coefficient (0.2126) indicates that the teachers who work on Thursday tend to get exhausted, but the effect is less than working on Friday.

TABLE VI. DISTRIBUTION OF BINARY VARIABLES

Variable	Exhaustion (122 samples)		Stress (113 samples)	
	Yes/1	No/0	Yes/1	No/0
Male	15 (12.30%)	107 (87.70%)	12 (10.62%)	101 (89.38%)
Age: $\leq$ 29	47 (38.52%)	75 (61.48%)	43 (38.05%)	70 (61.95%)
Age: 30-39	35 (28.69%)	87 (71.31%)	31 (27.43%)	82 (72.57%)
Age: $\geq$ 40	40 (32.79%)	82 (67.21%)	39 (34.51%)	74 (65.49%)
Monday	8 (06.56%)	114 (93.44%)	7 (6.19%)	106 (93.81%)
Tuesday	6 (04.92%)	116 (95.08%)	5 (4.42%)	108 (95.58%)
Wednesday	25 (20.49%)	97 (79.51%)	25 (22.12%)	88 (77.88%)
Thursday	33 (27.05%)	89 (72.95%)	31 (27.43%)	82 (72.57%)
Friday	34 (27.87%)	88 (72.13%)	33 (29.20%)	80 (70.80%)
Saturday	9 (07.38%)	113 (92.62%)	8 (7.08%)	105 (92.92%)
Sunday	7 (05.74%)	115 (94.26%)	4 (3.54%)	109 (96.46%)

TABLE VII. DISTRIBUTION OF CONTINUOUS VARIABLES

Score	Exhaustion (122 samples)		Stress (113 samples)	
	Weight	Height	Weight	Height
Mean	53.61	159.96	53.61	159.90
Standard Error	0.72	0.53	0.72	0.53
Median	51	159	51	159
Mode	46	160	46	157
Standard Deviation	7.99	5.80	7.99	5.73
Sample Variance	63.79	33.64	63.79	32.79
Kurtosis	-0.32	2.59	-0.32	2.66
Skewness	0.87	1.44	0.87	1.44
Range	29	29	29	29
Minimum	44	150	44	150
Maximum	73	179	73	179

TABLE VIII. RESULT FOR EXHAUSTION

No	Factor	Coef.	p-Value	t-Value	95% CI
	Intercept	0.328	0.467	0.729	[-0.563, 1.218]
1	Male	-0.029	0.708	-0.375	[-0.179, 0.122]
2	Weight	-0.002	0.380	-0.882	[-0.007, 0.003]
3	Height	0.007	0.111	1.608	[-0.002, 0.015]
4	Age: $\leq$ 29	0.145	0.360	0.919	[-0.167, 0.457]
5	Age: 30 to 39	0.080	0.584	0.549	[-0.207, 0.366]
6	Age: $\geq$ 40	0.103	0.500	0.677	[-0.199, 0.406]
7	Monday	-0.078	0.365	-0.909	[-0.249, 0.092]
8	Tuesday	-0.097	0.304	-1.034	[-0.282, 0.089]
9	Wednesday	0.104	0.148	1.455	[-0.038, 0.245]
10	Thursday	0.213	(**) 0.004	2.941	[0.069, 0.356]
11	Friday	0.254	(***) 0.001	3.543	[0.112, 0.396]
12	Saturday	0.070	0.398	0.848	[-0.093, 0.233]
13	Sunday	-0.138	0.114	-1.594	[-0.309, 0.034]

(*): $0.01 < p \leq 0.05$, (**): $0.001 < p \leq 0.01$, and (***): $p \leq 0.001$

2) Stress: The regression model is applied to 113 samples. The result is shown in Table IX. Five factors were found:

- Age $\leq$ 29: *normal affecting factor* ($p = 0.030$). The positive coefficient (44.9775) indicates that the teachers who are less than or equal to 29 years old tend to get stressed.
- Wednesday: *normal affecting factor* ($p = 0.030$). The positive coefficient (20.1024) indicates that the teachers who work on Wednesday tend to get stressed.
- Sunday: *normal affecting factor* ($p = 0.029$). The positive coefficient (27.0998) indicates that the teachers

who work on Sunday tend to get stressed.

- Thursday: *nearly-significant affecting factor* ($p = 0.005$). The positive coefficient (27.6259) indicate that the teachers who work on Thursday tend to get stressed.
- Friday: *nearly-significant affecting factor* ($p = 0.007$). The positive coefficient (25.9464) indicate that the teachers who work on Friday tend to get stressed.

TABLE IX. RESULT FOR STRESS

No	Factor	Coef.	p-Value	t-Value	95% CI
	(Intercept)	116.777	0.047	2.012	[1.653, 231.901]
1	Male	-0.088	0.993	-0.009	[-19.792, 19.616]
2	Weight	0.150	0.617	0.502	[-0.442, 0.741]
3	Height	-0.920	0.093	-1.698	[-1.994, 0.155]
4	Age: $\leq$ 29	44.978	(*) 0.030	2.203	[4.469, 85.486]
5	Age: 30 to 39	33.416	0.074	1.806	[-3.294, 70.125]
6	Age: $\geq$ 40	38.384	0.055	1.943	[-0.797, 77.565]
7	Monday	2.692	0.804	0.249	[-18.778, 24.163]
8	Tuesday	-2.020	0.864	-0.172	[-25.334, 21.294]
9	Wednesday	20.102	(*) 0.030	2.201	[1.984, 38.220]
10	Thursday	27.626	(**) 0.005	2.873	[8.553, 46.699]
11	Friday	25.946	(**) 0.007	2.762	[7.314, 44.579]
12	Saturday	15.330	0.143	1.477	[-5.254, 35.914]
13	Sunday	27.100	(*) 0.029	2.214	[2.823, 51.377]

(*): $0.01 < p \leq 0.05$, (**): $0.001 < p \leq 0.01$, and (***): $p \leq 0.001$

C. Discussion

Both the results of exhaustion and stress show that the nursery teachers who work on Thursday and Friday tend to get exhausted and stressed. It is probably caused by the fact that Thursday and Friday are the latest two days before the teachers can take the weekend holidays. Furthermore, although working on Friday is more exhaustive than on Thursday, working on Thursday is more stressful than on Friday. The results also show that the people under 30 years old get stressed easier than the others. In our survey, the people under 30 years old are the youngest participants (compared with 30 to 39 and over 30) and it is quite obvious that the young people often do not have good control on their anxiety, emotion, and stress. The deeper reasons that explain these results will be formally examined in future work. Furthermore, a new questionnaire can be re-designed to collect other promising factors including the information related to schools (e.g., the number of male/female teachers and children, public or private schools, etc.) and teachers (e.g., experience (acquired skills), self-confidence, salary, full/part-time, etc.).

VI. Conclusion

In this paper, we used professional devices to collect exhaustion and stress information from 36 nursery teachers working in Tokyo. We built a regression model and found the evidence that working on Thursday and Friday affects both the exhaustion and stress. While working on Friday is more exhaustive than on Thursday, working on Thursday is more stressful than on Friday. While working on Saturday does not affect either the exhaustion or stress, working on Sunday is a factor affecting the stress, but not the exhaustion. Gender, weight, and height do not appear as affecting factors. People under 30 years old get stressed easier than the others.

References

[1] National Police Agency, Government of Japan. Toukei (in Japanese). https://www.npa.go.jp/toukei/index.htm. Retrieved: August 15, 2019.

[2] Y. Takashi et al., "Overwork-related disorders in Japan: recent trends and development of a national policy to promote preventive measures". *Industrial Health*, vol. 55, no. 3, 2017, pp. 293-302.

[3] W. Rupert, "Japan: The worst developed country for working mothers?". *BBC News*, 2013. Available: https://www.bbc.com/news/magazine-21880124. Retrieved: February 02, 2020.

[4] Y. Nohara, "Low pay haunts Tokyo's nurseries despite massive demand for places". *Bloomberg*, 2016. Available: https://www.japantimes.co.jp/news/2016/08/16/national/social-issues/japans-nursery-school-teachers-opt-better-paying-jobs/#.XUaYlpMzbBJ. Retrieved: February 02, 2020.

[5] Ministry of Health, Labour and Welfare, "Nursery school related situation report", 2016. Available: https://www.mhlw.go.jp/stf/houdou/000013 5392.html. Retrieved: February 02, 2020.

[6] Y. Okumura, "School Choice with General Constraints: A Market Design Approach for the Nursery School Waiting List Problem in Japan". *The Journal of the Japanese Economic Association*, 2018. Online Access. Available: https://papers.ssrn.com/sol3/papers.cfm?abstract_id=3176853. Retrieved: February 02, 2020.

[7] A. Rudman and J. P. Gustavsson, "Burnout during nursing education predicts lower occupational preparedness and future clinical performance: A longitudinal study". *International Journal of Nursing Studies*, vol. 49, no. 8, 2012, pp. 988-1001.

[8] A. S. Antoniou, A. Ploumpi, and M. Ntalla, "Occupational Stress and Professional Burnout in Teachers of Primary and Secondary Education: The Role of Coping Strategies". *Psychology*, vol. 4, no. 3A, 2013, pp. 349-355.

[9] N. Barkhuizen, S. Rothmann, and F. Vijver, "Burnout and Work Engagement of Academics in Higher Education Institutions: Effects of Dispositional Optimism". *Stress and Health*, vol. 30, no. 4, 2014, pp. 322-332.

[10] L. Flook, S. B. Goldberg, L. Pinger, K. Bonus, and R. J. Davidson, "Mindfulness for Teachers: A Pilot Study to Assess Effects on Stress, Burnout, and Teaching Efficacy". *Mind, Brain, and Education*, vol. 7, no. 4, 2013, pp. 256-256.

[11] N. Khamisa, K. Peltzer, I. Dragan, and B. Oldenburg, "Work related stress, burnout, job satisfaction and general health of nurses: A follow-up study". *Journal of Nursing Practice*, vol. 22, no. 6, 2016, pp. 538-545.

[12] M. Mikolajczak, M. Raes, H. Avalosse, and I. Roskam, "Exhausted Parents: Sociodemographic, Child-Related, Parent-Related, Parenting and Family-Functioning Correlates of Parental Burnout". *Journal of Child and Family Studies*, vol. 27, no 2, 2018, pp. 602-614.

[13] P. Gkorezis, E. Petridou, and T. Krouklidou, "The Detrimental Effect of Machiavellian Leadership on Employees' Emotional Exhaustion: Organizational Cynicism as a Mediator". *Europe's Journal of Psychology*, vol. 11, no. 4, 2015, pp. 619-631.

[14] W. Liang, W. Zhen, J. Gaskin, and L. Wang, "The role of stress and motivation in problematic smartphone use among college students". *Computers in Human Behavior*, vol. 53, 2015, pp. 181-188.

[15] G. Mark et al., "Email Duration, Batching and Self-interruption: Patterns of Email Use on Productivity and Stress". *Conference on Human Factors in Computing Systems (CHI'16)*, 2016, pp. 1717-1728.

[16] A. M. Barbarin, L. R. Saslow, M. S. Ackerman, and T. C. Veinot, "Toward Health Information Technology that Supports Overweight/Obese Women in Addressing Emotion- and Stress-Related Eating". *Conference on Human Factors in Computing Systems*, 2018, No. 321.

[17] J. Adriaenssens, V. Gucht, and S. Maes, "Causes and consequences of occupational stress in emergency nurses, a longitudinal study". *Journal of Nursing Management*, vol. 23, no. 3, 2015, pp. 346-358.

[18] Garmin Ltd, www.garmin.com. Retrieved: February 02, 2020.

[19] Omron Corporation, https://www.omron.com. Retrieved: February 02, 2020.

Building Guidelines for UNESCO World Heritage Sites' Apps

Joatan Preis Dutra
Mobile Media Group
Bauhaus-University Weimar
Weimar, Germany
Leicester Media School
De Montfort University
Leicester, United Kingdom
e-mail: joatan.dutra@dmu.ac.uk

***Abstract*—Technological improvements and access provide a fertile scenario for the creation and development of mobile applications. This scenario of intense production of new software for mobile devices results in a myriad of apps providing information about almost all the cultural segments, including those dedicated to UNESCO World Heritage Sites (WHS). However, not all of the apps have the same efficiency. In order to have a successful app, its development must consider usability aspects aligned with reliable content. Despite the guidelines for mobile usability being broadly available, they are generic, and none of them concentrates specifically in cultural heritage. This article aims to fulfil this literature gap and discusses how to develop specific guidelines for a better WHS experience. It uses an empirical approach applied to an open-air WHS city: Weimar and its Bauhaus and Classical Weimar sites. To build the guidelines, this research compared literature-based guidelines to industry-based ones, extracted from a vast compendium of available apps dedicated to WHS. The instructions compiled from both sources have been comparatively tested by using two built prototypes from the distinctive guidelines.**

Keywords – Interface design; world heritage sites; usability; app; mobile devices.

I. INTRODUCTION

It is far behind the time when, in order to enjoy a historical and cultural experience, it was necessary to visit a museum or to buy a guide to check the information about the monuments and historical buildings in a city. Despite the importance of these institutions and tools, the technology allows the expansion of the concept one step further, transforming cities themselves in open-air museums, by using mobile apps accessible through smartphones that most people carry in their pockets. They can be used to converge information and recreate the museum experience in open-air spaces.

However, to make this experience effective, the apps must follow a particular set of rules, or they can end up influencing the tourism experience negatively by causing frustration when the user tries to retrieve the desired information. To make this experience enjoyable for the user, it is advised to follow guidelines and good practices during the development of an app for touristic purposes. This study goes beyond the touristic aspects and helps to define guidelines that are appropriately applied for WHS scenarios. This research considered a vast range of usability studies and explored the interactions between users and urban spaces. It also includes precise niche requirements for the chosen scenario such as usability applied to elderly groups, as they are an important target group for tourism in Germany.

From a content perspective, it is valid to mention the preparedness of UNESCO WHS. Every recognised site has a vast range of official information available, aiming for different audiences. For example, it is easy to find educational content, ready to be used inside classrooms. For this study, the set of available material related to heritage locations is defined as *target content,* and some of the discussions explore how it is possible to make it accessible and tailored for mobile devices.

It is necessary to say that, despite the popularity of mobile gadgets, the target content does not contemplate guidelines or suggestions for digital applications. It will be explored in Section II. The same section also shows why Germany is relevant as a scenario to develop guidelines for WHS apps, that can have an international application. The research uses a mixed-method approach to suggest the guidelines. It started with the analysis of apps available in the industry through a classification based on affordances [1], identifying features, elements and their use in the mobile application, as detailed in Section III. The analysis revealed one set of guidelines used to create one of the prototypes. Section IV shows how a systematic literature review was used to identify the available articles discussing the topic and, by analysing the content, to extract another set of guidelines used in a second prototype. After the compilation, each one of the guidelines was used to develop their own mobile app prototype, and both prototypes were submitted to a comparative A/B test. Section V deals with the implementation of the two prototypes and also with the evaluation process, comparing the results from both developed prototypes. In Section VI, the evaluation, implementation and results are discussed. In Section VII, a new set of recommended guidelines emerges, considering the evaluation results.

II. TARGET CONTENT

The focus of this research is on apps that deal with cultural heritage content. Germany is the 5th largest country with of "World Heritage Sites" from the UNESCO's list [2]. The country has 43 cultural sites spread across its territory. From those sites, two of them (Bauhaus and its Sites in Weimar and Dessau; and Classical Weimar) are situated in Weimar - a place where this research is based. These sites are easily accessible, being a perfect sample opportunity for in loco use. There is a vast amount of target content available for the two sites mentioned. It means the information was retrieved directly from official sources to build the two prototypes. By doing so, the test was concentrated on verifying the features, functionalities, and on different ways to display similar information on the app.

Also, Germany is well known for its technological potential. This scenario reflects on services using a digital format, available for different purposes, such as information, education, entertainment, just to mention a few, applied to multiple devices, such as mobile devices, web-based services, and interactive screens.

Taking Germany as a scenario for the empirical approach is a fair way to gain experience and access for innovative projects using mobile devices for cultural heritage.

III. INDUSTRY BASED GUIDELINES

There are many smartphones and tablets' models available on the market, with different features but also constraints. The iOS or Android OS together have more than 3 million published apps, embracing 80% of the German mobile market share. For that reason, the prototypes were developed using a platform that could be accessed by both OS: iOS and Android operating systems. For the same reason, the apps to be evaluated were retrieved from both official stores following the same criteria.

To retrieve the apps from each selected OS markets, a search string was applied, using the following combination of words:

1. UNESCO WHS in Germany
2. Official app market
3. Word search options:
   - UNESCO Germany
   - UNESCO Deutschland
   - World Heritage
   - Welterbe (World Heritage in German)
   - The name of the WHS for Germany, in English and German versions
4. When the WHS refers to "Old Town" or "Parks" of a city, the used search term is "City Name" + UNESCO
5. Dedicated WHS apps

In this work, a *dedicated WHS app* defines an app specially made for the WHS attraction. Generic touristic apps, on the other hand, usually cover multiple touristic attractions and not only the WHS site; the only exception is when the city centre (usually called as old town, inside the WHS context) is considered a WHS itself. In this case, a generic city touristic app may enter in the list, if in its home screen there is an indication of UNESCO or WHS. Following these search criteria, 29 apps dedicated to German WHS sites were retrieved by 25 July 2018.

Other apps were found following the beforementioned search criteria, but they did not offer specific WHS-related content and, therefore, were excluded from the analysis. In some cases, they were *clickbait* apps, using the WHS identification to encourage the users to download it, but promoting other sorts of content, such as touristic tours or *purchase-in app* features. In other cases, sweb-based apps had problems to load the pages. As they were not fully functional – thus not trustworthy to generate guidelines – they were also excluded from the final sample.

The final sample also included generic touristic apps where it was possible to find specific WHS information, despite this not being shown on their home screen. In these cases, it means one needs to go further into the app to discover if a WHS is mentioned or not.

A. WHS App Analysis

The selected apps were analysed and classified from an affordance perspective, observing their properties and usage from a user perspective. This enabled the identification of common features and tools used for the promotion of a WHS. It also allowed identifying unique features and the ones that could be part of the guidelines to build the prototype. The analysis extracted guidelines from layout, navigation, design, and content perspectives. From that, a WHS prototype app was built based on the state of the art observed in the industry (Table I).

The app affordances were analysed from the user perspective, by using the individual expert review technique, in which "an individual expert review involves a single practitioner who is asked to provide feedback on the usability of a UI." [2, p. 37]. After being mapped, the content was distributed under subcategories, adapted from a study about usability guidelines for mobile websites and applications [3], taking into consideration just the app functionalities. This approach allowed the identification of the usability guidelines, plus mapping the visual and content structure from the official apps for WHS in Germany.

B. Industry Overview Guidelines

The industry/market analysis of the available apps for WHS in Germany revealed a set of guidelines used to build a market-based prototype with the most common features and layout, creating an average model to be tested against a literature-review-based one (Figure 1).

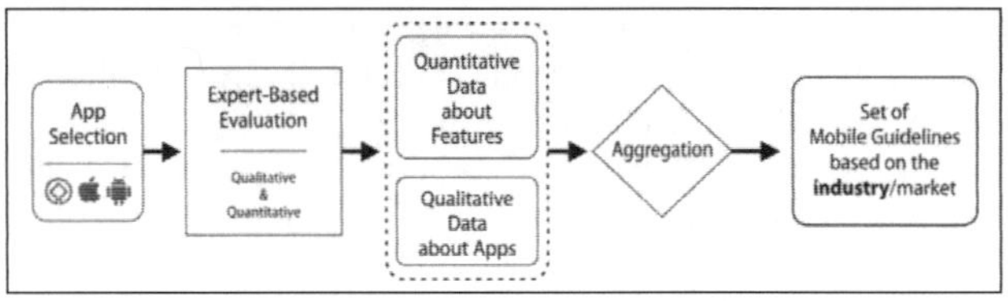

Figure 1. Schematics on the creation of the industry-based guidelines

The prototype following the industry-based guidelines combined the most popular elements presented on the evaluated apps, taking in consideration layout, navigation, design, content style, features and media. The guidelines considered only those elements that appeared in more than 50% of the apps (Table I). The guideline also followed the most prominent qualitative features in regards to elements that cannot be quantified, such as colour, layout disposition, etc.

TABLE I. INDUSTRY BASED GUIDELINES

		Total %
Layout		
L1	Place Content in one screen	41.38 %
L2	Vertical Scrolling	89.66 %
L3	Horizontal Scrolling	17.24 %
L4	Consistency between different sections	79.31 %
Navigation		
N1	Number of Taps to WHS Information	2 (average)
N2	Number of items on main navigation	6 (average)
N3	Navigation Menu visible	75.86 %
N4	One Level Navigation Menu	48.28 %
N5	More Levels	51.72 %
N6	Self-explanatory menu	55.17 %
N7	Enable gestures	48.28 %
N8	Presence of the Back button	72.41%
Design		
D1	Limited use of colours	68.97 %
D2	Wide range of use of colours	31.03 %
D3	Simple design	75.86 %
D4	Polluted design	31.03 %
D5	Use of icons	86.21 %
Content		
C1	Long text	86.21 %
C2	Short text	24.14 %
C3	Info at start screen	24.14 %
C4	No info at start screen	68.97 %
C5	Prevent information loss (when back)	89.66 %
C6	Provides action feedback	41.38 %
C7	Provides share options	20.69 %
C8	Nearby	3.45 %
C9	Tours	41.38 %
C10	Links to external content	41.38 %
Features and Media		
F1	Photo	96.55 %
F2	Photo 360°	6.90 %
F3	Map GPS	68.97 %
F4	Map Static	55.17 %
F5	Video	13.79 %
F6	Audio	44.83 %
F7	Animation Film	6.90 %
F8	AR	10.34 %
F9	VR	3.45 %
F10	Game	3.45 %

It is possible to point that, based on the sample, an average app based on what the industry is offering, would have the following characteristics:

1) Layout

- The content is spread beyond the initial screen, creating vertical scrolling (L2).
- The layout structure will be maintained across the sections (L4).

2) Navigation

- The number of taps to achieve a WHS content from the initial screen is two (N1).
- The number of items in the main menu would vary from four to six (N2).
- The navigation menu is always visible among the sections (N3).
- The content will be spread in different levels, leaving the user to explore further in each section (N5).
- The main menu is self-explanatory, with direct meaning sections (N6).

3) Design

- The use of colours is limited up to three (D1).
- The design is clean and not polluted (D2).
- The use of an icon reinforces the menu and content is present (D5).

4) Content

- The content utilises long text, usually more than two paragraphs (C1).
- No need for introductory or explanation text on the initial screen (C4).
- The prevention of content loss when backing from a section is ensured (C5).

5) Features and Media

- Use photo/illustration along with the text, to reinforce the content (F1).
- Providing GPS or static versions (F3, F4).

These guidelines were used to build the structure and layout of the market-based prototype and how its content was organised. The content was elaborated addressing the WHS in Weimar, retrieving target content available at the official touristic site of the city [4], and from the largest cultural foundation from Weimar [5].

IV. GUIDELINES FROM LITERATURE-REVIEW

This section covers the creation of the second set of guidelines for WHS apps, based on the literature review, to be compared with the app guidelines extracted from the market overview.

While the guidelines from the app market overview took an observational approach of affordances, aiming to generate a model that could represent the average content style and features present on the available WHS apps for Germany, the guidelines acquired from the literature review took into consideration a systematic approach to the academic articles. The literature-based guidelines were extracted from publications about mobile app usability, available on research databases. It also took into consideration existing usability models [6] - [10], and official guidelines for mobile development from the leading mobile OS companies (iOS and Android).

The generated guidelines took into consideration studies from the academia and the industry recommendations, connecting and combining different views and approaches on mobile interface design guidelines applied for WHS (Figure 2).

The systematic literature review took into consideration the guidelines from the mobile industry, with an added layer of confirmed guidelines on studies of mobile apps retrieved from academic publications, on platforms, such as: ACM [11], IEEE [12], JSTOR [13], SAGE [14], and Google Scholar [15].

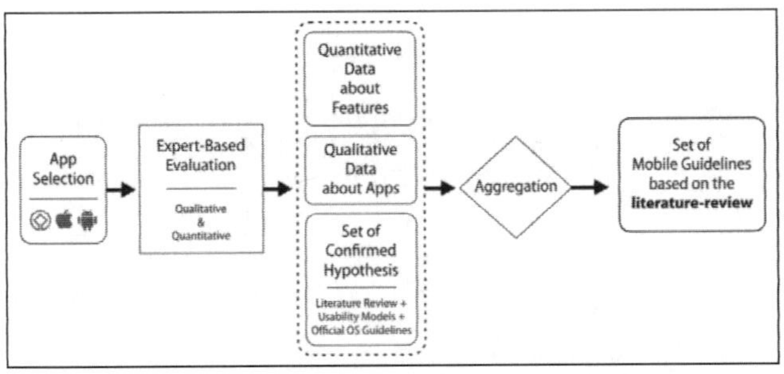

Figure 2. Schematics on the creation of the literature-based guidelines

In order to find academic studies and research outcomes that can contribute to the formation of literature-review guidelines for mobile apps dealing with cultural places, a set of search parameters were applied:

Search Strings:

- "Mobile usability" AND "Guidelines"
- "Mobile usability" AND "App"
- "Mobile usability" AND "Heritage"
- "Mobile usability" AND "Travel Guide"
- "Mobile usability" AND "City Guide"
- "App guidelines"
- "Mobile interface guidelines"
- Published material since 2013, covering five years of publication, considered enough for a literature review [16, p. 53].

The first 50 results in each search string on each platform were sorted by relevance and initially analysed based on their abstract/description to be selected or discarded for content analysis.

A. Selected papers

The aim of the reading selection from the literature review was to find guidelines and interface recommendations for mobile devices to build a literature-based prototype to be tested in comparison with the market-based one. With this goal in mind, studies done on mobile web sites were included, as they address the interface design on mobile screens. Medical and health studies were included just when they addressed mobile interface design and usability, and not therapeutic issues.

Also, studies covering mobile interaction with public spaces were included, as the prototype app will deal with interaction in the city centre of Weimar. The same applies for context-aware and location-based mobile interactions.

Taking into consideration the wide range of profiles of the Weimar's visitors, the selection also included studies on mobile interface for elderly users. Although the guidelines are not focused on educational features, studies on mobile learning were also included, as long as the interface was the research target. This decision was made because the city of Weimar also deals with teenager students visiting and learning about the heritage attractions of the city.

Overall, the analysis was concentrated on direct instructions that could be translated into guidelines. Vague recommendations, such as "create an appealing design" were not considered for being too open for different interpretations.

Based on their titles and abstract, 249 academic publications on mobile usability and mobile cultural heritage were selected, where only thirteen were not accessible due subscription and/or accessibility issues (despite five of them providing a two-pages preview), totalling a 5.2% rate of waste in the original selection, making the final number of selected academic works for reading equal to 236 publications.

The selected readings, apart from those dealing with app interface and usability, dealt with topics such as cultural heritage, mobile tourism, mobile health, mobile learning, older adults, just to mention a few examples. Based on the readings' keywords (when available), a word cloud was generated to illustrate the full range of selected topics (Figure 3).

Figure 3. Word cloud generated from the used keywords from the reading selection.

It can be seen in the word-cloud that the keyword *cultural heritage* does not have the same weight as *usability* or even *app,* for instance. As said, the word cloud was based on the keywords defined by the authors, and it reflects the lack of studies that are specifically dedicated to the relation between apps and WHS, compared to those related to generic apps.

Each one of the selected publications was read and analysed to find and extract guidelines that could be used for cultural heritage apps. However, the analysis was not restricted to the selection list and was extrapolated, taking in consideration relevant references cited by the publications selected for the sample.

As a procedure, when a guideline or recommendation was found, it was placed in a table following a similar structure as the guidelines extracted from the app-market-overview, adding new categories to correspond to the literature review findings. Overall, the literature-review based guidelines reinforced some and challenged other guidelines found on the industry-oriented overview, creating a new set of guidelines to be tested against the first prototype.

When a conflicting guideline was found (for instance: one author claiming that text should be long and another that it should be short), the one supported by the majority (more than one author endorsing it) was selected; in case of a tie (equal sum of authors supporting opposite views), an expert-based overview technique was implemented to select which one would be selected from the literature-review guidelines list, based on how closely related it was to the research topic.

The guidelines found during the analysis are shown in Table II, using the common ones with the market-based selection with the addition of new literature-based guidelines, distinguished with an asterisk (*) mark. It is possible to note that the literature-based guidelines have similar items with the market-based ones, but with more detailed orientations regarding the content.

TABLE II. SELECTED LITERATURE-REVIEW GUIDELINES

Code	Guidelines	References
Layout		
L1	Place content on one screen / minimizing-avoiding scrolling	[17] [18] [19] [20] [21] [22] [23] [24] [25] [26]
L4	Consistency between different sections (it may include the way the tasks are performed in different sections)	[18] [19] [20] [22] [24] [25] [27] [28] [29] [30] [31] [32]
L5 *	Orientation: provide session title	[25] [30]
L6 *	Providing search bar	[25] [29] [30]
Navigation		
N1	Number of Taps to WHS Information	[30]
N3	Navigation Menu visible	[25] [31] [32] [33]
N4	One Level Navigation Menu	[17] [23] [28]
N6	Self-explanatory menu	[17] [20] [23] [27] [30] [34]
N8 *	Presence of Back button	[25] [26] [32]
Code	Guidelines	References
Design		
D1	Limited use of colours	[20] [21] [22] [25] [26] [27] [29] [30] [35] [36]
D3	Simple design	[17] [19] [20] [22] [28] [29] [33]
D5	Use of icons	[17] [20] [21] [22] [23] [24] [26] [28] [29] [32] [33] [36] [37] [38] [39] [40] [41]
D6 *	Space between buttons or other clickable items	[19] [21] [23] [24] [25] [26] [27] [33] [42] [35] [39]
Content		
C2	Short text	[17] [18] [20] [22] [24] [28] [31] [25] [26] [32]
C3	Info at start screen	[30] [34] [38] [40] [43] [44]
C5	Prevent information loss (when back)	[17] [28] [29] [30] [31] [44]
C6	Provides action feedback (in some cases, confirmation before deleting/uploading)	[17] [25] [28] [29] [33] [40] [41]
C9	Tours / Routes	[45] [46]
C11 *	Focus / Only display essential information, no more than needed	[25] [31] [41]
C12 *	Clickable buttons with tactile feedback or sound (for Elderly)	[23] [26] [27] [33]
C13 *	Considering surrounding environment	[38] [40] [43]
C14 *	Provide notification of location-based (incorporated into the C17 guideline)	[43] [47] [48] [49]
C15 *	Use of visual clues for visited POI	[18] [25] [48]
C16 *	Screen font large (for Elderly) / optimal size (incorporated into the C17 guideline)	[18] [19] [21] [25] [26] [27] [33] [42]
C17 *	Allowing personalization / configuration	[26] [28] [29] [31] [50]
Features and Media		
F1	Use of Aesthetics graphics (related to "Photos" of market-based guidelines)	[20] [22] [23] [24] [25] [26] [32] [35] [36] [37] [39] [41] [50]
F9	Use of AR (if the app idea allows it)	[37] [51] [52]

The use of maps is one of the features that was not detailed in the literature-based guidelines. From the market-based research, the recommendation is to offer an offline map along with the GPS one. Still, such orientation was not confirmed by the literature, leaving this specific feature open and, as a consequence, allowing to test original ideas.

For the Augmented Reality (AR) feature, most of the selected studies addressed issues on using this technology, but just a few of them recommended it for a mobile application. Here, it is believed that AR can be indeed an appealing feature for a mobile app, but using such an environment demands an exclusive and sophisticated development which is not the purpose of this research.

Overall, when comparing both guidelines sets (Table III), it was possible to identify unique guidelines in each one, enabling the idea of an A/B test comparing a prototype based in each set of guidelines.

Despite the complexity and extension of the guidelines, some critical elements were not clearly identified in any guideline. However, the relevance requires them to be implemented and compared in the prototypes:

- **Content: List vs Grid content**
  List is when the options are listed in a (generaly) vertical sequence. *Grid* presents the content in a *tile* format, generally in square shape.
- **Map: icons**
  Displaying one map with generic *pin* icon, and others with personalised icons (according to content categories).
- **Map: marker information**
  When tapping/clicking on a pin on a map, the information may be displayed in the bottom of the screen, or as a centred floating banner.

The use of two different subtle prototypes created an opportunity to test other features, such those mentioned above, along with dedicated WHS content.

V. GUIDELINES INTO PROTOTYPES

Two prototypes were created, each one based on one set of guidelines built beforehand (industry and literature-review based). At this stage, considering the need to follow the guidelines as close as possible, the decision was made not to involve users during the design process, but to rely on an expert review approach [2, p. 37], leaving the involvement of users for later, when comparing and evaluating the prototypes.

To enable the comparative A/B test, two prototypes were developed:

- Prototype Red (Figure 4): industry-based guidelines, available at [53].
- Prototype Blue (Figure 5): literature-review based guidelines, available at [54].

The reason for calling the two prototypes "Red" and "Blue" was to set a neutral impression for the users/testers, not revealing their nature (industry or literature-review), neither their chronological development using letters, such as "A" and "B" – which could lead to the impression of "A" being the first version, and "B" a second-and-updated version. The chosen set of colours (red and blue) was also implemented to avoid conflict for possible colour-blind testers.

Figure 4. Prototype Red, with less content on the main menu, bigger tiles for pages and standard map icons.

Figure 5. Prototype Blue, with more items on the main menu, detailed tiles for pages and customised icons for the map.

VI. EVALUATION

In order to compare the two prototypes based on different guidelines, a task-based test and a comparative evaluation survey were implemented. The idea behind this approach is having different individuals performing a series of pre-defined tasks in both prototypes and answering a series of questions comparing features and formats presented in both versions.

Questionnaires are a well-known method to collect and summarise evidences [55] [56, p. 100], also helping to collect opinions and input from the users. They are efficient for a wide range of data collection, such as usability, user satisfaction and interface design [57, p. 30].

The questionnaire used in this work had a set of pre-defined answers to be chosen by the users, ideal to statistics, especially on user satisfaction [58]. It also offered open-ended questions to allow the testers to give personal inputs. This method was crucial to compare and analyse both sets of guidelines (industry vs literature-review) against each other and to extract an ideal set of guidelines for apps dealing with open-air world heritage sites.

A. Evaluation process

A questionnaire can be divided into four parts: introduction, participant information, information section and epilogue [57]. In the introduction, it is crucial to give general information about the test, carefully preventing it from producing a biased result. In this case, it explained that the test was meant to compare two different models of interface design. Within this context, the testers had an indication of the upcoming content of the test/questionnaire, but no other details regarding the origins or the differences between the prototypes were provided.

As participant information, the gender role was discarded on purpose as it was irrelevant for this study. The relevant information to understand the profiles were: age, which could be later related to the different groups of visitors; familiarity (or not) with the city of Weimar, showing if the results would change if a tester knows the locations or not; and the behaviour related to the use of apps, especially for travel and touristic activities, and the level of expertise in using them.

The selection of testers/participants aimed to find two different groups: people who knew the city of Weimar beforehand, and people who have never been in the city. The age groups had a wide range spread, going from the early '20s to late '40s. The differences brought an interesting perspective on how familiar the users were with the locations, and which features were prefered by individuals of certain group age. For this test, academics, students and professionals from a diverse set of areas of expertise were invited.

It is argued that even a modest number of five participants is enough to perform a usability test [59] [60], getting the necessary feedback to find usability problems when compared with a setting using a larger amount of testers. For the test, 35 participants confirmed the interest in performing the evaluation, with a final attendance of 30 participants.

B. Test settings

After designing the evaluation, an unmonitored / unmoderated setting was selected for the users to perform the tasks in an online evaluation. The unmonitored setting for assessments is not new in computer science [61]. Unmoderated tests can be perfectly applied for testing prototypes [62], and they bring a series of advantages by increasing the measurement precision [63]; no restriction of time [64] [65]; and simultaneous participation [61]. Also, unmonitored tests have a set of advantages in comparison to the monitored ones, which may intrusive to the task performance and time-consuming when having one tester at a time in the observational setting [57, p. 44].

The data collection of the evaluation was implemented by using *Google Forms*, as it is a free tool and covers all the needs relating to the type of questions and sets of data for further analysis.

C. Types of questions

Surveys commonly present two types of questions: open or close-ended. Open-ended questions give more freedom to the participants in answering without any influence, but they require more time and effort from them in creating their own answers and demanding interpretation of the collected data [66]. Close-ended questions are more suitable for quantitative usability data [67].

As the questionnaire has 69 questions in total, it used close-ended questions but with a possibility to an open-ended answer. Different types of questions were used, changing according to the desired data. Most of the questions were multiple-choice, with the option for the tester to add their own open-ended answer. In this way, the participants could always give their own input. Almost all the questions had a screenshot image from the app to contextualise the question.

D. Results

The evaluation questionnaire was divided into seven sections: About you, About the attractions, About the Red Prototype, About the Blue Prototype, Comparing the two versions (Red/Blue), About Weimar, and Final opinion. Among the questions (About the attractions), for example, the testers were asked if they could recognise the UNESCO's WHS logo after using the prototypes, confirming if they acquired this information by using the prototypes or if they already knew it. From the feedback, it was suggested that using the UNESCO's WHS logo helps to reinforce its branding, with 59% of the testers who recognised this symbol claiming they learnt if from the prototypes.

The "About Weimar" identified if the testers have been to Weimar beforehand, to verify if the familiarity with the locations and previous knowledge about the WHS site would affect the answers. However, the results were inconclusive in this regard. However, when checking if the prototypes could serve as an incentive for people to travel to

Weimar, the evaluation suggested that the users who have never been in the location were considering to visit the city after using the app. It allows one to conclude that dedicated apps can be a tool to promote the city.

The core-questions - "About the Red Prototype" and "About the Blue Prototype" and the comparisons - identified the testers' views on each one of the prototypes, but also inquired about exclusive features/pages, such as Routes, Settings and Right-Top-Menu available on the Blue Prototype only. In the end, as the final evaluation of each one of the implemented features, the testers answered a final question regarding which one of the prototypes they would prefer to use, resulting in 83.3% in favour of Blue Prototype (literature-based guidelines), and 16.7% for the Red Prototype (industry-based guidelines).

The exclusive features mentioned in Section IV (the ones not suggested from the found guidelines) were also tested. The results are detailed in Table III, which displays separately each one of the features tested and the guideline that originated it, divided into 'from industry-based', 'from literature-based', 'from evaluation' and the beforementioned ones, that are not from the guidelines.

It is also important to mention that, by making the literature review more inclusive - adding tailored outcomes for specific target groups, such as elderly people and studies on open-air media urban integration using apps – resulted in a more inclusive set of guidelines in general.

As seen, the results were mostly favourable to the literature-based prototype (blue version), confirming the found guidelines suggested by academics, reports, and official documentation for developers. These results can support the idea that, sometimes, the apps offered at the official stores might be closer related to the developers' taste and expertise than to the real needs and requirements of a niche sector.

TABLE III. SUGGESTED GUIDELINES

Guidelines		From Industry -Based	From Lit.- Based	From Evalu- ation
Layout				
1	Place Content in one screen / minimising-avoiding scrolling		X	
2	Consistency between different sections	X	X	
3	Orientation: provide session title		X	
4	Providing a search bar		X	
Navigation				
5	Number of Taps to WHS Information (up to 3)		X	
6	Number of items in the main navigation (up to 5)			X
7	Navigation menu visible	X	X	
8	One level navigation menu		X	
9	Offering visible (tabs) sub-menu navigation			X
10	Self-explanatory menu	X	X	
11	Presence of the Back button		X	
Design				
12	Limited use of colours	X	X	
13	Simple design	X	X	
14	Use of icons	X	X	
15	Space between buttons or other clickable items		X	
16	Use standard icons inside maps			X
Content				
17	Short text		X	
18	Info at start screen		X	
19	Tours / Routes		X	
20	Focus / Only display essential information		X	
21	Use of Aesthetics graphics		X	
22	Considering the surrounding environment		X	
23	Large font size		X	
24	Display the locations in a list format			X
25	Display more details on the locations' preview			X
26	Allow personalisation / configuration		X	
27	Centred pop-up for warnings and messages			X
28	Prevent information loss	X	X	
29	Provide action feedback		X	
30	Clickable buttons with tactile feedback or sound (for Elderly)		X	
31	Provide location-based notification		X	
32	Use of visual clues for visited locations		X	
Media and Features				
33	Photos & Gallery			X
34	Map GPS	X		
WHS Related				
35	Use of the WHS logo			X
36	Provide an "about WHS" info			X
37	Provide carefully curated content			X

VII. CONCLUSION

The main objective of this work was to set guidelines for the future development of apps applied for historical open-air locations, with emphasis on UNESCO World Heritage Sites.

From this analysis, some unique guidelines can be highlighted, such as, the best approach regarding the use of a large amount of text to describe each POI (Point Of Interest) - in this case, offering a short version, with the possibility to read further/expand; no use of audio or video, considering the surrounding noises while walking through the city; the recommendation of implementing thematic routes; and offering the possibility to change interface features such as text-size (especially for elderly groups),

POI warnings based on GPS and the presence of WHS related content, such as displaying the official WHS logo, curated content and explanation about the reasons the place was listed as WHS.

It can be argued that the found guidelines could be applied not just to dedicated apps to open-air WHS, but also to touristic apps in general. This assumption can be true, as touristic locations also require wayfinding and POI descriptions, alongside with the navigation, design, layout and content recommendations described in this research.

It is important to say that – as it happens in most of the independent projects – this research had a constrain of time and budget for the prototype development and testing. However, in the ideal scenario, the work could continue with the implementation of a commercial app based on the final guidelines and another round of tests with different demographics. Another improvement could be done in regards to inclusion, checking the extension of the elderly-friendly features and extending the user-friendly approach to various disabilities and special needs.

REFERENCES

[1] M. Bower, "Affordance analysis – matching learning tasks with learning technologies," *Educational Media International*, vol. 45, no. 1, pp. 3–15, Mar. 2008, doi: 10.1080/09523980701847115.

[2] C. Wilson, *User interface inspection methods: a user-centered design method*. Amsterdam ; Boston: Elsevier/Morgan Kaufmann, 2014.

[3] M. Shitkova, J. Holler, T. Heide, N. Clever, and J. Becker, "Towards Usability Guidelines for Mobile Websites and Applications.," 2015, pp. 1603–1617.

[4] "Kulturstadt Weimar - UNESCO World Heritage." https://www.weimar.de/en/culture/unesco-world-heritage/ (accessed Nov. 10, 2020).

[5] "Klassik Stiftung Weimar: UNESCO." http://www.klassik-stiftung.de/en/about-us/unesco/ (accessed Nov. 10, 2020).

[6] J. Nielsen, *Usability engineering*. San Francisco, Calif.: Morgan Kaufmann Publishers, 1994.

[7] B. Shneiderman and C. Plaisant, *Designing the user interface: strategies for effective human-computer interaction*, 5th ed. Boston: Addison-Wesley, 2010.

[8] S. Weinschenk and D. T. Barker, *Designing effective speech interfaces*. New York: Wiley, 2000.

[9] "ISO 9241-11:2018(en), Ergonomics of human-system interaction — Part 11: Usability: Definitions and concepts." https://www.iso.org/obp/ui/#iso:std:iso:9241:-11:ed-2:v1:en (accessed Nov. 10, 2020).

[10] R. Harrison, D. Flood, and D. Duce, "Usability of mobile applications: literature review and rationale for a new usability model," *J Interact Sci*, vol. 1, no. 1, p. 1, May 2013, doi: 10.1186/2194-0827-1-1.

[11] "ACM Digital Library." https://dl.acm.org/ (accessed Nov. 10, 2020).

[12] "IEEE Xplore Digital Library." http://ieeexplore.ieee.org/Xplore/home.jsp (accessed Nov. 10, 2020).

[13] "JSTOR." https://www.jstor.org/ (accessed Nov. 10, 2020).

[14] "SAGE Journals: Your gateway to world-class journal research." http://journals.sagepub.com/ (accessed Nov. 10, 2020).

[15] "Google Scholar." https://scholar.google.co.uk/ (accessed Nov. 10, 2020).

[16] R. Cottrell and J. F. McKenzie, *Health Promotion & Education Research Methods: Using the Five Chapter Thesis/ Dissertation Model*. Jones & Bartlett Learning, 2010.

[17] M. Shitkova, J. Holler, T. Heide, N. Clever, and J. Becker, "Towards Usability Guidelines for Mobile Websites and Applications," Osnabrück, Germany, 2015, pp. 1603–1617, Accessed: Nov. 10, 2020. [Online]. Available: https://aisel.aisnet.org/wi2015/107.

[18] A. Miniukovich, A. De Angeli, S. Sulpizio, and P. Venuti, "Design Guidelines for Web Readability," in *Proceedings of the 2017 Conference on Designing Interactive Systems*, New York, NY, USA, 2017, pp. 285–296, doi: 10.1145/3064663.3064711.

[19] C. Antoun, J. Katz, J. Argueta, and L. Wang, "Design Heuristics for Effective Smartphone Questionnaires," *Social Science Computer Review*, p. 089443931772707, Sep. 2017, doi: 10.1177/0894439317727072.

[20] B. A. Kumar and P. Mohite, "Usability guideline for mobile learning apps: an empirical study," *International Journal of Mobile Learning and Organisation*, vol. 10, no. 4, p. 223, 2016, doi: 10.1504/IJMLO.2016.079499.

[21] E. Kaur and P. D. Haghighi, "A Context-Aware Usability Model for Mobile Health Applications," 2016, pp. 181–189, doi: 10.1145/3007120.3007135.

[22] J.-M. Díaz-Bossini and L. Moreno, "Accessibility to Mobile Interfaces for Older People," *Procedia Computer Science*, vol. 27, pp. 57–66, 2014, doi: 10.1016/j.procs.2014.02.008.

[23] A. Petrovčič, S. Taipale, A. Rogelj, and V. Dolničar, "Design of Mobile Phones for Older Adults: An Empirical Analysis of Design Guidelines and Checklists for Feature Phones and Smartphones," *International Journal of Human–Computer Interaction*, pp. 1–14, Aug. 2017, doi: 10.1080/10447318.2017.1345142.

[24] S. Carmien and A. G. Manzanares, "Elders Using Smartphones – A Set of Research Based Heuristic Guidelines for Designers," in *Universal Access in Human-Computer Interaction. Universal Access to Information and Knowledge*, vol. 8514, C. Stephanidis and M. Antona, Eds. Cham: Springer International Publishing, 2014, pp. 26–37.

[25] N. Ahmad, A. Rextin, and U. E. Kulsoom, "Perspectives on usability guidelines for smartphone applications: An empirical investigation and systematic literature review," *Information and Software Technology*, Oct. 2017, doi: 10.1016/j.infsof.2017.10.005.

[26] P. A. Silva, P. Jordan, and K. Holden, "Something Old, Something New, Something Borrowed: gathering experts' feedback while performing heuristic evaluation with a list of heuristics targeted at older adults," 2014, pp. 1–8, doi: 10.1145/2693787.2693804.

[27] J.-O. Ropponen, "Usability of mobile devices and applications for elderly users," 2016, Accessed: Nov. 10, 2020. [Online]. Available: http://www.theseus.fi/handle/10024/120286.

[28] K. Y. Zamri and N. N. Al Subhi, "10 user interface elements for mobile learning application development," Nov. 2015, pp. 44–50, doi: 10.1109/IMCTL.2015.7359551.

[29] F. Nayebi, J.-M. Desharnais, and A. Abran, "An Expert-Based Framework for Evaluating iOS Application Usability," Oct. 2013, pp. 147–155, doi: 10.1109/IWSM-Mensura.2013.30.

[30] C. X. N. Cota, A. I. M. Díaz, and M. Á. R. Duque, "Developing a framework to evaluate usability in m-learning systems: mapping study and proposal," 2014, pp. 357–364, doi: 10.1145/2669711.2669924.

[31] R. Inostroza and C. Rusu, "Mapping usability heuristics and design principles for touchscreen-based mobile devices," 2014, pp. 1–4, doi: 10.1145/2590651.2590677.

[32] N. Jailani, Z. Abdullah, M. A. Bakar, and H. R. Haron, "Usability guidelines for developing mobile application in the construction industry," Aug. 2015, pp. 411–416, doi: 10.1109/ICEEI.2015.7352536.

[33] J. van Biljon and K. Renaud, "Validating Mobile Phone Design Guidelines: Focusing on the Elderly in a Developing Country," in *Proceedings of the Annual Conference of the South African Institute of Computer Scientists and Information Technologists*, New York, NY, USA, 2016, p. 44:1–44:10, doi: 10.1145/2987491.2987492.

[34] I. Costa *et al.*, "An Empirical Study to Evaluate the Feasibility of a UX and Usability Inspection Technique for Mobile Applications," Jul. 2016, pp. 595–599, doi: 10.18293/SEKE2016-127.

[35] H. Hoehle, R. Aljafari, and V. Venkatesh, "Leveraging Microsoft's mobile usability guidelines: Conceptualising and developing scales for mobile application usability," *International Journal of Human-Computer Studies*, vol. 89, pp. 35–53, May 2016, doi: 10.1016/j.ijhcs.2016.02.001.

[36] J. Ross and J. Gao, "Overcoming the language barrier in mobile user interface design: A case study on a mobile health app," *arXiv:1605.04693 [cs]*, May 2016, Accessed: Nov. 10, 2020. [Online]. Available: http://arxiv.org/abs/1605.04693.

[37] M. Hincapie, C. Diaz, M. Zapata, and C. Mesias, "Methodological Framework for the Design and Development of Applications for Reactivation of Cultural Heritage: Case Study Cisneros Marketplace at Medellin, Colombia," *Journal on Computing and Cultural Heritage*, vol. 9, no. 2, pp. 1–24, Jan. 2016, doi: 10.1145/2827856.

[38] G. Joyce, M. Lilley, T. Barker, and A. Jefferies, "Adapting Heuristics for the Mobile Panorama," 2014, pp. 1–2, doi: 10.1145/2662253.2662325.

[39] H. Hoehle, X. Zhang, and V. Venkatesh, "An espoused cultural perspective to understand continued intention to use mobile applications: a four-country study of mobile social media application usability," *European Journal of Information Systems*, vol. 24, no. 3, pp. 337–359, May 2015, doi: 10.1057/ejis.2014.43.

[40] P. E. Kourouthanassis, C. Boletsis, and G. Lekakos, "Demystifying the design of mobile augmented reality applications," *Multimedia Tools and Applications*, vol. 74, no. 3, pp. 1045–1066, Feb. 2015, doi: 10.1007/s11042-013-1710-7.

[41] B. Cruz Zapata, A. Hernández Niñirola, A. Idri, J. L. Fernández-Alemán, and A. Toval, "Mobile PHRs Compliance with Android and iOS Usability Guidelines," *Journal of Medical Systems*, vol. 38, no. 8, Aug. 2014, doi: 10.1007/s10916-014-0081-6.

[42] H. K. Kim, C. Kim, E. Lim, and H. Kim, "How to Develop Accessibility UX Design Guideline in Samsung," in *Proceedings of the 18th International Conference on Human-Computer Interaction with Mobile Devices and Services Adjunct*, New York, NY, USA, 2016, pp. 551–556, doi: 10.1145/2957265.2957271.

[43] A. Alkhafaji, M. Cocea, J. Crellin, and S. Fallahkhair, "Guidelines for designing a smart and ubiquitous learning environment with respect to cultural heritage," May 2017, pp. 334–339, doi: 10.1109/RCIS.2017.7956556.

[44] A. S. Ajibola and L. Goosen, "Development of heuristics for usability evaluation of m-commerce applications," 2017, pp. 1–10, doi: 10.1145/3129416.3129428.

[45] K. Baker and S. Verstockt, "Cultural Heritage Routing: A Recreational Navigation-based Approach in Exploring Cultural Heritage," *Journal on Computing and Cultural Heritage*, vol. 10, no. 4, pp. 1–20, Jul. 2017, doi: 10.1145/3040200.

[46] D. Gavalas *et al.*, "Scenic Athens: A personalised scenic route planner for tourists," Jun. 2016, pp. 1151–1156, doi: 10.1109/ISCC.2016.7543892.

[47] D. McGookin, K. Tahiroălu, T. Vaittinen, M. Kytö, B. Monastero, and J. C. Vasquez, "Exploring Seasonality in Mobile Cultural Heritage," 2017, pp. 6101–6105, doi: 10.1145/3025453.3025803.

[48] P. Galatis, D. Gavalas, V. Kasapakis, G. Pantziou, and C. Zaroliagis, "Mobile Augmented Reality Guides in Cultural Heritage," 2016, doi: 10.4108/eai.30-11-2016.2266954.

[49] C. T. Hermansson, M. Soderstrom, and D. Johansson, "Developing Useful Mobile Applications in Cross-Media Platforms," Jul. 2014, pp. 128–132, doi: 10.1109/IMIS.2014.59.

[50] A. Alkhafaji, S. Fallahkhair, M. Cocea, and J. Crellin, "A Survey Study to Gather Requirements for Designing a Mobile Service to Enhance Learning from Cultural Heritage," in *Adaptive and Adaptable Learning*, vol. 9891, K. Verbert, M. Sharples, and T. Klobučar, Eds. Cham: Springer International Publishing, 2016, pp. 547–550.

[51] M. C. tom Dieck and T. Jung, "A theoretical model of mobile augmented reality acceptance in urban heritage tourism," *Current Issues in Tourism*, Jul. 2015, Accessed: Nov. 10, 2020. [Online]. Available: http://www.tandfonline.com/doi/abs/10.1080/13683500.2015.1070801.

[52] N. Chung, H. Lee, J.-Y. Kim, and C. Koo, "The Role of Augmented Reality for Experience-Influenced Environments: The Case of Cultural Heritage Tourism in Korea," *Journal of Travel Research*, p. 004728751770825, May 2017, doi: 10.1177/0047287517708255.

[53] "Prototype-Red." https://www.justinmind.com/usernote/tests/34737592/34752103/35004322/index.html#/screens/d12245cc-1680-458d-89dd-4f0d7fb22724 (accessed Nov. 10, 2020).

[54] "Prototype-Blue." https://www.justinmind.com/usernote/tests/34737592/34752103/35245888/index.html#/screens/e86ffab7-a690-4860-b679-ee35d2a074f5 (accessed Nov. 10, 2020).

[55] J. S. Molleri, K. Petersen, and E. Mendes, "Survey Guidelines in Software Engineering: An Annotated Review," 2016, pp. 1–6, doi: 10.1145/2961111.2962619.

[56] J. Lazar, J. H. Feng, and H. Hochheiser, *Research methods in human-computer interaction*. Chichester, West Sussex, U.K: Wiley, 2010.

[57] N. A. Stanton, P. M. Salmon, L. A. Rafferty, G. H. Walker, C. Baber, and D. P. Jenkins, *Human Factors Methods: a Practical Guide for Engineering and Design*. 2017.

[58] A. de Castro and J. A. Macías, “SUSApp: A Mobile App for Measuring and Comparing Questionnaire-Based Usability Assessments,” 2016, pp. 1–8, doi: 10.1145/2998626.2998667.

[59] J. Nielsen, “How Many Test Users in a Usability Study?,” *Nielsen Norman Group*, Jun. 04, 2012. https://www.nngroup.com/articles/how-many-test-users/ (accessed Nov. 10, 2020).

[60] J. Sauro, “MeasuringU: Why you only need to test with five users (explained),” Mar. 08, 2010. https://measuringu.com/five-users/ (accessed Nov. 10, 2020).

[61] U.-D. Reips, “Internet-Based Psychological Experimenting: Five Dos and Five Don’ts,” *Social Science Computer Review*, vol. 20, no. 3, pp. 241–249, Jan. 2002, doi: 10.1177/089393020200300202.

[62] Nielsen Norman Group, “Selecting an Online Tool for Unmoderated Remote User Testing,” *Nielsen Norman Group*, Jun. 01, 2014. https://www.nngroup.com/articles/unmoderated-user-testing-tools/ (accessed Nov. 10, 2020).

[63] H. E. M. Feenstra, I. E. Vermeulen, J. M. J. Murre, and S. B. Schagen, “Online cognition: factors facilitating reliable online neuropsychological test results,” *The Clinical Neuropsychologist*, vol. 31, no. 1, pp. 59–84, Jan. 2017, doi: 10.1080/13854046.2016.1190405.

[64] A. Barak and N. English, “Prospects and Limitations of Psychological Testing on the Internet,” *Journal of Technology in Human Services*, vol. 19, no. 2–3, pp. 65–89, Mar. 2002, doi: 10.1300/J017v19n02_06.

[65] C. Caine, M. P. Mehta, N. N. Laack, and V. Gondi, “Cognitive function testing in adult brain tumor trials: lessons from a comprehensive review,” *Expert Review of Anticancer Therapy*, vol. 12, no. 5, pp. 655–667, May 2012, doi: 10.1586/era.12.34.

[66] U. Reja, K. L. Manfreda, V. Hlebec, and V. Vehorar, “Open-ended vs. Close-ended Questions in Web Questionnaires,” in *Developments in Applied Statistics*, Ljubljana: Fakulteta za družbene vede, 2003, pp. 159–177.

[67] S. Farrell, “Open-Ended vs. Closed-Ended Questions in User Research,” *Nielsen Norman Group*, May 22, 2016. https://www.nngroup.com/articles/open-ended-questions/ (accessed Nov. 10, 2020).

Development of a Wearable Vision Substitution Prototype for Blind and Visually Impaired That Assists in Everyday Conversations

Anna Kushnir
Socio-Informatics and Societal Aspects of Digitalization
Faculty of Computer Science and Business Information Systems
University of Applied Sciences Würzburg-Schweinfurt
Würzburg, Germany
e-mail: info@anna-kushnir.de

Nicholas H. Müller
Socio-Informatics and Societal Aspects of Digitalization
Faculty of Computer Science and Business Information Systems
University of Applied Sciences Würzburg-Schweinfurt
Würzburg, Germany
e-mail: nicholas.mueller@fhws.de

Abstract—**This paper introduces an idea of a Sensory Substitution Device (SSD), which supports everyday conversations by conveying to the user the emotional valence of its interlocutor. It describes the work in progress of a SSD prototype design that aims to remap visual stimuli into tactile information, by utilizing the Facial Action Coding System (FACS).**

Keywords-Non-verbal communication; Emotional valence; Visually impaired; Vision Substitution; Sensory Substitution Device.

I. INTRODUCTION

Everyday face-to-face communication situations use a variety of communication channels. In addition to the verbalized information, several non-verbal cues are communicated, which have to be interpreted by the communication partners. These include facial expressions, intonations or gestures. Sighted people can use all these communication channels, which allows them, for example, to interpret the facial expressions in order to understand their interlocutor better.

Blind and visually impaired people are limited in interpretation as they are not able to process the visual non-verbal information. This makes it hard to determine the emotional valence of the communication partner, which indicates whether an emotional status is positive or negative. Although the emotional valence can be determined through the interlocutor's intonation, it is only possible while the person is speaking. While a visual impaired person speaks, he or she is not able to determine the emotional valence, since the interlocutor is listening and, therefore, only non-verbal cues are transmitted.

A survey carried out with focus groups of blind people and disability experts proves that there are several key needs of non-verbal information, that blind people may need to access during social encounters [1]. These include, but are not limited to, the facial expressions of a person standing in front of the user. Based on this demand, the purpose of this work is to design an interface prototype that assists people with visual disabilities in everyday conversations. The proposed system is based on vision substitution and, therefore, it can be classified under Sensory Substitution Devices (SSDs).

The aim of the proposed SSD is to supply blind people with visual information by converting it into tactile representation in order to convey emotional valence of the user's interlocutor.

The paper is structured as follows. In Section II, related work is presented, and the research needs are derived. Section III describes the relationship between Emotions, Facial Action Coding System (FACS) and emotional valence. In Section IV, the prototype of the SSD and important design decisions are presented. Finally, Section V summarizes the paper and describes the next steps.

II. BACKGROUND AND RELATED WORKS

Most of the related works about vision substitution for blind and visually impaired people focus on navigation, reading texts, object recognition and face recognition. Lykawka et al., for instance, presented a tactile interface that allows users to navigate in environments including obstacles and to detect the movements of people and objects. The system converts the visual information into tactile feedback and conveys it with the help of a vibrotactile belt [2].

Bernieri et al. dealt in [3] with visually impaired people's mobility. The authors describe a prototype of a smart glove that complements the classic cane. The described glove provides vibrotactile feedback on the position of the next obstacle in the range.

In [4], a text reading system called FingerEye is proposed, which translates text into audio or braille.

Bhat et al. also presented a system that aids reading texts. Additionally, it assists in recognizing objects. Both stimuli are translated into audio output [5].

The interaction assistant ICare, described in [6], deals with choosing an appropriate face recognition algorithm to build an assistant for social interactions. It also describes the prototype, of which the output is also in audio.

While a lot of research has been done to meet a wide range of needs of people with visual disabilities, not enough attention has been given to the development of assistive devices that satisfy the need for access to non-verbal communication in social interactions. However, there are a few systems that deal with social interaction, among other functions, and are available for purchase.

Orcam MyEye 2.0 [7] is a wearable device, which is worn on the temple stem of eyeglasses and it combines several features. With the help of a camera on the front and a loudspeaker on the back, the device is able to read texts, recognize barcodes and time, identify goods by their barcodes and recognize people, by saving their name. All recognitions are translated into audio information and conveyed through a loudspeaker.

Mircrosoft SeeingAI [8] is an application for the mobile phone, which shares a lot of features with the Orcam MyEye. Moreover, it offers a feature, which recognizes and describes scenes, people and their emotions. All types of recognition are translated and represented by audio output. To enable the recognition and translation, a photo of the object to be analyzed has to be taken.

An important shortcoming of SeeingAI and Orcam MyEye is that the solutions provide only audio outputs. People with a visual impairment rely on their hearing to perceive their environment. Audio signals that are played by an assistance system during social interactions, such as face-to-face communication, could be perceived as disturbing as they may interfere with the hearing of one's own speech or the one of the communication partners. Moreover, SeeingAI is able to recognize people and emotions, but not to communicate these in real-time. Instead of this, the user has to take a photo first. Orcam and SeeingAI are, therefore, not sufficient solutions to support face-to-face communication.

What is needed is a system that communicates non-verbal cues in real-time to a blind person and whose output is based on a different sense than the hearing, on which verbal communication is perceived.

A common alternative to audio-vision substitution is to use vibrotactile feedback, which was already used for a haptic belt in the described work about navigation [2]. McDaniel et al. also presented a haptic belt to assist in communication situations [1]. The focus of the work is on communicating non-verbal cues, like the number of people in the visual field, the relative direction and distance of the individuals with respect to the user. The output of the belt is created and delivered to the user continuously and in real-time through the haptic belt with vibrotactile feedback. Experiments have shown that non-verbal communication can be successfully conveyed through vibrotactile cues.

III. EMOTIONS AND THE FACIAL ACTION CODING SYSTEM

Every emotion sends signals, which are most noticeable through our voice and facial traits. For this reason, the FACS is used as the basis for the emotional valence recognition in this project. FACS is an anatomically based system for describing all visually perceptible facial muscle movements. The system assigns Action Units (AU) to almost every visible movement of facial muscles [9]. A combination of certain AUs can be assigned to emotions. The emotions of anger, happiness, sadness, disgust, contempt, fear and surprise are considered universal and cross-cultural, according to Paul Ekman. These can be recognized through facial expressions using FACS.

To get back to the emotional valence, every emotion has a value that categorizes emotions into positive and negative ones. Thus, it is possible to deduce the emotional valence from the emotion. Happiness is seen as a positive emotion. In contrast, the rest of the universal emotions, except surprise, belong to the negative emotions. The emotion surprise is a special case as it lasts at most a few seconds. After that, it ends in fear, pleasure, anger or other emotions, depending on the quality and nature of what surprises us. Therefore, a surprise can lead to positive valency, as well as negative valency [10].

IV. PROTOTYPE CONSTRUCTION AND DESIGN

This section discusses the architecture of the prototype and design decisions made in this project. The prototype's architecture is formed by four main components:

- Camera unit
- Laptop (for emotional valence recognition)
- Wearable microcontroller
- Wearable haptic device

Figure 1 shows a simplified representation of the interaction of these components.

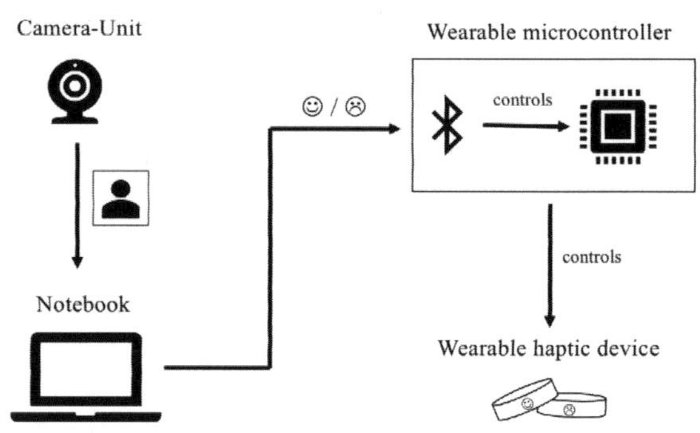

Figure 1. Prototype components interaction

The camera unit is recording the interlocutors face during the communication and sends the captured photos continuously and in real-time to the FaceReader Web API. A laptop is used to run the FaceReader Software, which analyzes and categorizes the photos with regard to the emotional valence. After categorisation, the FaceReader Web API sends the results to an Arduino nano board by using a Bluetooth module for the transmission. This microcontroller controls the haptic device consisting of a set of two vibrating rings. Depending on the emotional valence, either the ring which stands for a positive emotional valence or the one for the negative emotional valence will vibrate. In the following, the technical procedure and components of the system will be described in greater detail.

A. Camera-Unit

Currently the prototype is working with a Logitech Brio 4K webcam, which is able to make high quality pictures. Similar to the proposed face recognition device in [6], it is planned for the future work to use eyeglasses with an included camera or a portable camera, which can be attached on the temple of eyeglasses instead, to make the device more mobile. As an alternative, it is also conceivable to use the smartphone camera while the smartphone is in the breast pocket. However, the webcam is sufficient for the planned experiments with the system during the second quarter of 2020.

B. Notebook

The notebook is used to run the FaceReader software from Noldus [11]. In order to recognize the emotional valence of the interlocuter, it is not necessary to develop a software which will recognize faces and analyze facial expressions. This task can be undertaken by the FaceReader, which is an automatic analysis tool for facial expressions. It utilizes the FACS and is, therefore, able to recognize universal emotions and their intensity, which are described in Section III. The emotional valence is automatically calculated by the FaceReader during an analysis. It results from the difference between the intensity of the positive emotion and the intensity of the most pronounced negative emotion. Happy is the only positive emotion, while sad, angry, scared and disgusted are considered to be negative emotions in the calculation. A special case is the emotion surprised, which can be either positive or negative [12]. Due to the privacy aspects of having a camera recording during a conversation, we constructed the prototype as a closed-loop-system. This means the recordings are interpreted by the FACS software instantaneously and no video recording remains on the server.

C. Wearable microcontroller

The wearable microcontroller is an Arduino Nano V3.3 board which can be controlled via a Bluetooth module, the HC-05-6. The Arduino board can be placed around the neck and controls two vibration motors, which are part of the haptic device. Figure 2 shows a wiring diagram for these three components and Figure 3 shows how the device can be worn. For the power supply of the microcontroller, a power bank can be used. The Arduino Nano board was chosen because of its extensibility. During the second quarter of 2020, it is planned to expand the device with the seven universal emotions.

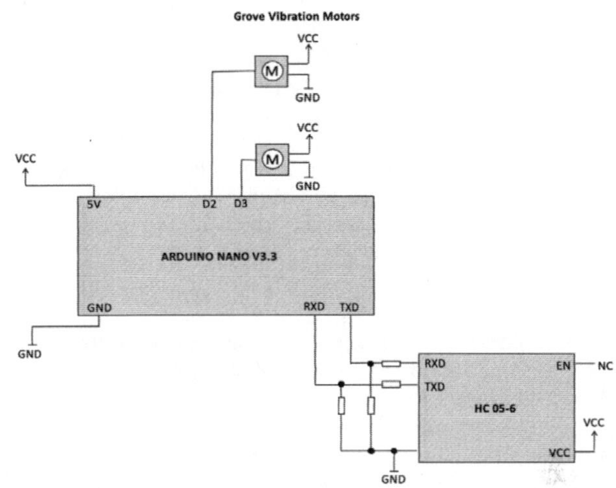

Figure 2. Wiring diagram of the wearables

D. Wearable Haptic Device

The goal is to create an interface that conveys the emotional valence in real-time, meaning that the signals should be conveyed during a conversation. As a result, these signals are also sent while the user is talking or listening to his communication partner. As described in Section II, vibrotactile cues for vision substitution have proven to be a good alternative to aural cues in terms of navigation and social interactions [1][2]. However, the crucial point why vibrotactile cues were chosen as the transmission method for this project is that they are received through a different sense than the hearing, to not interfere with the verbal

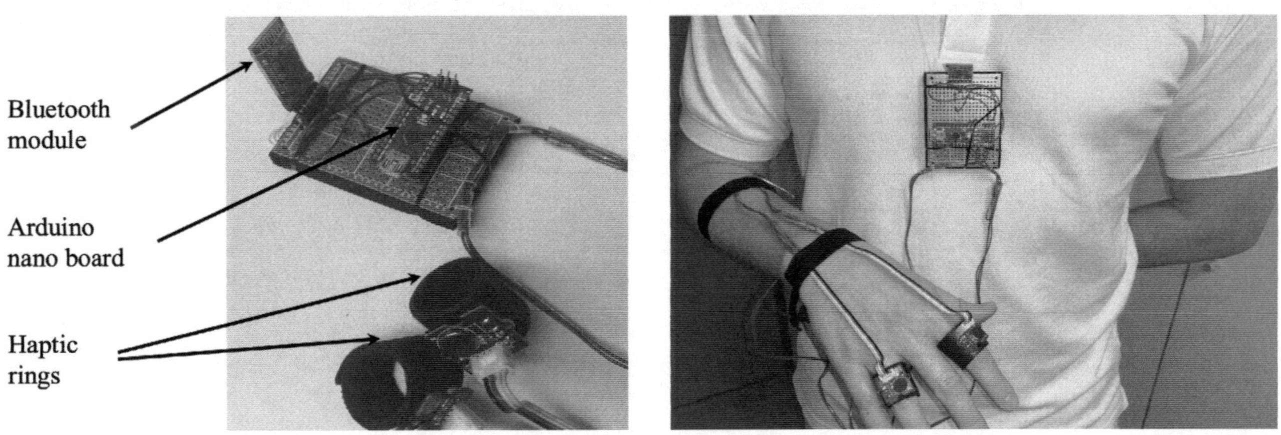

Figure 3. Haptic rings with Grove vibration motors connected to Arduino board with cables

communication. Some described systems in Section II have successfully used and tested vibrotactile cues in haptic belts or gloves [1][3]. Since SSDs for navigation use both vibrotactile cues in haptic belts and gloves, it follows that this also applies to communication for which only haptic belts were previously presented. To keep the device small, the system is based on a set of two Grove vibration motors attached to resizable rings which can be worn on the non-dominant hand. Thus, the camera-based recording of facial expressions, the conversion into emotional valence and, finally, the conversion into mute vibration movements on a hand, an unobtrusive signal transmission can be ensured. Additionally, the device is discreet, and the user is free to gesticulate with the other hand. Figure 3 shows the rings, each with a fixed motor connected to the Arduino nano board with cables. The cables are attached to the arm with two elastic bands so that the cables do not interfere with gesturing. In order to make the device more comfortable to wear, it is planned to create a wireless version in the future.

V. Conclusion and Outlook

This paper has introduced the idea and prototype of an SSD designed to assist people with visual impairment in daily face-to-face communication situations. This is made possible by recording the interlocutor during communication and determining the emotional valence in real-time, using the FaceReader software from Noldus. Subsequently, the recognized emotional valence is translated into tactile information and transmitted to the user via vibrating rings, which can be worn on the non-dominant hand.

Designing the prototype was the first step towards communicating the emotional state of the conversation partner to assist in everyday communications. The next steps will be to evaluate which tactile interfaces could also be used for the design of the prototype. For example, the vibration could be compared with the tactile stimuli heat and cold. In addition, it is planned to expand the prototype with the seven universal emotions, so that the user will be able to access a more detailed emotional state of the interlocutor. In the second quarter, the functionality of the overall system is to be experimentally validated as part of a master's thesis. It is planned to carry out the experiment in cooperation with visually impaired as well as blindfolded test subjects.

References

[1] T. McDaniel, S. Krishna, V. Balasubramanian, D. Colbry, and S. Panchanathan, "Using a haptic belt to convey non-verbal communication cues during social interactions to individuals who are blind", *IEEE International Workshop on Haptic Audio visual Environments and Games*, 2008, pp. 13–18, doi: 10.1109/HAVE.2008.4685291.

[2] C. Lykawka, B. K. Stahl, M. d B. Campos, J. Sanchez, and M. S. Pinho, "Tactile Interface Design for Helping Mobility of People with Visual Disabilities", *IEEE 41st Annual Computer Software and Applications Conference (COMPSAC)*, 2017, vol. 1, pp. 851–860, doi: 10.1109/COMPSAC.2017.227.

[3] G. Bernieri, L. Faramondi, and F. Pascucci, "A low cost smart glove for visually impaired people mobility", *23rd Mediterranean Conference on Control and Automation (MED)*, 2015, pp. 130–135, doi: 10.1109/MED.2015.7158740.

[4] Z. Liu, Y. Luo, J. Cordero, N. Zhao, and Y. Shen, "Finger-eye: A wearable text reading assistive system for the blind and visually impaired', *IEEE International Conference on Real-time Computing and Robotics (RCAR)*, 2016, pp. 123–128, doi: 10.1109/RCAR.2016.7784012.

[5] P. G. Bhat, D. K. Rout, B. N. Subudhi, and T. Veerakumar, "Vision sensory substitution to aid the blind in reading and object recognition", *Fourth International Conference on Image Information Processing (ICIIP)*, 2017, pp. 1–6, doi: 10.1109/ICIIP.2017.8313754.

[6] S. Krishna, G. Little, J. Black, and S. Panchanathan, "A Wearable Face Recognition System for Individuals with Visual Impairments", in *Proceedings of the 7th International ACM SIGACCESS Conference on Computers and Accessibility*, New York, NY, USA, 2005, pp. 106–113, doi: 10.1145/1090785.1090806.

[7] "OrCam MyEye 2", *OrCam*. [Online]. Available from: https://www.orcam.com/de/myeye2/ [Accessed: 2020.02.01].

[8] "Seeing AI | Talking camera app for those with a visual impairment". [Online]. Available from https://www.microsoft.com/en-us/ai/seeing-ai [Accessed: 2020.02.01].

[9] P. Ekman, *Emotion in the Human Face*, 2nd. edition. New York: Cambridge University Press, 1982.

[10] P. Ekman, *Gefühle lesen [In English: Emotions Revealed]*, 2nd. edition. Heidelberg: Spektrum Akad. Verl., 2010.

[11] Noldus Information Technology, "Free white paper on FaceReader methodology". [Online]. Available from: https://info.noldus.com/free-white-paper-on-facereader-methodology [Accessed: 2020.02.01].

[12] "FaceReader Webshop". [Online]. Available from: https://www.noldus.com/facereader-webshop [Accessed: 2020.02.01].

FatCombat: A Health Video Game for Education and Promotion of the Recommended Fat Intake Among Children

Ismael Edrein Espinosa-Curiel*, Edgar Pozas-Bogarin*, Janeth Aguilar-Partida*, Maryleidi Hernández-Arvizu*
and Edwin Emeth Delgado-Pérez†
* CICESE-UT3
Andador 10 #109, Ciudad del Conocimiento, 63197, Tepic, Nayarit, México
Email: ecuriel@cicese.mx, pozas@cicese.mx, amara@cicese.mx, maryleidi@cicese.mx
†Center for Studies and Research in Behavior
Universidad de Guadalajara (UdG)
Francisco de Quevedo 180 Arcos Vallarta, 44130, Guadalajara, Jalisco, México
Email: emeth.delgado@gmail.com

Abstract—**Overweight and obesity are frequently assumed to be the result of an energy imbalance caused by an excess in calories and fat intake. To help children learn about the different types of fat and their intake recommendations, we developed the health video game *FatCombat* (FC). In this game, players go inside the bodies of children to help them eat healthily by respecting fat intake recommendations. As a result of their actions, the heart can stay healthy and generate a constant flow of blood to the children's bodies. FC is based on knowledge of fat intake and integrates a set of behavior change techniques related to cognitive and behavioral theories used in children's health interventions. In this paper, we describe the design process for FC and report the results of a pilot study to evaluate the effect of FC on the knowledge children have of fat and to evaluate the user experience of FC players. Players of FC improved their knowledge of fats and the game provided high levels enjoyment.**

Keywords–Health video game; Children; Fat intake recommendations; Learning; Fat intake change.

I. Introduction

The prevalence of childhood overweight and obesity has reached alarming levels, affecting virtually all socio-economic groups, irrespective of sex and ethnicity, of both developed and developing countries [1]. Childhood obesity can profoundly affect children's physical health, social, and emotional well-being and self-esteem [2]–[4]. It can also contribute to increased premature mortality [5]. Childhood obesity is a multifactorial problem; however, it is frequently assumed to be the result of an energy imbalance caused by an excess in fat intake in children [5]. One possible solution to this problem is to eliminate as much fat as possible from children's diets; however, children need fat for adequate growth (e.g., it helps them absorb vitamins and minerals, provides fuel and insulates the body). Therefore, instead of reducing fat intake, to have adequate growth, children must learn how to intake the daily recommended amount of the four types of fat. Different fats have different effects on the body. While saturated and trans fats can raise blood cholesterol levels and increase the chance of getting heart disease, monounsaturated and polyunsaturated fats have several health benefits. In addition, children need to identify the types of fat contained in the food they usually consume in order to be more selective and improve their fat intake habits.

Health video games are an emerging strategy that can help fulfill these objectives of learning and changing behavior. These types of video games are innovative and enticing methods for attracting attention, educating, and promoting changes in the knowledge, attitudes and behaviors of players [6], [7]. The literature indicates that health video games can have positive effects on nutritional knowledge, physical activity, and eating attitudes and behaviors of children [6]–[8]. In particular, this type of video games can help children to increase their knowledge regarding nutrition definitions and eating rules [9], the five most important macronutrients of foods [10], and the U.S. Department of Agriculture MyPlate guidelines [11]. This type of game can also help increase the intake of healthy food, such as vegetables, fruits, legumes, and white meat [12]–[14], and reduce the intake of unhealthy food, such as sugar-containing snacks and beverages and processed snacks [13], [15], [16].

Some of the current nutrition health video games for children include knowledge related to fats. The video game "Fit, Food, Fun", for instance, includes a mini game structured like a quiz that compares protein, fat, carbohydrates, or calories between two food items. It also includes a mini game designed to estimate the content of sugar, fat, or salt in food [9]. Similarly, the video game "Alien Health" encourages students to discourse about the somewhat similar food items and to make an optimal choice, taking into account the protein, fats, carbohydrates, fiber, and vitamins/minerals of the food [10], [11]. In the game 'Fitter Critters", the player is responsible for the health of a virtual pet (Critter) and needs to complete quests to learn how food and activity choices influence their Critter's behavior and health. By choosing healthy foods without surpassing the fat, sugar, and caloric allotment, the Critter becomes healthier and is sick less [17]. The game "Creature 101" includes a mini game to learn about the role of taste, sugar, and fat in our diets. It also includes a mini game related to food and nutrition facts about sugar and fat contents of commonly consumed beverages and snacks [15]. In the "NutritionBuddy" video game, players collect food to make a well energy-balanced combination of food and beverages by keeping carbohydrates, fats, and proteins within the recommended limits [18].

II. Present study

Although the health video games described above include knowledge related to fats, to the best of our knowledge, there is not an explicit game designed to educate children about the different types of fat and their effects in the body, the daily fat intake recommendations for children, and the type and amount of fat that have the food frequently consumed by children. Therefore, we developed *FatCombat* (FC), a health video game that focuses on helping children understand and apply the nutritional concepts related to fats mentioned above. The FC elements and mechanics are based on nutrition knowledge and Behavior Change Techniques (BCT). FC is part of IFitKids, a platform that integrates nutrition mini games and components related to psychology, nutrition, and physical activity. In this paper, we describe the design process of FC and how BCTs were operationalized into the game elements to induce changes in the fat intake of players. We also describe the results of a pilot study to evaluate the effect of FC on the fat knowledge of children and to evaluate the user experience and usability of the game.

We organize this paper as follows. Section III describes the methodology we used to design FC. In Section IV, we describe our proposed health video game. Section V describes the evaluation of FC. Section VI reports the results of a pilot study to evaluate the effect of FC on the knowledge children have of fat and to evaluate the user experience of FC. Section VII discusses our findings. Finally, Section VIII provides some concluding remarks and some research directions for future work.

III. GAME DESIGN

To design FC, we used an iterative game design methodology based on the work of Macklin and Sharp [19]. Our methodology consisted of the following five steps (see Figure 1): (1) learning and behavioral change planning; (2) game design; (3) prototype development; (4) play-testing; and (5) evaluation. We conducted three cycles until we obtained the version of FC evaluated in this study. Next, we describe the activities conducted in each step.

- In Step 1, we conducted a literature review to position FC in the specialized serious game literature (e.g., [20]–[22]) and nutrition knowledge. In addition, we conducted several multidisciplinary design sessions with two nutritionists and a psychologist to establish and improve the learning objectives, target behaviors, behavior change objectives, and BCTs that could be integrated into the gameplay elements to support the behavior change objectives.
- In Step 2, we conducted multidisciplinary design sessions with the participation of two nutritionists, one psychologist, one expert on human-computer interaction, and three game designers. The session aimed to propose design ideas and game rules and mechanisms and define how to include the nutritional concepts and implement the selected BCTs into the gameplay elements. Based on these activities, we designed high-fidelity prototypes. We conducted 4, 2, and 2 multidisciplinary design sessions in cycles 1, 2, and 3, respectively. The number of sessions is higher in the first cycle because this is when we go from the idea to have a working prototype.
- In Step 3, we implemented in the video game engine Unity® a high-fidelity prototype based on the game design obtained in the previous step.

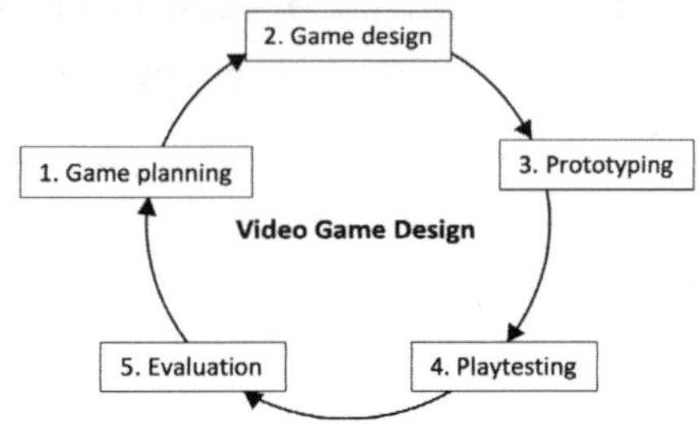

Figure 1. Process of designing FC

- In Step 4, children played with the prototype and later participated in a focus group where they were encouraged to talk about their game experience (e.g., instructions, activities, challenges, game flow, human-computer interaction, and amount of fun) and to draw new game elements or features. Some suggestions from cycle 1 were to improve the explanation of fats, the tutorial, the health indicators, and the feedback messages, as well as to clarify the mission and emphasize the role of fats in the game mechanics. The suggestions for improving and changing cycles 2 and 3 were to add a map, add difficulty levels, increase the reward coins, make the heart interactive, and add more fun elements. In cycles 1, 2, and 3 there were 6, 12, and 10 children participating, respectively. The age range of all participants was 8 to 11 years. Different children participated in each cycle. The playing duration was 10, 15, and 15 minutes for cycles 1, 2, and 3, respectively.
- Finally, in Step 5, we conducted a multidisciplinary session with the same participants of the Step 2 session to discuss and analyze the obtained results, the changes suggested for the game and the new requirements obtained in the previous step, and we elaborated a set of recommendations to improve the usability, enjoyment, player experience, game mechanics, game elements, and learning and behavior change strategies.

IV. FATCOMBAT

Players have to fill out a "welcome form", which creates a user-tailored profile, and then they are allowed to start playing. The requested data are gender and age in years and months. This information is used to estimate the recommended energy consumption, and based on this information, estimate the total number of grams of fat and the amount of each type of fat. FC includes a configuration section, where players log-in, play through the game's story, select and buy avatars, and select the next level from a map. In addition, FC includes an educational section, where the players learn about the importance of fat for adequate growth, the four types of fat and their effects on the body, fat intake recommendations, and the predominant types of fat contained in popular food (see Figure 2, top left and top right screens). Players should see this tutorial completely the first time they play. Then, they can see it again if they want to review the explanation. This section also includes a tutorial that explains the game goal, how to play the game, the game

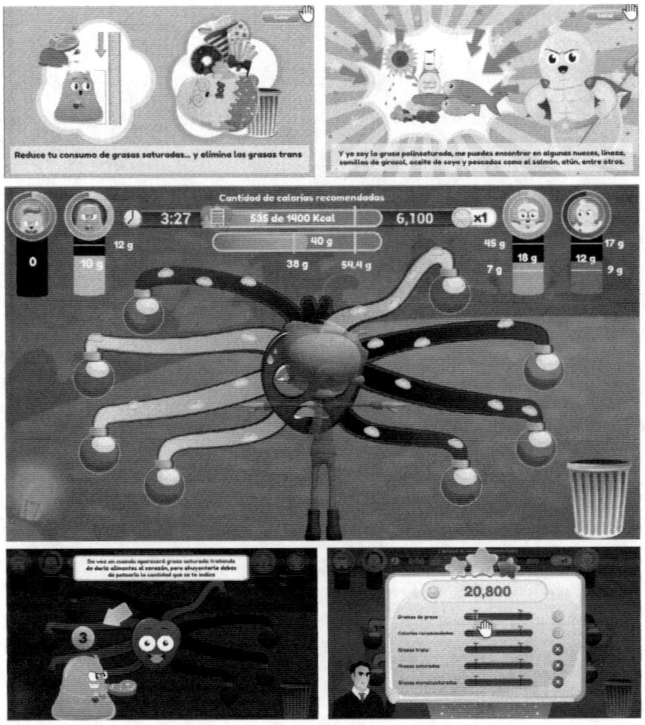

Figure 2. FatCombat's screens.

options and elements, the indicators, and the results section (see Figure 2, bottom-right screen).

A. *Active playing*

We designed FC as an active game to make it more fun, improve the user experience, and promote light physical activity [23]. Active games require physical activity beyond that of conventional hand-held games and rely on technology that tracks body movements or reactions for game progress [24]. FC players must perform basic physical movements, such as squats, jumps, lateral body movements, and arm movements to pick up the food. They also need to perform kicks and punches to prevent the avatars of trans and saturated fats from delivering food to the heart. To follow the body movements of the players, FC uses the Microsoft Kinect V2® sensor.

B. *FC gameplay*

The adventure of FC takes place in HealthyTown, a city controlled by a group of evil chefs who added fats that come to life within the children's bodies to the food. Dr. Yokuro Kokoro, the chief scientist of the city, realizes what is going on, so he assigns a secret agent (the player) the mission to go inside the bodies of children and help their hearts eat healthy, respecting the intake recommendations for calories, total fat, trans fats, saturated fats, monounsaturated fats, and polyunsaturated fats. The Food and Agriculture Organization of the United Nations (FAO) proposed the following daily fat intake recommendations for children aged between 2 and 18 years old [25]:

- Between 25% and 35% of Kcal should come from fat.
- Up to 1% of Kcal should come from trans fats;
- Up to 8% of Kcal should come from saturated fats;
- From 6% to 11% of Kcal should come from or polyunsaturated fats;
- The intake of monounsaturated fat depends on the total fat intake and the characteristics of dietary fat. Analyzing the possible combinations of fat consumption, we calculated that the recommended consumption range is from 5% to 29% of Kcal.

C. *FC mechanics*

In the game, food appears randomly, and players must decide whether the heart should consume it or not. For each food, the game shows a real picture and a tag that specifies the type and amount of fat that the food contains. The game has a database of 400 foods frequently consumed by Mexican children. The food included in the database was selected from interviews with children from 8 to 11 years of age and the opinion of two nutritionists. The fat quantity of the foods was obtained from the Mexican equivalent food system [26]. To make their decision, players must take into account the type and amount of fat that the food contains and the fat already consumed by the heart, which is specified in fat bars. In alignment with the recommendations mentioned previously, we integrated into the game six variables that influence gameplay (see Figure 2, middle screen). These variables are "total calories", "total fat", "trans fats", "saturated fats, "monounsaturated fats" and "polyunsaturated fats". A bar displayed on the user interface serves as a visualization of the "variables" levels, and each bar has an exclusive range depending on the variable.

When the player feeds the heart with food that contains saturated or trans fat, yellow or pinks fats will appear in the veins and the bars of these fats will increase. When the player feeds the heart with food that contains monounsaturated or polyunsaturated fats, green or blue fats will appear in the veins and, since these fats help clean the trans and monounsaturated fats, some yellow and pink fats will disappear and their bars will drop. The blood flow in the veins is determined by the amount of fat they have. Therefore, the more fat, the less blood flow. When the blood flow is low, it is reflected in the facial expressions of the heart. In addition, the avatars of the saturated and trans fats randomly appear and try to give the heart food with their type of fat (see Figure 2, bottom-left screen). For example, the saturated fats avatar gives the heart a dish of beef, and the trans fats avatar gives the heart a chocolate cake. The player must determine if the heart should be allowed to eat these foods. If the player does not want the heart to consume such food, he or she must defeat those fats by kicking or hitting them. FC has other scenarios in which questions related to fats, types of fat, and the types of fats present in popular food appear randomly. The player earns coins if he or she answers the questions correctly.

We included a curve of increasing difficulty across the 10 levels of the game to encourage players to have fun through the end of the video game. The learning objectives of the levels are incremental. For example, at level 3, in addition to the objective of level 3, players must meet the objectives of levels 2 and 1. The game levels are as follows:

- Level 1. Players need to ensure that the total calories and fat intake are within the recommended ranges.

- Level 2. Players have to prevent the heart from intaking food with trans fats.
- Level 3. Players need to ensure that the intake of saturated fats is less than the maximum amount allowed.
- Levels 4 and 5. Players need to ensure that the intake of monounsaturated and polyunsaturated fats is within the recommended range.
- Levels 6 and 7. The hints about the types and amounts of fat in the foods are hidden.
- Levels 8, 9, and 10. The bars showing saturated, monounsaturated, and polyunsaturated fats are hidden, and only the grams consumed are shown.

If the player meets the objective of the levels, he or she earns points and moves on to the next level. On the contrary, if he or she loses, the level must be repeated.

D. Behavioral change techniques

We integrated a set of BCTs in the gameplay elements of FC to induce changes in the fat intake behaviors of players. Figure 3 explicitly shows the relationship between the BCTs used and the gameplay elements. A BCT is defined as "an observable, replicable, and irreducible component of an intervention designed to alter or redirect causal processes that regulate behavior; that is, a technique is proposed to be an "active ingredient" [27]. BCTs are based on constructs of theories frequently used in health interventions, such as behavioral theory, cognitive theory, control theory, theory of planned behavior, and social cognitive theory. BCTs can be used alone, but the combination of several BCTs is frequently critical for effectiveness [28]. The BCTs integrated into the game show empirical evidence of the game's efficacy in aiding weight loss and addressing other kinds of dietary problems in children [29]. In the game, we integrated BCTs related to the explanation of the natural consequences of fat intake in order to shape knowledge by providing instructions on how to perform the planned behaviors. The game also provides an environment to substitute and practice new behaviors and includes game mechanisms to instigate the selected behaviors. To support the practice of the behaviors, FC includes prompts and clues that are reduced or eliminated in the last levels of the game. In addition, to guide the activities, the game includes goal setting, review, feedback and monitoring. The game also includes rewards to immediately reinforce short-term actions (e.g., maintain the blood flow) and long-term actions, such as level completion. The reward follows an incremental scheme. Finally, the game includes other elements associated with learning and behavior change, such as vicarious consequences, social comparison, and the player being centered as a role model. The work of Michie et al. [27] provides a broad definition of the BCTs operationalized in FC.

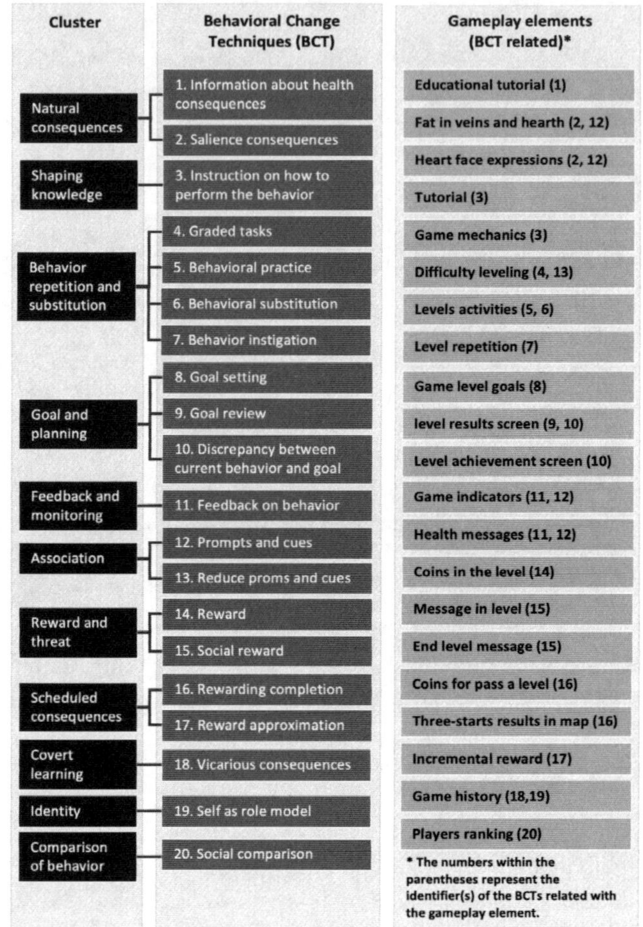

Figure 3. BCTs operationalized in the gameplay elements of FC

V. GAME EVALUATION

We conducted a pilot study to evaluate whether the game helps improve the children's knowledge about fats and to examine the user experience of the players. Although FC was also designed to generate changes in fat intake attitudes and behaviors related to players, we did not evaluate this due to the short duration of the evaluation study. A longer-term study is required to evaluate changes in the fat intake attitudes and behaviors of players. A total of 13 children (n=5 girls, n=8 boys) aged 8-10 (mean age 9.6, SD 1.12 years) from a primary school voluntarily participated in the experiment. Of the participants, 50% of the girls and 70% of the boys were overweight or obese. Before collecting the data, we obtained written authorization from school authorities and written consent from the parents for the children to take part in the study. Later, we applied a fat knowledge questionnaire. The questionnaire included seven general fat questions with 5 response options (e.g., *What is the type of fat that is solid at room temperature and is found in animal foods?*) and 10 questions about the types of fat various foods contain (e.g., *What type of fat does avocado mainly contain?*). Later, over a period of 25 days, the participants conducted six game sessions, with an average of 35 minutes per session (one session every two days). The total average time that the children played was 3.5 h. When the students finished the game sessions, we applied the fat knowledge questionnaire and a user experience questionnaire. The user experience questionnaire was based on two validated questionnaires [30], [31] and had 47 items grouped into 13 categories. For each item, we asked the participants to indicate on a 5-point Likert-type scale ranging from (1) "Totally disagree" to (5) "Totally agree" the level to which they believe the game accomplishes each of the

TABLE I. FAT KNOWLEDGE PRETEST AND POSTTEST RESULTS

Correct responses	*Mean*	*SD*[a]	*P*[b]
pretest	5.1	4.5	0.038
posttest	8.9	4.6	

[a] Standard deviation

[b] P value of<0.05 was considered to be statistically significant

questionnaire statements.

VI. Results

We compared the pretest and posttest levels of fat knowledge using the Wilcoxon signed-rank sum test. We used the Statistical Package for the Social Sciences (SPSS) version 25 software [32] to conduct the statistical analysis. From the statistical analysis results (see Table I), we identified that the players significantly improved their fat knowledge after playing the game (P=0.038). In relation to user experience, for each category, Table II, shows the number of items, an example of the statement, the median and interquartile range, and the percentage of participants who agreed that the game fulfills the statements in that category. The agreement percentage represents the result of dividing the number of responses with an evaluation of 4 or 5 by the total number of responses. The game received a median score of 4 or above in all dimensions, which reflects high levels of user experience, enjoyment, and usability. Most of the participants agreed that FC is fun and easy to use; has a clear story, goals, and dialogues; provides useful feedback; and has pleasing sounds and graphics. Another significant result is that most of the players agreed that the game adapts the difficulty to their capacity and skills, stimulates their curiosity, and allows them to be imaginative. They also agreed that the game helped improve their knowledge and constantly motivated them to advance to the next stage or level. These characteristics provide them with a good amount of immersion because most of the players agreed that they forgot about the passage of time, became unaware of their surroundings while playing the game, and could not wait to play again.

VII. Discussion

To best our knowledge, FC is the only nutrition health video game explicitly designed for education on and the promotion of the recommended fat intake among children. The obtained results show that children significantly improved their knowledge of fat after playing FC. The video games that include some knowledge about fat have also obtained favorable results in knowledge improvement and behavior change. The video game "Creature 101" [15] helped children to improve their eating behaviors, and the video games "Fit, Food, Fun" [9], "Alien Health" [10], [11] and "Fitter Critters" [17] helped to improve the general nutrition knowledge of children. However, because none of these studies evaluated the effect of the video game on children's knowledge about fats, we cannot be made a comparison against the results obtained by FC. The study conducted by Holzmann et al. [9] is the only that includes some questions to evaluate fat knowledge of children; however, they reported that players obtained a lower score in the knowledge of fat and oil after play the video game. These results are encouraging for further research on the ability of FC to teach about fats and improve fat eating.

Moreover, the high user experience and usability results of FC were in line with results from other health video games for children. These studies reported satisfaction and usability ratings ranging from 4.11 to 4.52 on a 5-point scale [13], [17], [33] which are similar than ratings observed in the present study. As satisfaction and usability appear to be correlated with knowledge gained, the high user experience and usability of FC has implications for its ability to impact fat knowledge. Two areas of improvement for the video game are autonomy and visual aesthetics because these were the subscales with the lowest rating. The first refers to the control that the players felt in the game elements and the support provided to players in the game so that they would know what the next steps in the game were. The second relates to the quality of the game's graphics and whether the players like them and find them pleasant. One limitation of this study is that it was conducted in a single school and with only a few participants. However, given that the objective of this study was not to generalize our findings but to achieve an overall impression of the usability of FC, we consider our results to be valuable for researchers exploring the design context of this type of serious game.

VIII. Conclusion and Future Work

In this paper, we present *FatCombat* (FC), an active health video game used for educating and promoting the adequate intake of different types of fat among children. Additionally, we describe how a multidisciplinary team used an iterative game design methodology to design FC. Finally, we describe how BCTs were operationalized into FC gameplay to induce changes in the fat intake of the players. These contributions can help game designers design new serious games for nutritional education and for encouraging changes in eating behaviors of children. From a pilot study, we identified that players of FC improved their knowledge of fats. In addition, we identified that the game provides high levels of user experience, enjoyment, and usability. For future work, we are planning to conduct additional design cycles in which parents, teachers, and children will be involved as co-designers to improve game design. In addition, we are planning to conduct a comparative study of using FC versus the traditional lecture way. Finally, we are planning to conduct a randomized controlled trial to evaluate more in-depth the effectiveness of FC to support player learning about fats and to evaluate its effects on fat intake intentions, fat intake auto-efficacy, and fat intake behaviors.

Acknowledgment

We thank the Consejo Nacional de Ciencia y Tecnología (CONACYT, Mexico) for financial support (grant number PDCPN-2015-824 awarded to CICESE). We thank the Colegio Real de San Juan for facilitating the evaluation of FC and all of the teachers, students, and parents who participated in this study. We also thank the participating experts and users who helped develop FC. Finally, we thank the graphics designer Laura Nayely Miranda Piña for participating in the design of the several graphical elements of FC.

References

[1] UNICEF-WHO-The World Bank Group, "Joint child malnutrition estimates - levels and trends," UNICEF, WHO & World Bank, Tech. Rep., 2019 edition.

TABLE II. USER EXPERIENCE RESULTS

#	Category	Items	Question example	Median(IQR)	Agreement
1	Goal clarity	2	The overall game goals were presented clearly.	5(1)	81% (21/26)
2	Feedback	3	I received feedback on my progress in the game.	5(1)	79% (31/39)
3	Challenge	3	The level of challenge in the game was adequate for me.	5(1)	77% (30/39)
4	Autonomy	2	I felt a sense of control in the game.	4(2)	65% (17/26)
5	Immersion	4	I cannot wait to play again	5(2)	71% (37/52)
6	Knowledge improvement	3	I understood the basic ideas of the knowledge taught in the game.	5(1)	77% (30/39)
7	Playability/Usability	9	I think it is easy to learn how to play the game.	5(2)	72% (84/117)
8	Narratives	3	I enjoyed the story provided by the game.	5(1.5)	74% (29/39)
9	Enjoyment	3	I think the game is fun.	5(1.5)	74% (29/39)
10	Creative freedom	3	I feel that my curiosity has been stimulated as a result of playing the game.	5(1)	77% (30/39)
11	Audio aesthetics	3	I enjoyed the sound effects in the game.	5(1)	79% (31/39)
12	Personal gratification	4	I am very focused on how to achieve the game's goals and get the rewards.	4(2)	77% (40/52)
13	Visual aesthetics	3	I enjoyed the game's graphics.	4(2)	62% (24/39)

Data are expressed as the median (interquartile range) of the participants' scores. The scores are (1) "Strongly disagree"; (2) "Agree", (3) "Undecided", (4) "Agree", (5) "Strongly agree".

[2] M. Kelsey, A. Zaepfel, P. Bjornstad, and K. Nadeau, "Age-Related Consequences of Childhood Obesity," Gerontology, vol. 60, no. 3, 2014, pp. 222–228.

[3] E. P. Williams, M. Mesidor, K. Winters, P. M. Dubbert, and S. B. Wyatt, "Overweight and obesity: Prevalence, consequences, and causes of a growing public health problem," Current Obesity Reports, vol. 4, no. 3, 2015, pp. 363–370.

[4] A. W. Harrist, T. M. Swindle, L. Hubbs-Tait, G. L. Topham, L. H. Shriver, and M. C. Page, "The social and emotional lives of overweight, obese, and severely obese children," Child Development, vol. 87, no. 5, 2016, pp. 1564–1580.

[5] K. Sahoo, B. Sahoo, A. K. Choudhury, N. Y. Sofi, R. Kumar, and A. S. Bhadoria, "Childhood obesity: causes and consequences," Journal of family medicine and primary care, vol. 4, no. 2, 2015, pp. 187–192.

[6] T. Baranowski et al., "Games for Health for Children: Current Status and Needed Research," Games For Health Journal, vol. 5, no. 1, 2016, pp. 1–12.

[7] A. S. Lu, H. Kharrazi, F. Gharghabi, and D. Thompson, "A Systematic Review of Health Video Games on Childhood Obesity Prevention and Intervention," Games for health journal, vol. 2, no. 3, 2013, p. 10.1089/g4h.2013.0025.

[8] H. Parisod et al., "Promoting children's health with digital games: A review of reviews," Games for Health Journal, vol. 3, no. 3, 2014, pp. 145–156.

[9] S. L. Holzmann et al., "Short-Term Effects of the Serious Game "Fit, Food, Fun" on Nutritional Knowledge: A Pilot Study among Children and Adolescents," Nutrients, vol. 11, no. 9, 2019, pp. 1–13.

[10] M. C. Johnson-Glenberg, C. Savio-Ramos, and H. Henry, "Alien health game: A nutrition instruction exergame using the kinect sensor," Games For Health Journal, vol. 3, no. 4, 2014, pp. 241–251.

[11] M. C. Johnson-Glenberg and E. B. Hekler, "Alien Health Game: An embodied exergame to instruct in nutrition and myplate," Games for Health Journal, vol. 2, no. 6, 2013, pp. 354–361.

[12] T. Baranowski et al., "Video game play, child diet, and physical activity behavior change: A randomized clinical trial," American journal of preventive medicine, vol. 40, no. 1, 2011, pp. 33–38.

[13] D. Marchetti et al., "Preventing adolescents' diabesity: Design, development, and first evaluation of "Gustavo in Gnam's Planet"," Games for Health Journal, vol. 4, no. 5, 2015, pp. 344–351.

[14] K. W. Cullen, Y. Liu, and D. I. Thompson, "Meal-Specific Dietary Changes From Squires Quest! II: A Serious Video Game Intervention," Journal of Nutrition Education and Behavior, vol. 48, no. 5, 2016, pp. 326–330.e1.

[15] D. Majumdar, P. A. Koch, H. Lee, I. R. Contento, A. d. L. Islas-Ramos, and D. Fu, "Creature-101: A serious game to promote energy balance-related behaviors among middle school adolescents," Games for Health Journal, vol. 2, no. 5, 2013, pp. 280–290.

[16] S. V. Sharma et al., "Effects of the quest to lava mountain computer game on dietary and physical activity behaviors of elementary school children: A pilot group-randomized controlled trial," Journal of the Academy of Nutrition and Dietetics, vol. 115, no. 8, 2015, pp. 1260 – 1271.

[17] K. L. Schneider et al., "Acceptability of an online health videogame to improve diet and physical activity in elementary school students: "Fitter Critters"," Games for Health Journal, vol. 1, no. 4, 2012, pp. 262–268.

[18] S. Michael, P. Katrakazas, O. Petronoulou, A. Anastasiou, D. Iliopoulou, and D. Dionisios Koutsouris, "Nutritionbuddy: a childhood obesity serious game," in 2018 Second World Conference on Smart Trends in Systems, Security and Sustainability (WorldS4), Oct 2018, pp. 5–8.

[19] C. Macklin and J. Sharp, Games, Design and Play: A detailed approach to iterative game design. Addison-Wesley Professional, May 2016.

[20] M. T. Baranowski et al., "Videogame mechanics in games for health," Games for Health Journal, vol. 2, no. 4, 2013, pp. 194–204.

[21] T. Baranowski, R. Buday, D. Thompson, E. J. Lyons, A. S. Lu, and J. Baranowski, "Developing games for health behavior change: Getting started," Games for Health Journal, vol. 2, no. 4, 2013, pp. 183–190.

[22] D. Thompson et al., "Serious video games for health how behavioral science guided the development of a serious video game," Simulation & gaming, vol. 41, no. 4, 08 2010, pp. 587–606.

[23] S. Y. S. Kim, N. Prestopnik, and F. A. Biocca, "Body in the interactive game: How interface embodiment affects physical activity and health behavior change," Computers in Human Behavior, vol. 36, 2014, pp. 376 – 384.

[24] A. G. LeBlanc et al., "Active video games and health indicators in children and youth: A systematic review," PLOS ONE, vol. 8, no. 6, Jun. 2013, p. e65351.

[25] Food and Agriculture Organization of the United Nations (FAO), "Fats and fatty acids in human nutrition. report of an expert consultation, 10-14 november 2008, Geneva," Tech. Rep., 2010.

[26] A. B. P. Lizaur, B. P. González, A. L. C. Becerra, and I. F. Galicia, Sistema Mexicano de Alimentos Equivalentes. Fomento de Nutrición y Salud, 2014.

[27] S. Michie et al., "The behavior change technique taxonomy (v1) of 93 hierarchically clustered techniques: building an international consensus for the reporting of behavior change interventions," Annals of Behavioral Medicine, vol. 46, no. 1, Aug. 2013, pp. 81–95.

[28] S. Michie, R. West, K. Sheals, and C. A. Godinho, "Evaluating the effectiveness of behavior change techniques in health-related behavior: a scoping review of methods used," Translational Behavioral Medicine, vol. 8, no. 2, Mar. 2018, pp. 212–224.

[29] J. Martin, A. Chater, and F. Lorencatto, "Effective behaviour change techniques in the prevention and management of childhood obesity," International Journal of Obesity, vol. 37, no. 10, Jun. 2013, p. 1287–1294.

[30] F.-L. Fu, R.-C. Su, and S.-C. Yu, "Egameflow: A scale to measure learners' enjoyment of e-learning games," Computers & Education, vol. 52, no. 1, Jan. 2009, pp. 101–112.

[31] M. H. Phan, J. R. Keebler, and B. S. Chaparro, "The development and validation of the game user experience satisfaction scale (guess)," Human Factors, vol. 58, no. 8, 2016, pp. 1217–1247, pMID: 27647156.

[32] IBM Corp., "IBM SPSS Statistics for Windows, Version 25.0," New York: IBM Corp, 2017.

[33] Y. Hswen, L. Rubenzahl, and D. S. Bickham, "Feasibility of an online and mobile videogame curriculum for teaching children safe and healthy cellphone and internet behaviors," Games for Health Journal, vol. 3, no. 4, 2014, pp. 252–259, pMID: 26192373.

Trust Me ! I Can be a Designated Driving Assistant

Misbah Javaid
School of ICT
Griffith University
Nathan, Queensland, Australia 4111
Email: misbah.javaid@griffithuni.edu.au

Vladimir Estivill-Castro
School of ICT
Griffith University
Nathan, Queensland, Australia 4111
Email: v.estivill@griffith.edu.au

Rene Hexel
School of ICT
Griffith University
Nathan, Queensland, Australia 4111
Email: r.hexel@griffith.edu.au

***Abstract*—*Autonomous vehicles* drive themselves by utilizing sensors and artificial intelligence. Evidence from surveys has shown that humans are captivated by *autonomous vehicles*, yet reluctant to give up control entirely to an *autonomous vehicle*. Inadequacy of humans trust has been identified as a pre-eminent factor behind the unacceptability of *autonomous vehicles* for driving. We propose that explanations describing behavioural decisions serve to upgrade human's sense of trust in the driving performance of *autonomous vehicles*. The contribution of our proposed research is tested by creating an interactive scenario with 34 human participants, in which we present a robot as a *driving assistant* of an *autonomous vehicle*. We incorporated the *driving assistant* with the capability to explain *traffic rules* and *traffic signs*. Moreover, the *driving assistant* is equipped with the ability to make decisions on uncertain road situations in terms of explaining, i.e., what should be a decision and why; keeping in view *traffic rules*. Additionally, the *driving assistant* has the ability to analyse and explain when to overstep a *traffic rule*, relative to a perceived hazard on the road. During the interactive scenario, the human participants performed a decision making task comprised of different *road problem-solving* scenarios with the *driving assistant*. We examined the effect of explanations from the *driving assistant* on humans' trust under two conditions (Condition 1): *no-error* and (Condition 2): *error-justification and correction*. Overall, the results show that during the decision-making task, the human participants trusted and conformed more with the *driving assistant's* decisions as compared to their own decisions. Furthermore, the human participants perceived the decisions of the *driving assistant* under Condition 1 more reliable, intelligent and trustworthy than under Condition 2. We conclude that explanations disseminating behavioural decisions are an effective communication modality that can help to improve humans trust and perceived agency (functional capability) of *autonomous vehicles*.**

Keywords*–*Human-Robot Trust; Explanations;Queensland Traffic Rules;Human-Robot Physical Interaction.

I. INTRODUCTION

Autonomous vehicles are the vehicles that can drive themselves using their sensors and artificial intelligence; therefore, they need no direct input from a human. The lack of control has caused fear and speculations about the reliability of *autonomous vehicles* [1]. Notably, the behaviour of autonomous vehicles is unpredictable to humans under uncertain road conditions, and makes humans think about what a vehicle will do and why? [1]. There is no doubt that autonomous vehicles predominantly offer many benefits i.e., road accidents will be reduced because, it is reported that more than 90 % of vehicle accidents involve human factors like distractions, fatigue, and misjudgement of the situation [2]. However, introducing such vehicles on the road also manifests different challenges. Evidence from investigations has shown that humans are captivated by *autonomous vehicles*, but reluctant to completely give up control entirely to *autonomous vehicles*. One of the foremost challenges for autonomous vehicles is the inadequacy of humans trust and humans have different concerns to justify their position behind the unacceptability. For example, what if a human wants to take back the control of a vehicle and the vehicle is incapable for that, or if some bad incident happens, who is going to take responsibility for the incident [1]. However, when people do have the possibility to take back the control, the quality of the take over action varies for different traffic situations [3] and this is likely to be related to a loss of situation-awareness [4]. Research has already begun to develop strategies to address these challenges and concerns. One way to give people the feeling that they are in control, while they are not actually in control, is to provide explanations. Especially, explanations that provide decision transparency, in terms of explaining a best decision based on a road condition. Moreover, explanations can also help humans track the performance and capabilities of *autonomous vehicles*.

We designed an experimental study based on an interactive scenario with 34 human participants, in which we present a robot as a *driving assistant* of an *autonomous vehicle*. The *driving assistant* is expert in identifying and explaining *traffic rules* and *traffic signs*. Moreover, the *driving assistant* has the ability to make decisions under uncertain road situations and can make some judgements to break *traffic rules* if perceive any hazard on the road. The *driving assistant* reveals the *transparency* of its decisions by generating relevant and meaningful explanations in terms of *how* a decision is made and *why* the decision is best according to the traffic situation; keeping in view traffic rules and regulations. Our main aim is to establish humans trust through explanations that will also keep the *human-in-the loop* by supplying the correct situation-awareness. The *driving assistant* provides explanations through communicating plausibly, and also provides other explanations when necessary i.e., explaining complicated terms. This strategy will not only allow the human participants to monitor the performance ability of the *driving assistant*, but also help them understand what is going on and consequently establish trust in the *driving assistant*. In general, explanations are given to impart, modify or clarify knowledge [5], to make things clear and understandable, and are often the core of any trustworthy relationship. Even in human-human interactions, unexpected and unforeseen circumstances can affect trust, and the loss of trust can be reduced by giving explanations [6]. In this sense, trust and explanations seem to be common partners in everyday life.

Revising the primary purpose of our study, we created an interactive scenario, in which human participants perform a decision-making task with a *driving assistant*, in a given time. The decision-making task is based upon *road problem-solving* scenarios. We told the human participants that the task is based on the collaboration with the *driving assistant*, and the final decision does not depend on the human participants' decision solely. We explained this to every human participant. First, human participants must choose an option, and then they can change the answer after listening to the *driving assistant's* explanations or to leave it as it was. For the proposed method, we set the focus of our inquiry through humans' acceptance and conformation to the *driving assistant's* answers, as a new objective measure of the trustworthy relationship.

If *autonomous vehicles* make the right situation assessments and provide the right explanations for their decisions, they will earn humans trust more. However, *autonomous vehicles* like other autonomous systems, can have some degree of errors or can be susceptible to misjudgement of traffic situations and that may have a significant adverse effect on humans trust towards the *autonomous vehicles*. From a performance standpoint, if *autonomous vehicles* can sense their errors and recover themselves automatically, they will be considered more efficient and reliable by humans. Similarly, providing appropriate explanations can reduce the negative effect of the situation [7]. Mapping it into real life, humans tend to trust humans if they can explain to us what do they do and why? This reflects how trust appears to work; it involves (more or less elaborate) explanations of a person or a thing that we may or may not trust. If we expect others to justify their failures to us, the same we expect from *autonomous vehicles*. Therefore, we manipulated the *driving assistant* to make a wrong judgement on some traffic scenarios, and produce inaccurate information by generating wrong explanations intentionally. A wrong explanation means that the *driving assistant* contradicts a traffic situation for some reason and produces wrong explanations. However, immediately corrects himself with a sophisticated justification for the error and sets out to understand the influence of *error-justification and correction* policy. In the time-sensitive task, if the *driving assistant* recovers from a failure and justifies the cause of the failure to the human participants, does it mitigate the possible adverse effects of the erroneous situations? Will human participants agree to rebuild trust in the *driving assistant*? By addressing these questions, the current study contributes to the design metrics of future *autonomous vehicles*. One more factor to consider is explanations modality; how the explanations should be communicated to humans according to their expectations and needs. For *autonomous vehicles* to communicate explanations to the humans, they need to construct a form of agency. The agency can be ascribed based on their ability to follow the same modalities as between human human interaction so that humans perceive the *autonomous vehicles* believable and trustworthy.

Speech is the most common mode of interaction, and many studies suggest the use of verbal statements to express information [8] for the development of humans trust in automation [9]. *Text to speech* voice exerts significant effects on humans' perception and trust in technology [10]. Therefore, the current research adopts a more direct form of communication for the provision of explanations as *English like sentences* in audio modality. We divided this paper into different sections. Section II investigates the literature on trust between humans and automation. Section III discusses the design of a robot as a *driving assistant*. Section IV describes the proposed study as well as hypotheses, experiment procedure, and measures of dependent variables. Section V details the results obtained based on our hypotheses. Section VI presents the discussion and the limitations of the study. Finally, Section VII considers the implications of the study while summarizing the conclusions.

II. Human-Automation Trust

Mayer [11] investigated that trustworthiness is based on the benevolence, perceived integrity and the ability of the given system. In this manner, Lee and See [12] also proposed a dynamic process model that guided how to build trust in automation and its impact on reliance. Their conceptual model provides insightful information about trust in automation and describes guidelines that can help in calibrating trust appropriately, thereby avoiding misuse and disuse of trust. If humans do not trust autonomous systems, the interaction between humans and systems may be affected and eventually lead to the abortion of future interactions [5]. Hoff and Bashir's model [13] also described three layers of trust. According to the model, during interaction with an automated system, trust is moderated by how a system performs during the task, its design features and the experience of the interaction itself. In this way, previous experience with a system helps to build trust in autonomous systems. In today's *semi-autonomous vehicles*, trust is aimed to be established by employing interfaces that display the automated function of the vehicle to provide humans with the transparency of the internal system [14]. McKnight [15] also suggested that trust in *autonomous vehicles* can be enhanced by focusing on certain factors, one of which is system transparency.

III. Robot as Driving Assistant

Pepper is a social robot with a height of 1.2 meters and is suited for easy Human-Robot Interactions. For perception, the *Pepper* robot has two cameras with a native resolution of 640*480 pixels. We chose *Pepper* robot for our study because, given the height of the robot, the top camera is a natural choice for our intercative scenario as it points toward the average height of a human. In our research, we created different flash cards. Each flash card contains an image and a *QR code*. A *QR code* is a quick response that can store a lot of helpful information and is similar to a barcode in matrix form. Although, a *QR code* is readable from any direction, however, the detection of the *QR code* depends on the resolution of the printed *QR code*. Hence, ensure that only high resolution *QR codes* are used. We used *QR codes* as compared to the *Nao marks* because a *QR code* is detected more accurately and allow to store a large amount of data.

During the experiment, the robot's behaviour was completely autonomous. To do this, all the explanations of the robot are preprogrammed in advance and stored in each *QR code* as an identifier for each image. We created a set of three explanations for each flash card, and the robot randomly

Figure 1. Images on the Flash Cards - (a) *TYPE - 1 (Traffic Rule)*, (b) *TYPE - 2 (Traffic Sign)*, (c) *TYPE - 3 (Road Problem Solving - Hazard Perception Scenario)*

chose any explanation. In addition, if a human will show a flashcard to the robot more than once, the explanation given previously will not be triggered again. We make the human participants think that they are interacting with an intelligent *driving assistant*, who is expert enough to remember *traffic rules* and recognise *traffic signs* and can make decisions on uncertain road situations accordingly, by generating a different set of explanations every time. The robot uses the *QR code* to identify the image and to generate different explanations according to the image printed on the flash card. The robot is directed by an executable *NAOqi*, which acts as a broker and starts automatically when *NAOqi OS* starts. *NAOqi* framework contains a *ALBarcodeReader* vision module, that is used to recognise and decode a barcode. The robot uses the *ALBarcodeReader* vision module, using *Python* (an interpreted language) to scan an image in the camera and find a *QR code* in the image. If a barcode is detected in the image, the module will try to decypher it and raise an event to trigger *ALTextToSpeech* (this is another module of the *NAOqi* framework), which enables the robot to speak. We created a separate database for the images printed on the flashcards, and the explanation for each image in *MySQL*. To keep a human in the loop, we also developed a *Graphical User Interface* in *Python* for human participants, that contains images with numbers. Every time, a human participant shows the image to the robot, the experimenter selects the same image on the *Monitor Screen*, so that the human participant can see the image and listen to explanations from the robot. There is an operator who monitors the robot and can control the physical movements of the robot. Also, the operator can make the robot speak as a result of unforeseen questions from the human participants.

A. Experiment Material

We made 105 flash cards with different images on *traffic rules*, *traffic signs* and *road problem-solving* scenarios. All the images and explanations were created by the *Queensland Department of Transport and Main Roads* [16]. We created three possible types of flash cards (35 of each type). Figure 1 shows an example of each type of flash card.

1) TYPE - 1 Flash Cards with Traffic Rules): Type 1 flash cards contain only *traffic rules* and are written in text format, as shown in Figure 1 (a). The primary goal with the *Type 1* flashcard is, we want a human to observe the reading ability (correctly reading without making any mistake) and ability of the *driving assistant* to produce correct and relevant explanations according to the image on the flashcard. Expected explanation from the *driving assistant* for *Type 1* flashcard is:

"Listen human carefully ! With only one working headlight, you cannot drive at night or in conditions of low visibility. Even in the daytime, you may get pulled over if you are seen with only one headlight. If your vehicle has other faults or your headlight has been out for a while, you may be fined."

2) TYPE - 2 Flash Cards with Traffic Signs: Figure 1 (b) shows a Type 2 flash card containing only *traffic signs*. The primary goal with the *Type 2* flash cards is we want a human to analyse that the *driving assistant* is not only capable of reading, but it also has a correct assessment of the *traffic sign* and then producing relevant and explanations according to its assessment. The *driving assistant's* explanation for the Figure 1 (b) is:

"School zone speed limits do not apply on public holidays or weekends. This sign means, you must keep a speed of 40 kilometers per hour in the morning from 8 am to 9:30 am and in the afternoon from 2:30 pm to 4 pm during school days only."

3) TYPE - 3 Flash Cards with Road Problem Solving Scenarios: Type 3 flash cards contain road problem solving scenarios, which are more similar to hazard perception scenarios. Figure 1 (c) shows *Type 3* flash card. If the *driving assistant* can read and explain *traffic rules* and correctly evaluates *road signs*, it does not necessarily mean that the *driving assistant* complies with *traffic rules* and can be trusted as a *driving assistant*. Many people think and admit that the *traffic ruless* are the guidelines for human drivers to drive a vehicle on the road. So, a good driver is the one who knows when to break a traffic rule so as to keep the situation safe and to avoid any accident on the road. Keeping in view, we have created the *road problem solving* scenarios, which are more about solving problems by making decisions under uncertain road conditions and communicating those decisions to humans in terms of relevant explanations. The main goal with *Type 3* flashcards is that we want humans to be able to assess that the *driving assistant* can do something meaningful in a complex situation.

"Giving way to emergency vehicles is foremost important as compared to yourself and other road users. If an emergency vehicle is coming towards you and is sounding an alarm or showing flashing red or blue lights, you must move out its path as soon as you can do so safely. However, giving a way to emergency vehicles should always be done with the utmost care and with the safety of yourself and all other road users as a priority. For pedestrians and other road users, this is correct but, in this scenario, I am driving an ambulance at 40 km/h speed I can see an old lady with her son is about to cross the road and I also saw a dog hiding behind the tree. The dog also wants to cross the road. I am sounding the horn, but the pedestrians do not seem to respond. The situation is not safe for me so I will reduce my speed to stop because there is no traffic on the road and wait for the pedestrians to cross the road first then, I will move on. Remember Human! Emergency vehicles often stop or slow down to check if they can pass through safely."

IV. Proposed Study

To explore the effect of explanations on the human participants' trust towards the *driving assistant*, we carried out an experimental study.

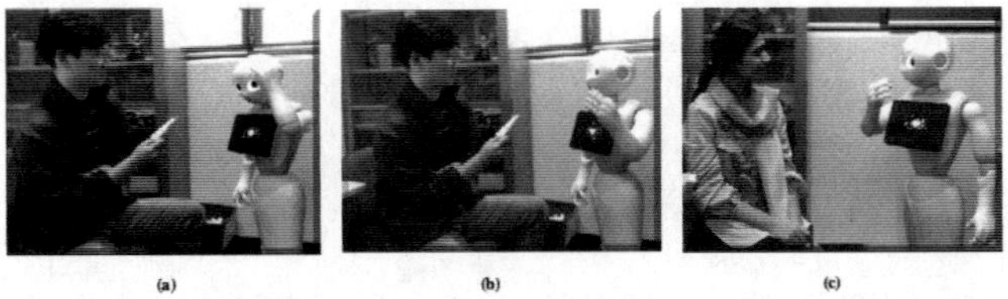

Figure 2. After a fauly behaviour, the *driving assistant* corrects himself (a) The *driving assistant* is scratching head and recalling the correct explanations (b) The human participant maintains eye contact with the *driving assistant* and is listening carefully to the explanations (c) The human participant is looking at the *driving assistant* with strange facial expressions.

Figure 3. The human participants are showing flash cards to the *driving assistant*.

A. Hypotheses

We aim to extend our line of research by posing the following hypothesis :

- *Hypothesis 1* - Humans would appreciate being informed of the *decision-transparency* of the *driving assistant* in terms of explanations and that would facilitate the establishment of trust.
- *Hypothesis 2* - Explanations that disseminate *error-justification and correction* (after the faulty behaviour), help to remedy negative effect of the erroneous situation and rebuild humans' trust in the *driving assistant.*
- *Hypothesis 3* - During a decision-making task, humans conform more with the *driving assistant's* decisions, as compared to their own decisions, when experiencing uncertainty in the environment.

B. Design of Experiment

We use a between-subjects design for our experiment, in which the human participants interact with a *driving assistant* in two possible conditions:

- *Condition 1 - control condition*: The *driving assistant* makes no mistake and provides *correct explanations*
- *Condition 2 - error-justification and correction*: The *driving assistant* makes an error intentionally and provides wrong explanations, but immediately corrects the error with a sophisticated justification.

During the decision-making task, the *driving assistant* did not directly answer by telling which option was correct. Rather, the human participants have to use their common sense to verify the correct option by listening carefully to the *driving assistant's* explanations. In *condition 2*, to justify its failure, the *driving assistant* generates different words along with gestures for example : *"I am sorry for wrong assessment and scratches head to show that it is recalling the correct explanations", "oh wait human, let me have a look again", AND "Sorry I don't agree with you human, my belief is...!"* (See Figure 2 (a), (b) and (c)). In this way, we also assessed the impact of *acceptance of mistake* from a *driving assistant* towards the human participants.

C. Humans' Conformation to the Driving Assistant as an Innovative Measure of Trust

In the field of human-robot interaction, many subjective measures of humans trust in robots have been developed and are mostly based on self-reports (i.e., questionnaires). The measures reflect a human's specific mental posture concealed in an apparent and clear opinion. Therefore, it is difficult to analyse those spontaneous opinions; mostly based upon the human's inner belief and are limited in their capacity to analyse further on which robot knowledge, the human has built its trust. One complementary approach in this perspective is *Media Equation Theory* [17], which illustrates that, when humans engaged in collaborative tasks with computers, they tend to accept computers as social entities unconsciously. Therefore, they trust the answers provided by the computer, and conform their answers according to it. We adapted the famous *Media Equation Theory* paradigm for our study. During the decision-making task, we measured human participants' conformation to the *driving assistant's* answers; generated in terms of explanations, to specific questions as an innovative measure of humans' trust in the *driving assistant.* In particular, we want to examine the humans' trust in the *driving assistant's* competency by assessing its correct situation awareness and (1) change their answers after getting explanations, (2) or reject the *driving assistant's* answers and stick with their own answer(s).

D. Procedure of Experiment

In the previous literature, human-robot trust has been measured either by objective measures (implicit) or by subjective measures (explicit). Objective measures can be retrieved from behavioural data (i.e. response time) unconsciously produced by individuals and subjective measures deals with self-reports and questionnaires retrieved from collected verbal data consciously produced by the individuals [18]. The former is limitedly developed in human robot interaction, while the latter is widely used. This study adopted the approach of combining survey(s) with an experiment to evaluate the humans' trust in the *driving assistant.* We conducted experiment in three stages.

1) Stage - 1 of Experiment: During *Stage 1*, we evaluated human participants' initial level of trust towards the *driving assistant*, by filling Human-Robot Trust questionnaire [19] as pre-interaction questionnaire.

2) Stage - 2 of Experiment: During *Stage 2*, initially, human participants selected six flash cards (three of each type i.e., *Type 1* and *Type 2*) and showed to the *driving assistant* sequentially and listened to the explanations. Following this, the human participants performed the decision-making task with the *driving assistant*, as per the following steps:

1) Human Participants selected three different flash cards of *Type 3* from a pile of flash cards.
2) Meanwhile, the *Monitor Screen* displayed the scenario, and the human participant after analysing, solved the scenario by selecting an option(s).
3) Following this, the human participant was given a chance to change its answers after listening to the

Figure 4. The human participants are selecting the correct option(s) according to the given scenario.

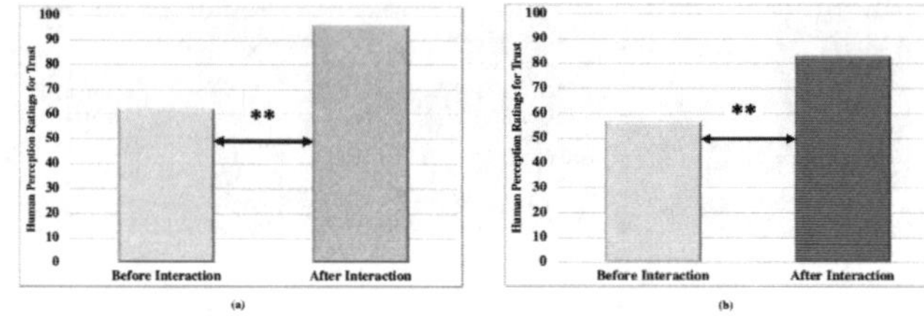

Figure 5. Difference in the trust level of human participants before and after interacting with the *driving assistant* (a) (Condition - 1) *no-error* (b) (Condition - 2) *error-justification and correction* - (**Correlation is significant at $p < 0.01$).

driving assistant's explanations, otherwise the answer was saved. For each scenario, we gave each human participant 150 seconds.

Figure 4 shows the human participants are solving the traffic scenarios.

3) Stage - 3 of Experiment: Trust is a dynamic attitude that changes over time [12] [19]. On the completion of the experiment with the *driving assistant*, as a possible clarification of the change in the humans' trust in the *driving assistant*, the human participants filled another Human-Robot Trust questionnaire [19] after interaction.

E. Measures

The independent variable was the explanations before and after interaction with the *driving assistant*. For quantitative assesment, subjective and objective analyses of the interaction were performed. The dependent variables are divided into two categories:

1) Human participants' trust, which is not directly observable, by using a 14-items subscale of the Human-Robot Trust questionnaire [19], which focuses specifically on the robot's functional capabilities, before and after interaction.
2) Impact of explanations was also analysed with the following questions:
   - do you believe the *driving assistant* "knows" the *Traffic Rules*?
   - Do you believe the *driving assistant* "follows" the *Traffic Rules*?
   - Do you trust in the *driving assistant*?

We video-recorded the experiment to examine the affective states and behavioural responses of the human participants towards the *driving assistant*, especially during the decision-making task.

F. Recruitment and Participation

This study was conducted in an Australian University, and there was a total of 34 human participants, (16 females and 18 males) with age ranging from 18 to 35 years old ($M = 18.2 \pm 4.59$). Since this was an individual activity, we kept a balance of human participants in each condition (17 human participants in *condition 1* and 17 human participants in *condition 2* as well). We recruited human participants through general advertising, using posters on university notice board, and communicating directly with students. Each human participant received an invitation letter for the main objective of conducting the experiment. We offered a gift card valued *AUD* 10 as a *token of appreciation* to every human participant.

V. Experiment Results

In this section, we present the results of the subjective and objective assessments of the effect of explanations on human participant's level of trust, set in the context of the human-robot collaborative scenario. Before conducting any analysis, we performed a reliability analysis (Cronbach's α) to assess the internal reliability of the Human-Robot Trust questionnaire [19] and it was $\alpha > 0.723$. An $\alpha > 0.7$ or higher is considered acceptable, indicating the reliability of the measuring scales. Following this, we performed a normality analysis using *Shapiro-Wilk Test* to check whether the dependent variable trust follows a normal distribution. The test reported a normal distribution.

A. Condition - 1 : Controlled Condition (No-Error)

We performed a parametric paired sample *t-test* to analyse the overall effect of the explanations from the *driving assistant*. After interacting with the *driving assistant*, we compared the trust levels of human participants, controlling the levels of trust reported before interaction. Results showed a significant difference ($t(16) = -7.512$, $p<0.001$), suggesting that the paired sample *t-test* is appropriate in this case. Figure 5 (a) shows a glimpse of the effect of explanations from the *driving assistant*, that reflects significant higher trust levels after interaction ($M = 96.41 \pm 4.63$), when compared with the trust levels reported before interaction ($M = 62.76 \pm 7.69$).

B. Condition - 2 : Error-Justification and Correction

With the help of parametric paired sample *t-test*, we analysed the effect of *driving assistant's* faulty behaviour on the human participants' trust. We examined human participants' trust towards the *driving assistant* when it produced an error but corrected himself immediately with that of before interaction. The results showed a significant difference (t (16) = -22.50, $p<0.001$), suggesting the suitability of dependent samples *t-test*. Figure 5 (b) shows significant higher trust levels towards the *driving assistant* after interaction ($M = 83.06 \pm 8.52$), when compared the trust levels before interaction ($M = 56.63 \pm 6.19$).

C. Impact of Explanations by General Question Items

No matter whether the *driving assistant's* behaviour is *error-free* or it makes mistakes in predicting the behaviour of other road users; because it immediately corrects himself by selecting and implementing the most appropriate response, therefore, it can help a human to drive. The human participants realised that the *driving assistant* was competent in detecting

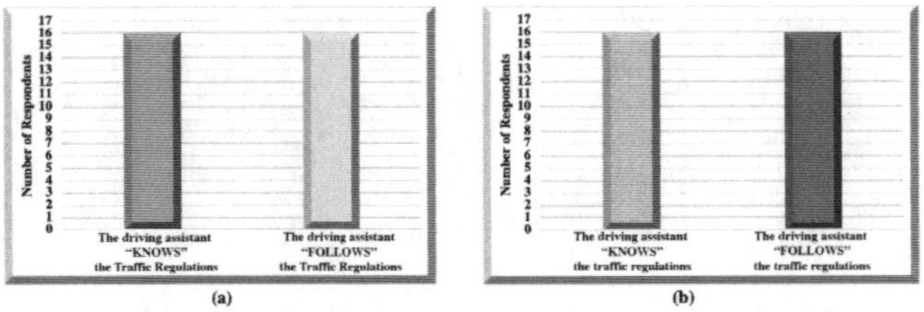

Figure 6. (a) Explanations with *no-error* (b) explanations with *error-justification and correction*.

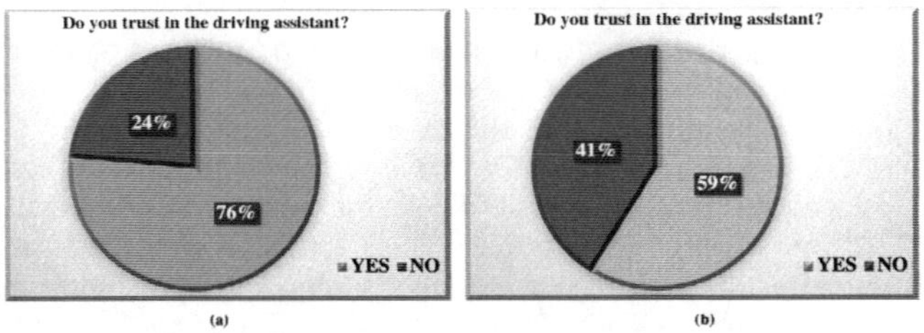

Figure 7. (a) Explanations with *no-error* (b) explanations with *error-justification and correction* policy.

	Mean	Standard Deviation
Explanations With No-Error	0.62	0.314
Explanations with Error-Justification and Correction	0.6	0.42

Figure 8. Conformation score for the group of human participants, N = 17 in each group.

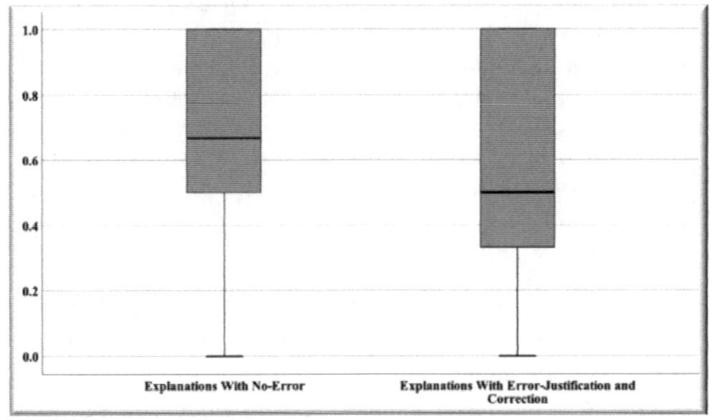

Figure 9. Human participants' conformation with the *driving assistant's* decisions.

Figure 10. After selecting the option(s), the human participants are verifying their selected option by asking from the *driving assistant*.

hazards, and also explained the right decision according to traffic rules and regulations. Even if it considered to break traffic rules, it was only to minimise the likelihood of an accident. Therefore, the *driving assistant* "knows" the traffic rules and "follows" the traffic rules (refer to Figure 7 (a) and (b)), it can be trusted to help humans to drive safely (refer to Figure 7). However, in general, the human participants who received explanations without errors trusted in the *driving assistant's* ability more.

D. Human Participants Conformation to the Driving Assistant

In addition, we also kept a record of the number of times the human participant changed an answer after listening to the *driving assistant's* explanations. If the human participant changed the answer after explanations, then we can say that the human trusted the functional capabilities of the *driving assistant*. Our method to calculate the conformation score was to divide the number of times a human participant changed its answer to the *driving assistant's* answer by the total number of times where the *driving assistant's* answer mismatched with the human participant's answer selected for the first time. Therefore, we got a reasonable score for the analysis ranging between 0 (no conformation) and 1 (full conformation). A score greater than or equal to 0.5 was considered as human participant's trust in the *driving assistant*, see Figure 8 for conformation score. Interestingly, human participants were willing to accept and conformed more to the *driving assistant's* answers as compared to their answers. To examine whether a group of human participants under *Condition 1* conformed more with the *driving assistant* or a group of human participants under *Condition 2*.

Descriptive analysis was performed to analyse the normal distribution of the conformation score, which revealed that the conformation score is not normally distributed. Hence, we performed (non-parametric) *Mann-Whitney U Test* for paired samples, which indicated no significant difference between the two groups ($Z = -0.090$, $p > 0.05$), as shown in Figure 9.

Maybe, the human participants relied more on the driving assistant's decisions, because they observed that it has some criteria or logical demonstration to apply knowledge of traffic rules rather than applying blindly. Furthermore, if the driving assistant considers to break a traffic rule, it is based on an evaluation of the danger of the situation. Some human participants identified the correct option(s), still they verified by asking from the driving assistant as shown in Figure 10.

VI. DISCUSSION

This paper conducted an experimental study to investigate whether a driving assistant characterized by the capability of providing explanations can earn the humans' trust. Specifically, we examined the effect of explanations under two conditions, i.e., (1) *no-error*, and (2) *error-justification and correction* policy. Overall, the human participants trusted the driving assistant in both conditions by supporting our *Hypothesis 1* and *Hypothesis 2*. However, the human participants under *Condition 1*, perceived the decisions of the *driving assistant* more intelligent and trustworthy. Figure 5 (a) visualizes a higher level of trust in the driving assistant. These findings motivate the acceptability of the autonomous vehicles in the human environment. By adding an extra layer of communication in terms of explanations in the design metrics of the autonomous vehicle can promote humans' trust towards them.

Especially, explanations that not only describe "what" should be a decision according to a traffic situation but also justify the decision by providing a sophisticated reason i.e., why is the decision best. As in our study, the humans' not only trusted the explanations given by the driving assistant but conformed more with it, supporting our *Hypothesis 3*. The driving assistant's explanations helped the human participants to scrutinize the information provided by him. The human participants have a fair understanding that the *driving assistant* has not only reasonable understanding of road rules but also has excellent ability to spot a hazard by visual scanning and detecting road-surface-based hazards. Furthermore, the driving assistant also prepares to respond i.e., to break a traffic rule to ensure that the situation is safe. Hence, humans understand and recognise the capability of the driving assistant as an expert, which was reflected during the decision-making task, the human participants' withdraw their answers and conform more to the driving assistant. This constitutes a pertinent measure to straightforwardly registering the human participants' trust in the *driving assistant.*

In addition, the strategy of *error-justification and correction* for autonomous vehicles can make humans comfortable in accepting mistakes made by it, if the consequences are not very severe. On the other hand, the strategy can also alert humans that they have to be attentive and aware of the surroundings because over trust can cause less visual attention of the road and also leads to slower reaction times when humans need to intervene in a case of an emergency. Most importantly, reactions to take-over control of the vehicle can also lead to low-quality decisions [20]. Therefore, explanations communicated in audio-modality can potentially help by keeping humans in the loop of driving assistant's decision-making process, thereby potentially avoiding a reduction in reaction times. We also noticed the human participants, after looking at the monitor screen, also scrutinize the flashcard to examine the image and to inspect whether the *driving assistant's* explanations are aligned with the image on the flashcards as shown in Figure 11. The human participants aimed at assessing the trust in the *driving assistant's* functional capabilities by considering it safe who knows how to recognise and respond to hazards. We also analysed the voices of the human participants, especially under *Condition 2* as wao, genius, intelligent and maintained an eye contact with the driving assistant.

In the end, we gave the human participants a chance to give their free opinion, and many of them wrote different comments for the performance and ability of the *driving assistant*: *"Such driving assistants can help people to follow the rules", "Although I said the driving assistant can be trusted to drive but it cannot be fully trusted because it makes mistakes and then corrects himself, but again that is a good thing", "The driving assistant not only knows the rules but it also knows how to apply the rules, which is surprise to know that it can perform so much", "Robots may not be able to make rapid decisions on empathy, but it makes decisions on facts and rules only", "I do support autonomous vehicles."*

A. Limitations

The current study used an interactive scenario with an autonomous *driving assistant*, to investigate the effects of explanations in improving humans' perceived agency (functional capability) and trust in *autonomous vehicles*. Although

Figure 11. (a) and (b) The robot is giving explanations and the human participants are looking into flash cards to scrutinize whether the *driving assistant's* explanations are aligned with the image on the flash card.

the interactive scenario allowed us to perform experimental control, it does not have sustainability in real traffic situations. There is a considerable difference between a stationary autonomous *driving assistant* that is prone to make little errors in making judgements of the traffic situations with that of an *autonomous vehicle* that makes errors in real road traffic situations. When such *autonomous vehicles* share roads with humans, the limit will become obvious. Hence, the perception and trust of the human participants in the *driving assistant* has limited impact without any danger. In our daily lives, not every situation requires explanations, and in most cases humans mainly need explanations for circumstances that do not meet their expectations. The same is true for *autonomous systems*; humans often need explanations for autonomous decisions, which can confuse them. For an *autonomous vehicle*, if it is always *error-free* and behaves as expected, there might be no need for explanations. This seems to be compatible with the trend in our results and the choice of our experimental study. The explanations in the study were simulated through *text-to-speech* commands along with necnecessary pauses, to create a natural tone in the voice of the *driving assistant* and enough to create a significant impact on the humans, which has been demonstrated by the results of this research. We expect if *autonomous vehicles* behave intelligently by understanding, which situations to be explained. This will contribute to upgrading humans trust.

VII. Conclusion

This main purpose of this study was to investigate the effects of explanations from a *driving assistant* in the level of human participants. In this perspective, we implemented an interactive scenario in which we presented a robot as an intelligent *driving assistant* of an *autonomous vehicle*. We enhanced the capability of the *driving assistant* to enable it to recognise and explain traffic rules and traffic signs. Moreover, the *driving assistant* has the ability to solve road problem solving scenarios by making decisions in uncertain road situations and is competent enough to break a traffic rule to minimise the likelihood of an accident.

During the design process, we make sure that the scenario should introduce some moments of distrust so that we could quantify the differential impact of *error-justification and cor-correction* policy on a human's level of trust. Overall, we analysed that the *driving assistant* is successful in earning the trust of human participants'. The appearance of fully *autonomous vehicles* on the roads seems to be very close. To date, humans have very low exposure to physically present *autonomous vehicles*, so their perception has been shaped by fictitious media. We expect that as the opportunity for interaction with real *autonomous vehicle* increases, findings from the study can serve to guide future work in the identification of specific *autonomous vehicles'* design standards. This research has the potential to promote the acceptability of *autonomous vehicles* in human environment by addressing the topic of trust through explanations.

References

[1] B. Schoettle and M. Sivak, "A survey of public opinion about autonomous and self-driving vehicles in the US, the UK, and Australia," University of Michigan, Ann Arbor, Transportation Research Institute, Tech. Rep., 2014.

[2] M. Peden, "The world report on road traffic injury prevention: getting public health to do more," Journal of Geneva, Switzerland: World Health Organization, 2005.

[3] Radlmayr et al., "How traffic situations and non-driving related tasks affect the take-over quality in highly automated driving," in Proceedings of the human factors and ergonomics society annual meeting, vol. 58, no. 1. Sage Publications Sage CA: Los Angeles, CA, 2014, pp. 2063–2067.

[4] D. Winter et al., "Effects of adaptive cruise control and highly automated driving on workload and situation awareness: A review of the empirical evidence," Transportation research part F: traffic psychology and behaviour, vol. 27, 2014, pp. 196–217.

[5] F. Nothdurft, F. Richter, and W. Minker, "Probabilistic human-computer trust handling." in SIGDIAL Conference, 2014, pp. 51–59.

[6] A. Glass, D. L. McGuinness, and M. Wolverton, "Toward establishing trust in adaptive agents," in Proceedings of the 13th international conference on Intelligent user interfaces. ACM, 2008, pp. 227–236.

[7] Khastgir et al., "Calibrating trust to increase the use of automated systems in a vehicle," in Advances in Human Aspects of Transportation. Springer, 2017, pp. 535–546.

[8] Visschers et al., "Probability information in risk communication: a review of the research literature," Risk Analysis: An International Journal, vol. 29, no. 2, 2009, pp. 267–287.

[9] P. Robinette, A. M. Howard, and A. R. Wagner, "Timing is key for robot trust repair," in International Conference on Social Robotics. Springer, 2015, pp. 574–583.

[10] L. Qiu and I. Benbasat, "Online consumer trust and live help interfaces: The effects of text-to-speech voice and three-dimensional avatars," International journal of human-computer interaction, vol. 19, no. 1, 2005, pp. 75–94.

[11] R. C. Mayer, J. H. Davis, and F. D. Schoorman, "An integrative model of organizational trust," Academy of management review, vol. 20, no. 3, 1995, pp. 709–734.

[12] J. D. Lee and K. A. See, "Trust in automation: Designing for appropriate reliance," Human Factors: The Journal of the Human Factors and Ergonomics Society, vol. 46, no. 1, 2004, pp. 50–80.

[13] K. A. Hoff and M. Bashir, "Trust in automation: Integrating empirical evidence on factors that influence trust," Human factors, vol. 57, no. 3, 2015, pp. 407–434.

[14] P. Pu and L. Chen, "Trust building with explanation interfaces," in Proceedings of the 11th international conference on Intelligent user interfaces. ACM, 2006, pp. 93–100.

[15] D. H. McKnight and N. L. Chervany, "Trust and distrust definitions: One bite at a time," in Trust in Cyber-societies. Springer, 2001, pp. 27–54.

[16] Department of transport and main roads. [Online]. Available: https://www.tmr.qld.gov.au [retrieved: March, 2020]

[17] C. Nass and Y. Moon, "Machines and mindlessness: Social responses to computers," Journal of social issues, vol. 56, no. 1, 2000, pp. 81–103.

[18] Gaudiello et al., "Trust as indicator of robot functional and social acceptance. an experimental study on user conformation to icub answers," Computers in Human Behavior, vol. 61, 2016, pp. 633–655.

[19] K. E. Schaefer, "The perception and measurement of human-robot trust," Ph.D. dissertation, University of Central Florida Orlando, Florida, 2013.

[20] Gold et al., "Take over! How long does it take to get the driver back into the loop?" in Proceedings of the Human Factors and Ergonomics Society Annual Meeting, vol. 57, no. 1. SAGE Publications Sage CA: Los Angeles, CA, 2013, pp. 1938–1942.

Enhancing Humans Trust and Perception of Robots Through Explanations

Misbah Javaid
School of ICT
Griffith University
Nathan, Queensland, Australia 4111
Email: misbah.javaid@griffithuni.edu.au

Vladimir Estivill-Castro
School of ICT
Griffith University
Nathan, Queensland, Australia 4111
Email: v.estivill@griffith.edu.au

Rene Hexel
School of ICT
Griffith University
Nathan, Queensland, Australia 4111
Email: r.hexel@griffith.edu.au

***Abstract*—To integrate robots into humans' environment, robots need to make their decision-making process transparent to increase humans' trust in robots. Explanations from a robot are a promising way to express "how" a decision is made and "why" the decision made is the best. We performed a user study investigating the effect of the explanations from a robot on humans' trust. Our setting consists of an interactive game-playing environment (the partial information game *Domino*), in which the robot partners with a human to form a team. Since in the game there are two adversarial teams, the robot plays two roles: the already mentioned partner with a human in a team, but also as an adversary facing the second team of two humans. The robot's explanations are provided in *human-understandable terms*. Explanations from the robot not only provide insight into the robot's decision-making process, but also help in improving humans' learning of the task. We evaluated the human participants' implicit trust in the robot by performing multi-modal scrutiny i.e., recording observations of facial expressions and affective states during the game-play sessions. We also used questionnaires to measure participants' explicit trust and perception of the robot attributes. Our results show that the human participants considered the robot with explanations' ability as a trustworthy team-mate. We conclude explanations can be used as an effective communication modality for robots to earn humans' trust in social environments.**

Keywords–Implicit Trust; Explicit Trust; Explanations; Human-Robot Physical Interaction.

I. INTRODUCTION

Social robots have moved from manufacturing environments and are now deployed into human environments, such as in hotels, shops, hospitals and as office co-workers. These robots complement humans' abilities with their own skills. Hence, robots are expected to cooperate and contribute productively with humans as teammates. In recent years, the technical capabilities of robotic systems have immensely improved, which has led to an increase in the autonomy and functional capabilities of existing robots [1]. As robots' abilities increase, their complexity also increases, but increased capability in robots often fails to improve the competency of a human-robot team [2]. Effective teamwork between humans and robots requires trust. In situations with incomplete information, where humans need to interact and work as teammates with a robot, humans trust in their robot teammate is crucial. In such cases, autonomous decision-making by the robot creates unpredictable and inexplicable situations for human teammates. Consequently, humans' lack of insight into the robot's decision-making process leads to humans' loss of trust in their robot teammate. In critical situations, such as *search-and-rescue* or to complete a time-sensitive task, humans cannot afford to lose trust in robot teammates.

We hypothesise that the explanations from a robot are a promising way to express *how* a decision is made and *why* the decision-made is the best. Robots shall be required to explain and justify their decisions to humans, and humans will tend to accept those decisions as they realise the reasoning behind them. We postulate that a robot's decisions (which generate the robot's actions) can be communicated through explanations to humans. These explanations will also make it possible for humans to perceive and accept the robot as a trustworthy teammate.

Trust is an important aspect for humans and robots to perform cooperatively as a team [3]. Trust directly affects humans' willingness to receive and accept robot-produced information and suggestions [4] [5]. The absence of trust in human-robot interaction leads to disuse of a robot [6]. Ensuring an appropriate level of trust is a challenge to the successful integration of robotic assets into collaborative teams because under-reliance or over-reliance on a robot can lead to misuse of the robot [2].

Humans are desirous of trusting other humans, particularly if explanations are provided. Trust appears to require explanations [7]. In essence, trust-building encompasses a more or less detailed understanding of the motives of a person we may or may not trust. We accept explanations, or we may cast a validity verdict upon them. Logically, trust and explanations seem to be mutual companions in everyday life.

Artificial intelligence researchers, within the area of expert systems, have also provided sufficient motivation to consider the contribution of explanations [8] to building humans trust [9] [10] and to the acceptability of these systems [11]. Hand-craft explanations have also shown to be promising in providing enough transparency to humans [12]. Robots have become increasingly important in human society, and it seems timely and essential to understanding how to promote their interactions with humans. An interaction, by definition, requires communication between humans and robots [13]. Hence, explanations can be used as an effective communication modality for robots, earning humans' trust in a social environment. By explanations, humans will also be able to track the performance and capabilities of the robots. Hence, a clear understanding of the robots' decision-making process can also lead to humans' desire for interaction and acceptability and will also help in establishing smooth and trustworthy human-robot interactions.

This study sets out to examine the effect of a robot's explanations on humans' level of trust. In addition, we refer to the explanations' approach as *English like sentences*, because in this way, humans can trace the performance of the robot. We expect that, when humans understand the behaviour of the robot, they will tend to trust the robot's actions and will work together as a team, to achieve a common goal.

For human-robot interaction, there has been a little empirical evaluation of the influence of explanations on humans' level of trust. Wang [9] used a different approach to increase transparency by using a simulated robot to provide explanations of its actions. Explanations did not improve the team's performance, although trust was identified as an influential factor only in the high-reliability conditions. Moreover, Wang [9] used an online survey because human participants were not present with a physical robot. Wang's analysis of the survey's responses indicates improvements in humans acceptance of the robot's suggestions. One of the disadvantages of conducting an online survey for evaluating humans' perception of a robot's attributes is that the human participants act only as observers. Such human perception is incomplete, since it is missing the robot's physical presence and interaction [2]. Thus, it is unclear what happens in settings where humans and a robot interact directly in the same environment. We focus here on a physical setting where the robot communicates via explanations. We investigate the change in humans' perception of the robot from a tool to a trustworthy teammate. By addressing this question, findings from our research can serve to guide future work in recognition of specific robots' design metrics.

We explore the influence of explanations on humans' trust. Our contribution consists of a *User Study* that takes a more socially relevant approach by focusing on the physical interaction between humans and an autonomous social robot. We chose *Domino*, a team-based partial-information game, to immerse interaction between humans and the social robot. Game-playing scenarios are useful and powerful environments to establish human-robot interaction [14] because games provide an external, quantifiable measure of the underlying psychological state of a human's trust [15]. Especially, multi-player game environments, not only maintain social behaviour when played in teams, but also develop trust dynamics among teammates to achieve the common goal of wining the game. Besides, we hope to enhance the intelligibility of the robot by augmenting it with the communication ability through explanations, to improve the clarity of its decision-making.

We selected *Domino* game as the basis for our experimental paradigm for the following reasons. A game of *Domino* involves two teams with two members of each team, where each participant has incomplete information (the hand of each player is not revealed to any other player), but cooperation is required by members of a team to achieve a win. We configured mix-teams of a human and a robot. The robot plays two roles: first, team partner with a human, and second, member of a human-robot team that competes with a team of two humans. Because each player has different tiles, each player has different resources. The environment in the game *Domino* is partially observable.

We want to examine the effect of explanations on the humans' level of trust in an environment where a robot makes decisions, and those decisions influence the outcome. The primary motivation behind this study is the interaction between humans and robots is changing from *master-slave* to *peer-to-peer*. Hence, to model effective human-robot interaction, the *human-in-the-loop* concept must be incorporated as frequently as possible. Hence, we adopted a *human-in-the-loop* approach by augmenting a robot with the capability of providing different types of explanations. Explanations shall make complex behaviour of the robot more understandable and intuitive for a human. We hope that explanations will lead to developing the humans' trust in the robot.

We divide this paper into different sections. Section II surveys the literature on trust and explanations in the context of human-robot interaction. Section III presents our human-robot interaction scenario followed by the design description of our robot as a team player. Section IV discusses the *User Study* in detail, as well as the experimental design and the measurement of dependent variables. Section V presents the results in detail, taking into account the proposed hypotheses. Section VI shows the correlation between the dependent variables. Section VII presents the discussion and finally, Section VIII considers the implications of this work on the human-robot interaction community.

II. Related Work

For decades, trust has been studied in a variety of ways (i.e., interpersonal trust and trust in automation). However, in human-robot interaction, there is much space to study the trust that humans attribute to robots. There have been a growing number of investigations and empirical explorations on different factors that affect human-robot trust [16] [17]. Hancock [4] reported on 29 empirical studies and developed a triadic model of trust as a foundation to provide a greater understanding of different factors that facilitate the development of humans' trust in robots. The model's three groupings of factors are first, robot-related factors (anthropomorphism, performance and behaviour), second, environmental-related factors (task and team related factors) [4] and third, human-related factors (i.e., demographic attributes of humans) [1].

Robot-related factors [4], especially robot performance-based factors, influence humans' trust most dramatically. Robot performance-based factors comprised of a robot's functional capability [18], etiquette in a robot (i.e., remained attentive of errors) [19] [20], especially how the robot casts the blame of error [2], its reliability and safety [5]. Previous research [5] also provides additional support to precisely address the significance of errors and feedback from error-prone robots. In a situation where the robot's low reliability was clearly evident, even from early stages of interaction, human participants continued to follow the robot's instructions.

Most of the previous investigations regarding the influence of explanations on humans' trust have been conducted in rule-based systems [10], intelligent tutoring systems [21], intelligent systems (i.e., neural networks, case-based reasoning systems, heuristic expert systems) [8] and knowledge-based systems [22].

Intelligent tutoring systems try to convey knowledge on an exclusive subject to a learning person. Nevertheless, intelligent tutoring systems cannot clarify their behaviour and remain restricted to particular tasks [23]. Expert systems [24] are systems that recommend answers to problems (i.e., financial decisions, industrial procedure investigations). The corresponding problems usually require a skilled human to solve them [7].

The rule-based expert system *Mycin* [25] was the first expert system to provide trace explanations of its reasoning to respond to *Why*, *Why-Not* and *How-To* queries, but the comparative benefits of these explanations were limited [8] [26]. Since *Mycin* was incapable to justify its advice, it was observed that physicians were reluctant to use it in practice [27].

Earlier work [28] confirmed that different types of explanations not only improved the effectiveness of context-aware intelligent systems but also contributed to stronger feelings of humans' trust. Although the main focus was on the influence of the *How-to*, *What-if*, *Why* and *Why-not* explanations. However, the results showed that *Why* and *Why-not* explanations were an excellent type of explanation, which effectively helped to improve the overall understandability of the system.

For human-machine trust, there has been little empirical evaluation of the impact of explanations [11]. Dzindolet et. al. [12] explored manually crafted explanations. Hand-crafted explanations have been shown to be effective in providing transparency and improved trust. However, since hand-crafted explanations were static and created manually, they fail to transfer the complexity of the decision-making to the team members. Nothdurft et. al. [29] [30] focused on transparency and the justification of decisions in human-computer interaction. Glass et. al. [31] studied trust issues in technical systems, analysing the features that may change the level of humans trust in adaptive agents. They claim that designers should "supply the user of a system with access to information about the internal workings of the system", but the evidence to substantiate such claim is limited.

The systems, as mentioned earlier, deliberately focused on the use of explanations to convey conceptual knowledge and acceptability of these systems, such as the reliability and accuracy of performance. However, the state-of-the-art may not resolve the problem of non-cooperative behaviour and trust of humans towards robots. To the best of our knowledge, there is still a gap in current human-robot interaction literature, and there is very little experimental verification that could show that explanations promote and certainly affect humans trust in and acceptance of robots.

Such systems, as mentioned earlier, deliberately focused on the reliability and accuracy followed by explanations to convey conceptual knowledge and their acceptability. However, the state-of-the-art leaves open the problem of non-cooperative behaviour and trust of humans towards robots. In particular, there is very little experimental verification that could show that explanations promote humans trust in robots.

It is important to realise that in addition to the physical appearance of a robot, human perception of the robot's attributes can also affect trust [2]. For example, prior to interacting with a robot, humans develop a mental model of the expected functional and behavioural capabilities of the robot. Nonetheless, the human's mental model evolves after interaction with the robot. The mismatch between the human's initial mental model and the later mental model creates a detrimental effect on the human's trust [32]. A human's mental model also defines the human's intentions for future use of robot [8]. Therefore, explanations are valuable because explanations can shape the humans' mental model.

Finally, we suggest that our approach that enables a robot to provide explanations for *transparency* and for *justification* of its reasoning is to be considered a robot's functional capability, which should be categorised as a robot-related factor.

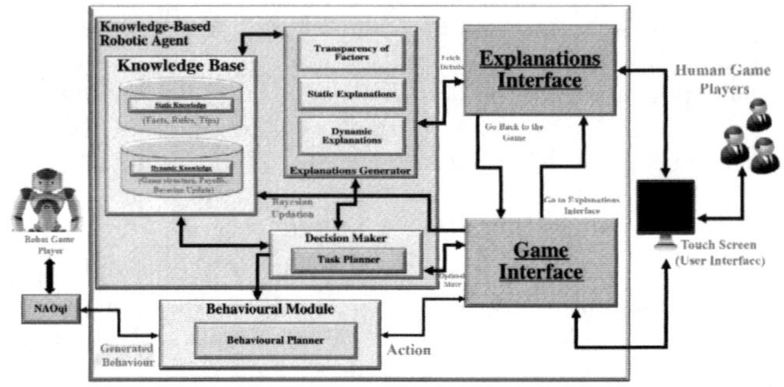

Figure 1. Complete architectural overview of our human-robot interaction scenario.

III. Human-Robot Interactive Scenario

Our human-robot interactive scenario is around a block-type game known as Spanish *Domino*. A match is between two teams with two players in each team, and it consist of several *hands*; in each *hand*, each of the four player receives seven random domino tiles. Game players take their turn clockwise and aim for their couple to have the first player to release all its *hand*. The *hand* is confidential to its owner. Thus, the decisions a player makes are with partial information. At each turn, a game player can perform only two actions,

1) to release a tile (by putting a tile with an endpoint matching one of the open ends of the current board), or
2) to *pass* (because to release a tile is impossible).

The game ends when no player can play a domino tile or when a player runs out of the domino tiles.

Domino is a non-deterministic game, because of the random shuffling and dealing of tiles to four players at the beginning of every game. This initial *hands'* aspect is an element of non-determinism, but after each player has received their *hand*, all actions are deterministic and successful. Figure 2 shows the complete set of domino tiles ranging from (0,0) to (6,6) as used in the study. Because each tile is different, all players have different resources, and team members must cooperate without full knowledge of their partners' resources or the opposing teams' resources.

During the match, the robot's behaviour is completely autonomous. Figure 1 shows the global architecture and the modules involved in our software for human-robot interaction [33]. Our *knowledge-based robotic agent* is capable of performing rapid updates of knowledge while playing the multi-player game of *Domino* with humans in the partial-information environment and in teams. Information becomes available to all players each time a player completes its turn; either by releasing a tile, or *passing*.

Bayesian inference is an effective way to deal with such partial observability. We incorporate *Bayesian inference* into our *knowledge-based robotic agent*. By using Bayesian inference, the *knowledge-based robotic agent* can update information about the environment (i.e., the current state of the game). The update is performed after an observation. An

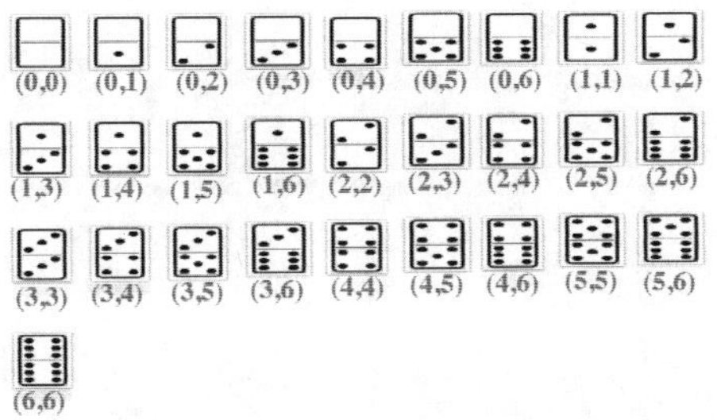

Figure 2. Complete Set of domino tiles used in the study ranging from (0,0) to (6,6).

observation provides new evidence, enabling the update of the belief representation. These observations are forwarded to the *Knowledge-Base* module.

The *knowledge-based robotic agent* controls the two roles of the robot: firstly, as an adversary with two humans and secondly, as a team partner with a human. Therefore, it displays cooperation with human team partners, but is goal oriented and competes with human opponents. We developed the explanation-generation mechanism on top of the game-playing mechanism.

We enable the robot to generates multiple *static* and *dynamic* explanations. The *static* explanations are based upon (1) *history and facts* about the game, (2) *rules of the game* and (3) *game-play tips*. While, *dynamic* explanations provide insight into the *knowledge-based robotic agent*'s decision-making process. These *dynamic* explanations would be suitable to answer *how-type* and *why-type* questions. Furthermore, *dynamic* explanations provide team members with the *transparency* for the different factors involved in the decision-making process of the *knowledge-based robotic agent*.

The mechanism for generating *dynamic* explanations is meaningful for the strategic aspect of the game.

IV. User Study

Using the human-robot interactive scenario discussed in Section III, we conducted a *User Study* to investigate the effect of a robot's explanations on the humans' level of trust and how much the explanations are effective in changing humans' perception of the robot attributes during an interactive task.

A. Hypotheses

Hypothesis 1 - Human participants would appreciate understanding about how the robot's decisions are made (*transparency*) and receiving informed *justifications* of the robot's choices in a partial information environment. Such human inclination will be reflected by an increase in humans' trust in the robot.

Hypothesis 2 - Explanations that provide *transparency* and supply *justification* for a robot's decisions in a collaborative (team-based) environment help in changing humans' perception of the robot attributes.

B. Variables

The independent variable is the explanations of the robot at the beginning of the first game and after the end of the match. For the quantitative assessment, both subjective and objective analysis of the interaction took place. The dependent variables fall into three categories to analyse the impact of explanations:

1) **Trust** - Human teammates' trust, which is not directly observable [34], by using a 14-items subscale of the Human-Robot Trust questionnaire [1] before and after interaction with the robot.
2) **Perception of Robot Attributes** - We used Godspeed questionnaire [35] [36] before and after interaction with the robot to evaluate human perception of the robot attributes related to trustworthiness [1]. We use the Godspeed questionnaire because it is a standardised measurement tool for interactive robots [35]. The Godspeed questionnaire uses a 5-point scale to measure five key concepts in human-robot interaction. (1) *Anthropomorphism* [37] is the characteristics of a human form. (2) *Animacy* [38] is the perception of a robot as a lifelike living entity. Perceiving things as living creatures allows humans to distinguish between humans and machines [38]. (3) *Likeability* [39] describes the first (positive) impression that humans make in their mind of others. Previous research investigated [40] that humans tend to consider robots as social agents; hence deal with them in a similar way. (4) *Perceived intelligence* [41] indicates how intelligent; the human participants judge the robot by its explanatory ability. (5) *Perceived safety* is the perception of danger attributable to the robot during the collaboration and the level of comfort the human participants' experience during the interaction [42].
3) **Previous experience of human participants** - Prior relationship with non-human agents such as pets [43] influence the interaction of a human with a robot. Thus, to examine other factors such as prior experience with robots, we evaluated human participants' demographical information with the following questions:
   - Do you have any prior physical experience with a robot?
   - Have you ever watched a television show or a movie that involves robots?
   - Do you have any prior relationships with non-human agents such as pets [43].

   We also showed two pictures, each with a social robot (i.e., *Nao* and *Pepper*) to human participants and assessed their initial impression of the robots. We also asked human participants to rate these images by classifying them as (1. human-like, 2. machine-like, 3. child-like, 4. toy-like, and 5. avatar). Trust between humans and animals may be a suitable analogy to trust between humans and robots [2]. To examine the nature of a human-animal relationship can help in increasing the understanding of how a human interacts with and trusts a robot [18].

C. Additional Measurement

Before starting the experiment, we instructed the human participants about the procedure of the experiment. The human participants were allowed to ask any relevant questions before starting the formal experiment. We asked the human participants to maintain a safe distance from the robot, so no human participant will push or damage the robot in any way.

In addition, no human participant can interrupt the robot and ask for explanations during a game.

The recognition of humans' affective states and emotions is one of the much-studied research questions at the moment [29] that can be recognised via vision-based, audio-based, and audio-visual recognition [44]. Therefore, we video-recorded the experiment to examine the affective states and behavioural responses of the human participants towards the robot. We also maintained a history at the backend of the system to record the moves played by the human participants. Also, we kept a history of the human participants examination and use of the robot's explanations. This record of explanation usage was used later to investigate, which type of explanations were accessed more i.e., *static* explanations or *dynamic* explanations.

D. Procedure of the Experiment

We adopted the approach of combining survey(s) with an experiment to evaluate the humans' perception and trust towards the robot. We experimented in three-stages.

*1) **Stage-1 of the Experiment:*** During Stage 1, we evaluated human participants' demographics, initial perception and trust towards the robot.

*2) **Stage-2 of the Experiment:*** Before starting the formal game activity, the robot greeted the human participants and provided verbal static explanations of how to play the game.

> ***"We will play the block-type game of Domino with double-six set of domino tiles. There are 28 tiles in the set ranging from (0,0) to (6, 6). There are four players in the game and each player will initially receive a set of seven random tiles. . . !"***

Next, human participants played repeated hands with the robot in teams, until reaching a pre-defined score. After the match, the human participants examined the explanations. Following the explanations session, human participants played more hands with the robot, until reaching a pre-defined score. The second game-playing session aims at observing the effect of explanations, and whether explanations improve a team's performance.

*3) **Stage-3 of the Experiment:*** Trust is a dynamic attitude that changes over time [1] [3]. On the completion of Stage 2 of the experiment, to elucidate the changes in trust by human participants and their perception of the robot, human participants filled out another human-robot trust questionnaire and Godspeed questionnaire. Changes in the level of trust and perception of the robot attributes will elicit the influence of explanations from the robot. At the end of the experiment, the robot thanked all the human participants for their participation.

E. Recruitment and Participation

This study was conducted in Griffith University Australia, and there were a total of 33 human participants, (15 females and 18 males) with ages ranging from 19 to 35 years old (M = 28.33 $\pm$ 4.58). We recruited human participants through general advertising, using posters on university notice board, and communicating directly with students. Each human participant received an invitation letter for the main objective of conducting the experiment. Along with the invitation letter, we also attached a brochure with a brief description of the *Domino* game. We expected all human participants to start

Figure 3. (a) Robot is explaining how to play the game (b) Player 2 is taking its turn (c) Human participants' are checking the robot's explanations (d) Player 3 is taking its turn after the explanations' session.

Cronbach's α for Scales used in the Experiment		
Sr. #	Scale	α
1	Shafear Human-Robot Trust Scale	0.729
2	Godspeed Questionnaire	0.893

Figure 4. Statistics for Cronbach's α for the customised scales used in the experiment.

with the same common-sense model of the task (i.e., the *Domino* game), which also helped us estimate what knowledge the human participants have already possessed about the task. Before taking part in the experiment, all human participants provided their consent.

We offered an *Aud* 10 gift card as a *token of appreciation* to every human participant. We configured human-robot matches, with four participants i.e., one robot and three humans in each team. There were 11 groups in total. Each group played two matches with the robot. A single match consists of a maximum of five hands in total, or until a pre-defined score is reached. Each group played two matches, the first match before the explanations' session and the second after the explanations' session.

V. Experiment Results

Prior to conducting any analysis, we performed a reliability analysis (Cronbach's α) to assess the internal reliability of the Human-Robot Trust Questionnaire [1] and Godspeed Questionnaire [35] [36]. An $\alpha > 0.7$ or higher is considered acceptable, which indicates the reliability of the measuring scale. Figure 4 shows Cronbach α for all the scales used in the experiment.

A. Effect of Robot Explanations on Humans' Trust

After performing the reliability analysis, we performed a normality analysis by applying the *Shapiro-Wilk test.* The *Shapiro-Wilk test* showed the dependent variable trust fit a normal distribution satisfactorily. Therefore, we performed a parametric paired sample *t-test* to analyse the effect of robot explanations. We compared the levels of trust that human participants had in their robot teammate after interaction,

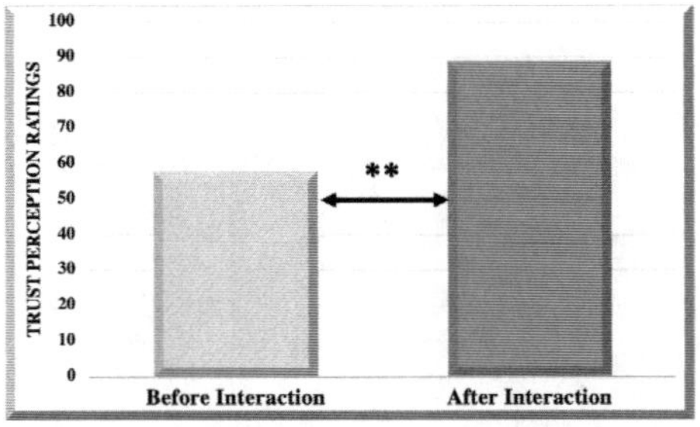

Figure 5. Difference in the level of trust of the human participants in the robot before and after interaction - (** $p < 0.01$).

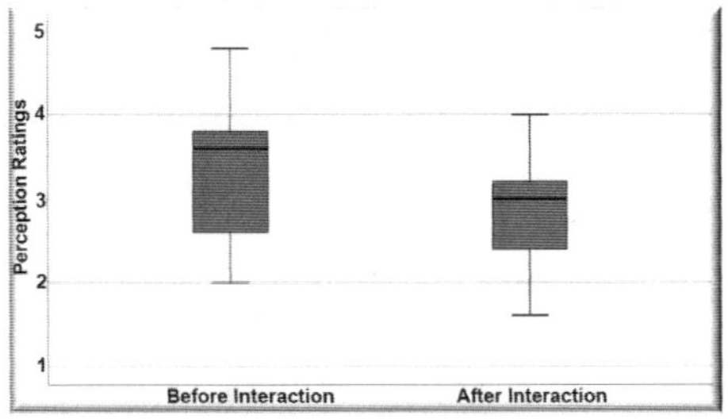

Figure 6. After interacting with the robot, the *anthropomorphism* ratings of the robot decreased.

controlling for the levels of trust reported before interaction. Results showed a significant difference ($t(32)$ = -7.729, $p<0.001$); Figure 5 displays much higher trust levels of human participants towards the robot after interaction (M = 89.27 $\pm$ 6.44), when compared with their respective trust levels before interaction (M = 58.24 $\pm$ 9.44). Overall, the analysis indicates that the robot is successful in earning the trust of the human participants' based on the notable distinction between the trust levels before interaction and after interaction.

B. Effect of Explanations in changing humans' perception of the robot.

We performed the *Shapiro-Wilk test*, which indicated that the Godspeed questionnaire follows a normal distribution. Following this, we performed paired sample *t-test* to scrutinize the effect of explanations from the robot in changing humans' perception of the robot.

1) Anthropomorphism: We analysed the decline in the degree of anthropomorphism after interacting with the robot: $t(32) = 4.389$, $p<0.001$ (refer to Figure 6). These values reflect that the humans' perception of anthropomorphism of the robot was reduced significantly after interaction (M = 2.9 $\pm$ 0.59) when compared with before interaction (M = 3.4 $\pm$ 0.79). The results indicate that the human participants considered the robot less human-like, less natural and less conscious.

2) Animacy: The robot's explanations created a positive effect on the perception of the robot's *animacy* : $t(32)$ = -4.884, $p<0.001$ (refer to Figure 7). We observed higher perception ratings of the robot's animacy after the interaction (M = 3.6 $\pm$ 0.71), when compared to before the interaction (M = 2.88 $\pm$ 0.50). The results show that the human participants appraise the robot as more interactive and responsive.

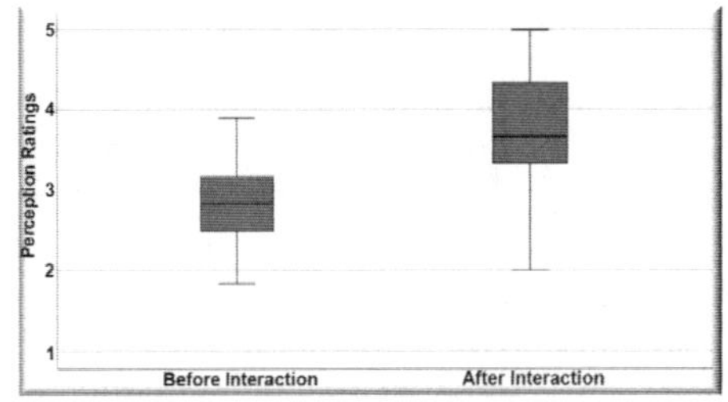

Figure 7. The *animacy* ratings of the robot significantly increased, after interacting with the robot.

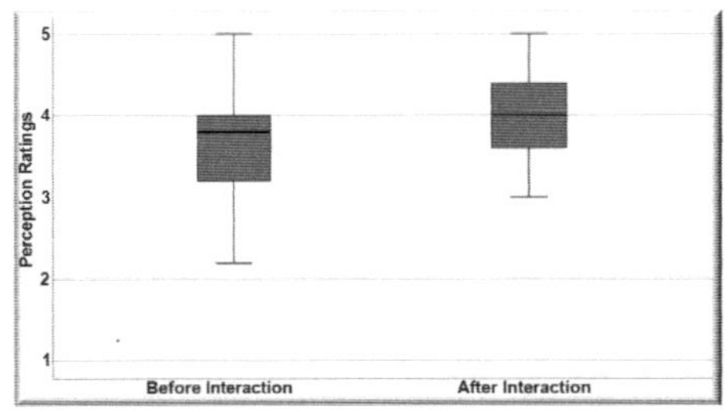

Figure 8. After interacting with the robot, the *Likeability* ratings of the robot greatly increased.

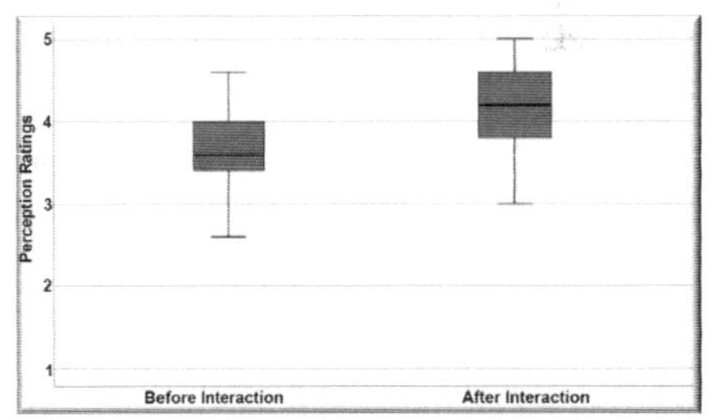

Figure 9. Difference in the perception ratings show the rise of the robot's *Perceived Intelligence*.

3) Likeability: Significant differences were found in the *likeability* of the robot : $t(32)$ = -3.522, p = 0.001. Figure 8 shows a significant difference in the perception ratings of the robot after interaction (M = 4.07 $\pm$ 0.55), when compared with the perception ratings before interaction (M = 3.60 $\pm$ 0.69). The results show that the human participants considered the robot pleasant and friendly.

4) Perceived Intelligence: Figure 9 shows the rise of the robot's perceived intelligence: $t(32)$ = -5.502, $p < 0.001$. We observed a significant difference between the pre-interaction ratings (M = 3.70 $\pm$ 0.41) and the post-interaction ratings (M = 4.23 $\pm$ 0.50). The results provide evidence that the human participants considered a robot with explanatory capability to be more intelligent, knowledgeable and competent.

5) Perceived Safety: Figure 10 shows that there is no significant differences between the perceived safety levels before and after interacting with the robot. Consequently, there were no significant changes in this aspect as a result of interaction with the robot.

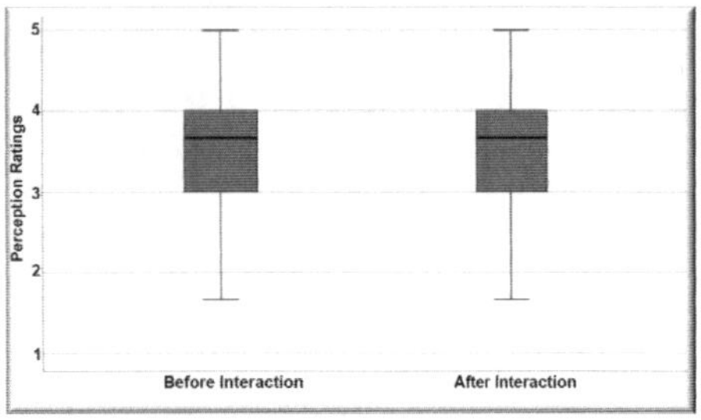

Figure 10. After interacting with the robot, there was no significant difference in the level of *Perceived Safety*.

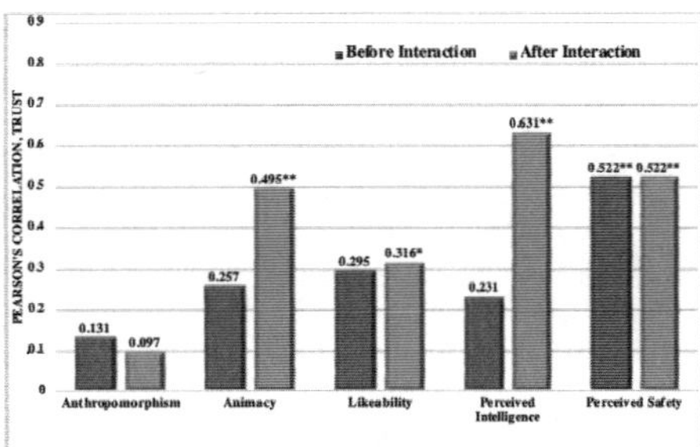

Figure 11. Correlation between trust and humans' perception of the robot, before interaction and after interaction - (⋆⋆Correlation is significant at $p < 0.01$, ⋆Correlation is significant at $p < 0.05$).

VI. Correlation Between Dependent Variables

We also conducted *Pearson's* (parametric) correlation to analyse (1) how much humans' trust and perception of the robot are correlated with each other and (2) how much trust impacts in changing humans' perception of the robot.

We found no significant correlation between the dependent variable *trust* and the *anthropomorphism* attribute. This result applies to both cases, before and after interacting with the robot.

Before interacting with the robot, we did not find any correlation between *trust* and *animacy, likeability* and *perceived intelligence* attributes of the robot. However, after the interaction, as *trust* increased, we observed a significant positive correlation between *trust* and the robot's *animacy, likeability* and *perceived intelligence* attributes. We also observed a significant positive correlation between *trust* and the *perceived safety* attribute before interaction with the robot, and it did not change after interaction with the robot.

VII. Discussion

Results from our preliminary analysis strongly support our *Hypothesis 1* by indicating that explanations increased human participants' trust in the robot. Moreover, explanations also improved the humans' perception of the robot attributes associated with trust, which is our *Hypothesis 2*. However, after interacting with the robot, the perception ratings of the *anthropomorphism* attribute decreased, and in a sense, our results partially support *Hypothesis 2*. Furthermore, for the *perceived safety* attribute, we did not see any difference in the perception ratings, neither before interacting nor after interacting with the robot. We suggest that the human participants considered that the robot in the experiments conditions was not dangerous at all.

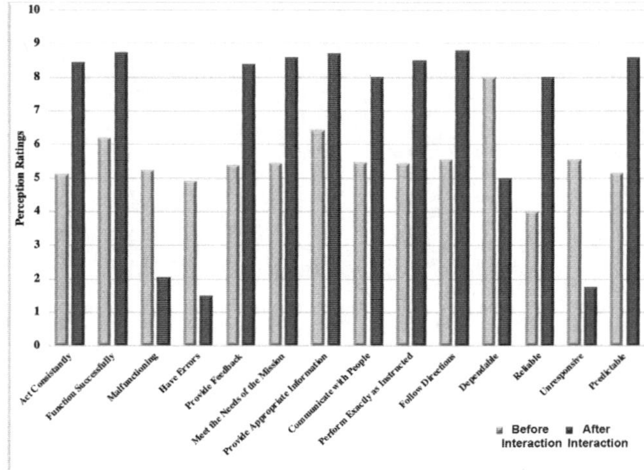

Figure 12. A summary of the quantitative data analysis results for trust.

Previous studies have shown the role of transparency in building trust [12]. However, transparency alone may not be sufficient to establish trust. Hence, we designed our explanations to provide not only *transparency* about the mechanism for the robot's decisions, but also communicate *justifications* for the underlying sophisticated reasoning. We aimed at explaining the robot's motive for each of the decisions. Additionally, we believe explanations provide the human participants' with an insight into the concrete and individual factors involved in the decision-making process of the robot. Therefore, in the current study, explanations not only improved the trust of human participants' but also changed their overall impression of the robot. The results help us gain insight into how to design explanations to increase humans' trust.

Furthermore, Figure 12 shows that items measuring the robot's explanatory ability: *Provide Feedback, Provide Appropriate Information* and *Communicate with People* are tightly connected with the outcome.

Similarly, Figure 13 displays an increase in the ratings of the attributes *animacy*, *likeability* and *perceived intelligence*. This increase reflects that human participants' adopted a model of the robot that is more interactive, competent, knowledgeable and intelligent. In terms of *anthopomorphism*, human participants showed more concern by lowering the level of ratings associated with anthropomorphism. Even if a robot looks like a human, humans do not consider its capabilities to be human-like. This is an interesting result, because regardless of the less anthropomorphic perception, human participants still trusted the robot.

Most of the human participants had their previous interaction with robots through fictitious media or movies; thus, we believe that our results are not biased (or affected) by the human participants' previous experience with a physical present robot. Similarly, we did not find any partiality or differences in the results, for no-pet ownership with respect to pet ownership.

We also examined human participants' multi-modal

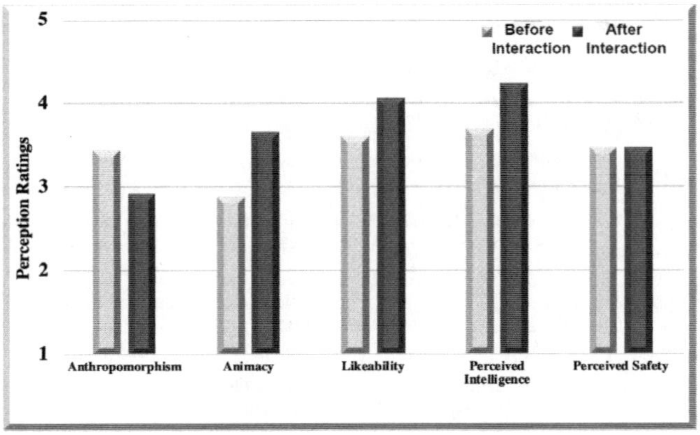

Figure 13. Summary of results for the quantitative data analysis of human participants' perception of the robot.

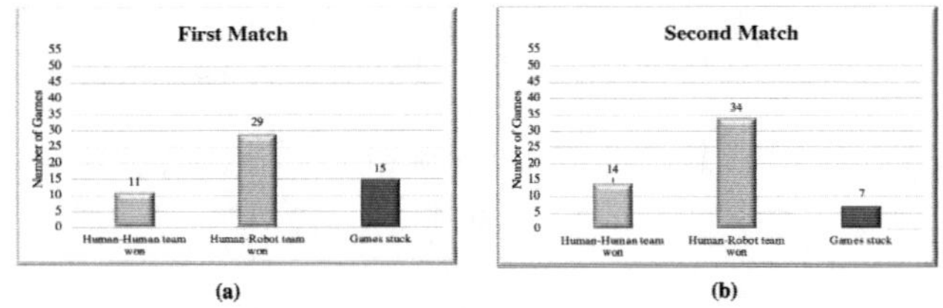

Figure 14. Change in the impression of the robot (a) before interaction (b) after interaction.

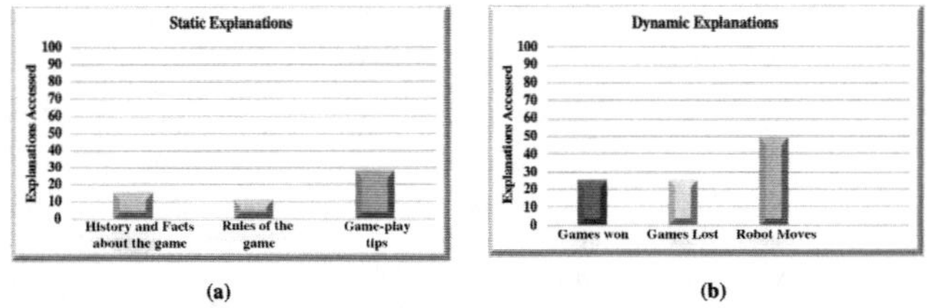

Figure 15. Change in the impression of the robot (a) before interaction (b) after interaction.

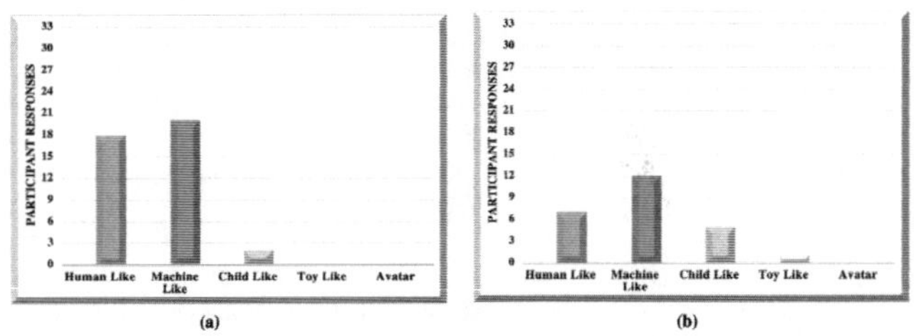

Figure 16. Change in the impression of the robot (a) before interaction (b) after interaction.

scrutiny i.e., facial expressions and affective states during the match and the explanations' sessions. We observed that human participants were unreserved, open to the robot, and even trying to cuddle it from a distance. When the robot was explaining the rules of the game, we noticed that human participants maintained eye contact with the robot, which is another signal of willingness to interact and affects trust. During the explanations' session, we observed human participants' facial expressions. These facial expressions show interest and engagement in explanations. We examined human participants' gestures and body movements while involved in a game. Players struggle to hide tiles, but reflected before making a move, were attentive towards the robot when the robot was speaking and describing its move and after the robot finished its turn, participants focused on the released tile, assimilating further the robot decision and play. As we mentioned, we provided the human participants with a brochure that briefly described the rules and mechanics of the *Domino* game. In addition, the robot also provided explanations for the mechanics of the game. Hence, our expectation is that all human participants starting playing ability is similar, and approached the matches with the same common-sense model. By evaluating the moves of the players stored in our records, we observed the implicit trust of human partners in a team. The records also show moves where humans exhibit cooperation and sacrifice also to their robotic partner.

Furthermore, the human participants' learning of the task domain enhanced, which is reflected by the increase in the number of games the human-human team won, after the explanations' session. We also investigated the human participants' use of strategies to select their moves, which was significantly improved and became visible in the second match. For example, the human participants considered playing random tiles in the first match. After the explanations' session, human participants' used some of the strategies i.e., preferred to play tiles with the highest points and put doubles on the board during the early stages of the hand.

In addition, we also kept a record of the number of times a human participant (partner/adversary) accessed explanations i.e., *static* or *dynamic*. We examined that the human participants (regardless of team partners or opponents) accessed the *dynamic* explanations more, to investigate the robot's decisions.

VIII. CONCLUSION

Overall, our results confirm that, in a team-based collaborative environment, the explanations that disseminate transparency and justification of a robot's decisions facilitate human-robot interaction.

Significant differences in the level of trust and perception of the robot, before and after the interaction, confirm that the robot has successfully earned the trust of the human participants through its explanations' ability. Besides, the strong correlation between trust and perception of the robot also suggests that the explanations helped change the overall impression of the robot.

To date, humans have rarely encountered physical robots in their lives, so their perception of robots may be affected by fictitious media. We expect that, as the opportunity for interaction with physically present robots increase, our study will be taken into account for future robot design metrics. Consequently, the findings of this study can be used to guide future work to determine specific robot design standards. So far, our work is the first to study the impact of explanations from a robot on humans' trust, by establishing peer-to-peer human-robot interaction. Overall, the results suggest that explanations can potentially relieve the issue of misusing or under-utilizing a robot, which usually happens in the "absence" of trust.

REFERENCES

[1] K. E. Schaefer, "The perception and measurement of human-robot trust," Ph.D. dissertation, University of Central Florida Orlando, Florida, 2013.

[2] N. Wang, D. Pynadath, S. Hill, and A. P. Ground, "Building trust in a human-robot team with automatically generated explanations," in Interservice/Industry Training, Simulation, and Education Conference (I/ITSEC), December 2015, pp. 1–12, paper No. 15315.

[3] J. D. Lee and K. A. See, "Trust in automation: Designing for appropriate reliance," Human Factors: The Journal of the Human Factors and Ergonomics Society, vol. 46, no. 1, 2004, pp. 50–80.

[4] Hancock et al., "A meta-analysis of factors affecting trust in human-robot interaction," Human Factors, vol. 53, no. 5, 2011, pp. 517–527.

[5] M. Salem and K. Dautenhahn, "Evaluating trust and safety in hri: Practical issues and ethical challenges," Emerging Policy and Ethics of Human-Robot Interaction, 2015.

[6] R. Parasuraman and V. Riley, "Humans and automation: Use, misuse, disuse, abuse," Human Factors, vol. 39, no. 2, 1997, pp. 230–253.

[7] W. Pieters, "Explanation and trust: what to tell the user in security and ai?" Ethics and information technology, vol. 13, no. 1, 2011, pp. 53–64.

[8] K. Darlington, "Aspects of intelligent systems explanation," Universal Journal of Control and Automation, vol. 1, no. 2, 2013, pp. 40–51.

[9] N. Wang, D. V. Pynadath, and S. G. Hill, "Trust calibration within a human-robot team: Comparing automatically generated explanations," in The Eleventh ACM/IEEE International Conference on Human Robot Interaction. IEEE Press, 2016, pp. 109–116.

[10] W. R. Swartout and J. D. Moore, "Explanation in second generation expert systems," in Second generation expert systems. Springer, 1993, pp. 543–585.

[11] L. R. Ye and P. E. Johnson, "The impact of explanation facilities on user acceptance of expert systems advice," MIS Quarterly, vol. 19, no. 2, 1995, pp. 157–172.

[12] Dzindolet et al., "The role of trust in automation reliance," International Journal of Human-Computer Studies, vol. 58, no. 6, 2003, pp. 697–718.

[13] M. A. Goodrich, A. C. Schultz et al., "Human–robot interaction: a survey," Foundations and Trends® in Human–Computer Interaction, vol. 1, no. 3, 2008, pp. 203–275.

[14] F. Correia, P. Alves-Oliveira, N. Maia, T. Ribeiro, S. Petisca, F. S. Melo, and A. Paiva, "Just follow the suit! trust in human-robot interactions during card game playing," in Robot and Human Interactive Communication (RO-MAN), 2016 25th IEEE International Symposium on. IEEE, 2016, pp. 507–512.

[15] A. M. Evans and J. I. Krueger, "The psychology (and economics) of trust," Social and Personality Psychology Compass, vol. 3, no. 6, 2009, pp. 1003–1017.

[16] E. Paeng, J. Wu, and J. C. Boerkoel, "Human-robot trust and cooperation through a game theoretic framework," in AAAI, 2016, pp. 4246–4247.

[17] R. E. Yagoda and D. J. Gillan, "You want me to trust a robot? the development of a human–robot interaction trust scale," International Journal of Social Robotics, vol. 4, no. 3, 2012, pp. 235–248.

[18] Billings et al., "Human-animal trust as an analog for human-robot trust: A review of current evidence," University Of Central Florida Orlando, Tech. Rep., 2012.

[19] C. A. Miller, "Trust in adaptive automation: the role of etiquette in tuning trust via analogic and affective methods," in Proceedings of the 1st international conference on augmented cognition, 2005, pp. 22–27.

[20] M. Salem, G. Lakatos, F. Amirabdollahian, and K. Dautenhahn, "Would you trust a (faulty) robot?: Effects of error, task type and personality on human-robot cooperation and trust," in Proceedings of the Tenth Annual ACM/IEEE International Conference on Human-Robot Interaction. ACM, 2015, pp. 141–148.

[21] J. R. Anderson, A. T. Corbett, K. R. Koedinger, and R. Pelletier, "Cognitive tutors: Lessons learned," The journal of the learning sciences, vol. 4, no. 2, 1995, pp. 167–207.

[22] S. Gregor and I. Benbasat, "Explanations from intelligent systems: Theoretical foundations and implications for practice," The Journal of MIS quarterly, 1999, pp. 497–530.

[23] J. R. Anderson, C. F. Boyle, and B. J. Reiser, "Intelligent tutoring systems," Science, vol. 228, no. 4698, 1985, pp. 456–462.

[24] P. Jackson, Introduction to expert systems. Addison-Wesley Longman Publishing Co., Inc., 1998, vol. 6.

[25] C. Lacave and F. J. Díez, "A review of explanation methods for bayesian networks," The Knowledge Engineering Review, vol. 17, no. 2, 2002, pp. 107–127.

[26] F. Sørmo and J. Cassens, "Explanation goals in case-based reasoning," in Proceedings of the ECCBR 2004 Workshops, 2004, pp. 165–174, 142-04.

[27] C. Yuan, H. Lim, and T.-C. Lu, "Most relevant explanation in bayesian networks," Journal of Artificial Intelligence Research, vol. 42, 2011, pp. 309–352.

[28] B. Y. Lim, A. K. Dey, and D. Avrahami, "Why and why not explanations improve the intelligibility of context-aware intelligent systems," in Proceedings of the SIGCHI Conference on Human Factors in Computing Systems. ACM, 2009, pp. 2119–2128.

[29] F. Nothdurft, S. Ultes, and W. Minker, "Finding appropriate interaction strategies for proactive dialogue systems—an open quest," in Proceedings of the 2nd European and the 5th Nordic Symposium on Multimodal Communication, vol. 110. Linköping University Electronic Press, August 6th-8th, 2014 2015, pp. 73–80.

[30] F. Nothdurft and W. Minker, "Justification and transparency explanations in dialogue systems to maintain human-computer trust," in Situated Dialog in Speech-Based Human-Computer Interaction. Springer, 2016, pp. 41–50.

[31] A. Glass, D. L. McGuinness, and M. Wolverton, "Toward establishing trust in adaptive agents," in Proceedings of the 13th international conference on Intelligent user interfaces. ACM, 2008, pp. 227–236.

[32] F. Nothdurft, F. Richter, and W. Minker, "Probabilistic human-computer trust handling." in SIGDIAL Conference, 2014, pp. 51–59.

[33] M. Javaid, V. Estivill-Castro, and R. Hexel, "Knowledge-based robotic agent as a game player," in Pacific Rim : Trends In Artificial Intelligence. Springer, 2019, pp. 322–336.

[34] Chen et al., "The role of trust in decision-making for human robot collaboration," in Workshop on Human-Centered Robotics, RSS, 2017.

[35] K. S. Haring, Y. Matsumoto, and K. Watanabe, "Perception and trust towards a lifelike android robot in japan," in Transactions on Engineering Technologies. Springer, 2014, pp. 485–497.

[36] C. Bartneck, D. Kulić, E. Croft, and S. Zoghbi, "Measurement instruments for the anthropomorphism, animacy, likeability, perceived intelligence, and perceived safety of robots," International journal of social robotics, vol. 1, no. 1, 2009, pp. 71–81.

[37] A. Powers and S. Kiesler, "The advisor robot: tracing people's mental model from a robot's physical attributes," in Proceedings of the 1st ACM SIGCHI/SIGART conference on Human-robot interaction. ACM, 2006, pp. 218–225.

[38] K. M. Lee, N. Park, and H. Song, "Can a robot be perceived as a developing creature? effects of a robot's long-term cognitive developments on its social presence and people's social responses toward it," Human communication research, vol. 31, no. 4, 2005, pp. 538–563.

[39] J. L. Monahan, "I don't know it but I like you: The influence of nonconscious affect on person perception," Human Communication Research, vol. 24, no. 4, 1998, pp. 480–500.

[40] M. Mori, K. F. MacDorman, and N. Kageki, "The uncanny valley [from the field]," IEEE Robotics & Automation Magazine, vol. 19, no. 2, 2012, p. IEEE Robotics & Automation Magazine.

[41] R. M. Warner and D. B. Sugarman, "Attributions of personality based on physical appearance, speech, and handwriting." Journal of Personality and Social Psychology, vol. 50, no. 4, 1986, pp. 792–799.

[42] D. Kulic and E. A. Croft, "Affective state estimation for human–robot interaction," IEEE Transactions on Robotics, vol. 23, no. 5, 2007, pp. 991–1000.

[43] M. L. Walter et al., "The influence of subjects' personality traits on personal spatial zones in a human-robot interaction experiment," in

Robot and Human Interactive Communication, 2005. ROMAN 2005. IEEE International Workshop on. IEEE, 2005, pp. 347–352.

[44] Z. Zeng, M. Pantic, G. I. Roisman, and T. S. Huang, "A survey of affect recognition methods: Audio, visual, and spontaneous expressions," IEEE transactions on pattern analysis and machine intelligence, vol. 31, no. 1, 2009, pp. 39–58.

Handedness Detection Based on Drawing Patterns using Machine Learning Techniques

Jungpil Shin
School of Computer Science and Engineering
University of Aizu
Aizuwakamatsu, Fukushima, Japan
Email: jpshin@u-aizu.ac.jp

Md Abdur Rahim
School of Computer Science and Engineering
University of Aizu
Aizuwakamatsu, Fukushima, Japan
Email: rahim_bds@yahoo.com

***Abstract*—Handedness detection has an effective role in classifying different criminal suspects into specific categories according to soft biometric properties. It determines human motor skills that are performed with the dominant hand while doing everyday activities such as writing and throwing. In this context, this paper offers a system that extracts the characteristics of a person's drawing patterns and uses these features to perform handwriting classifications with regards to handedness. For this, we collect left and right hand data and derive various types of parameters such as elapsed time, x-coordinate, y-coordinate, pen pressure, pen orientation, and pen height. We define different features like mean, maximum, minimum, writing pressure, speed, and Dynamic Programming (DP) for handwriting data for analysis. P-value and t-test are calculated for handwriting evaluation. Furthermore, handedness detection is achieved by using a Support Vector Machine (SVM) classifier. The result shows quite encouraging performance that highlights the effectiveness of the proposed system.**

Keywords–Handedness; Handwriting; Drawing Pattern; Support Vector Machine (SVM).

I. INTRODUCTION

Handedness is a complex characteristic in human behavior that reflects the domination of the brain that is related to quantitative change. The use of the dominant hand instead of the other hand makes it more efficient and comfortable for everyday tasks. This became increasingly evident during childhood and persists throughout life. Handedness can be used to identify a person's cognitive ability and personality concerning fine motor skills and manual functionality and help to find suspects in criminal investigations. Many scholars have explained that psychological traits i.e., developmental process, cognitive abilities [1] and personality [2] are related to hand preferences. In [3], Nicholls et al. proposed a cognitive ability scale and hand preference test, which are subtle and sensitive measures of hand performance. Gradient feature-based biometric traits, such as handedness, age, gender prediction suggested in [4]. This work is addressed how to automatically predict these soft biometric features from the handwritten text. Moreover, in [5], Morera et al. proposed an offline handwriting-based gender and handedness prediction system. From the handwriting, they introduced a deep network in order to solve demographic classification problems. However, handwriting recognition can cause some problems when writing with inter- and intra-individual variations. This can be assessed by analyzing the correlation between the writing velocities of each test for each participant. Pressure and stroke sequences, use of different pen types, or background noise are also major concerns. Wang and Chuang [6] proposed a pen-type input device to detect trajectories for handwriting digits and gestures. They extract time and frequency-domain features from acceleration signals and then identify important features by a hybrid system. We, therefore, focus on the detection of handedness based on drawing pattern by analyzing elapsed time, x-coordinate, y-coordinate, pen pressure, pen orientation, and pen height. We consider different statistical methods and DP distances as a feature for handedness analysis and we make a classification using the SVM classifier.

The rest of this paper is structured as follows. Section II describes the proposed methodology. In Section III, we describe the data acquisition process and analyze the results. Section IV concludes this paper.

II. METHOD OF HANDWRITING ANALYSIS

In this section, we explain the overall process of the handedness detection system. Figure 1 shows the basic flow diagram of the proposed system. Data is acquired using a pen tablet and processed for feature extraction. Then, we calculate the t-test and p-value for each feature. Finally, we classify handedness using different kernels of SVM.

A. Handwriting Feature Analysis

To extract the handwriting features, we create a reference model. In this work, T represents the length of each input data and N_T represents the length of the coordinate points of the reference model. t(n) is the elapsed time after the start of the test, p(n) is the writing pressure, x(n) is the positional coordinate in the horizontal direction, and y(n) is the positional coordinate in the vertical direction. The experimental data is acquired by following (1), where $n = 1, 2, 3, \ldots, N$.

$$S(n) = [t(n), p(n), x(n), y(n)] \tag{1}$$

The reference model is defined using (2) where $x_T(n_T)$ represents the positional coordinate in the horizontal direction and $y_T(n_T)$ is the positional coordinate in the vertical direction.

$$S_T(n_T) = [X_T(n_T), y_T(n_T)] \tag{2}$$

where $n_T = 1, 2, 3, ..., N_T$. To evaluate the differences between right handed and left handed persons, we obtained some statistical features that are shown in Table I. Moreover, we had measured the DP distance using the DP matching algorithm as a feature.

B. Dynamic Programming (DP) Matching

DP matching is a pattern recognition methodology used in many studies in the field of signature authentication and speech recognition [7][8]. It calculates the distance between sample data and input data which optimizes all route-to-route measurements through backtracking. In this study, the differences between the right handed person and left handed

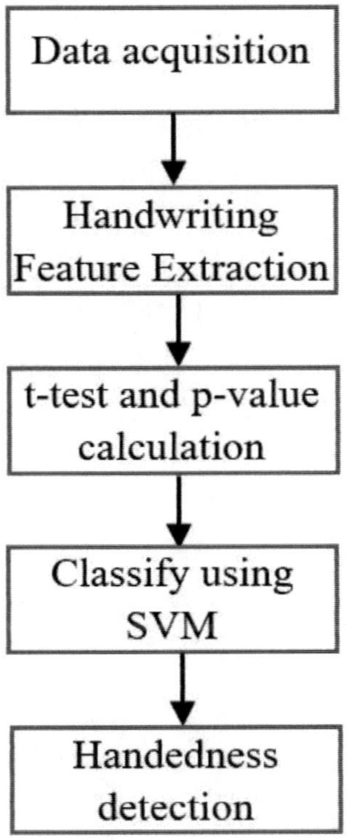

Figure 1. Basic block diagram of a handedness detection system.

TABLE I. STATISTICAL FEATURES FOR HANDEDNESS DETECTION

Feature	Equation
Average pressure	$P_{mean} = \frac{1}{N} \times \sum_{n=1}^{N} p_{(n)}$
Maximum pressure	$P_{max} = \max_{1 \le n \le N} (p_{(n)})$
Minimum pressure	$P_{min} = \min_{1 \le n \le N} (p_{(n)})$
Average velocity	$V_{mean} = \frac{1}{N} \times \sum_{n=1}^{N} \frac{\sqrt{\{x_{(n)} - x_{(n+1)}\}^2 + \{y_{(n)} - y_{(n+1)}\}^2}}{t_{(n+1)} - t_{(n)}}$

person are defined as the total cost DP_x of the optimum route and are calculated as the difference between the cost and the sample data. $d_{(i,j)}$ was measured by the distance between the x-coordinates of input data and reference data, as shown in (3) and (4). The cost C_x of DP matching was calculated from using (5).

$$d_{(i,j)} = x_{\gamma(i)} - y_j \tag{3}$$

$$g_{(i,j)} = d(i,j) + min \begin{bmatrix} C(i-1,j) \\ 2C(i-1,j-1) \\ C(i,j-1) \end{bmatrix} \tag{4}$$

$$DP_x = g(N_T, N) \tag{5}$$

$d_{(i,j)}$ defines the distance between the ith coordinate point of the sample data and the jth coordinate point of the input data. DP_y is defined similarly. After that, these analysis methods are used to recognize the differences between a right handed person and a left handed person.

C. Handedness Classification using SVM

Support Vector Machine (SVM) differentiates the advanced features into different domains based on the concept of finding a hyperplane [9]. In this work, we use different kernels, such as linear, polynomial, Radial Basis Function (RBF) to classify handedness. Table II shows the function of different SVM kernels.

TABLE II. DIFFERENT SVM KERNELS METHOD

SVM kernels	Functions
Linear	$f(X) = B(0) + sum(a_i * (X, X_i))$
Polynomial	$K(X_1, X_2) = (a + X_1^T X_2)^b$
RBF	$K(X_1, X_2) = \text{exponent}(-\gamma \|X_1 - X_2\|^2)$

III. Experimental Results

The experiment aims to classify handedness, provide handwriting features for analysis, and evaluate performance through machine learning techniques.

A. Data Acquisition Process

We used a liquid crystal tablet (Wacom Cintiq Pro 16) to collect handwriting data. Random participants are requested to draw and write characters that can be obtained as 6-dimensional data sets such elapsed time, x-coordinate, y-coordinate, pen pressure, pen orientation, pen height. The elapsed time since application startup (ms) and the x-coordinates and y-coordinates are represented by the pixel value. The writing pressure is represented by a 2^{15} scale; the value decreases as the writing pressure becomes weaker and the value becomes larger as the writing pressure becomes stronger. The pen orientation is represented by 90 degrees while the pen is positioned vertically on the surface of the board and the pen was at close to 0 degrees while it was horizontally aligned to the right of the board surface. As the tip of the pen points to the top of the display, the horizontal component of the height of the pen increases and the value decreases when pointing down. The value range is expressed between 0 and 1800, and the height angle can be calculated by dividing the value obtained by 10. However, these data were acquired as time-series data at an average of 40 ms. We used these parameters to detect and analyze the differences between handedness. Ten people (7 right handed and 3 left handed) participated in the handwriting experiment as we collecting data. Figure 2 shows some examples of handwriting samples in handedness detection. Samples 1 to 3 are continuous spiral writing, 4 to 6 writing a line in different directions, 7 is writing a square continuously, and 8 and 9 are dotted lines. The participants we asked to write the same character in the blank space in 10 and 11.

B. Results Analysis

We calculated handwriting characteristics from each sample data of each individual. Also, the t-test was performed and the p-value was calculated for each feature. Table III shows the results of the t-test analysis from each feature. In all results, the difference between right handed and left handed

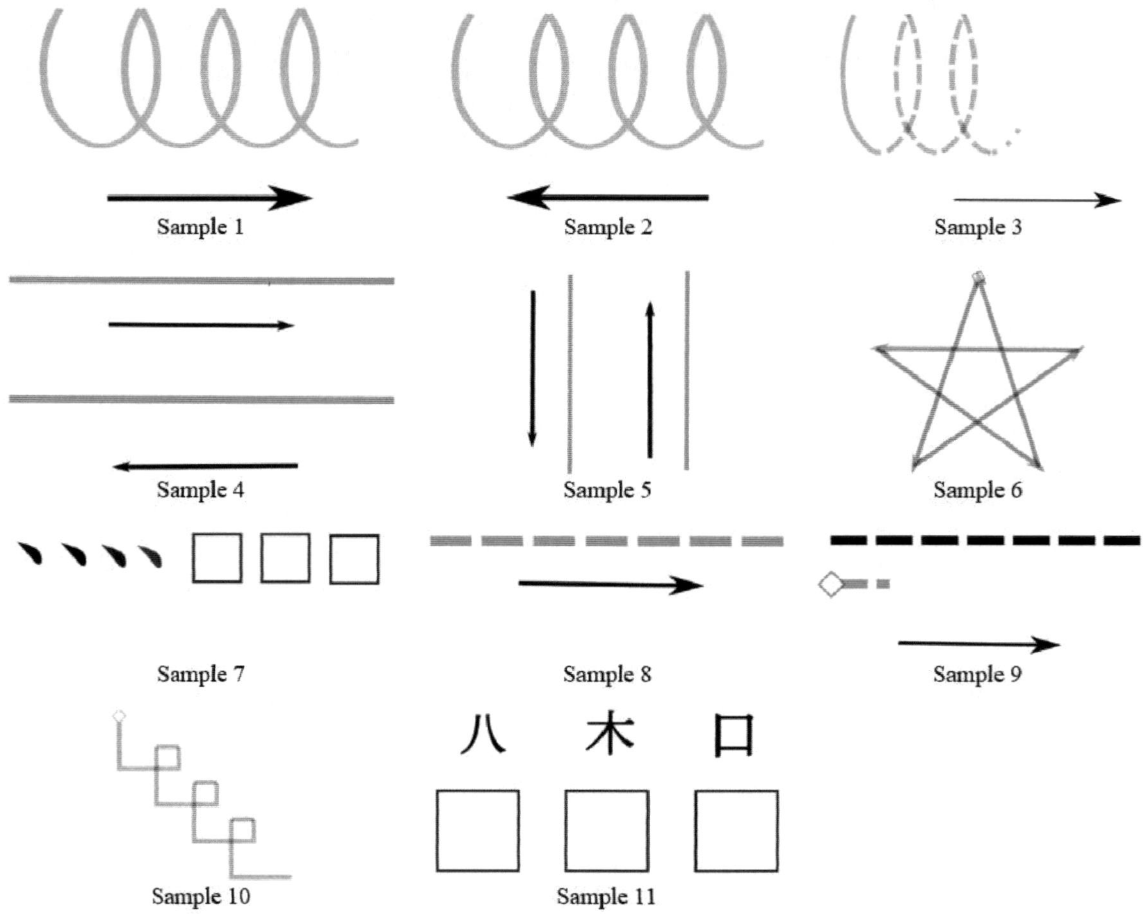

Figure 2. Example of handwriting samples in handedness detection.

individuals was significant at the 5% level. Finally, the results of significant differences were found to be the maximum pressure, the average pressure, and average velocity. For the classification process, we used and compared the different SVM classifications techniques shown in Table IV. The highest recognition accuracy at the highest pressure and the average pressure is about 95.20%. In the Polynomial kernel, we have achieved the highest accuracy in analyzing $Pmax$ and $Pmean$ features. Thus, a major difference between the right hand and the left hand has been observed from the pressure analysis of the pen. Table V presents the comparison of recognition accuracy with a state-of-the-art system.

IV. CONCLUSION

This work addresses the use of a statistical and DP distance feature to detect handedness. The SVM classifier is used to identify left hand and right hand individuals. We used built-in datasets in the experiments. There are 10 people who participated to create the dataset. We collected left handed and right handed data for each individual. We analyzed six parameter values, such as elapsed time, x-coordinate, y-coordinate, pen pressure, pen orientation, and pen height. From the results, we can say that the pressure of the pen is an important feature of distinguishing the handedness. The average classification accuracy of handedness is 95.20%. The obtained results reveal that the proposed system provides a significant improvement compared to the state of the art. In future work, we will explore more robust optical features and review various integrated feature identities and create a feature ranking to improve the detection of handedness.

REFERENCES

[1] M. Papadatou-Pastou, "Handedness and cognitive ability: Using meta-analysis to make sense of the data," in Progress in brain research, vol. 238, pp. 179-206, 2018.

[2] F. M. Bryson, G. M. Grimshaw, and M. S. Wilson, "The role of intellectual openness in the relationship between hand preference and positive schizotypy," Laterality, vol. 14, no. 5, pp. 441-456, 2009.

[3] M. E. Nicholls, H. L. Chapman, T. Loetscher, and G. M. Grimshaw, "The relationship between hand preference, hand performance, and general cognitive ability," Journal of the International Neuropsychological Society, vol. 16, no. 4, pp. 585-592, 2010.

[4] N. Bouadjenek, H. Nemmour, and Y. Chibani, "Age, gender and handedness prediction from handwriting using gradient features," in 2015 13th International Conference on Document Analysis and Recognition (ICDAR), IEEE, pp. 1116-1120, 2015.

[5] A. Morera, A. Sánchez, J. F. Vélez, and A. B. Moreno, "Gender and handedness prediction from offline handwriting using convolutional neural networks," Hindawi Complexity, 2018.

[6] J. S. Wang and F. C. Chuang, "An Accelerometer-Based Digital Pen With a Trajectory Recognition Algorithm for Handwritten Digit and

TABLE III. REPRESENTATION OF T-TEST ANALYSIS RESULTS

		Sample1	Sample2	Sample3	Sample4	Sample5	Sample6	Sample7	Sample8	Sample9	Sample10	Sample11
	right	21294.08	21335.62	22480	21056.85	21876.54	22048.46	21122	17229.08	17757.62	20119.23	20034.54
Pmax (R)	left	21614.17	21351.33	22880.33	20359.33	21832.17	22479	22384.83	16486.33	16715	18172.33	18296.33
	p-value	88%	92%	98%	47%	76%	68%	40%	88%	41%	26%	43%
	right	2206.62	2137.46	1938.46	787.23	872.46	2121.77	1948.923	96.38	18.77	1177.69	237.54
Pmin (R)	left	1448.83	667.67	940.33	767.33	791.67	1683.67	142.67	1	11.5	239.67	1
	p-value	26%	20%	46%	89%	100%	39%	27%	31%	68%	19%	26%
	right	18468.68	19408.64	20002.76	18338.79	19178.18	19660.54	19362.3	13618.27	14032.43	16254.72	15406.84
Pmean (R)	left	18971.08	19137.52	19861.17	17366.57	18547.55	19375.12	20359.69	13013.25	13166.97	14626.41	14065.96
	p-value	69%	80%	92%	44%	47%	99%	48%	76%	44%	20%	41%
	right	19089.92	18680.38	19557	17839.62	18198.23	19367.23	19253.31	15862.23	15769.54	15480.69	16707.46
Pmax (L)	left	22749.67	23335.67	24430	23152.5	23458.5	23355.17	23612.5	20590	20732.17	19727.67	22189
	p-value	2.39%	0.71%	0.54%	0.57%	1.48%	2.95%	1.97%	1.98%	2.04%	0.43%	1%
	right	595.85	1079	1029.77	1376.92	87.85	1043.46	1593.69	55.62	18	342.5	6.15
Pmin (L)	left	1812.83	2077.67	2131.33	443.33	98.83	2214.33	1444.83	232.67	1	1628.5	74.67
	p-value	10.42%	46.89%	15.82%	12.73%	7.58%	46.13%	78.34%	37.04%	40.62%	13.69%	19.34%
	right	16672.45	16337.96	17220.88	15330.92	15522.78	17341.71	17283.53	11605.87	11051.81	11796.97	12497.45
Pmean (L)	left	20535.54	20929.17	21960.79	19713.1	20558.53	21357.55	21525.28	16089.76	16205.18	15187.84	17069.56
	p-value	1.56%	0.55%	0.78%	0.91%	1.98%	3.57%	2.13%	0.80%	0.17%	0.83%	0.78%
	right	7425.67	2616	17273.58	8884.92	178365.1	2918	3521.5	84777.7	2378.83	2169.08	7652.83
DPx (R)	left	259435	252878.75	20743.25	377701.1	377818.38	17613.25	132931.12	251843.25	252063.62	126930.38	141956.62
	p-value	6.90%	4.71%	41.19%	1.13%	28.40%	15.51%	16.55%	27.99%	4.78%	18.33%	14.75%
	right	4157.77	5274.38	18875.69	3147.31	45864.08	10191.31	5444.38	2470.92	3707.54	769544.69	469589.46
DPy (R)	left	3215.43	3761.14	11564.14	3657.43	2219.71	3530.29	4472.71	2357.71	2423.86	428877.57	4369.71
	p-value	4.97%	25.98%	5.20%	52.74%	29.18%	44.19%	35.85%	86.13%	3.83%	14.13%	2.88%
	right	9058	2476.5	8170.92	2128.92	175808.25	2969.92	2763.92	84216.83	1975.08	1159.5	6197.67
DPx (L)	left	264135	254873.25	16478.75	377115.9	378215.75	10508.38	130495	250945.63	252336.13	126222.75	134194.63
	p-value	6.52%	6.98%	22.63%	1.99%	32.76%	13.35%	21.78%	33.15%	7.28%	22.93%	21.51%
	right	5673.77	4810.7	12835.15	3950.92	28878.23	3899.85	5749.23	1293.31	1870.23	769445.92	467958.46
DPy (L)	left	4243.43	4024.57	13409.57	4164.14	2014.29	3657.86	4168.86	1356.57	1859.86	428799.57	5555
	p-value	37.17%	41.98%	77.19%	87.69%	30.40%	73.74%	14.55%	88.00%	98.42%	14.15%	3.00%
	right	1.8	1.99	2.14	2.25	1.74	2.24	1.33	0.997	0.86	1.18	1.81
Vmean (R)	left	1.51	1.54	1.71	1.97	1.48	2.18	1.13	0.86	0.7	1.08	1.62
	p-value	29.15%	16.18%	20.70%	46.83%	43.65%	90.51%	24.40%	39.41%	25.54%	68.62%	48.46%
	right	1.51	1.62	1.83	1.82	1.43	1.66	1.05	0.71	0.67	0.93	1.35
Vmean (L)	left	1.59	1.56	1.7	2.04	1.63	1.9	1.22	0.9	0.91	1.83	2.29
	p-value	76.02%	84.95%	67.97%	61.26%	60.25%	50.98%	24.70%	20.28%	14.09%	0.04%	0.36%

TABLE IV. RECOGNITION ACCURACY USING DIFFERENT SVM KERNELS

	Linear	*Polynomial*	*RBF*
P_{max}(R)	66.70%	61.90%	61.90%
P_{min}(R)	42.90%	42.90%	61.90%
P_{mean}(R)	61.90%	42.90%	61.90%
P_{max}(L)	81.00%	76.20%	76.20%
P_{min}(L)	81.00%	81.00%	76.20%
P_{mean}(L)	71.40%	76.20%	71.40%
P_{max}	90.50%	95.20%	90.05%
P_{min}	61.90%	66.70%	61.90%
P_{mean}	90.50%	95.20%	90.50%
DP_x(R)	60.00%	65.00%	70.00%
DP_y(R)	65.00%	60.00%	75.00%
DP_x(L)	55.00%	65.00%	65.00%
DP_y(L)	55.50%	65.00%	65.00%
V_{mean}(R)	76.20%	71.40%	71.40%
V_{mean}(L)	71.40%	71.40%	71.40%

TABLE V. COMPARISON OF RECOGNITION ACCURACY.

Reference	*Handedness Recognition Accuracy*
Ref. [4]	90%
Ref. [5]	90.70%
Ref. [10]	95.97%
Proposed system	95.20%

Gesture Recognition," IEEE Transactions on Industrial Electronics, vol. 7, no. 59, pp. 2998-3007, 2012.

[7] J. Shin, "On-line cursive hangul recognition that uses DP matching to detect key segmentation points." Pattern Recognition, vol. 37, no. 11, pp. 2101-2112, 2004.

[8] W. D. Chang and J. Shin, "Dynamic positional warping: dynamic time warping for online handwriting," International Journal of Pattern Recognition and Artificial Intelligence, vol. 23, no. 05, pp. 967-986, 2009.

[9] I. Indyk and M. Zabarankin, "Adversarial and counter-adversarial support vector machines," Neurocomputing, vol. 356, pp. 1-8, 2019.

[10] E. Griechisch and E. Bencsik, "Handedness detection of online handwriting based on horizontal strokes," in 2015 13th International Conference on Document Analysis and Recognition (ICDAR), IEEE, pp. 1272-1277, 2015.

The Changing Nature of Childhood Environments

Investigating Children's Interactions with Digital Voice Assistants in Light of a New Paradigm

Janik Festerling
Department of Education
University of Oxford
Oxford, UK
e-mail: janik.festerling@education.ox.ac.uk

Abstract — **Based on the theoretical framework of the New Ontological Category Hypothesis (NOCH), this piece of doctoral research (work in progress) investigates the nature of children's interactions with commercial Digital Voice Assistants (DVAs), such as Alexa, Google Assistant, or Siri. In a nutshell, NOCH challenges the notion of anthropomorphism and argues that intelligently behaving machines, such as voice assistants, could become ontological categories in their own right within children's emerging understanding of the world. A methodological strategy is briefly outlined in order to explore NOCH with respect to children's relative self-disclosure, that is, how children self-disclose personal insights when they interact with DVAs, on the one hand, and humans, on the other hand.**

Keywords* – *voice assistants; children-machine interaction; anthropomorphism; cognitive development; mixed methods.

I. Introduction

The spread of commercial Digital Voice Assistants (DVAs), such as Apple's Siri, Amazon's Alexa, or the Google Assistant, has gained extreme momentum within a few years, not only in terms of total numbers (i.e. number of households using DVAs), but also regarding individual usage intensities (i.e. number of DVA-devices per household), or third party developers that enter the DVA-market [1][2]. Although today's DVAs are neither the only nor the most sophisticated manifestations of Artificial Intelligence (AI) in everyday life, these automated voice interfaces still remain one of the most tangible and recognizable embodiments of humanoid artificiality, and they are often present within the most intimate spaces of our home environments.

Although empirical insights regarding the nature of child-DVA interactions remain limited up to this point, a popular implicit or explicit theme in the growing body of preliminary research as well as journalistic commentaries is the anthropomorphism paradigm [3]–[8], which assumes that, as part of our human nature, we are sometimes inclined to treat and perceive non-human entities through a humanoid lens, either consciously or sub-consciously [9]–[12]. In the context of child-DVA interactions, this notion often translates into the general idea – not to say fear – that these machines could become children's 'imaginary' friends (e.g. [13]). But the question remains: How much imagination is required when you talk to DVAs? The short answer is *none*, because the fact that you talk to Alexa *et al.* is as real as the fact that an actual humanoid voice responds to your request. In addition, claiming that children's interactions with DVAs, in particular, and humanoid AI, in general, can be conceptually reduced to anthropomorphic behaviours and imaginative perceptions also means to ignore that children's cognitive development might give rise to unprecedented forms of understanding and perception when it comes to the human-machine interactions.

Hence, this piece of doctoral research, as it is outlined in this paper, argues that the anthropomorphism paradigm is not sufficient to grasp the evolving interactive relationship between children and DVAs on scientific grounds. Instead, the New Ontological Category Hypothesis (NOCH) by [14] is proposed as an alternative and exemplified in the contemporary context of DVAs. Lastly, a methodological strategy for its empirical investigation is briefly outlined.

This paper is organised as follows: Section II briefly introduces the anthropomorphism paradigm and explains its theoretical implications. Section III raises major criticisms and shortages of the anthropomorphism paradigm in the context of child-DVA interactions. Section IV proposes and explains NOCH as an alternative paradigm. Section V concludes the discussion before the next steps for future research are outlined in the last section, Section VI, of this paper.

II. Anthropomorphism: An Overview

A prevailing paradigm in human-machine interaction and related disciplines is anthropomorphism, arguing that our behaviours and perceptions that characterise interactions with other humans can also be present when we interact with non-human entities, such as machines. This section briefly summarises anthropomorphism's theoretical substructure and implications, before turning the reader's attention towards its shortages in the next section.

A. Origins and mechanisms of anthropomorphism

The human inclination to project some essence of humanness onto non-humanness, as firstly pointed out in early scholarly work by Charles Darwin, David Hume, or Sigmund Freud, remains a widely observable and reported phenomenon across different entities (e.g. animals, objects, or supranatural beings), and, of course, with varying degrees of prevalence and intensity throughout different historical, cultural, situational, and individual contexts [11][12]. Ever since the emergence of modern consumer technologies in the 20th century, this anthropomorphism paradigm has served as a popular framework to conceptualise those empirical observations in which human interactions with machines and media seemed to follow certain patterns of intra-human behaviours and perceptions (e.g. [9][15][16]).

When it comes to the underlying psychological mechanisms that supposedly drive this widely observable inclination of human nature, anthropomorphism has been explained as an inductive inferential process: when we encounter a non-human entity with an uncertain or ambiguous inner state of being, we attempt to imbue its opaqueness with our introspectively acquired certainty about human life and mentality by adjusting our behaviour and perceptions as if it was human [11][12]. Notably, this process can already be present during infancy and early childhood, when children project their inner idea of human life and mentality – even though these ideas might still be pre-mature from a developmental perspective – onto the objects they play with, often according to their vivid imaginations and fantasies, which is referred to as 'pretend play' or 'behaving-as-if-play' [10].

B. Extending anthropomorphism: a thought experiment

It must be emphasised that for children as well as adults anthropomorphism is not necessarily about confusing human and non-human entities; instead, it is about the creative control that is exercised over an entity that offers sufficient space for projection [10][17]. Hence, the reason why it would not make any sense to apply anthropomorphism to intra-human interactions is because, theoretically speaking, there is no space when one attempts to project humanness onto something that *is* indeed human. In other words, it would be odd to argue that when we interact with each other we do behave as if we were human, because, strictly speaking, we *are*.

This yields an interesting theoretical thought experiment: if we extend the basic notion of anthropomorphism, one reasonable implication – similar to the reasoning of the original Turing Test [18] – would be that human interactions with machines should become more humanlike as technology develops, all the way up to the (theoretical) stage of perfect resemblance when AI would be able to emulate all domains of human intelligence. At this (theoretical) stage – which would also go beyond a potential uncanny valley – the anthropomorphism paradigm would suggest that human-machine and human-human interactions follow (almost) indistinguishable patterns. Interestingly enough, this idea of 'perfect anthropomorphism' matches the notion embedded in most pop cultural future visions that became famous throughout the 20th and 21st-century, such as the supercomputer 'HAL 9000' in Stanley Kubrick's masterpiece '2001: A Space Odyssey', the crime-fighting car 'Kitt' in the TV-show 'Knight Rider', or, most recently, the charming virtual girlfriend 'Samantha' in Spike Jonze's science-fiction romantic drama 'Her'.

However, even today, while we still wait for general AI and humanoid supercomputers to arrive (or not), the anthropomorphism paradigm and its theoretical implications seem problematic for several reasons, which are discussed in the next section.

III. CHALLENGING ANTHROPOMOPHISM

This section challenges anthropomorphism with three points of criticism related to its theoretical substructure as well as its applicability in the context of DVAs.

A. The appreciation of non-human qualities

The first general point of criticism against anthropomorphism is that, due to its simplistic theoretical substructure, it fails to consider an important aspect, namely how we as humans might appreciate machines due to their non-human qualities – and not despite of them. In other words, instead of arguing that our interactions with machines will become more intimate and intense as we see more humanness in them, the opposite could be true, because we might prefer machines over humans whenever we appreciate certain aspects about their inner absence of humanness.

For instance, since the early 1970s, an extensive body of clinical research has shown how patients are more willing to self-disclose personal insights to a computer rather than a human physician [19]–[23], and a comprehensive meta-analysis confirmed this tendency of humans to self-disclose more personal insights through a computer interface compared to face-to-face interviews [24]. Furthermore, more recent research has been able to extend these findings to virtual agents, which were often able to establish higher levels of rapport and elicit more personal insights from participants compared to the human baseline condition [25]–[27]. Another very recent piece of experimental research has shown that, across different domains of intelligence, participants prioritised predictions and assessments that were labelled to be of algorithmic origin compared somebody else's or even one's own prediction and assessment, which suggests, that, at times, humans might be willing to attribute higher levels of trust to the computational power of contemporary machines, even when they are unfamiliar with the machines' inner working mechanisms [28].

Although both empirical aspects outlined above certainly allow for more than one theoretical explanation, this first point of criticism can be summarised as follows: contrary to the implicit notion of anthropomorphism, the breadth and depth of human interactions with machines might be enhanced by the perceived *absence* of humanness (e.g. moral judgement) and the *presence* of non-human machine qualities (e.g. superior computational power).

B. DVAs' limited scope for anthropomorphic projection

The second point of criticism refers back to an issue raised earlier in the introduction: how much imagination is required when we talk to DVAs? The short answer remains *none*, because, in light of the previous discussion, it would be as odd to argue that, when we interact with DVAs, we behave as if these machines were talking to us, because, strictly speaking, they *are*. But, even if one argues that human-machine interactions, which are restricted to voice-only communication, offer plenty of room for anthropomorphic projection (e.g. [29]), one should keep in mind that DVAs are endowed with *real* interactive features and pre-programmed personalities, which may not prevent anthropomorphism per se, but they certainly constitute impeding factors by reducing the potential scope for the imaginative forces of creative control. In fact, exploratory empirical findings reported by [30] show how children systematically probe DVAs in order to understand the inner nature of the machine. Although some of these reported probing behaviours (e.g. asking for DVAs' age or favourite colour, testing DVAs' sense of humour), and children's verbally expressed perceptions about DVAs (e.g. claiming DVAs possess emotions and feelings), seem anthropomorphic at first glance, the entirety of empirical findings by [30] does not suggest that children engage in strong pretend play, or behaving-as-if scenarios. Instead, children systematically attempt to reduce uncertainty by unfolding DVAs' opaqueness. And even if children report firm perceptions about DVAs' inner emotional states, this could be the result of a sincere experience-based judgement that a DVA has effectively communicated an emotional state, rather than expressing a pretended imagination of the DVAs' anthropomorphic inner state of being.

C. Developmental origins of what it means to be human

Lastly, and most importantly, the argument of anthropomorphism skips a decisive step: claiming that humans are inclined to project their inner idea of human life and mentality onto non-human entities, raises the question where these subjective ideas come from, and the consecutive critical question, how the emergence of somebody's internalised idea of what it means to be human may in itself be affected by interactions with non-human, but nevertheless humanoid entities, such as DVAs. As mentioned earlier (see Section II.A), our inner ideas of human life and mentality gradually mature as part of our development, when we learn – among other things – to recognise others as living kinds with intentions, mentality, intelligence, morality, emotions, or, in short, as humans [10]. However, cognitive development is subject to environmental stimuli, and therefore, changing childhood environments, that are increasingly characterised by humanoid manifestations of AI, could not only change how children think about these technologies, but also about themselves as humans [31]. This reasoning introduces the starting point of NOCH, which is discussed in the next section.

IV. New Ontological Category Hypothesis

In a nutshell, NOCH argues that children, who grow up in highly technologised environments, might conceptualise humanoid intelligently behaving machines as hybrid beings, between the cognitive domains of living humans, on the one hand, and non-living machines, on the other hand, therefore forming an ontological category in its own right within children's emerging understanding of the world. This section briefly summarises the theoretical substructure of NOCH and exemplifies how it can raise new perspectives around child-machine interactions, in general, and child-DVA interactions, in particular.

A. Developmental concept of ontologies

In general, human cognitive development describes the iterative process of developing an experience-based understanding of the world by linking the sensual experience of the present with the conceptualised experience of the past [32]. Although these emerging and constantly refined mental representations of reality become more sophisticated, nuanced, and engrained throughout infancy and childhood, their complexity always remains subsumable under a single system of cognitive boundaries, referred to as ontology, which allows for a basic categorisation of entities along the lines of their perceived features and attributes [32][33]. Hence, ontological categories translate into foundational distinctions between the broadest classes of physical existence, such as living and non-living beings, human and non-human living beings, natural and artefactual non-living beings, and so on [17][31][33]. Although research has shown how children may struggle to categorise entities with ambiguous characteristics into ontological categories [35]–[37], the argument of NOCH goes one step further: if certain entities remain 'lost' within a child's ontology, because they display characteristics that relate to multiple ontological natures from the perspective of the child (see Fig. 1), therefore preventing a clear categorisation, a *new* ontological category might be formed in order to overcome cognitive ambiguities [14].

In other words, from the perspective of children, who would have developed a new ontological category for intelligently behaving machines, the question whether Alexa *et al.* are humans or machines might seem as strange as the question whether an orange piece of paper is yellow or red, because, in both cases, the object (i.e. DVA) or quality (i.e. colour) in question would be perceived as something *in its own right* [38].

B. DVAs: A new ontological category?

Peter H. Kahn and his colleagues, the original authors of NOCH, conceived their idea in light of the technological achievements of the early 2010s [14], but their work predates many of the recent AI breakthroughs, as well as DVAs' tremendous commercial success, and, so far, there have been very few attempts to advance and apply their legacy (for one of the few exceptions see [5]), despite an array of intuitive reasons, why DVAs' humanoid omnipresence could indeed introduce an perceptual ontological change of today's childhood environments. Although an all-encompassing discussion is beyond the scope of this paper, the important point to make here is that, when it comes to the investigation of child-DVA interactions, NOCH urges us to at least consider that this unprecedented context – namely the permanent presence of a humanoid voice in a child's home environment, starting at birth, and lasting into maturity – might also raise unprecedented questions.

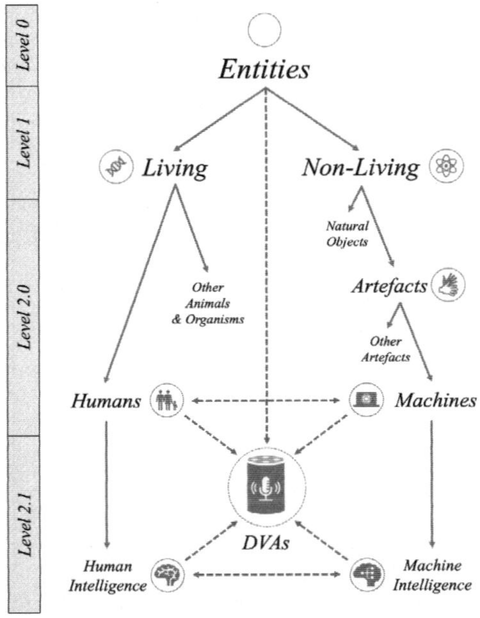

Figure 1. DVAs' embeddedness in children's ontological believe system according to NOCH (Source: compiled by the author, see [40])

In particular, it could explain why children might appreciate DVAs' humanoid (e.g. mastery of human language) as well as non-human qualities (e.g. absence of moral judgement) at the same time (see Section III.A), and why children's interactions with DVAs might not display strong notions of anthropomorphism, such as pretend play or behaving-as-if scenarios. Furthermore, NOCH also urges us to question common assumptions and arguments. For instance, when children use human attributes to characterise DVAs (e.g. she/her, he/his/him), according to NOCH, this would not necessarily imply that children anthropomorphise by projecting humanness onto these machines, because, as a new hybrid ontological category, Alexa *et al.* simply draw upon certain linguistic qualities from one of the ontological 'parent' categories, while remaining a distinct non-human (but nevertheless humanoid) category in their own right.

Another example: the feminist criticism that DVAs' female voices *cause* the reproduction of discriminating stereotypes in children (e.g. [39]), implicitly assumes that children directly associate and equalise the concept of human femininity with artificial femininity, as it is embodied by DVAs' female voices. However, if Alexa *et al.* were hybrid beings in their own right, from an ontological perspective, this assumption would require empirical validation, since it cannot be inferred from theory alone. Or differently spoken, and in line with the metaphor used earlier: if you do not like the colour yellow, can we simply assume that you do not like the colour orange either?

In sum, it may be left to the reader whether NOCH constitutes a paradigm shift that could overcome the implicit shortages of anthropomorphism. But it certainly raises new and potentially important questions in the context of child-DVA interactions, which might be worth investigating.

V. Conclusion

This paper constitutes a critical review and discussion of the anthropomorphism paradigm, which remains a popular implicit or explicit theme in the literature on human-machine interaction, in general, and child-DVA interactions, in particular. This paper contributes to the literature by raising the argument that NOCH serves as a fruitful theoretical lens for the conceptualisation and empirical investigation of child-DVA interactions, as they take place in children's natural home environments.

VI. Future Research

The next steps for future research are to develop a research design that allows for the empirical investigation of NOCH in the context of child-DVA interactions.

In particular, the research will focus on the empirical exploration of NOCH with respect to one particular dimension of child-DVA interactions: a comparison of the nature of children's self-disclosure when interacting with DVAs, on the one hand, and humans, on the other hand. This empirical focus seems to be of particular importance, because it sheds light on an important area of tension: as pointed out in the introduction, there is this concrete vision that children might develop close interactive relationships with intelligently behaving machines while growing up with them (e.g. [13][39]). If this notion is combined with the empirical findings reported earlier (see Section III.A), showing how humans are also inclined to appreciate machines' non-human qualities (e.g. absence of human moral judgement), and the theoretical implications of NOCH that children might accept, appreciate, or even prefer a confidant of hybrid ontological nature over a human alternative, this issue seems worthwhile investigating. In addition, given that DVAs, in particular, and, arguably, even AI, in general, will continue to rely on the depth and breadth of insights we are willing to reveal, investigating children's self-disclosure of personal insights would also have important implications for the future role of DVAs in our home environments, which is currently envisioned with a strong emphasis on leveraging user data through the customisation of services [42]. In order to compare the nature of children's self-disclosure when communicating with DVAs, on the one hand, and humans, on the other hand, a mixed methods research design with two major design components is proposed.

A. First design component

The first design component is supposed to explore the nature of children's self-disclosure by comparing how children share personal insights with a DVA, on the one hand, and with a real human, on the other hand. Although the collection of verbal data through DVAs has already been applied in preliminary research on DVA usage patterns [43]–[47], the future research referred to in this paper attempts to contribute to the literature by using a researcher-designed DVA-application (work-in-progress). For the analysis, the transcribed verbal data are supposed to be explored and compared with computational methods of psychological text analysis [48]–[50]. The focus of the analysis is to explore and compare children's self-disclosure patterns both within as well as between the DVA-condition and the human-condition (i.e. between subject comparison and within subject comparison).

B. Second design component

The second design component is supposed to complement the implicit weaknesses of the quantitative component by providing an in-depth panorama of selected cases, and in order to understand individual reasons and circumstances that might have caused the observed patterns of self-disclosure. Methods of data collection mainly include semi-structured interviews and observations during household visits, which are then used for qualitative means of data analysis in psychology, such as thematic analysis [51].

C. Additional remarks on future research

The target population of this research consists of normally developing children in industrialised English-speaking countries, who are in the concrete operational stage of their cognitive development (i.e. $\sim$ 5 to 10 years), and with or without prior domestic DVA exposure at the beginning of the study. The intended sample sizes are $n \rightarrow 50$ for the first component, and $n \rightarrow 10$ for the second component. The beginning of the data collection is scheduled for spring 2021.

ACKNOWLEDGEMENT

I would like to thank my academic supervisors for their great support so far.

REFERENCES

[1] B. Kinsella and A. Mutchler, "Smart Speaker Consumer Adoption Report." Voicebot & Voicify, 2019.

[2] B. Kinsella and A. Mutchler, "Voice Assistant Consumer Adoption Report." Voicebot, PullStrong & RAIN, 2019.

[3] K. Wagner and H. Schramm-Klein, "Alexa, Are You Human? Investigating Anthropomorphism of Digital Voice Assistants - A Qualitative Approach," in *Fortieth International Conference on Information Systems*, 2019, pp. 1–17.

[4] A. Purington, J. G. Taft, S. Sannon, N. N. Bazarova, and S. H. Taylor, "'Alexa is my new BFF': Social roles, user satisfaction, and personification of the Amazon Echo," in *Proceedings of the ACM CHI Conference on Human Factors in Computing Systems*, 2017, vol. Part F1276, pp. 2853–2859.

[5] A. Pradhan, L. Findlater, and A. Lazar, "Phantom Friend or Just a Box with Information: Personification and Ontological Categorization of Smart Speaker-based Voice Assistants by Older Adults," in *Proceedings of the ACM on Human-Computer Interaction*, 2019, pp. 1–21.

[6] J. Coughlin, "Alexa, Will You Be My Friend? When Artificial Intelligence Becomes Something More," *Forbes*, 2018. [Online]. Available: https://www.forbes.com/sites/josephcoughlin/2018/09/23/alexa-will-you-be-my-friend-when-artificial-intelligence-becomes-something-more/. [Accessed: 25-Jan-2020].

[7] I. Lopatovska and H. Williams, "Personification of the Amazon Alexa: BFF or a Mindless Companion," in *Proceedings of the 2018 Conference on Human Information Interaction & Retrieval*, 2018, pp. 265–268.

[8] N. Motalebi, E. Cho, S. S. Sundar, and S. Abdullah, "Can Alexa be your Therapist?: How Back-Channeling Transforms Smart-Speakers to be Active Listeners," in *Conference Companion Publication of the 2019 on Computer Supported Cooperative Work and Social Computing*, 2019, pp. 309–313.

[9] B. Reeves and C. I. Nass, *The media equation: How people treat computers, television, and new media like real people and places*. Stanford, CA, US: CSLI Publications, 1998.

[10] G. Airenti, "The Cognitive Bases of Anthropomorphism: From Relatedness to Empathy," *Int. J. Soc. Robot.*, vol. 7, no. 1, pp. 117–127, 2015.

[11] N. Epley, A. Waytz, and J. T. Cacioppo, "On Seeing Human: A Three-Factor Theory of Anthropomorphism," *Psychol. Rev.*, vol. 114, no. 4, pp. 864–886, 2007.

[12] A. Waytz, J. Cacioppo, and N. Epley, "Who Sees Human? The Stability and Importance of Individual Differences in Anthropomorphism," *Perspect. Psychol. Sci.*, vol. 5, no. 3, pp. 219–232, 2014.

[13] C. Biele *et al.*, "How Might Voice Assistants Raise Our Children?," in *International Conference on Intelligent Human Systems Integration. IHSI 2019. Advances in Intelligent Systems and Computing*, 2019, pp. 162–167.

[14] P. H. J. Kahn *et al.*, "The New Ontological Category Hypothesis in Human- Robot Interaction," in *HRI'11 - 6th Annual Conference for basic and applied human- robot interaction research*, 2011, pp. 159–160.

[15] C. Nass, J. Steuer, and E. R. Tauber, "Computers Are Social Actors," in *Proceedings of the SIGCHI Conference on Human Factors in Computing Systems*, 1994, pp. 72–78.

[16] C. Nass, B. J. Fogg, and Y. Moon, "Can Computers be Teammates?," *Int. J. Hum. Comput. Stud.*, vol. 45, no. 6, pp. 669–678, 1996.

[17] R. L. Severson and S. M. Carlson, "Behaving as or behaving as if? Children's conceptions of personified robots and the emergence of a new ontological category," *Neural Networks*, vol. 23, no. 8–9, pp. 1099–1103, 2010.

[18] A. Turing, "Computing machinery and intelligence," *Mind*, vol. 49, pp. 433–460, 1950.

[19] J. H. Greist, M. H. Klein, and L. J. Van Cura, "A Computer Interview for Psychiatric Patient Target Symptoms," *Arch. Gen. Psychiatry*, vol. 29, no. 2, pp. 247–253, 1973.

[20] J. H. Greist *et al.*, "A Computer Interview for Suicide-Risk Prediction," *Am. J. Psychiatry*, vol. 130, no. 12, pp. 1327–1332, 1973.

[21] R. Robinson and R. West, "A comparison of computer and questionnaire methods of history-taking in a genito-urinary clinic," *Psychol. Health*, vol. 6, no. 1–2, pp. 77–84, 1992.

[22] M. Ferriter, "Computer Aided Interviewing in Psychiatric Social Work," *Comput. Hum. Serv.*, vol. 9, no. 1–2, pp. 59–66, 1993.

[23] P. Kissinger *et al.*, "Application of Computer-Assisted Interviews to Sexual Behavior Research," *Am. J. Epidemiol.*, vol. 149, no. 10, pp. 950–954, 1999.

[24] S. Weisband and S. Kiesler, "Self Disclosure on Computer Forms: Meta-Analysis and Implications," in *Proceedings of the SIGCHI Conference on Human Factors in Computing Systems*, 1996, pp. 3–10.

[25] D. DeVault *et al.*, "SimSensei Kiosk: A Virtual Human Interviewer," in *13th International Conference on Autonomous Agents and Multiagent Systems (AAMAS 2014)*,

2014, pp. 1061–1068.

[26] G. M. Lucas, J. Gratch, A. King, and L.-P. Morency, "It's only a computer: Virtual humans increase willingness to disclose," *Comput. Human Behav.*, vol. 37, no. C, pp. 94–100, 2014.

[27] K. Yokotani, G. Takagi, and K. Wakashima, "Advantages of virtual agents over clinical psychologists during comprehensive mental health interviews using a mixed methods design," *Comput. Human Behav.*, vol. 85, pp. 135–145, 2018.

[28] J. M. Logg, J. A. Minson, and D. A. Moore, "Algorithm appreciation: People prefer algorithmic to human judgment," *Organ. Behav. Hum. Decis. Process.*, vol. 151, pp. 90–103, 2019.

[29] V. Turk, "Home invasion," *New Sci.*, vol. 232, no. 3104–3106, pp. 16–17, 2016.

[30] S. Druga, R. Williams, C. Breazeal, and M. Resnick, "'Hey Google is it OK if I eat you?,'" in *Proceedings of the 2017 Conference on Interaction Design and Children - IDC '17*, 2017, pp. 595–600.

[31] D. Bernstein and K. Crowley, "Searching for Signs of Intelligent Life: An Investigation of Young Children's Beliefs About Robot Intelligence," *J. Learn. Sci.*, vol. 17, no. 2, pp. 225–247, 2008.

[32] S. A. Gelman, "Concepts in Development," in *The Oxford Handbook of Developmental Psychology (Vol 1): Body and Mind*, vol. 1, P. D. Zelazo, Ed. New York, NY, USA: Oxford University Press, 2013, pp. 542–563.

[33] I. Gaudiello, S. Lefort, and E. Zibetti, "The ontological and functional status of robots: How firm our representations are?," *Comput. Human Behav.*, vol. 50, pp. 259–273, 2015.

[34] H. M. Wellman and S. A. Gelman, "Cognitive Development: Foundational Theories of Core Domains," *Annu. Rev. Psychol.*, vol. 43, pp. 337–375, 1992.

[35] J. L. Jipson and S. A. Gelman, "Robots and rodents: Children's inferences about living and nonliving kinds," *Child Dev.*, vol. 78, no. 6, pp. 1675–1688, 2007.

[36] J. M. Kory-Westlund and C. Breazeal, "Assessing Children's Perceptions and Acceptance of a Social Robot," in *Proceedings of the 18th ACM International Conference on Interaction Design and Children*, 2019, pp. 38–50.

[37] M. Scaife and M. Duuren, "Do computers have brains? What children believe about intelligent artifacts," *Br. J. Dev. Psychol.*, vol. 13, no. 4, pp. 367–377, 1995.

[38] P. H. Kahn, H. E. Gary, and S. Shen, "Children's Social Relationships With Current and Near-Future Robots," *Child Dev. Perspect.*, vol. 7, no. 1, pp. 32–37, 2013.

[39] UNESCO, "I'd blush if I could," 2019 [Online]. Available: https://en.unesco.org/Id-blush-if-I-could. [Accessed: 02-Mar-2020].

[40] J. Festerling and I. Siraj, "Exploring Children's Ontological Perceptions of Digital Voice Assistants: A Cognitive Developmental Perspective," unpublished manuscript.

[41] R. Gonzales, "Hey Alexa, What are you doing to my kid's brain?," *WIRED*, 2018. [Online]. Available: https://www.wired.com/story/hey-alexa-what-are-you-doing-to-my-kids-brain/. [Accessed: 25-Jan-2020].

[42] K. Hao, "Inside Amazon's plan for Alexa to for Alexa to run your entire life," *MIT Technology Review*, 2019. [Online]. Available: https://www.technologyreview.com/s/614676/amazon-alexa-will-run-your-life-data-privacy/. [Accessed: 25-Jan-2020].

[43] M. Porcheron, J. E. Fischer, S. Reeves, and S. Sharples, "Voice Interfaces in Everyday Life," in *Proceedings of the 2018 CHI Conference on Human Factors in Computing Systems - CHI '18*, 2018, pp. 1–12.

[44] S. B. Lovato, A. M. Piper, and E. A. Wartella, "Hey Google, Do Unicorns Exist?: Conversational Agents as a Path to Answers to Children's Questions," in *Proceedings of the 18th ACM International Conference on Interaction Design and Children*, 2019, pp. 301–313.

[45] E. Beneteau *et al.*, "Communication Breakdowns Between Families and Alexa," in *Proceedings of the 2019 CHI Conference on Human Factors in Computing Systems*, 2019, pp. 1–13.

[46] A. Sciuto, A. Saini, J. Forlizzi, and J. I. Hong, "Hey Alexa, What's Up?: A mixed-methods studies of in-home conversational agent usage," in *Proceedings of the 2018 Designing Interactive Systems Conference*, 2018, pp. 857–868.

[47] D. Beirl, N. Yuill, and Y. Rogers, "Using Voice Assistant Skills in Family Life," in *CSCL 2019 - 13th International Conference on Computer Supported Collaborative Learning*, 2019, pp. 96–103.

[48] Y. R. Tausczik and J. W. Pennebaker, "The Psychological Meaning of Words: LIWC and Computerized Text Analysis Methods," *J. Lang. Soc. Psychol.*, vol. 29, no. 1, pp. 24–54, 2010.

[49] S. M. Mohammad and P. D. Turney, "Crowdsourcing A Word–Emotion Association Lexicon," *Comput. Intell.*, vol. 29, no. 3, pp. 436–465, 2013.

[50] D. M. Blei, A. Y. Ng, and M. I. Jordan, "Latent Dirichlet Allocation," *J. Mach. Learn. Res.*, vol. 3, no. Jan, pp. 993–1022, 2003.

[51] V. Braun and V. Clarke, "Using Thematic Analysis in Psychology," *Qual. Res. Psychol.*, vol. 3, no. 2, pp. 77–101, 2006.

Exploring the Role of Children as Co-Designers – Using a Participatory Design Study for the Construction of a User Experience Questionnaire

Lea Wöbbekind, Thomas Mandl and Christa Womser-Hacker
Institute for information science and natural language processing
University of Hildesheim
Hildesheim, Germany
email: woebbek@uni-hildesheim.de, mandl@uni-hildesheim.de, womser@uni-hildesheim.de

***Abstract*—The evaluation of interactive products and systems based on hedonistic and pragmatic qualities is an important part of user-centered design. Human-Computer Interaction (HCI) research provides many validated and standardized questionnaires for usability and user experience assessment. However, these questionnaires are not suitable for children as younger users of digital products, as these surveys are developed and evaluated by usability professionals for adult users. Problems may arise due to the length, rating scales and difficulties to understand the content of user experience (UX) questionnaires. This paper focuses on the involvement of children in UX research as co-designers and describes the development of a semantic differential scale for measuring the user experience of children and teenagers (up to age 14). In order to involve children as users in UX studies, little attention has been paid to participatory research as a useful and innovative approach to do user experience research with children. Consequently, the usefulness of the implementation of a workshop with 6 children to develop and design a user experience questionnaire for an interactive learning app for children is discussed. It aims to get a better understanding of the effects of doing research with young teenagers. The results of the workshop show a UX questionnaire measuring UX on pragmatic as well as hedonistic qualities for a specific product. A first evaluation study demonstrates a high internal consistency of the scales.**

Keywords - participatory design; workshop; UX evaluation; semantic differential scale; pupils; user experience.

I. INTRODUCTION

Questionnaires can measure user experience quickly and in a simple way while covering a wide-ranging impression of a product. They are commonly used tools for user-centered evaluation of software and digital products. An important definition of user experience is introduced by the ISO 9241-210 and outlines user experience as "a person's perceptions and responses that result from the use or anticipated use of a product, system or service" [1]. It highlights emotional, hedonic, affective and aesthetic components and is typically characterized as fun, pleasure or negative feelings when interacting with a product [8]. Quantitative data about the user's perceptions of a product can be a helpful addition to other methods to assess the strengths and weaknesses of interactive products [7]. In particular, the research field of Child Computer Interaction has focused not only on how to design and evaluate products with and for children, but also on the modification and adaption of suitable survey methods for children and young adults [2][10]. Results show that user experience is not measurable with younger participants without modifications of already established (quantitative) methods [5][16]. Therefore, researchers need to work closely with the target group to identify useful approaches that encourage their perspectives and opinions. Methods need to be adjusted to children and young people´s strength, context and also culture. Therefore, this paper investigates the use of a participatory design study to construct a suitable and understandable UX semantic differential scale questionnaire for children up to 14 years based on the creation of common UX questionnaires [7]. The research question under consideration is whether young teenagers are able to participate in the construction of a questionnaire for a specific product. The development process involves the selection of semantic differential pairs, categories for item pairs, the overall length and a rating scale.

The rest of the paper is structured as follows. Section II describes related work. In Section III, the used method and challenges are illustrated in more detail, whereas Section IV presents findings and results. Section V summarizes the conclusion and future work.

II. RELATED WORK

The following section gives an overview of the related work regarding models of participatory design with children as well as the construction process of user experience questionnaires. Based on these approaches, this study combines the idea of children as co-designers in the construction process of one user experience questionnaire. Afterward, the questionnaire was applied in a user test study to evaluate its reliability.

A. *Participatory research with children*

The Child Computer Interaction community highlights the advantages of children as active participants in design as well as evaluation studies. The motive arises out of different needs, beliefs and contexts of uses of digital products of experts, adults and children [10][11]. Participatory research with children can mean many things. Normally, it takes the theoretical viewpoint that children are experts and having competencies in specific settings. The level of involvement varies. Listening to children's opinions, supporting them to reflect on their opinion and include their views into research processes is one approach to perform participatory research with children [13]. Different stages of participation can also mean that children as researchers identify and develop research questions, choose appreciate research methods, overtake the role of a researcher and are also included in the interpretation and evaluation of collected data [6]. The approach includes the design and development of a UX questionnaire in the context of a UX-workshop with 6 pupils from one class from a comprehensive school (grade 7, age between 12 and 13, m=3, f=3) in Germany. The pupils act as co-designers and are put in charge of the questionnaire creation. This approach is based on the construction process of many standardized UX questionnaires [3].

B. *Construction of UX questionnaires*

Good user experience is important for the success of interactive products. There is a large number of standardized UX questionnaires for measuring user's subjective perception and opinions of products and different components of UX. The AttrakDiff [3], as well as the User Experience Questionnaire (UEQ) [7], apply a semantic differential scale to measure UX, whereas the Modular Valuation of Key Components of User Experience (meCUE) [9] and the Visual Aesthetics of Websites Inventory (VisAWI) [14] consist of statements with a 7-point Likert scale. They have in common to quickly measure user experience, but are not suitable for the needs of children and teenagers. In general, UX questionnaires are developed within a workshop of usability professionals and validated in several user studies [12]. In the case of the German User Experience Questionnaire, the authors describe user experience based on aspects of pragmatic and hedonistic qualities. A set of 229 items were brainstormed and reduced in several studies to 80 items. 6 scales, as well as 26 items, were extracted by factor analysis. The scales include attractiveness, perspicuity, efficiency, dependability, stimulation and novelty [7]. In the research area of Child Computer Interaction, Hanna et al. [2] recommend the use of pairwise comparisons for the evaluation of interactive products with children. Zaman [16] introduced a pairwise comparison scale for the evaluation of UX with preschoolers. The author suggests that a pairwise comparison scale with 5 items leads to reliable answers from preschoolers in terms of system preferences, but the multidimensional of UX is not quantitatively measurable.

III. METHOD

The next sections report on the construction process of a UX questionnaire within a creative workshop by using participatory design. The workshop is divided into two parts. The first phase aims to give the pupils detailed and adapted information about the concept of user experience and UX questionnaires and the need to evaluate interactive systems within a user-centered design. Moreover, the UEQ [7] and its elements (number and order of items and scales) are explained and serve as an example for a UX questionnaire. This phase also includes a 30-minute testing time of an app under consideration on two mobile devices. After creating a profile and choosing one subject, the participants can play and use the different functions of the learning app [4]. The app itself consists of five different subjects. The user has to complete lessons to earn points. The collected rewards can be redeemed in several games. With this approach, the pupils get a better impression and understanding of the system. After this introduction follows the construction phase of the questionnaire. The task is to develop and design a questionnaire that includes all the necessary elements and items that are needed to evaluate the app. The pupils work together to find and discuss useful contrasting words and phrases for the evaluation of the learning app. In the beginning, the participants had difficulties to get started, as they cannot find words to describe the app. Therefore, the researcher asked the children again about their feelings and emotions when interacting with the app. It presented a starting point for further suggestions from the children. Figure 1 shows a translated version of the constructed UX Kids questionnaire.

Questionnaire for the Anton-App: Please give your opinion.

1. Learning development

		1	2	3	4	5	
1	easy	☆	☆	☆	☆	☆	difficult
2	suitable for learning	☆	☆	☆	☆	☆	Not suitable for learning
3	achieved study goals	☆	☆	☆	☆	☆	Not achieved study goals
4	Sufficiently for learning	☆	☆	☆	☆	☆	Not sufficiently for learning
5	It motivates to learn	☆	☆	☆	☆	☆	It does not motivates for learning
6	progress	☆	☆	☆	☆	☆	no progress

2. Overall impression of the app

7	exciting	☆	☆	☆	☆	☆	boring
8	It works well	☆	☆	☆	☆	☆	bad
9	It works fast	☆	☆	☆	☆	☆	slow
10	Fun	☆	☆	☆	☆	☆	serious
11	entertaining	☆	☆	☆	☆	☆	not entertaining

3. Design and appearance

12	well structured	☆	☆	☆	☆	☆	Not well structured
13	friendly	☆	☆	☆	☆	☆	Not friendly
14	joyful	☆	☆	☆	☆	☆	sad
15	colorful	☆	☆	☆	☆	☆	simple
16	tidy	☆	☆	☆	☆	☆	untidy

4. Are you satisfied with the Anton App?

Yes ☐ No ☐

5. Please explain why you are satisfied or not satisfied with the app.

Figure 1. The created UX questionnaire (translated version)

In the beginning, the brainstorming session is based on an oral discussion, whereas later the pupils use a whiteboard to write down randomized words and phrases. In the end, the pupils decide to organize antonyms in categories. The workshop took place during school time and lasted 2 hours with the absence of teachers. During the workshop, the researcher provided a passive role and did not participate in the discussion. To avoid further influence through the researcher, the shown presentation excludes judgmental statements about the app. In case of a possible failure of the workshop process, several slides with potential words and synonyms were prepared for discussion and selection with the participants. Observation, as well as writing notes, are used to document the development process by the researcher. Cronbach´s Alpha as an index for scale reliability is used to assess the questionnaire [15]. Regarding the selection and participation of children, teachers were given an introduction to the research topic. Written consent by parents or legal guardians was essential to participate in this study. Moreover, all children gave oral consent for each activity.

Examining the construction process and the interactions of the pupils, some challenges and effects appeared that need to be addressed. The workshop format illustrates that the role of the researcher is to be a contact person for questions or problems that might arrive during the construction process. It seems as the pupils are hesitant in the beginning and not sure how to start the brainstorming session. To support the discussion session, the researcher asked about their feelings and impressions of the app while interacting with it. In the following hour, the workshop is being maintained by word suggestions and discussion of opposing words or phrases, item pair by item pair by all children. For example, there is a long debate about the opposite of the word "fun". In the end, the pupils decide on the word "serious". The pupils decided on an approach to collect as many words as possible to evaluate the app and debate the usefulness of the words.

It appears that overall not more than 20 antonyms are being reviewed. Regarding the scale, the pupils discussed several options and decide on a 5-point Likert scale with stars, as they argue that it might be easier to understand and looks more aesthetic than points. To create greater comprehensibility of the questionnaire, the children consider adding words like good, medium and bad on top of the answer categories. They notice that giving an answer and competing the questionnaire, based on the contrasting items, already shows a tendency towards a word and therefore decide against this idea. As a result, it is questionable if the pupils fully understand the concept of a rating scale. Simplicity is also one reason to order pairs into positive (left side) and negative (right side) on the questionnaire. To provide extensive feedback, two additional questions were added. It consists of one closed question and one free text field for written responses. The workshop ends with the organization of words into categories, which is initiated by one pupil. It is questionable whether the concept of the workshop design is fully understood by the children, as finding words to evaluate the app seemed to be a difficult task. Nonetheless, the participants understood the need to design and adapt a questionnaire based on children's competences, as the understandability for younger pupils was taken into account during the brainstorming session and discussion of useful words.

IV. FINDINGS & DISCUSSION

The following section presents the findings of the study for the workshop results and the newly developed user experience questionnaire designed by children.

A. *Comparison to the User Experience Questionnaire (UEQ)*

All in all, the UX Kids questionnaire contains 16 antonyms in 3 categories. It includes "learning development", which deals with the quality of the content, if the system motivates or if it is adequate for learning. The category "overall impression of the app" contains item pairs for functionality, efficiency, fun and entertainment. The third category is called "design and appearance" and contains 5 items of color design and purpose. Additionally, an overall evaluation with one closed question: "Are you satisfied with the app?" and one free-text field for further explanations was added. Interestingly, not only the word selection but also an appealing design of the questionnaire seemed to be important. In comparison to the UEQ [7], many differences can be identified: The UX questionnaires differ in length, the number of items, rating scale and the number of scales. The UX Kids questionnaire also includes an overall evaluation question as well as a qualitative free-text field option to give a detailed review of the learning app. Interestingly, both questionnaires evaluate UX based on pragmatic as well as hedonistic qualities of an interactive product. Therefore, children view not only design and aesthetics as important factors for evaluating a learning app, but also the quality of content, usability and functionality. In particular, the content of a system is typically not part of UX instruments.

The comparison shows that children can take the role of an "expert" to do user experience research. It shows that a participatory approach can support children as co-designers to conduct user-centered studies, as the result consists of similar assumptions of the concept of user experience.

B. *Evaluation of the UX Kids Questionnaire*

To analyze the performance of the newly developed UX instrument, it is applied in a user test study to evaluate the UX of the learning app with 230 pupils from grades 6 and 7 of a comprehensive school in Germany. During a playtime of 20 minutes, the pupils explored the app on mobile devices in groups of three or four children. Afterward, the participants were asked to fill out the questionnaire in order to evaluate the app. 207 children completed the questionnaire and gave useful feedback about their opinion and possible improvements. Table 1 shows the Cronbach´s Alpha values for the full questionnaire and all three scales. The statistical analysis demonstrates a Cronbach's Alpha of 0.88 for the newly developed questionnaire, which proves the high internal consistency of the scales [15].

TABLE I. CRONBACH´S ALPHA PER SCALE

Scale	α
Overall	0.88
Learning development	0.75
Overall impression of the app	0.80
Design and appearance	0.71

V. CONCLUSION AND FUTURE WORK

This paper investigated the use of participatory design to construct a UX questionnaire for and with children and teenagers based on participatory design and early user involvement. The workshop approach shows that with an appropriate introduction to the topic of UX and evaluation, participatory design is a valuable method to do user experience research with children. Due to children's different perceptions, abilities and use context of interactive products, methods need to be adapted to their needs. Within a collaborative brainstorming session, the target group is able to do identify words and item pairs to evaluate the learning app and discuss them. Based on this research, it can be concluded that quantifying the user experience of younger users is possible within a participatory design study. The questionnaire is suitable to be used with qualitative methods to measure the multidimensional construct of UX of a specific product.

Further research involves the evaluation of the UX Kids questionnaire in user studies with pupils from a comprehensive school in Germany to verify the reliability and validity of the questionnaire with a statistical analysis and also with different learning applications. More research into suitable methods for measuring children's user experience is needed, as the participatory design study revealed some difficulties in regard to UX research with children. In particular, quantitative UX methods for younger children aged between 12 old and younger need to be explored and validated. Further research should also go more deeply into other possibilities to measure UX quantitative or in mixed methods approaches.

REFERENCES

[1] DIN EN 9241 210, Ergonomics of human-system interaction - Part 210. Human-centered design for interactive systems. Berlin: Beuth, 2011.

[2] L. Hanna, D. Neapolitan, and K. Risden, "Evaluating computer game concepts with children" Proceedings of the conference on Interaction design and children, 2004, pp. 49-56, doi:10.1145/1017833.1017840.

[3] M. Hassenzahl, M. Burmester, and K. Koller, "AttrakDiff: A questionnaire for measuring hedonic and pragmatic qualities" Human and Computer. Interaction in Movement, 2003, pp. 187-196, doi:https://doi.org/10.1007/978-3-322-80058-9_19.

[4] L. Heine and D. Hörmeyer. *Lerne einfach mit Spaß für die Schule!* [in English: *Learn easily and with fun for school!*]. [Online]. Available from: https://anton.app/de/ 2020.01.27.

[5] A. Hinderks, M. Schrepp, M. Rauschenberger, S. Olschner, and J. Thomaschewski "Konstruktion eines Fragebogens für jugendliche zur Messung der User Experience [in English: Construction of a questionnaire for teenagers and young adults for measuring user experience]" Conference Proceedings of Usability Professionals, 2012, pp. 78-83.

[6] G. Lansdown, "Can you hear me? The right of young children to participate in decisions affecting them" Working paper 36. 2005, Bernhard van Leer Foundation, The Hague, The Netherlands.

[7] B. Laugwitz, B. Held, and M. Schrepp, "Construction and evaluation of a user experience questionnaire" The 4th Symposium of the Workgroup Human-Computer Interaction and Usability Engineering of the Austrian Computer Society, Nov. 2008, pp. 63-76, doi: 10.1007/978-3-540-89350-9_6.

[8] E. Law, V. Roto, A. Vermeeren, J. Kort, and M. Hassenzahl, "Towards a shared definition of user experience" Extended Abstracts on Human Factors in Computing Systems (CHI EA) ACM, 2008, pp. 2395–2398. doi:https://doi.org/10.1145/1358628.1358693.

[9] M. Minge, M. Thüring, I. Wagner, and C.V. Kuhr, "The meCUE Questionnaire. A modular tool for measuring User experience" The 7th Applied Human Factors and Ergonomics Society Conference, Advances in Ergonomics Modeling, Usability & Special Populations, 2016, pp. 115-128.

[10] J. Read. "Children as participants in design and evaluation" Interactions, vol. 22, 2015, pp. 64-66, doi:https://doi.org/10.1145/2735710.

[11] J. Read, P. Markopoulos, N. Parés, J. Hourcade, and A. Antle "Child computer interaction" Extended Abstracts on Human Factors in Computing Systems (CHI EA) ACM, April. 2008, pp. 2419-2422, doi:10.1145/1358628.1358697.

[12] M. Schrepp, A. Hinderks, and J. Thomaschewski, "Applying the user experience questionnaire (UEQ) in different evaluation scenarios" 3rd international Conference of Design, User Experience and Usability. Theories, Methods and Tools for Designing the User Experience, June 2014, pp. 383-392, doi: 10.1007/978-3-319-07668-3_37.

[13] H. Shier, "Pathways to participation: Openings, opportunities and obligations" *Children & Society*, vol. 15, no. 3, 2001, pp. 107-117.

[14] M. Thielsch and M. Moshagen, "Erfassung visueller Ästhetik mit dem VisAWI [in English: Capturing visual aesthetics with the VisAWI]" Conference Proceedings of Usability Professionals, 2011, pp. 260-265.

[15] K. Wright, "An Introduction to Cronbach's α: It's the GLM (Again)!"Annual meeting of Southwest Educational Research Association, Feb. 2013, doi:10.13140/2.1.1816.8328.

[16] B. Zaman, "Introducing a pairwise comparison scale for UX evaluations with preschoolers," Human-Computer Interaction – INTERACT. Berlin, Heidelberg, vol. LNCS 5727, pp. 634–637, 2009.

Enabling Expert Critique at Scale with Chatbots and Micro Guidance

Carlos Toxtli
West Virginia University
Morgantown, United States
email: carlos.toxtli@mail.wvu.edu

Saiph Savage
West Virginia University
Morgantown, United States
email: saiph.savage@mail.wvu.edu

***Abstract*—Critique is important to improve creative work and help learners of design to grow. The "gold standard" of critique involves in-person discussion with experts who provide feedback. However, scaling expert critique is difficult as experts are scarce, have limited time and privacy concerns. Online alternatives, such as forums, rarely facilitate specialized critique. To enable at scale access to expert critique, we present Micro Apprenticeship Through Tutorials (MATT), a chatbot that micro-guides experts to critique in short bursts of time. This empowers more experts to critique as the activity becomes more accessible to their busy schedules. MATT's "bot aspect" also provides a mediated form of communication between experts and learners, helping to address experts' privacy concerns. Additionally, MATT helps to delegate critique work to experts in a way that can match experts' and learners' time constraints. We conduct a field experiment comparing MATT to current alternatives. We find that, contrary to other approaches, MATT's conversational micro-guidance facilitates leading a large number of experts to critique learners' creative work. We conclude by providing data-backed design implications to empower and facilitate at scale collaborations between experts and learners.**

Keywords–chatbot; mediated communication; feedback; experts.

I. INTRODUCTION

Feedback is essential to creative work. Creators can receive many kinds of feedback for their work, from informal reactions/kudos to more detailed, critical analyses. *Critique* is the most prestigious type of feedback a creator can receive because this feedback can truly help the person to improve their work. Critique is characterized by (1) identifying decisions made in the creative piece being analyzed; (2) relating those decisions to best practices; (3) and then describing how and why the decisions made support (or not) the best practices [1]. Critique is especially enhanced when done by experts who can more easily discuss the state of the art and connect the work to impactful societal outcomes [2][3].

Critique directly enhances creative work, and also helps the creators to learn new techniques and methods [4]. Critique is starting to be considered one of the most effective learning strategies [5].

In Section 2, we present how experts have historically provided critique to creative work within physical studios where experts were directly collocated with creators [6], individuals whom experts had usually never met before. Being physically together in a space with strangers helped experts to provide structured, spontaneous, open feedback, and facilitated an efficient exchange of information [7]. However, getting experts and creators together at the same time in one same physical space is hard [8]. Experts generally have limited time, complex schedules, and are distributed across the globe [9].

To overcome these difficulties, online platforms have emerged to support and act as a companion to physical studios [1]. These platforms aim to facilitate communication between experts and creators (who, in these settings, are considered to be "learners" due to the educational benefits associated with receiving critique). Such systems, however, assume that experts and learners have met previously offline at a design studio [10]. Consequently, these platforms fail at connecting individuals who have never physically attended a design studio, a space relatively foreign to most experts [11]. As a result, such platforms usually have a limited number of experts.

There are, however, many other tools that do facilitate interactions between experts and learners who have never met offline, e.g., online forums like Reddit. Here, learners can post photos/videos of their creative work; and then their peers or experts provide feedback to the creative artifacts [12].

However, experts on online forums generally get stuck in understanding what the creator tried to make. As a result, expert critique is rare [13][14]. Another problem is that experts usually have concerns about providing feedback on forums [1] and thus prefer not to participate in the activity due to fears of saying something wrong and damaging their reputation [15]. Reputation is a longitudinal social evaluator about a person's actions and can be used as a measure of trustworthiness [16]. Performing in a manner that is unexpected can damage an individual's reputation as well as the organization that the individual represents [17]. Critiquing the work of novices can become a risky activity for experts because they might not have experience interacting with learners and could accidentally do or say things outside the norms, damaging their reputation [18].

Given the difficulties of coordinating experts online, recent research [19] has focused on obtaining critique from nonexperts, e.g., crowd-workers. However, individuals also use critique to learn about best practices, new topics, and even to network [1], activities which crowd workers can rarely complete. Expert critique is, therefore, still needed and should be something that researchers aim to facilitate, especially at scale, to benefit and empower more learners.

To enable learners at scale access to expert critique, we introduce, in Section 3, MATT (Micro Apprenticeship Through Tutorials), a chatbot that guides experts to critique creative work, especially of novices starting to create designs. Figure 1 presents an overview of MATT. In a conversational way, MATT guides experts to critique learners' work. MATT's guidance helps experts to rapidly understand what the learner tried to make. This empowers experts to be able to focus more on critiquing the work instead of interpreting it.

MATT breaks down its guidance into a set of micro tasks embedded in the conversation it has with experts. These micro-tasks facilitate the participation of more experts as they do not have to invest a large portion of their day in the activity. Experts, instead, are empowered to provide feedback throughout their spare time. Each micro-task asks experts to provide feedback on a particular aspect of the design, always tying it back to best practices. By guiding experts to focus on specific design elements, MATT ensures quality feedback resembling a critique.

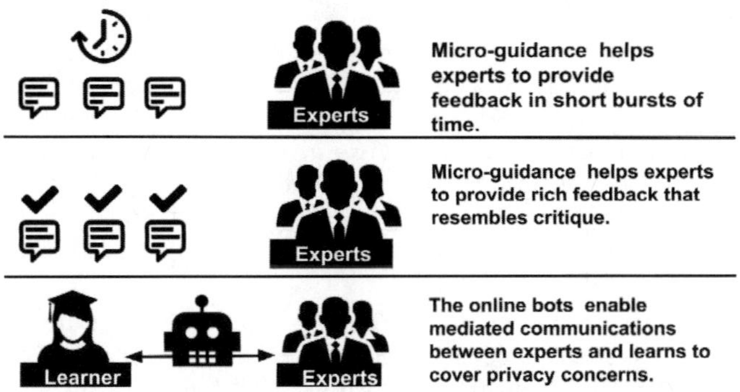

Figure 1. MATT integrates micro-guidance and mediated communication to enable experts to critique online.

It is important to note that most related platforms tend to assume that experts will work under prolonged and focused runs [20][21]. One of our design challenges is thus to create small tasks that experts can do in short bursts of time throughout their day. Micro-tasking also becomes important because, in our design, we consider that experts are volunteering their time and knowledge (prior work has identified that experts are more likely to participate in such activities if they are intrinsically motivated [22]; therefore, we limited providing them with monetary rewards and assumed they would volunteer their time). Given this setting, it becomes important not to burden experts. Through MATT, we broaden the design space of expert/learner systems to include the volunteer participation of specialists without requiring a large commitment. This enables providing specialized critique to a larger and broader number of learners.

Another of our design challenges is that experts can feel "insulted" from receiving guidance [23] (especially as they are allegedly the most knowledgeable in the area and they are volunteering in the activity). As a result, experts could be reluctant to follow directions on how they should critique. It is thus necessary to design guidance mechanisms that do not feel too imposing. We explore how such guidance can be designed via chatbots, which can provide structure without it feeling too commanding [24].

Our chatbot also acts as a proxy between experts and learners: learners first share with MATT their work; MATT then distributes the work to experts who are guided to critique the piece. Next, MATT presents to learners the feedback that experts produced to help them improve. By creating mediated communication between experts and learners, MATT helps to address experts' privacy concerns. Notice that privacy is a natural concern since any information sent by learners or experts (who many times are public figures) is susceptible to misuse when shared with strangers. MATT addresses this by providing a mediated communication channel via a chatbot.

In Section 4, we conducted a field deployment with MATT, where it coordinated a crowd of experts to critique the creative work of a large number of learners, which included posters, logos, and t-shirt designs. Through our study, we find that utilizing chatbots with micro-guidance empowers experts to provide feedback that approximates the gold standards of critique more closely. We finish by discussing in Section 5 the design implications of our work.

II. RELATED WORK

The design of MATT is based on two main areas: (1) platforms for generating critique; and (2) platforms for eliciting specialized information from people online.

A. Platforms for Generating Critique. For many disciplines, participating in the review of creative work is considered essential to develop skills in that area [1]. Many consider that being able to communicate with experts and use their feedback to improve is just as important as having particular knowledge and skills [25]. While the goal of critique varies across areas, its usefulness as an educational tool is consistent [26].

Related work has explored generating critique within online environments. However, given that even online, it is difficult to coordinate experts [27]-[29], most related work uses crowd workers to provide feedback to learners [30][31]. While learners do appear to value such feedback as it has helped them to make substantial adjustments to their work [32], crowd workers have still not been able to match the range and depth of expert feedback [19]; even when having access to more direction and examples of expert type critique [33]. We should, therefore, not see feedback from crowd workers as a replacement to expert feedback, but rather a supplement. Focusing on the educational aspect that expert critique provides to learners, this paper explores the potential of orchestrating specialists to critique the creative work of learners at scale.

Similar to a design studio where experts volunteer their time, MATT assumes that experts are working pro-bono. This design facilitates providing access to expert knowledge to a broader range of learners, especially those from marginalized communities. This is not an eccentric idea, given that many experts have an interest in social good [34], especially if it is part of a revolutionary program [22].

However, experts usually lack the time necessary to identify how to best help others [35]; it can be especially time consuming to find volunteering opportunities that effectively utilize their specialization. In this sense, MATT facilitates the volunteering process of experts by directly dispatching to them micro-volunteering opportunities that utilize their expertise.

B. Eliciting Specialized Information from People Online. Recently, we have seen the emergence of systems that ask people online to share specialized and specific information to benefit strangers [36]. Several human computation workflows have successfully driven strangers to share their knowledge to help others learn [37]. These studies have found that online strangers can indeed provide quality information [38], even when asked by bots [39].

Researchers have also started to investigate the type of feedback that is possible to manually obtain from different online sites, especially crowd markets, social networks, and forums [40]. The problem, however, is that in these platforms, much time is spent interpreting what the learner produced [14].

Figure 2. Overview of MATT's workflow: 1.- Learners submits to MATT their creative work. 2.- MATT finds an expert, sends the work to the expert, who is guided to review and provide micro-feedback approximating critique about the work. 3.- MATT then presents the micro-feedback from the expert to the learners who can use it to improve their work.

We motivate the design of MATT on some of the key findings of this previous research: it is possible to drive online strangers to provide useful information [38][40], even when asked by bots [39]. We hypothesize that if we integrate guidance, we could orchestrate experts to effectively critique the creative work of learners they have never met before at scale.

III. MATT

MATT is a chatbot that: (1) collects creative work from learners; (2) presents the creative work to experts and guides them to critique the work; and (3) then gives the critique back to learners to help them improve. Figure 2 presents an overview of how MATT functions.

To accomplish these three steps, MATT consists of two main components: 1) the "Learner Helper" module that collects learners' creative work, distributes the work to experts and then shares experts' feedback to learners; 2) " Expert Micro-Guidance" module that orchestrates experts to volunteer in short bursts of time quality micro-feedback that resembles online critique to help learners at scale.

A. Learner Helper Module

The goal of the Learner Helper component is threefold: 1) allow learners to submit their creative work easily; 2) find experts who can critique their work; 3) present back to the learner the feedback from experts. Figure 2 presents an overview of this workflow. Notice that the Learner-Helper acts as a proxy between learners and experts to address the privacy concerns of experts. Having mediated communication can also make it less awkward for an expert to reject reviewing a piece of work or say that they will review it once they are free. The learner would never know about the incident, but rather only MATT would be informed and would just search for another expert who can volunteer.

While there are many possible interfaces that could act as proxies between learners and experts, we consider a design that bootstraps on social media as it helps both learners and experts to easily share and receive critique from anywhere without needing to download or learn how to use new tools. Working on social media also facilitates finding people with particular specializations who can produce more relevant critiques [41], e.g., MATT can identify and recruit experts in "website design" based on the job title they present on their social media profile.

Our current design, therefore, considers that both learners and experts use social media, and we can utilize chatbots to act as proxies to connect these parties. We especially work within the Facebook messenger. Notice also that the design of MATT's Learner Helper module is based on intelligent conversational tutoring systems [42], which have shown to be effective for assisting learners.

B. Expert Micro-Guidance Module

MATT's Expert Micro-Guidance module focuses on orchestrating experts to produce, in short bursts of time, quality feedback that resembles critique. MATT, a chatbot on Facebook messenger, displays the learner's work to the expert and then asks the expert to complete small micro-tasks related to critiquing the learner's creative piece. The micro-tasks aim to guide experts to provide all the different types of feedback involved in a critique (especially identifying decisions the creators made in their design, and what are the best practices in each of the cases.) An example of these micro-tasks is to ask experts to provide feedback on the type of color used in the design and how it might or might not relate to best practices. Another similar micro-task is to ask an expert to "Provide feedback about the font type and size used, and how it relates (or not) to best practices."

The module has four features to enable this interaction.

1) Critique in Short Bursts of Time: Experts' time is limited, and experts also generally lack knowledge of how to effectively produce online critiques [35][43]. MATT tackles this problem by guiding experts to provide critique to creative work in short bursts of time by leveraging task decomposition from crowdsourcing. Crowdsourcing has studied how long and complex work can be done via micro-tasks that are quick to finish. A long review and analysis of a piece of work can also be finished in small steps using the same process. MATT changes the nature of online critique by enabling experts to do it in small bursts of time. This design helps experts to take advantage of the time that might otherwise be wasted. To guide experts, MATT asks them a set of questions related to their perspectives and analysis of the creative work. MATT is designed to help experts also recall points they had covered in their feedback previously to aid learners' growth. Each of MATT's question can be seen as a type of micro-task. These questions are based on prior work [1] that has defined guidelines or best practices to critique a piece of work. MATT empowers experts to critique in short bursts of time and at any point in time.

2) Critique Anywhere: MATT communicates via Facebook Messenger with experts. This design facilitates portability, and on-the-go experiences as experts can provide feedback wherever they use Facebook messenger, which can be on their desktop, their mobile device, or both. Experts can potentially provide feedback from anywhere, e.g., while waiting in line or on a shuttle.

We believe that these two functions enable more experts to participate in online critique, as they no longer have to invest consecutive hours at a physical desk reviewing work [44].

3) Privacy: MATT's mediated form of communication enables experts to remain anonymous to learners, which facilitates bringing experts' privacy. Our design builds upon privacy research that showcases that with anonymity, higher quality feedback is produced [45]. Our goal is that through MATT's mediated form of communication, experts will be more open and critical in their feedback, leading them to more deeply analyze creative pieces and consequently offering better learning opportunities to creators.

4) Conversational: MATT guides experts to produce critique within a conversational setting. We opted to use chatbots to guide experts because previous work had identified that they were viable sources for guiding strangers to provide specialized information [36] or to volunteer for a cause [46]. The conversational aspect of MATT might also help experts not to feel that MATT's guidance is too dictatorial. While previous work had identified that having chats incorporated into MOOCs did not necessarily increase student engagement [47], we adopt chat-based interfaces because they can help to create more "casual" environments that do not feel too "authoritarian" [48], which is important when working with experts who might feel they have the best knowledge and know-how of how to interact and provide feedback to novices.

IV. FIELD DEPLOYMENT

This paper hypothesizes that we can lead real-world experts to critique online by utilizing online mediated communication in the form of chatbots combined with micro-guidance. Our evaluation focuses on this claim: In the real-world, do chatbots micro-guiding experts enable a better approximation of the gold standard of studio design feedback? To respond to this question we conduct a real-world deployment of our tool and compare the feedback experts generated on MATT to two alternative interfaces: 1) chatbot lacking micro-guidance, i.e., a chatbot that simply asked experts to critique a piece of creative work without prompting experts on how to critique the piece; 2) online forum (we study online forums as they are a mediated communication channel that experts typically use to provide feedback [49]. Figure 3 presents an overview of these two interfaces and MATT.

Experts used either MATT or one of these two interfaces to provide feedback to learners. Learners were asked to create designs for real-world non-profits. We worked with non-profits because we were interested in having real-world usages of our tool, and this is one of the most common spaces where novice designers start to operate to build their portfolio [50]. Each learner produced one design, and each expert reviewed two designs from two different learners. Figure 4 presents examples of learners' work.

We recruited real word learners and experts using social media. To recruit learners, we posted on Facebook groups related to learning design, inviting people to our live deployment. Learners were offered the opportunity to potentially use new interfaces and obtain feedback from experts on their designs. To recruit experts, we used LinkedIn's search to find and invite individuals who stated they worked in design-related areas and identified themselves as experts. We recruited 153 learners and 76 experts. Each of our three interfaces was used by a total of 51 learners and 25 experts.

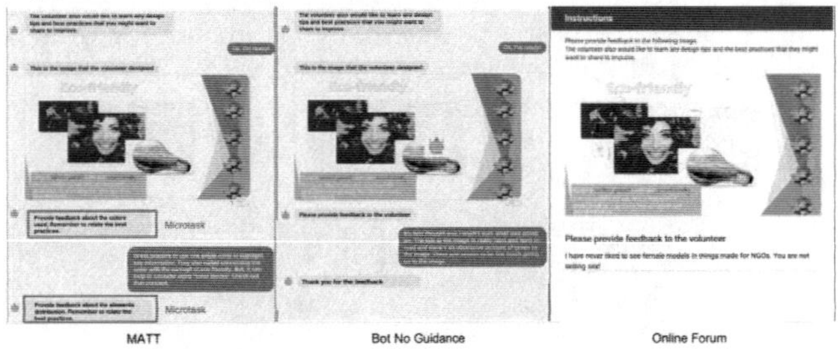

Figure 3. Feedback interfaces: 1) MATT, 2) Bot No-Guidance 3) Online Forum.

A. Categorizing Experts' Feedback

We were interested in understanding the type of feedback that experts in our real-world deployment generated. Our hypothesis was that experts using MATT would produce the most critiques. For this purpose, after experts provided feedback to learners' designs, we categorized their feedback according to the categories in the Feedback Typology of [1]. We recruited three college educated Upworkers [51] and asked them to categorize experts' feedback into either: *"reactive,"*, *"direction,"*, or *"critique"*, i.e., the feedback categories in the typology that [1] identified. We define each category in detail below.

Reactive Category: emotional or visceral feedback that does not provide information on how to improve the work. Examples: "That's wonderful! Great work!" or "Horrible!".

Direction Category: In this form of feedback, the individuals providing the feedback try to bring the design more in line with their own expectations of what the solution should be. The feedback provides direction but no reasoning behind it. Examples: "I would have..." or "I wish...".

Critique Category: This feedback is considered to be the gold standard of design studios as it helps learners to improve their work and learn new techniques along the way. This type of feedback focuses on identifying decisions made in the creative work, relating that decision to a best practice, and then describing how and why the decision made supports or does not support the best practices [3].

Two coders classified each of the feedback messages from experts into the category that represented the message the most (either critique, reactive, or direction). The two coders agreed on the classification of 90.1% of all the feedback produced by experts (Cohen's kappa =.89: Strong agreement). We then asked a third coder to act as a tiebreaker in cases of disagreement.

B. Results

Figure 5 presents the amount and type of feedback that experts generated in our real-world deployment with each interface. We observe that when using online forums and the chatbot without guidance, experts produced primarily reactive feedback. This result is in line with previous work that identified that experts online usually get stuck in interpreting the creative work by spending time trying to figure out what the goal of the designer was and consequently provide less critique [14][52]. We observe from Figure 5 that MATT was the interface that leads experts to critique the most in the real-world.

Figure 4. Examples of the produced creative work.

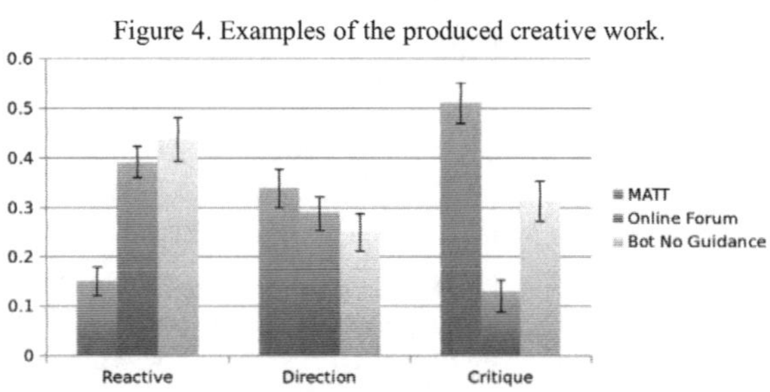

Figure 5. Overview of the type of feedback experts generated. Overall, experts using MATT generated the most critiques.

Given that we are primarily interested in whether MATT increases the amount of critique that a learner receives, we conducted a logistic regression predicting the likelihood that a piece of feedback would be classified as critique given its source (i.e., either from the MATT interface, Bot without Guidance interface, or the Online Forum). The logistic regression model showed that a piece of feedback was significantly more likely to be classified as critique when it came from MATT, compared to feedback from the online forum condition

(B=1.12, z=4.96, $p < .01$) or the Bot No Guidance condition (B=0.83, z=3.31, $p < .01$). The overall model was a statistically significant fit to the data, Likelihood Ratio Test χ^2 (2) = 26.33, $p < .01$.

We were also interested in understanding experts' perceptions of the interfaces. It could be that although MATT lead experts to critique more, experts got annoyed with MATT "bossing" them around. We had a post-survey that asked experts about their experiences with MATT and the alternative interfaces. Experts first provided their impressions via five level Likert questions and open responses.

Overall, experts enjoyed moderately the chatbot interfaces (mean=4.85 for MATT and for the chatbot without guidance). The forum interface was also enjoyed, but slightly less (mean=4.77). Experts considered all interfaces to be moderately easy to use (mean=4.8). Open-ended responses reinforced that experts felt that MATT helped them to produce meaningful feedback by directing the communication into what mattered: *"...Chatbots can direct communication efficiently which you don't really get with other technology [...] Suppose you want some information but are accidentally putting off the topic. The chatbot can steer you..."*

None of our experts expressed that MATT was too imposing. On the contrary, they felt that it presented a "sequential and clean" interface. Some experts expressed that the automated aspect of MATT made its guidance not feel too "bossy" because there was nothing personal about it. It was "just" a machine: *"Machines don't have feeling at all, so also nothing to feel on my side."* MATT's automation also helped experts to accept their guidance, as they felt that machines were made to help humans in their daily work. Thus, if a machine was trying to guide them, it must be for something beneficial: *They [machines] are just made to make human work easier [...] I felt the bot was steering towards meaningful communication. Just a good way to communicate..."*

Experts also felt that MATT addressed their privacy concerns (median = 5). Some seemed to especially like the format that MATT had for interacting with learners as they could help others while maintaining their privacy: *"I will get no benefits for not working anonymously. I don't want to be exposed to strangers... I just want to help. That's it...Chances of becoming more famous from doing this are too low to risk exposing my personnel details to strangers [...] I am completely satisfied with the bot [MATT], I am just providing feedback and not mentioning my personal information. So, providing feedback won't affect my privacy..."*

MATT's design also helped experts to not feel restricted in the feedback they shared. As one participant mentioned: *"If other people knew who I was by name, they might ask me later why I answered the way I did or tell other co-workers what I said or did here. I'd have to then explain myself."* Similar to conversing with "strangers at a bar," this type of mediated communication likely facilitates being more open.

However, some experts noted that there were instances where they would like to possibly meet with learners and further help them in their career growth (if the learner was willing). Experts' biggest requests for improving MATT involved adding different levels of privacy (e.g., being able to share where they worked with learners while keeping other information confidential). In the future, we will explore having more flexible privacy configurations.

Experts also mentioned that they would have liked to have a "better mental model" of the questions that MATT would ask them. In the future we will explore how we can better convene to experts the questions that MATT plans on covering. Perhaps here it is a matter of designing better conversations for MATT, so the questions feel more natural, and participants are not wondering about what will be asked next.

V. Discussion

In our real-world deployment of MATT, hundreds of learners and experts collaborated to produce creative work and share critique. Here, we reflect on open challenges and opportunities for systems that orchestrate experts to help learners, in particular, to provide useful feedback.

An interesting implication from our study is that interactive and guided mediated communication (i.e., MATT) was the most helpful in leading experts to critique. This result might be arising because the interactive aspect of MATT might have led experts to feel that they are working in a more conversational environment. Research has shown that "conversations" are an effective method to enhance learning [53]. It might be that this type of medium is also optimal for experts to express themselves and learn how to critique, and hence why MATT was the most optimal.

From our field deployment, we also observed that experts were empowered to provide quality feedback when working within a conversational type channel and when they focused their attention on specific features of the creative work (MATT's questions to experts were aimed at analyzing particular aspects of learners' work). We speculate that these conditions approximate the optimal conditions for critique that experts set for themselves in the design studio. Physical design studios facilitate *focus* (experts generally work on only one task at a time, inspecting one particular feature each time). Guided mediated communication through chatbots was also likely effective because it mitigated experts' time and task distribution concerns. Experts' were able to do the tasks in the time frame that they decided. Experts also had expectations of bots that seemed to facilitate the interactions. Some experts expressed how bots were there to help, and they were, therefore, willing to listen to the automated agent.

In our long-term vision of MATT, experts are given a platform where they can volunteer to share their knowledge in short bursts of time to support the learning process of any large crowd. We believe that it may be possible to lead experts to provide useful micro-feedback beyond our deployment of online critique. Opportunities include obtaining on-demand feedback for emergency response, accessibility, scientific discovery, citizen science, and a variety of other areas.

In MATT's design, the motivation of learners is clear: they gain support to improve their creative work. The incentives from experts are not as clear. Are experts motivated in providing feedback that impacts and helps the growth of other individuals or it simply to help in the creation of interesting creative work? Moving forward, we would like to explore the best way to motivate the continuous micro-participation of experts. This is especially important as having a large network of reliable experts can facilitate learning about any concept or topic. We believe there are important design opportunities in thinking about how to best match experts' intrinsic motivations with micro-volunteering opportunities and covering experts' privacy concerns.

A. Limitations

The insights from this work are limited by the methodology and population we studied. While our deployment allowed us to start to understand how experts engaged with systems like MATT, where a bot asks them to provide feedback to others, we cannot extrapolate to how experts would respond if this approach gained popularity and was widely used. In such a case, it might be relevant for these approaches to consider not pinging experts so frequently to avoid being ignored or labeled as spam. Additionally, while we recruited real-world experts and all creative work produced by learners resembled real-world creative projects, our results might not yet generalize to populations at large. Further analysis is needed to understand how systems that leverage experts and chatbots play out in helping learners to improve their work in different areas. Experiments that compare the type of feedback that experts generate for different areas would help quantify more broadly the effectiveness of using chatbots to guide expert critique. Future experiments that control for the social media platform or online ecosystem could be conducted to further understand what type of platform might facilitate accessing expert knowledge for on-demand feedback. Similar to [38][39], the goal of this paper was to shed light on how micro-guidance embedded in chatbots facilitated expert critique. Future work could conduct longitudinal studies and engage in in-depth interviews with experts to understand their motivations and perspectives of these types of systems and approaches. Future work could also explore how learners react and benefit from the feedback that experts provide with MATT as well as their overall impressions of such technology. Some interesting questions for future work to explore with learners: what type of skills does MATT help learners to improve? Does MATT help learners to make better design decisions after feedback (in what way)? Are learners improving because they follow experts' advice (in which case they are not really learning a skill, but rather using MATT to get support with their performance)? Do learners' career prospects improve in some measurable way?

VI. Conclusion and Future Work

In this paper, we introduced MATT, a chatbot that guides experts to critique the creative work of learners at scale. MATT embodies the vision that chatbots facilitate orchestrating experts to critique while addressing experts' privacy concerns and without creating an imposing environment on specialists. A field deployment provided evidence that MATT could guide experts to critique the creative work of hundreds of learners.

Future work lies in three main areas. First, further analysis is needed on best methods to combine chatbots and experts to improve the engagement of learners' long term, as well as workflows that enable crowds of learners and experts to best benefit from systems like MATT. Second, it will be important to devise mechanisms that can motivate experts to continuously micro-volunteer critique to learners. Third, in the long run, it will be important to design how experts and chatbots could help learners for more complex tasks. Experts are generally busy and consequently cannot do community work that is too time-consuming or demanding. This means that specialized social good work is generally not completed as the volunteers who do have the time lack the needed knowledge to complete the work [54]. We envision MATT's potential for combining crowds of experts, chatbots, and learners to complete complex volunteer work and create impactful change. In the future, we also plan to explore the impact of MATT on the type of creative work that learners produce and how they improve their work.

REFERENCES

[1] D. P. Dannels and K. N. Martin, "Critiquing critiques: A genre analysis of feedback across novice to expert design studios," Journal of Business and Technical Communication, vol. 22, no. 2, 2008, pp. 135–159.

[2] G. Fischer, K. Nakakoji, J. Ostwald, G. Stahl, and T. Sumner, "Embedding critics in design environments," The knowledge engineering review, vol. 8, no. 4, 1993, pp. 285–307.

[3] K. Luther et al., "Structuring, aggregating, and evaluating crowdsourced design critique," in Proceedings of the 18th ACM Conference on Computer Supported Cooperative Work & Social Computing. ACM, 2015, pp. 473–485.

[4] M. Fasli and B. Hassanpour, "Rotational critique system as a method of culture change in an architecture design studio: urban design studio as case study," Innovations in Education and Teaching International, vol. 54, no. 3, 2017, pp. 194–205.

[5] J. Corbin and A. Strauss, "Basics of qualitative research: Techniques and procedures for developing grounded theory," Sage Publications, 2008.

[6] K. H. Anthony, "Design juries on trial: The renaissance of the design studio," Van Nostrand Reinhold, 1991.

[7] S. Kiesler and J. N. Cummings, "What do we know about proximity and distance in work groups? a legacy of research," Distributed work, vol. 1, 2002, pp. 57–80.

[8] M. R. Louis, B. Z. Posner, and G. N. Powell, "The availability and helpfulness of socialization practices," Personnel Psychology, vol. 36, no. 4, 1983, pp. 857–866.

[9] J. Campbell et al., "Thousands of positive reviews: Distributed mentoring in online fan communities," in Proceedings of the 19th ACM Conference on Computer-Supported Cooperative Work & Social Computing. ACM, 2016, pp. 691–704.

[10] M. W. Easterday, D. Rees Lewis, C. Fitzpatrick, and E. M. Gerber, "Computer supported novice group critique," in Proceedings of the 2014 conference on Designing interactive systems. ACM, 2014, pp. 405– 414.

[11] L. D. Setlock, S. R. Fussell, and C. Neuwirth, "Taking it out of context: collaborating within and across cultures in face-to-face settings and via instant messaging," in Proceedings of the 2004 ACM conference on Computer supported cooperative work. ACM, 2004, pp. 604–613.

[12] J. S. Brown, "The social life of learning: How can continuing education be reconfigured in the future?" Continuing Higher Education Review, vol. 66, 2002, pp. 50–69.

[13] K. Luther and A. Bruckman, "Leadership in online creative collaboration," in Proceedings of the 2008 ACM conference on Computer supported cooperative work. ACM, 2008, pp. 343–352.

[14] Y. Kou and C. Gray, "Supporting distributed critique through interpretation and sense-making in an online creative community," PACMHCI, 2017.

[15] A. Xu and B. Bailey, "What do you think?: a case study of benefit, expectation, and interaction in a large online critique community," in Proceedings of the ACM 2012 conference on Computer Supported Cooperative Work. ACM, 2012, pp. 295–304.

[16] M. Anwar and J. Greer, "Reputation management in privacy-enhanced e-learning," in Proceedings of the 3rd Annual Scientific Conference of the LORNET Research Network (I2LOR-06), Montreal, Canada, 2006.

[17] T. Casserley and D. Megginson, Learning from burnout: Developing sustainable leaders and avoiding career derailment. Routledge, 2009.

[18] M. Rhee and M. E. Valdez, "Contextual factors surrounding reputation damage with potential implications for reputation repair," Academy of Management Review, vol. 34, no. 1, 2009, pp. 146–168.

[19] A. Xu, H. Rao, S. P. Dow, and B. P. Bailey, "A classroom study of using crowd feedback in the iterative design process," in Proceedings of the 18th ACM conference on computer supported cooperative work & social computing. ACM, 2015, pp. 1637–1648.

[20] H.-M. Lee, J. Long, and M. R. Mehta, "Designing an e-mentoring application for Facebook," in Proceedings of the 49th SIGMIS Annual Conference on Computer Personnel Research, ser. SIGMIS-CPR '11. New York, NY, USA: ACM, 2011, pp. 58–61. [Online]. Available: http://doi.acm.org/10.1145/1982143.1982175

[21] C. Toxtli, A. Monroy-Hernandez, and J. Cranshaw, "Understanding´ chatbot-mediated task management," in Proceedings of the 2018 CHI conference on human factors in computing systems, 2018, pp. 1–6.

[22] D. A. Joyner, "Scaling expert feedback: Two case studies," in Proceedings of the Fourth (2017) ACM Conference on Learning@ Scale. ACM, 2017, pp. 71–80.

[23] P. A. Kohler-Evans, "Co-teaching: How to make this marriage work in front ofthe kids," Education, vol. 127, no. 2, 2006, pp. 260–264.

[24] C. Beaumont, "Beyond e-learning: an intelligent pedagogical agent to guide students in problem-based learning," Ph.D. dissertation, University of Liverpool, 2012.

[25] K. Reily, P. L. Finnerty, and L. Terveen, "Two peers are better than one: aggregating peer reviews for computing assignments is surprisingly accurate," in Proceedings of the ACM 2009 international conference on Supporting group work. ACM, 2009, pp. 115–124.

[26] T. Barrett, "A comparison of the goals of studio professors conducting critiques and art education goals for teaching criticism," Studies in art education, vol. 30, no. 1, 1988, pp. 22–27.

[27] E. Foong, D. Gergle, and E. M. Gerber, "Novice and expert sensemaking of crowdsourced design feedback," Proc. ACM Hum.Comput. Interact., vol. 1, no. CSCW, Dec. 2017, pp. 45:1–45:18. [Online]. Available: http://doi.acm.org/10.1145/3134680

[28] D. Retelny et al., "Expert crowdsourcing with flash teams," in Proceedings of the 27th annual ACM symposium on User interface software and technology. ACM, 2014, pp. 75–85.

[29] R. Vaish, K. Wyngarden, J. Chen, B. Cheung, and M. S. Bernstein, "Twitch crowdsourcing: crowd contributions in short bursts of time," in Proceedings of the 32nd annual ACM conference on Human factors in computing systems. ACM, 2014, pp. 3645–3654.

[30] A. Xu, S.-W. Huang, and B. Bailey, "Voyant: Generating structured feedback on visual designs using a crowd of non-experts," in Proceedings of the 17th ACM Conference on Computer Supported Cooperative Work & Social Computing, ser. CSCW '14. New York, NY, USA: ACM, 2014, pp. 1433–1444. [Online]. Available: http://doi.acm.org/10.1145/2531602.2531604

[31] A. Xu and B. Bailey, "What do you think?: A case study of benefit, expectation, and interaction in a large online critique community," in Proceedings of the ACM 2012 Conference on Computer Supported Cooperative Work, ser. CSCW '12. New York, NY, USA: ACM, 2012, pp. 295–304. [Online]. Available: http://doi.acm.org/10.1145/2145204.2145252

[32] K. Luther et al., "Structuring, aggregating, and evaluating crowdsourced design critique," in Proceedings of the 18th ACM Conference on Computer Supported Cooperative Work & Social Computing, ser. CSCW '15. New York, NY, USA: ACM, 2015, pp. 473–485. [Online]. Available: http://doi.acm.org/10.1145/2675133.2675283

[33] M. D. Greenberg, M. W. Easterday, and E. M. Gerber, "Critiki: A scaffolded approach to gathering design feedback from paid crowdworkers," in Proceedings of the 2015 ACM SIGCHI Conference on Creativity and Cognition. ACM, 2015, pp. 235–244.

[34] H. Bussell and D. Forbes, "Understanding the volunteer market: The what, where, who and why of volunteering," International Journal of Nonprofit and Voluntary Sector Marketing, vol. 7, no. 3, 2002, pp. 244–257.

[35] E. Brady, M. R. Morris, and J. P. Bigham, "Social microvolunteering: Donating access to your friends for charitable microwork," in Second AAAI Conference on Human Computation and Crowdsourcing, 2014.

[36] J. Nichols and J.-H. Kang, "Asking questions of targeted strangers on social networks," in Proceedings of the ACM 2012 conference on Computer Supported Cooperative Work. ACM, 2012, pp. 999–1002.

[37] S. Weir, J. Kim, K. Z. Gajos, and R. C. Miller, "Learnersourcing subgoal labels for how-to videos," in Proceedings of the 18th ACM Conference on Computer Supported Cooperative Work & Social Computing, ser. CSCW '15. New York, NY, USA: ACM, 2015, pp. 405–416. [Online]. Available: http://doi.acm.org/10.1145/2675133.2675219

[38] J. Nichols, M. Zhou, H. Yang, J.-H. Kang, and X. H. Sun, "Analyzing the quality of information solicited from targeted strangers on social media," in Proceedings of the 2013 conference on Computer supported cooperative work. ACM, 2013, pp. 967–976.

[39] S. Savage, A. Monroy-Hernandez, and T. Hollerer, "Botivist: Calling volunteers to action using online bots," arXiv preprint arXiv:1509.06026, 2015.

[40] Y.-C. G. Yen, S. P. Dow, E. Gerber, and B. P. Bailey, "Social network, web forum, or task market?: Comparing different crowd genres for design feedback exchange," in Proceedings of the 2016 ACM Conference on Designing Interactive Systems. ACM, 2016, pp. 773–784.

[41] C. Grevet and E. Gilbert, "Piggyback prototyping: Using existing, largescale social computing systems to prototype new ones," in Proceedings of the 33rd Annual ACM Conference on Human Factors in Computing Systems. ACM, 2015, pp. 4047–4056.

[42] V. Rus, D. Stefanescu, N. Niraula, and A. C. Graesser, "Deeptutor: Towards macro-and micro-adaptive conversational intelligent tutoring at scale," in Proceedings of the first ACM conference on Learning@ scale conference. ACM, 2014, pp. 209–210.

[43] J. Sch et al., "A survey on volunteer management systems," in 2016 49th Hawaii International Conference on System Sciences (HICSS). IEEE, 2016, pp. 767–776.

[44] J. R. Kogan, "How to evaluate and give feedback," in The Academic Medicine Handbook. Springer, 2013, pp. 91–101.

[45] R. Lu and L. Bol, "A comparison of anonymous versus identifiable epeer review on college student writing performance and the extent of critical feedback," Journal of Interactive Online Learning, vol. 6, no. 2, 2007, pp. 100–115.

[46] S. Savage, A. Monroy-Hernandez, and T. Hollerer, "Botivist: Calling volunteers to action using online bots," in Proceedings of the 19th ACM Conference on Computer-Supported Cooperative Work & Social Computing. ACM, 2016, pp. 813–822.

[47] D. Coetzee, A. Fox, M. A. Hearst, and B. Hartmann, "Chatrooms in moocs: all talk and no action," in Proceedings of the first ACM conference on Learning@ scale conference. ACM, 2014, pp. 127–136.

[48] G. Ball and J. Breese, "Emotion and personality in a conversational agent," Embodied conversational agents, 2000, pp. 189–219.

[49] J. Luca and C. McLoughlin, "Using online forums to support a community of learning," in EdMedia: World Conference on Educational Media and Technology. Association for the Advancement of Computing in Education (AACE), 2004, pp. 1468–1474.

[50] A. Acus, "Volunteering in non-governmental organizations as social policy expression," Tiltai, no. 3, 2018, pp. 149–163.

[51] "In-demand talent on demand. Upwork is how." https://www.upwork.com/, (Accessed on 02/10/2020).

[52] R. Vahidov and R. Elrod, "Incorporating critique and argumentation in dss," Decision Support Systems, vol. 26, no. 3, 1999, pp. 249–258.

[53] R. Bellamy and K. Woolsey, "Learning conversations," SIGCHI Bull., vol. 30, no. 2, Apr. 1998, pp. 108–112. [Online]. Available: http://doi.acm.org/10.1145/279044.279170

[54] L. S. Hartenian, "Nonprofit agency dependence on direct service and indirect support volunteers: An empirical investigation," Nonprofit Management and Leadership, vol. 17, no. 3, 2007, pp. 319–334.

Mental Model Construction Process and the Time Variation

Toahiki Yamaoka
Faculty of Home Economics
Kyoto Women's University
Kyoto city, Japan
Email: tyamaoka6@gmail.com

***Abstract*— The purpose of this study is to grasp temporal characteristics of the structural and functional models of a mental model. The temporal characteristics were examined from a viewpoint of thinking and memorizing. Tests were performed using wooden blocks. As a result, it was determined that the structural model is useful for constructing mental models; understanding only the functional models is not enough. For example, when the structural model is shown at first in an operational screen or user manual, users can understand the structure of the products or systems quickly and can operate them easily.**

Keywords - mental model; construction process; time variation.

I. INTRODUCTION

Studies regarding temporal characteristics of mental models have not been addressed in previous studies [1][2]. As operational screens or user manuals of products become complicated and difficult to understand, a study of the temporal characteristics of mental models is very important. After users operate a product, such as a wi-fi router which is not familiar, they cannot usually memorize how to operate it because of temporal transition.

Mental models are important factors for users to successfully use products or systems. The mental model is defined as a system image in this paper. However, designers and engineers cannot understand how to design with mental models. The mental model consists of structural models and functional models. Structural models refer to how products or systems work and functional models refer to how to use the products and systems. The structural model shows the structure of products or systems, and the functional model shows the procedure of operation [3]-[8].

The provision of information in the structural models and functional models was examined in this study. The study details are described next. Participants were asked to construct blocks three times because of memorizing the final shape of the blocks.

1) Participants were showed information regarding the structural model (Section II).

2) Participants were showed information regarding the functional model first, followed by the structural model (Section III).

3) Participants were showed information regarding the functional model (Section IV).

4) Participants were showed the information regarding the structural model first, followed by the functional model (Section V).

The structural model, functional model and the combination of them can be evaluated by constructing the blocks without instructions.

The common information of the method is described as follows. 21 participants labelled from "A" to "U" participated in the studies. Only one participant answered only one task. The participants were students of Kyoto Women's University in Kyoto and not trained for the test. The tests were performed to determine the role of structural models and functional models in the memorization of a mental model. As memorizing two times is insufficient to memorize complicated structures and the order of constructing wooden blocks, a task was done three times in order to fully memorize the structure and the order of building the structure [9]. The number of successfully completed shapes constructed from wooden blocks was evaluated.

II. STUDY 1

Participants were shown the information regarding the structural model of the object.

A. Method

Five participants were asked to construct wooden blocks such as cubes, rectangles, etc. The participants were students of Kyoto Women's University and ranged in age from 21 to 24 years. The participants constructed a final shape according to the following instructions.

1) The first time, participants were shown the whole picture (the final shape) of the combination of cubes and rectangles (see Figure 1). They were then asked to construct the final shape showing the whole picture using wooden blocks.

2) The second time, the entire procedure in step 1) was repeated.

3) The third time, the entire procedure in step 1) was repeated once more.

4) The fourth time, participants were asked to construct the final shape without showing them the final shape first.

Five days later, they were asked to construct the final shape without any information.

B. Results and discussion

The five participants were able to construct the final shape (see Table I). Five days later, three participants could construct the final shape (see Table II). As the time to complete the final shape varied, Tables II, IV, VI, and VIII

Figure 1. The whole picture of shape.

TABLE I. RESULTS ON THE FIRST DAY

First day				
Participant	First time	Second time	Third time	Fourth time
	Constructing the blocks according the whole picture each time			No instruction
A	S	S	S	S
B	S	S	S	S
C	S	S	S	S
D	S	S	S	S
E	S	S	S	S
Average time (sec)	144	28	29	23

S: Success, F: Failure

TABLE II. RESULTS FIVE DAYS LATER

Five days later					
Participant	A	B	C	D	E
No instructions	S	**F**	**F**	S	S

S: Success, F: Failure

do not show the average time. Showing the whole picture (final picture) means providing a structural model of the mental model.

The results show that the structural model seems to be useful for constructing a mental model. After the participants took time to construct the wooden shape at first, they could put together the blocks easily because they had constructed the mental model (see Table I). As the structural model can make participants think according to these results, they can memorize by cue of thinking.

III. STUDY 2

Participants were shown information regarding the functional model first, and then the structural model.

A. Method

Six participants were asked to construct wooden blocks such as cubes, rectangles, etc. The participants were students of Kyoto Women's University and ranged in age from 21 to 22 years.

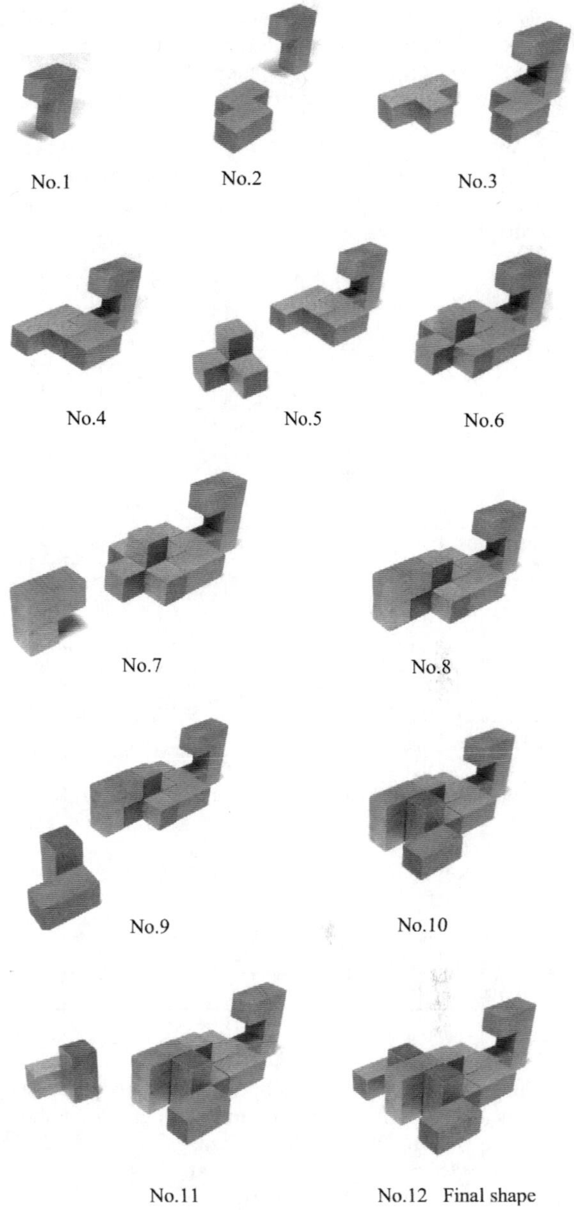

Figure 2. The shapes presented in order.

1) The first time, the participants were shown a part of the whole picture (final shape) combined of cubes and rectangles, in order. They constructed using the wooden blocks in order and completed the final shape (see Figure 2.)

2) The second time, the entire procedure in step 1) was repeated.

3) The third time, the participants were showed the whole picture of the combined cubes, rectangles etc. They

were asked to construct the final shape shown in the whole picture using wooden blocks.

4) The fourth time, they were asked to construct the final shape without showing the final shape first.

Five days later, they were asked to construct the final shape without any information.

B. Results and discussion

Three participants were able to construct the final shape. Five days later, two participants were able to construct the final shape.

TABLE III. RESULTS ON THE FIRST DAY

Participant	First day			
	First time	Second time	Third time	Fourth time
	The parts of whole picture presented in order (Figure 2.)		The whole picture	No instruction
F	S	S	S	S
G	S	S	S	S
H	S	S	**F**	**F**
I	S	S	**F**	**F**
J	S	S	S	S
K	S	S	S	**F**
Average time (sec)	77	37	68	176

The whole picture: Constructing the blocks according to the whole picture.
S: Success, F: Failure

TABLE IV. RESULTS FIVE DAYS LATER OF SIX PARTICIPANTS

Five days later						
Participant	F	G	H	I	J	K
No instructions	**F**	S	**F**	**F**	S	**F**

S: Success, F: Failure

Showing the parts of the whole picture presented in order means providing the functional model, while showing the whole picture (final shape) means the structural model (see Tables III and IV). The participants seem to be able to get the mental model by showing the whole picture which means the structural model compared with the results of study 2.

IV. STUDY 3

Participants were shown information regarding the functional model.

A. Method

Five participants were asked to construct the model using wooden blocks such as cubes, rectangles etc. The participants were students of Kyoto Women's University and ranged in age from 21 to 24 years.

1) The first time, the participants were shown a part of the final picture in order to combine the cubes, rectangles and so on. They put together the wooden blocks in order and completed the final shape.

2) The second time, the entire procedure in step 1) was repeated.

3) The third time, the entire procedure in step 1) was repeated once more.

4) The fourth time, they constructed the final shape without being shown the final shape first.

Five days later, the participants were asked to construct the final shape without any information.

B. Results and discussion

Only one participant could construct the final shape (see Table V). Five days later, only the same participant could construct the final shape (see Table VI). The procedure to construct blocks according to the functional model is difficult and does not successfully allow the users to make a mental model.

The structural model seems to be useful for users to understand the structure or function of systems according to the results of studies 1 and 2.

TABLE V. RESULTS ON THE FIRST DAY

Participant	First day			
	First time	Second time	Third time	Fourth time
	The parts of whole picture presented in order (figure 2.)			No instruction
L	S	S	S	**F**
M	S	S	S	**F**
N	S	S	S	**F**
O	S	S	S	S
P	S	S	S	**F**
Average time (sec)	64	37	32	22

S: Success, F: Failure

TABLE VI. RESULTS FIVE DAYS LATER OF FIVE PARTICIPANTS

Five days later					
Participant	L	M	N	O	P
No instructions	**F**	**F**	**F**	S	**F**

S: Success, F: Failure

V. STUDY 4

Participants were shown information regarding the structural model first, followed by the functional model.

A. Method

Five participants were asked to construct a shape using wooden blocks such as cubes, rectangles, and so on. The participants were students of Kyoto Women's University and ranged in age from 21 to 24 years.

1) The first time, participants were shown combined parts of the final picture, in order. They then constructed combined wooden blocks, in order, and completed the final shape.

2) The second time, the procedure in step 1) was repeated.

3) The third time, the participants were shown the final constructed object. They then constructed the final shape shown using the combined wooden blocks.

4) The fourth time, they constructed the final shape without being shown the final shape first.

Five days later, the participants were asked to construct the final shape without any information.

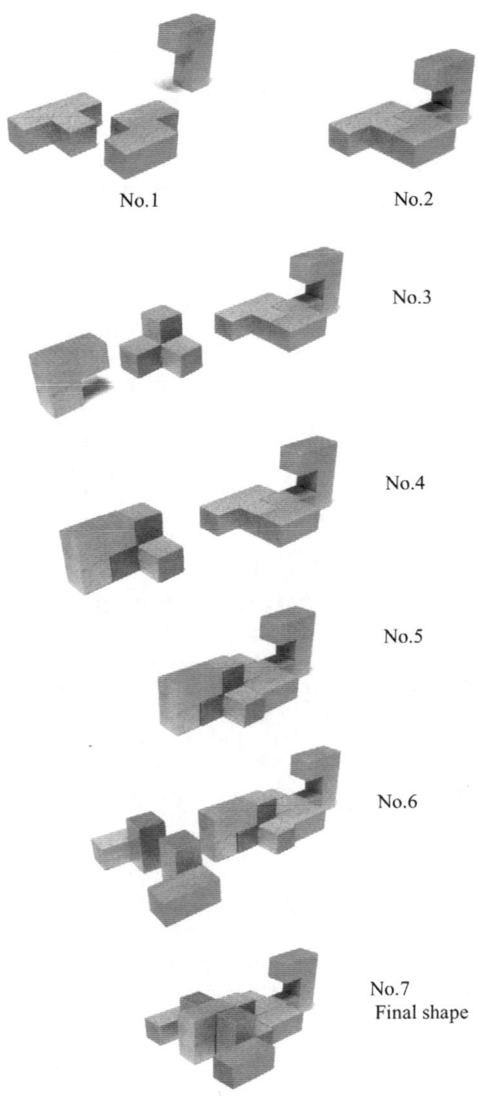

Figure 3. The grouped shapes presented in order.

B. *Results and discussion*

Four participants were able to construct the final shape (see Table VII). Five days later, only two participants were able to construct the final shape (see Table VIII).

The grouped parts of the whole picture presented in order represent both the functional model and the partial structural model. Since the procedure for users to read and understand each part and structure of the final shape was difficult, the idea to present one unit with some combined blocks seems to be useful. The structural model seems to be useful for users to understand the structure or function of systems according to the results of studies 1, 2 and 3.

TABLE VII. RESULTS ON THE FIRST DAY

	First day			
Participant	First time	Second time	Third time	Fourth time
	The grouped parts of the whole picture presented in order (Figure 3.)		The whole picture	No instruction
Q	S	S	S	S
R	S	S	S	S
S	S	S	S	S
T	S	S	S	**F**
U	S	S	S	S
Average time (sec)	51	27	61	40

The average time is calculated based on the data of participants Q,R,T and U.

TABLE VIII. RESULTS FIVE DAYS LATER

	Five days later				
Participant	Q	R	S	T	U
No instruction	**F**	**F**	S	**F**	S

S: Success, F: Failure

VI. DISCUSSION

The tasks evaluated in each study are presented in Figure 4. Showing the grouped parts of the whole picture presented in order represents the functional model and structural model. Showing the parts of the whole picture presented in order represents the functional model. Constructing the blocks according to the whole picture each time represents the structural model.

For the no instructions cases, Table IX shows the relationship between the structural model and the functional model to verify the results of the cases with no instruction on the first day and five days later.

The structural model influenced the construction of the mental model according to Table IX. The structural model easily allows users to memorize the structure according to the results of the four studies. So, the structural model is an important factor in constructing mental models. After we understand the structure or frame of systems, we can understand the substance of systems. Or, we can understand the substance of systems based on the context created by the functional model. The context can help users to convey the information of the system structure. Context helps users understand and memorize the structure of systems (see Figure 5.). Usually, the functional model causes trial and error to be used and creates the context as a result.

TABLE IX. THE RELATIONSHIP BETWEEN STRUCTURAL MODEL AND FUNCTIONAL MODEL FOR VERIFICATION OF NO INSTRUCTIONS

	First day			Five days later
	Structural model	Functional model	Validity for no instruction	Validity for no instruction
Study 1	✓	---	100%	60%
Study 2	✓	✓	60%	33%
Study 3	---	✓	20%	20%
Study 4	✓	✓	80%	40%

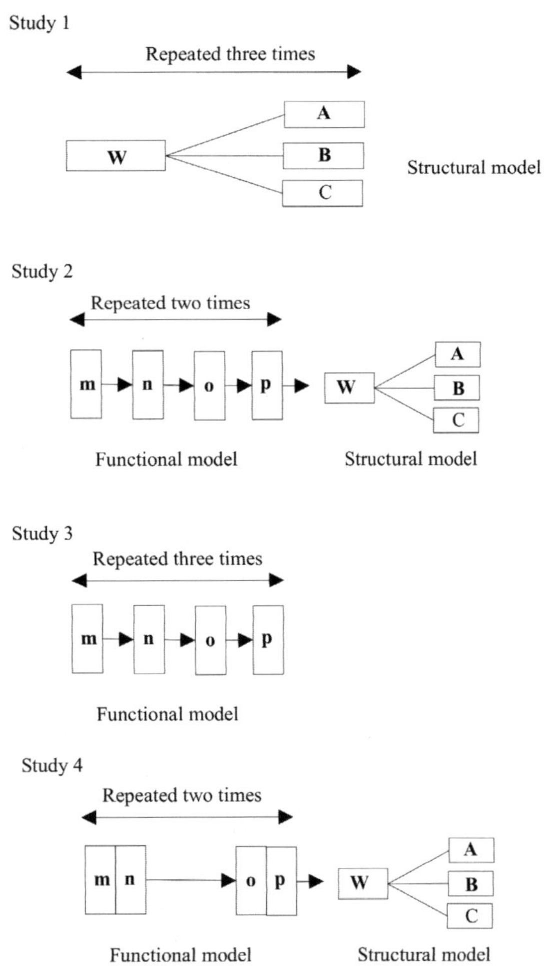

Figure 4. Study structure from study 1 to study 4.

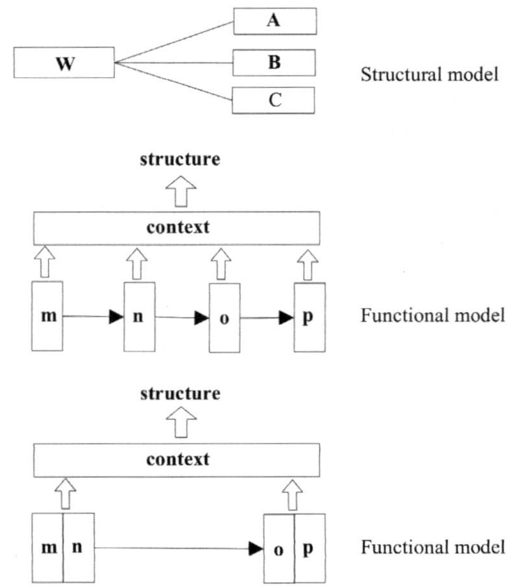

Figure 5. Relationship between structural model and functional model

When we read sentences in operational manuals to understand the operating procedure, we normally cannot memorize the content. This shows why the three participants in study 3 could not memorize. The reason participants in study 3 were not able to memorize and construct the blocks is because there was no context with the story which showed that the final shape was a scorpion.

Providing opportunities to think about system structure is very important for users. When the participants tried to look at the final shape in study 1, they were able to understand the system structure. Understanding the system structure means grasping the relationship among the parts of the system. They thought about the structure and were then able to memorize it. If the final shape was announced as a scorpion, some participants seem to be able to construct it easier because of a general idea of name which contains the shape and the function.

VII. CONCLUSION

Thinking about the structure is very important to construct the mental model. Operating according to the procedure without thinking about the structure, such as the examples found in operational manuals, seems not to be sufficient.

The conclusions based on the four studies are as follows.

(1) The structural model is useful for constructing a mental model.

(2) While functional models can create context using a story or other elements, they are also useful for constructing a mental model.

(3) Providing opportunities to think about the system structure is very important for users. Participants could not think or imagine the structure of the whole image (final shape) when they were using and understanding only the functional model.

(4) When the structural model was shown at first in the operational screen or user manual, users could easily understand the structure of products or systems and could easily operate them.

As user experience becomes an important factor to design products or systems, the mental model shoud be studied from the viewpoint of not only structural model and functional model, but also user experience.

ACKNOWLEDGMENTS

This work was supported by JSPS Kakenhi Grant number JP17K00739.

REFERENCES

[1] T. Yamaoka, "Examining the change of mental model from a viewpoint of time base and evaluation", The 4th International Conference on Ambient Intelligence and Ergonomics in Asia, October, 2019.

[2] L. Westbrook, "Mental models: A theoretical overview and preliminary study," *Journal of Information Science*, issue 6, vol. 32, pp. 563-579, 2006.

[3] J. Precee, Y. Rogers, H. Sharp, D. Benyon, S. Holland, and T. Carey, Human-Computer Interaction, Addison-Wesley, pp. 130-139, 1994.

[4] T. Yamaoka, "A basic consideration of evaluation method and construction model of mental model, " The 7th international conference on Kansei Engineering & Emotion Research (KEER2018), Kuching, Malaysia, 2018.

[5] T. Doi, "Mental model formation in user with high and low comprehension of a graohical user interface", *Journal of Human Ergology*, no.1, vol. 48, pp. 9-24, 2019.

[6] R. S. Bridger, Introduction to Ergonomics, third edition, pp. 554-557, CRC Press, 2009.

[7] J. P. Stephen, The Human-Computer Interaction handbook, pp. 63-75, CRC Press, 2008.

[8] C. D. Wickens, S. E. Gordon, Y. Liu, An introduction of Human Factors Engineering, Addison-Wesley Educational Publishers, p. 202, 1998.

[9] N. Katagiri, M. Hanatani, and T. Yamaoka, "Examining effective methods for constructing mental model," The 4th International Conference on Ambient Intelligence and Ergonomics in Asia, October, 2019.

Analysis Method for One-to-one Discussion Process for Research Progress Using Transition Probability of Utterance Types

Seiya Tsuji*, Yoko Nishihara*, Wataru Sunayama†, Ryosuke Yamanishi* and Shiho Imashiro‡

*College of Information Science and Engineering, Ritsumeikan University, Shiga, Japan
Email: {is0363ff@ed, nisihara@fc, ryama@media}.ritsumei.ac.jp
†School of Engineering, The University of Shiga Prefecture, Shiga, Japan
Email: sunayama.w@e.usp.ac.jp
‡Institute for Organizational Behavior Research, Recruit Management Solutions Co., Ltd. Tokyo, Japan
Email: shiho_imashiro@recruit-ms.co.jp

Abstract—**People in business companies and academic fields work in cooperation with others rather than working alone. They may discuss their progress with others, like co-workers and supervisors, to help them obtain the best results. Sometimes people may feel that such discussions are not conducted well. However, people do not evaluate the quality of each discussion every time because it is tough work for them; they usually do not have enough time for that. In the process of evaluating discussions, people might look back on their discussions and make a plan to have an improved discussion next time. This paper proposes an evaluation method for one-to-one research discussions. The method makes a model of the discussion process with transitions of utterance types. The labels of utterance types are assigned to each utterance in a discussion text manually. By calculating the transition probabilities between two labels, a matrix of transition probabilities is obtained. The transitions of labels with high probabilities are extracted from high quality discussions and connected to obtain a discussion process model. The model can be used for the evaluation of new discussions. We applied the proposed method to discussion texts and found that the obtained process model from high quality discussions had several loops of transitions which were connected loosely.**

Keywords–One-to-one discussion; Utterance type; Visualization; Process model; Transition probability.

I. INTRODUCTION

People in business companies and academic fields work in cooperation with others rather than working alone. It is important to discuss their working progress with others, like co-workers and supervisors, to help them obtain the best results. Such people can exchange their opinions and advise each other. These discussions make people understand not only what others think, but also ensure that members of the same team are in agreement about their work.

Discussions are sometimes not conducted well. This happens because discussions have a time limit and people often fail to arrive at a common understandings due to the difference in their thinking styles. However, people do not evaluate the quality of each discussion every time because it is tough work for them; they usually do not have enough time for that. In the process of evaluating discussions, people might look back on their discussions and make a plan to have an improved discussion next time.

This paper proposes an evaluation method for one-to-one research discussions between a student and his/her corresponding supervisor. The method makes a model of the discussion process with transitions of utterance types to evaluate future discussions. Note that we define a high quality discussion to be a discussion in which both the student and his/her corresponding supervisor understand their research progress. We believe that a high quality discussion should have characteristic transitions of utterance types.

The rest of this paper is structured as follows. In Section 2, we discuss related work. The proposed method is presented in Section 3, followed by our experiment in Section 4. Finally, we conclude in Section 5.

II. RELATED WORK

Our proposed method is a conversation analysis method. Previous methods cover not only general conversations [1], but also purpose-oriented conversations such as conversations for persuasion [2]. The proposed method targets the analysis of one-to-one discussions for research progress. A discussion on the topic of research progress tends to have loops of divergence and convergence. General conversations should be divergent conversations while purpose-oriented conversations should be convergent. A target discussion should be in the middle of the two types. Our hypothesis is that a loop appears in a model of the discussion process if the discussion is conducted well. Many conversational features are used in the conversation analysis. The number of utterances in a conversation is used for evaluating the quality of conversations [3]. The length of silent time in a conversation is also used for the evaluation of the quality of the conversation [4]. The proposed method uses utterance types in a discussion as the conversational features. While the two previous studies use quantitative features, the proposed method uses qualitative features, i.e., utterance types. If both features are used for conversation analysis, the analysis results will become rich.

There are some sets of utterance types for conversation analysis. The sets such as Switchboard-Dialog Act Markup in Several Layers (SWBD-DAMSL) [5] and Meeting Recorder Dialog Act (MRDA) [6] provide labels of utterance types. Those sets were prepared for analyzing specific conversations and discussions. Therefore, we also design a set of labels of utterance types by referring to our target discussions.

III. PROPOSED METHOD FOR EVALUATION OF DISCUSSION

The outline of the proposed method is described in this section. Firstly, a transcript of a discussion is prepared manually. One line includes a speaker's name and an utterance text.

Greeting, Confirmation, Question, Answer, Agreement, Repetition, Explanation, Opinion, Admiration, Suggestion, Understanding, Topic Shifting, Report, Degression, Soliloquy, Nodding, Request, Planning, Denial, Filler, Consultation, Response, Comment, Advice, Indication, Correction, Wondering, Surprise, Acknowledgement, Chatting, Additional Comment

Figure 1. Labels of Utterance Types.

Each utterance is assigned one utterance type label. A matrix of the transition of labels (i.e., utterance types) is obtained. Each cell of the matrix has a transition probability between two labels. Transitions with high probabilities are extracted from the matrix. The extracted transitions are connected if the same labels are included, and then a discussion process model is obtained. The model can be used to evaluate future discussions.

A. Preparing Transcripts of Discussions

We suppose that a research discussion should be conducted face-to-face. The research discussion is recorded by a voice recorder. The proposed method uses transcripts of discussion to make a model. One line of the transcript includes a speaker's name and an utterance text; the utterance text includes fillers. The length of sound in a word, the length of silent time, and any laughing time are not included. An utterance text includes several sentences before turn-taking occurs. Table I shows an example of a part of a transcript.

B. Assigning Utterance Type Labels to Utterances

Each utterance in the transcript is labeled with utterance types. Though an automatic labeling method has been proposed [7], the labeling accuracy is not enough. In our case, each utterance is labeled manually to ensure accurate labels. Though sets of labels for utterances have also been proposed [8], most of the sets of labels have their target discussions and conversations. We design a new set of labels for utterances of our target discussions, that is discussions for research progress.

Figure 1 shows labels of utterance types. These labels are designed by referring to the transcripts of discussions that will be described in Section IV. The utterance from a supervisor and the utterance from a student will be distinguished. The labels for the supervisor's utterances and the labels for the student's utterances will also be distinguished by a different ending added to the label. The proposed method uses $31 * 2 = 62$ types of labels in total.

When labeling utterance text, the already appeared utterance texts are also considered. An utterance text may not have enough information for labeling. If a student says "Yes" for a question from a supervisor, it means "Yes, you are right." But if a student says "Yes" for a proposal from a supervisor, it means "Yes, I will do it." The two "Yes"'s are different types of utterances.

Multiple labels may be assigned to an utterance text because a single utterance may have several roles. The corresponding ending to distinguish the speaker is also added to each label. In this paper, the ending for an utterance from a supervisor is set to T, while the ending for an utterance from a student is set to S.

C. Matrix of Transition Probabilities of Labels

A matrix of transition probabilities of labels is obtained by using the labels information on utterance texts. The transition probability of labels means a probability between labels. Suppose that the ith utterance text has a vector of labels $L(i)$ and the jth utterance text has a vector of labels $L(j)$ ($j = i+1$). $L(i)$ is described by (1).

$$L(i) = \{l_n | 0 <= n <= 61\}, \tag{1}$$

where n is the label index. l_n is 0 or 1. If the nth label is assigned to an utterance text, l_n = 1. Otherwise, $l_n = 0$. The frequency of transition from the label l_n in $L(i)$ to the label l_m in $L(j)$ is increased if both of l_n and l_p are not equal to zero. Let the frequency be $f_{n,m}$. Let the number of lines of the transcript be NL. $NL - 1$ is the number of turn-taking in a discussion. The transition probability $p_{n,m}$ from the label l_n to the label l_m is calculated by (2).

$$p_{n,m} = \frac{f_{n,m}}{NL - 1}, \tag{2}$$

where n and m are labels indices. By assigning the probability $p_{n,m}$ to each cell, a matrix of transition probabilities is obtained. Table II shows an example of a part of the matrix that is obtained from discussion texts (detailed in Section IV).

D. Discussion Process Model

A discussion process model is obtained by using the matrix of transition probabilities. Transitions of labels with probabilities more than a threshold T are extracted from the matrix. The extracted transitions are connected if the same label is included in two different transitions. The graph of connected transitions is the model to evaluate the discussions proposed in this paper.

IV. EXPERIMENT

We made discussion process models for high quality discussions and low quality discussions. We compared the two models and found the differences between the two models. We used eight transcripts of discussion between a supervisor and a student in our laboratory. The number of supervisors was two while eight students (four males and four females) were in the laboratory. Each of the supervisors had for students, respectively. The students were 21 to 22 years old and were enrolled in the College of Information Science and Engineering. The transcripts of the discussion were read by the 1st author and the 2nd author. The two authors divided the transcripts into two classes: a high quality discussion class and a low quality discussion class. Table III shows the details of the eight transcripts; the length of discussion, the number of utterances from a supervisor and the number of utterances from a student are described. The average length of discussion was 26 minutes and 58 seconds. The average number of utterances from a supervisor was 81 while that from a student was 71.5. The transcripts with IDs 1 to 4 were in the high quality discussion class while those with IDs 5 to 8 were in the opposite class.

A. Experimental Results and Discussion

Table IV and Table V show the top five label transitions with high probabilities in each transcript of the discussion. Table IV shows the transitions obtained from transcripts of a high quality discussion class. All of them had the transition $Answer\_S \rightarrow Question\_T$ in the top five transitions with the highest probabilities except in the transcript #4. It means that a supervisor gave a question and a student answered a question

TABLE I. EXAMPLE OF TRANSCRIPT OF ONE-TO-ONE DISCUSSION.

Speaker	Utterance	Label
T	はい、じゃあ、えっと、よろしくお願いします。(Well, let's start the meeting.)	挨拶 (Greeting)
T	えーっと、書き起こしが、まあ当然まだだと思ってるんですけども、えっと1人もらった？ (I'm sure that you have not made a transcription naturally. Did you get a recording data?)	質問 (Question)
S	はい。(Yes.)	回答 (Answer)
T	それは誰のん？(Who did you get it from?)	質問 (Question)
S	岡村さんから。(From Riko.)	回答 (Answer)
T	岡村さんからもらった、了解、了解。(You got it from Riko, OK.)	理解 (Understanding)
T	それはなん分ぐらいのデータ？(How long was the data?)	質問 (Question)
S	えっと、４５分ぐらいだったと思います。(Well, about 45 minutes)	回答 (Answer)
T	ながっ。(So long.)	感想 (Comment)
S	長かったです。(It's so long.)	反復 (Repetition)

TABLE II. EXAMPLE OF MATRIX OF TRANSITION PROBABILITIES.

/	Greeting_T	Question_T	Understanding_T	Suggestion_T	Confirmation_T	Answer_S	Repetition_S	Agreement_S	Question_S
Greeting_T	0	0	0	0	0	0	0	0	0
Question_T	0	0	0	0	0	0.082	0	3	0
Understanding_T	0	0	0	0	0	0	0	0	0
Suggestion_T	0	0	0	0	0	0	0	0.014	0.014
Confirmation_T	0	0	0	0	0	0.031	0	5	0
Answer_S	0	0.054	0	0.003	0	0	0	0	0
Repetition_S	0	0	0	0	0	0	0	0	0
Agreement_S	0	3	0	0.008	0.007	0	0	0	0
Question_S	0	0	0	0	0	0	0	0	0

TABLE III. USED EIGHT TRANSCRIPTS OF DISCUSSION. THE LENGTH OF DISCUSSION, THE NUMBERS OF UTTERANCES FROM A SUPERVISOR AND A STUDENT ARE SHOWN, RESPECTIVELY.

Discussion ID	Length (minutes : seconds)	# of utterances from a supervisor	# of utterances from a student
1	48:02	139	127
2	24:29	50	43
3	19:20	50	44
4	44:11	151	145
5	20:38	53	50
6	28:55	100	76
7	17:25	67	58
8	12:42	38	29
Average	26:58	81.0	71.5

frequently in a discussion. Table V shows the top five transitions of low quality discussion class. Though all of them had the same transition ($Answer\_S \rightarrow Question\_T$), there were other labels such as $Confirmation\_T$ and $Explanation\_T$. This means that the supervisor needed to confirm and explain to the student frequently in the discussion.

Table VI shows the top nine transitions of labels with high values of summation of probabilities in transcripts of high quality discussion and low quality discussion, respectively. The high quality discussion class has transitions such as $Answer\_S \rightarrow Question\_T$, $Agreement\_S \rightarrow Opinion\_T$ and $Answer\_S \rightarrow Understanding\_T$. The transitions indicated that the discussions were conducted smoothly. In contrast, the low quality discussion class has transitions such as $Question\_S \rightarrow Answer\_T$ and $Agreement\_S \rightarrow Explanation\_T$. The transitions indicated that the discussions were not conducted smoothly and so the supervisor and the student could not come to a common agreement.

Figure 2 shows the obtained model of the high quality discussion process. In the figure, there are loops consisting of some specific labels such as $Question\_T \leftrightarrow Answer\_S$, $Opinion\_T \leftrightarrow Agreement\_S$, and $Suggestion\_T \leftrightarrow Agreement\_S$. The small loops are connected to make a big loose loop.

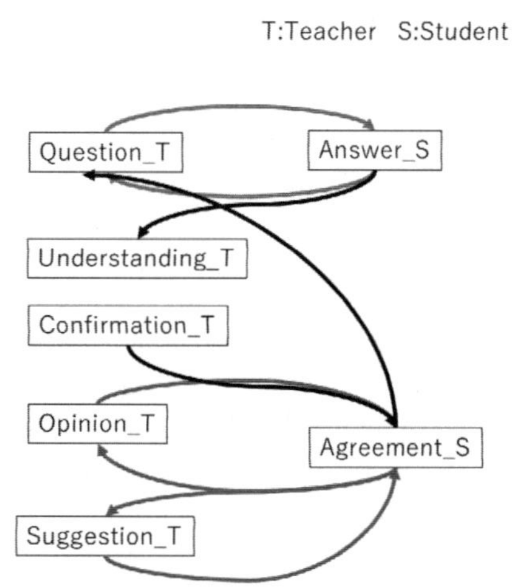

Figure 2. Process model of high quality discussion.

Figure 3 shows the obtained model of the low quality discussion process. In the figure, there are loops of some specific labels such as $Question\_T \leftrightarrow Answer\_S$ and $Suggestion\_T \leftrightarrow Agreement\_S$. Although some of the small loops are connected, all loops are not connected. Some of the transitions have dead-end paths like $Understanding\_S \rightarrow Opinion\_T$.

V. CONCLUSION

This paper proposed an evaluation method for one-to-one research discussions. We used the research discussion between a supervisor and a student who is studying for a graduation thesis at a university. The proposed method makes a discussion process model with transitions of utterance types. Labels of utterance types are originally designed for discussion analysis for research progress.

In this paper, we analyzed eight discussion texts. We

TABLE IV. TOP FIVE TRANSITIONS OF LABELS IN TRANSCRIPTS OF **HIGH** QUALITY DISCUSSION CLASS.

Discussion 1 Transition(Prob.)	Discussion 2 Transition(Prob.)	Discussion 3 Transition(Prob.)	Discussion 4 Transition(Prob.)
Answer_S → Question_T(0.074)	Answer_S → Question_T(0.098)	Answer_S → Question_T(0.069)	Opinion_T → Agreement_S(0.087)
Indication_T → Agreement_S(0.028)	Answer_S → Suggestion_T(0.036)	Agreement_S → Question_T(0.052)	Agreement_S → Opinion_T(0.084)
Question_S → Answer_T(0.025)	Suggestion_T → Agreement_S(0.036)	Suggestion_T → Agreement_S(0.052)	Suggestion_T → Agreement_S(0.032)
Understanding_S → Advice_T(0.025)	Nodding_S → Opinion_T(0.027)	Agreement_S → Suggestion_T(0.043)	Answer_S → Question_T(0.029)
Understanding_S → Question_T(0.021)	Answer_S → Understanding_T(0.027)	Confirmation_T → Answer_S(0.043)	Confirmation_T → Agreement_S(0.029)
Answer_S → Advice_T(0.021)	Opinion_T → Nodding_S(0.027)		

TABLE V. TOP FIVE TRANSITIONS OF LABELS IN TRANSCRIPTS OF **LOW** QUALITY DISCUSSION CLASS.

Discussion 5 Transition(Prob.)	Discussion 6 Transition(Prob.)	Discussion 7 Transition(Prob.)	Discussion 8 Transition(Prob.)
Understanding_S → Opinion_T(0.074)	Suggestion_T → Agreement_S(0.060)	Question_S → Answer_T(0.049)	Question_S → Answer_T(0.040)
Explanation_T → Understanding_S(0.074)	Agreement_S → Suggestion_T(0.042)	Confirmation_S → Answer_T(0.042)	Answer_S → Question_T(0.040)
Suggestion_T → Agreement_S(0.056)	Answer_S → Question_T(0.036)	Answer_S → Question_T(0.042)	Agreement_S → Suggestion_T(0.040)
Agreement_S → Explanation_T(0.037)	Explanation_T → Understanding_S(0.036)	Agreement_S → Suggestion_T(0.035)	Agreement_S → Confirmation_T(0.030)
Agreement_S → Suggestion_T(0.037)	Answer_S → Suggestion_T(0.030)	Suggestion_T → Agreement_S(0.035)	Confirmation_T → Agreement_S(0.030)
	Agreement_S → Advice_T(0.030)		Suggestion_T → Agreement_S(0.030)
	Advice_T → Agreement_S(0.030)		

TABLE VI. TRANSITIONS OF LABELS USED FOR MAKING DISCUSSION PROCESS MODELS FOR HIGH/LOW QUALITY DISCUSSION.

Transitions from **high** quality (Prob.)	Transitions from **low** quality (Prob.)
Question_T → Answer_S(0.125)	Question_T → Answer_S(0.083)
Answer_S → Question_T(0.058)	Suggestion_T → Agreement_S(0.044)
Opinion_T → Agreement_S(0.038)	Agreement_S → Suggestion_T(0.039)
Agreement_S → Opinion_T(0.037)	Question_S → Answer_T(0.035)
Suggestion_T → Agreement_S(0.027)	Answer_S → Question_T(0.031)
Confirmation_T → Agreement_S(0.022)	Explanation_T → Understanding_S(0.023)
Agreement_S → Question_T(0.020)	Understanding_S → Opinion_T(0.019)
Answer_S → Understanding_T(0.017)	Answer_S → Suggestion_T(0.017)
Agreement_S → Suggestion_T(0.017)	Agreement_S → Explanation_T(0.017)

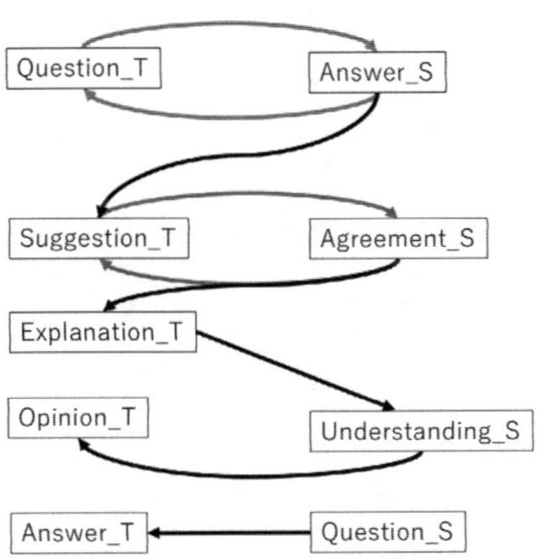

Figure 3. Process model of low quality discussion.

divided the texts into high quality and low quality discussion classes; each class had four texts, respectively. The obtained model from high quality discussions had several loops of transitions, which were connected loosely. In contrast, the obtained model from low quality discussions did not have loops of transitions. In the model for low quality discussions, the transitions between "understood by student" and "explanation by supervisor" were included. The transition in the model might mean that the supervisor and the student did not come to a common understanding.

As future work, we will try to evaluate the growth in the discussion skills of a student by using the proposed method. We will improve our method to conduct automatic labeling of utterances for analyzing many discussions.

ACKNOWLEDGMENT

This work was supported by Recruit Management Solutions Co., Ltd. Grant in Japan. We show our best appreciation.

REFERENCES

[1] W. Sunayama, "Discussion visualization on a bulletin board system," Data Science Journal, vol. 6, 2007, pp. 51–60.

[2] T. Hiraoka, G. Neubig, S. Sakti, T. Toda, and S. Nakamura, Construction and Analysis of a Persuasive Dialogue Corpus, Napa, California, USA, 2014, pp. 125–138.

[3] K. Toyoda, Y. Miyakoshi, R. Yamanishi, and S. Kato, "Estimation of dialogue moods using the utterance intervals features," the 5th International Conference on Intelligent Interactive Multimedia Systems and Services, vol. 14, 2012, pp. 245–254.

[4] Y. Nishihara, K. Yoshimatsu, R. Yamanishi, and S. Miyake, "Topic visualization system for unfamiliar couples in face-to-face conversations," International Journal of Service and Knowledge Management, vol. 2, no. 1, 2018, pp. 19–30.

[5] D. Jurafsky, E. Shriberg, and D. Biasca, "Switchboard swbd-damsl shallow-discourse-function annotation coders manual," University of Colorado, Institute of Cognitive Science, Tech. Rep. Draft 13, 1997.

[6] E. Shriberg, R. Dhillon, S. Bhagat, J. Ang, and H. Carvey, "The ICSI meeting recorder dialog act (MRDA) corpus," in Proceedings of the 5th SIGdial Workshop on Discourse and Dialogue at HLT-NAACL 200, 2004, pp. 97–100.

[7] Y. Nishihara and W. Sunayama, "Estimation of friendship and hierarchy from conversation records," Information Sciences, vol. 179, no. 11, 2009, pp. 1592–1598.

[8] D. Jurafsky, A. Bell, E. Fosler-Lussiery, C. Gir, and W. Raymond, "Reduction of english function words in switchboard," in Proceedings of the 5th International Conference on Spoken Language Processing (ICSLP 98), vol. 7, 1998, pp. 3111–3114.

Usability Testing in the National Information Processing Institute, Poland

Katarzyna Turczyn
National Information Processing Institute
Al. Niepodległości 188 b, 00-608 Warsaw, Poland
email: katarzyna.turczyn@opi.org.pl

Agnieszka Lepianka
National Information Processing Institute
Al. Niepodległości 188 b, 00-608 Warsaw, Poland
email: agnieszka.lepianka@opi.org.pl

***Abstract*—This article describes the specifics of usability research in public institutions using as example the work at the National Information Processing Institute in Poland. It describes the challenges faced by system creators, designers and researchers. It presents methods of preparing and conducting usability tests (preparation, execution and further steps after researches). The characterization of the systems created in the Institute shows the specifics of working with public systems and shares the insights from these researches. Based on the gathered information, the article proposes changes to improve the experience of systems' users. It presents good practices that the creators may follow during the design process, such as: naming, icons, charts, cohesion, searching, text editing and information architecture.**

Keywords - UX research; usability testing; information system; system design; National Information Processing Institute.

I. Introduction

The National Information Processing Institute (OPI PIB) is a public institution whose tasks include development of Information Technology (IT) systems for the Ministry of Science and Higher Education in Poland [1]. An inseparable element of system design and development at the Institute is research and testing, in particular usability tests, which facilitate the detection of errors on websites and applications as well as shortcomings in their architecture.

A. Method

The article is the result of qualitative research, the main element of which was the participant observation, which began when we started working at the Institute in 2018 as researchers in the User Experience (UX) research team at the Institute's Laboratory of Interactive Technologies. Data and information on which this article has been created was also collected thanks to many conversations with other OPI PIB employees, mostly other researchers working in the Institute several years longer, but also designers, analysts, developers and product owners. Working at the Institute and fulfilling our responsibilities also allowed us to analyse documentation and other available materials. In this case, Hastrup's sentence: "reality is lived, not talked or written" [2] is true. Thanks to the possibility of analysing our experiences, we are a little closer to reality than we would be by analysing only what we have heard or read.

The article is intended to approach the form of Geertz's thick description [3], trying to describe the broadest context of the topic.

B. Research Question

The aim of taking a closer look at the system development process at OPI PIB is to show the specificity of the job of a UX researcher in the public sector. An analysis of what takes place at the Institute in terms of usability testing has allowed us to indicate the pros and cons of the working environment in comparison to the ideal process of system design and development, as required by the principles and guidelines of User Experience. By looking at the current experiences, we will be able to identify some areas which could bring the process closer to the ideal if they are altered and optimised. The Institute's example allows us to take a closer look at how working on the software looks and, more precisely, how usability testing of this software looks in the public sector. The article can be a contribution to further work and reflection about the specifics of work in the public sector and how it differs from the private sector.

Section II introduces the research area, describing the systems produced at OPI PIB. Section III presents the way of conducting usability research in the Institute: preparation, execution and further steps after research. Section IV describes challenges faced by system developers and the results of usability tests. In Section V, we draw the conclusions from our qualitative research and present in-depth observations of research implementation at the National Information Processing Institute.

II. Research Area: A Description of the Systems and Challenges for Their Developers

Our work as researchers in the UX research team at the Institute's Laboratory of Interactive Technologies has allowed us to take a closer look at the following system development projects:

- Polish Graduate Tracking System (ELA) – a system for secondary school graduates, students and university employees; the system contains statistical data on graduates' earnings and employment obtained from the Social Security Institution (ZUS).
- POL-on – a database system on institutions related to higher education and science in Poland, designed for employees from the public sector, in particular university employees.

- Integrated System of Services for Science / Streams of Financing (ZSUN / OSF) – a system which facilitates submission of applications for funding in the science sector (for students, doctoral students, research workers) and the subsequent handling of these applications by public administration entities.
- Navoica – a free-of-charge educational platform with Massive Open Online Courses (MOOC) courses.
- Uniform Anti-Plagiarism System (JSA) – an anti-plagiarism platform for verification of dissertation and thesis content.

As the project descriptions above suggest, the direct recipient of the systems is the Ministry, and the systems' users are predominantly university employees (both administrative and research staff), as well as scientists, students, secondary school graduates and university graduates. The direct recipients of the system testing output, in turn, are employees of the Institute – the developers and creators of the systems.

The systems developed by OPI PIB are mostly database systems, mainly used by employees of the science sector. To a large extent, the systems reflect the processes that had been taking place at universities and their dean's offices before computers appeared, when paper forms and files played the key role. The development of the existing systems required the digitisation of data and the establishment of software to reflect the previously applied "paper-based" procedures. That is how the ZSUN / OSF grant application filing system was developed (among other systems). The current systems, for the most part, have not only grown out of paper procedures – they have also retained a lot of the legacy features. In Poland, electronic documents are not yet regarded as equal to paper documents because of, among other things, the attitude of employees of public institutions [4], not just due to the existing legal framework. Therefore, in one of the phases of system use (usually the final phase), the user is often required to print out a document to close out the process. This is the case of the JSA anti-plagiarism system, where the final scan report must be printed out. It seems fair to say that paper documents continue to determine the interface of the existing systems, at least to a certain extent.

The formats of documents and processes, including digital ones, depend on the legal conditions, laws and regulations. An example of a system determined by legal acts is the POL-on system. Each of its modules is conditioned by different legal sources, e.g., the "Employees" module is based on several acts of law [5]. We can therefore say that non-intuitive information architecture of some system elements, a lack of certain functionalities or the presence of illogical requirements within the system are sometimes not the fault of system developers, but a consequence of the legal framework.

Users of the systems developed by the Institute, despite their often similar motivations to use the system, differ from each other on many levels. The differences impact the final interface of the system. First of all, users have different levels of digital competence, varying even within one group such as the group of researchers applying for grants. Another element which contributes to the diversity is the variety of the fields of science represented by the researchers using the system: for example, some people find it easier to understand a legal text, while others find legal texts challenging.

The heterogeneity of system users also results from the disabilities they may have. The Institute creates public systems, which, according to the law in Poland, must comply with the requirements of WCAG 2.0 [6]. The WCAG guidelines are the relevant benchmark, and the websites, as well as applications developed by the Institute, are designed to be as responsive as possible to the needs of people with disabilities. Some of the systems are intended mainly for researchers. The JSA system is used primarily by supervisors and reviewers of dissertations, i.e., persons who hold a PhD degree or higher degrees. In the years 2000-2010, the average age of university-nominated professors in Poland was about 55 [7]. System design standards are changing, and elderly users often transfer their experiences from other media (newspapers, books, paper forms) to the portals and systems they are expected to work with [8]. Younger users are impacted by the website services they use, too. Additionally, at an advanced age people are more likely to experience problems with vision and motor skills. If systems are not adapted to the requirements of this group of users, the hardware barrier may be the consequence, for example, when the buttons and fonts are too small and when the user interface is too complicated [8].

Much of the work at OPI PIB consists in introducing changes, transformations, extensions to the systems which were developed when the standards and requirements were different from the current ones. As a result, the developers are facing limitations from the very start of their efforts. In order to maintain the coherence of the systems and to stay within the budgetary constraints of the project, they sometimes have to give up some ideas. It works similarly in all other companies on the market.

The systems developed by the Institute are mainly aimed at supporting the Ministry of Science and Higher Education, universities and academics in collecting information, managing projects, acquiring funds and broadening their competences. These system development projects are not market endeavours, in which the most important result is for the customer to buy a product or service. The users of the systems developed by OPI PIB sometimes have to use them for work (the POL-on system), and sometimes in order to acquire a grant (the ZSUN / OSF system). In this environment, some system developers may feel they are monopolists, which may trigger the risk of disregarding the needs and requirements of the users as the level of competition and motivation to continuously improve decreases. Regardless of what the system will look like, its users will still simply have to use it. For this reason, it is necessary to carry out research and analysis based on data from the end users of the systems [9].

III. Usability Testing in the National Information Processing Institute

Since 2014, the number of usability studies and research carried out by the Institute has increased significantly. The evolution in research has not only changed the number of studies, but also increased their diversity. New techniques, such as usability tests, focus group tests and in-depth interviews, have been added to the previously used workshop method. Additional tools, such as co and card sorting were also used. An important element that became a permanent part of the work of researchers at OPI PIB was the UX audit of systems for designers' and developers' needs.

However, the most frequently used research method at the Institute is still task testing, which takes place at the Institute's headquarters in a specially adapted testing room. Tests with one invited respondent allow the testing team to see how a potential user will use the product. Such tests [10] show how comprehensible the system is and where the critical points are that need to be modified in the first place. Moreover, this type of testing provides information on how intuitive the application and its system is, and whether it satisfies the needs of the users [10][11]. A big advantage of the tests is that the developers of the system are able to see live reactions of the respondents as they are interacting with the system. Furthermore, during task testing it is possible to ask in-depth questions which may have arisen during the test (this is a big advantage over tests conducted remotely). However, it is important to inform the recipients of test output that a single test will not answer all their questions, and that the number of tasks that can be performed during one session is limited. Consequently, test objectives and questions should be prioritised. As regards respondents, it is very important to ensure that they feel comfortable during the test, in particular if the respondent is a university employee who may feel that their knowledge and skills are being put to a test by an institution that supervises their work.

Focus groups are a less common data gathering technique at OPI PIB. It is used in the early stages of system design and in the redesign of existing systems. Thanks to a focus group interview with invited users or prospective users, it is possible to collect a large amount of information, insights, and translate them into conclusions and recommendations in a very short period of time (compared to other techniques) [11]. Focus groups often give direction to changes, provide information about users, their patterns of behaviour and expectations, enabling the researchers to use projection techniques and collaborative design [11]. The greatest risk in focus groups is associated with the role of the facilitator. Incorrectly facilitated tests may distort the results. If the facilitator is too withdrawn in the testing situation, one of the respondents may take over the role of the leader. Shy persons with little leadership energy may choose to avoid active participation in the conversation. Moreover, the Groupthink Syndrome can also occur. It is also a mistake to assume that focus groups can be the source of opinions about the entire population of users – in fact in only offers information about a segment of the population.

A. *Preparation*

The process of data gathering preparation at OPI PIB is presented in Figure 1. It concerns the implementation of the most frequently applied type of testing at the Institute, i.e., task-based usability tests in a test environment. The points on the vertical axis represent the degree of control over the process by the investigators and the probability of complications. The horizontal axis shows the course of the data gathering process in time. In the following section, the next steps of the research process will be discussed.

After learning about the needs and questions of the system's designers, the next step is the recruitment process. Due to the specific nature of the public institution in question, the recruitment of respondents is implemented by an external company selected in a tender. The complicated nature of the recruitment procedure further complicates the selection of the best external companies which, additionally, need to meet strict tender criteria. The time needed to prepare the tests makes it difficult to integrate them into different phases of project development, so sometimes the only solution is to carry out guerrilla research. The process takes time, allowing the researchers get to know the system, ask research questions and create test materials. In creating a scenario, apart from the golden rules presented by Iga Mościchowska in her book [11], two more rules are applied:

1) The test scenario is not only for the researchers – everyone should be able to understand the tasks, questions and their purpose, so that people not involved in the scenario's development have the opportunity to comment on it.

2) The respondent can look at the scenario during the test; he/she should not be able to find any hints or the facilitator's expectations in the scenario.

The form of the scenario itself and its layout depend on the type of test and the facilitator's preferences. However, the rigid rules of public institutions reduce any leeway: test materials are supposed to follow the established principles, and patience is required if researchers wish to introduce any changes.

As system developers are usually very busy, it can be challenging to ensure that all of them watch the focus group. Over the course of two years we have noticed a change in the approach to tests and test attendance at the Institute.

Information passed on to respondents covers two areas: first of all, practical information that will enable the respondents to arrive at the test location, e.g., a map with the location and the transportation suggestions. The second information area is any material and documents that the respondents will have to sign before starting the test procedure (e.g., respondent's consent).

OPI PIB has its own focus group room and one observation room. In the focus room, in the case of usability tests, two spaces are arranged. In the first one, the test is introduced, the house rules are presented, and a short introductory interview with the respondents takes place. The second area is where the computer workstation is located.

"Freezing" test versions can be a tricky point, which must be kept in mind, not only when reporting the test need to the project manager prior to the test. Unfortunately, errors can occur during testing, as can system malfunctions. Postponing tests and not delivering test versions on time happen relatively often. It works similarly in the public and private sectors.

Based on the above can claim that the highest probability of complications is in situations where researchers depend on other people, not technology. This is why the researcher's soft skills and good cooperation with project team members are so important. Unfortunately, despite the fact that these skills are highly relevant, it is not easy for entities from the public sector to ensure and provide employee training in this area.

B. *Implementation*

Usability tests lasting more than an hour and a half can be tiring not only for the respondent, but also for the observers and the facilitator. Unfortunately, the need and capacity to perform tests usually materialises when an advanced version of the system is ready (often a production-ready version). Stakeholders then want to test the entire system. Individual user sessions almost never take only half an hour – they are usually 60 to 90 minutes long. Unfortunately, it is challenging for the respondents to remain active and attentive for a long time. Although the optimal length of the test is of crucial importance, it is often subject to negotiations with the respondents at OPI PIB. The three pillars on which good research results are based are appropriately designed tasks, conversations and the test's overall atmosphere.

While creating the tasks, it is of key importance for all tasks to be natural and logical – they should minimize unnatural actions like logging out and logging in to another account. Tasks should not be interrupted with questions. There should be no suggestions to abandon a task before the respondent has expressed his/her wish to abandon the task. Importantly, the perception of the passing time is different for the observers and different for the person who is actually performing the task. Since the tested systems are often very comprehensive and have many functionalities, requests for reflection and questions to respondents are asked after a task or series of tasks, rather than after the completion of the whole test. Such conduct may yield more information than just the results of observation of the tasks performed. Employees of the science sector (users of previous versions of the system) may have many valuable reflections. This type of testing is no longer a classic usability test, but a hybrid with an in-depth interview, although in-depth interviews should typically take place before solution design.

The second foundation of good testing is the conversation. In the introduction, it is always a good idea to inform the respondents what the tests will look like and how long they will take [12], as well as telling them tell about the possibility of task interruption. The investigator should also allow the respondent to ask questions in order to make the respondent feel more confident in the new situation and speak more freely. The most important information to be conveyed to the respondent is that he or she is not going to be evaluated – this seems particularly important when working with employees of the science sector as they sometimes perceive our institution as superior and affiliated with the Ministry of Higher Education and Science.

As part of the third pillar of testing, the facilitator should radiate positive energy and develop a friendly and open test atmosphere. It is essential for the facilitator to be empathetic. The results of the test largely depend on the facilitator's involvement in building a positive, relaxed atmosphere conducive to the respondent's cooperation and information-sharing.

Insights from the tests and interpretations based on user feedback are provided in Section IV.

C. *After the Tests*

Before the test report is produced and after completion of testing, researchers at OPI PIB typically organise two summary meetings. The first one is informal and aims at discussing the results with the researchers involved in the project. The second one involves the stakeholders and is aimed at discussing the most important observations, and, if possible, should be organised within a short period of time after the end of the testing procedure. The meetings are also associated with the a need to build relationships between members of different teams, which would allow the project teams to work in a more agile and dynamic way, abandoning some procedures from the waterfall/cascade model and improving some standards of work within creative/UX teams [13][14]. After the report has been created, the first thing to do is to establish the date of its presentation, before the report is sent out to stakeholders. If there is no set date, the stakeholders may find it challenging to find time to meet later. It is a good idea to remember to send the report out to the stakeholders (mainly designers) before the presentation. This is sometimes due to the fact that the designers may be slightly anxious as to whether the report will show their work in bad light. They may also feel that their contribution is being evaluated.

It is good practice to determine the progress in introducing changes sometime after the test, as well as determining if the designers have all the information necessary to implement the necessary modifications. Their continuous interest in the subject increases the probability that the proposed changes will actually be implemented. The abundance of responsibilities and, to a larger extent, the formal procedures in place at the Institute, make it difficult for the stakeholders to meet regularly. As people work in different teams, official appointments for every meeting need to be made, in most cases involving leaders and managers whose availability is very limited. Although managerial presence at the meeting is not always necessary for the quality and efficiency of the meeting, meetings often cannot be held without them. These formal requirements are also responsible for a formal meeting atmosphere that hinders an unrestrained and free exchange of ideas. It is also likely that the physical work environment influences communication between teams. Open space office arrangements encourage conversations between employees, while at the OPI PIB people work in four different buildings.

IV. Challanges and Usability Tests Results

A. *Challenges for Researchers and Designers*

At OPI PIB, teams of UX researchers, UX designers and developers work across different departments. This specificity of work organization at the Institute means that people involved in the development of systems are separated from each other, and this undoubtedly hinders cooperation. As a result, researchers have a limited capability to monitor the further development of the product after the testing is completed. Therefore, it is important that the project team members cooperate closely and have frequent contacts to create product concepts together, co-design, co-develop and monitor further product use.

At OPI PIB, like in many other institutions and companies in Poland, UX testing is introduced at a fairly advanced stage of product development, triggering the risk of much higher costs of implementation of changes [15]. The benefits of early-stage UX testing include the ability to verify the identified target group, define the real needs of users, and investigate the initial concept of the system and its architecture.

The systems developed at OPI PIB are mostly commissioned by the Ministry of Science and Higher Education and are intended primarily for users from HEIs [16]. The systems are mainly based on regulations and laws, which directly affects the structure and functionality offered by these solutions, as well as imposing design constraints on developers and limiting the available options.

Due to the specificity and intended use of the systems designed and developed at OPI PIB, they are used mainly on desktop or laptop computers, so there has so far been no need to create mobile versions. However, the situation is now changing and new systems are being developed, designed also for users from beyond the academic community – therefore it is becoming necessary to develop mobile versions of the systems, too. In this respect, the public sector is beginning to operate like the private sector – "Mobile first" is beginning to apply.

Some of the systems created by the OPI PIB are digital versions of various types of paper forms and application forms. The designers face the challenge of creating functional and user-friendly forms ensuring an easy fill-out process. Unfortunately, despite the availability of digital versions, users still have to print out paper versions of forms as well.

Increasingly, stakeholders appear as observers in tests because they recognise tests as a great opportunity to see how users interact with the systems and what problems they encounter. Thanks to participation in such processes, stakeholders can count on receiving prompt feedback on their effort, without having to wait for the final report. Behind-the-scenes conversations in the viewing room also offer a good opportunity to discuss and exchange ideas on how to design systems, or how to redesign them. Thanks to such conversations, it is possible to learn about the limitations of both designers and users which for some reason did not surface at project meetings preceding the testing phase.

Remarks and comments from the post-test reports should ideally be introduced into subsequent versions of the system, with the critical points repaired of necessary. Unfortunately, this scenario is only implemented in 50% of the cases – not due to lack of involvement or bad will, but to a large extent due to the binding legal constraints.

B. *Usability Tests Results*

The numerous usability studies and conversations with end users we have conducted at the Institute have allowed us to outline the principles that designers should bear in mind when creating systems. Here are some of the recommendations:

1) Names, headings and keywords. Users quickly browse the website for specific keywords, sentences or paragraphs and skip most of the text. It is therefore important to organise the content, group the elements and assign headings, titles and labels to them in an appropriate way. The terminology used should be simple, clear and understandable to all system users.

In state institutions, some of the terminology that can be found on websites is borrowed from acts of law, regulations or technical documentation. This leads to lack of terminological clarity for users and difficulties in understanding the content. Some system designers have recognised this problem and the need to introduce plain language so that users with different levels of education and knowledge can understand the text. Consequently, public administration entities now employ a growing number of experts in their UX teams (UX writers).

2) Icons. They help users remember content more easily and quickly, making the message more interesting. It is important to remember that icons should be adequate to what the system is supposed to communicate to its users. In the case of database systems, icons can help users understand content more easily.

3) Diagrams and graphs. They should be understandable and legible. Remember to include explanations and legends. It is worth noting that the graph and its description should be visible on one screen at the same time so that the user does not have to scroll between the graph and its description. System developers know what information and data they want to present on charts and assume in advance that their preferred way of presenting data will be clear and legible for the users as well.

4) Short texts. Large blocks of lengthy text are not attractive and discouraging to users. Text should consist of short or medium-length sentences grouped into paragraphs. The content can also be split into bullet points. Furthermore, the users who would like to find out more need to be taken into account as well – include a link to a page with extended information.

5) White space. System developers often misinterpret system legibility as a lot of white space on the screen. Such an approach to design is often counterproductive, since users who interact with such a site assess it as poorly designed. Designers believe that by giving up illustrations and graphics, they can avoid the superfluous content characteristic of commercial websites overloaded with advertisements, pop-ups and banners. This misguided ascetic approach may cause the system to be perceived, on the one hand, as clear and transparent, but on the other hand – as overly rigid and official due to the excessive amount of white space. During the tests referred to in this paper, the respondents pointed out that in many systems designed at OPI PIB there is too much "vacant" space. They believed that the blank area could have been better utilized to accommodate more text and condensed content. A large amount of white space may mean that there is little meaningful content on the screen, and the user has to scroll down to find out more.

6) System coherence. It is important that all elements of the system should fit together and the construction of the site should be coherent. The design should be tailored to the needs and expectations of the user. Consistency of the components makes the design intuitive, easy to navigate, and easy to use. The systems developed at the Institute are comprehensive and complex. Due to changes in legal provisions and for other reasons they must be updated from time to time.

7) Searching, querying, sorting and display of results. User queries should be as easy as possible. It would be good if the search results covered the whole system, not only its selected part or category. Filters should be designed so that the user can select several variants of the same feature. Users should also be given to the possibility to enter keywords with spelling mistakes, typos and incorrect conjugation. It is very important to present the search results properly, displaying the searched information or its fragments in the format expected by the user. Unfortunately, public institutions do not always want to rely on the industry's best practice and solutions – instead, own solutions are created which are frequently neither proven nor tested. Perhaps such an approach is associated with the misconception that looking for own system solutions is a way to avoid being accused of plagiarism.

V. CONCLUSION

The aim of our research was to show the specificity of the UX research in the public sector in Poland and identify areas which could be change in order to bring the process of developing and designing systems closer to the ideal. After analysing the presented experiences and data and with a view to facilitate a further development of research activity at OPI PIB, the authors' aim is to ensure that the UX research of systems developed at the Institute are conducted at various stages of product development. During the tests and research conducted for this paper we noticed how important it is to apply different research techniques, appropriately matched to the given development phase of the system. An important task is also to change the attitude of designers and developers of systems to users. It is essential that system designers focus mainly on users and their needs, and that they take into account users' limitations.

In order to achieve these goals, internal seminars can help to present the work of UX researchers and the entire testing process. It is also beneficial to indicate how both system developers and users can profit from properly delivered testing. Effective communication of said benefits can be facilitated by issuing reports to provide stakeholders with more information about users and the testing procedure. It is also necessary to organize meetings with stakeholders as often as possible in order to talk about their needs and indicate possible solutions. It is important to give users a sense of security, support and space for their creativity. Communication is the foundation for creating systems that will match users' expectations. Furthermore, relations with other teams and the ability to communicate effectively and efficiently are important elements of the work of researchers. Additionally, researchers ought to continuously improve their competences and acquire new knowledge. It is of key importance that they continue to develop by attending training courses, reading professional literature or taking part in conferences where they can exchange their ideas and observations with other researchers.

REFERENCES

[1] National Information Processing Institute. *Research.* [Online]. Available from: https://www.opi.org.pl/en/Research.html 2020.01.30.

[2] K. Hastrup, "A Passage to Anthropology: Between Experience and Theory", London: Routledge, pp. 59, 1995.

[3] C. Clifford, "A Thick Description: Toward an Interpretive Theory of Culture", New York: Basic Books, pp. 3-30, 1973 in "The Interpretation of Cultures: Selected Essays".

[4] J. Janowski, "Elektroniczny obrót prawny", Translation: "Electronic legal transactions", Warszawa: Wolters Kluwer Polska, pp. 164, 2008.

[5] Polon. *Zestawienie danych o pracownikach*, translation: *Summary of employee data.* [Online]. Available from: https://polon.nauka.gov.pl/help/doku.php/terminy/pracownicy 2020.01.30.

[6] "Rozporządzenie Rady Ministrów z dnia 12 kwietnia 2012 r. w sprawie Krajowych Ram Interoperacyjności, minimalnych wymagań dla rejestrów publicznych i wymiany informacji w postaci elektronicznej oraz minimalnych wymagań dla systemów teleinformatycznych", translation: "Regulation of the Council of Ministers of April 12, 2012 on the National Interoperability Framework, minimum requirements for public registers and exchange of information in electronic form, as well as minimum requirements for ICT systems", Journal of Laws of 2012, item 526.

[7] O. Achmatowicz, "Blaski i cienie awansu naukowego w Polsce", translation: "The splendors and shadows of scientific advancement in Poland", Rocznik Towarzystwa Naukowego Warszawskiego", Warszawa, vol. 74, pp. 5-26, 2011.

[8] D. Batorski and A. Płoszaj, "Diagnoza i rekomendacje w obszarze kompetencji cyfrowych społeczeństwa i przeciwdziałania wykluczeniu cyfrowemu w kontekście zaprogramowania wsparcia w latach 2014-2020", translation: "Diagnosis and recommendations in the area of digital competence of society and counteracting digital exclusion in the context of programming support in 2014-2020", Warszawa, 2012 [Online]. Available from: http://www.euroreg.uw.edu.pl/dane/web_euroreg_publications_files/3513/ekspertyza_mrr_kompetencjecyfrowe_2014-2020.pdf 2020.01.30.

[9] E. Buie and D. Murray, "Usability in Government Systems: User Experience Design for Citizens and Public Servants", San Fransisco: Morgan Kaufmann, 2012.

[10] S. Krug, "Rocket Surgery Made Easy: The Do-It-Yourself Guide to Finding and Fixing Usability Problems (Voices That Matter)", CA: New Riders, 2010.

[11] I. Mościchowska and B. Roguś-Turek, "Badania jako Podstawa Projektowania User Experiencee", translation: "Research as the Basis of User Experience Design", Warszawa 2016.

[12] S. Krug, "Don't Make Me Think, Revisited: A Common Sense Approach to Web Usability", CA: New Riders, 2014.

[13] J. Gothelf and J. Seiden, "Lean UX: Designing Great Products with Agile Teams", CA: O'Reilly Media, 2016.

[14] L. Klein, "UX for lean startups: faster, smarter user experience research and design", CA: O'Reilly Media, 2013.

[15] I. Mościchowska, J. Rutkowska and T. Skórski, "Raport User Experience Design i Product Design w Polsce 2018", translation: "Report of User Experience Design and Product Design in Poland 2018", vol. 5, pp. 1-57, 2018. [Online]. Available from: http://raport2018.hci.org.pl/Raport_UxiPDwPolsce_2018.pdf 2020.01.30

[16] National Information Processing Institute. *Databases*. [Online]. Available from: https://www.opi.org.pl/en/articles/id/88.html 2020.01.30.

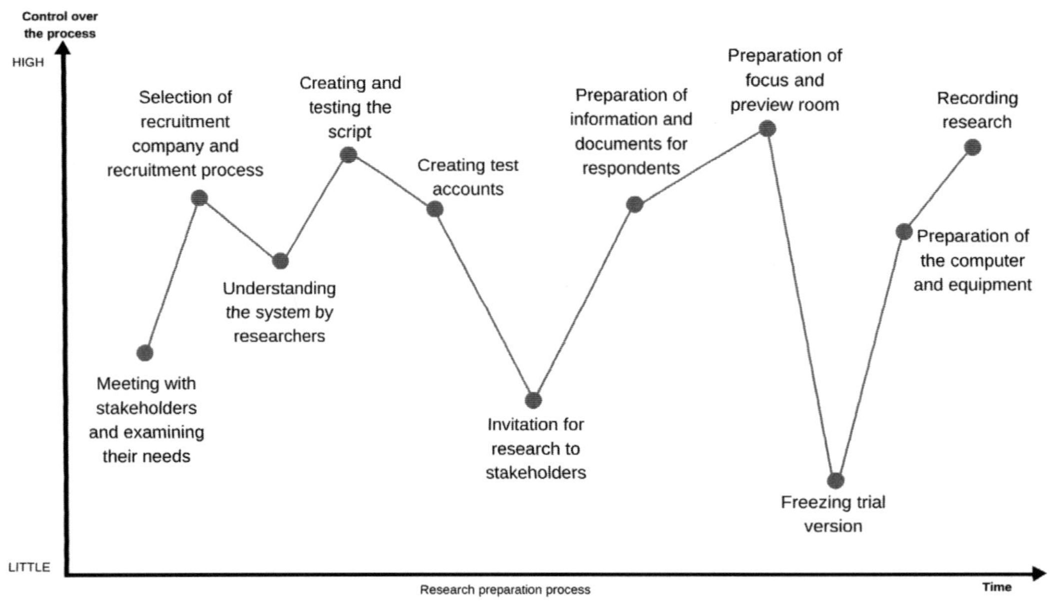

Figure 1. Research preparation process in the National Information Processing Institute in Poland.

Reactions to Immersive Virtual Reality Experiences Across Generations X, Y, and Z

Zbigniew Bohdanowicz, Jarosław Kowalski, Daniel Cnotkowski, Paweł Kobyliński, Cezary Biele
National Information Processing Institute
Warsaw, Poland
email: zbigniew.bohdanowicz@opi.org.pl, jaroslaw.kowalski@opi.org.pl, daniel.cnotkowski@opi.org.pl, pawel.kobylinski@opi.org.pl, cezary.biele@opi.org.pl

***Abstract*— Immersive Virtual Reality (IVR) may potentially effect considerable lifestyle changes in societies, comparable to those seen with the spread of smartphones. Questions arise as to the significance of IVR, and how people will respond to this type of innovation. The article presents the results of a qualitative study which assesses the reactions of adults from Generations X, Y and Z to IVR. 18 people aged 20-55 took part in the study; seven IVR applications were used. The study assessed participants' reactions, level of presence, affective response and susceptibility to cybersickness. The development potential of IVR was also considered. It was assumed that older generations would be less present in the IVR and their subjective assessment of satisfaction would be lower. The results of the study confirmed the hypothesis that, as people age, their level of presence in IVR decreases, but surprisingly, it emerged that satisfaction with being in IVR increases along with the age of the participants.**

Keywords - Immersive Virtual Reality; Generations; Presence; Immersion; Emotions; Adults; Qualitative Methods.

I. INTRODUCTION

The definition of presence in virtual space was formulated as early as 2005 by Slater and Sanches-Vives, as the degree to which people actually respond to stimuli in Virtual Reality (VR), at the level of basic psychological reactions as well as in terms of complex emotions and behaviors. The simplest way to describe it is that a person has the impression of being in a virtual space rather than in the place where they are physically present [1].

Currently, the development of VR technology is at an interesting stage where, on the one hand, simulations have reached a relatively high level of advancement and can provide a suggestive experience to the senses of sight and hearing, while, on the other hand, there are few people (at least in Poland) who have had actual contact with the technology. The new devices, introduced in 2016 (Oculus Vive in March of 2016, followed by others) opened a new level of VR-experience quality. High resolution vision, a wide scope of view, instant and smooth reaction to body movements and interactive controllers enabled simulation that had not been technically possible before. Therefore, to distinguish the experience offered by the generation of devices available since 2016, we shall refer to it as Immersive Virtual Reality (IVR).

In the near future, IVR is expected to become commonplace, as devices gradually become more comfortable, lighter, cheaper and simpler to use. It is likely that IVR technology will increasingly be used by people of all ages and will gradually become a more ordinary element of our lives. This impending technological change leads to questions about its use and its likely impact on people's way of life. Who will use it? Is the user group limited to younger people who feel at ease with adopting new technological solutions? Will older people take full advantage of the opportunities offered by IVR? Finally, how will the perceptions of this technology differ among people of different ages?

With these questions in mind, we decided to conduct the qualitative study which is presented in this article. The study evaluates the impressions of adult respondents after their first contact with IVR technology. In order to capture age-related differences, three age-differentiated groups of people were invited to participate in the study. In Section 2, groups representing generations labelled by sociologists as Generations X, Y and Z are described. Section 3 shows age-related differences in the reception of the IVR. Section 4 describes the dimensions on which experience of presence in the IVR is evaluated in the literature. The study objective, research questions and methodological details of the study are laid out in Sections 5, 6 and 7. The results are described in section 8, followed by discussion in Section 9 and conclusions in Section 10.

II. GENERATIONS X, Y, Z AND TECHNOLOGY

People of different ages may have diverse approaches to digital innovation, as Information Technology (IT) plays different roles across generations. The dynamic development of the industrial economy, particularly visible since the second half of the 20th century, has introduced a large number of changes to the world in which subsequent generations grew up. In order to better capture and describe these differences, sociologists have distinguished the following generations [2][3]:

- Generation X was born in the period between 1965-1980. Their younger years were spent in the 'analogue' world, without computers and the Internet. Computers appeared only later in their adult lives when they were either already working (in the case of people born around 1965) or in their late teens (the younger part of this generation). This generation became familiar with smartphones as grown-ups.

- Generation Y (Millennials) are those born between 1981 and 1996. Their childhoods coincide with the explosion of the Internet and personal computing. To them, computer literacy and Internet are natural, but in their childhoods, small, portable devices with high-speed Internet access (smartphones, tablets) were not yet widely available, so their childhoods resembled those of previous generations. Generation Y started to use portable devices as teenagers, so they gradually entered the digital world during adolescence.
- Generation Z are those born between 1997 and 2012. To this generation, the digital world and the Internet have always been available. They do not remember a world without mobile devices and broadband Internet access; the "pixel world" functions as a natural complement to the "real world".

Each of these generations experienced their initial contact with digital technology at a different stage of their lives, so it is likely that they will have differing opinions about being in a virtual world (Table 1.). One might suspect that the opinions on IVR expressed by Generation Z, born in a world dominated by digital technology and broadband Internet, would be different from those who had to learn to use digital devices when they were adults (Generation X and, to a lesser extent, Generation Y). Evaluation of how age affects users' behaviours and responses to IVR experience can be valuable from various perspectives. Estimation of this technology's potential within specific age groups may help to evaluate how IVR could influence the lifestyle of future societies. Software developers may also benefit from age-related insights, in order to prepare applications more adequately suited to the needs of specific age groups.

In order to verify whether there are any differences between the generations in their assessments of IVR experiences, three age groups were distinguished in the recruitment for the interview. These represent the first years of the X, Y and Z generations, as defined by sociologists and mentioned above. It should be noted that the generational changes described by sociologists from Western Europe and the USA arrived in Poland with a few years' delay.

III. Age-Related Differences In The Reception Of Immersive Virtual Reality

Due to intensified development and increasing availability of IVR technology, the number of research projects using this tool has grown rapidly. It should be noted that the general term 'Virtual Reality' (VR) may be applied to various experiences which differ from one another significantly. Sometimes, it defines an experience with a personal computer, some researchers designate experiences with basic Virtual Technology devices (before 2016) as VR, while others relate VR to the current IVR technology.

TABLE 1. PRESENCE OF A GIVEN TECHNOLOGY (TV, PERSONAL COMPUTER, INTERNET, SMARTPHONE) DURING CHILDHOODS OF SUBSEQUENT GENERATIONS.

Generation vs technology during childhood	**Gen X 1965-80**	**Gen Y 1981-96**	**Gen Z 1997-12**
TV (analogue) 1950-60 - USA, 1960-70 - Poland	yes	yes	yes
Personal Computer 1995 - Windows 95	-	yes	yes
Internet 1995 - civilian use	-	yes	yes
Smartphone 2007 - iPhone 2G	-	-	yes

In this article, we focus on the research projects done in 2016 or later, as the previous studies would have been carried out with earlier generations of VR technology, significantly inferior to the type available today. The vast majority of IVR research is conducted with young respondents. The first results currently available on the potential of IVR technology for older people [4] indicate that IVR may be accepted by this group of users. The usefulness of IVR is also studied on sample groups representing older generations in the context of training courses, for instance, which are aimed at improving the cognitive functions of older people [5] or the development of new tools to assess memory functions in older people [6]. Individual reports [7][8] indicate that performance levels in IVR may be lower among older people than among young people. However, there is no definitive research aimed at exploring how age impacts one's IVR reception. It is also interesting how the age of the users may affect one's approach to using IVR (e.g., the level of task completion), and how the same experience is evaluated, whether in terms of presence, subjectively perceived pleasure or effectiveness. It is also worth noting that all of the studies mentioned above focus on one experience (usually through a widely available application). In order to more effectively capture the potential differences in the reception of IVR, we believe it is necessary to use a wider range of experiences, preferably including experiences created specifically for the study [9].

IV. Dimensions For IVR Experience Evaluation

Being in a virtual space is a relatively new possibility. Scholarly sources do not yet have a well-established, universally accepted theory that describes the parameters of virtual reality experiences and their psychological dimensions. Among existing research there is work by

Slater [10], who suggests that the experience of immersion in a virtual environment should be described in two dimensions: Place Illusion (PI) and Plausibility Illusion (Psi). Slater assumes that PI pertains to the illusion of IVR being the same as actual reality, in terms of physical parameters. Therefore, the level of presence in the PI dimension depends on the physical features of the simulation (image quality, resolution, field of vision, natural simulation of head movements and other factors).

PI concerns the interpretation of events that take place in virtual reality. The level of presence in this dimension depends on the extent to which virtual events are perceived by the participant as actually occurring, whereby the participant will react to them as he/she would in the real world. Importantly, these two dimensions are independent of each other, i.e., it is possible to experience a presence at the PI level (where technical excellence in the simulation is high) while the Psi level is low (where events are interpreted as unrealistic and therefore do not engage the participant). The opposite situation may occur when, despite the low technical quality of the simulation, events are perceived as real (for example, this could be the experience of high involvement in a game running on a simple personal computer from the 1980s).

In 2018, a review of literature on immersion technology was published by Suh and Prophet [11]. Based on an analysis of 54 articles on the topic, the authors compiled a list of the most common dimensions used to describe the IVR experience. The analysis showed that the concepts used are similar in meaning to the definition of presence by Slater [10] in terms of PI and Psi. Alternative notions describing presence in IVR include Immersion (with its two dimensions: Physical Immersion and Mental Immersion) and Presence (with its three dimensions: Physical Presence, Spatial Presence and Social Presence). An important complement of Suh's and Prophet's work on the approach proposed by Slater, is a subjective evaluation of the IVR experience, measured by the intensity of one's affective reactions, such as Pleasure, Arousal, Dominance, and Positive/Negative Emotions.

Cybersickness is an important aspect of being in virtual reality. It describes a deterioration of well-being, resulting from a virtual world experience. Shafer et al. conducted a study proving that cybersickness occurs among players using IVR technology and is particularly common in games with higher levels of sensory conflict, like first person games [12]. This aspect of IVR experience would also be covered in the study.

V. THE STUDY OBJECTIVE

The study presented in this article was designed to evaluate the reactions of adults to their first experiences with IVR technology. In particular, the goal of the research was to compare the reactions of people of different generations (X, Y and Z). Our aim was to find out if the age at which at which a person first became familiar with digital technology has an impact on one's sense of presence during IVR experience and its evaluation.

Based on a literature review of virtual reality, we decided to describe this experience on the basis of two dimensions defining the sense of presence in virtual space, according to Slater's methodology [10], namely physical presence (PI) and reality of events (Psi). We assumed that a high sense of presence is manifested by the fact that the participant behaves in the virtual world as he/she would in reality: moves around freely, grips and manipulates objects, or reacts to stimuli in the same way as he or she would react in reality.

Based on the work of Suh and Prophet [11], the experience was also evaluated in terms of the respondent's affective reaction (Positive/Negative Emotions, Pleasure, Arousal, Dominance). We assumed that affective reaction is an indicator of subjective evaluation of the experience. A high level of positive emotions and feelings of pleasure following the experience indicate positive evaluation and satisfaction from experience, while negative emotions and unpleasant impressions indicate a negative evaluation.

Our study was also intended to find out if the respondents were affected by cybersickness during their IVR experiences. This issue was raised by the researchers and was the subject of a follow-up telephone conversation one day after.

VI. RESEARCH QUESTIONS

Following a review of the literature on the subject, we formulated the following questions concerning the relationship between age and reactions to an IVR experience:

Would the youngest respondents exhibit the highest levels of presence? How might the level of presence change as the age of the respondents increases?

Presence is understood here in two dimensions - as the physical presence (the freedom of movement, the speed of learning object manipulation) and as the sensed reality of the events in the virtual world (behaves similarly as one would in the real world).

VII. METHOD

The qualitative interview was conducted in June and July of 2019, in Warsaw. Each interview with a respondent took about 1.5 hours to complete and consisted of the following three stages:

1. Introduction. An initial conversation concerning the purpose and procedure of the research, the participants' interests and their previous experience with IVR. At this stage, the IVR equipment was also presented to the participant with information about how to operate it.
2. IVR experience. At this stage, seven different applications were used, one after another, in random order. The total time spent in the IVR was about 40 minutes.
3. Interview. At the beginning, questions were asked about the respondent's general impressions, the perceived attractiveness of the experience and about the elements that drew his or her attention. The respondent's impressions of the IVR experience were discussed in detail, with the respondent comparing the experience to reality, the factors

that make the experience "real" and the factors negatively impacting the feeling of presence. Questions were also asked regarding any difficulties or barriers the respondent felt, and about his or her interest in repeating the experience. The interview also discussed the future applications of the technology, the potential for its development and the expected benefits and risks associated with the dissemination of IVR.

In addition, the day after the study, the investigator called the participants to ask if they had noticed any changes in their mood and if they had any other observations about the experience that they would like to convey.

The qualitative interview format was selected as the most adequate method for exploring the subject of this study, as the topic had not yet been well researched. The use of qualitative interviews allows one to generate new hypotheses and define interesting avenues for future research. The data collected during the study were subjected to qualitative analysis for commonly-recurring themes, using the method of thematic analysis [13]. The study was carried out in compliance with rules governing the implementation of qualitative research; a moderator and an observer taking notes took part in the implementation of each study.

A. Respondents

The study involved 18 people (9 females and 9 males), all residents of Warsaw, Poland. The respondents were recruited in three age groups (50% F and 50% M):

- 6 people aged 20-25 (from Generation Z)
- 6 people aged 35-40 (from Generation Y)
- 6 people aged 50-55 (from Generation X)

The aim of the recruitment process was to invite individuals typical of their respective populations in terms of education (mostly secondary education), income and occupation (the dominant group were employed in the commercial and services sectors).

B. Equipment

To conduct the research, we used a computer set equipped with an Nvidia GTX 1070TI graphics card to ensure the smooth operation of the applications. The IVR set used in the study was an HTC Vive Pro with HTC Vive controllers, selected due to its image quality, wide field of view, easy-to-use goggles, built-in headphones and pupil spacing adjustment mechanism.

C. Stimuli

The study used seven applications that present different IVR environments. We selected the applications that demonstrate IVR's practical capabilities in a variety of uses. Games were deliberately not used, as these are generally marketed to younger target users and tend to be focused more on entertainment or competing for scores than on simulating reality. The applications were chosen to allow for diverse modes of transport and user interaction within the virtual environment. Only stable, high quality and smooth-running applications were selected for the study. The applications were presented to respondents in randomised order.

Two applications were created specifically with the Vizard environment [14] (Contemporary Loft Apartment and Walk the Plank), while the remaining applications were selected from publicly available software on the Steam platform. The 360° film was taken from YouTube. The experiences presented in the study were as follow:

1. *360° Video.* This 5-minute, stereoscopic 360° film shows short shots of places of natural interest. The film consists of several shots, including a flight next to a helicopter over a beach in a big city in the USA, a view of a sandy beach, swimming underwater with a turtle and diver, swimming on a boat in Thailand, and a rocky seaside beach with a pier. The film was played through the DeoVR Player application. While watching, the respondents were sitting in a chair, so the stimulus was an example of passive transport/passive locomotion. The aim of this simulation was to present the real world using IVR technology.

2. *Dreams of Dali.* This abstract world, inspired by the works of Salvador Dali, shows the nearly unlimited possibilities for creating spaces in Virtual Reality, which can be governed by entirely different laws than those in the real world. The application uses transport based on predefined points with a visual choice of a "gaze pointer". It was also possible to move, by walking in the physical world.

3. *Contemporary Loft Apartment.* The application simulates an environment familiar to the participants of the study (living in an apartment building), where free movement and interaction with objects is possible (e.g., lifting equipment). The participant could move physically by walking or moving his character, using the arrows on a controller. The environment was created in WorldViz [15].

4. *Walk the Plank.* This is a simulation of a suspended board which the user is supposed to walk on. The environment was created in Vizard software [14]. The reason for using this application was to test the respondents' reactions to the simulation of being at a high altitude.

5. *Droid Repair Bay.* This consisted of a robot repair station on board a spacecraft, set in a world inspired by the Star Wars series.

This application allowed for advanced interaction with the environment (control of devices, robots, manipulation of controllers).

6. *The VR Museum of Fine Art.* This is a virtual museum with outstanding works of art (sculptures and paintings) in their actual sizes. The user moves around the virtual museum on foot or by teleporting him/herself to a designated location. The application is distinguished by a very accurate representation of both the museum building and the collected works.

7. *Google Earth - Virtual Tour Landmarks.* This allows for a bird's eye view sightseeing tour of unique tourist attractions worldwide (including Rio de Janeiro, the Vatican, the Grand Canyon and Barcelona). The user can see the places from high above and hear sounds that are typical of a given location. He/she is only an observer and has no influence on the course of the tour.

VIII. Results

A. *Opinions on IVR prior to the study*

IVR is widely known in industry circles, but it does not yet evoke many specific associations outside of the IT environment. The respondents in this study had not had experience with IVR prior to the study. The experience was difficult for them to imagine in advance, and they did not know how to describe it; they had made assumptions based on previous experiences with 3D cinemas, sci-fi movies or friends' opinions about IVR games played on consoles in shopping centres. Some respondents associated IVR primarily with entertainment and computer games. Others expected the study to be a virtual simulation of the world and were curious to see how realistic it would feel.

B. *First Reactions*

Only one person rated the impressions from IVR's experience as average (a 25-year-old female). The remaining respondents, regardless of their age, said that their expectations had been significantly surpassed. Interestingly, the most enthusiastic reactions were recorded among the respondents from the oldest age group. While there appeared to be a high level of satisfaction from the experience based on the descriptions of impressions given by people from the younger group (20-25 year olds), the middle group (35-40 year olds) and the older group (50-55 year olds) in particular, expressed even more enthusiastic opinions. The oldest age group reacted very emotionally to the experience and specifically stated that it was something they had not expected, at all. The respondents felt their IVR experience was too short, and a few people even said that they did not want to return to reality: *"I didn't want to go back; I'm excited, I'm fascinated, It really exceeded my expectations".*

All respondents claimed that the time in IVR passed very quickly: *"I'd never say it took such a long time. I thought it was only 10-15 minutes, really. It finished too soon"* (M, 50). Everyone declared that they would like to repeat the experience, and several people said they wished to buy IVR devices for home use.

C. *The sense of presence*

Almost all respondents in the study used similar words to describe their IVR experience: *"You put on the goggles and simply move to another world"*. While younger people (aged 20-25) highlighted new functionality offered by this technology, the older age groups saw the study as a surprising and very emotional experience. One person described it thus: *"I didn't think the human mind could play such jokes on you, not at all. It seems to me that normally I stand with my feet firmly on the ground, and that I am in control of everything. And here, it turns out I am not. I close my eyes, or rather (...) I put on the goggles and I think I'm doing something different than I am doing in reality. So this study lets you go on a collision course with yourself, with what you expect and how you perceive reality."* (F, 51)

The sense of physical presence in IVR (PI) was experienced by all respondents. The graphic quality and the possibilities of interaction with the virtual environment were highly rated, as the controllers allowed those taking part in the study to move around freely and grip objects precisely. Everyone claimed that the mapping of head movements, the wide field of vision, the simulation of hand movements and capabilities for object manipulation were so convincing that they produced a sense of physical presence.

The applications themselves, however, aroused different levels of sense of presence. Sometimes it was just a sense of physical presence (PI dimension - 360° Video, Google Earth), whereas in some applications the respondents *also* felt an illusion of the reality of events (Psi - Dreams of Dali, the VR Museum of Fine Art, Walk the Plank, Droid Repair Bay).

The sense of presence depended on the interests of the respondents. Those keen on art got deeply immersed in the world of Salvador Dali:

"It was incredibly real.... I think somebody must've worked hard on making sure that the person who wears the goggles really feels as if they were in another world. Because I felt like I'd been teleported to another world. Everything was there actually, I had a feeling that wind was blowing in my face. I don't know why, but it was probably because of the realness of the experience of that other reality" (F, 51, commenting on her experience with Dreams of Dali).

In turn, those who liked entertainment and games were interested in the simulation of a service station on a spacecraft inspired by Star Wars: *"You get the feeling that you are genuinely involved in it (...) you're there and it feels fantastic"* (F, 40).

Despite positive subjective assessments from all of the respondents, our observation of their behavior led us to conclude that the older people explored the environment less intensely, and ventured to try out the interaction possibilities less frequently. As well, the older the respondents were, the more often they needed guidance from the researcher; they needed more time to get used to virtual reality and that process appeared more complicated.

The differences between people of different generations were particularly pronounced when using the Droid Repair Bay simulation. The youngest people in the study immediately looked around the room, actively explored it and quickly learned how to operate the devices. The oldest group (50-55 year olds) looked around to a lesser extent and were less at ease in their attempts to interact with the environment. It seemed that an attempt to interact with an object that could not be manipulated was perceived as an error and should therefore be avoided. Older respondents needed more frequent guidance from the investigator and advice on which actions were 'the right ones'. However, they also positively evaluated the application and said that they had felt present in the virtual world.

Based on the interviews with the respondents, we can conclude that the positive evaluations of the realism in the simulations were partly due to a large gap between low and incorrect expectations and the surprisingly high quality of the actual IVR experience. The experience was highly evaluated, though it was not ideal. Respondents mentioned a number of factors that reduced their sense of presence in the virtual worlds.

The lack of other people in IVR was brought up several times in the interviews. In particular, the youngest group (20-25 year olds) wished to see more interactive elements (including other people) in the assessed applications. In the opinion of the younger respondents, the presence of people – even those generated by the application – would have increased the perceived realism of the experience: "*Well, I guess other people were missing. And that's what real life is all about. I'm getting a ticket, I'm walking with it and into the coffee shop. The waiter's offering me something. It doesn't need to be a long experience, but it will produce the illusory impression that I'm really there*" (F, 25).

A full immersion in the virtual world was also hampered by stimuli from the outside world (the voice of the researcher, the weight of the goggles, the cable connecting the goggles with the computer) and imperfections of the applications. Sometimes pixels were visible in the image and the use of the controller was inconsistent across the applications. There were also some software errors and gaps, e.g., those enabling the user to pass through objects or walls. Such stimuli worked as "anchors", keeping part of the respondent's consciousness in the real world.

D. Affective Response

The descriptions of the respondents' reactions show a clear difference between traditional flat screen media and IVR. Virtual reality is not only perceived, but above all it is experienced. When describing their experiences, all of the respondents spontaneously talked about feelings and emotions. The content of the experience was of secondary significance. They used such words as: *pleasure, fear, anxiety, bliss, joy, horror, excitement, relaxation.*

In the youngest group (aged 20-25), the evaluation of the experience was positive or very positive, yet at the same time the respondents were not very surprised by what they saw – probably due to the fact that representatives of Generation Z have spent their lives in a world full of digital devices, and IVR is a natural expansion of an experience they already know. They were less emotional than the older group, and used words such as: "*cool; wow; I liked it; great*". People aged 35-40 (Generation Y) did not expect such a level of realism. To them, the IVR experience was both positive and emotional. Representatives of Generation Y use technology to a lesser extent than younger people, so the gaps between their expectations and actual impressions following the experience were greater than those seen among respondents from Generation Z. They used terms like: *I am excited, stunned; I'm literally trembling inside; I haven't experienced anything like that in my whole life.*

The experience was the most surprising to the oldest people involved in the study (50-55 year olds, Generation X). This group rated the experience very highly – we could even say they were enthusiastic, and their emotions seemed the strongest of all the respondents: "*I don't know if I want to go back to the real world (...) yes... I think I'm still in a state of great shock. | Clearly, I was overwhelmed in the way I hadn't expected*" (M, 55); "*That reality shocked me (...) the label 'reality' is truly justified. Through this study you've encouraged me to buy this device, seriously.* (M, 51); "*I'm fascinated at the moment. I was surprised at the realness of it*" (M, 50); "*I didn't want to go back because everything was so beautiful out there*" (F, 50).
One respondent (F, 50) described her experience as follows: "*I was very emotional about it. Even now I have tears in my eyes, because when I saw the sea, I was immediately emotional... I would like to go back to my holiday time. It was so...gosh, it was so emotional to me...incredibly emotional, that's for sure. It's the first time I've ever had one of those goggles on me. Honestly, it felt good for me there. It was cool*".

E. Cybersickness

The literature indicates cybersickness as a significant factor reducing satisfaction from IVR experiences [12]. For this reason, special attention was paid to this phenomenon in the course of the study. In addition to raising the question of cybersickness during the interview, the respondents were telephoned and asked follow-up questions concerning their mood during the day after the research.

It was surprising that the participants did not mention any negative feelings (such as dizziness, imbalance, discomfort or nausea) during the interviews, nor were they mentioned during the telephone conversations. Shifts in mood (if any) were caused by the intensity of the experience, though respondents did not describe them as a change for the worse.

This result may differ from observations described elsewhere in the literature, as most of the reports describing the phenomenon of cybersickness are based on IVR games, whereas in our study, games were deliberately excluded. Games are highly stimulating applications and often involve controlling one's own body movements in IVR with the buttons on a controller, which causes unpleasant feelings among a majority of adult users.

IX. Discussion

The study has shown differences in the perception of IVR by people at different ages. A look at IVR experiences through the lens of generational differences is an important complement to existing knowledge on human interactions with IVR. At the same time, the study has shown that there are a number of related topics that may be subject to research and analysis.

The first of them is user experience in IVR. So far, there have only been a few papers on this subject. The quality of user experience affects the user's satisfaction and performance in the virtual world. Another prospective research idea concerns social interactions within IVR. Most of the current research relates to the experience of one person who is in IVR on his/her own. It would be interesting to see how several people interact within one IVR simulation. What would be the similarities and differences compared to their social interactions in the real world? Yet another interesting perspective on IVR is to measure the acceptable cost of real versus virtual experiences, of similar content. The first publications concerning Willingness to

Pay (WTP) in IVR are already available, but the area is still new.

Furthermore, the definition of the dimensions through which IVR experiences are described may need to be updated. The quality of IVR simulations changes quickly, such that the theories proposed a few years ago may no longer apply to all aspects of the experiences being made available by today's technologies. Another interesting area is the analysis of factors influencing the level of presence (immersion) in virtual reality. Information about what affects amplification and what weakens presence in IVR can shed new light on our understanding of the phenomenon. Taking into account the results of this study, it can be expected that once the technical imperfections of the equipment are eliminated and the simulation is complemented with social aspects, the sense of presence in IVR would increase even further.

X. CONCLUSIONS

The results of the study suggest that the level of presence in IVR decreases with age. We observed that the older respondents moved around less freely in the virtual world and had more difficulty using interactive objects. In the case of the Generation X, there was a greater difference between their behaviors in reality and in the virtual world than in the case of the younger respondents. It is surprising, however, that the subjective evaluation of IVR did not decrease with the age of the participants. In fact, the oldest group evaluated the IVR experience at the highest level.

With regard to generational differences, one explanation of this outcome may be the fact that people from Generation X grew up in a world with far less ubiquitous digital technology. They have had to adapt to the use of digital devices and as adults may need additional technological education. Today, these people are primarily task-based IT users who use it more to perform specific tasks, rather than using it for fun and leisure. That is why they less frequently play computer games and may be less interested in the functionality of new devices. In addition, their previous experiences with technology may have left them convinced that new devices are usually difficult to operate and designed for the younger generations. It is likely that to Generation X, it was unexpected and very attractive that IVR turned out to be surprisingly easy to operate. In IVR, there is no need to learn an intermediate interface, such as an operating system, a keyboard or a mouse). In order to look around, one only needs to move one's head; in order to go forward, one needs to take a few steps; in order to grip an object, it is enough to clench one's hand on the controller. From this point of view, IVR responds well to the needs identified by Kowalski et al. (2019), in a study on the use of smart speaker assistants (Google Home) by older people. One of the needs identified is that the new technology should offer *"accessible design with low barrier of entry, unlike regular computers"* [5].

In the case of Generation Z, the reason for their relatively low evaluations of IVR experience (still high, but not enthusiastic) may be the fact that new technologies have always been present in their lives. Rather unsurprisingly, Generation Z perceived IVR as a very attractive technology. However, from their point of view, the rise of IVR is a fully expected stage of digital technology development. The evaluations of the middle-aged group are situated between the extremes described above, determined by the youngest (Generation Z) and the oldest (Generation X). What follows from the above is a practical recommendation for software developers who should account for the fact that the older the group of potential users, the easier an IVR application should be.

Another interesting conclusion is that IVR is distinct from other media we currently use. What is characteristic of IVR is the fact that it is experienced, rather than received or read, as in the case of conventional media. The respondents talked about their impressions of IVR as if they were reports from their real lives. They did not describe their impressions as they would have described a book, a film or a newspaper article. The most important elements were feelings and emotions. The content of the application was of secondary importance.

The results of the study indicate that IVR may already have many practical applications. It can be a substitute for travel, especially for people who find it difficult to travel longer distances in reality. Virtual spaces, such as the VR Museum of Fine Art used in the study, offer experiences very similar to an actual museum visit. For many people, IVR can also constitute an attractive form of entertainment.

Based on the results of the study, we can assume that IVR technology will continue to develop because it is highly attractive and generates positive reactions. Additionally, from a technical point of view, IVR devices are becoming increasingly comfortable: this year (2019) has seen the introduction of the first autonomous goggles; they do not require an external computer or a cable connection (the Oculus Quest). We believe that this process may facilitate further expansion of IVR technology.

REFERENCES

[1] M. V. Sanchez-Vives and M. Slater "From presence to consciousness through virtual reality," *Nature reviews. Neuroscience*, vol. 6, no. 4, pp. 332–339, Apr. 2005.

[2] M. Dimock, "Defining generations: Where Millennials end and Generation Z begins," *Pew Research Center*, vol. 17, 2019 [Online]. Available: http://tony-silva.com/eslefl/miscstudent/downloadpagearticles/defgenerations-pew.pdf

[3] M. McCrindle and E. Wolfinger, "The ABC of XYZ: Understanding the Global Generations." The ABC of XYZ, 2009.

[4] H. Huygelier, B. Schraepen, R. van Ee, V. Vanden Abeele, and C. R. Gillebert, "Acceptance of immersive head-mounted virtual reality in older adults," *Sci. Rep.*, vol. 9, no. 1, p. 4519, Mar. 2019.

[5] J. Kowalski et al., "Older Adults and Voice Interaction: A Pilot Study with Google Home," *arXiv* [cs.HC], 17-Mar-2019 [Online]. Available: http://arxiv.org/abs/1903.07195

[6] É. Ouellet, B. Boller, N. Corriveau-Lecavalier, S. Cloutier, and S. Belleville, "The Virtual Shop: A new immersive virtual reality environment and scenario for the assessment

of everyday memory," *J. Neurosci. Methods*, vol. 303, pp. 126–135, Jun. 2018.

[7] J. Chen and C. Or, "Assessing the use of immersive virtual reality, mouse and touchscreen in pointing and dragging-and-dropping tasks among young, middle-aged and older adults," *Appl. Ergon.*, vol. 65, pp. 437–448, Nov. 2017.

[8] A. Plechatá, V. Sahula, D. Fayette, and I. Fajnerová, "Age-Related Differences With Immersive and Non-immersive Virtual Reality in Memory Assessment," *Front. Psychol.*, vol. 10, p. 1330, Jun. 2019.

[9] S. A. McGlynn, R. M. Sundaresan, and W. A. Rogers, "Investigating Age-Related Differences in Spatial Presence in Virtual Reality," *Proceedings of the Human Factors and Ergonomics Society Annual Meeting*, vol. 62, no. 1. pp. 1782–1786, 2018 [Online]. Available: http://dx.doi.org/10.1177/1541931218621404

[10] M. Slater, "Place illusion and plausibility can lead to realistic behaviour in immersive virtual environments," *Philosophical transactions of the Royal Society of London. Series B, Biological sciences*, vol. 364, no. 1535, pp. 3549–3557, Dec. 2009.

[11] A. Suh and J. Prophet, "The state of immersive technology research: A literature analysis," Comput. Human Behav., vol. 86, pp. 77–90, Sep. 2018.

[12] D. M. Shafer, C. P. Carbonara, and M. F. Korpi, "Factors Affecting Enjoyment of Virtual Reality Games: A Comparison Involving Consumer-Grade Virtual Reality Technology," *Games Health J*, vol. 8, no. 1, pp. 15–23, Feb. 2019.

[13] V. Braun and V. Clarke, "Using thematic analysis in psychology," *Qualitative research in psychology*, vol. 3, no. 2, pp. 77–101, Jan. 2006.

[14] "Vizard | Virtual Reality software for researchers." [Online]. Available: https://www.worldviz.com/vizard-virtual-reality-software. [Accessed: 09-Aug-2019]

[15] "WorldViz - Virtual Reality Creation and Collaboration." [Online]. Available: https://www.worldviz.com/. [Accessed: 09-Aug-2019]

Detection of Safety Checking Actions at Intersections Significant for Patients with Cognitive Dysfunction

Tomoji Toriyama and Akira Urashima
Department of Electrical and Computer Engineering
Toyama Prefectural University
Imizu, Toyama, Japan
email:{toriyama, a-urasim}@pu-toyama.ac.jp

***Abstract*—Many elderly people have a high probability to become patients with cognitive dysfunction. They could show symptoms of attention disorder as well as execute function disorder. These symptoms may cause unsafe driving in their daily lives. The degree of these symptoms can be evaluated through neuropsychological examination. However, the correspondence relationship between these symptoms and unsafe driving is uncertain. To address this challenge, we are developing an unsafe-driving detection system, which requires a few small wireless sensors to be attached to a driver and a steering wheel. Because many patients with cognitive dysfunction show symptoms of attention disorder, it is generally assumed that they tend to be careless with safety checking actions. Based on this assumption, we analyzed driver's checking actions at intersections. In our experiments, 14 patients with cognitive dysfunction and 13 adults without cognitive dysfunction were evaluated while driving a real car. Video analysis of the experiment focused on left turn collision checking and left-right safety checking. Some results of the analysis indicate that the number of safety checking actions performed by patients with cognitive dysfunction is confirmed to be significantly lower than those by adults without cognitive dysfunction. Using the result of this analysis, we decided to use a sensor-based safety-checking action detection method based on calculations from wireless sensors. With this method, all safety checking actions at left-turn intersections were calculated. While the threshold value was decided between -37.5 to -27.5 degrees, some relationships regarding safety-checking between the patients with cognitive dysfunction and the adults without cognitive dysfunction are found using the chi-square test. The interactive evaluation system of safety-checking actions in intersections which enables the feedback for drivers can be constructed using the proposed sensors and evaluation method.**

Keywords - Cognitive dysfunction; Wearable Sensor; Safety Checking Action; Driving Skill.

I. INTRODUCTION

When a part of our brain is affected by apoplexy, a brain tumor or injury to the head, cognitive dysfunction symptoms, including attention disorder and execute function disorder, may appear. Although these symptoms can be improved through medical treatment, it may be dangerous for the patient to drive a car as part of his/her daily life, depending on the degree of the symptoms.

In Japan, under road traffic law, a driving license can be suspended or cancelled in cases of problems with recognition, judgement or operation which are identified through aptitude tests. However, there are no standard guidelines for judging the driving aptitudes of patients with cognitive dysfunction.

Shino et al. [1] revealed in their research that they found that the elderly drivers who belong to the Mild Cognitive Impairment (MCI) group had lower divided attention and alternating attention than the elderly of the non-MCI group. These elderly people were evaluated using Mini-Mental State examination Test (MMSE), Wechslor Memory Scale-Revised logical memory test (WMS-R) and the data from driving recorders.

Park et al. [2] investigated the association between unsafe driving performance and cognitive-perceptual dysfunction among elderly drivers. In this research, the authors revealed that unsafe driving performances are more prevalent among elderly drivers than among younger drivers and unsafe performances in steering operation are associated with cognitive-perceptual dysfunction. They compared these findings with the result from Cognitive-Perceptual Assessment for Driving (CPAD) and the data from virtual reality-based driving simulator research studies.

These research studies show that higher cognitive dysfunction is related to unsafe driving. Therefore, in some hospitals, neuropsychological examinations such as MMSE or WMS-R are used to evaluate the severity of the symptoms; however, the correspondence relationship between these symptoms and unsafe driving is uncertain [3].

Driving simulators are used to measure the reaction time to sudden dangers on the road and avoidance operations such as braking and steering [4]-[6]. However, such driving simulators do not provide a sense of acceleration and deceleration to the users, and the visual resolution and coverage angle of the display are limited. There simply is a certain gap between real and virtual driving.

To solve this problem, Tada et al. [7] used a real car and attached 3-dimensional acceleration and gyro sensors to the wrists of the drivers. The study revealed that there were some differences between the expert and the beginner drivers. By attaching these sensors to the toe and the head of the driver, it was clear that the general drivers' driving technique can be evaluated and more than 80% evaluation points corresponded with the point that was indicated by the safety driving instructor [8]. The system that was used in this experiment was commercialized [9]. However, this system was only used for evaluating the driving technique of general drivers under experimental conditions.

In order to adapt this system for cognitive dysfunction patients who want to restart driving, we have been developing an unsafe-driving detection system [10]. It is installed in real cars and captures the cognitive dysfunction driver's behaviors using wearable wireless motion sensors and a Global Positioning System (GPS) sensor. For lane changing operations, deceleration for planned slowdown [11], and safety checking when parking [12], the unsafe-driving detection system has demonstrated its ability to separate patients with cognitive dysfunction from adults without such dysfunction.

In this study, we focus on the differences in safety checking actions at intersections. Using the results of video analysis with patients' driving data acquired from experiments conducted on a specially designed private course, the method which enables us to separate the patients with cognitive dysfunction and adults without cognitive dysfunction was decided and the results are presented. In Section 2, we introduce several examples of research that support the background of the research field, and describe the positioning of our research. In Section 3, we describe the materials that were used in our experiment and the method concerning how to calculate an effective value to facilitate the analysis of driver behavior from the sensor data. In Section 4, we show the experimental design and the participants' information. In Section 5, video-based and sensor-based results are shown, respectively. In Section 6, we describe the results and considerations of the experiment. In Section 7, we conclude this research with future prospects.

II. RELATED WORKS

Using a real car, evaluations of unsafe driving caused by the symptoms of cognitive dysfunction have been conducted. To detect unstable driving, Sumida et al. [13] measured the triaxial angular velocity and acceleration of real cars at a driving school using a 3-dimensional acceleration sensor, a gyro sensor and GPS. Unstable driving was detected on both curved roads and straight roads. Chin et al [14] tried to facilitate safe behaviors with social support. In this research, only 3-dimensional acceleration sensors and gyro sensors were used to detect unsafe driving. In both studies, the authors used a real car with sensors. However, the motions of the car do not always represent unsafe driving. Bi et al. [15] revealed in their research that unsafe driving of elderly drivers can be detected with a sensor which included 3-dimensional acceleration and gyro sensors and was attached to both wrists of the drivers like a watch. However, the unsafe driving which can be detected with these sensors is limited to the behavior of some motions of the driver's arms.

III. THE CALCULATION OF SENSOR ANGLES TO DETECT SAFETY CHECKING ACTION

Figure 1 shows the small wireless wearable motion sensors used in our unsafe-driving detection system. The sensors are parts that were manufactured using the Objet system [9][10]. All sensors are synchronized and can measure triaxial angular velocity and acceleration. The black sensor box also holds the GPS sensor. Figure 2 shows the sensors attached to the driver's head, wrist and right leg toe, as well as the car's steering wheel and dashboard, to measure their movements. These sensors were used under the approval of the ethics committee of The Toyama Prefectural University, Japan. In this paper, we focus on the differences in safety checking actions at intersections, and only the sensor on the head and the car were used in this analysis. The relative yaw angle of the subject's head was used to evaluate the safety-checking action. This angle value was calculated from the head and car body yaw angle, and the calculation method of the yaw angle value is shown below.

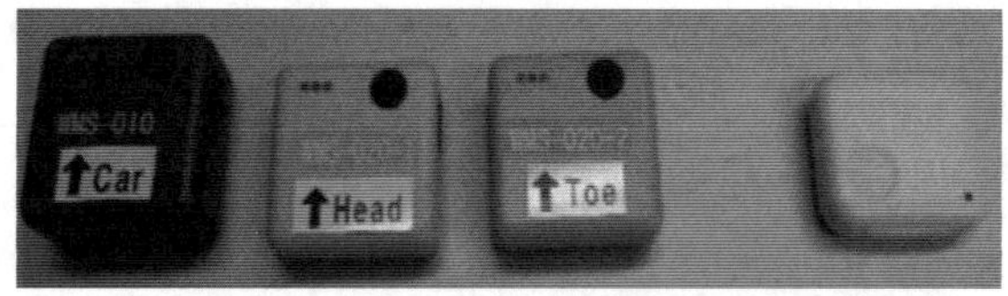

Figure 1. Wireless wearable motion sensors.

Figure 2. Attached position of sensors.

The sensor measures the three dimensional angular velocity (ω_x, ω_y, ω_z) and the three dimensional acceleration (a_x, a_y, a_z) at the interval time Δt. We adopt the kalman filter method to calculate the attitude of the sensor to the ground from those data. By defining four real numbers (t, x, y, z) in the quaternion which represents the sensor direction as the system state of the kalman filter, the sensor direction can be calculated by the iteration of the following steps:

<Prediction step>

As the sensor attitude changes by the angular velocity of the sensor, the predicted sensor attitude $\boldsymbol{x}_{k|k-1}=(t_{k|k-1}, x_{k|k-1}, y_{k|k-1}, z_{k|k-1})^T$ is given from the previous sensor attitude $\boldsymbol{x}_{k-1|k-1}=(t_{k-1|k-1}, x_{k-1|k-1}, y_{k-1|k-1}, z_{k-1|k-1})^T$ by

$$\boldsymbol{x}_{k|k-1} = \boldsymbol{F}\,\boldsymbol{x}_{k-1|k-1}, \tag{1}$$

where $\boldsymbol{F}$ is the state transition matrix which is calculated from the angular velocity and the interval time.

<Update step>

As the predicted sensor attitude can be corrected by the observed gravity direction, the updated sensor attitude $\boldsymbol{x}_{k|k}$ is calculated by

$$\boldsymbol{x}_{k|k} = \boldsymbol{x}_{k|k-1} + \boldsymbol{K}\,\boldsymbol{y}, \tag{2}$$

where $\boldsymbol{K}$ is the kalman gain, and $\boldsymbol{y}$ is the measurement residual which is calculated from the acceleration and the predicted sensor attitude. The updated sensor attitude $\boldsymbol{x}_{k|k}$ becomes the previous values of the next step.

We can calculate the sensor attitude $\boldsymbol{x}_{k|k}$ (k=1,2,3···) by the iteration of the above steps from the initial sensor attitude $\boldsymbol{x}_{0|0}=(1,0,0,0)^{\mathrm{T}}$, and the yaw angle θ_k for each of the steps is calculated from the sensor attitude by

$$\theta_k = \arctan\frac{2\left(t_{k|k}y_{k|k} + x_{k|k}z_{k|k}\right)}{t_{k|k}^2 - x_{k|k}^2 - y_{k|k}^2 + z_{k|k}^2}. \quad (3)$$

This yaw angle is clockwise, so the value of the car body sensor is increased when the car turns right, and vice versa. As the yaw angle is based on the ground, the head direction in the car is calculated by subtracting the yaw angle of the car body sensor from the yaw angle of the head sensor.

IV. Experiment through a Specially Designed Driving Course

A private course was designed at Toyama Driving Education Center, Japan, for the purpose of video analysis for safety-checking actions and acquiring the sensor data for objective evaluation. The experiment was conducted with the subjects equipped with wearable wireless sensors shown in Figure 1 while driving real cars on a private course. Figure 3 shows the top view of the private course designed for the experiment. The course includes several road types such as T-shaped, cross-shaped, and signalized/non-signalized, with/without stop sign, and roads with several kinds of speed limits. The course takes 10 - 15 minutes to drive. There are four types of turnings at T-shaped intersections (shown in Figure 4). In this study, type ①/② are called left/right turn at T-junction and type ③/④ are called right/left turn at branch. The intersections with turnings are selected for analysis because no safety checks were necessary at many of the intersections without turnings. Table 1 shows all types of intersections on the private course. In Table 1, ①, ②, ③, and ④ are denoted by LT, RT, RB, and LB, while the right and left turn at the cross intersections are denoted by RC and LC, respectively.

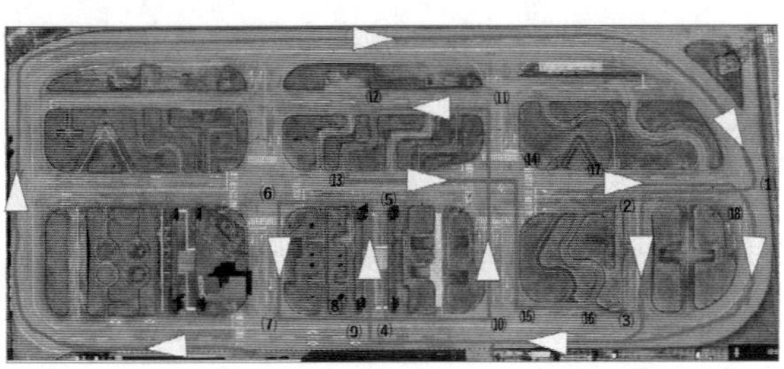

Figure 3. Specially designed private course.

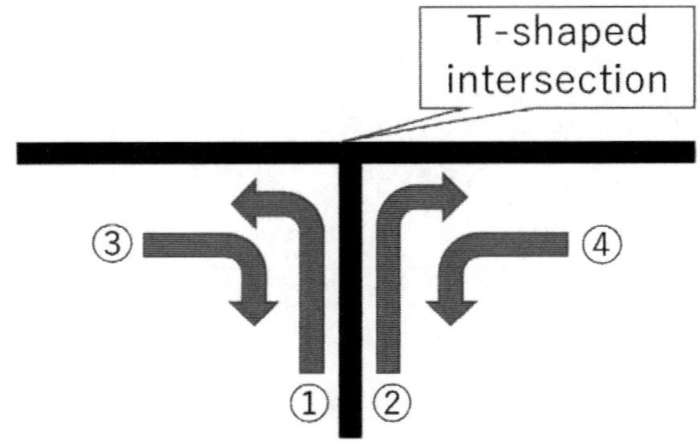

Figure 4. Types of in-out directions at T-shaped intersection on the course.

TABLE I. ATTRIBUTE OF EACH INTERSECTION

Intersection	1	2	3	4	5	6	7	8	9
Type	RB	LB	RT	RB	LT	LC	LT	LB	LT

Intersection	10	11	12	13	14	15	16	17	18
Type	LB	LC	LB	LT	RC	LT	LB	RT	RT

The subjects were males and females between 20 – 60 years old and consisted of 14 patients with cognitive dysfunction and 13 adults without cognitive dysfunction. All 14 patients had various cognitive dysfunction symptoms and were positioned border-line to be allowed to restart driving after the examination in the hospital. The experiments were conducted with all the sensors shown in Figure 1. Multiple video cameras were installed inside and outside the car to record the driving behavior in detail. These video cameras recorded a front, side, and back view of the cars and drivers.

V. Analysis using the Recorded Video

When crossing an intersection, checking for left-turn collision accident and left and right checking are essential. The former is necessary only when turning left since we have left-hand traffic in Japan, and the latter is necessary at all intersections except when checking for the left at RB, and the right at LB intersections. Therefore, 45 checking actions are necessary on the private course. From the preview of the video, the following hypothesis was established: the number of safety actions carried out by patients with cognitive dysfunction is significantly lower than the ones by adults without cognitive dysfunction. Experiments were conducted under the approval of the ethics committee of the Toyama Prefectural University. The video analysis for all 45 checking points was performed by six adult evaluators with valid driving licenses who are accustomed to driving in their everyday lives. These evaluators belong to the same organization as the authors and they are not related to this study. Table 2 shows the results of each evaluation by video analysis with T-test. One of the results indicates a significant difference ($p < 0.05$) and 2 results indicate a tendency of difference ($p < 0.1$) between the patients with cognitive dysfunction and the adults without cognitive dysfunction.

TABLE II. T-TEST RESULT

evaluator#	T-test (for all checking on all intersections)	T-test (for left checking on left-turn)
1	t(25) = 2.105, p = 0.023	t(25) = 1.912, p = 0.033
2	t(25) = 1.665, p = 0.054	t(25) = 2.206, p = 0.018
3	t(25) = 1.458, p = 0.079	t(25) = 1.806, p = 0.042
4	t(25) = 0.455, n.s.	t(25) = 1.158, n.s.
5	t(25) = 0.517, n.s.	t(25) = 0.906, n.s.
6	t(25) = 0.122, n.s.	t(25) = 0.546, n.s.

As a result of video analysis, it was clear that when the drivers check for left-turn collision, they also do left forward checking. Table 2 also shows the result of the T-test which calculated the significance of drivers' behavior focusing on the safety checking for left on left-turn. This result indicates that focusing on left side checking on left-turn leads to a significant difference between the patients with cognitive dysfunction and adults without cognitive dysfunction on safety-checking. Almost all of the safety checking actions at intersections are done before the entrance into the intersections and there is a tendency for the head angle to become bigger as the drivers approach the intersection.

For the reasons mentioned above, the safety checking detection sequence for left-turn intersections was decided to be as follows.

Step 1. Determination of the time range before and after the intersection.
To extract the sensor data including the safety-checking motion for left/right-turn from the data of the whole course, the time range before and after the target intersection is determined from GPS data according to the following criteria.
[start time: T_s] The time of GPS data nearest to the point that is 30 m before entering the target intersection or the point that is 5 m after exiting the previous intersection closer to the target intersection.
[end time: T_e] The time of GPS data nearest to the point that is 5 m after exiting the target intersection.

Step 2. Estimation of the straight-running direction before entering the intersection.
When the driver performs the safety checking before entering the intersection, it is thought that the car is going straight or has stopped and the direction of the car does not change. To extract such straight-running range, the straight-running direction of the car is estimated by the following steps.

(1) Calculate the weighted average direction d_0 from the yaw angle of the car as follows:

$$d_0 = \frac{\sum_{\{k|T_s \leq T_k \leq T_e\}} w0_k \theta_k}{\sum_{\{k|T_s \leq T_k \leq T_e\}} w0_k}, \quad (4)$$

where

$$w0_k = \frac{T_e - T_k}{T_e - T_s} \exp\left(-\frac{\left(\frac{d\theta_k}{dt}\right)^2}{\sigma_0^2} \right), \quad (5)$$

and T_k is the time of the data and σ_0 is the experimentally determined value from the standard deviation of the car yaw angle. In this weight value, the component before the exponential emphasizes the first section of the time region and the component of the exponential emphasizes the direction at the time of straight-running.

(2) Calculate the modified weighted average direction d_1 as follows:

$$d_1 = \frac{\sum_{\{k|T_s \leq T_k \leq T_e\}} w1_k \theta_k}{\sum_{\{k|T_s \leq T_k \leq T_e\}} w1_k}, \quad (6)$$

where

$$w1_k = \exp\left(-\frac{(\theta_k - d_0)^2}{\sigma_1^2} \right), \quad (7)$$

and σ_1 is the experimentally determined value from the angle region of the next step. This calculation pulls the angle d1 to the most frequently appeared angle near d_0, and the most frequently appeared angle means that the car was going into that direction for the most part.

Step 3. Extraction of the time range of the straight-running before entering the intersection.
Due to the influence of the sensor noise, the calculation error and the natural small steering offset of the car, the calculated direction of the car is not completely constant even if the driver thinks that the car is going straight. So, we determine the time range of the straight-running from the point when the car direction enters within ±5 degrees to the point when the car direction becomes more than ±15 degrees.

Step 4. Extraction of the angle of left-checking
The head direction of the car can be calculated by subtracting the car yaw angle from the head yaw angle. We define the angle of left-checking as the minimum of the head direction in the range of the straight-running before entering the intersection and the angle of the right-checking as the maximum of that.

The safety-checking angle that was calculated according to the above sequence may have the drift error which was caused by the sensor. To decrease the effect of the drift error, drivers head angle was reset when drivers looked toward the front every time they came close to the intersections.

VI. Detection with Unsafe-Driving Detection System

We processed the sensor data with the method shown in Section V and obtained the left-checking angles of the left turn. There are 27 subjects and 12 left-turn intersections in the course, but one intersection of one subject was excluded because he took the wrong turn at the intersection. In addition, in order to exclude cases when the car did not go straight for a sufficient amount of time before the intersection, we decided not to include data collected in cases when Step 3 of the previously mentioned method was less than 3 seconds. There were 18 cases that were under 3 seconds out of the 323 left-turn intersections; therefore, 305 cases were analyzed.

Assuming a threshold head angle can determine the safety checking actions, the relationship between the safety checking count was measured by the threshold angle and the driver's status. Patients with cognitive dysfunction or adults without cognitive dysfunction were tested from the threshold angle values of -60 to -15 degrees. Figure 5 shows the result of the chi-square test. It indicates that there is some relationship while head angle values are between -27.5 to -37.5 degrees. The T-test was performed to the ratio at which the person did their safety checking at the angle over/under -32.5 degree. Consequently, a significant difference was confirmed between the patients with cognitive dysfunction and adults without cognitive dysfunction $t(20) = 1.8276$, $p = 0.0413 < 0.05$.

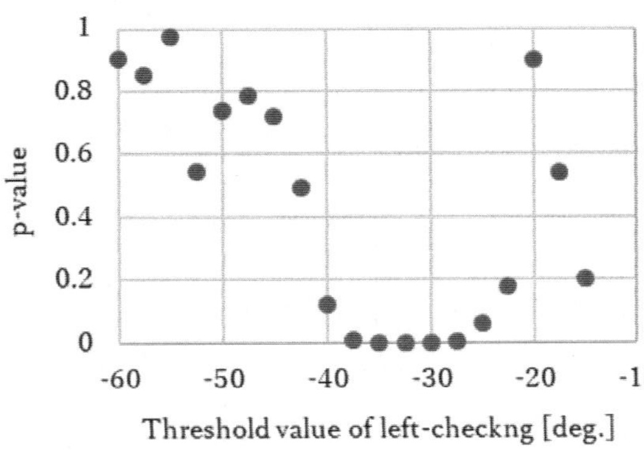

Figure 5. Wireless wearable motion sensors.

VII. Discussion

According to the results from the experiment, we conclude that the patients with cognitive dysfunction and adults without cognitive dysfunction can be separated by the head angle value just before the intersections. However, there are some differences between the results of the video-based subjective evaluations and the results of the sensor-based evaluations. The designed private course had various kinds of intersections in terms of shape, signalized/non-signalized, with/without stop sign, road width, speed limits, the time allowance to do safety-checking, and so on. By focusing on each feature, the differences between the two groups can be even clearer. The data is not sufficient for making satisfactory combinations with these features. Therefore, a further study that focuses on the effective combination of the features is expected to contribute to the supplement amount of data for distinguishing the two groups. It can also be concluded that the head angle movement threshold value calculated from the sensors can be used to separate the two groups. This study has not yet clarified the reasons for -37.5 to -27.5 degree as the best angle for separation. This leads to the hypothesis that the driver's safety checking is less than these values or includes many indirect checkings by way of the mirror or the checkings done with more eye movements and less head movements. This can be examined in a further studies using an eye-tracking system to analyze the driver's safety-checking actions in detail. In addition, the proposed safety checking action detection method may need changes. The angle calculation method which is shown in Section III may have a calculation error, because it calculates under the assumption that gravity acceleration is always constant and the direction is always 90-degree angle to the ground. This can cause errors when the car is accelerating or turning. Also, the accuracy of each parameter explained in Section V for detecting the safety checking action, requires adequate improvements for the effective detection. At the moment, manual resetting of the driver's head angle on every intersection is required. In order to reset automatically, the average head angle before the intersections can be used in future works.

VIII. Conclusion

This paper presented an unsafe-driving detection system. We conducted experiments equipped with video cameras and wearable wireless motion sensors using real cars. It was discovered that the safety checking actions of patients with cognitive dysfunction can be significantly confirmed by conducting a subjective evaluation and sensor based calculation with a basic set of checking actions.

Acknowledgment

We would like to thank Toyama Driving Education Center and Toyama rehabilitation Hospital and ATR-Sensetech Corporation for the cooperation in the experiments. This work was supported by JSPS KAKENHI Grant Number 15K01472.

References

[1] M. Shino, M. Nakanishi, R. Imai, H. Yoshitake, and Y. Fujita, Investigation of Driving Behavior and Cognitive Ability

Concerning Planning Process during Driving of Elderly Drivers, International Journal of Automotive Engineering, vol. 9, No. 3, pp. 138-144, 2018.

[2] S. Park et al., "Association Between Unsafe Driving Performance and Cognitive-Perceptual Dysfunction in Older Drivers," PM&R, vol. 3, no. 3, pp. 198-203, 2011, doi:10.1016/j.pmrj.2010.12.008.

[3] A. Schanke and K. Sundet, "Comprehensive Driving Assessment: Neuropsychological Testing and On-road Evaluation of Brain Injured Patients", Scandinavian Journal of Psychology, vol. 41, Issue 2, pp. 113-121, 2000.

[4] T. Tanaka et al., "Driver Agent for Encouraging Safe Driving Behavior for the Elderly", In Proceedings of the 5th International Conference on Human Agent Interaction (HAI '17), pp. 71-79, 2017, doi: 10.1145/3125739.3125743.

[5] I. Jonsson, M. Zajicek, H. Harris, and C. Nass, "Thank You, I Did Not See That: In-car Speech Based Information Systems for Older Adults, CHI '05 Extended Abstracts on Human Factors in Computing Systems, pp. 1953-1956, 2005, doi:10.1145/1056808.1057065.

[6] A. E. Akinwuntan, J. Wachtel, and P. N. Rosen, "Driving simulation for evaluation and rehabilitation of driving after stroke", J. of Stroke and Cerebrovascular Diseases, vol. 21, Issue 6, pp. 478-486, 2012, doi: 10.1016/j.jstrokecerebrovasdis.2010.12.001.

[7] M. Tada et al., "A Method for Measuring and Analyzing Driving Behavior Using Wireless Accelerometers", The IEICE transactions on information and systems (Japanese edition) J91-D(4), pp. 1115-1129, 2008 (in Japanese).

[8] M. Tada, M. Swgawa, M. Okada, K. Renge, and K. Kogure, "Automatic Evaluation System of Driving Skill Using Wearable Sensors and Its Trial Application to Safe Driving Lecture", The IEICE Technical Repport, vol. 108, no. 263, PRMU2008-88, pp.1-6, Oct. 2008 (in Japanese).

[9] Objet, https://www.sensetech.jp/service.html [retrieved:01/2020] (in Japanese)

[10] T. Toriyama et al., "A Study of Driving Skill Evaluation System Using Wearable Sensors for Cognitive Dysfunction", IEICE Tech. Rep., vol. 113, no. 272, WIT2013-48, pp. 29-34, Oct. 2013 (in Japanese).

[11] T. Toriyama, A. Urashima, and Yoshikuni, Detection System of Unsafe Driving Behavior Significant for Cognitive Dysfunction Patients, HCI International 2017 – Posters' Extended Abstracts. HCI 2017. Communications in Computer and Information Science, vol. 713, pp. 391-396, 2017.

[12] T. Toriyama, A. Urashima, and T Kanada, Detection of Checking Action on Parking Significant for Cognitive Dysfunction Patients, HCI International 2018 – Posters' Extended Abstracts. HCI 2018. Communications in Computer and Information Science, vol. 713, pp. 404-409, 2018.

[13] Y. Sumida, M. Hayashi, K. Goshi, and K. Matsunaga, "Evaluation of Unstable Driving Using Simple Measurement Device on Driving Behavior", Information Processing Society of Japan, vol. 57, No. 1, pp. 79-88, 2016 (in Japanese).

[14] H. Chin, H. Zabihi, S. Park, M. Y. Yi, and U. Lee, "WatchOut: Facilitating Safe Driving Behaviors with Social Support", In Proceedings of the 2017 CHI Conference Extended Abstracts on Human Factors in Computing Systems (CHI EA '17), pp. 2459-2465, 2017, doi: 10.1145/3027063.3053188

[15] C. Bi et al., "SafeWatch: A Wearable Hand Motion Tracking System for Improving Driving Safety", 2017 IEEE/ACM Second International Conference on Internet-of-Things Design and Implementation (IoTDI), Pittsburgh, PA, USA pp. 223-232,2017.

Smartphone Devices in Smart Environments: Ambient Assisted Living Approach for Elderly People

Roua Jabla
University of Sousse, ISITCom
4011 Hammam Sousse, Tunisia
e-mail: jabla.roua@gmail.com

Maha Khemaja
University of Sousse
4000 Sousse, Tunisia
e-mail: khemajamaha@gmail.com

Félix Buendía
Universitat Politècnica de Valencia
46022 Valencia, Spain
e-mail: fbuendia@disca.upv.es

Sami Faiz
University of Tunis El Manar
5020 El Manar, Tunisia
e-mail: sami.faiz@isamm.uma.tn

***Abstract*—One of the motivations for smart environment and Ambient Assisted Living (AAL) research works is the significant increase in the elderly population. In that sense, it is important to address the problems associated with aging and to provide solutions to support the elderly in their daily life. This paper aims to present an AAL approach able to identify ongoing elderly activities and their context through embedded smartphone sensors in a mobile smart environment. Based on the learned context of elderly people, the proposed approach addresses the elderly's needs and triggers the most appropriate service based on ontological reasoning so that it could interact with the elderly and, more importantly, seamlessly ensure their assistance. Finally, we validate the proposal through a questionnaire exploring elderly's views about service satisfaction. We found that our proposed approach has the potential to assist the elderly in their daily life, with the majority of elderly people being mostly satisfied with the provided services.**

Keywords-context-awareness; smart environment for elders; AAL; activity recongnition; ontology.

I. INTRODUCTION

The number of elderly people keeps on growing in today's societies. According to the World Health Organization (WHO), the elderly population will quickly increase in the upcoming years [1] and may reach about 2 billion in 2050 [2]. Since age-related declines and chronic diseases can severely impair elderly's ability to remember and adequately perform everyday activities, the fulfillment of their needs with relevant assistance with daily activities and with continuous caregiving is essential to promote healthy aging. Therefore, the rapid population aging, the importance of independent living and the fulfillment of elderly's needs, together motivate the development of smart environments for elders, which open up novel opportunities for enhancing their independence and their quality of life. The concept of smart environments that interact with the elderly has emerged to provide them support and assistance with their needs, preferences and surrounding context, in addition to helping elderly who are experiencing a disability or a decline in their health and their ability to remember and undertake activities of daily living. Assisting elderly's needs and reducing caregiver's burden without compromising safety and the sense of self-control could, therefore, be regarded as one of the main purposes of smart environments for elders. In this regard, such environment shall detect emergency situations or deviations in the elderly's routine, which can indicate a decline in their abilities. To cope with this, AAL has emerged to represent a promising approach where the aging issues are further addressed [3]. Owing to the fact that AAL systems represent support for aging in place and offer great potential to carry out tailored services to suit elderly's needs, they are able to guarantee the monitoring of the daily living activities performed by the elderly through data captured from heterogeneous sensors and context.

Moreover, context-awareness and recent advancements in mobile and wearable sensors help the vision of AAL to become reality. With AAL, context-awareness highlights a crucial feature that facilitates the decision-making in real-time according to elderly's circumstances and gain in accuracy. In order to support context-awareness and justify its effectiveness, another key feature in AAL is human activity recognition to detect the elderly-relevant activities. Activity recognition plays an important role in bridging the gap between sensor data and interpretation of necessary services that the elderly need.

Within this context, we propose, in this paper, an AAL approach that meets the requirement related to continuously monitoring, motivating and assisting elderly in different daily life situations and locations. The presented AAL approach acts as a mobile smart environment for elders to help them to be more integrated within their societies while being monitored and assisted indoors and outdoors. This mobile smart environment is illustrated with merging sensor data provided by different sensors embedded in smartphone devices to dynamically find out what services should be promoting for helping the elderly to continue to live an independent life.

The rest of this paper is structured as follows: Section II provides some background knowledge. In Section III, we review some related works that deal with support for the elderly in smart environments. Section IV presents an overview of the proposed AAL approach. We describe the implementation details and the potential scenarios and then, we present the main evaluation findings in Section V. Finally, conclusions are drawn in Section VI.

II. Background

Aging is associated with progressive problems and needs in different domains, such as psychology, physiology and societal environment. Preparing for a further aging society, it is essential to deeply explore these heterogeneous elderly's needs and problems. In this regard, we put forward Maslow's hierarchy of needs [4] to provide more effective solutions for the elderly. Tamang et al. [5] argue that Maslow's hierarchy provides a solid footing to understand the needs faced by elderly people seeing that each Maslow's level of need has relevance for elderly assistive technologies [6]. The hierarchy of needs proposed by Maslow categorizes human needs into 5 distinct levels, namely, physiological needs, safety needs, love and belonging needs, esteem needs and self-actualization needs.

III. Related Work

Many non-trivial issues should be addressed when monitoring elderly activities and providing assistive services. Within that context, recognizing daily activities, deploying sensors and providing tailored support services for the elderly in smart environments are well-researched problems. With this purpose, numerous solutions have been proposed in the literature for supporting the elderly in smart environments. For instance, Fahim et al. [7] proposed a daily life activity tracking solution for an aging society. The system monitors elderly activities through different kinds of sensors, such as Radio-Frequency Identification (RFID) Tags and cameras that are located in their homes. Then, it can generate reminders for scheduled tasks and for overlooked medicines. Alternatively, Mainetti et al. [8] described an AAL system to assist the elderly by tracking them during indoor and outdoor activities. In particular, the proposed system focuses on capturing elderly data for recognizing their behavioral changes, both in their home and city environment. When abnormal behavioral changes occur, the system triggers health care notifications. More recently, Huang et al. [9] explored context awareness, an ontology-based and a rule-based reasoning approach for risk recognition and assistance. They proposed a framework for smart home management based on numerous sensors located in the home, such as device, contact, position and camera sensors. The proposed framework offers safety assistance services according to the current user activity inferred through the reasoning process based on the Semantic Web Rule Language (SWRL) rules. Moreover, Jung et al. [10] presented a hybrid-aware model for elderly wellness service in a smart home. This model detects elderly health risk based on monitoring their activities and locations in the smart home. Elderly activity is monitored using biosensors in each location. After detecting elderly health status, appropriate treatment (e.g., music therapy, exercise and hospital checkup) is recommended for the elderly using an Expectation Maximization (EM) algorithm. Lately, Patel et al. [11] introduced a hybrid framework for human behavior modeling in AAL. The proposal employs machine learning and deep learning approaches to discover the user's activity in a smart home. For that, the authors employed different types of sensors, i.e., body, object, camera and environmental sensors. This proposed solution recognized user's actions to offer essential services like medical assistance or emergency response.

Following the aforementioned works, we observe that most of them have not taken into consideration the mobility of the elderly. For that reason, a common problem associated with these works discussed so far [7][9][10][11] is that they detect daily activities performed by the elderly in a single smart environment that is usually a smart home. They target a single smart environment since sensors, which are integrated with everyday objects and connected through networks, are exploited in elderly's smart home. In addition, they apply an activity recognition approach based on dense object sensors that are attached to such indoor objects. So, elderly activities are inferred by monitoring elderly-object interactions. On the other hand, the work of Mainetti et al. [8] supported elderly people in their indoor and outdoor activities by gathering ambient parameters through sensors included in wearable devices. Moreover, all these works are based on healthcare and medical services. They do not take into account more interesting services that fulfill current elderly needs to allow them to live safely and independently in their environments. Furthermore, none of the mentioned solutions really uncover the different needs of the elderly. There is a lack of research works that propose elderly need-related services within smart environment based on a good reference for elderly needs interpretation and services development.

In the context of an aging society, we present an AAL system to enhance and provide support for daily life of the elderly by sensing the surrounding environment and the elderly activity, and interpret these data to identify their situations and to infer services accordingly. Unlike the main solutions investigated in the literature, the gap of elderly mobility has been addressed by conducting a mobile smart environment in our work. As a consequence, our proposed solution encompasses heterogeneous smart environments through which an elderly can move, by using a mobile device and by applying sensor-based activity recognition. In other words, the exploitation of sensors embedded in mobile devices with the abandonment of object-attached sensors provides a mobile smart environment where the elderly mobility is supported. In this regard, our solution transparently collects and processes information about the elderly and the environment around them from the multitude of sensors built in their smartphones. In this way, the adopted sensor-based activity recognition does not require environment object sensors and ensures elderly mobility. And then, our solution identifies needed service with respect to the current elderly's situation that falls under a specific category of needs. These elderly's needs are put forward based on Maslow's hierarchy of needs already presented in the background section. Although services offered for the elderly in main AAL works cover only the healthcare and medical areas, our solution can improve the elderly relief and promotes more elderly-friendly care services by figuring out different needs addressed in the two lowest levels of Maslow's hierarchy. Apart from the need for health care that is fulfilled as a safety need, we focus on physiological needs, such as food, sleep, housing, transportation, etc.

IV. PROPOSED APPROACH

A. *Architecture Overview*

The main focus behind our proposed approach aims to assist the elderly users in a mobile smart environment and provide them with an appropriate service at the right time considering their preferences, current activity and surrounding environment. In that sense, this approach should allow a continuous monitoring of all incoming sensor data and an immediate prediction to detect a certain elderly's emergency or anomalous situation over a short period of time. Further, it necessitates to perceive any significant changes in elderly's context and manage the current elderly's needs to meet their context changes.

As a solution to this, we present a layered architecture overview as depicted in Figure 1 that summarizes the above discussed facts.

1) Context manager layer: Is responsible for continuously managing both static and dynamic elderly's context information. This lowest layer includes the following components:

a) Context collector: Refers to the process of gathering the sensed data in real-time to deal with the dynamic aspects involving contextual elements, such as elderly's activity, location and time.

b) Context pre-processor: Is in charge of analyzing the incoming sensor data. For both location and time sensor data, a high-level information is produced from a set of low-level information. And with respect to built-in accelerometer sensor data, the analysis process is to choose the better window size.

c) Constraint analyser: Interprets the elderly's profile that reveals their different preferences, requirements and health status.

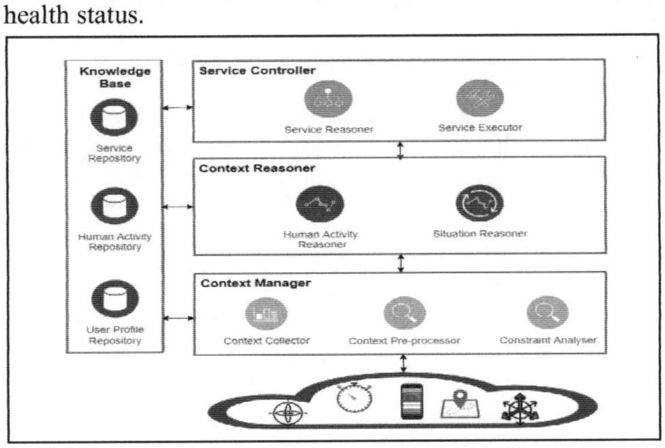

Figure 1. Architecture Overview.

2) Context reasoner layer: Supports reasoning mechanisms for activity recognition and then for situation identification regarding elderly's current context. This layer comprises two components as follows:

a) Activity reasoner: Is responsible for identifying the current activity of elderly using ontology reasoning and machine learning.

b) Situation reasoner: Is based on inference engine and uses rules on the available context information of an elderly to infer their current situation.

3) Service controller layer: Sustains the provision of personalized and adapted services to go with different elderly's needs and requirements. This layer includes the following components:

a) Service reasoner: Is responsible for determining which appropriate service should be executed through ontological inferences that are based on the current situation and elderly's profile.

b) Service executor: Is responsible for executing services that are earlier selected by "Service Reasoner" on the elderly's mobile device.

B. *Elderly service identification*

To support the proposed architecture, we focus on elderly service identification. To this end, we address the underlying needs of the elderly people based on Maslow's hierarchy previously discussed to offer certain assistive services for elders. Considering the most fundamental Maslow's levels in the view of prior study results [5], these services are fully provided to fulfill both Maslow's need levels that concern elderly physiological and safety needs. Thus, we can arrange our assistive services into two main categories to reach optimal elderly's satisfaction. The first category is elderly's physiological needs-related services and the second is elderly's safety needs-related services. In fact, both categories are often easily conflated, we investigate each of them in turn, as follows:

1) Elderly's physiological needs-related services: In addition to the basic human physiological needs, such as food, sleep, housing, transportation, etc., the eldely's physiological needs target also the daily care due to age-related problems. To moderate the side effect of unfulffiled physiological needs, a variety of elderly's physiological need-related services are developed to get over their physiological barriers.

a) Food recommendation service: Many elderly people cannot eat and drink unaided and need a special assistance. In this regard, we offer service that reminds elderly about eating at the right time. This service creates numerous reminders as notifications based on sensing and analyzing the current situation of elderly.

b) Exercise recommendation service: Elderly can carry out some physical activities that require moderate efforts, such as walking, biking, aerobics, etc. to maintain and improve their physical well-being. Hence, the increase of the efectiveness of well-being and falls-prevention needs further interventions for elderly into the behavioral patterns. To tackle that concern, we propose an exercise recommendation service that provides a reminder notification to encourage elderly to perform selected physical activity or exercise suggested by their doctors.

c) Entertainment recommendation service: While few studies, such as [12] along these lines have revealed that the entertainment needs of the elderly people is equally important for their well-being and joyful living, we provide entertainment recommendation service that selects the relevant entertainment media and delivers notification with the proposed media content, such as music, movie and so forth.

2) Elderly's safety needs-related services: Once physiological requirements are met, the safety needs, such as healthcare, emergency prevention, etc., arise. Elderly's safety needs-related services look forward to cover the demand of elderly people for life safety that refers to halth, emrgency and medical services.

a) Health recommendation service: Ensuring safe circumstances and protections for elderly, we aim to move when there are some anomalous events occurred as elderly's fall or inactivity and assure rapid and efficient help. To accomplish this aim, a health recommendation service raises alerts to an emergency contact, such as doctor, caregiver or family member when elderly is falling to the ground or has not arisen from bed for a long period in order to repond to an emergency event in a fast way.

b) Medication recommendation service: With age-related decline of memory and cognitive functionalities [13], elderly may forget to take the relevant medications at the appropriate times. For this attend, a medication recommendation service is offered to provide basic medical attention for people in old age. It yields an alert to remind them about their medicines at a pre-scheduled time to experience a healthy aging.

C. Elderly activity recognition

Tracking ongoing elderly's activity is regarded as a basis context information to better recognize their current situation in real-time and then providing the most relevant service from the aforementioned elderly's services. In this respect, we present a sensor-based activity recognition method based on mobile device using tri-axial accelerometer. We perform an online activity recognition on different activities, such as sitting, standing, walking, running, walking up/downstairs and falling, from the Heterogeneity Human Activity Recognition (HHAR) dataset [14]. The published HHAR dataset was employed as input to train a model. For inferring accurately, the actual elderly's activity, we enclose a knowledge-driven reasoning with a data-driven technique. Machine Learning (ML) algorithm as Random Forest is used to predict the initial activity label, where the accuracy of several ML algorithms (e.g., Random Forest Naïve Bayes, K-Nearest Neighbor) is well explored in previous work [15]. Then, a modular ontology, which represents the user's context, is applied for the purpose of enhancing and refining the predicted activity label derived from ML reasoning. This ontology was merged by means of activity recognition rules that are based on users' history as well as their current contexts.

D. Ontology and rules-based model

In order to process dynamic context, we provide a modular ontology for a semantic description of heterogeneous elderly's profiles with elderly's situation management and efficient service provisioning. Thus, we developed a modular ontology that offers a better selection of relevant service among a large number of services. The selection process of services is moving along a set of inference rules that are based on the current elderly's context, their needs and their inferred situations. This ontology consists of a set of interrelated ontologies, known as elderly, activity, sensor, device, process, situation, service, time and location. The general relationships among these different ontologies are depicted in Figure 2.

1) Elderly ontology: Is subclass of the context that represents and captures the elderly context within a changing environment. Figure 3 describes information about the elderly, which can alter the inferred service. An elderly has an elderly profile and an elderly constraint. Elderly profile is limited to some personal information, such as name, age, telephone, address and health status, as the elderly can be healthy or unhealthy (suffers from disease or disability). Also, it contains a medical profile that refers to the medical history of elderly including type of diseases, treatments and risk factors. As for the elderly constraint, it consists of two main branches: elderly preferences, which cover preferred entertainment content, preferred exercises (yoga, walking, biking, etc.) and preferred emergency contacts, and elderly requirements that deal with the elderly needs, such as what suggested exercises that elderly must perform.

2) Activity ontology: Describes the several physical activities that can be performed by an end user.

3) Sensor ontology: Manages perceived raw sensory data to monitor elderly's activities. It is built on top of SSN ontology [16] to represent mobile built-in sensors and their operations.

4) Device ontology: Defines knowledge about devices that are used to record raw sensory data.

5) Process ontology: Descibes different techniques that are used to interpret perceived raw sensory data and their relationships that make up activity recognition process.

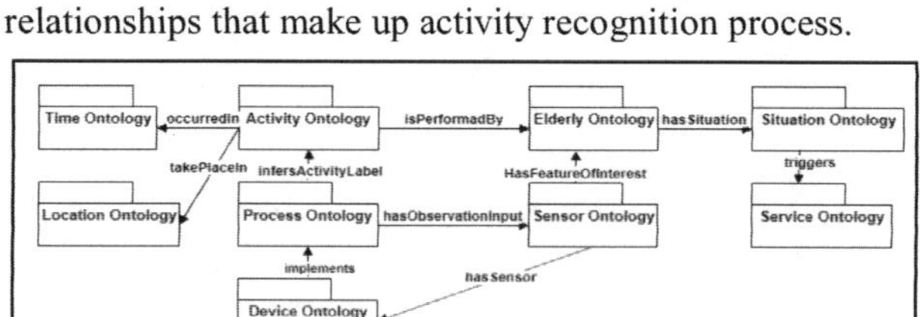

Figure 2. The core structure of our ontology and their relationships.

6) Situation ontology: Contributes to identify the possible situations depending on elderly contextual information to provide relevant service selection in order to meet their needs as closely as possible. As illustrated in Figure 4, situation consists of pertinent conditions that can be composed of the currently available context information to throughly understand elderly and improve their situation identification. A situation has different proprieties to characterize it, such as name, time, location and others. An elderly situation, which is sub concept of situation, can be either a daily situation binding a normal situation or a irregular situation related to urgent situation, such as, elderly's health issues.

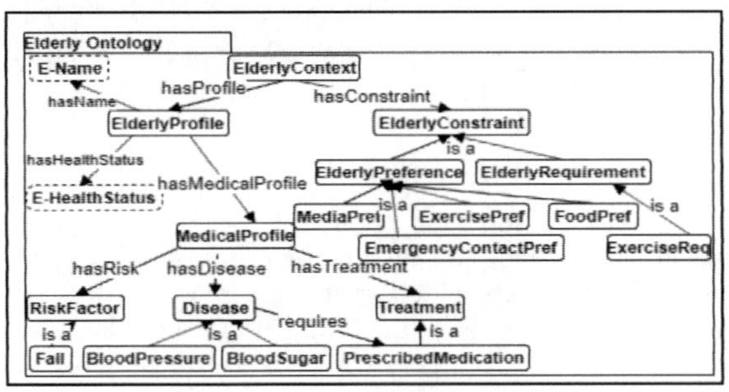

Figure 3. Excerpt of Elderly ontology.

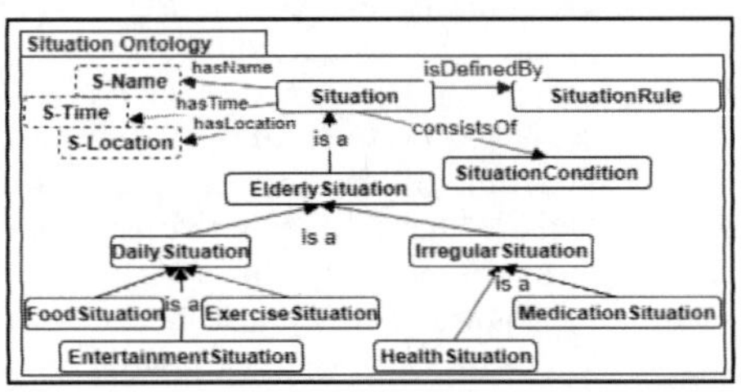

Figure 4. Excerpt of Situation ontology.

7) Service ontology: Provides a way for describing context-triggered services through the context and situation aware-based reasoning results. This sub-ontology for semantic service description adopts basic concepts and relations from a service ontology called OWL-S [17] since it is tailored to services in general along with the Web services and the semantic Web. It expands the OWL-S ontology to include additional features, such as elderly service, elderly service profile and elderly service model that extend, respectively, the OWL-S elements: service, service profile and service model. These elements are the core concepts of our service ontology as illustrated in Figure 5. An elderly service is triggered by an inferred situation. Each elderly service presents a profile to describe its characteristics by defining its name, input, output, precondition and intended purpose. Additionally, an elderly service profile can have a category. This elderly service category is divided into two basic categories: physological elderly services and safety elderly services. Moreover, elderly service is described by a model that deals with its internal structure. This elderly service model executes its own method, which defines the operational description related to the elderly service profile, to carry out the corresponding service.

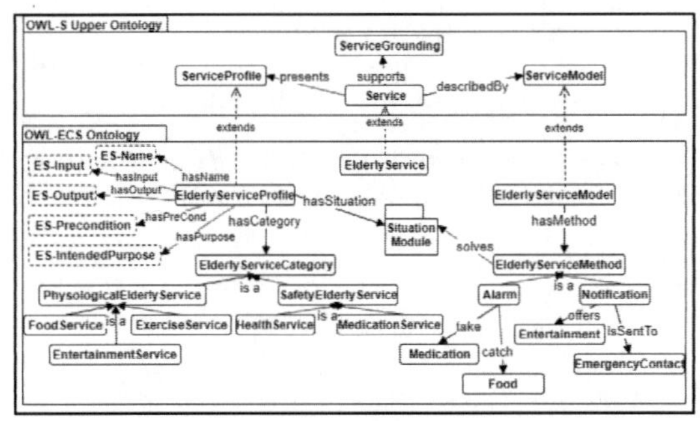

Figure 5. An excerpt of Service ontology.

8) Time ontology: Represents the time notion in the context, which can be used to indicate the time of performed activity.

9) Location ontology: Decribes the location of occurred activity.

V. IMPLEMENTATION AND POTENTIALS SCENARIOS

This section describes some implementation details of our approach, potential usage scenario and experimentation results.

A. Prototype implementation

First, we have implemented our modular ontology model based on OWL-DL using the Protégé tool. Second, Jena rule language as a syntax is used to express rules and to increase the expressivity of the ontology. The Jena inference rules are introduced to infer new knowledge that are related to the user's context, such as user activity, location and so on, the user's situations and user's needed services to adapt the interaction with the elderly and assist them. For instance, the Music service is an Entertainment situation that has Music as a media preference (see Figure 6). Then, we have developed a mobile application as a proof of concept. This application is basically implemented in Android environment and written in Java. For the purpose of activity recognition, we considered a hybrid activity recognition method, which combines data-driven on inertial sensor data from mobile devices and knowledge-driven. So, the implemented application is leveraging the smartphone's sensing capabilities as GPS and accelerometer for the localization and the detection of human activity, respectively. And finally, to validate the selection of appropriate needed service, our application integrated the modular ontology and a raft of inference rules discussed above.

B. Potential scenario

To demonstrate that our proposed prototype has the potential to infer current situations and determine relevant services for the elderly based on their profile information, their current physical activities, their current locations and time, we consider the following scenario depicting a typical real-life situation.

```
[Music-Service-rule:
(?EldCtx rdf:type uni:ElderlyContext)(?EldProf rdf:type uni:ElderlyProfile)
(?EldPref rdf:type uni:MediaPref)(?EldCtx uni:hasProfile ?EldProf)
(?EldCtx uni:hasConstraint ?EldPref)(?EldPref uni:E-MediaPrefName 'Music')
(?EldSit rdf:type uni:EntertainmentSituation)(?EldSit uni:S-Name 'Entertainment need')
(?EldProf uni:represents ?EldSit)(?EldServ rdf:type uni:ElderlyService)
(?EldServProf rdf:type uni:ElderlyServiceProfile)
(?EldServ uni:hasServiceProfile ?EldServProf)(?ProfileCat rdf:type uni:EntertainmentService
(?EldServProf uni:hasCategory ?ProfileCat)(?EldServProf uni:hasSituation ?EldSit)
->
(?EldServProf uni:ES-IntendedPurpose 'Music Service')]
```

Figure 6. An example of inference rule.

There are two elderly, named David and Sarah which are sitting in their living rooms during the morning after they had breakfast. But, they each have pretty different context profiles. First, David prefers cycling as physical exercise. He has a healthy status and has not any disease, risk factor and exercise requirement. Second, Sarah prefers walking as physical exercise. She has an unhealthy health status and suffers from diabetes disease. She adheres to Yoga as a regular physical exercise routine prescribed by her doctor and has not any risk factors. This situation provides an exercise need and the application triggers a notification service to convince David to get out and enjoy some cycling and to remind Sarah that she must make some Yoga as suggested by her doctor, as exhibited in Figures 7 and 8.

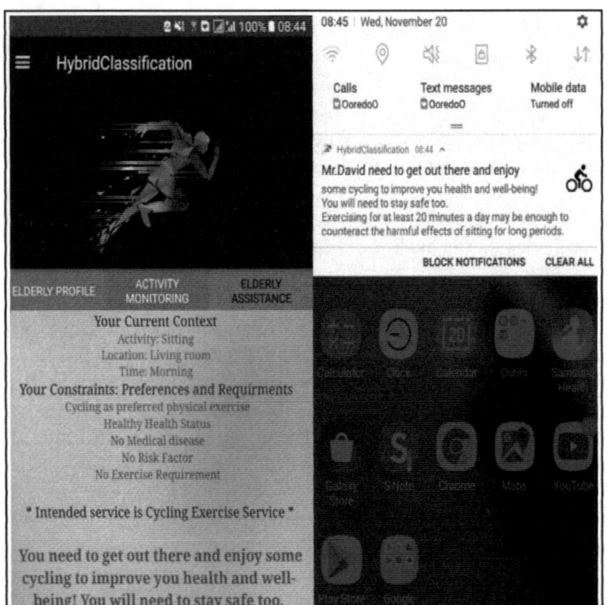

Figure 7. Interfaces for elderly assistance: Notification for Cycling service.

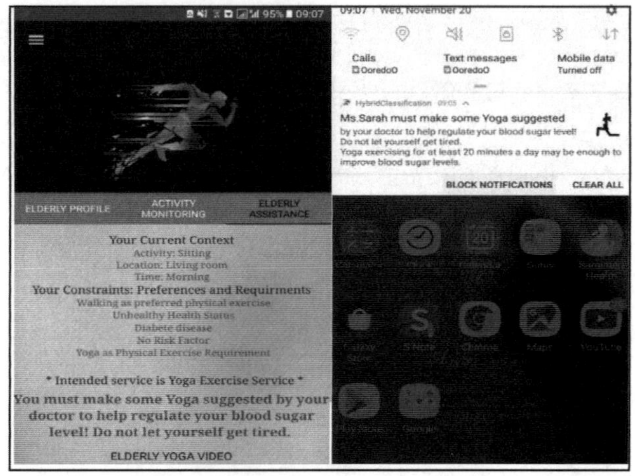

Figure 8. Interfaces for elderly assistance: Notification for Yoga service.

C. Evaluation and discussion

User satisfaction is commonly applied evaluation criterion for services in general. In our case, this criterion assesses the degree of elderly satisfaction with the provided services. Nevertheless, the evaluation of the elderly satisfaction from their perspectives is a critical step, which can be done with questionnaires. We decided to choose the Client Satisfaction Questionnaire-8 (CSQ-8) [18] as a reference to assess elderly satisfaction to evaluate and refine afterward our provided services for the elderly as optimally as possible. We chose CSQ since it offers a quick assessment of the client satisfaction of the services received. On this basis, our questionnaire that is conducted based on CSQ-8, consists of 8 questions ranging from Q1 to Q8. Each question should be answered using a response scale from 1 to 4, total score goes from 8 (great dissatisfaction) to 32 (great satisfaction). For the purpose of this evaluation, the questionnaire was completed by 10 elderly living alone who will use the application as an aid in their daily life and have heterogeneous context profiles. After receiving feedback from the elderly, we analyzed the collected responses outlined in Table I.

TABLE I. SCORES ON ELDERLY SATISFACTION QUESTIONNAIRE

Questionnaire	Scale Score			
	1	*2*	*3*	*4*
Q1. How would you rate the effeciency of services you have received?	0	4	4	2
Q2. Did you get the kind of service you expected?	1	4	3	2
Q3. To what extent has our application met your needs and intends?	1	5	2	2
Q4. Would you recommend our application a friend?	0	6	3	1
Q5. How satified are you with the amount of help and assitance you received through offered services?	1	3	3	3
Q6. Have the services you received help you to deal more effectively with your daily situations?	0	3	5	2
Q7. In an overall, general sense, how satisfied are you with the service you have received?	0	6	3	1
Q8. Would you reuse our application?	2	4	3	1

Based on the analysis results, the mean overall score for the questionnaire was 25.8. We concluded that the majority of elderly was mostly satisfied with the proposed application. The elderly were more satisfied with the provided services and less inclined to recommend the application to a friend or family member.

VI. CONCLUSIONS

The concept of smart environment for elders is still evolving, which may lack the mobility for elderly to simultaneously move around and maintain their daily assistance. Smartphone is a convenient device to provide mobility for assisting elderly. In this paper, we have presented an AAL system that monitors elderly in their mobile smart environments using smartphone devices in order to relieve burden of stress among elderly. The proposed system promotes services based on elderly's situations. These situations may vary based on the current elderly's needs, which are highly context dependent, and their profiles, such as their preferences, requirements, health status and so on. Moreover, we have introduced the experimental results of elderly test that show the effectiveness of our proposed system where a great number of elderly are satisfied. Despite that, we deemed indispensable to develop further new intelligent services for the elderly with a consideration of the rest of Maslow's hierarchy levels to undertake more robust evaluation results. Hence, we intend to shift our focus to the love and belonging level of Maslow's needs that could be met by socializing with others. We also plan to include other kind of smartphone sensors to keep a good control of the elderly's environment and to allow a faster response to the elderly's needs and situations at hand. Through this proposed approach, we aim to take on the history information of elderly to improve the evaluation results. Additionally, our future work includes evaluating our approach on more adequate population.

REFERENCES

[1] Eurostat, "Population projections 2008-2060: from 2015," deaths projected to outnumber births in the EU27, 2008.

[2] World Health Organization. WHO, "10 facts on ageing and the life course," 2008.

[3] H. Biermann, J. Offermann-van Heek, S. Himmel, and M. Ziefle, "Ambient assisted living as support for aging in place: quantitative users' acceptance study on ultrasonic whistles," JMIR Aging, vol. 1, no. 2, pp. e11825, 2018.

[4] A. H. Maslow, "A theory of Human Motivation," Psyhological Review, vol. 50, no. 4, pp. 370,1943.

[5] T. M. Tamang, "User-centered design of an interactive social service concept for elderly people," 2015.

[6] S. Thielke et al.,"Maslow's hierarchy of human needs and the adoption of health-related technologies for older adults," Ageing international, vol. 37, no. 4, pp. 470-488, 2012.

[7] M. Fahim, I. Fatima, S. Lee, and Y. K. Lee, "Daily life activity tracking application for smart homes using android smartphone," In 2012 14th International Conference on Advanced Communication Technology (ICACT), IEEE, pp. 241-245, 2012.

[8] L. Mainetti, L. Patrono, A. Secco, and I. Sergi, "An IoT-aware AAL system for elderly people," In 2016 International Multidisciplinary Conference on Computer and Energy Science (SpliTech), IEEE, pp. 1-6, 2016.

[9] X. YI. J. Huang, X. Zhu, and S. Chen, "A semantic approach with decision support for safety service in smart home management," Sensors, vol. 16, no. 8, pp. 1224, 2016.

[10] Y. Jung, "Hybrid-aware model for senior wellness service in smart home," Sensors, vol. 17, no. 5, pp. 1182, 2017.

[11] A. Patel, and J. Shah, "Real-time human behaviour monitoring using hybrid ambient assisted living framework," Journal of Reliable Intelligent Environments, pp. 1-12, 2020.

[12] N. Alm et al., "Engaging multimedia leisure for people with dementia," Gerontechnology, 2009.

[13] S. A. Small, Y. Stern, M. Tang, and R. Mayeux, "Selective decline in memory function among healthy elderly," Neurology, vol. 52, no. 7, pp. 1392-1392, 1999.

[14] A. Stisen et al., "Smart devices are different: Assessing and mitigatingmobile sensing heterogeneities for activity recognition," In Proceedings of the 13th ACM Conference on Embedded Networked Sensor Systems, pp. 127-140, 2015.

[15] R. Jabla, F. Buendía, M. Khemaja, and S. Faiz, "Balancing Timing and Accuracy Requirements in Human Activity Recognition Mobile Applications," In Multidisciplinary Digital Publishing Institute Proceedings, vol. 31, no. 1, pp. 15, 2019.

[16] M. Compton et al., "The SSN ontology of the W3C semantic sensor network incubator group," Web semantics: science, services and agents on the World Wide Web, vol. 17, pp. 25-32, 2012.

[17] D. Martin et al., "OWL-S: Semantic markup for web services," W3C Member Submission. World Wide Web Consortium, 2004.

[18] T. D. Nguyen, C. C. Attkisson, and B. L. Stegner, "Assessment of patient satisfaction: development and refinement of a service evaluation questionnaire," Evaluation and program planning, vol. 6, no. 3-4, pp. 299-313, 1983.

UI Design Pattern Selection Process for the Development of Adaptive Apps

Amani Braham
University of Sousse, ISITCOM
4011 Hammam Sousse, Tunisia
e-mail: amanibraham@gmail.com

Maha Khemaja
University of Sousse
4000 Sousse, Tunisia
e-mail: khemajamaha@gmail.com

Félix Buendía
Universitat Politècnica de Valencia
46022 Valencia, Spain
e-mail: fbuendia@disca.upv.es

Faiez Gargouri
University of Sfax
3029 Sfax, Tunisia
e-mail: faiez.gargouri@isims.usf.tn

***Abstract*—In User Interface (UI) development, UI design patterns constitute a crucial solution that helps to resolve design problems by reusing design knowledge. The diversity of patterns would require deep developer experience to select relevant patterns and would make it difficult to apply the right patterns. This paper proposes an ontology of UI design patterns that enables a potential UI design pattern selection process. We focus particularly on the capability of the Adaptive User Interface Design Pattern (AUIDP) framework in selecting relevant UI design patterns using both ontological and ranking reasoning. This is demonstrated through a service-oriented tool that recommends appropriate patterns. This tool is evaluated with regard to three main factors, including the tool's usefulness and practicality, the developed interface quality and the developer productivity. Results show that the tool enhances developer's accuracy in terms of selecting relevant patterns and hastens the UI development process.**

Keywords-Adaptive User Interface; Interface specification and design; UI design patterns; Ontology model.

I. INTRODUCTION

Currently, smartphones and mobile technologies are in the process of an ever-increasing development. The extensive use of mobile devices resulted in a notable increase in the application development industry. This makes the mobile application industry a multi-billion dollar industry [1]. With the increase in the number of mobile applications (a.k.a. apps), developers face a major challenge related to UI development. The statistics presented by Myers et al. [2] reported that the time required for developing user interfaces reaches 50% of the time needed for software development, and their corresponding source code includes 48% of the whole code. These user interfaces are intended to be used by various users with different profiles and needs, and also using different types of devices. A study conducted in [3] showed that 15% of the world's population has some kind of disability, which could be physical, cognitive, or sensory. The great variety of disabilities that users may be affected by has led to the emergence of adaptive interactive systems [4]. Hence, these systems open up new challenges, as users need adaptive user interfaces that fit their corresponding disabilities and requirements. Therefore, this kind of interface is becoming one of the most dominant part of adaptive systems. However, its development is not a trivial task; it presents a high complexity and takes a long time in such a way that developers often cannot fully cover disabled user's needs and preferences. Moreover, developing adaptive user interfaces requires a multidisciplinary team with a deep experience in using design knowledge, resolving design problems, as well as choosing the relevant design solution. Within this context, UI design patterns are introduced to support the design of adaptive user interfaces [5], since they attempt to educate designers to build user interfaces [6]. While hundreds of UI design pattern catalogues have been developed and published [7], they tend to be overlooked in practice. The major hurdle in considering these catalogues is how developers can recognize the relevant patterns for solving a specific design problem. This is due to the lack of tools for selecting existing UI design patterns. This might lead to applicability issues that create difficulties for developers to properly select and apply UI design patterns, and makes the design and development of adaptive user interfaces a time consuming and tedious task. Therefore, it becomes mandatory to find an intelligent way to handle, select and use relevant design patterns, to increase the reusability of design knowledge, to decrease the time and complexity of the design and development process and, finally, to improve the quality of adaptive user interfaces for users with disabilities.

To tackle the above mentioned challenges, the remainder of this paper presents the Modular UI DEsign Pattern (MIDEP) ontology that enables a potential UI design pattern selection process. This ontology is created using a specific method and augmented with a set of inference rules that provide intelligent support for developers to integrate relevant UI design patterns while developing user interfaces. The selection process is demonstrated through the AUIDP framework, which allows semantic reasoning over the proposed ontology in order to deliver UI design patterns that contribute to the process of developing adaptive mobile applications for users with disabilities.

The rest of this paper is organized as follows. Section II reports related works that deal with design patterns modeling methods and UI design patterns in software development. Section III presents an overview of the AUIDP framework. In Section IV, we introduce the UI design pattern selection process. Section V presents the design pattern selection process as a service-oriented tool. Section VI presents an evaluation of the developed tool considering three main factors. Finally, the last section outlines the conclusion and opens up further research orientations.

II. RELATED WORK

This section goes through existing literature in order to cover works related to design patterns modeling methods and UI design patterns in software development.

A. *Design patterns modeling methods*

The cornerstone of design pattern concept was laid by Christopher Alexander [8], in late 1970s, to deal with problems occurring in building architecture and it was initially defined as "a three-part rule, which expresses a relation between a certain context, a problem, and a solution". Such concept has been used in the Human Computer Interaction (HCI) field and exploited as an approach to design and evaluate interfaces [6]. Within this context, several works proposed their own collections of design patterns, offering solutions for specific design problems. The pattern collection presented in [9] is considered as one of the largest libraries that covers different kinds of applications including Web and mobile. Likewise, the Welie's catalogue [10] includes 131 patterns for interaction design and particularly for Web design. Besides, Neil's collection [7] comes with patterns for mobile applications. Furthermore, Mushthofa et al. [11] introduced a set of design patterns for designing websites. Despite the large numbers of catalogues, patterns are usually expressed in a traditional text-based representation with different and inconsistent pattern attributes. To tackle the heterogeneity issues, some standardization methods have been introduced. In this sense, pattern languages have been introduced [12]. Nevertheless, these representations are not a satisfactory solution since applying patterns requires a deep developer's comprehension in the context of use of each pattern. This barrier makes accessing patterns more difficult for developers. A machine-comprehensive representation is thus required. In [13], the authors introduce usability patterns models using ontologies. Furthermore, in [14] a formalization of Gang of Four's patterns (GoF) is modeled by means of ontologies. In [15], the authors reveal the formalization of Web design patterns based on ontologies. In [16], Kultsova et al. developed an ontological model of UI and interface pattern. However, all these works concern the representation of a set of patterns in a specific area, considering only its internal structure (e.g., patterns attributes, and their constraints).

B. *UI design patterns in software development*

The development of adaptive user interfaces has been investigated in various software development methods [17]. Nevertheless, there is a lack of effective design knowledge reuse. The capability of UI design patterns has been exploited in software development, since they allow developers to reuse design knowledge [18]. In this context, both works [19] and [20] are based on UI design patterns for mobile development and application development, respectively. Similarly, Coleti et al. [21] exploited the use of mobile design patterns to support the development of interfaces. However, in the aforementioned works, patterns are identified and analyzed manually by developers, which constitutes a tedious task. So, developers may face ambiguity in selecting the right patterns. Tools and techniques are then needed to retrieve relevant patterns and apply them to support the UI development process.

C. *Discussion*

In line with this literature review, the proposed work undertakes three main purposes: i) the specification of design patterns, ii) the selection of patterns according to specific design problems, and, iii) their applicability in UI development process. To this end, we provide a consistent and formal specification of UI design patterns by using ontologies. Furthermore, we present a framework that allows semantic reasoning to retrieve patterns and provides mechanisms to integrate patterns in the development of adaptive user interfaces for users with disabilities.

III. OVERVIEW OF THE AUIDP FRAMEWORK

The present framework contributes to the development of adaptive mobile applications for users with disabilities following a hybrid approach by combining model-based user interface development methods with pattern-based methods. The foundation of the proposed framework relies on the idea that the user interface can be fully modeled by a set of model fragments which is able to address a specific instance of UI design pattern. Therefore, within the AUIDP framework, UI design patterns constitute the basics for generating the final user interface. The overall overview of the AUIDP framework is depicted in Figure 1. It consists of four phases, including: UI design pattern selection, pattern instantiation, pattern integration, and, finally, user interface generation.

Furthermore, the AUIDP framework provides an environment for multidisciplinary teams to design and implement adaptive user interfaces in a consistent way by addressing particularly the following main aspects:

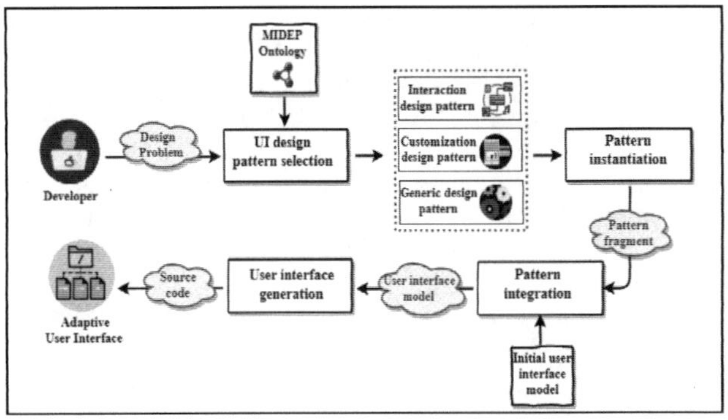

Figure 1. Framework overview.

- Open and accessible: The proposed framework puts UI design patterns at the fingertips of software developers/designers so they could be used in designing and developing the user interface.
- Modular: The user interface development process within the AUIDP framework is achieved by composing different UI design patterns.
- Code reuse: The developer has full access to the source code of the adaptive UI to be developed. Each UI design pattern that composes the interface is delivered with the source code corresponding to its design solution. This aspect speeds up the development process, fosters reuse and thus reduces the code that has to be developed.

In this paper, we focus on the UI design pattern selection process. A detailed description of the component that deals with the selection process is outlined in the next section.

IV. Overview of UI design pattern selection component

The purpose of this component is to automate the selection process of UI design patterns for specific design problems within the AUIDP framework. Handling this process requires mechanisms and methods for searching, classifying and selecting UI design patterns that will be further used in future work for developing user interfaces. In this regard, we rely on a rich repository of UI design patterns. However, the large number of UI design pattern and the complex relationships among them is becoming the primary impediment for recognizing relevant patterns. In addition to a textual description, a formal representation of UI design patterns is therefore required as input of the design pattern selection component. In the subsections below, we introduce the MIDEP ontology and the methodology used for the construction of this ontology; then, we examine the architecture of the component that is adopted for selecting relevant design patterns.

A. *MIDEP ontology*

The MIDEP ontology comprises knowledge about UI design patterns, since the AUIDP framework aims to support the design of adaptive mobile applications. This ontology mainly represents the best practices of UI development for users with special needs and uses information of design patterns that are introduced in [22]. In order to build the MIDEP ontology, we adopted the Neon methodology [23] since it can help to re-engineer non-ontological resources into ontologies, reuse existing ontologies, and thus assure modularity that would lead to consider the multidisciplinary aspect. In this regard, we identify the following three scenarios, which are extracted from a set of nine scenarios provided by the Neon method for building the MIDEP ontology:

- Neon's scenario 1: From specification to implementation.
- Neon's scenario 2: Reusing and re-engineering non-ontological resources.
- Neon's scenario 4: Reusing and re-engineering ontological resources.

Figure 2 illustrates the main steps considered when building the MIDEP ontology using a combination of the three aforementioned scenarios. A detailed description of each phase is outlined below.

1) Ontology requirement specification: The purpose of this phase is to introduce the ontology scope and motivation. It articulates the necessity of steps from step 1 to step 6 and gives as a result a global glossory of terms.

a) Specification: The MIDEP ontology is proposed as a modeling solution to tackle recurring design problems related to user interfaces. Within this step, we have identified a set of informal Computency Questions (CQs) which are used to evaluate the effectiveness of the ontology [24]. Some CQ examples are: What are the elements that compose a design pattern? What solution design pattern will provide? What are the relationships among design patterns and user interfaces? Which kind of design problem information could lead to better decision making for selecting relevant design patterns? Which kind of information could help to distinguish patterns that contribute to the same design problem?

b) Non-ontological resource selection: Several design pattern collections and catalogues have been developed. Within this step, patterns that can be used to deal with Web and mobile applications are reviewed, including the Tidwell's library [11], the Welie's catalogue [12], and Nilsson's collection [25].

c) Non-ontological resource re-engineering: For the aforementioned catalogues, we identified the attributes adopted for structure design patterns.

d) Ontology selection: An ontology named ONTO [26] for modeling the user interface is selected within this step.

e) Ontology resource re-engineering: Some concepts, terms and attributes are extracted from the ontology selected in the previous step.

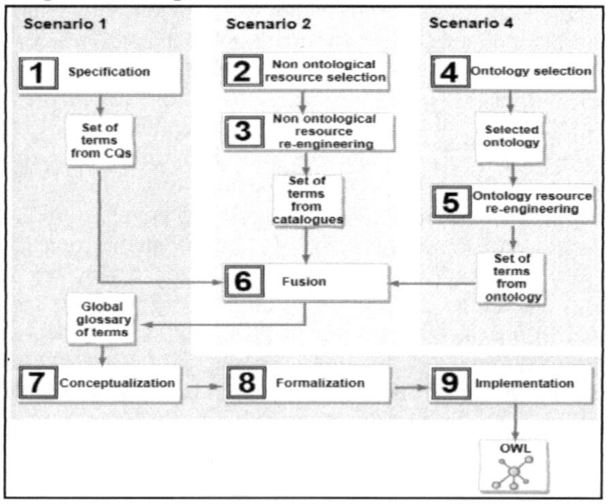

Figure 2. Process overview for building MIDEP ontology.

f) Fusion: This phase aims to blend terms of glossaries resulted from CQs, design pattern catalogues, and the selected ontology.

2) Conceptualization: It concerns mainly the definition of concepts and subconcepts, as illustrated in Figure 3.

3) Formalization: Once classes and subclasses are defined, a formal model is built. To this end we used Ontology Web Language version 2 (OWL2) as an ontology respresentation language.

4) Implementation: The concepts introduced previously are implemented using the Protégé editor tool.

B. Design pattern selection component architecture

This component incorporates two main modules, namely the reasoning engine and the ranking calculation engine. These modules interact among them to deal with the pattern selection process, as illustrated in Figure 4.

The reasoning engine component takes as input design problems that address mainly issues related to user characteristics, as well as interaction design issues [27]. User characteristic issues concern information about users, by whom the final interface is intended to be used, including user's disability, interest, goal, task, and need. Interaction design issues are information that comprise scattered data, bad contrast of colors, and useless interface elements. Once these issues are acquired from developers, the reasoning engine provides real time reasoning. It uses the MIDEP ontology in combination with a set of rules to decide on the UI design patterns that should be retrieved.

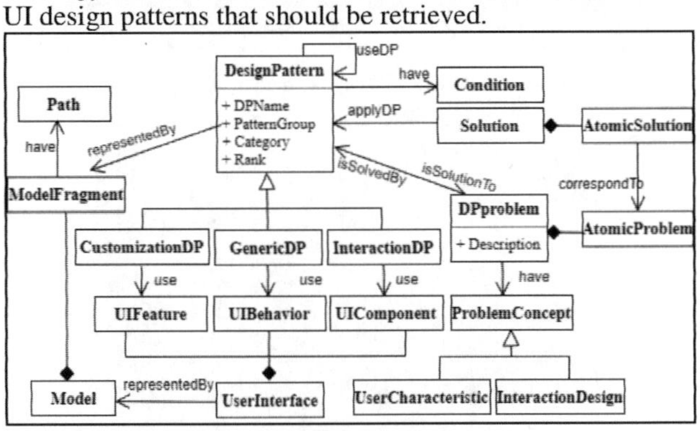

Figure 3. MIDEP Ontology model.

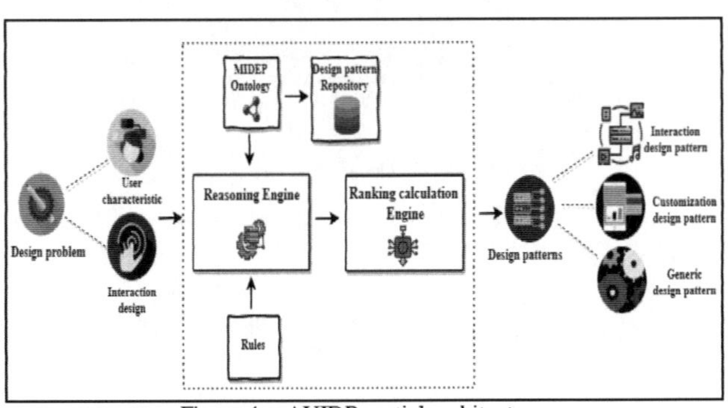

Figure 4. AUIDP partial architecture.

The ranking calculation engine is in charge of refining the set of design patterns resulted from the reasoning engine. It computes the similarity between the input design problem and the problem definition corresponding to design patterns retrieved from the reasoning engine. To this end, the ranking calculation engine applies the Cosine Similarity (CS) measure [28], since it allows computing the similarity of text documents. The CS values of each design pattern are calculated using (1), where patterns' problem and design problems are defined by a vector of terms and a frequency vector. For example, in (1), A and B are the frequency vectors of patterns' problem and design problems, respectively. This engine uses the obtained CS values to rank patterns, and generates the relevant UI design patterns that have the highest similarity scores.

$$CS(A,B) = \frac{\sum_{i=1}^{N}(A_i\ B_i)}{\sqrt{\sum_{i=1}^{N}(A_i)^2} * \sqrt{\sum_{i=1}^{N}(B_i)^2}} \qquad (1)$$

V. DESIGN PATTERN SELECTION AS A SERVICE

A. Implementation features

In order to implement the selection process, we developed a service-oriented tool including reasoning and ranking calculation services. It generates recommendations of design patterns according to specific design problems using a set of REpresentational State Transfer (REST) Web services. To this end, we used the generic reasoner that is considered as one of the inference engines supported by Jena and serves as the basis for OWL and Resource Description Framework Schema (RDFS) reasoners. It mainly exploits a rule-based engine for reasoning over the proposed ontology as well as for processing SPARQL queries.

B. Experiments and results

The procedure of design patterns selection phase within the developed tool can be introduced by the following experiment: A design problem "DP-1", that includes "LowVision" as users' characteristic issue and "FontSize" as interaction design issue, is considered in this experiment.

In the first step, the reasoning mechanism enables to obtain the design patterns' group, according to "DP-1". In this case, the reasoning engine triggers "rule 1" depicted in Figure 5. As a result, a set of design patterns corresponding to the selected pattern group is retrieved (Figure 6).

```
[rule1:

        (?ProblemConcept1 rdf:type uni:UserCharacteristicIssue)
        (?ProblemConcept1 uni:NameConcept 'LowVision')
        (?ProblemConcept2 rdf:type uni:InteractionDesignIssue)
        (?ProblemConcept2 uni:NameConcept 'FontSize')
        (?DPproblem1 rdf:type uni:DPproblem)
        (?designPattern1 rdf:type uni:FontSizeDP)
        (?designPattern1 uni:PatternGroup 'FontSizeDP')
        (?Solution1 rdf:type uni:Solution)
        (?Solution1 uni:IdSol '1')
        (?designPattern1 uni:isSolutionTo ?DPproblem1)

        ->
        (?DPproblem1 uni:isSolvedBy ?designPattern1)
        (?ProblemConcept1 uni:isConceptTo  ?DPproblem1)
        (?ProblemConcept2 uni:isConceptTo  ?DPproblem1)
        (?Solution1 uni:applyDP  ?designPattern1)
        (?Solution1 uni:SolutionDesc 'Apply FontSize DP')
]
```

Figure 5. Example of DP rules: Rule1.

DesignPatternName	Problem	PatternGroup	Category
"FontSizeSmall"	"non-disable user need small FontSize"	"FontSizeDP"	"CustomizationDP"
"FontSizeMedium"	"user with LowVision Medium need medium FontSize"	"FontSizeDP"	"CustomizationDP"
"FontSizeLarge"	"user with LowVision Severe need large FontSize"	"FontSizeDP"	"CustomizationDP"

Figure 6. Design patterns instances.

In the second step, a set of design pattern' instances generated by the reasoning engine will be refined in order to retrieve the most relevant design patterns. To this end, the ranking engine calculates the CS between the design patterns 'problem and DP-1. Table I presents the resulting CS values.

TABLE I. CS VALUES FOR DP-1

Value	Design Pattern		
	FontSizeSmall	***FontSizeMedium***	***FontSizeLarge***
CS	0.316	0.534	0.534

Finally, the ranking engine returns the patterns with the highest CS score. In this experiment, "FontSizeMedium" and "FontSizeLarge" are the relevant patterns that are recommended using our tool to resolve DP-1.

VI. EVALUATION

The developed service oriented tool for selecting design patterns was evaluated in terms of being effectively usable by the developer, considering the following factors: the usefulness and practicality of the tool, the application's interface quality, and developer productivity. These factors constitute the main requirements for the design pattern selection process. To assess these factors, three main research questions, were addressed as follows:

- RQ1: How can the tool assess the practicality for design patterns recommendation?
- RQ2: How well can the developed tool enhance the developer's accuracy in using design patterns?
- RQ3: How can the tool hasten the UI development process?

A. *Tool validation (RQ1)*

The usefulness and practicality of the proposed tool has been verified by the development of a hybrid application named Design Pattern Retrieve Application (DPRA) using Ionic [29]. This application includes a main menu for selecting the design problem, as illustrated in Figure 7. It further covers functionalities to allow a multidisciplinary team to view and extract relevant design patterns, as presented in Figure 8 and Figure 9, in order to resolve design problems.

B. *Developer based evaluation (RQ2, RQ3)*

1) Experimental setting: An experiment was designed in which two groups of software developers were invited to develop a location-based application that is able to track the user's current location and locate different points of interest. Each group consisted of four developers having University degrees in Computer Science and experience in creating hybrid applications using the Ionic framework. The first group, "Group-1", was asked to develop the application

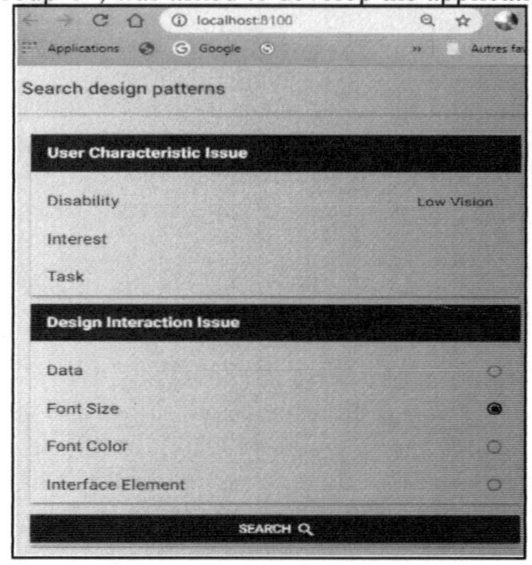

Figure 7. DPRA main menu.

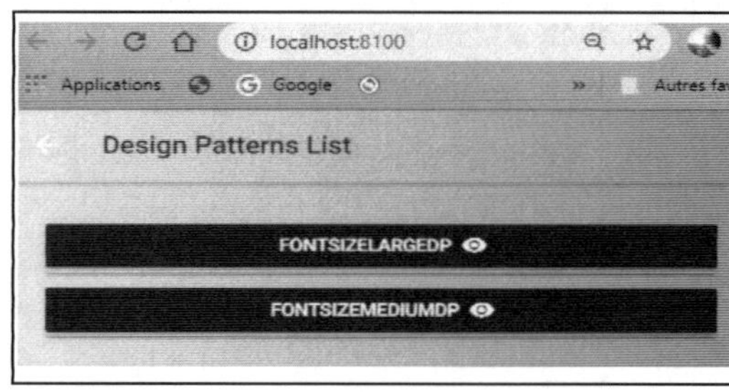

Figure 8. Design patterns list.

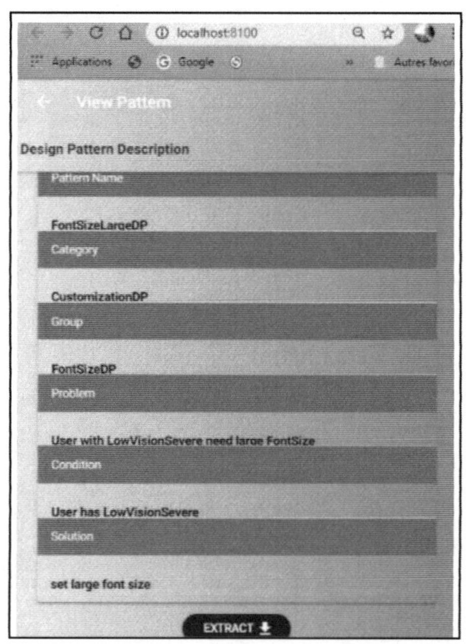

Figure 9. Design pattern Description.

without any tool. The second group, "Group-2", was provided the developed tool to support their application development. We conducted this study because we wanted to track the interface quality and developer productivity factors. The influence on the interface quality and developer productivity were inspected by measuring the accuracy of design patterns and by recording UI development time, respectively. The accuracy is calculated using (2) and scaled from 0 (0% accurate) to 1 (100% accurate), where the error rate is the percentage of failed developed interfaces. In (3), it is assumed that failed interfaces are interfaces that do not consider appropriate design patterns.

$$Accuracy = 1 - ErrorRate \quad (2)$$

$$ErrorRate = \frac{Number\ of\ failed\ interfaces}{Number\ of\ interfaces} \quad (3)$$

2) Results: The first step consisted in calculating the accuracy. In this case, the accuracy was about 33% for "Group-1" and about 88% for the second group, which is greater than the first accuracy value. These results outline that the set of design patterns recommended from the provided tool indeed enhances the accuracy of selecting relevant design patterns used in the development of UIs. Hence, the exploitation of the selected patterns makes the location-based application developped by the second group better than the application of the first one in terms of considering a good ergonomic design. The second step was to measure the amount of time for each group to fulfill the application development. Results show that the development time varied among the two groups: for "Group-1", the development took 9 days (12h/day, about 108 hours) while "Group-2", whose implementation method is based on the proposed tool, has taken only 5 days (12h/day, about 72 hours). The development time is dramatically reduced in the second group. This is due to the fact that the tool permitted "Group-2" to quickly identify relevant design patterns and extract their corresponding code and reuse it in the application's implementation instead of reinventing the whole application code. In general, these results indicate that the developed tool has a quite good impact on enhancing the interface quality, as well as on increasing developer productivity. Thus, the framework presented in this work allows a potential selection of design patterns. However, this framework has some limitations since the design pattern selection process is restricted to some UI design patterns. This lack can increase the development rework as well as the inability to adapt to changing disabled user's needs.

VII. CONCLUSION AND FUTURE WORK

In this work, we have presented an ontology for UI design pattern specification. Subsequently, we have introduced the AUIDP framework's main components, which concern the UI design pattern selection phase, including the reasoning and the ranking calculation engines. Such phase is implemented using a service oriented tool and evaluated considering the tool's usefulness and practicality, the interface quality, and the developer productivity. The experimental results, obtained in this work, consolidate the efficiency of the developed tool in terms of enhancing developer's accuracy in selecting relevant patterns and increasing developer productivity. As part of future work, we intend to generate adaptive UIs by using design patterns. So, we will target our emphasis on covering phases that follow the selection phase within the AUIDP framework. To address the limitation of the proposed framework, we will further extend the MIDEP ontology to cover the heterogeneity of design patterns and we will work on enhancing the developed service oriented tool functionalities.

REFERENCES

[1] Mobile application revenue generation. [Online]. Available from: https://www.abiresearch.com/press/tablets-will-generate-35-of-this-years-25-billion-/ [retrieved: December, 2019].

[2] B. A. Myers and M. B. Rosson, "Survey on user interface programming," In Proceedings of the SIGCHI conference on Human factors in computing systems, pp. 195-202, 1992.

[3] World Health Organization, World health statistics 2016: monitoring health for the SDGs sustainable development goals, World Health Organization, 2016.

[4] P. Brusilovski, A. Kobsa, and W. Nejdl, "The adaptive web: methods and strategies of web personalization," Springer Science & Business Media, 2007.

[5] M. Peissner, D. Häbe, D. Janssen, and T. Sellner, "MyUI: generating accessible user interfaces from multimodal design patterns," In Proceedings of the 4th ACM SIGCHI symposium on Engineering interactive computing systems, pp. 81-90, 2012.

[6] C. E. Wania, "Exploring Design Patterns as Evaluation Tools in Human Computer Interaction Education," MWAIS 2019 (9), 2019.

[7] T. Neil, "Mobile design pattern gallery: UI patterns for smartphone apps," "O'Reilly Media, Inc.", 2014.

[8] C. Alexander et al., "A pattern language," Gustavo Gili, pp. 311-314, 1977.

[9] J. Tidwell, "Designing interfaces: Patterns for effective interaction design," O'Reilly Media, Inc., 2010.

[10] M. van Welie, "Patterns in Interaction Design. [Online]. Available from : http://www.welie.com [retrieved: December, 2019].

[11] D. Mushthofa, M. K. Sabariah, and V. Effendy, "Modelling the user interface design pattern for designing Islamic e-commerce website using user centered design," In AIP Conference Proceedings, AIP Publishing LLC, vol. 1977, no. 1, pp. 020022, 2018.

[12] Y. Pan and E. Stolterman, "Pattern language and HCI: expectations and experiences," In CHI'13 Extended Abstracts on Human Factors in Computing Systems, pp. 1989-1998, 2013.

[13] S. Henninger and P. Ashokkumar, "An ontology-based infrastructure for usability design patterns," Proc. Semantic Web Enabled Software Engineering (SWESE), Galway, Ireland, pp. 41-55, 2005.

[14] H. Kampffmeyer and S. Zschaler, "Finding the pattern you need: The design pattern intent ontology," In International Conference on Model Driven Engineering Languages and Systems, Springer, Berlin, Heidelberg, pp. 211-225, 2007.

[15] S. Montero, P. Díaz, and I. Aedo, "Formalization of web design patterns using ontologies," In International Atlantic Web Intelligence Conference, Springer, Berlin, Heidelberg, pp. 179-188, 2003.

[16] M. Kultsova, A. Potseluico, I. Zhukova, A., Skorikov, and R. Romanenko, "A two-phase method of user interface adaptation for people with special needs," In Conference on Creativity in Intelligent Technologies and Data Science, Springer, Cham, pp. 805-821, 2017.

[17] I. Jaouadi, R. Ben Djemaa, and H. Ben Abdallah, "Interactive systems adaptation approaches: a survey," In Proceedings of the 7th International Conference on Advances in Computer-Human Interactions ACHI, pp. 127-131, 2014.

[18] P. Cremonesi, M. Elahi, and F. Garzotto, "User interface patterns in recommendation-empowered content intensive multimedia applications," Multimedia Tools and Applications, vol. 76, no. 4, pp. 5275-5309, 2017.

[19] T. Wetchakorn and N. Prompoon, "Method for mobile user interface design patterns creation for iOS platform," In 2015 12th International Joint Conference on Computer Science and Software Engineering (JCSSE), IEEE, pp. 150-155, 2015.

[20] C. A. Cortes-Camarillo et al., "EduGene: a UIDP-based educational app generator for multiple devices and platforms," International Journal of Human–Computer Interaction, vol. 35, no. 3, pp. 274-296, 2019.

[21] T. A. Coleti et al., "Design Patterns to Support Personal Data Transparency Visualization in Mobile Applications," International Conference on Human-Computer Interaction, Springer, Cham, pp. 46-62, 2019.

[22] A. Braham, F. Buendía, M. Khemaja, and F. Gargouri, "Generation of Adaptive Mobile Applications Based on Design Patterns for User Interfaces," In Multidisciplinary Digital Publishing Institute Proceedings, vol. 31, no. 1, pp. 19, 2019.

[23] M. C. Suárez-Figueroa, A. Gómez-Pérez, and M. Fernández-López, "The NeOn methodology for ontology engineering," In Ontology engineering in a networked world, Springer, Berlin, Heidelberg, pp. 9-34, 2012.

[24] M. Grüninger and M. S. Fox, "Methodology for the design and evaluation of ontologies," 1995.

[25] E. G. Nilsson, "Design patterns for user interface for mobile applications," Advances in engineering software, vol. 40, no. 12, pp. 1318-1328, 2009.

[26] M. Ansarinia. User Interface Ontolog. [Online]. Available from: https://old.datahub.io/dataset/ui [retrieved: December, 2019].

[27] W. Iftikhar et al., "User Interface Design Issues In HCI," International journal of computer science and network security, vol. 18, no. 8, pp. 153-157, 2018.

[28] A. Huang, "Similarity measures for text document clustering," In Proceedings of the sixth new zealand computer science research student conference (NZCSRSC2008), Christchurch, New Zealand, vol. 4, pp. 9-56, 2008.

[29] Ionic Framework. [Online]. Available from : https://ionicframework.com/ [retrieved: January, 2020].

Towards Context Adaptation in Ubiquitous Applications

Mohamed Sbai
Department of Science Computer
Faculty of Sciences
Tunisia
e-mail: mohamed.sbai155@gmail.com

Faouzi Moussa
Department of Science Computer
Faculty of Sciences
Tunisia
e-mail: faouzimoussa@gmail.com

Hajer Taktak
Department of Science Computer
Faculty of Sciences
Tunisia
e-mail: taktakhajer@gmail.com

Abstract—**Ubiquitous computing is considered one of the most impactful scientific achievements in the last decade. This conception created tremendous revolution in the end-user interactions through the concept of context-awareness. Ubiquitous computing offers a new opportunity to redesign the pattern of conventional solutions where it can easily tailor its processes upon existing contextual situations. Several theoretical architectures have been developed to enable context-awareness computing in pervasive settings. In order to exceed the limits of these related works, we will make a comparative study of these architectures and we will propose our solution. The objective of this article is to propose an adaptation architecture which aims to design and validate a contextual model for ubiquitous systems in order to offer services adapted to the preferences of the user.**

Keywords- Context; Ontology; Adaptation.

I. INTRODUCTION

The study of the literature shows that sensitivity to the context has become an essential element for the implementation of adaptive services in ubiquitous interactive applications. The context is no longer a pre-established and predefined model when designing interactive application systems, but rather a dynamic description of the current situations which can be discovered in the context data and which can change dynamically according to changes in requirements and user preferences. Therefore, context information tends to be incorrect because it does not exactly reflect the actual state of the observed entity, incomplete when certain aspects of the context are missing, or even ambiguous if several values are collected and do not entirely correspond to each other [1]. For example, two separate localization devices can provide values corresponding to overlapping regions, having different levels of precision or even being inconsistent if they present contradictory information. When the context information collected is imperfect and uncertain, there is a risk of basing a decision on incorrect information [2]. In addition, reasoning on uncertain information induces very high reasoning costs due to the complexity of the solutions to be implemented [3][4]. Ubiquitous applications must be able to run in different contexts of use depending on the user's environment, their profile, the terminal they are using, or their location.

In order to meet the different requirements for adapting to dynamic changes in contextual situations, we propose in this article our architecture for adapting to context in ubiquitous applications.

In this work, we distinguish four main components: the acquisition of the context, the representation, the reasoning and the application. Context acquisition functions allow interrogation of physical devices to obtain contextual data. Given the various characteristics of contextual information such as heterogeneity, dynamics and imperfections, it is essential to define a model to describe this data. In addition to context information, reasoning schemes are used to develop applications and services for specific needs.

The article is organized in several parts: In Section 2, we present a detailed study of the different approaches to contextual adaptation. In Section 3, we make a comparative study of these approaches. Section 4 positions our proposal in relation to related work. We describe later, in Section 5, our context modeling method. Then, we present in Section 6 our method of adaptation to the context. In Section 7, we present a performance study of our approach. Section 8 concludes the article and presents future work on the subject.

II. RELATED WORK

In recent years, many context-dependent infrastructures have been developed to manage ubiquitous systems. However, these infrastructures differ a lot in their architectures and implementations. They depend on the requirements of the systems and the process of acquiring, transforming and processing context information. These systems are different not only in architecture, which is generally organized in layers, but also in the model of the context adopted.

Pung et al. [5] proposed an architecture that provided context information to context dependent mobile services. This approach allowed applications to integrate several online services for their specific areas of context. It offered the ability to easily integrate and reuse components in the system such as new sensors. It also made it possible to abstract from the heterogeneity of the data sources.

Chen [6] proposed an architecture based on multi-agent systems. Its operation was essentially based on an intelligent agent called "Context Broker" who owned and managed a context model. This agent was composed of four main elements: the context knowledge base, a context reasoning engine, a context acquisition module and a private data management module. The major advantage of this architecture is the use of the ontology which, by definition, allows the sharing of data and the reasoning on its content.

Rouvoy et al. [7] proposed an architecture supporting self-adaptive mobile and context-aware applications. This architecture could be adapted to the dynamic changes of the environment (e.g., location, network connectivity) in order to satisfy the user requirements and device properties (battery, memory, CPU). The adaptation process defined is based on the principles of planning-based adaptation. This work has not taken into account the multimodal aspects for user-machine interaction and the contextual information that could be gathered by the distributed action mechanism.

More recently, Taing et al. [8] have proposed an architecture based on the Context Toolkit infrastructure; it supported the change of XML files and fire events to an unanticipated adaptation component that could be associated to fully described situations, including time, place and other pieces of context. This work used a transaction mechanism to ensure uniformly-consistent behavior for every smart object executing inside a transaction and supported only a notification as an action type without multimodality aspects that could be triggered as a result of situation identification and smart event detection.

Ghiani et al. [9] proposed an architecture that aimed to provide adaptable interfaces, allowing end users to easily and autonomously customize the behavior of their applications. It provided an environment for users to easily specify rules in the form of event / action pairs by limiting these rules to the contextual elements that are actually possible in the user's situation. However, this approach did not present adaptation rules as such.

Miñón et al. [10] proposed a system called "Adaptation Integration System". This system aimed to integrate accessibility requirements for people with disabilities by including adaptation rules in the development process.

III. DISCUSSION

After studying the related work, our comparison will be made on two fundamental criteria: the modeling of context elements and context adaptation parameters. At this level, we prove the need to use these two criteria while referring to the different roles of each in the response to the main context modeling objectives when designing a pervasive interactive application.

A. The first criterion: The modeling of context elements

The modeling of contextual elements is one of the important features for fostering and improving context sensitivity in pervasive environments. Indeed, this modeling is considered as an essential step for the design and development of interactive systems.

In Table I, we present a classification of all approaches according to their degree of modeling.

In Table II, we start our study by designating the set of contextual elements that were most often used in the context sensitivity. One element of the context is the one that describes the points of adaptation. It is part of the descriptions of the characteristics of the environment which describes reference parameters or preferences. The first step is to study the sensitivity to the context and to define the constituent elements of the current environment. These elements are used later in the adaptation phase (Section 6).

B. The second criterion: Context adaptation parameters

The design of interactive applications in pervasive environments requires consideration of the set of adaptation parameters (Table III). So, these applications can be used on terminals, by users, in specific environments and locations. In addition, these applications must deal with the dynamic change of context of use to achieve activities and achieve the appropriate objectives of users.

TABLE I. COMPARATIVE STUDY ON THE DEFINITION OF DATA STRUCTURES

Related Works	**Modeling approach**	**Complex structure definition**
[7][9][10]	-	No
[5]	+	Yes
[6][8]	++	Yes

TABLE II. COMPARATIVE STUDY OF CONTEXT ELEMENTS

Related Works	**Description of context-sensitive elements**						
	User	***Environment***	***Terminal***	***Location***	***Service***	***Activity***	***Time***
[5][6][8]	Yes	Yes	Yes	Yes	Yes	Yes	Yes
[7][9][10]	Yes	Yes	Yes	No	No	No	Yes

TABLE III. COMPARATIVE STUDY AT THE CONTEXT ADAPTATION PARAMETERS LEVEL

Related Works	**Context adaptation parameters**				
	Logical reasoning	***Management***	***Adaptation type***	***Adaptation technique***	***Action Mechanism***
[6][8]	Yes	Centralized	Integration	Reasonner	Centralized
[5]	No	Distributed	Reaction	Metamodel	None
[7][9][10]	Yes	Distributed	Integration	Formel object	Centralized

On the other hand, these approaches have limits in terms of modeling and adapting of the context. In the approach presented in [5], the modeling did not take into account neither the description of the relevant situations nor the adaptation actions. On the other hand, architecture makes it possible to describe the dependencies between the observable contexts through properties or by using the notion of inheritance. The limits of the approach presented in [5] consist of an object-oriented model for context management. This model is not easily extensible and offers limited expressiveness. In addition, access to relational databases takes time, which negatively affects the performance of the infrastructure. The limit of approaches [6][8] is the impossibility of recording the background history, which does not allow the use of learning algorithms to improve the treatment of the context. The model of entity association adopted is less expressive than the ontological model. To overcome the various limitations present in these approaches, we will present, in the following section, our proposed approach.

IV. CONTRIBUTION

After an in-depth study of the different architectures presented in the previous section, we note that an important challenge in the field of ambient computing concerns the optimization of the use of context management mechanisms and the adaptation of interactive applications to the diversity of ubiquitous environments. Our objective is to propose an adaptation architecture which aims to design and validate a contextual model for ubiquitous applications in order to offer services adapted to the preferences of the user. Our proposed architecture is formed by the following layers (Figure 1):

A. *Sensor*

Contains all data sources which can provide useful information for the context.

B. *Context processing*

Used to identify and model the context (User, Environment, Platform) from data of the various sensors.

C. *Adaptation control*

Allows us to detect adaptations and to implement them, it is made up of two modules: adaptation analysis and adaptation decision. The adaptation approach involves considering the different facets of the data context to adapt them to their needs. This is the basic concept that influences the process of the system.

D. *Interface generation*

Once the necessary elements of the interface are identified, the next step is to specify the graphical interface in terms of graphical objects and display. Indeed, the last step is devoted to automatic generation of the interface.

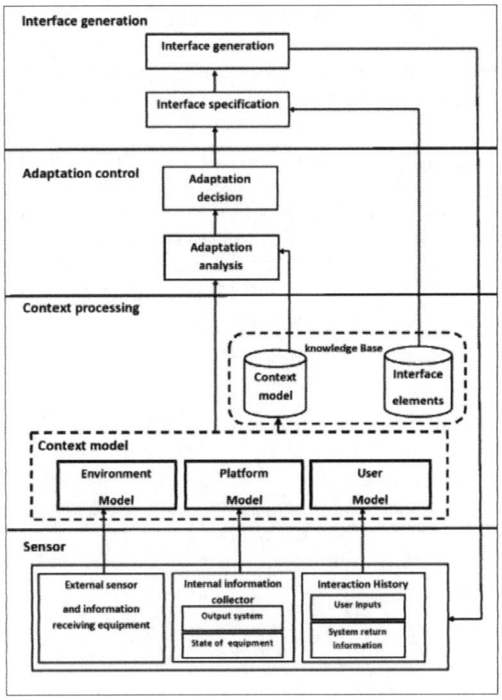

Figure 1. Proposed architecture.

V. CONTEXT MODELING

In this section, we present our context model based on ontology. To begin, we will present the core model of this ontology from a scenario. Then, we will detail all the ontologies of our domain. The main objective is to build a context model to support the functionalities of our context-aware adaptation platform. A context model for the adaptation platform must contain the usage contextual state: environment, platform, user context. It must be extensible by these applications. Our adaptation platform uses it to identify adaptation situations. It must find knowledge of contextual data, the state of execution of the platform, etc. This knowledge helps deploy the platform and the application.

A. *Scenario in a context-aware environment*

We consider, for example, users who use computing resources for daily activities in a context-aware environment. Olivier and David are teachers at the university. In the morning before leaving for work, one uses the tablet, the other uses the phone to consult the news and communicate with their family remotely by video chat. When they arrive at the university, they use their PC from their office for their research activities. They have access to some university services to work. In the afternoon, they have a lecture at another university. They take the company car to get there and they use the computer built into the car for navigation.

This scenario shows that changes in user activity or location will cause context changes. When they move from one place to another, the physical environments around them are different.

The computing resources available to them may change, for example, because of the available network connectivity. As they move from one activity to another, computing resources also change. For example, in the scenario, when they are in their offices, the resources of the university are accessible to them for their professional activities. These hardware or software resources are different from those available to them when they are at home.

B. Core ontology

In this section, we present our context model design starting with the highest level of abstraction. Our objective is to have a state of the current context of the users in their adaptation domain and to enable the identification of adaptation situations. After developing the generic context model based on the core ontology (Figure 2), we will introduce domain ontologies, their objectives, and describe each domain.

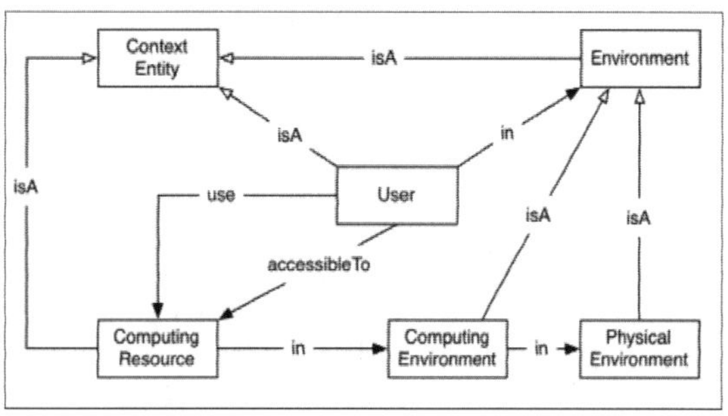

Figure 2. Core ontology: Relationships.

C. Domain ontologies

1) Domain "User"

This part of the ontology (Figure 3) describes the user's current situation and profile. This information is closely linked to information of a space-time nature (place, time, mobility). The adaptation platform needs to know which devices the user is using.

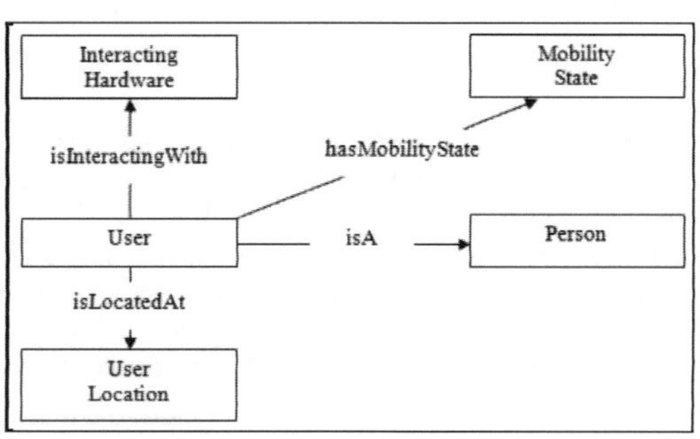

Figure 3. "User" ontology.

2) Domain "Environment"

A user of our platform is an individual who is surrounded by a set of physical elements and computer elements. The living environment of a user consists of the physical elements (light, location, etc.) and the computing resources (Smartphone, PC, etc.) which the user can access and which render services in the user's daily activities. The environmental ontology aims to describe these elements and their relationships (Figure 4).

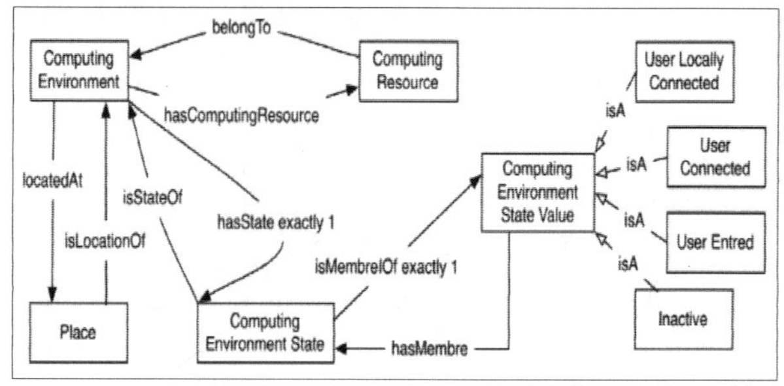

Figure 4. "ComputingEnvironment" ontlology.

3) Domain "ComputingResource"

The purpose of this ontology is to have knowledge of all the resources of the adaptation domain, i.e., their static and dynamic descriptions during the execution. We have identified four types of computing resources of interest for software adaptations: "Hardware", "Software", "Power", and "Network" (Figure 5).

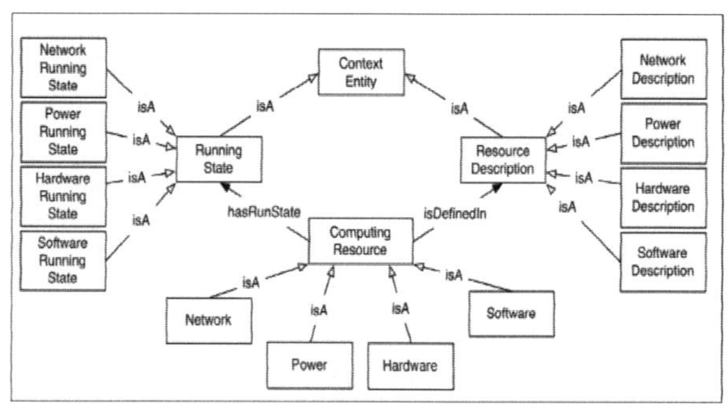

Figure 5. Structure of "ComputingResource" ontology.

VI. ADAPTATION CONTROL

This layer allows us to detect adaptations and implement them. It is composed of two modules: adaptation analysis and adaptation decision.

A. Adaptation analysis

This component of our adaptation platform must answer the following question: What is the current situation? This is the essential information we need to know and which will guide us to make the decision of adaptation.

Our platform enables the system to make adaptation decisions. Reasoning about situations is a very broad area of research. In context-aware applications, researchers define a situation as an external semantic interpretation of sensor data [11].

Next, we present our situation model. This situation model is designed to represent adaptation situations. We once again use an ontology to design this model because we want a semantic representation that is easy to extend and also a tool adapted to reasoning. An adaptation situation is either detected by a lack of resource adequacy, identified by the application, or identified by the platform. An adaptation situation is a result of the states of the current context.

Our goal is to design a model to support the identification of the situations defined by the application and those defined by the platform. An adaptation situation in our platform (Figure 6) corresponds to one of three broad categories: "GeneralASituation", "PlatformASituation" and "AppASituation".

The general situations ("GeneralASituation") correspond to an imbalance between the needs of the user and the resources available in the current environment. The platform adaptation situations ("PlatformASituation") are related to the structure and operating logic of the platform itself. The adaptation situations of the application ("AppASituation") are only detected to be transmitted to the application that will process them according to its business logic. The "PlatformASituation" and "AppASituation" categories are extensible. The platform and applications will be able to extend these situations according to their needs. A situation is linked to a description and a cause. The description is either a natural language description text or a context element state (user activity, environment, network presence, etc.). A situation of adaptation can be produced by a chain of reasoning from the state of the resources and the user or by a chain of reasoning from a logical reasoning on the ontology. Both cases correspond to an imbalance between the needs of the user and the resources available in the current environment.

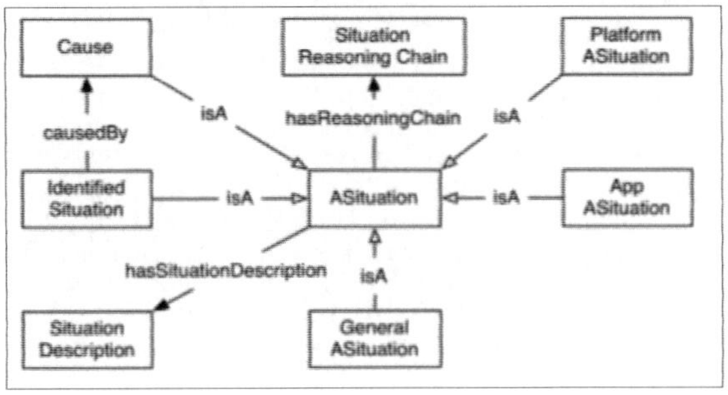

Figure 6. Situation Ontology.

B. Adaptation decision

Depending on the different types of adaptation platforms, the definition of the decision-making changes. For example, in Event, Condition, Action (ECA) -based platforms, decision-making means that when the platform captures context-change events, if these events meet the conditions set out in the predefined rules, an adaptation will be made by the defined actions in these same rules. For heuristic platforms like CAMPUS [11], a decision-making is equivalent to a software component parameterization according to the available resources. Our platform is based on semantic situations; this allows us to treat the context with a higher level of vision. The adaptation decision is to find a new application architecture (Figure 7) applicable in the current context to respond to the identified adaptation situation. When an adaptation situation is identified, a "new adaptation situation identified" notification is sent to the "decision makers".

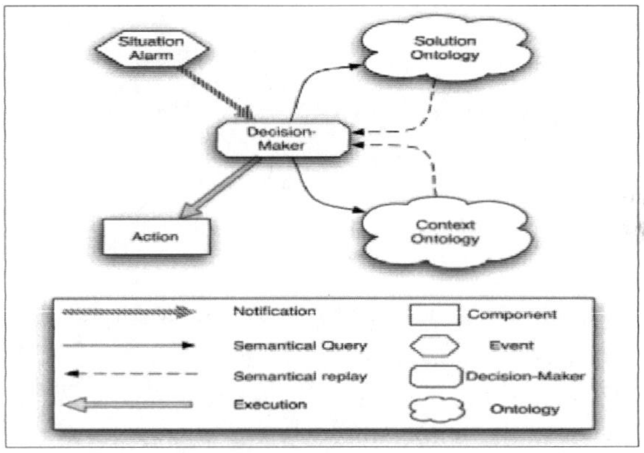

Figure 7. Architecture for Adaptation Decision Making.

The decision makers are notified of the addition of a new alarm "ASituation" in the knowledge base. (ASituation is the concept associated with adaptation situations). They are then in charge of the decision making adaptation for which they use both ontologies (situation and solutions) to reason and find a solution to the notification received.

The solution ontology contains knowledge of solutions related to situations and their causes. The situation ontology contains the situation information. When the "decision makers" have chosen a solution, it will deploy "Actions" to make the adaptation. An adaptation solution contains the processing logic specific to the associated situation.

VII. PERFORMANCE STUDY

In this section, we present the results of the performance study of our approach. First, in order to estimate the effectiveness of the adaptation, we measured the user satisfaction rate. In a second step, we measured the gain in memory space generated by the adaptation.

A. User satisfaction rate

We asked a panel of users to do a few tasks including browsing the Web pages they used to visit. After adapting these pages using our adaptation method, we asked them to locate specific information in the original page and in its adapted version. After completing these tasks, we asked them to respond to a questionnaire. In this questionnaire, the first four questions relate to navigation. The last question concerns the harmony of the structure of the Web page. A score is assigned to each question to assess the level of satisfaction of these users (8 being the highest score and 1 the lowest score). In Figure 8, we present the means of the scores obtained for each question posed to the panel of users. We note that the averages for the adapted version of the page exceed the averages for the original version.

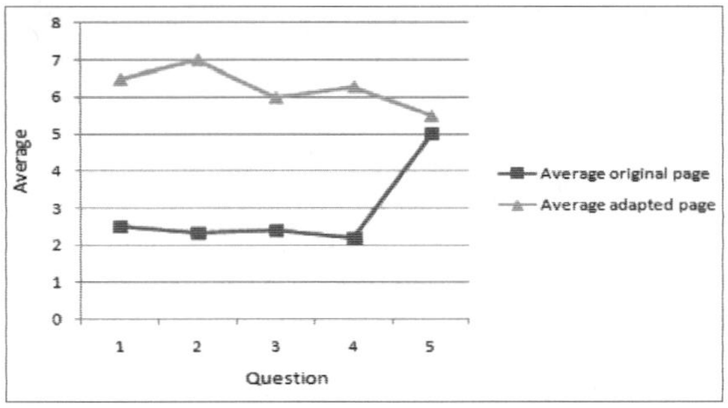

Figure 8. Satisfaction rate of users for the adaptation obtained.

B. Memory space used

In Figure 9, we present the results of the study of the memory space occupied before and after adaptation. The results show that adaptation plays an important role in reducing the memory space occupied by media objects.

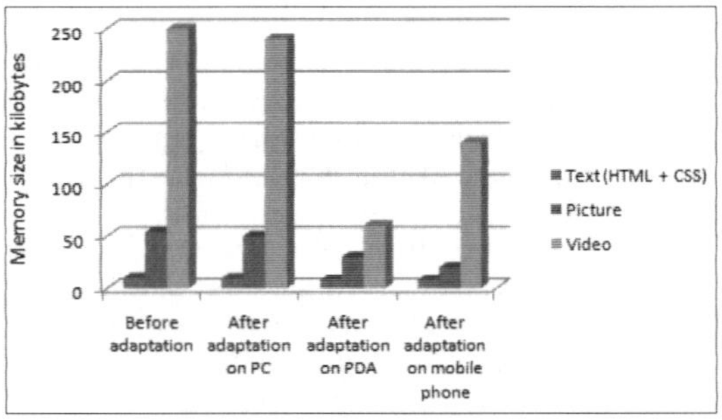

Figure 9. Component memory space before and after adaptation.

VIII. CONCLUSION AND FUTURE WORK

Building on recent advances in the world of mobile technology, pervasive environments are attracting growing interest. However, limitations linked to the resources of mobile terminals, the heterogeneity of devices and data, the multiplicity of requests and user preferences generate undesirable problems.

For that, the objective of this article is to propose an adaptation architecture which aims to design and validate a contextual model for ubiquitous systems in order to offer services adapted to the preferences of the user. In a mobile environment, decision-making cannot guarantee that the best solution will be chosen for a given adaptation situation during execution.

In future research, in order to choose a better solution, we will consider setting up a passive service responsible for long-term analysis of past (historical) decision-making without intervening directly in the adaptation cycle. This service could then refine decision making by adding adaptive situations in the ontology of situations and by associating them with specific solutions in the ontology of solutions. This new information being taken into account in future decisions, it could allow the learning decision-making system to evolve.

REFERENCES

[1] W. Dargie and T. Hamann. “A distributed architecture for reasoning about a higher-level context”. In IEEE International Conference on Wireless and Mobile Computing, Networking and Communications. (WiMob 2006), Canada, pp. 268–275, July 2006.

[2] A. Dey, G. Abowd, and D. Salber, “A conceptual framework and a toolkit for supporting the rapid prototyping of context-aware applications”. Special issue on context-aware computing in the Human-Computer Interaction Journal, April 2001.

[3] K. Henricksen and J. Indulska, “ Modelling and using Imperfect Context Ifnformation”. In Proc. 1st PerCom Workshop CoMoRea, USA, pp. 33–37, March 2004.

[4] A. Ranganathan, J. Al-Muhtadi, and R. Campbell, “Reasoning About Uncertain Contexts in Pervasive Computing Environments”. IEEE Pervasive Computing, vol. 3, pp. 10–18, April 2004.

[5] H. Pung and D. Q. Zhang, “A service-oriented middleware for buildfing context-aware services”, vol. 28, pp. 1-18, January 2005.

[6] H. Chen, "An Intelligent Broker Architecture for Pervasive Context-Aware Systems", PhdThesis, University of Maryland, Baltimore County, December 2004.

[7] R. Rouvoy, P. Barone, Y. Ding and F. Eliassen," MUSIC: Middleware Support for Self-Adaptation in Ubiquitous and Service-Oriented Environments”. In Software Engineering for Self-Adaptive Systems, Germany, January 2009.

[8] T. Taing, M. Wutzler and T. Spriner, “Consistent Unanticipated Adaptation for Context-Dependent Applications”. In Proceedings of the 8th International Workshop on Context Oriented Programming, Italy, pp. 33-38, July 2016.

[9] G. Ghiani, M. Manca, F. Paterno and C. Santoro, “Personalization of Context-Dependent Applications Through Trigger-Action Rules”. ACM Transactions on Computer-Human Interaction (TOCHI), vol. 24(2), April 2017.

[10] R. Miñón, F. Paternò, M. Arrue and J. Abascal, "Integrating adaptation rules for people with special needs in model-based UI development process", Universal Access in the Information Society, vol. 15, pp. 153-168, March 2016.

[11] E. Wei and A. Chan,"Campus : A middleware for automated context-aware adaptation decision making at run time". Pervasive and Mobile Computing, vol. 9, pp.35-56, February 2013.

A Cross Domain Lyrics Recommendation from Tourist Spots Reviews with Distributed Representation of Words

Yihong Han*, Ryosuke Yamanishi†, Yoko Nishihara† and Kenta Oku‡
*Graduate School of Information Science and Engineering, Ritsumeikan University, Shiga 525-8577, Japan
†College of Information Science and Engineering, Ritsumeikan University, Shiga 525-8577, Japan
Email: {is0387ps@ed, ryama@media, nisihara@fc}.ritsumei.ac.jp
‡ Department of Media Informatics, Ryukoku University, Shiga 520-2194 Japan
Email: okukenta@rins.ryukoku.ac.jp

Abstract—**In this paper, we propose a system for recommending lyrics similar to the context of the reviews of a tourist spot. The system is based on the technique of distributed representation of words. Instead of the metadata, such as genres and artists, the proposed approach takes the listening environment into consideration. By using the listening environment, it is possible to recommend music lyrics that fit the atmosphere of a tourist spot when the user enjoys the sightseeing. In this paper, the proposed system recommends the music that fits the atmosphere of a tourist spot by sharing the distributed representation beyond the domains of lyrics and reviews. The system uses a lyrics corpus to build the distributed representation model, and the reviews' vectors are calculated with the model. As a result, the tourist spot reviews are assumed to be types of lyrics. Based on the lyric-like vector representation of reviews, the similarity between reviews and lyrics can be calculated.**

Keywords–Music Information Retrieval; Lyrics; Context Aware Music Recommendation; Cross Domain Search.

I. INTRODUCTION

The user-system interaction for listening to music has dramatically changed with the use of web services. Subscription services for music enable us to bring almost an infinite amount of music everywhere. Users do not need to select the music before going out. We previously enjoyed music in places designed especially for music, such as live houses and concert halls. However, nowadays, we can listen to music in many places, such as when driving, being on a flight, or trekking. That is to say, music has now become more of a co-entertainment while doing some other activities though it was previously the main entertainment for places designed especially for music.

Based on this background, context-aware music retrieval can be a new style to enjoy music: listening to music while interacting with the environment surrounding the user. In this paper, we take music in tourism in consideration as a listening context for the music. Perhaps, some of us might experience listening to music which includes the name of a tourist spot in the lyrics. The experience of visiting a tourist spot is more impressive while listening to music related to it, e.g., "*San Francisco*" by Glantis in San Francisco, USA and "*Lovers in Japan*" by Coldplay in Osaka, Japan. It is expected that even listening to the music without the name of a spot in the lyrics also enhances the impressions toward the trip if the sentiment for the music corresponds to the atmosphere of the spot: for example, listening to "*Perfect*" by Ed Sheeran which is a relaxed love song in the airy and relaxed park in Vancouver "Stanley Park" and listening to "*Toxicity*" by System of a Down in an exciting city like Kabuki-Cho, Japan. It is reasonable to say that such experiences are similar to listening to the background music for each scene in movies. This paper can be positioned in the location-aware music recommendation field [1] [2].

In this paper, the goal is to enrich the tourism experiences with listening to music for the tourist spot. We propose a method to recommend music that has lyrics suitable for the tourist spot. In the proposed method, the reviews for the tourist spots are assumed as the general evaluation or the collective intelligence of experience toward the tourist spot. By using the reviews of the tourist sport as the query, the proposed method retrieves the lyrics for the spot: that is, cross-domain retrieval between tourist spots and music. The distributed representations of words are modeled using a lyrics corpus. As the reviews of tourist spots are vectorized with the distributed representation model, the reviews of tourist spots should be assumed as the lyrics. The lyrics that have higher vector similarity with the reviews of the tourist spots are retrieved: the lyrics retrieval with tourist spots should become enable.

Section II will introduce the related work. The description of the proposed method will be in Section III. Section IV will show the experiment results and the evaluation of the proposed method. Finally, Section V will summarize this paper.

II. RELATED WORK

Music Information Retrieval (MIR) has been widely researched. Music retrieval with humming [3] and music genre classification [4] [5] are typical research topics in the MIR field.

Music with singing can be considered as multimedia art and consists of acoustics and linguistics. That is, the affection towards music can be caused by the combination of "listening to acoustics" and "understanding lyrics." Let us focus on the related work for lyrics, which is the target of this paper. Tsukuda *et al.* [6] developed *Lyrics Jumper* that recommends artists whose lyrics have similar topics. Cai *et al.* [7] have proposed *MusicSense* that recommends the music while reading a document on the Web. In the work by Cai *et al.*, the affective words extracted from both lyrics and documents on the Web are used to relate the two types of domains with each other. Our proposed system does not focus on some specific words, but the overall similarity between lyrics and reviews by using the word distributed representation model.

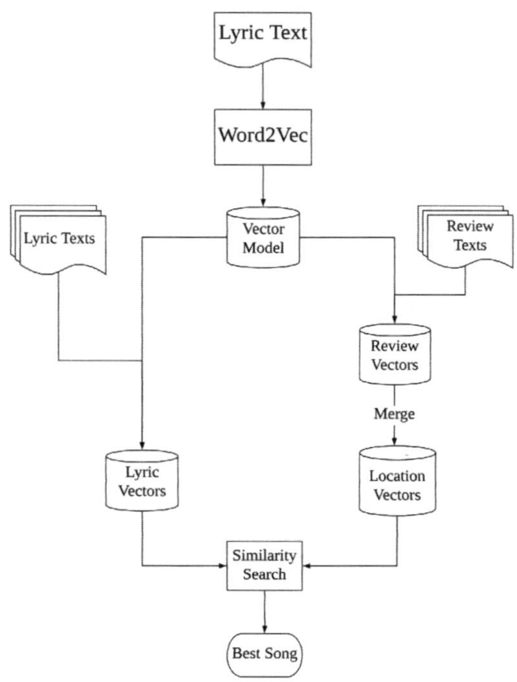

Figure 1. Flowchart of proposed method.

The music and location have been related to each other in several existing research works. Kaminskas *et al.* have proposed a location-aware music recommendation system while using a tag-based approach [8] and a knowledge-based approach [9]. In their tag-based approach [8], music and Point Of Interest (POI) are related to each other based on the tag given to those. Their knowledge-based approach [9] constructs the graph that semantically relates music with POI based on the knowledge with DBPedia and ranks the songs for a given POI. Moreover, a hybrid approach of a tag-based and knowledge-based approach has been proposed [10]. Our proposed method is considered as the lyrics-based approach in the above research context.

III. Proposed Method

In this paper, we propose a lyrics recommendation method based on the vector similarity between lyrics and reviews of tourist spots. The proposed method uses distributed representations of words [11] to quantify lyrics and reviews of tourist spots. We use an English lyrics corpus to build distributed representations as a model. The model is used for calculating the distributed representations vectors of lyrics and reviews of tourist spots. The mean vectors of a single tourist spot are calculated from all of the vectors concerning the reviews for the tourist spot. The method calculates the vector similarities between lyrics and tourist spot reviews. The lyric with the highest similarity to the given tourist spot is output as the recommendation result for the tourist spot. The concept of our method is, the texts of reviews for tourist spots are assumed as "pseudo lyrics." So, the lyrics and reviews can be unified into the same dimension and become comparable. Figure 1 shows an outline of the proposed method. Each process of the proposed method will be detailed in the next two sections.

A. *Words Distributed Representations Model*

We model a distributed representations with the lyric data fetched from a lyrics site "azlyrics" [12]. This paper focuses on English content, so we just choose English lyrics as the text corpus. All lyrics written in non-English language are omitted from the lyrics dataset. After the cleansing, there are 94,451 English lyrics remaining in the dataset. We use Word2Vec (Skip-Gram) [13] [14] framework to model word distributed representations as the primal study, though there are so many types of frameworks. We use this lyrics corpus on Word2Vec framework as the training data and get a distributed representation model that represents every word in the corpus as a 300 dimmensions vector. During the training, the parameter setup of Skip-Gram is as follows: $size = 300$, $window = 10$, $min\_count = 2$, $workers = 8$, $iter = 10$.

B. *Quantifying Lyrics and Tourist Spot Reviews to Vectors*

This section describes the general concept for the distributed representation for both lyrics and tourist spot reviews. Based on the distributed representation model described in Section III-A, the distributed representations vectors of lyrics and reviews for tourist spots can be obtained. In detail, for every word in lyrics and reviews, we fetch the word vector from the distributed representations model. Then, the mean vector of lyrics or reviews $\overline{\boldsymbol{V}}$ is calculated by summing all word vectors for each dimension and dividing the sum by the number of words in the lyrics or reviews (1) as follows:

$$\overline{\boldsymbol{V}} = \frac{\vec{v_1} + \cdots + \vec{v_i}}{N - \gamma}, \tag{1}$$

where, $\vec{v_i}$, N, and γ denote the vector of ith word, the number of words in a lyric or review text, and the number of words that only exist in review texts, respectively. Note, as the distributed representations model is trained from lyrics corpus, the words that only exist in review texts but do not appear in lyrics texts, will not get their vectors from the model. In the calculation of average vectors, we counted the number of these "not available words" and subtracted the number γ from the word number in the whole text. As a result, the number of "available words" is the divisor in the equation.

C. *Merging Vectors of Reviews for Tourist Spot to Spot Vectors*

In Section III-B, we obtain both vectors of lyrics and tourist spot reviews (hereafter, review vectors). Here, another process for the tourist spot reviews is detailed in this section. Tourist spot reviews are written by a human so they may include emotional expressions and subjective estimations. By merging reviews of the same tourist spot, the individuality and general properties of the tourist spot can be represented. Based on this consideration, we calculated the weighted arithmetic mean of each tourist spot. The mean vector of tourist spot s: $\overline{\boldsymbol{X_s}}$ is calculated using the following equation:

$$\overline{\boldsymbol{X_s}} = \frac{\omega_{s,1}\vec{x_{s,1}} + \cdots + \omega_{s,j}\vec{x_{s,j}}}{\omega_{s,1} + \cdots + \omega_{s,j}}, \tag{2}$$

TABLE I. EXAMPLES OF TOURIST SPOTS AND THE CORRESPONDING RECOMMENDED LYRICS. THE CONTENTS OF LYRICS WILL BE DETAILED IN TABLE II.

Tourist spots	Recommended lyrics ID
The Montcalm at the Brewery London City	84127
The Beekman A Thompson Hotel	84057
Conservatory Garden	55628
Riverside Park	74814
Hudson River Park	74814
Roosevelt Island	39663
Fort Troon Park	74814
New York Harbor	56837
Franklin D Roosevelt Four Freedoms Park	53520
Long Beach	54217

where, $\vec{x}_{s,j}$ and $\omega_{s,j}$ denote the vector of jth review and the number of words in jth review for tourist spot s, respectively.

A given tourist spot may have two types of reviews: short simple or long detailed reviews. By weighting the vectors of words using the number of words in the review, the contributions to the tourist spot expression should be differently evaluated depending on the length of the description. We suppose that the longer the review text is, the more information this review brings to the tourist spot expression. Hereafter, the mean vector of each tourist spot is named as "location vector."

D. Lyrics Recommendation Based on Similarity Between Lyrics and Spots

For a tourist spot s, we calculate the cosine similarity between its location vector and every lyrics vector. The lyric with the highest similarity for the tourist spot s is recommended as the lyrics toward the tourist spot s. The cosine similarity is calculated using the following equation:

$$\cos(\vec{X}_s, \vec{L}_k) = \frac{\vec{X}_s \cdot \vec{L}_k}{|\vec{X}_s| \times |\vec{L}_k|}, \tag{3}$$

where, $\vec{L}_k$ shows the vector of kth lyrics in the lyrics dataset. The proposed method recommends $\arg\max_k \cos(\vec{X}_s, \vec{V}_k)$ as the recommendation result for the tourist spot s.

IV. EXPERIMENT

The effectiveness of the proposed method is subjectively discussed through the lyrics recommendation experiments. In the experiment, we evaluate some tourist spots randomly selected from "TripAdvisor [15]". We take some of the recommendation results as examples to be discussed in detail. Also, we discuss the overall tendency of the recommendations.

This paper is a working in progress, so the objective evaluation for the recommendation will be our future work. The discussion may lead to the direction for the idea of our future objective experiments.

A. Results

TABLE I shows the recommendation results of each tourist spot in lyrics ID. TABLE II shows the list of lyric URLs for each lyrics ID on lyrics site "azlyrics."

Figure 2 shows the number of tourist spots corresponding to each of the lyrics, where the horizontal axis is the lyrics ID and the vertical axis is the number of tourist spots. In the figure, from left to right, the lyrics are sorted in the descending order.

TABLE II. EXAMPLES OF RECOMMENDED LYRIC ID AND ITS URLS. THE URL WAS RETRIEVED ON MARCH 16, 2020.

Lyric No.	Lyric URLs
59978	https://www.azlyrics.com/lyrics/mcfly/mcflythemusical.html
84127	https://www.azlyrics.com/lyrics/sunkilmoon/strangerthanparadise.html
92790	https://www.azlyrics.com/lyrics/whitestripes/littlecreamsoda.html
84057	https://www.azlyrics.com/lyrics/sunkilmoon/beautifulyou.html
80687	https://www.azlyrics.com/lyrics/slimdusty/themanfromthenevernever.html
55628	https://www.azlyrics.com/lyrics/lobo/whyisitme.html
35313	https://www.azlyrics.com/lyrics/gregoryalanisakov/fireescape.html
74814	https://www.azlyrics.com/lyrics/rodstewart/manhattan.html
56035	https://www.azlyrics.com/lyrics/lorettalynn/imshootinfortomorrow.html
39663	https://www.azlyrics.com/lyrics/idinamenzel/oneshortday.html
20655	https://www.azlyrics.com/lyrics/cowboyjunkies/arlington.html
56837	https://www.azlyrics.com/lyrics/luckyboysconfusion/likeratsfromasinkingship.html

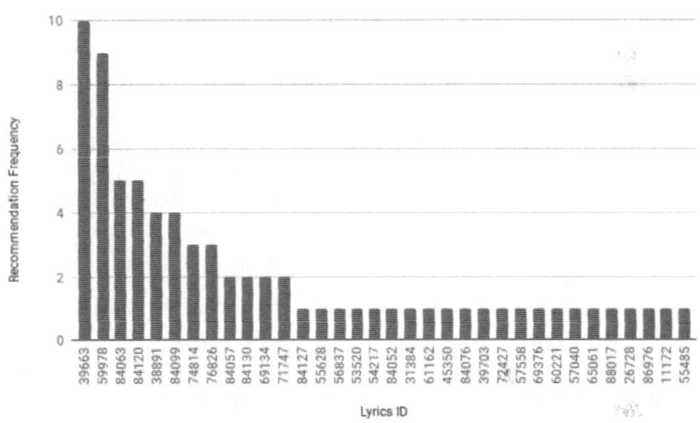

Figure 2. Number of locations corresponded to same lyric.

B. Discussions

From the experiment results, the tendency of the recommendations was found. Several tourist spots corresponded to the same lyrics. In TABLE I, the same lyrics "74814" was recommended to "Riverside Park," "Hudson River Park" and "Fort Troon Park." As these three locations are all parks, we supposed that the reason for this tendency was caused by the specific common features in the several tourist spots. To verify the assumption, we focused on the lyrics "39663" and "59978," which were recommended for the most spots. The tourist spots corresponding to the lyrics were studied in detail to find if there had been some similarity among them. The tourist spots recommended to lyrics "39663" and "59978" are each shown

TABLE III. TOURIST SPOTS CORRESPONDING TO LYRIC "39663"

Tourist spots	Locations
Roosevelt Island	State of New York, America
Bowling Green	Commonwealth of Kentucky, America
Governors Island National Monument	State of New York, America
SoHo	State of New York, America
West Village	State of New York, America
Meatpacking District	State of New York, America
Twin Peaks	State of California, America
Lincoln Park Conservatory	State of Illinois, America
Greenwich	London, England
Greenwich Park	London, England

TABLE IV. TOURIST SPOTS CORRESPONDING TO LYRIC "59978."

Tourist spots	Genre of location
Neue Galerie	Museum
Solomon R Guggenheim Museum	Museum
New York Historical Society Museum Library	Museum
Museum of Arts and Design	Museum
United Nations Headquarters	Organization
Broadway	Street
Radio City Music Hall	Theater
Le Puy du Fou	Theme Park
Westminster	Street

in TABLE III and TABLE IV, respectively.

As a result, it was suggested that the tourist spots corresponding to the same lyrics had specific common features. In TABLE III, there were a lot of spots located in the U.S.A., especially in the State of New York: for "Greenwich" and "Greenwich Park," the latter is inside of the former so substantially they should be almost the same spot. Generally, the tourist spots that corresponded to lyric "39663" were similar to each other in their location.

In TABLE IV, lyric "59978" was recommended to many museums and other historical places, such as "Radio City Music Hall" and "Westminster." Kaminskas mentioned that the recommendation result of music could be diversified with the matching of music and location information in his paper [16]: this is a common issue in this field. We will improve the method to recommend more diverse lyrics depending on the characteristics of tourist spots by using more specific features for each spot.

V. CONCLUSION

In this paper, we proposed a cross-domain lyrics recommendation system based on the distributed representation of words. The vectors of tourist spot reviews were generated by using the distributed representation model with lyrics corpus. Then, the tourist spot reviews were assumed as a type of lyrics in the proposed system. The system merged the vectors of tourist spot reviews to location vectors and calculated the similarity between location vectors and lyric vectors. The system finally selected the lyrics with the highest similarity to the arbitrary tourist spot as the recommendation result. During the experiment, we found a tendency that several locations corresponded to the same lyric in the recommendation results. We confirmed some commonalities among those locations corresponding to the same lyric through the survey. This discussion will help the future work of this research to achieve better recommendations.

This paper is still a work in progress, so the objective evaluation of the recommendation result will be one of the tasks in the future. Also, we should carry out subjective evaluation experiments to verify usability in real use cases.

ACKNOWLEDGMENT

This work is in part supported by KAKENHI #16K21482, #15K12151, and #19K12567. The data of lyrics is collected by Assist. Prof. M. Yoshida at Toyohashi Institute of Technology, Japan. We show our best appreciation.

REFERENCES

[1] Z. Cheng and J. Shen, "On effective location-aware music recommendation," ACM Trans. Inf. Syst., vol. 34, no. 2, April 2016. [Online]. Available: https://doi.org/10.1145/2846092

[2] M. Pichl, E. Zangerle, and G. Specht, "Improving context-aware music recommender systems: Beyond the pre-filtering approach," in Proceedings of the 2017 ACM on International Conference on Multimedia Retrieval, ser. ICMR ' 17. New York, NY, USA: Association for Computing Machinery, 2017, p. 201 - 208. [Online]. Available: https://doi.org/10.1145/3078971.3078980

[3] S. Pauws, "Cubyhum: A fully operational query by humming system," in Proceedings of ISMIR 2002, 2002, pp. 187–196.

[4] D. Wang, T. Li, and M. Ogihara, "Are tags better than audio features? the effect of joint use of tags and audio content features for artistic style clustering," pp. 57–62, 2010.

[5] E. Pampalk, A. Flexer, and G. Widmer, "Improvements of audio-based music similarity and genre classification," in Proceedings of the 6th International Conference on Music Information Retrieval, 01 2005, pp. 628–633.

[6] K. Tsukuda, K. Ishida, and M. Goto, "A lyrics-based music exploratory web service by modeling lyrics generative process," in Proceedings of the 18th International Conference on Music Information Retrieval, 2017, pp. 544–551.

[7] R. Cai, C. Zhang, S. Wang, L. Zhang, and W.-Y. Ma, "Musicsense: contextual music recommendation using emotional allocation modeling," in Proceedings of the 15th ACM international conference on Multimedia, 2007, p. 553 - 556.

[8] M. B. abd Marius Kaminskas and F. Ricci, "Location-aware music recommendation," International Journal of Multimedia Information Retrieval, vol. 2, no. 1, 2013, pp. 31–44.

[9] I. Fernández-Tobias, I. Cantador, M. Kaminskas, and F. Ricci, "Cross-domain recommender systems: A survey of the state of the art," in Proceedings of the 2nd Spanish Conference on Information Retrieval, 2012, p. 187 - 198.

[10] M. Kaminskas, F. Ricci, and M. Schedl, "Locationaware music recommendation using auto-tagging and hybrid matching," in Proceedings of the 7th ACM conference on Recommender systems, 2013, p. 17 - 24.

[11] T. Mikolov, W.-t. Yih, and G. Zweig, "Linguistic regularities in continuous space word representations," in Proceedings of HLT-NAACL, 2013, pp. 746–751.

[12] "AZLyrics - Song Lyrics from A to Z," https://www.azlyrics.com/, last accessed on 01/28/20.

[13] T. Mikolov, K. Chen, G. Corrado, and J. Dean, "Efficient estimation of word representations in vector space," CoRR, vol. abs/1301.3781, 2013.

[14] T. Mikolov, I. Sutskever, K. Chen, G. S. Corrado, and J. Dean, "Distributed representations of words and phrases and their compositionality," in Advances in Neural Information Processing Systems 26. Curran Associates, Inc., 2013, pp. 3111–3119.

[15] "Tripadvisor: Read Reviews, Compare Prices & Book," https://www.tripadvisor.com/, last accessed on 01/28/20.

[16] M. Kaminskas and F. Ricci, "Emotion-based matching of music to places," in Emotions and Personality in Personalized Services, J. Fagerberg, D. C. Mowery, and R. R. Nelson, Eds. Springer, 2016, pp. 287–310.

Time-Variable Analysis of Accommodation Reviews Based on a Hierarchical Topic Model

Yujiro Sato*, Ryosuke Yamanishi†, Yoko Nishihara†
*Graduate School of Information Science and Engineering, Ritsumeikan University, Shiga, Japan
†College of Information Science and Engineering, Ritsumeikan University, Shiga, Japan
Email: {is0309he@ed, ryama@media, nisihara@fc}.ritsumei.ac.jp

***Abstract*—Accommodation reviews are valuable resources for future guests to know the opinions of users who have already stayed at a particular place before. However, it is difficult for users to extract the information specific to each topic such as facilities, access, and breakfast. We consider that the seasonal features of accommodations are especially important to ensure a comfortable and enjoyable stay. This paper proposes a hierarchical topic analysis with time variation to extract seasonal features for accommodations. The proposed method extracts seasonally important words and shows the similarity of topics that the important words belong to between seasons. In this paper, we discuss the effectiveness of the extracted features as references for guests to choose accommodations.**

Keywords–review analysis; consumer decision support; hLDA.

I. INTRODUCTION

Since the mainstream of accommodation reservations is online, travelers need to decide on accommodation based on the information on the Web. Consumers-stated preferences for decision criteria are various [1]. In particular, the amount of reviews has been found to promote accommodation room occupancy [2]. However, it is hard to check a large number of reviews. We thus consider that the value of reviews would be increased by helping users to easily check the reviews.

According to Dickinger *et al.*, recommendations from friends and online accommodation reviews should be the most important factors that influence online hotel booking [3]. Online accommodation reviews have been widely studied [4], and such research enables us to use the analysis results by text mining to help travelers with their decision making. According to Vermeulen, negative as well as positive reviews increase the consumer awareness of the accommodation [5]. Also, they showed that positive reviews can improve consumer attitudes toward the accommodations.

This paper focuses on seasonal features in accommodation reviews. We believe that the value of each accommodation also depends on seasonal events held in the neighborhood. The presentation of seasonal features might become one of the determinants of accommodations. The tf-idf method is a well-known representative method providing word importance in documents and it is used in several applications such as documents classification [6]. The first step of our proposed method is extracting higher tf-idf words from monthly reviews of an accommodation. The second step is forming hierarchical topics that contain higher tf-idf words. Finally, comparing the analysis results of each month showed the seasonal features of the accommodation. In order to provide accurate information to the consumers, the category should be taken into consideration [7]. Features change according to the season for each category, and it influences the users' decision making. In the proposed method, a topic model (i.e., latent semantic analysis) is used for category acquisition. One of the topic models is an Unsupervised Learning method: Latent Dirichlet Allocation (LDA) [8]. Our purpose is to extract topics from the documents based on the assumption that a document has multiple topics. Han *et al.* analyzed hotel reviews using LDA [9]. This research has succeeded in extracting the relationships between emotions and evaluations by topic analysis of accommodation reviews. Another LDA extension method is hLDA (hierarchical Latent Dirichlet Allocation) [10][11]. The hLDA probabilistically estimates topics, assuming that the topics contained in the document have a hierarchical structure. Regarding the feature of accommodation reviews, Wang *et al.* defined a new problem in opinionated text data analysis called Latent Aspect Rating Analysis (LARA) [12]. This study focuses on the inclusion relation in the category of accommodation reviews. For example, the category for "meal" includes more detailed information such as "meal price" and "meal quality."

In this paper, we hypothesize that it is possible to extract the inclusion relations of topics in accommodation reviews by using hLDA. We incorporate the time change analysis of the accommodation reviews using the results of hLDA and important words extracted by using the tf-idf method. The problem tackled in this paper is when consumers are not able to know the seasonal features from information on the Web. The decision making of the consumers should become easier as this problem is resolved. In Section 1, we have introduced the background and the relevant studies. In Section 2, we will introduce the data to be used, and in Section 3, we will propose an analysis method. In Section 4, we will discuss the evaluation method, and in Section 5, we will discuss the results. Finally, we will discuss the prospects of this research.

II. DATA

In this study, we use 5,082,427 Rakuten Travel reviews (the data was retrieved on March 29, 2020 [13]). The data was collected from 29,400 accommodation reviews for the time period 1996 through 2016. The top 10% of accommodations with the highest number of reviews were used for our analysis.

The importance of preprocessing in natural language processing has been widely known [14]. With preprocessing, the accuracy of the analysis would be improved by narrowing down the parts-of-speech to be analyzed as the stop-words. In this paper, we analyze only nouns to extract the characteristics of accommodations. We exclude the following words from the analysis:

1) Nouns whose meaning can be not understood.

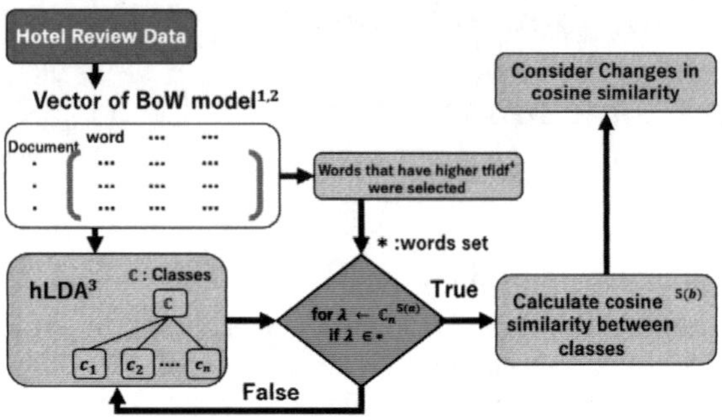

Figure 1. The framework of analysis procedure. In the figure, the index of procedure is shown as a superscript which is detailed in section III.

2) Nouns whose frequency is lower than three.
3) Days and symbols.

According to these procedures, we removed many noise nouns from the analysis: 8,817 of 10,979 nouns and 7,825 out of 9,674 nouns were each removed from the reviews of the accommodation #1 and #2, respectively.

III. THE PROPOSED METHOD

In the proposed method, hLDA, is usedfor a latent topic analysis, and the tf-idf method is used to extract seasonal features. Using both methods, we extract the latent topics depending on season in the reviews in a hierarchical structure. Extraction and consideration are performed according to the following procedure (see the subscript number in Figure 1).

1) The morphological analyzer extracts the nouns that appear in the document. For the Japanese documents, we use MeCab and NEologd as the morphological analyzer and the dictionary, respectively.
2) The extracted nouns are vectorized based on the Bag-of-Words model.
3) Using the vectors, the latent topics are hierarchically clustered.
4) The reviews are divided for each month in the calendar and 12 documents are generated. The tf-idf value is given to each noun that appears in each document.
5) The following processing (a) and (b) are executed for the top 10% nouns with tf-idf values excluding stop words.
    a) The tendency of nouns extracted in the same cluster is analyzed.
    b) Focusing on the clusters containing the arbitrary noun among plural months, the similarity among the clusters is calculated.

A. Hierarchical topic model

Accommodation reviews have two category types: large and small. Assuming that the structure of the categories can be extracted as topics, the hierarchical relationship of topics is constructed. Therefore, we focused on hLDA, which is an extension model of the LDA. The hLDA analyzes the hierarchical relationship of topics.

1) The nested Chinese Restaurant Process: The nested Chinese Restaurant Process (nCRP) is a stochastic process on a tree structure. This stochastic process is used for hLDA and is represented by the following metaphor using the Chinese Restaurant Process (CRP). The CRP is a distribution obtained by imagining a process by which N customers sit down in a Chinese restaurant with an infinite number of tables [11]. Let the customers be labeled as $1, 2, \ldots, N$ in the order they entered the restaurant. The first customer sits at the first table. The nth customer sits. The probability of sitting at the ith-table is determined by the following distribution (1);

$$p(c_n = i | c_{n-1}) = \begin{cases} \frac{n_i}{\gamma+n-1} & \text{(occupied table } i \text{),} \\ \frac{\gamma}{\gamma+n-1} & \text{(next unoccupied table),} \end{cases} \quad (1)$$

where, n_i is the number of customers currently sitting at ith-table, and γ is a meta-parameter that controls how often a customer chooses a new table versus sitting with others, which is relative to the number of customers in the restaurant.

In nCRP, a tree structure is formed based on CRP. nCRP is explained with the following metaphor. Suppose there are an infinite number of restaurants in the city, and each restaurant has an infinite number of tables. There is the restaurant at the root of the hierarchy, and each table at the restaurant specifies other restaurants. The first customer enters the root restaurant and selects the table according to the CRP. Then, the route to the next restaurant would be provided to the customer. The customer selects the table again according to the CRP. This procedure is infinitely repeated, and the path in the tree structure is constructed. All customers select a table, and a subtree consists of an infinitely deep tree branched infinitely. In this study, customers, restaurants and table seats each represents words, hierarchies, and topics.

2) Hierarchical Latent Dirichlet Allocation: In the generation process of hLDA, the tree structure is generated by nCRP. The hLDA is conducted according to the previous study [10], [11]. In the implementation of hLDA, it is necessary to set meta-parameters (α, γ, η, number of layers) in advance; affects" should be "affect " appropriateness " of the extraction results. We set $\gamma = 1.0$ and $\eta = 1.0$ referring to the previous study [10] for appropriate extraction for accommodation reviews. The main goal of this paper is to extract the feature of accommodation facilities, so it is desirable to know what is the specific criteria for the topic classification. Therefore, we set the number of layers in a hierarchy to three and the number of sampler iterations to 500. Only converged nouns are used in the analysis.

B. tf-idf

Essentially, tf-idf works by determining the relative frequency of words in an arbitrary document compared to the inverse proportion of the word over the entire document corpus [15]. In this study, since monthly reviews are used as a document set, nouns with high tf-idf values are assumed to be feature nouns representing seasons which rarely appear in other months.

C. Similarity among clusters

In this paper, we extract the nouns featuring the seasons by evaluating the change of the similarity among the clusters for each month constructed by using hLDA. The cosine similarity between the clusters for each month obtained by using hLDA

TABLE I. TOP FIVE NOUNS WITH HIGHER TF-IDF FROM ACCOMMODATION REVIEWS [TRANSLATED INTO ENGLISH BY THE AUTHORS]

	Accommodation #1	Accommodation #2
January	new year, new year's day, new year's end, mochi pounding, superlative degree	new year, new year's, sweets, special, anniversary
May	Golden Week, red snapper, spring, love, holiday	room temperature, Golden Week, weekend, grade, beauty treatment
August	Obon, Gassho, Rokusaburo Michiba, sweetfish, Noryo	pool, summer vacation, beach, sea bathing, barbecue
December	christmas, meal, breakthrough, specialty, superlative degree	Luminarie, christmas, winter, hospitality, special

is calculated. A cluster is formed by a collection of multiple nouns. Let each cluster for the months $m1$ and $m2$ be C_m and C_n. C_m and C_n are represented as (2) and (3), respectively;

$$C_m(1,\ldots,l) = \{W_1, W_2, \ldots, W_l\}, \quad (2)$$
$$C_n(1,\ldots,l) = \{W_1, W_1, \ldots, W_l\}. \quad (3)$$

The cosine similarity between these two sets is calculated by using (4);

$$cos(C_m, C_n) = \frac{\sum_{k=1}^{l} C_m(k) \cdot C_n(k)}{\sqrt{\sum_{k=1}^{l}(C_m(k))^2} \cdot \sqrt{\sum_{k=1}^{l}(C_n(k))^2}}. \quad (4)$$

IV. EXPERIMENT

The target months of analysis were narrowed down to the busy season of accommodations: January, May, August, and December. Table I shows the top five nouns in the two reviews with the higher tf-idf: note, the words are translated from Japanese into English by the authors. Parts of the hLDA analysis results are shown in Figure 2 and Figure 3; note that nouns that did not converge are excluded.

From Table I, other than the nouns that indicate the season itself, items suitable for evaluation such as "meals" and "events" are selected. In this paper, we analyzed the two accommodations randomly selected from the dataset described in Section II as examples for the kick-off of our research project.

We define the class to analyze as follows:

- Small cluster: a single cluster in third layer of hierarchy containing the nouns, e.g., C_{a1} and C_{a2} in both Figure 2 and Figure 3.
- Large cluster: multiple clusters with the same parent as the second layer of hierarchy cluster containing the noun, e.g., all small clusters of C_a an C_b in both Figure 2 and Figure 3.

The next step is to analyze the transition of similarity among months for each category of clusters. This method compares temporal changes in topics on large and small scales. Table II and Table III show the results.

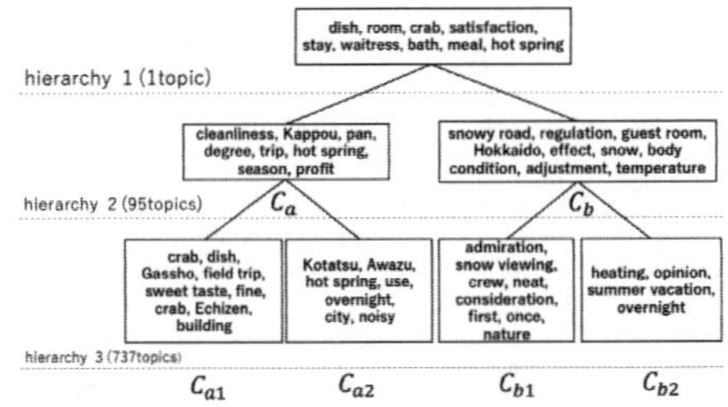

Figure 2. The result of hLDA for accommodation #1 in January.

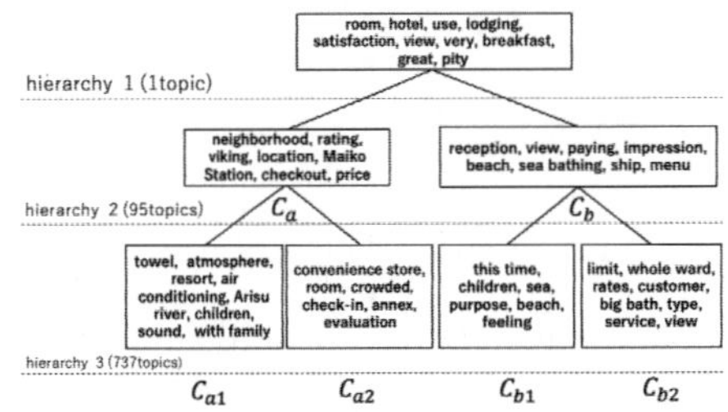

Figure 3. The result of hLDA for accommodation #2 in August.

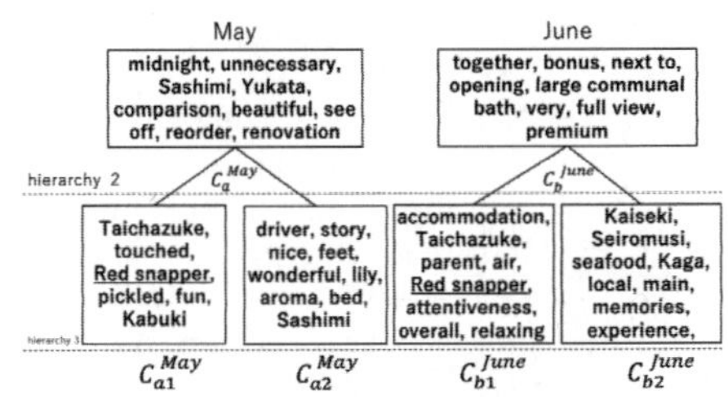

Figure 4. The Hierarchical structure for accommodation #1 in May and June including "red snapper."

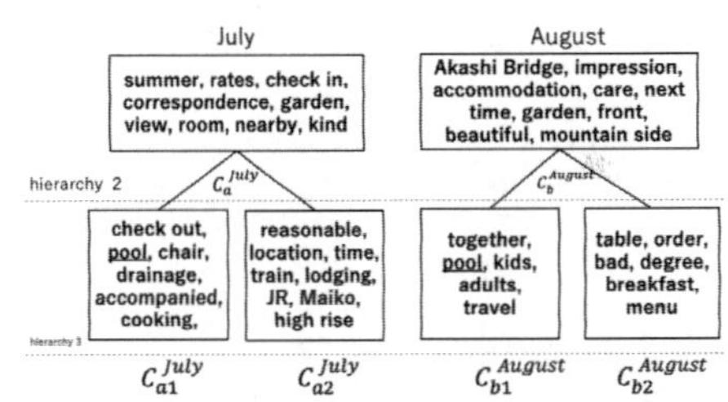

Figure 5. The Hierarchical structure for accommodation #2 in July and August including "pool."

V. DISCUSSION

A. hLDA extraction results

From "cleanliness" and "hot spring" in Figure 2, it can be seen that services and facilities were evaluated as the topics. In contrast, topics related to weather and environment such as "snow" and "temperature" were extracted from C_b. In C_{a1}, evaluations on meals, such as "crab" and "sweet" were extracted. As comparing C_{a2} with C_{b2}, it is clear that food-related topics were classified. C_{b1} had topics for services and environment, while C_{b2} had topics for temperature.

From C_a in Figure 3, it is shown that price and location were evaluated as topics. From "sea bathing" and "view" in C_b, it can be seen that outdoor and facility features were evaluated

TABLE II. THE COSINE SIMILARITY BETWEEN CLUSTERS INCLUDING "RED SNAPPER" WHICH IS EXTRACTED BY TF-IDF METHOD, IN THE REVIEW OF ACCOMMODATION #1 IN MAY.

Month	1	2	3	4	5	6	7	8	9	10	11	12
Large cluster	0.0	0.0	0.0	0.029	1.0	0.046	0.018	0.039	0.021	0.028	0.0	0.0
Small cluster	0.0	0.0	0.0	0.099	1.0	0.199	0.099	0.099	0.099	0.105	0.0	0.0

TABLE III. THE COSINE SIMILARITY BETWEEN CLUSTERS INCLUDING "POOL" WHICH IS EXTRACTED BY TF-IDF METHOD, IN THE REVIEW OF ACCOMMODATION #2 IN AUGUST.

Month	1	2	3	4	5	6	7	8	9	10	11	12
Large cluster	0.0	0.0	0.0	0.0	0.0	0.110	0.042	1.0	0.164	0.0	0.0	0.0
Small cluster	0.0	0.0	0.0	0.0	0.0	0.099	0.099	1.0	0.099	0.0	0.0	0.0

as the topics. "With family" and "beach" were classified into C_{a1} and C_{b1}, it is imagined that we can enjoy a family trip and swimming in the sea; we confirmed that some of the reviews described such experiences. As a result, it can be expected that we should be able to enjoy seasonal foods especially crab and hot pot and snowy weather in accommodation #1 in January. Also, it is expected that we should be able to enjoy swimming with our family in accommodation #2 in August.

B. Evaluation by Cosine similarity

We focus on "Red snapper", which is the specific noun in May in the review of accommodation #1. The similarity between classes including "Red snapper" beyond months is calculated. Table II shows the transition of the similarities between May and each month, respectively. From Table II, it was found that June showed the highest similarity to May, followed by August and April. Though each similarity was low in real values, the similarity can be used in the discussion for relative evaluation. Because it includes various topics in a large cluster, more conceptual changes can be seen. Since the similarity between May and April and the one between May and June are relatively high, it seems that seasonal topics are similar to each other on that combination of months. In the hierarchies of May and June that contain "Red snapper" in Figure 4, it can be seen that "red snapper dishes" were included in both the third layers. In fact, it is known that the season for "Red snapper" should be March through June and September through November. However, we can have the fish during all seasons if we do not mind the freshness, it becomes clear that it is a topic that attracted attention in May and June for this accommodation.

For accommodation #2, we focus on "pool" in August for a discussion. Table II shows the similarity between classes including "pool" beyond months. From the results, it can be seen that "pool" appeared from June to September.

In large clusters, the classes including "pool" between August and September showed the highest similarity. However, the similarity between July and August was relatively low, though "pool" generally shows popularity in the season. From Figure 5, it can be seen that family trips like "adults" and "kids" were in the same cluster as "pool" in August. In the actual reviews, family travel styles appeared more frequently in August than July. The season for family trips was suggested from the results. From the result of analysis, we found that the user group using the pool changed according to the season. The analysis revealed the seasons that attract attention and the seasons for family trips.

C. Weakness of the System

In this analysis, the review data was divided into months. Therefore, it can be said that this analysis method is weak for features that straddle the months and features for each one day. In addition, this analysis method does not completely extract features for irregularly held events and review sentences for questions. The background of this method is that it is assumed that it will help consumers to think about which month they will travel when making travel plans. Also, this method was adopted in consideration of the difference between the date of staying and the date of writing the review.

VI. Conclusion and Future Work

In this paper, we have shown the analysis and discussion of using hLDA to extract seasonal features from accommodation reviews. As a result, we were able to extract the seasonal characteristics of accommodation facilities in a hierarchical structure. However, we need to consider a more practical use. We will go to the big goal of "consumer decision support" as the next step of our research. The feature directions can be as follows: (1) hLDA hyperparameters for accuracy, (2) visualization of the results, (3) regional differences with time variation, and (4) find useful information for accommodation. The task (4) is considered to improve the services of accommodation facilities and dynamic pricing.

Acknowledgment

We show our apprication to Rakuten Dataset provided by Rakuten with a support of National Institute of Informatics Research Data.

References

[1] K. Kim, O.-J. Park, S. Yun, and H. Yun, "What makes tourists feel negatively about tourism destinations? application of hybrid text mining methodology to smart destination management," Technological Forecasting and Social Change, vol. 123, 2017, pp. 362–369.

[2] P. De Pelsmacker, S. Van Tilburg, and C. Holthof, "Digital marketing strategies, online reviews and hotel performance," International Journal of Hospitality Management, vol. 72, 2018, pp. 47–55.

[3] A. Dickinger and J. Mazanec, "Consumers' preferred criteria for hotel online booking," Information and communication technologies in tourism 2008, 2008, pp. 244–254.

[4] R. Filieri, "What makes an online consumer review trustworthy?" Annals of Tourism Research, vol. 58, 2016, pp. 46–64.

[5] I. E. Vermeulen and D. Seegers, "Tried and tested: The impact of online hotel reviews on consumer consideration," Tourism management, vol. 30, no. 1, 2009, pp. 123–127.

[6] B. Trstenjak, S. Mikac, and D. Donko, "Knn with tf-idf based framework for text categorization," Procedia Engineering, vol. 69, 2014, pp. 1356–1364.

[7] K. Berezina, A. Bilgihan, C. Cobanoglu, and F. Okumus, "Understanding satisfied and dissatisfied hotel customers: text mining of online hotel reviews," Journal of Hospitality Marketing & Management, vol. 25, no. 1, 2016, pp. 1–24.

[8] D. M. Blei, A. Y. Ng, and M. I. Jordan, "Latent dirichlet allocation," Journal of machine Learning research, vol. 3, no. Jan, 2003, pp. 993–1022.

[9] H. J. Han, S. Mankad, N. Gavirneni, and R. Verma, "What guests really think of your hotel: Text analytics of online customer reviews," 2016.

[10] D. M. Blei, T. L. Griffiths, and M. I. Jordan, "The nested chinese restaurant process and bayesian nonparametric inference of topic hierarchies," Journal of the ACM (JACM), vol. 57, no. 2, 2010, pp. 1–30.

[11] T. L. Griffiths, M. I. Jordan, J. B. Tenenbaum, and D. M. Blei, "Hierarchical topic models and the nested chinese restaurant process," in Advances in neural information processing systems, 2004, pp. 17–24.

[12] H. Wang, Y. Lu, and C. Zhai, "Latent aspect rating analysis on review text data: a rating regression approach," in Proceedings of the 16th ACM SIGKDD international conference on Knowledge discovery and data mining, 2010, pp. 783–792.

[13] "Rakuten dataset," URL: https://www.nii.ac.jp/dsc/idr/en/rakuten/ [accessed: March 2020].

[14] S. Vijayarani, M. J. Ilamathi, and M. Nithya, "Preprocessing techniques for text mining-an overview," International Journal of Computer Science & Communication Networks, vol. 5, no. 1, 2015, pp. 7–16.

[15] J. Ramos, "Using tf-idf to determine word relevance in document queries," in Proceedings of the first instructional conference on machine learning, vol. 242. Piscataway, NJ, 2003, pp. 133–142.

An Approach Towards Artistic Visualizations of Human Motion in Static Media Inspired by the Visual Arts

Anastasia Rigaki, Nikolaos Partarakis, Xenophon Zabulis
Institute of Computer Science, Foundation for Research and Technology – Hellas (FORTH),
Heraklion, Greece
e-mail: {rigaki, partarak, zabulis}@ics.forth.gr

Constantine Stephanidis
Institute of Computer Science, Foundation for Research and Technology – Hellas (FORTH),
Department of Computer Science, University of Crete
Heraklion, Greece
e-mail: cs@ics.forth.gr

Abstract— **The visualization of 3D human motion on a 2D canvas or display is employed by a wide spectrum of disciplines to abstract and provide insight on the motion of human subjects that is depicted by the 2D medium. Painters, illustrators and directors use motion lines, contrast, superimposition as well as juxtaposition of visual frames for a better conveyance of motion. The proliferation of digital cameras, motion sensors, combined with computer vision has enabled the 3D recording of human motion in a wide range of conditions. At the same time, applications of human motion visualization, such as illustrated safety or assembly instructions, still have a wide use in conventional depictions of human motion, namely 2D static depictions, whether these are presented on screen or on paper. Inspired by the depiction of human motion in the visual arts, we transfer pertinent visual approaches to the domain of human motion visualization. Our goal is to utilise these visualization techniques and create insightful visualizations of human motion recordings on static 2D media. To that end, we propose the MotiVo system that dynamically integrates multiple tools for the visualization of human motion. Based on these tools, we study basic approaches of human motion visualization and abstraction.**

Keywords-Motion visualization; Artistic Visualization; Motion capture; Image processing;Computer Vision.

I. INTRODUCTION

In visual arts, human motion and activity are often conveyed through still depictions or sculptures. Depiction of motion is an important part of artistic expression. Over the years, artists have depicted both motion (e.g., Claude Monet, En Plein Air, 1886) and lack of motion, (e.g., Johannes Vermeer's Woman Holding a Balance, 1664) as a way to stimulate interest [1]. We call *visual abstraction*, a drawing that encapsulates events lasting more than one moment and possibly occurring in more than one location. In essence, a visual abstraction is a manipulation of realistic imaging aiming to convey an understanding of the events occurring within a time-space interval. Motion is effectively conveyed in static media using superimposed and juxtaposed images. Pertinent techniques are based on the cognitive capability of the observer to "fill-in" missing information. In this way, the depiction encodes an event, taking place during a time interval rather than a photographic recording of a single moment. Superimposed forms are employed in the visual arts to summarize motion within a short time interval, taking place at a location (Figure 1).

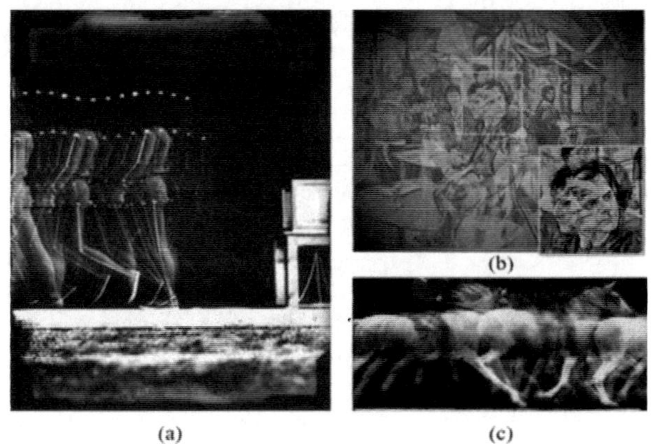

Figure 1. (a) *Man walking*, Marey 1891 (b) *Calder's Ascension*, Head 2017 (c) *Cheval blanc monté*, Marey 1886.

Juxtaposed illustrations are used in comics [2] and illustrated instructions to convey motion. Visualizing motion, as a sequence of juxtaposed key pose [3] depictions, provides a clear understanding of the illustrated motion. Annotations, such as motion lines, provide visual cues to motion and facilitate understanding (Figure 2).

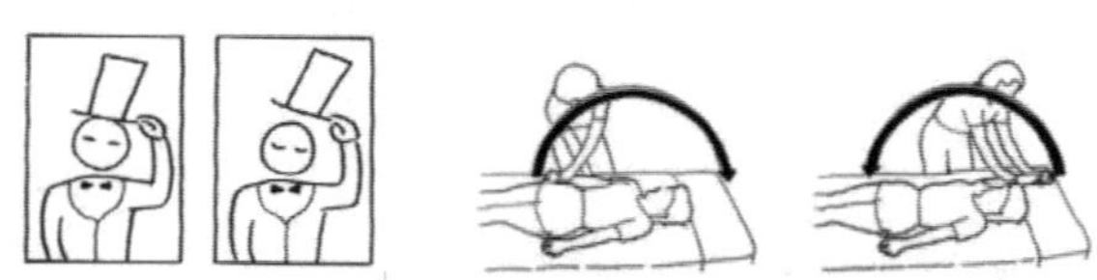

Figure 2. Juxtaposed illustrations encoding motion.

Representation of motion and activity in longer time intervals or scenes has been treated in art by manipulating time in the depiction, so that multiple time instances are seamlessly summarized, or "gracefully superimposed" without affecting the realism of depiction. For example, in Figure 3, it is the characteristic activity of each person depicted by each form in the painting rather than a photographic depiction of a moment. If the depiction would be literally considered, the depicted behaviours would probably not occur simultaneously. Instead, the painting summarizes the behavior of each character during the depicted event. The painter guides the observer to examine each form sequentially. The dominant stroke of light creates a salient visual path in the painting. Then, the attention [4] is guided by contrast changes in an elaborate visual path that visits the depicted characters and reveals the interaction among them.

Figure 3. *The Calling of St. Matthew*, Caravaggio 1599-1600.

Juxtaposition is also used in illustrated instructions (e.g., manuals) as an ordered representation of images combined with written information and graphical annotations, to direct the reader (Figure 4).

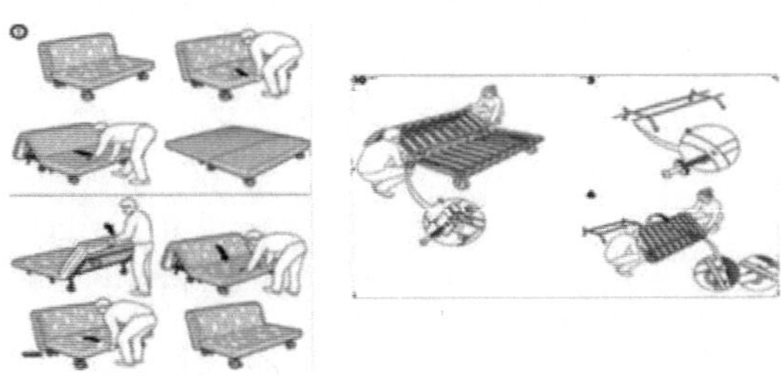

Figure 4. Motion and action visualization in instruction manuals.

Although this was conventionally a manual task for illustrators, nowadays technology is offering a plethora of tools for digital creativity. It is common for graphic designers and illustrators to use image-processing software in order to simplify authoring and enhance visualization. Though these tools are a commodity, they still require insight and art skills from the illustrator. The efficiency of communication and the abstraction of form is also noted as another inspirational aspect of story-telling visuals. Le Corbusier in a letter, he describes his project through suggestive drawings. The style reminds of the so-called "ligne claire" (clear line) [5], whose precursor is now recognized in Rodolphe Töpffer [6]. The technique is explained in: *"Le Corbusier obsessively draws "after" photographs as in an attempt to remove anything superfluous"*. The overlaps with Töpffer were particularly vivid in Le Corbusier's sketches of human body actions, creating figures with a dynamism and liveliness (Figure 5).

Le Corbusier's trademark line style transformed his architecrural representations to a graphic narrative communication tool.

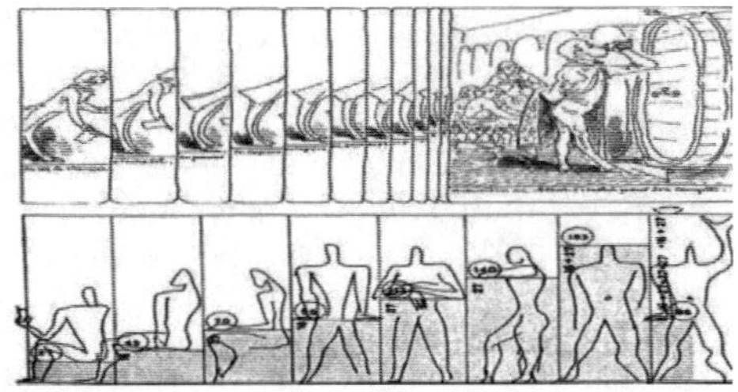

Figure 5. Reduction of complex photographs into drawings.

The goal of this research is to build over centuries of experience in the domains of the visual arts and implement a system that transfers artistic concepts in the digital world. Although there are techniques that offer a wide range of motion visualization tools, some of them focusing on Motion Capture (MoCap) whereas others work exclusively on motion visualizations, there is still need for an interactive and simple to use editor. Existing works are mostly targeted to one specific motion visualization technique that fits their work subject, nevertheless, there have not yet been presented works for general purposes. In this context, we present MotiVo, an interactive system that simplifies this process by offering a number of visualization tools and provides insightful and visually pleasant results requiring minimum expertise and knowledge from the user side. Using these tools, motion is visualized by parameters, such as the blending of key poses retrieved from an activity, the visualization of motion trajectories, the application of image filters to visualizations and their 3D and 2D combinations for hybrid depictions of motion.

The rest of the paper is structured as follows. In Section II, we summarize the related work. In Section III, we present system's input data and also give a brief description of how we acquired them. In Section IV, the *MotiVo* user interface and its tools are described. In Section V, there are presented some experimental results as well as we give some guidelines for a better experience according to an expert-based evaluation with the tools. Finally, we present our future work and draw some conclusions (Section VI).

II. RELATED WORK

A large number of existing studies in the broader literature have examined motion visualization techniques. Digital artists, such as T. Gremmler, use technology to produce artistic visualizations of motion. Gremmler has rendered a sequence of animations that illustrate the disciplined and defined movements of Kung Fu practice in the form of shapes, geometries, and abstract shapes. Human figures are reduced to a minimum of a simple sequence of lines, lines, and points, which adopt postures and pose throughout the video [7].

In this context, technical state-of-the-art is offering a number of alternative ways to digitize human motion, such as MoCap and Computer vision technologies [2][8]-[10].

These technologies provide accurate digitized representation of movement in 3D [11][12]. At the same time, in the domain of computer graphics, a wide range of visualization tools are available that allow the simplification of the production of 2D and 3D visualizations.

Key Probe is a key-frame extraction technique, relied on an algorithm appropriate for rigid-body and soft-body animations that converts a skeleton based motion or animated mesh to a key frame-based representation [13]. To select a representative moment from a performance, they introduce "Action Snapshot", a method based on information theory that automates the process of generating meaningful snapshots, by taking as input dynamic scenes as input and producing a narrative image as output [14].

3D visualization has also been proven valuable in the demonstration of Motion Capture (MoCap) data. Such an example is TooltY, a 3D authoring platform for demonstration of simple tool operations in 3D environments [15]. In sports, human motion visualization is used to display 3D models of swimmers by digitizing their motions and creating personalized virtual representations [16]. Lucent Vision is a visualization system developed for tennis. It uses real-time video analysis to extract motion trajectories and provides a variety of visualization options [17].

Action summarization is prevalent in the human motion visualization community, as it can produce motion effects in still image frames. "Action Synopsis" takes as input human movements, encoded either as MoCap animations or videos and presents motion in still images [18]. The work [19] creates compact narratives from videos, by composing foreground and background scene regions into a single interactive image, using a series of spatiotemporal masks.

Depth information of animations assists summarization of 3D animations in a single image. A method that extracts important frames from the animation sequence based on the importance of each frame is proposed, based on its contribution to overall motion-gradient [20].

Similar work has also been developed for the artistic motion visualization. In [21], simulates thick, dominant brush strokes, to place emphasis on important line features of an image. M.G Choi proposed an interface, where the user browses overall motion visualized by a unified medium in the form of 2D stick figure images [19].

All these proposals offer a wide range of motion visualization techniques but they lack in terms of intuition, interaction and ease of use. In this work, we identify a gap between motion digitisation and insightful, artistic motion visualization. We propose a bridging of these dimensions in a single workflow. To realise this approach, we implemented MotiVo, a 2D visualization editor. In this editor, two tools are presented for the production of motion visualizations. The first is based on video key frames. The second visualizes 2D motion trajectories computed by visual tracking. To further assist users, we include post-processing tools that enable the application of image filters to input visual assets and manual annotation of upon these assets. Finally, we propose a method to use 3D information about human and object motion to enrich the produced visualizations. Our editor does not only focus on motion visualization effects, but also facilitates users to extend the tools through their combination in order to generate unique representations of motion visuals.

III. ACQUIRING VISUALIZATION SOURCES DATA FROM IMAGE, VIDEO AND HUMAN MOTION

For the purposes of this research work, two types of potential digital input are of interest. The first type is still images and image frames acquired from video and the second type is MoCap data. In order to collect data for our case study, we use the following methodology. Initially, we recorded in a video format of a person performing typical activities, such as waving. The video stream was segmented to video frames and frames of interest were then extracted from the video stream to produce a summarization in frames of movements. Furthermore, the video stream was used as a source for the Open Pose Computer Vision library [22]. Using the Open Pose output in this research work, we isolated specific joints of the skeleton in order to produce the trajectories path for our visualization algorithm.

IV. THE MOTIVO APPROACH

A. *MotiVo tools*

1) Motion Blender

Motion blender creates a directional motion effect by overlapping key poses into a united content. Specifically, as a dataset, each user is able to import multiple strong key pose images, they consider as the main motions of an activity. This dataset differs for every user. The combination of all the frames summarizes the overall action. Besides the visualization of motion direction, the user can emphasize on each frame with varying contrast and color intensity volumes. The contrast intensity of each key pose is determined by a value selected by each user via the tool's User Interface (UI) sliders. The value range is between zero and one hundred, with zero to be the lowest contrast value whereas one hundred the maximum intensity.

Depending on the nature of activity, the emphasis on the each image frame may be differentiated. In many cases the most significant action is the initial, middle or the last one. For example, on hammering a nail, the dominant action could be the last key pose, which indicates exactly how to hit the top of the nail, therefore this key frame is highlighted the most. In contrast to the previous scenario, in dance choreographies the motion sequence can be evenly defined as important, thus the relative intensity of each key pose is uniformly visualized. Users on runtime can view the resultant image. The output is a single image that can be also saved as an asset in the current project and then be loaded by another MotiVo tool for further processing. A color image I at coordinates x, y has pixel value $c = I(x, y)$ where c has values {R, G, B}.We do not treat monochromatic (grayscale) differently. If such input is given, the monochromatic channel is replicated in all the RGB (Red Green Blue) bands and the image is treated as a color image.

Let n be the number of key frames selected by the user. We denote by I_i the corresponding images, where i is in $[1, n]$. In case of even distribution between contrast and volume of the image frames, for each I_i we average the corresponding pixel RBG values from the color arrays of each selected image (1). This can be achieved in case of all the number values are set evenly. The combined result is a visualization of all the images demonstrating a motion sequence (Figure 6).

$$I_s = \sum_{i=1}^{n} \frac{I_i(x,y)}{n} \quad (1)$$

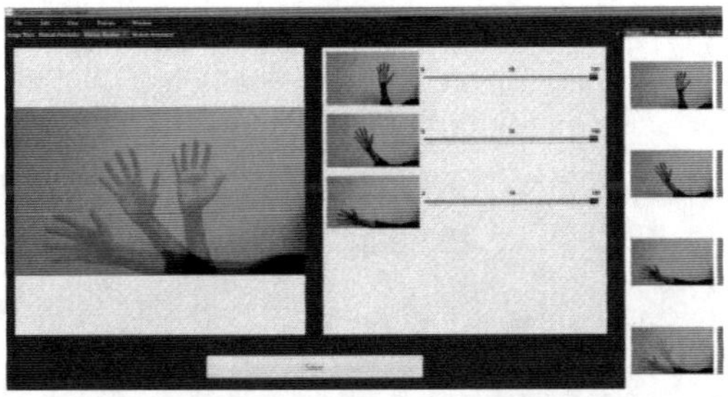

Figure 6. Averaged Motion visualization.

An extended approach of the previous scenario is the weighted visualization of human motions. In this version, users alter the UI slider values thus setting different weight value w_i for each image frame to denote the contrast intensity depicted in the final result (2). For lower weight values, the frames have low opacity volume in contrast to high weights values where the RGB values are greater. The effect of fading and overlapping motion allows the human eye to perceive easily the chronological order of the action (Figure 7).

$$I_s = \frac{\sum_{i=1}^{n} w_i * I_i(x,y)}{\sum_{i=1}^{n} w_i} \quad (2)$$

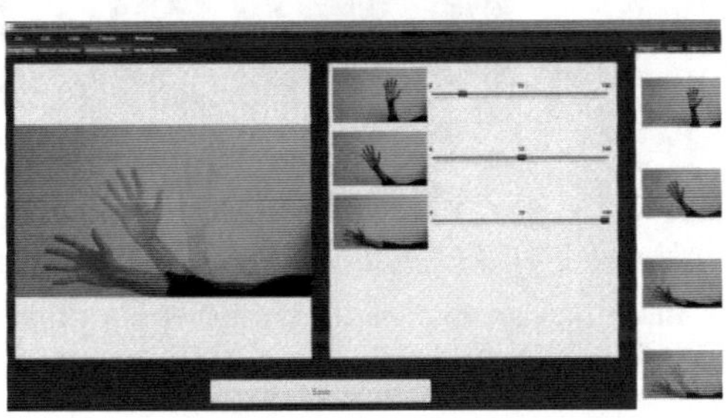

Figure 7. Weighted motion visualization.

Average and weighted visualization of Motion Blender were implemented using the Windows Presentation Foundation (WPF). In order to rectify the problem of CPU overhead in pixel operations, the algorithms, we developed, were optimized using parallel loops and direct memory access□

2) Motion Annotator

The second tool of MotiVo editor is Motion Annotator. This tool takes as an input, an image frame depicting a human action, (e.g., the produced image from Motion Blender) as well as a trajectory file containing the specific joints of the skeleton body as *(x, y)* coordinates in 2D space. The trajectory files are generated by the OpenPose output for a specific joint of interest, thus isolating the movement of this joint for visualization purposes. These *(x, y)* coordinates are visualized on the canvas of the loaded input image. The algorithm we have developed, highlights with artistic designs the specific coordinates provided by the 2D trajectory file. There are multiple ways of hi-fidelity artistic representations that can be depicted based on the trajectories (i.e., bullets, simple lines, comic style lines). The annotated points on the image frame denote the direction of the motion. For example, in the case of hand waving, by annotating the image with the retrieved points, it highlights the human hand trajectory during the activity (Figure 8).

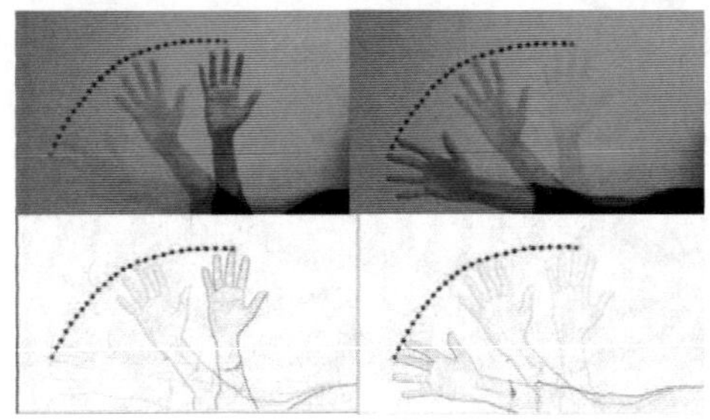

Figure 8. Motion annotations using Motion Blender (top) and Motion Annotator with trajectories extracted by Open Pose (bottom).

To smooth the visualized trajectories, we used composite Bézier curves. In computer graphics, a composite Bézier curve is a piecewise Bézier curve that is at least continuous. In other words, a composite Bézier curve is a series of Bézier curves joined end to end where the last point of one curve coincides with the starting point of the next curve [23].

3) Manual motion enhancer

In some cases, there is need for manual annotation of motion, especially where the context information is to be added to the visualization. To that end, we exploit the techniques used to create juxtaposed illustrations in comics. The manual motion enhancer is an editing component that allows users to load an existing image result from the project assets and manually enhance it by attaching ready to use concepts and icon sets (i.e., arrows, lines, etc.), such as those in comics (Figure 9).

4) Image filters

This tool receives as input an image file and provides a list of image filters that can be used image similar to the ones used in popular image processing software [10][24]. Currently a wide array image transformations, color operations and artistic transformations are available. An example of edge detection is presented in Figure 10.

Figure 9. Motion frames enhancement using iconsets

Figure 10. Edge detection filter.

5) *Scene composer*

The scene composer was inspired by the depictions of crafts in art and photography (Figure 11). Its goal is to abstract human motion and tools to the minimum ingredients.

Figure 11. Depiction of tools grip and usage in the visual arts (left, middle) and moment of interest for Scene Composer (right).

As a result, scene composer is capable of depicting the essential parts of the craft so as to assist human perception and understanding and improve the development of captivating visualization for information and education.

Scene Composer is a tool that takes as input an overview of the scene from a static moment in the course of a craft action, (e.g., passing the shuttle through a loom). This static motion frame is then used by a computer vision tracker, capable of tracking the position and orientation of hands and objects. An example of such a moment where both the hand posture and the tool orientation can be extracted (Figure 11).

In both cases, we march from the hypothesis that the tracker has already the geometry and texture of the object to be tracked, (e.g., a generic model of a hand or a 3D model of the tool to be tracked). In both cases, the tracker is estimating the Rotation and Translation and Scale of the object tracked (i.e., hand, or tool) and overlays the model on top of the given frame for abstraction and emphasis on the spatial arrangement of the critical actors in the scene. Scene composer is inspired by visualization in robotics, where they are used to create a human-comprehensible illustration of the model of that the robot has built for its environment. In Figure 12, an example of such a visualization is shown for the case where a robotic manipulator grips objects upon a table top. The visualization illustrates the location and poses that the robot has estimated regarding the objects on the table top (blue) and its own manipulator (red).

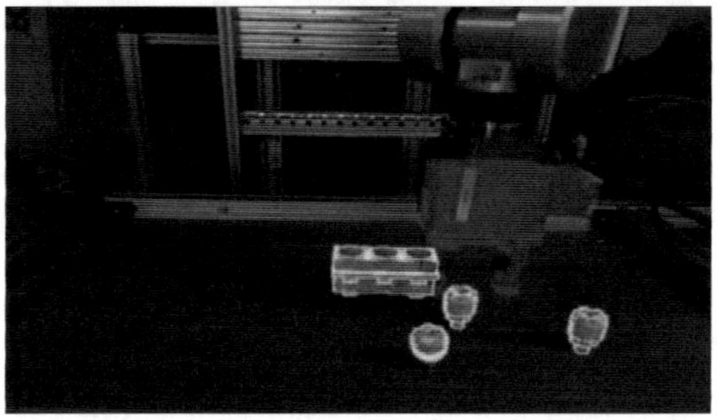

Figure 12. Illustration of object and robotic manipulator localization.

In Figure 13, the process of integrating information in static frames using the scene composer tool is illustrated. In the illustrations, on the right is the 3D model of the tool that is tracked and on the right the inference of the position of the tool at the imaged moment.

Figure 13. Visualization of tool usage.

B. *Extendable UI architecture*

The main requirement of the system-UI architecture of MotiVo was to use a plug-in based software development pattern where there is a distinction between the main system and visualization tools. This distinction was important so as to develop an extendable motion visualization system where new components are added as new visualization tools arise. In such a context, it was decided that the main system should support the creation of project files and the assignment of assets to these projects (images, videos, Biovision Hierarchy (BVH) files, image trajectories, etc.). All tools should be then loaded as window components and should be drag-drop enabled. Taking into consideration this main requirement, a dockable UI container architecture was selected, based on the one followed by Integrated Development Environments. In this architecture, components can be loaded and unloaded on the fly and new components can be loaded as plugins by integrating a new dockable window to the main window manager. Furthermore, this was considered a good option as one of the target groups of this tools are technical people with expertise on using dockable layouts. The only limitation is that typically such UIs may have a longer learning curve that simpler ones with the added value of extensibility and extensibility in the future. For the purposes presented above it was decided to structure the UI of MotiVo on top of the DevZest WPF Docking library [25].

V. EXPERIMENTS AND GUIDELINES

A formative evaluation was conducted in the context of the Mingei Innovation Action under the Horizon 2020 Programme of the European Commission [26]. The evaluation was based on images and videos of craft practitioner recordings in the context of the Mingei project. Based on these datasets, an expert-based evaluation was performed and several experiments were conducted with practitioners to assess our motion visualization strategies by using all the MotiVo tools. The outcome of those experiments formed a set of preliminary guidelines to address the needs of each individual tool.

Guidelines

In order the users to use MotiVo editor efficiently, we propose some guidelines based on an expert-based evaluation.

1) Motion Blender

After experimenting with weight values, we concluded that imaging settings play a significant role in the outcome.

Guideline 1: Prefer image sequences acquired through static camera.

Guideline 2: When working with a moving camera select a frame of reference where the camera is static and another one with multiple changes happening in the initial scene. This will improve the blending quality.

2) Motion Annotator

Guideline 1: The use of 2D trajectories can be sometimes be non-representative. The total number of Points *(x,y)* should be sufficient for the trajectory visualization to be precise. Despite the fact that we use Bezier splines to design curves, the input files content should be a good starting point for the Motion Annotator.

3) Manual motion enhancer

Guideline 1: Depending on the nature and style of the annotated image, users should choose graphic elements of similar style so as to fit the context.

Guideline 2: For comic style images, annotations should be comic styled or even multicolored whereas in the case of simple and minimal images, artistic arrows or other elements are the appropriate ones.

Guideline 3: Due to the fact that we are trying to visualize motion in 2D space, users are advised to adjust the projection on the annotation stickers so as to indicate the depth and direction of motion.

4) Image Filters

Guideline 1: Motion filters may be a powerful tool for post and pre-processing results. Experiment with motion filters to have an overview of the potential outcomes.

Guideline 2: When a motion blending fails you can facilitate motion filters to simplify the input of motion blender and thus get better Visualization results.

5) Scene Composer

Guideline 1: Make sure that source frames have sufficient information regarding the visualized-tracked object or hand (i.e., it is clearly visible).

Guideline 2: Avoid using frames where the position of the object can only be inferred through the position of the hand (non-occluded hand but occluded object).

6) Combined usage of tools

Guideline 1: Create richer motion Visualization by combining several MotiVo tools in the same Visualization project (Figure 14).

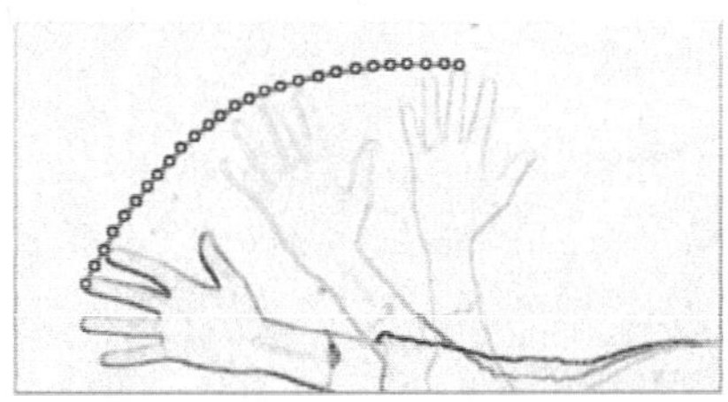

Figure 14. Visualization of tool usage through the estimation of hand and 3D model pose within the static motion frame

VI. CONCLUSION AND FUTURE WORK

This paper has presented an approach towards the visualization of data stemming from video recordings and visual tracking of human movement. Until now such visualizations were mainly targeted to the actual reproduction of motion in 3D or 2D space, such as for example the preview of MoCap output or the visualization of 2D pose estimations on top of the video or image sources.

Inspired by motion visualization in art, cinema and design we marched into implementing MotiVo, a motion visualization editor that is comprised of four distinct tools built on top of a plugin-based architecture capable of being extended and enriched in the future.

Based on the experience gained in this research work and the experiments performed in the context of implementing the visualization tools, it can be safely concluded that artistic visualization of human motion in 2D is technically feasible and can produce aesthetically pleasant results. Of course, human intervention is needed to orchestrate the appropriate selection of tools. This paper reports not only on the implementation of these tools, but

also through the experience during implementation and experimentation provides a set of best practice guidelines so as to get the most
[2] out of these tools.

The authors plan to enhance their approach by exploring the advances on style transfer algorithms to provide even better visualizations. Furthermore, the integration of 3D information to the static motion frames will enable the use of 3D data, in favor of motion analytics and visualization. Finally, video visualizations would be easily produced and even the isolation of the actors in a movement sequence would be facilitated, in order to reproduce them in another context, for example, in Virtual Reality (VR) training.

ACKNOWLEDGMENT

For this work, data stemming from the three pilot sites of the Mingei H2020 EU funded project (GA No. 822336) were used. The authors are grateful to project partner ARMINES for the acquisition of MoCap data.

REFERENCES

[1] S. Zeki, "An exploration of art and the brain," in *Inner Vision*, 2000.

[2] S. McCloud, "Understanding comics: The invisible art," *Northamp. Mass*, 1993.

[3] P. J. Kellman and T. F. Shipley, "A theory of visual interpolation in object perception," *Cognit. Psychol.*, vol. 23, no. 2, pp. 141–221, 1991.

[4] M. E. Chevreul, *The Laws of Contrast of Colour*, 1858.

[5] L. Arana and L. Miguel, "La Ligne Claire de Le Corbusier. Time, Space, and Sequential Narratives," presented at the Le Corbusier, 50 Years later, Valencia, 2015.

[6] C. L. Marcos, *Graphic Imprints: The Influence of Representation and Ideation Tools in Architecture*. Springer, 2018.

[7] "Kung Fu Motion Visualization," *Vimeo*. [Online]. Available: https://vimeo.com/163153865. [Accessed: 13-Jan-2020].

[8] C. M. Brigante, N. Abbate, A. Basile, A. C. Faulisi, and S. Sessa, "Towards miniaturization of a MEMS-based wearable motion capture system," *IEEE Trans. Ind. Electron.*, vol. 58, no. 8, pp. 3234–3241, 2011.

[9] M. Müller, T. Röder, M. Clausen, B. Eberhardt, B. Krüger, and A. Weber, "Documentation mocap database hdm05," 2007.

[10] D. A. Ross, J. Lim, R.-S. Lin, and M.-H. Yang, "Incremental learning for robust visual tracking," Int. J. Comput. Vis., vol. 77, no. 1–3, pp. 125–141, 2008.

[11] Dariush, M. Gienger, A. Arumbakkam, C. Goerick, Y. Zhu, and K. Fujimura, "Online and markerless motion retargeting with kinematic constraints," in *2008 IEEE/RSJ International Conference on Intelligent Robots and Systems*, 2008, pp. 191–198.

[12] C. Hecker, B. Raabe, R. W. Enslow, J. DeWeese, J. Maynard, and K. van Prooijen, "Real-time motion retargeting to highly varied user-created morphologies," in *ACM Transactions on Graphics (TOG)*, 2008, vol. 27, p. 27.

[13] K.-S. Huang, C.-F. Chang, Y.-Y. Hsu, and S.-N. Yang, "Key probe: a technique for animation keyframe extraction," *Vis. Comput.*, vol. 21, no. 8–10, pp. 532–541, 2005.

[14] M. Wang, S. Guo, M. Liao, D. He, J. Chang, and J. Zhang, "Action snapshot with single pose and viewpoint," *Vis. Comput.*, vol. 35, no. 4, pp. 507–520, 2019.

[15] E.Stefanidi, N. Partarakis, X. Zabulis, P. Zikas, G. Papagiannakis, and N. Thalmann Magnenat, "TooltY: An approach for the combination of motion capture and 3D reconstruction to present tool usage in 3D environments," in *Intelligent Scene Modelling and Human Computer Interaction*, Springer.

[16] C. Kirmizibayrak, J. Honorio, X. Jiang, R. Mark, and J. K. Hahn, "Digital Analysis and Visualization of Swimming Motion.," *Int. J. Virtual Real.*, vol. 10, no. 3, 2011.

[17] G. Pingali, A. Opalach, Y. Jean, and I. Carlbom, "Visualization of sports using motion trajectories: providing insights into performance, style, and strategy," in *Proceedings Visualization, 2001. VIS'01*, 2001, pp. 75–544.

[18] J. Assa, Y. Caspi, and D. Cohen-Or, "Action synopsis: pose selection and illustration," in *ACM Transactions on Graphics (TOG)*, 2005, vol. 24, pp. 667–676.

[19] M. G. Choi, K. Yang, T. Igarashi, J. Mitani, and J. Lee, "Retrieval and visualization of human motion data via stick figures," in *Computer Graphics Forum*, 2012, vol. 31, pp. 2057–2065.

[20] H.-J. Lee, H. J. Shin, and J.-J. Choi, "Single image summarization of 3D animation using depth images," *Comput. Animat. Virtual Worlds*, vol. 23, no. 3–4, pp. 417– 424, 2012.

[21] H. Yang and K. Min, "Importance-based approach for rough drawings," *Vis. Comput.*, vol. 35, no. 4, pp. 609–622, 2019.

[22] "GitHub - CMU-Perceptual-Computing-Lab/openpose: OpenPose: Real-time multi-person keypoint detection library for body, face, hands, and foot estimation." [Online]. Available: https://github.com/CMU-Perceptual-Computing- Lab/openpose. [Accessed: 13-Jan-2020].

[23] E. V. Shikin and A. I. Plis, *Handbook on Splines for the User*. CRC Press, 1995.

[24] N. Partarakis, M. Antona, E. Zidianakis, P. Koutlemanis, and C.Stephanidis, "Traditional Paintind Revided: The Ambient Intelligence Approch to Creativity"

[25] "GitHub - DevZest/WpfDocking: A docking library to integrate undo/redo-able tabbed docking, floating and auto hide window management into your application in minutes." [Online]. Available: https://github.com/DevZest/WpfDocking. [Accessed: 13-Jan- 2020].

[26] "The Mingei project." [Online]. Available: http://www.mingei-project.eu/. [Accessed: 20-Jan-2020]

An Approach for the Visualization of Crafts and Machine Usage in Virtual Environments

Evropi Stefanidi, Nikolaos Partarakis, Xenophon Zabulis
Institute of Computer Science, Foundation for Research and Technology – Hellas (FORTH)
Heraklion, Greece
email: {evropi, partarak, zabulis}@ics.forth.gr

George Papagiannakis
Institute of Computer Science, Foundation for Research and Technology – Hellas (FORTH) &
Department of Computer Science, University of Crete
Heraklion, Greece
email: papagian@ics.forth.gr

Abstract—**Despite the cultural, societal, economic and traditional significance and value of Heritage Crafts and Intangible Cultural Heritage, efforts towards their digital representation and presentation, and subsequently their preservation, are scattered. To that end, this paper proposes an approach for their visualization in Virtual Environments, within which the practitioner is represented by a Virtual Human, their actions through animations resulting from Motion Capture recordings, and objects through their 3D reconstructions. Our novel approach is based on a conceptual, twofold decomposition of craft processes into actions, and of the machines used into components. Thus, in the context of this paper, we have developed a pipeline that delivers a Virtual Environment, through which a wide range of users, from museum curators and exhibitors, to everyday users interested by a craft, can experience craft usage scenarios. Via our visualization pipeline, we claim that we deliver an efficient way of visualizing craft processes within Virtual Environments, thus increasing the usability and educational value of craft representation, and opening the way to a variety of new applications for craft presentation, education and thematic tourism. In the scope of this paper, we focus on the Heritage Craft of loom weaving; however, our approach is generic, for representing any craft, after its decomposition according to our technique.**

Keywords-Machine Usage Visualization; Heritage Crafts; Cultural Heritage; Motion Capture; Virtual Humans.

I. INTRODUCTION

Heritage Crafts (HCs) involve tangible craft artifacts, materials and tools, and encompass traditional craftsmanship as a form of Intangible Cultural Heritage (ICH). Intangible HC dimensions include dexterity, know-how, and skilled use of tools, as well as identity and traditions of the communities in which craftsmanship is, or was, practiced [1].

Regarding their digitization, the advances in the 3D digitization of the shape and appearance of physical objects (3D reconstruction) have enabled the digital representation of tangible CH elements. The selection of a digitization modality and approach is central for accurate digitization, and is facilitated by guidelines focused on the Cultural Heritage domain [2]. In order to digitize not only the tangible elements of craft, but also the actions of the practitioner, the representation of the craft needs to include intangible dimensions.

As a step towards digitizing and representing HCs, we propose a novel approach for their visualization in Virtual Environments (VEs), within which the practitioner is represented by a Virtual Human (VH), and objects through their 3D reconstructions. Practitioner actions are reproduced by animating the VH based on Motion Capture (MoCap) recordings. The appropriate simulation of VHs is an important aspect, since crafts are practiced by humans and machines are designed for use by them. At the center of the proposed approach is a conceptual, twofold decomposition of craft processes into actions, and of machines into components, which include their physical interface. This is essential in the systematic transfer of craft practice from the physical to the virtual domain, while retaining realism. In more detail, this decomposition must be meaningful to allow the semantic representation of craft processes.

Using this approach, we claim that we could model a multitude of craft instances and machines, by decomposing crafts to simple motion driven operations, and machines to fundamental machine components. Thus, our contribution lies in a novel method for the presentation, representation and preservation of HCs, from which a multitude of user groups can benefit: (i) craftsmen whose work will be preserved and represented, (ii) local communities in which the craft is practiced, (iii) museum curators and exhibitors for the presentation of various traditional crafts and (iv) people without a specialization regarding Heritage Crafts, who are however interested in a HC and wish to learn more about it (e.g., tourists, teachers, school groups).

In the context of this paper, we focus on the craft of loom weaving, and describe the application of our pipeline and decomposition methodology on this craft. Nevertheless, our approach could be used for the representation of a variety of crafts, after their segmentation according to our technique. The rest of this paper is organized as follows. Section II presents a discussion of related work. Section III describes how we designed the transition of loom weaving from the physical to virtual world. Section IV addresses the details of the design and implementation of our approach, while Section V presents our conclusions and future work. The acknowledgement and references close the article.

II. RELATED WORK

To the best of our knowledge, there is no similar work regarding the digital representation of Heritage Crafts – or crafts in general - via the utilization of Virtual Humans, MoCap and 3D reconstruction; nor did we find other work that proposes the conceptual decomposition of crafts and machines used. Our approach is an extension of the work we conducted in [3], which presented a pipeline for the demonstration of tool usage for handicrafts and hand-held tools, to the world of HCs. In this paper, we take our research a step further, by focusing on HCs, and including all the steps that are needed, including interaction with craftsmen, in order to deliver a successful result for accurate representation of a HC. Therefore, in this section we present the related work we found regarding: (i) Virtual Humans and their use and importance in 3D applications, and (ii) tools for tool usage demonstration.

With respect to VHs, they constitute an important aspect of 3D applications, since humans can familiarize themselves with human-like characters. They mainly play the role of narrators [4] and virtual audiences [5]. In the context of VEs, they have already been used for explaining physical and procedural human tasks [6], simulating dangerous situations [7], group and crowd behavior [8], and assisting users during navigation, by pointing relevant locations and positions and providing users with additional information [9]. They can also play the role of a tutor, acting as an embodied teacher, enabling an individualized instruction for a massive number of learners. In our approach, they are used to represent HC practitioners, by demonstrating craft processes.

Regarding tool usage demonstration, M.A.G.E.S ™ [10] is a platform facilitating just that, by introducing an SDK for VR surgical training. It also includes a plugin for manipulation of tools in VR environments, which allows developers to transform any 3D model of a tool (pliers, hammer, scalpel, drills, etc.) into a fully functional and interactive asset, ready to use in VR applications. After the tool generation, users can interact with it in the VE and use it to complete specific tasks following recorded directions. Another tool is ExProtoVAR [11], which allows non-technical users to generate interactive experiences in AR.

With respect to the related work, we propose a novel approach that utilizes the concepts of Virtual Humans and demonstration of tools in VEs, but in the context of presenting and representing Heritage Crafts, so as to aid in their representation and preservation. To that end, we utilize 3D reconstruction to digitize the machines and tools used for each craft, and MoCap recordings for the actions of the craftsmen. Moreover, we induce the motion of the tools and machines from the human motion, by applying mathematical formulas for the simulation of the tool motion, and for the correct attachment of the tools to the corresponding body parts which should use them. Our contribution also entails the segmentation of the craft process into its essential parts, and the decomposition of the machines used into basic parts which we call Fundamental Machine Components.

III. Designing the Transition of Loom Weaving from the Physical to the Virtual World

The proposed design process for the representation of machines entails the conceptual decomposition of craft processes into actions and machine components. To facilitate presentation, the use case of loom weaving is considered.

It is essential that craftspersons are centrally involved in the conceptual decomposition, to provide functional insight and emic understanding of the represented process. In this case study, we collaborated with the practitioner community of the Association of Friends of Haus der Seidenkultur (HdS), Krefeld, Germany [12] (Figure 1), within the context of the Mingei EU H2020 Innovation action [13]. HdS provided descriptions and testimonies and allowed us to record functional demonstrations (MoCap, Video) of the practitioners, so as to perform careful observation and analysis of the craft. At the same time, collaborative sessions enabled craft understanding and provided insight from the perspective of the practitioner, towards a meaningful decomposition. Context definitions for our use case were then created, which are provided below, and are visible in Figure 2.

Figure 1. Co-design session at HdS.

Figure 2. Loom components.

Yarn is a continuous length of interlocked fibers, produced by spinning fibers into long strands. *Warp and Weft* are the horizontal and vertical threads of a fabric. *Weaving* is the process of yarn transformation to fabric; vertical warp threads (warps) are held in tension on a loom, while weft is perpendicularly interlaced, fastened in-between elevated (upper) and lowered (lower) warps. A *loom* is a piece of machinery that facilitates weaving. The configuration of upper and lower warps (or the weave of the fabric), determines the structure of the woven fabric. *Shed* is the space due to the temporary separation of upper and lower warps. A *treadle* is a loom lever that mechanizes shed creation. A *shuttle* is a device used to interlace weft through upper and lower warps. Finally, a *beater* is a tool used to fasten the weft to the warp.

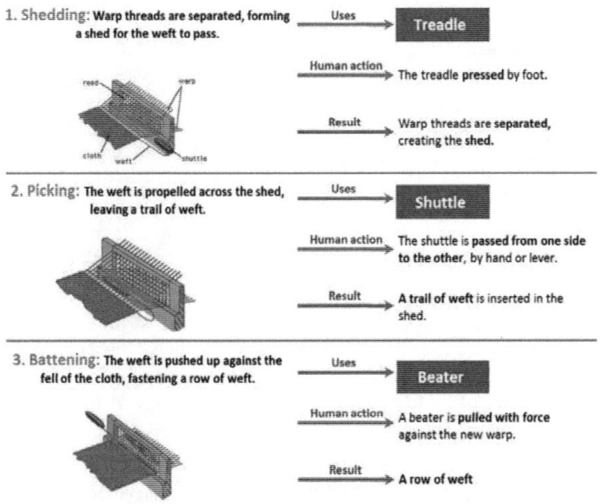

Figure 3. Storyboard of the three stages of weaving and the machine parts involved.

Central to the process is the *loom* machine, which retains warps at tension, to facilitate the thread-by-thread interlacement of weft through them. There are several types of looms. In the conventional loom, weft is introduced using a shuttle. Each thread of weft is fastened by a beat of the beater [14].

Regarding our approach, the weaving process was decomposed into 3 actions, repeated for each thread of weft [14]: (i) *Shedding*: warp threads are separated to form a shed, (ii) *Picking*: weft is passed across the shed using the shuttle, and (iii) *Beating*: weft is pushed against the fabric using the beater. The decomposed loom interface components are the shuttle, treadle and beater, depicted on the left side of Figure 2. Initially, textual descriptions were created collaboratively for each action, which also identified the machine interface components and human body parts used to operate them.

We thus developed an analytical way to visually and textually represent a process comprised of actions performed on objects and machine interface components. In this collaborative process, the need for a representation that is intuitive to the practitioner and analytical enough for a semantic representation of the process was identified. To that end, storyboards were selected as a methodological approach to address this need. The weaving process was encoded as a sequence of actions and reviewed by the community of practitioners, finally producing the storyboard visible in Figure 3.

This decomposition of the weaving process contains the interplay between human motion and components of the physical interface of the machine. To meaningfully represent the machine interface, we decompose it in elementary components, called Fundamental Machine Components (FMCs). These FMCs are rigged 3D models enhanced with functionality that simulates their motion, as described in Table I.

IV. Design and Implementation of our Approach

The proposed approach is generic towards the transfer of knowledge on machine usage to Virtual Environments. To that end, we segment the recordings of practitioners during machine usage into actions and categorize them by introducing them as items in a *Motion Vocabulary* (MV). At the same time, we decompose elements of the physical interface of Machines into FMCs. Thus, we call a *Motion Vocabulary Item* (MVI) an entity that represents an action, or part of an action, and contains a motion recording and possibly a reference to an FMC.

The steps of the pipeline for the proposed approach are the following:

- Involvement of craftspersons in the conceptual decomposition, to provide functional insight and emic understanding of the process to be represented.
- Decomposition of machine interface components.
- Acquisition of machine 3D model.
- MoCap of operators using the machine.
- Implementation of a VH.
- Segmentation of MoCap recording into a MV.
- Retargeting of recorded motion to the VH operating a 3D model of the machine. While human motion is recorded in MoCap files, we do not have MoCaps for the FMCs, because it is simpler and more cost-efficient to induce the machine motion by combining the mechanics of the FMC and the human motion from the MoCap. Moreover, in this way, we avoid the intervention and instrumentation of machines, which could alter their usage.
- Visualization of modeled process.

The following sections present the implementation of the proposed approach for the case study of loom weaving.

A. MoCap

The motion of practitioners was recorded in MoCap animation files, using a NANSENSE R2 [15] motion capture suit, during MoCap sessions.

B. Loom Model Acquisition

Often the machine is extremely difficult to reconstruct, due to its placement in the constrained environments of workshops and museums. As this was the case with the looms we had at hand, we used a basic loom model found at [16] to demonstrate our approach. Of course, any 3D model of the machine could be used.

C. Virtual Humans

The VHs that reproduce the recorded actions are 3D Avatars. In this case study, the VH was created in *Poser Pro 11*, and then imported to our development platform (*Unity3D*).

TABLE I. DECOMPOSITION OF LOOM WEAVING INTO STEPS

Steps	Action	Result	Design of the FMC[a]
Shedding	**Treadle** is pressed by **foot**.	**Warp threads** are separated, by the press of the **treadle**.	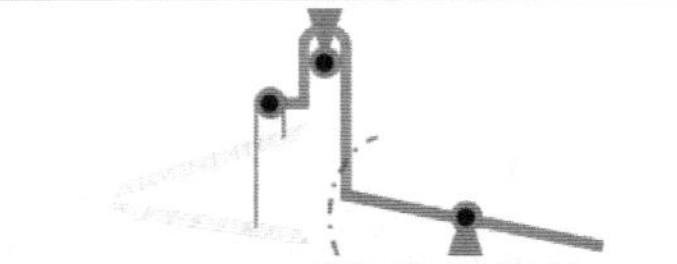
Picking	The shuttle is passed from one side to the other by **hand**.	A **row of weft** is created by a pass of the **shuttle**.	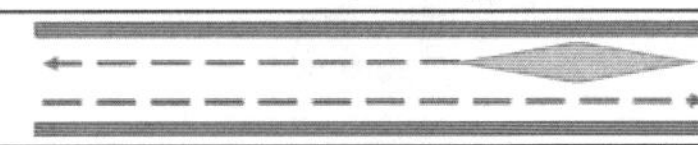
Battening	The **beater** is **dragged** with force on the new warp.	Weft row completed using the **beater**.	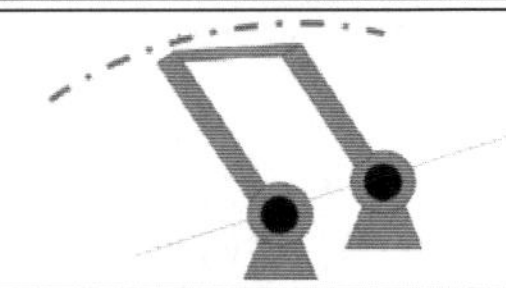

a. In the figures, dashed lines plot the feasible induced motion trajectories.

D. *Motion Vocabulary*

The next step entails the decomposition of the process of loom weaving into actions. Thus, we edited the MoCap animation files, to correlate the motion segments (MVIs) to the conceptually decomposed actions. These segments are considered building blocks of the weaving MV, which is the basis of sequences, or "sentences", encoding weaving processes.

E. *Loom Machine Abstraction*

We then proceeded with defining the elements of the physical interface of the loom as FMCs. Each one is comprised of (i) a 3D model of a machine part, and (ii) motion rules that represent the feasible, induced motion of the FMC during its operation.

F. *Association of Virtual Humans and FMCs*

Machine interface components, represented as FMCs, are associated with the VH body part(s) that are used for their operation (e.g., treadle with foot, shuttle with hand, beater with both hands). We first establish a pairing between the FMC and a point on the Avatar. Subsequently, the preferred grip posture is defined. For this purpose, we employ the following entities:

- Avatar A, with skeleton S, is comprised of joints and skin T. Skin T is a, possibly textured, deformable 3D surface, represented by a mesh of triangles. When A is animated, T deforms according to the motion of S.
- Two grip points, g_L, g_R on T encode the grip center for the left and right hand respectively. These points are selected with respect to the FMC, as objects may not always be held in the same way.
- Each hand has a reference frame based on orthogonal unit vectors. These are u_x^L, u_y^L, u_z^L, for the left and u_x^R, u_y^R, u_z^R for the right. The center of the frame is selected at an anatomically meaningful location.
- An FMC has a reference frame based on u_x^M, u_y^M, u_z^M, which are orthogonal unit vectors for the FMC. Each FMC is centered at its centroid.
- The FMC has a preferred usage position (e.g., grip, foot position). This position may not be unique.
- A posture p is comprised of (i) a configuration of the joints of A, (ii) a preferred location and (iii) orientation of A's body members, for FMC usage.
- An animation is a transition from a posture to another, represented by a sequence of states of the A's joints.

A *preemptive posture* is the preferred for A posture at the first moment of the FMC usage. A preemptive animation is an animation that brings A to the preemptive posture.

For our case study, we define the following concepts:

- Loom L is represented by a mesh of triangles, encoded by its vertices, l_v, and its triangles, l_t.
- *TRE, BEA, SHU* are FMCs for the treadle, beater and shuttle, respectively.
- Points b_L and b_R on the *BEA*, denote the grip locations of the left and right hands.
- Animations p_L and p_R, for preemptive usage postures for the *BEA*, for the left and right hand.
- Preemptive usage animations f_L and f_R for the placement of the left and right feet on *TRE*.
- Point d_a on *TRE* at the center of the area that the foot is pressing on the treadle. Preemptive usage postures s_L, and s_R encode shuttle grip by the left and right hand.
- Point u_s on *SHU* (shuttle centroid).
- MV for Loom Weaving MV_{LW} contains MVI_{TRE}, MVI_{BEA} and MVI_{SHU} which are the treadle, beater and shuttle animations (encoding human motion but not machine motion):
  - MVI_{TRE}: treadle pushed down and released.
  - MVI_{SHU}: shuttle pushed from left to the right and vice versa.
  - MVI_{BEA}: beater pulled towards the operator for a beat, then pushed away.

- Animation function *AN(A/FMC,* Posture) which animates either the *A* or FMC according to a MVI.

A scene is the VE where the *A*, FMCs and objects are instantiated, and the FMCs, *L*, and *A* are brought to the reference frame of the scene. This is achieved by appropriate *rotation R* (encoded as a 3x3 rotation matrix), a translation *t* (encoded as a 3x1 matrix) and a scaling *s* transformation for each component, once and prior to their import in the VE. Each 3D point, let *q*, of the object's 3D model undergoes transformation $R * sq + t$, where * denotes matrix multiplication. The transformations are individual for each of the FMCs, loom and *A*, and are denoted as R_T, s_T, t_T for the treadle, R_S, s_S, t_S for the shuttle etc.

G. *Induced Machine Motion*

Induced machine motion was simulated as follows:

1) Principle of induced motion.

Let avatar *A* at the preemptive usage posture of an FMC. We consider the execution of a *MVI* by *A*, during a time interval. The motion of the FMC due to the MVI is called *Induced Motion* of the FMC. We propose a synchronization method of the FMC's motion with that of the VH for each MVI, based on the feasible induced motion trajectory of the FMC.

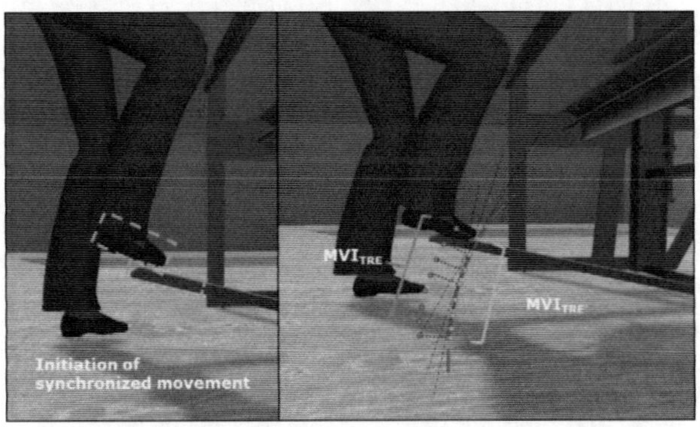

Figure 4. Visualization of the foot pressing the treadle.

2) Treadle Motion.

Treadle motion is performed by execution of MVI_{TRE} and denoted as $AN(A, MVI_{TRE})$. The treadle is moved when the bounding box of the *TRE* collides with the foot of the Avatar. The virtual motion is achieved through a function $TRE'=AN(TRE, MVI_{TRE}')$, where MVI_{TRE}' contains the projections of MVI_{TRE} to the motion trajectory of *TRE* (Figure 4).

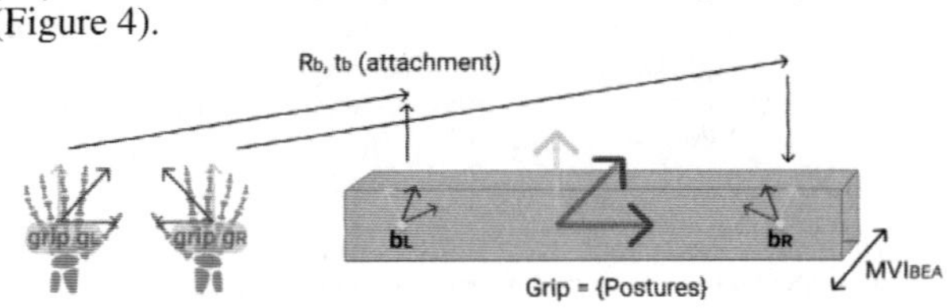

Figure 5. Attaching the hands on the beater.

3) Beater Motion.

The preferred posture of A's hands is reached by animating *A* using a preemptive animation, so that $A'=AN(A,p_L)$, $A'=AN(A,p_R)$. Hand motion is performed by MVI_{BEA}' through function $A'=AN(A, MVI_{BEA}')$ and loom motion through $L'=AN(L, MVI_{BEA}')$, where MVI_{BEA}' contains the projections of the grip points to the motion trajectory of *BEA* (Figure 5).

4) Shuttle Motion.

Shuttle motion MVI_{SHU} is simulated through function $A'=AN(A, MVI_{SHU})$, while the attachment of the shuttle to each of the hands of the Avatar is performed by $A'=AN(A', s_L)$ and $A'=AN(A', s_R)$ for the left and right hands respectively (shuttle is exchanged between the hands) (Figure 6). The motion of the shuttle is represented as $L'=AN(L, MVI_{SHU}')$, where MVI_{SHU}' is modeled as a constant linear motion, between the starting point of the *SHU* feasible induced motion trajectory and its ending point, and vice versa.

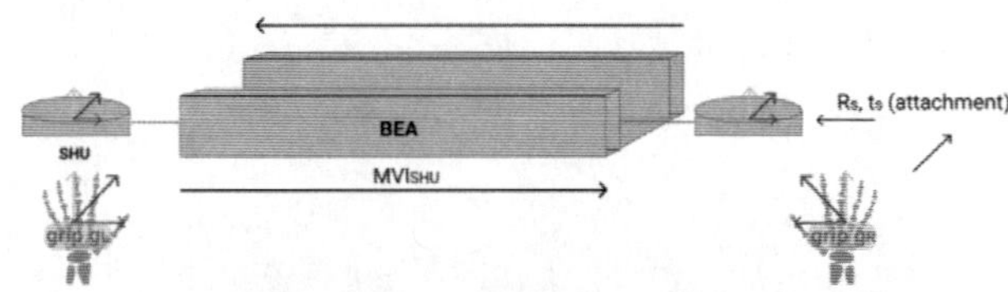

Figure 6. Attaching the hands on the shuttle.

Figure 7. Visualization of the result: the VH is operating the loom.

V. CONCLUSION

This work presented a novel approach for the representation of machine usage by Virtual Humans in Virtual Environments and described its implementation for the case of loom weaving. Resulting from our pipeline, the visualization of an Avatar using the loom are visible in Figures 7 and 8, with Figure 8 focusing on the treadle operation. The proposed approach allows for further configurations to facilitate the representation of other crafts including machine usage.

The application of our approach on the craft of loom weaving allowed us to have an initial validation of our pipeline, in the context of the described experiment; however, it is imperative, and part of our immediate future plans, to conduct an evaluation with craft experts, to have their verification. Subsequently, and after any necessary changes stemming from their feedback, we will evaluate our system with users from various target user groups, such as museum curators, exhibitors and non-craftspeople, such as tourists. Finally, we aim to further generalize our approach, by including new Fundamental Machine Components in our framework and studying new crafts and techniques.

The genericity of the approach stems from the reusability of the main components of the proposed pipeline. Motion Capture technologies can be used to record any human operation involving the usage of tools and/or machines. Furthermore, our approach of decomposing a machine in Fundamental Machine Components allows us to define different components used in different operations to achieve different results. The binding of such components with process-specific knowledge adds to the novelty and reusability of our approach.

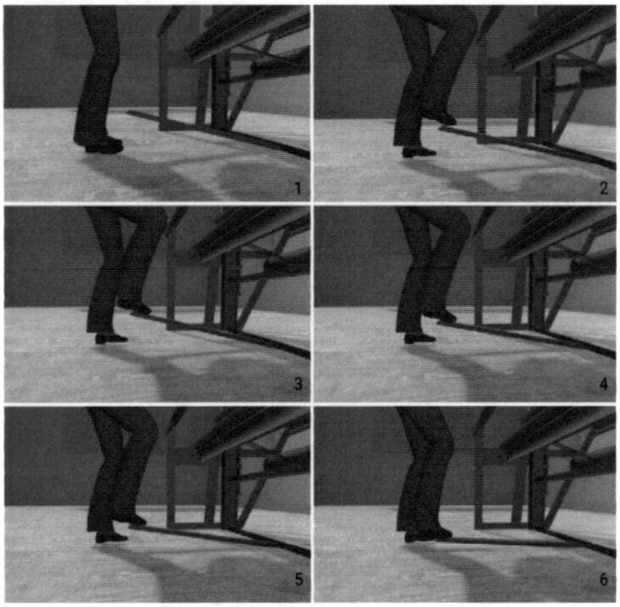

Figure 8. Detail of the foot of the VH operating the treadle while loom weaving.

As a second use case where the proposed approach is being applied, efforts are already being put towards representing the hand-based craft of mastic cultivation, practiced in the island of Chios, Greece, utilizing the pipeline described in this paper. Namely, after having performed Motion Capture of the mastic cultivators' movements, we are now in the process of segmenting the actions in their elementary parts, as well as digitizing the tools used with their corresponding motions. The overarching goal is the capability to represent and present a plethora of crafts, thus contributing to Heritage Craft presentation, representation and valorization. At the same time, our proposed pipeline presents opportunities for use cases that go beyond the field of Cultural Heritage, as it could be used to model various handicraft actions, e.g., using garden tools or assembling furniture, by decomposing them into their fundamental actions and components, according to our methodology.

ACKNOWLEDGMENT

This work has been supported by the EU Horizon 2020 Innovation Action under grant agreement No. 822336 (Mingei); the authors are grateful to project partner ARMINES for the acquisition of MoCap data and the practitioner community of the Association of Friends of Haus der Seidenkultur (HdS), Krefeld, Germany for their collaboration and support on understanding the craft of loom weaving.

REFERENCES

[1] UNESCO, "Text of the Convention for the Safeguarding of the Intangible Cultural Heritage," *UNESCO Paris, 17 October 2003*, 2003.

[2] "3D-ICONS, 'Guidelines & Case Studies,'". *3D-ICONS is a project funded under the European Commission's ICT Policy Support Programme, project no. 297194. 2014.*

[3] E. Stefanidi *et al.*, "TooltY: An approach for the combination of motion capture and 3D reconstruction to present tool usage in 3D environments," in *Intelligent Scene Modelling and Human Computer Interaction*, N. M. Thalmann, J. Zhang, and J. Zheng, Eds. Springer, in press.

[4] P. Zikas *et al.*, "Mixed reality serious games and gamification for smart education," in *European Conference on Games Based Learning*, 2016, p. 805.

[5] M. Chollet, N. Chandrashekhar, A. Shapiro, L.-P. Morency, and S. Scherer, "Manipulating the perception of virtual audiences using crowdsourced behaviors," in *International Conference on Intelligent Virtual Agents*, 2016, pp. 164–174.

[6] J. Rickel and W. L. Johnson, "Animated agents for procedural training in virtual reality: Perception, cognition, and motor control," *Applied artificial intelligence*, vol. 13, no. 4–5, pp. 343–382, 1999.

[7] D. Traum and J. Rickel, "Embodied agents for multi-party dialogue in immersive virtual worlds," in *Proceedings of the first international joint conference on Autonomous agents and multiagent systems: part 2*, 2002, pp. 766–773.

[8] Z. Paul, P. Margarita, M. Vasilis, and P. George, "Life-sized Group and Crowd simulation in Mobile AR," in *Proceedings of the 29th International Conference on Computer Animation and Social Agents*, 2016, pp. 79–82.

[9] L. Chittaro, R. Ranon, and L. Ieronutti, "Guiding visitors of Web3D worlds through automatically generated tours," in *Proceedings of the eighth international conference on 3D Web technology*, 2003, pp. 27–38.

[10] G. Papagiannakis, N. Lydatakis, S. Kateros, S. Georgiou, and P. Zikas, "Transforming medical education and training with VR using MAGES," in *SIGGRAPH Asia 2018 Posters*, 2018, p. 83.

[11] N. Pfeiffer-Leßmann and T. Pfeiffer, "ExProtoVAR: A Lightweight Tool for Experience-Focused Prototyping of Augmented Reality Applications Using Virtual Reality," in *International Conference on Human-Computer Interaction*, 2018, pp. 311–318.

[12] "Welcome to the 'Haus der Seidenkultur', Krefeld." [Online]. Available: https://seidenkultur.de/. [Retrieved: Jan, 2020].

[13] "The Mingei project." [Online]. Available: http://www.mingei-project.eu/. [Retrieved: Jan, 2020].

[14] A. Albers and N. F. Weber, *On Weaving: New Expanded Edition*. Princeton University Press, 2017.

[15] "Nansense - Professional Inertial Motion Capture Systems." [Online]. Available: https://www.nansense.com/. [Retrieved: Jan, 2020].

[16] B. L, "Counterbalance Loom." [Online]. Available: https://3dwarehouse.sketchup.com/model/a4d5115a90e3f5534cf6cee9a1fdf035/Counterbalance-Loom. [Retrieved: Jan, 2020].

Comparisons among Different Types of Hearing Aids

A Pilot Study on Ergonomic Design of Hearing Aids

Fang Fu
School of Design
Hong Kong Polytechnic University
Hong Kong SAR
Email: fang.fu@connect.polyu.hk

Yan Luximon
School of Design
Hong Kong Polytechnic University
Hong Kong SAR
Email: yan.luximon@polyu.edu.hk

***Abstract*—Hearing aids are widely used by people with hearing loss. In the current market, various hearing aids can be selected based on the users' demands. Previous research mostly concentrated on ear anthropometry and auditory function to explore fit and comfort of hearing aids. Even though Computer-Aided Design (CAD) simulation and virtual reality methods were used to examine the fit of earphones and specific hearing aids, how to achieve a proper fit for different types of hearing aids was not sufficiently studied. This study compares sizes and shapes among existing commercial hearing aids, and further proposes guidance in ear anthropometry for ergonomic design of hearing aids. Product parameters, including width, height, length, and weight, were measured for Behind-The-Ear (BTE) aids, In-The-Ear (ITE) aids, and In-The-Canal (ITC) aids individually. Selected hearing aids were fitted on the external ear of participants while recording their fit and comfort preferences. The findings of the study revealed the differences among BTE, ITE and ITC aids, and highlighted the anthropometric data for hearing aid design. Based on the findings of the study, potential research gaps were identified for future research.**

Keywords - hearing aids; product size and shape; fit and comfort.

I. INTRODUCTION

An ergonomic design is increasingly important with the cumulative demands of customers. Human-centered designs are especially applied in everyday used products, such as devices providing protections or achieving other functionalities. Hearing aid is one of these products in the health care industry. Hearing aids amplify the collected sound for people with hearing loss. These devices normally require long-time wearing by the users. Hence, resolving any fit issues between products and users is crucial when designing hearing aids.

Nowadays, different types of hearing aids, such as Behind-The-Ear (BTE) aids, In-The-Ear (ITE) aids, In-The-Canal (ITC) aids, and Completely-In-The-Canal (CIC) aids, are available to meet the different demands of customers. BTE aid consists of a plastic case at the backside of the ear, a clear tubing, and an earplug or an earmold. The aids are usually used for young children considering that the tubing and earplug parts can be adjusted along with the children physical growth [1]. ITE aid contains a small shell which fills outside the ear canal, which is considered as a relatively easy-to-handle device [1]. ITC aid is in a small case with a partial fit in the ear canal. The comparatively invisible sizes of ITC aids provide cosmetic appearance and efficient sound transfer for the users, but the devices are difficult to handle [1]. Figure 1 presents product shapes of three different hearing aids.

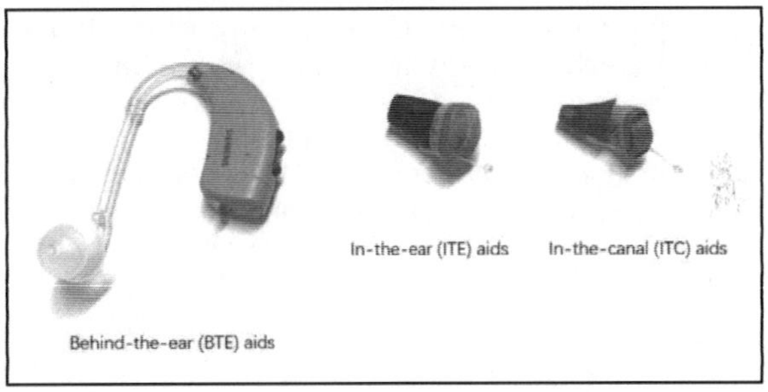

Figure 1. Different types of hearing aids

Fit evaluation has been studied for various products, such as shoes [2] and chairs [3]. For hearing aids, researchers have conducted various studies on the fit issues. Most of the previous research focused on ear anthropometry [4]-[6], auditory performance [7] [8], and cognition [9] for ear-related products, while physical fit of the product shape and size has not been systematically studied. Shapes of Bluetooth earphone were verified to influence users' comfort and fit perception [10]. However, the association between anthropometric data and design patterns has not been sufficiently evaluated. To address the design problem, there is a need to evaluate the fit for various hearing aids.

Evaluation methods, including CAD simulation and virtual reality, mock-up evaluation, and prototype evaluation, were the commonly used methods in design process [11]. CAD simulation models were applied to evaluate the product and related usability at the early designing stage. Ear-related products, such as earphone design [12] and ITC aids [13], were examined with CAD techniques. However, considering the different shapes and functionalities of ear-related products, methods to evaluate the fit of hearing aids have not been generalized comprehensively. Therefore, differences among different hearing aids should be studied for further research on ergonomic design of hearing aids.

This paper aimed at comparing sizes and shapes among different hearing aids. As a work-in-progress study, the findings can be useful to study fit evaluation of hearing aids in future research, and it also have referential significance for other ear-related product designs. The rest of the paper is structured as follows. In Section 2, three widely used types of hearing aids were selected and different parameters, such as length, width, height and weight, were compared along with the user experience of fit and comfort. In Section 3, we present the differences of sizes and shapes among these products, and the specific ear regions and parameters are discussed for designing different hearing aids. In the last section, we conclude the differences among selected hearing aids, identified anthropometric data with application in hearing aid design, and propose future work regarding the research topic.

II. Methods

In this paper, BTE Fun P, ITE Vibe Mini 8, and ITC Vibe Nano 8 aids (Siemens®) were measured and compared. Product parameters, including length, width, height, and weight, were measured to evaluate the product. These parameters can be compared with anthropometric data to seek proper fit. Participants were asked to wear each hearing aid for 5 minutes as shown in Figure 2. Fit and comfort perception of the participant was recorded. Contact area with the human ear was marked for further discussion on association between anthropometric data and product design.

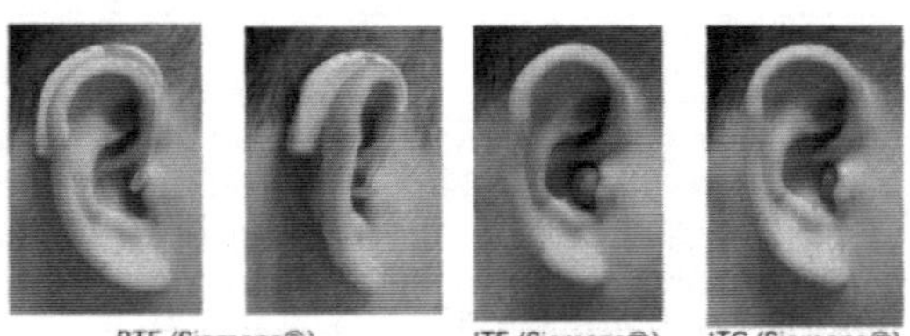

Figure 2. Fitting hearing aids on human ear

III. Results and Discussion

Despite the functionalities of different hearing aids, this study focused on the sizes and shapes of hearing aids from the fit and comfort perspective. The section showed the differences among BTE, ITE, and ITC aids based on the product shapes and sizes. While fitting different hearing aids with the human ear, reference ear regions were highlight for hearing aid design, and anthropometric dimensions were selected accordingly.

A. Differences among commericial hearing aids

Hearing aids normally require long-time usage, so the components with directly contacting external ear are vital for hearing-aid comfort and fit. Other product parameters, including size and weight, were investigated in the study. Comparison of sizes, weights, and components directly contacting the external ear are demonstrated in Table 1.

TABLE I. Hearing Aids

Type	***Hearing aids***	***Components contacting with human ear***	***Size***	***Weight***
BTE		Round earplug in soft plastic material; Tubing contacting the ear root.	Earplugs were designed with selectable sizes.	7.16g
ITE	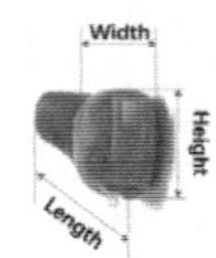	Special shape in direct contact with ear concha.	Width:8.71mm Height:12.97mm Length:19.88mm	1.42g
ITC	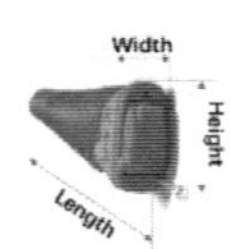	Special shape in direct contact with ear canal.	Width:5.72mmg Height:12.52mm Length:17.28mm	0.97g

Among the investigated hearing aids, BTE aids have the largest weight and size, followed by ITE and ITC aids sequentially. In the meanwhile, participants gave best scores on fit and comfort perception for BTE, followed by ITE and ITC aids in decreasing order. The parameters were difficult to compare directly, considering different aids need to fit with distinct ear region. Hence, there is a need to associate the product dimensions with anthropometric data to examine the comfort and fit. As for the product weight, load analysis can be conducted in specific ear region for the specific type of hearing aids.

B. Anthropometry for hearing aid design

Considering the fit issues, BTE, ITE, and ITC aids should be designed to match with specific ear regions individually, as presented in Figure 3. For BTE aids, tube and earplug were adjustable part, so the most important part in product design was the main body rested behind the ear. BTE should be designed considering ear root area and the back part of the ear, same as the support location of the aid. Ear root was also mentioned for earphone design in previous study [12]. ITE aids tightly fit with the ear concha, so the aid shape should be designed based on the concha shape in the contacted area. ITC aids fit with the entrance area of ear canal including part of the first bend of the canal, which was consistent with previous study [13]. Proper product size and shape can improve the comfort and fit perception during the usage of the hearing aids.

Thus, future research should focus on these areas to define the shape and size when designing different hearing aids.

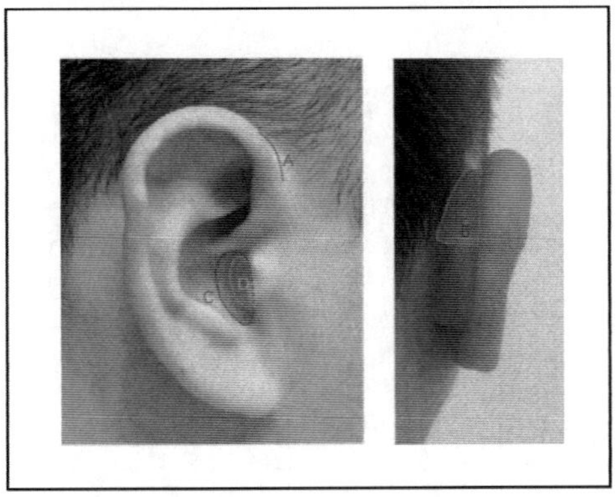

Figure 3. Ear reference area for designing hearing aids: Ear root (A) and back part of the ear (B) asscoiated with BTE aids; Ear concha (C) associated with ITE aids; Ear canal (D) associated with ITC aids.

To seek proper fit, anthropometric data were essential for designing distinct types of hearing aids. Related anthropometric dimensions can be used to define the product sizes. As the reference ear areas mentioned above, anthropometric dimensions were selected for hearing aid design. According to definitions of ear dimensions in the literature [14], different dimensions were chosen for specific hearing aids. Specifically, ear protrusion and pinna flare angle can be used for designing BTE aids; cavum concha length, center of concha to incisura intertragica length, and ear canal entrance circumference can be valuable for designing ITE aids; and ear canal entrance height, ear canal entrance width, ear canal entrance to 1st bend length, and ear canal 1st bend circumference can be applied in ITC aid design. To design the hearing aids products for different markets, these anthropometric dimensions can be applied to examine the product sizes.

IV. Conclusion and Future Work

This pilot study tried to compare the shapes and sizes of different hearing aids, and examined the application of ear anthropometry in hearing aid design from comfort and fit perspective. Generally, BTE aids have the largest size and weight but the highest fit and comfort perception, while ITC have the smallest size and weight but has the lowest fit and comfort perception. Different contact areas on the external ear were recorded with diverse types of hearing aids. Accordingly, anthropometric dimensions were selected for different hearing aids based on the literature. Based on the findings in the study, potential research gaps were identified for future research. With the preliminary findings in the study, next step is to apply CAD simulation to examine the fit of different hearing aids, and use prototypes to explore the users' experience. Future research can be conducted with larger sample size and more hearing aids in different markets to improve the fit of ear-related products with the use of CAD simulation technique.

Acknowledgment

The study was supported by Hong Kong RGC/GRF project B-Q57F.

References

[1] U.S. Food & Drug Administration. Hearing Aids. [Online]. Available from: https://www.fda.gov/medical-devices/consumer-products/hearing-aids. [retrieved: 28.11.2019].

[2] E. Y. L. Au and R. S. Goonetilleke, "A Qualitative Study on the Comfort and Fit of Ladies' Dress Shoes," Applied Ergonomics, vol. 38, pp. 687-696, 2007.

[3] M. Helander and L. Zhang, "Field Studies of Comfort and Discomfort in Sitting", Ergonomics, vol. 40, pp. 895-915, 2010.

[4] H. Jung and H. Jung, "Surveying the Dimensions and Characteristics of Korean Ears for the Ergonomic Design of Ear-Related Products," International Journal of Industrial Ergonomics, vol. 31, pp. 361-373, 2003.

[5] W. Chiou, D. Huang, and B. Chen, "Anthropometric Measurements of the External Auditory Canal for Hearing Protection Earplug," Advances in Safety Management and Human Factors, Springer, pp. 163-171, 2016.

[6] M. A. Mououdi, J. Akbari, and M. M. Khoshoei, "Measuring the External Ear for Hearing Protection Device Design," Ergonomics in Design, vol. 26, pp. 4-8, 2018.

[7] V. Rallapalli, M. Anderson, J. Kates, L. Sirow, K. Arehart, and P. Souza, "Quantifying the Range of Signal Modification in Clinically Fit Hearing Aids," Ear and Hearing, vol. 1, pp. 1-9, 2019.

[8] J. L. Vroegop, A. Geodegebure, and M. P. Schroeff, "How to Optimally Fit a Hearing Aid for Bimodal Cochlear Implant Users: A Systematic Review," vol. 39, pp. 1039-1045, 2018.

[9] E. Convery, G. Keidser, L. Hickson, and C. Meyer. "Factors Associated with Successful Setup of a Self-Fitting Hearing Aid and the Need for Personalized Support," Ear and Hearing, vol. 40, pp. 794-804, 2019.

[10] H. P. Chiu, H. Y. Chiang, C. H. Liu, M. H. Wang, and W. K. Chiou, "Surveying the Comfort Perception of the Ergonomic Design of Bluetooth Earphones," Work, vol. 49, pp. 235-243, 2014.

[11] S. Porter and J. M. Porter, "Product Evaluation Methods and Their Importance in Designing Interactive Artifacts," Human Factors in Product Design: Current Practice and Future Trends, Taylor & Francis, pp. 26-36, 1999.

[12] W. Lee, H. Jung, I. Bok, C. Kim, O. Kwon, T. Choi, and H. You, "Measurement and Application of 3D Ear Images for earphone design", Proceedings of the Human Factors and Ergonomics Society Annual Meeting, SAGE, vol. 60, pp. 1053-1057, 2016.

[13] S. S. Jarng and G. Ting. "CAD/CAM Method Application for Ear Shell Auto-Manufacturing," ICMIT 2009: Mechatronics and Information Technology, International Society for Optics and Photonics, vol. 7500, pp. 750008, 2010.

[14] W. Lee, X. Yang, H. Jung, I. Bok, C. Kim, O. Kwon, and H. You, "Anthropometric Analysis of 3D Ear Scans of Koreans and Caucasians for Ear Product Design," Ergonomics, vol. 61, pp. 1480-1495, 2018.

Detection of Strong and Weak Moments in Cinematic Virtual Reality Narration with the Use of 3D Eye Tracking

Paweł Kobyliński
Laboratory of Interactive Technologies
National Information Processing Institute
Warsaw, Poland
e-mail: pawel.kobylinski@opi.org.pl

Grzegorz Pochwatko
Virtual Reality and Psychophysiology Lab
Institute of Psychology, Polish Academy of Sciences
Warsaw, Poland
e-mail: grzegorz.pochwatko@psych.pan.pl

***Abstract*—Cinematic Virtual Reality (CVR) is a medium growing in popularity among both filmmakers and researchers. The medium brings challenges for movie and video makers, who need to narrate in a different way than in traditional movies and videos to keep viewers' attention in the right place of the 360-degree scene. In order to ensure an adequate pace of development, tools are needed to conduct systematic, reliable and objective research on narration in CVR. In the short paper, the authors for the first time fully report results of the initial empirical test of their recently developed Scaled Aggregated Visual Attention Convergence Index (*sVRCa*). The index utilizes 3D Eye Tracking (3D ET) data recorded during a CVR experience and allows measuring and describing the effectiveness of any system of attentional cues employed by a CVR creator. The results of the initial test are promising. The method seems to substantially augment the process of detection of strong and weak moments in CVR narration.**

Keywords–cinematic virtual reality; omnidirectional video; 3D eye tracking; visual attention; narration.

I. INTRODUCTION

Cinematic Virtual Reality (CVR) is a medium growing in popularity among both filmmakers and researchers. The recent rapid growth has been made possible by synergic progress in technology related to omnidirectional video cameras, VR headsets, computer hardware, software, and internet bandwidth. At this stage, some creators try to transfer old and tested narrative methods from traditional movies, while others have realized that they need to develop a new film language. Both educational and artistic CVR creators, who have sought advice regarding problems with guiding visual attention, have approached the authors of this short paper. Hence, these encounters constituted the real-life inspiration for this reported work in progress.

Since the viewpoint has been moved to the center of the movie set, participants, not directors, are in charge of the visual focus. This means the viewers are very probable to miss an important element of a story. Therefore, one has to rely more on light, spatial sound and arrangement of the scenery while building good narration. Setting actors around the camera and acting itself must be also different and thought over well.

In order to ensure an adequate pace of development, tools are needed to conduct systematic, reliable and objective research on narration in CVR. Visual attention is the crucial factor to measure if one wants to assure audience retention and make effectively entertaining, persuasive, or educational VR movies [1][2]. In the current short paper, the authors for the first time fully report results of the initial empirical test of their recently developed Scaled Aggregated Visual Attention Convergence Index (*sVRCa*). The quantitative index utilizes 3D Eye Tracking (3D ET) data recorded during a CVR experience. Theoretical basis of the *sVRCa*, among other variants of the Visual Attention Convergence Index (*VRC*), has been described in detail in [3] and [4].

The rest of the paper is structured as follows. Section II positions this work in relation to the other similar works in the literature. Section III presents the scaled aggregated visual attention convergence index. Section IV presents and discusses the empirical test. The work is concluded in Section V.

II. RELATION TO OTHER WORK

The method tested by the authors is by no means the first attempt to tackle the problem of measurement and improvement of CVR quality by addressing the issue of visual attention. Substantial work has been done to develop [5]-[7] and benchmark [8][9] computational models of visual attention prediction in order to advance optimization of such technical aspects as video compression [10], immersive media distribution formats [11], cashing for streaming [12], and artifact detection [6]. Attempts have also been made to analyze thoroughly the real viewing behavior in CVR [7][8][10][12]-[15].

On the other hand, some niche research is focused explicitly on the problem of storytelling in CVR. Ways of directing attention in CVR are proposed in [16]-[18]. The quality of narration is evaluated by viewers in [19]. Subjective questionnaires and recorded head orientation were used to assess the quality of video cuts and storytelling in [15]. Audience retention was analyzed in comparison with an "average YouTube video" in [20].

In contrast to the mentioned attempts, the authors report here a concise, timelined, near-continuous value, based solely on the measured positions of gaze fixations and computed without the need for prior computation of saliency maps or saliency optimization (neither theoretically- nor empirically-driven) [8][10][14]. The authors do not propose another measurement of video quality intended to improve its computational properties, neither by means of predicting nor mathematical optimization of visual attention. Moreover, the proposed method is designed to act differently than methods based on entropy measures [14]. Low values of the utilized *sVRCa* index do not necessarily relate to visual attention scattered randomly around the 360-degree scene (an unrealistic scenario in the case of narrated videos). Instead, the method may detect moments in which the values of index remain low, despite the order present in the visual attention pattern when different viewers look at distinct objects located at the opposite sites of the 360-degree video (a realistic scenario).

To the authors' best knowledge, the tested measure is the first reported one that is both objective in a quantitative, data-driven manner and, at the same time, indented to relate simply to a narration line chosen subjectively by a CVR video maker.

III. Scaled Aggregated Visual Attention Convergence Index

Values of the *sVRCa* index tell us if several people looked at the same or rather different virtual areas of the 360-degree scene during a chosen, short time interval. The index is based on Euclidean distances in 3D space and aggregates information about gaze fixations from a group of CVR experience participants.

The values are scaled to the range between 0 and 1, which is convenient for between-experiment comparisons. The authors have decided to fine-tune the simplified scaling proposed in [9] in order to make it more realistically constrained. The improved formula takes the assumption that the index takes approximately zero value when there are only two points of viewers' focus located at a maximum possible distance from each other, at the opposite sides of the virtual scene:

$$sVRCa \approx 1 - \frac{\sqrt{2}}{n}\frac{\sqrt{\sum_{i,j=1}^{n} \boldsymbol{D}_{ij}^{\;2}}}{2r} \in [0,1] \qquad (1)$$

D is the $n \times n$ distance matrix calculated from 3D positions of n detected gaze fixations (corrected for the headset positions in virtual space). In the case of CVR, the 360-degree video is displayed on the inner surface of a virtual sphere. r denotes the radius of the sphere (see [3] for details). In the future, it might be reasonable to find the exact scaling formula for sphere-constrained CVR experiences by means of mathematical optimization.

The full procedure requires computation of the index values for subsequent short time intervals and ordering the values into time series covering the whole time span of a 360-degree video. The time intervals should be long enough to catch enough fixations to enable calculation of the *sVRCa* values and short enough to approximate the precision of continuous measurement. Half-second intervals met the assumptions in the reported test.

The interpretation of the *sVRCa* values is relative to the intentions of a CVR maker. If the CVR designer had indented to focus people on a specific area or object at a given moment and the *sVRCa* peaked at a high level at that moment, it means success (provided the viewers did not focus on something else, which should be verified with the use of the same 3D ET data). If the creator had wanted the viewers to explore the scene at a given moment, high levels of the visual attention convergence at that moment mean failure and low levels mean success.

IV. Empirical Test

A. Materials

1) 360-degree immersive video

An educational video, aimed at a younger audience, contained a number of short scenes explaining professional work on a traditional 2D film set. The background commentary by a lector described the basic principles of setting the camera, lighting, and working with sound. Other narrative means included mainly changes of scenes, changes of lighting, and positioning of actors and props around the 360-degree scene. The film lasted about 17 minutes.

The tested CVR video and data collection were funded by the National Center for Film Culture (Lodz, Poland). The authors of the current paper had been asked to assess the efficiency of narration in this specific educational video, which gave them the first opportunity to test their recently developed methodology.

2) Software

To operate the experiment (displaying the CVR video, recording 3D ET and headset position data), the VIZARD 6 ENTERPRISE was used. All 3D ET data handling steps (i.e., fixation detection [21][22], data processing and analysis) were executed with the use of R [23] scripts coded from scratch. Gazes of angular speed below 30 degrees per second and lasting longer than 150 milliseconds were classified as fixations.

3) Equipment

HMD HTC VIVE has been equipped with a dedicated SMI eye tracker. 3D ET data were recorded synchronously with information about the location of the headset in 3D virtual space. The sampling frequency has been synchronized with the headset screen refresh rate of 90 Hz.

B. Participants

92 school children, 36 girls (Mage=14.1) and 56 boys, (Mage=14.2) participated in the study with the consent of a parent or a guardian. An ethical committee approved the procedure.

C. Context

The participants watched the 360-degree video separately, one by one, in controlled laboratory conditions. Only two people were present in the laboratory room: a participant and a trained experimenter. No external sounds or tactile stimuli distracted the viewing experience.

D. Results

Figure 1 illustrates the changes in the smoothed (Simple Moving Average over a 5 s window) and non-filtered *sVRCa* values (computed for half-second intervals) over the time span of the entire CVR educational video. Such visualization enables looking at the dynamics of the visual attention convergence results from the bird's eye view and grasping the general attentional pattern shaped by the properties of the narration employed in the immersive video.

We can observe that the visual attention convergence started from very low level; the viewers were looking around and not focused at any specific area of the 360-degree scene.

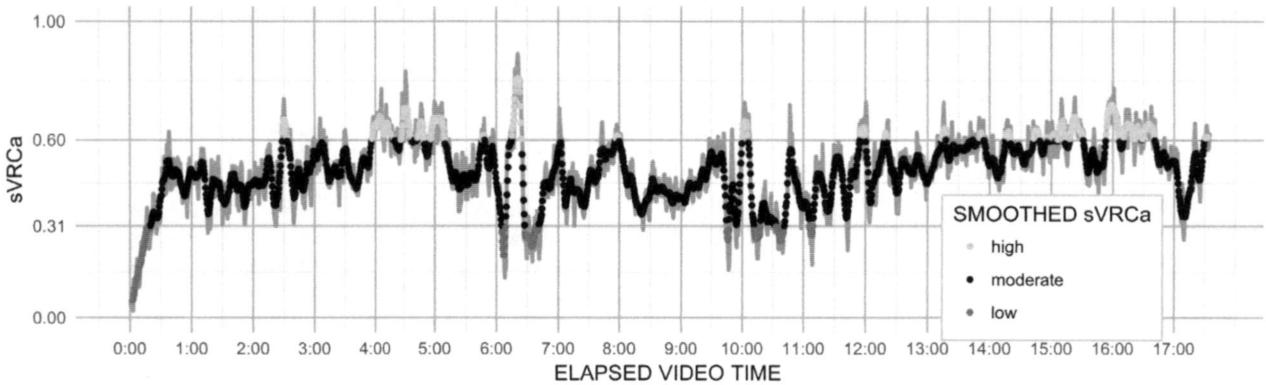

Figure 1. Changes in the values of both the non-filtered (grey) and smoothed (green, black, red) Scaled Aggregated Visual Attention Convergence Index (*sVRCa*) over the time span of the entire CVR educational video.

Then, the visual attention steadily converged towards moderate levels. Further in the video, there were relatively short fragments that provoked high and low levels of the visual attention convergence, between longer fragments characterized by moderate levels.

Table I presents chosen few examples of automatically detected high and low peaks in *sVRCa* time series within the detected fragments of the immersive CVR educational video. High peaks represent high levels of the visual attention convergence between the CVR participants at a given moment of the video. Low peaks represent low levels of the visual attention convergence. Colors denote values chosen for example *ex post* qualitative interpretation (Figures 2-4).

The procedure detected 24 high peaks within 24 short high-value fragments, as well as 7 low peaks within 7 short low-value fragments. The mean length of the automatically detected high-value video fragments was 7 seconds, exactly the same as in the case of the fragments with low *sVRCa*.

TABLE I. CHOSEN EXAMPLES OF DETECTED VIDEO FRAGMENTS AND PEAKS IN THE SCALED AGGREGATED VISUAL ATTENTION CONVERGENCE INDEX (*SVRCA*) TIME SERIES

Video fragment begins at:	Video fragment ends at:	Median *sVRCa*	Peak *sVRCa*	Peak type	Peak at:
06:16	06:25	0.75	0.89	**max**	**06:21**
15:18	15:31	0.64	0.75	**max**	**15:23**
04:43	04:50	0.63	0.72	**max**	**04:47**
10:34	10:41	0.27	0.22	**min**	**10:40**
06:28	06:41	0.28	0.19	**min**	**06:35**
06:06	06:09	0.22	0.14	**min**	**06:09**

Figure 2. The 4:47 frame corresponds to a high peak in the *sVRCa* (0.72). Yellow dots represent gaze fixations.

The cut-off thresholds for the smoothed *sVRCa* time series were calculated by dividing the empirical range of the original (non-smoothed) *sVRCa* values (0.02 to 0.89) into three even sub-ranges. 0.60 was the resulting value of the threshold above which the smoothed *sVRCa* values were classified as high (green in Figure 1), 0.31 was the value of the threshold below which the smoothed sVRCa values were regarded as low (red in Figure 1). The resulting detection of short video fragments allowed fast and simple determination of (quasi) local maxima and minima (in non-smoothed *sVRCa* time series) within the fragments.

E. Example Ex Post Interpretation of Detected Peaks

The *sVRCa* enabled us to determine candidates for strong and weak moments of the CVR video in the context of narration.

The 4:47 frame (green in Table 1) can be interpreted as a strong moment. A high value of the *sVRCa* (0.72) corresponds to participants' attention focused on actors in the depicted set and on an additional screen positioned above the set (Figure 2). All the distractors, members of the crew, camera, equipment, etc., were hidden in low light areas (we had actually two sets here: the set of the CVR, embracing the "set" of the depicted traditional 2D movie and all the surroundings; similarly actors of the CVR included "actors" and "crew" of the depicted 2D movie).

Another strong moment corresponds this time to a low *sVRCa* value (0.19). The 6:35 frame (blue in Table 1) represented a situation from the beginning of a scene. The stage was being prepared to show the role of lighting in the movies (Figure 3). There were many important elements around a participant. The CVR creator might have expected participants to look around the scene to figure out where the most important elements were.

Low *sVRCa* indicates weak moments as well. In the 10:40 frame (red in Table 1, index value: 0.22, Figure 4), instead of focusing subsequently on elements of lighting being described by the lector one at a time, participants focused on all of the elements of lighting and other, unrelated elements, like moving camera, members of the crew, etc.

Figure 3. The 6:35 frame corresponds to a low peak in the *sVRCa* (0.19). Yellow dots represent gaze fixations.

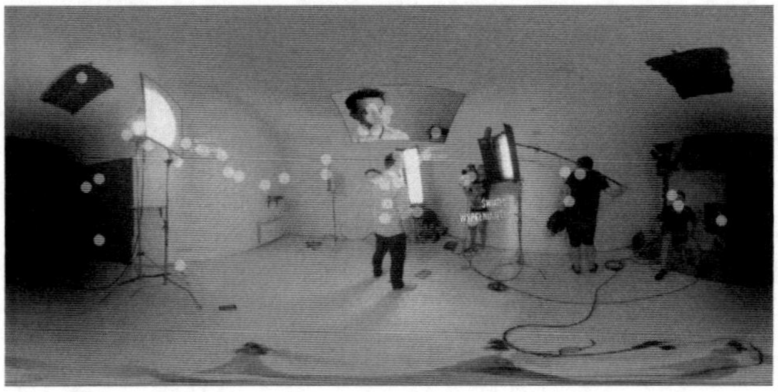

Figure 4. The 10:40 frame corresponds to a low peak in the *sVRCa* (0.22). Yellow dots represent gaze fixations.

V. Conclusion

The initial results of the test are promising. The method seems to substantially augment the process of detection of strong and weak moments in CVR narration. It delivers both the bird's eye view on the changes in reaction to narration and detailed information allowing either automated or point-by-point analysis of specific cuts, fragments, and moments in the immersive 360-degree video.

The authors propose a human-oriented measure, values of which reflect effectiveness of the process of attention directing along a narration line intended by a CVR experience creator. The method measures empirically the inter-viewer convergence in visual attention in order to give CVR creators feedback regarding whether they managed to converge the visual attention or whether they managed to dissipate it at any given moment of the video, according to their original creative intentions. Ideally, it is a CVR creator who should decide the qualitative interpretation of the quantitative measurement.

From a purely technology-oriented perspective, the need for the qualitative interpretation of the quantitative *sVRCa* values might be perceived as a limitation of the proposed method. However, the authors stand on the ground that, in the case of artistic pursuits, it is an artist, not a software system (not even a scientist), who should stay free to draw final conclusions from scientific data and be responsible for all the decisions as to the changes in the narration.

Regarding the next research steps, the authors find it indispensable to correlate the *sVRCa* time series with scenarios for videos, formulated *ex ante* by cooperating video artists in terms of precisely timelined sequence of cuts, attention-guiding cues, and other narrational tricks. Such a triangulation with data extracted from timelined scripts will not only advance the work on the methodology described in the paper. Above all, it will allow fully iterated feedback given by researchers to video makers in the real-life circumstances of CVR creation. It is even conceivable that the iterative feedback paradigm might be further developed into a semi-automatic software system that suggests ways to edit a video according to a desired flow of the *sVRCa* values [24].

The introduction of methodology, such as proposed and described in the paper, seems necessary to help CVR makers in the process of development and validation of the emerging

CVR narration language and means of expression [18]. There are no major objective obstacles for applying the proposed methodology in practice. Headsets equipped with eye trackers are recently available on the consumer market and it is even possible to approximate visual attention data directly from headsets' positions and rotations [25].

The authors hope the method could serve not only as feedback for CVR creators, but also as a criterion for other visual attention measures, physiological indices of attention (e.g., Heart Rate Variability (HRV)) or declarative, quantitative, and qualitative measures.

ACKNOWLEDGMENT

The tested CVR video and data collection were funded by the National Center for Film Culture (Lodz, Poland). The authors gratefully acknowledge the permission to use the data for scientific and publication purposes.

REFERENCES

[1] J. Blascovich et al., "Immersive virtual environment technology as a methodological tool for social psychology," Psychol. Inq., vol. 13, pp. 103–124, April 2002.

[2] D. M. Markowitz, R. Laha, B. P. Perone, R. D. Pea, and J. N. Bailenson, "Immersive virtual reality field trips facilitate learning about climate change," Front. Psychol, vol. 9, pp. 2364 (1–20), Nov. 2018, doi:10.3389/fpsyg.2018.02364.

[3] P. Kobylinski and G. Pochwatko, "Visual Attention Convergence Index for virtual reality experiences," Human Interaction and Emerging Technologies. IHIET 2019. Adv. Intell. Syst., vol. 1018, Springer, July 2019, pp. 310–316, doi:10.1007/978-3-030-25629-6_48.

[4] P. Kobylinski, G. Pochwatko, and C. Biele, "VR experience from data science point of view: how to measure inter-subject dependence in visual attention and spatial behavior. Intelligent Human Systems Integration 2019. IHSI 2019. Adv. Intell. Syst., vol 903. Springer, Jan. 2019, pp. 393–399, doi: 10.1007/978-3-030-11051-2_60.

[5] I. Bogdanova, A. Bur, and H. Hügli, "Visual attention on the sphere," IEEE T. Image Process., vol. 17, pp. 2000–2014, Nov. 2008, doi:10.1109/TIP.2008.2003415.

[6] S. Croci, S. Knorr, L. Goldmann, and A. Smolic, "A framework for quality control in cinematic VR based on Voronoi Patches and saliency," 2017 International Conference on 3D Immersion (IC3D 2017), IEEE, Jan. 2018, pp. 1–8, doi:10.1109/IC3D.2017.8251907.

[7] M. Xu, C. Li, Z. Wang, and Z. Guan, "Assessing visual quality of omnidirectional videos," IEEE T. Circ. Syst. Vid, vol. 29, pp. 3516–3530,, Dec. 2019, doi:10.1109/TCSVT.2018.2886277.

[8] J. Gutiérrez-Cillán, E. J. David, A. Coutrot, M. P. Da Silva, and P. Le Callet, "Introducing UN Salient360! Benchmark: a platform for evaluating visual attention models for 360-degree contents," 2018 Tenth International Conference on Quality of Multimedia Experience (QoMEX 2018), IEEE, Sept. 2018, pp. 1–3, doi:10.1109/QoMEX.2018.8463369.

[9] C. Ozcinar and A. Smolic, "Visual attention in omnidirectional video for virtual reality applications," 2018 Tenth International Conference on Quality of Multimedia Experience (QoMEX 2018), IEEE, June 2018, pp. 1–6, doi:10.1109/QoMEX.2018.8463418.

[10] E. Upenik and T. Ebrahimi, "Saliency driven perceptual quality metric for omnidirectional visual content," 2019 IEEE International Conference on Image Processing (ICIP 2019), IEEE, August 2019, pp. 4335–4339, doi:10.1109/ICIP.2019.8803637.

[11] V. Zakharchenko, K. P. Choi, and J. H. Park, "Quality metric for spherical panoramic video," Proceedings Volume 9970. Optics and Photonics for Information Processing X, SPIE, Sept. 2019, pp. 9970–11, doi:10.1117/12.2235885.

[12] N. Carlsson and D. Eager, "Had you looked where I'm looking: cross-user similarities in viewing behavior for 360-degree video and caching implications," Available from: https://arxiv.org/abs/1906.09779 (accessed Dec. 2019).

[13] I. Bogdanova, A. Bur, H. Hügli, and P.-A. Farine, "Dynamic visual attention on the sphere," Comput. Vis. Image Und., vol. 114, pp. 100–110, Jan. 2010, doi:10.1016/j.cviu.2009.09.003.

[14] V. Sitzmann et al., "Saliency in VR: how do people explore virtual environments?," IEEE T. Vis. Comput. Gr., vol. 24, pp. 1633–1642, Jan. 2018, doi:10.1109/TVCG.2018.2793599.

[15] C. O. Fearghail, C. Ozcinar, S. Knorr, and A. Smolic, "Director's cut - analysis of aspects of interactive storytelling for VR films," Interactive Storytelling. ICIDS 2018. Lect. Notes Comput. Sc., vol. 11318, Springer, Nov. 2018, pp. 308–322, doi: 10.1007/978-3-030-04028-4_34.

[16] S. Rothe, D. Buschek, and H. Hussmann, "Guidance in cinematic virtual reality - taxonomy, research status and challenges," Multimodal Technologies and Interaction, vol. 3, pp. 1–23, March 2019, doi:10.3390/mti3010019.

[17] A. Sheikh, A. Brown, Z. Watson, and M. Evans, ".Directing attention in 360-degree video," IBC 2016 Conference, IET Digital Library, Sept. 2016, pp. 29(9)–29(9), doi:10.1049/ibc.2016.0029.

[18] J. S. Pillai and M. Verma, "Grammar of VR storytelling: narrative immersion and experiential fidelity in VR cinema," The 17th International Conference on Virtual-Reality Continuum and Its Applications in Industry (VRCAI 2019), ACM, Nov. 2019, pp. 34(1)–34(6), doi: 10.1145/3359997.3365680.

[19] U. Świerczyńska-Kaczor, M. Żelazowska, M. Kotlińska, and J. Wachowicz, "Online interactive storytelling: evaluation of the viewer experience of 360-degree videos," Journal of Economics and Management, vol. 36, pp. 105–122, Feb. 2019, doi: 10.22367/jem.2019.36.06.

[20] D. Dowling, C. O. Fearghail, A. Smolic, and S. Knorr, "Faoladh: a case study in cinematic VR storytelling and production" Interactive Storytelling. ICIDS 2018. Lect. Notes Comput. Sc, vol. 11318, Springer, Nov. 2018, pp. 359–362, doi:10.1007/978-3-030-04028-4_42.

[21] A. T. Duchowski, Eye Tracking Methodology: Theory and Practice, Springer, 2007.

[22] D. D. Salvucci and J. H. Goldberg, "Identifying fixations and saccades in eye-tracking protocols,". ETRA '00 Proceedings of the 2000 Symposium on Eye Tracking Research and Applications, ACM, Nov. 2000, pp. 71–78, doi:10.1145/355017.355028.

[23] R Core Team, A Language and Environment for Statistical Computing, 2019, Available from: https://www.R-project.org (retrieved Dec. 2019).

[24] B. Huber, H. V. Shin, B. Russell, O. Wang, and G. J. Mysore, "B-script: Transcript-based B-roll video editing with recommendations," CHI '19: Proceeedings of the 2019 CHI Conference on Human Factors in Computing Systems, ACM, May 2019, pp. 81(1)–81(11), doi:10.1145/3290605.3300311.

[25] E. Upenik and T. Ebrahimi, "A simple method to obtain visual attention data in head mounted virtual reality," 2017 IEEE International Conference on Multimedia & Expo Workshops, IEEE, July 2017, pp. 73–78, doi:10.1109/ICMEW.2017.8026231.

Integrating Human Body MoCaps into Blender using RGB Images

Jordi Sanchez-Riera and Francesc Moreno-Noguer

Institut de Robòtica i Informàtica Industrial, CSIC-UPC
08028, Barcelona, Spain
Email: {jsanchez, fmoreno}@iri.upc.edu

***Abstract*—Reducing the complexity and cost of a Motion Capture (MoCap) system has been of great interest in recent years. Unlike other systems that use depth range cameras, we present an algorithm that is capable of working as a MoCap system with a single Red-Green-Blue (RGB) camera, and it is completely integrated in an off-the-shelf rendering software. This makes our system easily deployable in outdoor and unconstrained scenarios. Our approach builds upon three main modules. First, given solely one input RGB image, we estimate 2D body pose; the second module estimates the 3D human pose from the previously calculated 2D coordinates, and the last module calculates the necessary rotations of the joints given the goal 3D point coordinates and the 3D virtual human model. We quantitatively evaluate the first two modules using synthetic images, and provide qualitative results of the overall system with real images recorded from a webcam.**

***Keywords*–MoCap; 2D, 3D human pose estimation; Synthetic human model; Action mimic.**

I. INTRODUCTION

Motion Capture (MoCap) systems are used in industry and research to record real motions. The applications of such systems span from animating virtual characters or facial expressions, navigating into Virtual Reality (VR) environments, to modeling human-human/robot/object interactions. Professional MoCap systems are expensive, complex to use and need some dedicated space to record the motions, usually with multiple cameras. More modern systems just require to wear a suit which has reflective markers or motion sensors [1] [2]. These systems store the motions into files with a standard format that can be shared with other applications. However, due to the complexity of recording and processing the data from such systems, and that not everyone can afford to acquire a MoCap suite, it is not easy to find motion files processed by third parties. Or, even in the case we can find public repositories with motion files, as in [3] or [4], the motions we can find may not be those we need.

In order to make the MoCap recordings more affordable, there have been several attempts to find alternatives to reduce the complexity and time to process the recorded data. A good example can be found in [5], where the authors only need two calibrated cameras to infer 3D points given by a set of reflective markers on the human body. To eliminate the burden of having to wear body/cloth markers, Ganapathi et al. [6] propose a new system that uses depth images, therefore 3D locations come directly from the camera sensor device. This method, however, still needs a camera calibration process, which is a tedious task. More recently, Mehta et al. [7] eliminated the need of camera calibration, proposing a system able to infer 3D joint locations from a single RGB camera. At the same time, the irruption of Kinect camera has encouraged homebrew developers to program algorithms using the Application Program Interface (API) device library to achieve an inexpensive MoCap system for body [8] or faces [9]. Unfortunately, the official API library is only available on Windows platforms and some of the free alternative libraries are obsolete.

Similar to Mehta et al. [7], we propose an algorithm that is able to infer 3D body joint locations from a single RGB camera, and at the same time, we integrate it to a Blender 3D modeling software [10] that allows us to generate realistic renders using Makehuman [11] 3D human model. This allows easy saving and exporting captured motions into an industry standard motion file, which could be used by other software applications. Moreover, eliminating the need of a depth sensor device, as opposed to [6] [8], we can use our system both indoors and outdoors. As illustrated in Figure 1, our algorithm is composed of three modules. The first module takes the images from the camera and estimates the 2D joint articulations of the body. We then estimate the 3D human pose locations from the 2D detected joints, and finally the third module calculates the rotation of each joint to map from the virtual 3D human body joints to the 3D pose locations estimated by the second module.

The rest of the paper is organized as follows. In the next section, we discuss the related work for the first and second implemented modules. In Section III, we describe the developed algorithm as well as its integration to Blender. Then, in Section IV, we present the synthetic and real performed experiments, and, finally, in Section V, we draw the conclusions.

II. RELATED WORK

One of the key parts for a MoCap system is to have a reliable human pose detector. There are many works in literature on human pose estimators, that is why in this section, we will only review the most significant in 2D human pose detection and 3D human pose estimation.

A. 2D Human Pose Detection

When estimating 2D human pose from a single RGB image, there are two possible different approaches. One, known as bottom-up approach, consists into find the body joint locations and then trying to reason about the best configuration links that matches the observed body. The other one, known as top-down approach, starts from localizing the whole body region and later detecting the several body joints. A very popular bottom-up algorithm was introduced by Wei et al. [12],

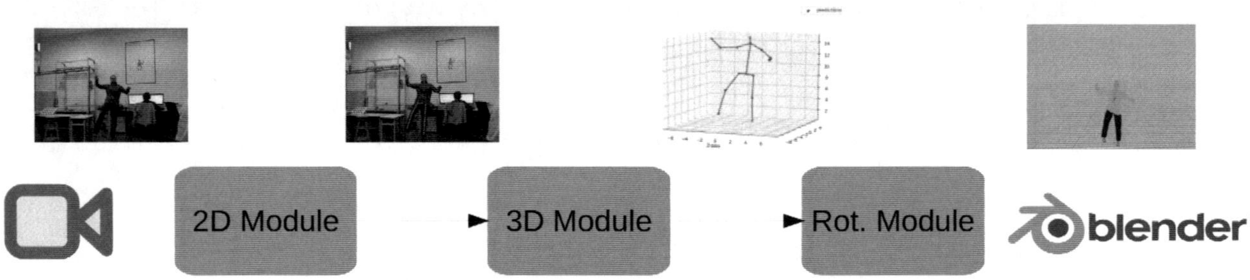

Figure 1. Pipeline of the proposed MoCap system.

and was improved by adding body parts optical flow in Cao et al. [13]. Both algorithms can run on several platforms, e.g., PC, phone, tablet, at very high frame rates. Top-bottom approaches can also detect 2D poses of multiple persons at high frame rates. Most of them first run a human detector [14] to localize body regions, however, these algorithms are prone to have problems when two persons overlap with each other. The most popular top-bottom algorithms are [15] [16], and their respective improved versions [17] [18]. Finally, another very popular approach [19] combines multiple bottom-up and top-down layers together, named hourglass, to detect the human pose at multiple resolutions. For our system, we decide to use the AlphaPose [16] method because it outperforms the other algorithms presented in this section, can also run in real time, and the skeleton that is retrieved is more similar to our 3D human skeleton model used in Blender, see Figure 2 a, b.

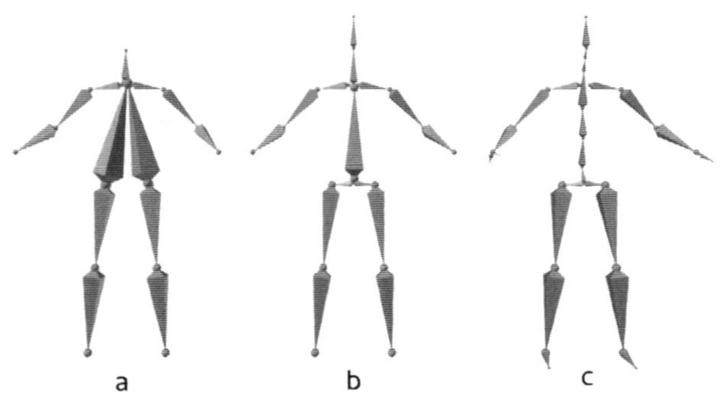

Figure 2. Different skeletons configurations. a) skeleton given by CPM [12] method, b) Alpha Pose skeleton used to compute angle rotations, c) skeleton used for Makehuman model to which captured motion is transferred.

B. 3D Human Pose Estimation

Estimating 3D human pose from a single RGB image is an important challenge. Most approaches assume that 2D joint locations are already known [20]–[22]. Some other approaches make use of additional extra cues, such as descriptors [23], stereo information [24] or even part models [25]. However, the most common used approach consists of combining 2D and 3D detections to make the 3D pose estimation more robust to errors [26]. One of the problems that arises when training these networks is the lack of labeled data. It is not easy to find ground truth for 3D human poses. For this reason, Zhou et al. [27] propose a method to combine labeled images with images in the wild. Chen et al. [28] go one step further and estimate directly 3D human pose from a single image using a synthetic dataset of 5M labeled images. These kind of networks are quite complex [29], and using extra information such as temporal correlations, can help to improve their performance [30]. Most recent algorithms, not only can find a 3D human pose estimate, but also can recover the whole body mesh [31] or even the shape parameters [32]. We decide to use the method described in Martinez et al. [20] due to its simplicity for training. The network described is relatively simple, and can be trained with thousands of samples instead of millions. Moreover, the network inference is very fast.

III. METHOD

The proposed MoCap system is divided into several interconnected modules. These modules will process the RGB images coming from a webcam, and finally will control a 3D human model through the Blender software. We first explain the modules responsible to infer 3D body joint positions from a single image. Then, we describe how these 3D joints are transformed into rotations for our 3D human model and, finally, how these rotations are passed to the render software.

A. Find 2D Joint Locations

We follow Alpha Pose [16] to obtain 2D human pose estimations from a single RGB image. The method is fast, outperforms other state-of-the-art algorithms, and the returned body pose is similar to the Makehuman 3D human model skeleton that we use in Blender. The method starts from some human region proposals, then these region proposals are passed through three different modules. The first one is the symmetric spatial transfer network that generates a set of pose proposals. The second one, a parametric pose non-maximum-suppression module, selects the most plausible pose estimations. And finally, the third one, the pose-guided proposals generator, is used to augment the training data and improve the network performance.

B. Infer 3D Joint Coordinates

Given a set of 2D points $x \in \mathbb{R}^2$ obtained in the previous module, we want to find a regression function that estimates the 3D points $y \in \mathbb{R}^3$ and minimizes the error over a set of 3D body poses. The regression function will be modeled by a neural network defined in Martinez et al. [20]. This network is composed of two consecutive blocks that contain a linear layer with batch normalization and a Rectified Linear Unit (ReLU) followed by a dropout layer. We use default parameters to train this network.

C. Animate 3D Human Model

Our 3D human model is controlled by a hierarchical structure called skeleton. This skeleton can be seen as a directed graph, where there is a root node and none or several children for each node. Each node is a segment where its start position defines the rotation pivot point and the end position is the start of the child node. For each node, also named bone or joint, a bind matrix M_{bj} encodes the joint position and rotation of the skeleton at rest pose. A pose matrix M_{pj} encodes the amount of rotation of each joint with respect to the rest of the skeleton pose. Thus, a skeleton pose $P(\theta)$ will be defined by a set of rotation parameters $\theta \in \mathbb{R}^{3K}$ for each one of the K joints that have direct correspondence with the 3D virtual model, Figure 2 c.

We want to calculate, for each joint of our skeleton, the rotation that matches a set of estimated 3D joint locations. The 3D joint locations, Figure 2 b, and our model skeleton, Figure 2 c, can have a different structure. Therefore, we can only find rotations for the skeleton joints that are equivalent in both structures. In order to calculate the rotations of each joint, we will define a source vector v_s and a target vector v_t. The source vector v_s will go from the the parent of the joint to the beginning of the child of the joint. The target vector v_t will be defined by the 3D point coordinates. If $v = v_s \times v_t$, $s = ||v||$ and $c = v_s \cdot v_t$, the rotation matrix to match the two vectors v_s, v_t is defined by:

$$R = I + [v]_x + [v]_x^2 \frac{1-c}{s^2}, \tag{1}$$

where $[v]_x$ is the skew-symmetric cross product matrix of v.

Before we can calculate the rotation matrix, it is necessary to have the two sets of 3D points in the same coordinate system. Therefore, the skeleton 3D joint locations need to be transformed from local X_j^L coordinates to world X_j^W coordinates. In the case that the skeleton joint has no father, we will use (2), otherwise we will use (3), where M_{Tf} is the M_T matrix already calculated for the father of the current bone.

$$X_j^W = M_{bj} \cdot M_{pj} \cdot X_j^L = M_T \cdot X_j^L \tag{2}$$

$$X_j^W = M_{Tf} \cdot M_{bf}^{-1} \cdot M_{bj} \cdot M_{pj} \cdot X_j^L \tag{3}$$

Finally, to obtain the skeleton joint coordinates in Blender coordinates, we need to use the defined world matrix M_w.

$$X_j^G = M_w \cdot X_j^W \tag{4}$$

D. Transfer Joint Rotations to Blender 3D Human Model

The final goal of the algorithm is to be able to transfer detected motion human poses from a videos or a webcam to a 3D human model in Blender. This will allow to store the motion into MoCap files or just simply use it as it is. To this end, we design a communication protocol between Blender and the image stream, using ZMQ library [33]. On one hand, we will have a process that will take the images from the stream and calculate the 3D joint coordinates of the body. On the other hand, we will have a Python script that will take the 3D joint locations from the stream as well as the rest of the 3D joint locations of the 3D human model and will calculate the body joint rotations. Therefore, we will use a server-client structure where the server will provide 3D joint locations at desired frame rate, while the client will be limited to listen to the data from the server.

IV. Experiments

We perform two different kinds of experiments. We generate two sets of synthetic data to train and evaluate the 3D human pose estimation, and then, we record several real sequences with a webcam to evaluate the whole algorithm performance.

A. Generate synthetic data

For training and evaluation purposes, we generate two different kind of datasets with Blender [10] and Makehuman [11]. The first dataset is used to train the 3D pose estimation module, while the second dataset is used to evaluate the overall performance of the proposed MoCap system. Note that for the 2D joint estimation module, a dataset is not needed since we use the weights trained from [16].

The first dataset consists of 6 human models (3 men and 3 women) with different shapes and sizes, performing a total of 54 motions obtained from Mixamo website [3]. Therefore, we have a total of 324 sequences of approximately 100 frames each. For each sequence, the ground truth for 3D joint locations as well as their 2D projections on a camera image are stored. We set the camera resolution to be of 640×480 for both datasets.

For the second dataset, we use 4 human models (2 men and 2 women) different from the ones used in the first dataset. We also use 10 motion sequences that were not included in the first dataset. In this case, the information gathered includes also the render RGB images of the sequences, apart from the 3D and 2D ground truth locations. To make the images more close to the real world, in each generated sequence, a random image is added as a background.

We also record five real sequences with a webcam at 640×480 image resolution to evaluate qualitatively the proposed MoCap system. Each one of the sequences is about 30 seconds long with a person performing different movements in the center of the image. The recorded images also have a person in the background of the scene, therefore, this person detection is removed from the image with a simple post-processing algorithm consisting in keeping the person with the biggest bounding box in the center of the image.

B. Evaluation

The images generated in the second dataset are passed to the Alpha Pose [16] detector network. This network returns the estimated 2D locations of 16 body joints, see Figure 2. The estimated locations are compared with ground truth locations using the PCKh@0.5 [34] measure. This measure calculates the percentage of correct keypoints when the threshold is 50% of the head bone link. The curves for the values of each action can be seen in Figure 4. We can observe that most of the actions have similar performance except for two actions: "teeter" and "picking up". In the case of "teeter" action, the motions of arms and legs are small but fast, making it seem like the person is shaking and this fact provokes several

(a) 2D joint detections

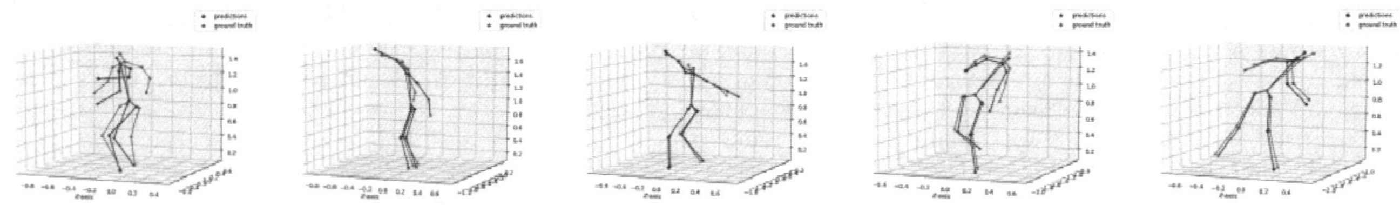

(b) 3D pose estimation

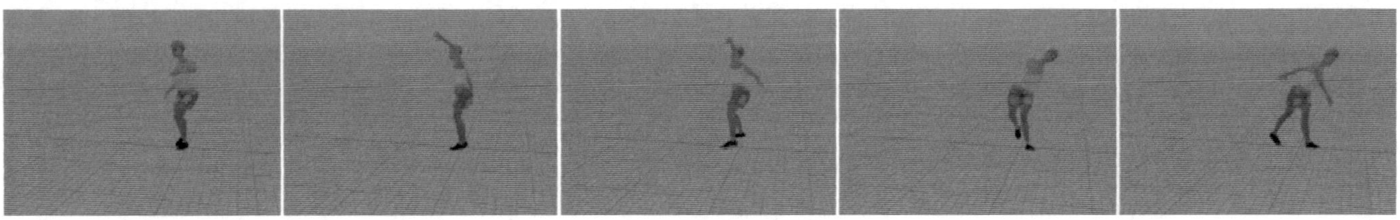

(c) Render 3D human model

Figure 3. Proposed algorithm on a synthetic sequence. a) 2D joint detections, b) ground truth 3D joint positions (in green) and the correspondent estimations by the 3D joint detection module (in blue), c) render images of the 3D human model. The input images are synthetized with Blender software. Ground truth is available.

TABLE I. MEAN PER JOINT POSITION ERROR (MPJPE) (m) FOR EACH SEQUENCE MOTION IN THE SECOND DATASET

	boxing	goalie throw	jumping jacks	looking around	picking up	talking	teeter	walking	walking 2	zombie kicking	average
error(m)	0.0961	0.0989	0.1299	0.1585	0.1399	0.0952	0.1416	0.1621	0.1535	0.1288	0.1304

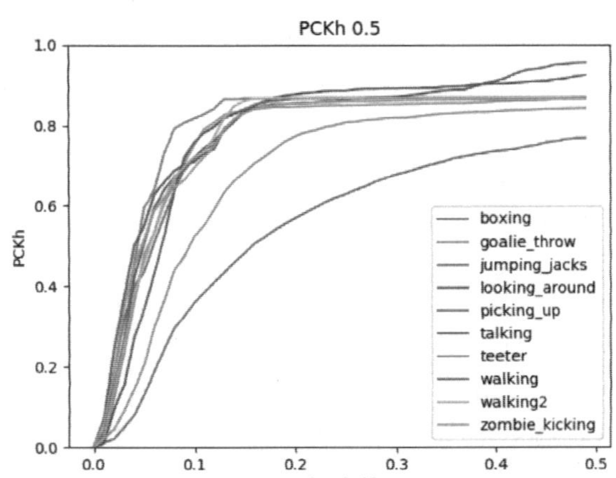

Figure 4. Percentage of correct keypoints at 50% of the head bone link for the different actions generated in the second dataset.

misdetections. In the case of "picking up" action, the model bends the upper part of the body occluding the other bottom half, making the 2D estimation module fail. However, the overall performance among all the actions is quite accurate.

Unlike the 2D joint detection module, the 3D pose estimation module is trained from the scratch. The reason for that is because we want to express the 3D joint positions with the Blender coordinate system for a simpler calculation of rotations. Therefore, the ground truth 2D and 3D joint locations are normalized according the new generated training dataset. This means that all sequences are reoriented taking the "hips" joints as reference, and values for all joints are rescaled to values from 0 to 1. Once the 3D joint estimation network is trained and weights are obtained, we proceed to evaluate the same 10 sequences as before. In this case, to evaluate the performance of the network, we use the Mean Per Joint Position Error (MPJPE) given in meters [35]. For evaluation, the ground truth 2D joint locations are replaced by the estimations obtained in the 2D joint estimation module. The results can be observed in Table I. The first thing to notice is that, while in the 2D detection model the actions "teeter" and "picking up" are the ones with worst performance, in the current 3D detection module the worst performance actions

(a) 2D joint detections

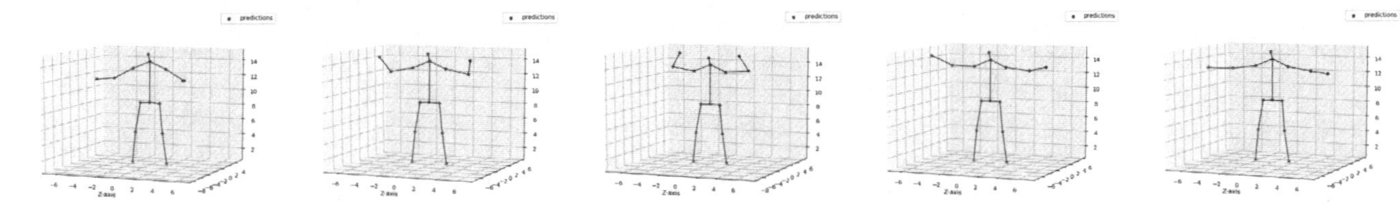

(b) 3D pose estimation

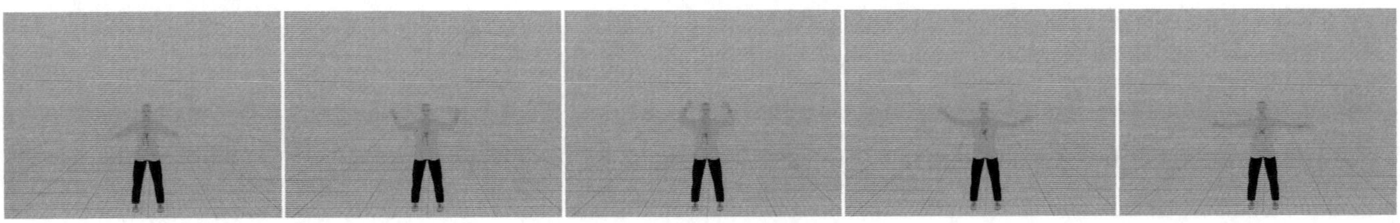

(c) 3D human model render

Figure 5. Results of the presented algorithm on the first real sequence.

are "walking" and "walking 2". Therefore, the errors from previous 2D detection module are not propagated as we could expect. The action with less error correspond to "boxing", which is the action where the model has less joints moving. The mean performance of all the actions is very low, with an error of 0.13 meters.

In Figure 3, we show the results for 5 frames of the sequence "goalie throw" for a woman actor. In each row, we present the results for each one of the proposed modules. The top row shows the results of the Alpha Pose algorithm. In the middle row, we show the ground truth 3D coordinates (in green), and the 3D estimated joint values (in blue). Finally, in the bottom row, we show a render model in Blender. We can observe that the original motion is very close to the render motion. In Figures 5 and 6, we show the results for two real sequences, when the actor is performing some random movements in the center of the scene. We can observe in the first row, that in the recorded images our 2D human pose detection module is able to find two different persons in the scene. Since for our proposed MoCap, we want only to focus on one person, we apply a simple image processing consisting in keeping biggest bounding box near to the center of the image. In the second row, we show the inferred 3D human position for the only person that we want to detect. In the third row, we show our virtual 3D model once calculated rotations are applied.

V. Conclusion

We presented a system capable of performing as a MoCap system with only a single RGB camera, with free source software that can run on several platforms. The system is based on three components that calculate 2D human body joint locations, then, from these locations, infer the 3D joint world coordinates, and finally, the 3D joints are transformed to joint body rotations for our virtual human model. The first two components are evaluated quantitatively with synthetic data, while the third component is only evaluated qualitatively. The overall system is also evaluated in real video images, with several sequences performed by a person. We show that we can mimic the movements of a person, with the potential to run the whole system in real time. In the future, we could use this MoCap system to perform dedicated actions for any kind of topic, and extract several ground truth data like in [36].

Acknowledgment

This work is supported by the Spanish MiNeCo under projects HuMoUR TIN2017-90086-R and Maria de Maeztu Seal of Excellence MDM-2016-0656. We also thank Marta Altarriba Fatsini for her support derivating the formulas to compute skeleton angle rotations.

References

[1] "XSens: MotionCapture," 2019, URL: https://www.xsens.com/ [accessed: February, 2020].

[2] "Vicon: MotionCapture," 2019, URL: https://www.vicon.com/ [accessed: February, 2020].

[3] "Adobe Mixamo," 2019, URL: https://www.mixamo.com/ [accessed: February, 2020].

[4] "CMU Motion Files," 2019, URL: http://mocap.cs.cmu.edu/ [accessed: February, 2020].

[5] J. Chai and J. K. Hodgins, "Performance animation from low-dimensional control signals," in SIGGRAPH, vol. 24, no. 3, 2005.

(a) 2D joint detections

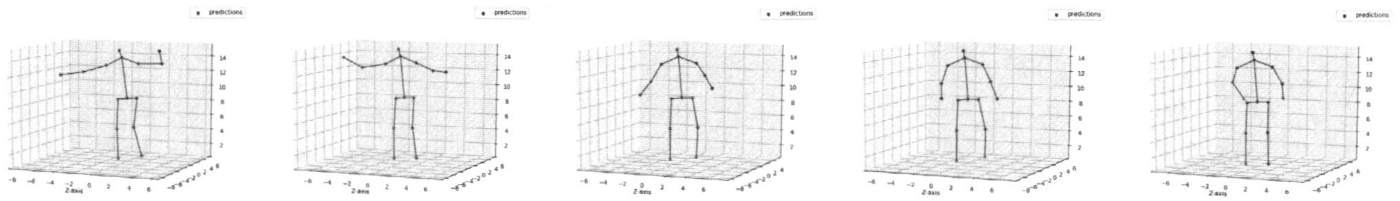

(b) 3D pose estimation

(c) 3D human model render

Figure 6. Results of the presented algorithm on the second real sequence.

[6] V. Ganapathi, C. Plagemann, D. Koller, and S. Thrun, "Real-time human pose tracking from range data," in ECCV, 2012.

[7] D. Mehta et al., "Vnect: Real-time 3d human pose estimation with a single rgb camera," in SIGGRAPH, vol. 36, no. 4, 2017.

[8] "Homebrew Mocap Studio," 2019, URL: https://www.youtube.com/watch?v=1UPZtS5LVvw [accessed: February, 2020].

[9] "Face Mocap Studio," 2019, URL: https://brekel.com/brekel-pro-face-2/ [accessed: February, 2020].

[10] "Blender," 2019, URL: https://www.blender.org/ [accessed: February, 2020].

[11] "Makehuman," 2019, URL: http://www.makehumancommunity.org/ [accessed: February, 2020].

[12] S.-E. Wei, V. Ramakrishna, T. Kanade, and Y. Sheikh, "Convolutional pose machines," in CVPR, 2016.

[13] Z. Cao, T. Simon, S.-E. Wei, and Y. Sheikh, "Realtime multi-person 2d pose estimation using part affinity fields," in CVPR, 2017.

[14] R. Girshick, "Fast R-CNN," in ICCV, 2015.

[15] L. Pishchulin et al., "Deepcut: Joint subset partition and labeling for multi person pose estimation," in CVPR, 2016.

[16] H.-S. Fang, S. Xie, Y.-W. Tai, and C. Lu, "RMPE: Regional multi-person pose estimation," in ICCV, 2017.

[17] E. Insafutdinov et al., "Arttrack: Articulated multi-person tracking in the wild," in CVPR, 2017.

[18] Y. Xiu, J. Li, H. Wang, Y. Fang, and C. Lu, "Pose Flow: Efficient online pose tracking," in BMVC, 2018.

[19] A. Newell, K. Yang, and J. Deng, "Stacked hourglass networks for human pose estimation," in ECCV, 2016.

[20] J. Martinez, R. Hossain, J. Romero, and J. J. Little, "A simple yet effective baseline for 3d human pose estimation," in ICCV, 2017.

[21] F. Moreno-Noguer, "3d human pose estimation from a single image via distance matrix regression," in CVPR, 2017.

[22] E. Simo-Serra, C. Torras, and F. Moreno-Noguer, "3d human pose tracking priors using geodesic mixture models," in IJCV, vol. 122, no. 2, 2017, pp. 388–408.

[23] E. Simo-Serra, C. Torras, and F. Moreno-Noguer, "DaLI: Deformation and light invariant descriptor," in IJCV, vol. 115, no. 2, 2015.

[24] J. Sanchez-Riera, J. Cech, and R. Horaud, "Robust spatiotemporal stereo for dynamic scenes," in ICPR, 2012.

[25] E. Trulls, S. Tsogkas, I. Kokkinos, A. Sanfeliu, and F. Moreno-Noguer, "Segmentation-aware deformable part models," in CVPR, 2014.

[26] C.-H. Chen and D. Ramanan, "3d human pose estimation = 2d pose estimation + matching," in CVPR, 2017.

[27] X. Zhou, Q. Huang, X. Sun, X. Xue, and Y. Wei, "Towards 3d human pose estimation in the wild: A weakly-supervised approach," in ICCV, 2017.

[28] W. Chen et al., "Synthesizing training images for boosting human 3d pose estimation," in 3DV, 2016.

[29] X. Sun, B. Xiao, F. Wei, S. Liang, and Y. Wei, "Integral human pose regression," in ECCV, 2018.

[30] M. Lin, L. Lin, X. Liang, K. Wang, and H. Chen, "Recurrent 3d pose sequence machines," in CVPR, 2017.

[31] R. A. Güler, N. Neverova, and I. Kokkinos, "DensePose: Dense Human Pose Estimation In The Wild," in CVPR, 2018.

[32] A. Kanazawa, M. J. Black, D. W. Jacobs, and J. Malik, "End-to-end recovery of human shape and pose," in CVPR, 2018.

[33] "ZMQ," 2019, URL: https://zeromq.org [accessed: February, 2020].

[34] M. Andriluka, L. Pishchulin, P. Gehler, and B. Schiele, "2d human pose estimation: New benchmark and state of the art analysis," in CVPR, 2014.

[35] L. Sigal, A. Balan, and M. J. Black, "HumanEva: Synchronized video and motion capture dataset and baseline algorithm for evaluation of articulated human motion," in IJCV, vol. 87, no. 1, 2010.

[36] A. Pumarola, J. Sanchez-Riera, G. P. T. Choi, A. Sanfeliu, and F. Moreno-Noguer, "3dpeople: Modeling the geometry of dressed humans," in ICCV, 2019.

Serious Games with Serious Aims

The Design and Development of a Serious Game for Construction Based Learners

Lauren Maher
Department of Informatics
Technological University Dublin
Dublin, Ireland
Email: seriousgamesresearcher@gmail.com

Shaun Ferns, Matt Smith, Mark Keyes
Technological University Dublin
Dublin, Ireland
Email: {shaun.ferns, matt.smith, mark.keyes}@tudublin.ie

Abstract— **For the purpose of this study, a serious game prototype has been designed and is currently being developed and tested with construction-based learners, to discover the effectiveness of serious games as educational tools within the industry. Serious games are commonly described as computer and video games that are intended to entertain learners while achieving a primary goal of education and training. Many studies and experiments have been carried out in order to test whether serious games have made it possible to play and learn simultaneously. Although the effectiveness of serious games as teaching and training tools is well established in the literature, some gaps have been identified. These include frameworks to transform traditional learning outcomes to game systems, serious game adoption and data collection, their relevance for affecting attitudinal change and the effectiveness of serious games in the construction sector. This study explores the effectiveness of upskilling training being delivered through the use of serious games rather than with traditional methods. In addition, there is a focus on the training of construction skills and the capacity for effecting attitudinal change within the construction industry. The research explores the opportunities provided by serious games to align with the learning characteristics of construction workers and to optimise the development of resources that achieve learning objectives effectively for this cohort.**

Keywords- Serious Games; Education; Training; Low-Energy; Construction; Data-Collection.

I. INTRODUCTION

The overarching aim of this study is to explore the possibilities of whether upskilling training can be delivered more successfully through the use of serious games than with traditional methods. This research is specifically interested in the effectiveness of using serious games for the training of construction skills and the capacity for affecting attitudinal change. This paper outlines the initial stages and steps taken to design and develop the serious game prototype, additionally, it describes the preparation process of our primary study, taking place in mid-2020.

The rest of the paper is structured as follows. Section II begins by stating the project background and motivation. Section III reviews current literature surrounding serious games and their effectiveness as educational and training tools. Section IV illustrates the methodology and data collection tools, chosen and utilised, in aid of this project. This section also demonstrates the results from the initial game design and development session and states the current stage of the project. Section V prepares for the next stage, which aims to test the serious game prototype with participants from our target audience. The potential challenges of future studies and how we plan to overcome these challenges are also presented within this section.

II. PROJECT BACKGROUND

In 2012, the European Union (EU) funded Build Up Skills Ireland (BUSI) [1] project conducted a skills-gap analysis of the Irish construction sector in relation to the capacity of the workforce for delivering low-energy buildings. One of the most significant conclusions of the report was an identified need for an introductory course on the principles of low-energy buildings for all building construction workers [2].

Build UP Skills QualiBuild (2013-2016), the follow-on project to BUSI, developed a Foundation Energy Skills (FES) course, with over 200 participants upskilled under a QualiBuild national pilot [3]. The focus of this course was knowledge of the underpinning principles of low-energy buildings and reinforcing the message of a need for a collaborative effort from all involved in the building construction process towards the achievement of quality standards. The FES programme focused on a pedagogical approach that would best address the identified knowledge gaps and need for attitudinal change amongst construction workers, which also considers the challenges, such as cost, equipment, space and time restrictions.

For the specific challenges of QualiBuild FES training, in upskilling an entire workforce, utilising serious games alongside traditional delivery methods offers greater flexibility of time and place. The potential contribution of serious games in construction skills training has not been explored in an Irish context to date. This study explores this potential for QualiBuild training and beyond.

III. REVIEW OF SERIOUS GAMES

Serious games include mixed media/reality and virtual environments created to meet user needs, through an interactive and engaging environment [4]. The significance of serious games has increased rapidly in recent years, with an inclination of technological aptitude, from people of all ages [4]. In any instance, when a video game purpose is learning rather than entertainment, it is typically referred to as digital game-based learning or serious games [2]. Serious games have become a growing market in the video games industry [4] as well as a field of academic research [5]. The serious games industry is constantly evolving to tailor user needs and is currently a multi-billion-dollar market [6], which uses video games, simulations, extended reality environments, and mixed reality/media as training and educational tools for a variety of industries such as military, healthcare, and aviation [7]. In response to the recent desire for serious games to be implemented as a new training and learning tool [8], we need to further understand the ability, advantages, and disadvantages of using serious games as an aid to learning. The aim of serious games being used as a teaching and training tool is not to replace classroom teaching, but to add an alternative option to help learners understand a subject in new ways [9]. Recent studies have shown that many students prefer to learn by doing, rather than listening and trying to take in information traditionally. One study published shows that "though students felt as if they learned more through traditional lectures, they actually learned more when taking part in classrooms that employed active-learning strategies" [8]. It has been demonstrated that serious games can simulate a variety of working conditions and scenarios while avoiding potentially dangerous situations and costly field training [10].

Recently, serious games have been compared and evaluated against written texts, regarding their ability to convey knowledge [9]. A primary advantage of serious games when compared to written texts is that serious games illustrate a virtual world that visualizes the subject matter and uses real-life situations in a learning environment. These components help the user to learn, remember and understand [10]. Serious games may enable students to bridge the gap between theory and practice. However, they are not without their concerns. Teachers can make learning engaging and interactive for the learner, but textbooks and printouts cannot [8]. Additionally, few studies have identified the negative aspects of utilising serious games, stating that exposure to high fidelity entertainment video games leads users to prefer serious games to be as visually realistic as possible [11]. As a result, when entertainment video game users hear the term "game", it could create unrealistic expectations in the learners [12], resulting in negativity during gameplay. Serious games often refer to the use of game design approaches when designing and developing a game [13]. Examples of this include incorporating a rewards system into the game to improve player motivation and enjoyment.

IV. METHODOLOGY

Our methodology has two goals: 1) to ease the comparison of serious games versus traditional learning methods and 2) to provide a systematic way to assess the effectiveness of using serious games as a teaching and learning tool. To achieve these goals, our approach covers the complete process of creating a serious game (Figure 1).

The target audience for this project is construction-based learners. Their age, gender, and experience within the industry are not necessarily contributing factors, as low-energy building training must be delivered to all construction workers regardless of these demographics. However, it should be noted that a large number of the construction worker demographics in Ireland are males, with an average age of 42 [14], therefore, our primary target audience is made up of males, aged 35-50. Our secondary target audience is construction-based learners of any age.

This study applies a dual methodology process. One of the primary methodologies chosen for the design and development of this project was an iterative design process. Iterative design is an adaptive process, whereby designers move through multiple cycles of conceiving an idea, creating a prototype that embodies the idea, running playtests with the prototype to see the idea in action and then evaluating the results. Based on those results, changes and refinements are made. The game is currently nearing the end of the Create Prototype Stage (Stage 3, Figure 1) and, in the coming weeks, will enter the first round of testing. Whilst developing the game, individual playtests are being carried out regularly, with participants of the same demographic as the target audience. Individual playtests provide initial data collection regarding the functionality of the game mechanics, to allow for refinement before the official playtest session takes place with the group of construction-based learners.

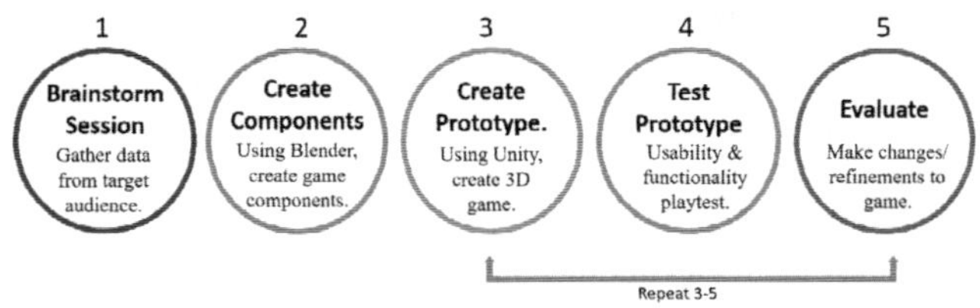

Figure 1. Iterative Design Process for Serious Game.

The second methodology chosen for the design and development of this project is a case study methodology. A case study was selected to determine the effectiveness, of using serious games to teach low-energy building principles and influence attitudinal change. At the end of the final playtest session, a set of two questionnaires will be presented to the participants. One questionnaire will focus on player demographics and personal details such as age, experience in the industry and experience with video games. The second questionnaire will gauge their knowledge and attitudes, related to the construction industry before and after gameplay. This method will allow the researcher to discover the success and failures of using serious games to teach construction-based learners low-energy building principles and allows comparison with current teaching and training methods.

The project in its entirety requires 3 sessions with our target audience. The initial fact-finding session, also referred to as Stage 1 (Figure 1), is used to determine the characteristics required for the game. Two additional playtest sessions will take place after game development.

These sessions will be used to assess the functionality and usability of the game and later will be used to test the success and failures of using serious games to teach low-energy building principles and their potential influence on attitudinal change within the industry.

Future studies in aid of this project, will test and evaluate the serious game with our target audience, to gather data regarding the effectiveness of using serious games to teach low-energy building principles and the potential impact of player attitudes. The playtest session, scheduled to take place towards the end of the project, will be evaluated by splitting the participant group in half. One half of the testing group will learn low-energy building principles using traditional methods, such as reading texts and attending a lecture. The other half of the participants will play the serious game with no additional help. This will enable the researcher to discover the possibilities of teaching low-energy building principles, using serious games over traditional methods. Both learning methods will be utilised, to try to deliver the same knowledge to all participants. Afterward, based on the data collected from the in-game data collection application and via questionnaires completed by the participants. User attitudes and knowledge obtained through the game can be measured and compared to prior knowledge and attitudes related to the construction industry.

The use of mixed-methods for the study will include, secondary analysis of existing literature and data and collection of primary quantitative and qualitative data. Proposed data collection tools to be used in aid of this study, are game testing sessions, an in-game data collection application, and participant questionnaires. The in-game data collection application tracks player data such as: how long the user spends in each level, interactions between characters, when a 'help' button is clicked and when a task is completed. Participants will be tested within the game in a variety of ways, these include, through decisions made by the user during gameplay, by having the player work through various scenarios within the game and through measuring player motivation and their desire to continue with the serious game. These methods of data collection have been chosen above others, as they are commonly used in game design and development. Previous studies, which have employed these tools have returned valuable results concerning serious game development and evaluation [8] [12]. These data collection tools, provide an opportunity to evaluate player responses in regards to the serious game. The use of these tools will ensure the game design and functionality meets the needs of the end-user and allows the research question to be answered.

A. Stage 1 – Brainstorm Session

An initial prototype design and development session, ('brainstorming') has been used as a way to connect with the target audience and discover their needs and wants regarding the serious game. The prototype design and development session took place, with a group of 8 male construction-based lecturers, aged 35-45. The participants have experience working and teaching in the area of low-energy buildings and have contributed to the FES Learners Handbook. Their involvement within the construction industry greatly influenced the decision of what characteristics the game should include. Initially, questionnaires were distributed and data collected highlighted a clear vision of the type of interaction to be included within the game, which topics would benefit from a more hands on approach and what type of graphics (realistic/cartoon) would appeal. Through this interaction, the following results were collected:

1) The common areas, concepts, and skills that construction workers struggle most with are as follows: continuity of insulation, the effects of badly installed insulation, thermal bridging, effective airtightness and systems thinking (Figure 2).

2) Topics identified concerned Unit 3 of the QualiBuild Foundation Energy Skills Training Handbook (building fabric, air-tightness, and wind-tightness) (Figure 2).

3) It was decided a realistic narrative-based game would best suit our desired learning objectives. Through creating a narrative style serious game, the user can decide on the character they wish to be and can interact with the other characters within the game to give them a sense of perspective and empathy.

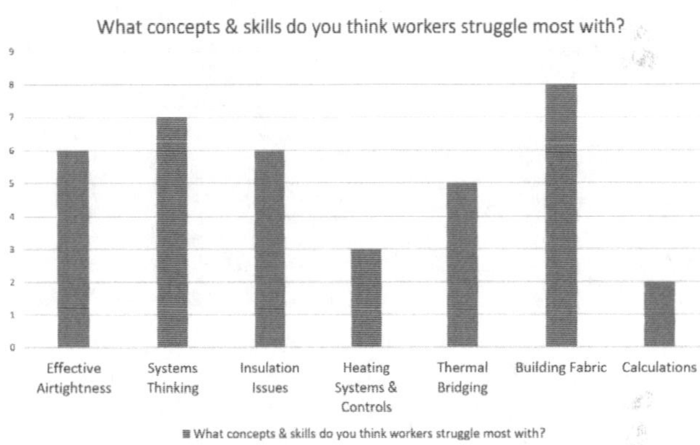

Figure 2. Results of Brainstorm Questionnaire

B. Stage 2 – Create Components

Through the collection of data, regarding areas that construction workers struggle with, it was made possible to determine the required learning outcomes for the serious game and to begin game design and development. Many elements within the game, were developed of which employ a multimodal approach to the presentation of course material, i.e., a combination of text, visuals, video, 2D drawings, and narration. A multimodal approach has been chosen as it creates a dynamic learning experience for the students. A multimodal approach was designed to help each student to achieve academic success in their way. Software and technologies were taken into consideration before the development of the game to ensure that it would be easily accessible and readily available for educational practitioners to continue using and adopting in the future.

C. *Stage 3 – Create Prototype*

Based on the data collected, the serious game prototype has been designed and is currently under development. The current game prototype allows the user to switch back and forth between first and third-person views and to interact and engage with different elements throughout the game (Figures 3 and 4). Examples of this include navigating and interacting with the 3D environment, entering the home, locating various documents and other interactive objects and engaging with family members within the home. The prototype allows the user to observe and interact with the learning objectives specified in section three of the FES Learners Handbook. The game enables the player to have interactive dialogues with other characters/ family members in the house, track user actions, allows the user to view the current score, hide and reveal window components such as walls, insulation, and cavities and locate problems from the pop-up checklist. It provides the user with an option to request help at any time by clicking on the 'help' button when clicked on, a pop-up builder appears to assist by filling in the knowledge gap required to continue with the game.

Figure 3. Gameplay First Person View

Figure 4. Gameplay Third Person View

V. FUTURE CHALLENGES

Stage four of the iterative design process for this project (Figure 1) will be held to collect and analyse data regarding the usability and functionality of the game. Using this data the game mechanics can be evaluated (Stage 5, Figure 1) and re-defined depending on the user experience and feedback. The next stage involves assessing future challenges, which may occur during the testing stage of this study. Potential challenges for future studies include time management, to ensure the game has been adequately tested and is ready for the future study/ playtest with the target audience. Another potential challenge is incentivizing participation, there is a known obstacle of finding enough construction student participants to warrant a sound, evidence-based research project. A final, potential challenge is the experience and emotional responses, of participants using entertainment video games. If the participants are frequent video game users, they may find the game uninteresting compared to entertainment video games. However, if the user has no prior video game experience, it might prove difficult for them to grasp navigating and playing at first instance. This challenge has been anticipated by the developer and therefore a 'walk through' level at the beginning of the game has been incorporated, to help the user to navigate through the game and use command keys in an easy, non-treating environment.

VI. CONCLUSION

In conclusion, it has been shown in the literature that the significance of using serious games as training and educational tools has increased rapidly in recent years. Through reviewing current literature regarding serious games in different learning contexts, their potential effectiveness and how they are designed and developed, it is clear that serious games for teaching and educating are a valued pedagogical method. However, in order to implement game-based learning as a successful training and learning tool, there is a need to further understand the opportunities and constraints. Gaps within the literature include frameworks to transform traditional learning outcomes to game systems and data collection regarding the effectiveness of serious games in the construction sector and their relevance for effecting attitudinal change.

A serious game prototype has been designed and is currently being developed and tested using an iterative design process. An initial prototype design and development session has taken place and data collected throughout this session has been evaluated and analysed to discover the needs and wants, regarding the serious game design. Prior involvement of the brainstorm participants, within the construction industry, greatly influenced the decision of which characteristics should be included within the game. Through data collected via questionnaires, it was evident which interaction types are needed within the game. These characteristics include a narrative, a family living in the home, intractable characters and issues that need resolving. Results from this session also included, which topics would benefit from a more hands approach and what type of graphics would appeal.

The next stage of this project is to complete the working prototype and begin testing with a group of construction-based students to successfully discover the effectiveness of using serious games to teach construction workers low-energy building principles and their capacity for effecting attitudinal change within the industry.

REFERENCES

[1] Build Up Skills Ireland "Analysis of the National Status Quo". IEE/11/BWI/460/S12-604350, available from: https://ec.europa.eu/energy/intelligent/projects/sites/iee-projects/files/projects/documents/build_up_skills_ie_status_quo_analysis_en.pdf, 2012

[2] A. D. Coster, "Final Report on the Assessment of the BUILD UP Skills Pillar II", Brussels: European Commission Available from: https://www.buildup.eu/sites/default/files/content/bus-d4.4finareport_on_assessment_april_2018_0.pdf, 2015.

[3] M. Keyes and S. Walsh, "Foundation Energy Skills Evaluation Report," QualiBuild, Retrieved Febuary 2020 from:http://www.qualibuild.ie/wp-content/uploads/2015/01/D3.3-QualiBuild-FES-Pilot-Evaluation-Report-Final_PU.pdf , 2016.

[4] J. Alvarez, J. Jessel and O. Rampnoux 'Origins of Serious Games' In Serious Games and Edutainment Applications, Springer London, 2011.

[5] U. Ritterfeld and R. Weber, "Video games for entertainment and education". In P. Vorderer, & J. Bryant (Eds.), Playing video games: Motives, responses and consequences, pp. 399-413, 2006.

[6] B.P. Bergeron, 'Developing Serious Games' Hingham, MA: Charles River Media; 2006.

[7] A. De Gloria, F. Bellotti and R. Berta, "Serious Games for education and training," International Journal of Serious Games, 2014.

[8] L. Deslauriers, L.S McCarty, K. Miller, K, Callaghan and G. Kestin, 'Measuring Actual Learning Versus Feeling of Learning in Response to being Actively Engaged in the Classroom'. Proceedings of the National Academy of Sciences of the United States of America, 2019.

[9] S. deFreitas and F. Liarokapis, "Serious Games: A New Paradigm for Education?", in Serious Games and Edutainment, Springer London, 2011.

[10] A. De Gloria, F. Bellotti and R. Berta, 'Serious Games for Education and Training'. International Journal of Serious Games, Vol. 1, 2014 .

[11] R. Hunicke, M. LeBlanc and R. Zubek "MDA: A Formal Approach to Game Design and Game Research", AAAI Workshop, Technical Report. 1, 2004.

[12] I. Roslina, and J. Azizah, Educational Games (EG) Design Framework: Combination of Game Design, Pedagogy and Content Modeling. 2009 International Conference on Electrical Engineering and Informatics, Selangor, Malaysia. 2009.

[13] R.E. Ferdig, 'The Design, Play and Experience Framework' In Handbook of Research on Effective Electronic Gaming in Education, Anonymous : IGI Global, pp.1010-1024, 2008.

[14] T. Conefrey and T. McIndoe-Calder "Where are Ireland's Construction Workers?" Quarterly Bulletin, Central Bank of Ireland . Ireland, Available from: https://www.centralbank.ie/docs/default-source/publications/quarterly-bulletins/quarterly-bulletin-signed-articles/where-are-ireland-s-construction-workers-(conefrey-and-mcindoe-calder).pdf?sfvrsn=4, 2018.

[15] M. Keyes, S. Ferns, R. Hickey, R. Ryan, J. Cussen, and D. Hynes, QualiBuild Train the Trainer: Lessons Learned from the Development of a Program for Training Trainers of Construction Workers in Ireland. Higher Education in Transformation Symposium, Oshawa, Ontario, Canada, 2016.

The Use of Virtual Reality in Mindfulness Meditation

Gabriela Górska*†, Daniel Cnotkowski*, Paweł Kobyliński*, Cezary Biele*
*Laboratory for Interactive Technologies, National Information Processing Institute
†Robert Zajonc Institute for Social Studies, Warsaw University
Warsaw, Poland
e-mail: gabriela.gorska@opi.org.pl, daniel.cnotkowski@opi.org.pl, pawel.kobylinski@opi.org.pl, cezary.biele@opi.org.pl

***Abstract*—Virtual Reality (VR) is widely used in different areas of research in psychology. Its use seems irreplaceable since it allows the simulation of many previously unreachable interactions in laboratory settings. In our research, we designed an environment to facilitate meditational training. We tried to prove that VR can support mindfulness through immersion. We also hypothesized that mindfulness meditation would show significantly higher results than relaxation on mindfulness-related constructs such as decentration and curiosity. The same effect would also be visible on positive mood or social skills questionnaires. A total of 80 participants took part in the research. However, the results did not support our hypotheses. Whether meditation or relaxation took place, with or without VR, none of these conditions seemed to differ significantly from one another. The psychometric issues related to the research are discussed as well as the qualities of VR that could have inhibited the effects of immersion, such as real world similarity, level of abstractness of the virtual environment, landscape, and virtual enhancement of transcendence.**

Keywords-Virtual Reality; Virtual Environment; meditation; mindfulness.

I. Introduction

The potential of Virtual Reality (VR) in science has been explored in various fields, e.g., in understanding clinical aspects of fear and anxieties [3] by provoking certain desired states in a safe laboratory environment. It is a widely used tool in therapy – for example, in short-term pain distraction [18], or in anxiety treatments, where VR is used as Virtual Reality Exposure Therapy (VRET) [34], as well as in Post-Traumatic Stress Disorder (PTSD) therapy [10] or in the treatment of arachnophobia [5]. In the current research, we would like to examine whether VR has the potential to be successfully used to enhance a meditative experience. In this article, "mindfulness", "meditative experience" and "meditation" will be used synonymously for ease of reading. However, we are aware of the complexity of what meditation actually is and that "mindfulness" represents only one type of a meditation-related state.

II. VR in Contemplative Studies

VR can create a stressful environment that is not accessible in real-world ethical studies, e.g., an immersive VR environment can be used to imitate a train station hit by several explosions [7]. By doing this, it can elicit fear, anxiety or, in general, a difficult emotional state under stress. In this way, the influence of meditation on emotions and processing stress can be checked in ethically approved, albeit stressful conditions. The aforementioned study confirmed a less anxious response to stressful stimuli in a group of meditators who underwent an 8-week-long meditation course prior to the experiment. However, it does not prove the utility of VR in enhancing an alternative state of mind.

VR has been checked as a tool supporting relaxation while meditating. For example, VR can be used in connection to neurofeedback to check the impact of meditation on a group of chronic pain patients [15]. As the patients became more relaxed, the view of a forest in VR changed to a less foggy, clearer, sunny and green image. This was not immersive VR though, as a stereoscopic VR viewer was used. Later in this article, we will describe the difference between relaxation and meditation in more depth, and the relation to relaxation in meditation.

Another example of a VR-meditation connection is a study using neurofeedback (specifically, electroencephalography, EEG) for focused attention and body-scan [24]. The study proves, amongst other things, that immersive VR, with or without neurofeedback, can give significantly better results in questionnaires related to meditation (self-reflection and relaxation) than the control conditions, in which the participants could observe the same view as the experimental group, albeit on a computer screen. As the VR design is crucial to this kind of research, it seems important to mention that the authors decided to keep the environment as simple as possible (the leaves on the trees were represented as triangles; the sky was left cloudless). The study proved immersive VR to be of some use as a meditation-enhancement tool even though the participants had to sit still.

Why would VR be effective in enhancing meditation? One of the most common types of meditation, mindfulness, has been researched for almost 30 years and started with an 8-week long meditation training program known as Mindfulness-Based Stress Reduction Program designed by Jon Kabat-Zinn [22]. Mindfulness meditation was conceptualized and later proved to work as an emotion processing strategy, along with suppression and positive reappraisal [6]. It has been commonly used as a relaxation method as well as part of therapeutic treatments [13][14]; it has also been shown to influence compassionate and empathetic thinking [4], stereotypical thinking [36], prejudices [27][28] and conflict studies [1]. Since VR has already been successfully shown to enhance meditative experiences, we decided to replicate this result using a brief meditation training session. We were interested in examining whether such a complex state as mindfulness meditation [16] can be influenced by a simple mindfulness training session and enhanced by a basic immersive VR environment. We wanted to explore in more depth the possibilities that VR gives to facilitate meditation, as well as try to identify any obstacles that modern technology meets when facing an alternative state of mind. It was interesting for us to see whether a brief training session gives any results as it did in several previous studies (see: [27] and [28], as examples).

III. RESEARCH HYPOTHESES

In our study, we decided to combine Virtual Reality with mindfulness meditation and compare the effects of both mindfulness and relaxation with or without VR. The goals were: 1) to investigate the possibilities of using Virtual Reality in meditative states (mindfulness meditation only) with the hypothesis that VR would enhance relaxation and detachment from the surrounding environment which may facilitate the experience for the meditators. This would be mirrored by higher scores on the subjective well-being scales, as well as on the meditation-related scale, especially in the experimental (mindfulness) group with VR; 2) to compare the influence of a short meditation vs. relaxation training session on subjective well-being and mindfulness-related states (such as decentration and curiosity of one's emotions and thoughts) with our hypothesis being, the experimental mindfulness groups would feel happier and more open to their thoughts and emotions after the training session than the relaxation groups; 3) to our knowledge, there is yet no study relating mindful meditation and VR with social processes, hence we decided to compare the influence of short meditation or relaxation sessions in social processing (such as empathic thinking, or seeing humanity as one in general). Our hypothesis was that the experimental mindfulness group would present more empathic thinking and would identify with all humanity more than the relaxation group.

IV. METHOD

A) *VR Environment*

The immersive VR environment used for the study was prepared by the authors in Unity 2018.3.8f1. The environment was created to imitate the natural surroundings as reliably as possible using the accessible assets. Figures 1 and 2 present the final form of the environment prepared for the study. The concept of the 'meditation island' was to facilitate achievement of meditative states, hence it was supposed to be calming, imitating a mountain lake view, enhancing the self-reflective nature of meditation. Participants could also hear sounds of a forest (including various bird species singing) regardless of their experimental group: those who did not meditate in VR had headphones with the background music on. The hardware that was used in the study was VR HTC Vive Pro with Stereo AudioTechnica mx 20 headphones, connected to an Intel Xeon based PC with the Nvidia GTX 1070 graphics card.

Figure 1. The mountain lake view of the 'meditative island'; the front view of the virtual environment.

Figure 2. The view on the mountains. The back view of the virtual environment.

B) *Experimental conditions*

The experiment was conducted using the between-subjects design. Participants were divided into four groups (2x2 design) with or without VR (VR, No VR); with mindfulness meditation instructions or simple relaxation instructions (meditation vs. relaxation group). The design is illustrated in Table I. Participants were randomly assigned to a certain group at the beginning of each study. Subsequently, they sat on a chair in an empty room, facing the same direction both in real and in VR, with VR hardware on, or with headphones only. Before starting the software, participants in all groups listened to the instructions delivered by professional mindfulness trainers. Under mindfulness conditions, participants were asked to observe their thoughts and emotions in a non-judgmental manner and let them go, as they would not be related to them, observing their bodies and breath. Under relaxation conditions, participants were taught to tense and relax certain body muscle groups step by step. After these instructions, participants were asked to continue these tasks during a VR experience or listening to the sounds of forest, which took exactly 15 minutes. Participants could freely observe the environment if they wished to. Afterwards, they were asked to fill in the questionnaires (listed below) and had time to ask questions. Figure 3 briefly outlines the study design.

TABLE I. EXPERIMENTAL CONDITIONS DESIGN

	With VR	Without VR
mindfulness meditation	Group 1 (N = 20)	Group 2 (N = 20)
relaxation	Group 3 (N = 20)	Group 4 (N = 20)

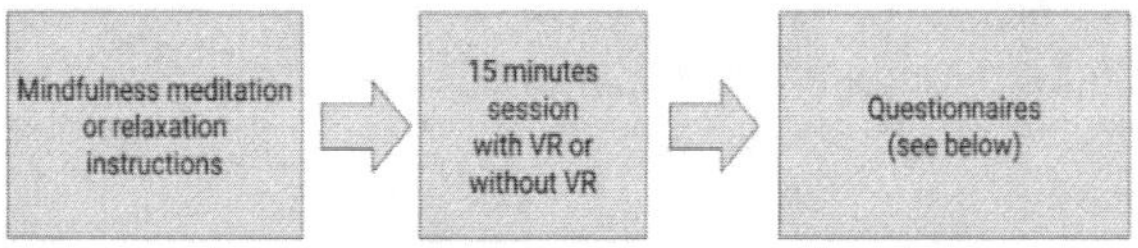

Figure 3. The study design.

C) *Measures*

In order to check our hypotheses, we decided to use several questionnaires translated into Polish: the Toronto Mindfulness Scale to measure the state of mindfulness meditation, the Positive Orientation Scale, the Depression Anxiety Stress Scale, the Satisfaction With Life Scale to check the influence of meditation on mood, and the Interpersonal Reactivity Index as well as the Identification With All Humanity scale to check the social processes.

Toronto Mindfulness Scale (TMS; meditation-VR group, mean = 3.60, SD = 0.48, relaxation-VR group, mean = 3.60, SD = 0.60, meditation-no VR group, mean = 3.59, SD = 0.50 and relaxation-no VR group, mean = 3.36, SD = 0.48). Since we did not use any objective measure of mindfulness as a state, we decided to use the Polish translation of the commonly used Toronto Mindfulness Scale prepared by one of the authors. The scale has been developed as a questionnaire measuring mindfulness as a state and consists of 13 questions with two subscales: Decentering and Curiosity [25]. The original scale had satisfactory results: high internal consistency as well as positive correlations with scales measuring life satisfaction and happiness, and negative correlations with scales measuring ruminations and anxieties. We used a Polish translation of the test with 13 questions grouped into two subscales with responses formed in a Likert scale from 1 („I definitely disagree with this statement") to 5 („I definitely agree with this statement"), as in the original version. We decided to use the TMS as we needed a measure to understand the potential differences between relaxation and mindfulness. The TMS is a commonly used questionnaire [35] that has been used in a pilot study and translated into Polish by one of the authors in collaboration with the Department for Social Sciences at the Pontifical University of John Paul II, , and trialed on a sample of 300 participants via an online research questionnaire using confirmatory factor analysis consisting of two subscales. In the current research, the internal reliability was checked using Cronbach's Alpha ($\alpha = 0.75$) which is a satisfactory level.

Positive Orientation Scale (POS; meditation-VR group, mean = 3.59, SD = 0.64, relaxation-VR group, mean = 3.63, SD = 0.54, meditation-no VR group, mean = 3.59, SD = 0.81, and relaxation-no VR group, mean = 3.59, SD = 0.66). The scale has been translated into Polish and proved to have significant internal validity and was well correlated with similar measures within the Polish population [29]. We used it to compare the results of the effects of meditation and relaxation on the TMS with the general tendency to stay positive-oriented. POS in a shorter 8-item version is a construct measuring self-esteem, life satisfaction and optimism within one factor. Our hypothesis was that those who score higher on the TMS would have a general tendency to see the world in a more positive manner as mindfulness meditation is shown to support positive reappraisal [1] [12]. The current research showed satisfactory internal reliability of the scale (Cronbach's α = 0.91).

Depression Anxiety Stress Scale (DASS; meditation-VR group, mean = 1.62, SD = 0.34, relaxation-VR group, mean = 1.81, SD = 0.35, meditation-no VR group, mean = 1.83, SD = 0.56, and relaxation-no VR group, mean = 1.70, SD = 0.31). The scale was prepared to detect the level of depression as a state and anxiety in a patient [32]. Polish translation has been commonly used for example to assess the emotional states of women with pregnancy pathologies [26]. Our hypothesis is that participants scoring higher in mindfulness meditation as a state should have a general tendency towards lower results in the DASS. The scale consists of 21 questions with three subscales: anxiety, depression and stress; answers indicating how often participants feel in a certain way from „never" to „almost always"; it has been shown to have a high level of internal reliability (Cronbach's $\alpha = 0.91$)

Satisfaction With Life Scale (SWLS; meditation-VR group, mean = 4.28, SD = 1.60, relaxation-VR group, mean = 4.03, SD = 1.28, meditation-no VR group, mean = 3.69, SD = 1.31, and relaxation-no VR group, mean = 4.13, SD = 1.07).The scale has been developed to measure self-evaluation of general life satisfaction and to continue the wide research on subjective well-being [33], translated to Polish in 2015 by Jankowski [20]. It is a 5-item scale using a 7-point response, from strongly disagree to strongly agree. In our research, the hypothesis was that the scale should correlate positively with TMS. The level of internal reliability is high (Cronbach's $\alpha = 0.9$).

Identity With All Humanity Scale (IWAH; meditation-VR group, mean = 3.10, SD = 0.69, relaxation-VR group, mean = 2.99, SD = 0.82, meditation-no VR group, mean = 3.23, SD = 0.83, and relaxation-no VR group, mean = 3.03, SD = 0.79). This scale was developed by McFarland, Webb, and Brown [40] to measure humanitarian concerns. It consists of 9-items asking participants about their identification with all humanity as a whole (e.g. „How close do you feel to people all over the world?"). The measure is linked to people's interest in international humanitarian actions. It was translated into Polish for the purpose of the study, with satisfactory internal reliability (Cronbach's α = .87). As the case study presents, long-term meditation practices can lead to body boundary dissolution and subsequently loss of the egocentric perspective [2], hence we assumed even a short meditation may lead to the loss of social identity while enforcing the sense of identity with all humanity. The hypothesis is that meditators should have higher results in the IWAH scale than the relaxation group.

Interpersonal Reactivity Index (IRI; meditation-VR group, mean = 3.23, SD = 0.40, relaxation-VR group, mean = 3.25, SD = 0.55, meditation-no VR group, mean = 3.32, SD = 0.42, and relaxation-no VR group, mean = 3.40, SD = 0.40). The commonly used questionnaire of 28 items (responses on a scale from 1 „[this sentence] does not describe me at all" to 5 „[this sentence] describes me very well") was developed to measure empathy on four subscales: FS – Fantasy Scale; EC – Empathic Concern; PT – Perspective Taking; PD – Personal Distress (Davies, 1980) [8][9]. A Polish translation has been used for the research on empathy with satisfactory results of internal reliability [21]. We decided to use the same test as it is a well-studied tool that takes into consideration emotional (PD and EC) and cognitive aspects of empathy (FS, PT). The mutual influence of empathy and mindful meditation is also widely studied in neuroscience [23] proving that there are some significant outcomes of intense contemplative training of compassion or empathy on subjective rating of the negative effects while watching a number of highly stressful movies. Hence, the hypothesis is that those who meditated would score higher on IRI, especially in PD and EC as these two are mostly related to meditation training, than the participants who relaxed their muscles only. The measure had a satisfactory level of internal reliability (Cronbach's α = 0.82, with the 21st item excluded as it had a negative correlation with the total scale; with 95% confidence intervals).

TABLE II. SAMPLE CHARACTERISTICS AND CHI-SQUARE ANALYSIS FOR METRIC DATA SUCH AS GENDER, EXPERIENCE WITH VR AND EXPERIENCE WITH MINDFULNESS MEDITATION IN RELATION TO MINDFULNESS VS. RELAXATION CONDITIONS.

		Total, *N* = 80	M*	R**	χ^2	*Df*	*p*
Gender	Female	58	55	63	0.21	1	0.65
	Male	42	45	37			
VR experience	None	54	58	40	4.33	3	0.23
	Some	46	42	40			
Frequency of meditation practice	None	26	25	27	0.00	1	1
	Some	74	75	73			

* Mindfulness condition, *n* = 40.
** Relaxation condition, *n* = 40.

TABLE III. SAMPLE CHARACTERISTICS AND CHI-SQUARE ANALYSIS FOR METRIC DATA SUCH AS GENDER, EXPERIENCE WITH VR AND EXPERIENCE WITH MINDFULNESS MEDITATION IN RELATION TO VR VS. NO VR.

		Total, *N* = 80	VR, *N* = 40	No VR, *N* = 40	χ^2	*df*	p
Gender	Female	59	50	67	1.86	1	0.17
	Male	41	50	33			
VR experience	None	54	52	55	0.00	1	1
	Some	46	48	45			
Frequency of meditation practice	None	26	17	35			
	Some	74	83	65	2.32	1	0.13

An even number of 80 participants enrolled in the study. The average age was 36.2, ranging from 25 to 61, with 33 males and 47 females. Participants were employees of the National Information Processing Institute and all of them were Polish. The study was advertised as an opportunity to explore virtual technology in the workplace. Participants were questioned about their experience of VR as well as their experience of meditation, including different kinds of meditation, and their age. 27 of them had no experience of any kind of meditation. The frequency of those who meditated also differed: 6 of them meditated daily while 15 meditated at least once a week with one person meditating 120 minutes daily. The rest of them rarely meditated or meditated only a few times a month. The VR experience divided the participants into four subgroups: those with no experience (55%), those who had used VR once (25%), those who had used it but rarely (16.25%) and those who used it often (3.75%).

In order to validate adequate randomization of our participants, we used Chi Square tests. We found that there were no significant interactions for either mindfulness vs. relaxation conditions, or VR vs. no VR conditions. The details can be found in Table II and Table III.

V. RESULTS

Our study was conducted to examine the three main hypotheses. The first one was that VR would enhance the effects of both (mindfulness and relaxation) training sessions, and this would be expressed through the feelings of general happiness and openness to personal experiences under VR vs. no VR conditions, especially under mindfulness conditions. Using two-way ANOVA analysis, we found no proof for the hypothesis. There was no significant effect of VR conditions on the dependent variables: for the TMS ($F(1,76) = 1.09$, $p = 0.30$), the POS

($F(1,76) = 0.01$, $p = 0.92$), the DASS ($F(1,76) = 0.30$, $p = 0.59$) and the SWLS ($F(1,76) = 0.68$, $p = 0.41$). The interaction effect of independent variables is not significantly related to the results on TMS ($F(1,76) = 1.02$, $p = 0.32$) either.

TABLE IV. RESULTS OF A TWO-WAY ANOVA ANALYSIS WITH TORONTO MINDFULNESS SCALE SCORES

Source	df	F ratio	P value
Mindfulness vs Relaxation	1	1.02	0.31
VR vs No VR	1	1.09	0.3
Interaction effect.	1	1.02	0.32

To check the effect of VR on subjective well-being we ran a two-way MANOVA and added the mood-related scales (the SOP, DASS and SWLS measures to the calculations): the main effect for the independent variables was not significant, $V = 0.02$, $F(3,76) = 2.17$, $p = 0.10$. Figure 4 presents the boxplots for TMS as a dependent variable and the two conditions, where the hypothesized tendency (the highest scores for meditation with VR group) is supported, however not significantly. The main effects for the TMS with the interaction effect on the 2x2 ANOVA are visible in Table IV.

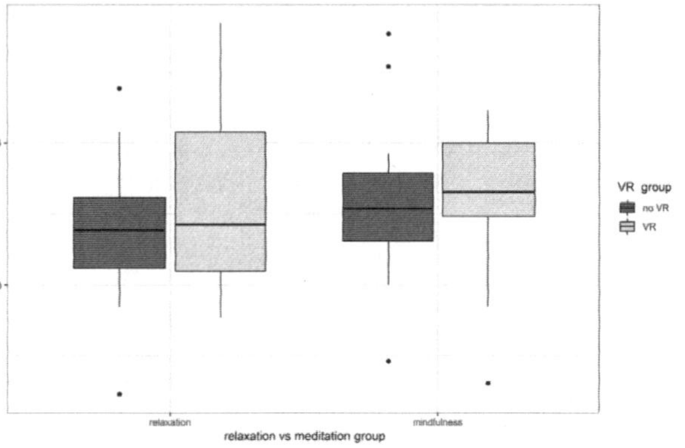

Figure 4. Boxplots for 2 x 2 experiment design.

TABLE V. MATRIX OF PEARSON'S CORRELATIONS FOR DEPENDENT VARIABLES.

	TMS	POS	DASS	SWLS	IRI	IWAH
TMS	1	.40**	.30**	-.05	.33**	.07
POS	.40**	1	-.26*	.62**	.23*	.38**
DASS	.30**	-.26*	1	-.44**	.25*	-.22*
SWLS	-.05	.62**	-.44**	1	.06	.24*
IRI	.33**	.23*	.25*	.06	1	.35**
IWAH	.07	.38**	-.22*	.24*	.35**	1

**. Correlation is significant at the 0.01 level.
*. Correlation is significant at the 0.05 level.

In order to check the external validity of the TMS as well as to further explore the possible explanations of the results, we measured the correlations between the dependent variables: TMS, POS, DASS, SWLS, IRI and IWAH. We found some correlations to be significant. The correlation matrix is displayed in Table V.

VI. DISCUSSION

A) *Main hypotheses*

The goal of the study was to check the potential influence and utility of Virtual Reality in contemplative training and to compare the effects of mindfulness training and relaxation training.

We hypothesized that VR conditions would enforce the results of mindfulness through immersion since Virtual Reality has been shown to support immersion in the digital world. This might help to create a safe but reliable experimental environment [7]. We found no proof for the hypothesis, undermining the potential of VR to achieve alternative states of mind. The results of ANOVA under VR conditions were not significant either as a main effect or as an interaction effect between both mindfulness and VR conditions. MANOVA analyses revealed a similar lack of significant results taking into consideration several dependent variables: TMS, POS, SWLS and DASS.

It was hypothesized that both meditation training sessions (with or without VR) would enhance the subjective well-being of participants more than the relaxation training. We assumed that mindfulness training would boost subjective well-being as well as decentration and curiosity of one's emotions more than relaxation. This would be observable via higher scores on the Mindfulness Toronto Scale (measuring curiosity and decentering), the Positive Orientation Scale (measuring general positive attitude to life), the Satisfaction With Life Scale and lower the results of the Depression Anxiety Stress Scale. The assumption is based on the research on mindfulness training: decentering is known to be a central characteristic of mindfulness but not of relaxation [11]. Mindfulness, on the other hand, is related to positive reappraisal and stress-coping processes along with other mindfulness-typical processes, e.g., attentional broadening [13]. However, there were no conclusive results to indicate that the mindfulness meditation group scored significantly higher than the relaxation group: the two-way ANOVA analysis revealed no significant main effects of mindfulness training vs. relaxation training. Also, MANOVA analyses, taking into consideration more than one dependent variable, showed no more statistically significant effects under mindfulness/relaxation conditions.

We also hypothesized that this mindfulness-related increase in general happiness and curiosity along with decentration would have an impact on social skills, such as empathy or group identity. This would be expressed in higher results of the Interpersonal Reactivity Index as well as of the Identity With All Humanity scale, as mindfulness has been proved to enhance social processing on various levels, e.g.. implicit bias [28]. However, we failed to prove this hypothesis. Our results showed no influence of either mindfulness meditation conditions, or of the interaction of both conditions on the two dependent variables related to social processing. In all of our calculations, we rejected a possible interference of demographic data proving well-randomized groups.

B) Possible explanations – mindfulness training

Since the results of experimental manipulation were not significant on any of the dependent variables, we may think of methodological errors that appeared in the study and should be taken into consideration in following studies. One of the possible objections against the study design was the briefness of the mindfulness training. Some researchers in contemplative studies argue that mindfulness is a complex and yet mostly unknown state [16]. We could conclude that a short intervention may not be sufficient to tackle such a complex alternative state of mind. On the other hand, one can argue that even shorter training sessions have already been successfully applied to meditation training with some significant outcomes [27], especially since TMS as a tool has been designed in such a way that it would capture the instant mental processes related to mindfulness (e.g., "I was curious to see what my mind was up to from moment to moment"). Moreover, the length of the training was exactly the same as the length of the training used in the TMS validation [25].

C) Possible explanations - self-reported measures

There is a growing body of evidence which suggests behavioral measurements give a better evaluation of the effects of mindfulness training than self-reported measures [16][17]. This strong objection is based on several issues, e.g., not having a clear definition of what mindfulness really is; self-reported measures not being able to tackle the profound correlations of mindfulness as well as not being able to capture the exact meaning of certain understandings of Buddhist teachings. However, in our research we have not only failed to prove TMS to be influenced by the experimental conditions but also other dependent variables seemed to be inexplicable by the experiment itself. In order to ensure that the lack of main effects or interactions is not related to gender, experience with VR or experience with meditation, we ran Chi-Square analysis that proved the factors were equally distributed over the groups. We decided to compare the dependent variables using Pearson's correlations in order to explore the lack of significant results. Surprisingly, there was a significant positive relation of TMS to the positive mood scale (POS) and the depression and anxiety-related scale (DASS). There was also a significant, positive correlation with the IRI but not with the IWAH scale, even though there was a significant, positive correlation between the last two variables. It is important to note, however, that there was only one average significant correlation (POS and SWLS; measures related to positive mood and life-satisfaction), with the rest of the correlations being weak or insignificant. These results may support our conclusion that maybe the self-related measures are not strong enough to efficiently measure the effects of such a complex process as mindfulness.

D) Possible explanations – VR design

An interesting aspect of the measurement that has not been reported is the spontaneous reaction of participants when exploring the VR meditation island. While conducting the study, we observed that participants paid particular attention to those details of VR that did not exactly match reality. Looking at the general research where VR is proposed to be a meditation-friendly environment, some of the virtual worlds had some similar features, e.g., a lake, trees, forest sounds (e.g., [31]) and they seemed to imitate a natural background. However, there were exceptions, e.g., [24], where the same objects (a tree, a lake, a piece of land, sunny weather) were constructed in the simplest way possible, instead of trying to imitate nature. We hypothesize that in such a way, participants acknowledge the differences between VR and the real world, yet they do not focus on the detailed differences between these two worlds, since they are trivial. Hence, for the next study, we suggest an environment that would symbolically resemble the natural environment rather than try to imitate it. We suggest this way may facilitate immersion through familiarizing participants to an imperfect world and letting them focus on the purpose of the study, rather than encouraging them to seek the hidden imperfections of a virtual world. On the other hand, we conceptualize that maybe even a predictable but very abstract environment could cause the same immersion without absorption by the imperfections of the world. In such a way, the virtual world would be obviously unrelated to the natural landscapes, but would still remain predictable, hence it could be a secure place to meditate in.

Analyzing the effects of mindfulness, self-transcendence is an often-omitted construct. Following the potential importance of transcendence in mindful meditation, it is crucial for future research using VR to take it into consideration. The authors of the *Mindfulness-To-Meaning Theory* [12] argue that self-transcendence is a natural effect of mindfulness meditation as it brings pleasurable emotions such as gratitude or compassion. It also lifts meditators to the next steps of meditation, the feeling of oneness, selflessness, and finally to the non-dual sense of subject-object relations. We hypothesize that maybe certain landscapes can facilitate the feeling of self-transcendence through a wide clear view, and hence the role of VR in self-transcendence should be carefully taken into consideration in future studies.

Finally, it should also be mentioned that maybe VR is not an effective or sufficient tool to enhance mindfulness experiences. We hypothesize that it could be a beneficial tool in promoting relaxation (i.e., through immersion) but not sufficient to enhance more complex mental states related to mindfulness such as decentration or non-judgmental observation of one's thoughts and emotions. Even the feeling of transcendence can be blurred by the virtual experience bringing a state of excitement or curiosity of the outside world rather than helping to understand the internal states leading to alternative states of awareness.

E) Generalization and study limitations

The study is not free from some limitations typical to the field of mindfulness, e.g., the effectiveness of a brief mindfulness training session remains questionable. On the other hand, we managed to develop a study of interest to VR enthusiasts and not only meditation enthusiasts – which is a common sampling problem since meditation may seem attractive to a very distinct group of people. Yet, another challenge stems from the fact that all the participants were Polish and the cultural upbringing might have influenced the results. Taking into consideration that mindfulness is relatively new in Poland (Polish Mindfulness Society was inspired by Jon-Kabat Zinn and developed in 2008; [19]), it is certainly important to compare the results controlling for cultural influences. Last but not least, individual differences could have affected the results of the study. We suggest adding some questionnaires related to openness to experience and neuroticism to the study in the future. Due to limited external validity as well as to a specific sample quality, we cannot generalize the results for a wider population.

VII. CONCLUSIONS

To sum up, our study failed to prove the main hypothesis - that even short mindfulness meditation can enhance subjective well-being along with decentration and curiosity to one's internal states, and in effect, it can also influence social skills such as empathy. Another hypothesis, that Virtual Reality would boost the effect of mindfulness, also failed. We found a few possible methodological explanations, i.e., that the mindfulness/relaxation training period could have been too short and brief. However, as some previous studies proved, even a short mindfulness intervention can be effective in the aforementioned states. We hypothesized that the virtual environment should be distinctively different from the real environment so participants can focus on their tasks, instead of directing attention to the imperfections of the virtual world. Following the comments of contemplative science, we also discussed the drawbacks of self-reported measures in studying such a profound state as mindfulness. Certainly, before we finally establish the role of mindfulness in human life, and the effect of Virtual Reality on it, some further evidence needs to be collected.

REFERENCES

[1] A. Alkoby, E. Halperin, R. Tarrasch, and N. Levit-Binnun, "Increased Support for Political Compromise in the Israeli-Palestinian Conflict Following an 8-Week Mindfulness Workshop", Mindfulness, vol. 8, no. 5, pp. 1345–1353, 2017.

[2] Y. Ataria, Y. Dor-Ziderman and A. Berkovich-Ohana, "How does it feel to lack a sense of boundaries? A case study of a long-term mindfulness meditator", Elsevier Enhanced Reader. Retrieved July 15, 2019 from https://www.sciencedirect.com/science/article/pii/S1053810015300295/pdfft?isDTMRedir=true&download=true.

[3] J. M. Baas, M. Nugent, S. Lissek, D. S. Pine and C. Grillon, "Fear conditioning in virtual reality contexts: a new tool for the study of anxiety", Biological psychiatry, vol. 55, no. 11, pp. 1056–1060, 2004.

[4] K. Birnie, M. Speca and L. E. Carlson, "Exploring self-compassion and empathy in the context of mindfulness-based stress reduction (MBSR)", Stress and health: journal of the International Society for the Investigation of Stress, vol. 26, no. 5, pp. 359–371, 2010.

[5] S. Bouchard, S. Côté, J. St-Jacques, G. Robillard and P. Renaud, "Effectiveness of virtual reality exposure in the treatment of arachnophobia using 3D games", Technology and health care: official journal of the European Society for Engineering and Medicine, vol. 14, no. 1, pp. 19–27, 2006.

[6] R. Chambers, E. Gullone and N. B. Allen, "Mindful emotion regulation: An integrative review", Clinical psychology review, vol. 29, no. 6, pp. 560–572, 2009.

[7] C. Crescentini, L. Chittaro, V. Capurso, R. Sioni and F. Fabbro, "Psychological and physiological responses to stressful situations in immersive virtual reality: Differences between users who practice mindfulness meditation and controls", Computers in human behavior, vol. 59, pp. 304–316, 2016.

[8] M. H. Davis, "A multidimensional approach to individual differences in empathy", JSAS Catalog of Selected Documents in Psychology, vol. 10, p. 85, 1980.

[9] M. H. Davis, Empatia. O umiejętności współodczuwania. Gdańsk: Gdańskie Wydawnictwo Psychologiczne, 1999.

[10] J. Difede et al., "Virtual reality exposure therapy for the treatment of posttraumatic stress disorder following September 11, 2001", The Journal of clinical psychiatry, vol. 68, no. 11, pp. 1639–1647, 2007.

[11] G. Feldman, J. Greeson and J. Senville, "Differential effects of mindful breathing, progressive muscle relaxation, and loving-kindness meditation on decentering and negative reactions to repetitive thoughts", Behaviour research and therapy, vol. 48, no. 10, pp. 1002–1011, 2010.

[12] E. L. Garland and B. L. Fredrickson, "Positive psychological states in the arc from mindfulness to self-transcendence: extensions of the Mindfulness-to-Meaning Theory and applications to addiction and chronic pain treatment", Current opinion in psychology vol. 28, pp. 184–191, 2019.

[13] E. Garland, S. Gaylord and J. Park, "The role of mindfulness in positive reappraisal", Explore, vol. 5, no. 1, pp. 37–44, 2009.

[14] P. R. Goldin and James J. Gross, "Effects of mindfulness-based stress reduction (MBSR) on emotion regulation in social anxiety disorder", Emotion, vol. 10, no. 1, pp. 83–91, 2010.

[15] D. Gromala, X. Tong, A. Choo, M. Karamnejad and C. D. Shaw, "The Virtual Meditative Walk: Virtual Reality Therapy for Chronic Pain Management", Proceedings of the 33rd Annual ACM Conference on Human Factors in Computing Systems, ACM, pp. 521–524, 2015.

[16] P. Grossman, "On measuring mindfulness in psychosomatic and psychological research", J Psychosom Res, vol. 64, no. 4, pp. 405-408, 2008.

[17] Y. Hadash and A. Bernstein, "Behavioral Assessment of Mindfulness: Defining Features, Organizing Framework, and Review of Emerging Methods", MindRxiv. Retrieved 15 September from http://dx.doi.org/10.31231/osf.io/z237a, 2018.

[18] H. G. Hoffman, D. R. Patterson, G. J. Carrougher and S. R. Sharar, "Effectiveness of Virtual Reality–Based Pain Control With Multiple Treatments", The Clinical Journal of Pain, vol. 17, pp. 229–235. Retrieved 10 October from http://dx.doi.org/10.1097/00002508-200109000-00007, 2001.

[19] P. Holas, *"Historia PTM"*, Polskie Towarzystwo Mindfulness, 2017. Accessed on: Jan 24, 2020. [Online]. Available: http://mindfulness.com.pl/o-nas/

[20] K. S. Jankowski, "Is the shift in chronotype associated with an alteration in well-being?", Biological Rhythm Research, vol. 46, pp. 237-248, 2015.

[21] A. Jerzmanowska, "Empatia oraz decentracja interpersonalna a radykalność postaw społecznych", Psychologia Społeczna, vol. 8, no. 1, pp. 67-79, 2013.

[22] J. Kabat-Zinn, Full catastrophe living: Using the wisdom of your body and mind to face stress, pain and illness, New York: Dell Publishing, 1990.

[23] O. M. Klimecki, S. Leiberg, M. Ricard and T. Singer, "Differential pattern of functional brain plasticity after compassion and empathy training", Social cognitive and affective neuroscience, vol. 9, no. 6, pp. 873–879, 2014.

[24] I. Kosunen, M. Salminen, S. Jarvela, A. Ruonala, N. Ravaja, and G. Jacucci, "RelaWorld: Neuroadaptive and Immersive Virtual Reality Meditation System", IUI for Entertainment and Health, Sonoma, CA, USA, March 7-10, 2016.

[25] M. A. Lau et al., "The Toronto Mindfulness Scale: development and validation", Journal of clinical psychology, vol. 62, no. 12, pp. 1445–1467, 2006.

[26] M. Lewicka, A. Wdowiak, M. Sulima, M. Wójcik and M. Makara-Studzińska, „Ocena nasilenia negatywnych emocji przy użyciu Skali DASS w grupie ciężarnych hospitalizowanych w oddziale patologii ciąży", Problemy Higieny i Epidemiologii, vol. 94, no. 3, pp. 459-464, 2013.

[27] A. Lueke and B. Gibson, "Mindfulness Meditation Reduces Implicit Age and Race Bias: The Role of Reduced Automaticity of Responding", Social psychological and personality science, vol. 6, no. 3, pp. 284–291, 2015.

[28] A. Lueke and B. Gibson, "Brief mindfulness meditation reduces discrimination", Psychology of Consciousness: Theory, Research, and Practice, vol. 3, no. 1, pp. 34–44, 2016.

[29] M. Łaguna, P. Oleś and D. Filipiuk, „Orientacja Pozytywna i jej pomiar: Polska Adaptacja Skali Orientacji Pozytywnej", Studia Psychologiczne, vol. 52, no. 1, pp. 77–90, 2011.

[30] S. McFarland, M. Webb and D. Brown, "All humanity is my ingroup: a measure and studies of identification with all humanity", Journal of personality and social psychology, vol. 103, no. 5, pp. 830–853, 2012.

[31] M. V. Navarro-Haro et al., "Meditation experts try Virtual Reality Mindfulness: A pilot study evaluation of the feasibility and acceptability of Virtual Reality to facilitate mindfulness practice in people attending a Mindfulness conference". PloS one, vol. 12, no. 11, e0187777, 2017.

[32] K. Nieuwenhuijsen, A. G. E. M. de Boer, J. H. A. M. Verbeek, R. W. B. Blonk, and F. J. H. van Dijk, "The Depression Anxiety Stress Scales (DASS): detecting anxiety disorder and depression in employees absent from work because of mental health problems", Occupational and environmental medicine, vol. 60, suppl. 1, pp. i77–82, 2003.

[33] W. Pavot and E. Diener, "Review of the Satisfaction With Life Scale", E. Diener, ed., Assessing Well-Being: The Collected Works of Ed Diener. Springer Netherlands, Dordrecht, pp. 101–117, 2009.

[34] M. B. Powers and P. M. G. Emmelkamp, "Virtual reality exposure therapy for anxiety disorders: A meta-analysis", Journal of anxiety disorders, vol. 22, no. 3, pp. 561–569, 2008.

[35] B. L. Thompson and J. Waltz, "Everyday mindfulness and mindfulness meditation: Overlapping constructs or not?", Personality and individual differences, vol. 43, no. 7, pp. 1875–1885, 2007.

[36] M. M. Tincher, L. A. M. Lebois, and L.E.W. Barsalou, "Mindful attention reduces linguistic intergroup bias", Mindfulness, vol. 7, no. 2, pp. 349–360, 2016.

A Study on Virtual Reality Work-Space to Improve Work Efficiency

Tianshu Xu
School of Knowledge Science, Japan Advanced Institute of Science and Technology
Nomi City, Japan
Email: xutianshu@jaist.ac.jp

Shinobu Hasegawa
Research Center for Advanced Computing Infrastructure, Japan Advanced Institute of Science and Technology
Nomi City, Japan
Email: hasegawa@jaist.ac.jp

Abstract—**Many people feel a lack of efficiency while working in an Open-Plan Work-Space because of ambient noise and low privacy. Although recent research has analyzed the application of virtual reality technology for the improvement of work efficiency, as far as we know, there are no studies focused on analyzing how to design a virtual reality environment that can maintain or improve work efficiency. This article proposes a Virtual Reality Work-Space solution to focus on work efficiency. The preliminary experiment of this research compared the proposed Virtual Reality Work-Space with the Open-Plan Work-Space and showed that the proposed workspace helped participants gain better work efficiency.**

Keywords - virtual reality; workspace; work efficiency.

I. INTRODUCTION

Open-Plan Work-Space (OPWS) is an office style that allows many employees to work simultaneously in a wall-less, partition-less environment. OPWS is characterized by a high sense of openness, low cost, encouraging cooperation, and improving the collective wisdom of the team. More and more companies have chosen this kind of office since its birth in the last century. Although OPWS has already proven its value, there still exist many shortcomings. For example, studies have shown that OPWS often produces adverse effects, such as noise, stress, conflict, high blood pressure, and high turnover rate, etc., among others [1][2]. The noise has the most apparent impact on work efficiency. Compared to quiet rooms, noise interference in OPWS reduces work efficiency by one third [3]. Not only is the OPWS full of auditory and visual interference, but also the low level of privacy protection causes psychological stress to employees and reduces work efficiency. Although many researchers have been working to solve these problems, they still cannot declare that these problems are entirely solved. The obvious point is that most of the proposals suggest creating an additional workspace that needs extra cost. For example, the proposal of providing employees with various additional spaces to alleviate the problem [4] will be very difficult in some countries with demanding space utilization requirements, such as Japan, and some companies are often unable to find enough space.

On the other hand, in response to the work efficiency reduction problem caused by auditory and visual interference in the environment, Microsoft has proposed a Virtual Reality Work-Space (VRWS) that supports typing. People can use this VRWS in the original OPWS without adding additional space costs [5]. Meanwhile, VRWS is a virtual personal space independent of OPWS, so it can also solve the psychological pressure caused by the lack of privacy protection of employees in the public environment. So, this research assumes that this technology has great potential to solve the problems in OPWS. However, no studies are showing how VRWS can be designed to maintain or improve work efficiency. On the other hand, there are some opinions that virtual reality technology cannot benefit the work itself [6].

Some VRWSs have already been used to support people's office work. Among them, the VRchat [7] and Oculus Virtual Desktop [8] are the leading examples of VRWS. VRchat is a virtual reality-based social platform with more than 2 million users. It allows users to interact with others as 3D character models. Oculus Virtual Desktop also has a huge user group, which is offering excellent image quality and some useful extra features to help users with their work. In this VRWS, only a virtual desktop is shown to them, as shown on the right side of Figure 1.

Figure 1. The scene of VRchat office and Oculus Virtual Desktop.

VRchat allows for custom VR environments, but there are no studies to show how VRWS can be designed to maintain or improve work efficiency. Thus, the design of the VR environment relies entirely on personal customization. Oculus Virtual Desktop even ignores VR environment design and shows the dim universe to the user. It is hard to believe that work efficiency would benefit from these kinds of VR environments. We believe that the VR environment can be a solution to improve or maintain work efficiency. It is different from existing ones, and the VRWS which we have suggested has a good environment that can improve work efficiency.

This research focuses on proving that VRWS can deal with work efficiency, and, at the same time, identifying the factors which, in virtual reality, affect work efficiency. In this article, the research consists of the following questions:

- What kind of VRWS may handle work efficiency?
- How to find the factors that affect work efficiency in VRWS?

The rest of this article is organized as follows. Section II describes the related work. Section III introduces the experimental design, result, and analysis in detail. The conclusion and future work are presented in Section IV.

II. RELATED WORK

In order to clarify the position of this research, this section introduces related work on previous OPWS and VRWS for targeted working spaces, and Semantic Differential as an evaluation method.

A. *OPWS and VRWS*

The environment of OPWS not only directly affects people's health and enthusiasm for work, but also affects work efficiency [1]-[3]. A pleasant office environment should be a cozy space that has no visual and auditory interference, good lighting, a controlled sound environment, and plenty of natural light [9]-[12].

According to our investigation, there is currently no research to confirm what VRWS design standards can maintain or improve work efficiency. Although there have been a couple of research works proposing solutions to improve the shortcomings of OPWS, it is not sure whether the solutions for OPWS can be applied to VRWS. The research tends to create a VRWS with excellent OPWS characteristics to maintain or improve work efficiency.

B. *Semantic Differential*

Semantic Differential (SD) was proposed by Osgood in 1957 as a method of psychological measurement [13]. The analytical method of the SD is to use "language" in semantics as the scale for experiments, and quantitatively describe the concept and structure of the research object through the analysis of various established scales.

The SD method for workspace can be summarized as follows: study the psychological response of participants in the space to various environmental characteristics of the target space, develop a "semantic" scale for these psychological responses, and then, evaluated and analyze all the description parameters of the scale to quantitatively describe the concept and structure of the space target.

Therefore, we adopt SD analysis to compare the quantification of different emotions obtained from the participants in both OPWS and VRWS. We obtain the difference between the two office environments on participants and we find the factors that impact work efficiency that exist only in VRWS.

III. EXPERIMENTAL DESIGN AND DISCUSSION

The purpose of this experiment is to compare the respective effects of OPWS with VRWS and explore whether VRWS can deal with users' work efficiency.

A. *Experimental Design of OPWS*

OPWS is very popular all over the world, and different types of work content will also produce OPWS with different characteristics. For example, the call center is a typical noisy OPWS because answering a call is an essential task in the call center. In this environment, working noise is unavoidable. There are also different types of OPWS. For example, librarians rarely worry about noise.

It was difficult to find a typical noisy OPWS in the area where the authors live. In order to control the experimental settings, we decided to use the Cave Automatic Virtual Environment (CAVE) system to simulate a typical noisy OPWS. The CAVE system is a projection-based virtual reality system, which consists of several projection screens surrounding the participants and it can produce a completely immersive virtual environment. At the same time, mini-speakers were arranged around the CAVE system to restore the simulated OPWS sound environment as much as possible. Therefore, the CAVE system used in this experiment can make the participants feel the real situation of a noisy OPWS very well.

The experimental arrangement of this study based on the CAVE system is shown in Figure 2. Five participants in the group performed experiments together in the CAVE system. There were five seats in the CAVE system, and a laptop and a mouse were placed in each seat to allow the participants to take the CAB test.

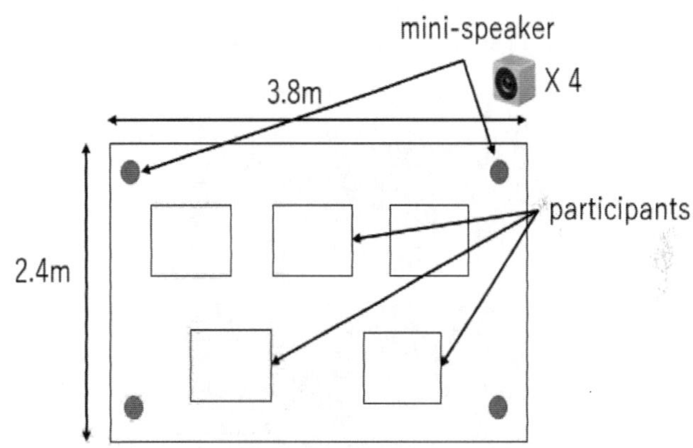

Figure 2. Experimental arrangements in the CAVE system.

For the content played in the CAVE system, the simulated OPWS chosen for this experiment was the mission center of National Aeronautics and Space Administration (NASA) [18]. One of the frequent activities in this content was to exchange information among employees. Figure 3 shows the scene in the OPWS condition.

Figure 3. The scene of the experiment in the CAVE system.

B. Experimental Design of VRWS

We assumed a VRWS with excellent OPWS characteristics, which was an environment without visual and auditory interference, good lighting, sufficient natural light, and privacy protection, with the expectation to maintain or improve work efficiency. In order to make VRWS met the above requirements, we did the following steps.

In order to avoid the visual and auditory interference from the environment, we decided to use a combination of Head Mounted Display (HMD) and noise-canceling earphones. The HMD could completely isolate the visual interference in the environment, and the muffler headphones could eliminate most of the auditory interference. Figure 4 shows the combination of HMD and noise-canceling earphones.

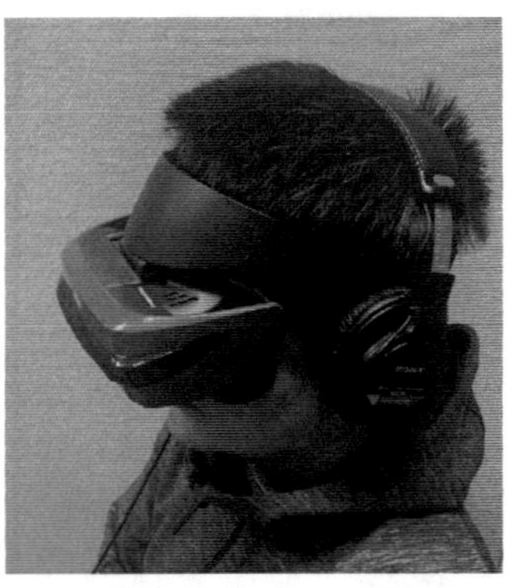

Figure 4. HMD and noise-canceling earphones.

In order to create a present lighting environment, in the initial design stage of the virtual model, we increased the brightness of the model and used natural light sources instead of ordinary light sources to make the light fill the entire virtual space.

For the requirement of enough natural light, we designed some large floor-to-ceiling windows to replace the walls on either side of the VRWS. For privacy protection, we designed VRWS as a personal workspace that could not be shared with others. In the VRWS experiment, an HMD with a computer and mouse was provided to the participants to complete the experiment. The HMD used in this experiment is Acer Windows Mixed Reality headset AH101. Each participant experimented alone in this setting. Through the above steps, we developed the VRWS, as shown in Figure 5.

Figure 5. The scene of the VRWS.

C. Comparative Experiments

A total of 20 people participated in the experiment, consisting of 9 females and 11 males, from 24 to 30 years old. The participants were fluent in English, but had no previous experience with VR systems and were recruited by an open call as a small part-time job for the experiment. The experiment invited the participants to share their opinions/feelings while working in specific environments rather than doing complicated problems. The complexity of the experiment might not affect the participants' motivation to join the experiment. In addition, the experiment was about 50 minutes for each participant, which was considered as a short experiment. The reward was 'thanks for their time', and that did not change their motivation much.

Before starting the experiment, we informed the participants about the experiment process, gathered data and got approval from them. Next, we assigned all participants randomly to groups A, B, C, and D. Each group consisted of five participants. Among them, groups A and C performed OPWS experiments before VRWS experiments. Groups B and D performed the experiments in the reverse order. The duration of each experiment was about 25 minutes and after the experiment, each participant was asked to fill a questionnaire. After the experiments, all the data and questionnaires were collected to compare OPWS and VRWS.

D. Cognitive Assessment Battery Test

In this experiment, each participant was required to complete his/her "work" in OPWS and VRWS. Therefore, we adopted the Cognitive Assessment Battery (CAB) test consisting of no language-based questions with only numbers and pictures. This test avoids deviation, such as caused by different understanding speeds and understanding difficulty in different languages.

The purpose of the CAB test was to measure people's logical thinking ability. Thus, in this "work" process, the participants were expected to concentrate on solving the test as an essential requirement. We assumed that there is a relationship between the CAB test results and work efficiency.

Every participant received an electronic test containing 45 questions for each experiment. The participants were requested to complete as many CAB tests as possible within 25 minutes. Participants could only answer the questions one by one. Each test question had four options. In order to rule out errors due to condition differences, the participants were requested not to use all tools except a mouse during the answering process in both settings. The questions were designed with reference to some related works [14][15]. Some examples of the CAB test questions are shown in Figure 6.

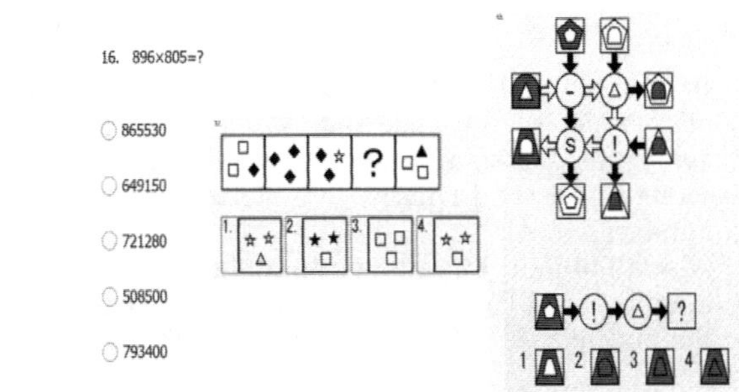

Mental arithmetic question. Logical reasoning question. Cipher question.

Figure 6. Examples of CAB test.

At the same time, these three kinds of test questions appeared in the same proportion in each set of test papers for each participant. The ratio of the test types is shown in Figure 7.

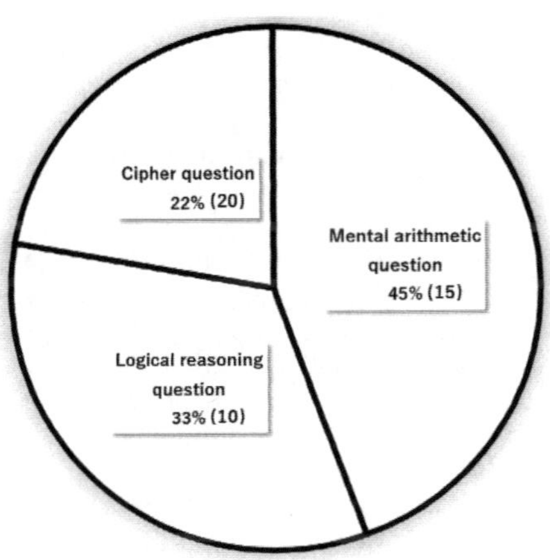

Figure 7. The ratio of the 3 types of questions in one CAB test.

E. Questionnaire

In order to use the SD method for evaluation, the expression phrases in the questionnaire were designed with reference to *Research on Emotional Engineering* [16] and *Versatility of Building Language Description* [17]. The set adjective pairs are shown in Table I. The reason for choosing these phrases is because they can express people's feelings where they are at the workspace.

The evaluation scale in this experiment was divided into seven levels. A small value was given for a negative evaluation, and a large value was given for a positive evaluation.

TABLE I. ADJECTIVE PAIRS FOR SD EVALUATION

1	*Broad view*	*Narrow view*
2	*Low psychological pressure*	*High psychological pressure*
3	*Free atmosphere*	*Non-free atmosphere*
4	*Comfortable*	*Uncomfortable*
5	*Well-lighted*	*Ill-lighted*
6	*Not tired*	*Getting tired*
7	*Natural feeling*	*Strange feeling*
8	*Grace*	*Graceless*
9	*Relaxing*	*Not-relaxing*
10	*Cheerful*	*Depressed*
11	*Easy to work*	*Hard to work*
12	*Not noisy in movement*	*Noisy in movement*
13	*Enjoyable*	*Not enjoyable*
14	*Not noisy in sound*	*Noisy in sound*
15	*Motivated*	*Unmotivated*
16	*Efficient*	*Inefficient*

F. Results

The more correct answers and the less time it took means the more efficiently the subjects worked. Similarly, the more correct answers per unit time one got, the more efficiently one worked. Thus, we calculated the difference between the number of correct results of the CAB test in each subject's OPWS and VRWS and the difference between the times taken in the two experiments.

For the questionnaire, the adjective pairs were compared with the average of the two groups' results. As shown in Figure 8, lower points are negative evaluations and higher points are positive evaluations.

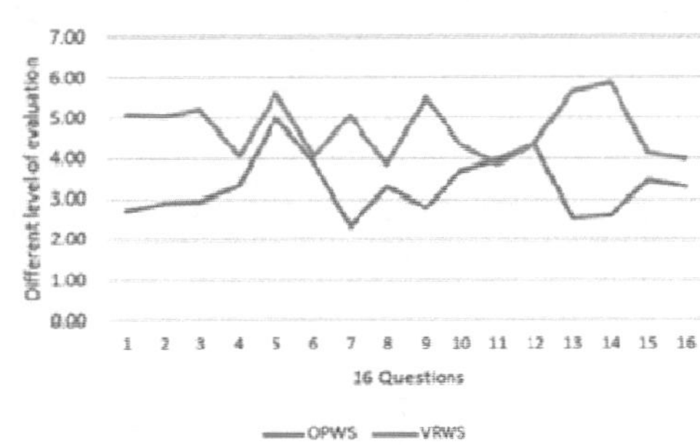

Figure 8. The average of the two groups' results.

In order to ensure the validity of this study, a student's t-test (t-test) was used to analyze the data further. In this study, SPSSAU [19] was used for data analysis.

Before performing the t-test, we needed to confirm the normality of the sample. Because the number of sample data from the CAB test and the questionnaire were all less than 50, the Shapiro-Wilk test was chosen. Through the Shapiro-Wilk test, although some sample data were considered to have no normality traits because their P-values were under 0.05, their absolute values of Kurtosis were all less than 10, and the absolute values of Skewness were all less than 3. So, even though some sample data were not the standard normal distribution, the data could basically be accepted as a normal distribution. Therefore, all the sample data can be considered to follow the normal distribution. So, we adopted the t-test to analyze the sample data. T-test results on the CAB test are shown in Table II, and t-test results on the questionnaire are shown in Table III.

TABLE II. T-TEST RESULTS ON CAB TEST

t-test				
Items	***Environment(average ± SD)***		***t***	***p***
	OPWS(N=20)	***VRWS(N=20)***		
Correct Answer	30.70 ± 3.85	32.25 ± 4.22	-1.214	0.232
Time Difference in Two Experiments	23.10 ± 2.61	21.60 ± 2.66	1.798	0.08

TABLE III. T-TEST RESULTS ON QUESTIONNAIRE

t-test				
Question Number	***Environment(average ± SD)***		***t***	***p***
	OPWS(N=20)	***VRWS(N=20)***		
Q1	5.30 ± 0.98	2.90 ± 1.25	6.753	0.000
Q2	5.10 ± 1.21	2.95 ± 1.00	6.13	0.000
Q3	5.05 ± 1.39	2.80 ± 1.20	5.476	0.00
Q4	4.65 ± 1.39	3.95 ± 0.89	1.901	0.066
Q5	3.00 ± 1.08	2.40 ± 0.94	1.878	0.068
Q6	4.10 ± 1.17	3.95 ± 1.10	0.419	0.678
Q7	5.70 ± 0.86	2.95 ± 1.15	8.568	0.000
Q8	4.70 ± 1.22	4.15 ± 1.14	1.476	0.148
Q9	5.20 ± 0.89	2.50 ± 1.15	8.301	0.000
Q10	4.30 ± 0.86	3.65 ± 1.23	1.938	0.06
Q11	4.00 ± 1.12	4.15 ± 1.35	-0.382	0.704
Q12	3.60 ± 1.64	3.60 ± 1.10	0	1
Q13	5.50 ± 1.10	2.35 ± 1.09	9.098	0.000
Q14	5.40 ± 1.39	2.10 ± 0.72	9.424	0.000
Q15	4.55 ± 1.43	3.85 ± 0.81	1.901	0.067
Q16	4.70 ± 1.42	4.00 ± 1.03	1.789	0.082

From Table II, we can see that the Correct Answer is non-significantly different ($0.1 < p$), and Time Difference is marginally significantly different ($0.05 < p < 0.1$).

From Table III, Q1, Q2, Q3, Q7, Q9, Q13, and Q14 are significantly different ($p < 0.01$). Q4, Q5, Q10, Q15, and Q16 are marginally significantly different ($0.05 < p < 0.1$). Also, Q6, Q8, Q11, and Q12 are non-significantly different ($0.1 < p$).

G. Findings

In this research, each experiment was conducted for about 25 minutes, so we guessed that the time was not long enough to make a significant differences in the number of Correct Answers and Difference in Time between the two experiments.

A small number of participants could not bear the noisy environment in OPWS. In order to leave as soon as possible, they completed the CAB test at the fastest speed possible while giving the correct answer as much as possible. Therefore, these participants believed that although they could not bear the unbearable interference in OPWS, from the perspective of the results, the work efficiency was improved.

From OPWS to VRWS, although it was more beneficial for participants to answer CAB tests, it was impossible to make difficult questions easier just because the environment become better, so the Correct Answers had no significant difference.

The results of Q14 shows an effect of sufficient separation of auditory interference by noise-canceling earphones. At the same time, we believe that the no auditory interference environment also has a positive effect on the results of many significant and marginally significant items.

The results of Q1, Q7, Q9, and Q13 indicate the floor-to-ceiling windows greatly improve the subject's vision. The virtual nature environment surrounding the VRWS gave the subjects a more natural feeling. Because of the floor-to-ceiling windows, it was easier for natural light to enter the room through the windows.

As shown in the results of Q2, Q3, and Q9, compared with the noisy environment of OPWS, the elegant and comfortable virtual environment design and private use features can play a role in preventing psychological pressure.

HMD must be worn when using VRWS. There might be a negative effect in the physical sense, but the impact was not significant from the results of Q4, Q10, Q15, and Q16. The CAVE system used in this experiment had good lighting effects, so the participants did not strongly feel the difference in lighting effects between the two experiments from the result of Q5.

There was no difference between Q15 and Q16 because wearing HMD could be an obstacle to face-to-face communication. When considering other network communication methods such as e-mail, HMD only caused communication failure in certain situations.

Most of the participants rejected the use of HMD for a long time. The main reasons were: the weight and volume of the HMD put an extra burden on long-term work, and virtual reality might cause vertigo. VRWS did not have sufficient input support and HMD cooling problems. These reasons have led to the results of Q6, Q8, and Q11.

The participants did not notice the visual interference problem in OPWS from the result of Q12. HMD is a display device wrapped around the eyes of the user, and the user could no longer feel the external visual interference, theoretically. Considering that the CAVE system was used to simulate OPWS in the comparative experiment, the busy scene in the noisy OPWS is displayed in 2D by several projection surfaces around the participants in the CAVE system, which might affect the psychological reality of visual interference. Thereby, they reduced the intensity of interference. Furthermore, the contrast effect between OPWS and VRWS in Q12 in the movement was not significant.

In previous VRWS work, it was not considered that VR environments could be a solution to improve work efficiency. However, this research and experiments showed that there is indeed a significant difference in some factors in the VR environment. The previous VRWS could not find these factors because of the simple VR environment. So, participants' work efficiency could not benefit from their VR environment. The research has also demonstrated those factors in the discussion section.

IV. Conclusion and Future Work

From the experiments, it is hard to confirm that VRWS could maintain or improve work efficiency. Aiming at work efficiency, the conclusions of OPWS related research maybe can be used as a design standard for VRWS. Through this research, we can know that VRWS has generally received higher evaluations and has more significant positive evaluations on Relaxing, Enjoyable, and Not noisy in sound. Using VRWS based on OPWS related research conclusions as design standard, compared to OPWS, people can get a wider virtual vision environment, can reduce the psychological pressure, feel a freer atmosphere, enjoy the office process more, and have a quieter office. Also, VRWS may be more comfortable, may have better lighting effects, help generate positive emotions, increase work enthusiasm, and increase work efficiency.

For future work, we first plan to improve the defects of the VRWS input. Because a person wearing the HMD cannot see the surrounding environment, it makes the use of the keyboard, paper, pen, and other tasks more difficult. Through the camera connected to the HMD, the keyboard, paper, and pen can be recognized and displayed in VRWS, which is convenient for users. This also means turning VRWS into Augmented Reality Work-Space (ARWS). In addition, for the virtual environment part of VRWS, we will consider the ability to customize it, which will further improve the practicality of VRWS and improve work efficiency.

References

[1] C. P. G. Roelofsen, "Performance loss in open-plan offices due to noise by speech", Journal of Facilities Management, vol. 6, no. 3, pp. 202-211, 2008.

[2] V. Oommen, M. Knowles, and I. Zhao, "Should health service managers embrace open plan work environments? A review," Asia Pacific Journal of Health Management, vol. 3, no. 2, pp. 37-43, 2008.

[3] J. Treasure, "The 4 ways sound affects us," The Speaker's Handbook, pp. 460, 2014.

[4] C. Candido, P. Chakraborty, and D. Tjondronegoro, "The Rise of Office Design in High-Performance, Open-Plan Environments," Buildings, vol. 9, issue. 4, pp. 100, 2019.

[5] J. Gruber et al., "Effects of Hand Representations for Typing in Virtual Reality," IEEE VR 2018 publication, pp. 151-158, 2018.

[6] https://www.theguardian.com/technology/2017/jan/05/i-tried-to-work-all-day-in-a-vr-headset-so-you-never-have-to, [retrieved: 03, 2020].

[7] https://store.steampowered.com/app/438100/VRChat/, [retrieved: 03, 2020].

[8] https://www.moguravr.com/virtual-desktop-4/, [retrieved: 03, 2020]

[9] G. W. Evans and D. Johnson, "Stress and open-office noise," Journal of Applied Psychology, vol. 85, no. 5, pp. 779-783, 2000.

[10] M. Humphries, "Quantifying occupant comfort: Are combined indices of the indoor environment practicable?" Building Research and Information, vol. 33, no. 4, pp. 317-325, 2005.

[11] J. A. Veitch, K. E. Charles, G. R. Newsham, C. J. G. Marquardt, and J. Geerts, "Workstation characteristics and environmental satisfaction in open-plan offices: COPE field findings," proceedings of Lux Europa, Berlin, Germany, pp 414-417, 2005.

[12] R. Karasek and T. Theorell, "Healthy Work: Stress, Productivity and the Reconstruction of working life," New York: Basic books, pp.72-108, 1990.

[13] C. E. Osgood, "Semantic differential technique in the comparative study of cultures," American Anthropologist, vol. 66, no. 3, pp. 171–200, 1964.

[14] S. Ellbin, N. Engen, I. H. Jonsdottir, A. I. K. Nordlund, "Assessment of cognitive function in patients with stress-related exhaustion using the Cognitive Assessment Battery (CAB)," Journal of Clinical and Experimental Neuropsychology, vol. 40, no. 6, pp. 567-575, 2018.

[15] A. Nordlund, L. Pahlsson, C. Holmberg, K. Lind, A. Wallin, "The Cognitive Assessment Battery (CAB): a rapid test of cognitive domains," International Psychogeriatrics, vol. 23, no. 7, pp. 1144-1151, 2011.

[16] N. Mituo, S. Isao, and I. Rituko, "The study of emotional engineering," human engineering, vol. 10, no. 4, pp. 121-130, 1974.

[17] K. Kitagawa, K. Yugo, and T. Tomoyuki. "The ambiguity of architectural language description," Transactions of AIJ. Journal of architecture, planning and environmental engineering, vol. 79, no. 697, pp. 669-676, 2014.

[18] https://www.youtube.com/watch?v=Y0yOTanzx-s, [retrieved: 02, 2020].

[19] https://spssau.com/front/spssau/index.html, [retrieved: 03, 2020]

AI – Based Approach for Mobile User Interface Adaptation

Hajer Dammak
University of Tunis El Manar
Faculty of Sciences of Tunis
Laboratory LIPAH-LR11ES14
Tunis, Tunisia
E-mail: hajer.dammak@fst.utm.tn

Meriem Riahi
University of Tunis
High National School of Engineers of Tunis (ENSIT)
Tunis, Tunisia
E-mail: meriem.riahi@ensit.rnu.tn

Faouzi Moussa
University of Tunis El Manar
Faculty of Sciences of Tunis
Laboratory LIPAH-LR11ES14
Tunis, Tunisia
E-mail: faouzi.moussa@fst.rnu.tn

***Abstract*— The technological evolution and the advent of smart mobile devices have profoundly changed the daily lives of users. Indeed, users are particularly focused on their smartphones in order to manage their activities, check their e-mails, follow the news, connect to social networks, etc. Despite the impressive technological evolution of smartphones, the user interface remains below expectations of users, especially in terms of adaptation. Parallel to the technological evolution, Artificial Intelligence (AI) has also progressed very significantly. This discipline can improve user-smartphone interaction. Indeed, Machine Learning (ML), for example, offers effective means to adapt the interface according to the habits and changes in the behavior of the user. The goal here is to dynamically reorganize the mobile interfaces by grouping the frequently used applications so they will be more efficiently accessible by users. In this sense, the smartphone's log files are used to make better data-driven decisions. These logs will be exploited in a ML approach to model the user's behavior and to propose adaptations. In this paper, we discuss the user feedback for the first results of grouping icons.**

Keywords-Adaptation; Mobile User Interface; User Behavior; Log File; Artificial Intelligence; Machine Learning.

I. INTRODUCTION

In mobile and ubiquitous computing, the context changes frequently, which can affect the functionality of the system. Therefore, the need for adaptation becomes a fundamental requirement. Many researchers tried to define adaptation. Kakousis et al. [1] defined adaptation as '*any kind of structural, functional or behavioral modification of a software component, with the aim of better fitting to a changing environment and satisfying a high-level overall objective*'. More formally, Capra et al. [2] defined it as '*the ability of the application to alter and reconfigure itself as a result of context changes to deliver the same service in different ways when requested in different contexts and at different points in time'*. In brief, adaptation is seen as a discipline that addresses the necessity to adjust information systems behavior in order to meet the specific user characteristics and the current context.

The literature shows a variety of definitions of the adaptive system. In a broader scope, it is a system helps the user in satisfying the need for information by adapting the system and/or the displayed information to the user's specific requirements.

It is important to mention that adaptation in the Web environment differs from adaptation in the ubiquitous environment. The first helps to reduce the information overload problem in order to satisfy the user information need by adapting the system and/or the displayed information to user' specific requirements. The latter helps to deal with the frequently changing context (known as context-aware system) and thus to adapt the system according to the user's current context or/and the user's behavior.

Furthermore, according to Brusilovsky [3], Kobsa [4], Torre [5] and Plumbaum [6], the adaptive system in the Web environment can be divided into three different tasks. The first task is the data acquisition and consists of collecting information about users. The second task is the representation and data mining task and it supports processing information and creating a user model. The last one is the adaptation task. It serves to adapt the application to the user's profile.

Generally, in the ubiquitous environment, the adaptation cycle of a context-aware system is based on Dey's approach [7]. It includes observations of the environment, the selection of adaptations and their executions. Several authors adopt the same adaptation cycle. The approach proposed by Da et al. [8] and Cheng et al. [9] contains four steps, namely: information Collecting, Analysis, Decision and Action (CADA). Joining the same spirit, Dobson et al. [10] and Kakousis et al. [1] define adaptation as a closed loop that includes three phases: (i) context detection and processing (ii) reasoning and adaptation planning (iii) action for adaptation. Based on these two approaches, we can conclude that the adaptation system in the ubiquitous environment has four tasks: context manager, planner, decision-maker and middleware.

The Human-Computer Interaction (HCI) discipline helps to improve the usability of User Interface (UI) and provides better interaction between users and systems. In other words, UI should be easily adapted to perform various tasks. The use of mobile applications is relatively new compared with the use of desktops and Websites. Desktop computers do not suffer from much interference from the external environment compared to mobile devices. Consequently, applying the traditional HCI adaptation methods for mobile applications is not efficient [11]. With the continuous growth of the number of mobile devices and applications, it becomes crucial to understand how the users interact with their devices and applications. The user can change effortlessly the purpose of a mobile device through the used applications. The smartphone can be transformed into Global Positioning System (GPS), musical instruments, credit cards, among others [12].

Smartphones are equipped with various applications. Some of the applications exist by default and some of them are installed by the user. However, many applications remain unused, or rarely used, while others are regularly used. In fact, some applications are frequently used and may not be considered as important applications while others are less used and may be considered as important ones such as social media versus e-mail application. . In this research work, we aim to create an adaptive Mobile User Interface (MUI) by adopting the grouping approach. We wanted to test the efficiency and the practicality of this method. The idea behind adopting this hypothesis is that we noticed that the grouping of applications is static and fixed by the device manufacturer. Consequently, we tried in this study to group applications in a dynamic and modifiable way.

In this work, we raise the following questions: How can we measure the importance of an application for a user: is it measured by the frequency of use, by the time spent on the application or by other criteria? How can we group the "frequently used applications" efficiently? By application's category or by user's category? How to monitor the interface with this new grouping? Where are we going to put the created grouping in the interface? Where is the most suitable icon's position? Do we need more than one grouping?

To answer all these questions, we propose, in this paper, a solution for adapting MUI based on ML through log files. The remainder of the paper is organized as follows: Section 2 gives an overview of the related works. Section 3 describes the proposed approach. Section 4 presents the experiment carried out in a case study while Section 5 discusses the feedback from users' evaluation. Finally, Section 6 concludes the paper and outlines future perspectives.

II. RELATED WORK

To understand the adaptation process in adaptive systems that occurs in runtime stages, many research works tried to classify the adaptation methods by referring to these questions: who, why, what and how the adaptation occurs [13]-[15]. Particularly, Almutairi and Alharbi [16] offer a graphical illustration of the adaptation taxonomy where they explain the 4 dimensions. The "WHY" dimension explains the reasons for launching an adaptation: the purpose of adaptation can be corrective, adaptive, perfective, extending or preventive. The "WHO" dimension describes the problem of adaptation from various actors (human and software) that are involved. In the "WHAT" dimension, the adaptation aims and objectives are classified. The "HOW" dimension supports applying adaptation by specifying the particular strategic approaches, decision mechanisms and implementation approaches.

In our case, we are aiming for an adaptive adaptation. However, we are especially interested in the "HOW" dimension. In the literature, different UI adaptation approaches exist. They are generally based on the user model. Except that this model is generally static and is previously defined. Consequently, it doesn't take into account the user's behavior changes and its evolution while using his mobile device. Thus, the idea of relying on the user's behavior via the log files seems interesting for the success of the adaptation process.

In the first part of this section, we point out the importance of log files in studying user behavior. In the second part, we enumerate research works that focus on collecting data from mobile devices using log files. The last part is dedicated to the contribution of AI and ML in the adaptation process.

A. Log File

When it comes to studying user interaction with mobile applications, we can distinguish three approaches in the literature for the usability studies: laboratory experiments, field tests and logs studies. In HCI research, behavioral logs arise from the activities recorded when the user interacts with devices. Dumais et al. [17] highlight approaches that are in contrast with log studies presented in two dimensions. The first one indicates whether the studies are observational or experimental. The second one indicates the naturalness, depth and scale of the resulting data (Table I).

TABLE I. DIFFERENT USER STUDIES IN HCI RESEARCH

	Observational	Experimental
Lab Studies		
Controlled interpretation of behavior with detailed instrumentation	In-lab behavior observations	In-lab controlled tasks, comparison of systems
Field Studies		
In the wild, ability to probe for detail	Ethnography, case studies, panels (e.g., Nielsen)	Clinical trials and field tests
Log Studies		
In the wild, little explicit feedback but lots of implicit signals	Logs from a single system	A/B testing of alternative systems or algorithms

Laboratory experiments represent the most controlled approach. The participants are brought into the laboratory and asked to perform pre-fixed tasks. Such experiments imply perceiving the participant performing the tasks and the evaluation of usability is realized during the interaction. The observed behavior happens in a controlled and artificial setting and may not represent the behavior that would be observed "in the wild" [18][19]. Consequently, collecting data in laboratory studies is expensive in terms of the time which limits the number of participants and systems that can be studied.

Data collection in field studies tends to be less artificial and less controlled than lab studies. The participants are in their real usage environments conducting their own activities and in general, they are periodically asked for additional information. Observation of users in their own environments allows gathering information including interruptions and distractions. As affirmed by Barbosa [20], this is an investigation of the reality of the users and not of assumptions. Field studies bring the benefit of understanding user's interaction and the influence of external factors on such interaction. Yet, collecting data in this approach is not an easy task. In fact, it may change the user behavior, as capturing user's interaction in the field is an intrusive method [21].

Contrary to lab studies and field studies, log studies appear as the most natural observation as the systems are used with no influence by experimenters or observers. Log studies provide a portrait of uncensored behavior. They give a more complete, accurate picture of all behaviors. Furthermore, logs have the advantage of being easy to capture at scale. They can easily include data from tens or hundreds of millions of people while laboratory and field studies typically include tens or hundreds of people. Logs are more about WHAT users are doing rather than WHY. In other words, there is less information about the user's motivation and user satisfaction. Furthermore, log data can be used to test hypotheses that researchers develop about user's behavior. In the case of mobile devices, we distinguish 2 types of log files:

- Log files-oriented application: traces generally the user's interaction with a particular application.
- Log files-oriented device: traces usage information, the context of use and data across arbitrary apps.

B. Data collection

We aim to adapt the MUI for Android devices based on the most frequently used applications. Thus, the data collection task is an important task to acquire the looked-for adaptation. To enhance our knowledge about collecting data, we tried to answer the following questions through our readings: What is the main purpose behind collecting data? What data is collected? How it is collected (approaches/methods)? Where is it stored? What are the types of logs (extension)?

For most of the research works, the purpose behind using log files is to develop methodologies and techniques to evaluate smartphones or application usability. Indeed, analyzing the interaction log file allows a better understanding of how the user behaves with his mobile device and applications.

Marczal and Junior [22] catalog a series of variables that are examined while studying user behavior. They classified the variables into interaction, context and device variables. The first category "determines the user behavior while the user interacts with the application". The second one "concerns the physical, social, temporal and technical environment where the interaction took place". The last category "represents the device characteristics with which the user interacted".

The log file can help to capture user interaction with applications accurately and efficiently. Otherwise, the challenge of restoring to such a file rests on the whole process of preparing the system from collecting data to extracting and interpreting the logged data. Thus, it would be easier to have a tool that can process a large amount of data. Table II summarizes the work of some researches around log files and data collection.

Fernandez and Hussmann [23] developed a tool EvaHelper that helps developers in the usability analysis of the mobile application. The authors simplify the developer's task of evaluating and processing of the automated data collection. The proposed methodology is based on 4 phases: preparation, collection, extraction and analysis.

Ma et al. [24] propose a toolkit that embeds into mobile applications the ability to automatically collect UI events as the user interacts with the applications. The events are fine-grained and useful for quantified usability analysis. The authors implement the toolkit on Android devices and evaluate it with a real deployed Android application by comparing event analysis with traditional laboratory testing.

Kluth et al. [25] modify the four-phased model of Fernandez and Hussmann [23] by adding an automatic critique phase. This phase allows the developer to get feedback in the form of a suggested improvement of usability issues analyzed.

For the same purpose of usability evaluation in a mobile application, [26] presents a solution for the need of applying cost-effective methods to such evaluation. The authors extend Google's API basic service named Google Analytics for Mobile Applications (GAMA) to collect specific low-level user actions. The solution allows lab usability testing, automating quantitative data gathering on one hand and logging real use after application release on the other hand. The mentioned work needs instrumentation of specific code to collect data.

Alternatively, Holzmann et al. [27] [28] present an open-source toolkit for Android that does not require any instrumentation of the application source. The toolkit allows automated logging of the mobile device to evaluate the efficiency of the MUI. It traces user interactions, the context of use and works across arbitrary applications on Android devices.

The commonly used log format for mobile systems is comma-separated-values, CSV. Researchers chose this format instead of XML to minimize the file size, knowing that XML needs additional tags to stock information.

We conclude that most of the works that use log files are application-oriented. They focus on evaluating the usability of a particular application. Rare are the works that are interested in evaluating the mobile device and that focus on the adaptation part.

C. Artificial Intelligence in Adaptation

AI can bring added value to the adaptation process. Initially, we need to clarify what AI really is. It can be several things such as doing smart things with computers or doing smart things with computers the way people do them. In the field of AI, imitating human approaches has been a long-standing effort as a mechanism to confirm our understanding.

The second field of study of AI is ML. It provides computers with the ability to learn autonomously, using a combination of methodologies developed by the statisticians and computer scientists, to learn relationships from data while also placing emphasis on efficient computing algorithms. Here, we do not try to model what is happening. Instead, we simply provide inputs and feedback on the outputs. With a learning algorithm, there is some procedure whereby the computer changes its approach to better match the desired output. Eventually, the machine learns what to do. Also, the resulting 'rules' may be opaque to semantic inspection: we can not necessarily intuit what rules are being used, even if the output is good [29].

The automated learning power of ML helps data scientists gain knowledge in a variety of applications such as computer vision, speech processing, natural language understanding, neuroscience, health and Internet of Things (IoT). The major challenge of using ML in big data is to perform the analysis in a reasonable time [30].

ML techniques are used in many fields for different purposes [31]: analyze and diagnose medical images in radiological medicine [32][33], predict the susceptibility of soil liquefaction [34] and forecast models of consumer credit risk [35]. The used techniques fall under one of two categories of supervised or unsupervised learning. In the first category, algorithms are trained using labeled data, while in the second category, algorithms are used against data which are unlabeled.

The following section explains how we use the ML in our approach to adapt the MUI based on user interaction.

TABLE II. RESEARCH WORKS USING LOG FILES FOR DATA COLLECTION

	[23]	[24]	[25]	[22]	[27]	[26]	[28]
Platform	Android	Android	iOS	Android + iOS	Android	Android	Android
Log format	CSV	-	-	-	CSV	-	-
Storage	Mobile device	Central server	Central server	Server	Mobile device	GAMA Server	Web Server
Instrumentation	√ (manually added code)	√ (requires code modificationl)	√	-	×	√	-
Type de collection	Triggered by the user		Auto	Auto (service)	Triggered by the user	Auto	Triggered by the user
Scaling	×	×	-	√	×	√	×
Collected data	Interaction data	Interaction info: UI events	Interaction info	• Interaction info • Mobility (GPS, data sensor)	• Context of use • Interaction info	Interaction info	• Visited apps' screenshot • Interaction info
Test / evaluation	Real world / lab	Lab	Lab	Real world	Real world	Lab + Real usage	Lab
Purpose	Usability analysis	Usability eval	Usability eval	Behavior analysis	UI eval	Usability eval	UI Evaluation
Object of study	Mobile apps	Mobile apps	Mobile apps	Mobile apps	Mobile device	Mobile apps	Mobile UI

III. PROPOSED APPROACH

Our research focuses on adapting MUI based on user behavior: the user interaction with mobile applications. Thus, we can manage the used apps by grouping them as "frequently used apps" in a dynamic and changeable way.

To reach our goal, we propose an approach based on 3 phases. As mentioned in Figure 1, the first phase is considered as field studies. It consists of training the model. The second phase is oriented log studies, i.e., real-world interactions. It consists of recommending to the user a set of apps mostly used and pre-judged as "important" by the model. The latter phase uses a fine-tuning, for continuous improvement and sends the noticed changes to the model so it can cope with them.

To train the model in the first phase, several steps should be followed. The first step focuses on collecting data from diverse mobile users. To accomplish this task, we use an open-source Android toolkit called Automate that supports field studies on mobile devices proposed by Holzmann et al. [27]. It allows the automated logging of mobile device usage in the background. It captures data related to user interactions, the context of use and works across arbitrary apps. This software does not require any instrumentation of the application source code. We are trying to gather an important amount of log files from volunteers, mainly students, from our university over a period of time. These files are stored in the external storage directory of each smartphone and are sent voluntarily by participants. We gather the log files and then we import them into our data store where we perform an offline analysis.

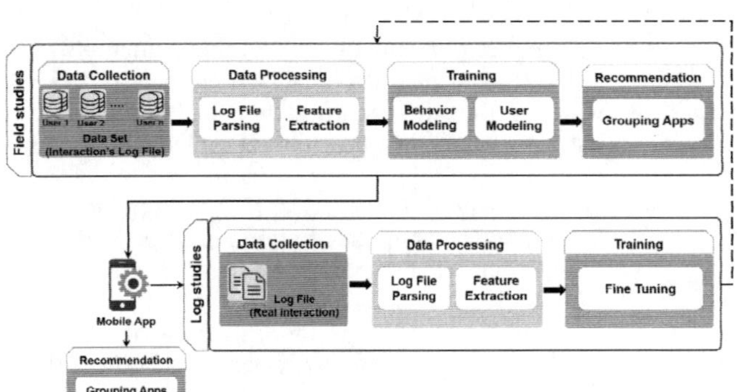

Figure 1. Proposed approach for the adaptation process.

The second step consists of processing the previously collected data by parsing the log files and extracting the most appropriate features. We can group the features to two main aspects: time and visit. The former takes into account information, such as the time spent per application (time linger), time of the last visit and time of the day (morning, afternoon). The latter takes into account information, such as the frequency of visits (number of visits per day) and the sequence of visited apps out of one session. A session, in this context, starts when the screen is turned on and the device returns from sleep mode and it lasts until the screen display is off again (returns to sleep mode) or when the device is turned off completely. The third step represents the AI module to train the data by applying ML techniques. At this stage, we apply an offline learning where we first use non-supervised algorithms to train the model and to identify the different clusters of user behavior. Second, we use supervised algorithms to classify the new entry.

In this study, we examine the following unsupervised ML algorithms:

- *Agglomerative clustering*: It is a subgroup of K-means clustering which is an iterative clustering algorithm that helps find the highest value for every iteration. Agglomerative clustering starts with a fixed number of clusters. It allocates all data into the exact number of clusters. This clustering method does not require the number of clusters K as an input. The agglomeration process starts by forming each data as a single cluster. This method uses some distance measure and reduces the number of clusters (one in each iteration) by merging process.
- *Hierarchical Clustering*: It is an algorithm which builds a hierarchy of clusters. The Hierarchical clustering Technique can be visualized using a Dendrogram which is a tree-like diagram that records the sequences of merges or splits. Hierarchical clustering methods summarize the data hierarchy, i.e., they construct a number of local data partitions that are eventually nested. The clustering outcome depends on the selected linkage strategy (single, complete, average, centroid or Ward's linkage) and the similarity measure being considered.

We also examine the following supervised ML algorithms:

- *Logistic Regression:* Linear regression attempts to fit a line to data that has only two levels or outcomes, whereas, logistic regression models the chance of an outcome based on a transformation known as a logit [36].
- *Support Vector Machine (SVM):* The Support Vector Machine algorithm uses training examples to create a hyperplane that separates the dataset into classes. The complexity of classes may vary, but the simplest form of the SVM algorithm has only two possible labels to choose from. To reduce misclassifications, a decision boundary is obtained while training the SVM algorithm. This decision boundary is known as the optimal separation hyperplane.

The last step recommends a grouping of the frequently used apps and places it on the most suitable place for the user as mentioned in Figure 2.

After training the model, we suggest installing the framework into the mobile device. This framework supports log studies, i.e., real-world interactions. Similarly, as the first phase, several steps should be followed. The first step consists of collecting the user's real time interactions. The second step consists of processing the gathered data, which will be forwarded to a real-time data analysis system for learning. The third step consists of fine-tuning the ML model. This step can be described as rotating TV switches and knobs to get a clearer signal. In fact, with fine-tuning, the learning of new tasks relies on the previously learned tasks. The fine-tuning ML predictive model is a crucial step to improve the accuracy of the forecasted results. It is essential to mention that, if we want to improve the accuracy of our forecasting model, we ought to enrich data in the feature set first.

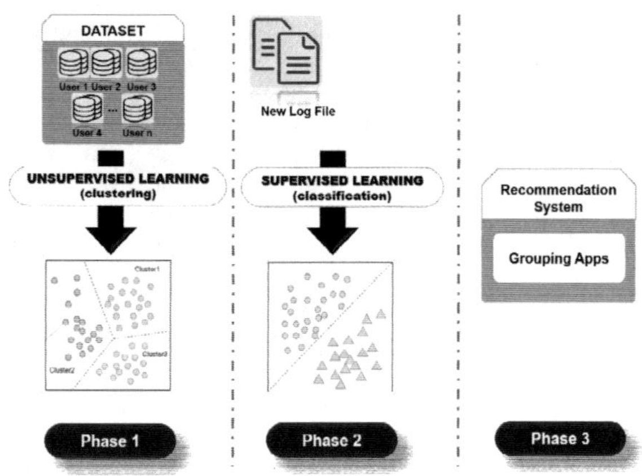

Figure 2. Leraning process of the proposed approach.

The idea of grouping the applications raises many questions. How many groups of applications should we create? Should we group according to the application's category or according to the user's category? How many applications per group? What is considered as the most suitable place for the user (bottom, up, left, right, in the middle)? Does the user prefer a group of applications or does he prefer them to be placed in the main widget? In the case of many widgets, in which widget should we place the recommended group? And if the widget is overloaded, what is the best decision to make?

We can notice that the user's feedback is important to evaluate the adapted interface. Thus, taking into account the user's interaction with the created grouping can improve the model. In fact, modifying the place of the group or re-adjusting it must be considered in the next generation of grouping.

IV. Case Study

As we mentioned previously, we used the toolkit named Automate proposed by Holzmann et al. [27] for collecting data. The resulting log file is in CSV format. As seen in Figure 3, the extracted log file contains overall interesting information like the sequence of opened apps, app usage duration, phone orientation, where the user clicked, etc. The given sample of log file shows the used application: Google Quick Search Box and WPS office.

```xml
<?xml version="1.0" encoding="UTF-8"?>
<session>
    <appUsage
    packageName="com.google.android.googlequicksearchbox"
    name="Google"
    startTime="1573929957560">
        <state
        name="[Tap to update]"
        className="android.widget.FrameLayout"
        duration="211"
        interactionCount="1"
        orientation="1"
        />
    </appUsage>
    <appUsage
    packageName="cn.wps.moffice_eng"
    name="WPS Office"
    startTime="1573929960194">
        <state
        name="[ WPS Office]"
        className="cn.wps.moffice.documentmanager.PreStartActivity"
        duration="2231"
        interactionCount="1"
        orientation="1"
        />
    </appUsage>
</session>
```


Figure 3. Excerpt from a log file.

These data can be used in many ways. Some use cases of log files processing can be:

- *User Behavior Analysis*: By studying the underlying patterns and styles of use of a user, we can detect personality traits and classify a user into a category, which can be used later for various recommendations or as input for other use cases.
- *Apps recommendations*: We can cluster users and log each type's most-used apps, then recommend the apps to a new user that has been classified as one of them but lacks some apps.
- *Sequence detection*: Some people have regular app patterns (exp: Mail then Social Media). If we can identify a user's pattern, we could make it so that apps can be loaded in advance into memory or get their notifications refreshed before the user actually clicks on the app, thus making it easier for him.
- *App grouping*: Like the apps recommendations, we could look into how the user groups their apps and propose a similar grouping to a new user, which could interest him.

We tested our approach on 3 users having different backgrounds and different attitudes. User#1 is an entrepreneur having an unpredictable lifestyle and actively toggling between work and fun every day. He has only 1 widget screen, where he put all his apps into multiple groups (professional, social, entertainment). User#2 is a Ph.D. student who has many widget screens and doesn't group her apps. User#3 is a startup CEO and has multiple widgets screen, but uses solely the home widget where he puts only productivity apps to focus on his work. Figure 4 shows screenshots of the main widget of the 3 users before and after grouping the used apps.

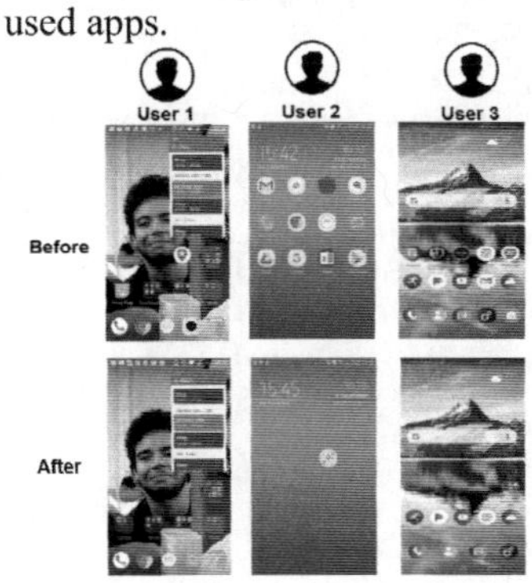

Figure 4. Screenshots before and after grouping the used apps.

These users have been using their configuration for a long time and they announced that they are satisfied with the way apps are arranged. After proposing a new layout, we asked them for their feedback. User#1 said that the grouping didn't go well with his needs as he initially grouped his apps based on his frequency of use and routine. User#2 completely refused the proposition as she just doesn't like to have groups. She prefers to set the most important apps in the main widget. User#3 said that, while the grouping made sense, it's ineffective to have one group when there are a lot of empty spaces in the home widget. We discuss the feedback from user evaluation in the next section.

V. Discussion

The given feedbacks highlight an important point: as much as the solution can technically be good, is it really useful? Although the users' evaluation feedback is negative toward the grouping method, nevertheless, this does not indicate that the conceptual model of the prototype is wrong or needs revision. It denotes that it is natural that people do not like significant changes in a very short time. The case study here drastically changed routine usage. Therefore, we are looking to make the approach more friendly to mobile users and thus by taking into account the periodicity and the frequency of adaptation.

VI. Conclusion

In this paper, we pointed out the importance of log files in the adaptation process in order to make the mobile user's experience better. We also presented use cases on how log files could be used and went in depth with suggesting grouping mobile apps. We presented a novel process-based AI where we use ML to understand user's behavior. It consists of recommending to the user a set of apps mostly used and pre-judged as "important" by the model. We used a case study to show a sample of adapted interfaces from different users with different attitudes. The user's feedback did not show a big interest in the grouping which brought us questioning usability versus utility. Furthermore, the given feedback points out that users do not like major changes in their devices. Thus, in future work, we will study and adjust the periodicity and the frequency of adaptation so the user can benefit from an ongoing interaction. Besides, we aim to consider the user mood for a smooth user experience. We will examine further the performance of many other ML algorithms. We intend to expand our experimentation to a wider, but specific, audience and we will be exploring utility-first solutions whose sole purpose is to improve the mobile user's interaction. In addition, we plan to explore users' implicit feedback to fine-tuning the model to get a more accurate adaptation.

References

[1] K. Kakousis, N. Paspallis and G. A. Papadopoulos, "A survey of software adaptation in mobile and ubiquitous computing", Enterprise Information Systems, vol. 4, no. 4, pp. 355-389, 2010.

[2] L. Capra, W. Emmerich and C. Mascolo, "Reflective middleware solutions for context-aware applications", International Conference on Metalevel Architectures and Reflection, Springer, Berlin, Heidelberg, pp. 126-133, September 2001.

[3] P. Brusilovsky, "Methods and techniques of adaptive hypermedia", User modeling and user-adapted interaction, vol. 6, no. 2-3, pp. 87-129, 1996.

[4] A. Kobsa, "Generic user modeling systems". User modeling and user-adapted interaction, vol. 11, no. 1-2, pp. 49-63, 2001.

[5] I. Torre, "Adaptive systems in the era of the semantic and social Web, a survey", User Modeling and User-Adapted Interaction, vol. 19, no. 5, pp. 433-486, 2009.

[6] T. Plumbaum, T. Stelter and A. Korth, "Semantic Web usage mining: Using semantics to understand user intentions", International Conference on User Modeling, Adaptation and Personalization, Springer, Berlin, Heidelberg, pp. 391-396, June 2009.

[7] A. K. Dey, G. D. Abowd and D. Salber, "A conceptual framework and a toolkit for supporting the rapid prototyping of context-aware applications", Human–Computer Interaction, vol. 16, no. 2-4, pp. 97-166, 2001.

[8] K. Da, M. Dalmau and P. Roose, "A Survey of adaptation systems", International Journal on Internet and Distributed Computing Systems, vol. 2, no. 1, pp. 1-18, 2011.

[9] B. Cheng et al., "Software engineering for self-adaptive systems : A research roadmap", Software Engineering for Self-Adaptive Systems, Springer Berlin Heidelberg, vol. 5525, pp. 1–26, 2009.

[10] S. Dobson et al., "A survey of autonomic communications", ACM Trans. Auton. Adapt. Syst., vol. 1, no. 2, pp. 223–259, 2006.

[11] A. H. Kronbauer and C. A. S. Santos, "Um modelo de avaliação da usabilidade baseado na captura automática de dados de interação do usuário em ambientes reais", In Proceedings of the 10th Brazilian Symposium on Human Factors in Computing Systems and the 5th Latin American Conference on Human-Computer Interaction, Brazilian Computer Society, pp. 114-123, October, 2011. [In English: "A usability evaluation model based on the automatic capture of user interaction data in real environments"].

[12] M. Böhmer, B. Hecht, J. Schöning, A. Krüger and G. Bauer, "Falling asleep with Angry Birds, Facebook and Kindle: a large scale study on mobile application usage". In Proceedings of the 13th international conference on Human computer interaction with mobile devices and services, ACM, pp. 47-56, August, 2011.

[13] D. Weyns and T. Ahmad, "Claims and evidence for architecture-based self-adaptation: a systematic literature review", In European Conference on Software Architecture, Springer, Berlin, Heidelberg, pp. 249-265, July, 2013.

[14] M. Salehie and L. Tahvildari, "Self-adaptive software: Landscape and research challenges". ACM transactions on autonomous and adaptive systems (TAAS), vol. 4, no. 2, pp. 1-42, 2009.

[15] L. Tang, H. Liu, J. Zhang, N. Agarwal and J. J. Salerno, "Topic taxonomy adaptation for group profiling". ACM Transactions on Knowledge Discovery from Data (TKDD), vol. 1, no. 4, pp. 1-28, 2008.

[16] A. Almutairi and M. Alharbi, "A Survey of Adaptation and the Best Approach for Ubiquitous Systems", International Journal of Computing and Digital Systems, vol. 6, no. 05, pp. 277-284, 2017.

[17] S. Dumais, R. Jeffries, D. M. Russell, D. Tang and J. Teevan, "Understanding user behavior through log data and analysis", In Ways of Knowing in HCI, Springer, New York, NY, pp. 349-372, 2014.

[18] J. Kawalek, A. Stark and M. Riebeck, "A new approach to analyze human-mobile computer interaction", Journal of usability studies, vol. 3, no. 2, pp. 90-98, 2008.

[19] C. Mayas, S. Hörold, C. Rosenmöller and H. Krömker, "Evaluating methods and equipment for usability field tests in public transport", In International Conference on Human-Computer Interaction, Springer, Cham, pp. 545-553, 2014, June.

[20] S. Barbosa and B. Silva, "Interação humano-computador", Elsevier Brasil, pp. 263-326, 2010.

[In English: "Human-computer interaction"].

[21] B. Brown, M. McGregor and E. Laurier, "iPhone in vivo: video analysis of mobile device use", In Proceedings of the SIGCHI conference on Human Factors in computing systems, ACM, pp. 1031-1040, April, 2013.

[22] D. Marczal and P. T. A. Junior, "Behavioural Variables Analysis in Mobile Environments", In International Conference of Design, User Experience and Usability, Springer, Cham, pp. 118-130, August, 2015.

[23] F. Balagtas-Fernandez and H. Hussmann, "A methodology and framework to simplify usability analysis of mobile applications", In Proceedings of the 2009 IEEE/ACM International Conference on Automated Software Engineering, IEEE Computer Society, IEEE Computer Society, pp. 520-524, November, 2009.

[24] X. Ma et al., "Design and implementation of a toolkit for usability testing of mobile apps", Mobile Networks and Applications, vol. 18, no. 1, pp. 81-97, 2013.

[25] W. Kluth, K. H. Krempels and C. Samsel, "Automated Usability Testing for Mobile Applications". In WEBIST, no. 2, pp. 149-156, 2014.

[26] X. Ferre, E. Villalba, H. Julio and H. Zhu, "Extending mobile app analytics for usability test logging", In IFIP Conference on Human-Computer Interaction, Springer, Cham, pp. 114-131, September, 2017.

[27] C. Holzmann, D. Steiner, A. Riegler and C. Grossauer, "An android toolkit for supporting field studies on mobile devices", In Proceedings of the 16th International Conference on Mobile and Ubiquitous Multimedia, ACM, pp. 473-479, November, 2017.

[28] A. Riegler and C. Holzmann, "Measuring visual user interface complexity of mobile applications with metrics". Interacting with Computers, vol. 30, no. 3, pp. 207-223, 2018.

[29] https://www.litmos.com/blog/articles/the-realities-of-artificial-intelligence-and-adaptive-learning, last access 03.12.2019

[30] L. Zhou, S. Pan, J. Wang and A. Vasilakos, "Machine Learning on Big Data: Opportunities and Challenges", pp. 350-361, 2017.

[31] Y. Seyedfaraz, "User Behavior Analysis using Smartphones". Ph.D. Thesis, 2017. https://thescholarship.ecu.edu/bitstream/handle/10342/6330/YASROBI-MASTERSTHESIS-2017.pdf?sequence=1&isAllowed=y

[32] R. C. Deo, "Machine learning in medicine", Circulation, vol.132, no. 20, pp. 1920–1930, 2015.

[33] S. Wang and R. M. Summers, "Machine learning and radiology", Medical Image Analysis, vol.16, no. 5, pp. 933–951, 2012.

[34] P. Samui and T. G. Sitharam, "Machine learning modelling for predicting soil liquefaction susceptibility", Natural Hazards and Earth System Science, vol. 11, no. 1, pp. 1–9, 2011.

[35] A. E. Khandani, A. J. Kim and A. W. Lo, "Consumer credit-risk models via machine-learning algorithms", Journal of Banking and Finance, vol. 34, no. 11, pp. 2767–2787, 2010.

[36] S. Kristin, "Logistic Regression", PM&R, vol.6, no. 12, pp. 1-28, 2006.

A Fuzzy Logic Approach for Dynamic User Interests Profiling

Abd El Heq Silem, Hajer Taktak, and Faouzi Moussa
Faculty of Sciences of Tunis, LIPAH LR11ES14
University of Tunis El Manar, El manar1
Tunis, Tunisia
Email: {hakou.silem, taktakhajer, faouzimoussa}@gmail.com

Abstract— **The user profile is the virtual representation of the user that holds a variety of user information such as personal data, interests, preferences, and environment. In literature, there are two different techniques for profiling user interests. The first one is based on the retrieval of text from the user browsing history; this technique has a high probability to generate a false interest from uninteresting websites. The second technique is based on user behavior (factors like scrolling speed or time spent) and navigation history. The proposed approach using the second technique does not use enough factors and calculates the weight of each factor via predefined ranges, which is not accurate for all users. This technique generates incorrect factor weight and false user interests. In this paper, we propose an approach that employs Fuzzy Logic with several factors (scrolling speed, time spent, and the number of visits) to automatically build and update the user profile from the user's browsing history. The target websites for this approach are websites that contain text content rather than visual content. This approach adapts the range of each factor according to the user habits using Fuzzy Logic, which improves accuracy and avoids a predefined factor range. Finally, we use an ontology-based model to store the user profile.**

Keywords-Context-Awareness; Fuzzy Logic; Fuzzy Logic System; User Profiling; User Behavior.

I. INTRODUCTION

Personalization systems are very important in computer science due to their ability to provide relevant content to the user and due to the growth of accessible information. The personalization system must act according to user preferences and interests (in other words, to provide content relevant to the user). To solve this problem, it is necessary to collect and store user personal information, preferences, and interests. This is called user profiling.

The user profiling process has two significant challenges. The first challenge is the creation of the user profile, called the cold start (the system has no information about the user to be used in the personalization). The second challenge is to keep the existing information in the profile up to date according to the user changing preferences. In literature, there are three main approaches [1][2] about user profile information collection:

- Explicit approach (static profiling): This approach collects data directly from the user using forms or surveys, which generate a very accurate profile at the beginning. This accuracy deteriorates over time, especially when the user does not fill in the new surveys.
- Implicit approach (dynamic profiling): this approach infers information about the user without the user's intervention, based on the browsing history and behavior. The problem in this approach is the cold start and the accuracy of inferred information about the user.
- Hybrid approach: combines the previous approaches to override their weaknesses and increase their benefits. It creates the profile of users using the explicit approach. Then, it maintains the profile updated using the implicit one.

The rest of the paper is organized as follows: In Section 2, we discuss some of the related works. Section 3 presents the Fuzzy Logic system. In Section 4, we discuss the user profile model, and Section 5 concludes the paper.

II. RELATED WORK

In literature, there are three main user profiling methods: the content-based, the collaborative, and the hybrid method [2]. The content-based methods create the user profile according to the user's behavior (detect interest from the behavior). Then, they select content with a strong correlation to the created profile. The collaborative methods are based on a similar rating of users. These methods create a profile for a group of users who have the same rating or similar taste and make a recommendation based on the group rating. The hybrid techniques combine the two previous methods to improve the strengths and overcome the weaknesses of each method.

Tchantchou et al. [3] propose a multi-agent architecture for user interest profiling and an improved algorithm for mapping the Conceptual Clustering Concept (ICCC). The user profile contains both explicit and implicit interests. Implicit interests are derived from the user browsing history using the ICCC algorithm. The architecture extracts the text from the visited webpages, removes stop words, and reduces each word to its stem. Then, it assigns weights to those stems according to the stem position and occurrence and creates the term vector of each website. After that, the architecture will map each website to a concept based on the ICCC algorithm and an ontology that contains a set of concepts and websites. Finally, it updates the profile of users with the new weights. This architecture does not use user behavior to detect user interest. It only uses the text extracted from visited webpages, which does not differentiate between interesting and uninteresting websites and it will generate false interests (if the user visits a set of random uninteresting websites in a session).

Moawad et al. [4] propose a multi-agent architecture for customization of Web search according to the user profile. The profile is built from the user's explicit information and interests (collected explicitly). The architecture implicitly updates the profile by capturing the interaction and the browsing history of the user. First, it retrieves the stems from webpages like the precedent work [3] (the authors add user action, such as copying and bookmark, to calculate the weight). Using the Wordnet ontology [5] (Wordnet ontology is a lexical database of English), the architecture recovers the first common topic between all the stems (of the same webpage) and creates a triplet (stem, topic, and weight of stem). Finally, the topic weight is calculated based on the weight of all its stems and the number of stems. In this work, the authors rely only on two actions to determinate the interesting webpages. Bookmarking or copying text from a webpage does not always mean that the user is interested in this type of content and vice versa (in many cases, users do not bookmark or copy text from interesting webpages). Therefore, the results of this technique are misleading and far from being reliable.

Singh et al. [6] propose a multi-agent architecture for the dynamic construction of the user profile according to user's browsing history, the scrolling speed, time spent, and user behavior at the desktop (such as applications and files opened). The architecture is a client/server architecture where the client-side is responsible for collecting user information (desktop and browsing behavior). It analyses that information to create the user profile (estimation of user interests). The server-side maintains and updates the profiles of all users provided by the client-side. Then, it groups these users according to their interests and provides content based on these groups. In this work, the authors detect the user's interest in a webpage using two factors: the scrolling speed and the time spent. The weight of each factor value is calculated based on a predefined range (for example, when the scrolling speed is between x and y, the weight will be z). This transformation of the value into weight is not always accurate and excludes the diversity in user habits.

Makvana et al. [6] and Wu et al. [7] extract user interest from the user's query. The authors in [7] proposed an approach to solve the polysemy problem through query expansion. The approach collects keywords from the query, title, URL, content (snippets), and time spent of clicked websites (websites resulting from the query). Then, it computes the weight of each keyword using co-occurrence. Finally, the approach creates the user profile with the pairs (keyword, weight). The approach proposed by Hawalah et al. [9] represents the user interest in a model with a keyword and weight (K_i, W_i) pair vector. Each time the user enters a query, the approach extracts keywords and searches them in the profile. In the absence of a keyword, the approach adds it with a predefined weight (W_i); otherwise, the approach adds a unit score to W_i. The weights of all keywords decrease over time (current time (t) and last update time (t_0)) by the following formula :

$$W_{i\_new} = W_{i\_old} \times \lambda \text{ where } \lambda = e^{\log_2 \frac{t-t0}{30}} \quad (1)$$

The two previous approaches [6][7] suffer from the same problems as the first approach [3], namely, they cannot distinguish between interesting and uninteresting keywords.

The architecture described in [9] creates the user profile through three phases. In the first phase, the architecture collects information such as visited websites, their content, time of the visit, and the duration. After the collection is done, the architecture fetches text from the webpages, removes all noise data from it (like HTML tags), tokenizes it, and removes stop words. Finally, each term is transformed into its stem. The resulting text is called a document. In the second phase, the architecture computes the TF*IDF weight (TF is the Term Frequency in a document, and IDF is the Inverse Document Frequency, which represents the number of documents containing the term divided by the total number of documents) of each term and creates a vector space that contains terms with weights. In the last phase, using cosine similarity, the architecture maps each visited website to the appropriate concept in the reference ontology. TABLE I summarizes the existing approaches.

The behavior of each user may differ from the others. Each user has their own reading speed (e.g., scrolling speed and the time spent). Therefore, the use of static intervals as in [5][8] is not practical since it does not take into account the diversity of users' behaviors. For instance, older users may spend more time than younger ones. This does not necessarily mean that they are more interested in this type of content, as it may occur due to reading difficulties. On the other hand, the existing solutions do not use factors [3][6][7] or enough factors [4][10] to determine the degree of user interest in a specific topic, which, in the meantime, affects the whole determination process and generates a false user interest.

To overcome this, we propose an approach that employs Fuzzy Logic. Instead of using a predefined range for all the users, each user's ranges will be calculated based on their browsing habits. We also introduce several factors to improve the detection process. Thus, this translates into high accuracy and adaptability. In this paper, we will consider the following aspects:

- We collect the browsing history with several parameters (factors) about each visited website, such as the time spent, the number of visits, and the scrolling speed.
- We apply the Fuzzy Logic in order to overcome the misinterpretation of factors weights and to provide better adaptability.

TABLE I. COMPARISON OF PROPOSED RESEARCHES.

Authors	Method	Profile constructed based on	Factors	Information collection approach	Profilin method
Tchantchou and Ezin [3]	Multi-agent architecture	Browsing history	N.A	Hybrid	Content-based
Moawad et al. [4]	Multi-agent architecture	Browsing history User Behavior	User Actions	Hybrid	Content-based
Singh and Sharma [6]	Client/server Multi-agent architecture	Browsing history User Behavior	Scrolling speed Time spent	Implicit	Content-based
Makvana et al. [7]	Approach	User queries User Behavior	Time spent	Implicit	Content-based
Wu et al. [7]	Approach	User queries	N.A	Implicit	Collaborative-based
Hawalah and Fasli [9]	Approach	Browsing history User Behavior	Time spent	Implicit	Content-based

III. THE FUZZY INFERENCE SYSTEM

In this phase, we attempt to build a Fuzzy Logic system to predict the user interest degree and to solve the problem of misinterpretation of factors weights.

Fuzzy Logic was proposed first by Lotfi Zadeh in 1994 [10]. Unlike the binary logic, it does not use exact values to represent a situation (0 or 1, like or dislike, true or false). This type of logic represents the situation with a continuous value from 0 to 1, which gives the computer the ability to represent the unclear idea of humans, e.g., in the describing of a room brightness, instead of using a dark or a bright room (0 or 1), we can represent the degree of light and say little bright (0.6), little dark (0.4), very dark (0), very bright (1).

The Fuzzy Inference System (FIS) transforms multiple independent inputs into one output using Fuzzy Logic, memberships function, and rules. FIS has four components, the fuzzifier, the inference engine, the rule base, and the defuzzifier, as shown in Figure 1 [11]–[17].

A. The Fuzzification

The fuzzification is the first phase in a Fuzzy Logic system that decomposes the crisp values into fuzzy sets. The fuzzification process has a few parameters to define. First, we define one or more imprecise fuzzy sets that divide the crisp values. Then, we represent the fuzzy sets using a membership function defined as follows:

$$(\mu_A : X \rightarrow \{0,1\} |\ X \in [values_{min}, values_{max}]) \qquad (2)$$

There are many membership functions, such as Triangular, Trapezoidal, Gaussian, and more. These functions assign the input value to one or more fuzzy sets with some degree of membership (Figure 2), e.g. if x = 40, the degree of membership of x is 0.3 in low and 0.3 in medium.

The above-mentioned misinterpretation of factor weight is generated from the predefined ranges. To resolve this problem using Fuzzy Logic, we calculate the range dynamically based on user browsing habits. The browsing values (e.g., scrolling speed) will be sorted by ascending order. Then, these values will be divided into three fuzzy sets that will be represented by the linguistic terms "low," "medium," and "high." These sets will generate three intervals, where each of them will range from the minimum value of the set to the minimum value of the next one.

When users finish their browsing session, we extract the collected values (of those factors). Each value will be classified according to the previously generated intervals in order to determine the user interest degree in this type of content. These new values will be added to the previous ones and used to update the intervals, as shown in Figure 3. This allows the system to adapt to the user behavior and guarantee a high level of accuracy as compared to the existing solutions.

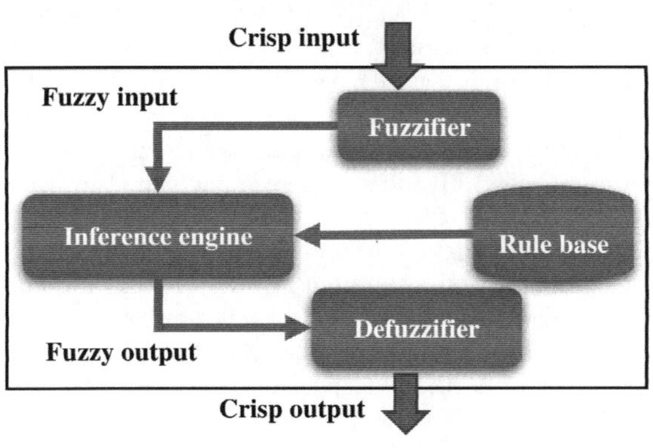

Figure 1. Fuzzy Logic system.

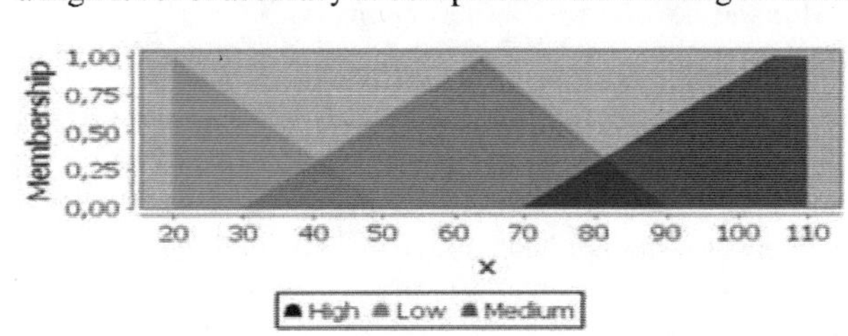

Figure 2. Triangular membership function example (Time spent in a Web site).

This adaptation transforms the captured value into a linguistic term to represent the right weight of this value (the linguistic term is more accurate than the value itself), which ensures the right detection of the user interesting topics. For example, let us consider two different users. Table A in Figure 4 shows the ranges of each user generated from the browsing habits. Now, let us assume that the two users will have the same browsing values for each factor (Table B in Figure 4). By using the fuzzification process on each factor value, we obtain different weights for each user according to the user's habits (Table C in Figure 4).

B. The Inference Engine

The Inference Engine is the core of the Fuzzy Logic system; this component is responsible for the calculation of one fuzzy output from a set of fuzzy inputs. The fuzzy output is calculated using a set of "IF.... THEN" rules built as follows:

IF *input1 is A* **AND** *input2 is B* **AND** *input3 is C* **THEN** *output is D*

The antecedent part of the rules contains the fuzzy inputs (input1 is A) obtained from the fuzzification process. A, B, and C represent one of the fuzzy sets of the first, second, and third variables, respectively (in our case, the variables are the factors such as scrolling speed, time spent, and the number of visits).

The consequence part of the rules contains the fuzzy output (output is D), which belongs to one of the following three fuzzy sets: uninteresting (range from 0 to 0.3), likely interesting (from 0.3 to 0.7), and interesting websites (from 0.7 to 1). The rules of the Fuzzy Inference Engine are presented in TABLE II ("I" represents Interesting, "LI" represents Likely interesting, and "UI" represents Uninteresting).

The Fuzzy Inference Engine maps the fuzzy inputs to the fuzzy output through two phases: first, it calculates the activation degree of each rule based on the fuzzified inputs. If the antecedent of the rule has more than one input, the engine applies the Fuzzy Logic operator (replace the and/or operator with the min/max between the two inputs) and composes those inputs. In the second phase, the engine aggregates the output of all rules into one fuzzy output. The aggregation is the union of all rule's outputs, which will be used in the next phase (the defuzzification).

C. The Defuzzification

The defuzzification is the inverse process of the fuzzification, which transforms the fuzzy output of the Fuzzy Inference Engine into a crisp value in order to make this result available to other applications.

The defuzzification is performed based on a decision-making algorithm that selects the best crisp value according to the fuzzy output. The two most used methods are the Center Of Gravity (COG), which return the center of the

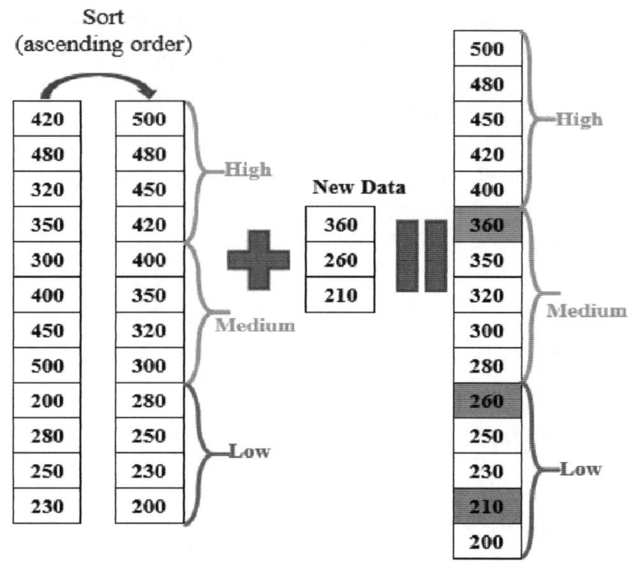

Figure 3. The adaptation process of intervals to user behavior.

fuzzy output area and the Mean Of Maxima (MOM), which returns the crisp value or the mean of crisp values with the highest degree. In this paper, we used the COG function in the defuzzification process because the values generated by this function tend to change smoothly when there are small changes in the values of factors (the second produces two values that are far apart with slight changes in factors values).

IV. USER PROFILE MODEL

The user profile is an essential component in this approach, which is why we must use a well-defined model to store it. This model describes the structure and the semantic relation between all information that exists in the profile.

There are several techniques to represent the user profile; we will discuss the more appropriate methods in our opinion based on the reviews of [17]–[20]. First, the Graphical models use modeling languages like Unified Modeling Language (UML) and Object-Role Modeling (ORM) to build the model. Then, it implements it using Structured Query Language (SQL), Non-Structured Query Language (NoSQL), or eXtensible Markup Language (XML) language. These models have a clear structure that makes it easy to retrieve information using queries in small data (queries become very complicated when the model contains a massive amount of data). Besides, these models do not support reasoning or context inference.

The Object-Oriented Models have the same principle as the Object-Oriented programming; they model the context and its relations with the others in a way similar to those (e.g., relations) between classes. The most important advantage of these models is the encapsulation (masks the context processing detail), and the reusability. However, it increases the number of needed resources and does not support reasoning.

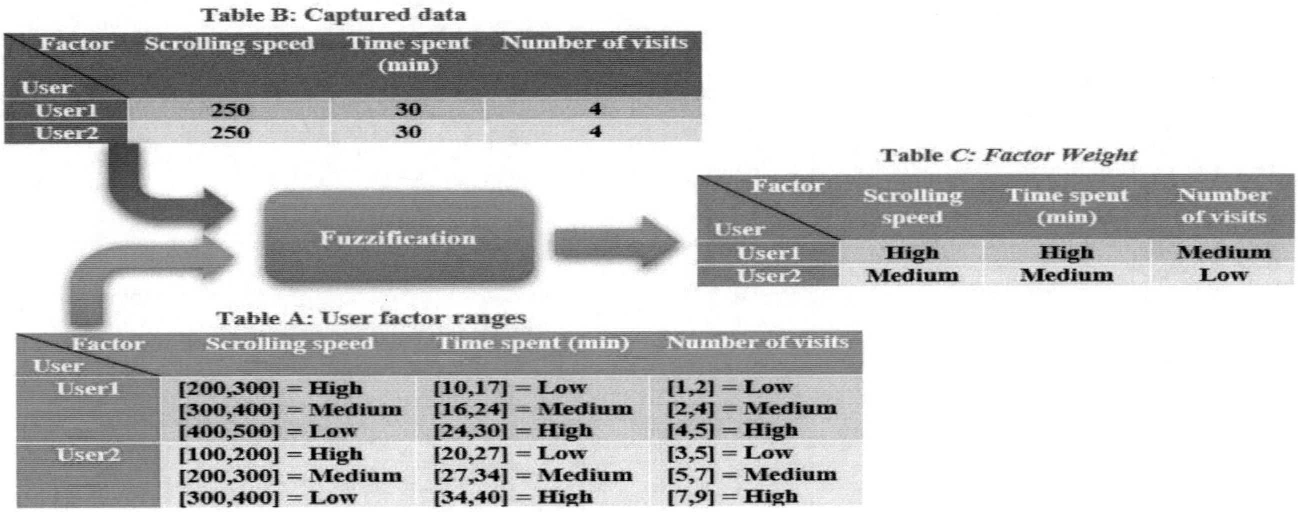

Table B: Captured data

Factor / User	Scrolling speed	Time spent (min)	Number of visits
User1	250	30	4
User2	250	30	4

Table C: Factor Weight

Factor / User	Scrolling speed	Time spent (min)	Number of visits
User1	High	High	Medium
User2	Medium	Medium	Low

Table A: User factor ranges

Factor / User	Scrolling speed	Time spent (min)	Number of visits
User1	[200,300] = High [300,400] = Medium [400,500] = Low	[10,17] = Low [16,24] = Medium [24,30] = High	[1,2] = Low [2,4] = Medium [4,5] = High
User2	[100,200] = High [200,300] = Medium [300,400] = Low	[20,27] = Low [27,34] = Medium [34,40] = High	[3,5] = Low [5,7] = Medium [7,9] = High

Figure 4. Fuzzification process.

The Logic-Based Models are based on binary logic. They use the facts, expressions, and rules to model the context (adds information as facts and removes/ modify it by rules). These models support reasoning and context inference. They have a very high degree of expressiveness and formality, and there are graphic tools for the development of this type of models. These models are heavily coupled with the application domain, which decreases their reusability.

The last one is the Ontology-Based models. These models represent the context with description logic such as Resource Description Framework (RDF), RDF Schema (RDFS), and Web Ontology Language (OWL). Those languages offer a high degree of expressiveness in the modeling of context and the modeling of relations between contexts. The ontology supports reasoning and inference (using inference engine like pellet), as well as separates the knowledge from the application, which increases the reuse and the share of knowledge between applications.

To model the user profile, we choose the ontology-based model for several reasons, such as the high expressiveness, many tools for implementation, the capability of reuse and share knowledge. Our ontology, represented in Figure 6, has two main classes:

- User Interests: contain user interest websites. This class has five attributes: URL of the website, scrolling speed, time spent, number of visits, interest degree calculated by our approach.
- Topic: represents the topic of the website. This class has only one attribute "Label" that represents the name of the topic (e.g., machine learning, sport).

The user profile model (classes, attributes, and the relation between classes) is created manually using Protégé [22] (a visual application to create an ontology) and maintained up to date automatically using the algorithm in Figure 5.

V. CONCLUSION AND FUTURE WORK

The user profile contains information about the user that helps the customization systems to provide data or service to the user's needs. In this paper, we propose an approach to automatically construct and update the user profile using a Fuzzy Logic system. This system solves the problem of factor weight misinterpretation and calculates the degree of interest of the user in specific topics. This paper contains the theory part of the system. This is a work in progress; the Fuzzy Logic system based on this approach is under development. As future works, we will develop the system, and perform the initial test with two users (we already have the data collected from those users) to prove the efficiency of this approach. Finally, we will discuss the possibility of increasing the number of factors.

```
Inputs: New_Site, Interest_degree;
SS: Scrolling speed, TS: Time spent, NV: Number of visits
Begin:
  Profile = Get_User_Profile ();
  IF (Profile.Site_Exist (New_Site)) {
    Old_Site = Profile.Get_Site (New_Site.URL);
    Profile.Update (Interest_degree);
    Profile.Update (New_Site.SS, Old_Site.SS);
    Profile.Update(Average (New_Site.TS, Old_Site.TS));
    Profile.Update(Average (Old_Site.NV++));
    IF (Profile.Missing_Topics (New_Site.Topics)) {
      Profile.Update_Attribute (New_Site .Topics);
    }
  } Else {Profile.Add (New_Site, Interest_degree);}
End.
```

Figure 5. Algorithm to update the user profile.

TABLE II. FUZZY INFERENCE ENGINE RULES.

Rule	IF			Then
	Scrolling speed	Time spent	Number of visits	Degree of interest
1.	High	High	High	I
2.	High	High	Medium	I
3.	High	High	Low	I
4.	High	Medium	High	I
5.	High	Medium	Medium	LI
6.	High	Medium	Low	LI
7.	High	Low	High	I
8.	High	Low	Medium	LI
9.	High	Low	Low	UI
10.	Medium	High	High	I
11.	Medium	High	Medium	I
12.	Medium	High	Low	LI
13.	Medium	Medium	High	I
14.	Medium	Medium	Medium	LI
15.	Medium	Medium	Low	LI
16.	Medium	Low	High	LI
17.	Medium	Low	Medium	LI
18.	Medium	Low	Low	UI
19.	Low	High	High	I
20.	Low	High	Medium	LI
21.	Low	High	Low	UI
22.	Low	Medium	High	LI
23.	Low	Medium	Medium	UI
24.	Low	Medium	Low	UI
25.	Low	Low	High	UI
26.	Low	Low	Medium	UI
27.	Low	Low	Low	UI

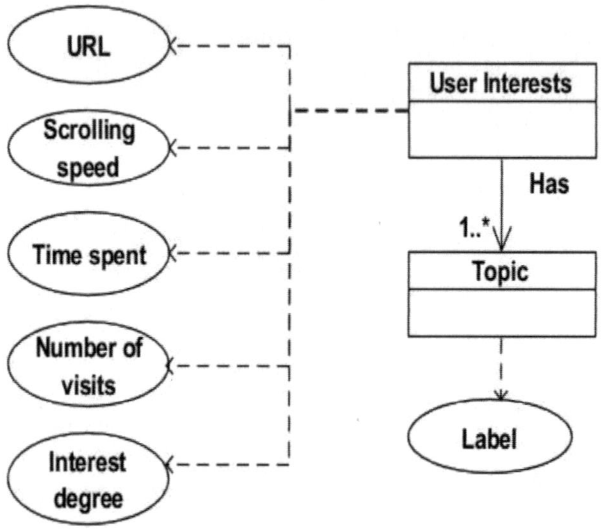

Figure 6. User profile model.

REFERENCES

[1] S. Kanoje, S. Girase, and D. Mukhopadhyay, "User Profiling Trends, Techniques and Applications," vol. 1, no. 1, p. 6, 2015.

[2] A. Cufoglu, "User Profiling - A Short Review," *Int. J. Comput. Appl.*, vol. 108, no. 3, pp. 1–9, Dec. 2014, doi: 10.5120/18888-0179.

[3] Y.-U. S. Tchantchou and E. C. Ezin, "An Improving Mapping Process Based on a Clustering Algorithm for Modeling Hybrid and Dynamic Ontological User Profile," in *2017 13th International Conference on Signal-Image Technology & Internet-Based Systems (SITIS)*, Jaipur, India, 2017, pp. 1–8, doi: 10.1109/SITIS.2017.12.

[4] I. F. Moawad, H. Talha, E. Hosny, and M. Hashim, "Agent-based web search personalization approach using dynamic user profile," *Egypt. Inform. J.*, vol. 13, no. 3, pp. 191–198, Nov. 2012, doi: 10.1016/j.eij.2012.09.002.

[5] "WordNet | A Lexical Database for English." [Online]. Available: https://wordnet.princeton.edu/. [Accessed: 24-Feb-2020].

[6] A. Singh and A. Sharma, "A Multi-agent Framework for Context-Aware Dynamic User Profiling for Web Personalization," in *Software Engineering*, Springer, 2019, pp. 1–16.

[7] K. Makvana, P. Shah, and P. Shah, "A novel approach to personalize web search through user profiling and query reformulation," in *2014 International Conference on Data Mining and Intelligent Computing (ICDMIC)*, Delhi, India, 2014, pp. 1–10, doi: 10.1109/ICDMIC.2014.6954221.

[8] X. Wu, Y. Fu, S. Tian, Q. Zheng, and F. Tian, "A hybrid approach to personalized web search," in *Proceedings of the 2012 IEEE 16th International Conference on Computer Supported Cooperative Work in Design (CSCWD)*, 2012, pp. 214–220.

[9] A. Hawalah and M. Fasli, "Dynamic user profiles for web personalisation," *Expert Syst. Appl.*, vol. 42, no. 5, pp. 2547–2569, Apr. 2015, doi: 10.1016/j.eswa.2014.10.032.

[10] L. A. Zadeh, "Soft computing and fuzzy logic," in *Fuzzy Sets, Fuzzy Logic, and Fuzzy Systems: Selected Papers by Lotfi a Zadeh*, World Scientific, 1996, pp. 796–804.

[11] Y. Bai and D. Wang, "Fundamentals of Fuzzy Logic Control — Fuzzy Sets, Fuzzy Rules and Defuzzifications," in *Advanced Fuzzy Logic Technologies in Industrial Applications*, Y. Bai, H. Zhuang, and D. Wang, Eds. London: Springer London, 2006, pp. 17–36.

[12] H. R. Berenji, "Fuzzy logic controllers," in *An introduction to fuzzy logic applications in intelligent systems*, Springer, 1992, pp. 69–96.

[13] D. Veit, "Fuzzy logic and its application to textile technology," in *Simulation in Textile Technology*, Elsevier, 2012, pp. 112–141.

[14] R. S. Jaiswal and M. V. Sarode, "An Overview on Fuzzy Logic & Fuzzy Elements," *Int. Res. J. Comput. Sci.*, vol. 3, no. 2, p. 6, 2015.

[15] A. K. Nandi, "GA-Fuzzy Approaches: Application to Modeling of Manufacturing Process," in *Statistical and Computational Techniques in Manufacturing*, J. P. Davim, Ed. Berlin, Heidelberg: Springer Berlin Heidelberg, 2012, pp. 145–185.

[16] S. N. Mandal, J. P. Choudhury, and S. R. B. Chaudhuri, "In Search of Suitable Fuzzy Membership Function in Prediction of Time Series Data," vol. 9, no. 3, p. 10, 2012.

[17] P. Cingolani and J. Alcalá-Fdez, "jFuzzyLogic: a Java Library to Design Fuzzy Logic Controllers According to the Standard for Fuzzy Control Programming," *Int. J. Comput. Intell. Syst.*,

vol. 6, no. supl, pp. 61–75, Jun. 2013, doi: 10.1080/18756891.2013.818190.

[18] T. Strang and C. Linnhoff-Popien, "A context modeling survey," in *Workshop Proceedings*, 2004.

[19] C. Perera, A. Zaslavsky, P. Christen, and D. Georgakopoulos, "Context Aware Computing for The Internet of Things: A Survey," *IEEE Commun. Surv. Tutor.*, vol. 16, no. 1, pp. 414–454, 2014, doi: 10.1109/SURV.2013.042313.00197.

[20] X. Li, M. Eckert, J.-F. Martinez, and G. Rubio, "Context Aware Middleware Architectures: Survey and Challenges," *Sensors*, vol. 15, no. 8, pp. 20570–20607, Aug. 2015, doi: 10.3390/s150820570.

[21] C. Bettini *et al.*, "A survey of context modelling and reasoning techniques," *Pervasive Mob. Comput.*, vol. 6, no. 2, pp. 161–180, Apr. 2010, doi: 10.1016/j.pmcj.2009.06.002.

[22] "protégé." [Online]. Available: https://protege.stanford.edu/. [Accessed: 12-Mar-2020].

The Benefits of Combining Paper- and Video- Based Prototypes for User Interface Evaluation

Hayet Hammami[†*], Fatoumata Camara[§], Gaëlle Calvary[*], Meriem Riahi[†] and Faouzi Moussa[†]
[*]Univ. Grenoble Alpes, CNRS, Grenoble INP, LIG
F38000 Grenoble France
Email: FirstName.LastName@univ-grenoble-alpes.fr
[†]Univ. of Tunis El Manar, Faculty of sciences of Tunis, LIPAH-LR11ES14
2092 Tunis Tunisia
Email: faouzimoussa@gmail.com, meriem.riahi2013@gmail.com
[§]HWR Berlin, Berlin Germany
Email: fatoumatag.camara@gmail.com

***Abstract*—The use of multiple User Interface (UI) designs for evaluation has been demonstrated beneficial for UI evaluation as it results in better feedback, both qualitatively and quantitatively. However, producing several designs is time-consuming. Moreover, the properties that the alternative UI must satisfy remain under-explored. The paper investigates the use of different prototype forms of the same design as support to evaluation instead of relying on alternative design solutions. We investigate two experimental conditions: (1) paper prototype first then video prototype, and (2) video prototype first then paper prototype. Results show that the combination of paper and video prototypes is well suited for UI evaluation, as feedback addresses all aspects of Human-Computer Interaction (HCI), namely, utility, usability, and aesthetics. When exposed to multiple prototypes, users develop an understanding of the functional core and of the interactive aspect of the system. The experiment outcomes indicate that, when evaluating the paper prototype first, then the video prototype, users tend to be more critical and provide more suggestions of improvements.**

Keywords–UI evaluation; Feedback; Prototyping; Video prototyping; Comparative evaluation.

I. Introduction

The number of UI designs used for evaluation influences responsiveness of users as well as the amount and quality of feedback. Therefore, submitting different design examples could help UI testers see issues clearly, identify concrete steps for improvement, and integrate novel ideas [1].

Many research papers addressed the use of multiple design alternatives for UI evaluation (comparative evaluation) [1]–[5]. These alternatives consist of design variations at several levels of abstraction, such as syntactic and semantic levels. They can be designed by the same designer(s) [2] [4], or obtained via targeted research such as the visual aspects or the content [1].

Comparative evaluation increases the amount of comments (reviews and suggestions), gives rise to more and stronger criticisms, and facilitates comparative reasoning. Consequently, showing multiple design alternatives to users for UI evaluation represents *a way to get the right design*.

Previous work clearly highlights that comparative evaluation has great benefits. However, producing alternative design(s) can be time-consuming and difficult, particularly considering that existing literature does not address criteria that should be considered for the generation of the alternative design(s).

In this work, we investigate the use of different prototype forms as support to evaluation. Our aim is to determine whether the use of different forms could be as beneficial as different designs so that it could be considered as an alternative to multiple designs for evaluation. In this paper, we report an experimental evaluation in which we used both paper and video as prototype mediums for UI evaluation.

The remaining of this paper is organized as follows. Section II presents related work about system prototyping. Section III describes the experiment and the design elaboration. Section IV reports results and observations from the experiment and Section V concludes the paper and presents future work.

II. Many faces of prototyping

Prototypes can be of different levels of fidelity and can take different forms. The right level of fidelity and appropriate form of a prototype depends on the design stage and evaluation needs. A prototype can be of low-fidelity, medium-fidelity or high-fidelity with respect to the final UI [6]. According to Greenberg [7], *"The determining factor in prototype fidelity is the degree to which the prototype accurately represents the appearance and interaction of the product"*.

Much of the often-cited literature emphasizes the use of low/medium fidelity prototypes [8] [9]. When assessing low fidelity prototypes, users feel more included in the design process and feel more free to criticize the design [10]. Oppositely, when evaluating high fidelity prototypes for the first time, users tend to focus on the details of the interface (e.g. color of icons, size of font) rather than on the overall structure [7]. Furthermore, it has been found that the usability data collected from low and high-fidelity levels are comparable [9] [10] [11].

Moreover, a prototype can take different forms, such as a sketch [8], a paper mock-up [4] or a tool to test [12]. Designers can also use presentation software like PowerPoint or Keynote [13], or videos [14] [15] in order to illustrate the dynamicity of interaction.

A. Paper prototyping

Techniques such as paper prototyping excel at representing static visual properties [15]. They are very used during the design process due to their low cost and efficiency. They can perform the role of sketching in order to develop, explore, communicate and evaluate the designer's ideas [2] [8].

Paper prototyping presents a fast and easy way to communicate and to test initial ideas early and quickly, e.g., brainstorming sessions. Paper prototypes help in getting substantive user feedback, promote rapid iterative development [10], and allow for easy and inexpensive modifications. Moreover, paper prototypes can be very helpful for usability testing as mentioned in Tohidi et al.'s work: "*the interaction designer communicates with the user largely by means of an "interactive sketch", such as a paper prototype*" [8].

B. Video prototyping

Video prototypes, on the other hand, are particularly well suited to assess interaction. Video prototyping is an established technique in HCI, which is typically used in early designs stages to enable software designers to evaluate the interaction prior to actual software implementation. Producing a video prototype is cheaper and less time-consuming in comparison to building a fully working prototype.

Video prototypes present great benefits [11] [14]–[17], for instance, they allow design exploration, evaluation and presentation [16] [17]. They also communicate and reflect the interaction design [15] and help capture and communicate the details of how users interact with software. Zwinderman et al. [18] compared the use of video prototypes and usability tests. They analyzed results regarding overall user experience (AttrackDiff), user acceptance (Unified Theory of Acceptance and Use of Technology (UTAUT)), and five "expectations" elaborated by the researchers in this work:

- Participants who use the product give more comments on the interface.
- Viewers of the video prototype make more comments on the context of use.
- Participants provide a similar number of comments as to when and where they use the application.
- Viewers of the video prototype suggest more new features.
- Participants who use the product suggest more improvements.

The conclusion of this study suggests that video prototypes help obtain feedback from users that is quite similar to that gathered when users test the final product.

In other works, researchers studied the impact of the visual fidelity-level of video prototypes on the amount and quality of feedback provided by users during evaluation. Dhilton et al. [11] compared feedback collected from using a low-fidelity video prototype (animated paper cut-outs) and feedback collected from using a high-fidelity video prototype (a video with real actors, edited to simulate computer output). The video prototype fidelity focused on the notion of realism of the video (Figure 1). Analysis considered attractiveness and usability of the concept (AttrackDiff), intent to use, understandability, ease of use and feasibility of the system presented (UTAUT). Additionally, during test sessions, users were asked to express likes and dislikes related to the system as well as suggestions for improvement. Dhilton et al.'s study concludes that the visual fidelity level of the video prototype does not affect

Figure 1. Low fidelity (left) and high fidelity (right) versions of the video prototype used in [11].

the amount and quality of user's feedback during evaluation sessions.

Both paper and video prototypes foster discussion regarding interface and interaction with stakeholders. Video prototypes represent a powerful tool as they produce feedback that can be compared to feedback from other techniques that might be more costly. Both paper and video prototypes are cheap to produce and have been proven beneficial for HCI evaluation. However, to the best of our knowledge, the combined use of paper and video prototypes as support to HCI evaluation has not yet been investigated (particularly as alternative to using multiple design alternatives).

In this work, we use a paper prototype and a video prototype to assess a commercial Website. We investigate the benefits of using both prototype forms presented together in the same evaluation session for UI evaluation. The main research question tackled here is the following: "does using different prototype types as support to HCI evaluation could be as beneficial as relying on alternative UI designs?".

III. Experiment

Our study focused on a commercial Web site for high-tech products. The case study was purely academic. The reason for this choice was that the e-commerce platform is widespread and familiar to many people, and thereby easy to explain.

A. Prototypes elaboration

The prototypes consisted of medium fidelity prototypes, designed using the Balsamiq Wireframes tool [19]. The UI illustrates essential features of the commercial Web site: menu, sub-menus, list of items on the home page, list of items for a specific category of products, details of a product, and content of the cart.

The paper prototype (Figure 2) consisted of four screenshots, illustrating four different pages of the Web site. Figure 2-A represents the home page of the Web site, Figure 2-B represents the page referring to the sub-category smartphones, Figure 2-C represents the page referring to the details of a selected product, and Figure 2-D represents the page referring to the cart. Using a tool like Balsamiq allowed us to assign hypertext links to different components of the interface in order to create functional widgets and navigate between the different pages.

The video prototype was then made by recording interaction through the same UI, using a video screenshot tool. There were no additional pages shown on the video. However, in some cases, the products displayed changed due to navigation in the list (Figure 3).

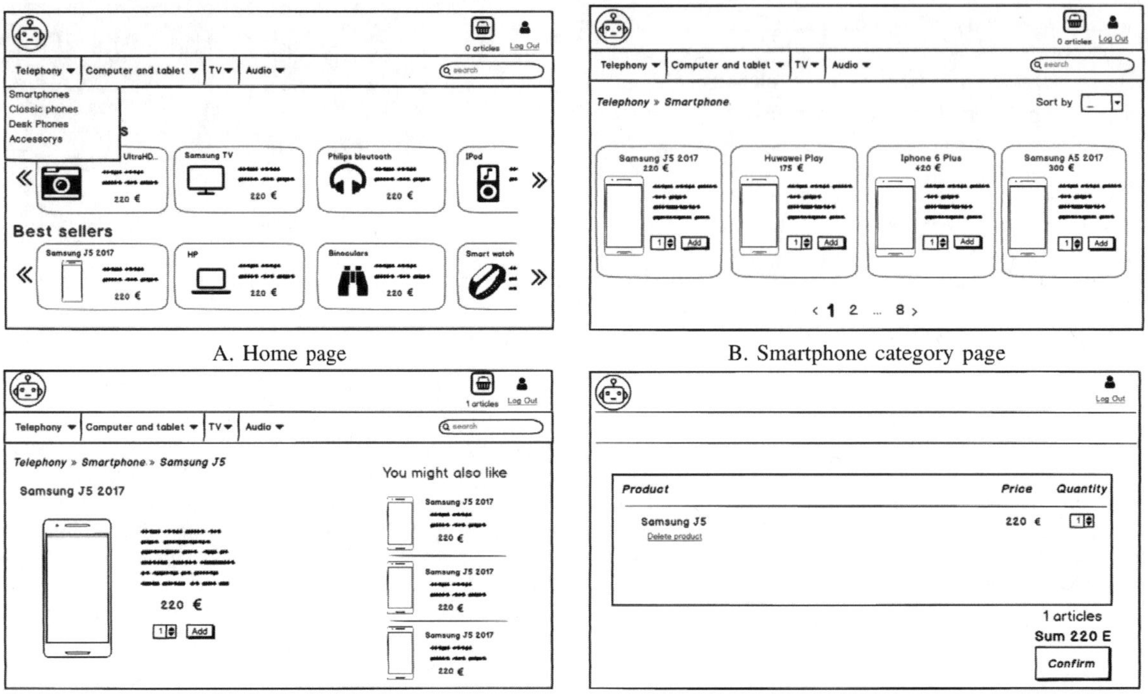

A. Home page

B. Smartphone category page

C. Article details page

D. Cart page

Figure 2. Paper-based prototype presented to users

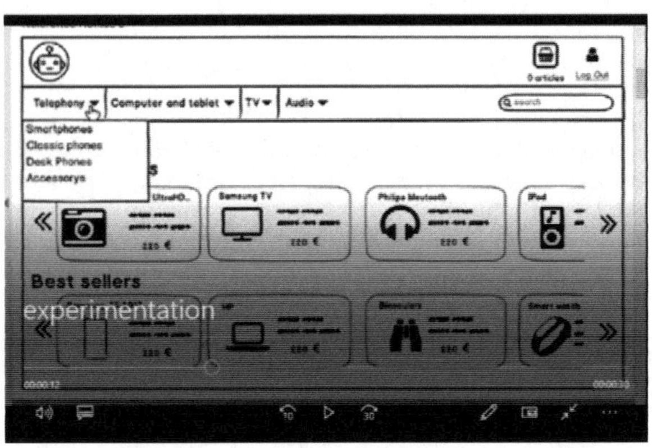

Figure 3. Video based prototype

B. Scenario

The video is 42 seconds long and features a user choosing and purchasing a smartphone through the Web site. The scenario goes as follows: the user starts by navigating through the home page of the Web site, browsing the deals and the best sellers' lists, then, he/she browses the menu to explore the different categories and sub-categories presented, and selects the sub-category "smartphone". Next, we see the user being redirected to the smartphone sub-category page, from where he/she can choose a product from the list and add it to the cart. After consulting the cart, we see the user changing his/her mind about the product that he/she selected. He/she deletes it from the cart and goes back to the home page to choose another item.

The same person who designed the UI was the one who ran the scenario for the video.

C. Participants

The technique used for our experiment is primarily a qualitative one, but which allows to collect quantitative data. With qualitative techniques, such as usability tests or interviews, the aim is to dig into topics (i.e., usability problems) while usually observing testers' reactions: as the name implies, the focus is more on quality rather than on quantity. Consequently, qualitative techniques require a low number of testers to get a fair overview over the addressed topics; for instance, as low as 5 participants for a usability tests [20]. Indeed, according to Nielson [20], "*with 5 users, we almost always get close to user testing's maximum benefit cost ratio*". However, it is important to mention that, to get statistically significant numbers, at least 20 participants should be included in the study. Folkler [21] suggest that 20 participants help obtain 95% of usability problems.

Our experiment involved 22 participants (11 women and 11 men, with a range of age between 22 and 58 years old). Participants included both HCI students and researchers as well as people with no knowledge at all in the field. The number of HCI students, females and males were equivalent for each group of participants.

Participants were asked about their online shopping frequency. 13 participants said that they often purchase products online, 7 participants said that they sometimes do online shopping, and 2 participants said that they rarely purchase products online.

D. Protocol

We considered two experimental conditions: paper prototype, then video prototype and video prototype, then paper prototype. Participants were divided into two groups of eleven participants, and were asked to observe and critique both prototypes. Each group tested one experimental condition:

- **Experimental condition 1: paper prototype, then video prototype:** participants were first provided with the paper-based prototype and asked to observe the UI without enforcing any time limit. After looking at the prototype, the participants were asked to evaluate it. As a second step, we replaced the paper-based prototype with the video and asked the participant to watch it. The video could be watched up to three times at most. It was up to the participant to re-watch. However, it was not allowed to pause the video while watching. After watching the video, the participants were asked if they had something to add regarding their first evaluation.
- **Experimental condition 2: video prototype, then paper prototype:** participants were first presented with the video then with the paper-based prototype.

E. Users feedback record

Participants were asked to provide feedback using their own words regarding three aspects: things they like, things they do not likee and improvements. To do so, they had to write their statements on magnetic post-its and place them as either 'like', 'dislike' or 'improvement' on a board (Figure 4).

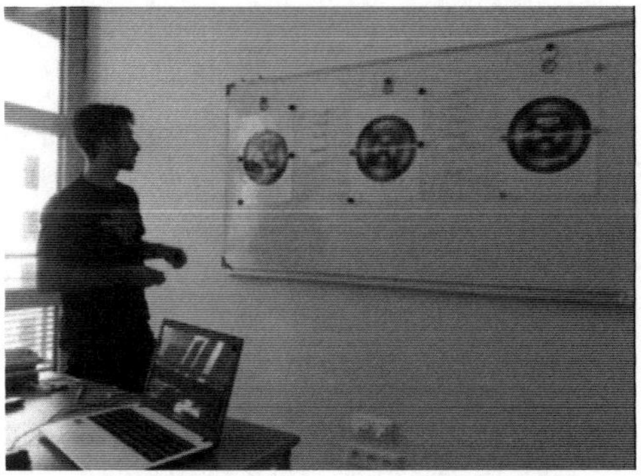

Figure 4. Participant expressing his opinions

Most of the time, participants tended to explain what they are writing and expressed their thoughts orally. Observations were recorded by note-taking throughout the experiment. Furthermore, we recorded the evaluation sessions via a Dictaphone.

IV. Results

This section presents the results of the experiment. We first classify users' feedback, then we discuss the impacts of the two types of prototyping on the UI evaluation.

A. Categorization of user's feedback

We collected, counted, and classified users' statements in three categories with respect to the ones that were considered to collect feedback: likes (positive comments), dislikes (negative comments) and suggestions for improvement. This first categorization was inspired by the taxonomy elaborated in [2], and used in [4]. We used it to study the user's willingness to criticize during evaluation sessions. Then, we gathered statements inductively according to three criteria commonly considered in UI evaluation: utility, usability and aesthetics, in order to study users' feedback.

The total number of statements collected for both groups was approximately the same: 106 for the first group (paper then video) and 104 for the second group (video then paper).

As indicated in Table 1, in both experimental conditions, the number of statements provided with the prototype being presented at first was significantly higher than the number of statements collected with the second prototype. Indeed, during the first step of the evaluation, regardless whether the paper or the video prototype was presented first, the number of statements was roughly the same.

TABLE I. NUMBER OF STATEMENTS.

	Step 1	*Step 2*	*Total number of statements*
Group 1 (Paper then video)	77	29	106
Group 2 (Video then paper)	79	25	104

B. Impact on user's willingness to criticize depending on the prototype presented and evaluation condition

In order to assess the impacts of presenting different forms of prototypes on participants' willingness to be critical, we compared the number of positive comments, negative comments and suggestions for improvement according to the order of prototypes presentation: paper then video (group 1) and video then paper (group 2).

Figure 5 shows how the total numbers of statements produced were classified. The first observation in Figure 5 is

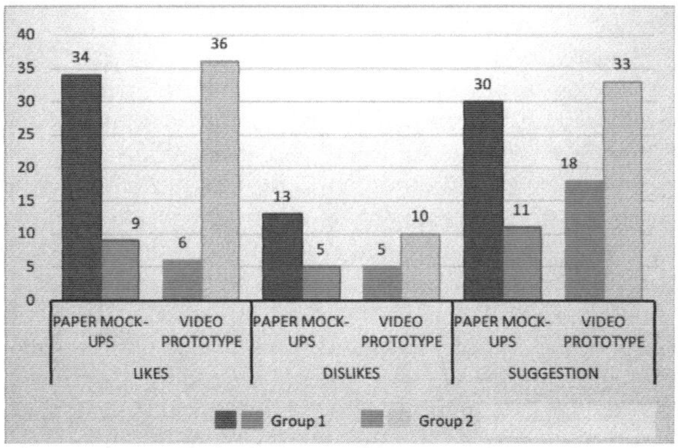

Figure 5. Numbers of positive comments (likes), negative comments (dislikes), and suggestions

that the number of likes and suggestions are higher than the negative comments for both groups. However, it is important to note that the number of dislikes added to the number of suggestions is higher than the number of likes for each prototype for both groups.

The number of dislikes is significantly lower than the numbers of likes and suggestions. This result can be explained by the overlap between dislikes and suggestions. Indeed, during the experiment, participants often hesitated to choose between dislikes and suggestions for many comments.

Examples of likes included feedback about the access to best sellers on the welcome page and the simplicity of the UI. Examples of suggestions included feedback about integrating a more sophisticated search function and using vertical instead of horizontal scrolling. Examples of dislikes included feedback about the lack of the navigation menu in the cart page and the lack of the "add" button in the best deals list.

An important observation is that the feedback collected in the second step of the evaluation for both groups consisted mainly in suggestions and negative comments. Indeed, reevaluating the same UI design, but, presented through a different type of prototype pushed users to be more critical and to provide more insights about improvements.

Overall, Overall, regardless of what prototype was presented first, users started by expressing their likes and appreciations of the prototype in question. However, users in the first group provided more suggestions in the second step of the evaluation than the second group. Seeing the video prototype after the evaluation of the paper prototype pushed users to be more critical and to provide more suggestions for improvements.

Based on these results, we can say that the experiment highlighted the positive aspects of the design, while also gathering an even greater number of insights for design improvement.

C. Impact on users' feedback depending on the prototype presented and evaluation condition

We qualitatively analyzed the data in order to relate participants' statements to utility, usability and aesthetics within each prototype and evaluation order. Feedback about utility addressed the system features, including comments such as deleting or adding a feature to the Web site. We considered usability as defined by the International Organization for Standardization (ISO): "The extent to which a product can be used by specified users to achieve specified goals with effectiveness, efficiency, and satisfaction in a specified context of use" [22]. Feedback regarding usability included, for instance, the possibility to add a product directly from the welcome page; the absence of the navigation menu in the cart page; the possibility to add several products to the cart at the same time; or, the absence of an information message once a product is added or deleted from the cart. Feedback about aesthetics considered the graphic design (e.g., colors, icons design, fonts, widget choices, etc.) and included statements about the choice of the icon chosen as the Web site logo and the colors used.

Figure 6 shows how the total number of statements produced were classified.

Results show that the paper prototype produced the highest number of feedback related to utility whilst the video prototype produced the highest number of feedback related to usability.

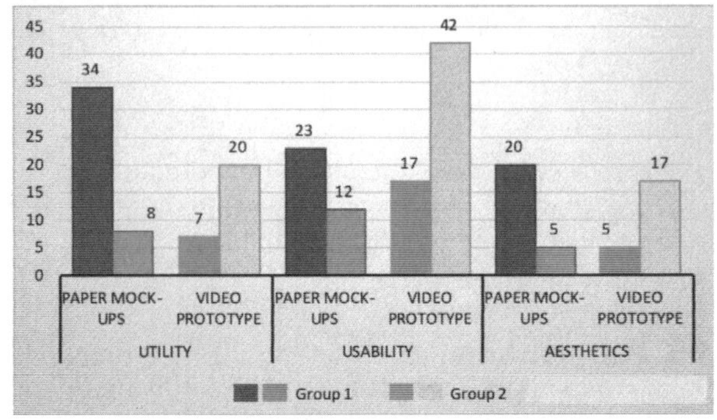

Figure 6. Numbers of statements according to utility, usability, and aesthetics.

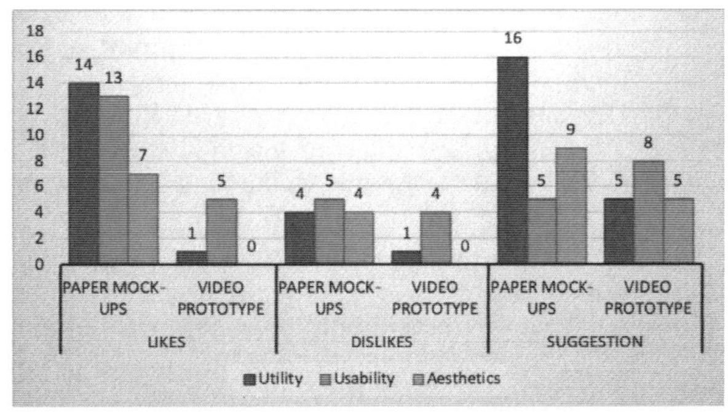

Figure 7. Numbers of statements according to utility, usability, and aesthetics for the first evaluation order (paper then video).

Finally, the numbers of feedback regarding aesthetics are roughly the same for the two prototypes over the two groups.

Furthermore, we summarize below the qualitative data providing indications according to the two mentioned classifications in order to compare the number of problems discovered and suggestions provided regarding each aspect (utility, usability and aesthetics) for each prototype for both groups.

Figures 7 and 8 show how the total numbers of statements produced were classified.

Results show that participants detected more problems and provided more suggestions in experiment condition 1 (paper

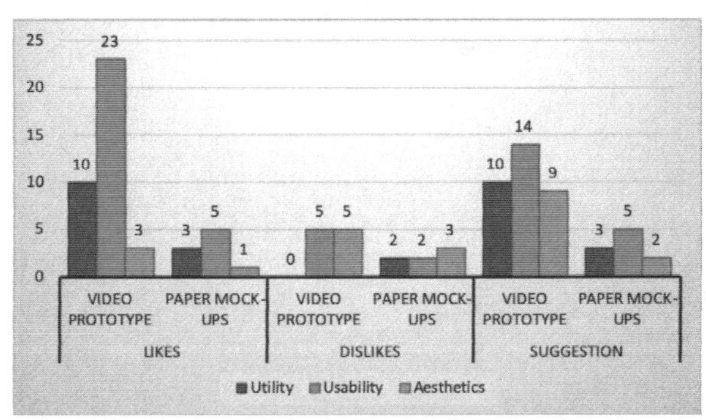

Figure 8. Numbers of statements according to utility, usability, and aesthetics for the second evaluation order (video then paper).

then video) than in experiment condition 2 (video the paper). For example, the number of likes regarding usability provided with the video prototype in the second group was similar to the number of dislikes and suggestions provided about this HCI aspect. However, in the first group, when comparing the number of likes with the number of dislikes and suggestions about utility, we find that the number of likes is considerably lower.

V. CONCLUSION AND FUTURE WORK

This study explores a different approach to UI evaluation, which could guide practitioners towards getting the design right while minimizing the cost of UI design.

We conducted an experiment which consisted in using a medium-fidelity paper prototype and a medium-fidelity video prototype as support to evaluation and tested two experimental conditions. Users successively evaluated either a paper prototype then a video prototype, or a video prototype then a paper prototype.

The results indicate that (1) using paper prototypes allowed users to focus on features offered by the system ; actually, users took time to explore the system features, as such, they developed an understanding of the functional core and criticized mainly utility. (2) Using a video prototype allowed users to focus more on the interaction with the system, i.e., how a user can perform a specific task; as such, by seeing the system 'in action', they developed an understanding of the interactive aspects of the system and focused on usability. (3) Regarding aesthetics, feedback provided by users was comparable within both groups.

Moreover, it is important to note that the order of prototypes presentation to users does matter since evaluating the video prototype after evaluating the paper prototype incites users to be more critical and to provide more suggestions of improvements.

Overall, the results indicate that evaluating one prototype is not enough. Over both evaluation conditions, when seeing the UI in a different prototype form, users discovered problems and provided suggestions of improvements that did not occur to them when evaluating the first prototype provided.

A general recommendation coming out of this study is to supplement video prototypes with paper prototypes at first for UI evaluation, in order to increase the evaluation benefits.

In future work, we are interested in comparing evaluation based on different types of prototypes and evaluation based on alternative design solutions in order to identify the most beneficial approach in terms of relevant feedback at a minimum cost.

REFERENCES

[1] H. B. Kang, G. Amoako, N. Sengupta, and S. P. Dow, "Paragon: An online gallery for enhancing design feedback with visual examples," in Proceedings of the 2018 CHI Conference on Human Factors in Computing Systems, 2018, pp. 1–13.

[2] M. Tohidi, W. Buxton, R. Baecker, and A. Sellen, "Getting the right design and the design right," in Proceedings of the SIGCHI conference on Human Factors in computing systems, 2006, pp. 1243–1252.

[3] S. Dow, J. Fortuna, D. Schwartz, B. Altringer, D. Schwartz, and S. Klemmer, "Prototyping dynamics: sharing multiple designs improves exploration, group rapport, and results," in Proceedings of the SIGCHI Conference on Human Factors in Computing Systems, 2011, pp. 2807–2816.

[4] H. Hammami, G. Calvary, M. Riahi, F. Moussa, and S. Bouzit, "Comparative evaluation? yes, but with which alternative ui?" Electronic Visualisation and the Arts (EVA 2017), 2017, pp. 1–7.

[5] R. S. Dicks, "Mis-usability: on the uses and misuses of usability testing," in Proceedings of the 20th annual international conference on Computer documentation, 2002, pp. 26–30.

[6] A. Coyette, S. Kieffer, and J. Vanderdonckt, "Multi-fidelity prototyping of user interfaces," in IFIP Conference on Human-Computer Interaction. Springer, 2007, pp. 150–164.

[7] S. Greenberg, "Prototyping for design and evaluation," November, vol. 30, 1998, p. 2004.

[8] M. Tohidi, W. Buxton, R. Baecker, and A. Sellen, "User sketches: a quick, inexpensive, and effective way to elicit more reflective user feedback," in Proceedings of the 4th Nordic conference on Human-computer interaction: changing roles, 2006, pp. 105–114.

[9] M. E. Wiklund, C. Thurrott, and J. S. Dumas, "Does the fidelity of software prototypes affect the perception of usability?" in Proceedings of the Human Factors Society Annual Meeting. SAGE PublicationsSage CA: Los Angeles, CA, 2016.

[10] M. Walker, L. Takayama, and J. A. Landay, "High-fidelity or low-fidelity, paper or computer? choosing attributes when testing web prototypes," in Proceedings of the human factors and ergonomics society annual meeting, vol. 46, no. 5. SAGE Publications Sage CA: Los Angeles, CA, 2002, pp. 661–665.

[11] B. Dhillon, P. Banach, R. Kocielnik, J. P. Emparanza, I. Politis, A. Rczewska, and P. Markopoulos, "Visual fidelity of video prototypes and user feedback: a case study," in Proceedings of HCI 2011 The 25th BCS Conference on Human Computer Interaction, 2011, pp. 139–144.

[12] H. Kim, C. Coutrix, and A. Roudaut, "Morphees+ studying everyday reconfigurable objects for the design and taxonomy of reconfigurable uis," in Proceedings of the 2018 CHI Conference on Human Factors in Computing Systems, 2018, pp. 1–14.

[13] P. I. Khella. Use keynote and powerpoint to prototype web and mobile apps. [Online]. Available: https://keynotopia.com/ (Retrieved: July, 2019)

[14] W. E. Mackay, "Using video to support interaction design," DVD Tutorial, CHI, vol. 2, no. 5, 2002.

[15] G. Leiva and M. Beaudouin-Lafon, "Montage: A video prototyping system to reduce re-shooting and increase re-usability," in Proceedings of the 31st Annual ACM Symposium on User Interface Software and Technology, 2018, pp. 675–682.

[16] W. E. Mackay, A. V. Ratzer, and P. Janecek, "Video artifacts for design: Bridging the gap between abstraction and detail," in Proceedings of the 3rd conference on Designing interactive systems: processes, practices, methods, and techniques, 2000, pp. 72–82.

[17] W. E. Mackay, "Video prototyping: a technique for developing hypermedia systems," in CHI'88 Conference Companion Human Factors in Computing Systems, vol. 5. Citeseer, 1988, pp. 1–3.

[18] M. Zwinderman, R. Leenheer, A. Shirzad, N. Chupriyanov, G. Veugen, B. Zhang, and P. Markopoulos, "Using video prototypes for evaluating design concepts with users: a comparison to usability testing," in IFIP Conference on Human-Computer Interaction. Springer, 2013, pp. 774–781.

[19] Balsamiq wireframes. [Online]. Available: https://balsamiq.com/ (Retrieved: December, 2019)

[20] J. Nielsen, "How many test users in a usability study," Nielsen Norman Group, vol. 4, no. 06, 2012.

[21] L. Faulkner, "Beyond the five-user assumption: Benefits of increased sample sizes in usability testing," Behavior Research Methods, Instruments, & Computers, vol. 35, no. 3, 2003, pp. 379–383.

[22] ISO, "Ergonomics of human-system interaction–part 11: Usability: Definitions and concepts," 2018.

Applying Design Thinking to Address Users ATM Deposits Needs

A Case Study on the Financial Sector

Arturo Moquillaza
Pontifical Catholic University of Peru
Lima, Peru
email: amoquillaza@pucp.pe

Joel Aguirre
Pontifical Catholic University of Peru
Lima, Peru
email: aguirre.joel@pucp.pe

Fiorella Falconi
Pontifical Catholic University of Peru
Lima, Peru
email: ffalconit@pucp.pe

Freddy Paz
Pontifical Catholic University of Peru
Lima, Peru
email: fpaz@pucp.pe

***Abstract*—Nowadays, people can use their nearest Automated Teller Machine (ATM) to perform different banking transactions, such as cash withdrawals, cash deposits, bill payments, and transfer of funds between accounts and other banks. However, the total of deposits and cash payments that are made are still low, since ATMs do not give change, and in that sense, everything depends on the total to be paid be equal to the bills the client has available to deposit. This is due to what Shy calls "the burden of receiving and carrying change". In this study, we used Design Thinking, as part of a development team, to address a problem as a challenge for the ATM channel of a well-known bank in Peru. As the problem, we found that the denominations an ATM could dispense generate a significant amount of not withdrawable change that makes people avoid the ATM, forcing to clients and not clients look for a human bank teller to make their operations. This bank adapted and incorporated Design Thinking into its Design practice inside and outside its corresponding division. A solution was proposed from the application of the methodology, giving encouraging results and motivating the financial customer to use other financial products to manage change in ATM cash operations.**

Keywords – Human Computer Interaction; Interaction Design; Self-Service; Automatic Teller Machine; Cash Deposit; Design Thinking; Cash Payment; Banking; Innovation.

I. INTRODUCTION

The introduction of Automated Teller Machines or ATM was intended to decongest the banking halls as people can now go to the nearest ATM to perform their financial operations [1]. Odusina opined that ATM is a technological product developed to enhance quick service and diversified financial services, such as deposits, withdrawals, funds transfer, and payments [2]. However, according to Shy, experts consider that paying with bills subjects the user to what is known as "the burden of receiving and carrying change". This burden is more substantial when the change is farther away from multiples of the available bills at an ATM, where customers look for smaller denomination coins [3].

About the "burden of receiving and carrying change" experienced by clients of banking institutions, this refers to the cost of obtaining cash, counting and receiving change after each transaction. Shy explains that there is a cost proportional to the difference between the available cash and the payment amount. Shy also explains that Knotek called this problem the "relative inconvenience of price" [3]. In that sense, it is expensive for clients to have the exact cash to make the payments that they must make in cash, and in addition, it is unlikely that the payment amount is in multiples of 10, and that no change is required at the end of the transaction. This means that, in the long run, clients end up entering the branch looking for a human teller to perform their deposit or cash payment operation. The first suggestion would be to allow ATMs to give change, but technical and economic restrictions consider this solution as unfeasible in the context of a well-known bank of Peru.

In the past, digital developments were traditionally dedicated to the IT (Information Technology) Departments, but since customer behavior is changing, it is not enough simply to offer new digital services, or just copy the existing ones of the competition [4]. The concept of Design Thinking has driven successful innovation in several industries [5]. Adopting Design Thinking enables bankers to bring customers into consideration so they can know what the clients need and how the service should be delivered to be the most beneficial for its users [6].

In addition, there is insufficient consideration of user centered design guidelines or methodologies in the design of the interfaces for embedded systems in the ATM. This factor is critical to overcoming the complex financial environment [7]. This paper presents a case study, held in BBVA Peru, a leading bank in that country, where a Design Thinking approach is applied to bring a solution for "the burden of receiving change" its customers face when performing deposits and cash payments at an ATM, and, therefore, enter the branch for assistance.

The conducted Design Thinking process consisted of four stages: Comprehension, Ideation, Prototyping, and Evaluation. This was part of a Design Challenge organized in BBVA Peru by Design UX division. The paper is organized as follows. Section II describes other successful cases where Design Thinking was applied in the banking industry. Section III describes in detail the problem that was addressed in this Design Challenge. Section IV describes, step by step, the process conducted. Section V concludes this work.

II. DESIGN THINKING IN THE BANKING INDUSTRY

According to Brown, Design Thinking is a human-centered approach to finding the best ideas and solutions [8]. In the literature, there is some evidence of the application of Design Thinking in the financial sector. Klepek [6] made a study of five banks that implemented this approach. In that study, he mentioned the following cases:

- The ANZ Banking Group developed [6] a cutting-edge mobile app for their employees and changed the organizational culture to be more user-centered.
- The Juniper Bank redesigned [6] its Web banking making it more user-friendly by changing its customer service strategy.
- The PNC Bank developed [13] a new concept of Virtual Wallet with a powerful visualization to help customers with their savings management.
- The Suncorp used Design Thinking [6] visualization to successfully merge with the insurance giant Promina with a 94% rate of employees who understood the new post-merge vision.
- The Bank of America brought the "keep the change" [12] idea that enables customers to transfer small amounts of cents from every purchase they make, enrolling more than eight million users.

However, this kind of cases where banks include customers in the innovation process, usually engage with a specific business division, such as retail banking, but rarely with divisions such as IT [9]. The Deutsche Bank understood this need and adopted Design Thinking allowing them to get final user feedback on quickly developed or incomplete prototypes of new services [9]. To align to these ideas, the BBVA is focusing on implementing Design Thinking in the IT divisions.

III. CONTEXT AND THE REAL PROBLEM

For the BBVA Peru Bank, as in the rest of local banks, the ATM channel is still the most used by its customers. Despite the fact that it has more than 300 deposit ATMs, more than 40% of its bank branches are still crowded. This affects the digitalization of the bank, having only 40% of the deposit and payments made through this channel because of "the burden of change".

According to Shy [3], when people face financial transactions that involve cash, they carry the burden of receiving and carrying their change (coins and low denomination bills). This is what he calls "the burden of change", based on his study [3]. Paying with cash subjects the clients to receiving and carrying change, depending on the payment amounts. Shy observed that people tended to change to debit and credit cards when the amount exceeded the threshold of $20. This affects directly the services an ATM could offer, such as payments in cash and cash deposits, making people employ other channels.

Following the adoption of Design Thinking started by other banks, a few years ago, it was adopted by BBVA as the way of working for all its Design teams worldwide, as part of its digital transformation process. In addition, Design Ambassador Programs are carried out for all teams of the organization. In this sense, in BBVA Peru, teams other than the Design team are applying Design Thinking or adaptations in their own design and development processes [10] [11]. According to this, the ATM developing team from BBVA Peru is adopting those approaches and others in order to find an innovative solution to problems and pain-points. In this context, the proposed challenge was to solve the "burden of change" that final users of ATM face at the time of depositing and paying. This burden makes the users decide to look for a human-teller and stop using the ATM channel.

IV. CASE STUDY: APPLYING DESIGN THINKING

Tim Brown mentioned that Design Thinking is a system of space rather than a predefined series of orderly steps [8]. This case study was developed in the context of a Design Challenge inside the Bank. For this case study, the Design Thinking approach used was the adaptation the BBVA made [10] and socialized via Design Challenges for the local Banks as BBVA Peru. This motivates every team to align to the objectives of the organization. These Design Challenges had the constraint that the teams must employ the methods and approaches the organization had. In this particular case, the constraint was to use Design Thinking to design an innovative solution for the ATM channel.

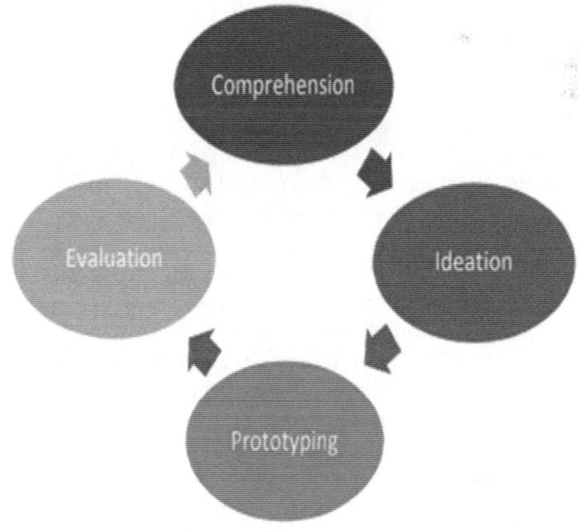

Figure 1. Phases of design thinking. Adapted from BBVA.

The following subsections, from A to D, detail the methods employed in this case of study. Subsection E details the results of the application. Finally, in subsection F, the experience is discussed. The phases followed were Comprehension, Ideation, Prototyping, and Evaluation, as we illustrated in Figure 1.

A. Comprehension

This phase consisted of two steps: the first one was about research and the second was about the analysis of the research made. The objectives of this last step, and in general of the first phase, were to empathize with the problem and obtain insight from the users. We detail methods and techniques we used in each step, as follows:

1) Research

a) Defining the Objective: The first step for the comprehension consisted in making the team aware of what they know, what they do not know, and who can give relevant information to the project. For this, a Field Study/Observation was held in two bank offices located at crowded avenues. We visited two bank branches that had a Deposit ATM inside. We observed that 3 out of 5 people who approached the ATM with cash in hands ended up performing their operations with a human teller. All the Service Payments were performed in the office instead of the ATM because the payment amount was not exact and the change was not withdrawable. On the other hand, all the users who made deposits showed familiarity and ease of use when performing this operation at the ATM. The customers who approached the branches did not know the operations that could be done at the ATM, in those cases the human teller helped them to migrate.

b) User Profile: Three user profiles were made to reflect the typical user of the Deposit Operation on ATMs. These profiles were ideated based on the users observed in the previous step. A man with technical studies who pay bills, a woman who manage the economy at home, and an elder woman not so familiar with technology and still carries cash. For all the profiles, gender and age were described, and why is important to talk to that profile.

c) Interviews: A semi-structured interview were conducted and addressed to people who matched the user profiles created. We selected six different final users, three young people, two men and a woman, with technical knowledge, two middle-age women, and one elder with low technical knowledge. The interview consisted in open questions about four main things, what they worry, what they wish, how they imagine the future, and what they need. The participants were customers from BBVA Peru and other leader banks in the country. We add time for a free conversation where each participant could talk about the problems they face when performing financial operations that involves cash and change in coins or bills. From all the interviewed customers, five out of six participants preferred using the ATM when carrying cash instead of the bank office, but all of them agreed on the idea of an ATM that can give the exact change with coins if possible.

d) Competitor Analysis: The last step of the research consisted in the analysis of other solutions that the competitors might have implemented already. Three leading local banks were analyzed and the BBVA Spain. The analysis was aimed to find which competitor offers a solution to the "burden of change". The results showed only one Peruvian bank that gives change in their ATM that dispense coins. This ATM with coins dispenser is also used in BBVA Spain; however, it is expensive to implement in the Peruvian context, and were given as a constraint for this experience.

2) Analysis

a) Empathy Map: The first step was empathizing with the final users and understanding their motivations in order to have a process guided by the user needs. The empathy map generated considering four aspects:

- What they think and feel. This aspect showed that clients were not comfortable with carrying cash after making operations. This affected to their sense of security directly. In addition, the fact that ATM dispense only multiples of twenty made them to prefer a bank teller to the self-service.
- What they see. Throw observation, the team could evidentiate what the final users actually see in their daily visits to an office bank. Crowded offices, ATM that captured bills occasionally, and in most of the cases, their relatives influenced into selecting the bank-teller as a better way to perform their transactions.
- What they hear. The bank-tellers always tell the users that using the mobile banking is easier and safer now, but the observed sample claimed that they did not feel that was true. In addition, they heard about fraud stories, other people complaining in social media and others having trouble with the ATM. On the other hand, they are aware of a new type of ATM that dispense coins and that more people employ a debit or credit card.
- What they decide to do. They only used the ATM when the office was really crowded. If the office seemed empty to them, they went straightforward to the bank-teller inside the office. However, they were opened to the idea of not entering the account number (hard to remember), to the idea of not going to the office, and to use another attention channel with the same services as in the office.

b) Insights Discovery: In the Empathy Map, we identified what the customer felt and thought, what he or she saw and heard, and what he or she actually decided to do. This lets us identify the greatest pain points of the final users interviewed, which are listed as follows:

- People would continue looking for a human teller while the ATM did not offer any solution to the "burden of change".

- The customers who paid at the ATM were not very digitized.
- The most important aspects for the clients to consider were security and fastness.
- The final users associated the word "change" with "money in cash" or "coins".
- There was inadequate communication between the bank and its customers about the available channels.
- The final user did not perceive the value of the ATM for deposit operations when he or she was at the office due to the insufficient ubiquity about this type of ATM.

B. *Ideation*

After analyzing the context and comprehending the final user's problem, it was necessary to define the exact necessity that would be solved. After that, the ATM team started the ideation of possible solutions. Finally, a meeting was held to converge all the different ideas.

1) Rethinking the challenge

a) New challenge: Based on the six insights discovered in the last phase of comprehension, and the constraint mentioned, the team defined the following specific challenge: *"How could we give alternative options to physical change, quickly and safely, to achieve greater digitalization of our clients and non-clients?"*

2) Generating Ideas

The ideation was started with a brainstorm performed between all the ATM team. For this collaborative idea-generation task, the team started with a divergent process, but later the ideas were filtered through a convergent process.

a) Divergence: All the member proposed different solutions; for instance, using typical operations, payments in advance and commission discounts, transfer change to a "savings account" without account number, integration with a "saving goals" program, convert the change into redeemable "bank points", and a complex system where the change is transformed into coupons.

b) Convergence: In this process, the team classified ideas by their relevance. For this, each member assumed a role in the judgment: one member assumed the role of a positive and optimistic customer, the second member assumed the role of a negative and pessimistic customer, and the third one assumed the role of an internal user of the bank who ensured that the business goals were met. At the end of the process, the team made an election of the most relevant ideas. One was discarded and, from the rest, the team took the top three into consideration for the solution: transfer to accounts without the need of account number, integration with a "saving goals" program, and using typical operations.

C. *Prototyping*

Once the ATM team formulated, filtered and selected ideas, the next step was prototyping. First, a low fidelity prototype was made. Here, the user interaction was needed so we could progress to the high fidelity prototype.

1) Low Fidelity

The low fidelity prototype was a result of a paper prototyping. All the workflow for this operation was drawn. Examples of this are shown in Figure 2 through Figure 4.

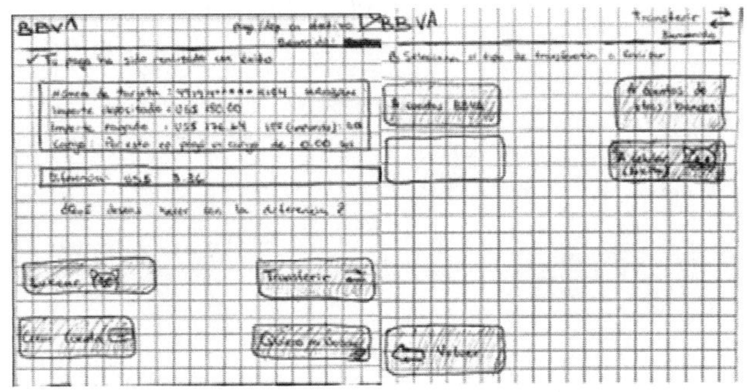

Figure 2. Low fidelity prototypes (I).

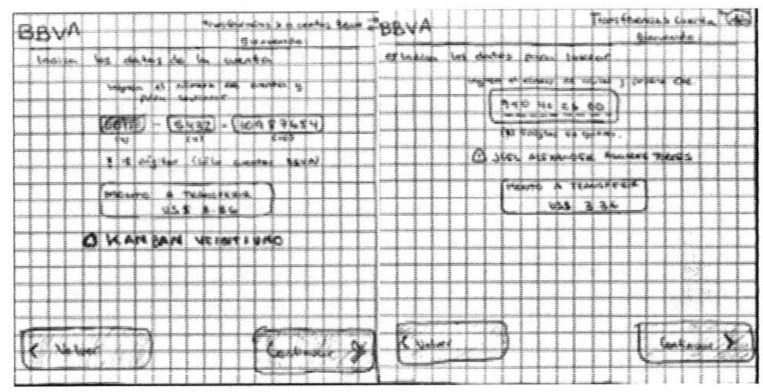

Figure 3. Low fidelity prototypes (II).

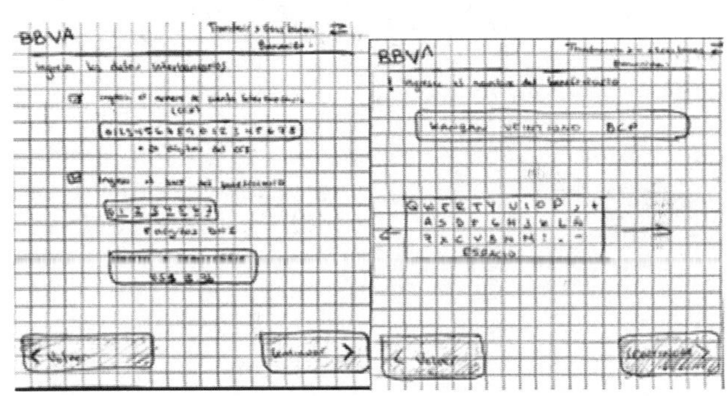

Figure 4. Low fidelity prototypes (III).

2) High Fidelity

The high fidelity prototypes were made taking into consideration what was found by evaluating the low fidelity prototypes. The team added a message for the user in order to notify in advance about the change they would receive. After finishing the operation, the team asked what the user would like to do with the change.

In Figure 5, we show how we notify the user differently for the payment amount and the deposited cash. With this information, the users will know in advance the amount of change they would receive, so they could make a better choice of what to do with this amount.

Figure 5. Notifying the user about the change.

Figure 6 shows the last screen of the payment operation where a sub-menu was introduced, giving the user options to manage the change. Also, we added messages to make clear to the user what would be done to their change. These options corresponded to the ideas selected in the last phase.

Figure 6. Asking the user what to do with the change.

D. Evaluation

This phase started with the elaboration of a list of activities. The users were recruited following the user profiles defined in the first phase of comprehension. The participants were internal users that were interested in the Design Challenge and wanted to collaborate.

1) User Testing

The user testing was held using the installations of the ATM laboratory of the BBVA Peru. Five final users were invited and asked to interact with the high-fidelity prototypes and complete a cash payment simulation where they had to transfer the change to a different account, but without using the account number, instead, they were asked to use another financial product that requires only a phone number.

For these tasks, the prototypes were displayed in a real ATM located in the ATM Laboratory. The "thinking aloud" method helped in the tests. The participants had to raise their voice and tell the evaluator their feelings and ask questions, if they had any.

After completing the operation proposed, the participants were asked about the first impressions they had, the positive and negative aspects they found, and a final appreciation on a scale from 1 to 5. In the evaluation phase, the users found some improvements were needed in the iteration of the prototype. These changes were focused on the button of "return of change", some text boxes that were confusing, and the last screen where the details of the completed transfer were shown in a non-friendly way. Figure 7 shows the participants during this evaluation.

Figure 7. User Testing.

2) Design Iteration

The participants liked the solution proposed. They found some confusing texts and images in the interfaces that had to be fixed through a design iteration. Some of the problems found in the interfaces were, for example, a button that confused the user with an image that might not relate correctly to the functionality of the button itself. Some texts were displayed repeatedly over more than one screen, and the final information about the change transfer was unclear to the user because a lot of unnecessary information was displayed. These errors are shown in Figure 8 and Figure 9, with a red circle to emphasize them.

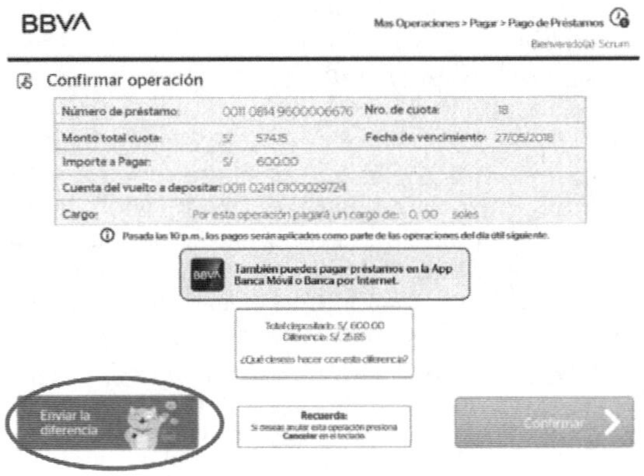

Figure 8. Problem in the button.

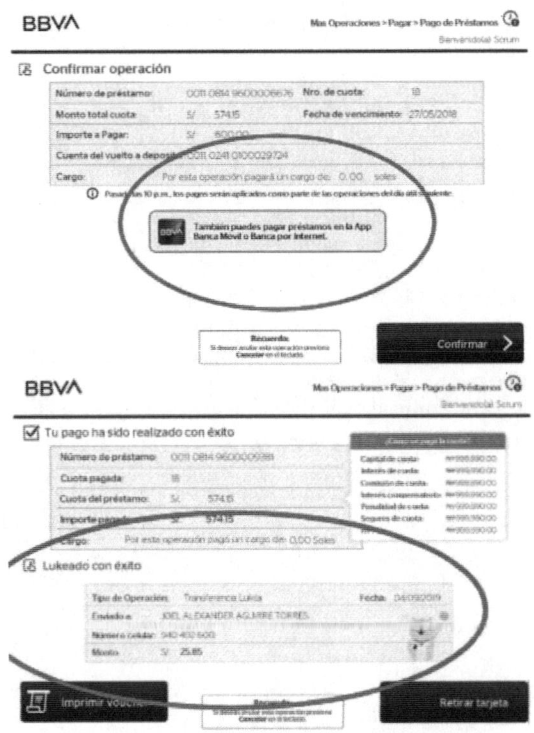

Figure 9. Problems in the text box and information.

E. Results and Valuable Final Proposal

A redesign was done after the user testing, so we could fix the problems they had. After another interaction the users had with the redesigned interfaces, we could finally accept a final proposal that really adds value. Figure 10 and Figure 11 show the final valuable proposal.

F. End of the Experience

The design experience using Design Thinking ended with the delivery of the prototypes in the context of the Design Challenge mentioned. After this, the most relevant projects were selected to be presented to a panel composed of all the departments of the bank, especially the business department. This project was selected as one of the finalists. In the presentation, the experience and everything learned was shared, and valuable feedback could be obtained from the business areas, as well as plans for future implementations of the presented work.

Figure 10. Valuable Final Proposal (I).

Figure 11. Valuable Final Proposal (II).

V. CONCLUSIONS

The Design Thinking approach allowed us to propose an innovative solution to the problems that users discovered, adding value to the prototypes. This assured that the final prototypes improved the experience of the final user because the whole design process was user-centered. At the end of the process, we made an analysis of the results and could identify what we learned.

In general, the participants of the evaluation found added value in the new proposed interfaces, considering using them according to their necessities. However, the participants opined that the solutions only solve the "burden of change" partially. They mentioned that, in the Peruvian context, the users who paid in cash expect their change to be in cash so they could use it somewhere else, for instance, transportation or groceries.

From this challenge, we learned that Design Thinking is an approach that seeks innovation. Adopting the approach proposed by the organization brought encouraging results and created an expectation in the impact it would have if we integrate it into the whole construction process. However, it is a constraint and different results could be delivered by adopting different design approaches, but this first step aligned with one of the principal strategies of the organization helped the ATM team to be more emphatic with the final customer.

ACKNOWLEDGMENT

We want to thank the DUXAIT research group for all their support throughout this experience. We also want to thank BBVA Peru, its Design team, and especially the development and discipline ATM teams in Engineering, with whom we constantly work, committed to improving the User Experience and the reliability of the ATM channel.

REFERENCES

[1] E. O. C. Mkpojiogu and E. A. Augustine, "The user experience of ATM users in Nigeria: a systematic review of empirical papers," International Journal of Science and Engineering Applications, June 2018, ISSN 1596-8303.

[2] A. O. Odusina, "Automated Teller Machine usage and Customers' Satisfaction in Nigeria," Type: Double Blind Peer Reviewed International Research Journal Publisher: Global Journals Inc, 2014, 14(4), ISSN: 2249-4588.

[3] O. Shy, "How the ATM Affects the Way We Pay," Federal Reserve Bank of Atlanta, Working Papers, February 2019, doi:10.29338/wp2019-02.

[4] P. Fehér, and K. Varga, "Using design thinking to identify banking digitization opportunities – Snapshot of the Hungarian banking system," 30th Bled E-Conference: Digital Transformation - From Connecting Things to Transforming Our Lives, BLED 2017, December 2017, pp.151–168, doi:10.18690/978-961-286-043-1.12.

[5] A. J. H. Chia, and J.-J. Lee, "Banking Outside-in: How Design Thinking is Changing the Banking Industry ?" IASDR 2019, October 2019.

[6] C. Klepek, "Design Thinking: The case of Banking Services," Proceedings of The 5th International Conference Innovation Management, Entrepreneurship and Sustainability, IMES 2017, pp.416–425, 2017, Available from https://www.ceeol.com/search/chapter-detail?id=544899

[7] J. Aguirre, A. Moquillaza, and F. Paz, "A User-Centered Framework for the Design of Usable ATM Interfaces," Lecture Notes in Computer Science (Including Subseries Lecture Notes in Artificial Intelligence and Lecture Notes in Bioinformatics), 11583 LNCS, July 2019, pp.163–178. doi:10.1007/978-3-030-23570-3_13.

[8] T. Brown, "Design Thinking," Interaction Design Foundation 1, Available from https://www.interaction-design.org/literature/topics/design-thinking, retrieved: January, 2020.

[9] C. Vetterli, F. Uebernickel, D. Stermann, and C. Petrie, "How Deutsche Bank's IT Division Used Design Thinking to Achieve Customer Proximity," MIS Carterly Excutive, March 2016.

[10] A. Moquillaza, F. Falconi, and F. Paz, "Redesigning a Main Menu ATM Interface Using a User-Centered Design Approach Aligned to Design Thinking: A Case Study," International Conference on Human-Computer Interaction, pp. 522-532, July 2019, Springer, Cham, doi:10.1007/978-3-030-23535-2_38

[11] BBVA, "Design Thinking. Serie Innovation Trends. BBVA Innovation Center," 2015, Available from https://www.bbva.com/wp-content/uploads/2017/10/ebook-cibbva-design-thinking_es_1.pdf, retrieved: January, 2020.

[12] Keep the Change Savings Program from Bank of America. Retrieved March 17, 2020, from https://www.bankofamerica.com/deposits/keep-the-change/

[13] Virtual Wallet is Checking & Savings. Together. PNC. Retrieved March 17, 2020, from https://www.pnc.com/en/personal-banking/virtual-wallet-overview.html

Trust Metrics to Measure Website User Experience

Andréia Casare, Tania Basso, Regina Moraes
University of Campinas - UNICAMP
Campinas, Brazil
email: casareandreia@gmail.com, {taniabasso, regina}@ft.unicamp.br

Abstract—**Trust in computational systems and online applications depends on technical, social and personal aspects. The technical ones, such as a strong computational infrastructure, adequate network bandwidth, sufficient storage space, among others, have been largely studied. Social issues, such as runtime security and data privacy are important for users to be protected from attacks by malicious people. However, there are personal aspects that impact the sense of trust, which depends on the user experience when interacting with those systems. This paper tackles this issue by proposing a study on measures that can determine the user experience when using an online system or application. The approach relies on a quality model to combine these metrics and compose a trustworthiness score. Seven websites are used in the experiments in two different contexts and, based on the set of measures that composes the quality model, the approach suggests the one that presents the highest user perception of trust in each context, that is the one with the highest score.**

Keywords–Trustworthiness; User experience; Quality model.

I. Introduction

The increasing use of online systems and applications by individuals in a globalized market has introduced new challenges in software development, including issues related to human-computer interaction. Nonetheless, challenges regarding nonfunctional requirements, such as security, privacy and trust can arise from the value of a business or even the need to improve the relationship with the consumer.

Trust is defined differently in distinct areas [1] and, inspired by the existing definitions, we can define it as the reliance of a client on a service, that it will exhibit some expected behaviour. Then, trustworthiness can be defined as the level in which a service meets a set of those requirements, i.e., the worthiness of services for being trusted. In some cases, trust is subject to individual interpretation and context of use.

Trust does not only involve technical aspects, such as data security, fault tolerance, but also human interaction aspects that should consider attributes of usability, accessibility and user experience. If the system presents a pleasant interface, good performance, easy to use and learn, providing in the tasks execution a good experience of use, it will have great chances of being reused and trusted.

In this context, the goal of this work is to define a set of metrics and to propose a way to combine several metrics to get a score for trustworthiness focused on the user perception. This work is part of a wider proposal, in which several metrics should be defined, validated and combined in order to translate the importance of each metric toward trustworthiness score, being able to translate the user's perception and allowing to evaluate and determine the user experience when using online systems or applications. Based on it, users can compare and choose systems that present higher level of trust from the perspective of the system user.

In order to obtain a trustworthiness score composed of heterogeneous metrics, a quality model is used in this work. The quality model was proposed in the ISO/IEC 25000 (SQuaRE) standard [2] as a way to formalize the interpretation of measures and the relationship among them. These models are built by a user / analyst, who knows in advance the context, the final scores, their units and scales. This way, it is possible to define how the measures should be aggregated in the analysis, and what procedures have to be used to homogenize their values, so they can be aggregated. It is possible to define one quality model for each considered property, and then, these different perspectives can be aggregated following a hierarchical structure.

The contributions of this work are: (i) the selection of a set of properties that can be used to measure a user experience; (ii) a user experience quality model to compose the properties' metrics and their relationship. The model was evaluated using seven real systems (websites) to demonstrate its usefulness.

The idea followed by this work is aligned with the interest of the Adaptive, Trustworthy, Manageable, Orchestrated, Secure, Privacy-assuring Hybrid, Ecosystem for Resilient Cloud Computing (ATMOSPHERE) project [3]. ATMOSPHERE is an Europe-Brazil collaborative project that exchange experiences and results with its members. By defining a user experience quality model, the resulted model can easily be integrated with other quality models defined in the ATMOSPHERE project and complement the trustworthiness score with a user experience measurement.

The paper is organized as follows: Sections II and III present, respectively, relevant concepts and related work that guided our study. Section IV presents the proposed user experience quality model and the methodology used to get the metrics and final trustworthiness score. Section V shows the results of experiments applying the quality model to calculate the trustworthiness score of two categories of e-commerce websites. Finally, Section VI presents the conclusions and future work.

II. Background

This section addresses, briefly, the issues that underpin this work. It discusses trust, user experience and quality model.

A. Trust

Trust and trustworthiness concepts have been studied in different areas, such as people social relationship and business environments. For example, Mayer et al. [4] proposed a model for defining trust including characteristics of the trustor, the trustee, and the role of risk. Their model is focused on trust in an organizational relationship. Venkatesh et al. [5] proposed a conceptual framework of online trust based on different views and requirements of different stakeholders (such as customers, suppliers, employees, partners, etc.). In a broader context, McKinght et al. [6] proposed a multidimensional model of trust in e-commerce. The model includes four high-level constructs (disposition to trust, institution-based trust, trusting beliefs, and trusting intentions), which are further delineated into 16 measurable subconstructs.

Although these concepts are differently defined in distinct areas, one of the common main goals in all definitions is to accurately assess the trust level as a robust basis for decision making (e.g., system adaptation), which turns out to be a very complex problem. A key problem is that the trust level is uncertain and may dynamically change. Mainly, it can be strongly dependent on the feeling of a user, when she / he is interacting with the system, i.e., the quality of the interaction between the human and the system. So, the user experience should be included among the properties that are used to compose the trustworthiness score of a system. Thus, establishing trust and building trustworthy services is a challenge and can benefit from research on the quality of the system interface and user experience.

B. User Experience

ISO 9241-210 [7] defines user experience as *the user's perceptions and reactions resulting from the use of a software product, system or service*. The user experience includes all of the user's emotions, perceptions, preferences, physical and psychological responses, behaviors, and achievements that occur before, during, and after the use. Therefore, user experience is a consequence of the features, performance, system interactivity or products that the user has had as a result of previous experiences, abilities and context of use.

C. Quality Model

Trustworthiness can be understood as a multi-dimensional construct combining specific attributes, properties and characteristics (for example, security, privacy, fairness, transparency, dependability, among others). All of them have other sub-attributes that increase the number of possibilities to be addressed.

Since several conflicting properties may be involved in the analysis, a Multi-Criteria Decision-Making (MCDM) based technique can be useful to define how to compute the global score of a service. In this work, Logic Score of Preferences (LSP) [8] was chosen due to its previous use in the dependability field. It comprises multiple aggregation blocks to define how the different elements should be used to produce a final score.

Usually, measures of services present distinct scales and dimensions. In order to apply LSP, the measures should be brought to the same scale before the aggregation. To do this, we used the normalization functions proposed in [9].

To use the LSP technique, it is necessary to first define a Quality Model [10], which is essentially a conceptual representation of attributes, weights, thresholds and operators that should express the requirements that the system should meet (for example, the tree structure in Figure 2). The blocks, in this work, represent (leaf or composite) attributes, which are aggregated (by the operators). Values at the bottom level (leaf attributes) are aggregated to calculate upper level values (composite attributes), towards the calculation of the final score of the system through a single 0-to-100 score. *Thresholds* are elements used in the normalization function to specify the range of acceptable input values of leaf-level attribute. *Weight* is an adjustable element which specifies a preference over one or more characteristics of the system (e.g., in certain contexts memory usage might be more important than throughput).

III. Related Work

The Human-Computer Interface (HCI) literature presents some works that consider usability, accessibility and quality of product as attributes / characteristics that influence the users' trust perception when using a website or application, as well as works that propose quality models for software measurement.

Few works address user experience related to trust. Most of them use the eye-track technology (e.g., the work of Djamasbi et al. [11], which examines the effect of images of faces on the visual appeal, efficiency, and trustworthiness of a page). The work most related to ours is the one from Ramadhan et al. [12]. The authors evaluate the user experience regarding factors that influence user trust through the design of website interface. They evaluated the three cryptocurrency websites most frequently accessed from Indonesia using methods, such as Performance Metrics, Post-Task Rating, Post-Session Rating, Experiential Overview and eye-tracking device. However, they did not use quality models to represent the multi-dimensional attributes nor calculate trustworthiness scores to help define the more trusted website.

Regarding quality models, Seffah et al. [13] proposed an hierarchical model of usability measurement, called Quality in Use Integrated Measurement (QUIM). It has 10 factors, which are decomposed into 26 sub-factors that are further decomposed into 127 specific metrics. Some factors are: efficiency, effectiveness, productivity, accessibility, trustfulness, among others. The metrics may be extracted from log files, video observations, interviews, or surveys. Lew et al. [14] proposed, based on ISO 25010, a framework for modeling requirements for quality, usability and user experience. The goal is to evaluate quality attributes of software and Web applications. Some attributes are accuracy, suitability, accessibility, and legal compliance. Hendradjaya and Praptini [15] proposed a quality model with attributes to evaluate e-government websites. The attributes are: functionality, reliability, usability, efficiency, portability and productivity. The measures were obtained through some specific Web tools and questionnaires.

Although these previous works [13]-[15] presented quality models related to usability and user experience and even presented some quality attributes related to trustworthiness (e.g., reliability, accessibility), they are not focused on this characteristic. Furthermore, although Seffah et al. [13] defined some metrics, their focus is only on usability. Hendradjaya and Praptini [15] also defined some metrics that go beyond usability, but they are specific for e-government and may not be generalized.

IV. User Experience Quality Model and User Trustworthiness Score Calculation

This section presents the quality model we defined, as well as the methodology used to get the metrics and the final user experience quality score. Also, it presents the results of applying the quality model on seven real websites of two different contexts - optics sellers and airlines.

The research methodology consisted of the following steps: (i) HCI literature review to select the software quality attributes that influence the user experience when interacting with a system; (ii) a Quality Model development with measures hierarchically represented by quality attributes (such as usability, accessibility, performance, among others) that will compose the confidence perception score; (iii) the selection of tools that are able to collect the selected metrics; (iv) the experiments performed on real websites relying on automatic tools that return values of performance, accessibility, among other metrics; (v) based on the Quality Model and the experiments results, a website reliable score is computed; (vi) the analysis and discussion of the experiments results.

In step (i), we identified the quality attributes that impact user confidence during her/his interaction with the website or Web application. The complete set of metrics identified so far can be seen in Figure 1.

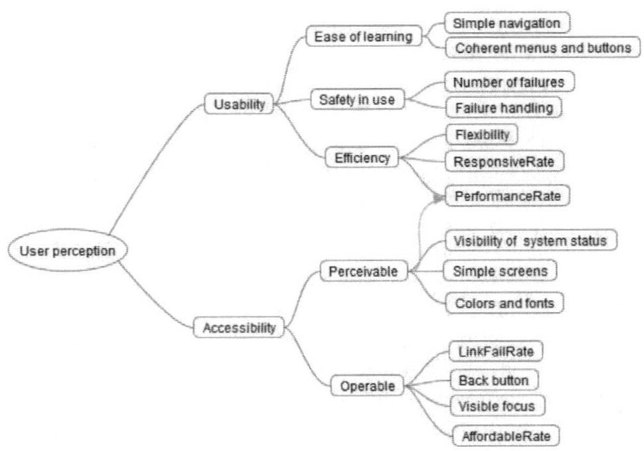

Figure 1. Quality attributes that influence trust

The attributes were grouped in two main categories: *Usability* and *Accessibility*. The *Usability* group is composed of *Ease of Learning* (regarding website navigation, menus and buttons coherence), *Safety in use* (regarding website failures), *Efficiency* (regarding website response, performance and flexibility).

The *Accessibility* group is composed of attributes *Perceivable* (regarding website design, as colors, screens and system status) and *Operable* (regarding website functions as buttons, links, focus, etc.).

From these quality attributes, we selected a subset to tackle in the present work, that is *PerformanceRate* (also called, in the quality model, *PerformancePageUp*, which refers to the time/rate to load the website), *AffordableRate*, *ResponsiveRate* and *LinkFailRate*. We first choose these metrics because they are objective measures and can be measured automatically by tools. The remaining attributes in Figure 1 will be assessed in future work, mainly to be dependent on user personal evaluation.

It is important to clarify that we decided, as a first stage, to consider only the attributes that can be measured by automatic tools because our main goal is to perform experiments that allow evaluating the quality model, the metrics and the scores calculation. It is obvious that, once we are interested in evaluating user perception, experiments with human users (for example, comparing whether the scores produced by the tools and human users match or not) would produce more solid results. However, we intend to extend the quality model and to perform experiments with users in a second stage.

Following the methodology, step (ii) defined a quality model to aggregate the several identified metrics. For now on, only the metrics to be tackled in this work were placed in the current version of the Quality Model, which is presented in Figure 2.

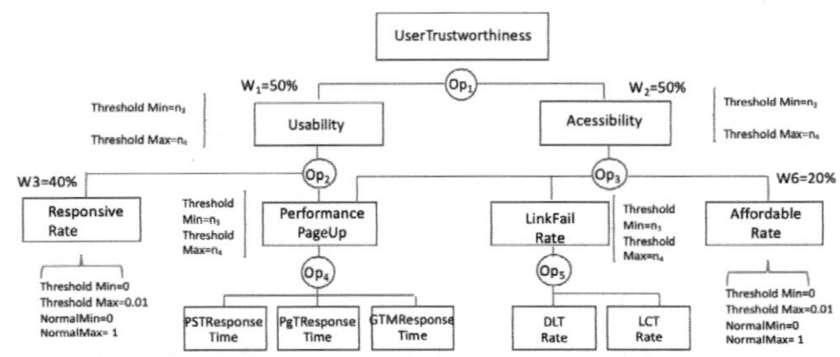

Figure 2. User Experience Quality Model

As mentioned in Section II-C, *UserTrustworthiness* is decomposed in composite and leaf attributes, which were aggregated based on operators. Some weights were defined for each attribute denoting the importance to represent *UserTrustworthiness* as a whole. For example, *Usability* and *Accessibility* collaborate both with fifty percent to compose *UserTrustWorthiness*. *Usability*, in turn, receives the collaboration of *ResponsiveRate* (40%) and *PerformancePageUP* (60%), and so on. This last attribute (*PerformancePageUp*) also collaborates with *Accessibility*, but, in this case, its importance is determined to be 30% (see Table III).

It is important to mention that the metrics configuration values (weighs, thresholds, normalization values, periodicity, operators) were defined by experts who integrated the ATMOSPHERE project teams. They worked on the layers to which a quality model refers, performing experiments during the framework layer development and defining the values based on these experiments. To the best of our knowledge, there are no previous works that also define these values, otherwise we would consider them to perform a more robust study.

Table I, Table II and Table III provide more details about the User Quality Model. In Table I, a description of each leaf metric is provided to give a broader view of the metric. In addition, details are provided about how the metric is computed, which type of data is each one of them, how and when it is collected, how it can be considered to improve the user experience and if the metric acts as *Benefit* (the higher the metric value is better) or *Cost* (the lower metric value is better).

Related to the leaf attributes configuration, Table II provides information about minimum (NMin) and maximum (Nmax) values that the attribute can assume and these values are used for normalization purpose (normalized between 0 - 1 range). It also provides the thresholds minimum (TMin) and maximum (TMax), the weight (W) of the attribute in the composition to the subsequent level attribute, the periodicity of

TABLE I. LEAF ATTRIBUTES METRICS DESCRIPTION (PARTIAL VIEW)

Metric Name	Description	How is it Computed ?	Type of data	How & When is it sent?	How is it used for adaptation	B(en) / C(ost)	Property
Responsive Rate	Check if the website is able to adapt to mobile devices	Extracted relying on Mobile Friendly Test Tool	1 (yes) / 0 (no)	On demand	Improving components and software development	B	Usability
PST Responsive Time	Measure the website performance (time to be up)	Extracted relying on PageSpeed Insights tool	0 up to 100	On demand	Compose the mean to obtain the performance metric	B	Performance

the calculation (CP), given in seconds (and, in this case, all of them are on demand (*On dem.*), and the operator (OP), which can be *Average* (Avg), *Min, Max, Sum* (S), through which the metrics will be aggregated.

TABLE II. LEAF ATTRIBUTES METRICS CONFIGURATION (PARTIAL VIEW)

Metric Name	N Min	N Max	T Min	T Max	W(%)	CP	OP
Responsive Rate	0	1	0	1	40%	On dem.	OP2 Max
PST Response Time	0	100	0	100	33.3%	On dem.	OP4 Avg

TABLE III. COMPOSITE ATTRIBUTES CONFIGURATION

Metric Name	T Min	T Max	W(%)	CP	OP
Performance Page Up	0	100	60% 30%	On dem.	Op2-N Op3-N
LinkFail Rate	0	100	20%	On dem.	Op3-N
Usability	0	100	50%	On dem.	Op1-N
Accessibility	0	100	50%	On dem.	Op1-N

In addition to the leaf attributes configuration, the composite attributes also need to be configured. So, Table III presents the configuration of composite attributes where the thresholds (TMin and TMax), the weight (W), the periodicity (CP) and the operator (OP) are specified. It is important to notice that, in this case, the operator refers to different operations, that can be:

- *Neutrality (N)*. Refers to the arithmetic mean and represents the combination of simultaneous satisfaction requirements with replaceability capability.
- *Simultaneity (S)*. This operation means that all requirements must be satisfied; it refers to a conjunction - i.e., the logical operator AND.
- *Replaceability (R)*. Is used when one of the requirements of the system has a higher priority replacing the remaining requirements; it refers to a disjunction - i.e., a logical operator OR - to perform aggregation.

V. CALCULATING METRICS AND SCORES: EXPERIMENTS AND RESULTS

This section presents the experiments regarding the application of the User Experience Quality Model in order to calculate user trustworthiness scores for some e-commerce websites.

A. Experimental setup

Step (iii) finds automatic tools to collect the metrics that were selected to compose the quality model. We found some freeware or open source and proprietary tools. This latter (proprietary) set was not considered in this work. Based on preliminary tests, the following tools were selected: *PageSpeed Insights* [16], *Pingdom Website Speed Test* [17] and *GTMetrix* [18] evaluate the performance of the website to be up; *Dead Link Checker* [19], *Xenu's link* [20] and *Screaming Frog* [21] inspect the links and count the broken ones; *Mobile Friendly Test* [22] verifies if the website is a responsive one; *ASES (Accessibility Evaluator and Simulator)* [23], *Nibbler* [24] and *Access Monitor* [25] verify the website affordable rate. All these tools are stable and freeware.

Step (iv) is reserved to run the tools on the chosen websites. For the experiments, the website selection is based on the website type (e-commerce) of two business segment (optics sellers and airlines) and the website size with up to 10,000 URLs to allow the experiments control. We selected four optics websites and three airline websites. The companies names or respective websites are not mentioned because they have commercial license. So, we will refer to the optics websites as Opt1, Opt2, Opt3, Opt4 and the airline websites as Air1, Air2 and Air3, without any special order.

B. Results and discussions

In the experiments, we applied the selected tools to extract the following metrics of the websites: performance of the page up (*PageSpeed, Pingdom* and *GTMetrix*); amount of broken links (*Dead Link Checker*, *Xenu's link* and *Screaming Frog*); responsiveness (*Mobile Friendly Test*); affordable rate (*ASES, Nibbler* and *Access Monitor*). The next subsections present the results for each metric, including the trustworthiness score calculation.

1) Performance: To measure the performance of each website, nine experiments were performed using different machines, Internet networks and Web tools. For each website, we executed three tests using a desktop machine, processor I5 and Windows 7, accessing the wired network of the university administrative sector; three tests using a notebook, processor I5 and Windows 10, accessing the university WiFi network, and three tests using a notebook, processor I5, Windows 10, accessing a 15-megabytes wireless network at home.

All the tools used to measure the performance returned a value between 0 up to 100, which is normalized to 0 - 1 range for the calculation. In case of a *Benefit* attribute, the higher the value, the better the performance contribution to the score. Table IV shows the measurements obtained in the nine tests on the first website (*Opt1*). For all the other websites, a similar table has been created but for the sake of space and better presentation they are not included in this paper and we opted to present only a summary table. However, all the tables from these experiments can be found in our institutional website [26].

TABLE IV. PERFORMANCE MEASUREMENTS - WEBSITE OPT1

Test #	PageSpeed	Pingdom	GTMetrix	Remarks
1	82	67	48	Desktop
2	85	67	48	Desktop
3	80	67	48	Desktop
4	86	67	48	Notebook wifi
5	87	67	48	Notebook wifi
6	85	67	48	Notebook wifi
7	86	67	48	Notebook wifi - home
8	85	67	48	Notebook wifi - home
9	81	67	48	Notebook wifi - home

Table V summarizes the measurements obtained in the nine tests on each optics website, using the same tools and configurations. Table VI summarizes the tests for airline websites.

The performance score is calculated using the normalized measurements average:

$$PerformancePageUp = (AVG(PageSpeed) * W + AVG(PingDom) * W + AVG(GTMetrix) * W) \quad (1)$$

For example, for *Opt1*, PerformancePageUp = 0.8411 * 0.3333 + 0.67 * 0.3333 + 0.48 * 0.3334 = 0.6637.

Considering only the performance attribute, the *Opt2* website is considered better than the other three optics websites and the best considering both e-commerce segments, as its score is the highest. Among the airline websites, *Air1* is better than the other two. It is important to notice that the metrics collected by a tool, in any case (considering the same tool and the same website), are very similar when one considered different computers and networks configurations. Higher differences are recorded by the *PageSpeed* tool (*Opt3, Air2* and *Air3* websites) pointing out that this tool is more sensitive to the computational resources used by the user.

2) Broken links: To check the number of website broken links, one experiment was carried out using a notebook, a processor I5, and Windows 10, accessing a 15-megabytes wireless home network. Three tools were used that returned the total number of the website links and the number of defective links. In this case, only one experiment was performed using each tool, because this measurement is not impacted by the computational environment or network. Table VII shows the scores returned from the test of the *Opt1, Opt2, Opt3* and *Opt4*.

The broken link rate is calculated based on the maximum rate obtained by any of the tools, i. e., it is calculated as:

$$LinkFailRate = MAX(DeadLInkChecker(broken\_links/total\_links), Xenu'sLink(broken\_links/total\_links)). \quad (2)$$

Using expression (2), the *Opt1* score for Link Fail Rate is 8.46%, the scores of *Opt3* is 5.45%, *Opt3* is 1.66% and *Opt4* 0.55%. As this metric is a *cost* one (i.e., lower value is better for the score), *Opt4* presented better score for this attribute (broken link) in the optics segment and also considering both segments. The metrics collected by all tools are very similar for *Opt3* website but differ significantly for the other websites. Investigating why this difference happens, we observe some restrictions. *Dead Link Checker* is limited to 2000 links, so this justifies the difference observed for the *Opt4* website. *Screaming Frog* was not able to inspect the *Opt3* website even after several attempts. We could not identify this problem.

Considering the airline websites, we can better observe the limitation of *Dead Link Checker* tool in Table VIII, which stops the analysis of all the websites when 2000 links are inspected. For this reason, we ignored its results and considered the maximum rate among the other two tools. The best airline website related to broken links is *Air1* with 2.9% of broken links, followed by *Air2* (4.47%) and *Air3* (4.96%) .

3) Responsiveness: To verify if the website is ready to run on mobile devices, one experiment was carried out using a notebook, processor I5, Windows 10, accessing a 15-megabytes wireless network. The *Mobile Friendly Test* tool is the only stable tool identified to collect this metric. All the websites used in the experiment (both segments) are ready for mobile devices (i.e., they are responsive). In this case, this metric should be 0 (non responsive) or 1 (responsive).

4) Affordable rate: The affordable rate score is given in percentage and calculated using the normalized measurements average:

$$AffordableRate = (AVG(ASES) * W + AVG(Nibbler) * W + AVG(AccessMonitor) * W) \quad (3)$$

Table IX and Table X present the results for applying the tools to the optics sellers and airline websites, respectively. In Table IX, the highest score is computed for *Opt2*, with approximately 0.7% and the lowest one for *Opt1* with approximately 0.5%. In Table X, the scores are very close, however, *Air1* presented the highest one (approximately 0.75%).

5) Trustworthiness score calculation: Considering the measurements that were obtained for the attributes of the Quality Model, the score of the next level (i.e., Usability and Accessibility) can be calculated. *Usability* is composed of *Responsive Rate* and *Performance Page UP* using the operator *Neutrality* (arithmetic mean), applying the *weight* (W) of each one of them (0.4 and 0.6, respectively) as follows:

$$ScoreUsability = (MeanResponsiveRate * W + MeanPerformancePageUp * W) \quad (4)$$

For example, the usability score for *Opt1* website = (1 * 0.4 + 0.6637 * 0.6) = 0.79822. Table XI presents the score

TABLE V. PERFORMANCE MEASUREMENTS - OPTICS SELLERS WEBSITES

Website Name	PageSpeed			Pingdom			GTMetrix			Score
	Min	Max	Avg	Min	Max	Avg	Min	Max	Avg	
Opt1	81	87	84.11	67	67	67	48	48	48	0.6637
Opt2	100	100	100	81	81	81	73	74	73.33	0.8477
Opt3	61	75	68.66	68	68	68	63	65	64.55	0.6707
Opt4	43	48	45.11	69	70	69.22	56	59	57.33	0.5722

TABLE VI. PERFORMANCE MEASUREMENTS - AIRLINE WEBSITES

Website Name	PageSpeed			Pingdom			GTMetrix			Score
	Min	Max	Avg	Min	Max	Avg	Min	Max	Avg	
Air1	82	94	87.77	67	67	67	59	59	59	0.7126
Air2	19	23	20.11	63	63	63	48	50	48.66	0.4392
Air3	9	12	10.11	63	63	63	52	53	52.77	0.4196

TABLE VII. AMOUNT OF TOTAL AND BROKEN LINKS - OPTICS WEBSITES

Tool	Opt1 Total/ Broken links	Opt2 Total/ Broken links	Opt3 Total / Broken links	Opt4 Total / Broken links
Dead Link Checker	1830 / 155	383 / 6	1785 / 15	2000 / 2
Xenu's link	552 / 39	403 / 22	1748 / 29	8593 / 47
Screaming Frog	1168 / 23	2 / 0	1697 / 2	7866 / 3
Score	0.0846	0.0545	0.0166	0.0055

TABLE VIII. AMOUNT OF TOTAL AND BROKEN LINKS - AIRLINE WEBSITES

Tool	Air1 Total / Broken links	Air2 Total / Broken links	Air3 Total / Broken links
Dead Link Checker	2000 / 58	2000 / 53	2000 / 22
Xenu's link	69482 / 262	2974 / 133	9748 / 484
Screaming Frog	93995 / 340	2498 / 61	7738 / 126
Score	0.029	0.0447	0.0496

of all optics sellers websites. The airline websites have their usability score presented in Table XII.

Accessibility score is composed for *Performance Page Up* (but now its weight is 0.3), *Link Fail Rate* and *Affordable Rate*. It is important to note that, in the composition of accessibility score, one of the measures, the *Link Fail Rate*, is a *Cost* attribute, so we use its complement in the calculation expression and *Performance Page Up* is now weighted as 30% to compose the accessibility score, since its importance for accessibility is lower. The expression to calculate the

TABLE IX. AFFORDABLE RATE - OPTICS SELLERS WEBSITES

Tool	Opt1 %	Opt2 %	Opt3 %	Opt4 %
ASES	61.19	76.42	79.54	64.17
Nibbler	62	78	67	78
Access Monitor	33.8	57.8	56.4	50.2
Score	0.5233	0.7074	0.6765	0.6412

TABLE X. AFFORDABLE RATE - AIRLINE WEBSITES

Tool	Air1 %	Air2 %	Air3 %
ASES	85.6	83.34	78.31
Nibbler	87	87	89
Access Monitor	52.8	44.4	48
Score	0.7513	0.7158	0.7177

accessibility score is:

$$ScoreAccessibility = MeanPerformancePageUp * W \\ +(1 - MeanLinkFailRate) * W \\ +MeanAffordableRate * W \quad (5)$$

For example, *Opt1* website accessibility score = 0.6637 * 0.3 + (1 - 0.0846) * 0.2 + 0.5233 * 0.5 = 0.64384. Table XI and Table XII present the accessibility scores for the optics sellers and airline websites, respectively.

Following the Quality Model, the last calculation (the top of the Quality Model tree) is the user trustworthiness score. The aggregation is guided by *Operation 1* (OP1), which was configured as *Neutrality*. So, the user trustworthiness score is computed as follows:

$$UserTrustworthinessScore = (UsabilityScore * W) \\ +(AccessibilityScore * W) \quad (6)$$

For example, *Opt1* website user trustworthiness score = 0.79822 * 0.5 + 0.64384 * 0.5 = 0.72103. The user trustworthiness score for the optics sellers websites are presented in Table XI and Table XII presents the same score for airline website.

Comparing the user trustworthiness scores obtained, we

observe that, considering the selected attributes as the ones which impact the user perception of trust, *Opt2* is the website that has the highest chance to please the users during their interaction, followed by *Air1* website. The worst website in this selection is *Air3* website which presents the smallest score among all.

TABLE XI. USABILITY, ACCESSIBILITY AND USER TRUSTWORTHINESS SCORES - OPTICS SELLERS WEBSITES

Attributes	Opt1	Opt2	Opt3	Opt4
Usability	0.79822	0.90862	0.80242	0.74332
Accessibility	0.64384	0.79711	0.73614	0.69116
User Trustworthiness	0.72103	0.85286	0.76928	0.71724

TABLE XII. USABILITY, ACCESSIBILITY AND USER TRUSTWORTHINESS SCORES - AIRLINE WEBSITES

Attributes	Air1	Air2	Air3
Usability	0.82756	0.66352	0.65176
Accessibility	0.78363	0.68072	0.67481
User Trustworthiness	0.80559	0.67212	0.66328

In general, considering both segments, the order for user trustworthiness score (from highest to lowest score) is: *Opt2, Air1, Opt3, Opt1, Opt4, Air2 and Air3*. We could observe that *Opt2* website presents the best trustworthiness score being almost 22% better than *Air3* website (the worst one). In the middle, *Opt3* presents a score 10.5% smaller and *Opt1* 15.2% smaller when compared to *Opt2*. Observing the airline websites, the best is *Air1*, but its score is almost 6% worse when compared to the *Opt2* (the best score).

Also, considering both segments, it is important to notice that *Opt2* is the best when we observe the attribute *Performance Page Up*. It is not the number one in the other three attributes, but also it is not the worst one in any of the attributes. Moreover, *Performance Page Up* is an important attribute in the current version of the Quality Model, since it is considered as component of the Usability attribute and the Accessibility attribute scores as well. *Air1* is the best in Affordable Rate and *Opt4* is the best in the broken link rate. Even being better in these attributes, neither *Air1* nor *Opt4* websites are able to overcome the *Opt2* website trustworthiness score due to the importance of *Performance Page Up* attribute for the context. *Opt1* presents the smallest score in the *Affordable Rate* and the highest *broken link* score.

VI. CONCLUSIONS

This work presented a definition of a set of metrics with the aim of obtaining a score for the user perception regarding trust. It is part of a wider proposal, in which several metrics should be defined, validated and combined following a methodology toward trustworthiness score calculation. The trustworthiness score should translate the user's perception when using online applications. This score will allow users to compare and choose systems that present a high level of trust.

Using the use case composed by four optical sellers and three airline websites, it was possible to calculate the trustworthiness scores and allow users to select the more trustworthy websites among the same business segment. Moreover, it was possible to observe the importance of the proposed mechanism to obtain the score (the quality model) as it balances the results based on the importance of the attributes and not only one attribute or another, neither the amount of attributes with the best scores only.

Future work will tackle more complex metrics, which are more subjective and will require some tests with the users, to evaluate usability and accessibility. It is our intention to perform usability tests using the think aloud technique and accessibility evaluation by an expert based on the World Wide Web Consortium (W3C) [27] recommendations among other evaluation techniques.

ACKNOWLEDGMENT

This work has been partially supported by the project ATMOSPHERE- Adaptive, Trustworthy, Manageable, Orchestrated, Secure, Privacy-assuring Hybrid, Ecosystem for Resilient Cloud Computing (https://www.atmosphere-eubrazil.eu/ - Horizon 2020 grant agreement No 777154 - MCTIC/RNP) and by the project ADVANCE - Addressing Verification & Validation Challenges in Future Cyber-Physical Systems (https://www.advance-rise.eu/ - call H2020-MSCA-RISE-2018, number 823788).

REFERENCES

[1] D. Artz and Y. Gil, "A survey of trust in computer science and the semantic web," Web Semantics: Science, Services and Agents on the World Wide Web, vol. 5, no. 2, 2007, pp. 58–71.

[2] International Organization for Standardization, "Systems and software engineering — systems and software quality requirements and evaluation (square) — guide to square," 2014, URL: https://www.iso.org/standard/64764.html [Last access on September, 2019].

[3] ATMOSPHERE, "Adaptive, trustworthy, manageable, orchestrated, secure, privacy-assuring hybrid, ecosystem for resilient cloud computing," 2018, URL: https://www.atmosphere-eubrazil.eu/ [Last access on January, 2020].

[4] R. C. Mayer, J. H. Davis, and F. D. Schoorman, "An integrative model of organizational trust," Academy of management review, vol. 20, no. 3, 1995, pp. 709–734.

[5] V. Shankar, G. L. Urban, and F. Sultan, "Online trust: a stakeholder perspective, concepts, implications, and future directions," The Journal of strategic information systems, vol. 11, no. 3-4, 2002, pp. 325–344.

[6] D. H. McKnight, V. Choudhury, and C. Kacmar, "Developing and validating trust measures for e-commerce: An integrative typology," Information systems research, vol. 13, no. 3, 2002, pp. 334–359.

[7] International Organization for Standardization, "Ergonomics of human-system interaction — part 210: Human-centred design for interactive systems," 2010, URL: https://www.iso.org/standard/52075.html [Last access on February, 2020].

[8] J. Dujmovic and R. Elnicki, "A DMS cost/benefit decision model: mathematical models for data management system evaluation, comparison, and selection," National Bureau of Standards, Washington DC, No. GCR, 1982, pp. 82–374.

[9] M. M. Friginal, Jesus, D. de Andres, and J.-C. Ruiz, "Multi-criteria analysis of measures in benchmarking: Dependability benchmarking as a case study," The Journal of Systems and Software, no. 111, 2016, pp. 105–118.

[10] I. IEC, "Software Product Quality Requirements and Evaluation - SQUARE," ISO/IEC, User Guide, 2005.

[11] S. Djamasbi, M. Siegel, T. Tullis, and R. Dai, "Efficiency, trust, and visual appeal: Usability testing through eye tracking," in 2010 43rd Hawaii International Conference on System Sciences. IEEE, 2010, pp. 1–10.

[12] B. A. Ramadhan and B. M. Iqbal, "User experience evaluation on the cryptocurrency website by trust aspect," in 2018 International Conference on Intelligent Informatics and Biomedical Sciences (ICIIBMS), vol. 3. IEEE, 2018, pp. 274–279.

[13] A. Seffah, M. Donyaee, R. B. Kline, and H. K. Padda, "Usability measurement and metrics: A consolidated model," Software quality journal, vol. 14, no. 2, 2006, pp. 159–178.

[14] P. Lew, L. Olsina, and L. Zhang, "Integrating quality, quality in use, actual usability and user experience," in 2010 6th Central and Eastern European Software Engineering Conference (CEE-SECR). IEEE, 2010, pp. 117–123.

[15] B. Hendradjaya and R. Praptini, "A proposal for a quality model for e-government website," in 2015 International Conference on Data and Software Engineering (ICoDSE). IEEE, 2015, pp. 19–24.

[16] PageSpeed Insights, "Increase the speed of your web pages on all devices," 2020, URL: https://developers.google.com/speed/pagespeed/insights/ [Last access on January, 2020].

[17] Solarwinds Pingdom, "Pingdom website speed test," 2018, URL: https://tools.pingdom.com/ [Last access on January, 2020].

[18] GTmetrix, "How fast does your website load? find out with gtmetrix," 2020, URL: https://gtmetrix.com/ [Last access on January, 2020].

[19] Dead Link Checker, "Free broken link checker," 2013, URL: https://www.deadlinkchecker.com/ [Last access on January, 2020].

[20] Xenu, "Xenu's link sleuth," 2020, URL: https://xenu-link-sleuth.br.softonic.com/ [Last access on January, 2020].

[21] Screaming Frog, "A website crawler and log file analyser tools," 2020, URL: https://www.screamingfrog.co.uk/ [Last access on January, 2020].

[22] Mobile Friendly Test, "Is your webpage mobile-friendly?" 2020, URL: https://search.google.com/test/mobile-friendly [Last access on January, 2020].

[23] ASES, "Site accessibility evaluator and simulator," 2020, URL: http://asesweb.governoeletronico.gov.br/ases/ [Last access on January, 2020].

[24] Nibbler, "Test any website," 2020, URL: https://nibbler.silktide.com/ [Last access on January, 2020].

[25] Tenon, "Access monitor," 2020, URL: https://wordpress.org/plugins/access-monitor/ [Last access on January, 2020].

[26] Faculty of Technology, "Software engineering department," 2020, URL: http://www.ft.unicamp.br/∼regina [Last access on January, 2020].

[27] World Wide Web Consortium, "Leading the web to its full potential," 2020, URL: https://www.w3.org/ [Last access on February, 2020].

How Users Perceive Authentication of Choice on Mobile Devices

Akintunde Jeremiah Oluwafemi
Computer and Information Sciences Department
Towson University
Towson, USA
e-mail: aoluwa2@students.towson.edu

Jinjuan Heidi Feng
Computer and Information Sciences Department
Towson University
Towson, USA
e-mail: jfeng@towson.edu

***Abstract*—When interacting with an application, users expect to complete the desired tasks securely with minimal interference from the actions required to ensure security and privacy. Previous research confirmed that there is a tradeoff between the security and usability of an application. Although numerous user studies examined various authentication methods, such as alphanumeric password, graphical password, and biometrics, very limited research investigated users' performance and perception when they were allowed to choose the authentication method(s) for a specific application. This study investigates how users interact with and perceive the 'authentication of choice' method when using a mobile device. 75 participants completed an online study that compared three different authentication designs: alphanumeric username and password, one-factor authentication of choice, and two-factor authentication of choice. The result of the study confirms the tradeoff between security and usability in the design of authentication mechanisms. The result also indicates that the 'authentication of choice' approach has the potential to offer a solution that provides the desired balance between usability and security.**

Keywords-Access control; Authentication of choice; Usability; Security.

I. INTRODUCTION

Security can be defined as the concepts, techniques, technical measures, and administrative measures used to protect information assets from deliberate or advertent unauthorized use, destruction, disclosure, or alteration [1]. With the continuous increase in security threats, it is crucial to incorporate security measures into the system design to ensure the security of both the system and the information that resides in the system. Authentication is the process of identifying an individual process or entity that is attempting to log in to a secure domain. One goal of authentication design is to ensure users can perform their primary tasks securely with minimal interference [2][3]. Previous research confirmed the tradeoff between the security and usability of common authentication methods currently in use. A particular measure that improves the security of the authentication mechanism usually has a negative effect on the usability of the system [4].

Due to the huge variation in the user abilities and preferences, the nature of tasks and devices, and the context of use, the authentication process should not be one-size-fits -all. An authentication method that is usable for a specific user in a particular context may not be usable for other users in another context. For the same reason, an authentication method that is considered by some users to be sufficiently secure may not be secure enough for other users. When choosing an authentication method, the user's preference between the security and usability of the authentication method may affect their decision. To make a system usable and secure, system developers need to go beyond the traditional human-centered design techniques and adopt design techniques that allow users to make decisions [5].

Although numerous user studies had examined various authentication methods, such as alphanumeric password [6] [7], graphical password [8][9], and biometrics [10] [11], very limited research investigated users' performance and preference when they were allowed to choose the authentication method(s) for a specific application [12] [13]. We conducted an online empirical study to provide preliminary understanding of the 'Authentication of Choice' (AoC) approach in the context of mobile devices. Authentication of choice is an authentication concept that allows users to select their preferred authentication method(s) out of various methods provided. Three different authentication designs were examined: traditional alphanumeric username and password, one-factor authentication of choice, and two-factor authentication of choice. Preliminary results of the study including the participants' preference over the three authentication designs and the specific authentication methods chosen under the 'authentication of choice' conditions were reported in [14]. This paper presents the performance measures including login time and failed login attempts. More importantly, we present and analyze participants' response to a series of questions that reveals their perception of usability and security in the context of mobile devices as well as how their perception affected their decision when using the 'Authentication of Choice' methods.

The rest of the paper is structured as follows. Section II reviews the literature on authentication methods currently in use and the study related to authentication of choice. We discuss the research methodology for this study in Section III of the paper and the result of the study in Section IV. We addressed the result of the study in Section V of the paper and the conclusion in Section VI.

II. RELATED WORK

There are different authentication methods currently in use. In this section, we review the literature on common authentication methods.

A. Authentication on Mobile Devices

There has been a rapid increase in the use of mobile phones. It was reported in 2016 that almost two-thirds of the world's population has a mobile phone [15]. Mobile devices have improved the quality of life by providing a variety of services anytime and anywhere. However, the mobility and portability of mobile devices pose a significant threat to the privacy and security of the information stored on the device [16]. User authentication is one of the security measures to mitigate the threat to security and privacy of the information on mobile devices. The most popular authentication approach on mobile devices is knowledge-based authentication methods, such as Personal Identification Number (PIN), password, and pattern or graphical passwords. More recently, fingerprint authentication and facial authentication have been widely adopted as well [17].

B. Authentication Methods

There are various authentication methods currently in use. These authentication methods are broadly categorized into four groups based on the factors required for authentication:

I. Knowledge-based Authentication

Knowledge-based authentication uses the information that users must know to verify their identity to the system. Authentication methods in this category require users to be able to recollect some information before gaining access to the system. This is done in form of challenge and response, in which the user responds to the challenge with something he knows [18]. Examples of knowledge-based authentication include numeric password, also referred to as PIN, alphanumeric password, or graphical password. Knowledge-based authentication methods are the most popular form of authentication because they are relatively easy to implement and have lower operating costs [19]. The major limitation of this type of authentication is the memorability requirement. Users have to commit information to memory and recollect the information during the authentication process. This memorability problem does affect the usability and security of knowledge-based authentication methods [18]. Users find it difficult to remember password or PIN and many end up writing down their passwords or choose simple passwords that may result in the compromise of the system security.

II. Inherent factors authentication

Inherent factors authentication, also known as biometrics, uses the physiological or behavioral traits of the user for authentication. These traits include fingerprint, iris, retina, voice, face, signature, typing patterns, physical movement, etc. [20]. To enroll users for biometric authentication, the feature to be used will be captured, processed, and stored in the computer as a baseline to compare with the newly captured biometrics during authentication [21].

Biometric authentication is relatively more usable and secure compared to knowledge-based authentication [22]. One of the challenges of the biometric authentication approach is that once the factor is compromised, the factor will remain compromised forever. There is no way that the user can change his fingerprint like in the case of knowledge-based or possession-based authentication [22]. Another problem with inherent factor authentication is that the user's environment can affect the efficacy of the authentication method [23]. For instance, a health worker in the emergency room wearing gloves and masks may not be able to use fingerprint or face recognition for authentication until they remove their gloves or face mask.

III. Possession-based Authentication

The possession-based authentication, also known as token-based authentication, relies on what users have or possess for authentication. Examples of possession include a token, smart card, common access card, etc. This authentication approach can be used on the stationary computer as a stand-alone device, plug into the computer through the USB port, or installed on a mobile device as an application. The token is widely used in mobile devices. This can be stand-alone hardware or software-based token. The token has a unique cryptographic secret embedded in it that can be used to authenticate using the challenge-response handshake system [24]. If the token device is broken, the key becomes invalid [25]. This authentication approach is relatively more acceptable to users compared to other authentication methods, but it is more difficult to manage, and the device can get lost, stolen or shared [26].

IV. Location-based Authentication

Location-based authentication involves using the geographical location of the user or device to authenticate and validate access to the information system. A common implementation of this approach is when banks deny customer transactions on their debit or credit card in an unauthorized location until the customer calls the bank to provide additional validation. This authentication approach can provide an additional level of security for the system by preventing access from unauthorized areas, but it is not easy to implement and has to be combined with another authentication approach to identify a specific user [27]. Location-based authentication requires a large number of databases and access towers to function effectively [28].

C. Multifactor Authentication Method

Multifactor authentication is a combination of two or more authentication methods to authenticate a user. This was introduced because of the insufficient level of security provided by single-factor authentication [29]. Multifactor authentication provides a higher level of security especially for government and military systems as well as other critical information systems [30]. Combining two or more factors of authentication increases the security of the system, but does affect the usability of the system [31].

D. Authentication of Choice

There is no perfect authentication method that can accommodate the needs of all users [32]. A system designer cannot design a universally accessible authentication method for users without knowing their abilities and disabilities [12]. People have different preferences for authentication methods based on their cognitive skills or physical abilities [13]. Systems are usually designed with one authentication method selected out of a variety of authentication methods that are currently in use. To enhance the security of the system, some systems adopted two-factor authentication that requires a higher workload from the user [32]. In either one-factor or two-factor authentication, providing the freedom of choice in selecting the authentication method(s) preferred by the individual user may improve the usability and the security of the system [14]. To date, there is no known research on the authentication of choice approach. We conducted the following study as an initial attempt to fill in this gap by collecting preliminary data on user performance, preference, and perception of AoC methods on mobile devices.

III. METHODOLOGY

The study was conducted electronically. A within-group design was adopted with three conditions for authentication:

- Alphanumeric username and password
- One-factor AoC: In this condition, participants chose one authentication method out of five options: alphanumeric password, PIN, fingerprint authentication, facial recognition, and One Time Password (OTP).
- Two-factor AoC: In this condition, participants chose two authentication methods out of the five options listed above.

A. Participants

75 participants completed the study. Participants did not receive any financial or other types of incentives for taking part in the study. The participants for the study were selected randomly. The age of participants varies, with 47 participants in the age range of 18-30 years, 18 in the range of 31-40 years, 8 in the range of 41-50 years and 2 above 50. Out of the 75 participants, 43 claimed they were male while 32 claimed to be female. 71 of the participants were professionals working in various fields, such as business, education, science, engineering and IT, and healthcare. Three participants were students. One participant did not identify his/her career. Regarding educational background, 31 participants claimed to have a high school diploma, 33 participants had bachelor degree and 11 participants had postgraduate degrees. The level of information security experience of the participants varies: 28 participants claimed themselves as experts, 23 with intermediate knowledge, and 23 with basic level of experience. One participant did not respond to this question.

B. Event Manager Application

An Android-based mobile device application called 'Event Manager' was developed to provide a realistic setting for this study. The 'Event Manager' supports five authentication methods and provides a calendar for managing daily schedule. The calendar function was chosen because it was available on almost all mobile phones and its' security and privacy related expectation was representative of many tasks conducted on mobile devices on a daily basis. The five authentication methods supported are commonly adopted on mobile devices:

- Alphanumeric username and password
- PIN
- Fingerprint authentication
- Facial recognition
- One-Time-Password (OTP)

The design of the application followed general usability guidelines and underwent several rounds of refinement based on users' feedback. The home page and the registration page of the application are demonstrated in Figure 1 (a and b). Users can create three types of accounts on the application using the same email:

Type 1 (T1): Alphanumeric username and password
Type 2 (T2): One-factor AoC out of five options
Type 3 (T3): Two-factor AoC out of five options

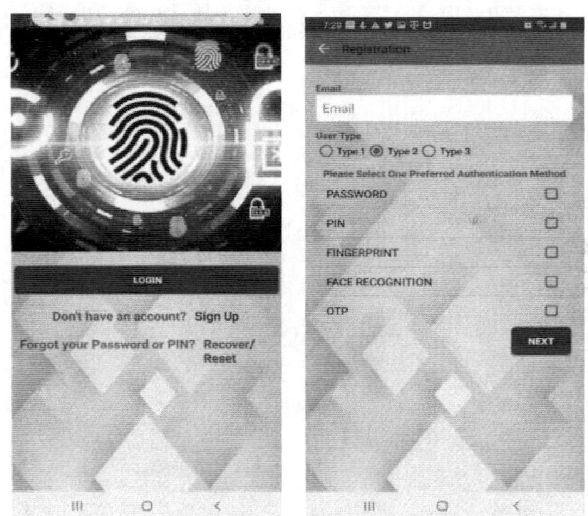

Figure 1. (a) Home page and (b) Registration page.

C. Procedure

This study was conducted electronically. Instructions for the study and the questionnaire link were sent out to participants via email. After providing consent to take part in the study, participants first downloaded the 'Event Manager' app from Google Play and installed it on their Android phones. Then, each participant created and logged into an account under all three conditions. After they logged into an account, they added or revised an event on the calendar. The order of the three conditions was counterbalanced among the participants to control the learning effect. After the participants completed the tasks under all 3 conditions, they answered a questionnaire via a Google Form. The questionnaire collected participants' demographic information, their general attitude toward security and privacy, their security-related practice on their mobile devices, and their preference and perception towards the AoC approach. The authentication methods chosen during the two AoC conditions, the time it took to login, and the outcome of the login attempt were automatically logged by the application.

IV. RESULTS

In this section, we discuss the result of the study using the data obtained from the Event Manager application and the questionnaire completed by participants.

A. *Login time and failed attempts*

A One-Way Repeated Measures ANOVA test using login time as the dependent variable and condition as the independent variable suggests that there is significant difference in the login time under the three conditions ($F(2, 148) = 56.80$, $p < 0.001$). Post hoc Least Significant Difference (LSD) tests suggest that the participants took significantly longer time to login under the alphanumeric username/password condition than the one-factor AoC condition ($p < 0.001$) and the two-factor AoC condition ($p < 0.05$). Participants also took significantly longer time to login under the two-factor AoC condition than the one-factor condition ($p < 0.001$).

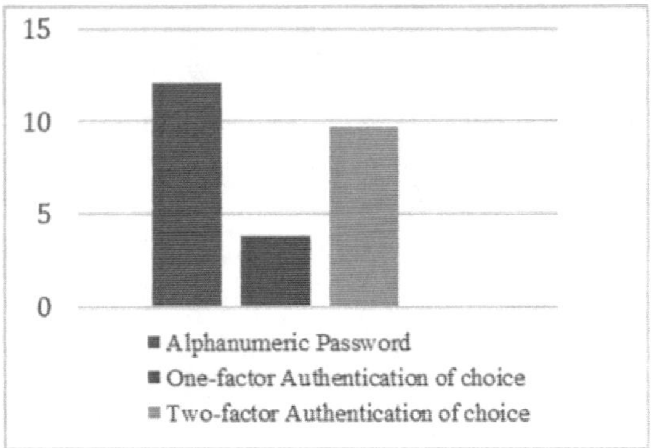

Figure 2. Login time for the three authentication conditions.

Failed login attempts rarely occurred during the study. There were five instances of incorrect alphanumeric password, two instances of unrecognized fingerprint, and two instances of unrecognized face.

B. *Attitude toward security and usability*

Participants were asked to rate the importance of security and privacy of their information; 67 (89%) participants claimed that it was very important, 5 (7%) claimed it as fairly important while 3 (4%) claimed it as important. When asked about the importance of security of their mobile phone, 69 (92%) participants rated it as very important, 4 (5%) as fairly important, 1 (1%) as important while the remaining 1 (1%) as slightly important.

Participants rated the level of importance regarding the security and ease of use of the authentication method on their mobile phone. Table I illustrates the number of participants that ranked the importance of security and ease of use at a specific level. Out of 75 participants, 69 (92%) believed security is very important and the remaining 6 (8%) claimed that is it fairly important. 63 (84%) participants claimed ease of use is very important, 6 (8%) participants claimed it as fairly important and the remaining 6 (8%) claimed it as important.

TABLE I. PARTICIPANTS RANKING OF SECURITY AND EASE OF USE

Level of Importance	Security	Ease of use
1 (Not at all)	0	0
2 (Slightly important)	0	0
3 (Important)	0	6
4 (Fairly important)	6	6
5 (Very important)	69	63

Participants were asked whether they would choose ease of use over security regarding mobile phone authentication. Out of 75 participants, 47 strongly disagreed, 10 disagreed, 5 were neutral, 7 agreed and 4 strongly agreed.

C. *Current practice regarding mobile phone authentication*

67 (89%) participants normally secured their phone while 8 (11%) did not. Table II illustrates the number and percentage of participants that used a specific authentication method to secure their phones.

TABLE II. PARTICIPANT AUTHENTICATION METHOD PREFERENCE

Authentication method	# of participants	# of participants
Alphanumeric password	27	36%
PIN/ Passcode	67	89%
Gesture /Pattern	40	53%
Fingerprint	59	79%
Facial authentication	48	64%

D. *User perception of authentication on mobile phones*

Based on their perception, participants selected an authentication method that they believed was the most secure and one they believed was the easiest to use on mobile phones. Table III illustrates the number of participants that rated the two elements at a specific level.

TABLE III. AOC BASED ON SECURITY AND EASY OF USE

Methods	Most Secure	Easiest of use
Alphanumeric password	2	2
PIN	2	6
Fingerprint	50	42
Facial authentication	18	23
Gesture/Pattern	1	2
Voice authentication	2	0

As illustrated in Table IV, the majority of the participants chose fingerprint as the most secure (67%) and the easiest to use (56%) authentication method. The second on the list is facial authentication, with 18 participants choosing it as the most secure and 23 participants as the easiest to use. All the other methods received much fewer votes on both perspectives. No participant chose OTP to be the most secure or easiest to use.

Participants were asked to rank four criteria for selecting an authentication method on a mobile phone, namely efficiency, ease of use, security, and memorability. Table IV illustrates how participants ranked the four criteria. Security was chosen to be the top rank criteria when selecting an authentication method by 56 (75%) participants, followed by the ease of use, efficiency, and memorability.

TABLE IV. CRITERION RANKING

Rank	Efficiency (quick)	Ease of use	Security	Memorability
Top rank	8	11	56	0
2nd rank	20	28	16	11
3rd rank	31	26	3	15
4td rank	16	10	0	49

Participants ranked their preference towards the three authentication conditions. The results were reported in [6]. Participants overwhelmingly preferred the one-factor AoC condition over the other two conditions. 63 participants chose the one-factor AoC as their top choice while 9 selected the two-factor AoC and 3 selected the alphanumeric password method. To further understand their preference, we asked participants to select the possible reasons behind their ranking. Four possible reasons were provided: efficiency, ease of use, security, and memorability. Participants could check multiple reasons that applied. Table V illustrates the number of participants that selected each condition as their top preference and the number of participants in that group who selected each specific reason.

TABLE V. TEST CONDITIONS CHOICE BASED ON CRITERION

	Alphanumeric password as top preference	One-factor AoC as top preference	Two-factor AoC as top preference
Number of participants	3	63	9
Efficiency	2	34	3
Ease of use	2	51	3
Security	2	54	7
Memorability	0	28	1

Among the 63 participants who chose one-factor AoC as their top preference, 54 participants selected security and 51 selected ease of use as one of the reasons for their decision, suggesting that the two factors are the dominant factors in the decision making process regarding the selection of authentication approach on mobile phones.

Finally, we asked participants whether two-factor AoC improves the security of the system, requires too much time for authentication, is difficult to remember, or difficult to use. We asked these questions to evaluate their perception of the two-factor AoC approach.

TABLE VI. PERCEPTIONS OF TWO-FACTOR AOC

Perceptions	1 Strongly Disagree	2 Disagree	3 Neutral	4 Agree	5 Strongly Agree
Improves Security	0	2	5	11	56
Takes too much time	17	25	11	13	8
Difficult to remember	29	29	11	5	0
Difficult to use	21	34	11	7	1

Among the 74 participants who answered these questions, 67 agreed that using two-factor AoC improved the security of the authentication process. When asked whether two-factor AoC took too much time, 42 participants disagreed, 11 were neutral and 21 agreed. 58 participants disagreed that the two-factor AoC was difficult to remember, 5 agreed and 11 were neutral. 55 participants disagreed that using two-factor AoC made the authentication process difficult, 8 agreed and 11 were neutral.

V. DISCUSSION

The results suggested that, on a mobile phone, both the one-factor authentication and the two-factor authentication are significantly more efficient than the alphanumeric password method. The participants highly valued security and privacy both from the general perspective and in the specific context of mobile phone usage.

The study revealed an interesting contradiction between users' perception about security and their actual security decision. 92% of participants rated security as very important in general and 75% chose security as their most important criteria when selecting an authentication method for their mobile phone. However, 84% of the participants prefer one-factor AoC over two-factor AoC even though 89% of them agreed that two-factor AoC could improve the security of the device. This finding suggests that users should not be expected to choose the most secure authentication method available even though they highly value security. The reason could be attributed to the classic tradeoff between security and usability. In this study, 51 out of the 63 participants who chose one-factor AoC as their top preference selected 'ease of use' as one of the reasons for their decision. So, between one-factor and two-factor authentication, it seems that most users would prefer the one-factor AoC due to its efficiency and reduced cognitive load.

One-factor AoC may not support the level of security protection desired or required by many institutions, businesses, or individual users. In those cases, is it feasible to require two-factor AoC? The finding of the study provides a positive answer to that question. Although the participants overwhelmingly preferred one-factor AoC over two-factor

AoC, their perception about two-factor AoC is highly positive. 89% of the participants thought two-factor AoC could improve security. 71% and 92% of the participants were fine with the efficiency and memorability of two-factor AoC, respectively. 87% thought the general usability of the two-factor AoC was acceptable. Therefore, when one-factor AoC is not an option, it is quite likely that users would adopt two-factor AoC and find it usable.

As a preliminary investigation of the authentication of choice approach, this study has several limitations that need to be addressed through future research. First, the study only involved Android users and the results may not be generalizable to users of other platforms. Second, the authentication methods supported were either knowledge-based or biometrics. Possession-based and location-based authentication methods were not examined. Third, because the participants logged into each account only once during the study, the result only applies to the very initial interaction with the different authentication options. We are planning a one-month longitudinal study to examine the AoC approach in a more realistic setting.

VI. CONCLUSION

This study provided insights about user performance, preferences, and perception of the authentication of choice approach on mobile devices during their initial interaction with this approach. The efficiency and the user subjective perception suggest that the AoC approach has the potential to serve as a usable and secure authentication solution on mobile devices. Although users overwhelmingly prefer the one-factor AoC over two-factor AoC, they are likely to adopt the two-factor AoC when a higher level of security protection is desired or required. Future research is needed to confirm the findings of this study on other platforms and longer period of user interaction.

VII. ACKNOWLEDGMENT

We sincerely appreciate Edward Miklewski for his assistance in data collection and our appreciation goes to all the participants of this study.

VIII. REFERENCES

[1] E. Davidson, B. McCredie, and W. Vikelis, IBM Dictionary of Computing. Edited by G. McDaniel. 10th ed. New York, NY: McGraw-Hill, 1994.

[2] R. Clarke, Sufficiently Rich Model of (id)Entity, Authentication and Authorization http://www.rogerclarke.com/ID/IdModel1002.html#MAc, [retrieved: November, 2020].

[3] A. Beautement, M. A. Sasse, and M. Wonham, "The compliance budget: Managing security behavior in organizations," In Proceedings of the workshop on new security paradigms, pp. 47-58, 2010. doi: 0.1145/1595676.1595684.

[4] K. P. Yee, User Interaction Design for Secure Systems. In Proceedings of the 4th International Conference on Information and Communications Security, Singapore, pp. 278-290, 2002.

[5] L. F. Cranor and N. Buchler, "Better Together: Usability and Security Go Hand in Hand," in IEEE Security & Privacy, vol. 12, no. 6, pp. 89-93, 2014. doi:10.1109/MSP.2014.109

[6] R. Anderson, J. Yan, A. Blackwell, and A. Grant, Password memorability and security: Empirical results. IEEE Security and Privacy, 2(5), pp. 25–30, 2005.

[7] J. Yan, N. H. Zakaria, D. Grifths, and S. Brostof, Shoulder surfing defense for recall-based graphical passwords. In: Proceedings of the seventh symposium on usable privacy and security (pp 6:1– 6:12), 2011. New York, NY, USA: ACM. https://doi.org/10.1145/20788 27.2078835, [retrieved: November, 2020].

[8] R. Dhamija and A. Perrig, "Deja Vu: A User Study Using Images for Authentication," in Proceedings of 9th USENIX Security Symposium, pp. 45-58 , 2000.

[9] A. M. Eljetlawi and N. Ithnin, Graphical Password: Comprehensive Study of the Usability Features of the Recognition Base Graphical Password Methods. Convergence and Hybrid Information Technology, pp. 1137-1143, 2008.

[10] A. H Mir, S. Rubab, and Z.A Jhat, Biometrics Verification: a Literature Survey. Journal of Computing and ICT Research, Vol. 5, Issue 2, pp. 67-80, 2011.

[11] S. Cohen, N. Ben-Asher, and J. Meyer, Towards information technology security for universal access. In: Stephanidis, C. (ed.) Universal Access in HCI, Part I, HCII 2011. LNCS, vol. 6765, pp. 443–451. Springer, Heidelberg.

[12] P. Fairweather, V. Hanson, S. Detweiler, and R. Schwerdtfeger, From assistive technology to a web accessibility service. In Proceedings of the 5th International ACM Conference on Assistive Technologies (ASSETS). ACM, pp. 4-8, 2002.

[13] M. Belk, C. Fidas, P. Germanakos, and G. Samaras, Security for diversity: Studying the effects of verbal and imagery processes on user authentication mechanisms. In IFIP TC13 Conference on Human-Computer Interaction (INTERACT). Springer, pp. 442-459, 2013.

[14] A. J. Oluwafemi and H. D. Feng, Authentication of Choice on Mobile Devices: A Preliminary Investigation. Human-Computer Interaction international conference 2020, in press.

[15] S. Kemp, Digitalin 2017: Global Overview.' We Are Social, 2017, https://wearesocial.com/specialreports/digital-in-2017-global-overview [retrieved: November, 2020].

[16] R. Marcin, S. Khalid, R. Mariusz, T. Marek, and A. Marcin, User Authentication for Mobile Devices. 12th International Conference on Information Systems and Industrial Management (CISIM), Sep 2013, Krakow, Poland. pp.47-58, ff10.1007/978-3-642-40925-7_5ff. ffhal01496111

[17] P. S. Teh, N. Zhang, and S. Tan, Strengthen user authentication on mobile devices by using user's touch dynamics pattern. J Ambient Intell Human Comput, pp 4019-4039, 2020 https://doi.org/10.1007/s12652-019-01654-y,[retrieved: November, 2020].

[18] C. Katsini, M. Belk, C. Fidas, N. Avouris, and G. Samaras, Security and Usability in Knowledge-based User Authentication: A Review, 2016. 10.1145/3003733.3003764.

[19] B. W. Lampson, Computer Security in the Real World, IEEE Computer, vol. 37, no. 6, pp. 37 - 46 , 2004. ISO 9564-1:2011

[20] S. C. Fang and H. L. Chan, Human identification by quantifying similarity and dissimilarity in electrocardiogram phase space. Pattern Recogn. 42, pp. 1824–1831, 2009. https://doi.org/10.1016/j.patcog.2008.11.020, [retrieved: November, 2020].

[21] F. L. Podio and J. S. Dunn, Biometric Authentication Technology: from the Movies to Your Desktop, ITL Bulletin , 2001.

[22] C. Stephanidis and M. Antona, UAHCI/HCII 2013, Part I, LNCS 8009, pp. 195–204, 2013. Springer-Verlag Berlin Heidelberg

[23] D. Bordea, Selecting a two-factor authentication system. Network Security, p. 17-20, 2007.

[24] R. Sandhu and P. Samarati, Authentication, access control, and audit. Computing Surveys (CSUR), Vol. 28, 1, pp. 241-243, 1996.

[25] A. Habtamu, Different Ways to Authenticate Users with the Pros and Cons of each Method, Norwegian: Norsk Regnesentral, pp. 350-364, 2006.

[26] R. Sailer, X. Zhang, T. Jaeger, and L. Van Doorn, "Design and Implementation of a TCGbased Integrity Measurement Architecture", Proceedings of the 13th Conference on USENIX Security Symposium - Volume 13, SSYM'04, USENIX Association, Berkeley, CA, USA, pp. 16–16, 2004

[27] S. Holtmanns, V. Niemi, P. Ginzboorg, P. Laitinen, and N. Asokan, Cellular Authentication For Mobile And Internet Services, Wiley, UK, 2012.

[28] R. K Konoth, V. Van der Veen, and H. Bos, How anywhere computing just killed your phone-based two-factor authentication. In Proceedings of the International Conference on Financial Cryptography and Data Security, Christ Church, Barbados, 22–26 February 2016; Springer: Berlin, Germany, pp. 405–421, 2016.

[29] R. K Banyal, P. Jain, and V. K. Jain, Multi-factor authentication framework for cloud computing. In Proceedings of the Fifth International Conference on Computational Intelligence, Modelling and Simulation (CIMSim), Seoul, Korea, pp. 105–110, 2013.

[30] E. De Cristofaro, H. Du, J. Freudiger,, and G. Norcie, A comparative usability study of two-factor authentication. arXiv preprint arXiv:1309.5344, 2013.

[31] K. Renaud, Quantification of authentication mechanisms - a usability perspective. Journal of Web Engineering, 3(2), pp. 95-123, 2004.

[32] A. Jain, A. Ross, and K. Nandakumar, Introduction to biometrics. Springer 2011 edition, pp. 947-954, 2011.

Rule-based Intelligent System for Dictating Mathematical Notation in Polish

Agnieszka Bier
Faculty of Applied Mathematics
Silesian University of Technology
Gliwice, Poland
email: agnieszka.bier@polsl.pl

Zdzisław Sroczyński
Faculty of Applied Mathematics
Silesian University of Technology
Gliwice, Poland
email: zdzislaw.sroczynski@polsl.pl

***Abstract*—The paper describes the design and implementation of the system for dictation of mathematical expressions in Polish. The details of the developed solution environment are presented, as well as the workflow scheme of the actual natural language parser. In order to test the dictation engine, we have extended the Equation wizard editor, developed initially as a classic desktop application for MS Windows operating system. Preliminary experiments prove the system works efficiently and accepts even complex expressions and can, therefore, be used as a basis for the novel approach to editing mathematical documents by people with disabilities. The proposed solution provides an efficient interface for input of mathematical content and may be easily adapted to human-computer interaction systems for educational purposes.**

Keywords*—*Natural language; Mathematical notation; Assistive technologies; Verbalization.

I. INTRODUCTION

People with different kinds of disabilities, such as mobility or visual impairment, often encounter difficulties with editing mathematical equations. As most popular tools use document description languages such as LaTeX and MathML, or editors with graphical user interface, they require visual control, as well as the effective and precise manipulation of the keyboard, mouse or touch screen.

In the following sections, we present details of design and implementation of a system translating the spoken version of mathematical notation into the structural and formal description language. The output from the translation system can be passed further to e-learning applications, desktop publishing or algebra manipulation mathematical software.

The rules of the translation engine are fine-tuned to Polish language and, therefore, the system fills the gap in the solutions available to people with sight or motion disabilities in Poland.

The structure of the translation system contains the "Equation wizard" visual editor, enhanced with App Tethering technology by the extra "Mobile assistant" application. The actual voice recognition is performed by a mobile device, which works as the terminal for the server – the visual editor. The results of recognition can be displayed on-the-fly by the mobile assistant app. This way, we have integrated the environment for testing translation rules from spoken to structural notation with minimal effort. Moreover, the mobile multi-platform clients can be the starting platform for various assisting educational projects.

The paper is organized into five sections. In Section II, we provide a short review of the state-of-the-art contributions for editing/verbalizing mathematical formulas, with particular interest in widely used standards for writing mathematical content and parsing to spoken language. Section III concerns the design and implementation details of the proposed solution. In Section IV, some experimental results and user experience are presented. We conclude the paper with a brief discussion on further development of the system in Section V.

II. RELATED WORK

There are many alternative methods of presentation and editing mathematical content: automatic recognition of printed expressions [1], recognition of handwritten equations, editing with visual editors (WYSIWYG), editing with the use of document description languages (LaTeX, MathML), editing with the use of specialized notations and software (for example Braille dot language), verbalization (translation to/from the spoken, natural language version) [2]–[9]. Contemporary computer systems implement the voice input and natural language processing with increasing success rates and user satisfaction level [10]–[12]. It is worth noting that the understanding of commands and sentences of natural language in general tasks can be just statistically exact, while for the mathematical notation things get much more complicated – every single sign, letter or number matters a lot, and possibly can change the meaning of the whole expression [13].

A. Description languages

There are two main description languages used to encode two-dimensional mathematical notation into linear form. The first one is LaTeX – de-facto standard for scientific and educational documents. The main advantages of LaTeX are popularity and consistent syntax, which allows editing of even very complex equations by hand.

The second one is MathML, compatible with XML specification, and therefore used in Internet applications. Some Internet browsers render MathML natively (Firefox, Chrome); for the rest (Internet Explorer) the end-user can install a plugin for that purpose. MathML uses two different layers of notation: the presentation layer, which describes the visual appearance of the equation, and the content layer, which describes the meaning of the expression. Although these two layers can be mixed in one document, the majority of applications utilizes only the presentation layer. This way, MathML suffers from ambiguities at the same level, as LaTeX does. The resolving of ambiguities in the encoded mathematical notation is the key issue for further processing and translating the given equation into another media.

In our framework and "Equation wizard" editor, we use dedicated internal language, which helps to preserve the context of the equation parts. We call it EQED (EQuation EDitor) format. It can be also easily translated into the internal object tree, representing the equation in the rendering engine of the editor. On the other hand, we provide filters for import and export of LaTeX and MathML notation.

B. Math verbalization

There are no formal rules for the verbalization of mathematical content. Some common spelling suggestions are given in numerous mathematical schoolbooks and scientific works, as well as the tradition during teachers education [14][15]. Mathematical publications in Polish very seldom include natural language description of the equations, so the only source of unified de-facto standard in this area is the pronunciation used during maths lessons or university language centers' publications [16]. Moreover, spelling maths is mostly parallel with visual presentation on the blackboard, so any ambiguities are resolved immediately. On the other hand, people with sight disabilities have no such visual aid and the maths verbalization designed for them requires much more precise syntax [17][18], including the terminating signs for most of the subexpressions. The maths verbalization in English is certainly the most common and comprehensive [19][20], however other languages still need extended elaboration [21][22].

III. Dictating Mathematical Content

Proper conversion from spoken language to formal, structured mathematical notation is an important issue, which could make the education of physically disabled people much easier. Moreover, common mathematical education could benefit as well, as speech based interfaces became popular nowadays.

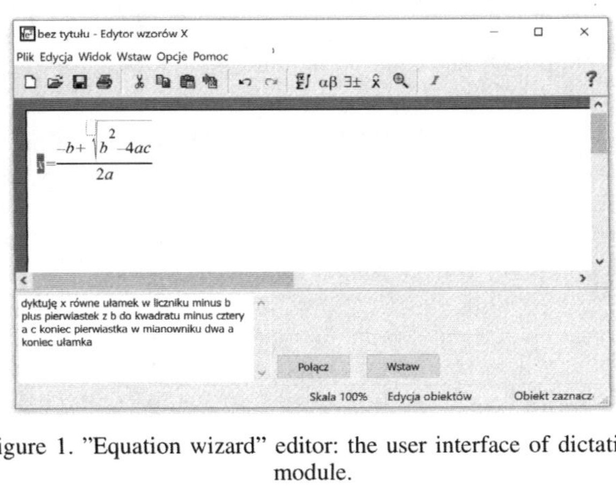

Figure 1. "Equation wizard" editor: the user interface of dictation module.

In order to test the dictation engine, we have extended the "Equation wizard" editor, developed initially as a classic desktop application for MS Windows operating system.

The user interface of the dictation module is shown in Figure 1. The natural language description of the mathematical notation appears in the multi-line text widget and the operator is able to paste it into the main window of the editor, invoking the translation process. This mode resembles more or less a debugging console and for the future production-ready versions of the software it should be altered to provide the complete voice driven human-machine interface. Eventually, this interface should include commands for the manipulation of the parts of the equation as well.

Because of the lack of Polish language native support in MS Windows voice recognition engine, there was the need for an extra software solution. Therefore, we have integrated the supplementary multi-platform application for mobile operating systems (iOS and Android). Both of the mentioned operating systems support dictation in Polish, although there are some differences, especially when spelling numbers. The quality of recognition for particular words also differs and is below standard results for the sentences, because in the natural language description of mathematics every sign and single letter has significant meaning and placement. Nevertheless, the results of the dictation were satisfactory enough to perform some tests on rather complicated equations.

The "Mobile assistant" application provides the result of the recognition in the graphical form, which can be considered as a substitute of the editor module. Some screen shots of the user interface of this assistant application are shown in Figure 2.

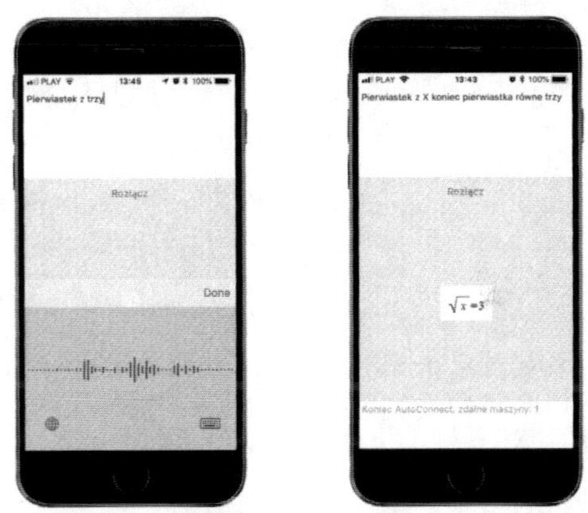

Figure 2. "Mobile assistant" application: the user interface during dictation in iOS (left) and after the recognition and visualization of the results (right).

A. App Tethering

App Tethering is the technology which allows to easily extend the existing applications developed in RAD Studio [23] with the network connectivity, regardless of the operating system used. The "Equation wizard" editor has been enhanced this way with the use of the supplementary mobile apps mentioned above.

The main aim of App Tethering is to provide the novel mobile interface for classic desktop application, which is also our case. The classic MS Windows desktop application could work as a server, responding to the information changes in the mobile terminal and possibly returning the result data.

App Tethering technology:

- operates at Windows, MacOS, Android and iOS platforms,
- allows to exchange the data (resources) between platforms,
- can be introduced into any application based on RAD Studio Run-Time Library (RTL) with the use of:
  - IP connections in the same subnet,
  - classic Bluetooth connections,
- provides an automatic search for connected applications,
- allows to run remote procedures,
- ensures easy exchange of the data,
- introduces simple network protocol and is easy to implement with ready to use high level software components.

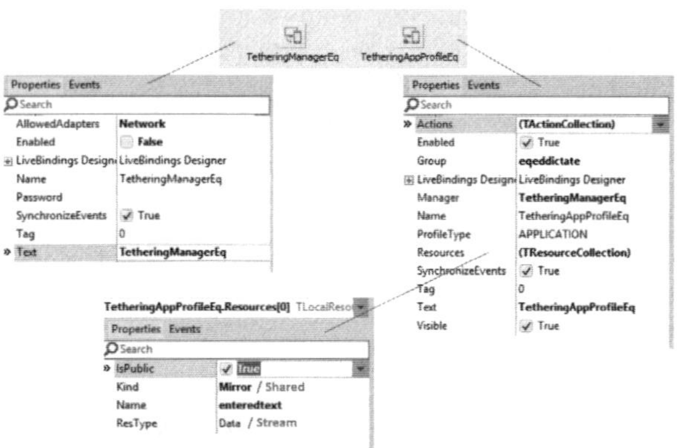

Figure 3. App Tethering: software components flowchart.

The exemplary setup of the App Tethering components and source code snippets are given in Figure 3 and Figure 4, respectively.

```
procedure TMainForm.ResourceReceived(
  const Sender: TObject;
  const AResource: TRemoteResource);
begin
 MemoEqDictate.Text:='dyktuje␣' +
       AResource.Value.AsString.ToLower;
end;
...
TetheringAppProfile.Resources.
          FindByName('eqpicture').Value :=
                            EqPictureStream;
```

Figure 4. App Tethering: source code snippets for resource exchange.

B. Parsing the verbal form of mathematical expressions

A parser designed for automatic recognition of the structure of the mathematical expression given in spoken form is incorporated into the main engine of the "Equation wizard" editor. The core of the equation editor uses a tree-like data structure to represent the expression being manipulated in the main window. The leaves of the tree contain specialized objects representing particular parts of the equation i.e. simple symbols (as letters or numbers) or two-dimensional templates (as for example fractions, roots and integrals). Recursive traversal through the entire tree gives the possibility to translate, edit, move or alter parts of the expression. Moreover, the core engine offers an interface for expression import and export using the internal domain-specific language (EQED, based on LaTeX), MathML or plain LaTeX. In previous experiments, this engine was extended with the verbalization and search modules, ensuring the export of the equation with natural language, with possible multi-language support [2][24].

The import of the natural language form of an equation is the next level achievement for the "Equation wizard" environment. The parser environment processes the input from the natural language into the graphical, visual representation in the following steps:

- the acquisition of the input description string in the natural language (there is the requirement of the compatibility with the rules for Polish verbalization engine at the moment, which is convenient for testing) with the use of an assistant mobile application and speech recognition engine from the mobile operating system (iOS or Android),
- transfer of the input description string into the recognition module in the "Equation wizard" application, working as server in this mode,
- the actual translation with the set of replacement rules described as pairs of natural language phrase and the corresponding EQED internal format command,
- backward scanning for the corrections of the keywords without explicit termination mark,
- the transfer of the result string encoded with EQED commands to the standard import module of the equation editor in order to visualize it and edit,
- the final visual appearance of the dictated equation is returned to the assistant mobile application and shown to the user.

The translation rules have the following format:

`natural_language_phrase~EQED_internal_format`,

where ~ (tilde sign) is a separator. The left side is the part to search for and the right side is the corresponding notation in EQED format. Some exemplary rules are presented in Figure 5.

Symbols `#`, `@` and `$` were introduced to maintain subexpressions which do not have an explicit termination command or require pairing of possibly nested symbols as brackets. These symbols are processed at the final stage of parsing.

The current version of the parser supports different variants of the spoken notation, making the dictation as natural as possible. The main inconvenience, however, is the requirement to provide the termination command for the majority of subexpressions.

```
pierwiastek stopnia~\EQEDroot{
pierwiastek z~\EQEDroot{\EQEDplain{}}{
pod pierwiastkiem~}{
koniec pierwiastka~}
do kwadratu~#}{\EQEDnplain{2}}
do potegi~#}{\EQEDnplain{
otworz nawias~$EQEDbrackets{\left(}{
zamknij nawias~}{\right)@
```

Figure 5. Example rules for translation Polish verbalized mathematical notation into structural form.

IV. EXPERIMENTAL RESULTS

We have performed a series of experiments involving four experts, with the use of different operating systems for the assistant mobile application (Android and iOS). The experts were familiar with the "Equation wizard" editor user interface and editing rules, knew the rules of verbalization of the mathematical notation and could check it live before dictation experiments. There were over a dozen dictation attempts of different equations by every expert. All these circumstances were undoubtedly helpful to build the dictation commands in the proper form (see some exemplary results in Figure 6). Especially, the overall high level of experience in editing mathematical content was decisive for rather high success rate (about 70%). On the other hand, the requirement to spell the whole equation at once (temporary for current beta solution), could certainly make the dictation extremely difficult for not prepared user.

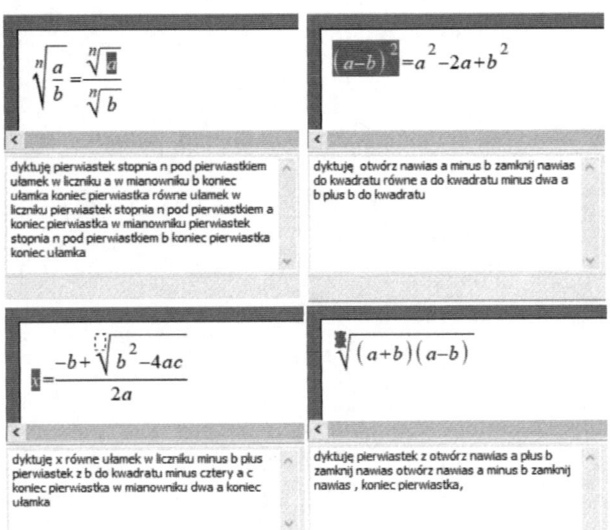

Figure 6. Examples of successfully dictated equations with the visualization in "Formula wizard" editor.

V. CONCLUSION

In this paper, we have described the design of the natural language to structural mathematical notation translation system. The main language of the tests was Slavic language – Polish, which significantly differs from the western languages, especially when it comes to numerals and details of mathematical notation.

The usage of the existing engine and graphical equation editor ("Equation wizard") for rendering and processing of the mathematical notation increased the effectiveness of the translation. Several preliminary experiments proved that the system works smoothly for the current, limited list of translation rules. Nevertheless, some of the mathematical expressions in the test suite were relatively complex and careful dictation gave very promising results for them.

It is worth to note that translation rules could be profiled according to specific features of speech recognition modules from the mobile operating systems. The introduction of some editing voice commands would certainly make the system more user friendly in real life examples for the people with motion disabilities. The last improvement could be a closer integration with mobile operating system, i.e., usage of smart glasses interface, sharing the results with other applications, e-mail or messaging clients.

REFERENCES

[1] Z. Sroczyński, "Priority levels and heuristic rules in the structural recognition of mathematical formulae," *Theoretical and Applied Informatics*, vol. 22, no. 4, p. 273, 2010.

[2] A. Bier and Z. Sroczynski, "Adaptive math-to-speech interface," in *Proceedings of the Multimedia, Interaction, Design and Innnovation*, ser. MIDI '15. New York, NY, USA: ACM, 2015, pp. 7:1–7:9. [Online]. Available: http://doi.acm.org/10.1145/2814464.2814471

[3] A. Bier and Z. Sroczyński, "Rule based intelligent system verbalizing mathematical notation," *Multimedia Tools and Applications*, vol. 78, no. 19, pp. 28 089–28 110, 2019.

[4] J. Cuartero-Olivera, G. Hunter, and A. Pérez-Navarro, "Reading and writing mathematical notation in e-learning environments," *eLearn Center Research Paper Series*, no. 4, pp. 11–20, 2012.

[5] D. Attanayake, J. Denholm-Price, G. Hunter, E. Pfluegel, and A. Wigmore, "Speech interfaces for mathematics: Opportunities and limitations for visually impaired learners," in *IMA International Conference on Barriers and Enablers to Learning Maths: Enhancing Learning and Teaching for All Learners*, 2015, pp. 1–8.

[6] M. Isaac *et al.*, "Improving automatic speech recognition for mobile learning of mathematics through incremental parsing." in *Intelligent Environments (Workshops)*, 2016, pp. 217–226.

[7] A. Mazzei, M. Monticone, and C. Bernareggi, "Using nlg for speech synthesis of mathematical sentences," in *Proceedings of The 12th International Conference on Natural Language Generation*, 2019, pp. 463–472.

[8] A. Szesz Junior, L. Ribeiro Mendes, and S. de Carvalho Rutz da Silva, "Math2text: Software para gerao e converso de equaes matemticas em texto - limitaes e possibilidades de incluso," *RISTI*, no. 37, pp. 99–115, 2020.

[9] P. Sojka, V. Novotn, E. F. Ayetiran, D. Luptk, and M. tefnik, "Quo vadis, math information retrieval," in *Proceedings of Recent Advances in Slavonic Natural Language Processing*, 2019, pp. 117–128.

[10] D. Polap, "Voice control in mixed reality," in *2018 Federated Conference on Computer Science and Information Systems (FedCSIS)*. IEEE, 2018, pp. 497–500.

[11] J. Kowalski *et al.*, "Older adults and voice interaction: A pilot study with google home," in *Extended Abstracts of the 2019 CHI Conference on Human Factors in Computing Systems*, 2019, pp. 1–6.

[12] I. Tautkute, T. Trzciński, A. P. Skorupa, Ł. Brocki, and K. Marasek, "Deepstyle: Multimodal search engine for fashion and interior design," *IEEE Access*, vol. 7, pp. 84 613–84 628, 2019.

[13] R. Fateman, "Handwriting + speech for computer entry of mathematics," *Style, Benjamin L. Kovitz, Manning Publications Company*, 2004.

[14] ——, "How can we speak math?" Computer Science Division, EECS Department, University of California at Berkeley, Tech. Rep., 2013.
[15] T. Sancho-Vinuesa *et al.*, "Automatic verbalization of mathematical formulae for web-based learning resources in an on-line environment," *INTED2009 Proceedings*, pp. 4312–4321, 2009.
[16] R. Szopa and D. Zuziak, *Selected Texts on Higher Mathematics*, ser. Academic Textbooks, No 1837. SUT Press, 1994.
[17] S. Bocconi, S. Dini, L. Ferlino, C. Martinoli, and M. Ott, *ICT Educational Tools and Visually Impaired Students: Different Answers to Different Accessibility Needs*. Berlin, Heidelberg: Springer Berlin Heidelberg, 2007, pp. 491–500. [Online]. Available: https://doi.org/10.1007/978-3-540-73283-9_55
[18] A. Salamonczyk and J. Brzostek-Pawlowska, "Translation of MathML formulas to Polish text, example applications in teaching the blind," in *Cybernetics (CYBCONF), 2015 IEEE 2nd International Conference on*. IEEE, 2015, pp. 240–244.
[19] D. Attanayake, J. Denholm-Price, G. Hunter, E. Pfluegel, and A. Wigmore, "Intelligent assistive interfaces for editing mathematics." in *Intelligent Environments (Workshops)*, 2012, pp. 286–297.
[20] D. Attanayake, G. Hunter, J. Denholm-Price, and E. Pfluegel, "Novel multi-modal tools to enhance disabled and distance learners' experience of mathematics," *ICTer*, vol. 6, no. 1, pp. 1–10, 2013.
[21] M. Maćkowski, P. Brzoza, M. Żabka, and D. Spinczyk, "Multimedia platform for mathematics' interactive learning accessible to blind people," *Multimedia Tools and Applications*, pp. 1–18, 2017.
[22] P. Riga, G. Kouroupetroglou, and P.-P. Ioannidou, "An evaluation methodology of math-to-speech in non-English DAISY digital talking books," in *International Conference on Computers Helping People with Special Needs*. Springer, 2016, pp. 27–34.
[23] Z. Sroczyński, "Internet of things location services with multi-platform mobile applications," in *Proceedings of the Computational Methods in Systems and Software*. Springer, 2017, pp. 347–357.
[24] A. Bier and Z. Sroczynski, "Towards semantic search for mathematical notation," in *2018 Federated Conference on Computer Science and Information Systems (FedCSIS)*. IEEE, 2018, pp. 465–469.

NICER: Aesthetic Image Enhancement with Humans in the Loop

Michael Fischer
University of Würzburg
Würzburg, Germany
email: m.fischer@informatik.uni-wuerzburg.de

Konstantin Kobs
University of Würzburg
Würzburg, Germany
email: kobs@informatik.uni-wuerzburg.de

Andreas Hotho
University of Würzburg
Würzburg, Germany
email: hotho@informatik.uni-wuerzburg.de

***Abstract*—Fully- or semi-automatic image enhancement software helps users to increase the visual appeal of photos and does not require in-depth knowledge of manual image editing. However, fully-automatic approaches usually enhance the image in a black-box manner that does not give the user any control over the optimization process, possibly leading to edited images that do not subjectively appeal to the user. Semi-automatic methods mostly allow for controlling which pre-defined editing step is taken, which restricts the users in their creativity and ability to make detailed adjustments, such as brightness or contrast. We argue that incorporating user preferences by guiding an automated enhancement method simplifies image editing and increases the enhancement's focus on the user. This work thus proposes the Neural Image Correction & Enhancement Routine (NICER), a neural network based approach to no-reference image enhancement in a fully-, semi-automatic or fully manual process that is interactive and user-centered. NICER iteratively adjusts image editing parameters in order to maximize an aesthetic score based on image style and content. Users can modify these parameters at any time and guide the optimization process towards a desired direction. This interactive workflow is a novelty in the field of human-computer interaction for image enhancement tasks. In a user study, we show that NICER can improve image aesthetics without user interaction and that allowing user interaction leads to diverse enhancement outcomes that are strongly preferred over the unedited image. We make our code publicly available to facilitate further research in this direction.**

Keywords*—*aesthetic image enhancement; user-centered.

I. INTRODUCTION

With the ever-increasing amount of images taken, it is logical that the casual user neither has the knowledge, time, nor patience to manually edit all images towards pleasing versions. This, combined with the fact that photography can benefit greatly from image enhancement, explains the availability of numerous simple-to-use image enhancement applications. Fully-automatic enhancement software that can be found in most smartphone photo applications is usually intransparent, leaving users with a result that neither was created in an explainable way nor necessarily correlates with their individual perception of aesthetics. Semi-automatic approaches often let the users select a single, pre-defined image filter that usually combines different properties, such as higher contrast and higher saturation. This, evidently, takes control from the user.

We argue that it is beneficial for both, fully- and semi-automatic image enhancement methods, to be able to incorporate the user's individual perception of aesthetics **before**, **during**, and **after** the enhancement process. We hence propose the **N**eural **I**mage **C**orrection & **E**nhancement **R**outine (NICER), which allows exactly this. It consists of two neural network based components: An Image Manipulator first applies a set of learned image operations (e.g., contrast, brightness) with variable magnitude onto the unedited source image while a subsequent Quality Assessor then assesses the resulting enhancement quality. NICER iteratively optimizes the parameters of the enhancement operations to maximize the Quality Assessor's aesthetic score. Due to the iterative approach, users can modify the Image Manipulator's parameters before, during, and after the optimization process, directing the enhancement procedure towards subjectively more appealing local optima. While other enhancement tools merely provide preview options for the current filter setting, NICER's semi-automatic mode allows for an interactive back-and-forth between the user and the automatic optimization and hence facilitates human-computer interaction in image enhancement applications.

Although the flexible architecture of our approach makes it possible to exchange each component with a specifically tailored version (from, e.g., training on a user's photo collection), NICER can enhance images in a no-reference setting, without any previous info about the user's liking. In a user study, we show that the visual appeal of NICER's fully-automatic enhancement results already is superior to the original images. We further show that interweaving user interactions and the automatic enhancement process results in highly diverse images that are subjectively perceived superior. Our main contributions are

1) NICER, a novel way of incorporating human aesthetic preferences into the image enhancement process,
2) a user study assessing NICER's performance, and
3) a publicly available repository containing our source code and trained models [1].

The rest of this paper is organized as follows: Section II presents related work on human-centered image enhancement. Section III introduces the methodology and components of NICER. Section IV then assesses NICER's enhancement quality in a user study. We conclude this contribution in Section V and outline starting points for future research.

II. RELATED WORK

The research area of learned perceptual image enhancement has received ample attention in recent works, particularly so after the emergence of neural image assessors [3]–[6]. However, most approaches do not consider user preferences and enhance the image in a black-box fashion, leaving users

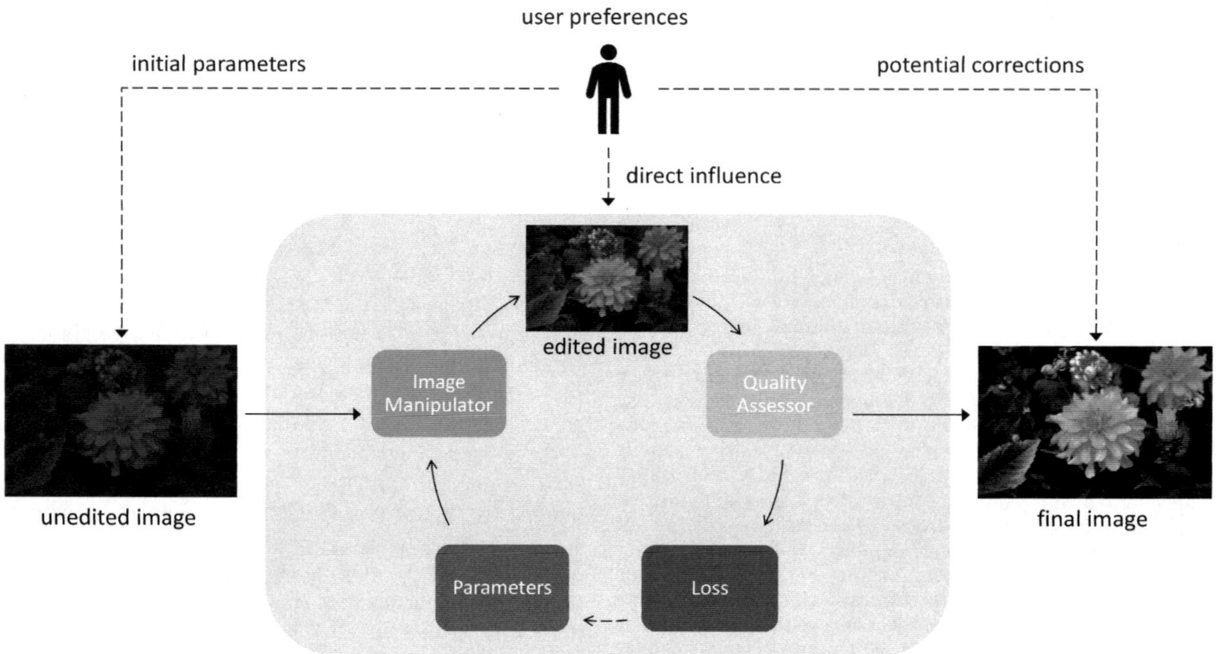

Fig. 1. NICER's optimization workflow. If desired, users can interfere with the enhancement routine before, during or after the image optimization. However, user interference is voluntary and not necessary for a successful enhancement. The dashed line between loss and parameters implies that the loss does not directly affect the parameters but instead is backpropagated through the architecture. Sample image from [2].

with a potentially sub-optimal result that has not been tailored to their personal liking.

The few methods that *do* personalize image enhancement rely on a given photo collection that has already been retouched to the user's liking. In [7] and [8], users are directly asked to create this photo collection during the setup phase of their approaches, which is both inconvenient and time-consuming. Similarly, Hu et al. [9] use Generative Adversarial Networks to learn a latent space from a pre-enhanced photo collection and then sample from this space to edit unseen images. In [10], styles are grouped into clusters of certain enhancement presets. New users are then assessed and matched against the enhancement cluster that best suits their preferences. This approach is most useful for large, cloud-based solutions, where many users are averaged and less suitable for individual, personal image enhancement.

Generally, the mentioned approaches do not explicitly consider the user's individual preferences for the image optimization routine, but rather implicitly use the overall information encoded in the edited image collection. We argue that such an already edited photo collection is a requirement that might not always be fulfilled (especially for casual users) and further claim that sampling from the style-space might not necessarily yield an edit that is well-suited for a particular image content. Contrary to the previously mentioned approaches, our method does not rely on a pre-enhanced photo collection that implicitly represents the user's preferences in an abstract style-space. Although one could train the Quality Assessor to be sensitive to personal preferences by using custom photo collections, this is not necessary for NICER to work correctly. Instead, we give the user the freedom to individually guide the optimization by directly interfering with the optimization routine. The higher amount of (voluntary) interaction can be seen as drawback and benefit at once: While users might put more effort into getting enhanced images than in fully-automatic enhancement approaches, our method really allows for the individual preferences to be set per image, instead of relying on a globally estimated preferred enhancement style. Moreover, using a general purpose Quality Assessor and letting users guide the optimization eliminates the need for a pre-enhanced photo collection, making NICER a ready-to-use, no-reference approach without time-consuming setup.

III. NICER

In this section, we introduce NICER, our proposed approach for user-centered image enhancement. The structure of our approach is shown in Figure 1 and was motivated by the idea of using a perceptually motivated loss function to increase enhancement appeal [11] [12]. The pipeline consists of the Image Manipulator, that applies a set of image filters to an unedited source image, and the Quality Assessor, that estimates the aesthetic quality of the Image Manipulator's outcome. Using differentiable components allows us to iteratively optimize the Image Manipulator's filter parameters with respect to the Quality Assessor's score using gradient descent, resulting in a no-reference, automatic image enhancement. The optimization procedure modifies the filter parameters in each iteration towards the nearest local score optimum and allows user interference in every enhancement step. If a user changes parameters during optimization, NICER continues from the new parameter settings towards a different local optimum and thus enables the user to interactively and individually alter the image editing style.

A. *Image Manipulator*

The Image Manipulator ψ_F is used to apply a set of n image editing filters F $= \{f_1, f_2, ..., f_n\}$ to the image I. The only requirement of the Image Manipulator is differentiability with respect to its image filter parameters K $= \{k_1, k_2, ..., k_n\}$, $k_i \in \mathbb{R}$, as these are optimized via gradient descent. While, in general, any image filter can be used, NICER implements six common photographic filters: Contrast (Con), Saturation (Sat), Brightness (Bri), Shadows (Sha), Highlights (Hig), Exposure (Exp), and two artistic filters: Local Laplacian Filtering (LLF) [13] and Non-local Dehazing (NLD) [14].

We implement the Image Manipulator as a Context Aggregation Network (CAN), a Fully Convolutional Neural Network with dilated convolutions [15] that has been shown to be well-suited for image enhancement tasks [16]. As the CAN is able to approximate a large variety of image filters [16], it is a very flexible and general, yet differentiable enhancement model.

NICER adapts the CAN24 model by Chen et al. (cf. Table I), as it provides a good trade-off between accuracy and speed [16]. Between layers one to eight, a leaky rectified linear unit (Leaky ReLU) [17] activation is applied, with a negative slope of 0.2, while the last layer uses no activation function. We exclude Batch Normalization, as it showed no significant improvements in approximation accuracy or performance.

Each image filter intensity $k \in [-1, 1]$ is fed into the network by concatenating it to each pixel of the input image. During training, we apply one image operation per sample and let the CAN learn the relationship between the input and target output. At inference time, multiple image filters can be set, as the network interpolates correctly and applies the filters simultaneously [16].

In order to learn our proposed image operations, we use the MIT-Adobe FiveK dataset [2] with a 50/50 train/test split, resulting in 2500 images per set. We employ the GNU Image Manipulation Program (GIMP) [18] to create two manipulated versions (filter intensity $\pm 100\%$) of each original image for the six photographic filters (Sat, Con, Sha, Hig, Bri, Exp) as ground truth. To create the ground truth for the filters LLF and NLD, we use the implementations from [13] and [14], respectively. Note that for NLD, we only use positive values (i.e., $+100\%$), as negative values would haze the image, which is usually undesired in image enhancement. We then train the Image Manipulator as in [16].

TABLE I
CAN24 ARCHITECTURE OVERVIEW

Layer	1	2	3	4	5	6	7	8	9
Convolution	3×3	3×3	3×3	3×3	3×3	3×3	3×3	3×3	1×1
Dilation	1	2	4	8	16	32	64	1	1
Padding	1,1	2,2	4,4	8,8	16,16	32,32	64,64	1,1	-
Receptive Field	3×3	7×7	15×15	31×31	63×63	127×127	255×255	257×257	257×257
Width	24	24	24	24	24	24	24	24	3

The trained Image Manipulator can apply any set of filter intensities onto a source image. This enables users to initially set or modify filter intensities and provides a way of manually controlling the image editing process, if desired.

B. *Quality Assessor*

Once the Image Manipulator ψ_F has edited the image I with the current filter intensity combination K, the Quality Assessor is used as a metric M to rate the manipulation's outcome with a score $S = M(\psi_F(\text{K}, \text{I}))$, which is then optimized by NICER. The Quality Assessor must meet several criteria:

1) Full differentiability with respect to its input.
2) The Quality Assessor's score prediction must correlate with the human notion of aesthetics. This is especially necessary in the automatic enhancement mode, as NICER will optimize for this score.
3) S must be deterministic, i.e., same for identical images.

We use a neural network based model called Neural Image Assessment (NIMA) [4] as Quality Assessor, as it complies with the above desiderata and achieves state-of-the-art performance on aesthetic image assessment. NIMA fine-tunes a pre-trained Convolutional Neural Network for image classification; in our case VGG16 (conf. D, [19]), as it achieved best cross-dataset performance in [4]. The network's output consists of ten nodes that correspond to ten quality score buckets $\{1, 2, ..., 10\}$, where 10 is the highest aesthetic rating. NIMA then feeds the obtained logits through a Softmax function to create a rating distribution, which is the score S.

We train NIMA with the Aesthetic Visual Analysis (AVA) dataset [20], whose content ranges from blurry, low-quality snapshots over artistic imagery and advertisements to high-quality photography. $80\,\%$ of the dataset is used for training and the remaining $20\,\%$ are equally split into validation and test set. We follow the training procedure in [4].

We find that training solely on the original AVA dataset yields a Quality Assessor that is insensitive to illumination changes, as they are highly under-represented in the dataset. Therefore, we re-train NIMA's dense layer with 3000 images that are manually edited towards bad lightning and whose ground truth scores are decreased to indicate the reduction of aesthetics that comes with poor illumination.

Additionally, we introduce a preprocessing step called Adaptive Brightness Normalization (ABN) to make all initial images have similar brightness. ABN computes the perceived image brightness $P = \sqrt{0.241R^2 + 0.691G^2 + 0.068B^2}$ using the mean red, green, and blue pixel intensities [21]. With $P \in [0, 255]$, ABN normalizes the brightness to the range

128 ± 30. If the image is too bright ($P > 158$), ABN evens out the original histogram by linearly transforming the pixel values and clipping its left and right side by $5.0\,\%$. This percentage is reduced if the Structural Similarity [22] is less than 0.8. If $P < 98$, ABN brightens up the image by converting it to the HSV color space and increasing the V-value by 20. As this often introduces unwanted noise, ABN reduces the shift factor if the Peak Signal-to-Noise Ratio [23] between the corrected image and the original version is above 30. ABN also checks for intended uses of white and black backgrounds, e.g., in product photography. For this, ABN randomly samples $5\,\%$ of the image's pixels and checks if more than $60\,\%$ of the sampled pixels are black or white. If this holds true, the image is not modified to avoid washed out background colors.

C. Optimization Loop

The overall enhancement process of an image now works as follows: The image is normalized using ABN and fed through the Image Manipulator, which applies a set of filters with initial parameters (zero, if not set by user) to the image I. The image aesthetic of the resulting image is then scored by the Quality Assessor. We now calculate the gradients of the score w.r.t. the filter parameters K to optimize the parameters via gradient descent towards the nearest local optimum. This naturally ensures an iterative process a user can interact with before, during, and after the optimization converges.

To optimize the image, NICER uses a loss function that maximizes image beauty while balancing the ratio between aesthetic gain and induced image change [11]. We hence formulate the optimization loss as

$$\mathcal{L}(\mathrm{K}, \mathrm{I}) = \underbrace{\mathrm{EMD}(\mathbf{p}_t, \mathbf{p}_d)}_{L_{QA}} + \underbrace{\gamma\, L_2(\mathrm{K})}_{L_{IM}}, \tag{1}$$

where L_{QA} is the loss that maximizes the Quality Assessor's score and L_{IM} is a weighted regularization term ($\gamma = 0.1$) to penalize large parameter changes by the Image Manipulator, which might not be intended by the user. More specifically, we define L_{QA} to be the Earth Mover's Distance (EMD) [24] between the predicted rating distribution and a desired distribution that corresponds to a highly aesthetic image. In our implementation, a one-hot encoded target vector for the largest score bucket would force the Quality Assessor to extrapolate towards a "perfect" image, which it has never seen during training. Therefore, we use a realistic target distribution $\{0.0, 0.0, 0.0, 0.0, 0.0, 0.01, 0.09, 0.15, 0.55, 0.20\}$ that could also be found in the AVA dataset. For Quality Assessors that output a single scalar, $L_{QA} = -S$ can be used to maximize the score S. NICER uses Stochastic Gradient Descent (SGD) with Nesterov Momentum of 0.9 and a learning rate of 0.05.

D. Human in the Loop

Our approach allows users to intervene with the optimization process at multiple stages: A user can set initial filter intensities **before** the optimization loop. Adding the L_2 regularization term to the global enhancement loss ensures that the optimized parameters do not diverge too far from the initial filter intensities set by the user. Also, by setting the regularization weight γ, the user can control NICER's "diversity", i.e., the strength with which divergence from the initial filter parameters is penalized. A high γ could, e.g., be used for fine-tuning an already (subjectively) beautiful image.

A user can modify the filter parameters **during** the optimization loop, since the gradients are calculated w.r.t. the current parameters. Setting new parameters may lead to a new local score optimum that the image is optimized towards. NICER also provides the option of fixing desired parameter values, which prohibits further intensity updates for a filter and thus ensures that the outcome is to the user's individual liking.

A user can finally modify the parameter settings **after** the optimization has converged. This is especially helpful if the optimization yields an image that scores high regarding the Quality Assessor, but tweaks are necessary to increase the image's subjective visual appeal.

IV. EXPERIMENTS

In this section, we conduct a user study to qualitatively assess the performance of NICER. First, we show that the fully-automatic enhancement without any user interaction improves the quality of the original images. Second, we demonstrate that user interactions can produce different enhancement outcomes that improve the image's subjective appeal.

A. Without User Interaction

While NICER is specifically designed to incorporate users into the optimization process, it is also able to automatically enhance images without any interactions. Showing that fully-automatic enhancement results are perceived as more aesthetic than the original images gives us a "lower-bound" that can then be further improved by allowing user interactions.

In the user study, 51 subjects sit at a workstation and are instructed to rate NICER's automatically optimized images (using $\gamma = 0.1$), comparing them to the unedited images and versions that are obtained by choosing random filter intensities. To this end, we use 500 randomly sampled images from [2] and let each participant rate 30 image tuples which results in a total of 1530 image ratings. The subjects are asked to rank the images on a low-to-high scale, with the original reference image centered in the middle of the scale.

The results show that our method is preferred over the random baseline in $93.0\,\%$ of all cases. The subjects prefer our enhancement result over the unedited original image in $53.7\,\%$ of all cases. To quantify the relative ratings, we map the low-to-high scale to the interval $[0, 10]$, where the original image has a score of 5 and the other ratings are scaled such that the best or worst rating has a score of 0 or 10, respectively. The normalized rating histograms are shown in Figure 3. NICER's images receive a mean rating of 5.3 and a median of 5.23. A 1-sample Wilcoxon test [26] shows that the median is significantly different from the original's normalized rating 5 in a confidence interval of $1\,\%$. This suggests that our fully-automatic results on average are perceived more beautiful than the unedited images. The high variance of the

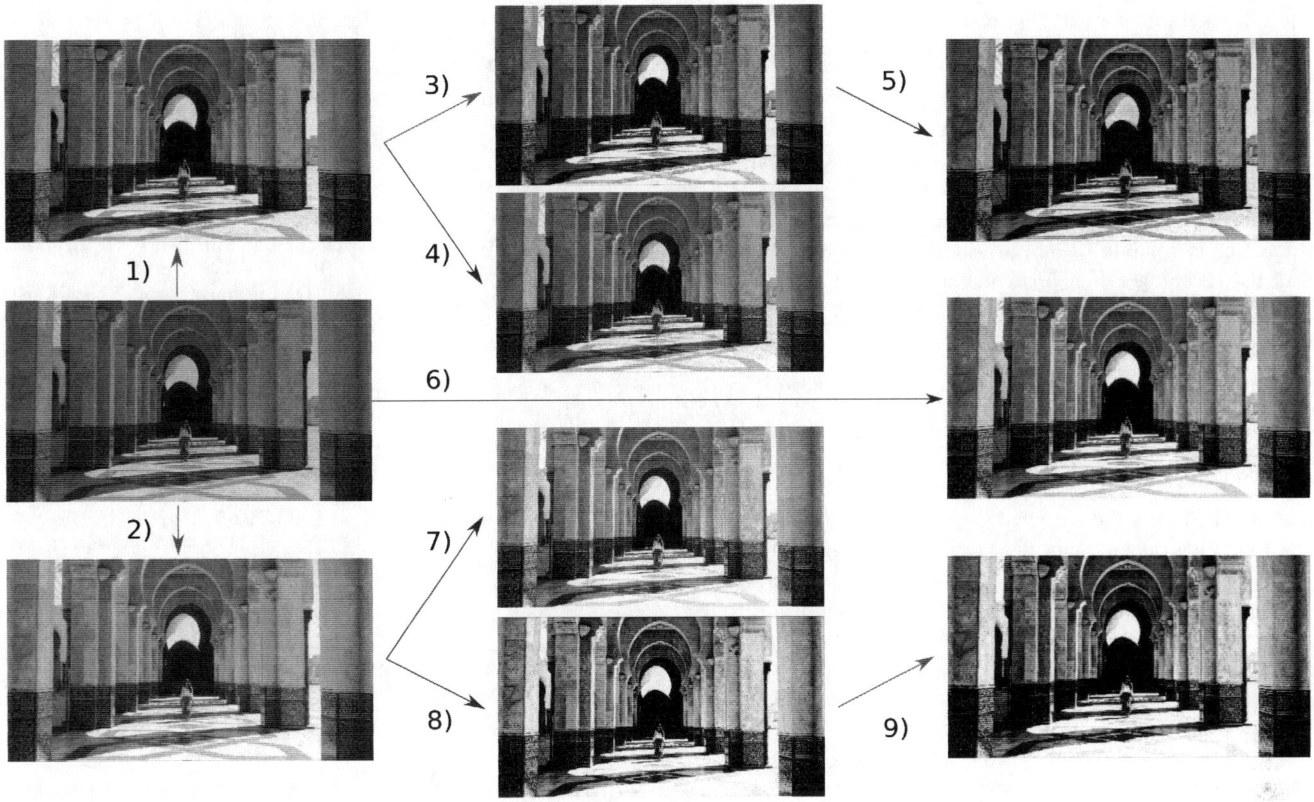

Fig. 2. The original image (left column, middle row) with user-defined enhancements (red arrows) and auto-enhancement (blue arrows, default 50 steps, $\gamma = 0.1$). The transformations (given in %) are: **1)** Con = Sat = 20, fixed. **2)** Bri = 8, Sha = -13, Hig = 18, Exp = 24. **3)** Con = Sat = 20 fixed, NLD = 75 fixed, Exp = 20. **4)** & **6)**: Auto **5)** Auto, $\gamma = 0.5$. **7)** Auto, stopped by user after 10 steps. **8)** NICER, $\gamma = 0.005$. **9)** User post-correction, Hig reduced from 79% to 40%. Image from [25].

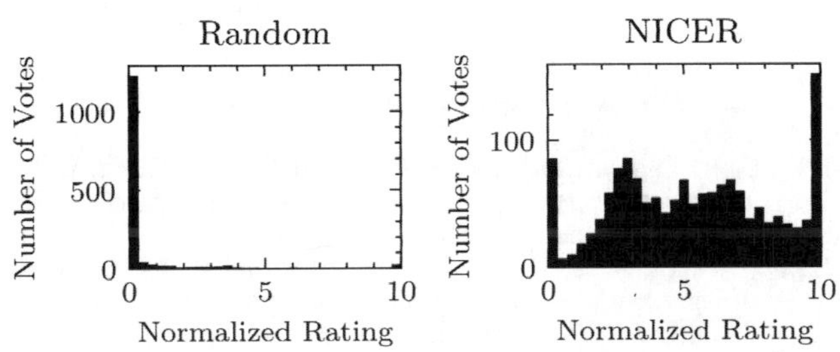

Fig. 3. Normalized rating histograms for the random enhancement and NICER's automatic enhancement results. The original image always has a score of 5.

automatic enhancements' rating results ($\sigma^2 = 2.87$) supports our hypothesis that the perception of image beauty varies greatly across subjects. To showcase NICER's full potential, we investigate the effects of directly involving the subjects in the enhancement process.

B. *With User Interaction*

We have shown that NICER can obtain promising results without user interaction. This section shows how different interactions before, during, and after the optimization loop produce remarkably different enhancement outcomes. To this end, subjects choose interaction routes from NICER according to their personal liking, starting from a baseline image. In NICER, users have different interaction possibilities: manually change filter settings, fix single filter intensities such that they are not optimized any further, or automatically optimize the image from the current parameter settings for one or multiple steps. Additionally, they can set the regularization weight γ. One set of possible interactions is shown in Figure 2, with not only four different outcomes that involve at least one automatic enhancement step (4, 5, 7, 8), but also the automatically edited version without user interaction (6). In this experiment, some subjects prefer routes that lead to more saturated looks, while others like high contrasts or slightly tinted images better. A substantial $97.9\,\%$ of the subjects agree that the achieved optimization results are better than the unedited starting image (left column, middle row). Routes that involve at least one of NICER's automatic enhancement steps are preferred by $68.1\,\%$. This shows that combining automatic enhancement with user guidance is a valid approach that yields subjectively more beautiful results. Fully automatic approaches do not necessarily lead to results that are subjectively aesthetic, which is why NICER enables users to intervene with the optimization process at any time and encourages users to bring their individual, preferred style into the enhanced image.

V. Discussion and Conclusion

In this paper, we have presented a new method called NICER to interactively edit and enhance images that allows for the incorporation of user preferences before, during, and after the enhancement process. The trained models and the source code for NICER are available online [1].

NICER, being a first implementation of the presented general framework, has certain caveats and weak points that we intend to address in the future: NICER runs in reasonable time on a modern machine with a graphics card (1.36 s for the full enhancement of a 1080p image), but might benefit from further optimization when used in hardware-constrained environments like smartphones. As a first optimization, our enhancement routine rescales images to a width and height of 224 pixels during the parameter optimization and only applies the found parameters once to the full-sized image at the end of the optimization cycle. A further speedup could be achieved by using a more lightweight Quality Assessor. While the Image Manipulator could theoretically be replaced by a differentiable image filter library (e.g., Kornia [27]), we explicitly renounced from doing so, as using a neural network makes it possible to not only learn single image filters, but whole editing styles. This is especially helpful for casual users, who often lack the photographic vocabulary to describe their desired outcome and hence rely more on intuitive terms, such as "moodiness", or the indicated settings for a "sunset" atmosphere.

We evaluated our results in a user study and found that NICER's fully-automatic enhancement results usually outperform the unedited images. In a second experiment, we have shown that NICER's enhancement results in combination with user interaction were favored by virtually all participants. In the future, we plan to conduct further in-depth user studies to examine the effects of different Image Manipulators and Quality Assessors on NICER's enhancement quality.

Since our approach allows users to intervene with the enhancement process before, during, and after optimization, NICER offers a first step towards user-centered image editing without reference images. Overall, we found our method and implementation to be a promising start in this direction.

References

[1] M. Fischer, K. Kobs, and A. Hotho. (2020). NICER: Neural Image Correction and Enhancement Routine. https://github.com/mr-Mojo/NICER, (visited on 10/11/2020).

[2] V. Bychkovsky, S. Paris, E. Chan, and F. Durand, "Learning photographic global tonal adjustment with a database of input / output image pairs," in *IEEE CVPR*, 2011, pp. 97–104.

[3] Z. Yan, H. Zhang, B. Wang, S. Paris, and Y. Yu, "Automatic photo adjustment using deep neural networks," *ACM TOG*, vol. 35, no. 2, pp. 1–15, 2016.

[4] H. Talebi and P. Milanfar, "Nima: Neural image assessment," *IEEE Transactions on Image Processing*, vol. 27, no. 8, pp. 3998–4011, 2018.

[5] X. Fu, J. Yan, and C. Fan, "Image aesthetics assessment using composite features from off-the-shelf deep models," in *IEEE ICIP*, 2018, pp. 3528–3532.

[6] S. Kong, X. Shen, Z. Lin, R. Mech, and C. Fowlkes, "Photo aesthetics ranking network with attributes and content adaptation," in *ECCV*, Springer, 2016, pp. 662–679.

[7] S. B. Kang, A. Kapoor, and D. Lischinski, "Personalization of image enhancement," in *IEEE CVPR*, 2010.

[8] Y. Murata and Y. Dobashi, "Automatic image enhancement taking into account user preference," in *IEEE CW*, 2019, pp. 374–377.

[9] Y. Hu, H. He, C. Xu, B. Wang, and S. Lin, "Exposure: A white-box photo post-processing framework," *ACM TOG*, vol. 37, no. 2, pp. 1–17, 2018.

[10] A. Kapoor, J. C. Caicedo, D. Lischinski, and S. B. Kang, "Collaborative personalization of image enhancement," *International journal of computer vision*, vol. 108, no. 1-2, pp. 148–164, 2014.

[11] H. Talebi and P. Milanfar, "Learned perceptual image enhancement," in *IEEE ICCP*, 2018, pp. 1–13.

[12] P. D'Oro and E. Nasca. (2019). An empirical evaluation of convolutional neural networks for image enhancement, [Online]. Available: https://github.com/proceduralia/pytorch-neural-enhance (visited on 10/11/2020).

[13] M. Aubry, S. Paris, S. W. Hasinoff, J. Kautz, and F. Durand, "Fast local laplacian filters: Theory and applications," *ACM TOG*, vol. 33, no. 5, pp. 1–14, 2014.

[14] D. Berman, S. Avidan, and T. Treibitz, "Non-local image dehazing," in *IEEE CVPR*, 2016, pp. 1674–1682.

[15] F. Yu and V. Koltun, "Multi-scale context aggregation by dilated convolutions," *arXiv preprint arXiv:1511.07122*, 2015.

[16] Q. Chen, J. Xu, and V. Koltun, "Fast image processing with fully-convolutional networks," in *IEEE ICCV*, 2017, pp. 2497–2506.

[17] B. Xu, N. Wang, T. Chen, and M. Li, "Empirical evaluation of rectified activations in convolutional network," *arXiv preprint arXiv:1505.00853*, 2015.

[18] The GIMP Team. (2020). GIMP - GNU Image Manipulation Program, [Online]. Available: http://www.gimp.org (visited on 10/11/2020).

[19] K. Simonyan and A. Zisserman, "Very deep convolutional networks for large-scale image recognition," *arXiv preprint arXiv:1409.1556*, 2014.

[20] N. Murray, L. Marchesotti, and F. Perronnin, "Ava: A large-scale database for aesthetic visual analysis," in *IEEE CVPR*, 2012, pp. 2408–2415.

[21] D. R. Finley. (2020). Hsp color model — alternative to hsv (hsb) and hsl, [Online]. Available: http://alienryderflex.com/hsp.html (visited on 10/11/2020).

[22] Z. Wang, A. C. Bovik, H. R. Sheikh, and E. P. Simoncelli, "Image quality assessment: From error visibility to structural similarity," *IEEE Transactions on Image Processing*, vol. 13, no. 4, pp. 600–612, 2004.

[23] Q. Huynh-Thu and M. Ghanbari, "Scope of validity of psnr in image/video quality assessment," *Electronics letters*, vol. 44, no. 13, pp. 800–801, 2008.

[24] E. Levina and P. Bickel, "The earth mover's distance is the mallows distance: Some insights from statistics," in *IEEE ICCV*, 2001, pp. 251–256.

[25] Pexels GmbH. (2020). Pexels, [Online]. Available: https://www.pexels.com (visited on 10/11/2020).

[26] B. Rosner, R. J. Glynn, and M.-L. T. Lee, "The wilcoxon signed rank test for paired comparisons of clustered data," *Biometrics*, vol. 62, no. 1, pp. 185–192, 2006.

[27] E. Riba, D. Mishkin, D. Ponsa, E. Rublee, and G. Bradski, "Kornia: An open source differentiable computer vision library for PyTorch," in *The IEEE Winter Conference on Applications of Computer Vision*, 2020, pp. 3674–3683.

Social Media Usage in Supporting Children with Cognitive Disabilities and Their Caregivers from Saudi Arabia: A Qualitative Analysis

Reem Nasser Alshenaifi[1,2] and Jinjuan Heidi Feng[1]
[1]Department of Computer & Information Sciences, Towson University, Towson, MD, USA
[2] Department of Computer Science, Majmaah University, Al-Majmaah, Saudi Arabia
Email: ralshe1@students.towson.edu, jfeng@towson.edu

Abstract— **This study investigates the use of social media in supporting and empowering Saudi caregivers of children with cognitive disabilities. Through interviews with 13 caregivers, we examined their motivations and concerns around using social media in relation to their children or students' conditions. We also investigated the role of social media during the COVID-19 pandemic. We found that caregivers used social media with caution to seek information and emotional support, to spread awareness, and to communicate and build communities. Our findings also suggest that caregivers face a great deal of challenges in security and privacy, social stigma and negative discussions, misinformation, as well as lack of resources. We propose recommendations to the government, specialists, and parents that could lead to more effective use of social media to support children with cognitive disabilities and their caregivers in Saudi Arabia.**

Keywords-Social Media; Cognitive Disabilities; Children; Saudi Arabia; Accessibility.

I. INTRODUCTION

Caregivers across the world face challenges when raising a child with a disability. Therefore, they are constantly in need of information and social support to navigate through these challenges [1]. Social media has become a desirable means for spreading awareness, advocating for rights, establishing communities, acquiring information, and much more [2]-[4]. Numerous studies have confirmed the substantial value of social support and community belonging for individuals with disabilities and their caregivers. However, existing literature mainly focuses on Western users. In fact, public perceptions around disabilities differ across cultures [5]. Saudi caregivers, in particular, face unique challenges which might not exist in the Western context due to differences in social and cultural customs and values [6].

Saudi users have shown an increasing interest in using social media in the past decade. Previous studies emphasized its significant role in empowering members of Saudi society. These empowerment opportunities cover many aspects of their lives, ranging from establishing new forms of cross-gender communications [7] and possibly examining potential spouses [8] to facilitating interaction skills among adult users with autism [9]. Social media has helped women, specifically, in their integration into entrepreneurship [10], their participation in political activities and rights campaigns [11], as well as facilitating their inclusion in research and humanitarian studies [12]. However, to date, there is no research that investigated how social media was used to support children with cognitive disabilities and their caregivers from Saudi Arabia. We, therefore, conducted a study of online interviews as our initial effort to fill in this gap. Knowledge in this area can provide insights for educators and social workers to improve their services and support for families with children with cognitive disabilities. It can also help designers and developers of social media platforms implement features that accommodate the special needs of this population. Finally, government and non-profit organizations may benefit from this body of knowledge when developing policies and practices related to children with cognitive disabilities.

The structure of the paper is as follows: Section II presents an overview of the related work; Section III describes the methodology we used to conduct this research; Section IV presents the findings in four main themes; Section V discusses the results, their implications, and the limitations of our study; Section VI introduces our conclusions and further work.

II. RELATED WORK

Researchers have explored the value of social media in promoting public awareness around disability, as well as in building relationships and establishing communities. A recent work by Auxier et al. [13] found that Twitter is an effective means for establishing political action and awareness campaigns. Similarly, Li and Brady indicated that social media platforms can be effective tools for users, especially disability rights activists and people with disabilities, to promote public awareness, address accessibly issues, and encourage taking corrective actions [14]. In regard to building communities, Hashemy studied the use of social media platforms among 17 Canadian high school students with Autism Spectrum Disorder (ASD) to find that social media platforms, particularly Facebook, are widely used to share information and connect with others [15].

An individual's disability does not only affect them, but also affects their caregivers. As many studies noted, parents of children with disabilities are in a desperate need for information and social support. Kirby et al. found that parents of children with developmental disorders have the majority of postings on an online message board [16]. Their analysis of the posts identified multiple themes, including assistance seeking and experience sharing. Several studies investigated the role of social media in supporting caregivers of children with disabilities [2][3]. For example, Ammari et al. conducted research on parents of children with special needs in the

United States and found that they relied mainly on Facebook and Yahoo groups for acquiring information and obtaining social support [3]. Furthermore, their study indicated that their participants experienced more freedom and less judgment online compared to real world scenarios. These studies only involved Western users; more research is needed to explore how users from substantially different cultures, such as the Saudis, interact with such technologies. Studies particularly addressing disability-related matters in Saudi Arabia are very scarce.

III. METHODS

We conducted in-depth semi-structured interviews, following the procedures elaborated by Lazar et al. [17]. The interview questions were grouped into five main categories: (1) demographics and background, (2) general use of social media applications, (3) social media use related to children with cognitive disabilities, (4) government support, (5) the role of social media during the COVID-19 pandemic.

A. Interview Procedure

Thirteen participants were interviewed for the study. Participants were recruited through the 'snowball' technique recommended for highly conservative countries, such as Saudi Arabia [8][12][18]. Among the 13 participants, 12 were female. Five were specialists working with children with cognitive disabilities and their families, six were parents of children with cognitive disabilities, and two were siblings. The ages of the interviewees ranged from 19 to 44 years; eight participants had an undergraduate degree, while four had graduate degrees and one had a high school diploma. The conditions of the children that the participants cared for included ASD, Attention Deficit Hyperactivity Disorder (ADHD), Down syndrome, severe cognitive disabilities (unspecified), dyslexia, Cerebral Palsy, learning disabilities (unspecified), and brain atrophy. Interviews were conducted online through social media applications, such as Snapchat, WhatsApp, and Skype, by using voice call and/or instant messages. Interviews lasted between 40 and 120 minutes. The participants were given the freedom to choose the language of the interview. Two interviews were conducted in English while 11 interviews were conducted in Arabic (the native language of the participants as well as the first author).

B. Data analysis

In preparation for the analysis, the first author carefully transcribed and translated the interviews into English. We conducted thematic analysis following the approach proposed by Braun and Clarke [19]. The interview transcripts were coded in NVivo12 [20] using an inductive approach, which is suitable for areas of research, such as ours, that have not been thoroughly investigated.

In the first phase of analysis, the first author open-coded the transcripts and organized the codes into themes. Then, the second author reviewed the codes and themes and discussed with the first author all cases of disagreement until the disagreements were resolved. At last, the two authors worked together to finalize the main themes and sub-themes.

IV. RESULTS

We present our findings in four main themes: motivations, difficulties and challenges, opportunities for enhancements (desires), and social media use during the pandemic. The main themes and their subthemes are illustrated in Figure 1.

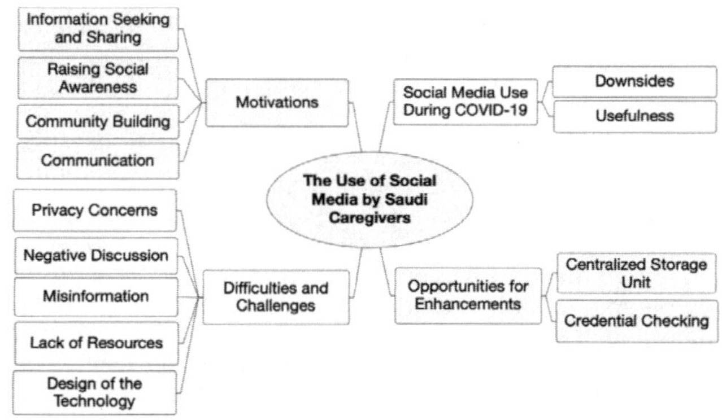

Figure 1. Thematic map, showing four main themes and their sub-themes.

A. Motivations

Participants used social media for four reasons: seeking and sharing information, raising social awareness, expanding communication, and building communities.

1) Information Seeking and Sharing

Twelve participants reported that they used social media to acquire or share general knowledge and resources about their child's disability. Family members increased their use of social media in relation to their child's condition after their initial diagnosis, while specialists used it more intensively after joining the field of special education. For example, four parents shared their experiences of how social media helped them in gaining knowledge regarding their children's conditions. P4, who has four children, the youngest with autism, expressed how unaware she was about autism before her child's diagnosis and that she sought information on YouTube to educate herself: *"Once I knew about my son's condition, I opened the YouTube immediately to get information about his disability, how to look after him, and how to enhance his case."* While P4 chose to surf YouTube for educational videos, P11 chose to follow some accounts on Twitter: *"I added several accounts that my child's specialist recommended me to follow right after she diagnosed him with ADHD and Dyslexia."* In this excerpt, it is promising to see healthcare providers encouraging parents to educate themselves and directing them to reliable accounts on social media. This is particularly important for parents who believe that their healthcare provider is the only source of information: *"I only communicate with specialists who follow my son's condition in the hospital." (P13)*

Some participants were approached by other caregivers of children with cognitive disabilities in an attempt to learn more about their own child's condition and its symptoms: *"The question I usually receive is how I knew my son is autistic." (P10).* P7 shared that searching the internet, Facebook and forums in particular, helped her to self-diagnose her sister and to find available governmental services: *"I learned there are cases called learning difficulties, which is what my sister was suffering from, and then I knew that there was a governmental establishment which tested her and sent her to the appropriate school."* Additionally, all 5 specialists indicated that social media is a great avenue to *"connect with specialists who have a great deal of experience in [the] field." (P1)*

Interestingly, out of seven family members who used the platforms for the acquisition and dissemination of information, only three individuals shared information publicly. Out of these individuals, two are current graduate students living in the United States where their children received their diagnoses. This reflects a reservation in public sharing, which may be caused by fear of public criticism, lack of awareness, or privacy concerns. P11 commented on such a common practice: *"I don't share anything in public [...], but I give advice privately to anyone whom I know have children with the same condition."*

2) Raising Social Awareness

The wide use of social media as a means of spreading social awareness has been acknowledged in many Western studies. In this study, only five out of 13 participants used social media to spread public awareness. Still, we found promising signs of using social media for this purpose among Saudi caregivers. Three participants used it to advocate for their children/students as well as to promote and defend their rights. Twitter, according to our participants, is the most used and suitable platform for advocacy as they exploit some of its known features to accelerate the spread of their message. These features include the use of "hashtagging" and retweeting. P3 shared her experience in sharing a hashtag that was directed to the government to change a regulation related to registering children with disabilities in daycare centers:

> *"The Ministry of Labor changed the criteria of beneficiaries of the daycare services so that more than half of the children were excluded from the service. Families and specialists released a hashtag #ايقاف_اشعار_قبول_ذوي_الاعاقه [#TurnningOff_admission_childrenWithDisabilities] calling for returning to the old criteria. We tweeted and retweeted until the decision was made by the custodian of the two holy mosques, King Salman, to restore the old regulations."*

While P3 has had a positive experience, P8, the father of an autistic daughter, feels "*helpless*" in that technology had not supported him in communicating his voice due to the lack of public engagement. He stated: *"We need more awareness and cooperation of the competent authorities to spread awareness. I post hashtags on Twitter, but unfortunately, they are usually deleted after two or three hours because they lack the participation of tweeters."*

In the same token, P3 wished she "*had a louder voice*" through having a great number of followers, so that her *"posts were more valuable and influential in terms of media awareness and true implementation on the ground."*

3) Communication

Participants discussed the role of social media in supporting two-way communications. Twelve participants used social media to get connected with professionals or parents who had children with similar conditions. The purpose of communicating was mostly about providing and obtaining social support, specifically informational support. All five specialists stated that they use WhatsApp to communicate with parents. Some specialists used social media to continuously monitor children's progress beyond their daycare center: *"I use social media to check on the children's progress in training and learning needed skills." (P2)*

Participants reported that they mainly communicated through private social media communities, such as in WhatsApp groups, or through private one-to-one communication. P1 stated that she shared information and communicated with her collogues through a WhatsApp group, while communicates individually with the parents of her students. She said: *"I do not share any information outside the scope of my colleagues' WhatsApp group [...]and I send [information] to each mother separately."*

Moreover, we found that the nature of the relationship between two entities, whether they have a personal or non-personal relationship, had a substantial role in determining the platform used for communication. For instance, WhatsApp is preferred for interpersonal communications, whereas Twitter is a favorite for impersonal communications. We observed that platform preference was based on various factors, including security as well as the supported interaction features within each platform. For example, P2 expressed that she felt secure using WhatsApp: *"WhatsApp is linked with phone numbers of the users; it is more reliable."*

4) Community Building

All specialists were part of online groups that brought them together in professional settings to share general advice and resources. However, only three out of eight family members belonged to online groups. P4 felt confused and lost after her son was diagnosed with autism, and she sought emotional and informational support from other parents online:

> *"I started to look for people who have a child with the same condition as my son's. I was asking about how to deal with him and improve his skills. I was confused and shocked ...."*

While three parents shared their positive experiences with online gatherings, five participants stated that they were not part of any online groups.

B. Difficulties and Challenges

Saudi caregivers face barriers that hinder them from fully exploiting the potentials of social media. Five major barriers identified in the interviews include: privacy concerns, negative discussion, misinformation, lack of resources, and design of technology.

1) Privacy concerns

Ten participants expressed worries regarding their privacy when using social media. P9 believed that the degree of security and privacy varied across platforms and that she trusted Twitter more than other platforms: *"Twitter is excellent in security and privacy, where in Telegram, as an example, fears exist from hacking and suspicious links."*

Regardless of her own view, P7's family did not approve of her sharing information about her sister's condition online because they did not want to reveal her case to others. She expressed: *"My family prefer not to talk about my sister's condition in front of anyone."* Her family also disallowed her sister from using certain applications on her smart phone for fear of violating her privacy and sharing her private information with strangers: *"They try to keep my sister away from using Snapchat, Facebook, or Twitter because she can be easily contacted by strangers and fake accounts"*.

Similarly, P3 believed that *"as everyone can use anything on social media, our intellectual property is vulnerable to theft"*, and referred to her experience by saying: *"I've shared a number of self-designed posters with my students; then, one day I was surfing Instagram [...] and was shocked to see my work being displayed for sale in one of the commercial accounts on Instagram."*

Furthermore, the response from six participants revealed an interesting contradiction where they stated that they were not concerned about their privacy; Yet, they did not share any information about themselves or about the children they cared for on social media.

> *"I am not concerned, if someone posts something, he knows it can be circulated a lot on social media, so each user is responsible and bears the consequences of his actions. For me, I am very cautious and do not share things I do not wish to spread." (P1)*

It is clear that there was great concern among parents about sharing basic information about their children, such as their disability treatments and training updates with other parents. Three out of five specialists stated that they communicated with their students' mothers individually through WhatsApp as there was no group that brought them together. *"I do not guarantee that each mother is okay with me sharing information related to her child's case. I do not have a group for all the mothers together since some of them refused the idea." (P1)*

2) Negative discussion and comments

Sharing negative experiences may be seen by some as a way to relieve personal stress, to find emotional support, or to show solidarity with other caregivers. However, most participants expressed their displeasure at sharing such experiences. P1 explained her reason for disapproving of such posts: *"In Snapchat, a mother of an autistic son always shares about her son's constant crying; sharing such experiences negatively affects other parents who have children with Autism, [...] other mothers might lose hope that their children will improve over time."*

While most participants were against posting any negative posts, P11, on the other hand, believed it could open the door for discussion and criticism, which might help in raising public awareness: *"I think that they are published to be criticized and to spread awareness."*

P3 took a middle place between the two opinions, where she thought that someone should not post bad behaviors about a specific child, but talk about these behaviors scientifically for the purpose of spreading the knowledge needed.

Furthermore, being concerned about social stigma negatively affected the caregivers' engagement level. Some became passive users, where they only read and browsed information. For instance, P4 chose YouTube to search for answers instead of asking someone she personally knew as she was afraid of public judgment: *"I feel embarrassed when I ask questions on WhatsApp. Also, because I do not want anyone to look at me or at my son with pity or to diminish his value."*

While P7 believed social media could be a great avenue for sharing and raising public awareness, she stopped sharing or asking public questions about her sister's condition out of respect for her parents' desire because they were afraid that by sharing her condition, she might get judged or bullied: *"they are afraid talking about her in social media may let people bully her and call her names or treat her differently."*

Another reason behind refrainment of sharing was the fear of being blamed. P4 stated "*blaming them[parents] as they are the reason of their child's disability"* as the most negative attitude that bothered her in social media discussions. Similarly, P10 shared that people on social media always criticized and blamed her for the way she was raising her son: *"My son is Autistic. I will get attacked, people will tell me that I did not hug him enough and even I am spoiling him too much [..] it used to put me in tears."*

In addition to the challenges they already face as caregivers of children with disabilities, the fear of online judgment and exposure to negative comments adds an extra layer of complexity to fully adopting social media platforms.

3) Misinformation

The caregivers reported that seeking credible information could be a challenge. Some specialists showed their resentment about spreading false statements that might mislead parents: "*They call autism "disease," and this thing is wrong because it is a disorder and has no cure!" (P1).* In the same token, P7 questioned the credibility of social media content and referred to her experience on Instagram about an advertisement announced as an educational event for families of children with disabilities:

> *"According to the post, if the family attended, they would be provided with information about the children's conditions and methods of treatment; so, I, my sister, and my brother went to find out that the program was all about distributing cake and brochures. It was just an advertisement which is often found on this platform."*

Misinformation about health treatments can actually put children with disabilities in danger. Therefore, concerns around using generalized treatment plans or fake medications were a major theme in the specialists' responses. One participant shared, in pain, one of her student's experiences:

> *"I have a case of a child who has paralysis. His mother travelled to meet a traditional healer after she had seen his ads and clips on social media. The medication was in the form of burning her son's skin [a form of moxibustion]. The mother said I paid him a lot of money. The worst part is my son is still not able to walk." (P6)*

Some participants also expressed worry about the credibility of social media accounts. For example, some questioned the credibility of the qualifications presented in a user's profile. P1 wondered: *"[how can someone] identify themselves in their bio as specialists of autism, learning difficulties, delayed speech, etc. This is incorrect! No one can be a specialist in all tracks."* Therefore, participants wished that the identities of users, especially those who identify themselves as specialists and health care providers, could be verified.

4) Lack of resources

The majority of our participants believed that there was scarcity in the available resources to support them and their children. In addition to the general lack of resources related to cognitive disabilities, two problems are especially pressing, namely the scarcity of related information in Arabic and online communities.

To deal with the shortage of educational resources, especially in Arabic, P12 had to search for information in English because she *"did not find much information in Arabic [...] about dyslexia ..."* Besides the lack of Arabic language resources and Arabic content makers in the way that caregivers aspired to, most of the attention and effort was devoted to certain disabilities. All caregivers have expressed that there was *"more interest in Down syndrome"* compared to other conditions.

With regard to the scarcity of online communities, P11, when asked about why she was not a part of any online group, answered: *"simply because no one had created one and invited me to join."* In a similar way, P2 stated that she communicated with the mothers of her students separately since there was no group to bring them together.

The lack of resources and online engagement around topics related to children with cognitive disabilities affected the level of awareness within the society, which in turn discouraged some participants from publicly sharing their children's cases:

> *"Honestly, I feel people in our society don't know what dyslexia is. I remember one time I was talking to a friend about my daughter's condition. Later my friend came to me saying that she did not notice anything different about my daughter and that she looked "normal!" [..] I don't want to tell other people that my daughter is dyslexic. I'm afraid by doing so I will cause her harm [..]. I do not share any information about my child on social media. They see a person with dyslexia as a sick person."*

5) Design of the technology

Several parents complained about some of the inherent features within the nature of social media platforms, such as constant advertisements as well as abbreviating information especially when using Twitter. A mother shared her frustration with distracting ads hindering her ability to stay focused: *"social media platforms display ads in an irritating way. I wish if they were Ads-free; those ads distract my attention." (P11)*

Another element of social media design that some participants did not like is the abbreviation of information. The problem is particularly frustrating on Twitter due to the limit of 140 characters for each tweet. *"The abbreviation of the information is done in an aggressive way where it becomes too short, misleading, and unclear." (P9)*

C. Opportunities for Enhancements

While the overall experience of using social media among Saudi caregivers was positive, they expressed a desire for certain features or functions on social media that might boost their level of confidence and improve accessibility.

One proposed feature was a centralized storage unit where all the files related to a specific topic shared within a social media platform can be easily accessed: *"I hope there is a place to keep all the files scattered here and there in one center and classify them according to the conditions, functional goals, etc.; as a file bank which has a search engine." (P1).*

Having an account verified will encourage users to trust and engage in online interactions. As clarified by P9: *"I use twitter in relation to the child's care because it includes a number of authenticated accounts [...] their accounts verified with the Twitter blue checkmark."* Although social media platforms offer verification, only certain groups of people have the privilege to get their accounts verified, mostly celebrities and public figures. Participants expressed their desire in expanding social media credential checking, especially when the account owner claims to be a health care worker: *"Check credentials of people who claim they are who they are! For example, on Instagram, you will see actual doctors and fake ones, you will see actual speech therapists and people who took one course and called themselves speech therapists." (P10)*

D. Social Media Use During COVID-19

Participants shared the benefits as well as the downsides of using social media during the novel COVID-19 pandemic. Using social media during the COVID-19 pandemic has brought many benefits to the children and their caregivers, such as raising virus awareness, facilitating distance learning, and seeking social support. Participants stated that social media helped them *"learn about the disease and know how to protect [themselves and their] family. As, on social media, [they] can find the most important guidelines and instructions about [COVID -19]." (P4).*

Eight participants praised the role that social media played during the pandemic in facilitating the continuation of the learning process. Social media served as an alternative solution for sharing educational materials with parents, especially with the absence of a specialized educational platform: *"The center my daughter attends did not provide any online courses and was completely shut down. My daughter's teacher sent me a package of activities via WhatsApp to implement them with my daughter." (P8)*

Furthermore, some participants used social media for social support. P10 stated that she turned to a group of mothers on Facebook for support when she could not find her son's favorite snack due to the pandemic:

> *"I reached out to other special needs parents for emotional support, as my son has his daily breakfast meltdown because he doesn't see his favorite PJ sandwich. They all reached out to arrange for me to get some peanut butter and they sure did."*

Finding social support through social media not only for the parents, but also for the children themselves is valuable: *"my daughter misses her teacher [...] she always brings the phone [...] and repeats her name to call her. She calls her with an audio or video call through Snapchat." (P8)*

Regarding the downsides, specialists stated that, during this tough time, they were unable to maintain long and direct communication with their students through social media. Thus, they fell short in adequately training them and evaluating their behavior goals and that they mainly relied on the children's mothers to train and evaluate their progress: *"I cannot evaluate children correctly; the training of children is not done fully and adequately by the mother due to limitations of understanding." (P9)* Another downside of social media during this time was the dissemination of misinformation around the novel Coronavirus. Two participants believed that *"social media is the reason for increasing the anxiety level among people by promoting rumors and spreading information about infected people and deaths which caused panic among people." (P5)*

V. DISCUSSION

The findings suggest that social media has the potential to empower Saudi caregivers and meet their informational and social needs. Caregivers increased their use of social media in regard to their child's condition after the initial diagnosis, which is consistent with parents from the United States [21]. Caregivers from Saudi Arabia tend to prefer private over public sharing of information due to privacy concerns. This private sharing is maintained within private social media groups or one-to-one communications. While they share general information within social media channels, they are hesitant to ask private questions regarding their child's condition due to fear of social stigma. Therefore, they prefer the passive format of communication to find answers, suggesting the importance of effective searching and filtering functions. This finding is consistent with an early study in which blind users felt hesitant to use their social networks as a Q&A avenue to their vision-related questions [22].

The subject of our study "cognitive disabilities among children" is considered relatively sensitive matter to discuss specifically in the Saudi Arabian context [23], where privacy is highly appreciated and tied with core cultural values, such as honor and modesty [18]. In our study, privacy concerns among participants goes beyond concerns for maintaining self-identity and honor to fear of public judgment and social stigma. In fact, several participants mentioned that they have hidden their children's disabilities from others, especially when the child is a girl and has an *"invisible disability"*, such as dyslexia. More research is needed to investigate caregivers' online interaction with cyberbullying and the content shared that is considered culturally inappropriate and could cause negative reactions. While fearing stigmatization also exists in Western context [24], families and children with disabilities experienced less judgment online [3][25].

The participants of this study revealed promising signs and positive examples of using social media, especially Twitter, to advocate on behalf of their children and influence policy changes. However, there is still lack of public engagement around topics related to disability. For decades, there were many misconceptions around disability and social exclusion practices within the kingdom; however, this has gradually started to change as a result of establishing a new governmental vision in 2016 entitled "Vision 2030" that emphasizes the rights of people with disabilities [26]. As a result, many initiatives to reform and promote the rights of persons with disabilities have taken place, such as the Authority for the Care of Persons with Disabilities and the *Mowaamah* program. All of these newly established programs and authorities have accounts on social media channels, especially on Twitter, to reach out to beneficiaries and raise public awareness. This is a promising effort that might encourage openness and information sharing. Still, substantial effort is needed to boost the public engagement level. Adopting more comprehensive mechanisms to spread awareness among society will be beneficial, such as funding seminars and conferences and other online and offline awareness activities. The government may also need to publicize their national efforts and online activities as many of our participants were unaware of them. We also recommend the allocation of funding to develop social media content in Arabic to address the lack of Arabic resources.

Many studies conducted in Western context confirmed the significant value of online communities in supporting their members [2][3][27]. However, only three out of eight family members in our study belonged to online groups. This may indicate low engagement in online communities among Saudi parents and family members of children with cognitive disabilities. Their limited engagement may be due to the scarcity of dedicated online communities and/or privacy concerns. To encourage community engagement, we recommend incorporating online communities as a part of educational centers' technological plans. We also urge social activists of parents, teachers, and health workers to initiate special interest communities. Additionally, the government could legislate data privacy policy to protect the rights of caregivers and their children on social media. Further research is needed to analyze other dimensions of caregivers' engagement behaviors: e.g., understanding barriers of actively participating in online communities and the nature of online discussion that stimulates their participation.

As an initial effort to explore this topic, the study has several limitations. Participants voluntarily reached out to us to be part of the study; therefore, the data sample is subject to self-selection bias. Those who volunteered may be more comfortable and open to share information about themselves and their children/students. As we mainly relied on social media channels for recruiting participants, caregivers who do not use social media were under-represented. Finally, our study oversampled female caregivers. Thus, our results might not be reflective of the whole population. In our future work, we aim to mitigate these limitations through using different methods and data sources (e.g., social network analysis) and triangulating results between the current study and future work.

VI. CONCLUSION AND FUTURE WORK

In this paper, we studied how Saudi caregivers of children with cognitive disabilities use social media to support their needs as well as their children's. We found that participants used social media to seek emotional and informational support, raise awareness, communicate with professionals and other parents, and build online communities. However, they encountered obstacles which hindered them from fully exploiting the advantages of social media, such as privacy concerns, misinformation, and lack of resources. We introduced several recommendations to the government, specialists and parents to help mitigate challenges faced by caregivers of children with cognitive disabilities on social media and enhance their user experience and online engagement.

ACKNOWLEDGMENT

We would like to express our sincere appreciation to our participants for taking part in this study. Special thanks to Nourah Alshenaifi for her help with recruiting participants.

REFERENCES

[1] J. W. Gowen, D. S. Christy, and J. Sparling, "Informational needs of parents of young children with special needs," Journal of Early Intervention, vol. 17, no. 2, pp. 194–210, 1993.

[2] B. A. DeHoff, L. K. Staten, R. C. Rodgers, and S. C. Denne, "The role of online social support in supporting and educating parents of young children with special health care needs in the United States: A scoping review," Journal of Medical Internet Research, vol. 18, no. 12, p. e333, 2016, doi: 10.2196/jmir.6722.

[3] T. Ammari, M. R. Morris, and S. Y. Schoenebeck, "Accessing social support and overcoming judgment on social media among parents of children with special needs," in Proceedings of the 8th International Conference on Weblogs and Social Media, ICWSM 2014, 2014, pp. 22–31.

[4] A. C. Wright and S. Taylor, "Advocacy by parents of young children with special needs: Activities, processes, and perceived effectiveness," Journal of Social Service Research, vol. 40, no. 5, pp. 591–605, 2014.

[5] S. Mohamed Madi, A. Mandy, and K. Aranda, "The Perception of Disability Among Mothers Living With a Child With Cerebral Palsy in Saudi Arabia," Global Qualitative Nursing Research, vol. 6, p. 2333393619844096, 2019, doi: 10.1177/2333393619844096.

[6] M. S. Al-Jadid, "Disability in Saudi Arabia.," Saudi Medical Journal, vol. 34, no. 5, pp. 453–460, May 2013.

[7] S. Nassir and T. W. Leong, "Conducting Qualitative Fieldwork with Ageing Saudis," in Proceedings of the 2018 on Designing Interactive Systems Conference 2018 - DIS '18, 2018, pp. 427–439, doi: 10.1145/3196709.3196820.

[8] A. Al-Dawood, N. Abokhodair, H. El Mimouni, and S. Yarosh, "'Against Marrying a Stranger': Marital Matchmaking Technologies in Saudi Arabia," in DIS 2017 - Proceedings of the 2017 ACM Conference on Designing Interactive Systems, 2017, pp. 1013–1024, doi: https://doi.org/10.1145/3064663.3064683.

[9] A. Mashat, M. Wald, and S. Parsons, "Improving Social and Communication Skills of Adult Arabs with ASD through the Use of Social Media Technologies," in International Conference on Computers for Handicapped Persons, Springer International Publishing, 2014, pp. 478–485.

[10] A. A. AlArfaj and E. Solaiman, "Investigating commercial capabilities and trust in social media applications for entrepreneurs," in Proceedings of the 9th International Conference on Communities & Technologies-Transforming Communities, 2019, pp. 65–75, doi: 10.1145/3328320.3328390.

[11] E. Thorsen and C. Sreedharan, "#EndMaleGuardianship: Women's rights, social media and the Arab public sphere," New Media & Society, vol. 21, no. 5, pp. 1121–1140, May 2019, doi: 10.1177/1461444818821376.

[12] S. Nassir and T. W. Leong, "Traversing Boundaries: Understanding the Experiences of Ageing Saudis," in Proceedings of the 2017 CHI Conference on Human Factors in Computing Systems, 2017, vol. 2017-May, pp. 6386–6397, doi: 10.1145/3025453.3025618.

[13] B. E. Auxier, C. L. Buntain, P. Jaeger, J. Golbeck, and H. Kacorri, "#HandsOffMyADA: A Twitter Response to the ADA Education and Reform Act," in Proceedings of the 2019 CHI Conference on Human Factors in Computing Systems - CHI '19, 2019, pp. 1–12, doi: 10.1145/3290605.3300757.

[14] H. Li and E. Brady, "#accessibilityFail: Categorizing Shared Photographs of Physical Accessibility Problems," in Proceedings of the 18th International ACM SIGACCESS Conference on Computers and Accessibility - ASSETS '16, 2016, pp. 277–278, doi: 10.1145/2982142.2982186.

[15] S. T. Hashemy, "Usability and accessibility of social media among Canadians with high functioning autism," (Master's thesis, Library and Archives Canada, Montreal, Quebec), 2011.

[16] A. Kirby, L. Edwards, and A. Hughes, "Parents' concerns about children with specific learning difficulties: Insights gained from an online message centre," Support for Learning, vol. 23, no. 4, pp. 193–200, 2008.

[17] J. Lazar, J. H. Feng, and H. Hochheiser, Research Methods in Human-Computer Interaction. Morgan Kaufmann, 2017.

[18] N. Abokhodair and S. Vieweg, "Privacy & Social Media in the Context of the Arab Gulf," in Proceedings of the 2016 ACM Conference on Designing Interactive Systems - DIS '16, 2016, pp. 672–683, doi: 10.1145/2901790.2901873.

[19] V. Braun and V. Clarke, "Using thematic analysis in psychology," Qualitative Research in Psychology, vol. 3, no. 2, pp. 77–101, Jan. 2006, doi: 10.1191/1478088706qp063oa.

[20] B. Edhlund and A. McDougall, NVivo 12 essentials. Lulu. com, 2019.

[21] T. Ammari and S. Schoenebeck, "Networked Empowerment on Facebook Groups for Parents of Children with Special Needs," in Proceedings of the 33rd Annual ACM Conference on Human Factors in Computing Systems, 2015, pp. 2805–2814, doi: 10.1145/2702123.2702324.

[22] E. L. Brady, Y. Zhong, M. R. Morris, and J. P. Bigham, "Investigating the appropriateness of social network question asking as a resource for blind users," in Proceedings of the 2013 conference on Computer supported cooperative work - CSCW '13, 2013, p. 1225, doi: 10.1145/2441776.2441915.

[23] M. S. Al-Jadid, "Disability in Saudi Arabia.," Saudi Medical Journal, vol. 34, no. 5, pp. 453–460, 2013.

[24] S. E. Green, "'What do you mean "what's wrong with her?"': Stigma and the lives of families of children with disabilities," Social Science and Medicine, vol. 57, no. 8, pp. 1361–1374, 2003, doi: 10.1016/S0277-9536(02)00511-7.

[25] K. S. Sweet, J. K. LeBlanc, L. M. Stough, and N. W. Sweany, "Community building and knowledge sharing by individuals with disabilities using social media," Journal of Computer Assisted Learning, vol. 36, no. 1, pp. 1–11, Feb. 2019, doi: 10.1111/jcal.12377.

[26] Government of Saudi Arabia, "Vison 2030 Kingdom of Saudi Arabia," Report, 2016. [Online]. Available: https://vision2030.gov.sa/download/file/fid/417. [Accessed: 02-Nov-2020].

[27] J. Meng, L. Martinez, A. Holmstrom, M. Chung, and J. Cox, "Research on Social Networking Sites and Social Support from 2004 to 2015: A Narrative Review and Directions for Future Research," Cyberpsychology, Behavior, and Social Networking, vol. 20, no. 1, pp. 44–51, Jan. 2017, doi: 10.1089/cyber.2016.0325.

Design Guidelines for Educational Games Targeting Children

Emma Nilsson, Åsa Cajander
Uppsala University
Uppsala, Sweden
e-mail: emmalaura.nilsson@gmail.com,
asa.cajander@it.uu.se

Marie Sjölinder, Olov Ståhl, Erik Einebrant
RISE – Research Institutes of Sweden
Stockholm, Sweden
e-mail: marie.sjolinder@ri.se, olov.stahl@ri.se,
erik.einebrant@ri.se

***Abstract*—There exists a wide range of frameworks with design guidelines within child-computer interaction and educational games. However, hardly any frameworks can be found that combine both these areas. This work aims to develop accessible and easily applicable design guidelines aimed towards educational games for children. A literature review was conducted within the areas of games, educational games, and child-computer interaction. From the publications, 42 guidelines within educational games and child-computer interaction were elicited. The guidelines were applied and tested on a healthcare application. Based on the outcome of the evaluation, formulations of the guidelines were updated and resulted in a new, more easily applicable compact version of the framework, named the Educational Games for Children (EGC) framework, presenting 24 guidelines within educational games for children.**

Keywords - educational games; child-computer interaction; design guidelines; game design.

I. INTRODUCTION

Applications aiming at educating and preparing children require consideration of several design aspects. When designing educational games, both motivation to use, and achievement of intended learning goals are important aspects. While guidelines regarding games, educational games and child-computer interaction are all well documented areas [1]-[5] it is more difficult to find guidelines that combine these areas, all relevant when developing and designing educational games for children. Guidelines and recommendations in the academic literature are also often complicated for practitioners to access and there is a need for accessible easy to use guidelines in the area [3].

The aim with this work was to define a framework for guidelines when developing and designing educational games for children. This work was a first explorative step towards developing a tool that easily can be used by designers of educational games. The work was conducted in an iterative way alongside with the development of an educational game for children. Initially, a literature study within the areas of games, game-based learning (educational games) and child-computer interaction was conducted. Based on the literature study, a first draft of a framework for guidelines was created. In the next step, this first version of the framework was tested on the COSMO@HOME project, an ongoing project that develops a healthcare educational game to prepare children for Magnetic Resonance Imaging (MRI) procedures. Based on an evaluation and interviews with game designers in the COSMO@HOME project, the guidelines were modified, and a final version of the framework was created.

The paper starts by presenting the results from the literature study, describing the area of game-based learning and education (Section 2), followed by a section about child-computer interaction (Section 3). Section 4 elaborates on existing frameworks and their advantages and disadvantages, in relationship to the suggested framework. In Section 5, a first version of the suggested framework is described. In Section 6, insights from evaluating the framework are presented and applied to create an updated version of the guidelines. Lastly, Sections 7 and 8 comprise a discussion, conclusion, and future work.

II. GAME-BASED LEARNING AND EDUCATIONAL GAMES

Since the beginning of 1980, computer games and TV games have been used not only for entertainment but also for learning, and during the early 1990s, games were brought to academia to be researched as beneficial. The area of educational games is still discussed today, and was questioned from its early beginnings due to the detrimental impact computer and TV games in general were considered to have on children. Opinions such as *waste of time and money* were common, but so were the cognitive effects games were thought to have on children [6]. These might well be opinions that we still can hear today, but the views on games are nowadays more nuanced, and the area of games has become a popular research topic. Researchers have argued that games are a unique way to engage and motivate people in learning and education [7][8].

To understand how a game can be a tool for learning, we first need to define the concept of a game and the different parts that build it. Kapp [9] defines a game in the following way:

"A game is a system in which players engage in an abstract challenge, defined by rules, interactivity, and feedback, that results in a quantified outcome often eliciting an emotional reaction."

Through feedback and interaction, coupled with challenge, the player will interact and engage with the game. The game, that is defined by the rules of its system, and that is designed as an abstract version of a larger system, will result in a quantifiable outcome that in turn will give rise to an emotional reaction from the player. These are, according to Kapp, the factors that will promote learning and engagement [9]. The concept of gamification uses these elements to bring further meaning and motivation for a certain task. Kapp [9] defines the term as:

"Gamification is using game-based mechanics, aesthetics and game thinking to engage people, motivate action, promote learning, and solve problems."

As in learning, games also use typical techniques that can be found in educational psychology. Techniques, such as giving points, feedback, and encouragement to collaborate are common practice for teachers as well as typical elements of a game. What gamification adds to learning is, according to Kapp [9], another layer of interest that both engages and motivates the player to learn. Appreciation sounds given after completed tasks can be an effective way of encouraging the user [10], as well as points and badges [3][10][11].

There are several advantages of using games for learning. As a game can be used to model parts of the real world it makes it possible for people to play around with and visit an abstract reality of a real life setting or place, but in a simplified form [9]. However, many aspects of real life are complex and do not necessarily enrich the experience of a game. The concept of purchasing different artifacts is, for example, a common act a player can perform in games, and being able to acquire better tools etc can enrich the game for players. Yet other actions associated with the concept of buying, such as standing in line, counting your money, and packing your goods do not enrich the experience. These kinds of real-world concepts can both make the game less interesting and overwhelming [9]. Other educational settings that games can be used for is to understand the effects of one's actions, since the player can get immediate feedback during play [9]. In this way, players can learn about concepts in the real world and how their actions can result in certain outcomes.

A. Motivation and Learning

Winn [2] states that the intended learning goals should be central and primarily set clear as the development of a game is started. Setting these goals can then help the designer throughout the development phase as they provide a practical way of measuring the intended learning outcome.

A significant motivation for using educational games in learning is the engagement and joy they bring to the user [11]. Motivation is crucial for engagement and is fostered by several factors in games, such as challenges and feedback but is also connected to other elements such as graphics and the storyline of the game. Provision of good audio and sound quality are also important within educational games [5]. A study conducted by Linek [5] showed that lack of good sound quality can cause a greater degree of disruption than poor image quality. Kapp [9] discuss the concept of internal and external motivation which is referred to as intrinsic motivation and extrinsic motivation. Extrinsic motivation is experienced when the focus is put on the reward or the outcome of a certain task. Intrinsic motivation on the other hand, is when the activity is the main purpose and not the reward upon completion [12].

Providing choice is another way to create motivation [5]. Choice makes the player feel powerful in the game-situation and is a way of engaging the player even more. Further, Chiasson and Gutwin [13] imply that providing the feeling of control has been seen as a good way of enhancing engagement. Choice can be incorporated in many ways, such as selecting game paths, but also through the ability to customize avatars, items, and other appearances of the game [3][11]. Winn [2] implies that it is important to balance the number of available choices, so as not to overwhelm the player early in the game. Choices within games should progress during the game as the player is learning and becoming more comfortable with it.

Role-playing games have also been seen as beneficial for learning as they are a way to address engagement [11]. By letting the player take on a role, for example through an avatar, the player becomes more involved in the game-play and emotional engagement and motivation is created.

B. Feedback and Rewards

Clear goals and rules within the game are important for the player, and are also important for creating intrinsic motivation [5]. If the player does not know what to do or if the goals of the game are unclear, it creates frustration and becomes unmotivating. Feedback is an important tool for learning through games and it can optimize learning by directly giving the player tips and tricks with respect to the performance and actions within the game [5]. Feedback can be incorporated in many ways, one of which is by using pedagogical characters often referred to as animated agents [3][13]. According to the Touchscreen Interaction Design Recommendations for Children (TIDRC)-framework and research done by Chiasson and Gutwin [3][13], this can improve learning outcomes, even though it is important to ensure they are not too intrusive [13].

Rewards are typical components of games and are a good way of encouraging and motivating the player [3][11][13]. Winn [2] implies that is important to balance the number of awards to better maintain player motivation.

This work suggests that rewards should be given more frequently when the challenge is greater, or when the learning curve is steeper. Further, the TIDRC-framework recommends being careful with the frequency of rewards given as this can rule out the intrinsic motivation of users [3]

C. Challenge

One of the challenges when creating a game for a broader user group is to find the right level of challenge that will keep players with different skills entertained. One way to handle this is to use levels that change during gameplay according to the skills of the user [9]. Either the level can be set for the whole game beforehand, or it can be used and evolved throughout the game until the end. Kapp [9] points out that levels can help the user to learn certain skills that are required to achieve the main goal. For example, to slay a dragon requires skills such as swinging a sword or dodging attacks from an enemy. These and other skills can be practiced by using the concept of levels. When creating educational games, Kapp [9] suggests creating three levels of interaction: easy, intermediate, and difficult. Linek [5] also points out the importance of adapting the level of challenge to optimize learning. If a user finds a game too easy to play it can quickly become unchallenging and unmotivating. Additionally, lack of motivation can also appear if the player instead finds the game too challenging and difficult to master [5]. Another way for the player to test and practice skills is to master obstacles and quests [11]. Abdul [11] implies that these moments of challenge improve learning since the player is forced to employ skills that they have already been trained in.

III. Child-Computer Interaction

Children's media usage is increasing [14]. The time exposure to media, such as computers, is a general concern at the same time that computers creates opportunities for children to learn and experience things in a new way [4]. Gelderblom and Kotzé [15] found that computers even supported children's development in writing, verbal creativity, mathematics, and language, among others. The use of computers, given that the experience is developmentally appropriate, could benefit construction of knowledge, as they encourage children in active learning. The use of computers could also be an opportunity to experience virtual environments where children can learn and acquire knowledge in other contexts at the same time as being provided with challenge and fantasy, which creates curiosity. By using the interactive opportunities of computers, children can effectively be given feedback, which can speed up their development in learning new things [15].

Designing interfaces for children creates different challenges to designing for adults. Children, as they are in their developmental stage, have different cognitive, social, and physical needs and skills than adults. These are the three main aspects in which children's development can be divided and categorized [10] and all of them need to be considered when creating technology for children [10]. Cognitive abilities of children usually cover reading and understanding, but also their attention skills. Physical abilities in the area of human-computer interaction usually refer to the fine motor skills needed when interacting with different devices such as computers, video games, or smartphones. Socio-emotional abilities in this context are connected to social-sharing and customization [3].

A. Cognitive Abilities

Using technology requires mental processing, such as perception, attention, information handling, and decision making, and is tightly coupled with the area of cognition [4]. As children have different needs and skills to adults, designers for children's technology should be aware of the differences between child and adult users.

Reading knowledge: In many applications and games, instructions are given in text. Menus and choices available are commonly written in text, which can clearly be a challenge for children of pre-reading age. Navigating through menus can also be challenging for younger children as it may still be an unknown and abstract concept for them [10]. Even older children may experience written instructions as challenging, which is why audio and animation can be a useful tool to support their understanding of instructions. Due to the limitations of children's reading capacity, it cannot be expected that games can be learnt through text instructions unless they are easy enough to follow and understand. Further, it has been suggested that in-app tutorials should be avoided, since there is a tendency that children may not read or remember instructions given in this way. A better solution is to provide guidance whereby the user can be active [3]. Further, Chiasson and Gutwin [10] also suggest that the interface should be intuitive enough to be used without instructions, or that child-users are given guidance until the intended task is understood. This is usually referred to as scaffolding [10].

Graphics: An alternative to written text and instructions is graphical metaphors and interfaces where minimal use of text is required, especially for the youngest users. Giving instructions in speech with corresponding pictures and animations can also help the users to both remember and understand the instructions. This is also a good way of catching the attention of the user [10]. As children usually have less experience with computer interfaces than adults, many of the typical visual representations and symbols are not yet common knowledge for child-users. Icons such as "stop" or "play" can be abstract for a novice user and should not be expected to be familiar icons for a child [3][10]. Therefore, icons and symbols should be represented by pictures and concepts recognizable and intuitive for children. Gelderblom and Kotzé [4] also formed a guideline of this based on Piaget's theory of Cognition. This states that children's knowledge is structured in schemes which can be reorganized and adapted to environmental change as the child becomes older. To understand and acquire a new skill, therefore, demands that prior schemes and knowledge fit the presented information. Due to this, it is also important for designers to consider and acknowledge the existing schemes and knowledge of the intended user. Interactive components such as buttons should also be designed in a way that show that they are clickable. One way is to give buttons a 3D-looking design [10]. Another way to differentiate certain items is to make them stand out from the background using distinct outlines, colours, and backgrounds. Another recommendation within the TIDRC-framework is to avoid too-complex backgrounds as these may confuse the child integrating with the system [3].

B. *Physical Abilities*

Several design choices have to be considered when forming the more practical components and possible interactions within software for children. Children's developing physical and motor skills put other requirements on the usual gestures used when integrating with a device. Chiasson and Gutwin [10] found that touch screen devices rather than computers are better and more appropriate tools for children. Even though touchscreen devices are a good choice for child users, there are limitations to these. As mentioned, the interaction of these devices is often limited by the motor skills of a child and thereby not all available touchscreen gestures can be implemented.

Primarily, the gestures used within the interface should be consistent throughout the game [10][11][16]. Typical gestures such as *drag-and-drop*, *rotate*, *pinch*, *double-tap,* and *spread* should be avoided [3], as well as gestures that require an object being dragged a longer distance. Ways to overcome some of the challenges that may come with these gestures are to allow partial gesture completion, accepting both single and multi-touch, and increasing the time between taps in the double tap gesture [3][10]. Another aspect to consider when designing interfaces for children is to avoid targets being too small and also ensure that the distance between targets are long enough to deal with outbound touches. Another good solution is to increase the active area of targets [3].

IV. Existing Framework and Guidelines

The MDA-framework, from 2004, is one of the earlier formal approaches to describe how games are built and, thereby, how they can be understood and evaluated. MDA stands for Mechanics, Dynamics, and Aesthetics which represent different game layers, from hard coded objects and components (mechanics) to all actions a player can perform within the game and with the objects (dynamics). These two concepts give rise to different feelings and impressions that the player gets from playing the game (aesthetics) [17]. The MDA-framework has become one of the most widely used and accepted theories within game design for decomposing and evaluating games [1]. While the theory has been popular and appreciated, it has also become a topic of discussion.

Walk et al. [1] found two main aspects of weaknesses within the MDA-framework as discussed in the academic literature. Primarily, they questioned the absence of visual design aspects of games as the MDA-theory merely focuses on mechanics. Because of this, the authors found that the theory is not applicable to gamified content or experience-oriented design as it focuses more on functionality. Further, Walk et al. [1] found that the framework is barely applicable to narrative designs as those components are hard to break down into the main concepts of MDA. Instead, the authors [1] suggested a new, updated version of MDA to address its weaknesses, namely, the DDE-framework, which stands for Design, Dynamics, and Experience. The DDE-framework was an attempt to further define the concepts within the MDA theory.

Another alternative to the MDA-framework was presented by Winn [2], who also found weaknesses with the MDA-framework. He argued that the framework was difficult to apply on serious games that have requirements other than just entertainment. Optimizing fun within a serious game can be challenging as it also needs to fulfil requirements for more serious outcomes. To address these weaknesses of MDA and to create a framework more suitable for serious games, Winn suggested an extended version of MDA called the DPE-framework. DPE stands for Design, Play, and Experience. These three main concepts are built on sub-categories or "layers" within learning, storytelling, gameplay, and user experience.

With respect to design recommendations for children, Soni et al. [3] created a set of guidelines – the TIDRC-framework. Building on evidence-based studies, the authors created their own framework consisting of 57 recommendations elicited from the literature. The recommendations were grouped into categories important within the field of child development: cognitive, physical, and socio-emotional abilities, considering children in the age-span 2 to 11 years.

V. Developing a New Framework Targeting Educational Games for Children

Guidelines regarding games, game-based learning, and child-computer interaction are all well documented areas. Yet, it is more difficult to find guidelines that combine these areas, which are all relevant when developing and designing educational games for children. The early and frequently used game theories MDA [17], DDE [1], and DPE [2] work well for breaking down game elements to understand their components and functions [2]. The game-design part of the guidelines in this work is mainly inspired by the DDE- and DPE-frameworks. Other important insights have been obtained by analyzing guidelines for educational games and game-based learning, which narrows down the general game-design principles even more. Designing for children is, however, different to designing for adults [17].

Therefore, it was also of interest to examine the literature about child-computer interaction.

Guidelines from the literature were collected continually into a 3x4 table. The guidelines were structured into specific columns based on the area to which they belonged, either game-based learning or child-computer interaction. Further, these columns were separated by rows to sort the guidelines into specific aspects of game design. The left-most column categorizes the guidelines into game design within the areas of Design, Dynamics, and Experience [10]. This column, describing educational games, suggests guidelines specifically elicited from game-based learning theory. The column named child-computer interaction suggests design recommendations specifically aimed for children as users. A compressed version of the constructed framework is presented in Table 1 below.

TABLE I. COMPRESSED VERSION OF THE THEORETICAL FRAMEWORK OF DESIGN PRINCIPLES FOR EDUCATIONAL GAMES AND CHILD-COMPUTER INTERACTION.

Guidelines within:		A. Educational games	B. Child-computer interaction
Game Design	Design		
	Dynamics		
	Experience		

Design: The first row describes all components and design choices implemented in a game that are under direct control of the designer. Examples of such components are colours, characters, and story elements incorporated in quests and obstacles.

Dynamics: In the second row of the table, guidelines within dynamics and interaction are given. Dynamics within a game refer to the runtime behaviour of the implemented design-components when input is given from a player. One common example in games is when the player can collect money or select clothes for its avatar.

Experience: The last row provides guidelines within the area of Experience within game design. As other game design researchers [1][2][17] have renamed the "Aesthetics" area of MDA in their framework, the same adjustment has also been implemented in this framework. Experience in this framework stands for, as the title implies, the experience and reactions of the player.

VI. EVALUATING THE FRAMEWORK

Within an ongoing project, an application for children to be used before undergoing an MRI-scanning procedure was developed. By preparing children in their home environment, the amount of sedation can be lowered and through that, the discomfort of patients is reduced, as well as the costs associated with preparing and sedating children. The application COSMO@HOME consists of games and interactive exercises to prepare the children, and to convey important learning goals. For example, increase the understanding of the size of the MRI-scanner and its sounds, the need for lying still for a long period of time, and information about not being allowed to bring metal objects into the MRI-scanner.

The framework was evaluated and tested on the COSMO@HOME application to investigate how useful and usable the framework was. A walkthrough of the application was conducted by an expert by reviewing and comparing the application with the guidelines. User testing with children was continually made within the COSMO@HOME project. In April 2020, user testing was conducted by the project group at the University Hospital Leuven (KU Leuven). Eight children participated in the user tests, ranging from four to nine years old. The average age of the children was 6.5 years. Results from the tests have been examined to detect possible similarities between the findings from the walkthrough and experiences from the user tests. Finally, interviews with two game designers/developers within the COSMO@HOME project were made to obtain further insights about the framework.

To highlight the implications, that the evaluations had on the framework, the outcome of the evaluations is presented in relationship to the different aspects of the framework. Topics that were brought up during the interviews were mainly in the areas of designing for children and learning through games. The interviewees also evaluated the framework and provided feedback about structure and applicability. Based on the findings from the different evaluation methods, a new version of the framework was created to increase the usability of the guidelines.

The experience from the walkthrough showed that most of the guidelines were applicable to the application. However, some guidelines were easier to apply than others, which was also pointed out by the interviewees. The guidelines that had more concrete recommendations – for example, "Avoid too-small targets, especially on the edge of the screen" – were easier to identify with regard to whether the application met the recommendation or not. More abstract guidelines, such as "Incorporate a reasonable level of challenge; not too easy or too hard" or "Designers should be aware of individual differences and preferences", were more challenging to apply. The perception of these guidelines can be both subjective and dependent on the intended user group; although it was possible to reason about the guideline with respect to the application, it was harder to clarify whether the recommendations were met or not.

The experience of evaluating the application via the walkthrough was that written guidelines can be applied and used to reason about design choices in educational games for children, and that concrete recommendations are easier to apply. Although more abstract or generic guidelines can work as good reminders or aspects to reason about, it is harder to answer whether such a recommendation is met or not.

To create a framework of guidelines that can be used in an easy and accessible way by designers was also an important aim of this study. By applying the framework to the application, important indications were given about which design choices of the framework and updates of guidelines should be made to make them easier to use.

The first version of the guidelines consisted of 17 guidelines within educational games and 25 guidelines within child-computer interaction, to give a total number of 42 guidelines. The guidelines were divided into two columns in the two research areas. The number of guidelines and the distribution of these into two columns, which spanned over three pages, were not favourable for giving a good overview of the framework. To create a more usable and accessible framework, some guidelines were excluded, and some were pulled together to compress the first version of the framework.

The columns in the framework worked well to clarify which guideline corresponded to which research area – either educational games or child-computer interaction. However, many of the guidelines acknowledge similar aspects, and the benefit of dividing the guidelines in the framework was not particularly useful when applying to the evaluation. Therefore, another improvement for the updated framework was to merge the current columns into one. The order in which the guidelines were presented by the game design components: *design, dynamics,* and *experience* was changed to start with recommendations that were more abstracts or generic, and end with more specific guidelines. The new version of the guidelines instead followed the order: *experience, dynamics,* and *design.* To summarize, updates regarding the design and formulations of the guidelines for the second version were:

- New order of game design components into experience, dynamics, and design.
- A merging of the two columns and presenting the guidelines together.
- Grouping of similar guidelines near each other to improve the structure of the framework.
- Summary of recurrent guidelines to shorten the framework and not to repeat concepts.
- Reformulation of some of the guidelines to provide a better understanding.
- New layout of the framework to improve the overview.

Changes according to the bullets mentioned above resulted in a new version with 24 guidelines presented as the Educational Games for Children (EGC) framework; see Figure 1.

VII. Discussion

In this work, theories and guidelines from 16 peer reviewed publications within the field of games, game-based learning, and child-computer interaction were combined into a new framework in the specific field of educational games for children, called the EGC-framework. The final product presents 24 guidelines in an accessible format, concerning important aspects to consider for educational games with children as users.

One of the main challenges was to combine and design a framework that incorporates the three different research fields that are all relevant for educational games targeting children. To make the framework easy to use and follow, it was decided not to group the guidelines with respect to their research fields, but rather to which aspect within a game they refer to.

It is important to keep in mind that the framework is not intended to be used as a checklist but rather as a means to reflect and be aware of aspects to consider when developing educational games for children. However, it can give an indication of how well a game meets these recommendations, and detect which aspects could be given further consideration. The guidelines are intended to give advice based on previous research, and it is possible to apply them before, after, or during game development.

VIII. Conclusion and Future Work

In conclusion, this work suggests that it could be beneficial to combine guidelines and theories from different areas. The walkthrough showed that it worked well to apply the framework of design guidelines in the development of an educational game for healthcare, and that it was also possible to evaluate how well the game met the recommendations.

Moreover, findings from the user tests conducted at the University Hospital Leuven supported several aspects and findings that were also acknowledged by the walkthrough. Through interviews with designers/developers within the COSMO@HOME project it was confirmed that the framework is able to provide insights and acknowledge aspects when developing an application within this particular field.

One final important conclusion is that the framework should not be seen as a checklist but rather as a way in which to reflect and acknowledge important aspects within game-based learning and child-computer interaction.

A next step is to evaluate the framework based on the field trials with the children in the COSMO@HOME project. Another next step to further develop the framework is to systematically review it in future projects. This could be done by letting developers use the framework when designing a game within the field, and continuously evaluate the usefulness and usability of the framework. Interviews could be conducted to get concrete feedback, and after being updated, another usability test of the framework could be performed. Future research within the field of educational games for children can contribute with further recommendations, but also broaden the field by including different aspects, for example, regarding research about socio-emotional needs in relationship to social interaction and social sharing.

DESIGN-GUIDELINES FOR EDUCATIONAL GAMES FOR CHILDREN

EXPERIENCE

1) Consider the intended learning goals of the game early in the development process.
2) Designers should be aware of individual differences and preferences to address self-expression and engagement.
3) Provide the feeling of control to empower and engage the player.
4) Implementing fantasy and roleplay creates enjoyment and the feeling of escapism which in turn can support engagement and learning.
5) The cultural context of the end users should be considered.

DYNAMICS

6) Provide clear goals and rules within the game.
7) Provide choice to address engagement but make sure it is balanced within the game.

Cognitive aspects

8) Provide scaffolding & guidance with positive feedback and feedback by giving hints, tips and tricks. Provide immediate feedback to avoid impatience.
9) Show current state for when the system is processing (buffering) or when the system is waiting for input to avoid impatience.
10) Provide customization to enhance intrinsic motivation and self-expression.

DESIGN

11) Use rewards to motivate and engage but be careful with too frequent rewards not to overweight the intrinsic motivation. Do also make sure to balance the number of rewards along the gameplay and the level of challenge or when the learning curve is steeper.

Motor aspects

12) Touchscreen is a good choice for younger users rather than a computer and mouse interaction.

Gestures

13) Use consistent gestures throughout the app.
14) Avoid too small targets, especially on the edge of the screen. Do also provide enough of distance between targets and increase the active area around them.

Avoid gestures as:

a. *drag & drop* (use "sticky-drag-and-drop" instead.
b. *rotate, pinch* and *spread* for younger users <4.
c. *double tap* gesture or allow longer delay between the taps.

Accept gestures as:

d. partial gesture completion, single- and multi-touch.

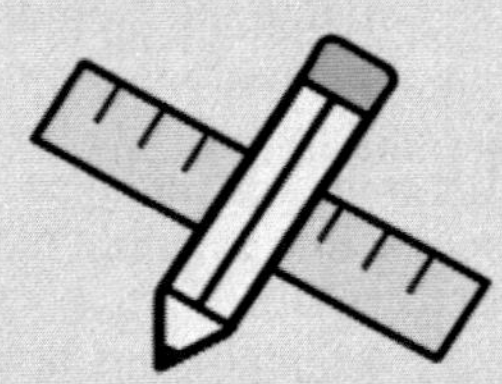

Cognitive aspects

15) Design buttons and clickable items in a 3D- or a clickable-looking way to differentiate these from the background by using different colors and outlines.
16) Avoid visually complex backgrounds as it can create confusion and use a neutral color palette to lower the cognitive load.
17) Limit the behavior of interactive elements to their sole purposes not to draw attention from their core functions.
18) Use content specific metaphors and meaningful icons and minimize abstract concepts (e.g. "left" and "right") or symbols.
19) Avoid menus and submenus as it can be challenging for children in the pre-reading age and difficult to understanding this kind of navigation.
20) Entertainment "click-ons" and hotspots can keep the child engaged and entertained between tasks but use these carefully as they may distract from learning.
21) Use good quality audio and visual cues instead of text to support understanding. Audio supported by animations can help to uphold the attention.
22) Expand the complexity and the level of challenge along the users learning curve in order to optimize learning. Provide levels to increase challenge in a natural way.
23) Preschoolers tend to appreciate challenge with short term awards (e.g. collecting items rather than longer problems/quests with long term rewards).
24) Three-dimensional images and virtual worlds can teach and let children explore new environments and objects.

Figure 1. The updated version of the guidelines – the Educational Games for Children (EGC) framework

Acknowledgment

The COSMO@HOME project was funded by EIT health. The authors would like to thank all project members and participants in the COSMO@HOME project.

References

[1] W. Wolfgang, M. Barret, D. Görlich, "Design, Dynamics, Experience (DDE): An Advancement of the MDA Framework for Game Design,", pp. 27-45, 2017, DOI: 10.1007/978-3-319-53088-8_3.

[2] B. Winn, "The Design, Play, and Experience Framework," vol. 2, pp. 1010-1024, 2009, DOI: 10.4018/978-1-59904-808-6.

[3] N. Soni, A. Aloba, K. S. Morga, and P. J. Wisniewski, "A framework of Touchscreen interaction design recommendations for children (TIDRC): Characterizing the gap between research evidence and design practice," *Proc 18th ACM Int Conf Interact Des Child IDC 2019*, pp. 419-431, 2019. DOI: 10.1145/3311927.3323149.

[4] H. Gelderblom and P. Kotzé, "Designing technology for young children: What we can learn from theories of cognitive development," *ACM Int Conf Proceeding Ser*, pp. 66-75, 2008 DOI: 10.1145/1456659.1456668.

[5] S. B. Linek, "As you like it: What media psychology can tell us about educational game design," pp. 606-632, 2011.

[6] P. Felicia, Improving Learning and Motivation through Educational Games, Information Science Reference, 2011.

[7] S. Kelle, R. Klemke, and M. Specht, "Design patterns for learning games," *Int J Technol Enhanc Learn*, vol. 3, 2011, DOI: 10.1504/IJTEL.2011.045452.ß

[8] A. Amory, "Game object model version II: A theoretical framework for educational game development," *Educ Technol Res Dev*; vol. 55, pp. 51-77, 2007, DOI: 10.1007/s11423-006-9001-x

[9] K. Kapp, The gamification of Learning and Instruction. Pfeiffer, 2012.

[10] S. Chiasson and C. Gutwin, "Design Principles for Children's Technology," vol. 7, 2005.

[11] A. Abdul Jabbar and P. Felicia, "Gameplay Engagement and Learning in Game-Based Learning: A Systematic Review," *Rev Educ Res*, vol. 85, pp. 740-779, 2015, DOI: 10.3102/0034654315577210

[12] T. W. Malone, "Toward a theory of intrinsically motivating instruction," *Cogn Sci*; vol. 5, pp. 333-369, 1981, DOI: 10.1016/S0364-0213(81)80017-1.

[13] S. Chiasson and C. Gutwin, Design Principles for Children's Technology, vol. 7, 2005.

[14] Ofcom, The office of communication UK. Children and Parents: Media Use and Attitudes, pp. 5, 2020.

[15] H. Gelderblom and P. Kotzé, "Ten design lessons from the literature on child development and children's use of technology," *Proc IDC 2009 - 8th Int Conf Interact Des Child*, 2009, DOI: 10.1145/1551788.1551798.

[16] V. Celis, J. Husson, V. Vanden Abeele L. Loyez, L. Van den Audenaeren, P. Ghesquiére, A. Goeleven, J. Wounters and L. Geurts, "Translating preschoolers' game experiences into design guidelines via laddering study," ACM int conf proceeding ser, 2013, DOI: 10.1145/2485760.2485760.2485772

[17] R. Hunicke, M. Leblanc, and R. Zubek, "MDA: A formal approach to game design and game research," *AAAI Work - Tech Rep*, 2004.

How-To: Instructional Video

Recommendations for the Design of Software Video Trainings for Production Workers

Maximilian Tandi
Dept. of text linguistics and technical communication
Human-Computer Interaction Center
RWTH Aachen University
Aachen, Germany
e-mail: m.tandi@tk.rwth-aachen.de

Lorena Niebuhr
Dept. of text linguistics and technical communication
Human-Computer Interaction Center
RWTH Aachen University
Aachen, Germany
e-mail: l.niebuhr@tk.rwth-aachen.de

Eva-Maria Jakobs
Dept. of text linguistics and technical communication
Human-Computer Interaction Center
RWTH Aachen University
Aachen, Germany
e-mail: e.m.jakobs@tk.rwth-aachen.de

***Abstract*— This paper gives an overview of design aspects of software instructional videos resulting from a literature review. The goal is to identify design dimensions and recommendations for instructional videos for software training and to make the results usable for the production of Computer-Aided-Design/-Manufacturing (CAD/CAM) instructional videos as part of a training concept within a Research and Development (R&D) project. The qualitative analysis provides four key design dimensions: (1) didactic design, (2) influence of the object, (3) material-technical implementation and (4) linguistic-visual design of the instruction. Recommendations were examined for similarities and differences and, if necessary, supplemented with findings from studies on particular aspects. The guidelines' recommendations are mainly influenced by contextual factors. Fewer design solutions are discussed at a linguistic or visual level. The results provide valuable input for the design of instructional videos as learning materials for CAD/CAM software training in professional contexts.**

Keywords-instructional videos; software video training; digital education; CAx systems; digitalization in industry sectors.

I. Introduction

Instructional videos present a solution process for specific tasks, enable users to act independently [1] and support Demonstration-Based Training (DBT) [2]. Multimedia products are increasingly discussed as a suitable means of knowledge transfer in a rapidly changing technical world. They can be produced quickly due to technical developments [3] and they use a familiar form of knowledge transfer (instruction) with new means. They are among the most used tools in the 21st century for the efficient, independent solution of activity-related tasks [4]. In addition to private use, there is a growing interest in the use of instructional videos in professional fields. Instructional videos have a high potential for companies (e.g., software training). As a blended learning format, they facilitate to make training and education of employees more efficient; employees are given the opportunity to acquire knowledge in a self-regulated way [5].

Within the R&D project "WerkerLab - A modular training concept for Small and Middle-sized Enterprises (SMEs) in the production technology environment" a training concept that prepares workers in SMEs for the use of CAD/CAM systems and for requirements of Industry 4.0. is developed. A major part of the modular training concept is the use of instructional videos. Therefore, a literature-based orientation framework for the production of CAD/CAM training videos is developed. This framework will then be enriched by the perspectives of workers and trainers from industrial project partners. Based on this framework videos will be produced and evaluated. The goal was to identify requirements for the design of instructional videos in this field of application. The results are presented in a systematic manner with reference to four design dimensions: didactic design, influence of the object, material-technical implementation and linguistic-visual design of the instruction. The latter part focuses on the central aspect of instruction and its implementation. From the perspective of communicative usability [6], questions of linguistic and visual design are considered in particular. The paper addresses three research questions:

- RQ1: Which design dimensions of instructional videos are considered in the research literature?
- RQ2: Which design aspects are discussed? Which recommendations are given?
- RQ3: How are aspects of communicative usability taken into account?

In the following, the theoretical framework that guides the literature evaluation is established (Section 2), followed by the description of the methodological procedure (Section 3). The evaluation is based on the four design dimensions mentioned above (Section 4). After a discussion in Section 5, the article closes with a conclusion and outlook for further research (Section 6).

II. Theoretical Framework

This paper addresses instructional videos from a linguistic point of view and refers to it as a communication pattern (A). Their main purpose is to instruct. Instructing is understood as a linguistic design task that takes didactic principles into account (B) and must meet the requirements of communicative usability (C).

A. *Instructional videos as a communicative format*

This paper treats instructional video as a communicative tool (or genre) for solving recurring problems (in this case lack of knowledge to operate CAD/CAM software). The design of the tool is oriented towards an overall goal (mediation or acquiring knowledge about software operation) and its pattern is conventionally agreed upon [7][8]. The design is limited by external parameters: the object (here production software), contextual factors (e.g., the domain or industry in which the software is used, with its values and conventions, and the cultural-economic context), as well as situational factors (conditions for video use, e.g., embedding in didactic measures). Other restrictions concern the material-technical implementation as well as the users. The design pattern encompasses different levels [7][8]: the topic hierarchy (main topic, secondary topics), structuring and sequencing of content and design solutions, the types of actions (instructing, naming target states) with typical linguistic and visual means as well as a typical average length.

B. *Instructing*

According to action theory, instructing is a directive writing or speaking act [9: 255]. They are intended to enable people to acquire (long-term) procedural (how-to) knowledge in order to independently carry out action steps and achieve a desired target state. Ballstaedt [9] defines action as the intentional change of a state by an agent.

From the perspective of learning psychology (and theories of comprehensibility that are based on it), actions (and their mediation) are framed by goals, conditions, consequences and potential disturbances [10]. The learning process is more efficient if the learner knows about the purpose of the action and the context. Every action has initial conditions that must be described [9]. Initial state S1 requires action A (rule: name conditions, then describe action). Every action has its consequences, it changes the initial state S1 and transfers it into a state S2. State S2 gives feedback whether action A was successful or not. S2 must therefore be described, even if it is not directly observable. Instructions always contain series of the sequence S1, A and S2 [9]. They need to be described in the order in which they are to be executed. Actions can be hindered by disturbances. Instructions must describe what the target state looks like when an action step has been carried out successfully and name potential disturbances and offer problem-solving options for them. This can also be done by means of supplementary measures (further sources of information) [11].

Instructions must describe goals, conditions and consequences in the correct order to avoid mistakes, which can sometimes be costly or even dangerous. They must be segmented in the right granularity and sequenced in a logical manner [11]. The content structure of an instruction is hierarchical, consisting of a main action with several subactions [9]. The hierarchically highest action represents the superordinate activity, which is implemented via actions and operations [9: 256]. The level of detail depends on the target group and its requirements. Experts understand process descriptions without a detailed level of instruction (high-level instructions); intermediate experts or laypersons require instructions in small steps (low-level instructions).

The quality of the target naming and the description of initial and target states are relevant for success. Beginning and end of the instruction are functionally assigned. A task-oriented heading at the beginning, e.g., helps the recipient to mentally establish a meaningful context. Based on the representation of sub-goals (action-target state scheme) the user can verify whether he has executed an action step correctly.

A special component of instructions are warnings. Their intention is to induce the user to "refrain from certain actions or to carry them out imperatively in order to avoid unwanted consequences" [9: 259]. Since product liability exists in Europe and America, warnings in technical documentation are legally relevant and writing acts are mostly standardized. Established components are information on the severity of the hazard, the type and source of the hazard, the consequences of the hazard and measures to counteract it.

C. *Communicative Usability*

The concept of communicative usability complements other forms of usability (e.g., cognitive or ergonomic) [6]. It focuses on the use of communicative modes in digital communication and interaction contexts and sees language as the most important modality of interaction between humans and machines [6][12]. The quality of design is measured by the extent to which linguistic-visual means support the user in fulfilling higher-level (pragmatic, hedonistic or affective) interests of action and the resulting hierarchies of goals and tasks. The reception of instructional videos as part of professional training is motivated pragmatically - the acquisition of skills is part of the professional activity.

Communicative usability considers communicative artifacts in their embedding in superordinate contexts of action, which are influenced by domain-specific, socio-cultural as well as temporal-spatial aspects [6].

Based on the theoretical framework, four perspectives are used to analyze the literature: Aspects of the didactic design (purpose: transfer procedural knowledge), impact of the object (CAD/CAM software, use in SMEs producing tangible goods) and its contextual embedding, the material-technical implementation as well as the linguistic-visual implementation of the instruction. The starting point is the assumption that the first three factors mentioned above significantly expand or limit the scope of design for the instruction itself.

III. Methodological Approach

The literature search and selection (corpus building) was done in four steps. Step 1: The search included the following terms: instructional video, video tutorial, video instructions, how-to video, recorded demonstration. The search was carried out in the databases Scopus, Web of Knowledge and

Google Scholar. For reasons of manageability it was limited to German and English articles published between 2004 and 2019. In a second step, the results - 13317 findings - were limited to publications that discuss video tutorials as learning material and software use. The resulting corpus comprises 67 publications. In step three, the corpus was limited to contributions to video tutorials for software in the production area or as part of training courses that give design recommendations for their production. The adjusted corpus contains 13 publications. In step four, two subcorpora from this cleaned-up corpus were formed. Subcorpus 1 comprises contributions that formulate design recommendations in the form of guidelines (n=4). Subcorpus 2 includes individual studies on the topic (n=9).

The two subcorpora were evaluated qualitatively [13] - firstly the guidelines, then case studies. The evaluation was based on the dimensions of didactic design, influence of the object, material-technical implementation and linguistic-visual design of the instruction. The determined categories within the main categories (dimensions) were transferred into a category system. Five subcategories were determined for the dimension didactic design, three subcategories were determined for the dimension influence of the object, seven subcategories were determined for the dimension material-technical implementation. The dimension linguistic-visual design of the instruction was initially divided into two categories - user guidance and instruction. Three subcategories were determined for the category user guidance. The category instruction comprises four subcategories. The design recommendations were compared in terms of similarities and differences.

IV. DESIGN RECOMMENDATIONS FOR INSTRUCTIONAL VIDEOS

A. *Didactic design*

All evaluated guidelines discussed didactic requirements for instructional videos [1][2][4][14]. Taken the fact that instructional videos convey knowledge about action processes, they have didactic elements per se. In the literature mainly five design aspects of didactic design are discussed: (1) relevance of types of knowledge, (2) the user's prior knowledge, (3) knowledge application, (4) self-efficacy, (5) autonomy of the learning material.

Relevance of the types of knowledge: All guidelines address the types – conceptual knowledge and procedural knowledge [1][2][4][5][14]. They emphasize their dependence on the learning content [1]: it makes a difference whether basic mathematical knowledge should be taught or whether the user should learn how to set up a tool in the tool database. In the first case, the focus is on teaching conceptual knowledge. In the second case, the learning material mainly provides procedural knowledge [1]. Software training is designed to teach the user the sequence of necessary steps (procedural knowledge). Swarts [4] emphasizes that processes are simultaneously demonstrated (procedural knowledge) and explained (conceptual knowledge). Plaisant and Shneiderman [14] call this hybrid of both types of knowledge "instructional information".

User's prior knowledge: During the learning process, new information is incorporated into existing knowledge [2]. The evaluated guidelines emphasize that learning success depends on how the user's prior knowledge is activated [1][2] and on how much prior knowledge the addressee has [2]. Van der Meij [15] recommends the use of Advanced Organizers for the activation of prior knowledge. They should show "initial and final states" [15: 1370] of the action in order to clarify the learning goals and purpose of the video. This preview of the task supports orientation and the development of a bigger picture (Guideline preview the task [1]). Users with little prior knowledge benefit from added instructional support, i.e., design solutions that additionally support the learning process such as markers. Users with a lot of prior knowledge need less instructional support, it rather hampers their learning process.

Knowledge application: Instructional videos provide knowledge for the autonomous solution of action-related tasks. The literature emphasizes the value of using practical exercises [1][2][15][16]. Practical exercises support retention (i.e., they help to anchor knowledge in long-term memory) and give the user the opportunity to check whether he can solve the problems on his own ([1] Guideline 8; hereafter referred to as "G.1-8"). The video should explain the problem and the way to solve it, which should be the starting point for practical exercises. During the application the learner should be able to consult the video again and solve the task without having to resort to other teaching materials/staff.

Self-efficacy: Two guidelines address affective aspects of learning [2][4]. An affective design "helps users engage with and feel comfortable about a message". [4: 196]. During the instruction the user should develop the feeling of being able to solve the task successfully (perceived self-efficacy) [2][4][15][16]. The user should have the feeling to be able to reach the target state by following the instructions. The instructor has to be convincing (confidence and expertise) [4] and not deviate from the previously determined solution. Important information should be repeated, the speaker should explain confidently (script, practice before recording) and confidently execute actions in in the interface.

B. *Influence of the object*

The evaluated literature focuses on instructions for acquiring operating knowledge for software. The target group receives the videos in order to gain knowledge for a specific "task domain" [2], e.g., to achieve better performance in university studies or in everyday working life. The object (software, operating tasks) is part of the task domain. Considered are aspects of (1) content selection, (2) content segmentation and (3) content sequencing.

Content selection: The selection of content should take the application context (task domain) into account as well as characteristics of the target group [14] in order to serve the interests of the user best. To anchor the learning content in the (professional) domain of the user has a motivating effect [2][16]. Also, content (problem, solutions, target states) should be oriented to the users' core tasks [2]. Content in instructional videos should be representations of sequences of actions. Only essential information relevant to the learning objective should be given [1][4]. Relevant content is always up to date. Brenner & Walter [17] emphasize the updating of content as an essential and continuous task of producers.

Content segmentation: Instructional videos should not exceed a certain duration (see 4.C.). If the content to be conveyed cannot be presented in a given time, it must be divided into segments [1][2]. Segmentation means the division of the superordinate content into smaller but self-contained tasks.

Content sequencing: The learning content in the video must be sequenced. The sequencing of the actions demonstrated should be based on the correct order in which the user has to solve the problem [1]. The object (e.g., software) usually determines which content must be learned first and what must be learned later. If a video is divided into several segments, and the sequence of those is not determined by the object, the presentation sequence should follow the simple-to-complex principle (problems that are easier to solve are presented first and more complex problems later) [2].

C. *Material-technical implementation*

Instructional videos are complex multimedia products that are produced with technical aids. In the literature the technical implementation is dealt with extensively. The following design aspects are addressed: (1) duration of the video, (2) coordination of image and sound, (3) user control, (4) quality of the visual recording, (5) screencapture, (6) quality of the auditory recording and (7) voice-over.

Duration of the video: The most discussed technical design aspect in the literature is the duration of the video [1][2][14][16][18][19]. Guidelines and individual studies agree that videos should be kept as short as possible (G. 7). Differences can be seen in the exact determination of length. Plaisant and Shneiderman [14] do not address the length of an entire video, but rather the length of individual segments that ideally last 15-30 seconds but should not exceed 60 seconds. The exact number of such segments needed to form an instructional video is not given. In contrast, guideline [1] specifies a maximum length of 3 minutes. Guo, Kim, and Rubin [18] find that shorter videos have a more engaging effect and suggests keeping videos shorter than 6 minutes. If a topic cannot be dealt with in a given length, it should be divided into shorter videos to not overwhelm the user with too much information.

Coordination of image and sound: Information in videos are multi-coded (visual, verbal, auditory) and must be orchestrated. The majority of the guidelines [1][4][14] consider this and recommend that the actions performed on the visual level should be presented simultaneously with the content-related information on the auditory level. The user is cognitively relieved as he/she does not have to keep out-of-date information active on one coding level while waiting for the presentation of information on another coding level [1]. Swarts [4] goes into more detail and recommends that sound should slightly precede image.

User control: User control allows the user to independently navigate through the video and to determine their learning pace individually. This should be realized by allowing the recipient to use the following functions via the video player software: starting, pausing, stopping, repeating, fast-forwarding/rewinding and (chapter) skipping [1][2][4][14][20]. Recommended interface elements are buttons and an interactive timeline. To enable the user to move through the content in a self-determined way, segmented content (sections) should be labelled and be directly selectable. Individual segments can be marked by short breaks, the insertion of black screens or title slides [1][2][4][14].

Quality of visual recordings: The quality of the visual recording is taken into account by most guidelines [1][4][14]. The visibility of the actions and objects that are manipulated is a prerequisite for users to be able to follow the processes. The literature recommends the image in the video to be as stable as possible. The resolution of the video should be at least Near HD (vertical resolution = 720P). The visibility of objects and the readability of texts must be guaranteed by using a zoom effect [1][14]. However, the zoom area should not overlay important elements [1][14].

Screencapture: Usually, video recordings are edited. Among other things, the producers decide whether or not to adapt the screen recordings. Two guidelines [1][14] take this into account. They recommend to always show the entire interface in the video without cropping the edges (G. 2). In practice, the user is guided by what he has seen in the video. Hence, it is important that the video shows what the user will see later in practice. If it differs, the user will have problems orientating.

Quality of auditory recordings: In contrast to the visual quality, the auditory quality is hardly discussed. Only [4] states that information presented in video must be of sufficiently high quality to ensure that the user can understand everything. Swarts [4: 202] speaks of "high resolution audio".

Voice-over: If there is a voice-over narration in the video, it can be performed either by a computer or a human. The explanations should be spoken by a human voice [1][4]. The learning process would be facilitated by a human voice (G. 2), as users perceive it as more natural and appealing.

D. *Linguistic and verbal realization of the instruction*

With regard to implementation, in the following, a distinction is made between the framing of the instruction (user guidance) and the instruction itself.

1) User guidance

The majority of the recommendations in the guidelines relate to user guidance, i.e., how the instruction is framed communicatively or how the beginning and end of the video are designed. The framing pursues different goals: (1) accessibility of the information, (2) directing attention and (3) narration.

Accessibility of information: Instructional videos must ensure the accessibility of information; relevant information must be easy to find. A distinction can be made between external (finding the video itself) and internal (in the video) accessibility. If a learner is looking for a video, he/she must be able to judge whether the video is suitable for his/her purposes based on the title (G. 1). Therefore, the title should be well chosen. With the help of a table of contents, an index or by using keywords the learner can assess in detail the relevance of the topics covered within a video.

At the beginning of the video, in the title sequence, the learning objective should be formulated and afterwards a short overview of the content should be given [1][4]. It is important to cover all announced contents [4]. A preview can be used as a tour through the components of the main screen [14]. However, detail should not be described in advance.

User attention: The user's attention can be directed visually and/or audibly. Especially visual signals and markers are recommended in all guidelines. Elements in the interface can be highlighted by the cursor or in editing process by e.g., circles or arrows [1][2][4][14]. Auditory signals and markers can be edited in the form of a voice-over and can indicate content or details [1][2][4][14].

Narration: Narration is the reproduction of an event in oral or written form. Instructional videos for software can be understood as screen capture with narration [1]. It is important that all communicative modes (video, audio and text) are well coordinated [1, 4]. The spoken narration should be a human voice (G. 2). The language should be personal [1][2][18] and functional (G. 4). The ideal speaking rate is a bit lower and should be supported by natural pauses in speech. The speaking rate should follow the shown action sequences [1][2][18].

2) Instruction

The presentation of the instruction itself requires design decisions on different levels: sequencing, wording, visual, auditory.

Sequencing the instruction content: The sequencing of the instruction and sub-actions follows the sequence of actions that must be performed to get from the (superior) initial state to the (superior) target state [1]. The process from the superordinate beginning to the superordinate goal should be divided into manageable, meaningful sequences. Those sequences should also have a clear beginning, a clear middle section, a clear end and should comprise three to five subactions. This is described as a three-part division [1]: (1) the starting state or the problem to be solved, (2) the solution path, and (3) the target state (see similarly [9][11]).

Wording: The Guidelines recommend few aspects concerning the wording in instructions. The vocabulary should be adapted to the user group [1]. Technical terms and foreign words should be defined and explained; abbreviations should be avoided [14]. They should be explained in a tour through the user interface. Technical vocabulary should be explained during the demonstration and in context, according to the just-in-time principle (G. 4) [1]. The narrator should address the learner directly and use the personal pronoun *you* to emphasize that the objectives of the video are relevant to the learner [1]. Plaisant and Shneiderman [14] apply the criteria of simplicity, directness and precision to language. Active language should be used and sentences kept short and simple. The imperative is best suited to describe the visual demonstration [1].

Visual parts: The visualization of the instruction should represent the entire interface that the user sees in front of him when he performs the task himself (G. 2). High resolution and stable images should ensure that all relevant information is clearly visible at all times [1][4]. If good visibility or legibility cannot be guaranteed a zoom effect can be used. Otherwise the complete interface should always be visible. The pace of the demonstration has to follow the pace of action in the real performance but also has to consider the pace of the learner [1][2][4]. Actions in the video must be executed fluidly and correctly [4]. Consequences of user actions has to be made clear [1][4][14]. The cursor should be highlighted with an animated circle that changes color depending on the performed action (right or left click) [14].

Auditory parts: All guidelines mention the high relevance of auditory parts for the reception of the instruction [1][2][4][14]. The spoken description should begin shortly before the visual demonstration, so that users can make a mental model of the actions to come [4]. During the visual demonstration, the spoken explanation should firstly describe what is being shown. On the other hand, it should give reasons for what is shown, explain why something is done [1][4][14]. It should contextualize the actions, place them in a higher level of action. The speaker should use the interface at the same time to ensure synchronicity of the auditory and visual parts [14]. In addition to the spoken instruction, other auditory components such as sound effects play a subordinate role. Sound effects should be used e.g., to highlight mouse clicks or scrolling audibly [14].

V. Discussion

Communicative usability and the guidelines see the embedding in and dependence of the communicative instructional video on superordinate contexts of action that are shaped by the domain. The embedding in professional contexts and the pragmatic motivation of the guidelines are particularly evident in the focus on learning purpose-related knowledge about action sequences and the recommendation to apply this knowledge in practice. The recommendations show that the scope for designing instructional videos is primarily influenced by external parameters.

In contrast to the communicative usability approach [6], the guidelines, do not measure quality by how linguistic-visual means support the user in fulfilling higher-level interests of action, but rather by how the didactic design and the material-technical implementation relieve the user cognitively and make the learning process effective [1].

The focus in the recommendations is primarily on "technical guidelines" [14], which are intended to provide users with easy technical access to the learning content. In this respect, there is a consensus on the technical and media requirements that instructional videos must meet in order to effectively support the learning process. Details regarding the exact duration of a video differ.

Regarding the linguistic-visual implementation of the instruction, recommendations for user guidance include considerably more aspects than recommendations for instructing as a linguistic action. Although there is an awareness that the beginning and closing of the video is crucial for learning success, linguistic-visual aspects are only addressed superficially. The guidelines mainly discuss material-technical conditions as factors influencing the design of the instruction.

In contrast to individual studies, the guidelines have a greater claim to general validity; they address software training in general - not for specific products. The applicability of the guidelines should always be checked in the context of the interface to be presented and the target group [14].

The guidelines focus on conveying best practice recommendations. In industry, however, a failure-oriented approach is also used to convey how action should not be taken. This is, e.g., also part of warning. This approach is not found in the literature and there is no research that contrasts both approaches. Warnings play a subordinate role in the guidelines, although it is legally relevant [9]. Only [4] mentions that warnings should be issued at the beginning.

VI. CONCLUSION

Research on the production of instructional videos for professional purposes and design solutions includes best practice as well as research-based approaches. There are already "key notions of accepted thinking" [1] that provide guidance for the production and evaluation of well-designed, efficient software instructional videos.

Design requirements for instructional videos for software training are characterized by three main factors: Didactic purposes, influence of the object and technical-material conditions. The literature primarily addresses questions of didactic design and/or technical-material implementation. The communicative usability of instructional videos, i.e., the extent to which the linguistic-visual design supports the learner in the appropriation of content has rarely been addressed.

This article provides an overview of design dimensions as well as aspects and corresponding recommendations discussed in the literature. It aims to sensitize producers of instructional videos for CAD/CAM software training for established design requirements. In the research project WerkerLab, the results of this contribution will be presented to practitioners (workers and trainers) in order to evaluate the relevance of the identified recommendations from a practical point of view and, if necessary, to add new aspects. Preliminary results of interviews with practitioners already suggest that context factors such as video production costs are more relevant for practitioners than described in the literature.

ACKNOWLEDGMENT

This research and development project is funded by Europäische Fonds für regionale Entwicklung (EFRE) (funding number EFRE-0801580) and implemented by the LeitmarktAgentur NRW - Project Management Agency Jülich (PtJ). The authors are responsible for the content of this publication.

EUROPÄISCHE UNION
Investition in unsere Zukunft
Europäischer Fonds für regionale Entwicklung
EFRE.NRW
Investitionen in Wachstum und Beschäftigung

REFERENCES

[1] H. van der Meij and J. van der Meij „Eight Guidelines for the Design of Instructional Videos for Software Training," in Technical Communication. vol. 60, pp. 205-228, 2013.

[2] J. Brar and H. van der Meij, „Complex Software Training: Harnessing and Optimizing Video Instruction," in Computers in Human Behavior. vol. 70, pp. 475-485, 2017.

[3] A. Mogos and C. Trofin, „You Tube Video Genres. Amateur How-to Videos versus Professional Tutorials," in AUDC. vol. 9, pp. 38-48, 2015.

[4] J. Swarts, „New Modes of Help: Best Practices for Instructional Video," in Technical Communication. vol. 59, pp. 195-206, 2012.

[5] D. Horvat and O. Som, „Wettbewerbsvorteile durch informationsbasierten Wissensvorsprung [Competitive benefits through information-based knowledge advantage]," in R. Wagner (eds.): Industrie 4.0 für die Praxis. Springer Gabler, Wiesbaden 2018.

[6] E.-M. Jakobs, „Kommunikative Usability [Communicative Usability]," in K. Marx, M. Schwarz-Friesel (eds.): Sprache und Kommunikation im technischen Zeitalter. Berlin, Boston: de Gruyter, pp.119–142, 2012.

[7] B. Sandig, „Formulieren und Textmuster. Am Beispiel von Wissenschaftstexten [Formulation and text patterns. Using the example of scientific texts]," in E.-M. Jakobs (ed.): Schreiben in der Wissenschaft. Frankfurt am Main u.a., pp. 25-44, 1997.

[8] E.-M. Jakobs, „Hypertextsorten [Hypertext types]", in ZGL 31 (Themenheft "Deutsche Sprache im Internet und in den neuen Medien"), pp. 232-273, 2003.

[9] S.-P. Ballstaedt, Sprachliche Kommunikation: Verstehen und Verständlichkeit [Understanding and comprehensibility]. Narr Francke Attempto: Tübingen, 2019.

[10] S.-P. Ballstaedt, Wissensvermittlung. Die Gestaltung von Lernmaterial [Knowledge transfer. The design of learning material]. Beltz PsychologieVerlagsUnion: Weinheim, 1997.

[11] S. Göpferich, „Textproduktion im Zeitalter der Globalisierung. Entwicklung einer Didaktik des Wissenstransfers [Text production in the age of globalization. Development of a didactics of knowledge transfer]", Studien zur Translation vol. 15. Stauffenburg: Tübingen 2008.

[12] M. Ziefle and E.-M. Jakobs, "New challenges in human computer interaction: Strategic directions and interdisciplinary trends," in Proc. 4th Int. Conf. Competitive Manuf. Technol., pp. 389–398, 2010.

[13] P. Mayring, Qualitative Inhaltsanalyse: Grundlagen und Techniken [Qualitative content analysis: basics and techniques]. Beltz: Weinheim, 2015.

[14] C. Plaisant and B. Shneiderman, „Show Me! Guidelines for Producing Recorded Demonstrations," in Proc. of 2005 IEEE Symposium on Visual Languages and Human-Centric Computing, pp. 171-178, 2005.

[15] H. van der Meij, „Advance organizers in videos for software training of Chinese students," in Britisch Journal of Educational Technology. vol. 50., pp. 1368-1380, 2019.

[16] H. van der Meij, „Developing and Testing a Video Tutorial for Software Training," in Technical Communication. vol. 61. pp. 110-122, 2014.

[17] G. Brenner and C. H. Walter, „Individualized Learning with Instructional Videos in Engineering Simulation Education," in Proc. of 50th Computer Simulation Conference, pp. 1-7, 2018.

[18] P. J. Guo, J. Kim, and R. Rubin, „How Video Production Affects Student Engagement: An Empirical Study of MOOC Videos," in Proc. of the first ACM conference on Learning @ scale conferences, pp. 41-50, 2014.

[19] L. Ponzanelli et al., „Too Long; Didn`t Watch! Extracting Relevant Fragments from Software Development Video Tutorials," in Proc. of the 38th International Conference on Software Engineering, pp. 261-272, 2016.

[20] J. S. Chabura, J.M. Leake, and W. B. Hall, "Development of Instructional Software for Demonstrating CAD/FEA Integration Best Practices", in Proc. Of the 59th Meeting of the Engineering Design Graphics Division of ASEE, pp. 168-176, 2004.

Embodied Conversational Agent for Emotional Recognition Training

Karl Daher*, Zeno Bardelli†, Jacky Casas*, Elena Mugellini*, Omar Abou Khaled* and Denis Lalanne†
*University of Applied Sciences and Arts Western Switzerland, Fribourg, Switzerland
Email: firstname.lastname@hes-so.ch
†University of Fribourg, Switzerland
Email: firstname.lastname@unifr.ch

***Abstract*—Avatars are known in the world of video games, where heroes with specific characters, attributes and powers are assigned to players. However, avatars are evolving and reaching domains like companions, assistants and tutors. These avatars now use speech, facial expression, body language or text to interact with humans. When we say interaction, we say emotional expression and empathy. Avatars are still short in the emotional and empathic world; they cannot express nor share emotions. In this paper, we research the emotional avatar world, and we present the Anthropomorphic Chatbot for Emotion Recognition (ACER), an empathic friend companion designed for children. The goal of ACER is to teach children about emotions by expressing them through facial expressions and body language while texting through a chat. An experiment was held to test the avatar effect. Qualitative and quantitative results show users positive emotions tending towards having a chat with ACER with facial and body expressions instead of only ACERs chatbot.**

Keywords–HCI; ECA; Conversational agent; Avatar; Emotions.

I. INTRODUCTION

Humanising technology, having a human-computer interaction similar to human-human interaction, is driving researchers and companies in recent years to develop Artificial Intelligence (AI). We can mention AI-driven conversational agents, known as chatbots, avatars, assistants, and humanoid robots with human-like functionality and purpose. Chatbots started in 1950 with Alan Turing wondering if a computer system can communicate in an equivalent way as a human [1] which later led to the Turing test used to test AI-driven conversational agents. In practice, chatbots are programs that allow the user to interact with the machine using natural language. Chatbots development is a growing field, especially with intelligent personal assistants like Siri and Cortana, which are well known to most. The applications of those agents are manifold: they can act as virtual assistants to help the users within an online store by answering their questions, or by booking him a flight online to checking their balance of a bank account [2]. There are also great possibilities in the areas of customer service, but also health [3] and coaching [4].

The most common category of chatbots involves interaction via keyboard, through an interface similar in every way to that of a chat program, and the conversation consists of an exchange of orders. However, those characteristics undermine the naturalness of the conversation itself. In a conversation between two human beings, there is much more than just a conversational expression between the two parties. There are numerous communicative behaviours complementary to the meaning of words, divided into two categories, verbal and non-verbal communication. We can cite, for example, the tone, frequency, and amplitude of the voice or pauses between words from the verbal category. On the other hand, the non-verbal communication category beholds other ways of interaction, where it is generally defined as the aspect of communication that is not expressed in words [5]. For example, facial expression, hand gestures, head movements, gaze, and body posture are involuntary and voluntary behaviours that are an integral part of a conversation between two humans.

Chatbots using text as a means of communication convey emotions in a way that is not practicable, albeit the evolution made in chatbots to support emojis and Graphics Interchange Format (GIFs). Nevertheless, these chatbots still fall short of human-human communication; the result of chatbot-human communication is still direct, cold, impersonal, and unrealistic. To overcome these limitations, many people have explored the possibilities provided by Embodied Conversational Agents (in short ECAs). ECAs employ gestures as the body, hands, and legs movements, mimics as the facial expressions macro-micro expressions and speech to communicate with the users [6]. These features make the interaction more realistic and more humanised. However, researchers and developers are still testing prototypes to find the ideal avatar that can be perceived and treated as human by the user. In this vision, the work on including emotions and empathy within machines started to evolve, but yet many drawbacks and dilemmas still exist and need more deepen exploration and examination. Machines should be able to show empathic capabilities and understand its users and their needs [7].

Within the spectrum of avatars, emotions, and chatbots, we present Anthropomorphic Chatbot for Emotion Recognition (ACER), an embodied conversational agent to teach emotion recognition. ACER's long term goal is to become a friend and a tutor. He is designed for kids and people facing difficulties in understanding and expressing emotions. Alexithymia is "conceptualised as a cluster of cognitive traits which include difficulty identifying feelings and difficulty describing feeling to others" [8] and it is present in "approximately 10% of the population with significantly higher incidence levels within autistic populations 50%" [9]. The goal of ACER is to teach how emotions are expressed using facial expressions and body language while using a chat as a communication tool. In this article, we will present the related work for conversational agents and avatar in general, then briefly present empathy and emotions. Moreover, we present avatars that include and use empathy and emotions, and we end with an analysis and synthesis. In Section 3, we present the prototype, where we develop the architecture and its usage. Further, we give the details of the experiment in Section 4, followed by the qualitative and quantitative results in Section 5. We wrap up this article in Section 6 presenting the future work, and the conclusion in Section 7.

II. State of the Art

In the early 2000s, the problem of Embodied Conversational Agents (ECAs) was studied by researchers. Many articles have been written proposing scenarios for the use of such virtual entities and what features they need to have in order to be as credible as possible. In the next sub-sections, we will present research over conversational agents and avatars, following an introduction about empathy and emotions, adding avatars that use empathy and emotions, and ending this section with an analysis and synthesis.

A. Conversational agents and avatars

One of the first conversational agents with an avatar was Gandalf [10]. Gandalf is a virtual humanoid who allows simple conversations. Equipped with a face and a hand, it integrates expressions and gestures in its dialogues. Besides, it reacts adequately to misunderstandings, showing uncertainty and hesitation. Gandalf uses a microphone and sensors to perceive the movement of the user's body and eyes. In this way, it is also able to read non-verbal aspects of communication.

Another early example is Real Estate Agent (Rea) [11][12]. It has a database containing data and images about homes and apartments in Boston. It can then share this information with the user, acting just like a virtual real estate agent. Its creators are committed to providing it with various features to make a conversation with her as natural as possible. It is capable of superficial small talk. It can take a turn during a conversation and also to both use and react to non-verbal communicative behaviours. For example, it can understand when the user raises a hand to ask a question.

A way to design a chatbot with an avatar, speech synthesis, and speech recognition is described by Angga et al. [13]. A conversation takes place as a cycle of separate operations. The user speaks into the microphone, and the program translates the audio into text. At this point, the chatbot API generates the appropriate response, always in the form of text. The text is used both to generate the spoken response and the 3D avatar's behaviour.

The search for realistic behaviour has been the subject of study by Cassell and Vilhàlmsson [14]. In this case, it was not for conversational agents, but rather avatars of users in a three-dimensional virtual world. Important details are the movement of the mouth associated with what is said, the ability to speak and continuous, and involuntary movements like raising eyebrows, head inclination, and blinking eyes. Emotions can also be expressed both by facial expression and body movements. Bringing all these elements together is essential to achieve a credible avatar that can communicate more than just words.

B. Empathy and emotions

Empathy is an essential factor in everyday life; it fosters strong relationships and collaborations between individuals [15]. Machines, robots, chatbots, and avatars that adopt the concept of empathy earn more trust towards the human [16]. The concept of empathy is defined in many ways in research, Omdah divided empathy into two parts, affective empathy, and cognitive empathy [17]. Cognitive empathy is the understanding of other's emotional states, while affective empathy is the response to other emotional states. Another psychological definition of empathy is "putting yourself in the shoes of others", where it is elaborated as taking the position of the other mentally, trying to feel the emotional states he is going through based on personal experience [18]. While Davis defined empathy as the following: "Empathy is a set of constructs having to do with the responses of one individual, to the experiences of another. These constructs specifically include the processes taking place within the observer and the affective and non-affective outcomes, which result from those processes" [19]. When talking about empathy, communication has to be considered, where interaction is included. Roa-Seïler and Craig mention that empathy is an interaction between two individuals who share each other's experiences and feelings [20]. An interaction can cause a continuous development of emotions, thanks to the relationship between the interactants [21] at the same time emotions can affect our behaviours, choices, mood, and our well being in every-days life [22]. Paul Ekman pointed out the six basic categories of emotions that consist of anger, disgust, fear, happiness, sadness, and surprise. These emotions are shared among all humankind around the world and are universal across many cultures [23]. The emotional state of the individual is usually expressed by the face and the body language. However, it becomes biased toward the emotion expressed by the body when both convey conflicting emotional information [24]. Empathy and emotions are two essential research subjects to have an empathic machine.

C. Avatars, empathy and emotions

Modern avatars are starting to include emotions, human-like capabilities, empathy, and emotional behaviours, from the text expressed to the speech tonality, moving towards the gesture shown by the body or the facial expressions that are programmed. However, all still have many drawbacks and major challenges, like shortage of quality training data, the balance between emotion level and content level responses, a fully end-to-end experience, or even modelling emotions throughout conversations [2].

Poggi et al. [25] wrote about Greta, a virtual talking head. It is capable of conducting social conversations. When Greta expresses something, the process of generating behaviour has three phases. First, it generates the sentence with which to respond, based on factors like personality, culture, emotions and age. Then it uses a sort of tag system to identify the right non-verbal behaviour, and finally, it expresses it through her avatar.

It is believed that the display of a conversational agent improves interaction for the user. The reason is that an anthropomorphisation of the chatbot takes place. In order to verify the correctness of the information, an experiment was conducted in which a conversational agent acted as a tutor, instructing users on how to use an interface [26]. In particular, the agent was presented in three formats: with a realistic human avatar, with a monkey cartoon-like avatar, and without an avatar. In both cases with the avatar, the agent proved to be more efficient.

The usefulness of ECAs in Clinical Psychology is being studied [27]. The field is in an early stage, so there are mostly prototypes not ready for evaluation. Most of the proposed treatments deal with autism, particularly for training social skills. It is not yet clear whether ECAs are effective, but there

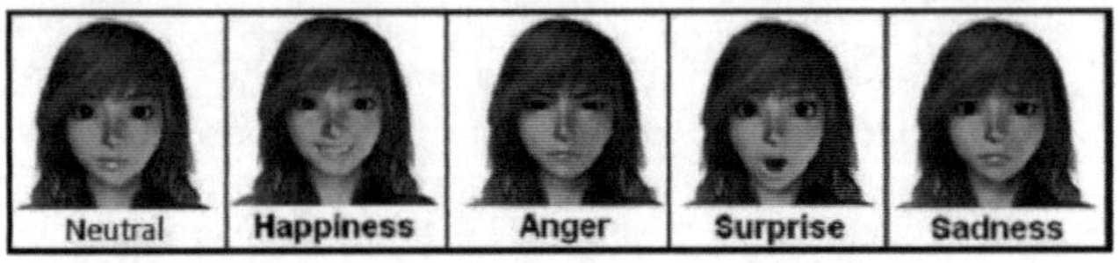

Figure 1. Facial expressions of the avatar [32]

is certainly a great interest in developing new technologies of this kind.

However, the display of a virtual agent is not always considered positive. A very realistic appearance can influence users' expectations upwards. The more advanced it seems, the more complex and realistic the interaction is expected to be. When these expectations are regularly disappointed, the impression on the agent is very negative [28]. Moreover, according to another study, it turns out that users can better receive a chatbot without an avatar because it does not cause the famous uncanny valley effect [29].

Samuela, another avatar developed by Roa-Seïler [30], has the purpose of being part of the "home of the future", it lives with the owner and can deliver comfort and encouragement. A cooking companion application was developed using Samuela allowing people to choose between different dishes. Samuela has a female face and style. It has a pretty character, a female voice. It is emotionally expressive, can respond to questions, is useful, helpful in every-days life, and acts like a companion. Samuela is excepted to have human behaviour [20].

An empathic companion was developed at the National Institute of Informatics in Tokyo, Japan [31]. This companion consists of a character-based interface that is used to accompany the user in the setting of a virtual job interview. The user physiological signals are taken into consideration in real-time, and the response of this interface is the states that the human is going through. These states are analysed from the physiological signals.

In 2012, a pedagogical agent was developed [32]. This agent has characteristics like facial expressions and body gestures. The users used the mouse-clicking to interact with the avatar while reading, and the avatar motivates them accordingly. The purpose of the avatar was to motivate and encourage the user to make more reading effort. The facial expressions of the avatar can be seen in Figure 1.

The technology aims towards solving practical problems we face. The research was developed for the people who have schizophrenia, who have difficulties in recognising emotions in other facial expressions. These difficulties decrease their abilities for social interaction and thus their integration. For this purpose, the authors created a virtual realistic-looking avatar for assessment of emotion recognition deficit. The experiment held took into consideration the avatar and static images into the recognition of the set of facial expressions [33].

Another important domain where researchers are trying to find solutions is eldercare. The goal is to automate and facilitate elderly lives and at the same time, keep emotional bonding and empathic interactions around them. A research was conducted to create an autonomous conversational agent system that can simulate human-like affective behaviour and act as a daily companion for adults at home. This avatar includes speech recognition, text to speech, and a graphical touch interface. The primary purpose of the companion is to support older adults with many functionalities like locating objects, creating reminders, and orientations with household activities [34].

These days with the technology evolving and the ability to create applications on the Apple App Store or Google Play Store, we find many applications that were developed to help children with difficulty in recognising emotions. In particular, there are several applications for smartphones and tablets that set themselves precisely this goal. Sung et al. [35] did research work testing the various iOS and Android applications available, in particular about facial emotion recognition. Here are a few examples:

- Autimo (developed by Auticiel) offers three different mini-games: associate photos of people with the same expressions, find a different expression among many and guess the emotion shown in a photo.
- CopyMe (developed by Games Studio) uses the web-cam to asks the user to mimic the expression shown in a simple picture.
- Emotions 2 (developed by I Can Do App) contains images of people with different expressions. With these images, it offers five types of exercises, including associating the photos to a scenario or a label based on a scenario.

The essential features for these applications are ease of use and immediate feedback, to keep the user's interest and degree of gratification high.

D. Analysis and Synthesis

In this state of the art, a review was created on many conversational agents and avatars, targeting mainly the avatars developed with emotion and empathic interaction. Each of the systems presented has its advantages as well as disadvantages. With the advancement of the technology, these avatars will continue to develop and become more complex, especially in their graphical side as well as their conversational and understanding capabilities, moving towards human-like companions. The research conducted led that the world of avatars is advancing since its early days. Now, this advancement will keep evolving; we can see that some of the oldest companions use text as a way of communication and interaction. On the other, we find others avatars that use static images to represent facial expressions.

Moreover, videos have been used to support facial or body movements. Lately, we found agents that use body gestures and facial expressions combined. The aim is to combine all interaction techniques to make avatars as affective and human-like as possible. For that, in the next section, we will present ACER, an avatar designed for kids, that fusion the communication and interaction techniques used by the human. ACER utilise facial and body language as well as text chats to interact with the user. ACER aims to become a tutor to teach kids about emotions and how is it expressed in the face and the body language while interacting using text. ACER is designed to have different interaction methods combining the multiple methods seen in state of the art. ACER is designed to become a friend able to handle a conversation about specific topics and expressing it through emotional responses using his empathic behaviour.

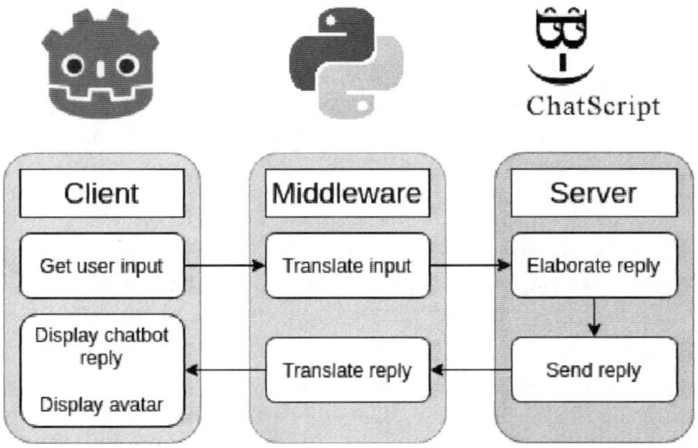

Figure 2. Architecture of ACER, role of its components and message exchange via TCP tunnel. The logos from left to right represent the Godot Game Engine, the language Python and the ChatScript Engine.

III. THE PROTOTYPE ACER

ACER is an embodied conversational agent whose task is to help children to train themselves to recognize emotions. Its name is an acronym for Anthropomorphic Chatbot for Emotion Recognition. It can show six emotions: calm, happiness, anger, sadness, fear, and disgust. ACER is still a prototype; its purpose is to show how such software could work and to provide a complete framework from which to start. In the following sections, we will first describe the architecture of the prototype and then explain how it works in practice.

A. Architecture

ACER runs on Linux operating systems and consists of three software running at the same time. They are a local server that hosts the chatbot, a client and middleware to communicate between the two. Communication between the parties is done via Transmission Control Protocol (TCP). Figure 2 summarises the architecture and the exchange of messages. It also indicates the language or engine used to develop the components.

The task of the server is to host the chatbot. In practice, it is the place where user input is examined, and answers are processed. To write the server for ACER, ChatScript, a powerful chatbot engine, was used. ChatScript is a free and open-source chatbot engine created and maintained by Bruce Wilcox. Among its salient features are natural language processing, relatively compact and clean syntax, word generalisation, topic encapsulation, and pattern matching. The server manages both ACER's replies and emotions. The emotion model is still basic. In practice, each response that the chatbot can give is tagged with an emotion corresponding to it. Since the bot communicates in plain text, the convention is that each response begins with a 3-letter tag that indicates the emotion. In addition, the 4th character is a hyphen to improve readability while browsing the chatbot script file.

To develop the client, we used Godot, a free and open-source game engine. The reasons for using a game engine are the availability of means both to create an interface and to display an avatar and the ease of interaction between the different components. The client basically takes care of receiving the user's input to send it to the chatbot and show the response. It can be divided into three components: the chat,

Figure 3. The chatbot client showing a calm ACER conversating with the user.

Figure 4. Guess the emotion? The facial expressions of ACER from left to right, top to bottom: calm, happiness, sadness, anger, fear, disgust.

the avatar, and the window that is prompted when asking the user to match the facial expression with the emotion of ACER. The first two of those components are shown in Figure 3.

The chat looks like a classic client. At the bottom, there is space to input text messages and send it, while above a scrollable window for messages history. Each time a message is sent or received the scrollbar reaches the bottom. The bot messages have a different colour.

The avatar is a kid with a hat and glasses. Its cartoon look is meant to appeal to children. Depending on the emotion it simulates, it adopts a different animation for the expression of the emotions. In addition to animations related to emotions, it has one to greet the user when he opens the program or is about to leave. The emotion and animation switching is triggered when the client receives a message from the server. We check the tag contained in the reply, and if it corresponds to an emotion different than the current one, the switch happens. The 3D model and its animations have been downloaded from Mixamo, a store of 3D models. Adobe Incorporated created them. However, due to compatibility issues, the avatar that the user sees in the client window is not a three-dimensional model. These are pre-rendered images, so it is actually a two-dimensional animation.

The last component of the client is the window mentioned above (see Figure 4). When it appears, the user must click on the face with the expression associated with the emotion simulated by the avatar. The window appears when the bot changes emotion and is positioned so that neither the last text received nor the avatar is hidden. After the user clicks, a symbol appears to immediately give feedback on whether the answer was correct (green check) or not (red cross).

Finally, there is the middleware written in Python. Since ChatScript only receives messages in a specific format that it is not clear if achievable using GDScript, Godot's scripting language, this program receives messages from the client and adapts them for the server. It also takes care of restarting the server, selecting the right chatbot, and building it.

B. *Usage*

In order to run ACER, it is necessary to run the three software separately in the following order: server, middleware, and client. From here on, the user needs to watch only the client. After a few seconds of loading, the client opens, showing ACER greeting the user with both gestures and text message. At this point, the conversation can begin. Every time ACER changes emotion based on the text, the avatar will show a different animation, and a window will appear asking the user to compare a facial expression with the current body language expression of the bot in addition to the discussion context. The top left corner shows the results of the session, indicating how many correct answers and the number of questions there were.

The interface is designed to be intuitive and straightforward so that a child can use it. The only interactive elements are the window to enter text and faces of the bot with expressions when it pops-up. Regarding the recognition of non-verbal communication, ACER works on three levels.

The idea is to have a conversation as natural as possible, in any subject possible, yet for this prototype, the subjects were limited for more accuracy during the experiment. ACER tries to lead the conversation so that it is clear to the user what kind of answers they can give. For example, it gives multiple options or asks questions that can only be answered by yes or no. Below is a small example of the discussion that can be held with ACER.

IV. EXPERIMENT

In order to subject ACER to an initial test, we conducted an experiment with 20 users. This preliminary study aimed at testing the user experience, the prototype testing was conducted with people aged between 21 and 30 years old that were recruited from the authors' circle of acquaintance. This group of people was chosen for a mature evaluation of the first prototype. In particular, we were interested in the empathic and emotional reactions of the users. The goal of this test was to verify the added value of the avatar by analysing the user experience. Due to COVID-19 lockdown circumstances in Switzerland, test sessions were organised remotely via desktop sharing and video conferencing software. Future testing will be conducted on children to evaluate the effectiveness of the system.

The experiment consists of using ACER for five minutes with two different modes. The first mode includes the usage of ACER chatbot only, by that we mean the user will have a chat with ACER without having any facial or body language responses. ACER will be changing his emotions based on the discussion and the user will have to guess which emotions ACER is having. The chats were aimed at certain subjects to reduce the scope, and not have a haphazard discussion.

The second mode includes ACER's facial expressions as well as its body language. The user will be able to chat with ACER, but this time ACER will share its emotions through facial and body language expressions. Whenever ACER changes emotion, the user will have to know which emotion ACER is expressing. In this way, ACER will be able to tutor the user using it about how emotions are expressed. The chat is part of the prototype, as described in Section III. Thus, in this experiment, the facial and body expressions were removed. Since the situation is quite unusual during the COVID19 crisis, the tests were carried out remotely using a videoconferencing tool.

After each mode, each of the users was asked to fill a survey which evaluates the qualitative and quantitative aspects of the emotions felt towards ACER. Positive and negative emotions are to be evaluated in the next section. For the quantitative survey, meCUE 2.0 [36] questionnaire was used to evaluate the key components of the user experience. On the other hand, another survey was prepared to understand the qualitative emotional effects of the embodied ACER chatbot compared to the text-only ACER chatbot.

V. RESULTS

In this section, we present the results of the experience which hold the meCUE 2.0 [36] questionnaire for the quantitative analysis and the qualitative survey where users are asked about their personal interaction with ACER. Details can be found in Table I. The questionnaire meCUE 2.0 is dedicated to the user experience of interactive technical products, in our case ACER. The questionnaire is divided into multiple modules; we are interested in module III User emotions to study the emotional effect of the body language and facial expressions addition to ACERs chatbot.

A. *Qualitative Analysis*

A questionnaire about how ACER is perceived was submitted to the subjects. They had to state if they agree with several sentences with respect to the chatbot without the avatar and the chatbot with it. The questions and the distribution of answers are summarised in Table I.

In general, it can be seen how the avatar version has generated better impressions for each of the sentences. 90% of the users thought that learning from the avatar has a positive effect, while only 35% stated the same for the text-based chatbot. More than half of the users said that the interaction with ACER is natural in both cases, showing appreciation for how easy it is to converse with a chatbot. Still, the percentages scored are 55% without the avatar and 80% with the avatar. The 95%, respectively the 75% of the users said that the chatbot with avatar has a personality, respectively looks clever and competent. Those numbers are 35%, respectively 35% for the chatbot without avatar. To 10 people over 20, the chatbot without avatar is boring, but only one person said the same about the chatbot with the avatar. Finally, the text-based conversational agent looked emotionless to 75% of the users, while the embodied conversational agent only made that impression in 20% of the subjects.

B. *Quantitative Analysis*

According to the measurements made with module III of the meCUE 2.0 questionnaire, the chatbot with the avatar

TABLE I. SUBJECTS WERE ASKED IF THEY AGREE WITH THOSE SENTENCES WITH RESPECT TO THE CHATBOT WITHOUT AVATAR AND THE CHATBOT WITH AVATAR.

Sentence to agree with	No Avatar	Avatar
Learning from ACER has a positive effect.	35%	90%
The interaction with ACER is natural.	55%	80%
ACER has personality.	35%	95%
ACER looks clever and competent.	35%	75%
ACER is boring.	50%	5%
ACER looks emotionless.	75%	20%

causes more positive emotions and less negative emotions in users. In terms of mean and standard deviation, over a scale of 7, the results were the following: positive emotions without avatar $\bar{x} = 3.31$, SD= 1.26, with avatar $\bar{x} = 3.37$, SD= 1.25; negative emotions without avatar $\bar{x} = 2.14$, SD= 0.84, with avatar $\bar{x} = 1.95$, SD= 1.10. We also performed two-tailed t-test with $p = 0.05$ to verify if the difference is statistically significant. For positive emotions, we obtained that the t-value is 0.20283, while the p-value is 0.840349. For negative emotions, we obtained that the t-value is 0.45388, while the p-value is 0.652497. There is no statistical difference. Even if the avatar with the body language and facial expressions achieved a better result, we could not state that it is better than the text-based chat. One of the reasons for not achieving a statistical result might be the small population size.

Nevertheless, the overall analysis shows a mean result of 2.0 over 5 for the text-based avatar, while embodied ACER had an overall score of 2.9 over 5. This difference is presented in different metrics and features received from the questionnaire, first in terms of usability we can see a clear difference between a 4.68 and a 5.63 score over 7 for the usability of the embodied agent over the text-based. Another feature, commitment shows a 4.08 for text-based and 4.62 for embodied ACER.

The results of the meCUE questionnaire show that all the features of the embodied ACER received a score higher than the text-based ACER. More participants will be recruited in the future to have a larger dataset and more precise result.

VI. CONCLUSION AND FUTURE WORK

In this article, we researched avatars that use emotions and empathy for defined purposes. From state of the art, we were able to synthesise that it is still a growing field and research is yet improving and developing. Avatars, among all other technologies, still fall short when compared to humans. With the aim of humanising technology, these avatars need to have human abilities each in their way based on its purpose. Avatars in state of the art use many ways of communication like text, speech, facial expression or body language sometimes these techniques are combined.

In the aim of having empathic avatars, avatars that can express its emotions based on the context of a conversation, we designed ACER, a friend and a tutor. ACER, the Anthropomorphic Chatbot for Emotion Recognition training, a companion with a tutoring purpose is designed to train humans to understand the emotional expressivity of the facial and body language while chatting with a chatbot. The design of ACER was made to be easy to use and easy to understand. An experiment was conducted where the user is asked to connect body language and facial expressions emotions according to the conversation being held. Quantitative and qualitative results show that the users tend to have a conversation with ACER with its body and facial representation rather than only ACER text-based chat. Although still in the prototype stage, ACER has all the bases to grow.

Inspired by several smartphone applications, ACER is proposed as a new tool to help people, and children in particular, with difficulty in reading non-verbal language. ACER allows them to relate expression, body language, and context of a discussion. As a next step towards improving user experience and testing, ACER will be tested with kids and people facing emotion recognition problems to improve the quality of interaction. ACER provides a solid foundation; many technical improvements are set for development. First, we will start with the chatbot, where the server will have more fluency and broader topic scope discussions. More into chat, ACER will be designed to have an empathic behaviour when discussing with the user, being able to analyse the emotion that the user is feeling through the text provided. Another improvement that we are aiming for is to make ACER personalised. For example, it will save the discussions for each user, analyse and learn from them. First, the chatbot brain will develop over time, and the second analysis will be made to see the progression of the user. Design-wise, we would like to improve the ACERs presentation by personalising the shape of ACER and the design of the application. Quizzes and games will be integrated for long term interaction purposes. In this way, the user will be able to get rewarded as well as test his abilities. Levels and complexity of the game and quiz will be adapted to the learning process and capabilities of the user. Another fundamental tool that we would like to add is speech recognition, where the user will be able to interact with ACER either through text or using speech. From a more technical point of view, it would be interesting to port the program to other operating systems and devices, in particular on smartphones, since they are the most accessible devices by kids. A design for ACER on a smartphone will be needed because of privacy concerns and performance matters of smartphones.

Another point that is set for the future is to replace the pre-rendered animations with a real three-dimensional model. It would allow a smooth scrolling between the animations thanks to interpolation, and above all, it would make the program smaller in terms of size on disk. Indeed, many images are needed to maintain high-quality animations. The loading time would also be faster. Finally, we can imagine these three-dimensional models to be rendered in the virtual world using Virtual Reality (VR) where ACER will be having more specifications as height and size and having more real interaction with the user.

REFERENCES

[1] A. M. Turing, "Computing machinery and intelligence," in Parsing the turing test. Springer, 2009, pp. 23–65.

[2] T. Spring, J. Casas, K. Daher, E. Mugellini, and O. Abou Khaled, "Empathic response generation in chatbots." in SwissText, 2019.

[3] K. Daher, J. Casas, O. Abou Khaled, and E. Mugellini, "Empathic chatbot response for medical assistance," in Proceedings of the 20th ACM International Conference on Intelligent Virtual Agents, 2020, unpublished.

[4] J. Casas, E. Mugellini, and O. A. Khaled, "Food diary coaching chatbot," in Proceedings of the 2018 ACM International Joint Conference and 2018 International Symposium on Pervasive and Ubiquitous Computing and Wearable Computers, 2018, pp. 1676–1680.

[5] U. Hess, "Nonverbal communication," Encyclopedia of Mental Health, 12 2016.

[6] E. Andre and C. Pelachaud, Interacting with Embodied Conversational Agents, 07 2010, pp. 123–149.

[7] K. Daher, M. Fuchs, E. Mugellini, D. Lalanne, and O. Abou Khaled, "Reduce stress through empathic machine to improve hci," in International Conference on Human Interaction and Emerging Technologies. Springer, 2020, pp. 232–237.

[8] L. Ricciardi, B. Demartini, A. Fotopoulou, and M. Edwards, "Alexithymia in neurological disease: A review," The Journal of neuropsychiatry and clinical neurosciences, vol. 27, 02 2015, p. appineuropsych14070169.

[9] J. R. Absher and J. Cloutier, Neuroimaging personality, social cognition, and character. Academic Press, 2016.

[10] K. R. Thórisson, "Gandalf: An embodied humanoid capable of real-time multimodal dialogue with people," in First ACM International Conference on Autonomous Agents, 1997, pp. 536–537.

[11] J. Cassell, "More than just another pretty face: Embodied conversational interface agents," Communications of the ACM, vol. 43, no. 4, 2000, pp. 70–78.

[12] T. Bickmore and J. Cassell, "Social dialogue with embodied conversational agents," in Advances in natural multimodal dialogue systems. Springer, 2005, pp. 23–54.

[13] P. A. Angga, W. E. Fachri, A. Elevanita, R. D. Agushinta et al., "Design of chatbot with 3d avatar, voice interface, and facial expression," in 2015 International Conference on Science in Information Technology (ICSITech). IEEE, 2015, pp. 326–330.

[14] J. Cassell and H. Vilhjálmsson, "Fully embodied conversational avatars: Making communicative behaviors autonomous," Autonomous agents and multi-agent systems, vol. 2, no. 1, 1999, pp. 45–64.

[15] A. Paiva, I. Leite, H. Boukricha, and I. Wachsmuth, "Empathy in virtual agents and robots: a survey," ACM Transactions on Interactive Intelligent Systems (TiiS), vol. 7, no. 3, 2017, p. 11.

[16] S. Brave, C. Nass, and K. Hutchinson, "Computers that care: investigating the effects of orientation of emotion exhibited by an embodied computer agent," International journal of human-computer studies, vol. 62, no. 2, 2005, pp. 161–178.

[17] B. L. Omdahl, Cognitive appraisal, emotion, and empathy. Psychology Press, 2014.

[18] L. Rameson and M. Lieberman, "Empathy: A social cognitive neuroscience approach," Social and Personality Psychology Compass, vol. 3, 01 2009, pp. 94 – 110.

[19] M. H. Davis, Empathy: A social psychological approach. Routledge, 2018.

[20] N. R. Seïler and P. Craig, "Empathetic technology," in Emotions, Technology, and Design. Elsevier, 2016, pp. 55–81.

[21] C. Marinetti, P. Moore, P. Lucas, and B. Parkinson, Emotions in Social Interactions: Unfolding Emotional Experience, 10 2011, pp. 31–46.

[22] R. J. Dolan, "Emotion, cognition, and behavior," science, vol. 298, no. 5596, 2002, pp. 1191–1194.

[23] P. Ekmann, "Universal facial expressions in emotion," Studia Psychologica, vol. 15, no. 2, 1973, p. 140.

[24] H. Meeren, C. Heijnsbergen, and B. Gelder, "Rapid perceptual integration of facial expression and emotional body language," Proceedings of the National Academy of Sciences of the United States of America, vol. 102, 12 2005, pp. 16 518–23.

[25] I. Poggi, C. Pelachaud, F. de Rosis, V. Carofiglio, and B. De Carolis, "Greta. a believable embodied conversational agent," in Multimodal intelligent information presentation. Springer, 2005, pp. 3–25.

[26] R.-J. Beun, E. De Vos, and C. Witteman, "Embodied conversational agents: effects on memory performance and anthropomorphisation," in International Workshop on Intelligent Virtual Agents. Springer, 2003, pp. 315–319.

[27] S. Provoost, H. M. Lau, J. Ruwaard, and H. Riper, "Embodied conversational agents in clinical psychology: a scoping review," Journal of medical Internet research, vol. 19, no. 5, 2017, p. e151.

[28] M. S. B. Mimoun, I. Poncin, and M. Garnier, "Case study—embodied virtual agents: An analysis on reasons for failure," Journal of Retailing and Consumer services, vol. 19, no. 6, 2012, pp. 605–612.

[29] L. Ciechanowski, A. Przegalinska, M. Magnuski, and P. Gloor, "In the shades of the uncanny valley: An experimental study of human–chatbot interaction," Future Generation Computer Systems, vol. 92, 2019, pp. 539–548.

[30] N. Roa-Seïler, P. Craig, J. A. Arias, A. B. Saucedo, M. M. Díaz, and F. L. Rosano, "Defining a childs conceptualization of a virtual learning companion," in INTED2014 Proceedings. IATED, 2014, pp. 2992–2996.

[31] H. Prendinger and M. Ishizuka, "The empathic companion: A character-based interface that addresses users' affective states," Applied Artificial Intelligence, vol. 19, 03 2005, pp. 267–285.

[32] G.-D. Chen, J.-H. Lee, C.-Y. Wang, P.-Y. Chao, L.-Y. Li, and T.-Y. Lee, "An empathic avatar in a computer-aided learning program to encourage and persuade learners," Journal of Educational Technology & Society, vol. 15, no. 2, 2012, pp. 62–72.

[33] S. Marcos-Pablos, E. González-Pablos, C. Martín-Lorenzo, L. A. Flores, J. Gómez-García-Bermejo, and E. Zalama, "Virtual avatar for emotion recognition in patients with schizophrenia: A pilot study," Frontiers in human neuroscience, vol. 10, 2016, p. 421.

[34] C. Tsiourti, M. B. Moussa, J. Quintas, B. Loke, I. Jochem, J. A. Lopes, and D. Konstantas, "A virtual assistive companion for older adults: design implications for a real-world application," in Proceedings of SAI Intelligent Systems Conference. Springer, 2016, pp. 1014–1033.

[35] A. Sung, A. Bai, J. Bowen, B. Xu, L. Bartlett, J. Sanchez, M. Chin, L. Poirier, M. Blinkhorn, A. Campbell et al., "From the small screen to the big world: mobile apps for teaching real-world face recognition to children with autism," Advanced Health Care Technologies, vol. 1, 2015, pp. 37–45.

[36] M. Minge, M. Thüring, I. Wagner, and C. V. Kuhr, "The mecue questionnaire: a modular tool for measuring user experience," in Advances in Ergonomics Modeling, Usability & Special Populations. Springer, 2017, pp. 115–128.

3D Virtual Try-On System Using Personalized Avatars: Augmented Walking in the Real World

Yuhan Liu[1], Yuzhao Liu[1], Shihui Xu[1], Jingyi Yuan[1], Xitong Sun[1], Kelvin Cheng[2], Soh Masuko[2] and Jiro Tanaka[1]
[1] Waseda University, Kitakyushu, Japan
[2] Rakuten Institute of Technology, Rakuten, Inc., Tokyo, Japan
E-mail: liuyuhan-op@akane.waseda.jp, liuyuzhao131@akane.waseda.jp, shxu@toki.waseda.jp, jingyyuan@toki.waseda.jp, sunxitong@akane.waseda.jp, kelvin.cheng@rakuten.com, so.masuko@rakuten.com, jiro@aoni.waseda.jp

Abstract— **Despite the convenience offered by e-commerce websites for consumers to purchase clothes online, consumers still have difficulties imagining what they might look like. To address this problem, we propose a holographic 3D virtual try-on system that enables users a novel experience where they can view garments fitted onto their own personalized virtual body. The garment models are generated from the garment images from online shopping websites. Users can animate their dressed virtual body in a real-life scene in Augmented Reality. We have conducted a user study to compare our proposed system with an image-only shopping system and have validated the effectiveness of our system.**

Keywords-Virtual try-on; Virtual garment modeling; Augmented reality.

I. INTRODUCTION

With the continuous development of e-commerce technology, the number of consumers purchasing clothes online is increasing [1]. Consumers usually have the desire to try on garments in order to assess if they are suitable or not before purchasing. However, when shopping online, consumers have the problem of not being able to try them on. They might worry how well the clothes will fit on their own body. Furthermore, it is difficult for customers to imagine what they might look like with various postures (i.e., standing, walking, posing, etc.) or in different settings.

To address these problems, we propose a 3D virtual try-on system using personalized models (Figure 1). (a) We generate the virtual model of users based on their own body and face information. (b) We gather some garment information and realize the 3D garment visualization using Cloth-weaver [5]. (c) We customize the garment model for each user and match the garment model to their personalized virtual avatar. (d) We enable users to view their own personalized body model fitted with virtual garment. (e) These models can also be visualized in a real-life scene and together with animated motions. To understand the user's acceptability, we conducted a user study to evaluate the value and convenience of our system.

The main contributions of this paper can be summarized as follows:

- Virtual garment models generation based on online garment images;
- A method for users to view the virtual garment interactively and immersively in 360 degrees and enabling users to check the garment by augmenting the motion of a personalized user body in the real-world.

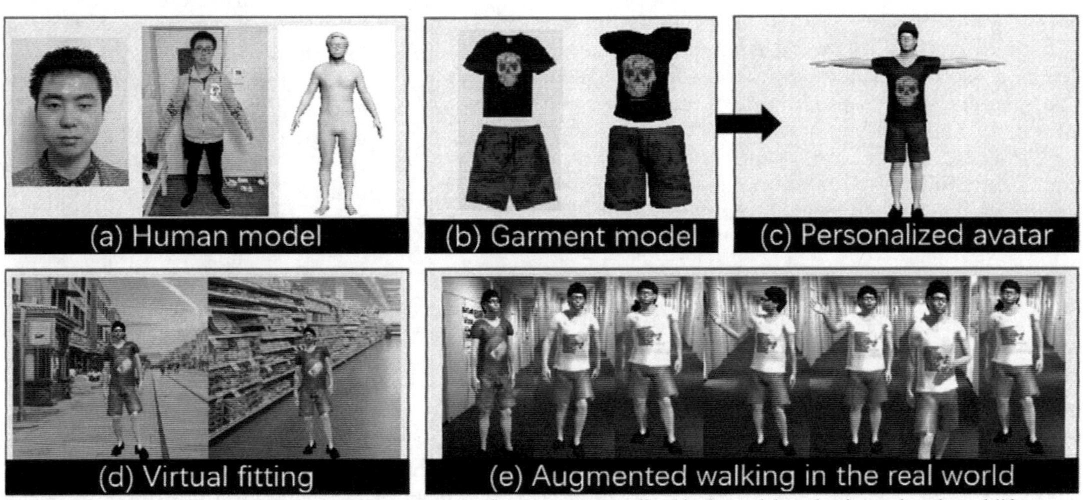

Figure 1. Our system allows users to view virtual garment fitted onto personalized body models and animate them in real-life scene.

The rest of the paper is organized as follows. In Section 2, a brief review of previous research on 3D virtual try-on, garment modeling and virtual avatar is presented. In Section 3, we describe the system design, including human model personalization, garment model generation and 3D virtual try-on system. In Section 4, we present our evaluation result. In Section 5, we conclude our paper with a brief summary and discusses future work.

II. RELATED WORK

A. *Virtual try-on*

Earlier work on virtual try-on are mostly conducted in computer graphics [11][12][14]. Previous work focused on two types of virtual try-on: 2D overlay virtual try-on and 3D virtual try-on.

- **2D overlay virtual try-on**:
  Hilsmann et al. [15] retextured garment overlay for real-time visualization of garments in a virtual mirror environment. Yamada et al. [2] proposed a method of reshaping the garment image based on human body shapes to make fitting more realistic. However, like many other retexturing approaches, they operate only in 2D without using 3D information in any way, which lacked the ability for users to view their virtual self from arbitrary viewpoints.

- **3D virtual try-on**: 3D garment models perform precise garment simulation rather than just a 2D overlay. Protopsaltou et al. [20] created a virtual dressing room, where customers can view garments fitted onto their virtual body. Li et al. [21] proposed a multi-part 3D garment model reconstruction method to generate virtual garments for virtual fitting on virtual avatars.

Recently, virtual try-on combined with Augmented Reality (AR) or Virtual Reality (VR) technologies can give consumers a more realistic try-on experience. Consumers can get a better sense of what they look like when wearing the products. Several fashion firms utilized AR technology in the form of a mobile application, including Uniqlo and Gap [22]. Using VR technology, consumers can feel like they are physically in a virtual fitting room. Several fashion retailers have provided this kind of shopping experience, such as Alibaba and Dior [22].

B. *Garment modeling*

Unlike 2D images, 3D garment model performs precise garment simulation. Most garment modeling works focus on modeling 3D garment for a virtual character. Some garment-retargeting methods transform garment designs from one character to another. For example, Pons-Moll et al. introduced a system using multi-part 3D model of clothed bodies for clothing extraction and retargeting the clothing to new body shapes [16]. Pattern-based methods simulate the garment creation process in real life, while garment modeling tools, such as Marverlous Designer [25], offer garment modeling and editing in pattern design. Pattern-based methods require professional knowledge of garment design and are difficult for non-experts. To address the problem of digitizing garments, Zhou et al. created virtual garments from a single image [10]. Chen et al. captured real garment with a depth camera and built a coarse shape from its raw RGBD sequence using the RGB color information and depth information [17].

C. *Virtual Avatar*

Most virtual try-on systems provide virtual fitting experiences on a default virtual avatar, rather than one generated from user's own body [13]. The default virtual avatar can be modified by users based on the individual preferences and could be personalized if the consumers upload their facial image [23][24]. This type of virtual avatar does not reflect consumers' true body shape.

The absence of "true fit" may disappoint customers when shopping online. For our system, we propose to create virtual personalized models for each user, which can reflect their body shape and facial appearance, making their try-on experience more accurate, engaging, and increasing the customer's confidence when making purchasing decisions on garments online.

III. SYSTEM DESIGN

Our 3D virtual try-on system is composed of human model personalization, garment model generation and 3D virtual try-on.

1) *Human model personalization:* we personalize users virtual avatar using their face image and 360-degree body shape video. 2D face image is used for generating a face model of users, while 360-degree body shape video is used for generating the body model of the user. We then integrate the body model and face model into their personalized virtual avatar.
2) *Garment model generation:* in order to provide users a better visualization of online clothes, we generate 3D virtual garments based on 2D images of clothes. To realize 3D garment visualization, we map the garment texture to prepared garment model templates.
3) *3D virtual try-on:* we combine VR (Virtual Reality) and AR (Augmented Reality) technology to simulate try-on experience for users.
   - **VR fitting:** users can view their personalized avatar fitting different clothes in several virtual scenes.
   - **Augmented walking**: users can view their avatar doing daily life activity in their real environment.

Figure 2 gives an overview of our proposed system pipeline. Our system uses three elements as input: a single face image with a full-frontal face, a short video of the user's full body, and a 2D garment image from online shopping websites.

- *Garment model generation:* (a) Mapping the 2D garment image into the 3D garment model templates and generating the 3D garment model based on online images.
- *Human model personalization*: (b) Generating the 3D human model based on the face image and recorded video.
- *3D virtual try-on:* (c) Matching the 3D garment model to the human model. (d) **VR fitting:** Users choose different clothes to try on. Users can change the pose and animation of the human model in different virtual scenes. **Augmented walking**: Users can animate personalized virtual body walking or do some natural activities in the real world.

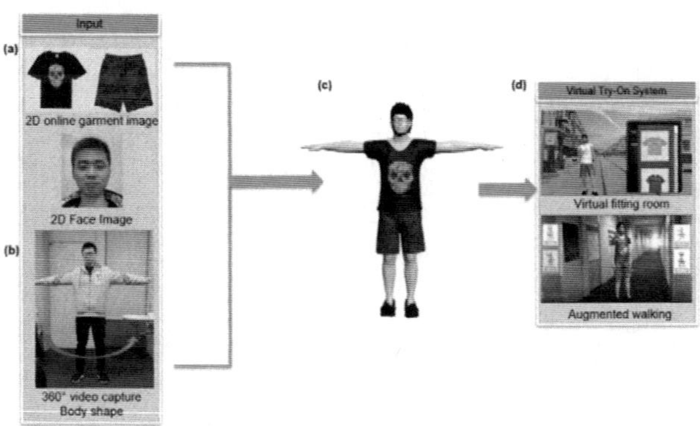

Figure 2. System Overview

A. Human Model Personalization

Due to the lack of "physical fitting" in online shopping experience, consumers may have a gap between actual and perceived body size, which may make it difficult to examine "true fit" on their own body and influence their purchase selection while shopping online. Therefore, virtual human body should have an appropriate 3D representation corresponding to the real user's human body shape and face features. This would give a better representation of the user and allows for a more accurate clothes fitting, as well as for virtual human body animation. We generate human body models based on Alldieck's work [4] and generate face models based on Deng's method [3]. Also, a hair model library is prepared, and the most similar hair model is matched to the face model we generated.

B. Garment Model Generation

In order to provide users with better garment product visualization, we allow users to view garments from various angles and directions when users are shopping online. Our approach uses garment image information from existing shopping websites (i.e., H&M [18], Zara [19]) to create a virtual garment library. Textures are extracted from the garment image and mapped onto the 3D garment model. The final 3D garment is shown in Figure 3. We mainly focus on these two parts: garment model templates used in our system and 3D modeling and texturing approaches.

Figure 3. Generate 3D garment model based on the information from shopping website.

1) 3D Garment Model Templates

Garments are created using the traditional 2D pattern approach. We build several 3D templates of virtual garment models for the personalized human model using Cloth Weaver, which is a Blender template library. It allows us to simulate the methods of traditional garment designs. The 2D pattern is discretized into a triangular mesh. Next, we can design and modify the 2D pattern, and then use the reference line to automatically fit the flat pattern to the corresponding part of the body (Figure 4).

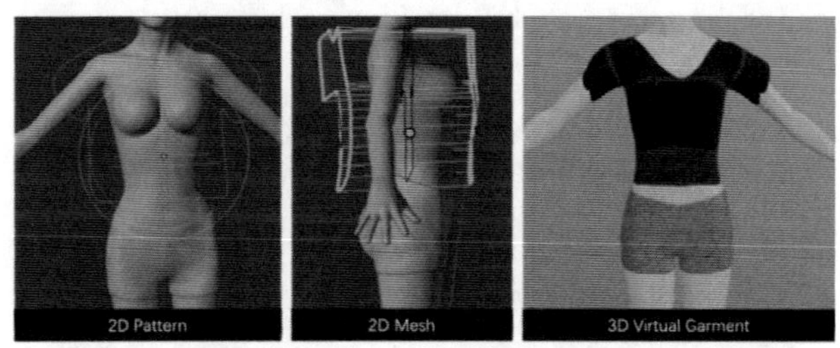

Figure 4. 2D patterns creation and positioning around generic body.

These are used as the basis for creating a variety of garment models (Figure 5). We simulated several types of clothing for female bodies and male bodies. For females, we prepare them with long sleeves, T-shirt, long pants, dress and skirt for fitting. For males, we prepare them with t-shirts, long sleeves and half pants for fitting.

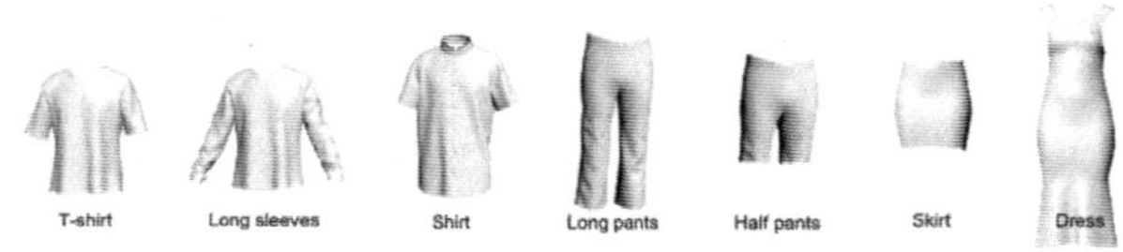

Figure 5. Some 3D garment templates provided for users

2) Texture Mapping

We collected garment images from existing shopping websites (H&M, ZARA, etc.) and mapped these clothes images to generated 3D garment model templates (Figure 6). We segmented different parts of the garment from a single garment image. The segmented clothes can be divided into three main parts: left sleeves, right sleeves, and the front of clothes. The 3D mesh of a generated garment template can be extended into a 2D reference mesh in 3ds Max [26]. To map the Web garment image into a 3D virtual garment template, we map the different segmentation parts from the garments image to its corresponding parts on the garment template. In this way, we can generate 3D garment model with texture.

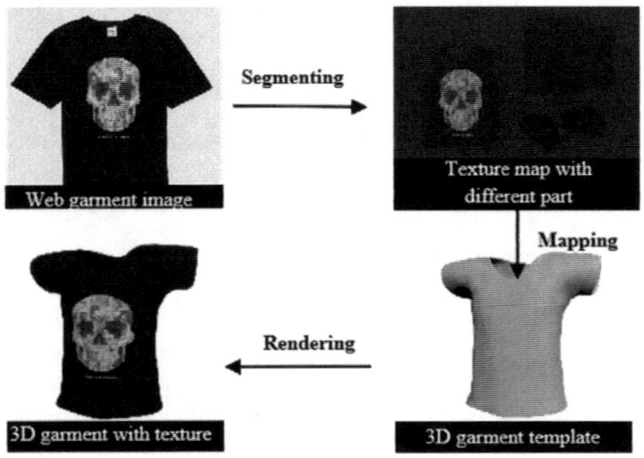

Figure 6. Mapping Web garment image to generated 3D garment templates

The garment can be customized in various ways to match the desired design. The most obvious change is the customization of appearance and color, which is achieved by modifying the texture of the cloth. Therefore, we collected garment images from online shopping websites as textures and created a garment model library for users (Figure 7).

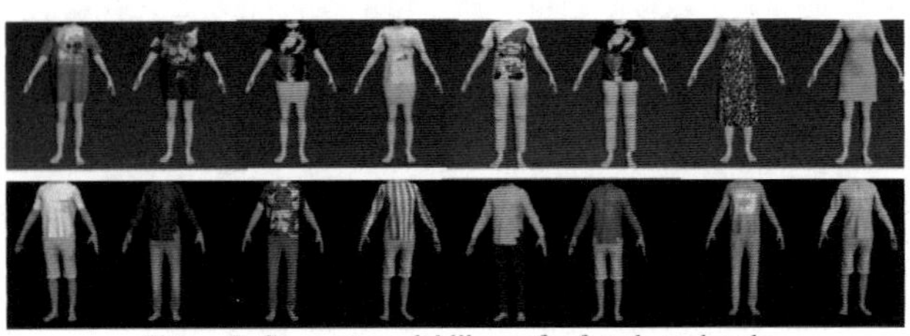

Figure 7. Garment model library for female and male

C. 3D Virtual Try-on

We gather various garment information from online websites and enhance the online shopping experience for users. Our system was developed using Unity3D [27] on Windows10 and we deployed our system on Android smartphones. The 3D virtual try-on system consists of two parts: virtual fitting and augmented walking.

1) Virtual Fitting

Virtual reality relies on an entirely digital environment, which can provide an immersive and interactive shopping experience for users.

We prepared a variety of fitting scenes for users, such as on the street, in the office and at the supermarket. Users can view the virtual garment based on the different virtual scenes, giving them an idea of what they would look like for various occasions or purposes (Figure 8).

Figure 8. Fitting scenes.

2) Augmented walking

In our daily life, when users shop at the physical (offline) shops, they often check the attributes of clothes through various motions, such as twisting the body or raising the arm to help the user confirm the fit of the clothes. However, when shopping online, users cannot visualize the details of the garment. Compared to the offline try-on experience, the traditional online shopping purchasing environment lacks the capability for users to try-on garment on their own body and check whether the clothes fit on them in various postures. Therefore, we propose a dynamically interactive method that allows users to animate their dressed human body in 360 degrees and enables users view their virtual body walking in the real-life scene.

A. Overview of Augmented Walking

The implementation of the augmented walking framework aimed to animate the personalized avatar of users in the real world (see Figure 9 for its overview). Figure 9 shows the workflow of animating the personalized virtual avatar in the real world.

- *Personalized virtual avatar*: we integrate the virtual human model and clothes model in 3ds max and export the virtual avatar as .fbx file.
- *Skeleton Binding and Skinning*: we upload the personalized virtual avatar to Mixamo [7] which is a Web-based services for creating 3D human models' animation. We bind the skeleton to the virtual avatar and skin it using Mixamo.
- *Animate virtual avatar*: to attach the animation to personalized avatar, we use animator controller in Unity [28] to control the virtual avatar and perform various animation.
- *Augmented walking in real world*: we realize the augmented walking using Vuforia Augmented Reality SDK [6].

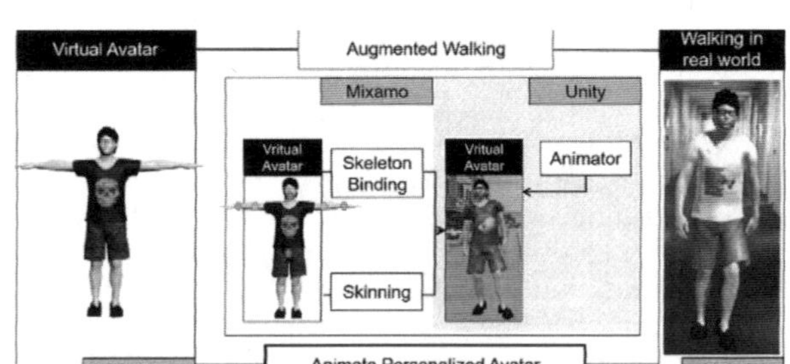

Figure 9. Implementation of augmented walking

B. Daily Life Animation

We fitted our generated human model with garment models and created walking and pose animations, as Figure 10 shows. Using Mixamo, the motions we generate are very lifelike actions, such as waving/shaking hands, walking, sitting, turning around, etc.

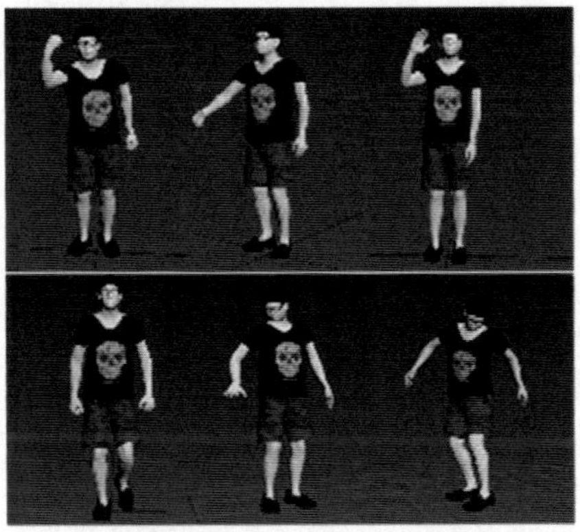

Figure 10. Postures of personalized human model

C. Augmented walking

Augmented walking enables users to view the dressed human model in a dynamic and interactive way from different perspectives (as Figure 11 shows). Therefore, users can have a better understanding of whether the garment is suitable or not while moving.

Figure 11. Views personalized model in different perspectives

Most of the previous work focused on fitting with a static body model [13][14]. So far, there is a lack of research exploring virtual try-on with motion. Therefore, we provide dynamic interaction with the virtual human model. To realize the augmented walking of the virtual human model in a real-life scene, we use Vuforia Augmented Reality SDK to detect the ground plane and place the user's virtual body into the real-life scene, in life size.

Our system enables users to view a life-size personalized virtual body with garment models and posing or walking augmented in the real-world so that they can get a sense of the real fit and get a sense of what they will look like wearing clothes with motion in a real-life scene. Figure 12 demonstrates different users animated with their virtual body with augmented walking or posing in the real-life scene.

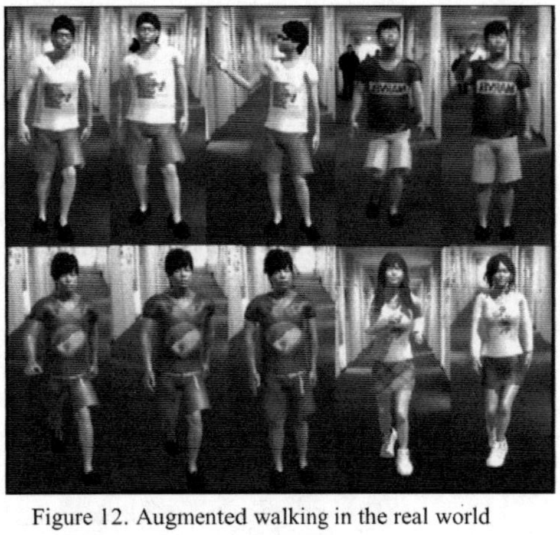

Figure 12. Augmented walking in the real world

IV. EVALUATION

A. Evaluation Design

We have conducted an initial experiment to evaluate our system. The objective of our experiment is to assess whether our 3D virtual try-on system in augmented reality benefits users' experience when online shopping, thereby helping users make better purchasing decisions. To investigate users' attitude toward the traditional shopping experience and 3D virtual try-on with augmented walking experience, we conduct a user study with two conditions. The Experimental Conditions are indicated below.

- *Virtual try-on condition:* simulate the shopping experience with our 3D virtual try-on system.
- *Image only condition:* simulate typical online shopping experience with only images of garments online.

We hypothesized that the former condition would lead to a higher rating than the latter.

B. Participants

A total of 10 college students participated in both condition 1 (*Virtual try-on condition*) and condition 2 (*Image only condition*). College students aged 18-30 years are usually targeted by AR/VR applications, as they are more likely to try new technologies and they are proactive in online shopping for fashion products. Hence, we invited N=10 participants (7M, 3F) to complete our evaluation, with an average age of 22.5 years.

C. Procedure

For each participant, we personalized their human model based on their 2D face image and 360-degree body videos. Each participant simulated the shopping experience with two different conditions. The order of the conditions was randomized. After each task, participants were asked to rate their experience (from 1 "strongly disagree" to 7 "strongly agree") in our questionnaire, indicated on a 7-point Likert scale. At the end of the experiment, we interviewed participants to gather their preferences and open-ended feedback.

D. Measures

We measured enjoyment, convenience, and user behavior for the two conditions. We also measured whether augmented motion in the real-life scene enhances user's shopping experience. The questionnaire and measurement items are shown in Table 1.

TABLE I. QUSTIONNAIRE AND MEASRUEMENT ITEMS

Items	Statements
Enjoyment	**a.** Using the system, shopping experience was enjoyable for me.
Convenience	**b.** I can get a sense of how the outfit might look for the various occasions.
	c. I can get a sense of how I look wearing these clothes.
Augmented Walking	**d.** Seeing a model of me walking in the real-world enhanced my shopping experience.
	e. Having a model walking in a real environment helps me understand more about the appearance of the clothes.
User Behavior	**f.** I want to use this system when I buy some clothes online in the future.

E. Results

We separate the result into two sections: analysis of the rating from questionnaires and thematic analysis of the participants' comments.

We analyzed the result in terms of users' enjoyment, convenience, augmented walking and user behavior.

(1) **Enjoyment:** As Figure 13 shows, we found a significant main effect on participants shopping enjoyment. A repeated measures t-test revealed a statistically significant difference between the various conditions $P<0.01$. Participants' rated the enjoyment significantly higher in the virtual try-on condition.

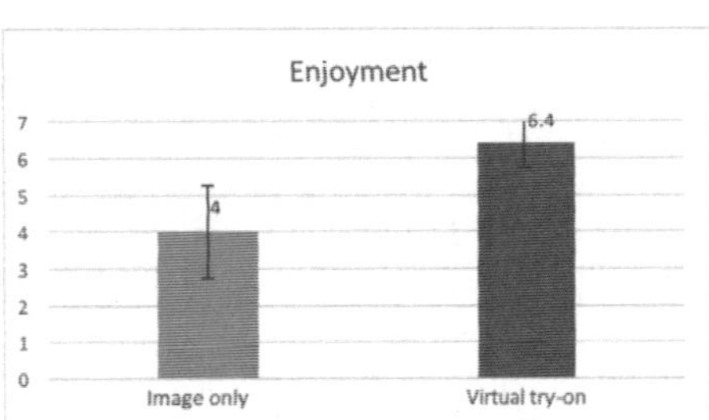

Figure 13. Participants rated their Experiences more enjoyable in the virtual try-on condition.

(2) **Convenience:** We analyzed the user convenience through the two questions below: A. *I can get a sense of how the outfit might look for the various occasions.* We found that participants rated the virtual try-on condition ($p< 0.01$) significantly higher than the other condition (Figure. 14). B. *I can get a sense of how I look wearing these clothes.* We also found that participants rated the virtual try-on condition ($p< 0.01$) significantly higher, meaning that it gave users a better feeling for how these clothes look like on their body (Figure 15).

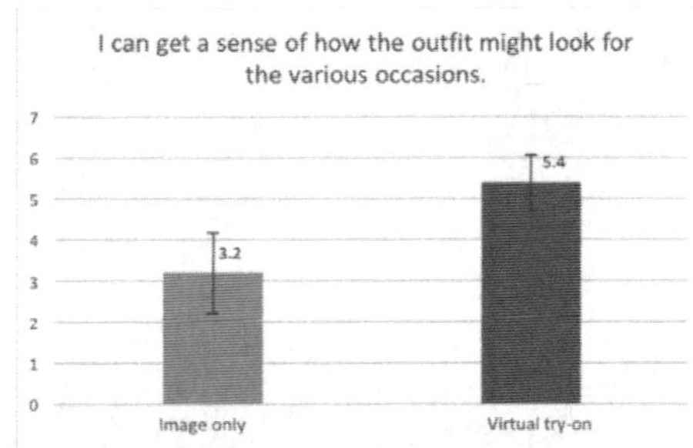

Figure 14. Participants rated they feel easier to get a sense of how the outfit might look for the various occasions in the virtual try-on condition.

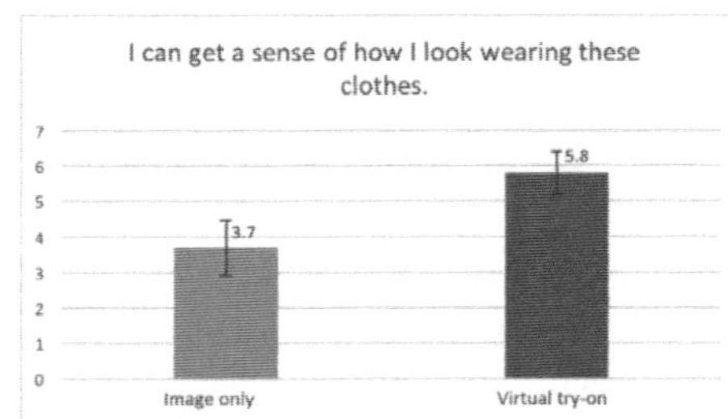

Figure 15. Participants rated that virtual try-on condition gave users a better feel for how these clothes look like on their body.

(3) **Augmented Walking:** To understand if the 3D virtual try-on system within the AR scene enhances the user's experience, we prepared two statements:

d. Seeing a model of me walking in the real-world enhanced my shopping experience. Figure 16 summarizes participants' opinions in the virtual try-on condition.

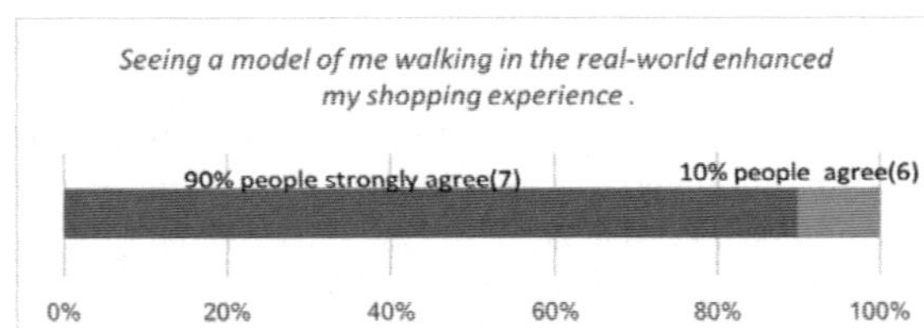

Figure 16. All participants agree that seeing own model in the real-world enhanced their shopping experience. 9 out of 10 participants strongly agree with it.

e. Having a model walking in a real environment helps me understand more about the appearance of the clothes. Figure 17 summarizes participants' opinions in the virtual try-on condition.

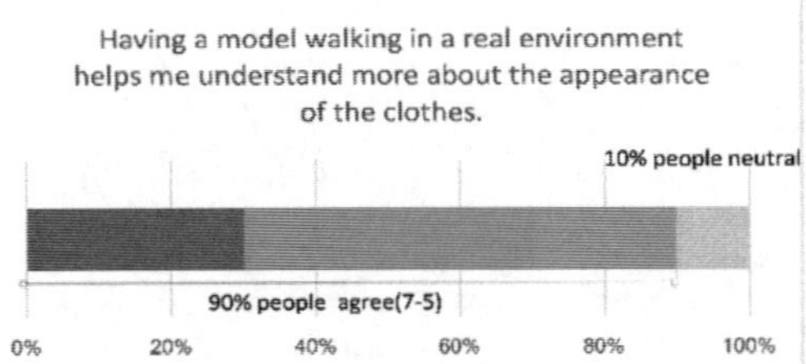

Figure 17. Most participants agree that the model walking in the real environment helps them understand more about the appearance of the clothes.

In conclusion, all the participants agreed that augmented walking may enhance their shopping experience. 9 out of 10 participants rated that the virtual model walking in the real environment helps them understand more about the appearance of the clothes. The main reasons given were, for example, the real environment is very realistic which helps them to view the appearance of the garment model. Moreover, for the participants, the virtual models walking in the real-life scene are very interesting and can improve their enjoyment of online shopping process. At the same time, augmented walking can also provide a better 3D visualization for users. The dynamic fitting display can show the shape of the clothes when they are in motion and increases the number of clothes attributes that can be observed.

(4) **User Behavior:** In summary, all participants preferred the virtual try-on condition, for both enjoyment and convenience. We also analyzed the user behavior about whether they want to use the virtual try-on system in the future or not. Results suggested that 9 out of 10 participants wanted to use this system in the future (Figure 18).

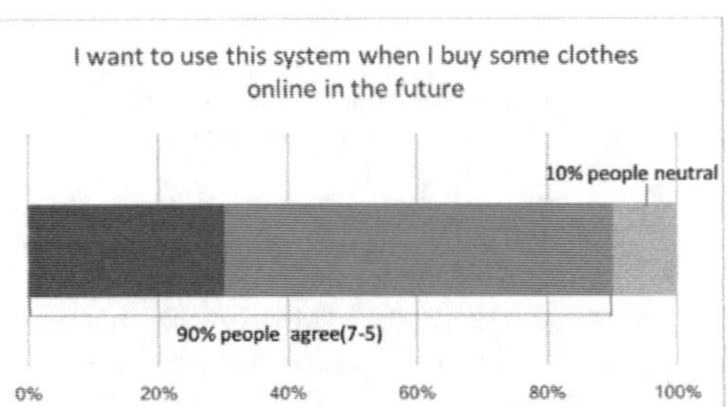

Figure 18. Most participants want to use this system when they buy some clothes online in future.

F. Qualitative Results

At the end of the experiment, open-ended feedback was sought from participants, and a thematic analysis was performed on participants' responses and their feeling of using our 3D virtual try-on system.

Most participants thought that the virtual avatar augmented walking in real world offers them a sense of wearing clothes on their own body, which can provide users with a better understanding of the detail of the clothes. Moreover, augmented walking allows users to visualize their personalized model in real world, increasing their shopping enjoyment. P6 mentioned that the augmented walking makes them feel like they are looking into a mirror. P7 said that augmented walking in the real world can help them observe more details of clothes.

Most participants thought that our system was interesting. Our system can enhance users' experience and narrow their selections when shopping online. For instance, P1 mentioned: "shopping online is difficult because the model's body shape is pretty, while actual people in real life don't have such a perfect body. This system shows how the clothes look like on my body in the real-world which makes me have confidence when buying clothes." Similar comments were received from P3 and P4.

Furthermore, the 3D virtual try-on system gives users outfit ideas and provides more clothing information to users. P3 thinks that 3D virtual system provides various virtual scenes to help users with selecting clothes, especially for special occasions. P6 mentioned that the 3D garment model allows him to see himself wearing clothes in 360 degrees and obtain additional clothing information than just looking in a mirror. P7 said the virtual model walking in the real world may help them to check how they look like in the real wearing conditions.

We also received comments about future improvement; P3 suggested that the material of clothes could be improved to look more like real fabric, and P9 thought that it would be better to use motion capture to simulate real movement of users' moving in the real world. The free comments from participants are summarized below in Table2.

TABLE II. CONCLUSION OF FREE COMMENT

Keyword	Conclusion and Comments
Augmented walking	**Judging of fitting:** Wearing clothes doing some activities in the real world provides users with better understanding of the detail of clothes, which allows to better judge of fitting. **Humanoid motion:** Using motion capture technology to capture user's movement may offer users a better sense of "real me".
Garment model	**Information visualization:** The 3D virtual try-on system gives users outfit ideas and provides more clothing information to users (muti-direction and muti-angle). **Realistic garment:** Garment material can be more like real fabric.
Shopping experience	The 3D virtual try-on system can narrow users' selections of clothes and increase their purchase confidence. Increases the enjoyment of shopping experience.

V. CONCLUSION AND FUTURE WORK

In this paper, we have presented a 3D virtual try-on system to facilitate consumers in getting a better sense of how they would look when purchasing clothes online. To allow users to assess how well the displayed products match their actual body, we personalized users' own virtual avatar corresponding to real user's human body shape and face features. Based on online garment images, we generated 3D virtual garment to personalize the human body. Users can fit their 3D user models with a selection of virtual garments, and view the animated body in the real-life scene, as well as various virtual scenes, to get a better sense of the dynamic effects of the clothes. An initial evaluation reveals that the virtual try-on system was more enjoyable and more convenient than the typical experience of using images only. Augmented walking provides an interactive, dynamic virtual try-on experience for users, which provide users with better understanding of the detail of clothes. The virtual avatar wearing clothes in the real world can provide a better sense of "true fit", which helps users better judge of fitting. Furthermore, most of the participants would prefer using this system for online shopping in the future. They think that this system can increase their purchase confidence and solve the fit problem when shopping online.

However, our system still has certain limitations that can be improved. In the future, we plan to enhance our clothing animations and cloth simulation methods to provide users with a more realistic virtual try-on effect. Motion capture can also be used to better simulate user's walking motion, in order to provide a more realistic and more interactive fitting experience.

REFERENCES

[1] C. Garcia Martin and E. Oruklu, "Human friendly interface design for virtual fitting room applications on android based mobile devices, " Journal of Signal and Information Processing3, vol. 3, pp. 481-490, 2012. DOI:https://doi.org/10.4236/jsip.2012.34061

[2] H. Yamada et al., "Image-based virtual fitting system with garment image reshaping. In 2014 International Conference on Cyberworlds, " IEEE, pp. 47-54, 2014. DOI:https://doi.org/ 10.1109/CW.2014.15

[3] Y. Deng et al., "Accurate 3D Face Reconstruction with Weakly-Supervised Learning: From Single Image to Image Set, " In Proceedings of the IEEE Conference on Computer Vision and Pattern Recognition Workshops, 11pages, 2019. Retrieved from https://arxiv.org/abs/1903.08527

[4] T. Alldieck et al., "Video based reconstruction of 3d people models, " In 2018 IEEE/CVF Conference on Computer Vision and Pattern Recognition, pp. 8387-8397, 2018. DOI:https://doi.org/10.1109/CVPR.2018.00875

[5] Cloth-Weaver, https://clothweaver.com/. [retrieved: Oct, 2020]

[6] Vuforia Engine, https://developer.vuforia.com/. [retrieved: Oct, 2020]

[7] Maximo, https://www.mixamo.com/. [retrieved: Oct, 2020]

[8] L. Chen et al., "Encoder-decoder with atrous separable convolution for semantic image segmentation, " In computer vision (ECCV 2018), pp. 833-851, 2018. DOI:https://doi.org/10.1007/978-3-030-01234-2_49

[9] H. Tanaka and H. Saito, "Texture Overlay onto Flexible Object with PCA of Silhouettes and K-Means Method for Search into Database, "MVA, pp. 5-8, 2009.

[10] Z. Bin et al., "Garment modeling from a single image, " In Computer graphics forum, pp. 85-91, 2013. DOI: https://doi.org/10.1111/cgf.12215

[11] X. Han et al., "Viton: An image-based virtual try-on network, " In 2018 IEEE/CVF Conference on Computer Vision and Pattern Recognition, pp. 7543-7552, 2018. DOI:https://doi.org/10.1109/CVPR.2018.00787

[12] M. Sekine et al., "Virtual fitting by single-shot body shape estimation, " In Int. Conf. on 3D Body Scanning Technologies. Citeseer, pp. 406-413, 2014.

[13] Warehouse, https://www.warehouselondon.com/row/homepage. [retrieved: Jan, 2020]

[14] P. Decaudin et al., "Virtual garments: A fully geometric approach for clothing design," In Computer Graphics Forum, pp. 625-634, 2006. DOI:https://doi.org/10.1111/j.1467-8659.2006.00982.x

[15] A. Hilsmann and P. Eisert, "Tracking and Retexturing Cloth for Real-Time Virtual Clothing Applications, " In Proceedings of the 4th International Conference on Computer Vision/Computer Graphics CollaborationTechniques Springer-Verlag, Berlin, Heidelberg, pp. 94–105, 2009. DOI:https://doi.org/10.1007/978-3-642-01811-4_9

[16] G. Pons-Moll et al ., "ClothCap: seamless 4D clothing capture and retargeting, " ACM Transactions on Graphics vol. 36, 15pages, 2017. DOI:https://dl.acm.org/doi/10.1145/3072959.3073711

[17] X. Chen, B. Zhou, F. Lu, L. Wang, L. Bi and P. Tan, "Garment modeling with a depth camera, " ACM Trans. Graph. vol. 34 , 12 pages. 2015. DOI:https://doi.org/10.1145/2816795.2818059

[18] H&M, https://www.hm.com/. [retrieved: Oct, 2020]

[19] ZARA, https://www.zara.com/. [retrieved: Aug, 2020]

[20] D. Protopsaltou et al., "A body and garment creation method for an Internet based virtual fitting room, " In Advances in modelling, animation and rendering, pp. 105-122, 2002. DOI: https://doi.org/10.1007/978-1-4471-0103-1_7

[21] D. Li et al., "Automatic three-dimensional-scanned garment fitting based on virtual tailoring and geometric sewing." Journal of Engineered Fibers and Fabrics, vol. 14, 16 pages, 2019. DOI: https://doi.org/10.1177/1558925018825319

[22] H. Lee and K. Leonas, "Consumer experiences, the key to survive in an omni-channel environment: use of virtual technology, " Journal of Textile and Apparel, Technology and Management, Vol. 10, pp. 1-23, 2018.

[23] M. Yuan, I. R. Khan, F. Farbiz, S. Yao, A. Niswar and M. H. Foo, "A mixed reality virtual clothes try-on system, " IEEE Transactions on Multimedia, vol. 15, pp. 1958-1968, 2013 DOI: https://doi.org/10.1109/TMM.2013.2280560

[24] N. Magnenat-Thalmann, B. Kevelham, P. Volino, M. Kasap and E. Lyard, "3d web-based virtual try on of physically simulated clothes, " Computer-Aided Design and Applications, vol. 8, pp. 163-174, 2011. DOI: https://doi.org/10.3722/cadaps.2011.163-174

[25] Marvelous Designer, https://www.marvelousdesigner.com/. [retrieved: Oct, 2020]

[26] 3ds Max, https://www.autodesk.co.jp/products/3ds-max/overview/. [retrieved: Sep, 2020]

[27] Unity3D, https://unity.com/. [retrieved: Oct, 2020]

[28] Animator Controller, https://docs.unity3d.com/Manual/class-AnimatorController.html , [retrieved: Oct, 2020]

Rethinking the Fashion Show: A Personal Daily Life Show Using Augmented Reality

Shihui Xu[1], Yuhan Liu[1], Yuzhao Liu[1], Kelvin Cheng[2], Soh Masuko[2], and Jiro Tanaka[1]

[1] Waseda University, Kitakyushu, Japan
[2] Rakuten Institute of Technology, Rakuten, Inc., Tokyo, Japan
e-mail: shxu@toki.waseda.jp, liuyuhan-op@akane.waseda.jp, liuyuzhao131@akane.waseda.jp, kelvin.cheng@rakuten.com, so.masuko@rakuten.com, jiro@aoni.waseda.jp

***Abstract*—At present, most fashion shows are professional and exclusive in nature and are not easily accessible to the general public. Ordinary people are usually excluded from these events and have few chances to participate in fashion shows in their daily lives. In addition, setting up a fashion show can be frustrating because the garments for fashion shows are often specially designed and difficult to obtain for ordinary people. In this paper, we attempt to rethink the design of fashion shows and discuss how future fashion show could be redesigned. We proposed an Augmented Reality (AR) personal daily life show, which enables users to virtually attend a fashion show that is customized for themselves, and in their own environment. Personalized avatar is created for each user as a virtual fashion model in the fashion show. Furthermore, the avatar is enhanced with animations and can interact with physical objects in the real environment. We have conducted an evaluation and results show that such personal daily life show can improve user's experience and narrow the gap between apparel show and user's own life.**

Keywords-fashion show; Augmented Reality; personalized fashion.

I. INTRODUCTION

Fashion show is a crucial part of the fashion industry and is defined as a showcase, presenting fashion designers' new collections of clothes and accessories to audiences of consumers, buyers, journalists, influencers, etc. [1]-[3]. The purpose of the fashion show is not only to exhibit fashion designers' collections to the public, but also to include its practicality as a distribution channel [1][4]. Since the first modern fashion show at Ehrich Brothers, New York City in 1903, fashion shows have been adopted by upscale fashion brands as promotional events [3].

Although fashion shows have superiority in distribution channel and advertising, they have their limitations. Firstly, consumers cannot participate at fashion shows themselves. Clothing is an involved product category, it is difficult to evaluate, and needs to be seen in person and tried on because it is highly related to personal ego [5]. Considering the purpose of fashion show is to present clothing to consumers, it is crucial to include general consumers in fashion shows so that they could see the clothing by themselves. Second, there is a gap between the current fashion show and daily life of the consumers. Current fashion shows prefer catwalks to showcase the apparels, which require specially built stages and are rarely seen in consumer's daily life. In addition, apparels of fashion show are not widely applicable for general consumers. So that general consumers can hardly benefit from the current fashion show.

Recently, fashion show has incorporated technologies such as Augmented Reality (AR) and Mixed Reality (MR), attracting the attention of more audiences. For example, UK wireless company Three teamed up with designers to show off a fashion show augmented with 3D special effects through network and AR head-mounted display at 2019 London Fashion Week [6][7].

However, these technologies are applied in merely eye-catching strategies. The essential issue of how to effectively use these technologies to solve the problems of current fashion show to make fashion show a more extensive channel for general consumers has not been explored.

Thus, to bring consumers into a completely new area of fashion show, it is important to rethink the design of fashion show and related technologies for meeting consumers' demands. Therefore, two research questions are proposed. First, how might we redesign the future fashion show? Second, what is the role of AR technology to facilitate consumers' shopping in the future fashion show?

In this paper, we present a novel AR fashion apparels show system named personal daily life show to explore the above questions and to solve the existing problems of current fashion show. The novelties of the personal daily life show are:

1. Generation of life-sized personalized 3-dimentional human avatar of the user self.
2. 3D apparel modeling from 2D shopping website images.
3. Interaction of the personalized virtual avatar with the real physical environment.

The contributions of this work include:

1. The conceptual design and a proof-of-concept prototype implementation of personal daily life show.
2. Quantitative and qualitative evaluation of personal daily life show and how it is effective in narrowing the gap between fashion show and user's own life.

The rest of this paper is organized as follows. Section II describes the related works on which our work is built. Section III describes the concept, design features and usage scenario of personal daily life show. Section IV goes into finer details with respect to the implementation of personal daily life show. Section V introduces the evaluation. Section VI gives the discussion of this work. The conclusions close the article.

II. RELATED WORKS

We have examined related works in terms of the AR and MR technologies in fashion industry and virtual avatar in fashion show.

A. *AR/MR Technologies in Fashion*

In fashion industry, the use of AR and MR technologies can be used to narrow the gap between online and brick-and-mortar shopping experience [8]. For example, Virtual try-on system provides virtual garments trial experience for consumers through AR and VR technologies, overcoming the lack of fitting experience of online shopping [9]. The apparel company Gap created an app called DressingRoom [10], which allows customers to virtually try on clothing on a dummy human model through a smartphone. Combining 3D modeling technologies, the London College of Fashion has created an app named Pictofit [11], adopting virtual avatar of the users and enabling users to browse clothes with their own avatar in AR environment. In contrast with DressingRoom, in Pictofic consumers can use their own avatar to try on clothing, undergoing mental simulation of the fitting with the garments during the process, leading vivid mental imagery and high purchase intention. However, both DressingRoom and Pictofit are limited to the virtual static human model, lacking dynamic view of clothing try-on. Users can only see the standing virtual model, with no interaction other than changing clothes.

The use of see-through type head-mounted displays (HMDs) with AR technology enables a more intuitive and immersive shopping experience compared to conventional e-commerce systems. With spatial computing, AR has the potential to provide a sensory and immersive virtual boutique shopping experience wherever the user is. For example, H&Moschino and Warpin [12] created a virtual fashion shop using MR head-mounted display, where users were able to watch 3D videos and sounds surrounding different garments. Portal is an AR fashion show application launched by MESON [13], making it possible to watch a brand's new seasonal items fitted with hundreds of 3D virtual human models in real-world through smartphone, tablet or AR glasses. But Portal adopts professional models instead of consumers themselves, causing a low correlation with consumers. In addition, the models in Portal is static and clothes could not be changed.

B. *Avatar in Fashion Show*

Previous research has investigated the design and development of avatar in AR and VR system. Avatars have been widely used in most virtual worlds and games. An avatar represents a user self and it allows the user to experience the virtual world by manipulating the avatar [14][15].

In this paper, we mainly focus on how people perceive their avatars in fashion show related system. For instance, Stephen Gray proposed a VR fashion show in which users can have a virtual model of the same shape as their own bodies [16]. The avatar can be fitted with virtual clothing and walk catwalks in a virtual environment. However, the avatar can only reflect the body shape of the user, without the face features of the user. Besides, the interactivity is limited. Users can only watch the performance of their avatar. Recently, virtual avatars have appeared in real-world fashion show using projection an AR technology. Central Saint Martins and Three launched a fashion show where a 3D life-size avatar of a famous model could walk in AR on the runway at 2020 London Fashion Week [17]. The audiences can watch the catwalks of virtual avatar by smartphone. In this system, the avatar is embedded with the motion capture animations of model self. But it is generated by professional and expensive setup, so that there is only one avatar and one dress available.

III. PERSONAL DAILY LIFE SHOW

This section describes the concept and design of personal daily life show and the scenario of its usage.

A. *Concept*

One of our major design decisions was to not design for a runway catwalk fashion show. Instead, we focus on closing the gap between fashion show and the general consumers, bringing the fashion show into users' life and displaying the lifestyle of users. While we agreed that the runway catwalk fashion show has great commercial value for fashion industry, we decide to design a fashion show from which consumers can directly benefit. In our concept, we focused on making the fashion show available for users anywhere in their life, which means users can experience a fashion show in their real environment.

Another major design decision was to let the user participate in the show instead of just being an audience. In order to allow users to see their own performances while participating in the show, we adopted users' personalized avatar as the show model. We think it is important to allow users to engage with the show, which could increase the engagement and enjoyment of users.

Based on above decisions, we defined the personal daily life show enabling general consumers to watch the fashion apparels on their own life-sized personalized avatar, which is overlaid on user's real environment and can interact with the real environment using AR technology. Furthermore, instead of having models only walking and posing, as in current fashion shows, our personalized avatar can perform human-like daily activities, such as walking around in the real-world, and interacting with real-world objects. A main consideration for the design of personal daily life show was to depict the scene of user's daily life, increasing the self-relevance of users during the show experience and facilitating consumers to imagine themselves fitted with fashion apparels in their own life.

B. Design

Based on the concept proposed above, we designed a proof-of-concept prototype of personal daily life show for further investigation. Figure 1 shows the pipeline of the personal daily life show.

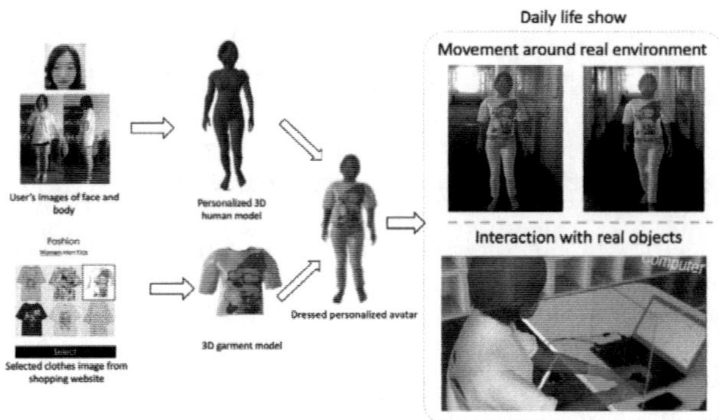

Figure 1. Pipeline of personal daily life show

The novelties and features of personal daily life show include the following items.

1) Adopting users' personalized avatar as models in the show.

In order to create a fashion show with the user, while enabling the user to watch the show at the same time, we propose to make a life-sized personalized avatar for each user and adopt the user's personalized avatar as the model of the fashion show. Thereby, users can watch the fashion apparels exhibited on their own personalized avatar and get the imagery of trying on the apparels on themselves. The personalized avatar is customized according to photos of user's body and facial appearance.

2) Providing virtual 3D apparel models based on 2D apparel images from shopping website.

The apparels of fashion show are usually difficult to obtain and purchase. To solve this problem, we provide users with 3D virtual apparels so that they could virtually fit the apparels on their personalized avatar. In addition, the 3D virtual apparels are generated according to the 2D apparels images from online shopping websites. In this way, users can easily purchase the apparels that appears in the fashion show. Besides, if they are satisfied with the apparel, they can purchase it using online shopping.

3) Enabling user's personalized avatar to interact with real environment using AR technology.

To close the gap between fashion show and user's daily life, we made use of AR technology to visualize and superimpose the personalized avatar in user's real environment. And users can make the user's personalized avatar interact with the real environment, such as walking and doing daily activities like a real person. By doing so, we intend to simulate the daily life of the user, giving user a fashion show experience that is associated with their own life and providing the user further information about how they will look like in their daily life.

C. Scenario

We propose a usage scenario illustrating how the personal daily life show can benefit the general consumers when online apparels shopping. And at the same time, users can also browse the clothes of online shopping website in a more intuitive and engaged way by the personal daily life show system.

When the user uses the system for the first time, before the user starts shopping on the apparels website, she can upload the images of her face and body to create a personalized avatar which reflects the face appearance and body shape of the user.

The user can then browse the shopping website of apparels to select the clothes she wants to view. Our system will generate the 3D model of the clothes selected by the user. Next, our system will provide a personalized avatar of herself fitted with the 3D clothes model to the user.

By wearing a see-through type AR head-mounted display (HMD) with a depth camera, users can launch the show where they are. Once the show is launched, the real-world environment of the user will be mapped by the HMD using the built-in depth camera. After that user can see the life-sized personalized avatar of herself superimposed onto the real environment through the HMD.

The user can interact with the system to make the personalized avatar interact with the real environment, similar to what a real person would do in their daily activities.

IV. Implementation

In this section, the implementation details of the personal daily life show will be described. The implementation contains the hardware, development environment, pre-processing and daily life show.

A. Hardware

The prototype system was built with a see-through type AR HMD, Microsoft HoloLens, with a 2GB CPU embedded [18]. HoloLens features four "environment understanding" sensors, a depth camera with a 120 * 120-degree angle of view, which is used for computing the real-world meshes in our system.

B. Development Environment

The software was developed using the Unity 3D game engine (2017.4). And a cross-platform toolkit for building Mixed Reality experiences for Virtual Reality (VR) and Augmented Reality (AR), MRTK, was used for building the application. This framework allowed us to rapidly prototype the personal daily life show system that supports spatial awareness and various interaction cues.

C. Pre-processing

After the pre-processing, a dressed personalized avatar with motions embedded will be available, which can be used in the fashion show as an apparel model.

1) Generation of personalized avatar

Figure 2 shows the process of the personalized avatar generation.

Our approach to generate the personalized avatar is to model the user's face and body separately and combine the two parts together. For the face modeling, our approach only uses a single frontal image of the user's face. By making use of existing face modeling technology, Avatar SDK [19], the photorealistic face model can be generated.

With body modeling, a front image and a side image of the user's body are required to build a body model of the user. By uploading the body images to 3DLOOK [20], the body model of the user can be generated.

The face model and body model are combined by replacing the head part of generated body model with the face model. This is done in a 3D modeling software.

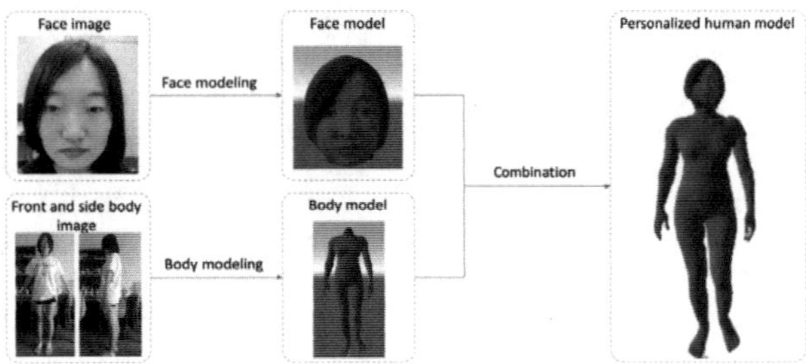

Figure 2. Generation of personalized avatar

2) Generation of 3D apparel model

Methods used to generate garment models from images are widely used in virtual try-on systems. Our aim is to handle the clothe images from online apparel shopping websites. However, it is difficult to process all the images on such large collections. Therefore, we focused on dealing with simple clothes images that have a unique or similar background color.

Our approach to generate garment model is to create 3D garment templates for each personalized avatar and map the 2D garment images to the garment templates, which are created from online apparel websites. The 3D garment templates are created for each personalized avatar using Cloth Weaver. The 2D garment images are then mapped onto the generated 3D garment model templates in 3ds Max. In doing so, 3D garment models can be created that matches online shopping website images.

3) Fitting apparel model to personalized avatar

With the generated 3D garment model, we fitted the garment model to user's personalized avatar by adjust the size and position of the 3D garment model within 3ds Max, which result in a dressed personalized avatar.

4) Attaching motions to personalized avatar

By embedding motions to the personalized avatar of users, they can be animated to mimic how we would normal move about in our daily activities. In order to embed motions to the personalized avatar, the personalized 3D avatar is rigged as a humanoid. We then select motion capture animations that mimics human actions, and attach them to the rigged personalized avatar.

a) Motion capture animations

Motion capture animations are the animation clips which record the movement of people or objects, widely used in games and movies. To make the personalized avatar act naturally and closer to real life, we chose to prepare motion capture animations that can reflect human's daily activities, such as sitting, walking, and standing.

The motion capture animations used in our system were sourced from Mixamo [21].

b) Rigging of Personalized Avatar

Rigging is the process of creating a skeleton for a 3D model so it can animate. Before the motion capture animations can be used, the personalized avatar need to be rigged.

The rigging process can be done in a 3D modeling software like 3ds Max or Maya, but it is time consuming using this method. Auto-rig software is currently available, which enables users to rig a 3D character by assigning several joints. We used the auto-rig function of Mixamo to rig the personalized avatar in our system, as the Figure 3 shows. By aligning several joints (i.e., chin, two elbows, two wrists, two knees and groin) to the 3D personalized avatar, Mixamo will help do the rigging process automatically. We can also choose different levels of skeleton details to optimize the performance of our personalized avatar.

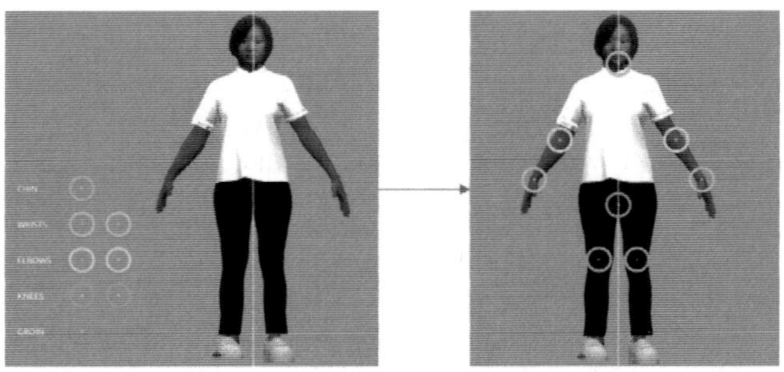

Upload the model to Mixamo **Assign joint points**

Figure 3. Rigging of the personalized avatar

c) Attaching the motion capture animation to rigged personalized avatar.

After rigging, we attached the prepared motion capture animation to the personalized avatar via Unity Animator Controller, which allows humanoid models to utilize multiple kinds of motion capture animations. Figure 4 shows a few examples of personalized avatar with various kinds of motions.

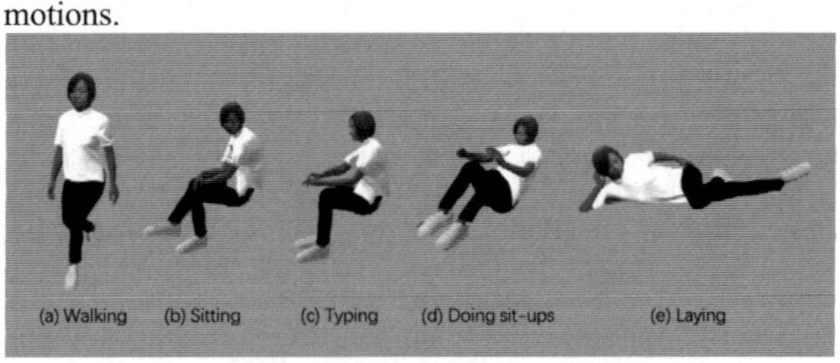

Figure 4. Personalized avatar with motions

D. *Daily Life Show*

The implementation of daily life show includes the avatar's movement around the real environment and avatar's interaction with real objects.

1) *Movement around the real environment*

In this section, the implementation of the avatar's movement around the real environment is explained. As shown in Figure 5, the implementation of avatar's movement includes specifying the destination, calculation of distance between avatar and destination, and avatar's response to the environment (walking or standing).

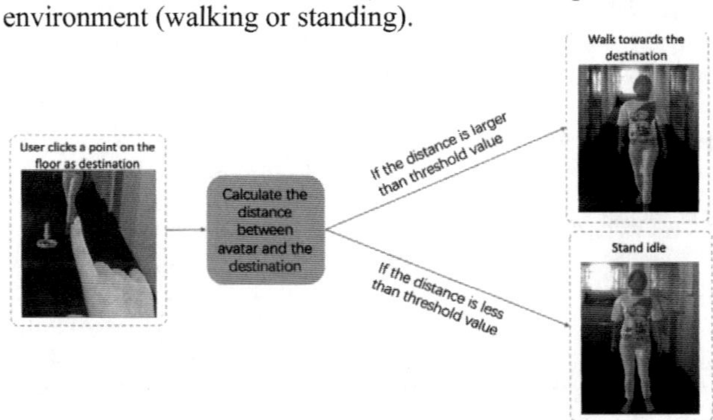

Figure 5. Avatar's movement around the real environment

a) *Specifying the destination*

The movement of avatar is triggered by user's specifying a destination on the floor by performing an "air-tap". "Air-tap" is a built-in gesture provided by HoloLens, which refers to straightening the index finger and then tapping down. The users can gaze on the floor and make an "air tap" gesture towards the floor. A virtual arrow will then appear as the indicator of destination of the movement.

b) *Calculation of distance between avatar and destination*

We calculate the distance between the avatar's current position and the destination at every frame. The calculation is done by updating the position information of the avatar.

c) *Response of avatar*

If the distance be between avatar and destination is larger than the pre-determined threshold value, which means the avatar need to move, we set the motion of the avatar to be "walking" motion. This is one of the animations that is already embedded in the avatar in pre-processing, and which sets the avatar in motion towards the destination. In this case, the avatar appears as walking towards the destination.

If the distance between avatar and destination is less than the threshold value, the position of avatar will not be changed. However, the avatar will perform the standing motion, which is also embedded in avatar in pre-processing.

2) *Interaction with real objects*

The implementation of avatar's interaction with real objects is illustrated in Figure 6. It consists of specifying real object for interaction, object detection in AR, and avatar's interaction with real object.

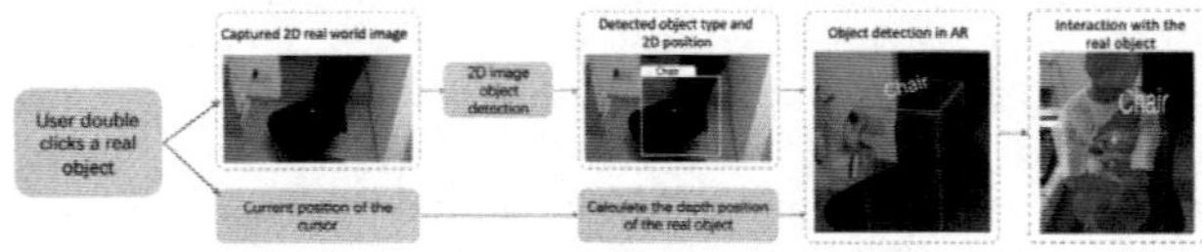

Figure 6. Avatar's interaction with real objects

a) *Specifying real object for interaction*

Users can specify which real object to interact by "double taps" to trigger the personalized avatar's interaction with real objects. "Double taps" means performing the "air-tap" gesture twice. The users can make the virtual user interact with real object by gazing at the real objects and performing the "double taps" gesture towards the real object. When the "double taps" gesture is recognized by HoloLens, it captures a screenshot of current view of real world and record the current position of the cursor for next step's object detection in AR. However, the limitation of "double taps" is that sometimes it will be misidentified as "air-tap" gesture because of the limited recognition speed of HoloLens.

b) *Object detection in the AR environment.*

In this step, we recognize the type of real object to interact with and compute the 3D position of the real object in the AR environment. To recognize the objects in the AR environment, we first recognize the objects' type by using 2D images object detection model, then calculate the 3D position of real object in AR environment.

Before object detection in runtime, we first train the model used to recognize the objects in 2D images. As a proof of concept, we chose several everyday objects, i.e., chair, bed, sports mat, computer. For each real object, we captured 50 images from multiple perspective as the database to train model. The images were uploaded to Azure Custom Vision and trained on webserver. After training, we can publish the model and can access it through APIs.

At runtime, after user performs double clicks, the captured 2D images of real-world view will be sent to the server for 2D object detection processing using Azure Custom Vision APIs. From this, we can get the type of object and its 2D position in the image. With the recorded 3D cursor position combined with detected 2D position from captured image, we could calculate the 3D position of the real object in AR with depth information through Camera.ViewportPointToRay API. After getting the type and position of the real object in AR, our system could draw a cube with a type label in the AR environment to demonstrate object detection results for the users. For example, Figure 6 shows an example where a chair is detected, in which case a cube with a "chair" label is drawed at the position of the chair.

c) *Avatar's interaction with real object.*

Knowing the 3D position and type of the real object, the avatar is then able to interact with the real object.

The type of real object that is recognized determines the type of motion that the avatar should perform. Different kinds of real object correspond to different kinds of motion. For instance, chair type objects will trigger the personalized avatar to do a sitting motion, whereas bed type objects will trigger the personalized avatar to perform a laying down motion. The position of the personalized avatar is determined by the distance between the real object and the current position of the personalized avatar. If this distance is less than a threshold value, the personalized avatar's position will be unchanged. If the distance is more than the threshold value, we set the position of the personalized avatar to the same position as the real object.

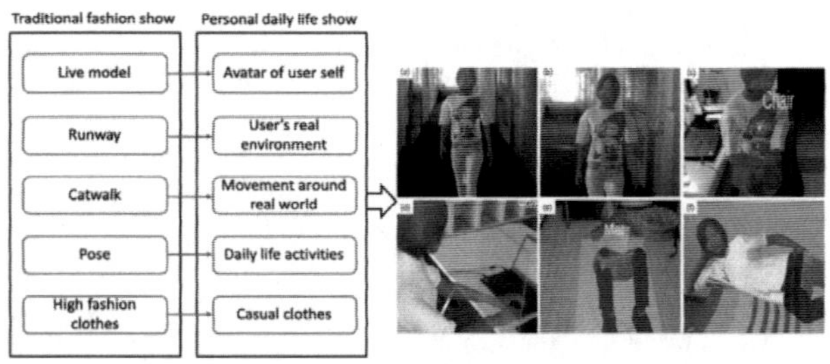

Figure 7. Personal daily life show. (a) Walking in real environment. (b) Standing in real environment. (c) Sitting on a chair. (d) Typing on a computer. (e) Doing sit-ups on a sports mat. (f) Laying on a bed.

With the movement and interaction of avatar, the users can conduct a fashion show in their real environment. Figure 7 shows a system image of personal daily life show. Compared with traditional fashion show, the personal daily life show uses an avatar of the user self rather than a live fashion model. In addition, instead of walking on the catwalks and making poses on the runway, the avatar can move and perform daily activities within user's physical environment.

V. EVALUATION

To assess our system, we conducted a user study in terms of quantitative and qualitative aspects. As previous work has already verified that the personalized avatar has positive effect on user's evaluation towards shopping experience, we will not re-evaluate personalized avatar redundantly. Instead, we are interested in evaluating the impact of interactivity of virtual avatar in AR fashion show system.

A. *Experimental Design*

The experiment follows a one-factorial design. In this case, our independent variable is the interactivity level of personalized avatar of user: static, in-situ animated and real-world-interactive. The conditions are:

1. Static personalized avatar: users can watch a static standing personalized avatar of themselves.
2. In-situ animated personalized avatar: the personalized avatar can make different animations on the same spot in front of the user, such as walking, sitting, typing, doing sit-ups. User can change the animation of personalized avatar.
3. Real-world-interactive personalized avatar: the personalized avatar can move around the real environment and make interaction with real objects, such as sitting on a chair, typing on a computer, doing sit-ups on a sports mat and so on.

B. *Experiment Environment and Set-up*

We set up our experiment in an office room with accommodation appliances, including tables, chairs, computers and a sports mat. The area of the room is about 50 square meters.

The device used in the experiment is see-through type head-mounted display HoloLens.

C. *Participants*

Twelve female students from a graduate school were recruited in the experiment. We focused on women participants because previous work [22] had examined women represent the largest apparel segment. All the participants had knowledge about fashion and had purchasing experience online, and 10 out of 12 had AR experience and learnt about human-computer interaction.

D. *Task and Procedure*

Before the experiment began, to reduce the impact caused by the unfamiliarity of device and hand gestures, each participant was required to be trained to use HoloLens and learn the basic gestures used in HoloLens. After training, each participant was informed about the experiment contents by a short video with explanations.

The experiment was a within-subject design. Each participant was asked to experience the fashion show of the personalized avatar using all three conditions. During each condition, each participant had 10 minutes to browse 20 apparel items. The clothes types were T-shirt, shirt, oversize T-shirt, skirt, tight skirt and pants. Participants were able to browse the next item by clicking on the personalized avatar.

TABLE I. QUESTIONNAIRE FOR QANTITATIVE EVALUATION

No.	Question	
	Aspect	*Description*
1	Likeness of avatar	I feel the avatar looks like me.
2	Affection to avatar	I like the avatar.
3	Interest	I think the show is interesting.
4	Engagement	I feel engaged in the show.
5	Future application	I would like to use the system in the future.
6	Assistance	I think the system is helpful for viewing apparels.
7	Relevance to real life	I feel the show is close to my life.

To minimize the effect of learning and transfer across treatments, we randomly assigned the test order and apparel items of the 3 conditions for each participant.

During the experiment, participants were asked to report their thoughts and feelings through think-aloud protocol.

After completing all three conditions, each participant was asked to complete a questionnaire to evaluate the three conditions in terms of likeness of the personalized avatar, affection to the personalized avatar, interest, engagement, future application, assistance and relevance to users' real life using 7-point Likert scale. The questions are described in Table 1.

Afterwards, participants were interviewed about our system. The whole experiment was captured by voice recording and dictation notes.

E. Results

From the experiment, we were able to collect two kinds of data, quantitative data from the questionnaires and qualitative data from the transcriptions of think-aloud sessions and interviews.

We conducted quantitative analysis for the former data and qualitative analysis for the latter data, which are described in detail below.

1) Result 1: Quantitative Analysis

In quantitative analysis, we aimed to examine if there was a significant difference between users' evaluation of each condition and the way in which these differences could be explained. As each participant tested all three conditions (within-subjects design), we analyzed the quantitative data using a one-way repeated measures ANOVA, comparing the effect of each condition on the user experience of the interface. We also conducted a Tukey's HSD test as a post-hoc test for pairwise comparisons.

TABLE II. RESULTS OF ANOVA

Aspect	ANOVA	
	F-value	*p-value*
Likeness of avatar	0.084	0.919
Affection to avatar	4.333	0.021*
Interest	10.164	<0.001***
Engagement	16.148	<0.001***
Future application	6.547	0.004**
Assistance	5.481	0.009**
Relevance to real life	8.589	0.001**

The one-way ANOVA with repeated measures revealed significant effects of conditions on users' ratings on user experience except for the likeness of avatar. TABLE II shows the results of ANOVA. Based on the results, we further conducted Tukey's HSD test to investigate pairwise comparisons between each condition. The results are visualized in Figure 8. We categorized the results in terms of the main issues below.

a) There is no significant influence of interactivity on the perceived likeness of the avatar, but the users tend to adore the real-world-interactive avatar (Q1, Q2).

We tested interactivity level's influence on users' ratings of personalized avatar. From the comparisons, even though participants evaluated that the perceived likeness of the personalized avatar was not related to the interactivity level, we observed that the participants tended to prefer real-world- interactive personalized avatar to the other two conditions (static personalized avatar and in-situ animated personalized avatar). The received scores of real-world-interactive avatars were significantly higher than static avatar (p = 0.016). The results showed that there was a trend that participants adored the personalized avatar with high interactivity level, especially the real-world-interactive avatar.

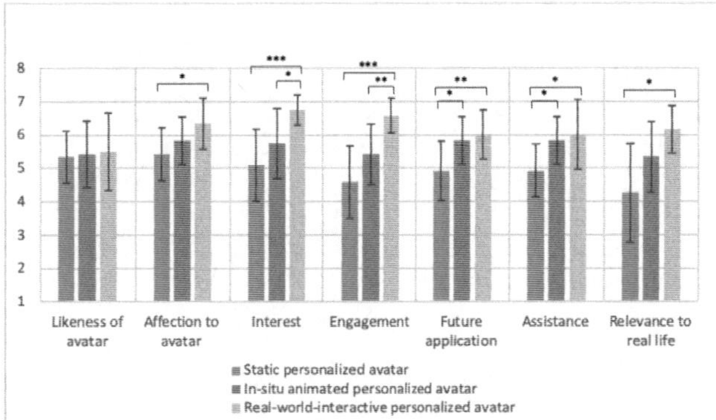

Figure 8. Visualization of quantitative analysis. (***p<0.001, **p<0.01, *p<0.05)

b) Real-world-interaction positively affected participants' interest and engagement (Q3, Q4).

One of the most interesting results of the analysis was that the user experience of the apparels show could be significantly improved by real-world-interactive personalized avatar, while only adding daily life motions to the personalized avatar was not obviously effective. We evaluated user experience from participants' interest and engagement, with significant differences found in both items. From a post-hoc test, we noticed the condition with real-world-interaction was distinct from the other two conditions. In the case of interest, the real-world-interactive condition showed significantly higher scores than static condition (p < 0.001) and in-situ animated condition (p = 0.029). In the case of engagement, participants felt more engaged in condition with real-world-interactive personalized avatar than static personalized avatar (p < 0.001) and in-situ animated avatar (p = 0.006). Besides, the post-hoc test suggested that participants did not perceive differences between static and in-situ animated conditions in terms of interest (p = 0.188) and engagement (p = 0.062).

c) Showing apparels using avatar with daily life motions is more helpful and more likely to be chosen for future use (Q5, Q6).

We also evaluated the effectiveness in terms of assistance and future application. The comparisons revealed that participants inclined to the conditions with motions, whether in-situ animated or real-world-interactive. From the assistance aspect, participants evaluated the condition with static personalized avatar as least helpful, compared with condition with real-world-interactive avatar (p = 0.011) and condition with in-situ animated avatar (p = 0.036). And from the aspect of future application, the post-hoc test showed that participants were more pleased to choose condition with real-world-interactive avatar (p = 0.005) and condition with in-situ animated avatar (p = 0.020) for future purchase of apparels than condition with static avatar. There was no significant preference between in-situ animated condition and real-world-interactive condition (p = 0.864), and both are likely to be adopted by the participants in the future.

d) Daily life motions can bring the feelings of participants' own life (Q7).

We identified that the conditions with real-world-interactions received higher scores in the relevance of participants' own life. The comparisons showed that participants felt the fashion show was significantly closer to their own daily life when the personalized avatars were enabled to interact with the real environment, compared with the static avatar (p = 0.001). Even though there is no significant difference between the condition with in-situ animated avatar and the condition with statically standing avatar, the received average score of the former condition was higher than the latter condition. This trend could also imply the daily life motions have a positive influence on user's perception about the relevance of the show and their own life, especially when the daily life motions are companied with interactions with the real-world.

2) Result 2: Qualitative Analysis

The qualitative data from the think-aloud sessions and interviews were transcribed and analyzed. In the qualitative analysis, we aimed to investigate the users' thoughts in more depth and discover the hidden characteristics beyond the quantitative analysis. The collated qualitative data is shown in TABLE III.

a) Avatar's interaction with real environment is important, especially the movement around the real environment.

As seen in the quantitative analysis, we also verified the importance of enabling avatar to interact with the real world in the qualitative analysis. Participants said that the personalized avatars' interactions with real environment provided imagery of their own daily activities. For example, P8 said, "Looking my avatar walking around the room makes feel like walking by myself." P2 also mentioned, "My avatar is typing on my computer, just like that I usually do in my office." Making the avatar move around freely in the real environment is crucial because it could facilitate users to view avatar's performance from different perspectives without having to move. P7 said, "I could imagine myself walking back and forth when instructing my avatar to walk. But I do not need to actually move at all." P11 also said, "With the movement of avatar, I can observe the apparels from different degrees of view while just standing still at a point."

b) Users enjoy engaging with the show, rather than just watching the show as audience.

TABLE III. QUALITATIVE RESULTS

Keyword	Description
Avatar's interaction	"Looking my avatar walking around the room makes feel like walking by myself." "My avatar is typing on my computer, just like that I usually do in my office." "I could imagine myself walking back and forth when instructing my avatar to walk. But I do not need to actually move at all." "With the movement of avatar, I can observe the apparels from different degrees of view while just standing still at a point."
Engagement with the show	"I feel the time is too long when I can just look at a static model." "I want to leave this session (static avatar) and go to next one." "I feel enjoyable when I can interact with the show, and this kind of experience is like playing a game."
Interface	"The 'click' is easy to use." "Using gestures is very interesting." "I want my avatar to do sports, but she just walks away." "I feel hard to let the avatar sit on the chair. It did not respond. Is there something wrong?"

From the think-aloud process, we observed that participants were eager to interact with the show. Insufficient interactions may make users feel bored during the show. For example, P12 said, "I feel the time is too long when I can just look at a static model." P11 also said, "I want to leave this session (static avatar) and go to next one." We also found that adding user interaction to the show could bring hedonic value. Participants tended to seek fun during the interactive experience. P9 reported, "I feel enjoyable when I can interact with the show, and this kind of experience is like playing a game."

c) The interruptive interaction interface may hinder the performance of the real-world-interactive avatar.

Despite verifying the real-world-interactive avatar in the apparels show, participants' evaluations to the interaction were heavily influenced by the interaction interface. For example, participants were confused with the two kinds of hand gestures, leading to undesired effects. During the experiment, P3 said, "I want my avatar to do sports, but she just walks away." The reason was that P3 used the wrong gesture. And in some cases, the time to wait for the avatar to respond could be longer than expected due to network delay. For instance, P4 said, "I feel hard to let the avatar sit on the chair. It did not respond. Is there something wrong?" Because of the above reasons, some participants felt difficult to make the avatar interact with the real environment, so that they could hardly perceive the hedonic value and practical value of the real-world-interaction.

VI. DISCUSSION

In this section, we summarize our findings of the study and discusses its implications for future fashion show design in general. We also report the plans of our future work as well as the limitations of current study.

A. *Avatar for apparels exhibition should be embedded with motions, and interaction with real world is preferable.*

As we have seen in both the quantitative and qualitative results, users prefer their personalized avatar animated. Avatars that are embedded with motions attract more affection from users, which may indirectly increase the fondness of using the whole system. Especially where motions of the avatar are related to the real environment, users show an obvious preference for the avatar. Furthermore, the real-world-interaction can close the gap between virtual apparels and users' own real life.

Therefore, when designing avatar for apparels exhibition, it is important to consider including real-world-interaction and animated avatar. When it is hard to enable the avatar to interact with real environment, having only in-situ animation is also effective to a certain degree.

B. *Let users interact with the show while avoiding complicated interactions*

From our analysis, we discovered that users are eager to participate in the show, such as interacting with the avatar and the environment. Users may feel tedious if there is no way to interact. Enabling users to participate more with the show, for instance manipulating and controlling the avatar, would improve the show experience.

However, complicated interaction should be avoided in order to prevent users getting confused. When users are stuck by the complex interaction interfaces, they tend to give up, they would usually lack confidence to try again. Despite adding interactions is crucial, the interface should be designed very carefully. Simple and user-friendly interaction interfaces are necessary. Complicated interaction interfaces will hinder the benefit of interaction.

C. *Limitations and Future Work*

As a proof-of-concept, we designed only a limited set of real-world-interaction, which cannot represent all the daily activities in users' daily life.

As future work, we will continue to include more real-world-interactions and investigate the interaction interface in the AR fashion apparel show to coordinate the interaction among users, virtual avatars and real environment. We are also interested in making the avatars aware of the real environment and react to it based on the user's behaviors.

VII. CONCLUSION

In this paper, we proposed a novel fashion show system, personal daily life show, using AR technology. It has three key features: (1) Adopting users' personalized avatar as the fashion show model (2) Providing virtual 3D apparel models based on 2D apparel images from online shopping website (3) Enabling user's personalized avatar to animate and interact with the real-world environment using AR technology.

We conducted an evaluation using both quantitative and qualitative analysis to verify our system. The results showed that the real-world-interaction of personal daily life show can significantly improve the experience of the show and narrow the gap between user's real life and the show.

REFERENCES

[1] K. W. Lau and P. Y. Lee, "The role of stereoscopic 3D virtual reality in fashion advertising and consumer learning," Advances in Advertising Research, vol. 4, pp. 75–83, 2015.

[2] Fashion show. https://en.wikipedia.org/wiki/Fashion_show. Accessed 17 October 2020.

[3] V. Pinchera and D. Rinallo, "Marketplace icon: the fashion show," Consumption Markets & Culture, vol. 0, pp. 1-13, 2019.

[4] S. Majima, "From haute couture to high street: the role of shows and fairs in twentieth-century fashion," Textile History, vol. 39, pp. 70-78, 2008.

[5] A. K. Kau, Y. E. Tang, and S. Ghose, "Typology of online shoppers," Journal of consumer marketing, vol. 20, pp. 139–156, 2003.

[6] Magic leap & three UK power 5G Augmented Reality fashion show at London Fashion Week. https://magic-leap.reality.news/news/magic-leap-three-uk-power-5g-augmented-reality-fashion-show-london-fashion-week-0193914/. Accessed 17 October 2020.

[7] Magic Leap brings mixed reality to the catwalk for London Fashion Week. https://www.wareable.com/ar/magic-leap-fashion-show-gerrit-jacob-london-fashion-week-6987. Accessed 17 October 2020.

[8] M. Blázquez, "Fashion shopping in multichannel retail: the role of technology in enhancing the customer experience," International Journal of Electronic Commerce, vol 18, pp. 97-116, 2014.

[9] H. Lee and Y. Xu, "Classification of virtual fitting room technologies in the fashion industry: from the perspective of consumer experience," International Journal of Fashion Design, Technology and Education, vol. 13, no. 1, pp. 1-10, 2020.

[10] Gap tests new virtual dressing room. https://www.gapinc.com/en-us/articles/2017/01/gap-tests-new-virtual-dressing-room. Accessed 17 October 2020.

[11] Pictofit. https://www.pictofit.com/. Accessed 17 October 2020.

[12] H&Moschino AR Fashion Experience by Warpin. https://www.youtube.com/watch?v=vB22CQMfsOs. Accessed 17 October 2020.

[13] PORTAL with Nreal. https://www.youtube.com/watch?v=2fVh9u8RBXI&list=PL-VKm55vWiVZXQWOMsXbuP7dsJ8SW_Fdm&index=5&t=0s. Accessed 17 October 2020.

[14] N. Ducheneaut, M. H. Wen, N. Yee, and G. Wadley, "Body and mind: a study of avatar personalization in three virtual worlds," In Proceedings of the SIGCHI Conference on Human Factors in Computing Systems (CHI '09) ACM, April 2009, pp. 1151–1160.

[15] R. Schroeder, "The social life of avatars: presence and interaction in shared virtual environments," Springer Science & Business Media, 2012.

[16] S. Gray, "In virtual fashion," in IEEE Spectrum, vol. 35, no. 2, pp. 18-25, Feb. 1998.

[17] Fashion fuelled by 5G. http://www.three.co.uk/hub/fashion-fuelled-by-5g/. Accessed 17 October 2020.

[18] Microsoft HoloLens. https://en.wikipedia.org/wiki/Microsoft_HoloLens. Accessed 17 October 2020.

[19] Avatar SDK. https://avatarsdk.com/. Accessed 17 October 2020.

[20] 3DLOOK. https://3dlook.me/. Accessed 17 October 2020.

[21] Mixamo. https://www.mixamo.com/. Accessed 17 October 2020.

[22] A. Merle, S. Senecal, and A. S. Onge, "Whether and how virtual try-on influences consumer responses to an apparel web site," International Journal of Electronic Commerce, vol. 16, no. 3, pp. 41-64, April 2012.

Hybrid Control and Game Design for BCI-integrated Action FPS Game

Supachai Tengtrakul and Setha Pan-ngum
Department of Computer Engineering
Chulalongkorn University
Bangkok, Thailand
e-mail: 6170289321@student.chula.ac.th, setha.p@chula.ac.th

Abstract— **Despite years of research, the fundamental issues of Electroencephalography (EEG) remain one of the most prominent problems for Brain-Computer Interface (BCI) game design, resulting in BCI games that look very lacking compared to other games in the market. This paper presents a new hybrid game control that is a combination of 4 methods of interaction: a Steady-State Visually Evoked Potential (SSVEP)-based BCI that utilizes a state-of-the-art Riemannian-based classifier, a mouse, a keyboard and an eye tracker. This paper also presents an action First-Person-Shooting (FPS) game that works together with the control to deliver satisfying BCI game experience. This game features 3 mechanics that assist the BCI control: slowing down time, highlighting an SSVEP stimulus that is being looked at and activating an SSVEP command automatically if players fail to do so in exchange for not receiving some rewards. From the test result from 10 subjects, we found that all subjects can issue commands through the eye tracker adequately at first, but the performance degraded over time. SSVEP commands had a 60.5% successful manual activation rate and it took around 3.569 seconds for each successful manual activation. Despite some inconveniences seen from the result, 90% of the subjects still found the game enjoyable, and 10% felt neutral toward the game.**

Keywords-BCI; EEG; SSVEP; Games; Riemannian-based classification.

I. INTRODUCTION

Brain-Computer Interface (BCI) gives us a mean to control a computer without moving by monitoring our brain activity. There are several techniques used to monitor the brain activity, and one of them is Electroencephalography (EEG) [1]. EEG monitors the brain activity through electrodes mounted on the scalp, so the procedure is completely non-invasive and can be applied repeatedly to anyone without risks or limitations [2]. These advantages, combined with the ease of setting up offered by dry electrodes, make EEG-based BCIs undoubtedly the most suitable BCIs for gaming application.

BCI games have a lot of benefits. They can be used to help patients recover from incidents of stroke and traumatic brain injuries, treat seizure disorders, help children and adolescents who have Attention-Deficit and Hyperactivity Disorder (ADHD) [3] or improve the quality of life of people with severe disabilities. Even for normal players, BCI games can provide Neurofeedback (NF) functionality that can modify the game experience to best suit players' emotional state and improve players' attention and cognitive skill when played regularly [4]. However, the gaming industry has never adopted BCIs in any full-featured game [5] since it has fundamental issues that make it not viable compared to the traditional input devices. The first issue is that the number of commands available for players can be very limited, depending on the approach we choose to process EEG. Another issue is high intersubject variability which leads to unreliability, the need for calibration and the phenomenon called BCI illiteracy, which prevents some people from using a BCI effectively [1].

Among several EEG-based BCI approaches, one of the most reliable ones is Steady-State Visually Evoked Potential (SSVEP) [3]. This approach uses visual stimuli that flicker at the frequency of 6 Hz or above to evoke brain responses [6]. EEG at the same frequency and its harmonics will become very dominant and easy to detect once subjects start focusing on a stimulus, and it will continue to dominate as long as subjects continue focusing. This means that SSVEP can support many commands, can support continuous input, has high susceptibility to artifacts [5], requires little to no time for calibration [7] and has a low chance to find a subject with BCI illiteracy [1]. However, this approach comes with a few issues. The first issue is that it cannot control in-game movement efficiently [5]. The second issue is that the accuracy of SSVEP classification has never been perfected and will only diminish the more stimulus frequencies are being used [8]. The last issue is that each subject's reaction toward the stimuli can be wildly different. Some people, especially the elderly, can find them annoying [1] while some people can find them tiresome or uncomfortable after constantly looking at them [9]. The most extreme case is that it can trigger a seizure in people with epilepsy, so every test requires a subject's medical history checking beforehand [10].

Using an SSVEP-based BCI with other input devices can mitigate some of the issues. For example, the study by Stawicki et al. [8] shows that a spelling application controlled by an SSVEP-based BCI and an eye tracker works better than the same application controlled by the BCI alone. Unfortunately, this idea has not gained a lot of traction in BCI game research community yet [5].

For the reasons mentioned above, we developed a new hybrid game control that uses an SSVEP-based BCI, a mouse, a keyboard and an eye tracker together. We also developed an action First-Person-Shooting (FPS) game that features several mechanics to facilitate the BCI control. Both work together to bring BCI game experience closer to the game experience provided by other games in the market.

This paper is organized into 6 sections. Section 2 describes the EEG signal acquisition and the development of the signal processor. Section 3 describes the design and development of the game. Section 4 describes the procedure of the experiment. Section 5 presents the result and discussion before Section 6 finally concludes this paper.

II. BCI Approach

A. Signal Acquisition

EEG signals are acquired through G.SAHARA active dry electrode system and G.MOBILAB+ from G.TEC [11]. Since SSVEP can be detected strongly in the occipital region of the brain [6], the electrodes were mounted at the following positions according to the international 10-20 system: Oz, O1, O2, POz, PO3, PO4, PO7 and PO8. The electrodes are connected to G.MOBILAB+ which is responsible for acquiring EEG signal at the sampling rate of 256Hz.

B. Signal Processing

According to the report on the progress of BCI games by Kerous et al. [5] and our survey, we found that the SSVEP classification method usually used in later studies is Canonical Correlation Analysis (CCA)-based classification. However, in the updated review of classification methods by Lotte et al. [12], we found another type of method called Riemannian-based classification. This type of classification can be applied to several BCI approaches and gives a performance that rivals or even surpasses the previous state-of-the-art method. For SSVEP, the first implementation was proposed by Kalunga et al. [13], and the result showed that it can outperform 2 CCA-based state-of-the-art methods proposed by Lin et al. [14] and Nakanishi et al. [15].

This classification method involves mapping a band-passed signal directly onto a Riemannian manifold and using Minimum Distance to Riemannian Mean (MDRM) algorithm to classify the signal. Essentially, this means estimating a covariance matrix from the band-passed signal, then finding the distance between the covariance matrix and the matrices that represent each class before finally classifying the signal into the closest class. The representative matrices are derived from all covariance matrices in the same class during a training phase. There are 3 variations of the method presented in the paper. The first one does not use the full MDRM algorithm, trading accuracy for speed. The second one uses the full algorithm, trading some speed for accuracy. The last one uses the full algorithm and an outlier signal removal method called Riemannian potato for maximum accuracy. We chose the first one to make our BCI as responsive as possible and compensate for the accuracy by limiting the number of stimulus frequencies to only one and utilizing an eye tracker to determine what stimulus is being focused on instead. This can mitigate the error that can happen during SSVEP classification, which, in turn, improves the accuracy and reliability of our BCI significantly, as seen in the work of Stawicki et al. [8].

We chose to implement this classifier on Matlab [16]. The original work by Kalunga was not implemented for real-time applications as it uses 4 seconds of signal for each iteration and requires 5 iterations before it can give a definite answer. Since G.MOBILAB+ uses a 256Hz sampling rate, 4 seconds of signal means 8,192 samples (1,024 x 8 channels) which is too much for real-time processing, so we reduce it to 2.5 seconds. We do not want to reduce it any further as requiring a lot of data might be the characteristic of this classifier. Still, 5,120 samples remain a lot for real-time processing, so we decided to give Matlab 0.25 seconds to complete each iteration. We also remove the voting process completely and reassign that task to the game instead. This allows the game to dynamically adjust the voting process to suit the current context, which can be very beneficial for continuous input.

III. Game Approach

A. Game Design

To demonstrate that the new hybrid control has more capability and imposes less restriction on the game design, we design the game with 2 goals in mind. First, the game must feature every kind of command that has ever been in an FPS game. Second, the game must feature unique mechanics to facilitate the BCI control that cannot be implemented with non-hybrid BCI control.

The core gameplay of FPS games is always the same since its earlier days, namely, players must progress through levels/maps and kill enemies. The innovation for the genre in terms of control comes from expanding more on this core gameplay. Regarding progressing through levels/maps, the most basic things that players need are movement, environment interaction and resources. In old games like Doom (1993) [17], movement is limited to walking and jumping, environment interaction is just pressing the right door switch, and resources only come in the form of pickups scattered around a level that can be utilized only when players walk right through them. However, in modern games like Far Cry 5 [18], movement can be sprinting, crouching or sliding, environment interaction can be talking to someone to receive a side quest, and resources can be items stored in the inventory that can be utilized anytime. Regarding killing enemies, the most basic things that players need are weapons. In Doom (1993) [17], players can only kill enemies with guns. However, in newer games like Borderlands [19], players can also kill enemies with a melee attack, a throwable item like a grenade or the special ability of the character that they chose.

Every command we have mentioned can be categorized into 5 types: movement, weapon, environment interaction, item and ability. Item and ability can be combined into one type since not every item and ability is meant for taking out enemies and both of their usages are limited by either quantity, cooldown or mana point. The real fifth type comes from in-game menu which is mandatory for every game. These 5 types are more than enough to serve the core gameplay of progressing through levels/maps and killing enemies. Therefore, they are enough for any FPS game.

Which command can be activated by SSVEP depends on whether or not it has at least one Head-Up Display (HUD) associated with it. However, as stated in the downsides of SSVEP, making every HUD become stimuli can be very annoying or tiresome for some players. Therefore, we need to do that only for the commands that require continuous input or the commands that do not, but should, require some degree of focus to activate. For the rest of HUD-associated commands, we decided to have players activate them by looking at a HUD and pressing a universal command button instead. The eye tracker that we use in this study is Tobii Eye Tracker 4C [20] which is capable of eye blink detection. This allows the game to know where players are looking at when they are blinking which can be translated into some additional commands as well.

The commands in movement type usually do not have any HUD associated with them. These commands should not require a lot of focus from players to activate as each of them is usually used in combination while players are focusing on more important tasks. Therefore, it is best to let players activate them easily through a mouse and a keyboard.

The second type is weapon which usually comes with a HUD: a crosshair for shooting or aiming down sight, an ammo count for reloading, a weapon icon for changing weapon, etc. We decided that aiming down sight should be activated by closing one eye to imitate how we aim a gun in real life. The rest of the commands, except shooting, can be activated by looking at a HUD and pressing a universal command button. Shooting is an exception because it shares the same HUD with aiming down sight and it needs both single and continuous input for automatic and semi-automatic weapons. Therefore, our solution is to make the command able to be activated by 2 methods: aiming at an enemy or focusing on a stimulus. The game also needs to slow down time for players when they are trying to focus because this command is more likely to be used during a hectic situation which can make focusing a lot harder.

The third type is item/ability, which needs a HUD to inform players whether an item/ability is available to use or not, meaning that every command in this type can be activated by looking at a HUD and pressing a button. However, we thought that there needs to be another way to activate these commands. Since some items/abilities tend to be used more often than others, having players closing one eye a little longer than usual to use the most essential item/ability immediately without the need to look at any specific HUD might improve gameplay significantly.

The fourth type is environment interaction, which needs a HUD to avoid confusion since most objects, or even doors, in most games are non-interactable. We decided that there should be 2 methods to activate this command: looking at a HUD and pressing a button or focusing on a stimulus. The latter would be used to depict an object that requires some effort to interact with. This also requires the game to slow down time for players if the interaction happens during a hectic situation.

The last type is in-game menu, which consists of every command related to in-game menus such as a pause menu, an inventory, a map, a weapon wheel, etc. We decided that it is best to let players control every in-game menu, except the weapon wheel, with a mouse and a keyboard since they can be wildly different in each game. The weapon wheel is an exception because its functionality is always the same; open, select an option and close which can be easily translated into holding a button, looking at an option before releasing the button.

From what we have described, a mechanic that facilitates the BCI control has already been mentioned, slow motion. This mechanic can already satisfy our goal since it needs an eye tracker, making it unable to be implemented with non-hybrid BCI control. However, due to the high intersubject variability of BCIs [1], we decided to add 2 more mechanics to improve the reliability, automatic activation and reward for manual activation. The game will activate an SSVEP command automatically at the end of the slow motion and give players some rewards if they can activate the command manually before the slow motion ends.

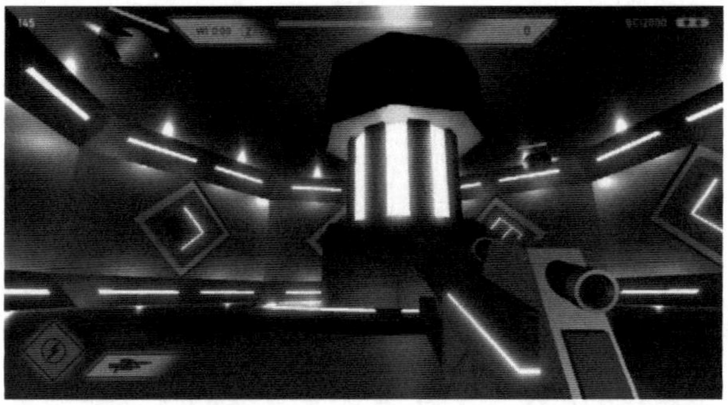

Figure 1. The screenshot of our game, Core Defender.

When combining this mechanic and the activation methods we have summarized together, we came up with a single-player FPS game called Core Defender, as seen in Figure 1. In this game, a player must use everything at his/her disposal to fight off 3 waves of enemies that want to crash into the core in the middle of the room. There are 2 weapons available: an assault rifle and a sniper rifle. The assault rifle can change between 3 ammo types: red ammo that does well against red enemies, yellow ammo that does well against yellow enemies and orange ammo that does well against both. If the player uses red or yellow ammo against the correct enemies, the player will be granted bonus scores. The sniper rifle, on the other hand, has only one ammo type and grants the player bonus scores all the time. Its shot is so powerful that it can destroy any enemy in a single hit. Besides the weapons, the player can also use the ability to turn on a laser grid around the core and slow down time. Turning on the laser grid can help the player destroy every enemy near the core, but it is limited to 2 times throughout the game. Slowing down time lasts for 8 seconds and players must wait for a cooldown to use it again. This ability is essential because it must be activated every time before the player can fire the sniper rifle or turn on the laser grid. If the player can activate one of those commands before the ability ends, the game will reward the player with a faster cooldown. Between each wave, the player has a choice to repair the core in exchange for some scores or skip to the next wave immediately. Regardless of how well the player plays, the core's health will always be reduced at the end of each wave to raise the stake for the player who wants the highest scores possible.

From the gameplay we have described, we can list every command available and summarize how each of them can be activated as follows:

- Using a mouse and a keyboard: move, look, open/close the assault rifle mode selection menu (Figure 2).
- Aiming at an enemy: fire the assault rifle.
- Pressing a universal command button when looking at a specific HUD: change weapon, use/cancel slowing down time.
- Closing one eye: aiming down sight.
- Closing one eye longer than usual: use/cancel slowing down time.
- Focusing on a stimulus when slowing down time is active: fire the sniper rifle, activate the laser grid.
- Focusing on a stimulus when slowing down time does not have to be active: fix the core, skip the wait time between each wave.
- Looking: select an option in the assault rifle mode selection menu (Figure 2).

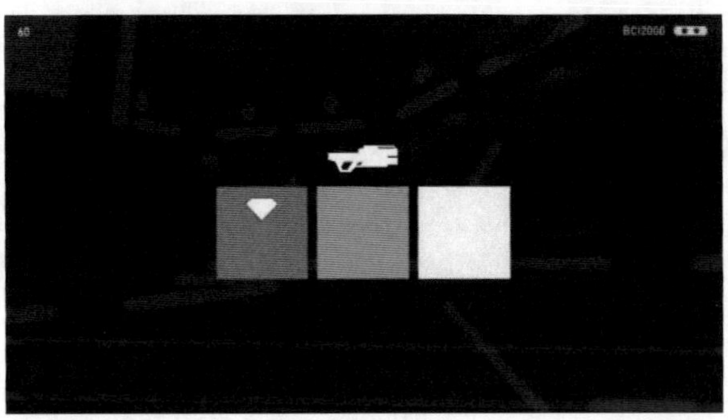

Figure 2. A screenshot showing the assault rifle mode selection menu.

B. *Stimulus Design*

Another thing that is crucial for bringing out the best performance of an SSVEP-based BCI is the stimuli. According to the report by Zhu et al. [21], using LED or fluorescent lights to display the stimuli can evoke stronger brain responses from a subject than using a monitor. Using a pattern reversal graphic instead of a simple flickering graphic can help us get a stronger brain responses as well. However, it is one of our goals to make the game as easy to set-up as possible and to make the stimuli look consistent with the rest of the game in terms of the aesthetic. Therefore, we cannot use those options which leaves us with 3 factors that we need to consider: frequency, color and visibility.

The frequencies used in most researches are usually in the range of 12-25Hz [21]. We decided to use 15Hz because, according to the study by Pastor et al. [22], the brain response reaches the greatest amplitude around this frequency.

The report by Zhu et al. [21] also wrote about the impact that stimulus color has on the performance of a BCI when using red, blue or yellow stimuli. However, none of those colors performs exceptionally well at 15Hz and the report stated that it required further study, so we chose the color that is used most among the studies that use the same type of graphic for their stimuli: white. The final design of our stimuli can be seen in Figure 3. Both second and third stimuli can appear at the same time.

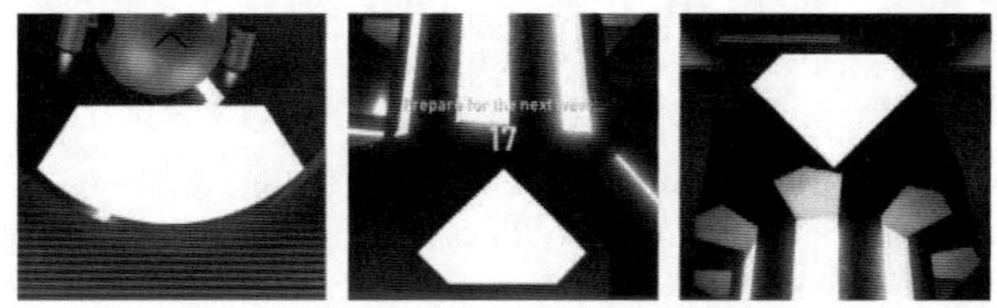

Figure 3. The SSVEP stimuli that appear in the game.

Visibility is another factor that may become an issue in our study. Since the stimuli are white and displayed on a computer screen, they can be barely visible to the player when his/her in-game character is in a bright environment or looking directly at a light source. To solve this issue, we use a mechanic called stimulus highlighting, as seen in Figure 4. The game will utilize the eye tracker to darken everything on the screen except the stimulus that is being looked at.

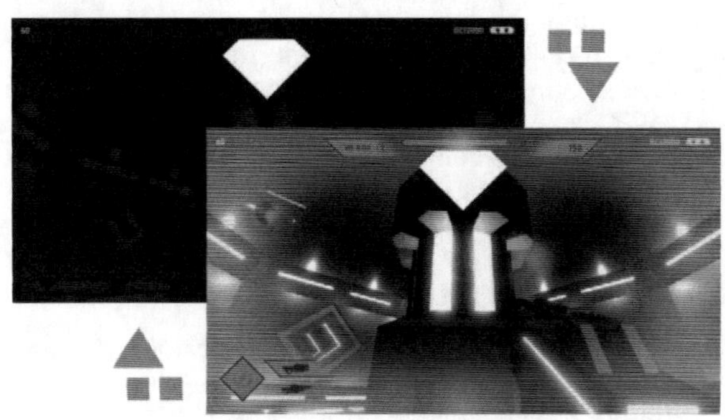

Figure 4. A screenshot showing stimulus highlighting.

C. *Game Development & BCI Integration*

The game was developed on game engine Unity 5 [23] for Windows platform and was integrated with 2 other components: Tobii Eye Tracker 4C and signal processor.

The integration with Tobii Eye Tracker 4C was done through a low-level Software Development Kit (SDK) called Stream Engine SDK [24]. Even though there is Tobii Unity SDK [25] available, we cannot use it since it does not provide a crucial feature that is eye blinking detection.

The integration with the signal processor was done through a software suite called BCI2000 [26]. BCI2000 consists of 4 modules: a source module, a signal processing module, an application module and an operator module. The first 3 modules can be swapped in and out freely while the last one stays the same to make sure that those 3 modules work together properly. For the source and signal processing module, we use the modules that come with BCI2000 to receive the signal from G.MOBILAB+ and send it to our classifier in Matlab. For the application module, however, there is currently no module that can communicate with Unity directly, so we use a dummy application with the sole functionality of sending and receiving User Datagram Protocol (UDP) messages instead. These messages can be sent across 2 computers or sent to other programs on the same computer through the localhost address. Despite the performance overhead, we chose remote communication because it allows us to test the game anywhere by simply installing the game on a target computer.

IV. EXPERIMENT

The experiment was performed on 10 male subjects who had never been diagnosed with epilepsy. Most subjects' age ranged from 21 to 26, except 1 subject who was 46. The test environment was dimly lit to increase the effectiveness of SSVEP stimuli and contained as few electrical sources as possible to minimize the number of artifacts in the EEG signal.

The experiment consisted of 3 main steps. The first step was testing the eye tracker, which involved calibrating the eye tracker and testing every eye tracker-related command. The test was done by having a subject activate each command 10 times and report to us how many attempts it took to activate each of them. During this step, any commands that were triggered when the subject had no intention to use any commands would be recorded as false triggering. The second step was testing the BCI which involves mounting electrodes, calibrating the BCI and testing every BCI command. The test was done by having the subject activate each command 10 times before moving on to the next one. The time it took to activate each command or whether the subject activated it manually or not would be recorded by the game. The last step was playing which involved playing the game from start to finish at least once. The data about SSVEP activation that the game recorded would not contribute toward the BCI test result because, after a long test, we wanted the subjects to have fun with the game so they may not focus on the stimuli as hard when they did not feel the need to get faster slow-motion cooldown that manual activation provided. All subjects were told about the prize that they would receive if they won and got 80% of the possible score before the game started.

After the experiment was completed, every subject must do a questionnaire. This questionnaire is adapted from the core module of Game Experience Questionnaire developed by Poels et al. [27] which aims to assess game experience in 7 aspects: competence, sensory and immersion, flow, tension, challenge, negative affect and positive affect. Every question must be answered on a scale of 0 to 4; 0 means strongly disagree, 4 means strongly agree. The subject can also provide additional feedback if he/she wishes to do so.

V. RESULTS AND DISCUSSIONS

A. *Eye Tracker*

Before the test began, we asked the subjects to close one eye to observe how well they can do it. Out of 10 subjects, there was only 1 who could keep the other eye open the entire time, which was below our expectation. Nonetheless, the result shows that the worst average first attempt rate of the commands that are activated by closing one eye is 70%, meaning that 70% of the time the subject can use the commands on the first attempt. The most attempts for a single command come from a different subject which is 3 attempts for aiming down sight. The worst average first attempt rate of the commands that do not involve closing one eye is 86.667%, and the worst false trigger rate is 7.407%. Overall, 10 subjects have an 86.5% average first attempt rate for the commands that are activated by closing one eye, a 96.333% average first attempt rate for the commands that are not and a 4.128% average false trigger rate. These data are enough to conclude that every subject can use eye tracker-related commands adequately during the test step.

TABLE I. THE RESULT OF THE BCI TESTING

	Shooting the Sniper Rifle			**Activating the Laser Grid**			**Skipping**			**Fixing the Core**			
	Manual	*Auto*	*Delay (sec.)*	*Manual*	*Auto*	*Delay*	*Manual*	*Auto*	*Delay*	*<8 sec.*	*>=8 sec.*	*Fail*	*Delay*
Sub. 1	7	3	1.764	5	5	2.41	4	6	2.421	6	2	2	2.792
Sub. 2	9	1	4.478	3	7	5.1	9	1	3.095	2	4	4	1.942
Sub. 3	9	1	4.042	7	3	2.355	10	0	3.542	8	0	2	2.265
Sub. 4	6	4	3.778	6	4	2.383	8	2	2.223	9	1	0	4.946
Sub. 5	5	5	3.045	8	2	2.531	7	3	3.684	8	2	0	3.992
Sub. 6	7	3	4.736	3	7	3.928	4	6	3.658	1	6	3	7.85
Sub. 7	6	4	2.752	5	5	3.703	8	2	2.669	6	4	0	3.672
Sub. 8	8	2	4.492	1	9	6.7	6	4	5.078	4	3	3	5.65
Sub. 9	7	3	3.088	2	8	1.992	6	4	2.808	2	5	3	5.567
Sub. 10	7	3	3.519	9	1	3.031	6	4	3.111	8	2	0	1.964
Avg.	7.1	2.9	3.569	4.9	5.1	3.413	6.8	3.2	3.229	5.4	2.9	1.7	4.064

B. BCI

The differences between the results of each command are far above our expectations. As seen in Table I, shooting the sniper rifle yields moderately good results with a 71% average manual activation rate and 3.569 seconds average activation time, while activating the laser grid and fixing the core are significantly worse. It is important to note that the activation time does not take Auto and >=8 sec. columns into account. We think that there are 3 potential causes. The first one is that the subjects might feel more pressured when trying to activate these commands. Activating the laser grid must be used during enemy waves, and the subjects must focus while they see enemies approaching from multiple angles. Fixing the core is a unique command because it has no automatic activation. Compared to other commands that have 8 seconds for manual activation, this command can fail completely if it is not activated manually within the time between enemy waves. The second cause might be the size of the stimulus which is noticeably smaller than the stimulus of shooting the sniper rifle. One subject also said that the position of the stimulus (upper screen) made it a bit harder to focus when compared to the stimulus of skipping that looks the same but is located in a different area (lower screen). The last cause, which we think affects every command in general, is the performance of the Riemannian-based SSVEP classifier. As mentioned before, this classifier in the original work requires 4 seconds of signal for each iteration. Applying that directly to our work might result in an average activation time that is well above 4 seconds. However, modifying the classifier to use only 2.5 seconds as we did might affect the accuracy and lower the manual activation rate, which is a trade-off that is worth looking into more in the future.

C. Playing Session

From 10 playing sessions, 453 enemies were destroyed in total, and 176 of them were destroyed by the sniper rifle which is equal to 38.852%. 60% of the subjects used the sniper rifle more than 40% of the time, and 50% of those used the sniper rifle more than the assault rifle. These results show that most subjects felt confident enough to use SSVEP commands during an action whether the BCI worked reliably enough or not.

TABLE II. THE RESULT OF THE QUESTIONNAIRE

	Avg. Score	Result (Positive/Negative)
Competence	2.8	Positive
Sensory & Immersion	3	Positive
Flow	3	Positive
Tension	2.3	Negative
Challenge	3.2	Positive
Negative Affect	1.42	Positive
Positive Affect	2.9	Positive

D. Questionnaire

We averaged the scores of every question in each category across every subject and the result can be seen in Table II. The max score of 4 can be either positive or negative, depending on the category. As can be seen, the subjects generally have positive impressions toward the game in every aspect except one, tension. The questions in the tension category focus on whether the subjects felt annoyed or frustrated by the eye tracker and BCI control or not. The average score of the eye tracker control is 2.1, and the average score of the BCI control is 2.5. When comparing the eye tracker score to the results of the previous test, it clearly shows that most subjects experienced facial fatigue during the real playing session. Despite all these negative results, most subjects still enjoyed the game and felt that they could control the game well enough, which are reflected in the positive affect and competence score.

VI. CONCLUSION AND FUTURE WORK

A new hybrid control, which is a combination of SSVEP-based BCI, an eye tracker, a mouse and a keyboard, has been presented. The BCI utilizes the Riemannian-based classifier proposed by Kalunga et al. [13] in the hope of making the BCI reliable enough to control FPS games. An action FPS game that features several mechanics to facilitate the BCI control has also been presented. Those mechanics are slow motion, automatic SSVEP activation, highlighting stimulus and reward for manual activation.

The performance of the BCI is inconsistent. The results were decent for some commands, but far below our expectation for others. This might be because we reduced the signal window used for each iteration from 4 seconds, as originally proposed, to 2.5 seconds. Furthermore, we found that most subjects cannot close one eye perfectly and experienced facial fatigue during the real playing session, which makes eye tracker-related commands more frustrating to use. Despite these issues, the mechanics of the game still helped the subjects gain enough control of the game to find it enjoyable and created enough incentive for the subjects to use BCI commands.

In future studies, we would like to focus on finding the optimal signal window that maintains both speed and accuracy for the classifier. We will also make activating commands by closing one eye not mandatory for aiming down sight since it is not related to the BCI and it hurts the overall game experience more than enhances it.

REFERENCES

[1] B. Allison et al., "BCI Demographics: How Many (and What Kinds of) People Can Use an SSVEP BCI?," IEEE Transactions on Neural Systems and Rehabilitation Engineering, vol. 18, no. 2, pp. 107-116, Apr. 2010, doi: 10.1109/TNSRE.2009.2039495.

[2] M. Teplan, "Fundamental of EEG Measurement," Measurement Science Review, vol. 2, pp. 1-11, Jan. 2002.

[3] R. Parafita, G. Pires, U. Nunes, and M. Castelo-Branco, "A spacecraft game controlled with a brain-computer interface using SSVEP with phase tagging," 2013 IEEE 2nd International Conference on Serious Games and Applications for Health (SeGAH), Vilamoura, May 2013, pp. 1-6, doi: 10.1109/SeGAH.2013.6665309.

[4] K. P. Thomas, A. P. Vinod, and C. Guan, "Enhancement of attention and cognitive skills using EEG based neurofeedback game," 2013 6th International IEEE/EMBS Conference on Neural Engineering (NER), San Diego, CA, Nov. 2013, pp. 21-24, doi: 10.1109/NER.2013.6695861.

[5] B. Kerous, F. Škola, and F. Liarokapis, "EEG-based BCI and video games: a progress report," Virtual Reality, vol. 22, no. 2, pp. 1-17, Oct. 2017, doi: 10.1007/s10055-017-0328-x.

[6] C. Ming, G. Xiaorong, G. Shangkai, and X. Dingfeng, "Design and implementation of a brain-computer interface with high transfer rates," IEEE Transactions on Biomedical Engineering, vol. 49, no. 10, pp. 1181-1186, Oct. 2002, doi: 10.1109/TBME.2002.803536.

[7] R. Singla, "Comparison of SSVEP Signal Classification Techniques Using SVM and ANN Models for BCI Applications," International Journal of Information and Electronics Engineering, vol. 4, no. 1, pp. 6-10, Jan. 2014, doi: 10.7763/IJIEE.2014.V4.398.

[8] P. Stawicki, F. Gembler, A. Rezeika, and I. Volosyak, "A Novel Hybrid Mental Spelling Application Based on Eye Tracking and SSVEP-Based BCI," (in eng), Brain Sci, vol. 7, no. 4, pp. 35, Apr. 2017, doi: 10.3390/brainsci7040035.

[9] H. Gürkök, A. Nijholt, and M. Poel, "Brain-Computer Interface Games: Towards a Framework," Entertainment Computing - ICEC 2012, Berlin, Heidelberg, Sep. 2012, pp. 373-380.

[10] G. Harding, A. J. Wilkins, G. Erba, G. L. Barkley, and R. S. Fisher, "Photic- and pattern-induced seizures: expert consensus of the Epilepsy Foundation of America Working Group," (in eng), Epilepsia, vol. 46, no. 9, pp. 1423-1425, Sep. 2005, doi: 10.1111/j.1528-1167.2005.31305.x.

[11] G.Tec Medical Engineering. G.Saharasys & G.Mobilab+. Product. available: https://www.gtec.at. last accessed: Oct. 2020.

[12] F. Lotte et al., "A Review of Classification Algorithms for EEG-based Brain-Computer Interfaces: A 10-year Update," Journal of Neural Engineering, vol. 15, no. 3, pp. 31005, Feb. 2018, doi: 10.1088/1741-2552/aab2f2.

[13] E. K. Kalunga et al., "Online SSVEP-based BCI using Riemannian geometry," Neurocomputing, vol. 191, pp. 55-68, Feb. 2016, doi: https://doi.org/10.1016/j.neucom.2016.01.007.

[14] Z. Lin, C. Zhang, W. Wu, and X. Gao, "Frequency recognition based on canonical correlation analysis for SSVEP-based BCIs," IEEE Transactions on Biomedical Engineering, vol. 54, no. 6, pp. 1172-1176, Jul. 2007, doi: 10.1109/TBME.2006.889197.

[15] M. Nakanishi, Y. Wang, Y. T. Wang, Y. Mitsukura, and T. P. Jung, "A high-speed brain speller using steady-state visual evoked potentials," (in eng), Int J Neural Syst, vol. 24, no. 6, pp. 1450019, Sep. 2014, doi: 10.1142/s0129065714500191.

[16] Math Works. Matlab R2018b. Software. available: https://www.mathworks.com. last accessed: Oct. 2020.

[17] Id Software. Doom (1993). Video game. available: https://store.steampowered.com. last accessed: Oct. 2020.

[18] Ubisoft. Far Cry 5. Video game. available: https://store.steampowered.com. last accessed: Oct. 2020.

[19] Gearbox Software. Borderlands. Video game. available: https://store.steampowered.com. last accessed: Oct. 2020.

[20] Tobii Tech. Tobii Eye Tracker 4C. Product. no longer available. detail: https://gaming.tobii.com. last accessed: Oct. 2020.

[21] D. Zhu, J. Bieger, G. Garcia-Molina, and R. Aarts, "A survey of stimulation methods used in SSVEP-based BCIs," Computational Intelligence and Neuroscience, vol. 2010, pp. 702357, Jan. 2010, doi: 10.1155/2010/702357.

[22] M. A. Pastor, J. Artieda, J. Arbizu, M. Valencia, and J. C. Masdeu, "Human cerebral activation during steady-state visual-evoked responses," (in eng), J Neurosci, vol. 23, no. 37, pp. 11621-11627, Dec. 2003, doi: 10.1523/jneurosci.23-37-11621.2003.

[23] Unity Technologies. Unity 5. Software. available: https://unity3d.com. last accessed: Oct. 2020.

[24] Tobii Tech. Stream Engine SDK. Software development kit. available: https://vr.tobii.com/sdk/develop/native/stream-engine. last accessed: Oct. 2020.

[25] Tobii Tech. Tobii Unity SDK for Desktop. Software development kit. available: https://developer.tobii.com/tobii-unity-sdk. last accessed: Oct. 2020.

[26] Schalk Lab. BCI2000. Software. available: http://bci2000.org. last accessed: Oct. 2020.

[27] K. Poels, Y. A. W. de Kort, and W. A. Ijsselsteijn, D3.3 : Game Experience Questionnaire (development of a self-report measure to assess the psychological impact of digital games). Eindhoven: Technische Universiteit Eindhoven, 2007.

Literature Review on Accessibility Guidelines for Self-service Terminals

Yuryeon Lee, Hwaseung Jeon, Hyun K. Kim
School of Information Convergence
Kwangwoon University
20 Kwangwoon-ro, Nowon-gu, Seoul, 01897, Republic of Korea
e-mail: {tkdenddl74, stella668, hyunkkim}@kw.ac.kr

Sunyoung Park
School of Software
Kwangwoon University
20 Kwangwoon-ro, Nowon-gu, Seoul, 01897, Republic of Korea
e-mail: tjsdud9151@gmail.com

***Abstract*— In the age of informatization, the informatization equipment domain is expanding worldwide. The introduction of self-service terminals has accelerated the development of the unmanned service industry, and currently, people interact with self-service terminals in various places. Although informatization using products and services related to information and communication is conducted at a significantly high speed, research on the accessibility of self-service terminals among users with physical and cognitive disabilities is insufficient. Therefore, we examined the laws and guidelines on accessibility to self-service terminals, compared and analyzed the characteristics of each guideline, and highlighted the factors to be supplemented based on the types of disabilities and User Interface (UI) functions.**

Keywords-self-service terminal; kiosk; guideline; accessibility; disability.

I. INTRODUCTION

In the age of information, a significant amount of data is being processed rapidly and accurately worldwide, thus expanding the field of information equipment [1]. The trend of using touch-screen technology in self-service terminals has continued to grow, and self-service technology is becoming increasingly prevalent and crucial [2]. In addition, the introduction of self-service terminals has accelerated the development of the unmanned service industry, and the services replaced by self-service terminals are gradually expanding into high value-added industries [3]. In addition, improvement in the functionality and costs of touch-screen technology has led to self-service terminals becoming increasingly integrated into our daily lives. People now interact with self-service terminals at various places, such as local grocery stores and airport check-in counters [4].

Although informatization using products and services related to information and communication is conducted at a significantly high speed, there are growing concerns regarding the information gap. The primary cause of this gap is the limitation of physical and cognitive access, which is a result of insufficient consideration of users with physical and cognitive disabilities [5].

Therefore, in this study, we aim to analyze the trends of products and services related to information and communication and to improve the accessibility of products and services related to information and communication. So we examine international guidelines on accessibility to self-service terminals based on the types of disabilities and User Interface (UI) functions. In the study results, we present the characteristics of each accessibility guideline and the supplementary factors of the guidelines to be developed later.

In Section II, accessibility guidelines and laws are introduced, and classification criteria are explained. Section III deals with the guidelines and statistical results on the type of disability, and Section IV explains the insights that can be obtained through statistical results. Finally, Section V summarizes the study.

II. METHOD

A. Guidelines and Law Clauses Survey

We examined new laws and guidelines that emphasize the importance of accessibility to prevent discrimination against people with disabilities while using Information Technology (IT) devices. Among a total of 12 guidelines and laws, five were selected in consideration of the law's enforceability, the importance of literature, and the relevance of kiosk accessibility. In these laws and guidelines, items related to self-service terminal accessibility have been selected. Specifically, 78 items from the Guidelines for Public Access Terminal Accessibility (PATA) [9], 13 items from Section 508 of the Rehabilitation Act (RA) [10], 49 items from The US Air Carrier Access Act (ACAA) [11], 16 items from the 2010 Americans with Disabilities Act (ADA) Standards for Accessible Design [12], and 13 items from the European Accessibility Act (EAA) [13] were selected. Based on the judgment that common items are important in terms of accessibility, 21 items from PATA, 7 from RA, 21 from ACAA, 14 from ADA, and 5 from EAA were selected as common items, as shown in the graph below (Figure 1).

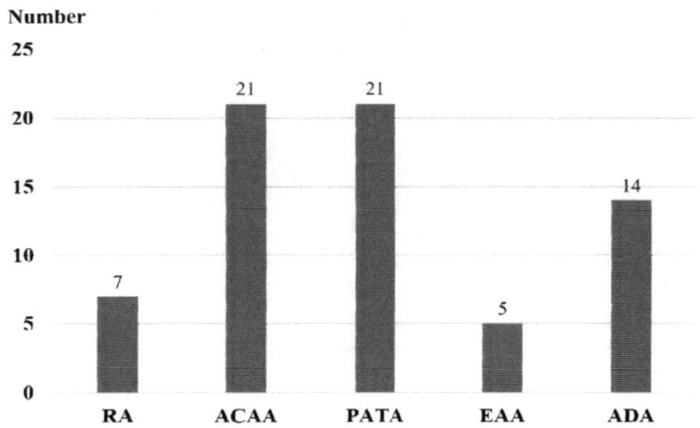

Figure 1. Number of Guidelines.

B. *Classification Criteria*

The self-service terminal accessibility guidelines were classified based on accessibility functions used in the previous studies [5]-[7] and reclassified in detail based on UI functions (Table 1). As a result of examining previous studies, the recommendation of manufacturer and service provider (F) deals with the physical part, unlike other provisions.

TABLE 1. ACCESSIBILITY AND UI FUNCTION

Accessibility function	UI function
Complement of color identification ability (A)	Avoid color coding
	Contrast
Complement of reaction time (B)	Sufficient time
Complement and replacement of hearing (C)	Volume control
Complement and replacement of vision (D)	Identification of input control
	Tactile information
	Input keypad
	Braille
	Text-size enlargement
	Audio output
Complement of cognitive ability (E)	Display seizure
Recommendation of manufacturer and service provider (F)	Display visibility
	Privacy
	Possibility of operation without assistive technology
	Floor or ground space
	User identification method
Complement hand or arm movement (G)	Fine motor control alternatives

The types of disabilities in the study were limited to three: visual impairment, hearing impairment, and physical disability, which are determined to affect the operation of self-service terminals. When more than one type of disability was present per clause, it was repeatedly calculated while determining statistics related to the disability type.

III. RESULT

A. *Percentage of Disabilities by Guidelines*

The study results show that among the types of disabilities, provisions related to visual impairment accounted for the highest proportion, whereas those related to hearing impairment accounted for the lowest proportion. The number of provisions related to visual impairment was highest in ACAA and lowest in EAA. Meanwhile, provisions related to hearing impairment were highest in the Guidelines for PATA and lowest in EAA. Similarly, provisions related to physical disabilities were highest in the Guidelines for PATA and lowest in EAA (Figure 2).

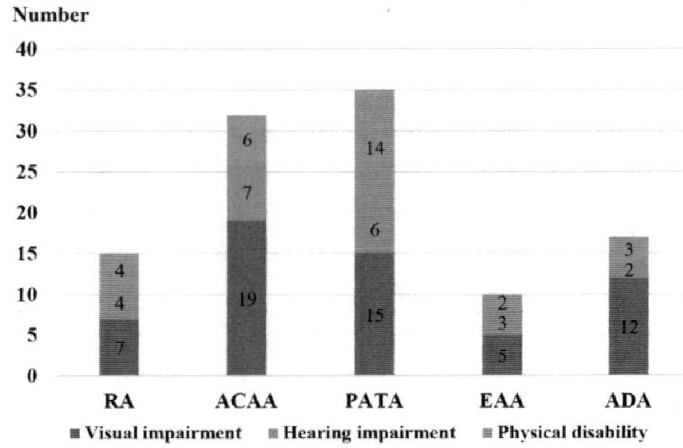

Figure 2. Percentage of Disabilities by Guidelines

B. *Percentage of Disabilities by Accessibility Function*

The study results show that the most common provisions related to visual impairment are complement of color identification ability (A) and complement and replacement of vision (D). Additionally, recommendation by manufacturer and service provider (F) and complement of reaction time (B) are not included in provisions for hearing impairment. Meanwhile, complement of cognitive ability (E) and complement hand or arm movement (G) have similar proportions of the three disability types (Figure 3).

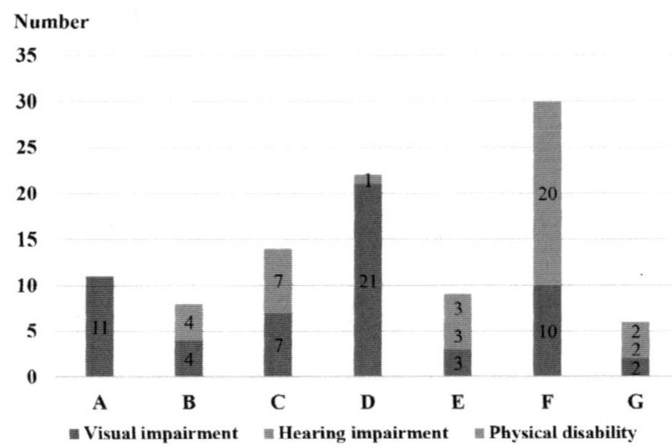

Figure 3. Percentage of Disabilities by Accessibility Function

C. *Percentage of Guidelines by Accessibility Function*

The complement of color identification ability (A) and complement and replacement of hearing (C) items are included in all the five guidelines and law clauses; however, the rest are included in only a few. The complement hand or arm movement (G) item is included in only two guidelines and has a low percentage. Similarly, the complement of cognitive ability (E) item is included in three guidelines and has a low percentage.

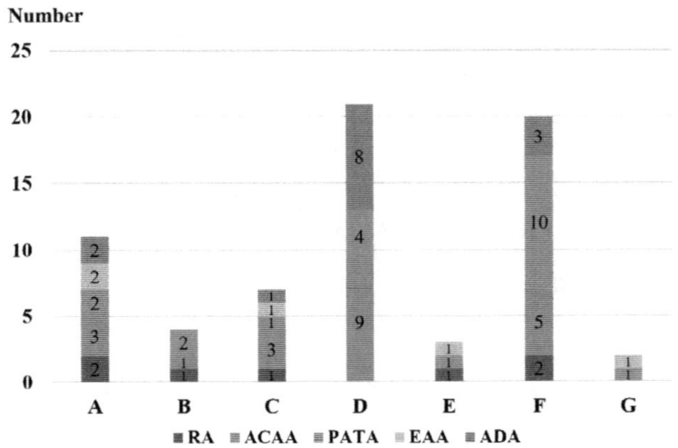

Figure 4. Percentage of Guidelines by Accessibility Function

The complement and replacement of vision (D) item is significantly included in the ACAA and ADA Standards for Accessible Design; however, it is completely excluded in the RA and EAA. In addition, the recommendation of manufacturer and service provider (F) item was primarily noted in PATA (Figure 4).

IV. DISCUSSION

The statistics of the graph presented in Figure 2 show that there are many provisions related to visual impairment, whereas those related to hearing impairment and physical disability are relatively fewer. The results also show that more factors are related to visual impairment, compared to hearing impairment and physical disability, because of the characteristics of self-service terminals that use touch-screen technology. The most important provisions related to physical disabilities are included in the PATA; however, the other guidelines have relatively fewer provisions related to physical disabilities. To develop future guidelines, it is necessary to promote provisions related to physical disabilities, such as installation location, passageways, and touch-screen interaction. In fact, most mobile devices provide touch-screen interaction, which can be particularly problematic for people with physical disabilities. Moreover, studies focusing on the design of touch-screen interfaces for users with physical disabilities are insufficient. The recommendation of manufacturer and service provider (F) item was considered a notable factor of visual impairment and physical disability, because there are many provisions for installation sites and spaces.

The statistics of the graph presented in Figure 4 show that the complement of color identification ability (A) and complement and replacement of hearing (C) items are included in all five guidelines; however, the others are included in only some guidelines. Therefore, it was determined that the specific factors for each guideline differed. In addition, the complement hand or arm movement (G) item is included only in the PATA and the EAA. Therefore, they must be considered and included in future provisions of other guidelines. The complement and replacement of vision (D) and complement of color identification ability (A) items related to vision were primarily noted in the ACAA and the ADA Standards for Accessible Design, whereas the recommendation of manufacturers and service providers (F) item was primarily noted in PATA. Hence, the ACAA should be analyzed for guidelines related to vision, while the PATA should be analyzed for guidelines related to kiosk manufacturing.

Other disabilities were not considered in this study because the types of disabilities were limited to visual, hearing, and physical disabilities, which are related to the operation of self-service terminals. Future studies may also focus on mental disabilities, such as intellectual disabilities.

Statistical calculations were conducted based on the number of guidelines; however, detailed evaluation methods are required to accurately evaluate the self-service terminal accessibility guidelines. For example, ANOVA can be used to evaluate the difference for each guideline, and Fisher test can be used to perform a post-test.

V. CONCLUSION

In this study, international guidelines related to self-service terminal accessibility were examined and classified based on three types of disabilities and seven accessibility functions.

Based on statistical information, we determined the UI functions and types of disabilities that characterize each guideline, as well as the percentage of the types of disabilities, according to the accessibility function.

The study results show the characteristics of the overall self-service terminal accessibility guidelines and the factors to be supplemented. This information will be useful for future studies aiming to further develop the self-service terminal accessibility guidelines.

ACKNOWLEDGMENT

This research was supported by the Ministry of Science and ICT (MIST), under the National Program for Excellence in SW (2017-0-00096), and supervised by the Institute for Information & Communication Technology Promotion (IITP). Moreover, this work was supported by the National Research Foundation of Korea (NRF) grant and funded by the Korean government (MIST) (No. 2018R1C1B5086269).

REFERENCES

[1] Y. Sung et al., “Correlation between cognitive function and ability to use kiosk (KIOSK) in seniors 65 years and older,” Journal of the Korean Age-Friendly Industry, vol. 11, no. 2, pp. 135-142, 2019.

[2] E. Jokisuu, M. McKenna, A. W. Smith, and P. Day, “Improving touchscreen accessibility in self-service technology,” In International Conference on Universal Access in Human-Computer Interaction, pp. 103-113, 2015, Springer, Cham.

[3] H. Lim, D. Ryu, and D. Park, "Kiosk Industry Analysis: Adoption Effects and Market Prospects," Korea Business Review, vol. 24, no. 1, pp. 21-48, 2020.

[4] S. N. Duff, C. B. Irwin, J. L. Skye, M. E. Sesto, and D. A. Wiegmann, “The effect of disability and approach on touch screen

performance during a number entry task," In Proceedings of the Human Factors and Ergonomics Society Annual Meeting, vol. 54, no. 6, pp. 566-570, 2010, Sage CA: Los Angeles, CA: SAGE Publications.

[5] J. Jo, S. Lee, and S. Park, "A study on evaluating accessibility of public institution kiosks: focusing on accessibility," Regulations on Informatization Policy, vol. 11, no. 1, pp. 51-73, 2004.

[6] H. K. Kim, and J. Park, "Examination of the Protection Offered by Current Accessibility Acts and Guidelines to People with Disabilities in Using Information Technology Devices," Electronics, vol. 9, no. 5, 742, 2020.

[7] H. K. Kim, C. Kim, E. Lim, and H. Kim, "How to develop accessibility UX design guideline in Samsung," In Proceedings of the 18th International Conference on Human-Computer Interaction with Mobile Devices and Services Adjunct, pp. 551-556, 2016.

[8] L. Anthony, Y. Kim, and L. Findlater, "Analyzing user-generated youtube videos to understand touchscreen use by people with motor impairments," In Proceedings of the SIGCHI conference on human factors in computing systems, pp. 1223-1232, 2013.

[9] Guidelines for Public Access Terminals Accessibility. Available online: http://universaldesign.ie/Technology-ICT/Irish-National-IT-Accessibility-Guidelines/Public-Access-Terminals/Guidelines-for-Public-Access-Terminals-Accessibility/ [retrieved : July 2020].

[10] Section 508 of the Rehabilitation Act. Available online: https://www.fcc.gov/general/section-508-rehabilitation-act [retrieved : July 2020].

[11] The U.S. Air Carrier Access Act. Available online: https://www.transportation.gov/tags/air-carrier-access-act [retrieved : July 2020].

[12] 2010 ADA Standards for Accessible Design. Available online: https://www.ada.gov/2010ADAstandards_index.htm [retrieved : July 2020].

[13] European Accessibility Act. Available online: https://eur-lex.europa.eu/legal-content/EN/TXT/?uri=CELEX%3A32019L0882 [retrieved : July 2020].

Developing Positive Attitudes Towards Cooperative Problem Solving by Linking Socio-emotional and Cognitive Intentions

Masato Kuno
Kyoto University
Kyoto, Japan
Email: kuno@ii.ist.i.kyoto-u.ac.jp

Yoshimasa Ohmoto
Shizuoka University
Shizuoka, Japan
Email: ohmoto-y@inf.shizuoka.ac.jp

Toyoaki Nishida
Fukuchiyama University
Fukuchiyama, Japan
Email: toyoaki.nishida@fukuchiyama.ac.jp

***Abstract*—We focus on problem-solving situations in which people cooperate with virtual interactive agents. The final goal is to achieve high-quality problem solving through a problem-solving process in which people recognise agents as effective collaborators and actively cooperate with the agents. It is known that trust, which is the basis of cooperation, has both affective and competent aspects. However, because the impression of agents tends to focus on the ability side, it is necessary to make the people recognise that the ability and emotional sides of agents are not separate but are integrated. In the proposed method, we apply the Alternate Estimation by representing Global and Local (AEGL) goal-oriented behaviour model, which adjusts the behaviour of an agent that show the agent's ability side and the emotional side by estimating the causes of the human behaviour. We demonstrated how both behaviours change consistently through interaction with people. In this study, we designed an experimental agent model to realise the proposed model. The people and agents are asked to perform cooperative decision-making tasks by exchanging opinions and adapting to each other's behaviour. The results suggest that the relationship between the ability and affective functioning of the agents eases tension and that people feel more comfortable talking to the agents.**

Keywords–human-agent interaction; cooperative problem.

I. Introduction

Today, agents are developed to cooperate for solving problems. When solving complex problems with no optimal solution, if people think alone, their view is narrow, and they will not be able to generate a solution. If people speak with other people and exchange opinions, their opinions stimulate them to produce various ideas. However, not everyone can be a good collaborator.

Kwon et al. argued that a situation in which self-disclosure and intimacy with collaborators are triggered is a precondition for a sense of community and that a sense of community is the final product of successful collaborative learning [1]. If people feel uncomfortable interacting with a partner who is unfriendly and difficult to talk to, they are not likely to interact willingly.

On the other hand, if they find a partner who is likeable and easy to talk to, they are expected to cooperate with him/her without resistance and to consider his/her opinion to be valid. They will be able to compare opinions efficiently and have a broader perspective regarding problem solving. As a result, good quality satisfactory problem solving can be achieved.

However, such a partner does not always exist in the scene of problem solving. Therefore, an agent who can be called on as a partner at any time and who is easy to talk to and likeable is expected to be available as a collaborator.

The final goal of this study is to realise good, satisfactory problem solving through a process in which people recognise agents as effective partners and actively cooperate with them. However, it is difficult to induce people to actively cooperate even in situations in which people must cooperate with other people.

Chi et al. categorised student engagement behaviours into four patterns: interactive, constructive, active, and passive [2]. This classification suggests that a gap exists between the passive and interactive states, in which students produce knowledge by talking with others. Therefore, to induce people's willingness to cooperate, it is necessary for people to feel that it is easy to talk to agents and to be friendly with them to overcome the gap. This study focuses on this aspect.

In collaborative learning where learners discuss and exchange opinions with each other to solve problems, social interaction is important for the learners' positive attitude towards cooperation [3]. The following two types of social interactions are typical during collaborative learning [4] [5]:

- Cognitive interaction: Discussions related to the task itself or the metacognition of the collaborators; and
- Socio-emotional interaction: Shared emotions about the task and pronounced expressions of positive and negative emotions.

First, cognitive interaction with other learners implies an active exchange of ideas for the solution of the problem. Smooth cognitive interactions can stimulate discussion of the problem and enhance people's evaluations of the agents' abilities. A previous study has shown that a group of learners who share their thoughts and understanding through cognitive interaction engage in a deeper level of the learning process than a group of learners who do not actively share their thoughts and understanding [6]. A study by Maltz et al. also demonstrated that people continue to accept system suggestions when they trust the system's capabilities [7]. Thus, if the partner makes appropriate and accurate statements about the task, the learner trusts his/her partner's ability, and the learner's positive attitude towards cooperation is expected to be induced.

Second, socio-emotional interaction is related to the expression of emotions in a social context. In other words, the interaction aims to 'build trust and belonging by getting to know each other'. Kwon et al. argued that socio-emotional interaction has the effect of smoothing out the behaviour of the members and protecting them from friction [1]. Kreijns et al. further argued that socio-emotional interaction facilitates overall interaction and increases the efficiency of cooperative learning [8]. In conclusion, socio-emotional interaction may increase the familiarity with other learners and induce smooth and low-resistance interaction. In addition, socio-emotional interaction is thought to have the effect of increasing the learners' positive attitudes by synergistically inducing total interaction including cognitive interaction.

From the above discussion, cognitive and socio-emotional interactions have the effect of giving people positive impressions about the competence and familiarity of the other learner, respectively. In this study, we induce agents to perform cognitive and socio-emotional behaviours to that people can recognise agents as collaborators and interact with them without resistance.

In the case of people, it is obvious that they have emotions in addition to their abilities. However, the fact that agents have emotions (including intention) is not obvious, since because their abilities are often emphasised due to their strong associations with machines. In this regard, Dennett proposed an idea called 'intentional stance', which refers to the idea that robots and agents have intentions when people interact with them [9]. Dennett stated that people do not usually think that robots and agents have intentions. A comparison of interactions between people and agents that induce intentional stance and those that do not induce intentional stance demonstrates that people who interact with the former interact more actively, even in situations unrelated to the task [10].

In conclusion, it is possible that the two functions of an agent are understood by people separately. If these two functions are not understood as a whole, people cannot perceive an agent's intention consistently. As a result, people cannot perceive the agent's abilities and emotions towards the inconsistent behaviour of the agent, and thus, they cannot induce positive attitudes towards the cooperation of the agent. We aim to demonstrate how agents behave with consistent intentions by inducing people to perceive that their cognitive and socio-emotional behaviours are related to each other. For this purpose, the cognitive and socio-emotional intentions of the agents are represented by the model, and both intentions are updated with consistency. Thus, we propose generating both cognitive and socio-emotional behaviours of agents using the AEGL model developed by Omoto et al. [11]. The AEGL model has the characteristic of combining the intentions of both people and agents, estimating their intentions alternately. Because cognitive and socio-emotional behaviours of people are consistent, it is expected that the cognitive and socio-emotional intentions of agents, which are updated based on the estimated intentions of people, are also consistent. In other words, it is expected that people can perceive how the two intentions are integrated and combined with people's intentions.

In this study, as a first step towards the realisation of the above-proposed method, the cognitive and socio-emotional behaviours of agents are generated in parallel. In the generation of socio-emotional behaviours, we suggest the relationship between the agents' socio-emotional behaviours and cognitive behaviours so that humans can recognise the relationship between them. Specifically, the AEGL model is not used, but a simple model that mimics the AEGL model is used to generate agents' behaviours. We then asked the agents and people to solve problems by cooperating and observed how the relationship between the agents' cognitive and socio-emotional behaviours affects people.

The goal of this study is to induce people to feel that agents are easy to talk with and are familiar to them. That is, we aimed to reduce the resistance that people feel to cooperating with an agent and to increase the subjective liking of the agent. These effects support people's willingness to cooperate with agents. When people feel comfortable and familiar with agents, they are more likely to speak with the agents and accept their opinions.

This paper is organised as follows. Section 2 introduces the related work. Section 3 provides an overview of the proposed method. Section 4 describes the experiments conducted in this study. Section 5 presents the results of the experiment. Section 6 describes the results of the experiment and future tasks. Section 7 concludes the work.

II. Related Work

Previous studies have shown that treating emotional interactions in addition to task-oriented interactions in dialogue systems and agents can increase people's satisfaction [12] and induce positive perceptions of interactions [13].

For example, Kumar et al. investigated the effect of having tutor agents support students in their studies while performing socio-emotional behaviours in addition to cognitive behaviours [14]. The tutor agents work on socio-emotional behaviours using interaction strategies based on the three categories of 'showing solidarity', 'showing tension release', and 'agreeing'. The rules for generating the behaviours are predefined, and the cognitive and socio-emotional behaviours of the agents were triggered using different interaction strategies with the input of task progress and interaction states. The tutor agents generated cognitive and socio-emotional behaviours separately, and the students did not perceive these behaviours to be linked to each other. Thus, although the questionnaire results indicated that the agents who performed the socio-emotional behaviour were friendlier than those who did not perform the socio-emotional behaviour, we did not find that the students had the impression that the agents were easy to talk to or friendly, and we did not obtain any indicators that revealed students' positive attitudes towards cooperation.

In contrast, in this study, agents used the same intention model to generate these behaviours, and the agents always behaved according to their intentions during the interaction. Furthermore, the parameters of one intention model were used as input to the other, and the goal was to make the participants perceive that the agent's cognitive and socio-emotional behaviours do not follow different interaction strategies, but that they are acting based on consistent intentions.

A study that considers the generation of behaviours based on the estimated intentions of people is the work by Zhou et al. [15]. Zhou et al. proposed a neural model that can detect emotions in people's speech and generate conversations by learning from a large set of conversational data. In the study by Zhou et al., emotions were detected by the trained model and the agent's optimal emotion was expressed based on the trained model. However, this study used the AEGL model to present the agents' goal orientation, assumed the same two-layered intention model for people and agents, and alternately updated the intention model based on the real-time cognitive and socio-emotional behaviours of the people during the interaction. Then, people can observe how the agents change their behaviour based on the intentions and emotions of the people during the interaction and can predict the agents' intentions. By making people strongly aware of the cognitive and socio-emotional intentions of agents, people can expect consistent intentions.

III. Proposed Model

The goal of this study is to induce the effect of the ease of talking and familiarity with an agent to support people's willingness to cooperate with the agent. For this purpose, we attempted to induce people to recognise the relationship between agents' abilities and emotional functions. The proposed model differs from previous studies in that both cognitive and socio-emotional behaviours are simply output in parallel, and both types of behaviour are output using the AEGL model developed by Omoto et al. [11]. The AEGL model, in which the intentions of people and agents are alternately estimated and combined, is used to output the agent's cognitive and socio-emotional behaviours in parallel so that people can perceive how the two intentions are combined with the people's intentions. In the following, we describe the details of the proposed model.

A. AEGL Model for Cognitive and Socio-Emotional Behaviour Generation

First, an overview of the AEGL model developed by Omoto et al. is presented in Figure 1. In the AEGL model, the intention of the people is inferred from their verbal and nonverbal behaviours. However, various intentions are inferred from the observed behaviour of the people. In the AEGL model, the relationship between behaviour and intention is represented by two different levels of concreteness: global purpose and local objective. That is, the two-layered relational intention model, with global purpose and local objective, is used to infer human intentions. The local objective is the categorisation of the actual observed behaviours and represents a temporal objective. For example, the observed behaviours, such as 'laugh' and 'eye contact', can be categorised into the category 'synchronize'. Therefore, 'laugh' and 'eye contact' are related to the local objective called 'synchronise'. However, the global purpose expresses a longer-term purpose. For example, temporary objectives, such as 'synchronise' and 'show attention', are thought to lead to the long-term purpose of 'showing acceptance'. Therefore, 'synchronise' and 'show attention' are related to the global purpose called 'showing acceptance'. In this way, the task-specific global purpose and local objective are represented as nodes, and each node has its own parameters.

Omoto et al. assumed the above intention models for both agents and people and updated the parameters of both intention models alternately with people's behaviours as input. Figure 1 presents an overview of the update, and Figure 2 reveals the details of the update.

1) First, the agent outputs the behaviour based on the parameters of the local objective.
2) Next, the agent observes the behaviour of the people, updates the parameters of the local objective in the people's intention model, and then updates the parameters of the global purpose of the people.
3) The parameters of the people's global purpose and the agent's global purpose are merged, and the agent updates the parameters of the local objective based on the parameters of the global purpose.
4) The agent then outputs its next behaviour based on the parameters of its updated local objective.

Omoto et al. stated that, by making people observe an agent's trial and error behaviour, people can infer the unobservable internal state of an agent [10]. By doing so, the agent's intentions are inferred by people, and their intentional stance is induced. Therefore, by outputting the cognitive and socio-emotional behaviours of agents using the AEGL model, it is possible to induce people to estimate the process by which agents produce their task behaviour and emotional expressions. Moreover, it can make people recognise that the agent has intentions regarding competence and emotional aspects.

In this study, we apply the feature of the AEGL model of inducing people to estimate the internal state of the agent and attempt to induce people to estimate the association between the agent's cognitive and socio-emotional intentions. An overview of the proposed model is illustrated in Figure 2. In the proposed model, cognitive and socio-emotional intentions are inferred from people's behaviour, and the next cognitive and socio-emotional behaviours of agents are determined in parallel. Both actions are output as a single behaviour of an agent. Because task-related behaviours and emotional behaviours of people are consistent, the cognitive and socio-emotional intentions of the agents, which are updated based on the estimated people's intentions, are also considered consistent (dotted arrows in Figure 2).

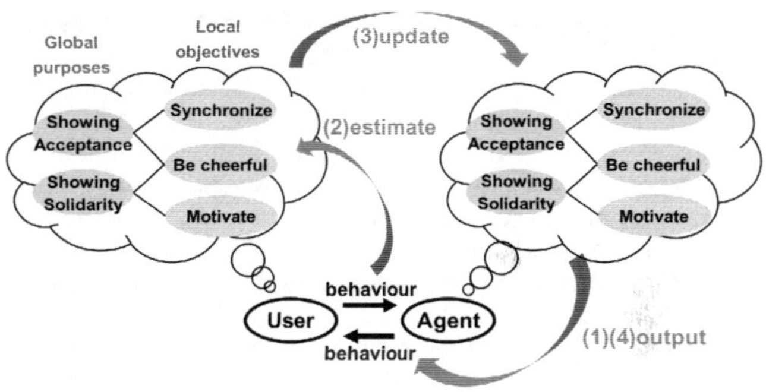

Figure 1. AEGL model.

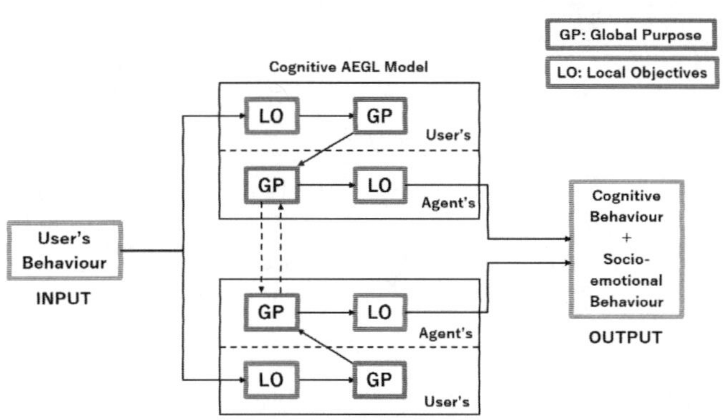

Figure 2. Agent model in this study.

B. Experimental Socio-emotional Behaviour Generation Model

The goal of this study is to facilitate people to perceive the relationship between agents' cognitive and socio-emotional behaviours so that they feel that it is easy to talk to and be familiar with the agents. In this study, we designed an experimental agent model that mimics the proposed model, and we investigated the effects of the relationship between agents' cognitive and socio-emotional behaviours on people. Specifically, the agent's cognitive behaviour, to which the AEGL model has already been applied in Ohmoto's study, is generated using the rule-based model, which is described later for simplicity. The socio-emotional behaviours of agents to which the AEGL model has not been applied in the previous studies are generated based on a simple behavioural model that mimics the AEGL model, which is also described later. Such a simple experimental agent model can also present the structure of the interaction in which cognitive and socio-emotional behaviours are performed in parallel during the interaction. Thus, we can induce people to feel that the agents perform each behaviour based on consistent intention, and people can recognise the relationship between each behaviour. The cognitive behaviours of the agents are generated from verbal and non-verbal behaviours of people based on predetermined rules. Cognitive behaviours, such as 'proposal', 'dividing labour', and so on, are triggered by the rule base on the observed task-related behaviours of the people.

The socio-emotional behaviours of the agents are generated using the behaviour generation model depicted in Figure 3. This model differs from the AEGL model in two respects. One aspect is that only the agent's intention model is assumed, and the other is that the local objective layer does not exist. In this model, the parameters related to the emotional state of people are set, and the connection between the parameters and their verbal and non-verbal behaviours is predetermined. Thus, based on the verbal and non-verbal behaviour of people during the interaction, parameters related to people's emotional state, such as 'nervous' and 'favourability', are updated. The socio-emotional intentions, such as 'showing tension release' and 'showing acceptance', are selected according to the values of these parameters, and the specific behaviours, such as 'praise' and 'acknowledge', are output for each intention. The five basic behaviours to express intentions other than 'seeing users attitude' are based on Kwon's classification of socio-emotional interactions [1].

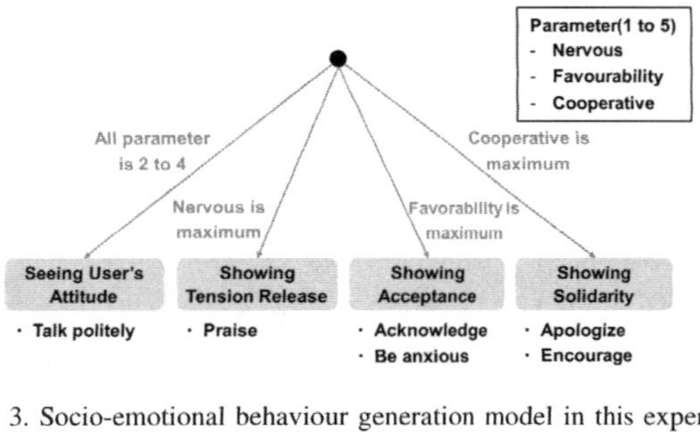

Figure 3. Socio-emotional behaviour generation model in this experiment.

C. Role of the Agent

In the proposed model, the following two agents are used to develop a positive attitude towards cooperation. The cooperative agent takes the same position as the people and interacts with them to engage in collaborative problem solving. This agent generates behaviours using the AEGL model. The teacher agent knows the details of the task that neither the people nor the cooperative agent knows and offers knowledge in response to their questions. This agent is not directly involved in solving the problem but leads the way in ensuring the task goes smoothly. In this study, we used two agents based on the work by Ohmoto et al. [16]. One of the reasons was to reduce the psychological resistance to interaction by having people observe interactions between agents. By doing so, we aim to induce people to learn how to interact with agents and reduce their psychological resistance to the interaction. The other reason is that this study is based on a cooperative learning situation in which learners in the same position work together to solve problems. Therefore, we aim to promote an equal discussion between the people and cooperative agents and to smooth the progress of the task by having a separate agent as a teacher who maintains the knowledge of the task. In the next section, we provide an overview of the evaluation experiments using this experimental model.

IV. EXPERIMENT

For the realisation of the proposed model, we designed the experimental model and conducted experiments in which people and agents were asked to perform cooperative problem solving. The purpose of this experiment is to generate both cognitive and socio-emotional behaviours of the agents in parallel and to observe the effects of the link between these behaviours on people. For this purpose, we adopted experimental tasks that require cooperation and assistance between people and agents. The task is performed in such a way that they help each other and show socio-emotional behaviours, such as gratitude and apology. In this way, we can evaluate the degree of familiarity and ease of talking of the agents based on their behaviour and physiological indices.

A. Task

1) Task Overview: For the task, we use a tower defence game. The player and agent communicate with each other to place a tower in position to prevent an enemy attack. The game was developed using Unity, and the player can move the character in the virtual world using a controller. The player interacts with the agent in the virtual world by speaking. Interactions involve three parties: the player, cooperative agent, and teacher agent. In the experimental group, the socio-emotional behaviour of the cooperative agent throughout the task is generated by the experimental model in Section 3-B. In the control group, the cooperative agent does not perform any socio-emotional behaviour. The experimental model of Section 3-B is not used for cognitive behaviour, but both groups generate rule-based behaviours based on the goal of completing the game. The game overview is illustrated in Figure 4.

2) Rule: The player works with the cooperative agent to discuss and determine how to place the towers to allow the player to defend his/her position against the enemy. The placement of the towers is costly and must be within the cost limitations. Players need to discuss and consider the placement of towers that can efficiently defeat enemies, considering trade-offs, such as the tower attack power versus cost. Players can

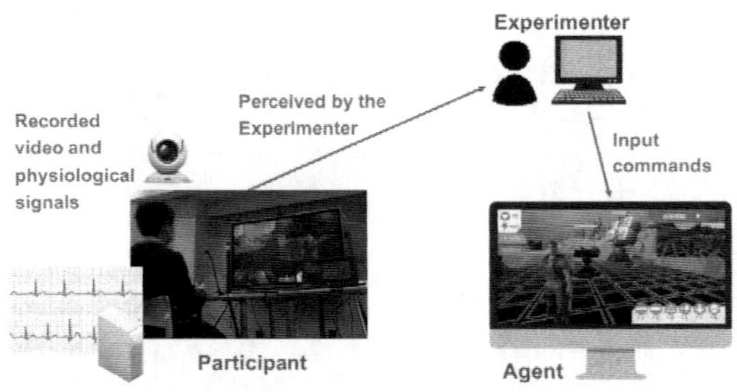

Figure 4. Experimental setup.

also strengthen and repair towers. The player and cooperative agent can communicate with the teacher agent and ask questions about the effects of the tower and types of enemies. The player and two agents talk to each other using voice chat.

To succeed in this task, the player and cooperative agent must work well together. For example, differences exist in the ability to strengthen and repair towers, and the players and agent must discuss and choose an action depending on the situation. When socio-emotional behaviours are displayed, such as thanking the partner for his/her help, praising the partner for his/her skill, and apologising for the failure of the tower, we believe that the player will become more familiar with the agent and more willing to interact and cooperate more actively.

B. Wizard-of-Oz

The experimental model used in this study was realised using the Wizard-of-Oz (WoZ) method. The experimenter observed the verbal and non-verbal behaviours of the players during the task and manually increased or decreased the parameters of the players associated with the behaviours based on predefined rules. For example, the 'cooperative' parameter increased if the player acted to encourage the cooperative agent, and the 'showing acceptance' parameter decreased if the player rejected the suggestion of the cooperative agent. The experimenter manually selected the behaviour of the cooperative agent from among the behaviours expressing socio-emotional intentions according to the highest parameters. The physical behaviours of the agents were performed manually by the experimenter using a controller, and the real-time speech of the experimenters was changed to be perceived as the agents' speech using a voice changer. The reason for not using the recorded audio is to respond immediately to changes in the player's behaviour.

C. Participants

In this experiment, 15 students who were not involved in information engineering were subjects. Participants ranged in age from 19 to 32 years old with an average age of 22.53 (variance of 10.65), including 12 males and three females.

D. Experimental Setup

Eight participants were set up as the experimental group, and seven participants were in the control group. An overview of the experimental setup is illustrated in Figure 4. Participants interacted with the agents through a monitor and controlled their avatars in the game using an Xbox controller. The perceptions of the participants' actions and statements and the manipulations of the agents were assessed by the experimenters based on the above model for each group of agents. The video images of the participants' upper body during the experiment were captured using a web camera, and the time series of the heart rate and Skin Conductance Response (SCR) were obtained using a Polymate biometric analyser.

After the game, a questionnaire was conducted to obtain the participants' subjective evaluations. The physiological indices obtained in this study were missing the heart rate data and SCR data for two participants, and for another three participants, the SCR data exhibited little response, so we concluded that they were not appropriate for use in the analysis. Therefore, considering the small number of participants, we included participants whose data were correctly obtained for each analysis.

The analyses in Sections 5-C, 5-D, and 5-E were performed on eight subjects in the experimental group and seven subjects in the control group. The analysis in Section 5-A was performed on six subjects in the experimental group and seven subjects in the control group. The analysis in Section 5-B was performed on five subjects in the experimental group and five subjects in the control group.

V. RESULTS

A. Cardiac Sympathetic Index and Cardiac Vagal Index

To estimate the internal state of the participants during the task, the Cardiac Sympathetic Index (CSI) and Cardiac Vagal Index (CVI) were calculated from the participants' heart rate data. The CSI and CVI are indices designed by Toichi et al. [17]. The long-axis component L and the short-axis component T were calculated from the distribution of the heart rate intervals in the Lorenz plot analysis, where T/L is CSI, and $log(L \times T)$ is CVI. These are indicators that can detect the heightened sympathetic and parasympathetic nerves. Hayashi et al. found that the stress state is higher when the sympathetic nervous system is high, and the relaxed state is higher when the parasympathetic nervous system is high [18]. In this analysis, we evaluated the participants' stress state in terms of their ease of talking with the agents and their resistance to cooperation.

We hypothesised that the change in the internal state of the participants would be more pronounced after the speech of the cooperative agent. Thus, we calculated the CSI and CVI of the participants for 30 seconds after normal speech (excluding socio-emotional speech) by the cooperative agent and analysed them separately as statistical data. The agent's socio-emotional speech was 'acknowledged', 'apologies', 'be anxious', 'encourage', and 'praise'. First, the average CSI for 30 seconds after normal speech for the entire task was 1.58 for the experimental group and 1.78 for the control group, with Welch's t-test showing a significant difference between the groups at p = 0.0001 (t = -4.38, p = 1.29*e-05). The average CVI is 5.33 for the experimental group and 5.12 for the control group, with Welch's t-test showing a significant difference between the groups at p = 0.001 (t = 3.67, p = 0.00025; Figure 5).

Therefore, to capture the temporal variation of CSI and CVI values, we calculated the average CSI and CVI 30 seconds after the cooperative agent's speech during the first and last 5 minutes of the task for each participant (Figures 6 and 7). A two-way analysis of variance (ANOVA) for the averages of CSI indicates no significant differences between groups or over time. We also analysed the CVI and found a significant interaction at the significance level of $p < 0.05$ ($F = 7.34$, $p = 0.02$), and an effect of temporal variation exists in the control group at a significance level of $p < 0.05$ ($F = 5.98$, $p = 0.033$).

The above analysis suggests that participants' internal states were particularly affected after the speech of the cooperative agent. The experimental group exhibited lower post-speech CSI values and higher CVI values throughout the task (i.e., the participants were at a relatively low level of tension and excitement and were relaxed). In the control group, the CVI value after the speech decreased and approached a tense state as the task progressed, whereas no decrease was found in the experimental group. This suggests that the socio-emotional speech of the cooperative agent suppresses the participants' tension and enhances their relaxation, removing some of their psychological resistance to cooperating with the cooperative agent, whereas under normal circumstances, the participants' tension and excitement levels increase as the task progresses.

Finally, to investigate whether the socio-emotional speech of the cooperative agent directly affects the internal state of the participants, we calculated the CSI and CVI values for 30 seconds after the socio-emotional and normal speech of the cooperative agents in the experimental group and compared them. The average CSI is 1.71 after the socio-emotional speech and 1.64 after the normal speech, and the paired t-test was performed with no significant difference found ($t = 0.25$, $p = 0.81$). The average CVI is 5.60 after socio-emotional speech and 5.34 after normal speech. A similar test was performed, and no significant difference was found ($t = 0.80$, $p = 0.44$).

The results suggest that, although socio-emotional speech does not affect participants immediately, the accumulation of socio-emotional speech may change the influence of the agent's normal speech. In other words, by performing cognitive and socio-emotional behaviours in parallel, the socio-emotional behaviour supports the cognitive behaviour in suppressing the participants' tension.

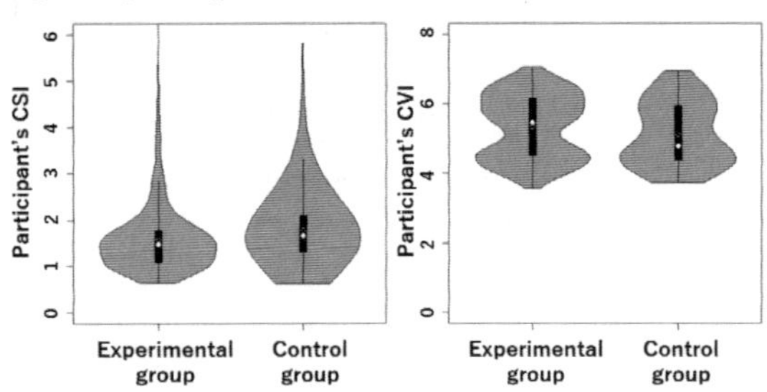

Figure 5. CSI, CVI average for 30 seconds after cooperative agent's speech for the entire task.

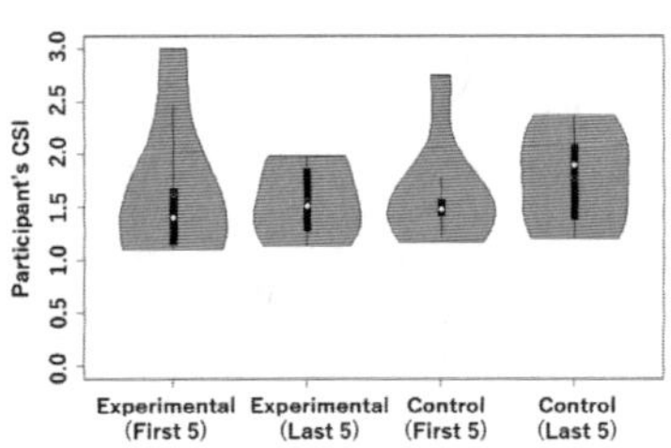

Figure 6. CSI average over time for 30 seconds after the cooperative agent's speech in the first and last five minutes in each group.

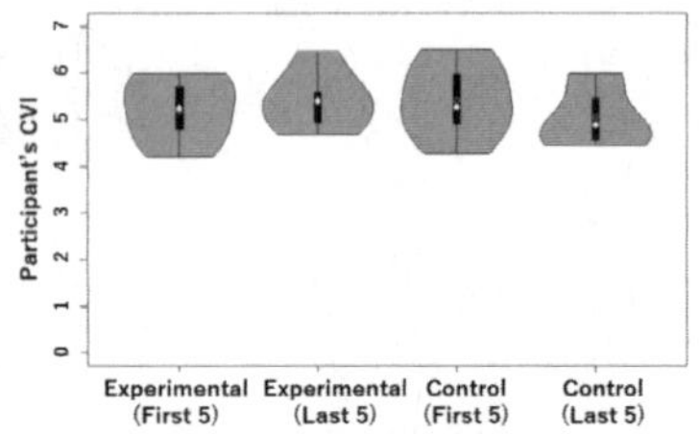

Figure 7. CVI average over time for 30 seconds after cooperative agent's speech in the first and last five minutes in each group.

B. Skin Conductance Response

To estimate the internal state of the participants during the task, we measured their SCR. The SCR is an electrical measure of sweating caused by mental tension and excitement, and it is expected that SCR can be used to estimate mental stress and emotion. Lin et al. showed that higher subjective stress results in a higher SCR value [19]. In this study, we focused on the effect of the cooperative agent's speech on the stress state of the participants by examining the change in the SCR value 30 seconds after the cooperative agent's speech during the task. In terms of the participants' stress state, we assessed the degree of resistance to cooperation and the ease of talking with the agents.

There is a delay in the reaction of the SCR and a delay in returning to the original value after a reaction. Therefore, it is reasonable to examine how the values vary concerning a certain threshold in the SCR analysis. For each participant, we calculated the average of the SCR for 30 seconds after each speech of the cooperative agent and set the average of the bottom 20% of values in the speech as the baseline for that participant. Then, we analysed the variation in SCR values 30 seconds after the speech based on a baseline +0.5 threshold.

First, we analysed the SCR response rate of the cooperative agent's normal speech, considering the speech to be responsive if the SCR value exceeded the threshold within 30 seconds after the speech. Thus, we found 330 responsive and 91 nonresponsive speech results in the experimental group, and 364 and 77 in the control group, respectively. We performed the chi-square ($\chi 2$) test to compare the response rates between groups, finding no significant differences in the response rates ($\chi 2 = 2.11$, $p = 0.15$). To investigate the response of the SCR in each group, we focused on the speech with an SCR. We first calculated the number of seconds that the SCR value exceeded the threshold within 30 seconds after speech and then compared the averages between groups (Figure 8). The average of the experimental group is 7.72, and the average of the control group is 8.48, which is the result of Welch's t-test. The significance level is $p < 0.05$, with the control group having a significantly longer time ($t = -2.01$, $p = 0.045$).

This result indicates that the control group tends to have a longer reaction time than the experimental group. This suggests that participants in the control group tend to pay too much attention to the cooperative agent's speech and become tense. However, the participants in the experimental group were not too tense and were able to relax in response to the agent's speech.

C. Participants' Speech

We measured the participants' socio-emotional speech and compared the speech with that of the experimental and control

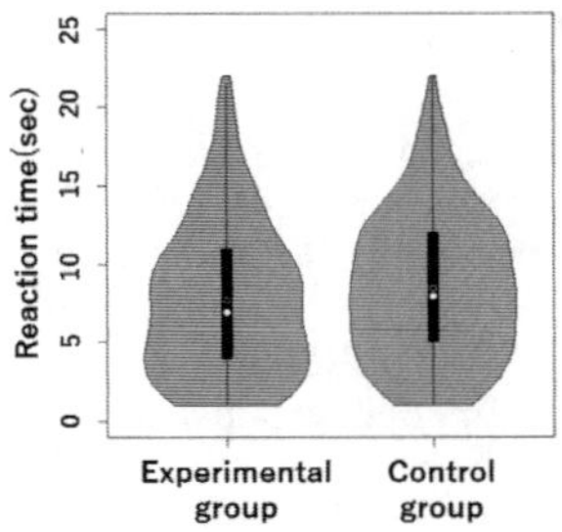

Figure 8. Results of analyses on SCR.

groups. Based on the categorisation of socio-emotional interactions by Kwon et al., we measured five types of speech: 'acknowledge', 'apologies', 'be anxious', 'encourage', and 'praise' [1]. The annotations were done manually by the experimenter after observing the video of the experiment. The chi-square ($\chi 2$) test was used in the evaluation statistics.

We measured the number of socio-emotional and other normal speech in the task for each group and compared the proportion of socio-emotional speech between groups. The results are listed in Table I. The results reveal that the number of instances of socio-emotional is high in the experimental group at a significance level of $p < 0.001$ ($\chi 2$ = 12.05, p = 0.00052).

Next, participants' cognitive speech other than socio-emotional speech was measured for 5 minutes after the start of the task, 5 minutes before the end of the task, and in the middle of the other tasks, and the number of instances of speech between the experimental and control groups was compared. The two-way ANOVA was used as a statistical measure.

The results of that average are presented in Table II. The results indicate no significant difference between the groups (F = 3.85, p = 0.072) and no significant interaction (F = 3.00, p = 0.067), but the cognitive speech of the experimental group increased in the middle part of the task. The mean mid-task time (s) was 1376.875 for the experimental group and 1321 for the control group, and Welch's t-test found no significant difference (t = 3.17, p = 0.10).

These results suggest that the familiarity and ease of talking to the cooperative agent felt by the participants were exhibited in the participants' behaviour in the form of increased socio-emotional speech. Furthermore, the recognition of the link between the cognitive and socio-emotional speech of the cooperative agent may have led to an increase in the participants' cognitive speech.

TABLE I. NUMBER OF SPEECHES OF PARTICIPANTS IN THE TASK

	Socio-emotional	Normal
Experimental group	40	538
Control group	7	381

TABLE II. NUMBER OF COGNITIVE SPEECHES OF PARTICIPANTS IN THE TASK

	First 5	Middle	Last 5
Experimental group	14.25	70.50	16.00
Control group	13.14	46.00	14.71

D. Participants' Speech Latency

The latency between the end of the cooperative agent's speech and the start of the participant's speech was measured, and the speech latency was compared between the experimental and control groups. We assessed the participants' familiarity and ease of talking with the cooperative agent by observing whether participants respond to the cooperative agent's speech in a fast-paced way.

A two-way ANOVA was used to evaluate the participants' speech latency. To capture the temporal changes in speech latency, we focused on the first and last 5 minutes of the task. The latency averages were calculated for each participant in each situation. The results are displayed in Figure 9. The results of the analysis reveal that the average of the experimental group is 1.51 seconds for the first 5 minutes and 0.95 seconds for the last 5 minutes. The average of the control group is 1.73 seconds for the first 5 minutes and 1.38 seconds for the last 5 minutes. A two-way ANOVA was applied, corresponding to each participant. A main effect between groups was found at a significance level of $p < 0.05$ (F = 4.68, p = 0.0498), and the experimental group exhibited a shorter speech latency than the control group. The main effect of the temporal change was found at a significance level of $p < 0.01$ (F = 12.27, p = 0.0039).

As the task progressed, the speech latency became shorter in both groups, but it was particularly short in the experimental group. We assumed that the long speech latency indicates that the participants found it challenging to communicate with the cooperative agent and that they did not consider the suggestions and opinions of the cooperative agent to be valid. The short speech latency indicates that they were actively attempting to communicate and cooperate with the cooperative agent.

In both groups, as the task progressed, the speech latency decreased because participants felt that the cooperative agent was easier to communicate with and more effective as a partner; thus, the speech latency decreased. However, in the experimental group, the latency of speech was shorter because participants felt more familiar with the agent and felt it was easier to talk to the cooperative agent due to the link between the cooperative agent's cognitive and socio-emotional behaviours.

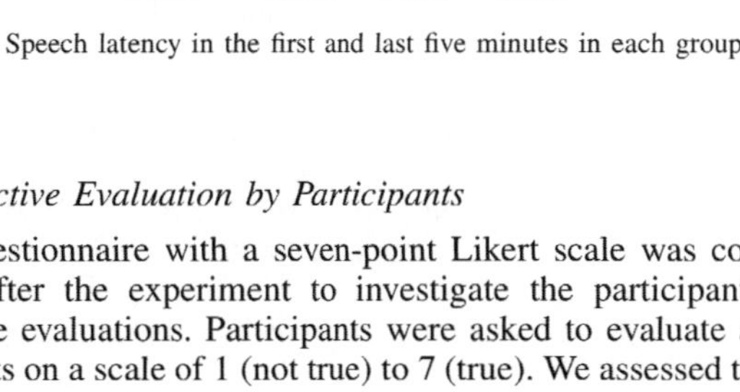

Figure 9. Speech latency in the first and last five minutes in each group.

E. Subjective Evaluation by Participants

A questionnaire with a seven-point Likert scale was conducted after the experiment to investigate the participants' subjective evaluations. Participants were asked to evaluate all statements on a scale of 1 (not true) to 7 (true). We assessed the answers to the following 12 statements about the cooperative agent.

- Q1: I took a liking to the agent.
- Q2: The agent was reliable.
- Q3: I felt easy to talk with the agent.
- Q4: The behavior of the agent was natural.
- Q5: I found the agent's behaviour human-like.
- Q6: I felt the value of the cooperation with the agent.
- Q7: I was willing to the cooperation with the agent.
- Q8: I could understand the way of thinking of the agent.
- Q9: The agent understands my way of thinking.
- Q10: I felt accepted by the agent.
- Q11: I felt relieved by the agent.
- Q12: I felt solidarity with the agent.

The answers to each statement were analysed, and the results of some of the statements are summarised in Figure 10. In the following section, we describe the content of each statement and the results of the answers.

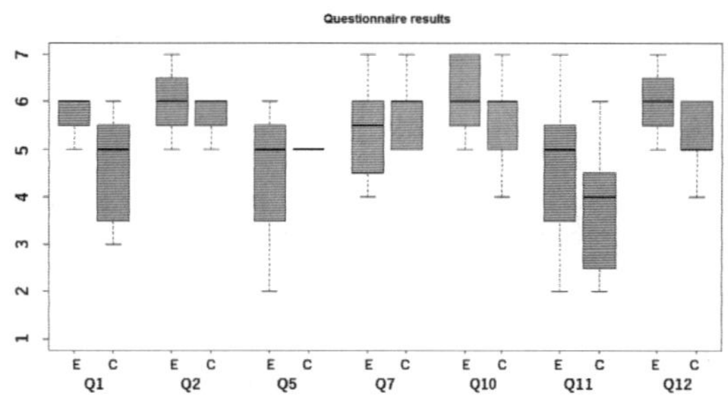

Figure 10. Questionnaire results (left: experimental group, right: control group).

- Q1: I took a liking to the cooperative agent.
  We assessed the participants' subjective liking for the cooperative agent. We performed the Mann-Whitney U test on the answer results and found a significance level of $p < 0.05$, resulting in high favourability in the experimental group.
- Q2: The cooperative agent was reliable and Q7: I was willing to the cooperation with the cooperative agent.
  We assessed the subjective trust in the cooperative agent and the participants' positive attitude. There was no significant difference in the answer results between the groups.
- Q5: I found the cooperative agent's behavior human-like.
  We used a voice changer for the cooperative agent's speech; however, if the participants were aware of WoZ, their perception of the cooperative agent's humanity could have been greatly enhanced. The actual answers obtained in both groups are close to the median, which suggests that the participants were not aware of the use of the WoZ technique using the voice changer.
- Q10: I felt accepted by the cooperative agent. /Q11: I felt relieved by the cooperative agent. /Q12: I felt solidarity with the cooperative agent.
  These statements assessed the participants' subjective perceptions of each socio-emotional intention expressed by the cooperative agent. As a result, although no significant difference was found between groups, the experimental group exceeded the average of the control group.

VI. DISCUSSION

A. *Effect of Link of Socio-emotional and Cognitive Behaviour*

Sections 5-A and 5-B demonstrate how the link between the cognitive and socio-emotional behaviours of the cooperative agent affect the internal state of the participants. The results reveal that the participants tend to be less tense and more relaxed in response to the cooperative agents' speech. This tendency supports the participants' willingness to cooperate with the cooperative agent and that the participants' psychological resistance to the cooperation with the agent was reduced. Furthermore, the results in Section 5-A suggest that the socio-emotional behaviour of the cooperative agents did not directly affect the participants but that cognitive behaviour, based on socio-emotional behaviour, was effective in reducing the participants' tension. This suggests that it is important to perform both behaviours in parallel.

The above psychological changes may have led to the changes in the participants' behaviour observed in Sections 5-C and 5-D. The increase in the participants' socio-emotional speech is thought to be due to a decrease in the participants' psychological resistance to sharing and expressing their emotions as a result of feeling more familiar with agents and because it was easier to talk to the cooperative agent. Furthermore, the participants' cognitive speech also increased in the middle part of the task, which suggests that familiarity with the cooperative agent may have affected the participants' willingness to cooperate. The decrease in the latency of the participants' speech may be because they became less stressed when interacting with the cooperative agent and thus responded more quickly.

The results of the questionnaire demonstrated that the participants in the experimental group were more favourable towards the cooperative agents. As a result of the participants' recognition of the link between the cognitive and socio-emotional behaviours of the cooperative agent and because they felt less tension and burden when interacting with the cooperative agent, their subjective favourability towards the cooperative agent was likely to increase. However, this study failed to develop more cooperative attitudes, such as trust and active cooperation, among participants towards the cooperative agent.

B. *Constructing an Ideal Proposal Model*

In this study, the analyses of the CSI, CVI, and SCR indicated that the participants in the experimental group tended to be more relaxed. According to the questionnaire results, the participants in the experimental group more strongly perceived the socio-emotional intentions of showing tension release, acceptance, and solidarity expressed by the cooperative agent. Thus, the socio-emotional intentions adopted in the experimental model used in this study were relatively well conveyed to the participants. Considering the purpose of the proposed model, which is to induce participants to feel the intentionality of the cooperative agent using the AEGL model, the types of adopted intentions were appropriate. However, room for improvement still exists in terms of the failure to develop the participants' positive attitudes, and it is necessary to continue to investigate optimal intentions.

In the experimental model, we aimed to generate the cognitive and socio-emotional behaviours of the cooperative agent in parallel, so that the participants perceive the link between the behaviours and experience familiarity and the ease of talking with the cooperative agent. However, we could not induce the participants' trust in the cooperative agent and strong positive attitudes towards it. Therefore, there is room to devise more effective ways to link the cognitive and socio-emotional behaviours of the cooperative agents. In this study, we did not implement the link in the model. However, it is possible to induce participants to feel a stronger consistency of the agent's behaviour by implementing the model using the intention parameter state to update the other intention parameters.

VII. Conclusion and Future Work

The final goal of this study was to induce people's positive attitudes towards cooperation with agents in cooperative problem-solving situations. To achieve the final goal, we aimed to induce people to feel that agents are easy to talk with and that they are familiar with the agents, which supports their positive attitude towards cooperation. Therefore, we proposed an agent model in which cognitive and socio-emotional behaviours are output in parallel using the AEGL model. The AEGL model was used to demonstrate that the agents behave based on consistent intentions and to induce people to recognise the integrity of their behaviours and to induce positive attitudes. As a first step towards the realisation of the proposed model, we designed an experimental agent model to simulate the link between cognitive and socio-emotional behaviours and aimed to make the agents feel easy to talk with and friendly to people. For the task, we used a tower defence game.

As a result, we found a change in the psychological state of people who became less nervous about the agents' speech and a change in the behaviour of people who were presumed to feel more comfortable talking to the agents. In addition, based on the socio-emotional speech of the agents, the positive effects of cognitive speech on people were increased.

The next task is to create a method to link the cognitive and socio-emotional behaviours of agents based on the findings of this experiment. Further consistency between cognitive and socio-emotional intentions in the model would further allow people to recognise the agent as a single entity with intentions and induce people's willingness to cooperate.

Acknowledgment

This work was supported by JST CREST Grant Number JPMJCR17A5, Japan.

References

[1] K. Kwon, Y.-H. Liu, and L. P. Johnson, "Group regulation and social-emotional interactions observed in computer supported collaborative learning: Comparison between good vs. poor collaborators," Computers & Education, vol. 78, 2014, pp. 185–200.

[2] M. T. Chi and R. Wylie, "The ICAP framework: Linking cognitive engagement to active learning outcomes," Educational Psychologist, vol. 49, no. 4, 2014, pp. 219–243.

[3] S. Järvelä, H. Järvenoja, J. Malmberg, J. Isohätälä, and M. Sobocinski, "How do types of interaction and phases of self-regulated learning set a stage for collaborative engagement?" Learning and Instruction, vol. 43, 2016, pp. 39–51.

[4] P. Dillenbourg, M. Baker, A. Blaye, and C. OMalley, "The evolution of research on collaborative learning," In P. Reimann and H. Spada, Learning in humans and machines. Towards an interdisciplinary learning science, 1995, pp. 189–211.

[5] R. Toni and L.-G. Lisa, "Socially shared regulation in collaborative groups: An analysis of the interplay between quality of social regulation and group processes," Cognition and Instruction, vol. 29, no. 4, 2011, pp. 375–415.

[6] P. Näykki, J. Isohätälä, S. Järvelä, J. Pöysä-Tarhonen, and P. Häkkinen, "Facilitating socio-cognitive and socio-emotional monitoring in collaborative learning with a regulation macro script–an exploratory study," International Journal of Computer-Supported Collaborative Learning, vol. 12, no. 3, 2017, pp. 251–279.

[7] M. Maltz and J. Meyer, "Cue utilization in a visually demanding task," Proceedings of the Human Factors and Ergonomics Society Annual Meeting, vol. 44, 2000, pp. 283–283.

[8] K. Kreijns, P. A. Kirschner, W. Jochems, and H. Van Buuren, "Determining sociability, social space, and social presence in (a) synchronous collaborative groups," Cyber Psychology & Behavior, vol. 7, no. 2, 2004, pp. 155–172.

[9] D. C. Dennett, "The intentional stance," MIT Press, 1989.

[10] Y. Ohmoto, T. Suyama, and T. Nishida, "A method to alternate the estimation of global purposes and local objectives to induce and maintain the intentional stance," in Proceedings of the Fourth International Conference on Human Agent Interaction, 2016, pp. 379–385.

[11] Y. Ohmoto, T. Suyama, and T. Nishida, "Extended method to alternate the estimation of global purposes and local objectives in multiple human-agent interaction," The Eleventh International Conference on Advances in Computer-Human Interactions, 2018, pp. 212–217.

[12] H. Prendinger, J. Mori, and M. Ishizuka, "Using human physiology to evaluate subtle expressivity of a virtual quizmaster in a mathematical game," International Journal of Human-Computer Studies, vol. 62, no. 2, 2005, pp. 231–245.

[13] H. Prendinger and M. Ishizuka, "The empathic companion: A character-based interface that addresses users'affective states," Applied Artificial Intelligence, vol. 19, no. 3-4, 2005, pp. 267–285.

[14] R. Kumar, H. Ai, J. L. Beuth, and C. P. Rosé, "Socially capable conversational tutors can be effective in collaborative learning situations," in International Conference on Intelligent Tutoring Systems. Springer, 2010, pp. 156–164.

[15] H. Zhou, M. Huang, T. Zhang, X. Zhu, and B. Liu, "Emotional chatting machine: Emotional conversation generation with internal and external memory," in Thirty-Second AAAI Conference on Artificial Intelligence, 2018, pp. 730–738.

[16] Y. Ohmoto, J. Karasaki, and T. Nishida, "Inducing and maintaining the intentional stance by showing interactions between multiple agents," in Proceedings of the 18th International Conference on Intelligent Virtual Agents, 2018, pp. 203–210.

[17] M. Toichi, T. Sugiura, T. Murai, and A. Sengoku, "A new method of assessing cardiac autonomic function and its comparison with spectral analysis and coefficient of variation of r–r interval," Journal of the Autonomic Nervous System, vol. 62, no. 1-2, 1997, pp. 79–84.

[18] R. Hayashi and S. Kato, "Proposal of design policy of therapy robots system based on relaxation state," in 2017 IEEE 6th Global Conference on Consumer Electronics (GCCE). IEEE, 2017, pp. 1–3.

[19] T. Lin, M. Omata, W. Hu, and A. Imamiya, "Do physiological data relate to traditional usability indexes?" in Proceedings of the 17th Australia conference on Computer-Human Interaction: Citizens Online: Considerations for Today and the Future, 2005, pp. 1–10.

UX Evaluation of a Mobile Application Prototype for Art Museum Visitors

Pekka Isomursu*, Minna Virkkula**, Karoliina Niemelä*, Jouni Juntunen*** and Janne Kumpuoja***
*School of Media & Performing Arts
**Business Department
***Information Technology
Oulu University of Applied Sciences,
Oulu, Finland
e-mail: firstname.lastname@oamk.fi

Abstract — **In this paper, we discuss user experience evaluation of a prototype mobile application for art museum visitors. The application acts as a personal, virtual museum guide that interacts with the physical surroundings using, e.g., image recognition and Augmented Reality (AR). The study included several techniques of early User Interface (UI) design exploration. Our additions to the AttrakDiff method revealed a deeper layer of user insight that otherwise would have gone unnoticed. Based on our study, we have drawn several design implications that we believe are not only usable in further development of our application, but also useful to others. Some of our key findings were that the application should have a supporting role only, subordinate to the actual exhibition, and the role of good, versatile, and up-to-date content is crucial.**

Keywords - user experience; user evaluation methods; case study; user study; interaction with physical objects.

I. INTRODUCTION

The smARTplaces project [1], co-funded by the European Union, aims to revolutionize the way culture and art can be perceived and consumed using digital technology and new forms of cultural mediation. In the project, we have developed a mobile application called smARTapp (Figure 1) where one can learn about the institutions, art works and local projects through, e.g., exclusive videos, Augmented Reality (AR) features, and a game called Storyworld [2].

In this paper, we discuss user evaluation of a new application, to be integrated in smARTapp. We call it Your Personal Art Tour (YPAT). YPAT focuses on enhancing the experience of a visit to an exhibition. Since YPAT is still under development, a lo-fi prototype that worked on a mobile phone and included the basic functionality with a rudimentary user interface (Figure 2) was used in this study.

In the following sections, respectively, we describe related work, YPAT in more detail, and user experience (UX) evaluation setup and procedure. We then discuss the results in detail, and end with conclusions and future work.

II. RELATED WORK

A. *User Experience*

Traditional usability evaluations mainly focus on user cognition and user performance when interacting with products or services [3]. According to ISO 9241-210:2010 (clause 2.15), UX is defined as a person's perceptions and responses resulting from the use and/or anticipated use of a product, system or service [4]. User experience focuses on lived experience. Therefore, in UX evaluation we need to concentrate on how the experience of a system subjectively feels to the user. It is associated with emotional, experimental, affective, hedonic, and aesthetic variables. Context-dependence is also an important aspect of user experience [5]-[7].

Figure 1. Front page of smARTapp for iOS and Android phones [8].

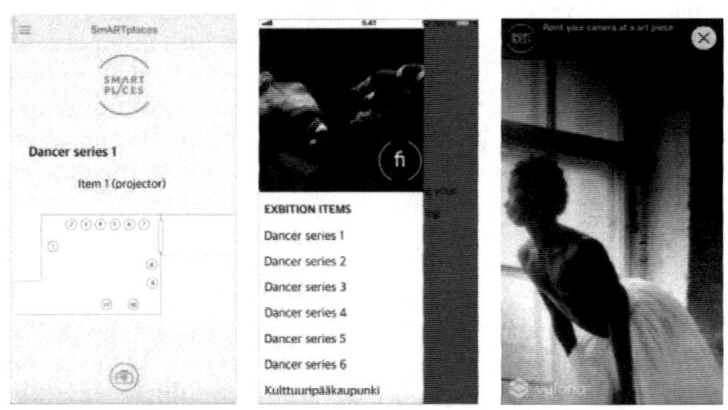

Figure 2. Screen shots of the lo-fi prototype of YPAT, used in user tests.

Hassenzahl [9] has proposed a model of user experience that divides the attributes of a product into pragmatic and hedonic attributes. Based on this model, he has developed two questionnaires, AttrakDiff and AttrakDiff 2 that can be used to measure the user's experience of different attributes in the product. AttrakDiff questionnaires use a seven-step Semantic Differential Scale to assess pragmatic and hedonic attributes as well as the attractiveness of the system under scrutiny. The attributes are arranged into word-pairs (semantic differentials) that have opposite meanings (e.g., *confusing - clear, good - bad*) [9]-[12].

Pragmatic quality, in this context, means clarity of interaction and usability of the application. Attractivity means aesthetic quality in general. Hedonic quality attributes are divided into two groups: Identity, measuring how well the user's self-perception resonates with the product, and Stimulation, measuring perceived potential of the application for reaching the user's individual goals.

B. *Mobile Museum Applications and Their Research*

Using mobile technology for enhancing museum experience is not a new idea per se. There are many applications that offer different types of support to enhance the experience during either a physical or a virtual museum visit, or in learning about art world in general. Typically, the art-oriented apps use image recognition technology, each with a particular twist. Some use AR, some even make the whole tour virtual. The applications vary a lot in their focus and technology. Our focus is in making a pleasant user experience for the whole "life cycle" of the museum experience, starting from the planning of the visit and ending with support for activities after the visit [13]-[15].

Applications like Magnus [16] try to become "Shazam of art". Magnus has used, e.g., crowdsourcing to build a database of more than 10 million images of art. It aims to help prospective art buyers. Magnus shows prices from galleries and auctions, and exhibition histories of galleries, museums, etc. Smartify [17] is more geared towards museumgoers. It teams up with individual museums to create digitized versions of their collections, also adding an educational angle.

Ree and Choi [18] have done user research on using mobile technology with museum visitors. The results were somewhat mixed. As the biggest challenge, they identify encouraging visitors to use the mobile experience. Several problems, such as intrusiveness, isolation, head-down effect and technical problems should be improved to use their mobile application. On the other hand, the usability and the degree of satisfaction of using the application were relatively high in their research.

A study by Rung and Laursen [19] shows that there is a growing potential for using mobile applications in museums. However, as this is a new(ish) approach for most museum visitors, mobile applications must be developed as user-friendly as possible and make a strong connection with the physical space.

III. YOUR PERSONAL ART TOUR (YPAT)

Using image recognition and Augmented Reality, YPAT is designed to enhance the experience of visiting art museums. In the physical space, an artwork is recognized with a mobile phone camera, and additional information, such as text, video, audio or web content, is displayed either in some "traditional" format or as Augmented Reality. The information provided can be pre-existing or created specifically for the app. A floor plan and a tour map help in navigation. Overall, YPAT aims to a personalized experience that resembles having a personal, live guide during the visit.

As discussed, mobile applications that enhance the experience of visiting a museum or an art gallery already exist, even commercially. Therefore, it is of crucial importance that YPAT not only has the functionality but also has its user experience at a very high level. Building blocks are readily available for the development of mobile applications that use enhanced technologies, such as image recognition and Augmented Reality. Instead of re-inventing the wheel, with YPAT we use proven technology of commercial development platforms (e.g., React Native [20] and Vuforia [21]) that can easily be adapted to our needs. We can then focus our project resources better to creating a product with excellent user experience and usability.

Image recognition can be done in several different ways, usually either in device or on some external server [22]. Server-side image recognition is better when there are thousands of reference images that need to be compared to a mobile camera image since the processing power of mobile devices is somewhat limited. In the case of YPAT the number of images that need to be recognized is relatively small, so an in-device approach was chosen. The camera image is compared against a point cloud that is stored in the device. If similarity is detected, the application returns a corresponding AR view - or some other pre-defined function - on the phone display.

IV. UX EVALUATION

A. *Evaluation Setup*

In our research project, our objective was to apply the user centric design process and involve the users to the development of YPAT, our mobile application for art museum visitors. In a user study that we conducted, we focused on the UX evaluation of YPAT. During that time, YPAT had a rudimentary user interface (UI) and the basic functionality working. The aim of the user study was to gain knowledge on people's behavior, interaction and how the users feel when using the developed application prototype in a museum environment. We wanted to find the best combination of features, content and UX.

To create an authentic yet controllable test environment, we created our own "art museum". We used a part of the art collection of our university as the exhibited items. The exhibition included drawings and photographs hung on the walls of a space normally dedicated to exhibit works of our students. We also included images of artworks projected on the wall, in order to see if they would be harder for YPAT to recognize than the physical artworks. The environment, although limited in size, provided all key elements needed to make the tests realistic. We felt that evaluating interaction and user perceptions in a real-world context was crucial for getting valid user feedback.

We recruited in situ 31 participants (14 males and 17 females). They included both students and staff with age range of 20 to 50+ years with bias towards cultural studies and occupations. Typically, they visited museums 2 to 5 times in a year. The age range is quite wide, but we did not focus on age differences at this early stage, although we do indicate some such differences in the results.

B. Procedure

We conducted the user study with a mixed methods research design combining several methods, e.g., observation, a questionnaire (in 3 parts, including a modified AttrakDiff questionnaire), and semi-structured interview [15].

At the beginning of every user observation, a brief introduction was given about the YPAT application. The first task to the participants was to walk freely at the gallery, using the prototype version of YPAT (Figure 3). Participants used one of the two test phones where the prototype application had been installed. They were followed while they took their time to look at the artworks and test YPAT by themselves. We also asked them to think aloud while using YPAT.

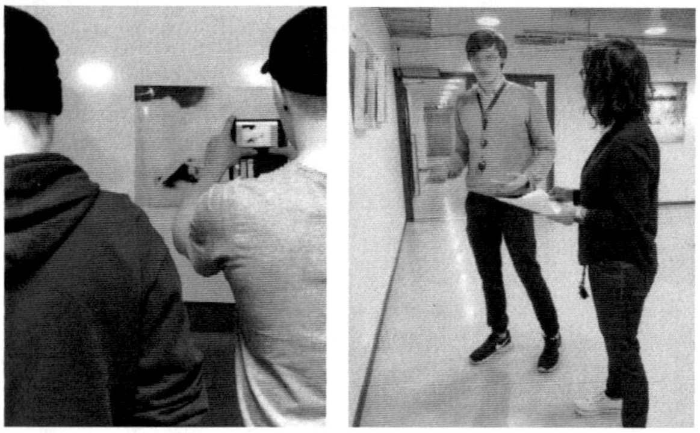

Figure 3. Scenes from user evaluation in progress.

After the participants had tried the application on their own, we would guide them to try features that they had possibly missed. Meanwhile, they were asked additional questions on the concept ideas. If at some point they got stuck with the UI, we first let them try to solve the problem by themselves, but if that did not happen, we would then instruct them. The study also included a semi-structured questionnaire that was filled in after the participants had used YPAT. Finally, a brief interview was run to elaborate on their answers to the questionnaire. In some cases, when there were two people tested at the same time and they knew each other, we let them try the app together as a pair. We noticed that this would spark a lively discussion on the app and its features, both while they were trying YPAT and during the final interview after they had individually filled in the questionnaire.

In the questionnaire, the participants first gave demographic information and their prior experience in visiting art museums. We also asked about their phone model to recognize if there were any correlations between ease of use and the participants' phone UI. The questionnaire also included a modified AttrakDiff questionnaire [15][23] with 15 statements related to application concept idea and a 7-point scale for attribute pairs (Figures 4 and 5).

As YPAT at that stage was only a lo-fi prototype with a rudimentary UI, we felt that the attributes for the hedonic quality used in AttrakDiff were rather meaningless for the participants at that point. It would have been hard for them to grasp, e.g., how *stylish*, *premium*, or *professional* user experience the final YPAT would offer. Therefore, we modified the AttrakDiff questionnaire by omitting the hedonistic attributes and only used attributes for pragmatic quality and appeal.

In addition, as we had to translate the questionnaire to Finnish, we found that the connotative meanings of three attribute pairs in English overlapped with each other when translated to Finnish, i.e., a word in Finnish might have similar connotations to more than one of the English words and vice versa. We ended up using two attribute pairs in Finnish language to cover the key connotative meanings of three pairs in English, namely *pleasant - unpleasant*, *attractive – ugly*, and *likeable - disagreeable*. These were substituted with Finnish *miellyttävä – epämiellyttävä* and *viehättävä – ruma*.

We also added two new attribute pairs, namely *innovative – ordinary*, and *engaging – boring* (in Finnish). We wanted to use these exact words since in the project plan a set goal was to develop an *innovative* application that would *engage* museum audiences in new ways. With the addition, we would get direct feedback on this goal. We consider *engaging – boring* to measure attractivity, and *innovative - ordinary* to measure pragmatic quality, although the latter has a hedonistic dimension as well.

We also wanted to dive a step deeper into the quantitative feedback from AttrakDiff than what the original method allowed. After a participant had filled in the questionnaire s/he was asked to select 3 attribute pairs (Figure 4) that s/he felt most certain about and then justify the selection. This revealed a deeper layer of user insight that otherwise would have gone unnoticed. It helped us better understand the users' reasoning in grading the attributes and what the most relevant and descriptive attributes in this case were.

As YPAT interacts with physical pieces of art in its environment, we found it to be crucial that the application was evaluated in a gallery environment. This gave a lot of insight to issues related to control and performance.

The methods and process that we used worked very well together. Data from direct observations gave us understanding how participants interacted with the lo-fi prototype as well as ideas on what part and features of YPAT the participants were interested in. From the interviews and open-ended questions that followed, we collected valuable insight and ideas for new features. We were able to exploit rather brief (ca. 30 minutes) user sessions to their fullest and gather plenty of versatile and easy-to-analyze user data that we could use in further development of YPAT. We can conclude that our methods mix and the process we followed worked well in real-life early phase development work.

V. UX Evaluation Results

A. Results of subjective ratings with modified AttrakDiff

Summarizing the user answers to our modified AttrakDiff questionnaire, Figure 4 shows that the participants were most certain about the app to be simple, practical, and manageable (shown in darkest colors in the figure). To a large extent, they thought the app also to be straightforward, pleasant, good, and very motivating. They were least certain whether the app was inviting – rejecting or appealing – repelling. They had most diverse opinions on whether the app was engaging or boring. The diversity with engaging – boring might be due to the fact that the app was still a prototype. When answering, some of the users might have thought of the actual prototype at hand whereas others might have thought of the final product of which the prototype gave just an indication. When asked why the participants chose simple and practical, their reasoning was that they could easily begin to understand the basic functionality and content of the application. Also, the users said that it was easy to take the application into use, as well as interact and learn with it. The reasoning for choosing the attribute motivating was that the application tempted the user to find out more information about the works of art and their background, such as information on the artist and related work.

"Innovative = I haven't seen this before,
Predictable = I quickly learned how it works,
Engaging = I wanted to start exercising right away."

In Figure 5, the darkest color shows the median answer for each attribute, and the lighter color shows the 90% range of the answers. From the figure we can see that overall, the participants felt rather positive about YPAT as the medians are mostly on the left side of the table. A notable exception is that the participants found the app to be more technical than human (although not with high certainty, as can be seen from Figure 4). When asked about this, the users did not necessarily see the app being technical as a negative thing. Since the app used new technology, such as AR, it simply gave a technical impression.

The questionnaire ended with open questions related to first impressions, likes and dislikes, possible new functionality or content and, lastly, a possibility for the participant to add anything at all that s/he still wanted to say. As at this point, they had used the app, discussed it with the moderator, and filled in most of the questionnaire, they had formed a good understanding of what the goals of the app development were. Thus, we got excellent additional comments on the user experience as well as on features that could be added to the app.

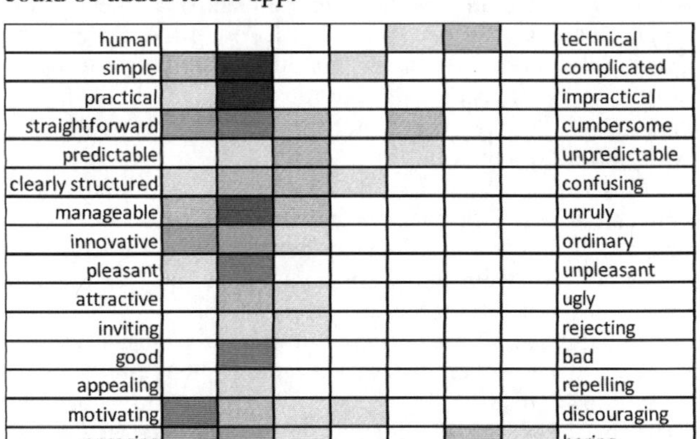

Figure 4. Participants were most certain of the answers marked dark.

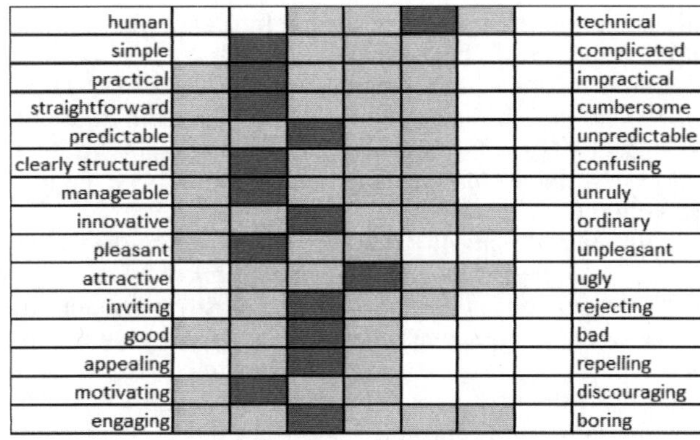

Figure 5. Median (darker) and 90% range (lighter) of the answers.

From the user evaluation of AttrakDiff attribute pairs, we can conclude that, overall, the test users found the app to be rather pragmatic and attractive. This is a very promising indicator for the success of the finalized application. The design implications that we gathered give us a good direction to further development.

B. *Design implications*

To further develop YPAT, consistent themes and findings from the study were translated into design implications. The implications suggest that the following aspects should be considered when designing a personal digital art guide in the museum context:

- Supporting role of the application: at the exhibition, physical works of art are the focus of attention.
- Varying contexts of use: user journey with the application can start at different points and with different goals.
- Content is king: the role of good content is crucial for the success of the application.
- Considerations on interaction and technology: we found plenty of improvement ideas related to technology and interaction.

Next, we discuss these design implications in more detail.

1) Supporting role of the application

Our first major finding and an important guideline for further design was that at the museum the users want to focus on the art physically around them, and not on their phone application. Also, the users mentioned how important it is that the application gives freedom to choose the objects that they find most interesting and study them at their own pace. Human museum guides are unapproachable to many as people tend to be shy and often wish to study the exhibition in peace, but still wish to get extra information. YPAT gives freedom to choose the objects that the user finds most interesting and focus on them without any hurry.

"Simplicity and practicality are important, because I want to be at the museum, not on my smart phone"

2) Varying contexts of use

The application must take into account different contexts of use. The users not only wanted to use the application during the museum visit, but also before and after it, with different focus in each context.

Before visiting an exhibition, people wanted to get to know the basics of the exhibition(s) and plan their own tour. For example, users could identify the works of art they would wish to see, and the app could tailor a personal tour accordingly.

"I would plan my own tour", "I would search the object from the (interactive) floor plan"

The use of the application would be most versatile during the visit. For example, an interactive map would show the location and where to go next and give more information about the exhibited works of art, as well as practicalities, such as where the amenities are located. An augmented audio guide would include image recognition with camera and a possibility to bookmark favorites for closer study after the visit.

To store information for later use was considered a useful feature. After the museum visit, the user might wish to learn more about selected favorites – or just simply remember which works of art s/he found especially interesting. People were also interested in having social aspects included in the application. Enabling easy and fun ways for social activity and sharing during and especially after a visit was listed as an important function. Quick social sharing could happen during the visit, but also afterwards. After the visit the user could better afford a longer and deeper social engagement since it would not interfere with the physical experience at the museum. The importance of social sharing emerged especially with the younger (student) participants.

One detailed idea for social sharing that emerged is e-postcards provided by the museum, to be shared via email or social media. Another idea was the possibility to give recommendations to users with similar interests.

Our user evaluation revealed three alternative starting points for the user journey with the application:

1. Start by planning own tour beforehand.
2. Start at the exhibition by scanning a work of art with the phone camera to get information.
3. Start from an interactive map at the exhibition.

Additional entry scenarios exist, such as starting by finding the amenities at the museum, but the above-mentioned three starting points were the ones emerging strongly from the user data. The UI of YPAT should be designed so that access to all three is easy and intuitive.

3) Content is king

Without versatile content, the application, no matter how good its technology and usability will get, is worthless. The users were clearly interested in additional information about the works of art that especially interested them: the subject and characters, the artist's own thoughts, where else can one see works from the same artist, etc.

Our study also showed that the application encourages the user to the consumption of additional information. This is due to making the information readily and interestingly available, reducing the need for the use of web search engines or similar. We found this to be more important to the older study participants.

Content should be hierarchical: one should easily get an overview and then be able to dive into details, according to personal interest. By content, we do not mean just data, but also a variety of functions that provide information to the user. These include interactive map and audio guidance.

Video content that would be consumed during the museum visit should be kept short, a minute at the maximum. This finding is related to the fact that the users wish to focus on the physical world during their visit. When watching videos after the visit this time restriction does not apply.

4) Considerations on interaction and technology

As the app was still a prototype during user evaluation, it is natural that we found a lot of technical details that need improvement. For example, there needs to be indicators when the camera is scanning, when it recognizes an image, and which image seen on the display is recognized. We also found some straight-forward bugs, such as the app sometimes showing information about a wrong image.

Some users tried to find the limits of the implemented technology: what happens when there are several works of art in camera view at the same time, how tilted can the viewing angle be, what if the object is only partially visible, etc. This gave us very valuable information for further development.

In a museum environment, issues with user embarrassment should be considered. Users do not want the application to disturb others. For example, it is good to give the user control of audio usage and volume before showing videos or starting guidance and perhaps force the use of headphones. Also, the user should not be overloaded with unnecessary information, such as push notifications.

As discussed earlier, in a museum the user prefers to focus on art itself and not on her phone. Using audio helps in getting eyes off the device.

Interaction with the physical works of art should be smart and feel natural. The user needs to feel s/he is in control, not the application. Perhaps a bit surprising finding was that the application recognized the works of art even too quickly, already before the user had pointed the phone camera directly towards the object. This caused confusion. Image recognition (or failure of it) must be clearly indicated on the phone display. Using AR to point the identified object on the display would be good. Another issue with the camera was that the users changed the orientation of the phone to better match the dimensions of the artwork with those of the camera display, but our prototype was made to work only with portrait orientation.

Battery consumption of the prototype was quite heavy. It consumed 7-10% of battery capacity during a 15-20-minute test period that included heavy usage of the camera. This needs to be taken into consideration in the coding and procedural structure of the final application.

The light in an art museum is often constant, at least in most of its exhibition space. This makes image recognition much easier than, e.g., outdoors with constantly changing light conditions. Image recognition worked very well in our tests for 2D objects on the walls. However, sculptures and other 3D objects would be more challenging. We did not include handling of them in YPAT at this point.

VI. Conclusion and Future Work

Our user evaluation confirmed that the YPAT prototype has potential. The feedback was generally positive even though the UI was rudimentary. The users were able to easily learn and interact with the app, and they liked the features we had. However, the visual appearance and elements for interaction need to be improved. We got a lot of ideas for improved and new functionality as well as simple bug fixing.

Whatever the functionality, the application should have a supporting role only, subordinate to the actual exhibition. Besides working on the application itself, a lot of work needs to be done to get good quality (and interactive) content for the application continuously in the future. Since the content would change with every exhibition, tools and instructions should be created that make content creation and putting it into the system as easy as possible. This is especially true with special types of content, such as AR. Also, support for social activity and sharing especially after the visit should be available.

There are especially plenty of opportunities for new functionality with an interactive floor plan. Adding gamification elements to the app is another track that came up in user evaluations and is worth studying closely. Although the prototype did not include a chatbot several test users said it would be an interesting feature. Also, recognition of 3D objects should be addressed in future versions of YPAT. Copyright issues may be a problem in the future since it would be logical for the app to use images of the original works of art.

Acknowledgment

We gratefully acknowledge that smARTplaces is co-funded by the Creative Europe Programme of the European Union [24].

References

[1] smARTplaces Project Web site. Available from: https://smartplaces.eu/ 2020.10.14

[2] smARTplaces Application Web site. Available from: https://smartplaces.eu/explore-the-new-smartplaces-app/ 2020.10.14

[3] ISO/IEC CD 25010.2 standard. International Standardization Organization (ISO). Switzerland

[4] ISO DIS 9241-210:2010. Ergonomics of human system interaction - Part 210: Human-centred design for interactive systems (formerly known as 13407). International Standardization Organization (ISO). Switzerland

[5] E. Law, V. Roto, M. Hassenzahl, A. Vermeeren, and J. Kort, "Understanding, Scoping and Defining User eXperience: A Survey Approach," ACM SIGCHI Conference on Human Factors in Computing Systems (CHI'09), pp. 719-728, 2009.

[6] N. Bevan, "Classifying and Selecting UX and Usability Measures," International Workshop on Meaningful Measures: Valid Useful User Experience Measurement (VUUM), Reykjavik, Iceland pp. 13-18. E. L-C. Law, N. Bevan, G. Christou, M. Springett, and M. Lárusdóttir, Eds. 2008.

[7] J. Isleifsdottir and M. Larusdottir, "Measuring the User Experience of a Task Oriented Software," International Workshop on Meaningful Measures: Valid Useful User Experience Measurement (VUUM), Reykjavik, Iceland pp. 97-102. E. L-C. Law, N. Bevan, G. Christou, M. Springett, and M. Lárusdóttir, Eds. IRIT, 2008.

[8] smARTplaces Application at Google Play Store. Available from: https://play.google.com/store/apps/details?id=de.menschortweb.smartplaces 2020.10.14

[9] M. Hassenzahl, M. Burmester, and F. Koller, "AttrakDiff: Ein Fragebogen zur Messung wahrgenommener hedonischer und pragmatischer Qualität," In J. Ziegler & G. Szwillus, Eds. Mensch & Computer. Interaktion in Bewegung, pp. 187-196, Stuttgart, Leipzig: B.G. Teubner, 2003.

[10] A. Colley, M. Pakanen, S. Koskinen, K. Mikkonen, and J. Häkkilä, "Smart Handbag as a Wearable Public Display - Exploring Concepts and User Perceptions," AH 2016, February 25-27, 2016, Geneva, Switzerland, pp. 1-8, ACM. ISBN 978-1-4503-3680-2/16/02

[11] H. Väätäjä, T. Koponen, and V. Roto, "Developing Practical Tools for User Experience Evaluation – A Case from Mobile News Journalism," ECCE 2009, Helsinki, Finland, pp. 1-8, ACM, 2009.

[12] M. Hassenzahl, "The thing and I: Understanding the relationship between users and product," In Funology: From usability to enjoyment, M.A. Blythe, K. Overbeeke, A.F. Monk, P.C. Wright, Eds. Kluwer, The Netherlands, pp. 31-42, 2003.

[13] C. Coates, "How Museums are using Augmented Reality," MuseumNext. Available from: https://www.museumnext.com/article/how-museums-are-using-augmented-reality/ 2020.10.14

[14] C. Shin et al., "Unified Context-Aware Augmented Reality Application Framework for User-Driven Tour Guides," Int. Symposium on Ubiquitous Virtual Reality, pp. 52-55, IEEE. 2010.

[15] P. Isomursu, M. Virkkula, K. Niemelä, J. Juntunen, and J. Kumpuoja, "Modified AttrakDiff in UX Evaluation of a Mobile Prototype," Int. Conference on Advanced Visual Interfaces (AVI '20), pp. 1-3, ACM ISBN 978-1-4503-7535-1

[16] Magnus Application Web site. Available from: http://www.magnus.net/ 2020.10.14

[17] Smartify Application Web site. Available from: https://smartify.org/ 2020.10.14

[18] B. Rhee and Y. Choi, "Using Mobile Technology for Enhancing Museum Experience: Case Studies of Museum Mobile Applications in S. Korea," Int. Journal of Multimedia and Ubiquitous Engineering vol. 10, no. 6, (2015), pp. 39-44 http://dx.doi.org/10.14257/ijmue.2015.10.6.05

[19] M. H. Rung and D. Laursen, "Adding to the Experience: Use of Smartphone Applications by Museum Visitors," The Transformative Museum Conference, Roskilde University, Roskilde, Denmark, ed. / Erik Kristiansen, pp. 314-324, 2012.

[20] GitHub Web site for React Native. Available from: https://github.com/facebook/react-native 2020.10.14

[21] Vuforia development Web site. Available from: https://developer.vuforia.com/

[22] T. Guo, "Cloud-based or On-device: An Empirical Study of Mobile Deep Inference," IEEE International Conference on Cloud Engineering (IC2E), pp. 184-190, 2018.

[23] Attrakdiff Web site. Available from: http://www.attrakdiff.de/ (ver. 10.12.2019). 2020.10.14

[24] Home page of Creative Europe Programme of the European Union. Available from: https://ec.europa.eu/programmes/creative-europe/ 2020.10.14

Comparison of Input Methods and Button Sizes in Augmented Reality Devices

Sunyoung Park
School of Software
Kwangwoon University
Seoul, Republic of Korea
e-mail: byi9151@kw.ac.kr

Yuryeon Lee
School of Information Convergence
Kwangwoon University
Seoul, Republic of Korea
e-mail: tkdenddl74@kw.ac.kr

Hwaseung Jeon
School of Information Convergence
Kwangwoon University
Seoul, Republic of Korea
e-mail: tkdenddl74@kw.ac.kr

Hyun K. Kim
School of Information Convergence
Kwangwoon University
Seoul, Republic of Korea
e-mail: hyunkkim@kw.ac.kr

Muhammad Hussain
Dept. of Industrial and
Management Engineering
Incheon National University (INU)
Incheon, Republic of Korea
e-mail: mhussain@inu.ac.kr

Jaehyun Park
Dept. of Industrial and
Management Engineering
Incheon National University (INU)
Incheon, Republic of Korea
e-mail: jaehpark@inu.ac.kr

***Abstract*— Augmented-Reality (AR) has already been applied to many areas and applications, but there is still a lack of research on the appropriate interface considering the usability of AR devices. At present, the main input methods of HoloLens can be classified into two categories: hand (gesture) and clicker. In this work, participants wear HoloLens and perform target selection works. We measure the task completion time, user satisfaction score and error rate to check the effects of the input methods, button sizes, and distances. The Latin Square design was used to minimize the effect of the order. Then, a questionnaire was conducted after each treatment. In this paper, we compared the performance changes by input methods, button size, and distance in HoloLens. There was a significant difference in input method, distance and button size. Task completion time and user satisfaction were better with the large button than the small button, and the error rate was higher with the large button. In task completion time and user satisfaction, the clicker performed better than the hand. The task completion time and the user satisfaction were better in 80 cm and 100 cm than 60 cm.**

Keywords-Augmented-reality; interface; Button-size; Hololens; Input method; Distance.

I. INTRODUCTION

Augmented-Reality (AR) refers to a computer interface technology that enables users to perceive mixed images by combining a virtual world composed of computer graphics with the real world in the form of virtual reality. Users interact with computers while manipulating them as virtual objects by their actions in real-time [1]. AR is already being used in a wide range of areas, such as education psychology, entertainment, retail, construction, cultural heritage, tourism, etc. with many different applications, such as training, skill learning, maintenance, repair, quality control, or safety awareness [2]. Previous studies have conducted performance evaluations according to the user input method of AR devices, analyzed the strength and weakness of the input method, and proposed an improved interface [3]. Research was also conducted to explore various safety problems that can occur while operating various Internet of Things (IoT) devices in the Augmented-reality environment, and to provide design guidelines to prevent them [4]. In the previous usability study using Virtual-Reality (VR) devices, large buttons (3° 50′) and small buttons (1° 55′) were found to have differences in terms of button input time and error rate, and the large button was recommended [5]. However, in the case of AR devices, it was thought that there would be a difference between the results of VR devices in that the background behind the buttons is the real world and the distance between the user's eyes and the button's visible distance is adjustable, and this research was conducted because there is still a lack of research on the interface considering the usability of AR devices. The rest of the paper is structured as follows. Section II presents the experimental design. Section III describes the results and Section IV offers the conclusion and future work.

II. EXPERIMENTAL DESIGN

Participants in our study conducted experiments using HoloLens, and the task was to repeatedly select targets from different variances. Participants in the experiment consisted of people who had no problem with the experiment and were not familiar with the use of HoloLens.

A. *Participants*

The research group consisted of 12 male and 12 female participants (Average age: 21.21 years old, Standard deviation: 1.26) who had no experience in using augmented reality except smartphone-based augmented reality and had no physical or visual problems. Participants were recruited using the university intranet, all Asian, and were given incentives to encourage participation. 11 of them had experience using VR devices and 22 of them were right - handed. Due to COVID-19, it was difficult to recruit participants of various age groups, so the participants were recruited as university students in their 20s.

B. *Apparatus*

The experimental device used the HoloLens Development Edition [6], which can mix holograms with the real world to make them sound like they are part of the world. The resolution of the instrument is HD 16:9 light engine and generates a 2.3M total light point. The HoloLens native user interface moves the cursor as the head moves and recognizes simple hand gestures within the angle of view of the camera on the front. The prototype Application runs on HoloLens and is implemented using Unity [7] and C#. HoloLens was light and comfortable to wear, easy to use, provided sufficient computing power, and was studied in many areas [8]. So, it was considered suitable for experimentation.

C. Tasks

This study repeats the target selection work, using HoloLens. Prototypes have a total of nine buttons and exist in the panel in the form of a 3 x 3 array. There are two sizes of buttons, and the size of small buttons is set to 1° 55′ 4″ based on the long side of the 3 x 4 keyboard of a smartphone or feature phone. Microsoft recommended against ever presenting holograms closer than 40 cm [9]. So, we constructed the experiment with a distance of 1.5, 2, and 2.5 times the distance of 40 cm. For the large buttons, it is set to double the small buttons, and the field of view is set as 3° 49′ 48″ [10] (Figure 1, Table 1). The distance was set at 60, 80 and 100 cm (Figure 2), and the subjects conducted the experiment with two types of input methods: hand and clicker. The participants repeatedly clicked the button that turns red among the 9 buttons, and then clicked the button 4 times (Figure 3) for 12 treatment conditions (2 Button sizes x 3 Distances x 2 Input methods) repeating 5 sets.

TABLE 1. BUTTON SIZE ACCORDING TO FOV AND DISTANCE

FOV	Distance	Size of Button
3° 49′ 48″	60 cm	3.68 cm
	80 cm	4.90 cm
	100 cm	6.14 cm
1° 55′ 4″	60 cm	2.00 cm
	80 cm	2.68 cm
	100 cm	3.35 cm

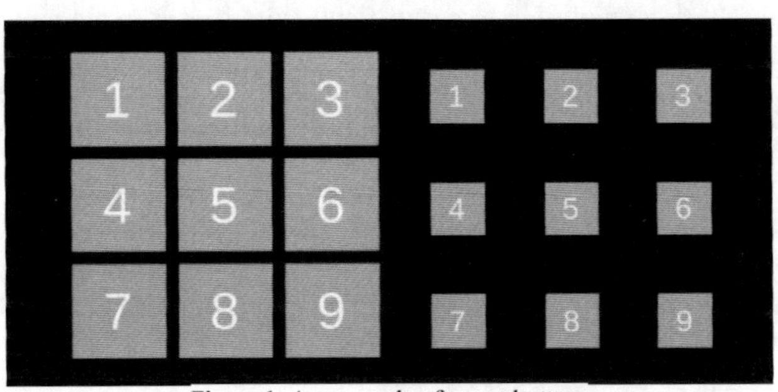

Figure 1. An example of target buttons
(left: large buttons, right : small buttons)

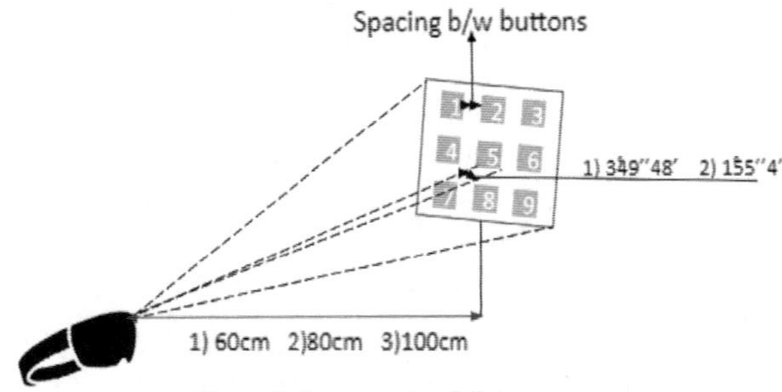

Figure 2. An example of distances

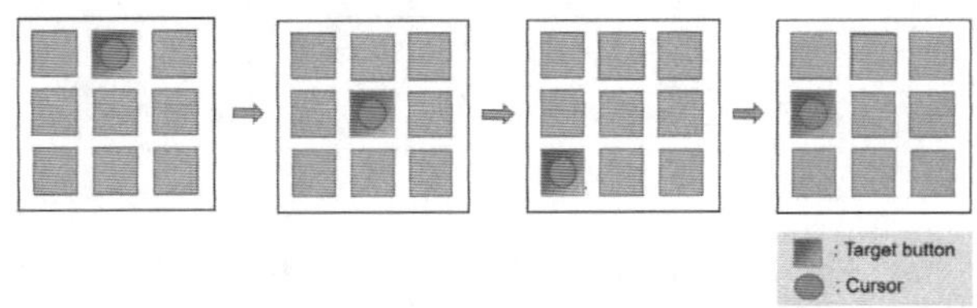

Figure 3. Sequence of target button selection

D. Procedure

All participants listened to the explanation of the experiment before the experiment, wrote the consent form and personal information, and pressed the button. Since, HoloLens is not a familiar equipment to subjects, we explained how to use it to carry out the experiment smoothly, went through simple practice, and then proceeded with this experiment. This experiment consists of a total of 12 treatment conditions, and the experiment was conducted with Latin square design to prevent learning effects. Each treatment condition repeats 5 sets of four button selection tasks, resulting in a total of 240 (12 test conditions x 4 random button selection x 5 sets = 240 tasks). The total time was less than 90 minutes. After performing each treatment condition, the subjects were given a break of about two minutes, and then user satisfaction was evaluated. A five-point Likert scale was used to evaluate user satisfaction for each test condition (1-Strongly disagree, 2-Disagree, 3-Neither agree nor disagree, 4 Agree, 5-Strongly agree). The subjects could take a rest whenever they wanted, and if they had difficulty in continuing the experiment, they could give up the experiment. In Section 2, we described the experimental design, including participants, apparatus, tasks, and procedure.

III. Result

Repeated measurement ANalysis of VAriance (ANOVA) showed that there are performance differences according to button size, distance, and input method.

TABLE 2. RESULTS OF ANOVA BETWEEN BUTTON SIZE, DISTANCE, INPUT METHOD

	Task Completion time		User Satisfaction		Error Rate	
	F	p	F	p	F	p
Button Size(A)	334.13	0.00	29.10	0.00	5.95	0.02
Distance(B)	51.92	0.00	10.08	0.00	0.85	0.36
Input Method(C)	402.86	0.00	33.81	0.00	1.73	0.19
A X B	20.63	0.00	3.89	0.05	0.00	1.00
A X C	9.34	0.00	0.59	0.44	1.73	0.19
B X C	15.80	0.00	0.18	0.67	0.21	0.65
A X B X C	12.89	0.00	0.01	0.93	1.90	0.17

There were statistically significant differences in button size, distance, and input method, interactions task completion time and user satisfaction (Table 2). Tukey's range Test (Tukey HSD) was used for post-test, and R, a programming language for statistical calculations and graphics, was used as an analysis tool.

A. Task Completion Time

2 (Button size) x 3 (Distance) x 2 (Input method) Repeat Measurement analysis of Variance (ANOVA) showed statistically significant differences in task completion time among button size, distance, and input method ($p<0.000$, $\alpha = 0.05$).

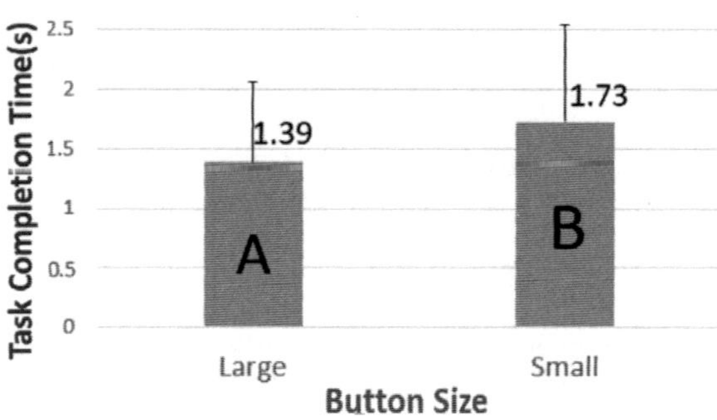

Figure 4. Task completion time according to button size (Error bars refer to standard deviation)

Task completion time for the large button was 1.39 s (±0.667) and for the small button was 1.73 s (±0.809). The task completion time was statistically significant in the button size ($p < 0.000$, $\alpha = 0.05$). Longer time was required to select the small button (1° 55′ 4″) than the large button (3° 49′ 48″) (Figure 4).

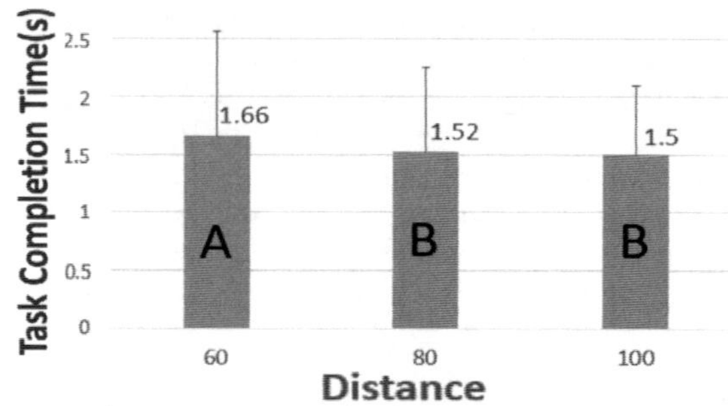

Figure 5. Task completion time according to distance (Error bars refer to standard deviation)

Task completion time for distance 60cm was 1.66 s (±0.906) and for distance 80cm was 1.52 s (±0.738) and for Distance 100cm was 1.5 s (±0.596). The average task completion time increased with the distance in the following order 100cm, 80cm, 60cm. Task completion time was statistically significant in the distance in A (60 cm) and B (80 cm,100 cm) ($p < 0.000$, $\alpha = 0.05$) (Figure 5).

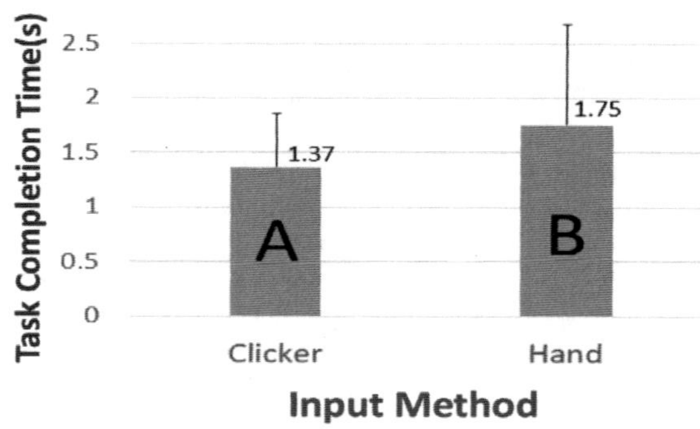

Figure 6. Task completion time according to input method (Error bars refer to standard deviation)

Task completion time for using the clicker was 1.37 s (±0.488) and for using the hand was 1.75 s (±0.921). The task completion time was statistically significant in the input method ($p < 0.000$, $\alpha = 0.05$). Longer time was required to using the hand than using clicker (Figure 6). In addition, there were statistically significant differences in interaction between button size and input method ($p < 0.01$, $\alpha = 0.05$), interaction between distance and button size ($p < 0.000$, $\alpha = 0.05$), interaction between the distance and input method ($p < 0.000$, $\alpha = 0.05$). There was also a statistically significant difference in the interaction of button size, distance, and input method ($p < 0.000$, $\alpha = 0.05$).

B. User Satisfaction

2 (Button size) x 3 (Distance) x 2 (Input method) Repeat Measurement analysis of Variance (ANOVA) showed statistically significant differences in user satisfaction score among button sizes ($p < 0.000$, $\alpha = 0.05$), distances ($p < 0.001$, $\alpha = 0.05$), and input method ($p < 0.000$, $\alpha = 0.05$).

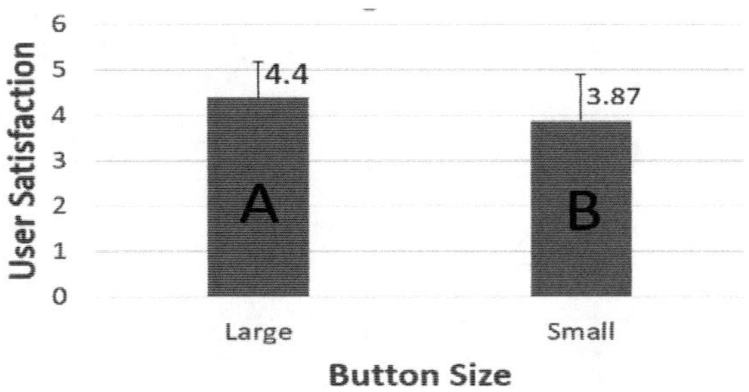

Figure 7. User satisfaction according to button size
(Error bars refer to standard deviation)

The user satisfaction score for the large button was 4.40 (±0.778) and for the small button was 3.87 (±1.03). The task completion time was statistically significant in the button size ($p < 0.000$, $\alpha = 0.05$). The user satisfaction score was higher in the large button than in the small button (Figure 7).

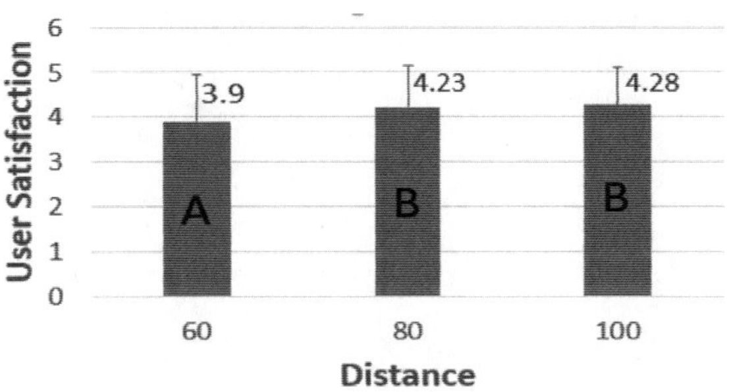

Figure 8. User satisfaction according to distance
(Error bars refer to standard deviation)

The user satisfaction score for distance 60 cm was 3.90 (±1.06), for distance 80 cm was 4.23 (±0.923) and for distance 100 cm was 4.28 (±0.817). The user satisfaction score was better in the order 100 cm, 80 cm, 60 cm. User satisfaction score was statistically significant in the distance in A (60 cm) and B (80 cm, 100 cm) ($p < 0.05$, $\alpha = 0.05$) (Figure 8).

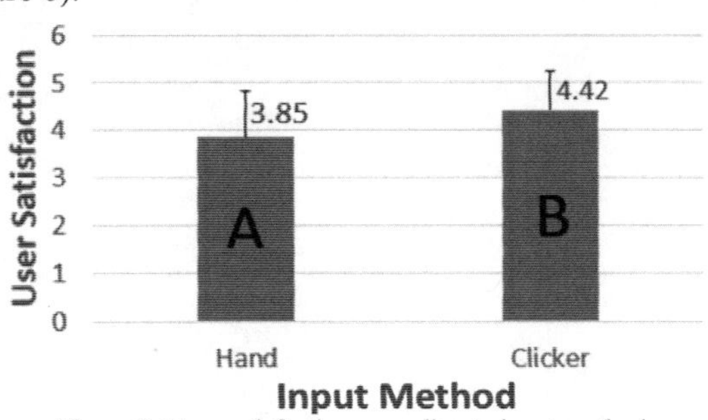

Figure 9. User satisfaction according to input method
(Error bars refer to standard deviation)

The user satisfaction score for using the hand was 3.85 (±0.978) and for using the clicker was 4.42 (±0.833). The user satisfaction score was statistically significant in the input method ($p < 0.000$, $\alpha = 0.05$) (Figure 9). In addition, there were statistically significant differences in interaction between button size and distance ($p < 0.05$, $\alpha = 0.05$).

C. *Error rate*

2 (Button size) x 3 (Distance) x 2 (Input method) Repeat Measurement analysis of Variance (ANOVA) showed statistically significant differences in error rate among button size ($p < 0.05$, $\alpha = 0.05$).

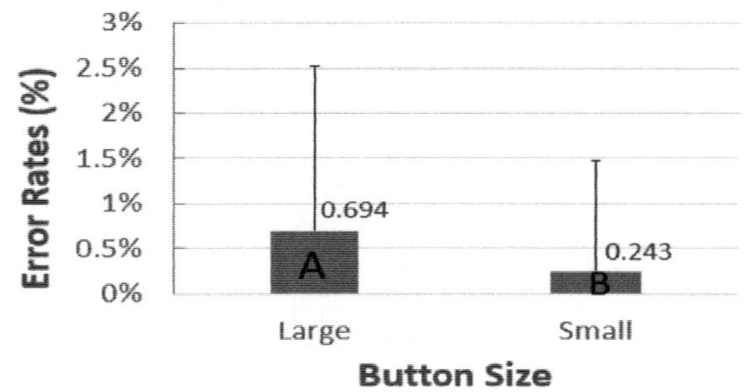

Figure 10. Error rate according to button size
(Error bars refer to standard deviation)

The average error rate for the large button was 0.694% (±1.83) and for the small button was 0.243% (±1.23). The error rate was statistically significant in the button size ($p<0.05$, $\alpha=0.05$). There was a higher error rate with the small button than with the large button (Figure 10). In Section 3, we described results of task completion time, user satisfaction, and error rate according to button size, distance, and input method.

IV. CONCLUSION AND FUTURE WORK

We compared the performance changes by two input methods (hand, clicker), two button sizes (large, small), and three distances (60, 80, 100 cm) in HoloLens. Three factors (Task completion time, Error rate, User satisfaction) were measured by conducting experiments on a total of 12 treatment conditions. There were statistically significant differences in task completion time, user satisfaction and error rate. Task completion time and user satisfaction were better in the large button than the small button, and the error rate was higher in the large button. In task completion time and user satisfaction, the clicker performed better than the hand. The task completion time and the user satisfaction were better in 80 cm and 100 cm than 60 cm. The results of this study are thought to help determine the appropriate target distance, size, and input method for AR devices. However, all participants were in their 20s and there is a limitation since only three variances (button size, distance, input method) are considered. In future studies, we would like to recruit participants of more diverse ages and conduct experiments with more variances in mind.

ACKNOWLEDGEMENT

This research was supported by the MIST (Ministry of Science and ICT), under the National Program for Excellence in SW (2017-0-00096), supervised by the IITP (Institute for Information & communications Technology Promotion). Also this work was supported by the National Research Foundation of Korea (NRF) grant funded by the Korea government (MSIT) (No. 2018R1C1B5086269).

REFERENCES

[1] H. J. Suh, "Relationships among presence, learning flow, attitude toward usability, and learning achievement in an augmented reality interactive learning environment", The Journal of Educational Information and Media, vol. 14(3), pp. 137-165, 2008.

[2] R. S. Vergel, P. M. Tena, S. C. Yrurzum, and C. Cruz-Neira, "A Comparative Evaluation of a Virtual Reality Table and a HoloLens-Based Augmented Reality System for Anatomy Training", IEEE Transactions on Human-Machine Systems, 2020.

[3] A. Hamacher, J. Hafeez, R. Csizmazia, and T. Whangbo, "Augmented Reality User Interface Evaluation – Performance Measurement of Hololens, Moverio and Mouse Input", *International Association of Online Engineering*, 2019.

[4] A. Hamacher, J. Hafeez, R. Csizmazia, and T. Whangbo, "Augmented Reality User Interface Evaluation – Performance Measurement of Hololens, Moverio and Mouse Input", International Association of Online Engineering, [retrieved: October, 2020], https://www.learntechlib.org/p/208272/.

[5] M. Choe, Y. Choi, J. Park, and H. K. Kim, "Comparison of Gaze Cursor Input Methods for Virtual Reality Devices", International Journal of Human–Computer Interaction, vol. 35(7), pp. 620-629, 2019.

[6] E. Miller and S. Paniagua, "HoloLens (1st gen) hardware", 2019, Microsoft Docs, https://docs.microsoft.com/en-au/hololens/hololens1-hardware [retrieved: July, 2020].

[7] Unity, Unity Platform, 2020, https://unity.com/products/unity-platform.

[8] M. G. Hanna, I. Ahmed, J. Nine, S. Prajapati, and L. Pantanowitz, "Augmented reality technology using Microsoft HoloLens in anatomic pathology", Arch Pathol Lab Med, vol. 142, pp. 638-644, 2018.

[9] F. Harrison, "Comfort", 2020, Microsoft Docs, https://docs.microsoft.com/en-us/windows/mixed-reality/design/comfort [retrieved: July, 2020].

[10] H. K. Kim, J. Park, Y. Choi, and M. Choe, "Virtual reality sickness questionnaire (VRSQ): Motion sickness measurement index in a virtual reality environment", Applied ergonomics, vol. 69, pp. 66-73, 2018.

Factors Affecting Motion Sickness in an Augmented Reality Environment

Hwaseung Jeon[1], Sunyoung Park[2], Yuryeon Lee[1], Hyun K. Kim[1]
[1]School of Information Convergence, [2]School of Software
Kwangwoon University
20 Kwangwoon-ro, Nowon-gu, Seoul, 01897, Republic of Korea
e-mail: {stella668, byi9151, tkdenddl74, hyunkkim}@kw.ac.kr

Muhammad Hussain, Jaehyun Park
Department of Industrial and Management Engineering
Incheon National University (INU)
119 Academy-ro, Yeonsu-gu, Incheon 22012, Republic of Korea
e-mail: {mhussain, jaehpark}@inu.ac.kr

***Abstract*—This study aims to evaluate the factors affecting motion sickness in the Augmented Reality (AR) environment. Motion sickness is due to a difference between actual and expected motion. When people use Virtual Reality (VR), they experience symptoms of motion sickness due to the inconsistency in vision and body movements. To measure the motion sickness, a VR Sickness Questionnaire (VRSQ) measurement index is used. The experiment was conducted with the following settings. The study group consisted of 12 female and 12 male participants with no health problems. They performed the task of repeatedly selecting specific buttons. It consisted of a total of 240 button selections (12 treatment (two methods of selection × two button sizes × three distances) × 4 choices × 5 sets = 240 tasks). The Latin Square design was used to minimize the effect of order. Then, a questionnaire was conducted after each treatment. ANOVA (ANalysis Of VAriance) was performed to check if there were differences in Oculomotor, Disorientation, and VRSQ total score. There was a significant difference in selection method and distance of VRSQ Oculomotor. It is recommended to use physical buttons and to have a distance of 100 cm from the target to reduce the motion sickness in AR environment.**

Keywords-Augmented reality; simulator sickness questionnaire; virtual reality sickness questionnaire.

I. INTRODUCTION

Over the past decades, Augmented Reality (AR) technology is developed and used in many fields. AR allows the user to see the real world, with virtual objects superimposed upon or composited with the real world [1]. There are many cases of motion sickness in Virtual Reality (VR) environment. There are many kinds of factors that cause motion sickness. Studies show that motion sickness varies depending on age. Older participants had a greater likelihood of simulator sickness than younger participants [2][6]. It is also related to the amount of time exposed to VR environments. VR sickness is also affected by visual stimulation locomotion and exposure times [6]. The longer the exposure time, the more pronounced the motion sickness symptoms [3].

However, there are not many studies dealing with motion sickness in AR environments. As a method to measure the degree of motion sickness of AR, a VR Sickness Questionnaire (VRSQ), which was developed according to the VR environment, is utilized. The goal of this study is to check the factors affecting motion sickness in the AR environment.

Section II introduces VRSQ measurement, Section III introduces how the user test was conducted, Section IV explains the limitation of the study, and Section V concludes this paper.

II. VRSQ

A typical tool for measuring motion sickness in a cyber simulator is SSQ (Simulator Sickness Questionnaire). SSQ includes 16 symptoms that are divided into three components [4]. In this study, VRSQ tools were selected to measure motion sickness in the AR environment. VRSQ is a motion sickness measurement specialized for VR environments [5]. VRSQ consists of nine symptoms (General discomfort, Fatigue, Eyestrain, Difficulty focusing, Headache, Fullness of head, Blurred vision, Dizzy (eyes closed), Vertigo), which are divided into two factors (Oculomotor, Disorientation) (Table 1). In this study, one index was used per nine symptoms. VRSQ scores can be calculated using the following formula (Table 2).

TABLE I. COMPUTATION SCORE OF VRSQ

VRSQ symptom	Oculomotor	Disorientation
1. General discomfort	O	
2. Fatigue	O	
3. Eyestrain	O	
4. Difficulty focusing	O	
5. Headache		O
6. Fullness of head		O
7. Blurred vision		O
8. Dizzy (eyes closed)		O
9. Vertigo		O
Total	[1]	[2]

TABLE II.

Components	Computation
Oculomotor	([1]/12)*100
Disorientation	([2]/15)*100
Total	(Oculomotor + Disorientation score)/2

III. CASE STUDY

A. Experimental design

1) Participants

The study group consisted of 12 female and 12 male participants with a corrected vision of 0.6 or higher, with no physical or visual health problems (average age: 21.2 years old, standard deviation: 1.26 years old). Since there may be differences between genders, 12 female and 12 male were chosen in consideration of gender balance. The participants were all Korean and had no experience in using AR devices. We recruited the university students who are thought to be interested in AR devices. There were 11 people who had experience using VR devices. Twenty-two of them were right-handed and two were left-handed. All of them conducted the experiment with their own hands.

2) Apparatus

The AR environment was configured using Microsoft Hololens (1st generation) developer edition. Its Holographic resolution 2HD 16:9 light engines producing 2.3M total light points. There are two ways to perform a task (Figure 1). The first thing is to use finger gestures. 1) Gaze at the hologram which want to select. 2) Point the index finger straight up toward the ceiling. 3) Air tap: lower the finger, quickly raise it. The second is to use a clicker. To select a hologram, button, or other element, gaze at it, then click.

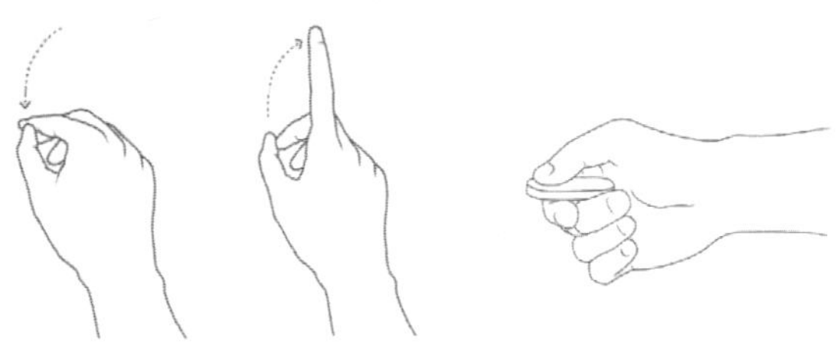

Figure 1. Finger gesture and clicker

3) Tasks

After wearing the Hololens HMD, finger gestures and clickers were used to perform the task of repeatedly selecting specific buttons. Nine buttons are marked in an array of 3×3. Buttons consist of two sizes and three distances (Table 3).

TABLE III. SETTINGS OF BUTTONS

FOV	Distance (cm)	Size of button (cm)
3°49"48'	60	3.68
	80	4.90
	100	6.14
1°55"4'	60	2.00
	80	2.68
	100	3.35

The small button was set to a 1°55'4" field of view based on the length of the large side of the mobile phone's 3×4 keyboard. The large button is set to twice the size of the small button and its field of view is 3°49'48" (Figure 2).

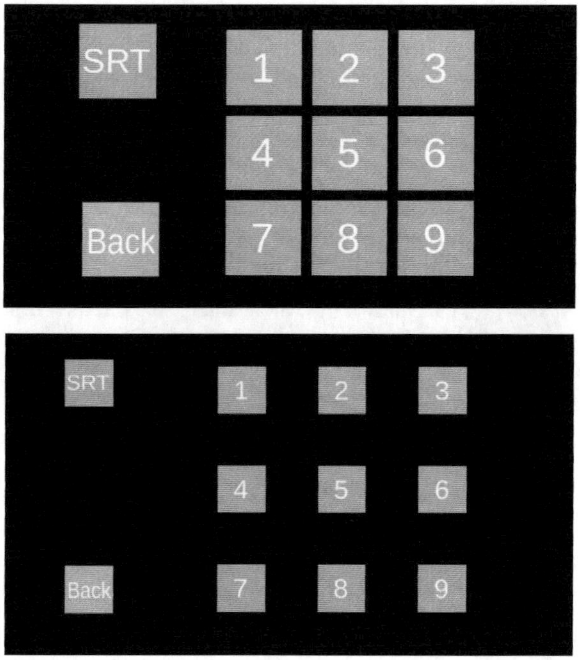

Figure 2. An example of target buttons (up: large buttons, down: small buttons)

4) Procedure

Participants were asked to perform tasks consisting of two selection methods (finger gestures, clickers), two button sizes, and three distances (60 cm, 80 cm, 100 cm) and respond to SSQ. The manufactured application was run through Hololens. The experiment lasted about 90 minutes, including break time.

First, the purpose and contents of the experiment were introduced. They were also explained that if participants feel severe motion sickness, they can rest and stop at any time. And It is evaluating the device, not the ability of the participants. Before starting the experiment, the subjects had a chance to practice until they got used to the device (Figure 3).

Second, participants performed a task consisting of 12 treatments (two methods of selection × two button sizes × three distances = 12 treatments). Each treatment consisted of five sets and one set was to select four randomly highlighted buttons. Thus, it consisted of a total of 240 button selections (12 treatment × 4 choices × 5 sets = 240 tasks). The Latin Square design was used to minimize the effect of order.

Finally, a questionnaire was conducted after each treatment. Motion sickness levels were assessed through the difficulty level and SSQ of performing the task. The score was based on a five-point recurve scale (1 = not at all, 2 = slightly, 3 = normal, 4 = moderately, 5 = very).

Figure 3. A person wearing the HMD equipment and clicking the buttons

B. Result

1) ANOVA with VRSQ

Analysis of variance (ANOVA) was performed to check if there were differences in Oculomotor, Disorientation, and VRSQ total score depending on the method of selection, the size of the buttons, and the distance. As a result of the analysis of variance, items with a P value of 0.05 or less were analyzed Tukey post-analysis (Table 4).

TABLE IV. EFFECT TESTING BETWEEN SELECTION METHOD, SIZE, DISTANCE

	VRSQ		VRSQ-Oculomotor		VRSQ-Disorientation	
	F	P	F	P	F	P
Selection (A)	2.97	0.09	5.62	0.02	0.11	0.75
Size (B)	1.90	0.17	2.66	0.10	0.45	0.51
Distance (C)	3.95	0.05	5.91	0.02	0.71	0.40
(A)×(B)	0.94	0.33	1.10	0.30	0.40	0.53
(A)×(C)	0.05	0.82	0.16	0.69	0.10	0.93
(B)×(C)	0.79	0.38	1.00	0.32	0.26	0.61
(A)×(B)×(C)	0.00	0.95	0.13	0.72	0.18	0.67

Differences were found in Oculomotor depending on the method of selection and the distance (Figure 4). In Oculomotor, the P value of Selection was 0.0185 ($p<0.05$), and there was a significant difference in the use of finger gesture and clicker as a result of post-analysis. The VRSQ Oculomotor score of finger gesture selection is 74.02 and the score of clicker is 65.1.

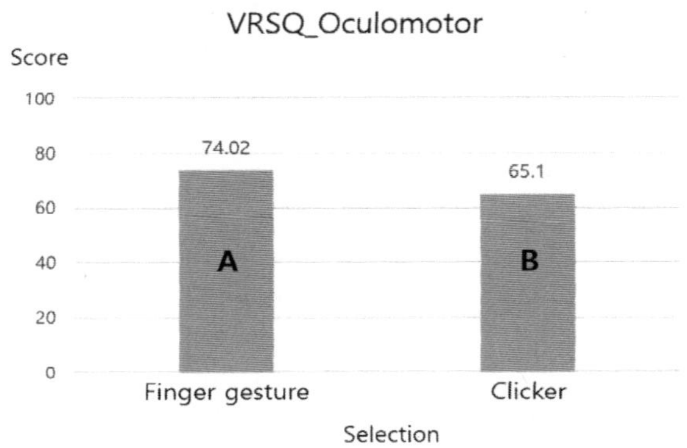

Figure 4. VRSQ_Oculomotor scores for Selection methods (Different letters indicate a statistically significant difference).

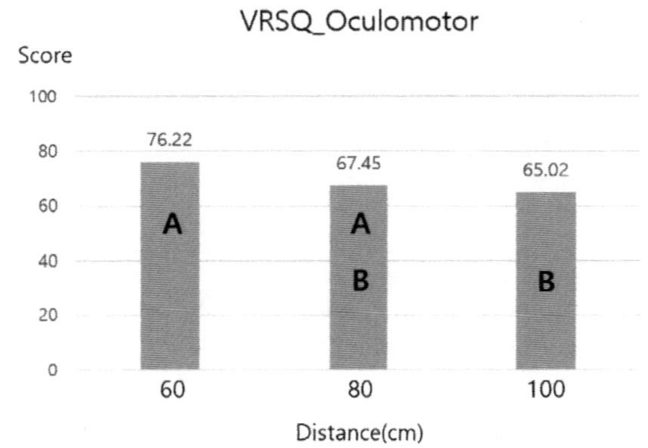

Figure 5. VRSQ_Oculomotor scores for Distance (Different letters indicate a statistically significant difference).

In addition, the P value of Distance was 0.0157($p<0.05$) and there was a significant difference between 60 cm and 100 cm (Figure 5). The VRSQ Oculomotor score of distance 60 cm is 76.22, and the score of 100 cm is 65.02. There were no significant differences in the disorientation score and VRSQ total score according to the selection methods, button sizes, and distances.

IV. DISCUSSION

As a result of the data analysis, two methods of selecting buttons indicated significant differences.

There was a study that measured motion sickness in two ways to select a target: direct selection to select a target with physical buttons and automatic target selection to stare and select for a certain period of time [5]. In this study, both SSQ and VRSQ scores for the choice method using physical buttons were significantly lower. The study also showed that the physical button, the clipper method, had a low motion sickness score.

There was a significant difference between 60 cm and 100 cm in the distance between the target and the subject. The 60 cm VRSQ Oculomotor score was 76.22 and the 100 cm score was 65.02 points. The button at a distance of 100 cm caused less motion sickness. Therefore, when producing contents of AR environment, it is recommended to use physical buttons and to have a distance of 100 cm from the target.

In the case of finger gesture, the finger must be within the camera radius to be recognized. So, the experiment was carried out with the arms stretched forward, and the fingers were in the field of view. Depending on the movement of the eyes, the hands had to move together and the subjects had to pay attention to it. However, the clicker was connected by Bluetooth, so it could be operated comfortably without raising its arms. Due to these differences, eye movements would have varied depending on how buttons were selected, so the degree of motion sickness must have been different.

The experiment was carried out standing in place, facing one direction. Although the position of the buttons changed slightly depending on the view, body movements were generally not required. This may have affected directional loss scores.

This study did not identify differences in the effects of motion sickness by gender. Gender differences need to be checked in further studies.

V. CONCLUSION

SSQ uses a 4-point Likert scale (0=not at all, 1=slightly, 2=moderately, and 3=very). However, in this study, there were limitations in converting to scores using 1-5 scales. Because the numbers on the scales were different, it was difficult to apply the SSQ calculation method.

24 subjects cannot represent all populations. Furthermore, the age of 24 participants was early 20s. So, it could not confirm previous research that there was a difference in the degree of motion sickness depending on age. It is necessary to recruit subjects of various ages for further research.

The task of selecting buttons in an AR environment was carried out and the motion sickness was measured using the VRSQ tool. Twenty-four participants carried out a task consisting of nine buttons, two button selection methods, two button sizes and three distances. VRSQ, which has increased efficiency in VR environment compared to the previous SSQ, is utilized.

This study revealed that Oculomotor among motion sicknesses in AR environment is related to the method and distance of button selection. To provide better usability, motion sickness in the AR environment needs to be improved. This study can suggest the possible user interface element of AR environment to reduce motion sickness.

ACKNOWLEDGMENT

This research was supported by the MIST (Ministry of Science and ICT), under the National Program for Excellence in SW (2017-0-00096), supervised by the IITP (Institute for Information & communications Technology Promotion). Also, this work was supported by the National Research Foundation of Korea (NRF) grant funded by the Korea government (MSIT) (No. 2018R1C1B5086269).

REFERENCES

[1] Azuma and R. T. “A survey of augmented reality”, Presence: Teleoperators & Virtual Environments, vol. 6, no. 4, pp. 355-385, 1997.

[2] Brooks et al. “Simulator sickness during driving simulation studies”, Accident analysis & prevention, vol. 42, no. 3, pp. 788-796, 2010.

[3] D. Saredakis et al., “Factors associated with virtual reality sickness in head-mounted displays: a systematic review and meta-analysis”, Frontiers in Human Neuroscience, vol. 14, 2020.

[4] H. K. Kim, J. Park, Y. Choi, and M. Choe, “Virtual reality sickness questionnaire (VRSQ): Motion sickness measurement index in a virtual reality environment.” Applied ergonomics, vol. 69, pp. 66-73, 2018.

[5] J. Lee, M. Kim, and J. Kim, “A study on immersion and VR sickness in walking interaction for immersive virtual reality applications”, Symmetry, vol. 9, no.5, pp.78, 2017.

[6] L. F. de Souza Cardoso, F. C. M. Q. Mariano, and E. R. Zorzal, “A survey of industrial augmented reality”, Computers & Industrial Engineering, vol. 139, no. 106159, 2020.

[7] M. Choe, Y. Choi, J. Park, and H. K. Kim, “Comparison of Gaze Cursor Input Methods for Virtual Reality Devices”, International Journal of Human–Computer Interaction, vol. 35, no. 7, pp. 620-629, 2019.

[8] N. Dużmańska, P. Strojny, and A. Strojny, “Can simulator sickness be avoided? A review on temporal aspects of simulator sickness”, Frontiers in psychology, vol. 9, no. 2132, 2018.

[9] R. S. Kennedy, N. E. Lane, K. S. Berbaum, and M.G. Lilienthal, “Simulator sickness questionnaire: An enhanced method for quantifying simulator sickness”, The international journal of aviation psychology, vol. 3, no. 3, pp. 203-220, 1993.

[10] R. Qiao and D. Han, “A Study on the Virtual Reality Sickness Measurement of HMD-based Contents Using SSQ”, Journal of Korea Game Society, vol. 18, no. 4, pp. 15-32, 2018.

Customized Gamification Design in Augmented Reality Training for Manual Assembly Task

Diep Nguyen

UniTyLab
Heilbronn University
Max-Planck-Str. 39
74081 Heilbronn, Germany
Email: diep.nguyen@hs-heilbronn.de

Gerrit Meixner

UniTyLab
Heilbronn University
Max-Planck-Str. 39
74081 Heilbronn, Germany
Email: gerrit.meixner@hs-heilbronn.de

***Abstract*—User engagement in training has always been a concern of organizations, especially in manual assembly and maintenance works. There are many techniques in training design and user experience design to create a captivating environment for the trainees. One of those is to use game mechanisms to stimulate playful experience. On the other hand, Augmented Reality is the technology that can provide significant benefits for manual assembly and maintenance training by providing real hands-on experience, the ability to manipulate 3D objects which are superimposed into the real world in a real-time manner. The combination of these two concepts is believed to optimizing the user's efficiency and experience. While there has been some research into this direction, the work is still nascent and the consideration for individual differences has not yet emerged to the picture. In this paper, we propose a gamified design for manual assembly training that takes different types of the user into account. However, we do not propose a new general design but rather want to experiment with a new approach that considers various user groups.**

Keywords–Gamification; Augmented Reality; Gamified Augmented Reality; Gamified Training; Human-Computer Interaction.

I. Introduction

Augmented Reality (AR) is the technology that can provide significant benefits for manual assembly and maintenance training by providing real hands-on experience on the task. AR allows the user to experience the physical world in combination with virtual content in real-time [1]. Whether it is examining a defect machine part or replacing a component, manual assembly and maintenance work that require the manipulation of objects have always been the key interest in the use of AR application. There are numerous examples both in industrial and academic settings that have provided sufficient evidence for this claim. The first and foremost is the pioneer industrial AR application from Boeing in 1992. The application aims were to assist and increase worker efficiency in the assembling aircraft wire bundles [2]. Another example is the ARVIKA project funded by the German Ministry of Education and Research. The project puts AR technologies in the center for research and developing several head-worn AR-based solutions in various fields like design, production, and maintenance operations [3].

On the other side, user engagement in training has always been a concern of organizations. There are many techniques in training design and user experience design to create a captivating environment for the trainees. One of those is gamification. Gamification is defined as "the use of game design elements in non-game contexts" [4]. Although this is the most common and widely accepted definition amongst academia, the debate over a consensus is still open. In the context of this work, we limit ourselves to the above term from Sebastian Deterding. To make it more clear, gamification is different from another similar context such as "serious games" or "exergames". While the first describes an end product as a game with an ultimate purpose which is higher than pure entertainment; the latter stands for exercise-game, which is self-explaining, in which one does exercise while plays the game.

The combination of these two concepts, AR and gamification, is believed to optimizing the user's efficiency and experience. While has been some research into this direction, the work is still nascent and there is much left to be explored. Most systems provide a single design approach to the user with no customization, which is not inclusive or optimal for the user. The users may have to go through the same procedural training, but their experience does not have to be the same. Therefore, our main contribution in this paper is the gamification design for different user types. However, in this paper, we do not propose a new general design for customized gamification in AR training systems since it would diminish the users and their individual needs. We rather want to experiment with a new approach that considers various user groups. Although our system demonstrates on a computer assembly use case, it could be used as an example for all other manual tasks which share similar characteristics: being procedural, having pre-designed content, requiring the manipulation of physical objects and tools.

The paper is organized as following: motivation is presented in Section II. Section III provides an overview of existing works. Section IV and V respectively describe the application design and gamification design. Section VI concludes the paper with a brief conclusion and future work.

II. Motivation

Apart from fancy promising effectiveness of changing people's behaviors by good motivation and engagement, the use of gamification in industrial production is far from matured or beyond the lab-based trial. Despite all its benefits, gamification is predicted to fail to live up to its expectations [5]. Gamification is all about design for people's motivation and engagement. Thus, gamification can be and should be personalized, tailored based on one's preferences for the best results.

However, all the existing works dismiss the role of the individual in designing gamified training. The common practice is a stereotype. It assumes that all users are treated as one group instead of individuals with different characteristics and approaches. For example, when the rewarding mechanism is deliberately used for the wrong users it could lead to "over-justification". "Over-justification" is a term in psychology to describe the situation where a high intrinsic motivated person gets demotivated by extrinsic recognition [6]. Once the user gets used to received rewards, the absence of it potentially may promote negative effects.

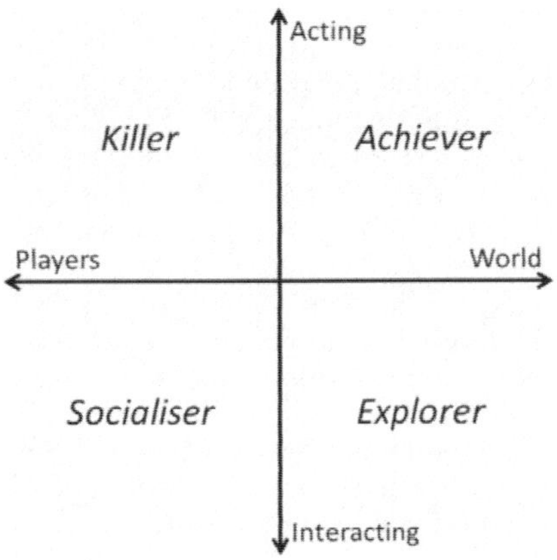

Figure 1. Bartle taxonomy of player types [7].

Game academic Richard Bartle proposed a classification of player types named after himself - the Bartle taxonomy [7]. These categories are the Achiever, the Explorer, the Socializer, and the Killer. Although it's tempted to fix a player into a specific category, it's more than one type that ignites the player's motivation. As demonstrated in Figure 1, the Achiever and the Killer types are somewhat similar in their competitive nature while the remained two focus on interacting with the surrounding world and people. It is important to understand the players to meet their needs, instead of stereotypes.

III. RELATED WORKS

AR for manual assembly tasks and maintenance training is finding its way into daily practices. It is because of the tremendous benefit of hands-on or on-the-job training experience. AR enables the possibility of manipulating assembly components, which are superimposed into the real world, in a real-time manner altogether with additional 3D instructional information. In designing AR training applications, it is not uncommon to borrow concepts or design guidelines from other well-established disciplines such as education and training design. That is to say, gamification is one of those.

The use of game-like design first was intended to engage and motivate students to learn. Taking an example from the historic role playing AR game "Re-living the Revolution" from Schrier [8]. A player is pre-assigned to a specific historic role and spot, after that, a GPS-enabled handheld device will guide the participants to the real site through a real site map with augmented information about the historic event related to their roles. A completed action results in items about the role and spot. Her results showed that students had developed better skills in problem-solving, collaboration via working together with other students to accomplish the given quest. Reports have been continuously stated the positive and promising results that businesses, and organizations learn from applying gamification.

Despite its fame, gamification is still a new trend in the context of industrial training. The unique characteristic of this field is that the employee's concentration on the task at hand is non-negotiable. Neglecting this requirement may result in injuries, damages to the equipment, and products themselves. One pioneer work on industrial gamification in the particular domain of assembly tasks is the Industrial Playground from Oliver Korn [9]. Korn and his research team transformed a traditional assistive system for the impaired worker at a manual assembly station into a gameful design one. And instead of a stationary monitor, projectors were used to project the design interfaced into users' working surface, which is directly in the users' field of view. The assembly process was animated as a Tetris game. Each brick, which was color-coded from green to red to indicate one's performance, represented for a work step. Basing on this base project, further studies were conducted and indicated promising results [10] [11]. Not only the workers showed openness and acceptance for the new design, but their performance was also improved.

Another work that combines AR and industrial gamification is a manual assembly training, procedural guidance for changing a robot arm batteries, from Nguyen [12]. The design of gamification is represented by a points system, progress bar, and signposting element. Each action that the user has to perform worth's a point while a training step, which consists of one or many actions, is visualized through the progress bar. While the target users of the system are novices, signposting provides an in-situ hint over which components should be targeted. In this experiment, the participants were separated into two groups who underwent an identical training process except one with the gamification design while the other did not. The participants performed the training task with a Head Worn Display (HWD), the Microsoft HoloLens, in a controlled environment to ensure everybody was exposed to (nearly) the same environmental conditions. The results showed a more homogeneous effect in user engagement through the task when the game design is present.

Brauer et al. recently presented an application that combined Gamification and AR to support the warehouse process with order picking [13]. Even though it is not an assembly task, this work is a very rare investigation about isolated individual game design elements' effectiveness. For order picking, the user must navigate through the warehouse in the specifically designed path and follows a fixed sequence of actions. Therefore, to some extent, it shares the nature of procedural work such as assembly. The design elements which are under investigation are leader-board and badge. The participants use also the Microsoft HoloLens to pick up 10 orders in the warehouse. After each picking, the user will receive performance feedback either displaying on a leader-board, receiving a badge, or nothing (no gamification support). Results revealed that the gamification is significantly improved user performance and motivation in opposition to non-gamification design.

IV. Application Design

The proposed training system is a mobile AR application that runs on Android platform. The test application is run on Samsung Galaxy S9 [14], which supports ARCore [15] and allows using the phone's camera for AR applications .

The application is used for training users on how to perform an entire assembly and disassembly of a computer which includes a motherboard, power supply, the Central Processing Unit (CPU), the Random-access Memory (RAM), Hard Disk Drive, Video Card, Optical Drives. The application contains three main modules: Assembly, Disassembly for procedural training, and Component Learning.

A. Procedural Training

The assembly and disassembly training is procedural training in nature. The assembly/disassembly module is a complete step-by-step instruction for AR training. The application could later be used in various areas, both private and business sectors, for example, to support IT specialists in their training and to teach them how to completely assemble and disassemble a computer. There are 47 assembly steps and 32 disassembly steps. There are three main actions throughout the process: removing a component, putting a component in the right position, pushing /pressing a component. At the beginning of the training, short guidance is displayed to show the user the meaning of the symbol:

- The blue hand with index finger pointing out: pushing/pressing on the component.
- The red hand: showcase the direction that the corresponding action should be performed.
- A screw driver/screw: indicating the needed tools.

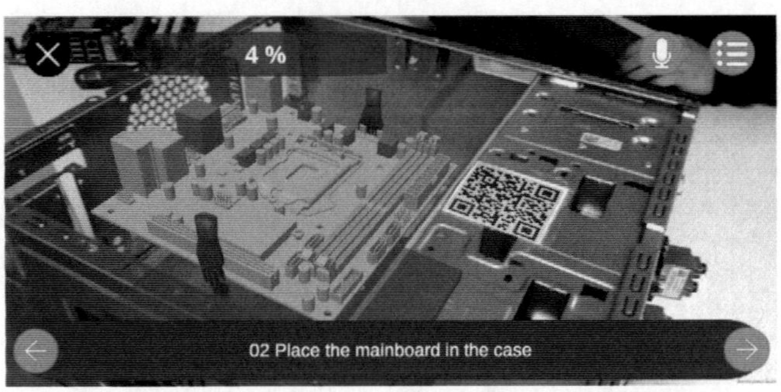

Figure 2. Training step display with multiple instruction components.

A step instruction as in Figure 2 includes five main components: text description of what needs to be done, a CAD model of the assembly components, a 3D model of the required tool, a hologram of the target destination, and the in-situ guidance of the corresponding action.

To navigate directly to a specific step in the assembly or disassembly, one can use the "Steps Selection" function. This function allows the user to directly start a specific assembly step without having to click through all previous steps. This is useful, for example, when one wants to practice a specific assembly/disassembly step directly.

To simplify the navigation between the screens and between the training steps, voice control is integrated into the system. So there are two possibilities to navigate within the application. On the one hand via the navigation buttons contained in the individual screens, and the other via various specific voice commands, such as "Exit". This voice command would take you back to the main menu.

B. Component Learning

The "Learning" function of this system is particularly interesting for this area. This function offers the user the possibility to get to know the individual hardware components of the computer. The learning module is built using the object recognition function. Whenever a component is placed into the field of view of the mobile camera, a detailed description of the component is displayed. It describes the elements in the detail of what it is and what are the functionalities. A 3D model database of all the computer components was built in advance for extracting the learning content.

V. Proposed Gamification Design

A. Points System

The points system works in such a way that a certain number of points (50, 100, or 200) are awarded per assembly step. The number of points depends on how quickly an assembly step has been carried out. The faster it is carried out, the higher the score. A certain amount of time is given for each assembly step, which is the pre-recorded average time of 5 novice users who are the target users of the system. This recorded time corresponds to the best time (200 points). Whenever the user finishes a step, the corresponding score will be added up to the trophy which reflects the overall performance. For example, if the user performs slower than the best time but faster than twice the best time, 100 points are awarded for the step, anything slower than twice the best time will score 50 points. After each step, the score is animated to the big cup and added to the previous score. The lower progress bar is color-coded to indicate the user performance at each step and the time left to reach the corresponding score. In the upper part of the screen, there is a timer, which shows the currently required time per assembly step (restarted after each step). The second is a trophy, which represents the total number of points and which changes to a silver or gold trophy the higher it is.

B. Badges

Besides, it is possible to preserve unique achievements. These are awards when a certain goal has been achieved. Such a goal can be for example the achievement of a Gold Cup or the completion of a certain number of assembly steps. Once a goal has been reached, the corresponding achievement as in Figure 3 is displayed for two seconds.

C. Leader Board

As soon as the whole assembly or disassembly process is finished and thus the total number of points, as well as the final cup, is defined, they are placed on the high-score screen.

Figure 3. User achieves different badges when a certain goal has been achieved.

D. Competitive mode vs Non-competitive mode

As discussed in section II and III, we bring the player types into consideration for providing customized user experiences. A user can select either the "Competitive Mode" or the "Normal Mode" for his training session depending on his characteristics. By allowing the freedom of choice, the hypothesis is that the user will experience the most suitable gamified design for his dominant characteristic. The application offers a choice between two modes each time the assembly and disassembly instructions are started.

The "Competitive Mode" (Figure 4) is designed for users who are highly competitive, predominantly Achiever and Killer. In this mode, the user will experience the points system, badges, and also leader board. Regarding the competitive nature of a user, he can set a user name at the beginning of the training in order to compete with others on the leader-board. The training then is designed with time pressure. Each step is pre-set with a time limitation to get either a gold, silver, or bronze trophy as described in the points system section. This will provide a sense of competition with others which suits the player type.

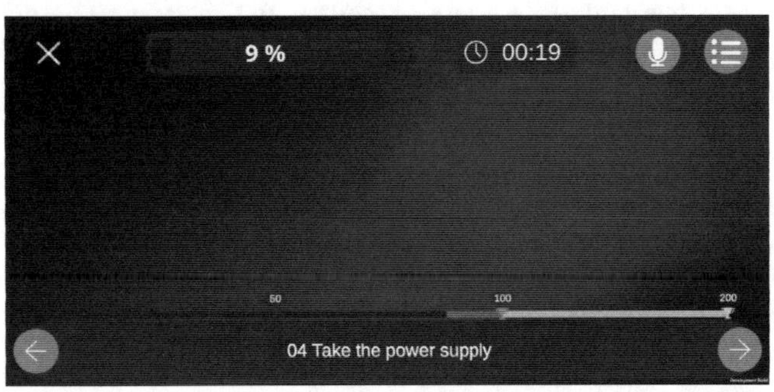

Figure 4. Competitive Mode

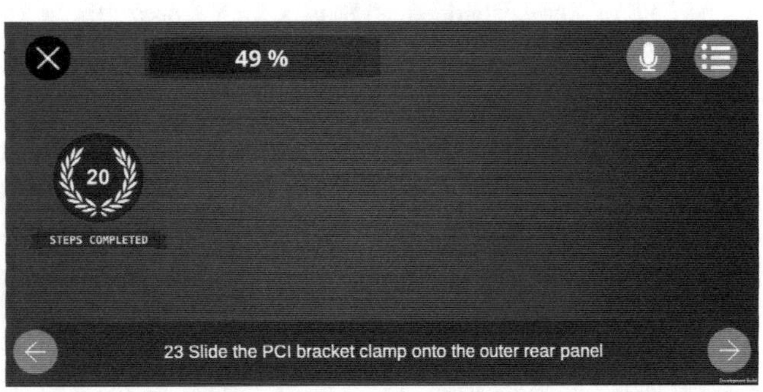

Figure 5. Non-competitive Mode .

In "Normal Mode" (Figure 5), there are no time limits and therefore no points or leader board. This mode is intended for users who are not looking for competition. The badges are available in this mode also. This allows us to simulate the sense of achievement without pressing users into the competitive mode.

VI. Conclusion and Future Work

In this paper, we addressed the problem of considering individual differences in gamification design for AR manual assembly training. We introduce an approach to gamifying the training process with the integration of player types concept. It provides the ability to select a play mode that allows the training to be modified, visualized to fit one's predominant nature. The ultimate goal is to embolden motivation and user engagement.

The proposed design approach will be tested in the next step. We will evaluate its effectiveness as well as its impact on the user's performance. It is interesting to figure out if there is a difference in user experience when the users are left aware and unaware of the choices.

References

[1] R. T. Azuma, "A survey of augmented reality," Presence: Teleoperators and Virtual Environments, vol. 6, no. 4, 1997, pp. 355–385.

[2] P. Thomas and W. David, "Augmented reality: An application of heads-up display technology to manual manufacturing processes," in Hawaii International Conference on System Sciences, 1992, pp. 659–669.

[3] W. Friedrich and W. Friedrich, "ARVIKA: Augmented Reality for Development, Production and Service," The 1st International Symposium on Mixed and Augmented Reality (ISMAR), 2002, pp. 3–4.

[4] S. Deterding, "Gamification: Designing for motivation," Interactions, vol. 19, no. 4, Jul. 2012, p. 14–17.

[5] B. Burke, "The Gamification of Business," Gartner Inc., Tech. Rep., 2013.

[6] F. Groh, "Gamification: State of the art definition and utilization," in Proceedings of the 4th seminar on Research Trends in Media Informatics, 2012, pp. 39–46.

[7] R. Bartle, "Hearts, clubs, diamonds, spades: Players who suit muds," Journal of MUD Research, 06 1996.

[8] K. Schrier, "Revolutionizing history education : using augmented reality games to teach histories," Master's thesis, Massachusetts Institute of Technology, Cambridge, MA., 2009.

[9] O. Korn, "Industrial playgrounds: How gamification helps to enrich work for elderly or impaired persons in production," in EICS'12 - Proceedings of the 2012 ACM SIGCHI Symposium on Engineering Interactive Computing Systems, 2012, pp. 313–316.

[10] O. Korn, M. Funk, S. Abele, T. Hörz, and A. Schmidt, "Context-aware assistive systems at the workplace," in Proceedings of the 7th International Conference on PErvasive Technologies Related to Assistive Environments - PETRA '14. New York, New York, USA: ACM Press, 2014, pp. 1–8.

[11] O. Korn, M. Funk, and A. Schmidt, "Design approaches for the gamification of production environments: a study focusing on acceptance," in the 8th ACM International Conference, 07 2015, pp. 1–7.

[12] D. Nguyen and G. Meixner, "Gamified Augmented Reality Training for An Assembly Task: A Study About User Engagement," in Proceedings of the 2019 Federated Conference on Computer Science and Information Systems, 2019, pp. 901–904.

[13] P. Brauer and A. Mazarakis, "AR in order-picking – experimental evidence with Microsoft HoloLens," Mensch und Computer, no. September, 2018.

[14] G. Gottsegen, "Your galaxy s9 just unlocked a new kind of app: Arcore," May 2018, URL: https://www.cnet.com/news/samsung-galaxy-s9-google-arcore-support/ [accessed: 2020-10-19].

[15] "Build new augmented reality experiences that seamlessly blend the digital and physical worlds," URL: https://developers.google.com/ar [accessed: 2020-10-19].

Development and Promotion of Educational Materials on Human-Centered Design

Jun Iio
Chuo University,
Shinjuku-ku, Tokyo 162-8478, Japan
Email: iiojun@tamacc.chuo-u.ac.jp

Ayano Ohsaki
Advanced Institute of Industrial Technology,
Shinagawa-ku, Tokyo 140-0011, Japan
Email: ohsaki-ayano@aiit.ac.jp

Rika Waida
JVC KENWOOD Design corporation,
Setagaya-ku Tokyo 158-0097, Japan
Email: waida-rika@jvckenwood.com

***Abstract*—Human-Centered Design (HCD) is the design principle that focuses on the users of services, systems, or products. The idea of HCD was proposed more than two decades ago, and it has been widely adopted in the Information Technology (IT) and design industries. However, entry-level educational materials are needed to increase the popularity of the concepts among consumers and students who study engineering and industrial design. The Human-Centered Design organization (HCD-Net) is a specific non-profit organization that promotes the concept of HCD in the Japanese industry. It has a Working Group (WG) whose members have been tasked to develop the required entry-level educational materials on HCD and to promote them to the industry. This paper describes some of its activities. As per the HCD cycle itself, we distinguish between the development and the promotion of the materials. The results of their efforts have been of great value to the people who have to teach the HCD concepts to newcomers.**

Keywords–Human-centered design; Educational materials; HCD cycle.

I. Introduction

Human-Centered Design (HCD) is the concept of a design process where the designers design their services, systems, or products focusing on the users of them. That is, HCD is considered as the user-oriented design process. The concept of HCD was proposed more than two decades ago, and it was standardized by the International Organization for Standard (ISO) as ISO 13407 in 1999. Also, it was integrated into ISO 9241 in 2010 (ISO 9241-210:2010), adding the concept of User eXperience (UX). Subsequently, it has been updated to ISO 9241-210:2019 in 2019 [1].

In Japan, a non-profit organization, the Human-Centered Design Organization (HCD-Net), was established in 2004 [2]. HCD-Net aims to assemble knowledge on HCD and to promote methods and skills regarding HCD. Due to their long-term efforts, the concept of HCD has been widely adopted among experienced engineers, especially in Information Technology (IT) and design industries. However, it is still not popular among consumers. Surprisingly, and unfortunately, even students who study engineering and industrial design are not so familiar with the HCD concepts [3]. Therefore, entry-level educational materials are needed for training newcomers to perform in accordance with HCD processes.

Although there are many training services, educational materials, books, and seminars for the higher-level training on HCD activities, unfortunately, we have few items that can be used as the educational material for introducing basic knowledge of HCD. Hence, entry-level educational materials on HCD are needed.

Several Working Groups (WGs) were established in HCD-Net to fill the gap between entry-level and high-level education due mainly to the lack of educational materials. The members of these WGs have been actively working to achieve their goals. "The fostering teachers WG" was established in June 2016, and it meets monthly for face-to-face discussions. In addition to the meetings, several events have been held by the WG and the work has been actively progressing [4]–[7].

The rest of the paper is structured as follows. In Section 2, we present the basic idea of the HCD process. In Section 3, literature reviews are described. In Section 4, the WG's strategies are illustrated. Then, in Section 5, we discuss how the HCD process worked in the WG's activities and the value of the educational materials delivered as their work. Finally, we conclude in Section 6.

II. The HCD Process

Before explaining the WG's activity further, we describe the basic idea of the HCD process to better understand the character of the WG's work.

The HCD standard is a process standard, i.e., the standard defines several processes to realize an efficient design from the viewpoint of a user. The general phases of the HCD process can be explained with the following steps: (quoted from [8]).

1) *Specify context of use: Identify who the primary users of the product, why they will use the product, what are their requirements and under what environment they will use it.*
2) *Specify Requirements: Once the context is specified, it is the time to identify the granular requirements of the product. This is an important process which can further facilitate the designers to create storyboards, and set important goals to make the product successful.*
3) *Create Design solutions and development: Based on product goals and requirements, start an iterative process of product design and development.*
4) *Evaluate Product: Product designers do usability testing to get users' feedback of the product. Product evaluation is a crucial step in product development which gives critical feedback of the product. The important point is that this cyclical process must be repeated several times to satisfy the service level of the users' requirements.*

WG members are in charge of creating the entry-level materials and of training the trainers who can teach the basic concepts of HCD by using their materials. The fact that their activities themselves were based on the concept of HCD should

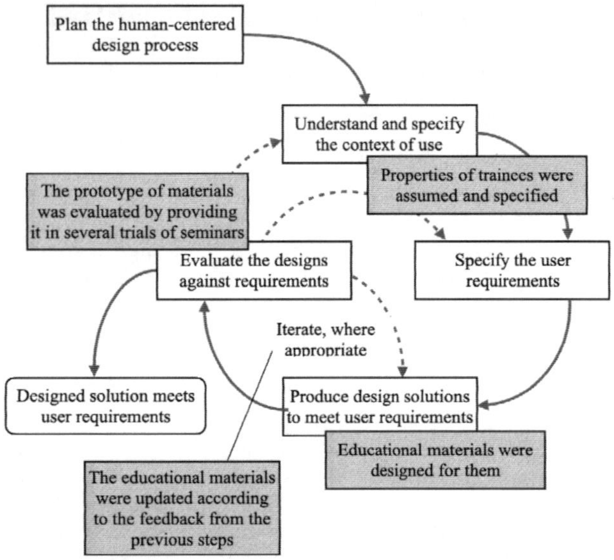

Figure 1. The WG's activities along with the concept of HCD defined in the ISO 9241-210.

be noted; that is, the designing process of their products was as follows: 1. Properties of trainees were assumed and specified. 2. Educational materials were designed for them. 3. The prototype of materials was evaluated by providing it in several trials of seminars. 4. After that, the educational materials were updated according to the feedback from the previous steps. Figure 1 illustrates the processes defined by ISO 9241-210 and the cases adopted to WG's activities in each step, respectively.

III. LITERATURE REVIEW

As the concept of HCD is more widely recognized, HCD education is gathering more and more interest from engineers in various fields. Instructors in this field are paying special attention to how to teach UX concepts. Some case studies in universities and professional training colleges have been reported. However, it still remains unclear how to help newcomers understand HCD in the real business field.

Ito *et al.* [9] reported their implementation of the e-learning course on the basics of HCD. They were working for a computer-electronics manufacturer, and their e-learning course was intended to prevent miscommunication regarding user interfaces among the employees. It was a good example of HCD education conducted in the enterprise.

Gonzalez *et al.* [10] surveyed 140 students who were members of the Human Factors and Ergonomics Society (HFES) and analyzed 40 UX job postings. The results show that there is a discrepancy between the skills the UX industry expects students to have, and the skills HFES promotes for a career in UX. They recommended a focus on increasing HFES's relevance to students interested in future UX careers. Vorvoreanu *et al.* [11] also reported on the UX education for undergraduate students at university.

The concept of "design thinking" is a similar idea to UX design. Wrigley *et al.* [12] focused on surveying the design thinking education provided as Massive Open Online Courses (MOOCs). MOOCs are open to the public and most can be participated in for free via the Internet. Therefore, anyone who wants to learn about design thinking can acquire the knowledge by accessing the courses presented on their web-sites.

Dirin and Nieminen [13] studied the relevance of User-Centered Design (UCD) education to a mobile application development course implemented in a university. They analyzed the feedback from students and concluded that UCD education had a significant role in the development and improvement of students' capabilities on consulting and user study research.

We can find many other cases where HCD or UCD processes were introduced to education programs in various fields; Adam *et al.* [14], Organ *et al.* [15], and Carter *et al.* [16] reported cases in health and medical education, Harvey *et al.* [17] reported a case in fashion education, Wilson *et al.* [18] discussed the possibility of applying the UCD approach to the training environment for aircraft maintenance personnel, and Bowie and Cassim [19] argued for the HCD methodology in contemporary communication design education. These papers reveal the presence of a potential need for HCD education in various domains.

Additionally, there are some studies on designing or evaluating a curriculum by incorporating HCD processes similar to our approach, in creating their educational materials. Altay [20] pointed out that there is a similarity between the learner-centered approach in education and the user-centered approach in design disciplines. Altay illustrates this by adopting a user-centered approach within the human factors course as one of the learner-centered instructional methods. Reich-Stiebert *et al.* [21] explored robot design education by means of the HCD approach. They investigated students' preferences regarding the design of educational robots and evaluated the course according to the results. Chen *et al.* [22] reported on the results of evaluating the curriculum using a method of creating student personas in the field of resource engineering education.

IV. THE WG'S STRATEGIES

The starting point for the WG's activities was the textbook published as the first of the HCD book series. Based on the contents of the book, the WG considered two strategies; one was to develop presentation slides and guidebooks as the educational materials, and another was to foster trainers who could provide seminars to newcomers who were not familiar with HCD.

Under these strategies, the WG created two prototypes of the educational materials for engineers and salespeople. Furthermore, some simulated seminars were conducted to acquire feedback and opinions to brush-up the materials.

A. Educational Materials for Engineers

The first target was newbie engineers who were not familiar with the concept of HCD. The WG published a beta-version of the presentation slides in June 2017, after several discussions by the WG members. After collecting some feedback, the materials were updated, and version 1.0 of the educational materials were published in May 2018.

The presentation materials have 42 slides, which are intended for conducting a seminar of approximately one-and-a-half hours. An overview of the contents is as follows:

1) Case studies
2) The concept of human-centered design
3) Usability
4) Introducing the HCD cycle

5) Appendix (good practices)

Figure 2 shows some examples of the educational materials. The upper left of the figure is the cover page, the upper right shows an example from the case studies, the lower left illustrates the HCD cycle, and the lower right is the cover of the appendix.

As it can be seen from the small icon at the corner of the cover page (see the upper left of Figure 2), the materials are published under the license of Creative Commons (CC BY-NC-SA 3.0). Therefore, everyone can share, redistribute, modify, and create deliverables based on this product, if they follow the conditions defined by the CC-license. This licensing strategy is especially helpful for future trainers, who the WG also wants to encourage because those educators are allowed to modify educational materials as they like.

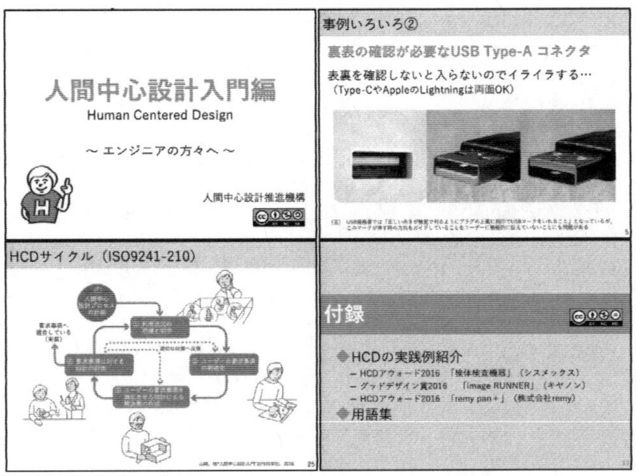

Figure 2. Examples of the presentation slides for training engineers.

B. Educational Materials for Salespeople

After finishing the creation of the entry-level educational materials on HCD for engineers, the WG started a discussion on another version of the educational materials. The members of the WG considered that the people in the front office who had contact with their customers had to know the HCD concepts. Especially in the case of 'business to business (B2B),' such businesses require customers' understanding and cooperation. Hence, the WG decided on salespeople as the next target for education on the idea of HCD.

At the beginning of the preparation work, the WG invited some salespeople and producers who were using HCD processes and worked directly with their customers in their daily business activities. The WG members had several interviews with them to get to know their mental thought processes, how they worked with their customers, etc. Also, they invited salespeople who did not know the HCD to attend an entry-level HCD lecture, so that the discussions could be fruitful for both sides.

Although the base materials were those for engineers, minor modifications were made to the original ones. There were two significant changes; one is that the thoughts of the customer-orientation investigation were introduced instead of the case studies. The other was that the discussion on the positioning of the HCD was added before the conclusions. The latter part also mentions the User eXperiences (UX), because the UX is also a key topic for discussing HCD-related issues with customers. The overview of the contents for salespeople is as follows:

1) Considering the view of the customer-oriented
2) The concept of the human-centered design
3) Usability
4) Introducing the HCD cycle
5) Positioning of the HCD
6) Appendix (good practices)

The education materials of the HCD for salespeople were released in May 2019 (version 1.0).

C. Guidebooks

In addition to providing the presentation slides, the WG also supplies a guidebook on how to conduct efficient training on HCD. Generally, it is not easy to run seminars along with the presentation materials when they were created by other individuals. Therefore, guidebooks to run training courses for trainers using two versions (for engineers and salespeople) of educational materials are also provided.

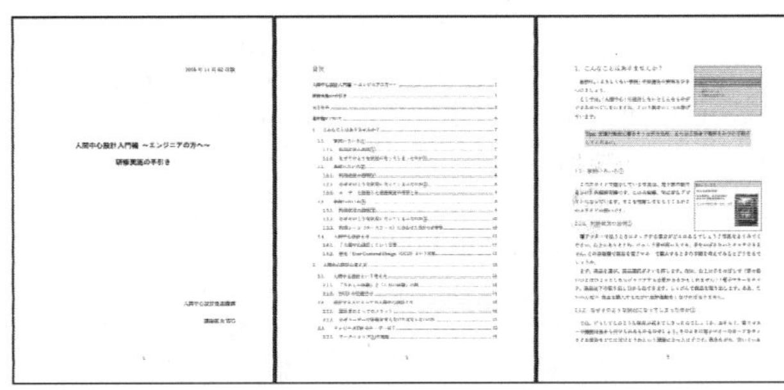

Figure 3. Examples of the guidebook for training engineers.

Figure 3 shows some examples of the guidebook for the educational materials for training engineers. The left of the figure is the cover page, the middle shows the table-of-contents, and the right shows one of the instructional pages.

As it can be seen on the right in Figure 3, the instructions are described for all presentation slides. The guidebook helps novice trainers by giving some additional information on how to teach the topics, etc. All the educational materials (presentation slides) and complementary guidebooks are uploaded to the server hosted by HCD-Net. These can be downloaded from [23] (for engineers) and from [24] (for salespeople).

D. Simulated Seminars (Trial Events)

To evaluate the prototype of the educational materials and lectures, the WG held five simulated seminars. Table I shows a list of trial events officially announced by HCD-Net.

TABLE I. THE LIST OF TRIAL SEMINARS.

ID	*Target*	*Version*	*Date*	*Participants*
1	Engineer	alpha	Mar 4, 2017	18 pros and beginners
2	Engineer	beta	Aug 29, 2017	10 pros and beginners
3	Engineer	ver. 1.0	May 25, 2018	21 pros and beginners
4	Salesperson	beta	Jan 19, 2019	18 pros and beginners
5	Engineer & Salesperson	Modified	Dec 19, 2019	26 (mainly) beginners

The target of the first three seminars (ID 1, 2, 3) was the version for engineers. Lectures based on the alpha version, the beta version, and version 1.0 were examined in each trial, respectively. The next one (ID 4) was for salespeople. At that time, the beta version of lectures for salespeople was confirmed. We asked for HCD professionals to participate in those trials (from ID 1 to ID 4). Therefore, we could hear various opinions from not only beginners but also from professionals. Furthermore, the trial seminars were helpful for those professionals because most of them were in charge of human resource development, and they had motivation to take the contents of the entry-level workshops back to their companies.

V. Discussions

As described in the previous section, the WG created the educational materials and the guidebooks in accordance with the HCD processes. In this section, the compliance with such methods, and the values of the WG's products are discussed.

A. How the HCD Process Worked in the WG's Activity

Looking back, in this section we consider how the four steps in the HCD cycle were applied to the WG's activities. We recall that the HCD cycle has four steps: specifying context of use, specifying requirements, creating design solutions and development, and evaluating products.

1) Specify Context of Use: As we described in the introduction of this paper, our study aimed to create entry-level educational materials and to encourage the instructors who present the training in their organizations. Considering the situations and experiences of each WG member [4][5], the WG decided on engineers as the first target group of trainees, and then salespeople as the second target group of trainees.

2) Specify Requirements: Because the educational materials are essentially designed to accompany the explanations of the textbook, the important part of the WG's work was to decide which components should be selected. Furthermore, the course time was considered very short. At the beginning of the WG's discussion, it made the assumption that the entry-level education on HCD would be conducted in one or two hours. Therefore, the members tried to not make the contents of the materials too complicated. Also, the members discussed what the participants of the lectures would consider important for their studies and their future careers. That is one of the essential points of the WG's activity in the view of the HCD concept.

3) Create Design Solutions and Development: The WG's process for making the materials was iterative, requiring at least two cycles.

The first cycle started with the prototype of the educational materials for engineers. The product was firstly published in its beta version. The WG then collected feedback and comments at the trial seminars (see Section 4.4). After that, the materials were published as version 1.0, and currently, it has been updated to version 1.1.

The second cycle was based on the first one. The prototype of materials for salespeople was started from the latest version of that for engineers, and then updated according to the WG's interviews and feedback from trial seminars. It was published as the beta version, and updated to version 1.0, as well.

4) Evaluate Product: Evaluation by the potential users is a very important process in the HCD cycle. In the WG's activities, the members also considered it the principal process. As described previously with the trial events run to evaluate the materials during the design phase, the WG remained focused on the evaluation process.

The WG's main work in 2019 was the evaluation, improvement, and investigation of which organizations were really utilizing their materials. Several new members, who were users of the materials, joined the WG in 2019. The educational materials and the guidebooks were updated according to the results of interviews conducted with them and feedback from questionnaires.

B. Value of the Educational Materials

The aim of the WG was to prepare entry-level educational materials and to foster instructors who can teach newcomers not yet familiar with the concept of HCD. Therefore, by providing the educational materials, it tried to fill the gap between newbies and experienced engineers, designers, and salespeople.

A review from Amazon's sales listing of the textbook states that: "It is not easy to understand only by reading. It will be worth reading if some lectures were provided using this book as its textbook." We had to agree with this comment. Hence, our decision to provide lectures on the entry-level HCD knowledge with these materials and guidebooks.

During the work conducted in 2019, the WG collected several opinions and impressions of the products from the new members. All of them mentioned that it was useful, but there was still some room for improvement. As the materials were provided under the CC-license, the users could modify the contents, so that it could become suitable for their own courses.

VI. Conclusions and Future Work

The members of the human resource development WG, which was set up in HCD-Net to implement the entry-level educational materials on HCD and to foster lecturers who can train newcomers in each organization, have been working actively during recent years. This paper described their activities and provides an overview of their results. The most significant feature of their work was the fact that their outcomes, that is, the HCD educational materials themselves, were designed according to HCD processes.

The educational materials they created are intended for two different target groups; one for engineers and another for salespeople. Firstly, the training materials for engineers were designed. After that, based on the first prototype, the revised ones for salespeople were created. Guidebooks for conducting the training were also created to accompany the educational materials to make it easier for the lecturers to present these materials.

The WG's main activities in 2019 were conducting interviews with the users, delivering questionnaires to them, and improving the educational materials according to the feedback, as described in the last part of Section 4.1. However, more in-depth analysis of the feedback remains to be done as part of their future work.

Several evaluations were conducted as part of the HCD cycles. In particular, we carried out a series of simulated seminars and interviews with users of the prototype versions.

However, the lectures using these educational materials should be more widespread if we want to let the HCD concepts penetrate into all of the industries. More and more promotions will be needed, and they remain our future work. Furthermore, more evaluations to improve educational materials should be conducted. It will be an ongoing task as part of the WG's future activities.

REFERENCES

[1] "ISO 9241-210:2019 Ergonomics of human-system interaction – Part 210: Human-centred design for interactive systems," https://www.iso.org/standard/77520.html, [retrieved: Sep, 2020]

[2] Z. Liu, "User Experience in Asia," *Journal of Usability Studies,* vol. 9, no. 2, pp. 42–50, 2014.

[3] B. B. Hong, E. Bohemia, R. Neubauer, and L. Santamaria, "Design for Users: The Global Studio," *The 20th International Conference on Engineering and Product Design Education* (E&PDE18), London, UK, 6–7th September, 2018.

[4] H. Yasu *et al.*, "Framework of Education to Promote HCD among Organizations, — Learning from Case Studies —," *Bulletin of Human Centered Design Organization,* vol. 12, no. 1, pp. 13–19, 2016.

[5] H. Yasu *et al.*, "Framework of Education to Promote HCD among Organizations — Proposal and Evaluation on Action Plans for Each Trainee —," *Bulletin of Human Centered Design Organization,* vol. 13, no. 1, pp. 19–24, 2017.

[6] R. Waida *et al.*, "Teaching Materials of HCD Introductory Course for Practitioners – Activities of Making the Beta Version," *Bulletin of Human Centered Design Organization,* vol. 14, no. 1, pp. 24–28, 2018.

[7] A. Kambayashi *et al.*, "Teaching Materials of HCD Introductory Course for Practitioners: Activities of Official Version for Engineers and the Beta Version for People in Contact with Customers," *Bulletin of Human Centered Design Organization,* vol. 15, no. 1, pp. 9–14, 2019.

[8] "User-centered design," From Wikipedia, the free encyclopedia. https://en.wikipedia.org/wiki/User-centered_design, [retrieved: Sep, 2020]

[9] J. Ito, A. Ikegami, and T. Hirayama, "Practice of Promoting HCD Education by a Consumer Electronics Manufacturer," *M. Kurosu (Ed.): Human Centered Design, HCII 2009,* LNCS 5619, pp. 594–600, 2009.

[10] C. A. Gonzalez, M. Ghazizadeh, and M. Smith, "Perspectives on the Training of Human Factors Students for the User Experience Industry," *Proceedings of the Human Factors and Ergonomics Society Annual Meeting,* vol. 58, no. 1, pp. 1807–1811, 2014.

[11] M. Vorvoreanu, C. M. Gray, P. Parsons, and N. Rasche, "Advancing UX Education: A Model for Integrated Studio Pedagogy," *Proceedings of the Computer Human Interaction, CHI 2017,* May 6–11, Denver, CO, USA, 2017, DOI: http://dx.doi.org/10.1145/3025453.3025726

[12] C. Wrigley, G. Mosely, and M. Tomitsch, "Design Thinking Education: A Comparison of Massive Open Online Courses," *The Journal of Design, Economics, and Innovation,* vol. 4, no. 3, pp. 275–292, 2018.

[13] A. Dirin and M. Nieminen, "Relevance of UCD Education to Software Development – Recommendation for Curriculum Design". *Proceedings of the 8th International Conference on Computer Supported Education (CSEDU 2016),* no. 2, pp. 112–120, 2016.

[14] M. Adam, S. A. McMahon, C. Prober, and T. Bärnighausen, "Human-Centered Design of Video-Based Health Education: An Iterative, Collaborative, Community-Based Approach," *Journal of Medical Internet Research,* vol. 21, no. 1:e12128, 2019. DOI: 10.2196/12128

[15] D. Organ *et al.*, "A systematic review of user-centred design practices in illicit substance use interventions for higher education students," *European Conference on Information Systems 2018: Beyond Digitization – Facets of Socio-Technical Change,* Portsmouth, UK, 23–28 June. 2018.

[16] J. Carter, Y. J. Bababekov, and M. D. Majmudar, "Training for our digital future: a human-centered design approach to graduate medical education for aspiring clinician-innovators." *npj Digital Medicine*, vol. 1 no. 1, 2018. https://doi.org/10.1038/s41746-018-0034-4

[17] N. Harvey, P. Ankiew, and F. van As, "Fashion design education: effects of users as design core and inspirational source." *Proceedings PATT 37: Developing a knowledge economy through technology and engineering education,* pp. 203–211, Malta, 3–6 June. 2019.

[18] C. Wilson, W. Bennett Jr., S. Guarino, K. Bove, and T. L. Cain, "Applying a User-Centered Design Approach to Developing Game-Based Training Environments for Aircraft Maintainers," *End-User Considerations in Educational Technology Design,* pp. 217–238, 2018. DOI: 10.4018/978-1-5225-2639-1.ch01

[19] A. Bowie and F. Cassim, "Linking classroom and community: A theoretical alignment of service learning and a human-centered design methodology in contemporary communication design education," *Education as Change,* vol. 20, no. 1, pp. 126–148, 2016.

[20] B. Altay, "User-centered design through learner-centered instruction," *Teaching in Higher Education,* vol. 19, no. 2, pp. 138–155, 2014. DOI: 10.1080/13562517.2013.827646

[21] N. Reich-Stiebert, F. Eyssel, and C. Hohnemann, "Exploring University Students ' Preferences for Educational Robot Design by Means of a User-Centered Design Approach," *International Journal of Social Robotics,* 2019. https://doi.org/10.1007/s12369-019-00554-7

[22] K. C. Chen *et al.*, "Creating a Project-based Curriculum in Materials Engineering," *Journal of Materials Education,* vol. 31, no. 2, pp. 37–44, 2009.

[23] Human Centered Design Organization, "HCD training materials for engineers ver. 1.1," https://www.hcdnet.org/hcd/column/materials_01/hcd-1177.html [retrieved: Sep, 2020]

[24] Human Centered Design Organization, "HCD training materials for salespeople," https://www.hcdnet.org/hcd/column/materials_01/hcd-1307.html [retrieved: Sep, 2020]

Using the Pepper Robot in Cognitive Stimulation Therapy for People with Mild Cognitive Impairment and Mild Dementia

Berardina De Carolis,
Valeria Carofiglio,
Ilaria Grimaldi,
Nicola Macchiarulo
Department of Computer Science
University of Bari
Bari, Italy
email: name.surname@uniba.it

Giuseppe Palestra
Hero srl
Martina Franca, Italy
email: giuseppepalestra@gmail.com

Olimpia Pino
Department of Medicine and Surgery
University of Parma
Parma, Italy
email: olimpia.pino@unipr.it

***Abstract*—Social Assistive Robotics (SAR) has successfully been used in healthcare interventions from the functional and socio-emotional points of view. In particular, they have been used in therapeutic interventions for elderly people affected by cognitive impairments. This paper reports of our research aiming at investigating the role of the social robot Pepper in aiding therapists during cognitive stimulation sessions for elders with Mild Cognitive Impairment (MCI) and Mild Dementia (MD). To this purpose, an experimental study was performed with a group of 8 participants in a 3-weeks cognitive stimulation program. To assess and monitor the results, each session was video recorded for further analyses. The collected videos were analyzed by three human raters, in order to evaluate them in terms of participation and engagement operationalized as eye gazes, number of correct answers and displayed emotions. Results show that Pepper has been positively accepted by the seniors, who were very attentive and involved in session tasks, during which the participants have rarely experienced negative emotions. Moreover, some correlations between the gathered data also emerged that emphasize the effectiveness of the proposed approach. In particular, seniors with lower impairment experienced less happiness; however, they were very engaged during the training with the robot.**

***Keywords*—Social Assistive Robots; Cognitive impairment; Cognitive Stimulation; Elderly people.**

I. INTRODUCTION

With the rapid growth of the older population worldwide, dementia and cognitive impairments are increasingly important issues in elderly care. Alzheimer's Disease International estimates that 24.4 million people worldwide suffer from dementia and that the number of patients will increase to 82 million by 2040. People suffering from dementia and cognitive impairments present problems with memory, thinking and behavior, and symptoms usually develop slowly and get worse over time [1] with devastating effects on the psychological well-being of the individuals.

MCI is an intermediate stage between the cognitive decline associated with typical aging and more severe serious forms of dementia. Individuals with MCI frequently show memory loss or forgetfulness and may have issues with other cognitive functions, such as language, attention or visuospatial abilities. MCI treatments aim to reduce existing clinical symptoms or to delay the progression of cognitive dysfunction and prevent dementia. The potential evolution of this disease makes it unavoidable to provide such people with increasing assistance over time. Therefore, it is especially relevant to offer them timely and engaging cognitive training to slow the progression of their decline, while significantly cutting down the associated socio-economic costs. The increasing attention for cognitive rehabilitation and neuropsychological interventions, in this case, is justified by the poor outcomes obtained with pharmacological treatments. Non-pharmacological treatments to these problems focus on physical, emotional and mental activation.

There is growing evidence that cognitive interventions may be associated with small cognitive benefits for patients with MCI and dementia. Based on recent trials, computer training program has particular positive effect on cognition and mood [2]. In particular, cognitive stimulation and rehabilitation therapy focus on protocols in which different types of tasks are used for recovering and/or maintaining cognitive abilities, such as memory, orientation and communication skills [3]. Also, motor activities are important to help individuals with dementia to rehabilitate damaged functions or maintain their current motor skills for preserving autonomy over time. According to some studies carried out on older subjects with MCI, several positive effects of physical exercise on cognition, executive function, attention and delayed recall are showed. This cognitive and physical training require a trained therapist that besides supporting the patient through their execution has to give feedback during the therapeutic session and keep track of the user's performance in order to monitor the progress over time [4]. In particular, humanoid robots seem promising since they can support more engaging interactions with users, and there have already been some work exploring the use of robots for aiding cognitive treatments [5].

Currently, there is a focus on humanoid robots and tablets to investigate how seniors with MCI relate with and perceive serious games accessed through humanoid robots, as part of a training program aimed to improve their cognitive abilities.Interestingly, few investigations exist currently that explore the impact of robots as tools to provide cognitive training for the elderly. Recently, Socially Assistive Robotics (SAR) is being effectively used in dementia care and several commercially available robots have been employed with satisfactory results in cognitive stimulation and memory training [6]–[8].

Following these findings, in collaboration with a local association ("Alzheimer Bari" ONLUS), we set up an experimental study aiming at evaluating the effectiveness and acceptance of SAR technology in providing therapeutic interventions to people suffering from cognitive changes related to aging and dementia. In this paper, we focus on the results of this pilot study in which we used Pepper, a semi-humanoid robot developed by SoftBank Robotics, as support to psychotherapists in cognitive stimulation sessions. The experiment and its protocol have been co-designed with therapists, following the paradigm of cooperative and participatory design, in dedicated sessions in order to make how Pepper administered the tasks as similar as possible to the method adopted by the human therapists in their training sessions [9]. After this preliminary phase, the intervention protocol was defined and the robot was programmed to execute the planned exercises used during the training sessions. In total, we planned to run 4 sessions with Pepper as a tool to convey the planned therapeutic intervention. Unluckily, due to the COVID-19 emergency, we had to suspend the experiment one session earlier. Each session was video recorded, with the consent of participants and their legal representative, to be subsequently analyzed by three expert raters to evaluate them in terms of participation and engagement through eye gazes [10], the number of correct answers and expressed emotions. From the analysis of the obtained results, we can conclude that Pepper is a fairly good technology for cognitive stimulation because it expands the accessibility of control synthesis for social robots for people of all programming skill levels across many domains. In general, all the seniors participated actively in the experiment experiencing more positive than negative emotions during the intervention, and the correlation analysis showed that individuals with lower MCI expressed less happiness even if the eye gaze estimation showed that they were more engaged by the robot. These results encourage us to to continue the current work, also carrying out the comparison with a control group in which the same stimulation protocol will be executed without the use of social robots.

The paper is structured as follows. In Section II, motivations and background of the research are reported. Section III describes the study and reports its results. Finally, in Section IV, conclusions and possible future works are discussed.

II. Motivations and Background

Cognitive Stimulation Therapy (CST) is a short-term, evidence-based, group, or individual intervention program for people with mild to moderate dementia or Alzheimer's disease. The goal of CST is to stimulate people with dementia through a series of themed activities designed to help them continue to learn and stay socially engaged. SAR describes a class of robots that is the intersection of assistive robotics (robots that aid a user) and socially interactive robotics (robots that communicate with a user through social and nonphysical interaction) [11].

One goal of an effective SAR system is to establish a relationship with the user that leads toward intended therapeutic goals. SAR has successfully been used in Human-Robot Interaction research (HRI) by including social robots in healthcare interventions by virtue of their ability to engage human users in both social and emotional dimensions [12].

The integration of robotics into both formal and informal MCI care opens up new possibilities for improving the lives of patients and alleviating the burden on caregivers and healthcare services. Early studies have shown that SAR has the advantage of improving mood, social relationships among patients and emotional expression of individual dementia sufferers [13]. Several investigations on the effects of robot therapy, using commercially available animal type robots has been investigated in [14] [15]. Other research aims instead at the creation of assistive humanoid robot therapists, using NAO robots [6].

Researchers [8] also investigate how patients with dementia relate to humanoid robots and perceive serious games accessed through it, as part of a training program aimed to improve their cognitive status. Here, it has been observed that elders became more engaged with Pepper along with sessions and there was a positive view towards the interaction with it.

In [3], NAO has been used to reproduce physical exercises to a group of seniors. NAO was also employed in individual and group therapy sessions [6] [16] to assist the therapist with speech, music, and movement. Indeed it has been argued that Pepper is easy to use by the patients with dementia, relatives, and caregivers, it brings patients with dementia in a more positive emotional state and in music sessions stimulating patients to recall memories and talking about their past [17].

In the CST intervention reported here, we used Pepper as a social robot.

III. The Experimental Study

This section describes the study performed to investigate how seniors with MCI relate to and perceive the CST program performed with the aid of the social robot Pepper. The CST program during which the experiments were conducted lasted 3 weeks, with weekly meetings of about 35 minutes. Eight subjects were selected for the experimental study among the members of the Alzheimer Bari" ONLUS Association according to their MMSE score (Mini-Mental State Examination) and their willingness to take part in the study.

A. Material

1) The Robot Platform: The robot platform used in the current study is Pepper, a semi-humanoid robot developed by SoftBank Robotics (Figure 1). It is an omnidirectional wheeled humanoid robot 1.21 m tall, with 17 joints and 20 degrees of freedom. The interactivity is the key feature of Pepper. It has multimodal interfaces for interaction: touchscreen, speech, tactile head, bumper, and 20 degrees of freedom for motion in the whole body. The robot is equipped with several LEDs that can be programmed to change colors and intensity to

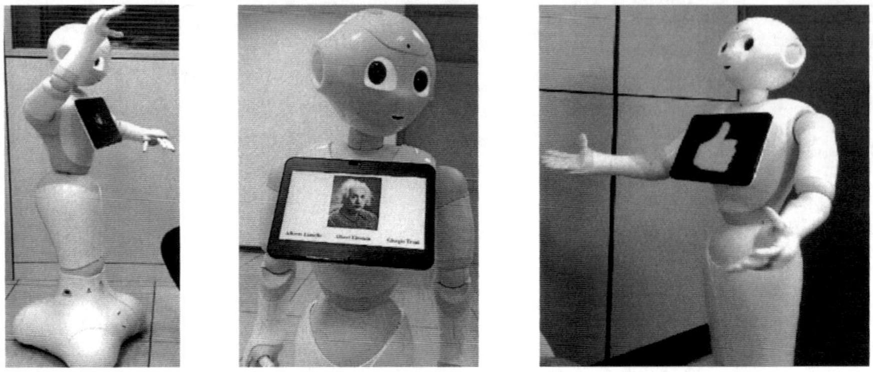

(a) (b) (c)

Fig. 1. (a) An example of physical exercises. (b) Memory training (c) Positive feedback.

signal and support communication. It is equipped with four directional microphones in its head that allow it to detect the origin of entries and thus to turn its face to whoever is talking. These microphones can eventually be used to analyze the voice tone and therefore interpret the emotional state of the interlocutor. Pepper can operate in complex environments thanks to its 3D video camera and the two HD cameras that allow it to identify movements and recognize the emotions on the faces of its interlocutors. The robot is equipped with 20 motors that allow it to move its head, back and arms. In addition, it has several sensors to provide information on the distance of objects placed up to 3 meters, in addition to its three cameras (two RGB and one 3D inserted in its head). Pepper has also tactile sensors on the head and hands, which are used for social interaction. The LEDs located in the eyes can take one of any RGB color: this feature is particularly useful when it is necessary to simulate emotions by changing the color of the eyes. Pepper has also a tablet to display videos, images and allowing the user to interact with it.

2) Neuro-psychological Evaluation: For the evaluation of the neuro-psychological state, the Mini Mental State Examination (MMSE) [18] was administered 1 week before starting the experimental phase to all the members of the association willing to participate in the study. The MMSE score was used to select seniors in order to have a group as homogeneous as possible.

3) The Tasks: The tasks to be performed during the CST program with Pepper were selected by the staff of specialized therapists of the center essentially from the volumes of "A gym for the mind" [19] and were adapted to Pepper communicative capabilities.

Three sets of cognitive stimulation tasks were created, all designed to be carried out in a group format. Each weekly session was planned to last between 30 and 40 minutes, according to the therapists' estimation of the duration of the patients' attention during the exercises. In Table I the exercises for each session are reported.

The opening and closing of each session with recreational activities were designed to make the therapy sessions less

TABLE I
DESCRIPTION OF THE EXERCISES FOR EACH SESSION.

Session 1	*Session 2*	*Session 3*
Motor imitation	Motor imitation	Motor imitation
Word completion	Memory of prose	Visual-verbal associative memory
Verbal associative memory	Verbal associative memory	Memory of prose
		Verbal associative memory

stressful for patients. The motor imitation task was chosen to open each session since it was evaluated as pleasant by all seniors in the group. In Figure 1a, Pepper is showing some movements to be imitated by seniors. For visual-verbal associative and word completion tasks, two levels of difficulty have been designed specifically to the type of exercise they have been associated with. During each session the levels of the activities to be carried out were performed one after the other, increasing the difficulty level. The tasks were based on vocal, visual, and touch-based interaction (through the tablet placed on Pepper's torso) in order to avoid some errors due to natural language understanding, such as: a) false positives: when the patient gives a wrong answer, but Pepper takes it as right, giving positive feedback and passing directly to the next question; b) false negatives: when the patient answers exactly, but the robot interprets it as wrong. For these reasons, the correctness of the answers to Pepper's questions was handled directly by the therapists by touching a different sensor on Pepper's head (for the correct answers it was decided to use the sensor closest to Pepper's face and for the wrong ones the last sensor behind the head and the central sensor was used to repeat the questions). In general, if the participant's answer was correct, Pepper reinforced it with positive feedback, showing a thumbs up on the tablet and body movements manifesting how happy it was with that response (Figure 1a). In the case of a wrong answer, Pepper encouraged the patient to try again without using negative words (e.g., bad, wrong).

Further support was given by the LEDs positioned in Pepper's eyes and used to provide either positive (green eyes) or negative feedback (red eyes) basing on the answers provided. If the subject answered correctly, after complimenting the patients, the robot moves on to the next step of the task and, after a short pause, it moves on to the next question. After three wrong answers to the same question, before moving on to the next question, the robot communicates the correct answer.

Figure 1b shows an example of a Visual-Verbal Associative Memory Task in which Pepper shows on the tablet the image of a famous person and asks for his/her name. The interaction between the robot and the patients is vocal.

B. Context and Environment Settings

The study was carried out with the collaboration of the "Alzheimer Bari" ONLUS Association in Bari, Italy. It was founded in 2002 and offers memory training and cognitive stimulation courses to subjects who have been diagnosed with mild or mild-moderate cognitive impairment (MCI), bringing together family members, doctors, psychologists, socio-health workers, and other figures all involved in various aspects of the management of Alzheimer's Disease patients and their family members. They also offer physiotherapy cycles, music laboratory, artistic and laboratory activities. Furthermore, assistance is provided to the patients' family members, who are also distinctly followed by neuro-psychologists and educators during the sessions dedicated to loved ones. Patients often follow multiple courses per week, in order to perform an intervention program as complete as possible, based on the stage of their illness.

The choice of the experiment room was important. We selected, according to the suggestion of the therapists, the room in which usually patients carried out musical sessions. In general, the seniors participated with joy in these exercises and then this environment for them represented a place where they had positive experiences. In addition, the chosen room is large enough to contain the two therapists, the patients and the robot, guaranteeing to the latter enough space to perform the movements, which, in the presence of obstacles, would not have been allowed by its safety sensors. The patients were seated in front of therapists and Pepper, and behind a wall, there was the technician in order to solve technical problems arising during the exercises with the robot.

Pepper was positioned about one meter away from each patient, respecting its range in which it manages to be engaged and perceive the people around it. Besides the Pepper's internal video camera located inside its mouth (which allowed to better capture the faces of the patients), another video camera was positioned in the room in order to have a front view of patients' faces and to be able to analyze the entire group behavior. Figure 2 shows the setting of the environment.

C. Participants and Procedure

The study involved 8 elderly people (see Table II for a description) enrolled among the population of members of the "Alzheimer Bari" ONLUS, considering as a condition of patient inclusion an MMSE score between 13 and 26.2, since patients with these scores can make progress with CST.

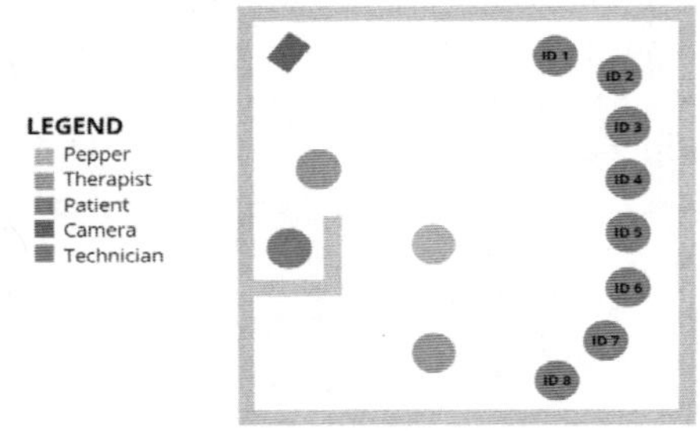

Fig. 2. The environment setting.

The group included participants with MCI, MD and two with subjective cognitive impairment. Among the users of the Association, the subjects eligible for the experimental study were contacted to ask them to participate. A week before the experiment, the therapists carried out neuropsychological assessments on future participants in the experiments. Before running the CST with Pepper, participants and their relatives received detailed information about the study and subsequently signed a consent to be video recorded during the experiments. The consent was also signed by their legal representatives.

TABLE II
PARTICIPANTS' MMSE

ID	*Gender*	*Age*	*MMSE*
1	F	89	23.4
2	F	77	26.2
3	M	82	24.1
4	M	89	21.1
5	M	82	13.0
6	F	79	13.2
7	F	69	20
8	F	72	17

In the same week, Pepper was presented to the Association for the first time to favor familiarization for the successive sessions. In the first five minutes of each session, the therapists put the elderly at ease, then Pepper was introduced already active, to avoid negative emotions and connected to the unanimated look of the robot. Once placed in the center of the room, Pepper greeted the elderly and conversed with them for a few minutes (directed by the technician who was sat on his hidden desk and exploited the Wizard of Oz technique). Subsequently, the set of exercises planned for that day was implemented. In the absence of answers, it encouraged patients to answer, asking the question again and helping them if necessary. Therapists intervened only to touch the sensor corrected on its head to direct the feedback provided by Pepper to each answer and to move on to the next question. At the end of each experimental session, the robot greeted the participants and was led out of the room to leave the patients with the therapists for a few minutes. The cognitive stimulation program lasted for 3 weeks, one day per week, performing a battery of tasks of about 30 minutes per day.

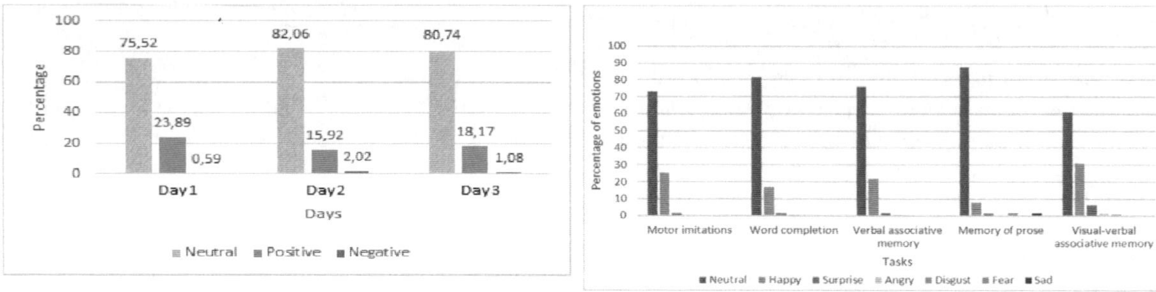

Fig. 3. (a) Valence of experienced emotions in each session. (b) Experienced emotions for each exercise.

D. Measurements

We collected the video-recording of the 3 sessions. Recordings were segmented in order to have one video for each exercise. In order to measure the number of correct answers, eye contact and emotions experienced by each participant during each session, three expert observers (two women and one man, of average age 37.67 y.o.) were selected. They had an almost perfect agreement index (0.83), calculated through the Fleiss' kappa [20].

To count the number of correct answers, they had the set of correct answers for each exercise. Subsequently, the total time each senior looked at Pepper during each exercise of the session was calculated. To annotate basic emotions (angry, disgust, fear, happy, sad, surprise, and neutral) expressed by the seniors the annotators were first trained on the Facial Action Coding System (FACS) [21].

E. Results

From the analyses of correct answers, we can say that the patients participated actively in the experiment. Overall, it has been noted that patients, in general, experienced problems with the prose memory exercise since the percentage of correct answers has been 0.2% in contrast to the average of the other exercises (55%), this type of task is inherently difficult and, in our opinion, the voice of the Pepper robot did not facilitate the story comprehension. Since this exercise was present only in the second session, we can ascribe to this the lower engagement in this day of the CST. As far as emotions are concerned, the level of negative emotions experienced by the seniors during the entire experiment is acceptable (0.59% for Session 1, 2.02% for Session 2 and 1.08% for Session 3). Considering the videos, it has been noticed that these emotions emerged when subjects disagreed with the statements made by the other participants and not towards Pepper. Besides the "neutral" state (on average 79.44% per day), seniors experienced more positive emotions (on average 19.33%) than negative ones. Figure 3a shows the valences of the emotions recognized in each session of the CTS. Analyzing the emotional experience for each task (see Figure 3b), during the visual-verbal associative memory one the maximum "happy" rate was achieved (30.75%), followed by the motor imitation task (25.32%). The observers also recorded the eye gaze of each participant's towards Pepper, by considering this a measure of engagement [22]. Figure 4a and Figure 4b show the engagement of seniors for each session and for each exercise, respectively. The session in which participants resulted most engaged in the interaction is the third one. In particular, during that session, they showed more engagement in the motor imitation task, in which they paid attention to Pepper for 76.53% of the exercise duration. The tasks on visual-verbal associative memory were also particularly successful (74% on average).

The Pearson coefficient was calculated to observe linear correlations between the results of the behavioral observations and the neuro-psychological evaluations' scores. In particular, seniors with a lower MCI tended to experience mostly neutral emotions (r=0.70) and were less happy (r=-0.80); this could be attributed to the need for separate sessions for them with tasks more stimulating. Positive correlations emerged between the eye gaze engagement estimation and the MMSE scores (r=0.42).

IV. Conclusions and Future Work

In this paper, we presented the results of an experimental study carried out in the context of rehabilitation interventions for reducing cognitive decline in the elderly people with MCI and mild dementia based on the use of the Social Robot Pepper. The reported study aimed at investigating how this technology can be used to support therapists in training programs for improving subjects' cognitive status. The evaluation and feedback from participants showed also that the system was appreciated and that the seniors involved in the study approached Pepper as a human and perceived it as a stimulus to go to the centre for the rehabilitation program. For example, participants talked to the robot as an entity having its own personality. Results obtained so far are encouraging but we must recognize some limitations. First of all we could not make a comparison with a control group as planned, due to the COVID-19 emergency. A second limitation concerns the sample size in that the research was implemented with only one group of people, which is not homogeneous for cognitive disease. Therefore, future work should involve a larger sample considering also a greater number of trials extended over more sessions. This will allow to make comparisons between people with different level of cognitive impairment and gender also

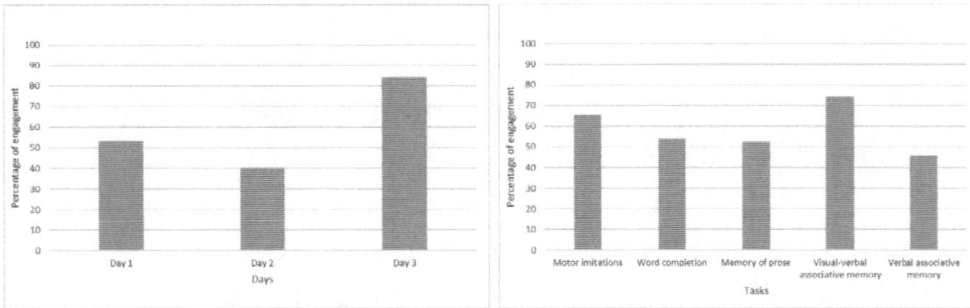

Fig. 4. (a) Percentage of Engagement in each session. (b) Percentage of Engagement in each exercise type.

exploring the effect of cognitive training on non cognitive functions, as mood and distress.

A further aspect that we plan to develop in the future, is the automatic analysis of engagement and emotions with the purpose of adapting the robots behaviour to the users for increasing their engagement in the rehabilitation program. It is desirable that robots applied to real world applications perform their activities in reactive but flexible manner. Thus, a robot architecture capable to adapt to human interaction is very suitable. Although the current paper concerns specific tasks, other abilities can be included. Besides, the investigation is a very common application of SAR, projected mainly for rehabilitation purposes.

ACKNOWLEDGMENT

The authors thank the "Alzheimer Bari" ONLUS, the therapists C. Lograno and C. Chiapparino for their support, and all the seniors who participated in the study.

REFERENCES

[1] W. M. van der Flier and P. Scheltens, "Epidemiology and risk factors of dementia," *Journal of Neurology, Neurosurgery & Psychiatry*, vol. 76, no. suppl 5, pp. v2–v7, 2005.

[2] C. Cooper *et al.*, "Systematic review of the effectiveness of non-pharmacological interventions to improve quality of life of people with dementia," in *Database of Abstracts of Reviews of Effects (DARE): Quality-assessed Reviews [Internet]*. Centre for Reviews and Dissemination (UK), 2012.

[3] O. Pino, "Memory impairments and rehabilitation: evidence-based effects of approaches and training programs," *The Open Rehabilitation Journal*, vol. 8, no. 1, 2015.

[4] N. Rouaix *et al.*, "Affective and engagement issues in the conception and assessment of a robot-assisted psychomotor therapy for persons with dementia," *Frontiers in psychology*, vol. 8, p. 950, 2017.

[5] M. Law *et al.*, "Developing assistive robots for people with mild cognitive impairment and mild dementia: a qualitative study with older adults and experts in aged care," *BMJ open*, vol. 9, no. 9, p. e031937, 2019.

[6] M. Valentí-Soler *et al.*, "Social robots in advanced dementia," *Frontiers in Aging Neuroscience*, vol. 7, 05 2015.

[7] O. Pino, G. Palestra, R. Trevino, and B. De Carolis, "The humanoid robot nao as trainer in a memory program for elderly people with mild cognitive impairment," *International Journal of Social Robotics*, vol. 12, no. 1, pp. 21–33, 2020.

[8] M. Manca *et al.*, "The impact of serious games with humanoid robots on mild cognitive impairment older adults," *International Journal of Human-Computer Studies*, p. 102509, 2020.

[9] E. A. Björling and E. Rose, "Participatory research principles in human-centered design: engaging teens in the co-design of a social robot," *Multimodal Technologies and Interaction*, vol. 3, no. 1, p. 8, 2019.

[10] K. Kompatsiari, F. Ciardo, D. De Tommaso, and A. Wykowska, "Measuring engagement elicited by eye contact in human-robot interaction," in *2019 IEEE/RSJ International Conference on Intelligent Robots and Systems (IROS)*, 2019, pp. 6979–6985.

[11] M. J. Matarić and B. Scassellati, "Socially assistive robotics," in *Springer handbook of robotics*. Springer, 2016, pp. 1973–1994.

[12] G. Kim *et al.*, "Structural brain changes after traditional and robot-assisted multi-domain cognitive training in community-dwelling healthy elderly," *PloS one*, vol. 10, no. 4, p. e0123251, 2015.

[13] A. A. Vogan, F. Alnajjar, M. Gochoo, and S. Khalid, "Robots, ai, and cognitive training in an era of mass age-related cognitive decline: a systematic review," *IEEE Access*, vol. 8, pp. 18 284–18 304, 2020.

[14] T. Tamura *et al.*, "Is an entertainment robot useful in the care of elderly people with severe dementia?" *The Journals of Gerontology Series A: Biological Sciences and Medical Sciences*, vol. 59, no. 1, pp. M83–M85, 2004.

[15] T. Shibata and K. Wada, "Robot therapy: a new approach for mental healthcare of the elderly–a mini-review," *Gerontology*, vol. 57, no. 4, pp. 378–386, 2011.

[16] F. Martín, C. E. Agüero, J. M. Cañas, M. Valenti, and P. Martínez-Martín, "Robotherapy with dementia patients," *International Journal of Advanced Robotic Systems*, vol. 10, no. 1, p. 10, 2013.

[17] R. De Kok *et al.*, "Combining social robotics and music as a non-medical treatment for people with dementia," in *IEEE Int. Symposium on Robot and Human Interactive Communication (RO-MAN)*, 2018, pp. 465–467.

[18] M. F. Folstein, S. Folstein, and P. R. McHugh, "Mini-mental state:a practical method for grading the cognitive state of patients for the clinician," *Journal of psychiatric research*, vol. 12, no. 3, pp. 189–198, 1975.

[19] D. Gollin, A. Ferrari, and A. Peruzzi, *Una palestra per la mente. Stimolazione cognitiva per l'invecchiamento cerebrale e le demenze (A gym for the mind. Cognitive stimulation for brain aging and dementia)*. Edizioni Erickson, 2007, 2011.

[20] J. Fleiss, "Measuring nominal scale agreement among many raters," *Psychological bulletin*, vol. 76, no. 5, p. 378—382, November 1971. [Online]. Available: https://doi.org/10.1037/h0031619

[21] E. Friesen and P. Ekman, "Facial action coding system: a technique for the measurement of facial movement," *Palo Alto*, vol. 3, 1978.

[22] Y. I. Nakano and R. Ishii, "Estimating user's engagement from eye-gaze behaviors in human-agent conversations," in *Proceedings of the 15th International Conference on Intelligent User Interfaces*, ser. IUI '10. New York, NY, USA: Association for Computing Machinery, 2010, p. 139–148.

Privacy-Aware Digital Mediation Tools for Improving Adolescent Mental Well-being: Application to School Bullying

Maria Gaci, Isabelle Vonèche-Cardia and Denis Gillet

School of Engineering
École Polytechnique Fédérale de Lausanne (EPFL)
Lausanne, Switzerland
email: maria.gaci@epfl.ch, isabelle.voneche-cardia@epfl.ch, denis.gillet@epfl.ch

Abstract—**In human-computer interaction, self-disclosure of sensitive information regarding distressing experiences requires the establishment of a trust channel between the user and the digital tool. As privacy and security have been identified as factors that contribute to increased levels of trust, they could be utilized to design digital tools that encourage and empower adolescents to disclose school bullying. This work-in-progress paper presents an interdisciplinary research project aimed at combining appropriate levels of usability and security to design a privacy scheme for adolescents in order to provide a digital solution that will help anti-bullying intervention at schools in Switzerland and beyond. The process for designing the interaction and interface of the digital tool is presented in the context of interviews with domain experts. Furthermore, participatory design workshops with Swiss teachers and students are used to inform the key trustful features that the tool should exhibit.**

Keywords–Human-Computer Interaction; Privacy; Trust; Security; Child-Computer Interaction.

I. Introduction

Bullying, delinquency, substance abuse, depression, and social isolation are some not uncommon distressing experiences that adolescents can encounter during their development [1]. These experiences affect their mental health, development, and wellbeing. School bullying is one of the most prevalent and complex of these experiences and can result in bullycide (suicide due to bullying) [1]. According to two surveys conducted in the Swiss cantons of Valais and Geneva in 2012 and 2013, school bullying affects one to two students per class, or 5-10% of all adolescents in Switzerland [2].

By definition, school bullying is "a systematic abuse of power in interpersonal relations exerted by one or more children" [3] [4]. It is a form of violence exerted by the wrongdoers (referred to as bullies) to the target individuals (referred to as victims) through different forms, such as physical, verbal, or cyber (involving the use of electronic technology) [3]. Various approaches exist for solving bullying conflicts such as the Shared Concern Method [5], yet the identification of the conflicts still remains a challenge as it relies on self-disclosure.

One of the major issues related to the identification of school bullying is the reluctance of adolescents to report their experiences to teachers, parents, or support teams at schools. In fact, it is estimated that less than 15% of students report school bullying conflicts [6]. According to [7], students perceive several barriers to self-disclosing, such as fear that their bullies might perpetrate more frequent or severe attacks, fear of peer disapproval, negative self-thoughts (e.g., feeling weak/undermined), and preference for autonomy or "dealing with it oneself." Moreover, several studies have indicated that teacher's negligence, passive role in intervening and failure to maintain a positive classroom climate directly affect students' decisions to self-report [8]. Witnesses to bullying are also often reluctant to disclose their observations due to fear of retribution and uncertainty about intervention [9].

In spite of research demonstrating that self-disclosure reduces bullying in schools [10] and the fact that higher levels of self-disclosure are recorded when a privacy-oriented approach is adopted in digital environments [11], no digital solutions currently exist in Switzerland. As such, this project aims to design a digital tool for adolescents aged 12–16 years old that will act as a mediator for disclosing school bullying. This digital tool is being developed in collaboration with a Non-Governmental Organization (NGO), and its validation will be performed in public secondary schools in Switzerland in collaboration with their health service teams.

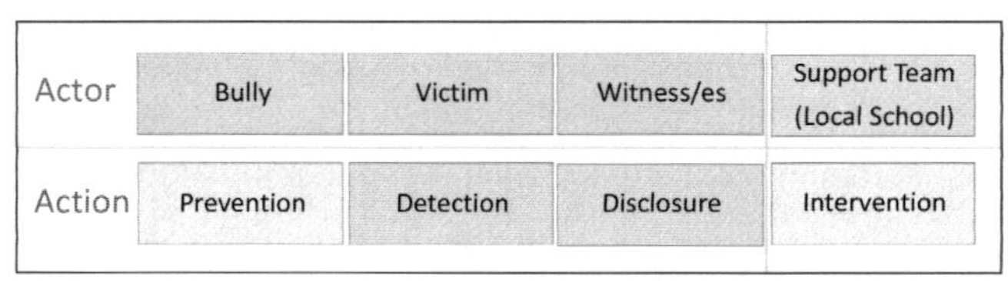

Figure 1. The actors and the actions targeted by the digital tool.

Our tool will serve as a means for the detection and disclosure of school bullying conflicts. Its goal is to encourage adolescents to self-report instances of bullying by providing an interface and means of communication with which adolescents are comfortable, i.e. a mobile application. The application should act as a catalyst to inspire students to seek face-to-face discussions with a human mediator like a teacher or member of the health services team. In order to create a closed-loop model, however, prevention and intervention will also be slightly targeted. Prevention will be targeted by increasing awareness regarding bullying in schools through testimonials. Temporary digital intervention will be provided through tailored advice available in the mobile application. The actors and the actions targeted by the digital tool are illustrated in Figure 1.

This ongoing research project aims to contribute to the field of Human-Computer Interaction (HCI) and eHealth by providing insights to the following research questions: *How should digital tools be designed in order to encourage adolescents to disclose distressing experiences, such as school bullying? What are the key trustful features that such digital tools should exhibit?* The paper describes the general framework of the project, and the process followed for the initial design of the prototypes of the digital tool for self-disclosing school bullying.

The paper is organized as follows: Section II presents a brief review of literature on the topics of self-disclosure and privacy, existing anti-bullying solutions, and the current limitations. Section III presents the development methodology of the anti-bullying digital tool. Section IV presents the design of the digital tool in accordance with the feedback gathered from domain experts and the target audience of adolescents. Finally, Section V briefly summarises the current state of the project.

II. Literature Review

A. Self-disclosure and Privacy

In 2019, the world's population was composed of 1.2 billion adolescents [12]. Despite the fact that this age group comprises 16 percent of the world population, research studies have emphasized the lack of scholarly work focusing exclusively on them [13]. This insufficient knowledge results in little guidance on the unique requirements, opportunities, and challenges when designing interactive tools for this target group [14]. One of the most effective practices for understanding the needs of adolescents and designing creative interfaces for them is the organization of participatory design workshops [15] [16], an approach that aims to actively engage and include adolescents as co-designers.

Research on the topic of self-disclosure has demonstrated its importance in maintaining psychological, physical, and spiritual well-being [17]. Some of the conditions identified by [17] under which people are willing to disclose personal information are: the specific need for physical "private places", the need for privacy more generally, the identity of the person to whom one might disclose himself, and the relation between the two.

Digital interaction also favors self-disclosure [18]–[21]. Medical patients have reported a higher number of symptoms and negative behaviors when interviewed through a digital tool rather than face-to-face [19]. Furthermore, participants claim to provide more honest and candid answers when digital means were utilized [20]. Higher disclosure rates have also been recorded in studies eliciting sensitive information through digital means rather than face-to-face or using pen-and-paper [21]. The same applies to scenarios where individuals may feel particularly vulnerable to the consequences of self-disclosure [21]. Finally, rates of self-disclosure through digital interfaces have been observed to be higher for individuals who perceive their health condition to be stigmatized [11].

When comparing digital and face-to-face interactions, privacy, and anonymity were among the top factors listed affecting subjects' willingness to disclose sensitive information [18] [21]. Higher rates of self-disclosure were recorded when people communicated in a visually anonymous manner rather than non-anonymously. Furthermore, increased willingness to answer sensitive questions and decreased errors associated with sensitive topics were recorded when privacy-enhancing data collection modes were employed.

Recent studies by [22] and [23] have demonstrated a preference for embodied conversational agents (e.g., virtual agents) rather than human interviewers. Four principal reasons were determined to affect the individuals' preference: (i) lack of judgment, criticism, and reactions (verbal or nonverbal), (ii) ease of providing answers due to the digital interface (texting enables participants to formulate their answers at their own pace), (iii) personal comfort due to reduced negative feelings, such as anxiety, embarrassment, or guilt, and (iv) protection of personal information and privacy.

Individuals tend to more likely disclose their experiences if they are doing so to someone who is perceived to be trustworthy [17]. Hence, the establishment of trust is required for individuals to feel comfortable in self-reporting sensitive information. Due to the complexity of trust as a social phenomenon, major questions arise with how to establish trust and how to reliably signal that trust through different interfaces and interactions [24]. According to [25], there are four elements that ease the communication of trust through digital interfaces: (i) design quality (site organization, visual design), (ii) up-front disclosure and transparency, (iii) comprehensive and current content, and (iv) connection to the rest of the web.

As privacy is significant to encouraging self-disclosure, attempting to establish trust requires a thorough security and privacy model [26]. Trust models, like [27], which combine aspects of usability and security have been demonstrated to impact users' levels of trust. The above model is composed of six building blocks, namely: (i) security (authentication, data access control, data integrity, software change procedures, and physical security), (ii) usability (perception issues, motor accessibility, and interaction design issues), (iii) privacy (user anonymity and data confidentiality), (iv) reliability and availability (vulnerability to denial-of-service attacks, connection to the internet, quality of service), (v) audit and verification mechanisms (cryptographic methods, audit trails, use of trusted agents), and (vi) user expectations (product reputation, prior user knowledge, knowledge of technology).

B. Existing Solutions

Recently, increasing emphasis has been placed on the design and evaluation of digital tools for adolescents. These digital tools not only help adolescents understand the nature of bullying but also serve as sources of positive intervention. The existing approaches can be categorized into two major groups: (i) as approaches for the prevention and (ii) as approaches for the disclosure of the bullying cases in schools. Below, existing solutions for each approach are presented along with a brief analysis of the mechanisms utilized by each of them to give an overview of the emerging technologies in this field.

1) Prevention-oriented Approaches: FearNot! [28], StopBully [29] and #StopBully [30] are interactive mobile apps aiming to develop the behavioral competence of victims and witnesses necessary to avoid and deal with future bullying situations. All three mobile apps educate and raise awareness by presenting real-life situations that the players have to respond to. The mechanisms utilized by the apps to teach effective responses to bullying are as follows:

- *Storytelling* is utilized by FearNot! to present the user with a virtual environment that improvises real-life bullying situations. Three-dimensional agents in a virtual school are designed to foster empathy and emotional involvement of the users. The story is gradually built in response to the suggestions of the users in the various episodes through artificial intelligence techniques.

- *Games* are a mechanism utilized by StopBully and #StopBully for delivering educational content to players. The games provide players with challenges that they have to solve to gain points and progress to higher levels. Both games are educational with cartoon-like characters and environments.
- *Videos*, *animated comics* and *quizzes* are utilized by #StopBully to train players on bullying. Videos and comics present the friendship of four characters, which is broken when one of them becomes a bully. The knowledge acquired through the videos and comics is put into practice through quizzes. There are different types of quizzes, such as multiple-choice, rearrange the letters, type an answer, etc.

2) Disclosure-oriented Approaches: STOPit Solutions [31] and Anonymous Alerts [32] are two similar incident reporting apps for students experiencing distress in schools. Both apps are available as mobile and web versions, and they provide digital solutions for two types of users — students and teachers — as described below.

- Students can utilize the platforms provided by the two apps mentioned above to anonymously report bullying cases by attaching videos, photos, and screenshots to the report. The apps also enable students to customize the incident type, location, and language. An anonymous messaging channel is also available to enable students to seek immediate help along with an emergency button that alerts the severity of the incident.
- Teachers can utilize the incident management platform to receive real-time updates on incident reports sent by students and parents. The platform enables them to monitor the reports and forward them to local authorities in case immediate action is required. Teachers can also run analytic and trend reports to identify patterns of bullying in their school.

These approaches, while effective in some contexts and for some problems, are not sufficient for our intended application and audience.

C. Limitations

In summary, digital solutions are available for adolescents to disclose bullying acts, yet some gaps exist: the existing solutions focus on one of the actors or specifically in one action. Moreover, there is limited research in the field of HCI on how trust can be established by design between adolescents and digital tools when self-disclosing sensitive mental health experiences. Finally, there exists limited analysis of how privacy and anonymity affect the disclosure of distressing experiences among adolescents, as they could be also utilized to promote spam or to practice additional bullying.

III. Methodology

To develop digital tools that nudge adolescents (victims, witnesses, and bullies) into disclosing bullying experiences in schools, a design thinking process [33] is being followed. The goal is to gain an empathetic understanding of the issue of bullying in schools, necessary for designing an effective solution for adolescents to disclose such experiences. The design thinking process is composed of four stages (Ideating, Prototyping, Implementing, and Validating), but as the project is still ongoing, only the initial two stages of the process are described in this paper.

Multiple iterations of this process were used to re-frame the issue of bullying in a human-centric way. Ideas regarding features and functions that the digital intervention should encompass were gathered through engagement with experts in the field as well as future users, as described below:

Initially, the process of requirements elicitation was conducted through unstructured interviews with domain experts, educators, and bullying mediators. Interviews were designed to be broad and open-ended to gain a deeper perspective on domain-specific practices, goals, and concerns related to bullying in public schools in Switzerland. The aim of the interviews was also to identify factors that might influence the adoption of new solutions in the specific context. Six one-hour meetings were held in the span of one year.

Research studies have demonstrated that focus groups are a successful data collection technique for interaction design for adolescents [14]. Thus, focus groups were organized both face-to-face and online (due to COVID-19) during the spring semester of the 2019-2020 academic year. As the project targets adolescents, the focus groups were organized with students in public secondary schools in Switzerland. The focus groups aimed to gather a wide range of opinions, viewpoints, and insights by the users, as well as raising issues that were not previously identified. Adolescents age 12–16 were encouraged to engage in interactive group discussions regarding the design of the digital tools and, participatory design workshops were organized to propose the initial paper-based prototypes. A teacher and/or mediator already familiar with the students of each focus group (hereafter referred to as teacher *T1* and *T2*) were present and moderated the sessions. Two female and five male adolescents were part of the first focus group, and four female and one male adolescent were part of the second focus group (hereafter referred to as student *S1* – *S12*). Students were recruited on a voluntary basis by their teachers.

During the interactive group discussions, adolescents described the bullying situation in their respective schools mentioning the methods that they can currently use to disclose instances of bullying, i.e., talking directly to teachers, calling a mediator, and sending an email. Students mentioned an initiative for dropping anonymous letters in designated boxes in the schools' halls, yet the project was never finalized. The principal issue identified with the current approaches was the fact that "the students do not dare to talk" (*S4*), as "everyone is different and some students are at ease talking to people that they know, but some of them are at ease when anonymous" (*S10*). Hence, anonymity emerged as an important aspect when disclosing distressing experiences, as students: i) were afraid of how adults would react, ii) were afraid of the fact that adults might judge them, or iii) were feeling intimidated due to the sensitivity of the topic. As such, in addition to requesting extra-curricular programs for raising awareness about bullying in schools, participants requested an anonymous digital channel for self-disclosure.

During the participatory design workshops, adolescents were involved in brainstorming sessions regarding design possibilities. Participants imagined the application would "play the role of a mediator that the students can write to, if they trust it, as the information is confidential" (*S11*). The application would further help them "feel less lonely because usually when students are bullied, they are left in the loneliness and they do not really want to have contact with people" (*S12*). Besides, the application would help students feel "reassured" (*S4*) and "send small messages every day asking how they were feeling" (*S6*). The main feature of the application was voted to be anonymity, as "an anonymous application cannot judge the students" (*S4*). Adolescents thought that the user should enter a *"pseudonym"* (*S4*) and an optional phone number, but no additional personal information or password to guarantee *anonymity by design*. When the students were asked to brainstorm on the series of interactions offered in the application, they mentioned the selection of a "role, such as victim or witness" (*S3*) and "form of bullying, such as verbal or physical" (*S5*), so that the application could pose the appropriate questions according to the needs of the student. Several students from both focus groups suggested that a chatbot might be used to customize the experience. Moreover, they suggested that the chatbot might be able to decide if the user was in danger and the appropriate measure that the user should take. The questions posed by the chatbot should be "convincing" (*S4*) so that the user is encouraged to request help from the support team, but must also be able to decide what information he/she would like to disclose. Finally, adolescents stated that they would "trust the chatbot" (*S12*) because their perception was that "Artificial Intelligence does not make mistakes" (*S3*).

IV. Tool Design

Taking into consideration the feedback from the domain experts and the ideas of the students and teachers during the participatory design workshops on the features that the digital tool for self-disclosing bullying should exhibit, a mobile application will be developed. The architecture, features that will enhance usability, and the security considerations for the application based on the trust model presented in Section II-A are presented below.

A. Architecture

The requirements elicitation process with the experts and future users enabled the selection of the appropriate type of digital tool, namely a mobile application, for two main reasons. Firstly, according to initial interviews with domain experts, adolescents in the school setting are primarily bullied by their peers, and portable devices that enable students to disclose information quickly and privately were recommended. Thus, even though the larger screen size of a computer-based tool enables better readability, better visual acuity, and higher usability, these benefits are a drawback to privacy, as bystanders may be able to read the content on the screen from different distances [34]. Secondly, according to initial interviews with the different parties, the majority of students in Switzerland have access to mobile phones, although students are not allowed to utilize them during lecturing.

A hybrid mobile application will be developed using the React Native framework to support multiple mobile operating systems. The application will be structured in two main layers of infrastructure: the mobile device and the remote school. Initially, the bullying information disclosed by the user will

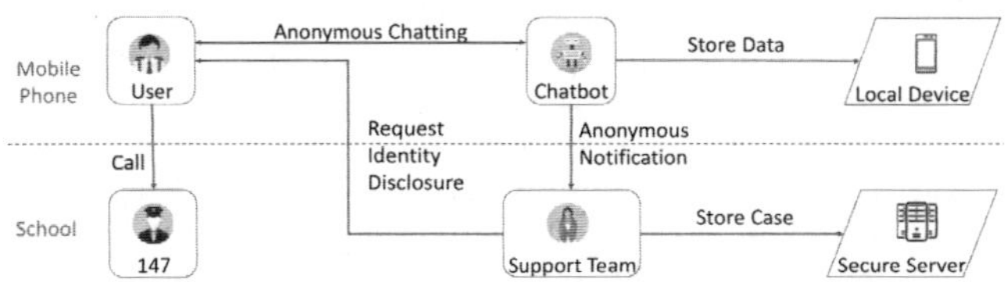

Figure 2. The architecture of the app for self-disclosing bullying in schools.

be anonymously stored in the mobile device. If the user agrees to disclose the information with the support team, their information will be shared with the support team of the specific school and stored in a secure local server. A human mediator will then contact the user anonymously and request the user to disclose their identity to provide face-to-face help. Students can also utilize the app to directly and securely contact third-parties, such as 147 (the consultation service for young people in Switzerland) or the police department. A simplified version of the architecture of the application is illustrated in Figure 2. The figure depicts: (i) the two layers of infrastructure, (ii) the interaction of users with the chatbot and the support team, and (iii) the storage of data on the local device and the remote server.

B. Usability

Chatbots were requested by students during the focus groups as a means to automate the disclosing process by "providing emergency support 24/7" (*T1*). As research has also demonstrated that they could be utilized to enable users to access information about bullying at any time and improve school cohesion [35], they will be included in the app. Students suggested that the chatbot will firstly ask generic questions to familiarise themselves with the user and then gradually perform a self-assessment task to determine the role of the user (i.e., victim, bully, witness). According to the students, this approach would also "increase the trust level" (*S12*) towards the application. The chatbot will provide immediate support in the form of advice ("Would it be possible to talk to your parents about this issue?" - *T2*) and try to nudge the user to disclose the case and seek help from a human mediator. It will never disclose information without the consent of the user unless the user explicitly mentions *suicide*, in which case due to legal requirements in Switzerland, the anonymous chat will be automatically forwarded to the support team. The chatbot will be programmed to run locally on the mobile device, so the costs and benefits of rule-based versus AI implementations are being evaluated. An illustration of a possible conversation with the chatbot is shown in Figure 3.

Avatars were suggested by the students as an option for creating immersive digital tools and have been demonstrated to be an effective mechanism to interact with users for anti-bullying education [36]. As such, users will be able to customize the appearance and characteristics (e.g., gender, age, name) of the avatar according to their preferences. The goal will be to enable users to personalize the experience in the application by creating distinct avatars that they "trust" (*S11*) and "feel comfortable having digital conversations with" (*S12*).

An interesting feature identified during the focus groups was continuously tracking the mental state of the adolescent through regular reminders. Students proposed an automated notifications system that "will contact the user if he/she has not connected to the app for a specific amount of time" (*S6*) (the amount of time can be configured in the settings of the application). Through the notifications, the chatbot will ensure that the mental health of the user is not at a critical level, and it will "show interest" (*S11*) aiming to decrease the feeling of solitude and negligence. Furthermore, reminders will also be sent to teachers and the support team if the case has been neglected for a long time.

Figure 3. The User Interface of the app for self-disclosing bullying in schools. (The original prototypes were designed in French and translated to English for clarification purposes.)

The results of the interviews and focus groups gave insights into the importance of creating a community feeling. An effective way to endorse a feeling of community within the app is through sharing personal experiences, thus a *Temoignages* (testimonials) page has been created. Adolescents have the option of choosing to disclose anonymously in the school group their experience and receive support from their peers through the *heart* button. To avoid additional bullying and spamming, the shared experience needs to be validated by the team of the local school. By sharing experiences on a dedicated page, the application aims to raise awareness regarding the negative aspects of bullying, as well as to show empathy to the bullying targets.

Text and voice calls are the only modalities for sharing experiences. No videos or pictures can be shared in the application as "they might infringe the privacy of witnesses" (*T1*). Users have the option of disclosing bullying either with the support team or with a specific teacher. A list of teachers who are willing to participate in the program will be included in the app, as focus groups indicated that some students are "more comfortable and trusting with specific individuals who they already know" (*S9*). Emergency contact numbers will be included in the application if the child wishes to make phone calls and receive external help by third parties (147 or police department).

C. Privacy and Security

Initial interviews with domain experts suggested that the bullying reports should be handled by the designated team at each local school. As such, an appropriate group signature scheme [37] will be selected to ensure credential/membership authentication. The group signature scheme will ensure that the local school can verify that the bullying report was sent from an authenticated adolescent, however, it will not reveal his/her identity. A fully-anonymous system is being evaluated by distributing a group member secret key to all the identified adolescents [38] with no possibility of signature tracing through the use of special trapdoors. QR codes will be posted in each school in order to redirect users automatically to the local school support team.

The implementation of an end-to-end encrypted messaging channel will enable students and the support team of the local school to communicate in real-time, using cryptographic protocols such as Signal [39]. Thus, the support team can provide help without being aware of who the student is if the student wishes to remain anonymous during the process. Furthermore, the encryption of the chat will ensure the security of the sensitive information disclosed in the application.

Offline capabilities will be considered in order to ensure the availability of digital tools for adolescents. The offline version will offer limited functionalities, and it will enable automatic syncing once the device is connected to the internet.

An emergency delete button will be included, in case the user wishes to delete all the data saved in his local device and restart the application from the beginning. Finally, the option of deleting individual messages exchanged with the human mediator will be included to give individuals control over their personal data.

D. Trust

The authors of [27] suggested that usage of trust models facilitates the successful deployment of new technologies, hence, their trust model was referenced to design the digital tool for self-reporting bullying in schools. Usability and security were carefully incorporated, and the features of the tool are compliant with the six building blocks enumerated in Section II-A:

- Security: Integration of group signature schemes to authenticate users provides enhanced security in the app. Furthermore, users will have complete control over the personal data provided in the app.

- Usability: The user interface was designed in collaboration with teachers, experts, and adolescents in order to address the needs of all types of users.
- Privacy: The tool will be fully anonymous, and no identifiable data will be collected. User data will be stored locally on the device until the user agrees to contact a human mediator.
- Reliability and availability: The tool will be open-source and provided for free to students and teachers.
- Audit and verification mechanisms: End-to-end encryption of the user messages will be provided to ensure the security of sensitive data.
- User expectations: The tool is being developed by a public institution in Switzerland, and as a result, it will follow the Swiss guidelines for the protection of personal data. The simple design of the features proposed during the workshops also aims to conform with prevailing norms of mobile user interfaces.

The trust model will be validated in the future through testing with adolescents and teachers, and it will be iteratively improved to better meet the needs of the project.

E. Summary

In summary, the outcome of the focus groups and the participatory design workshops reveals that the participants, on the whole, agreed that the digital tool for bullying scenarios should be designed as a means for adolescents to receive support rather than as a means for filing bullying complaints. Therefore, participants suggested that the tool should be carefully designed to act as a companion for adolescents by providing advice through an intelligent chatbot, regularly showing interest through notifications, and ensuring privacy through anonymity.

Unlike the existing solutions presented in Section II-B2, participants suggested that the digital tool addresses all actors involved in a bullying scenario, namely the victims, the witnesses, and the bullies. The reasoning behind the suggestion was that the tool should raise awareness about bullying in schools and support should be provided to all adolescents.

The majority of participants preferred a chatbot over directly contacting a human. Several reasons were echoed for such a preference such as the lack of judgment, the general perception that Artificial intelligence cannot make mistakes, and the ability to provide immediate support. Another view presented by the participants was the personalizing of the experience in the tool tailored to one's needs through the ability to customize the behavior and the appearance of the chatbot.

The main advantage of the tool was revealed to be the fact that students can receive support while remaining anonymous. This would break the barrier of taking the first step into self-disclosing bullying and increase the level of trust between the adolescents and the digital tool. While some students indicated that they would be more comfortable talking to people they were familiar with, all participants agreed that an additional channel for disclosing bullying in their schools would be necessary, as adolescents are different from each other.

Finally, students believed that bullying prevention is best achieved through extra-curricular events in their schools, hence the main target of the tool should remain detection and disclosure. Prevention could be slightly targeted to raise awareness through testimonials. Interviews with experts revealed that intervention should be handled by a human mediator. Yet to create an incentive for the student to utilize the tool, it was decided that the chatbot would provide circumstantial advice and repeatedly encourage students to talk to a human through an anonymous channel.

V. CONCLUSION AND FUTURE WORK

This paper aims to present the design process of an interactive digital tool for the self-disclosure of adolescents who are involved in bullying conflicts in schools. As adolescents belong to the group of the population that is not well understood, participatory design workshops were organized in public secondary schools in Switzerland to identify the key trustful features that the digital tool should exhibit. The results of this study indicate that: i) secure chatbots that assess the emotional state of the users and react accordingly ii) features that tailor the user experience such as avatars and notifications, and iii) features that foster a feeling of privacy, are aspects that should be taken in consideration when prototyping interfaces for sensitive mental health data.

The current existing solutions for disclosing bullying are not aligned with the feedback received from the students during the focus groups organized for this study. The disclosure-oriented approaches presented in Section II-B2 act primarily as a reporting system for negative activity in schools and heavily rely on the vulnerable individuals taking the initiative to file a report. Based on the interviews with the experts in the field, this approach can act as a barrier for adolescents to take the first step and disclose bullying in schools. As such, the idea is to assure users that the goal of the digital tool is to provide support to vulnerable individuals rather than solve bullying conflicts. This approach will nudge adolescents into gradually disclosing sensitive information (regardless if they are victims, witnesses, or bullies) and it was referred to be more favorable and efficient by the students who participated in the focus groups.

Based on the literature review presented in Section II demonstrating that self-disclosure reduces bullying in schools, trust is required for individuals to feel comfortable self-disclosing sensitive information, and privacy is an important aspect for establishing a trust channel, a hypothesis has been formulated in order to be tested in the future. The hypothesis is that *by designing privacy-aware medical applications, adolescents will be more inclined to disclose the distressing experiences that will contribute to improved mental health and will help develop sustainable behavior among adolescents.* Initial focus groups and participatory design with adolescents in Switzerland seem to support the hypothesis, yet additional research is required to test and validate it.

Considerably more work will need to be done in the future to evaluate the initial prototypes designed during the participatory design workshops. A natural progression of this work is to implement the digital tool based on the feedback gathered from the adolescents and the experts. As soon as a minimum viable product will be available, the features of the tool will be tested firstly with the experts and teachers who will contribute to devising several conversation scenarios for training the chatbot. Secondly, the tool will be tested with the students of the focus groups to validate the assumptions about the tool's requirements. Finally, the tools will be validated through iterations on the design of the tool from the feedback received through A/B testing in public schools in Switzerland.

To conclude, this research project will not only contribute to various disciplines within Computer Science such as Human-Computer Interaction, Computer Security and Cryptography, e-Health, and Social Computing, but it will also deliver digital solutions that will be available for immediate utilization in public schools in Switzerland and abroad.

ACKNOWLEDGMENT

This EPFLinnovators project has received funding from the European Union's Horizon 2020 research and innovation programme under the Marie Skłodowska-Curie grant agreement No. 754354. Special thanks to the domain experts from the NGO and the support team for school health, teachers and the students in the two secondary schools in Switzerland for their inputs and feedback during the participatory design workshops.

REFERENCES

[1] APA, "Developing adolescents: A reference for professionals," Washington, DC: American Psychological Association, 2002.

[2] RTS. One to two students per class are victims of bullying in Switzerland. [retrived: Oct, 2020]. [Online]. Available: https://www.rts.ch/info/suisse/6718365-un-a-deux-eleves-par-classe-sont-victimes-de-harcelement-en-suisse.html (2015)

[3] K. Rigby, The Method of Shared Concern: A positive approach to bullying in schools. Aust Council for Ed Research, 2011.

[4] A. Pikas, "New developments of the shared concern method," School Psychology International, vol. 23, no. 3, 2002, pp. 307–326.

[5] J.-P. Bellon and B. Gardette, School bullying: defeating it, it's possible: The shared concern method. ESF sciences humaines, 2018.

[6] A. Castillo. How to prevent bullying at school. [retrived: Oct, 2020]. [Online]. Available: https://www.letemps.ch/economie/prevenir-harcelement-scolaire (2018)

[7] M. J. Boulton, L. Boulton, J. Down, J. Sanders, and H. Craddock, "Perceived barriers that prevent high school students seeking help from teachers for bullying and their effects on disclosure intentions," Journal of adolescence, vol. 56, 2017, pp. 40–51.

[8] K. I. Cortes and B. Kochenderfer-Ladd, "To tell or not to tell: What influences children's decisions to report bullying to their teachers?" School psychology quarterly, vol. 29, no. 3, 2014, p. 336.

[9] I. Oh and R. J. Hazler, "Contributions of personal and situational factors to bystanders' reactions to school bullying," School Psychology International, vol. 30, no. 3, 2009, pp. 291–310.

[10] W. P. Murphy, J. S. Yaruss, and R. W. Quesal, "Enhancing treatment for school-age children who stutter: Ii. reducing bullying through role-playing and self-disclosure," Journal of fluency disorders, vol. 32, no. 2, 2007, pp. 139–162.

[11] S. A. Rains, "The implications of stigma and anonymity for self-disclosure in health blogs," Health communication, vol. 29, no. 1, 2014, pp. 23–31.

[12] Adolescents overview. [retrived: Oct, 2020]. [Online]. Available: https://data.unicef.org/topic/adolescents/overview/ (2019)

[13] S. Yarosh, I. Radu, S. Hunter, and E. Rosenbaum, "Examining values: an analysis of nine years of idc research," in Proceedings of the 10th International Conference on Interaction Design and Children, 2011, pp. 136–144.

[14] E. S. Poole and T. Peyton, "Interaction design research with adolescents: methodological challenges and best practices," in Proceedings of the 12th International Conference on Interaction Design and Children, 2013, pp. 211–217.

[15] Z. Ashktorab and J. Vitak, "Designing cyberbullying mitigation and prevention solutions through participatory design with teenagers," in Proceedings of the 2016 CHI Conference on Human Factors in Computing Systems, 2016, pp. 3895–3905.

[16] G. M. McCarthy, E. R. Rodriguez Ramírez, and B. J. Robinson, "Participatory design to address stigma with adolescents with type 1 diabetes," in Proceedings of the 2017 Conference on Designing Interactive Systems, 2017, pp. 83–94.

[17] S. M. Jourard, The transparent self. Van Nostrand Reinhold Company, 1971.

[18] A. N. Joinson, "Self-disclosure in computer-mediated communication: The role of self-awareness and visual anonymity," European journal of social psychology, vol. 31, no. 2, 2001, pp. 177–192.

[19] J. H. Greist, M. H. Klein, and L. J. Van Cura, "A computer interview for psychiatric patient target symptoms," Archives of General Psychiatry, vol. 29, no. 2, 1973, pp. 247–253.

[20] M. Ferriter, "Computer aided interviewing and the psychiatric social history," Social Work and Social Sciences Review, 1993.

[21] S. Weisband and S. Kiesler, "Self disclosure on computer forms: Meta-analysis and implications," in Proceedings of the SIGCHI conference on human factors in computing systems, 1996, pp. 3–10.

[22] M. D. Pickard, C. A. Roster, and Y. Chen, "Revealing sensitive information in personal interviews: Is self-disclosure easier with humans or avatars and under what conditions?" Computers in Human Behavior, vol. 65, 2016, pp. 23–30.

[23] G. M. Lucas, J. Gratch, A. King, and L.-P. Morency, "It's only a computer: Virtual humans increase willingness to disclose," Computers in Human Behavior, vol. 37, 2014, pp. 94–100.

[24] L. F. Cranor and S. Garfinkel, Security and usability: designing secure systems that people can use. O'Reilly Media, Inc., 2005.

[25] A. Harley, "Trustworthiness in web design: 4 credibility factors," Utg. av Nielsen Norman group. url: https://www. nngroup.com/articles/trustworthy-design, 2016.

[26] K. S. Jones, "Privacy: what's different now?" Interdisciplinary Science Reviews, vol. 28, no. 4, 2003, pp. 287–292.

[27] L. J. Hoffman, K. Lawson-Jenkins, and J. Blum, "Trust beyond security: an expanded trust model," Communications of the ACM, vol. 49, no. 7, 2006, pp. 94–101.

[28] M. Sapouna et al., "Virtual learning intervention to reduce bullying victimization in primary school: a controlled trial," Journal of Child Psychology and Psychiatry, vol. 51, no. 1, 2010, pp. 104–112.

[29] C. Raminhos et al., "A serious game-based solution to prevent bullying," International Journal of Pervasive Computing and Communications, vol. 12, no. 2, 2016, pp. 194–215.

[30] H.-F. Neo, C.-C. Teo, and J. L. H. Boon, "Mobile edutainment learning approach: #StopBully," in Proceedings of the 2nd International Conference on Digital Technology in Education. ACM, 2018, pp. 6–10.

[31] STOPit Solutions. [retrived: Oct, 2020]. [Online]. Available: https://stopitsolutions.com

[32] Anonymous Alerts. [retrived: Oct, 2020]. [Online]. Available: https://www.anonymousalerts.com/webcorp/

[33] H. Plattner, "An introduction to design thinking process guide," The Institute of Design at Stanford: Stanford, 2010.

[34] J. F. Jones, S. A. Hook, S. C. Park, and L. M. Scott, "Privacy, security and interoperability of mobile health applications," in International Conference on Universal Access in Human-Computer Interaction. Springer, 2011, pp. 46–55.

[35] A. Latham, K. Crockett, and Z. Bandar, "A conversational expert system supporting bullying and harassment policies." vol. 1, Jan 2010, pp. 163–168.

[36] R. Aylett et al., "Unscripted narrative for affectively driven characters," IEEE Computer Graphics and Applications, vol. 26, no. 3, 2006, pp. 42–52.

[37] D. Chaum and E. Van Heyst, "Group signatures," in Workshop on the Theory and Application of of Cryptographic Techniques. Springer, 1991, pp. 257–265.

[38] Y.-k. Lee, S.-w. Han, S.-j. Lee, B.-h. Chung, and D. G. Lee, "Anonymous authentication system using group signature," in 2009 International Conference on Complex, Intelligent and Software Intensive Systems. IEEE, 2009, pp. 1235–1239.

[39] K. Cohn-Gordon, C. Cremers, B. Dowling, L. Garratt, and D. Stebila, "A formal security analysis of the signal messaging protocol," in 2017 IEEE European Symposium on Security and Privacy (EuroS&P). IEEE, 2017, pp. 451–466.

Letter and Word Prediction for Virtual Braille Keyboard

Krzysztof Dobosz

Department of Algorithmics and Software
Silesian University of Technology
Gliwice, Poland
Email: krzysztof.dobosz@polsl.pl

Łukasz Prajzler

Department of Algorithmics and Software
Silesian University of Technology
Gliwice, Poland
Email: lukapra442@student.polsl.pl

Abstract—**The aim of this work was to study whether word prediction can be applied to virtual Braille keyboards and can improve typing text by visually impaired smartphone user. First the keyboards' advantages and disadvantages were compared to choose one to extend with word prediction mechanism. Next the method was proposed and implemented in a form of a mobile application. Due to Braille code's structure, it was possible to apply not only word, but also a letter and dot prediction. Finally, both number of dots and letters necessary for predicting letters and words respectively within the shortest time were studied. This work verified that prediction in on-screen Braille keyboards is possible and brings noticeable benefits in typing speed. The most important observation is that just after the first dot (or blank place) it is worth searching the suggested letters and words.**

Keywords–Text entry; Braille code; Letter prediction; Word prediction; Virtual keyboard.

I. INTRODUCTION

The rapid development of mobile technology in the 21st century resulted in smartphones and tablets. Interaction began to use touch and gestures on the surface of the touch screen. This has opened up many new opportunities for users of mobile devices. Anyone can customize the touch application interface to suit their needs. Thanks to this improvement, smartphones have become an essential part of the lives of many people around the world, also for people with visual impairments. The need for an external keyboard to interact with the device has been eliminated. In the era of ubiquitous smartphones, the study of text input methods on touch screens for people with visual disabilities has become a new area of research. Many methods of entering text using Braille and implemented as virtual keyboards have been developed. Their main disadvantage is their low writing efficiency.

The aim of this thesis was to study whether word prediction can be applied to virtual Braille keyboards and how this affects the efficiency of text input methods.

The rest of this paper is organized as follows: Section II presents related work on virtual Braille keyboards, Section III analyzes the problem of prediction and describes the proposed method. Section IV assesses the effects of the applied prediction. This contribution is concluded in Section V, which also outlines the starting points for future research.

II. BACKGROUND

A very well-known layout by people with visual disabilities is that of the six cells in the Braille system. In the *BrailleType* [1], the interface consists of 6 buttons ordered in 2 columns. They are placed on the edges and corners of the screen to allow for their easier localization. Dots are chosen one by one in any order with audio confirmation. Concurrently, similar project - the *LeBraille* [2] was developed. It enriches Braille typing by audio and vibration feedback. However, interaction with virtual keyboards imitating hardware keyboards is more complex for people with visual disabilities and often requires a lot of cognitive effort from them, such as remembering the positions of the virtual keyboard keys [3], [4]. Another text entry method - the *SingleTapBraille* [5], relies on six dot interface. First tap represents a first dot in a left column. It can be performed anywhere on the screen. The coordinates of the following taps are gathered and relying on their values a Braille symbol is created. Factors which influence the relations between dots are: the coordinates of each dot, the distance between dots, the number of dots in every symbol.

Two fingers are used in *TypeInBraille* [6], where two dots type dots at the same time row-by-row. This method additionally uses swipes to confirmed letters, enter space, and delete the last entered letter. In the *SBraille* [7], the user can enter text row by row. It is enough to gesture with the thumb to make all the necessary gestures. First, the user has to divide the screen into two parts by moving the diagonal line across the screen with his thumb. Then, taps are used to select a left or right point, or gestures to indicate a full or empty line.

In the approach called *Perkinput*, the user touches the screen with three fingers at the same time, the device registers and remembers their position [8]. Next, the user enters three dots at once, column by column. First, the left column were entered, then, the right one. Another column-by-column approach, the *BrailleEasy* method for one-handed Brailing is a custom keyboard called BrailleEasy to input Arabic or English Braille codes [9]. Its implementation extends the character set to support all special characters, capital letters and numbers. Another method using three fingers is *OneHandBraille* [10]. Here, neighboring dots are replaced with swipes.

Single continuous swipe for one Braille symbol can be done instead of all taps on the screen of a mobile device [11]. Evaluation using a theoretical CLC (Curve-Line-Corner) model [12] resulted with high performance. However, this method has not been verified in practice. Similar approach represents the *EdgeBraille* [13]. It is a keyboard which gathers data from six points. These points are located on the corners and long edges of the screen. The user has to enter a continuous line connecting the points to enter a letter. Selecting the dot second time deactivates it. In the *BrailleKey* the screen was divided into four big buttons [14]. Top two are used for entering text: single tap – first row, double tap – second row, long press – third row. Left and right buttons are used for entering left and right Braille symbol columns respectively. Bottom buttons – enter and delete - are used for text editing. Space is entered by double tap on enter. However, the most efficient, practically confirmed solution is *BrailleTouch* [15]. The application interface includes six virtual buttons corresponding to Braille dots. The smartphone has to be hold horizontally and the touchscreen has to be facing away from the user. This approach provides fast, eyes-free text input, where the user's fingers hit the right places on the touch screen very accurately. Some of the mentioned methods have been adapted for use in the air using image recognition technique [16], [17]. The independence from the plane of typing is a great advantage, but a big inconvenience is fast tiredness of hands, when the user types a long text.

The second research area closely related to text input is a word prediction. Word prediction often does not have a visible effect on typing proficiency when used with a standard keyboard. However, some results of studies presented that word completion or word prediction programs would increase typing speed when used with an on-screen keyboard that also requires looking away from the source document [18]. Word prediction systems can reduce the number of keystrokes required to form a message in a letter-based AAC (Augmentative and Alternative Communication) system [19]. The work [20] suggests that predictive performance can be improved by using higher-order n-gram prediction techniques. Next one demonstrates that phrases can be offered instead of words, although the user should interprets them rather as suggestions than predictions [21]. Finally, other solution adds to static text prediction of letters and words also phonetic and similarity algorithms to reduce the user's typing error rate [22]. However, some studies indicate that the effectiveness of using word prediction software to increase typing speed may vary due to the severity of physical disability or pre-intervention typing rate [23].

The purpose of this work was to verify whether prediction in on-screen Braille keyboards is possible, and whether it brings noticeable benefits in typing speed.

III. PREDICTION FOR BRAILLE KEYBOARDS

A. Analysis

A feature which can increase typing speed and has not been studied before is letter prediction. To be able to apply a such feature, all dots should not be entered all at once. The most desired text entry method is one which enables to do that one by one. After comparison of multiple advantages and disadvantages of existing Braille text entry methods, i.e. number of gestures, fingers and hands (Table I) - the *BrailleEnter* [24] solution was chosen. In this approach, the users must tap or press on a touchscreen six times sequentially to represent a letter. The user can tap or press anywhere on the screen without any concern about the location of interactions. Tap means inactivated Braille dot, and press - the activated dots. First of all, it can be used with only one hand, what is very convenient for users, who can type even while walking and holding a cane or a dog lead in second hand at the same time. Secondly, the user does not have to localize certain points on the screen and the dots are entered in a standard order.

TABLE I. COMPARISON OF GESTURES IN EACH METHOD.

Method	*Min. gestures*	*Max. gestures*	*No. fingers*	*No. hands*
BrailleTouch	1	6	6	2
BrailleKey	2	4	4	2
BrailleEnter	6	6	1	1
BrailleType	2	6	1	1
Perkinput	2	2	3	1
EdgeBraille	1	1	1	1
TypeInBraille	2	4	3	1
SingleTapBraille	1	6	1	1
OneHandBraille	1	3	1	1
SBraille	3	3	1	1

Additionally, this method is relatively fast and has a very small error rate and both of these features can be improved by using letter prediction.

The next problem to solve is how to present suggestions for letters and words to use when typing. In standard keyboard, the user can see all the suggested words while typing, so he can immediately choose one of them, if the desired one is among the suggestions. In virtual Braille keyboards it is obviously impossible. The only one possibility is emitting the words by voice using Text-To-Speech technology.

B. The Proposed Method

In this method active dot is represented by long press, inactive by single tap as in the *BrailleEnter*. The user can tap anywhere on the screen and uses only one finger to interact with the interface. A letter is entered dot by dot, column by column. The prediction is applied just after typing the first dot, but if the user wishes, instead of verifying the all the suggestions, he can continue typing remaining dots, so the search results are more restricted and more accurate. Following gestures are used to operate the prototype application of the method:

- *single tap* – adding an empty dot to the braille pattern search sequence,
- *long press* – adding a raised dot to the Braille pattern search sequence,
- *swipe right* – reading aloud next suggestion from the list to the user according to the alphabetical order,
- *swipe left* – reading aloud next suggestion from the list to the user opposite to the alphabetical order,
- *swipe down* – accepting suggested letter or word,
- *swipe up* – clearing currently being entered letter or word.

The search results create a closed loop, so after hearing the first suggestion from the list, the user can go directly at the end of the list just by swiping left. The following algorithm presents start of the process of typing letter 'M' and possible choices to be performed by the user.

1) The user performs long press, the list is filled with letters whose Braille sign begins with raised dot. The first suggested letter is letter 'A'. The user has following choices:
    - *swipe right* - the next suggested letter is 'B',
    - *swipe left* - the next suggested letter is 'Z',
    - *single tap* - continue typing.

2) The user can swipe to reach the desired letter. However knowing alphabet order the user knows that this letter is in the middle of alphabet, so it may take a lot swipe gestures. The user performs single tap, the list is filled with letters whose Braille sequence begins with "10", so the search results list is reduced. The first suggested letter is "A". Still the user has the following choices:
   - *swipe right* - the next suggested letter is 'C',
   - *swipe left* - the next suggested letter is 'Z',
   - *long press* - continue typing.

The full path of restricting the search results list after entering consecutive dots while typing letter 'M' is presented in Figure 1. Word prediction system works the same way. After typing first four letters the system suggests a word. The words are taken from the list of five thousands the most popular English words and are ordered descending, according to their occurrence frequency in English language. The user can swipe right to check next suggestion, swipe left for previous one or continue typing. The word is chosen by swiping down. In case the user is distracted or has to abandon typing for a moment, both letters and words are frequently being repeated every 10 seconds. Swiping up clears a letter which is currently being entered. If no letter is currently being entered, swipe up clears the initial word sequence.

IV. EVALUATION

A. Procedure

The evaluation procedure consisted of three parts. First, the number of gestures needed to enter each letter of the English alphabet was counted. Then, using the selected letter prediction method, typing of single words was tested. Finally, when both the letter and word prediction methods were chosen, final tests using a pangram were performed.

Before proceeding with testing, theoretical considerations were performed. Relying on each gesture duration and their amount in each investigated method, average time for every method was estimated after several trials:

- tap - 0.104 s.,
- long press - 0.771 s.,
- swipe - 0.114 s.,
- double tap - 0.215 s.,
- letter speech - 0.278 s.,
- word speech - 0.543 s.

Next, total number of gestures necessary for typing each letter using each method was calculated introducing a measure - GPC (Gestures Per Character). One sentence was selected to perform the final test. This sentence was a pangram that contains every letter of alphabet to perform the most reliable evaluation. The pangram was tested using following methods:

- basic *BrailleEnter* method,
- letter prediction applied after 1st dot,
- letter prediction applied after 2nd dot,
- letter prediction applied after 3rd dot,
- using both letter after the 1st dot and word prediction.

The set of data for letter prediction was just a set of every letter of English alphabet and its Braille sign representations.

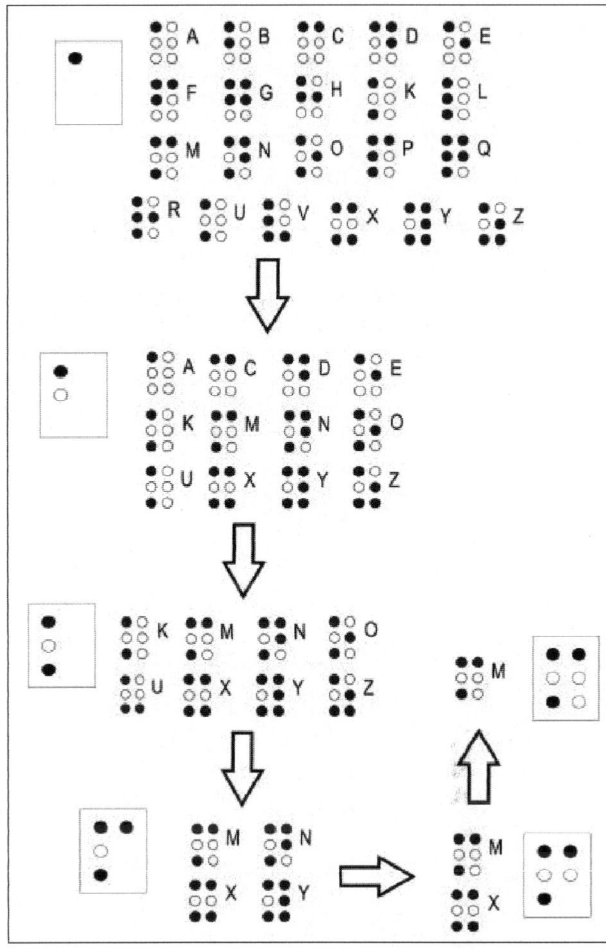

Figure 1. Steps for limiting a character set.

The list of 5000 the most popular English words was taken from the Corpus of Contemporary American English [25]. A sentence used for the final performance was a very popular English pangram *"The quick brown fox jumps over the lazy dog"*.

B. Letter Prediction

First average typing time for each letter was measured. Occurrence of each letter in the sentence was counted and multiplied by the average typing time of the letter. Swipe gestures for reviewing words suggestions and average time of letter speech, as well as double tap for entering spaces were added to the estimations. Then, all types of gestures and actions which occur in the sentence were counted. The numbers of each of them in each of the approaches were multiplied by the average timing calculated. Then, the results were summed up. Comparison of duration of each approach to the prediction is presented in Table II. The number of swipe gestures is always equal the number of suggested letters. In both approaches to the estimation, the best result was achieved, where prediction is applied after 2nd dot. Slightly worse scores obtained method, where prediction is applied after the 3rd dot. Next, estimated values were verified using the research tool in a form of mobile

TABLE II. AVERAGE TOTAL GESTURES TIME[S] AND GPC VALUE.

Gesture	$1^{st}dot$	$2^{nd}dot$	$3^{rd}dot$	$4^{th}dot$	$5^{th}dot$	*BrailleEnter*
tap	0.02	0.07	0.11	0.15	0.21	0.28
press	0.62	1.04	1.48	1.96	2.31	2.55
swipe	0.62	0.34	0.26	0.19	0.14	-
speech	1.52	0.83	0.63	0.47	0.34	-
time	2.78	**2.28**	2.48	2.77	3.00	2.83
GPC	6.46	**5.00**	5.27	5.69	6.23	6.00

application. After performing the experiments, the comparison of duration of letter prediction methods and *BrailleEnter* method clearly proves that application of letter prediction can significantly increase typing speed. The results and average times for each letter and method are presented in the Table III. The best time for each letter was bold.

TABLE III. AVERAGE TIMES OF LETTER TYPING WITH PREDICTION.

Letter	$1^{st}dot$	$2^{nd}dot$	$3^{rd}dot$	$4^{th}dot$	$5^{th}dot$	*BrailleEnter*
A	**0.61**	1.22	2.21	3.14	3.88	3.70
B	**1.04**	1.90	2.97	3.51	3.79	4.10
C	**1.47**	2.54	3.91	3.40	3.60	4.08
D	**2.05**	2.05	4.34	4.44	4.52	3.98
E	**2.97**	4.21	3.81	4.13	4.47	3.71
F	4.62	**3.47**	4.24	3.95	4.25	4.52
G	4.54	**3.84**	5.00	4.61	5.06	4.90
H	4.52	**3.91**	4.43	4.41	5.07	4.43
I	**0.49**	1.32	2.68	3.57	3.87	4.05
J	**0.93**	2.18	3.95	4.40	4.41	4.68
K	5.67	5.02	3.15	**3.13**	3.87	4.05
L	6.92	6.11	**3.81**	4.02	5.10	5.22
M	7.04	6.14	4.12	**3.82**	4.25	4.89
N	6.21	5.71	5.15	**4.51**	4.78	5.17
O	4.97	5.24	6.02	4.09	4.14	**3.98**
P	**4.76**	6.05	4.85	5.22	5.96	5.29
Q	**4.47**	4.94	6.28	5.94	7.53	5.92
R	**3.90**	4.69	6.47	5.20	5.73	5.26
S	**1.31**	3.33	3.70	4.43	5.11	4.99
T	**1.84**	3.93	4.67	5.66	6.18	5.39
U	**3.44**	5.09	7.10	4.69	4.96	4.39
V	**2.95**	3.27	5.01	5.60	6.36	5.26
W	**0.93**	2.61	3.93	4.70	6.22	5.11
X	**2.46**	3.56	5.48	6.24	5.23	5.27
Y	**1.67**	2.86	4.54	4.86	6.23	5.46
Z	**1.20**	2.81	3.89	5.16	5.74	4.58
Avr	**3.19**	3.80	4.45	4.49	5.01	4.70

The best typing speed was obtained for a method, where letter prediction is applied just after typing the first dot. These results are confirmed by analysis of normalized data, where the results are even better. However, not for every letter this method appeared to be the best. Time necessary for typing letters 'K', 'L', 'M', 'N', 'O' was higher than for the remaining letters, what is more for the first 4 of them this method appeared to be the most time consuming. The list of predicted letters was quite long due to relying only on the first dot while creating it and these letters were in the middle of the list. That is the reason why they required more time and more swiping gestures and the total number of required gestures to entering them was the highest from all the gathered data and varied from 10 to 12. Letter 'O' as the only one from the whole alphabet was entered the fastest using only the basic *BrailleEnter* method.

Table II does not reflect exactly the results of total direct letter time measurements, presented in Table III. First of all, direct letter times are much greater than the ones derived in calculations. Secondly, the order of best timing methods is not the same as in the letter measurements. However, after taking into account some circumstances, it can be seen that the results are reliable. The divergences are caused by the fact that in gestures measurements only the time when finger touches the screen was taken into account. While typing a letter, there are multiple factors which can influence typing speed, among them are: duration of putting up and down a finger, temporarily slowdown of the device, human error. After taking into consideration these factors it can be seen that the results are similar.

Finally, the task was to choose the best letter prediction method for further tests. This application does not assume setting fixed number of dots necessary to predict letter, only the minimal number. The results show that the highest typing speed is obtained when applying letter prediction already after the first dot. However, due to the fact that some letters achieved better results after higher number of dots, it may be more efficient, if in case of these letters more dots will be typed. And here can be seen that a big benefit for potential users would be freedom of choice. For users who are familiar with Braille code, this method would be definitely better choice. On the other hand, there are many visually impaired people who do not know the Braille code. Applying letter prediction after the first dot allows them for entering text relatively fast without the necessity of learning in details the Braille code. What is more, this method decreases the possibility of mistyping or entering a wrong letter a lot. If the first dot is incorrect, it can be easily and quickly corrected.

C. Word Prediction

The same as with letter prediction, this part began with theoretical analysis. In this case again, knowing number of each gesture in each letter and duration of each gesture, estimated typing time of each word was calculated. However, taking into account the differences between time calculation and experiments results, and knowing the average duration of typing each letter, second calculation which instead of analyzing each letter components in detail uses already measured average time for each of the typed letter.

The next task was to estimate typing time of one word. To achieve that average number of each action for each method was multiplied by the average duration of each action. The results are presented in Table IV.

TABLE IV. AVERAGE DURATION OF ACTIONS IN EACH METHOD OF WORD PREDICTION.

Gesture	*3 letters*	*4 letters*	*5 letters*	*6 letters*	*BrailleEnter*
tap	-	0.03	0.04	0.07	0.16
press	2.31	2.89	3.57	4.11	5.78
swipe	5.53	3.61	4.08	4.45	6.27
letters	6.81	7.96	9.35	10.33	15.29
words	13.03	1.63	1.15	1.00	-
total	27.69	**16.11**	18.18	19.95	27.50
estimation	29.51	**18.35**	20.83	22.47	31.81

The results are quite similar to the GPC results. For instance, it can be seen that average scores are the best for word prediction applied after 4th letter (one before last row). Afterwards, the average word entry duration was estimated using already measured letter entry time. Number of each letter occurrence in each method for all words was calculated and multiplied by the certain letter average duration. These results are presented in the last row of Table IV. After analysis of GPC metric and both types of time estimation it can be seen that the results are very similar to each other. Word prediction applied after 4th letter appeared to be the best.

D. Final evaluation

The final test was also preceded with theoretical considerations and estimation. First the pangram sentence is analyzed using GPC metric, than typing time is estimated using two approaches. The same as with word evaluation, first approach uses average duration of each gesture, the second uses estimated duration of the gestures and measured letter entry duration. For evaluation purposes it was assumed that only first 6 suggested words are checked. If there are no hits among them, the whole word is being typed. To perform estimation the most optimistic scenario was taken into account and it was assumed that all words are found in the database and they are correct just with the first word proposal. The mobile research tool was supplied with another feature – entering space after double tap, to allow typing whole sentences.

The first estimation consisted in counting all types of gestures and actions which occur in the sentence (Table V). The best results are obtained for the approach with letter prediction applied only after the second dot. The worst score again belongs to letter prediction after the first dot. The difference is very big here, it is over 20 seconds.

The second estimation consist in using measured average typing time for each letter presented in Table III. Occurrence of each letter in the sentence was counted and multiplied by the average typing time of the letter. Swipe gestures for reviewing words suggestions and average time of word speech, as well as double tap for entering spaces were added to the estimations. In this case the best results were obtained for approach, where both letter and word prediction are applied (one before last row in the Table V).

Measurements prove that application of both letter and word prediction can significantly improve typing speed in Braille virtual keyboards on touchscreen devices. Approach with letter prediction applied after the 1st dot and word prediction applied after the 4th letter obtained the best result(last row in the Table V). That is 20.15s (2.46 WPM). Slightly worse result was obtained for approach, where only letter prediction after the first dot was applied. Basic *BrailleEnter* method scored the worst result (284.9s equals 1.77 WPM). Application of both letter and word prediction improved typing speed by almost 80 seconds what is a very good result, especially that this score is for only one sentence.

Some remarks were made during the experiments. First, it should not be forgotten that letter prediction evaluation showed that some letters were typed faster after applying prediction after higher number of dots than one. If this piece of knowledge was taken into account, the typing speed for some letters could be increased by 1 to over 3 seconds. Secondly, in case of used pangram only 3 words were long enough to apply the word prediction. What is more, each of these words was only 5 letters long. Two of these words were found in the database and suggested as the firsts on the lists. In case of the third word, the word found in the database was exactly the same as the first 4 typed letters, and there was necessity to type additional letter "s" at the end of the word to create a plural form. It shows that the word prediction did not influence in this case the typing speed a lot – the difference in time between two the fastest approaches is only about 9 seconds.

TABLE V. ESTIMATED DURATION OF ACTIONS FOR THE PANGRAM.

Gesture	1^{st}dot	2^{nd}dot	3^{nd}dot	words	*BrailleEnter*
tap	0.06	2.50	3.95	0.52	10.09
press	22.36	35.47	51.66	20.82	87.12
double tap	1.72	1.72	1.72	1.72	1.72
swipe	23.48	13.00	9.92	21.20	-
letters	52.27	31.69	24.19	50.87	-
words	-	-	-	-	-
total	105.46	**84.37**	91.43	96.76	98.93
2nd estimation	119.24	142.21	165.72	**112.05**	162.80
measurement	214.25	246.25	255.02	**205.17**	284.90

V. Conclusion and Future Work

The aim of this work was to study whether typing speed on virtual Braille keyboards can be improved by using letter and word prediction algorithms. First, the existing Braille text entry method worth to be improved was selected. Afterwards, the prediction mechanism was chosen. Several variants for letter and word prediction were designed and implemented as complete research tool in a form of mobile virtual keyboard. Next letter and word prediction were analyzed, including gestures count, different gestures types and their duration. Obtained results confirmed that prediction in on-screen Braille keyboards is possible and brings noticeable benefits in typing speed. The most important observation is that just after the first dot (or blank place) it is worth searching the suggested letters and words. Obtained result equals 2.46 WPM is better than 1.77 WPM for reference *BrailleEnter* method.

In the future, the experimental virtual Braille keyboard can be extended with multiple additional features to increase typing speed even more. For instance, there are many advanced word prediction algorithms which could be applied to both improve accuracy of predicted words.

Acknowledgment

This work was co-financed by SUT grant for maintaining and developing research potential.

References

[1] J. Oliveira, T. Guerreiro, H. Nicolau, J. Jorge, and D. Gonçalves, "Brailletype: unleashing braille over touch screen mobile phones," in IFIP Conference on Human-Computer Interaction. Springer, 2011, pp. 100–107.

[2] A. R. Façanha, W. Viana, M. C. Pequeno, M. de Borba Campos, and J. Sánchez, "Touchscreen mobile phones virtual keyboarding for people with visual disabilities," in International Conference on Human-Computer Interaction. Springer, 2014, pp. 134–145.

[3] H. Tinwala and I. S. MacKenzie, "Eyes-free text entry on a touchscreen phone," in 2009 IEEE Toronto International Conference Science and Technology for Humanity (TIC-STH). IEEE, 2009, pp. 83–88.

[4] M. N. Bonner, J. T. Brudvik, G. D. Abowd, and W. K. Edwards, "No-look notes: accessible eyes-free multi-touch text entry," in International Conference on Pervasive Computing. Springer, 2010, pp. 409–426.

[5] M. Alnfiai and S. Sampalli, "Singletapbraille: Developing a text entry method based on braille patterns using a single tap," Procedia Computer Science, vol. 94, 2016, pp. 248–255.

[6] S. Mascetti, C. Bernareggi, and M. Belotti, "Typeinbraille: a braille-based typing application for touchscreen devices," in The proceedings of the 13th international ACM SIGACCESS conference on Computers and accessibility, 2011, pp. 295–296.

[7] S. Lee, J. S. Park, and J. G. Shon, "Sbraille: A new braille input method for mobile devices," in Advances in Computer Science and Ubiquitous Computing. Springer, 2017, pp. 528–533.

[8] S. Azenkot, J. O. Wobbrock, S. Prasain, and R. E. Ladner, "Input finger detection for nonvisual touch screen text entry in perkinput," in Proceedings of Graphics Interface 2012, 2012, pp. 121–129.

[9] B. Šepić, A. Ghanem, and S. Vogel, "Brailleeasy: One-handed braille keyboard for smartphones." Studies in health technology and informatics, vol. 217, 2015, pp. 1030–1035.

[10] K. Dobosz and M. Szuścik, "Onehandbraille: an alternative virtual keyboard for blind people," in International Conference on Man–Machine Interactions. Springer, 2017, pp. 62–71.

[11] K. Dobosz and T. Depta, "Continuous writing the braille code," in International Conference on Computers Helping People with Special Needs. Springer, 2018, pp. 343–350.

[12] X. Cao and S. Zhai, "Modeling human performance of pen stroke gestures," in Proceedings of the SIGCHI conference on Human factors in computing systems, 2007, pp. 1495–1504.

[13] E. Mattheiss, G. Regal, J. Schrammel, M. Garschall, and M. Tscheligi, "Dots and letters: Accessible braille-based text input for visually impaired people on mobile touchscreen devices," in International Conference on Computers for Handicapped Persons. Springer, 2014, pp. 650–657.

[14] N. S. Subash, S. Nambiar, and V. Kumar, "Braillekey: An alternative braille text input system: Comparative study of an innovative simplified text input system for the visually impaired," in 2012 4th International Conference on Intelligent Human Computer Interaction (IHCI). IEEE, 2012, pp. 1–4.

[15] M. Romero, B. Frey, C. Southern, and G. D. Abowd, "Brailletouch: designing a mobile eyes-free soft keyboard," in Proceedings of the 13th International Conference on Human Computer Interaction with Mobile Devices and Services, 2011, pp. 707–709.

[16] K. Dobosz and K. Buchczyk, "One-handed braille in the air," in International Conference on Computers Helping People with Special Needs. Springer, 2018, pp. 322–325.

[17] K. Dobosz and M. Mazgaj, "Typing braille code in the air with the leap motion controller," in International Conference on Man–Machine Interactions. Springer, 2017, pp. 43–51.

[18] D. Anson et al., "The effects of word completion and word prediction on typing rates using on-screen keyboards," Assistive technology, vol. 18, no. 2, 2006, pp. 146–154.

[19] K. Trnka, J. McCaw, D. Yarrington, K. F. McCoy, and C. Pennington, "User interaction with word prediction: The effects of prediction quality," ACM Transactions on Accessible Computing (TACCESS), vol. 1, no. 3, 2009, pp. 1–34.

[20] G. W. Lesher et al., "Effects of ngram order and training text size on word prediction," in Proceedings of the RESNA'99 Annual Conference. Citeseer, 1999, pp. 52–54.

[21] K. C. Arnold, K. Z. Gajos, and A. T. Kalai, "On suggesting phrases vs. predicting words for mobile text composition," in Proceedings of the 29th Annual Symposium on User Interface Software and Technology, 2016, pp. 603–608.

[22] R. d. S. Gomide et al., "A new concept of assistive virtual keyboards based on a systematic review of text entry optimization techniques," Research on Biomedical Engineering, vol. 32, no. 2, 2016, pp. 176–198.

[23] J. Tumlin and K. W. Heller, "Using word prediction software to increase typing fluency with students with physical disabilities," Journal of Special Education Technology, vol. 19, no. 3, 2004, pp. 5–14.

[24] M. Alnfiai and S. Sampalli, "Braillecenter: A touch screen braille text entry method for the blind," in ANT/SEIT, 2017, pp. 257–264.

[25] M. Davies. Corpus of contemporary american english, word frequency data. [Online]. Available: https://www.wordfrequency.info/

FocalVid : Facilitating Remote Studies of Video Saliency

Sahand Shaghaghi*, Bryan Tripp*, Chrystopher Nehaniv*† Alexander Mois Aroyo†, and Kerstin Dautenhahn†*
*Department of Systems Design Engineering
†Department of Electrical Engineering
University of Waterloo, Waterloo, Canada
Email: {s2shagha, bptripp, cnehaniv, aaroyo, kdautenh}@uwaterloo.ca

***Abstract*—Humans selectively use only a small fraction of the vast sensory data that arrives at their receptors. In vision, eye movements are an important part of this selection process. Eye movements arise from interacting bottom-up and top-down factors, including social factors, and they provide important information about cognitive processes. Tracking eye movements often requires very specialized hardware that is suitable for laboratory based studies, but less practical for online studies with remote participants. Recently, a proxy for eye movements was introduced, which facilitates large online studies of overt attention. In this approach, participants' mouse-clicks reveal parts of a static image sequentially. Mouse-click locations can be recorded accurately and reliably, without the need for a calibration procedure, and mouse-click locations were found to correlate strongly with gaze locations. However, while eye movements are often studied using static scenes, they are also affected by motion cues, and by more complex task-related dynamics. To facilitate the online study of such influences, we adapted the mouse-based approach to dynamic scenes, by continuously recording the location of the mouse cursor, and continuously revealing only part of the display surrounding the cursor. While our platform has been developed primarily to support large, remote video saliency studies, the same approach could be used to study overt attention, e.g., in computer games, or to study more complex interactions, such as co-operative tasks performed over video chat. This paper describes our platform, FocalVid, which will be made open-source on acceptance.**

Keywords*–eye tracking; visual saliency; video saliency; mouse-contingent interface; Web design.

I. Introduction

In human-human interactions, gaze behavior and visual preference choices are crucial since they influence and regulate the dynamics of the interaction. Similar dynamics are also present in Human-Computer-Interaction (HCI) scenarios. It is important to fully understand the dynamics of gaze interactions in these scenarios. Increasingly online studies are conducted with remote participants, in addition to laboratory in-person studies. Thus, it is timely to explore methodologies which facilitate seamless recording of gaze and visual saliency for a broader participant base that can be used across a variety of hardware and operating systems. The presented methodology makes it possible to explore remote human-human or human-robot interactions by allowing the researchers to observe and record participants' visual selection data for various scenarios involving video saliency, overt attention scenarios and co-operative remote tasks. Such gathered data is valuable not only in the field of HCI, but also in fields of computer vision, ergonomics, user experience design and Human-Robot Interaction (HRI) to name a few since it will ultimately enable researchers to make design choices based upon gaze and human visual preferences.

Eye movements and gaze patterns influence the dynamics of social interactions. Eye movements/fixations and gaze patterns are intertwined. Eye movements lead to instances of gaze, but not all eye movements necessarily lead to socially meaningful gaze instances. Theories [1] and models that have been discussed in the literature [2] attempt to make sense of these gaze patterns in social interaction, exploring the intricacies of gaze behavior in mutual gaze, joint attention, dyadic and triadic interactions. There is a need for new tools to further explore different aspects of these models and theories. Here, we introduce FocalVid as an effort towards this end. FocalVid facilitates recording of visual attention patterns of articipants while viewing videos in remote settings.

The correlation between visual selection and hand movements [3], and also the close correlation between gaze and cursor locations [4]–[8] have been established previously. This chain of correlations is the main rationale behind (computer) mouse-contingent methodologies, including FocalVid, which utilizes participants' controlled cursor movements on a visual canvas to record proxies for gaze behavior. Up to now, eye movement tracking has been conducted predominantly using expensive equipment in controlled laboratory environments to record participants' eye movements [9], which is limited in reach and typically cannot be used for remote, e.g., crowd-sourcing studies [10]. FocalVid departs from this approach by making use of a mouse-contingent methodology, which allows the participants' presence in a closed interaction loop involving the participant and the scenario unfolding in a video that they observe, facilitating broader participant reach due in remote participation.

The presented platform is not only useful in the study of gaze, but it is also useful in a multitude of experimental scenarios such as: video saliency studies, video game usability studies, and platform usability studies. The rationale that FocalVid is based on closely correlates with the concept of visual saliency [11], exploring the utilization of the bottom-up saliency concept [12]–[14] to establish a relationship between visual features and gaze directions. The field of visual saliency is interested in points of attention in 2D and 3D scenes [15]. Such a relationship then makes it possible to evaluate the findings gained with FocalVid against available findings from the field of human visual saliency studies which could be used to evaluate and benchmark the presented system. Our approach extended the methodologies designed by Kim et al. [4], Jiang et al. [16], and Jansen et al. [17] through the redesign and extension of those approaches with the addition of video playback. Such context has not been explored in detail previously, and is a novel contribution of the present work. As such, the main contribution of this study is the presentation of a system that would make it possible to record participant visual selection for any given video scenario.

The remainder of this article is structured as follows. Section II discusses related work, followed by a description of the design and implementation of FocalVid (Section III). Results of initial system tests are presented in Section IV and discussed in Section V. Section VI concludes the article.

II. Related Work

Related works are categorized into thematic areas: gaze, visual perception and visual saliency which has close ties with visual perception. Efforts relating to mouse-contingent methodologies are also reviewed which directly relates to the system designed in this study.

A. Gaze, Visual Perception and Eye-tracking methodologies

There is a rich history of research in the field of vision which deals with eye movements, gaze, and visual perception. There have been various attempts at the recording of eye movement in the past 60 years [18]. These attempts initially used more intrusive apparatus and since have moved toward less intrusive solutions [19, p. 9]. Initially, eye movements recording devices needed to be connected to the sclera such as the apparatus designed by Yarbus [20]. He developed an apparatus to accurately record eye movements using suction caps which attach to the sclera. Eye movement recording solutions have generally become less intrusive [9], often using cameras and infrared illumination to improve contrast between the pupil and surrounding tissue, but they still typically require expensive specialized hardware. There have been two new approaches that have challenged this tendency. Both of these approaches are moving in the direction of more broadly accessible methodologies and systems:

1) Appearance-based tracking: This approach attempts using visible-light cameras to track participant's eye movements. This method of eye tracking makes it possible to conduct remote studies using embedded Webcams in participants' personal computers [21]–[23].
2) Mouse-contingent tracking: This approach is the main focus of this study. These methodologies utilize cursor location to determine participant's visual selection. We elaborate on those issues in more detail in Section II-C.

B. Visual Saliency

Visual saliency refers to "bottom-up factors that highlight image regions that are different from their surroundings" [24, p.1], which make these regions in the visual field of interest to viewer. As such, there is a connection between visual saliency and eye movements: If a feature is highly salient, then there is a high likelihood of eye movement patterns whose trajectory dwells in that feature's spatial distribution within the field of view. One of the goals of the research field of visual saliency is the creation of models that could anticipate these highly salient features. These models are either hand-crafted [12][14][25][26] or, recently, deep-learning based [27]–[29]. Visual saliency explores detection for both static and dynamic scenarios [15]. Static scenarios mainly deal with static images and dynamic scenarios mainly deal with videos. Even though there are commonalities between the two settings, observation patterns differ for these two instances: The duration of viewing is different in the two, and dynamic cases have the extra element of motion with respect to the observer.

A necessity in the field of visual saliency is benchmark annotated data which models could be trained and tested against. This could either be in the form of eye-tracking benchmark data or crowdsourced benchmark data. Initially, it was customary to use smaller eye-tracking datasets for the training of hand-crafted models, but with the move to deep learning based models, larger databases are needed. Methodologies such as SALICON [16] become of use in these cases since such a methodology allows for the gathering of benchmark data from a broader participant base using services like Amazon Mechanical Turk [22]. As such, the creation of systems that make this type of data gathering possible would be of value, especially relating to video saliency where such solutions still are not readily available.

C. Mouse-contingent Methodologies

A current focus of the field of eye-tracking is the development of methodologies for more efficient collection of eye movements [4, p.4]. Such methodologies, including mouse-contingent ones, would then enable researchers to conduct experiments with a broader reach. Mouse-contingent methodologies make use of computer mouse and cursor location, which can be reliably recorded, and encourage co-origination of eye and mouse movements in various ways. These methodologies enable researchers to conduct saliency and usability studies through online platforms, which can be a significant advantage over time-consuming in-person laboratory experiments with expensive specialized software and hardware. Mouse-contingent methodologies have their roots in psychology studies. A seminal study investigates the use of bubble-shaped visual windows [30] for the evaluation of recognition tasks. Both visual windows and visual scotomas [31] have been explored extensively in the field of visual perception psychology which has lead to the moving-window approach in the field of HCI. An early example of such an approach is RFV viewer [17]. There have been some renditions and improvements of this model ever since [32][33] with the newest additions being SALICON [16], and Bubbleview [4]. These platforms are all designed with static images in mind and hence this creates the need for the design of a platform that could be utilized for video saliency.

III. Method

In this section, the FocalVid system design (Figure 1) is detailed. First, the fundamental moving visual window components of the system are detailed (Section III-A), followed by details regarding system interface (Section III-B) culminated by system implementation details (Section III-C).

A. Controlling Video Visibility via Mouse Movements

Here, much like BubbleView [4], the concept of bubbles was investigated as a base for the proposed platform [30][34]. This concept was then expanded upon by the incorporation of opacity, visual moving windows, and addition of the "graded regions of stimuli" [17] in the form of concentric circles. Our approach makes use of opacity instead of blurring used by Kim et al. [4].

Our platform displays a video behind a semi-transparent layer. This layer is nearly opaque over most of the video frame, but it is more transparent around the mouse-cursor

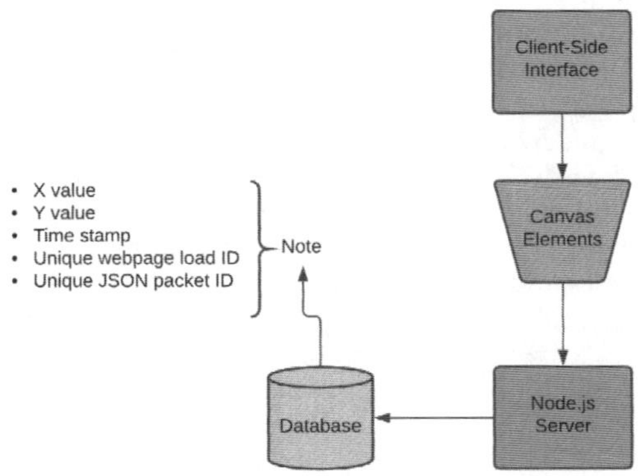

Figure 1. FocalVid system diagram.

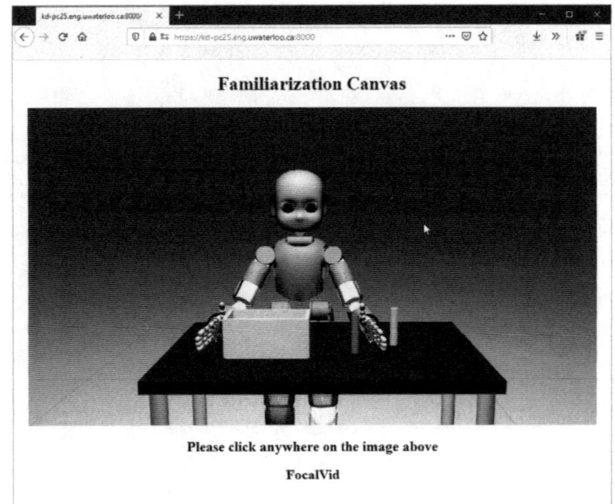

Figure 3. Get ready page: Here participants are asked to move their cursors inside the boundaries of the present image and then click in order for the experiment to begin. This is done so that participants' cursor is located on the canvas when the experiment begins.

location. The transparency is greatest within a small circle around the cursor location, and increasingly opaque in circles of increasing radius (Figure 2). This pattern reflects humans' higher visual acuity closer to the fovea, and approximately radially symmetric [35] decreases in acuity approaching the periphery. The result is that the video can be seen most clearly when gaze is centred on the cursor position. Participants must co-ordinate mouse and gaze to clearly see any part of the video. Importantly, partial transparency farther from the cursor allows detection of salient cues, but greater transparency at the centre encourages correspondence between gaze position and cursor position.

In our initial implementation described in this article, the circle sizes and transparencies are chosen by trial and error, with the goal of maximizing correspondence between natural gaze and mouse-cursor position. In the example of Figure 2, we have intentionally made the circles too large, to illustrate that this makes it too easy to see much of the scene without having an intention to move the cursor. To reduce the visual complexity of the display, as well as the complexity of the parameter space, the radii of circles always increase in uniform steps. We use a small number of circles, because displaying greater numbers of circles is more computationally demanding. Note, circle sizes and transparencies can be adjusted for the implementation of specific experiments, and might depend, among other factors, on the content displayed in the videos and/or associated research questions with regard to the type of data researchers intend to collect.

Figure 2. Details relating to radial bubbles.

B. Experiment Interface

The interface is Web-based, and implemented with HTML and JavaScript. The first page shows a short video (unrelated to the main experiment) and allows participants to freely practice using the interface without being evaluated.

The second page displays the first frame of the experimental video, in order to familiarize the participants with the general scene and points of interest, until the participant is ready to begin the experiment (Figure 3). The participant must move the mouse into the video canvas and click to begin. This ensures that the participant's attention is on the canvas when the experiment begins.

The third page presents the main experiment interface (Figure 4). This page includes one HTML canvas, with two layers. The bottom layer displays the video, and the top layer contains the semi-transparent overlay (Figure 2).

When the main experiment page has finished loading, a timer starts, and the video plays automatically. Cursor positions are detected via JavaScript "mousemove" events, time-stamped using the timer, and stored in a database. "mousemove" events report updates to the cursor location when the cursor is moved. When the video ends, the interface loads a final "thank you" page, and the experiment is complete.

C. Implementation Details

The implementation uses JavaScript, both in the client browser, and in a Node.js environment on the server. The client-side interface makes a secure HTTPS connection with a Node.js server, using the fetch method. The system continually transmits timestamped cursor positions to the server. Each instance of the experiment is assigned a unique ID, which is bundled with the cursor data, allowing multiple experiments to run in parallel.

The system stores data using NeDB [36], a widely-used NoSQL database that is compatible with Node.js. NeDB stores data in a simple JSON text file. The database stores x and

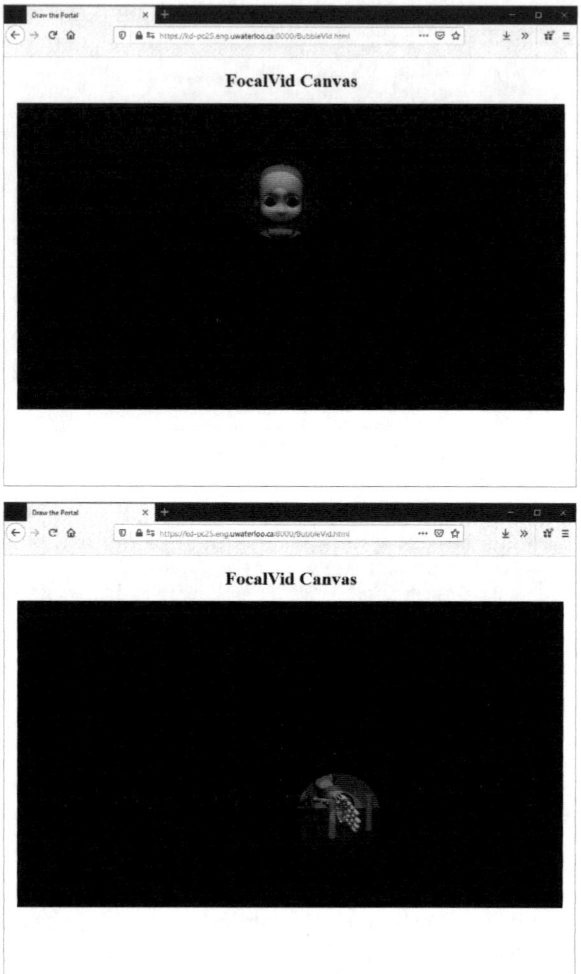

Figure 4. The main experiment page. Here participants' cursor is centered on the most inner circle of the co-centered circles. With the movement of the cursor, positioning of the concentric circles is altered, bringing into focus different elements in the video. In the upper figure the robot's head is focused on. In the lower figure the robot's left hand is focused on.

y coordinates of the cursor, timestamps of the coordinates, a unique identifier for each Webpage load, and a unique identifier for each JSON object. These JSON objects are continuously logged into the database. The unique identifier is created using the crypto API in the client-side platform. This API accommodates some cryptographic methods including random key generation.

IV. RESULTS

To technically test the system and confirm that it works as expected in a realistic experimental scenario, with a variety of hardware and browser software, the authors served as 'participants' in a mock experiment. We used FocalVid to view a video (with the duration of 20 seconds) of a simulated iCub robot [37] performing a sorting task. We viewed the same video twice, once focusing on the robot's face (task 1), and the other time focusing on the robot's left hand, which was moving objects into a box (task 2). iCub is an open-source humanoid robot broadly used by researchers.

Figure 5 shows an example trajectory (horizontal and vertical mouse positions versus time stamp) from the task 2. The cursor pauses from time 3064 (ms) to 5232 (ms), at a location on the robot's left hand.

Recorded mouse-contingent data was then used to produce a heatmap (Figure 6). Heatmaps are a visualization method used to visualize density distributions of points in 2D and 3D settings [38]. This then further confirms that the system is recording the proper mouse-contingent data at the proper timestamp. Here, a random frame from the viewed video was chosen for analysis. A heatmap of the recorded cursor data belonging to all viewing instances was then produced using the Seaborn library [39] in Python. This heatmap presentation illustrates the kernel density estimation for the logged cursor points in relation to the video frame. As seen in Figure 6, there are two major areas of interest aligning with the robot's face and the robot's left hand which is moving objects into the box. Outlier data points can be observed as well.

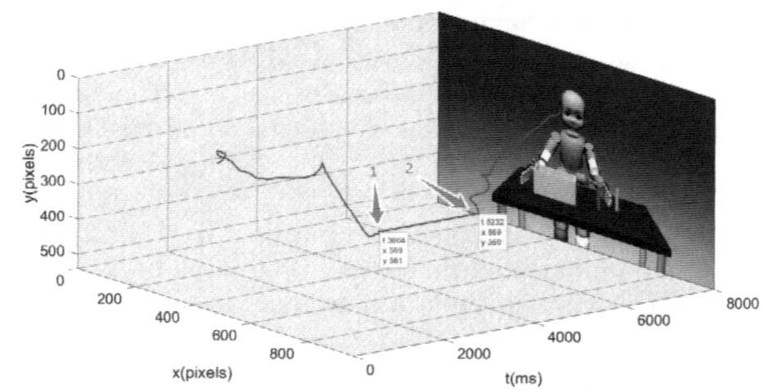

Figure 5. Data log visualization of recorded mouse-contingent cursor locations using FocalVid. The axes of the 3D graph represent x, y pixel coordinates in the video canvas and t, the time in milliseconds since the start of the video. Note that x & y refer to mouse locations in relation to the video frame and t refers to the timestamp belonging to that cursor location recording. An example of dwell of the cursor and hence the clearest visual region on the robot's left hand could be seen in this instance.

As another element of the technical evaluation of the system, to test the participant cursor and interface correspondence with the logged data, an additional set of recordings was made

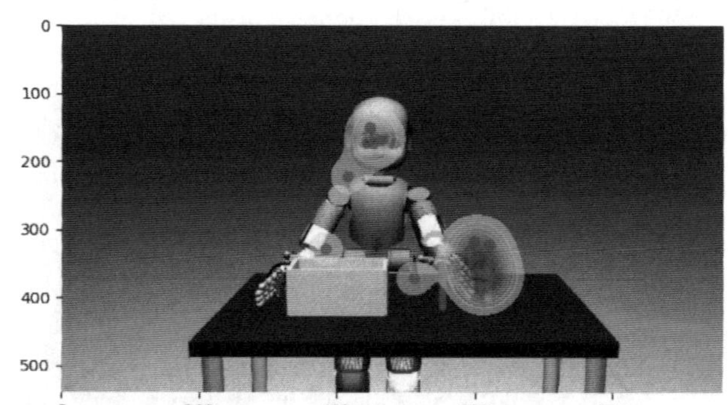

Figure 6. Heatmap of the mouse-contingent points recorded through the first two experiments using the authors. Here the data adjacent to a single frame was processed. Two major clusters could be seen, one belonging to the face area of interest (AOI) and the other belonging to the left hand AOI. Notice that the hand AOI does not fully align with the hand location, possibly due to presence of other highly salient features in the vicinity of hand, etc.

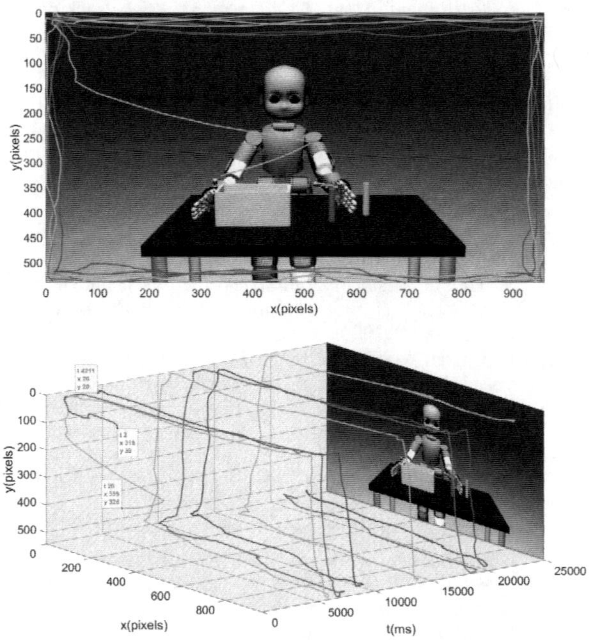

Figure 7. Three samples of the ten "4corners" experiment iterations conducted, plotted side by side. Note that the mouse movements could start immediately at the beginning of the experiment or with a delay, depending on participants' initial reaction time.

using the authors while viewing the same iCub video, assigned with a new task ('4corners'): The authors were instructed to move their mouse in a clockwise direction, attempting to get as close as possible to the four corners of the video frame in sequence starting from the upper left hand corner followed by the upper right hand corner and so forth. Example trajectories can be seen in Figure 7. The corner point cursor data for the ten recorded experimental instances were then extracted from this plot. Note that there was some variance around the targets, as is expected generally. In this case the variance was self-selected, as the authors were not given instructions about how to trade off speed and accuracy, or any other task constraints.

The final experiment conducted was the single point experiment. The rationale for this experiment was to assess the consistency of the system's performance across different operating systems, different browsers and screens. What was tested was if dwell on a specific point in the video frame would be accurately transmitted and recorded in the database. Authors were tasked with an experimental setup in which they were instructed to hover the mouse over the upper left hand edge of the yellow box present in the iCub video scenario. In order to achieve precision, cursor pointer was enabled in the interface. Results were positive attesting to the correct transmission of the data to database, with single cursor location being recorded for the entirety of the time cursor was positioned on the yellow box's edge.

V. DISCUSSION

This presented platform makes use of *opacity* instead of more widely used *blurring* for the purpose of distinguishing foveal vs. peripheral vision. Blurring more accurately approximates the difference in human perceptual abilities between the fovea and the periphery. However, our goal is not to approximate these differences, but simply to co-ordinate mouse and gaze locations. Because opacity makes the underlying image harder to see, we have found in pilot experiments that it strongly encourages mouse motion close to the gaze position. It will be an important next step to quantify this tendency, by comparing mouse and gaze positions in a larger study, using an accurate eye tracker.

VI. CONCLUSION AND FUTURE WORK

As laid out in this methodology paper, FocalVid could be used to record and analyze participants' mouse-contingent visual selection data which can be used in laboratory studies, but importantly, is likely to be highly advantageous for online studies with remote participants. In this article, we detailed the completed components of the presented system. It should be noted that the presented system is functional as it stands to record and conduct the needed analysis of the data. The immediate expansions would elevate FocalVid to a better-suited tool for other researchers, with its capability to produce meaningful simplified outputs that they then could use towards their research.

A limitation of our approach is that mouse movements are slower than eye movements, for a given degree of accuracy [40]. This difference will limit our approach with respect to rapidly changing scenes. There are also other limitations associated with the presented system which should be taken into consideration when using the FocalVid interface:

- Participants can have different mouse types (travel mouse vs. professional mouse), which affects cursor tracking capabilities. These different mouse types could lead to variability in points of interest tracking precision. This should be taken into consideration when using FocalVid.
- Participants can have different computer screens with different sizes, contrast ratios and dynamic range. Differences in screens lead to different visibility in the semi-transparent region. Calibration protocols might be needed to compensate for this.
- Participants can have computers with different processing power capabilities. Processing power minimum requirements should be in place for participants.

In addition to these system limitations, there is an innate variability associate with participant populations which should be taken into consideration when using the FocalVid interface:

- Participants have different hand-eye coordination abilities (e.g. older persons may have deteriorated hand-eye coordination compared to younger participants, and other participants may suffer from conditions that impair hand-eye coordination). This variability should be taken into consideration while using the FocalVid platform.
- Participant environmental setting cannot be controlled precisely in remote studies (some participants might be much more distracted due to environmental factors). As such, attention evaluation protocols should be put in place in conjunction with this system to assess participant attention and engagement in the task.

The system limitations could be mitigated by future system improvements such as inclusion of a screen contrast calibration process for the present system. Participant variability limitations could be mitigated by incorporation of specific experimental conditions and participant selection criteria while utilizing the FocalVid platform.

Immediate future works relating to this project could be classified into time stamping improvements, in-depth system verification and data analysis additions. The client-side components of the presented system are processing intensive which could lead to a possibility of lags between produced time-stamp and video playback. Work is underway to improve upon the time-stamping method such that in addition to the present time-stamp, frame count for viewed video frames is also recorded to the database so that lags could be identified and adjusted for in the data processing step.

As part of the immediate future steps relating to this project, experimental participant data would be gathered and analysed. The authors are planning on testing of the gathered data against the already labeled Hollywood2 dataset [41]. Regarding data processing, semantic segmentation [42]–[45], and spatiotemporal data clustering and visualization [46]–[48] could be explored. Long-term system verification could be in the context of diversification of testing case scenarios to assess broader system functionality.

ACKNOWLEDGMENT

This work was supported by University of Waterloo's Social and Intelligent Robotics Research Lab (SIRRL). This research was undertaken, in part, thanks to funding from the Canada 150 Research Chairs Program.

REFERENCES

[1] M. Argyle and M. Cook, *Gaze and Mutual Gaze*. Cambridge U Press, 1976.

[2] M. Jording, A. Hartz, G. Bente, M. Schulte-Rüther, and K. Vogeley, "The "Social Gaze Space": A taxonomy for gaze-based communication in triadic interactions," *Frontiers in psychology*, vol. 9, p. 226, 2018.

[3] M. Schulte-Mecklenbeck, R. O. Murphy, and F. Hutzler, "Flashlight–Recording information acquisition online," *Computers in human behavior*, vol. 27, no. 5, pp. 1771–1782, 2011.

[4] N. W. Kim, Z. Bylinskii, M. A. Borkin, K. Z. Gajos, A. Oliva, F. Durand, *et al.*, "BubbleView: An interface for crowdsourcing image importance maps and tracking visual attention," *ACM Transactions on Computer-Human Interaction (TOCHI)*, vol. 24, no. 5, pp. 1–40, 2017.

[5] M. C. Chen, J. R. Anderson, and M. H. Sohn, "What can a mouse cursor tell us more? correlation of eye/mouse movements on web browsing," in *CHI '01 Extended Abstracts on Human Factors in Computing Systems*, ser. CHI EA '01, Seattle, Washington: Association for Computing Machinery, 2001, pp. 281–282. DOI: 10.1145/634067.634234.

[6] Q. Guo and E. Agichtein, "Towards predicting web searcher gaze position from mouse movements," in *CHI '10 Extended Abstracts on Human Factors in Computing Systems*, ser. CHI EA '10, Atlanta, Georgia, USA: Association for Computing Machinery, 2010, pp. 3601–3606. DOI: 10.1145/1753846.1754025.

[7] K. Rodden, X. Fu, A. Aula, and I. Spiro, "Eye-mouse coordination patterns on web search results pages," in *CHI '08 Extended Abstracts on Human Factors in Computing Systems*, ser. CHI EA '08, Florence, Italy: Association for Computing Machinery, 2008, pp. 2997–3002. DOI: 10.1145/1358628.1358797.

[8] J. Huang, R. White, and G. Buscher, "User see, user point: Gaze and cursor alignment in web search," in *Proceedings of the SIGCHI Conference on Human Factors in Computing Systems*, ser. CHI '12, Austin, Texas, USA: Association for Computing Machinery, 2012, pp. 1341–1350. DOI: 10.1145/2207676.2208591.

[9] A. Al-Rahayfeh and M. Faezipour, "Eye tracking and head movement detection: A state-of-art survey," *IEEE Journal of Translational Engineering in Health and Medicine*, vol. 1, pp. 2 100 212–2 100 212, 2013.

[10] D. Lagun and E. Agichtein, "Viewser: Enabling large-scale remote user studies of web search examination and interaction," in *Proceedings of the 34th International ACM SIGIR Conference on Research and Development in Information Retrieval*, ser. SIGIR '11, Beijing, China: Association for Computing Machinery, 2011, pp. 365–374. DOI: 10.1145/2009916.2009967.

[11] S. Treue, "Visual attention: The where, what, how and why of saliency," *Current opinion in neurobiology*, vol. 13, no. 4, pp. 428–432, 2003.

[12] L. Itti, C. Koch, and E. Niebur, "A model of saliency-based visual attention for rapid scene analysis," *IEEE Transactions on pattern analysis and machine intelligence*, vol. 20, no. 11, pp. 1254–1259, 1998.

[13] R. J. Peters, A. Iyer, L. Itti, and C. Koch, "Components of bottom-up gaze allocation in natural images," *Vision research*, vol. 45, no. 18, pp. 2397–2416, 2005.

[14] N. Bruce and J. Tsotsos, "Saliency based on information maximization," in *Advances in Neural Information Processing Systems*, MIT press, 2006, pp. 155–162.

[15] A. Borji, "Saliency Prediction in the Deep Learning Era: An Empirical Investigation," *arXiv:1810.03716 [cs]*, Oct. 2018.

[16] M. Jiang, S. Huang, J. Duan, and Q. Zhao, "Salicon: Saliency in context," in *Proceedings of the IEEE Conference on Computer Vision and Pattern Recognition*, IEEE, 2015, pp. 1072–1080.

[17] A. R. Jansen, A. F. Blackwell, and K. Marriott, "A tool for tracking visual attention: The restricted focus viewer," *Behavior research methods, instruments, & computers*, vol. 35, no. 1, pp. 57–69, 2003.

[18] K. Holmqvist, M. Nyström, R. Andersson, R. Dewhurst, H. Jarodzka, and J. Van de Weijer, *Eye tracking: A comprehensive guide to methods and measures*. OUP Oxford, 2011, ISBN: 0-19-162542-6.

[19] J. R. Bergstrom and A. Schall, *Eye Tracking in User Experience Design*. Elsevier, 2014, ISBN: 0-12-416709-8.

[20] Alfred L. Yarbus, *Eye Movements and Vision*. Plenum Press, 1967.

[21] S. Baluja and D. Pomerleau, "Non-intrusive gaze tracking using artificial neural networks," in *Advances in Neural Information Processing Systems*, 1994, pp. 753–760.

[22] P. Xu, K. A. Ehinger, Y. Zhang, A. Finkelstein, S. R. Kulkarni, and J. Xiao, "Turkergaze: Crowdsourcing saliency with webcam based eye tracking," *arXiv preprint arXiv:1504.06755*, 2015.

[23] C. Shen, X. Huang, and Q. Zhao, "Predicting eye fixations on webpage with an ensemble of early features and high-level representations from deep network," *IEEE Transactions on Multimedia*, vol. 17, no. 11, pp. 2084–2093, 2015.

[24] A. Borji, D. N. Sihite, and L. Itti, "Quantitative analysis of human-model agreement in visual saliency modeling: A comparative study," *IEEE Transactions on Image Processing*, vol. 22, no. 1, pp. 55–69, 2012.

[25] T. Judd, K. Ehinger, F. Durand, and A. Torralba, "Learning to predict where humans look," in *2009 IEEE 12th international conference on computer vision*, IEEE, 2009, pp. 2106–2113, ISBN: 1-4244-4420-9.

[26] W. Kienzle, F. A. Wichmann, M. O. Franz, and B. Schölkopf, "A nonparametric approach to bottom-up visual saliency," in *Advances in Neural Information Processing Systems 19*, B. Schölkopf, J. C. Platt, and T. Hoffman, Eds., MIT Press, 2007, pp. 689–696.

[27] S. S. Kruthiventi, K. Ayush, and R. V. Babu, "Deepfix: A fully convolutional neural network for predicting human eye

fixations," *IEEE Transactions on Image Processing*, vol. 26, no. 9, pp. 4446–4456, 2017.

[28] J. Pan, E. Sayrol, X. Giro-i-Nieto, K. McGuinness, and N. E. O'Connor, "Shallow and deep convolutional networks for saliency prediction," in *Proceedings of the IEEE conference on computer vision and pattern recognition*, 2016, pp. 598–606.

[29] J. Pan, C. C. Ferrer, K. McGuinness, N. E. O'Connor, J. Torres, E. Sayrol, *et al.*, "Salgan: Visual saliency prediction with generative adversarial networks," *arXiv preprint arXiv:1701.01081*, 2017.

[30] F. Gosselin and P. G. Schyns, "Bubbles: A technique to reveal the use of information in recognition tasks," *Vision research*, vol. 41, no. 17, pp. 2261–2271, 2001.

[31] J. M. Henderson, K. K. McClure, S. Pierce, and G. Schrock, "Object identification without foveal vision: Evidence from an artificial scotoma paradigm," *Perception & Psychophysics*, vol. 59, no. 3, pp. 323–346, 1997.

[32] R. Bednarik and M. Tukiainen, "Validating the restricted focus viewer: A study using eye-movement tracking," *Behavior research methods*, vol. 39, no. 2, pp. 274–282, 2007.

[33] P. Tarasewich, M. Pomplun, S. Fillion, and D. Broberg, "The enhanced restricted focus viewer," *International Journal of Human-Computer Interaction*, vol. 19, no. 1, pp. 35–54, 2005.

[34] J. Deng, J. Krause, and L. Fei-Fei, "Fine-grained crowdsourcing for fine-grained recognition," in *Proceedings of the IEEE Conference on Computer Vision and Pattern Recognition*, IEEE, 2013, pp. 580–587.

[35] L. C. L. Silveira and V. H. Perry, "The topography of magnocellular projecting ganglion cells (M-ganglion cells) in the primate retina," *Neuroscience*, vol. 40, no. 1, pp. 217–237, 1991, ISSN: 03064522. DOI: 10.1016/0306-4522(91)90186-R.

[36] L. Chatriot, *Nedb*, https://github.com/louischatriot/nedb, 2018. (visited on 10/25/2020).

[37] E. M. Hoffman, S. Traversaro, A. Rocchi, M. Ferrati, A. Settimi, F. Romano, *et al.*, "Yarp based plugins for gazebo simulator," in *International Workshop on Modelling and Simulation for Autonomous Systems*, Springer, 2014, pp. 333–346.

[38] A. Pryke, S. Mostaghim, and A. Nazemi, "Heatmap visualization of population based multi objective algorithms," in *International Conference on Evolutionary Multi-Criterion Optimization*, Springer, 2007, pp. 361–375.

[39] M. Waskom, *Nedb*, https://github.com/mwaskom/seaborn, 2020. (visited on 10/25/2020).

[40] L. E. Sibert and R. J. K. Jacob, "Evaluation of eye gaze interaction," in *Proceedings of the SIGCHI Conference on Human Factors in Computing Systems*, ser. CHI '00, The Hague, The Netherlands: Association for Computing Machinery, 2000, pp. 281–288, ISBN: 1581132166. DOI: 10.1145/332040.332445.

[41] W. Wang, J. Shen, F. Guo, M.-M. Cheng, and A. Borji, "Revisiting video saliency: A large-scale benchmark and a new model," in *Proceedings of the IEEE Conference on Computer Vision and Pattern Recognition*, IEEE, 2018, pp. 4894–4903.

[42] L.-C. Chen, G. Papandreou, I. Kokkinos, K. Murphy, and A. L. Yuille, "Deeplab: Semantic image segmentation with deep convolutional nets, atrous convolution, and fully connected crfs," *IEEE Transactions on Pattern Analysis and Machine Intelligence*, vol. 40, no. 4, pp. 834–848, 2017.

[43] T. Zhu and D. Oved, *BodyPix - Person Segmentation in the Browser*, https://github.com/tensorflow/tfjs-models/tree/master/body-pix, 2020. (visited on 10/25/2020).

[44] A. Garcia-Garcia, S. Orts-Escolano, S. Oprea, V. Villena-Martinez, P. Martinez-Gonzalez, and J. Garcia-Rodriguez, "A survey on deep learning techniques for image and video semantic segmentation," *Applied Soft Computing*, vol. 70, pp. 41–65, 2018.

[45] Y. Li, J. Shi, and D. Lin, "Low-latency video semantic segmentation," in *Proceedings of the IEEE Conference on Computer Vision and Pattern Recognition*, IEEE, 2018, pp. 5997–6005.

[46] X. Li, A. Çöltekin, and M.-J. Kraak, "Visual exploration of eye movement data using the space-time-cube," in *International Conference on Geographic Information Science*, Springer, 2010, pp. 295–309.

[47] K. Kurzhals and D. Weiskopf, "Space-time visual analytics of eye-tracking data for dynamic stimuli," *IEEE Transactions on Visualization and Computer Graphics*, vol. 19, no. 12, pp. 2129–2138, 2013.

[48] K. Kurzhals, F. Heimerl, and D. Weiskopf, "Iseecube: Visual analysis of gaze data for video," in *Proceedings of the Symposium on Eye Tracking Research and Applications*, ser. ETRA '14, Safety Harbor, Florida: Association for Computing Machinery, 2014, pp. 43–50. DOI: 10.1145/2578153.2578158.

A Dashboard for System Trustworthiness: Usability Evaluation and Improvements

Diego Camargo, Felipe Nunes Gaia, Tania Basso, Regina Moraes
University of Campinas - UNICAMP
Campinas, Brazil
email:{kmargod, felipegaia.comp}@gmail.com, {tbasso@cotil, regina@ft}.unicamp.br

Abstract—**Dashboards are used to organize and display important information in a way that must be well-arranged, understandable and easy to read. Thus, the success of the dashboard depends on its usability. In this paper, we present the design and usability evaluation of a dashboard developed for the visualization of system trustworthiness properties, the relationship among them and their relevance in the composition of a trustworthiness score over usage time. The evaluation was performed to understand and support the usability regarding human perception in its operation. Security and Information Technology (IT) specialists feedback was sought throughout the process and was obtained from a usability testing and a questionnaire for user interaction satisfaction. Results revealed usability concerns regarding design and content, which led to improvements that were implemented in the dashboard.**

Keywords—Dashboard; Trustworthiness; User experience; Usability.

I. INTRODUCTION

A dashboard is a tool used for information management and business intelligence. Data dashboards organize, store, and display important information from multiple data sources into one, easy-to-access place.

If a dashboard is properly designed, it can help to understand the semantics of visualized information. Then, data can be easily transformed by a user to information and knowledge used for specifying tasks. On the contrary, improper design of a dashboard can lead to difficulties in its use, incomprehension of visualized data and unsuitable tasks specifications. Consequently, users avoid or quit using the dashboard [1].

In this work, we present a dashboard for trustworthiness assessment and a usability evaluation on it. The dashboard presents a trustworthiness score of a cloud application, as well as the scores of intermediate trustworthiness properties (e.g., security, privacy, dependability, isolation, scalability, among others). It allows users to interact with the monitoring and assessment of these properties and to input or modify the configuration values (e.g., weights, thresholds) to improve their scores. The dashboard was developed in the context of the ATMOSPHERE (Adaptive, Trustworthy, Manageable, Orchestrated, Secure, Privacy-assuring Hybrid, Ecosystem for Resilient Cloud Computing) project [2], a collaborative project between Europe and Brazil, whose main objective is to provide a solution for assessing the trustworthiness of cloud applications that handle large volumes of data.

The usability evaluation is an extension of a previous work [3]. We conducted a usability assessment of the dashboard with specialists through usability testing and satisfaction questionnaires in two rounds. After each round of usability testing, we revised and improved the dashboard in response to usability weakness findings before the next round of testing, until the majority of participants expressed high satisfaction. Even so, other improvements have been made to address minor usability concerns.

This paper is organized in six sections. After the first, the Introduction, Section 2 presents Background that is mandatory to understand the paper, including the dashboard importance. Related Work is presented in Section 3 and Section 4 presents the Usability Evaluation of the dashboard. Section 5 presents some Discussions and the Improvements that were performed according to the evaluation process. Conclusions and Future Works follow in Section 6.

II. BACKGROUND AND RELATED WORK

This section addresses, briefly, the issues that underpin this work. It discusses the need of dashboards, as well as describes the trustworthiness dashboard used in this study and usability tests.

A. The need of dashboards

Nowadays, large volumes of information are generated by several devices connected to the Internet. Companies and even governmental organizations are interested in holding these data because it is a source of very important information that can, for example, affect the operational efficiency of that organization, increase profits, identify customers profiles, and cut unnecessary expenditures that waste the budget. In this scenario, data mining has received a lot of attention due to its strong ability of extracting meaningful information from data.

Besides mining the data, it is necessary to present the process results to users and analysts. One of the tools used for this purposes is a dashboard. It helps to summarize data obtained by the data mining process, providing a quick view of results or actual state of the activities.

Dashboards are nowadays widely used for monitoring and analysis of business processes. Numerous companies such as IBM [4], SAP [5], Tableau Software [6], to name a few well-known vendors, offer complete Business Intelligence (BI) or information visualization solutions. Nevertheless, these

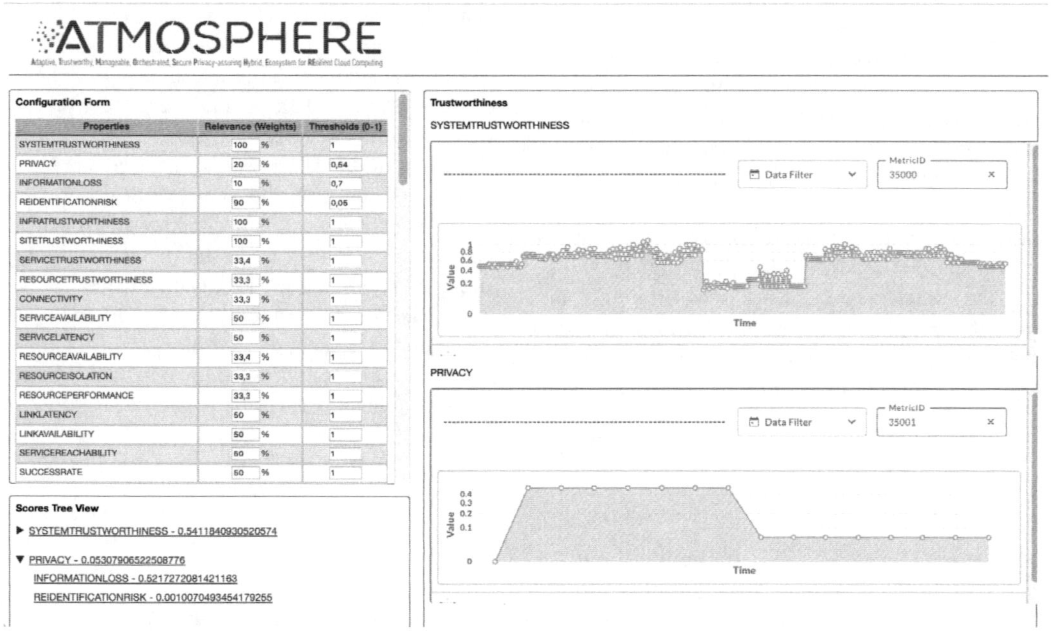

Figure 1. A first release of the trustworthiness dashboard [3]

approaches do not always integrate with specific applications, which requires a specific dashboard development.

B. The dashboard for trustworthiness assessment

As mentioned before, we developed a dashboard to present the scores of trustworthiness properties (and also intermediate scores from attributes composing the properties) for applications in cloud environment. It was developed to show the information provided by a specific solution, which could not be integrated to standards dashboards approaches.

The dashboard is based on quality model [7]. Basically, in this model, the root represents the **trustworthiness score**. The leaves represent a set of quantifiable **attributes** chosen to characterize the system (e.g., memory usage, throughput). When these attributes represent input measures, they must be normalized by applying adequate functions. For that, the definition of **thresholds** is necessary once they specify the maximum and minimum values for the inputs of the leaf-level components of the quality model.

The values for each component are influenced by an adjustable element **weight**, which specifies a preference over one or more characteristics of the system, according to established requirements (e.g., in certain contexts memory usage might be more important than throughput). The final score is computed using the aggregation of the weighted values of the attributes, starting from the leaf-level towards the root attributes, using **operators** that describe the relation between them. A first release of this dashboard was presented in [3]. More details about its requirements can be found in that reference.

It is important to mention that the input measures are provided by the *Trustworthy Data Management Services (TDMS)*. TDMS is a component of the ATMOSPHERE project similar to a database service in cloud systems dealing with mechanisms for data storage, access and management and it also considers trustworthiness properties. The trustworthiness-related information is obtained and stored according to definitions of quality models, including their weights and thresholds. More details of quality TDMS can be found in [8].

The dashboard for trustworthiness assessment was implemented using the Metabase tool [9] because it is open source and can be used for deployment on any system that is running Docker. As the dashboard requires user interaction and Metabase is not able to update information into the database, we developed a dynamic form that obtains the quality model configuration data defined by the users and saves (or updates) them in the database through REST services.

Figure 1 shows the first release of the trustworthiness dashboard. In the upper left corner, the *Configuration Form* allows users to select the attributes and configure weights, thresholds and periodicity of data collection. In the bottom left corner, the *Scores Tree View* allows the navigation through the scores. This navigation (drill down) is provided by a recursive algorithm implementation.

The calculation of the scores is made by the properties and the dashboard presents the historical scores according to the time configuration. The user evaluates the scores through the respective charts and can change the configuration (weights and thresholds) if necessary to better represent the trustworthiness composition.

C. *Quality Models*

Data privacy is one of the properties that makes up a trustworthiness system. Figure 2 illustrates the privacy quality model used in this work. Two main attributes are considered to compose data privacy: the re-identification risk and the information loss. Re-identification risk is the probability of discovering an individual by matching anonymized data with publicly available information. Information loss is the amount of information that can be obtained about the original values of variables in the input dataset. Both measurements are obtained through the use of anonymization techniques tools. More details about the privacy quality model and its attributes (thresholds, weights, normalization values) can be found in the work of Basso et al. [10].

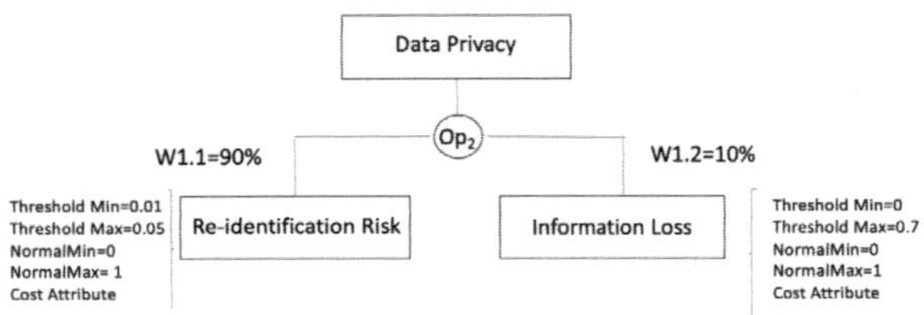

Figure 2. Privacy Quality Model Instance [10]

Figure 3 illustrates the main attributes of the other quality model used in this work. The System Trustworthiness Quality Model defines all the attributes involved in the trustworthiness score of a cloud-based application. Mainly, it is composed of the following (sub) quality models:

- Infra Trustworthiness- responsible to assess the trustworthiness of the cloud infrastructure (hardware and software resources available);
- Data Management Trustworthiness - where the trustworthiness of storage data is described;
- TDPS (Trustworthy Data Processing Services) - responsible to define the attributes of the services that are running to provide the expected results to the users.

The (sub) quality models are composed using a neutrality operator aiming at obtaining the score of trustworthiness of the system under analysis. Each one, per se, is a complex quality model composed of several attributes and sub-attributes that, for sake of simplicity, we did not represent in Figure 3. However, we briefly describe these attributes below.

The Infra Trustworthiness Quality Model is composed of the Site and the Virtual infrastructure trustworthiness. The Site is composed of Services, Resources and Connectivity and several sub-attributes, i.e., Service Availability, Service Latency, Resource Availability, Resource Performance, Resource Isolation, Link Latency and Link Availability. Some of them have their scores assessed at runtime (for example, Service Availability) and others as static metrics (for example, Resource Isolation).

Virtual Infra Trustworthiness is related to the cloud virtualisation services and resources and it is composed of used and free Central Processing Unit (CPU) and Memory, scalability capacity and CPU Isolation.

Data Management Trustworthiness is defined to assess the score related to data storage and recovery. This score is strongly influenced by the engine used and in the context of the ATMOSPHERE project, based on Vallum [11] or in a more common engine (i.e., MySQL). In any case, it has as attributes Performance (Response Time, Throughput and Bandwidth), Security (Attestation and Confidentiality), Fault Tolerance (Replication) and Data Privacy.

The TDPS is related to services provided by the application. In this context, each service has its own score and the TDPS general score is a composition of all the services executed by the user application. The attributes considered in this case are Fairness, Transparency, Stability and Data Privacy.

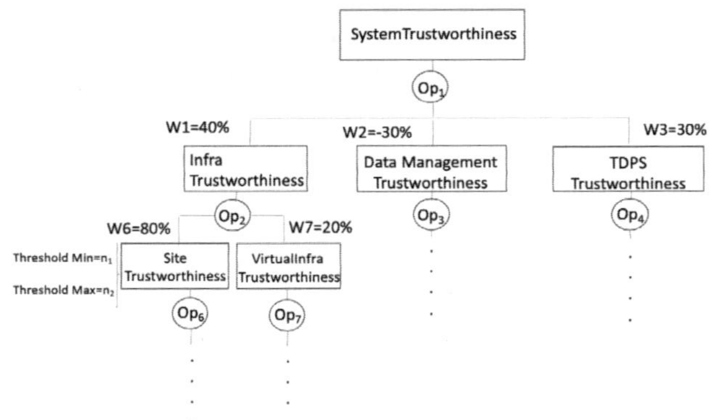

Figure 3. System Trustworthiness Quality Model Instance

Both these quality models (Privacy and System Trustworthiness) are displayed in the tree structure of the dashboard (see Figure 1 - lower left corner). An expanded view of the tree with the attributes and sub-attributes can be seen in Figure 5.

D. *Usability Testing*

As the dashboard is a data visualization tool, it must provide easy use and understanding of information semantics. Otherwise, the produced visualizations can be misguiding and, as a consequence, may lead to wrong conclusions. In addition, if users have difficulties in using the dashboard they can avoid or never use it. Thus, usability is an important issue that must be addressed while developing this tool.

The concept of usability is related to software quality, in terms of ease of use and learning. Brazilian Norm (NBR) 9241-11 [12] defines usability as a measure in which a product (software and hardware) can be used by specific users, in a specific context of use, to achieve specific objectives with effectiveness, efficiency and satisfaction. Nielsen [13] defines usability as a set of factors that qualify the user's interaction with the software (e.g., user control, easy to recall, efficiency, among others). These factors are related to the ease of use and learning to use the system.

According to Barnum [14], usability testing is *the activity that focuses on observing users working with a product, performing tasks that are real and meaningful for them.* There are two types of methods that can be used to assess the usability of interfaces: inspection (or analytical) methods and empirical methods. Inspection methods are those in which one or more evaluators examine the interface, judging it for usability problems, without the need to verify the interaction of real users with the system (for example, evaluation based on heuristics). Empirical methods, on the other hand, are those in which real users participate, interacting with the system being evaluated, while evaluators perform the analysis of such interaction and the problems found [15].

A *Questionnaire* is a widely used technique designed for the assessment of perceived usability, used as support for inspection and empirical methods mentioned above. Typically, a questionnaire has a specific set of questions presented in a specified order using a specified format with specific rules for producing scores based on the answers of respondents [16].

It is important to mention that there are some other techniques for usability testing, such as *heuristic evaluation, cognitive walkthroughs, and think aloud.* These techniques are out of the scope of this work, but they should be addressed in future work.

E. Related Work

Usability testing techniques have been applied to evaluate dashboards in the most diverse contexts. For example, Chrisna et. al [17] conducted a study that included user observations, heuristic assessment and a survey among users for a Business Intelligence (BI) application. Magdalena et al. [1] defined a strategy, based on user testing and heuristic evaluation, to provide improvements and, consequently, increase the use of the BI dashboard in their company (one of the biggest airlines in Indonesia). Lavalle et al. [18] presented an interactive dashboard to allow non-expert users to be guided towards specific data visualizations regarding tax collection. They used a questionnaire to evaluate the dashboard usability. Read [19] used the think aloud technique to develop a dashboard. Based on user behavior and comments about the system that were noted by the research team, the evaluation helped to understand the usability of the (navigational) menu layout for the design of the system.

It is obvious that each dashboard is designed and constructed according to the specific business needs from the company or organization, including data and users profiles, which requires respective specific usability evaluations. To the best of our knowledge, there is no dashboard for trustworthiness evaluation in cloud computing applications, neither a study regarding dashboard usability in this context. This work aims to help fill this gap.

III. USABILITY EVALUATION

In order to evaluate and improve the trustworthiness dashboard, we performed two sprints of evaluation. In the first sprint, a preliminary (pilot) test was performed with three specialists on security and privacy. Based on this evaluation, some improvements were implemented in the dashboard interface to prepare a more complete validation with a larger number of users. In the second sprint, 22 IT specialists, including professionals involved in the ATMOSPHERE project, evaluated the dashboard interface. It is important to mention that, before this whole process, the validation methodology was designed and submitted to the Research Ethics Committee (*Plataforma Brasil*) for the necessary authorization.

The validation methodology is composed of (i) a user testing, which specifies a dashboard usage scenario so that users exercise the scenario and answer some essay questions; (ii) two multiple choice questionnaires. We decided to use both these evaluation techniques because they are effective for reaching a wide audience, since the professionals interviewed are from different countries. Also, their cost is low and they are quite time-saving.

Regarding the user testing, a document explaining how the dashboard works was sent to the users. It describes the quality models (the dashboard uses their structure to the hierarchical representation of scores) and defines a scenario for users to interact, in a controlled manner, with the dashboard. The goal is that, after exercising the dashboard, the users answer some questions about the experience. To perform these tests, we made available two quality models (privacy and infrastructure) and respective component attributes. These quality models have already been validated through case studies in the ATMOSPHERE project.

The scenario for exercising the dashboard suggests at least the following actions: (i) change the weight of Information Loss attribute to 0.2 (20%) and Reidentification Risk to 0.8 (80%); (ii) See and write down the score of the Link Latency attribute; (iii) See and write down the score of the Service Trustworthiness attribute. Then, the users reported their impressions about the dashboard through questions such as: (i) "Did you have any problem when using this dashboard? If so, which ones?" (ii) "Do you suggest any change to improve this dashboard? If so, which ones?" (iii) "Would you use that dashboard again? Why?"

Regarding the two multiple choice questionnaire, the first one is about the user profile. It has six questions to mainly understand the user's experience as IT (Information Technology) professionals, as well as their experience in Human-Computer Interaction (HCI) domain. The second questionnaire is focused on the interface usability, composed of ten questions to evaluate the strengths and weaknesses of the dashboard interface. These questions were based on Nielsen's heuristics (usability) [20] and heuristics for information visualization [21]. Each question is a statement with a rating on a four or five-point scale of "Strongly Disagree" to "Strongly Agree" or "Very Easy" to "Very Difficult" and the answers were scored as a Likert scale on strength of agreement. Some questions statements from the second questionnaire are: (i) "the use of the dashboard configuration form for setting the parameters is simple." (ii)

"The symbols used in the tree structure make the hierarchy of attributes clear". Tables I and II present the questions and respective answers for the four and five-point scale questions, respectively.

IV. Discussions and Improvements

As mentioned before, we performed two sprints of evaluation. In the first sprint, three specialists in information security and privacy were selected. We selected these professionals because they are familiar to trustworthiness and the quality models used in the experiments (see Section II-C). Their age, in average, is 40 years; 100% work in IT more than three years; 33% never worked before in the HCI domain and 67% never worked directly but frequently use material of this domain; 33% work sometimes with system's Front-End and system's requirements while 67% work with these matters frequently; 67% work with system's testing sometimes while 33% use to work with systems testing frequently.

Based on the questionnaire results, all the evaluators agree that the dashboard interface is nice, presents adequate volume, intuitive configuration form and results are ease to understand through the charts. On the other hand, based on the user testing, i.e., through the exercise of the predefined scenario, all evaluators had some problems to navigate in the Quality Model tree structure. One of them was really not able to realize how to navigate, i.e., to open the structure and see the scores. So, navigation seems to be the most significant interface problem. One of them commented that "The tree did not appear on her/his screen, making it difficult for him/her to find the tree". A second comment is "The need to click the arrow to open the tree is not intuitive". Both comments complain about the navigation through the tree, pointing the need for improvements in that specific part of the dashboard. Some improvements were implemented trying to make the tree navigation more intuitive before continuing with a more wide evaluation (the second sprint).

In the second sprint, 25 IT professionals acted as evaluators. It includes professionals working in IT companies (32%), research (36%), professors (4%) and undergraduate IT students (28%). Their age, in average, is 32 years; 68% work in IT more than three years; 23% have already worked in the HCI domain; 68% work with system's Front-End and 73% work with system's requirements while 64% work with these matters frequently.

Based on questionnaires results, the majority of the evaluators (approximately 73%) agree that the dashboard interface is nice, presents adequate volume of data (approximately 55%), intuitive configuration form (50%) and results are ease to understand through the charts (64%). However, similarly to the sprint 1, the evaluators still had some problems to navigate in the Quality Model tree structure.

Although a minority (approximately 30%) of the respondents stated that the tree structure navigation is difficult and the symbols used in this structure are not intuitive, some comments and suggestions were made as a result of the user testing. Three evaluators suggested that the submit button could be fixed in the display field, avoiding the scroll, which would improve the usability. At least four evaluators commented about the difficulty on navigating through the tree and suggested improving the symbols to make them more intuitive. Two of them mentioned that the quality model should be clearer in the tree structure.

The majority of the comments were about the large volume of data displayed on the dashboard, which at least 10 evaluators found excessive. They suggested to improve the charts reducing (i.e., grouping) information and removing the data markers. Also, a considerable number of evaluators commented about the difficulty in understanding the meaning of the information displayed on the dashboard. Although the evaluators are familiar with IT context and technologies, the information about trustworthiness is quite specific. Even though we sent a document explaining how the dashboard works, at least 9 respondents stated that they needed a lot of effort to understand the properties, weights and thresholds. Two of them suggested the use of chart legends.

A summary of the results from the two sprints is presented in Tables I to IV.

Table I shows the questionnaire statements with a rating on a four-point scale. The statements refer to the evaluation of the interface and the volume of data presented in the dashboard. About 76% of the evaluators agree/strongly agree that the dashboard has a friendly interface and 60% agree/strongly agree that the volume of data is adequate. However, we considered that 40% of disagree/strongly disagree answers is a considerable percentage to indicate that improvements regarding the volume of data must be done.

Table II shows the statements with a rating on a five-point scale, also from the questionnaire. The statements refer mostly to navigation through the dashboard, the tree structure and the presentation of the charts. 48% of the respondents found that navigation through the dashboard was easy/very easy, while 24% found it difficult and 28% found that the level of difficulty is medium. Regarding the configuration form, 52% found that it was easy/very easy to use, while 28% found that it is difficult/very difficult to use and 20% classified the level of difficulty as medium.

When asked for the navigation in the tree structure, 52% found it easy/very easy, 32% found it difficult/very difficult and 16% found the level of difficulty as medium. However, about the symbols used, 32% classified them as easy/very easy to use, the same percentage for medium classification. And the majority of the evaluators (36%) found it difficult/very difficulty to use. This is a strong indication that these symbols must be improved.

Finally, regarding the charts evaluation, 56% found them easy/very easy to understand, while 32% found them difficult/very difficult. 12% found that the level of understanding is medium.

Table III presents the results from the two-point scale questions, which were answered by the evaluators as part of the user testing. In this evaluation, 68% stated that they would use the dashboard again; 44% stated that they

TABLE I
ASSESSMENT RESULTS (FOUR-POINT QUESTIONS)

Statement	Strongly Agree	Agree	Disagree	Strongly Disagree
The dashboard interface is friendly (for example, colors, easy viewing)	16%	60%	16%	8%
The volume of data displayed is adequate (i.e., the dashboard does not have excessive information)	16%	44%	36%	4%

TABLE II
ASSESSMENT RESULTS (FIVE-POINT QUESTIONS)

Statement	Very Easy	Easy	Medium	Difficult	Very Difficult
Navigation through the dashboard was ...	20%	28%	28%	24%	0%
The use of the configuration form for setting the parameters was ...	20%	32%	20%	24%	4%
The navigation in the tree structure to view the scores of the attributes was ...	20%	32%	16%	24%	8%
The symbols used in the tree structure made the hierarchy of attributes.... to use	20%	12%	32%	16%	20%
The results presented in the form of charts based on the history of the scores let the understanding ...	12%	44%	12%	20%	12%

TABLE III
ASSESSMENT RESULTS (USER TESTING TWO-POINT QUESTIONS)

Question	Yes	No
Would you use the dashboard again?	68%	32%
Did you have any problem when using the dashboard?	44%	56%
Do you suggest any change to improve the dashboard?	64%	36%

TABLE IV
ASSESSMENT RESULTS (USER TESTING ESSAY COMMENTS)

Category	Comments (%)
Understanding	37%
Volume of Data	37%
Navigation	44%
Charts	26%

had problems when using the dashboard and we considered this a high percentage and indicates that the problems must be investigated; 64% suggested improvements to the dashboard. We considered most of these suggestions and the improvements are described in the next subsection. Table IV summarizes the problems and suggestions pointed out by the evaluators through essay questions.

We received in total 27 essay comments. We classified them in 4 categories: *Understanding*, which refers to the understanding of the meaning of the information displayed in the dashboard; *Volume of Data*, which refers to the amount of information displayed in the dashboard; *Navigation*, referring to the navigation through the tree structure and the pages of the dashboard; and *Charts*, which refers to the visualization of the charts. As we are dealing with essay comments, some of them were classified in more than one category.

A. Usability improvements for the dashboard

Based on the evaluation, we provided the improvements to the dashboard. Figure 4 shows the latest release.

The first improvement is about the submit button, in the Configuration Form (upper left corner). We removed the scroll and now it is fixed, facilitating its visualization. The scroll is only for the properties. Also, in the Configuration Form, we added a help system where the user can position the mouse over the "?" symbol or the property itself and a popup will open with information and details about that property (see Figure 4, where a popup example is shown with the "The name of trustworthiness metric" message). This would facilitate the use of the dashboard by less expert users.

Regarding the excessive information on chart visualization, first, we removed the data markers, which left the chart cleaner. We also optimized some queries to group information. One example of query optimization is presented in Table V, where it is possible to observe the use of DISTINCT, AVG and GROUP BY clauses, which better organize and reduce the amount of information.

Another improvement for chart visualization is the addition of caption for the x-axis of the chart. In Figure 4, we can observe the dates throughout the metrics (December 1, 2019, December 8, 2019 and December 15, 2019 for System Trustworthiness property and August 1, 2019, September 1, 2019, October 1, 2019, November 1, 2019 and December 1, 2019 for Privacy property). These dates can be configured dynamically by the user, which can specify a period for visualization.

To improve the tree structure navigation, we decided to replace the symbols. It is possible to observe that, in Figure 4, bottom left corner, we used the plus and minus ("+", "-")

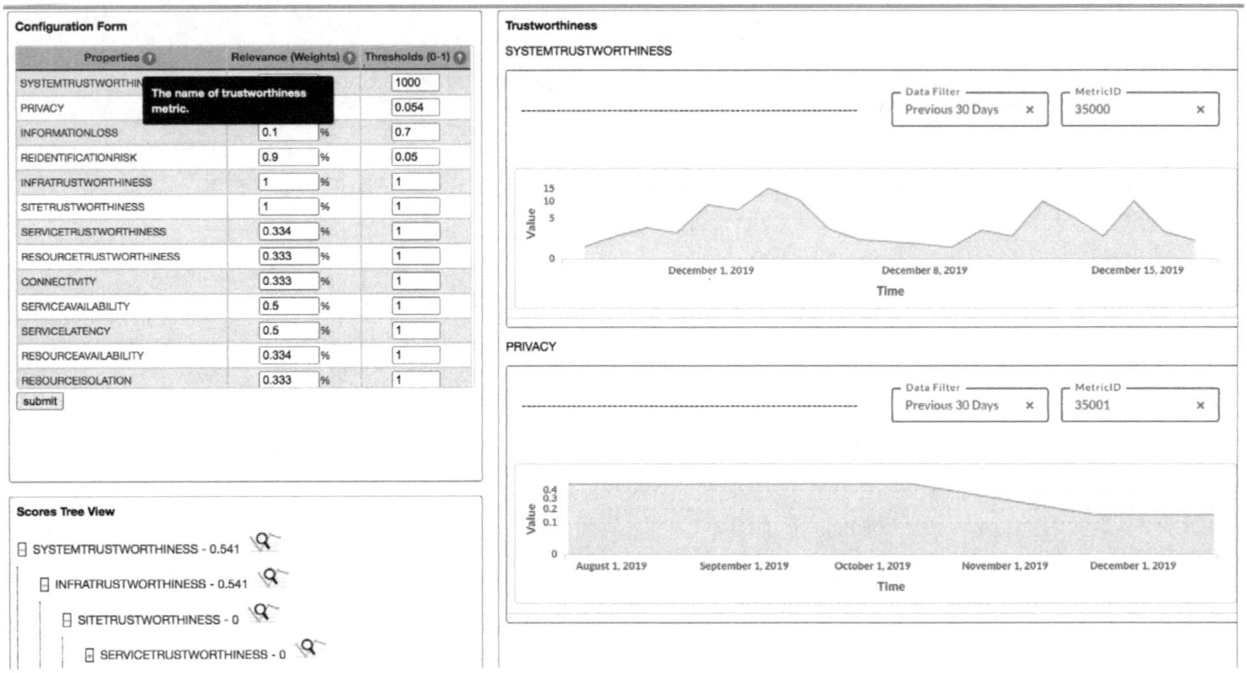

Figure 4. Improved dashboard based on the usability evaluation

TABLE V
EXAMPLE OF QUERY OPTIMIZATION FOR CHART VISUALIZATION IMPROVEMENT

Before	After (optimized)
SELECT 'MetricData'.'metricId' AS 'metricId', 'MetricData'.'valueTime' AS 'valueTime', 'MetricData'.'value' AS 'value' FROM 'MetricData' WHERE 'metricId' IS NOT NULL AND {{filter}} LIMIT 2000	SELECT distinct 'MetricData'.'metricId' AS 'metricId', CAST('MetricData'.'valueTime' as date) AS 'valueTime', AVG(cast('MetricData'.'value' as decimal(10, 2))) AS 'value' FROM 'MetricData' WHERE 'metricId' IS NOT NULL AND {{filter}} GROUP BY 'valueTime', 'metricId' LIMIT 2000

control symbols to expand or collapse the branch, i.e., to show and hide subgroup properties when navigating through the hierarchy. We believe that these are more universal symbols and the users are more familiar with them.

We also introduced a shortcut icon for charts (a magnifying glass with a chart) on the right side of each property in the scores tree view. This allows users to select a specific chart to be visualized while navigating or having a general view of the tree.

Finally, we reduced the number of decimal places in the score in order to make the tree visualization clearer. Figure 5 shows an example of expanded tree, where each property has its own shortcut icon.

B. Impacts on ATMOSPHERE project

It is important to mention that the dashboard and respective usability evaluation provided some improvements in the ATMOSPHERE project regarding the maturity level of some requirements and adaptation scenarios.

The ATMOSPHERE project produced a realtime platform that self-adapts when the score threshold is reached [8] and the dashboard was used as a front-end of it. The use of the dashboard with adequate usability allowed to validate adaptation scenarios in a visual way and, consequently, in a faster way too. For example, when the value of the privacy property is greater than the threshold assigned in the configuration form, the platform can use an adaptation plan that reduces the value of re-identification risk and/or information loss sub-properties and, consequently, the value of privacy too. Using the dashboard, these values are updated automatically in the interface, identifying to user the adaptation. Previously, the validation was performed by scripts and analysis of log files, which required a lot of time.

With respect to the project requirements, they required a experimental evaluation of different interfaces during the development and the evaluation of each one helped to improve the development of the components, as they were better designed and tested. At this point, we can say that the

Figure 5. Expanded tree and shortcuts to the respective properties charts

dashboard and the usability evaluation process performed in this work helped the development of the project, accelerating the validation and integration of components.

V. Conclusions and Future Work

This work presented a usability evaluation of a dashboard for assessing the trustworthiness of cloud applications that handle large volume of data. We applied questionnaires and usability tests to perform this evaluation.

The results and the improvements highlighted the importance of mixed-methods evaluation of usability as a part of the design of the dashboard. The different profiles of users (but all of them active in the IT universe) offered an efficient way to assess the needs of users, generate ideas and develop a more viable product for use. This could be done iteratively, through two sprints. When we talk about product viability, it is worth mentioning that the usability evaluation process can help improve the system requirements identification and maturity, as well as help define testing scenarios.

Since the improvements required by the respondents users did not demand huge changes and significant software development skills, we can state that, for the experiments in this work, the use of user-centered evaluation to mitigate potential usability challenges can easily help increasing user satisfaction and adoption of the dashboard. However, it is important to mention that the dashboard is in the early stage of its development. For late stages, it is recommended the use of other complementary techniques because the end stages of dashboard development can mask potential functional problems that will prevent proper usage and lead to misinterpretation of results.

So, as future work we intend to identify and apply different usability evaluation techniques together with usability testing to identify specific usability issues and room for improvement.

Acknowledgment

This work has been partially supported by the projects ATMOSPHERE (https://www.atmosphere-eubrazil.eu/ - Horizon 2020 No 777154 - MCTIC/RNP) and ADVANCE (http://advance-rise.eu/ - Horizon 2020-MSCA-RISE No 2018-823788).

References

[1] R. Magdalena, Y. Ruldeviyani, D. I. Sensuse, and C. Bernando, "Methods to enhance the utilization of business intelligence dashboard by integration of evaluation and user testing," in *2019 3rd International Conference on Informatics and Computational Sciences (ICICoS)*. IEEE, 2019, pp. 1–6.

[2] ATMOSPHERE, "Adaptive, trustworthy, manageable, orchestrated, secure, privacy-assuring hybrid, ecosystem for resilient cloud computing," 2018, URL: https://www.atmosphere-eubrazil.eu/ [accessed October, 2020].

[3] D. Camargo, F. N. Gaia, T. Basso, and R. L. Moraes, "A dashboard for system trustworthiness properties evaluation," in *Anais do XXI Workshop de Testes e Tolerância a Falhas [Testing and Fault Tolerance Workshop]*. SBC, 2020, pp. 1–14.

[4] IBM, "Accelerate your journey to ai with a prescriptive approach," 2020, URL: https://www.ibm.com/br-pt/analytics [accessed October, 2020].

[5] SAP, "Introducing sap customer data platform," 2020, URL: https://www.sap.com/index.html [accessed October, 2020].

[6] Tableau, "Get a full picture of your business, inside and out," 2020, URL: https://www.tableau.com/ [accessed October, 2020].

[7] ISO, "International organization for standardization. systems and software engineering — systems and software quality requirements and evaluation (square) — guide to square," 2014, URL: https://www.iso.org/standard/64764.html [accessed October, 2020].

[8] T. Basso, H. Silva, L. Montecchi, B. B. N. de França, and R. Moraes, "Towards trustworthy cloud service selection: monitoring and assessing data privacy," in *XX Workshop de Testes e Tolerância a Falhas (WTF 2019)[Testing and Fault Tolerance Workshop]*, Gramado, RS, Brazil, 2019, pp. 7–20.

[9] Metabase, "Have questions about your data? metabase has answers," 2020, URL: https://metabase.com [accessed October, 2020].

[10] T. Basso, H. Silva, and R. Moraes, "On the use of quality models to characterize trustworthiness properties," in *International Workshop on Software Engineering for Resilient Systems*. Springer, 2019, pp. 147–155.

[11] Vallum Software, "A nextgen network monitoring & management solution without the complexity and cost," 2020, URL: https://vallumsoftware.com [accessed October, 2020].

[12] ABNT - Brazilian Association of Technical Standards, "Ergonomic requirements for office work with visual display terminals (vdts) part 11:guidance on usability (abnt nbr iso 9241-11:2011)," 2011, URL: https://www.abntcatalogo.com.br/norma.aspx?ID=86090 [accessed October, 2020].

[13] J. Nielsen, *Usability engineering*. Morgan Kaufmann, 1994.

[14] C. M. Barnum, *Usability testing essentials: ready, set... test!* Morgan Kaufmann, 2020.

[15] J. Nielsen, "Usability inspection methods," in *Conference companion on Human factors in computing systems*, 1994, pp. 413–414.

[16] J. Sauro and J. R. Lewis, "Standardized usability questionnaires," in *Quantifying the user experience*, vol. 8. Morgan Kaufmann, 2012, pp. 198–212.

[17] C. Jooste, J. Van Biljon, and J. Mentz, "Usability evaluation for business intelligence applications: A user support perspective," in *South African Computer Journal*, vol. 53, no. Special issue 1. South African Computer Society (SAICSIT), 2014, pp. 32–44.

[18] A. Lavalle, A. Maté, J. Trujillo, and S. Rizzi, "Visualization requirements for business intelligence analytics: A goal-based, iterative framework," in *2019 IEEE 27th International Requirements Engineering Conference (RE)*. IEEE, 2019, pp. 109–119.

[19] A. Read, A. Tarrell, and A. Fruhling, "Exploring user preference for the dashboard menu design," in *2009 42nd Hawaii International Conference on System Sciences*. IEEE, 2009, pp. 1–10.

[20] J. Nielsen and R. L. Mack, *Usability Inspection Methods*. John Wiley & Sons, Inc., 1994.

[21] T. Zuk, L. Schlesier, P. Neumann, M. S. Hancock, and S. Carpendale, "Heuristics for information visualization evaluation," in *the 2006 AVI workshop on BEyond time and errors: novel evaluation methods for information visualization*, 2006, pp. 55–60.

Potentials and Challenges of Using Mixed Reality in Mining Education

A Europe-Wide Interview Study

Lea M. Daling, Christopher Eck, Anas Abdelrazeq, and Frank Hees
Chair of Information Management in Mechanical Engineering (IMA)
RWTH Aachen University
Aachen, Germany
email: {lea.daling, christopher.eck, anas.abdelrazeq, frank.hees}@ima-ifu.rwth-aachen.de

Abstract—**Mining engineering and its educational sector are continuously affected by different transformations. In this regard, the number of students is constantly declining. Universities and educational institutions are struggling for financial resources to maintain the attractiveness of mining education. In particular, real-life experience gained through excursions is indispensable for the success of mining education, but also expensive to offer. A possible solution to meet these challenges is the usage of Mixed Reality based tools in teaching. This technology allows otherwise hardly accessible or dangerous scenarios to be experienced directly in the classroom. This paper presents the results of a European-wide interview study, in which the potential, chances and risks of the technology for the field of mining education are questioned. From the results, first indications for the use of Mixed Reality tools and further demands for research are derived.**

Keywords-Mixed Reality; mining education; digital teaching; interview study; MiReBooks project.

I. INTRODUCTION

In the recent past, there have been major changes in the industry, which had a significant impact on the mining sector [1]. In the context of declining the economic importance of mining in many countries, unprofitable mining operations are closed down and state-controlled mining operations are increasingly being privatized. Moreover, the declining social acceptance of the raw materials industries deteriorates the public image of the mining industry, as it is seen as "a dangerous and environmentally damaging low technology industry"[1].

Despite the steadily increasing demand in the sand, gravel and quarry industry and the growth in minerals production, mining is becoming less and less attractive for students [2]. Although the mining sector continues to offer attractive job prospects, study numbers continue to decline. In addition, it is evident that the main focus of public investment is on growing and economically promising courses of study, which is why mining departments are suffering from severe financial cutbacks [1].

To prevent further decline and make mining engineering more attractive, industry and research have to cooperate closely and develop concrete measures [2]. Shields and colleagues emphasize, that especially in the education of mining engineers, we have to face the challenges of a new world in order to meet both present and unforeseen challenges [3]. Subsequently, engineering education has to enable new and broader perspectives "by incorporating the complexities of environmental, economic and social realities along with systems engineering, enabling technologies and physical constraints" [3]-[5]. In addition, knowledge should be provided in a holistic and transdisciplinary manner, and thus also transnationally [6].

This holistic knowledge also includes the acquisition of interdisciplinary skills beyond technical knowledge [7]. Allenby states in 2011: "while most engineers are technically competent, they lack communications ability and they do not understand the context within which they are expected to perform professionally" [8]. Moreover, mining engineering graduates often have little understanding of how to transfer their theoretical knowledge into practice [9].

Taking these requirements into consideration, the MiReBooks (Mixed Reality Books) project was launched in 2018 [10]. MiReBooks is a project funded by the European Institute of Innovation & Technology (EIT) Raw Materials that consists of a pan-European consortium with over 14 partners. The project addresses the current problems in the field of mining education. In particular, the focus is on increasing the attractiveness of mining engineering as a field of study. To this end, measures to increase the quality of studies are being developed. Within the project, the transfer of theoretical knowledge into practice is of particular importance. In a situation in which mines are hardly accessible and excursions are very expensive and time-consuming, teaching institutions have to find new methods to facilitate the transfer of knowledge. Thus, MiReBooks produces a series of Virtual Reality (VR) and Augmented Reality (AR) based interactive mining handbooks as a new digital standard for higher mining education across Europe. The project aims to change the way students are taught by empowering teachers to engage their students more effectively and provide them with a wider repertoire of content and better understanding.

This paper gives an overview of the potentials and threats of using Mixed Reality (MR) based technologies in mining education. For this purpose, an interview study with 39 participants (teachers and students) was conducted to assess the need, possible application scenarios and the opportunities and risks of MR in teaching. Section 2 presents the current state of MR tools in education. In Section 3, the method and framework of the interview study is presented. The results are presented in Section 4. Subsequently, a discussion of the main findings and an outlook can be found in Section 5.

II. Mixed Reality in Education

After more than twenty-five years of educational research, MR tools are increasingly finding their way into education [11]. Describing a continuum between reality and virtuality, MR enables to merge physical and digital worlds [12]. Thus, technologies such as AR or VR can be subsumed under the framework of MR. Within the context of teaching, AR augments the real world by placing virtual content (such as 3D models) into the field of view or provides further digitally displayed information (e.g., through annotations) to a real setting [13]. VR enables the user to experience the feeling of presence in a fully modelled, virtual environment [12].

According to Dede and colleagues, these media offer new "opportunities for enhancing both motivation and learning across a range of subject areas, student developmental levels, and educational settings" [11]. In addition, they state that MR experiences enable situated learning, which is widely acknowledged as a powerful didactic concept [14]. Thus, MR offers to experience and learn how to deal with problems or situations that are similar to the real world. Especially in mining education, students could experience important procedures and processes that are usually hardly accessible in the real world. Other promising fields of application are, for instance, in the education of engineers [15] and medical specialists [16].

By providing these opportunities, MR is able to further address the crucial factor of knowledge transfer [17][18]. Students can build a strong connection between their theoretical knowledge and a practical task or workflow. Thus, a replication of real processes in simulated environments can support the training of relevant behavior for performance in work or personal life [15]-[19]. In addition to that, collaborative forms of MR can foster communication and problem-solving skills by enforcing interaction with other students to jointly perform a task [20]. This can even be offered time and place independent. As a result, MR is expected to be able to address current challenges in mining education, such as:

1. offering experiences in otherwise hardly accessible settings [11][21],
2. enhancing motivation and learning and thus making mining more attractive for students [11][14][21],
3. fostering knowledge transfer and enhancing the development of professional skills [17][18],
4. allowing students to control their learning processes more actively [22],
5. and enabling a lasting learning-effect through game-based formats and the possibility of immediate feedback for actions and decisions [23].

The positive effects of MR in education were also confirmed by lecturers, who considered the use of the technology to be helpful [24].

However, there is still little knowledge on how and when to use these media in mining courses [10]. Questions relating to which applications are particularly suitable to be presented in MR or which positive and negative effects can be expected from their use remain unclear.

Based on twelve MR-based test lectures at different partner universities of the MiReBooks project (four on open pit bench blasting, three on hard rock underground drift development, two on hauling in mining, and another three on continuous surface mining), a broad qualitative interview study was conducted. Within these lectures, different sets of hardware components were presented (standalone and computer-connected VR headsets; such as HTC Vive (virtual reality headset developed by HTC and Valve), Oculus Go and Oculus Quest, AR-enabled smartphones and a local-network-based solution for connecting different VR headsets). During the test lectures, classical teaching materials were used (presentation slides, whiteboards, blackboard) and combined with small breakout sessions to provide MR-based experiences. Within the interview study, we addressed teachers and students with or without experiences with MR. Thus, we assessed general requirements in mining courses and aimed to find out which strengths and threats are associated with using MR based technologies in mining education.

III. Method

A. Study Design

Within the interviews, different perspectives of both teachers and students were considered. Furthermore, the aim was to interview not only those who already had experience with MR in the course of the test lectures. The majority of students and teachers in the field of mining have no previous experience with MR. Therefore, this target group was also considered in the present study. In summary, we interviewed four different target groups. We aimed at collecting feedback from experienced teachers, who conducted the test lectures, as well as inexperienced teachers, who did not use MR technologies in any lecture before. Furthermore, experienced students who took part in the test lectures, as well as inexperienced students were interviewed.

The experienced group of teachers and students, who conducted or took part in a MR-based test lecture, were asked in particular about their experiences with MR. The interviews with the experienced teachers were especially focused on their reflection of the test lecture, with special emphasis on the necessary preparation and optimal teaching conditions. The questions to experienced students served primarily to obtain feedback on how they perceive the use of MR in comparison to classical lectures. Furthermore, they were asked about perceived advantages, disadvantages and possible difficulties using MR. Inexperienced teachers were asked which media they currently use, whether they would be interested in using MR and what would be necessary to enable them to give their own lectures with such technologies. Inexperienced students were asked about their experiences with current teaching methods. Subsequently, they were asked whether it is possible to provide more realistic insights in mining processes through the use of MR. Additionally, we asked about potential meaningful application areas and student's general expectations with regard to benefits or threats using MR. All interview guidelines included questions on the effective communication of learning content, areas of application and opinions on problems.

The interview guidelines and number of questions varied between experienced teachers (10 questions), inexperienced teachers (12 questions), experienced students (8 questions) and inexperienced students (11 questions). The interviews were conducted either face to face or in written form. The average duration of an interview lasted between 15 to 30 minutes, where the written answers were often rather brief. The interviews were then anonymized and transcribed in order to analyze the entire data in a qualitative content analysis using software.

B. *Participants*

In total, 39 participants took part in the study. Overall, three experienced and three inexperienced teachers, as well as 21 experienced and twelve inexperienced students from five different universities all over Europe (Germany, Austria, Estonia, and Sweden) were interviewed for the study. The participants were recruited via project partners and posters of the project. Participation in the interviews was voluntary. Participation in test lectures was also voluntary. All students were from different semesters and study courses. The requirement for students to participate in the interviews was that they were currently enrolled in a mining-related subject. The teachers should also have experience in mining-related teaching.

C. *Qualitative content analysis*

The purpose of content analysis is to analyze communication that has been recorded for example in texts, images or other symbolic material. For this, a systematic, rule-guided and theory-based approach is used, which allows to draw conclusion about specific aspects of the communication [25]. The key to this is the definition of precise categories that capture the substance of the investigated content.

There are deductive methods in which a-priori categories are defined, according to which the contents are later sorted and analyzed. Other methods proceed inductively and extract the categories completely from the data itself. In general research practice, the existing categories from the interview guidelines are used first. Second, further subcategories are derived inductively on the basis of the data [26].

Since the aim was to generate new hypotheses about the potential and risks of using MR in mining education through the qualitative research approach and to open up new fields of research by dealing with pre-structured interviews in an interpretative way, the deductive-inductive categorization approach described by Kuckartz was chosen [26].

After reading the material carefully, the interview statements were coded for the first time according to categories that corresponded to the direction of the questions in the guidelines. As a result, irrelevant information could be excluded and longer answers could be subdivided into different units of meaning, whereby multiple coding of a sentence was possible. Subsequently, the coded statements within the categories were grouped by meaning, divided into different subject areas and described with the use of short summaries. These summaries served as a basis to define specific and clearly distinguishable criteria by which all data should be re-coded and finally analyzed.

Some of the categories were reorganized in order to make them more suitable to grasp the substance of the statements made. This form of revision of categories is intended, since the development of categories can be seen as a continuing iterative process in which, the categories are reflected upon and rearranged.

Because the answers, especially in the written interviews, were very short, covered very different questions and therefore did not form a coherent narrative, we refrained from preparing case-related thematic summaries suggested by Kuckartz [26]. Instead, the different categories and sub-categories of each interviewed group were summarized and examined.

The following section provides an overview of the derived categories and sub-categories and summarizes the related statements.

IV. RESULTS

A total of four main categories were defined. First, an overview of (1) media currently used in teaching is given. Secondly, the (2) changes in the learning experience resulting from using MR are presented. Three subcategories were formed in this section, which can be seen in Table I. Another main category describes (3) possible use cases for the use of MR. Three further subcategories summarize for which target group the use of MR is particularly suitable, in which use cases benefit can be expected from the use of MR and when the use of MR appears to be particularly helpful. The fourth main category summarizes the (4) Lessons Learned resulting from the Test Lectures. The derived subcategories can be found in Table I.

TABLE I. OVERVIEW OF DERIVED CATEGORIES

Categories	Sub-categories
Currently used media	Classical methods and media
Changes in the learning experience	General benefits of MR
	Guidance through the lecture
	Individual learning needs
Application scenarios	Target group
	Use cases
	Alternative to field trips
Lessons learned from test lectures	Preparation for conducting MR lectures
	Technical aspects
	Integration of MR in the lecture
	Financial aspects
	Availability of MR content

A. *Currently used media*

In the course of the interviews with inexperienced students and teachers, questions were asked about the media currently used during lessons. The possible responses were semi-structured, as respondents could either choose from existing categories or add additional information. Students stated to use pictures and graphs, followed by texts and manuals (9), excursions and visits to mines (8) and videos and films (8). Only half of them stated to use 3D animations. Similar statements were also made by the inexperienced professors, who used all media except for 3D animations, which were rarely used. The teachers were also asked about the use of haptic objects like equipment, which all of them affirmed.

B. Changes in the learning experience

One of the aims of the study was to find out in what way the learning and teaching experience changes through the use of MR. Aspects included to what extent the technology helped to provide a more practical knowledge, what is perceived as more or less helpful during the test lecture and at which point potential problems arise.

1) General benefits of MR

A large majority of 18 students who had previously attended the lectures agreed that the MR technology used was of immense benefit for practical understanding, or at least has great potential. The reasons given for this were that the used technology conveyed a feeling of reality and of actually being present in the situation, which led to a much better imagination of the machines and processes presented.

According to the respondents, the 360° videos, e.g., from the perspective of a machine operator, provide a more practical perspective and a potentially faster transfer from theory to practice. This experience of a more practical understanding through the use of the technology in the test lectures largely met the expectations of the inexperienced students (8) and teachers.

More skeptical points of three experienced students referred to the fact that they already had knowledge about the presented content. Thus, they stated that real experiences cannot be replaced by MR and that the shown examples had little or no advantages over videos.

2) Guidance through the lecture

When asked about the test lecture, three teachers and nine students found it difficult to ensure that all students follow and understand the lessons equally while using MR.

These statements mainly refer to the VR glasses used, which restricted the eye contact between teacher and student. Whenever the teacher was unable to track the student's position within the virtually displayed environment, they reported that it was difficult to ensure that students pay attention to the relevant aspects of the content presented.

For this reason, and since the impressions and amount of information can be "overwhelming" (as one experienced student and one inexperienced teacher put it), it was considered very important by many respondents that some form of helpful guidance through the situations is provided.

One of the teachers observed during the test lectures, that the material is not always self-explanatory and therefore "students still need guidance during their VR experience". Other reasons why students might be "lost" are that they want to play around with the technology and try out everything first, rather than deal with the actual content.

3) Individual learning needs

Three experienced students said that students first need some time to get used to the new technology. Otherwise, it may be difficult to listen to the lecturer at the same time.

An experienced teacher pointed out that everyone has their own pace and type of learning. What he liked about MR was that it opens up different "paths" of teaching. "Therefore, virtuality offers a more individual learning environment", in which things can be learned independently at their own pace.

The freedom to discover and learn new things through their own actions seemed to be particularly exciting and important for some of the experienced students (5). For them, the interaction with the virtual environment could have been even more extensive, e.g., through the possibility of movement or additional tasks.

C. Application scenarios

The following section summarizes feedback on possible application scenarios. Moreover, it is presented for whom and in which contexts the use of MR is perceived as most beneficial.

1) Target group

In terms of the optimal target group, a large proportion of respondents (two experienced and one inexperienced teacher, ten experienced and three inexperienced students) agreed that the greatest benefit from the use of the technologies exists among students who have not yet had any real practical experience, for example, have never been in a mine.

According to students who took part in the test lecture, the learning effect might be significantly lower for students in higher semesters who have already visited mines several times during internships and excursions. This in turn corresponds to a teacher's impression that it was difficult to convey the content in an understandable and interesting way despite the differences in knowledge between the students. Another experienced teacher said that the benefits of MR highly depend on the content, which probably differs between bachelor and master students. Nevertheless, it was stated that both can still benefit from MR due to improved visualization.

2) Use Cases

There were many different answers to the question, which application areas for MR the interviewees could imagine. Safety trainings or demonstrations for a public target audience were named as use cases outside of a lecture. With regard to lecture content, different forms of visualizations and simulated scenarios were listed: e.g., underground mining, open pit mining or blasting, but also smaller practical processes, such as displaying the functioning or operation of machines.

In general, particularly from the statements of the respondents from the test lectures, it can be derived that the teaching methods to be chosen and the technology used will depend strongly on the content to be taught. Although all experienced professors shared the opinion that MR provides added value by creating a feeling of reality, they emphasized that classical lectures, laboratory experiments or field demonstrations will still be essential in teaching students. According to the experienced professors (2), classical methods like calculations on a blackboard or the use presentation slides remain a better choice when it comes to teach scientific basics and principles or theoretical subjects, such as algorithms.

An inexperienced professor has particularly stressed that it would not be appropriate to teach content digitally, when a real use of instruments (such as measuring equipment) is needed. Both experienced and inexperienced respondents see the benefit of MR more in use cases, in which it can fulfil its illustrative function for otherwise hard to imagine processes. Compared to presentation slides or videos, MR might lead to a more in-depth understanding of the matter.

3) Alternative to field trips

A possible advantage of MR is that it could replace classical excursions to a certain extent through its realistic representation. However, both professors and students made contradictory statements in this regard, since real excursions are still considered an important part of education. Fields of application are therefore rather as a "virtual add-on" prior or after excursions enabling students "to have a feel of the process even before visiting", for example underground mines or providing additional information about a situation through an overlay of an already known situation. Since some sites for excursions are perceived as very expensive, far away or dangerous, the technology could also be used to introduce such rather special subjects.

D. Lessons learned from test lectures

The test lectures and the interviews with the different groups also contributed to clarify under which conditions MR can be used optimally and beneficially for teaching and what is necessary achieving this.

1) Preparation for conduction MR lectures

The teacher's preparation for the test lectures was mainly about familiarizing oneself with the technique in order to "foresee mistakes that students could do while being in VR". According to their own statements, all three inexperienced teachers would depend on external support in the preliminary stages of conducting their own MR lectures. This could be personal workshop trainings, or online offers like web platforms, because they need someone to show them "how to use the media".

In response to the question of how to prepare for the test lecture in comparison to a classical lecture, the professors said that they needed time to familiarize themselves with the technology used and the new teaching materials, e.g., 360° videos. One teacher stated that he received help from a PhD student for this.

2) Technical assistance during the lecture

The experienced (3) and inexperienced teacher (1) shared the opinion that some technical assistance is required to take care of the devices before, during and after the lecture. That means, "setting up the systems, bringing the systems to a classroom, putting them away, charging them", as well as solving technical issues currently still occur during the lecture. These personnel do not necessarily need to know anything about the content itself, but taking the responsibility for the technical functioning would ensure that the professor can focus completely on teaching of the content.

Possible technical issues, such as lack of synchronization or unstable Wi-Fi connection, were perceived as problematic, especially if students cannot have the same learning experience as others. One student therefore suggested to have a backup plan, such as following the experience on a screen or to provide material as a follow-up at home.

3) Amount of time

Based on their experience, the teachers said that in a 90-minute lecture, the MR experience should not exceed 30 minutes, otherwise it could bore the students or overwhelm them: "Too much VR might distract students from the considered topics. They need time to reconsider received portions of information, make appropriate notes, have contact with the lecturer, and ask questions." One suggestion, for example, was to show four to six 360° videos with a length of two to four minutes. A single five-minute video would be of little use and the technical effort would be considered too high. Another aspect worth considering, regarding the duration of MR use, is that (4) experienced students and (1) inexperienced students may find dizziness or cyber sickness a problem, especially if they are not yet used to the technology.

Some students also perceived switching between the presentation slides and the MR glasses as somewhat disruptive during the test lecture.

4) Frequency of use

The experienced professors expressed that the frequency of using MR depends very much on the respective contents and should therefore be decided flexibly and on a case-by-case basis.

After the test lectures, some students (6) shared the opinion that the use of MR can significantly improve teaching, but can also reduce the quality of the lectures if the technology is not integrated into the structure in a meaningful and purposeful way, for example, by reducing "the time you can talk with the students". In contrast, the prior explanation of the theory, in order to subsequently provide an immersive insight through MR, was a positively perceived example of the test lectures.

5) Amount of devices

As stated by one of the experienced teachers, the number of devices "depends on the media used and how many is available". Two of the three professors and two students said that each student should have his own device at his disposal, otherwise the rest would get bored and the constant change would be seen as inconvenient. An alternative approach would be to use "one HTC Vive per 10 students for a 90-minutes lecture" and to mirror the experience on a screen.

6) Financial aspects

The cost of purchasing and maintaining equipment was considered as possible problem, which was estimated to be quite high. Directly related to this was the for now unanswered question of whether the university or the students themselves would purchase the equipment and thus be responsible for ensuring that the equipment would be available in a functional state for the lectures.

7) Availability of MR content

An experienced professor stated that the use of MR mainly depends on how quickly he can create his own MR content for the lecture. One experienced student stated that a prerequisite for its benefits was easy access to MR teaching materials. This was justified with the argument that the use of MR technologies in a virtual excursion could otherwise become too expensive.

The results of the qualitative content analysis are summarized and discussed in the following section.

V. Discussion

The aim of the interview study was to identify possible potentials and obstacles for the use of MR in mining education. For this purpose, 39 persons with and without experience with MR were interviewed about their experiences and expectations. The aim was to determine whether MR-based education can be considered a possible approach for meeting the current challenges in the mining sector. The results of the interviews provide first indications for the design and use of MR in mining education and point out further research gaps.

By interviewing different target groups, it was possible to ensure that relevant perspectives on the topic were covered. In further surveys, experts from mining operations should be involved in order to obtain their opinion on the transferability of MR-based content.

The findings are presented and discussed below, starting with the students' perspective and then for the teachers' perspective. Overall, the potential of MR-based teaching was seen by students and teachers. The learning advantages of MR can be clearly seen in the statements of experienced students. The students had the impression to get a more practical and deeper understanding of the content through the use of MR technologies. It was emphasized that the better visualization of objects, processes and the feeling of presence in virtual environments was perceived as beneficial in comparison to classical teaching materials. In current teaching, 3D simulations are only used in a few cases so far, but are considered helpful by students and teachers.

At this point, it was emphasized that inexperienced students are most likely to benefit from MR-based experience, e.g., to get an overview of the structure of a mine or to estimate the real size of machines. The advice of experienced students suggests that the use of MR in, e.g., master's programs is more likely to be used for advanced processes - for example, to be able to observe blasting in slow motion. Another relevant aspect relates to the possibility of individualized learning. Thus, different levels could be realized by the mentioned possibilities to go through learning experiences at individual pace and with individual prerequisites.

With regard to the teachers' perspective, it should be ensured during the lecture that there are opportunities for interaction with the students. Otherwise, there might be the danger of a loss of control over the lecture or the challenge to direct student's attention to the relevant aspects of the content. Interaction can either directly be integrated in the MR experience using arrows, annotations or external control of the headsets. Alternatively, it is possible to offer the teacher a control mode on the PC screen so that he/she does not have to wear a head mounted display.

Various aspects should be ensured when preparing an MR-based learning experience. The teachers pointed out that the technologies should be used in a very content-oriented way and be integrated in existing teaching concepts. The inexperienced professors agreed that the benefits of MR technologies depend on what content and how it is used. They rather saw it as a meaningful virtual extension to classical teaching concepts, such as lectures, experiments or excursions. For the creation of MR-based learning experiences, guidance should be offered on choosing the appropriate medium for a respective learning goal.

Furthermore, a need for some technical assistance was pointed out, in order to be able to fully concentrate on the students and the lecture. In any case, both students and teachers should be given the opportunity to get used to the technology. This can avoid that someone feels insecure and cannot concentrate on the content.

The selection of devices and time slots in which MR is used depends highly on the content. However, many teachers emphasize that uncontrolled use of MR can be overwhelming: Therefore, before using MR, teachers should always reflect on the learning goal to be achieved. This is supported by the statements of the experienced students, expecting MR to be beneficial only if it is well integrated into teaching.

VI. Conclusion

The aim of this work is to derive possible advantages and disadvantages of using MR technologies in mining education. In summary, the following implications can be derived for the challenges mentioned above. Especially experienced teachers saw the potential of MR in offering experiences in otherwise hardly accessible settings. This means for the further elaboration of the topic and future research that transparency about the possibilities of MR technologies should be established. Especially in case of teachers or students who had already experienced MR in class, they were able to imagine further scenarios.

Regarding the possibility of enhancing motivation, providing better learning experiences and thus making mining more attractive for students, MR and its application in mining education shows great opportunities, but must definitely be further investigated. Only if MR is accepted by teachers and used efficiently, it can contribute to the achievement of learning goals and thus be attractive for students. An important step is to guarantee low-threshold tools and platforms in order to use MR for teaching purposes. Prototypical applications should be publicly available and accessible throughout Europe.

The interview result shows that MR seems to offer new ways of fostering knowledge transfer. Concerning the development of professional skills, there should be more research on collaborative solutions and scenarios in MR to enforce communication between students. Nevertheless, this approach should be discussed and validated by involving experts from industry.

ACKNOWLEDGMENT

This work is part of the project "Mixed Reality Books (MiReBooks)" and was funded by the EIT RAW Materials. The author is responsible for the contents of this publication.

REFERENCES

[1] H. Wagner, "How to address the crisis of mining engineering education in the western world?," Min. Res. Eng., vol. 8(04), 1999, pp. 471–481.

[2] J. M. Galvin and F. F. Roxborough, "Mining engineering education in the 21st century — Will universities still be relevant?," The AusIMM Annual Conf. Ballarat, March 1997.

[3] D. Shields, F. Verga, and G. A. Blengini, "Incorporating sustainability in engineering education," Int. J. of Sus. in Higher Ed., vol. 15(4), 2014, pp. 390–403.

[4] S. Costa and M. Scoble, "An interdisciplinary approach to integrating sustainability into mining engineering education and research," Journal of Cleaner Production, vol. 14 Nos 3/4, 2006, pp. 366-373.

[5] R. LaSar, K. C. Chen, and D. Apelian, "Teaching sustainable development in materials science and engineering," Materials Research Society Bulletin, vol. 37 no. 4, 2012, pp. 449-454.

[6] B. Nicolescu, Transdisciplinarity - Theory and Practice, Cresskill, NJ: Hampton Press, 2008.

[7] E. DeGraaff and W. Ravesteijn, "Training complete engineers: global enterprise and engineering education," European Journal of Engineering Education, vol. 26 No. 4, 2001, pp. 419-427.

[8] B. Allenby, The Theory and Practice of Sustainable Engineering, Upper Saddle River, NJ : Pearson Prentice Hall, 2012.

[9] M. Scoble and D. Laurence, "Future mining engineers – educational development strategy," Proceedings of the First International Future Mining Conference, Sydney, 19-21 November 2008, pp. 237-242.

[10] H. Bertignoll, M. L. Ortega, and S. Feiel, "MiReBooks – Mixed Reality Lehrbücher für das Bergbau-Studium (MiReBooks—Mixed Reality Handbooks for Mining Education)", Berg Huettenmaenn Monatsh vol. 164, 2019, pp. 178-182.

[11] C. J. Dede, J. Jacobson, and J. Richards, "Introduction: Virtual, augmented, and Mixed Realities in Education," In D. Liu, C. J. Dede, R. Huang, and J. Richards (Eds.) Virtual, Augmented, and Mixed Realities in Education. Singapore: Springer, 2017, pp. 1–19.

[12] P. Milgram and H. Colquhoun, "A taxonomy of real and virtual world display integration," In Y. Ohta and H. Tamura (Eds.) Mixed reality: Merging real and virtual worlds, Berlin: Springer, 1999, pp. 5–30.

[13] R. Azuma et al., "Recent Advances in Augmented Reality," IEEE Computer Graphics and Applications vol. 21(6), 2001, pp. 34–47.

[14] L. Dawley and C. Dede "Situated learning in virtual worlds and immersive simulations," In J. M. Spector, M. D. Merrill, J. Elen, and M. J. Bishop (Eds.), Handbook of research for educational communications and technology, 4th ed., New York, NY: Springer, 2013, pp. 723-734.

[15] N. Schiffeler, A. Abdelrazeq, V. Stehling, I. Isenhardt, and A. Richert, „How AR-e your Seminars?! Collaborative learning with augmented reality in engineering education," INTED2018 Proceedings, Valencia, Spain, 2018, pp. 8912-8920.

[16] J. Birt, Z. Stromberga, M. Cowling, and C. Moro, "Mobile Mixed Reality for Experiential Learning and Simulation in Medical and Health Sciences Education," Information, vol. 9 (2), 2018.

[17] G. Norman, K. Dore, K., and L. Grierson, "The minimal relationship between simulation fidelity and transfer of learning", Medical Education, vol. 46(7), 2012, pp. 636–647.

[18] B. W. Mayer, K. M. Dale, K. A. Fraccastoro, and G, Moss, "Improving transfer of learning:Relationship to methods of using business simulation", Simulation & Gaming, vol. 42(1), 2011, pp. 64–84.

[19] K. Fraser et al., "Emotion, cognitive load and learning outcomes during simulation training", Medical Education, vol. 46(11), 2012, pp. 1055–1062.

[20] N. Schiffeler, V. Stehling, M. Haberstroh, and I. Isenhardt, "Collaborative Augmented Reality in Engineering Education", In M. Auer and B. K. Ram (Eds.), Cyber-physical Systems and Digital Twins, Cham: Springer, 2020, pp. 719-732.

[21] A. Abdelrazeq, L. Daling, R. Suppes, Y. Feldmann, and F. Hees, "A Virtual Reality Educational Tool in the Context of Mining Engineering - The Virtual Reality Mine," 13th annual International Technology, Education and Development Conference (INTED2019), Spain, 11-13 March 2019, pp. 8067-8073.

[22] Q. Guo, "Learning in a Mixed Reality System in the Context of "Industrie 4.0"," Journal of Technical Education, vol. 3, no. 2, pp. 91-115, 2015.

[23] Hochschulforum Digitalisierung, „The Digital Turn – Hochschulbildung im digitalen Zeitalter, (The Digital Turn – Higher Education in the digital age)," Arbeitspapier Nr. 28. Berlin: Hochschulforum Digitalisierung, 2016.

[24] L. Daling, C. Kommetter; A. Abdelrazeq, and M. Ebner, "Mixed Reality Books: Applying Augmented and Virtual Reality in Mining Engineering Education," In V. Geroimenko (Ed.), Augmented Reality In Education: A New Technology for Teaching and Learning. Springer, 2020, in print (ISBN 978-3-030-42155-7).

[25] P. Mayring, Qualitative Inhaltsanalyse. Grundlagen und Techniken (Qualitative content analysis. Foundations and techniques), 12th. Ed., Weinheim: Beltz, 2015.

[26] U. Kuckartz, Qualitative Inhaltsanalyse: Methoden, Praxis, Computerunterstützung (Qualitative content analysis: methods, practice, computer support), 3. Ed., Weinheim, Basel: Beltz Juventa, 2016.

International Academy, Research,
and Industry Association (IARIA)
412 Derby Way
Wilmington, DE 19810

ISBN 978-1-7138-2177-9

CURRAN ASSOCIATES INC.
proceedings
.com